Lecture Notes in Artificial Intelligence 13086

Subseries of Lecture Notes in Computer Science

More information about this subseries at http://www.springer.com/series/1244

Haizhou Li · Shuzhi Sam Ge · Yan Wu ·
Agnieszka Wykowska · Hongsheng He ·
Xiaorui Liu · Dongyu Li ·
Jairo Perez-Osorio (Eds.)

Social Robotics

13th International Conference, ICSR 2021
Singapore, Singapore, November 10–13, 2021
Proceedings

 Springer

Editors
Haizhou Li (iD)
Department of Electronic
and Communication Engineering
National University of Singapore, Faculty
of Engineering
Singapore, Singapore

Yan Wu (iD)
A*STAR Institute for Infocomm Research
Singapore, Singapore

Hongsheng He (iD)
Department of Electrical Engineering
and Computer Science
Wichita State University
Wichita, KS, USA

Dongyu Li (iD)
School of Cyber Science and Technology
Beihang University
Beijing, Beijing, China

Shuzhi Sam Ge (iD)
The National University of Singapore
Singapore, Singapore

Agnieszka Wykowska (iD)
Center for Human Technologies
Istituto Italiano Tecnologia
Genoa, Italy

Xiaorui Liu (iD)
Qingdao University
Qingdao, China

Jairo Perez-Osorio (iD)
Social Cognition Human-Robot Interaction
Istituto Italiano di Tecnologia
Genoa, Italy

ISSN 0302-9743   ISSN 1611-3349 (electronic)
Lecture Notes in Artificial Intelligence
ISBN 978-3-030-90524-8   ISBN 978-3-030-90525-5 (eBook)
https://doi.org/10.1007/978-3-030-90525-5

LNCS Sublibrary: SL7 – Artificial Intelligence

This Springer imprint is published by the registered company Springer Nature Switzerland AG
The registered company address is: Gewerbestrasse 11, 6330 Cham, Switzerland

Preface

The 13th International Conference on Social Robotics (ICSR 2021) was held as a hybrid conference (onsite and online) in Singapore, during November 10–13, 2021, with the theme of "Robotics in our everyday lives", emphasizing the increasing importance of robotics in human daily living.

Marking the return of ICSR 11 years after it was first held in Singapore, this edition was jointly organized by the Chinese and Oriental Languages Information Processing Society (COLIPS), the National University of Singapore (NUS), the Singapore Chapter of IEEE Systems, Man and Cybernetics Society and the Teochew Doctorate Society, Singapore (TDSS). It was supported by the Robotics Horizontal Technology Programme Office (R-HTPO) of the Agency for Science, Technology and Research, Singapore (A*STAR), and the Robotics and Autonomous Systems Department of the A*STAR Institute of Infocomm Research (I^2R).

The International Conference on Social Robotics brings together researchers and practitioners working on the interaction between humans and intelligent robots and on the integration of robots into the fabric of our society. Out of a record total of 129 submitted manuscripts reviewed by a dedicated international team of Senior Program Committee and Program Committee members, 64 full papers and 15 brief research reports were selected for inclusion in the proceedings and presented during the technical sessions of the conference. In addition to paper presentation sessions, ICSR 2021 also featured three keynote talks, five workshops, and a robot design competition. The keynote talks were delivered by three renowned researchers – Giorgio Metta of the Italian Institute of Technology, Italy, Oussama Khatib of Stanford University, USA, and Nadia M. Thalmann of Nanyang Technological University, Singapore.

We would like to express our sincere gratitude to all members of the Steering Committee, International Advisory Committee, and Organizing Committee and to all volunteers for their dedication in making the conference a great success. We are also indebted to members of the Senior Program Committee and the Program Committee for their hard work in the rigorous review of the papers. Lastly and most importantly, we are grateful for the continued support of ICSR by the authors, participants, and sponsors, without which the conference would not be possible.

October 2021

Haizhou Li
Shuzhi Sam Ge
Yan Wu
Agnieszka Wykowska
Hongsheng He

Organization

General Chairs

Haizhou Li   National University of Singapore, Singapore
Sam Shuzhi Ge   National University of Singapore, Singapore

Program Chairs

Yan Wu   A*STAR Institute for Infocomm Research, Singapore
Agnieszka Wykowska   Istituto Italiano di Tecnologia, Italy
Hongsheng He   Wichita State University, USA

Finance and Sponsorship Chair

Lei Wang   KLASS Engineering and Solutions, Singapore

Award Chairs

Britta Wrede   Universität Bielefeld, Germany
Emily Cross   Macquire University, Australia
Tetsuo Ono   Hokkaido University, Japan
Yong Liu   A*STAR Institute of High Performance Computing, Singapore

Invited Session Chairs

Marcelo Ang   National University of Singapore, Singapore
Pey Yuen Tao   Singapore Institute of Manufacturing Technology, Singapore

Workshop Chairs

Keng Peng Tee   MooVita Pte Ltd., Singapore
Maartje de Graaf   Universiteit Utrecht, The Netherlands
Mariacarla Staffa   Università degli Studi di Napoli Federico II, Italy

Panel Chair

Yong Liu   A*STAR Institute of High Performance Computing, Singapore

Competition Chairs

Amit Kumar Pandey   beingAI Limited and euRobotics, France
Ruud Hortensius   Universiteit Utrecht, The Netherlands

Publication Chairs

Dongyu Li   Beihang University, China
Jairo Perez-Osorio   Istituto Italiano di Tecnologia, Italy
Xiaorui Liu   Qingdao University, China

Publicity Chairs

Alessandra Sciutti   Istituto Italiano di Tecnologia, Italy
Han Wang   Nanyang Technological University, Singapore
Xiaonan Wang   National University of Singapore, Singapore

Virtual Conference Arrangement Chairs

Siqi Cai   National University of Singapore, Singapore
Thommy Eriksson   Chalmers University of Technology, Sweden

Local Arrangement Chair

Jiang Rui   National University of Singapore, Singapore

Local Arrangement Co-chair

Tianying Wang   A*STAR Institute of High Performance Computing,
                       Singapore

Steering Committee

Shuzhi Sam Ge   National University of Singapore, Singapore
Oussama Khatib   Stanford University, USA
Maja Mataric   University of Southern California, USA
Haizhou Li   National University of Singapore, Singapore
Jong Hwan Kim   Korea Advanced Institute of Science and Technology, South
                       Korea
Paolo Dario   Scuola Superiore Sant'Anna, Italy
Ronald C. Arkin   Georgia Institute of Technology, USA
John-John Cabibihan   Qatar University, Qatar

International Advisory Committee

Abderrahmane Kheddar	CNRS-AIST, Japan, and CNRS-LIRMM, France
Adriana Tapus	ENSTA Paris, France
Alan Richard Wagner	Pennsylvania State University, USA
Arvin Agah	University of Kansas, USA
David Feil-Seifer	University of Nevada, USA
Markus Vincze	Technische Universität Wien, Austria
Mary-Anne Williams	University of New South Wales, Australia
Miguel Ángel Salichs	Universidad Carlos III Madrid, Spain

Senior Program Committee

Alireza Taheri	Sharif University of Technology, Iran
Alireza Nemati	Qingdao University, China
Andreea Niculescu	A*STAR Institute for Infocomm Research, Singapore
Ayse Kucukyilmaz	University of Nottingham, UK
Dimitri Ognibene	Università degli Studi di Milano-Bicocca, Italy
Dongyu Li	Beihang University, China
Jairo Perez-Osorio	Istituto Italiano di Tecnologia, Italy
Kyveli Kompatsiari	Istituto Italiano di Tecnologia, Italy
Luis Fernando D'Haro	Universidad Politécnica de Madrid, Spain
Maartje de Graaf	Universiteit Utrecht, The Netherlands
Michael Chuah	A*STAR Institute for Infocomm Research, Singapore
Nicolas Spatola	Istituto Italiano di Tecnologia, Italy
Pauline Chevalier	Istituto Italiano di Tecnologia, Italy
Pey Yuen Tao	Singapore Institute of Manufacturing Technology, Singapore
Qinyuan Ren	Zhejiang University, China
U-XuanTan	Singapore University of Technology and Design, Singapore
Xiaolong Liu	Johns Hopkins University, USA
Xiaopeng Zhao	University of Tennessee, USA
Xiaorui Liu	Qingdao University, China

Program Committee

Abdollah Eydi	Amirali Rasaeifard
Ahmad Zibafar	Ana Müller
Aikaterini Bourazeri	Anna Belardinelli
Alessandra Rossi	Ansgar Koene
Alexandra Bacula	Azadeh Shariati
Ali Amoozandeh Nobaveh	Bob Schadenberg
Alireza Esfandbod	Boyoung Kim
Ameer Helmi	Carmelo Calafiore

Cesar Lucho
Chek Sing Teo
Damith Herath
Dongjie Zhao
Eduardo Sandoval
Ehsan Saffari
Fengpei Yuan
Filipa Correia
Fujian Yan
Giulia Perugia
Guillem Alenyà
Haiyue Zhu
Hannah Bradwell
Hui Liu
Jamy Li
Jani Even
JeeLoo Liu
Jiawei Ge
Jing Qi
Joao Ramos
Joel Stephen Short
Kheng Hui Yeo
Kimberly Garcia
Kirsikka Kaipainen
Kolja Kühnlenz
Kritika Johari
Lidia Al-Zogbi
Linda Lastrico
Lisa Armstrong
Loriane Koelsch
Lucas Morillo-Mendez
Marcela Munera
Mariacarla Staffa
Mario Rodríguez-Cantelar
Maryam Alimardani
Mehdi Hellou
Michael Kam
Mohammad Mokhtari
Mohammad Hossein Mashaghi
Mojtaba Ahangar Arzati
Mojtaba Shahab
Myounghoon Jeon

Neelu Gurung
Neziha Akalin
Nisha Raghunath
Nur Beril Yapici
Omar Eldardeer
Pamela Carreno
Pourya Aliasghari
Qin Zhu
Ramanpreet Pahwa
Ravi Tejwani
Roshni Kaushik
Rui Zheng
Ruodan Zhou
Salar Basiri
Sarah Levitan
Scott Brown
Sebastian Wallkotter
Serena Marchesi
Seyed Mohammad Jafar Zolanvari
Seyed Ramezan Hosseini
Shuai Guo
Silvia Rossi
Siqi Cai
Sofia Thunberg
Sonja Stange
Swee See
Taha Aksu
Tatsuya Nomura
Teck Chew Ng
Timothy Bickmore
Tom Williams
Vivienne Jia Zhong
Wanyue Jiang
Wei-Po Lee
Wesley Chan
Xiaocong Li
Yixiao Wang
Yuzhe Wang
Zeynab Rokhi
Ziggy O'Reilly
Ziming Liu

Local Arrangement Committee

Boyuan Liang	A*STAR Institute for Infocomm Research, Singapore
Daiying Tian	Beijing Institute of Technology, China
En Yen Puang	A*STAR Institute for Infocomm Research, Singapore
Guiju Ping	Nanyang Technological University, Singapore
Haitao Yang	National University of Singapore, Singapore
Jiadong Wang	National University of Singapore, Singapore
Jiali Li	National University of Singapore, Singapore
Jiuqiang Deng	University of the Chinese Academy of Sciences, China
Kaiqi Yang	National University of Singapore, Singapore
Kang Nie	University of the Chinese Academy of Sciences, China
Qi Diao	Beijing Institute of Technology, China
Serena Marchesi	Istituto Italiano di Tecnologia, Italy
Wei Qi Toh	A*STAR Institute of High Performance Computing, Singapore

Sponsors

Gold

Silver

Arcadia
Computing Innovation

speech◑cean

Contents

Rehabilitation and Therapy

Social Perception of Robots

Brief Research Reports

Stereotypes and Biases in HRI

Women *Are* Funny: Influence of Apparent Gender and Embodiment in Robot Comedy

Nisha Raghunath, Paris Myers, Christopher A. Sanchez,
and Naomi T. Fitter[✉]

Oregon State University (OSU), Corvallis, OR 97331, USA
{nisha.raghunath,myerspar,christopher.sanchez,fittern}@oregonstate.edu

Abstract. Previous robotics work has identified significant effects of perceived gender and embodiment on human perceptions of robots, but these topics have yet to be investigated in the context of robot comedy. The presented study explored the effects of gender and embodiment on audience members' perceptions of a robotic comedian. Participants ($N = 153$) observed either an audio-only clip or a video of a robotic comedian, with either a male or a female voice. We measured self-reported ratings of robot attributes. Results showed that neither gender nor physical form influenced joke humorousness or robot attribute ratings, however those who viewed a video of the robot reported feeling more connected to the comedian. These findings suggest that, unlike in past studies of human comedy to date, gender stereotypes and physical appearance may not affect perceptions of robot comedy performance.

1 Introduction

Female human comedians experience different responses from an audience than their male counterparts, but it is difficult to investigate what factors may underlie these differences in a controlled setting. Robotic comedians, which can be designed to behave and look identical to one another, offer one promising way to begin isolating these factors. Further, human responses to robots based on apparent gender and presented form factor are important to understand in social robotics generally (e.g., to inform appropriate robot design for various situations). We propose that audience attitudes toward robotic comedians' manipulated characteristics (i.e., gender and embodiment) may extend to human comedians, and that the understanding of differing perceptions across these attributes can inform future social robotic applications.

Previous work on robot comedy has manipulated robot interaction behaviors (e.g., eye contact with the audience [14] and timing of joke delivery [29]), finding both factors to be significant and favorable to the audience. More generally in social robotics, studies have established marked differences in both the perceived personality traits and occupational roles of robots based on apparent gender [4,20]; however, to our knowledge, no studies have explored effects of perceived robot gender in the comedy context. Our work attempts to address

© Springer Nature Switzerland AG 2021
H. Li et al. (Eds.): ICSR 2021, LNAI 13086, pp. 3–13, 2021.
https://doi.org/10.1007/978-3-030-90525-5_1

this gap by investigating the effects of perceived gender of a robotic voice and a physically embodied robot on ratings of comedic success, closeness feelings, and other perceived attributes. Key contributions of this work include insights on what effect (if any) apparent gender has on comedic success (holding all other factors constant), what inherent attributes may be linked with perceived gender of robotic comedians, and how embodiment (i.e., observing a physical robot vs. a disembodied robot voice) influences perceptions of the artificial comedian.

2   Related Work

Key topics informing the present work include gender in comedy, gender in robotics, robot comedy, and effects of robot embodiment on human opinions.

Gender in Comedy: Netflix has hosted upwards of 270 comedy specials (in English) from 2012 to the present day, of which only approximately 20% featured female comedians [21]. According to Levitt [17], this gender discrepancy reflects a real-world discrepancy in the number of stand-up comedy time slots booked by men versus women and gender non-conforming individuals. Why are female comedians so underrepresented in the comedic landscape? A controversial explanation is offered by Greengross and colleagues: men are funnier [12]. Their meta-analysis of 28 studies measuring men's and women's humor production ability (HPA) via independent, blind judges in a image/cartoon captioning task revealed that 63% of men were scored higher than their female counterparts with a combined effect size of $d = 0.321$ [13]. In comedic performance settings, possible mechanisms for differences in perceived humor ability across sex are historical differences in accepted male and female roles in society (e.g., females being discouraged from using humor and performing comedy in public) [13], gender stereotypes (e.g., women being more concerned about others and men being more competent and dominant) [6], and visual cues (e.g., a person presenting as a particular gender) [26]. Robots offer a unique opportunity to explore differences in perception of humorousness and other characteristics via fine manipulations of robot attributes. Further, it is possible that apparent gender could affect robot success in humorous day-to-day social interactions.

Gender in Robotics: Previous literature indicates that people extend stereotypes based on perceived sex to robots, relying on human-human norms to explain human-humanoid interactions [4,19]. For example, robots manipulated to appear masculine are perceived to have more agency (e.g., seeming more assertive, more dominant, more authoritative) and less communion (e.g., seeming less friendly, less polite, less affectionate) than feminine robots [8]. Similarly, robots with a female appearance tend to be regarded as inviting, warm, and interactive, while robots with a male design were regarded as tough and challenging [4]. This automatic and unconscious tendency to interact with robots as one would with other humans (i.e., by applying social categories) is an extension of the computers-as-social-actors (CASA) approach [7,18]. This approach shows that a robot's voice, demeanor, and motions all function as social cues to communicate gender [7,22,25]. These attributes can additionally interact with stereotypical gender roles to impact humans' perceptions of robots; female-voiced computers are perceived as less dominant and serious when delivering evaluations compared to male-voiced computers, for example [20]. Regardless of apparent robot gender, studies indicate that humans prefer and respond more positively to robots that have congruent gender and occupational roles [27]. For example, female robots are more likeable, seen to have more behavioral control, and are accepted more when presented as a healthcare robot [27]. At the same time, the gender of a robot does not appear to affect perceived eeriness, regardless of a robot's role in a situation [1]. Based on the robust finding that humans perceive and treat robots as they would another human, it is plausible that humans' expectations for female comedians also extend to robots, and that female robotic comedians would be perceived less favorably than male robotic comedians.

Robot Comedy: Past robot comedy work includes initial efforts to equip robots with appropriate gaze, capable gesture, and abilities to "read the room." To investigate whether robots could perform these aspects of stand-up comedy, Katevas and colleagues manipulated both gesture and gaze of robotic comedians to examine their effects on live audience responses, finding evidence that the reciprocal give-and-take between comedian and audience were key to a well-received performance [14]. Other robot comedy work used audience polling and audio processing to track audience enjoyment of jokes [15]. Recently, a robot comedy study demonstrated that a robotic comedian with good timing was perceived as significantly funnier, and that the ability to adapt to its audience's reactions improved their opinions of the jokes [29]. Preliminary results from yet another study show promise for a robotic comedian's ability to "read the room," or analyze audience facial behavior, and improvise reactions (e.g., respond to grimaces with "What? Too soon?") [11]. To our knowledge, no past studies have investigated whether a robotic stand-up comedian's gender affects audience perceptions.

Effects of Embodiment: In previous studies evaluating human opinions of embodied vs. disembodied robots, experimenters have defined an embodied robot as one that has a physical form (i.e., not a screen-based image) and is located in the same room as the participant (i.e., not remotely located). Humans find embodied robots (vs. disembodied robots) more appealing and perceptive, and tend to empathize more with them [16,30]. Embodied robots are also regarded as more helpful, watchful, and enjoyable compared to videos of robots [24,30]. Importantly, however, Wainer and colleagues could not definitively state that participants favored embodied robots – only that embodied robots will be perceived as more "present" [30]. Taken together, this past work indicates that differences in robot embodiment will likely impact perceptions, but it is not clear how onlooker perspective will vary, especially in terms of preference and scales not previously explored in the comedy application space. Because of the influence of embodiment in past work, we decided to study the effects of embodied vs. disembodied robotic comedians (a coarse manipulation of embodiment) as a second variable of interest which, to our knowledge, has yet to be explored in the realm of robot comedy.

3 Methods

To study the effects of perceived gender and embodiment of a robotic stand-up comedian, we employed a 2×2 between-subjects factorial study design. Apparent robot gender (i.e., male or female as communicated by voice) and robot type (i.e., audio-only vs. video of a NAO robot [10]) were completely crossed, and observer opinions were measured with approval from our university ethics board.

The robot's comedy routine originated from a pilot study which presented 18 jokes (written in collaboration with a group of semi-professional comedians) to participants. Viewers rated each joke using the Joke Rating Scale (further described below). The same group of comedians also advised on the vocal and choreographic delivery of the jokes.

The top-performing 10 jokes were subsequently compiled into the roughly 4.5-minute comedy set used in the present study. Because of the order-dependent nature of comedy performance, all conditions used the same overall jokes and joke order. For the gendered voices, we used Amazon Polly's "Joey" voice as the male voice and "Joanna" as the female voice. Gender was manipulated via auditory cues only (i.e., voice characteristics) to control for visual cues. The embodiment condition modulated whether the robot was visible by presenting either an audio-only recording or a video. Both modalities closely parallel common methods for enjoying stand-up comedy; in addition to watching live performances, comedy fans commonly consume pre-recorded videos (e.g., Netflix comedy specials) and audio-only tracks (e.g., comedy albums).

Hypotheses: We were broadly interested in how human observers' perceptions of a robotic comedian, and their connection to it, varied as a function of apparent gender and physical form. Given the lack of closely aligned prior research, we proposed the following exploratory hypotheses based on the related work discussed in Sect. 2: (1) a female-voiced robot will be perceived as warmer than a male-voiced robot, (2) a male-voiced robot will be perceived as funnier and more competent than a female-voiced robot, and (3) video of an embodied robot will lead to more social closeness feelings than the audio-only condition.

Participants: Previous research involving robotic comedians has not reported result effect sizes. Therefore, we used a medium effect size of $f^2 = .25$ in an a priori power analysis using G-Power 3.0.10 with power set to 0.80 and error probability $\alpha = .05$, which resulted in an overall suggested sample size of 128. 157 adult undergraduate students were recruited from Oregon State University. Data were excluded from participants who failed to complete the study or who took longer than 2.5 standard deviations from the mean time taken to complete the study. These exclusions left 153 participants ($M = 22$ years old, $SD = 6$, 115 female, 35 male, 2 non-binary, 1 non-reported gender) for analysis. Participants received course credit for the study.

Procedure: We administered the study as a 30-minute Qualtrics survey, through which participants were randomly assigned to one of the four conditions: male × voice audio, male × robot video, female × voice audio, and female × robot video. After providing informed consent, participants completed demographic questions including the Ten Item Personality Inventory (TIPI) and the

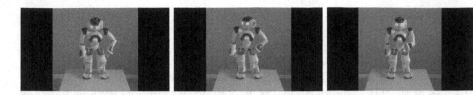

Fig. 1. Keyframes from one joke in the male video condition stimulus corresponding to each sentence of the following joke: "I saw a foxy robot the other night. She was smokin'! Naturally, we called tech support right away."

Negative Attitudes toward Robots Scale (NARS). Participants then observed the assigned robot comedy set recording, which they were able to replay an unlimited number of times. Figure 1 shows example keyframes from one of the jokes included in the study stimuli, along with the joke text. After they finished observing the comedy set, participants were asked to rate the performance using the Joke Rating Scale (JRS), Inclusion of Other in the Self (IOS) scale, anthropomorphism subscale of the Godspeed questionnaire, and the Robotic Social Attributes Scale (RoSAS), all of which are described in more detail below. Respondents also provided open-ended feedback about performance characteristics that affected their responses.

Measurement: The initial portion of the survey gathered basic demographic information, as well as the TIPI and NARS scales. Participants also indicated on a scale of one to five how much previous experience they had with robots and with comedy. The TIPI was included in this survey to briefly measure participant personality on 10 nine-point Likert scales from Strongly Disagree to Strongly Agree [9]. The NARS questionnaire was used to measure participants' evaluations of and attitudes toward robots prior to exposure to one in the present study using 7-point Likert scales from Strongly Disagree to Strongly Agree [23].

The JRS was adopted from past work on acceptability of robot jokes to measure the primary dependent variable: self-reported ratings of how funny the robot comedy performance was [28]. These ratings used seven-point Likert scales from Strongly Disagree to Strongly Agree, and the average score served as a rating of humorousness. The RoSAS was administered to collect data about participants' perceptions of the robotic comedian's social attributes on three factors: warmth, competence, and discomfort on the standard nine-point Likert scales [5]. The IOS measured participants' connection with the robotic comedian after observing the comedy set. Participants selected one of seven Venn diagrams that they felt best portrayed their relationship with the comedian, which ranged from separate circles (1) representing the self and other to almost completely overlapping circles (7) [2]. Participants answered manipulation check questions about the robot's gender (i.e., female, female-androgynous, androgynous, male-androgynous, male, no gender, or unsure) as well as anthropomorphism using one standard subscale of the Godspeed questionnaire [3].

4   Results

To test our hypotheses, we conducted a 2 (robot gender) × 2 (robot embodiment) factorial ANCOVA to analyze the main dependent variable: humor ratings (i.e., average JRS scores). The NARS subscales, the extroversion and openness subscales of the TIPI, and participants' experience with robots were included as covariates. In addition to the primary analysis, we also conducted exploratory analyses to investigate the effects of these factors and covariates on participants' ratings of the robot's social attributes (i.e., RoSAS subscale scores), and their connection with the robotic comedian (i.e., IOS scores). Participants' free-response data was also analyzed for recurring themes and insights into possible motivations behind quantitative results.

Quantitative Results: 125 of the 153 participants were able to correctly identify the robot gender, indicating that the majority were able to discern our manipulation. Of the 24 who did not report the correct gender, 22 responded with either "no gender," "unsure," or some form of androgyny (e.g., male- or female-androgynous). Only two participants explicitly reported perceiving a female when the robot was manipulated to be male, or vice versa.

Neither the embodied nor disembodied condition elicited average anthropomorphism ratings above a three, and these scores were not significantly different from one another, demonstrating that participants did not regard the robotic comedians as very human-like, $t(144) = -1.35$, $p = .18$.

The ANCOVA evaluating the effects of robot gender and embodiment on JRS scores (as described in Table 1) revealed that the first NARS subscale (i.e., questions about robot interaction scenarios) significantly covaried with participants' joke ratings, $F(1, 140) = 6.75$, $p = .05$, $\eta_p^2 = 0.03$. After controlling for the covariate, neither robot gender nor type were significant predictors of joke ratings. Another ANCOVA revealed that RoSAS subscale ratings significantly covaried with the NARS subscales. The RoSAS warmth subscale covaried with the third NARS subscale (i.e., emotions in interactions with robots), $F(1, 139) = 5.87$, $p = .02$, $\eta_p^2 = 0.04$, as did the RoSAS competence subscale, $F(1, 137) = 8.10$, $p = .005$, $\eta_p^2 = 0.06$. The RoSAS discomfort subscale covaried with both the first NARS subscale, $F(1, 139) = 11.22$, $p = .001$, $\eta_p^2 = 0.08$, as well as the second, $F(1, 139) = 11.65$, $p < .001$, $\eta_p^2 = 0.08$. After controlling for the appropriate covariates for each RoSAS subscale, the ANCOVA again demonstrated that robot gender and type did not predict differences in RoSAS reports.

Table 1. Means and standard deviations of study questionnaire responses, formatted as $M(SD)$.

	Female	Male	Audio	Video
JRS humorousness	4.26 (1.47)	4.13 (1.33)	3.98 (1.45)	4.14 (1.33)
RoSAS warmth	3.75 (1.88)	3.58 (1.66)	3.83 (1.73)	3.96 (1.78)
RoSAS competence	4.92 (1.76)	4.76 (1.79)	4.53 (1.79)	4.98 (1.75)
RoSAS discomfort	3.20 (1.46)	3.25 (1.62)	3.44 (1.45)	3.01 (1.60)
IOS closeness	1.83 (1.11)	1.66 (0.84)	1.60 (0.89)	1.90 (1.06)

Table 2. Free-response coding frequencies. Each code belongs to one of the three numbered themes of interest, and the "+" and "−" columns show the number of respondents who commented on each theme in a positive or negative manner.

Theme	Code	+	−
1	Gender perception based on joke content	12	0
1	Gender perception based on looks or form	7	0
1	Gender perception based on voice	12	0
2	Sound made by the robot/robot motors	9	8
2	Comparison of robot/robot voice to a human comedian	12	35
2	What feels/appears human vs. robotic in the system	14	59
2	Like or dislike of robots/AI	7	9
2	Comments on gestures/body language	16	12
2	Fear of robots/robots takeover	5	5
3	Format (e.g., video vs. in-person vs. audio-only)	16	2
3	Enjoyment of the set	30	48
3	Perceptions of the jokes as "dad jokes"	1	0
3	Joke content (e.g., funny v.s. not funny)	53	37
3	Relatability	15	34
3	Joke writing/delivery (e.g., forced, natural)	10	48

An exploratory ANCOVA of IOS scores showed that NARS subscales one (i.e., situations of interactions with robots), $F(1, 139) = 7.15$, $p = .008$, $\eta_p^2 = 0.05$, and three (i.e., emotions in interactions with robots), $F(1, 139) = 4.90$, $p = .03$, $\eta_p^2 = 0.03$, were significantly related to participants' self-reported connection with the robotic comedian. After controlling for these subscales, there was no evidence for an effect of robot gender, but the analysis did show that robot embodiment significantly predicted IOS scores, $F(1, 139) = 4.50$, $p = .04$, $\eta_p^2 = 0.03$.

Qualitative Results: Participants' free-response data regarding how robot performance characteristics influenced their ratings were coded for 15 facets using a positive or negative coding system, which was created for this study based on related work [4,14,20,29]. The responses to these facets were grouped to form three overarching themes: 1) gender perception, 2) robot attribute perception, and 3) comedic/humor perception (see Table 2).

Overall, all participant comments relevant to the gender perception category were positive ($N = 31$ responses). Opinions were much more negative, however, for the remaining two categories. Participants expressed approximately double the number of negative opinions ($N = 128$) as they did positive ($N = 63$) regarding the robot's attributes. Of the 128 negative comments, 94 pertained to comparisons between the robotic comedian and a human comedian. Facets that comprised the comedic/humor perception responses suggest that participants did not enjoy the comedy set ($N = 48$) and were most displeased with the joke writing/delivery ($N = 48$).

5 Discussion

The goal of the current study was to determine the effects of a robotic comedian's gender and physical appearance on human observers' connection to it, perceptions of it, and perceptions of its jokes. We manipulated the gender and embodiment communicated by a robotic comedian delivering a comedy set in a 2×2 between-subjects factorial design. Given that previous literature has established the effects of each factor individually, we predicted that a female-voiced robot would be perceived as warmer than a male-voiced robot, that a male-voiced robot would be perceived as funnier and more competent than a female-voiced robot, and that a video of the robot performing would lead to greater perceived connection on the observer's part than an audio-only clip of the performance.

Contrary to our first hypothesis, we did not find a main effect of gender (or robot embodiment) on warmth ratings or any other RoSAS subscale ratings; female-voiced robots were not perceived as warmer than male-voiced robots. This lack of quantitative evidence contradicts previous literature that female robots are regarded as more inviting [4]. Interestingly, participants' free-response data revealed that of those who shared that they found the robot "relatable" ($N = 15$), 80% identified the comedian as female, with one participant noting that they "sometimes wonder why most robots [have] female voices. Maybe it's sexist?" It is possible that while the same stereotypical gender norms typically attributed to robots may not apply in a comedy context, they do exist overall. Perhaps, then, the content (i.e., the jokes delivered) served to negate the usual gender stereotypes because females are not typically associated with a comedian role, resulting in no perceived warmth differences between the robot genders [6,13].

We also did not find a main effect of gender or robot type on joke ratings; male and female embodied and disembodied robots did not differ in observer ratings of funniness, though 74 participants reported that the jokes were of good quality ($N = 53$) and/or relatable ($N = 21$). While this result is incongruous with the previous literature stating that people tend to find males funnier than females, the finding is also an interesting discovery pertaining to past reported differences between male and female comedians [12]. A possible explanation is that human male comedians possess different characteristics that cannot be replicated by robots, which evoke greater humor ratings from observers than do female comedians/robots. Indeed, of the $N = 31$ participants who inferred robot gender based on the joke content ($N = 12$; rather than based on appearance ($N = 7$) or voice ($N = 12$)), $N = 20$ of them commented on it being male; one participant noted that while they relied on the perspective of the jokes to determine gender, they "wouldn't make the same association with a human [comedian]." Free-response data suggests that one differentiating characteristic is a joke delivery style that the robot could not achieve – specifically vocal differences ($N = 23$; e.g., "monotone and was not natural," "the voice makes it very rigid"). In fact, many participants ($N = 26$) categorically noted that the robot's voice did not compare to a human comedian, and mentioned it and the jokes being "forced," "scripted," or "unnatural" ($N = 48$). Future studies may compare human perceptions of human male and female comedians to robot male and female comedians to investigate to what extent these measurable traits (e.g., voice pitch, inflection, human vs. digital voices) explain the lack of difference in humor ratings for robots.

As hypothesized, observers reported feeling more connection with embodied robotic comedians than they did with audio-only clips of the same comedy sets, further supporting that humans find embodied robots more appealing and enjoyable [16, 24, 30]. Consistent with this, participants' free responses suggest that embodied robots are more enjoyable and relatable to watch in a stand-up comedy context (e.g., "The movement of the whole body was fascinating to watch. [It] held my visual focus throughout the video"). Among the participants who viewed a video of the embodied robotic comedian, many responded positively toward its gestures and/or body language ($N = 16$), while others noted that the movement made the robot more personable ($N = 11$). In contrast, more than half of the participants who observed the audio-only comedy set commented that it was limited ($N = 29$ of 48; e.g., "I thought with how the robot was speaking it was hard to hear the emotion in his speech"). This finding provides evidence that humans may favor embodied robots over disembodied ones – a fact that Wainer and colleagues could not ascertain beyond humans perceiving them to be more present [30].

Key Strengths and Limitations: To our knowledge, previous literature in the general robotics domain has only detailed the effects of robot gender and embodiment on human perceptions separately, and never in the context of robot comedy. Our study was designed to address this gap by utilizing a fully crossed design. It should be noted that while we were able to achieve a sample size that satisfied our *a priori* power analysis suggestion of $N = 128$, all participants were recruited from an online university sample pool. Therefore, it is possible that the typical university-aged individual has a particular taste in stand-up comedy not satisfied by the jokes used in this study. Similarly, it is possible that the jokes were not understood by all observers, given that they were written to be from a robot's perspective, instead of a human's. Finally, because participants used their personal devices to complete this study remotely and online, it is possible that they were not as attentive to the task as they may have been if the study had been conducted in a laboratory setting.

Conclusions and Future Work: Despite these shortcomings, this study's results shed light on human perceptions toward robots in a social context and inform future designs of studies and robotic systems. While stereotypical gender norms may constrain human perceptions of male vs. female robots in other contexts such as healthcare and manufacturing, it appears that robotic comedians are not likewise limited. Importantly, as expected, humans' preference for embodied robots in contexts where connection is integral to the experience (e.g., comedy) was supported by this study's results. In this study, we only manipulated gender through use of auditory cues (i.e., Amazon Polly's "Joanna" female voice vs. the "Joey" male voice). In future studies, it could be useful to explore the effects of changes in physical appearance of the robotic comedian as well. For example, it would be interesting to see if a robotic comedian with an overtly female form elicits different reactions and ratings from than the audience than does an overtly male form. Future directions for research in this area would also benefit from 1) exploring the upper and lower limits of accepted embodiment for robots in robot comedy, 2) normalizing and/or utilizing well-known and liked comedy sets to factor out the individual differences in joke preferences, and 3) conducting studies in person and perhaps in a larger group setting to simulate typical live stand-up comedy environments.

References

1. Appel, M., Izydorczyk, D., Weber, S., Mara, M., Lischetzke, T.: The uncanny of mind in a machine: Humanoid robots as tools, agents, and experiencers. Comput. Hum. Behav. **102**, 274–286 (2020)
2. Aron, A., Aron, E.N., Smollan, D.: Inclusion of other in the self scale and the structure of interpersonal closeness. J. Pers. Soc. Psychol. **63**(4), 596 (1992)
3. Bartneck, C., Kulić, D., Croft, E., Zoghbi, S.: Measurement instruments for the anthropomorphism, animacy, likeability, perceived intelligence, and perceived safety of robots. Int. J. Soc. Robot. **1**(1), 71–81 (2009). https://doi.org/10.1007/s12369-008-0001-3
4. Carpenter, J., Davis, J.M., Erwin-Stewart, N., Lee, T.R., Bransford, J.D., Vye, N.: Gender representation and humanoid robots designed for domestic use. Int. J. Soc. Robot. **1**(3), 261 (2009). https://doi.org/10.1007/s12369-009-0016-4
5. Carpinella, C.M., Wyman, A.B., Perez, M.A., Stroessner, S.J.: The robotic social attributes scale (RoSAS) development and validation. In: Proceedings of the ACM/IEEE International Conference on Human-Robot Interaction (HRI), pp. 254–262 (2017)
6. Eagly, A.H., Steffen, V.J.: Gender stereotypes stem from the distribution of women and men into social roles. J. Pers. Soc. Psychol. **46**(4), 735 (1984)
7. Echterhoff, G., Bohner, G., Siebler, F.: Social robotics and human-machine interaction: current research and relevance for social psychology. ZEITSCHRIFT FUR SOZIALPSYCHOLOGIE **37**(4), 219–231 (2006)
8. Eyssel, F., Hegel, F.: (S)he's got the look: gender stereotyping of robots. J. Appl. Soc. Psychol. **42**(9), 2213–2230 (2012)
9. Gosling, S.D., Rentfrow, P.J., Swann, W.B., Jr.: A very brief measure of the big-five personality domains. J. Res. Pers. **37**(6), 504–528 (2003)
10. Gouaillier, et al.: The NAO humanoid: A combination of performance and affordability. CoRR arXiv:0807.3223 (2008)
11. Gray, C., Myers, P., Fitter, N.T.: Read the room, robot! Exploring audiovisual methods to improve the effectiveness of robotic comedians. In: Proceedings of the IROS Workshop on Social AI for Human-Robot Interaction of Human-Care Service Robots (2020)
12. Greengross, G., Miller, G.: Humor ability reveals intelligence, predicts mating success, and is higher in males. Intelligence **39**(4), 188–192 (2011)

13. Greengross, G., Silvia, P.J., Nusbaum, E.C.: Sex differences in humor production ability: a meta-analysis. J. Res. Pers. **84**, 103886 (2020)
14. Katevas, K., Healey, P.G., Harris, M.T.: Robot comedy lab: experimenting with the social dynamics of live performance. Front. Psychol. **6**, 1253 (2015)
15. Knight, H., Satkin, S., Ramakrishna, V., Divvala, S.: A savvy robot standup comic: online learning through audience tracking. In: Proceedings of the ACM International Conference on Tangible and Embedded Interaction (TEI), Work-in-Progress Workshop, pp. 1–7 (2010)
16. Kwak, S.S., Kim, Y., Kim, E., Shin, C., Cho, K.: What makes people empathize with an emotional robot? The impact of agency and physical embodiment on human empathy for a robot. In: Proceedings of the IEEE International Symposium on Robot and Human Interactive Communication (RO-MAN), pp. 180–185 (2013)
17. Levitt, A.: Statistics show dudes still get majority of bookings at stand-up comedy shows. https://www.chicagoreader.com/Bleader/archives/2018/01/10/statistics-show-dudes-still-get-majority-of-bookings-at-stand-up-comedy-shows
18. Nass, C., Moon, Y.: Machines and mindlessness: social responses to computers. J. Soc. Issues **56**(1), 81–103 (2000)
19. Nass, C., Steuer, J., Tauber, E.R.: Computers are social actors. In: Proceedings of the SIGCHI Conference on Human Factors in Computing Systems, pp. 72–78 (1994)
20. Nass, C.I., Moon, Y., Morkes, J., Kim, E.Y., Fogg, B.: Computers are social actors: A review of current research. Human Values and the Design of Computer Technology, pp. 137–162 (1997)
21. Netflix (2021). https://www.netflix.com/browse
22. Nomura, T.: Robots and gender. Gend. Genome **1**(1), 18–25 (2017)
23. Nomura, T., Suzuki, T., Kanda, T., Kato, K.: Measurement of negative attitudes toward robots. Interact. Stud. **7**(3), 437–454 (2006)
24. Pereira, A., Martinho, C., Leite, I., Paiva, A.: iCat, the chess player: the influence of embodiment in the enjoyment of a game. In: Proceedings of the International Joint Conference on Autonomous Agents and Multiagent Systems, pp. 1253–1256 (2008)
25. Powers, A., Kiesler, S.: The advisor robot: tracing people's mental model from a robot's physical attributes. In: Proceedings of the ACM SIGCHI/SIGART Conference on Human-Robot Interaction (HRI), pp. 218–225 (2006)
26. Quinn, K.A., Macrae, C.N., Bodenhausen, G.V.: Stereotyping and impression formation: how categorical thinking shapes person perception. In: The SAGE Handbook of Social Psychology, pp. 68–92. Sage, Thousand Oaks (2007)
27. Tay, B., Jung, Y., Park, T.: When stereotypes meet robots: the double-edge sword of robot gender and personality in human-robot interaction. Comput. Hum. Behav. **38**, 75–84 (2014)
28. Tay, B.T., Low, S.C., Ko, K.H., Park, T.: Types of humor that robots can play. Comput. Hum. Behav. **60**, 19–28 (2016)
29. Vilk, J., Fitter, N.T.: Comedians in cafes getting data: evaluating timing and adaptivity in real-world robot comedy performance. In: Proceedings of the 2020 ACM/IEEE International Conference on Human-Robot Interaction (HRI), pp. 223–231 (2020)
30. Wainer, J., Feil-Seifer, D.J., Shell, D.A., Mataric, M.J.: Embodiment and human-robot interaction: a task-based perspective. In: Proceedings of the IEEE International Symposium on Robot and Human Interactive Communication (RO-MAN), pp. 872–877 (2007)

Cross-Cultural Timeline of the History of Thought of the Artificial

Gabriele Trovato[1]([✉]), Nikolaos Mavridis[2], Alexander Huerta-Mercado[3], and Ryad Chellali[4]

[1] School of International Liberal Studies, Waseda University, Tokyo, Japan
gabriele@takanishi.mech.waseda.ac.jp
[2] Interactive Robots and Media Lab, Al Ain, UAE
[3] Pontificia Universidad Católica del Perú, Lima, Peru
[4] Nanjing University of Technology, Nanjing, China

Abstract. The current world landscape in opinions and attitudes about robotics is highly variegated in different parts of the world. This landscape is a result of the sum of the effects of multiple factors, which date from millennia ago, as waves of philosophical thought, religion and historical events overlapped and allegedly influenced the concept of human and of the artificial. This paper provides a survey of such factors, and attempts to trace possible lines between causes and consequences. The analysis seems to indicate the presence of a West/East split which marks the main differences in intending the role of social agents, humanoids, transhumanism and labour automation.

Keywords: History of robotics · Culture · Humanoids

1 Introduction

Worldwide research in robotics is aware of the different approaches in the development and diffusion of these new technologies. Typically Asia, and in particular Japan, are seen as poles of advancement, especially regarding the realisation of humanoids, whereas Western countries are less akin to the purpose of replicating humans. This is happening despite the origin of the concept of robot came from Europe (the Czech word *robota* meaning "forced labour"). Kaplan [1] debated the reason why the Western world is more afraid of the humanoid, and concluded that Westerners are fascinated and afraid by new machines, while in Japan machines do not seem to affect human specificity."

One limitation of this analysis is that the fear of the humanoid goes beyond the proposed concept, and sometimes touches neurological reasons (uncanny robots appearance) or concrete worries (fear of losing jobs). Therefore, it is necessary to distinguish in which aspects automation is seen negatively.

A vast literature covered comparative studies of human-robot interaction; however, the core of this literature mainly revolves around West v East (where West often means the US, and East typically only means Japan). A more extensive analysis is thus necessary, digging into history in all different parts of the world.

© Springer Nature Switzerland AG 2021
H. Li et al. (Eds.): ICSR 2021, LNAI 13086, pp. 14–23, 2021.
https://doi.org/10.1007/978-3-030-90525-5_2

As Nisbett [2] stated, the differences between East and West in cognition, due to differing ecologies, social structures, philosophies, and educational systems, trace back to ancient Greece and China. In fact, some similarities among these ancient cultures are present, involving puppets and automata. Millennia later, the landscape has completely changed as civilisations parted ways of thought. What happened in between is the research question of the present contribution.

In different parts of the world, different lines of thought arrived to opposite conclusions regarding robots, and in particular humanoids. Multiple factors, tracing back to philosophy, history, religion and society, apparently prompt or hinder the development and the application of robots in societies nowadays. The goal of this paper is to connect the threads that lead the past to the present, and understand where are the criticalities.

2 The Part Ways – West to East

2.1 Latin America

While there is no trace of the idea of automation in Aztec, Maya and Inca civilisations, one interesting note in pre-Columbian Americas is the tale of the revolt of the objects (Fig. 1), depicted in Moche civilisation (150 to 700 A.D:, pre-Inca civilization present in the northern coast of Peru) [3], which parallels the current view of revolting robots. This odd episode reveals the fear of lack of control of the world order, which is based on fragile balance of nature and is maintained by sacrifices [4].

Mesoamerican civilisations shared many common traits, one of them being the use of human sacrifices, originating from the belief of a pact of blood with gods, who shed blood first for the humanity [5]. The relevant aspect of this fact is the human specificity in sacrifice: it was not possible to spare a human and obtain the same favour from the gods. Sacrifices were most common in Mexico, although also in South America studies [6] mention the taxonomic differentiation of wild and domestic species in sacrifices.

When immigration from other continents began, African Witchcraft and Turanic Shamanism were also imported and blended up with Christianity as well. Through the principle of resemblance, a humanoid doll or a similar representation is believed to generate an impact on a living person, operated by a shaman [7]. These kinds of practices are still executed nowadays. The connection of human figures with spirits slightly resemble animism of Eastern religions.

Fig. 1. Detail of the "Revolt of the Objects" from Moche culture.

On the other hand, Spanish conquest has added the cultural layer of Christian Catholicism in its most strict form (the Inquisition). The use of actuating a crucifix to help confirming a defendant guilty [8] represents the only real precedent - a negative one - of automation in Latin America.

2.2 Europe and Western Culture

The idea of machines traces back to Ancient Greece: artificial servants like Hephaestus's helpers, made by the gods to serve the gods [9], autonomous ships, the legendary bronze giant Talos, and the myth of Pygmalion [10]. Some automata were actually built: such as the "magic" opening of temple doors when a fire was lit in an altar: their purpose was to surprise and amuse [11]. Besides automata, from the writings of Herodotus [12] we also know about puppets moved by strings being used in religious festivals in Egypt and later in Rome. One famous episode: in 44 B.C., at the funeral of Julius Caesar, Marc Antony made use of a puppet actuated by a mechanical device. It was rotated to show the knife wounds and incite the emotional reaction of the angry mob.

The advent of monotheism view brought concepts borrowed from Judaism, like the desacralisation of nature [13] and the rejection of magic, which tend to make robots and automated objects appear like mere machines, which should be seen suspiciously for their autonomy. This might be the background that leads to the tale of the golem, present in Jewish folklore since only the 16th Century. The golem, a man-made creature built from clay or mud, went out of control and had to be destroyed. This story represents an example of hubris, is allegedly at the origin of the fear of man-made creatures called Frankenstein complex [14], which was reproduced in similar stories (Fig. 2). A first attempt at regulation of machines autonomy, however, comes from Europe, with the famous Three Laws of Robotics by Asimov [15].

While Israel developed in its own peculiar way (see the set of rules existing about the Sabbath, prompting the need of home automation), Christian countries developed on the top of the pre-existing beliefs. The production of automata related to the concept of "enchantment of technology" [16]. Though the Middle Ages and later, mechanical angels and fire-breathing devils were designed, patronised by the Catholic Church [17].

Conversely, while the Church never prohibited the advancement of technology and the realisation of machines, some aspects of the faith may be interpreted in opposition to the concept of intelligent machines. The dualistic view of soul renders a machine "soulless", and the concept of body as a gift from God, in common with the other monotheistic religions (e.g. "body is a gift from Allah/God"). This may lead to more conservative views regarding the possibilities of "enhancing" the human body.

Nevertheless, Western culture was influenced by concepts present in Genesis (1:26–28): "mankind is created as an "image of God" and receives the mission to "fill the Earth and subdue it" and to rule over the animals. As a consequence, the study of the created nature itself was a legitimate way of understanding God [13].

After the Renaissance, the power of creation has "shifted from gods to humans" [17], and anthropocentrism became a central thought also in philosophy. It is worth to mention the influential role of Descartes: his passive mechanical thoughts of the separation between body and soul, in which the body is regarded as soulless. In the res *cogitans/res extensa* dualism, animals are mere machines unable to think, while man masters and owns nature [18].

The emphasis on science led to the Industrial Revolution, in which we can find the episode of Luddism in the UK, in which protesting groups destroyed textile machinery. The fear of losing jobs was based on concrete evidence, although new jobs were eventually created.

The advent of the two World Wars, which particularly hit Europe, left a deep trace that is visible in Western philosophy and arts, in a pessimistic view of man's tendency to go against his self-interest with an immense destruction power [19]. Science-fiction arguably reinforced the Frankenstein Complex with this new awareness.

Fig. 2. Four creatures which went out of human control: from left to right the Golem, the Creature from Frankenstein, Pinocchio and Terminator.

2.3 Middle East

The peculiarities of this area as opposed to the Ancient World take place with the rise of Islam. It's the Arabian golden age that had a world-wide impact on science. Ismail al-Jazari, a scholar who lived in the 12th Century in present day Turkey, described fountains and musical automata [20]. Rosheim [21] stated that the Arabs were interested not only in dramatic illusion but also in manipulating the environment for practical applications.

The Middle East is characterised by the traits of the monotheistic religions, and the philosophical thought evolved in the same direction of distance between man and God. For example, Islamic scholar Mohammad-Ali Taskhiri also discussed the concept of dignity, intended as a state to which all humans have equal potential, as long as they live a life pleasing to the eyes of God [22]. The consequence is that a robot should be able to tell right from wrong, matching its dignity to the one of a human and complying the religious laws [23].

The most peculiar issue with Islam is due to iconoclasm. Islam prohibits the depiction of living beings, either animal or human, especially in sacred spaces, as depicting them would be considered same as adopting the role of creator [24].

In the Middle East, society rules and state laws are often blended with religious beliefs, and the understanding of cultural norms of the country is particularly necessary for ensuring technology acceptance [25], as the attempt to take power over nature by science or techniques could be seen as an offense against Allah's omnipotence [26]. Iconoclasm, however, is not necessarily a common issue to all the Islamic world and shall not be generalised: even in Persia, depiction of humans has been widespread in certain historical periods, and the Middle East does not represent the most populous area of Muslims.

2.4 India

The Indian subcontinent, one the largest Islamic areas by population, has always had a completely opposite approach regarding the embodiment of the sacred compared to the Middle Eastern Islamic approach. This can be seen in theology in the mystical symbolism of the traits of the human face [27]. The Bhagavad Gita scripture states a God with a form is necessary due to the human use of senses.

Since ancient times, puppet shows have been a tool to convey stories regarding Hindu gods and Puranic legends [28], and the use of Murti is widespread. The construction of automata with human/animal figures is documented (the tiger of the Islamic ruler Tipu Sultan [29] in Fig. 3, left).

In the ancient Vedic civilisation, there were already references of machines in ancient texts (the Sanskrit term Yantra may be translated as machine). In particular, in Yoga Vasishta [30] it is mentioned that an Asura named Sambarasura created three robots without sentiments, and in the Mahabharata [31] there is a reference of a gigantic human-like machine named Kumbhakarna.

Hinduism conceives God as a multiplicity and accepts different ways of worship. We argue that this inclusive nature of Hinduism towards other religions) and the multi-culturality of the populations in the Indian subcontinent may help acceptance of robots, in particular if employed in a religious application.

Especially in Hindu Tantric, rituals are of preeminent importance, as repetition and chanting of mantra are performed over and over again, while the concept of "vain repetitions" has been bitterly criticised, for instance, by Christian Protestants [32]. Being a repetitive action, it may lead to tedium [32]: we argue that, a philosophy in which the action of ritual itself is more important that the content may prompt the delegation of ritual. The Ganapati Bappachi Robotic Aarti [33] is an example of such delegation to a robotic arm.

Fig. 3. Tipu's Tiger: automata made for an Islamic Sultan (left); extreme anthropomorphism in Japanese onigiri (right).

2.5 East Asia

East Asia is tied to India for having received the influence of waves of spirituality and ideals [34]. In Asian countries it is possible to encounter different shades of people's religion, as Confucianism, Buddhism, Taoism and Shinto are not reciprocally exclusive, and influenced each other.

Taoism is the oldest among these religions, and is one that encourages people to concentrate on the present real world rather than on the afterlife. Conversely, the dream to become "immortal Taoist sages in a fairyland" is an ultimate goal for the Taoist [35]. Weng et al. debate whether this dream can be helped by the use of robotics. Another interesting aspect of Taoism is the concept of harmony between man and nature, in which "man must control his own conduct without violating the law of nature" [13]. Unlike Europe, dominated by anthropocentrism, this relationship implies that man is born from nature.

From Buddhism originated the concept by Mori [36] that robots have the Buddha-nature and the potential for attaining Buddhahood, deserving the same compassion that all living beings receive. Also related to Buddhism we can find historical traces, in southern China, Korea and Sri Lanka, of the use of shadow puppets [37]. China has a long tradition of shadow puppets, whose connotations were not always positive (like in the case of bringing back alive the spirit of the dead on a shadow screen [28]).

Confucianism then dominated society in Sinosphere, and its approach to science, which emphasises collectivism and pragmatism [38]. This can be seen in contemporary times, as the push to modernisation [39] is also bringing automatisation of labour.

Japan is a special case within East Asia because of the many components that built up its culture and of the prominent role in robotics.

Deriving from the Confucian animistic conception of religion, that ascribes souls to all living and non-living objects, and the harmony of Taoism, Shinto, puts emphasis on nature worship and leads to the belief that inanimate things are sacred objects at its core [40]. Shintoist Japan has an additional peculiarity as anthropomorphism has been a trait present since the 12th Century, proven by the animals depicted in the Chōjū-jinbutsu-giga scrolls [41], and is visible nowadays from the degree of objects that - literally - have a face (Fig. 3, right).

3 Discussion and Conclusion

In this last part, we summarise the data collected from all the sources, and try to draw lines between the main factors examined and the criteria of attitude towards robots, which is relevant today as may represent cultural barriers to the concrete application in the societies.

Macro cultural areas are synthesised in Fig. 4. As categorisation of cultural areas is highly inconsistent in Sociology and Anthropology, for our analysis we adapted areas defined in [42]. This representation is necessarily simplified and not inclusive of exceptions within each group.

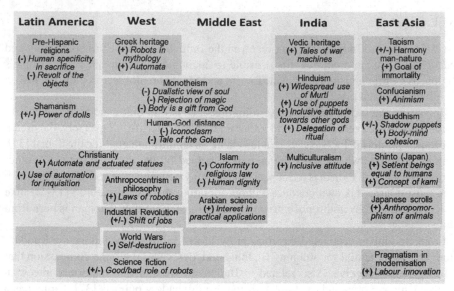

Fig. 4. The cross-cultural timeline. In vertical, cultural groups with each block indicating a topic, and specifically an aspect which may have caused a positive (+) or negative (-) effect into some aspect of attitude towards robots.

We consider four important criteria, partially corresponding to previous research by Dihal [43], on which the approach towards robots is radically different across the world nowadays, and discuss them in Sect. 3.1.

3.1 The Four Criteria

A. Social: robots as mere tools v robots as social agents

Factors that influence this aspect of the attitude seem to revolve around the concept of soul: whether it is in every object, or a separate entity from the body, and whether an object with social capabilities would possess a moral, or rather be considered magic, with its possible negative connotations. In other words, in Western perception, a conversational robot who displays emotions may be regarded as a fraud. In these regards, the Eastern philosophies and the Native American connection of human figures with spirits provide a much more favourable terrain for robots to be credible social agents.

This can be seen in Japan, where 8 million Gods and spirits exist in natural environments [35], and the leading role of Japan in developing social companions (Aibo, Kirobo, Lovot, Pepper, etc.).

B. Human-likeness: Frankenstein complex v development of humanoids

Two are the main factors: anthropocentrism and the distance from God. In all the cultures where the human being is considered unique (including Mesoamerica), its replacement is more difficult, including with an artificial version of it. Moreover, if humans are inferior to gods, their ability to replicate themselves may be insufficient, implying that a man-made humanoid robot will be faulty. These complications may be even more critical when depiction of human figures is associated with a negative perception: iconoclasm should be considered as an additional barrier for the development of humanoids, as their making would be open to a wrong interpretation.

C. Human biology: Bio-conservatism v Transhumanism
The main concept related to the modification of human biology (which is opposed in Bio-conservatism and advocated in Transhumanism) seems to be deriving from the concept of body - intended as a gift from the monotheistic God - which should not be altered, or rather as part of nature, as in Taoism. These opposing stances may influence the boundaries of what is considered "natural" when dealing with Cybernetics. It is worth mentioning the strict stance of the Catholic Church in these matters.

D. Labour: robots as job stealers v robots as job helpers
History may be the main factor that influences this aspect: the concrete change of society caused by new technologies is evident. The fear of unemployment caused by automation is a common concern despite that the original purpose (and etymology) of modern robots is labour. In case of the Middle East and East Asia, the philosophical attitude towards science may as well have a positive impact in the application of modern robotics. However, rather than cultural areas, single countries may adopt different approaches depending on their own pragmatism. Moreover, the attitude of first developers of technologies and the one of late adopters can be different as well. A late adoption of a technology may bring distortions as well as new possibilities. The future employment of robots in the societies will depend on a combination of these factors.

3.2 Overall View

An overall view of the cross-cultural timeline seems to indicate a "West/East split", with the sharpest division occurring between the Middle East and India, considering the many aspects in common within the two sides.

The greatest difference regarding the concept of human, which acts as a underlying factor, could be synthesised with the "metaphysical triangle" [26, 44], measuring the distance among the components God/Man/Nature. A greater separation between the profane and the divine, and the active role of man may have fuelled the invention of robots in the West, but at the same time put a limit to the innovation, which application in the most extreme senses was taken over by the East.

This collection of implications cannot be considered evidence, but rather as hypotheses, which contribute to shed some light to the background of the evolution of robotics worldwide. As for the concrete direction of future research, the authors suggest, when designing and employing robots in different parts of the world, to consider case by case the implications within the four criteria A/B/C/D of the new technology, and deduct the risks and opportunities.

Acknowledgements. The first author would like to thank Prof. Nathan Sidoli, Prof. Fabrizio Speziale, Mr. Mohammad Shidujaman, and Mons. Lucio Adrián Ruiz (Secretariat for Communication of the Holy See) for the prolific discussions that helped the conception of this paper.

Funding. This work was supported by Ministry of Internal Affairs and Communications (MIC) of Japan (Grant no. JPJ000595).

References

1. Kaplan, F.: Who is afraid of the humanoid? Investigating cultural differences in the acceptance of robots. Int. J. Humanoid Rob. **1**(3), 465–480 (2004)
2. Nisbett, R.: The Geography of Thought: How Asians and Westerners Think Differently...and Why. Free Press, New York (2004)
3. Quilter, J.: The Moche Revolt of the objects. Lat. Am. Antiq. **1**(1), 42–65 (1990). https://doi.org/10.2307/971709
4. de Ayala, F.G.P., Hamilton, R.: The First New Chronicle and Good Government: On the History of the World and the Incas Up to 1615. University of Texas Press (2009)
5. DK. The Religions Book: Big Ideas Simply Explained, 1st edn. DK, New York (2013)
6. Alaica, A.K.: Partial and complete deposits and depictions: social zooarchaeology, iconography and the role of animals in Late Moche Peru. J. Archaeolog. Sci. Rep. **20**, 864–872 (2018)
7. Benavides, Ó.S.: 'Despierta, remedio, cuenta…': adivinos y médicos del Ande/Mario Polia Meconi. Fondo Editorial de la Pontificia Universidad Católica, Lima, 1996. Anthropolog. Depart. Ciencias Soc. **15**(15), 375–377 (1997)
8. Malachowski, A.: "Una corta historia sobre la inquisición." Anita Malachowski, 16 Oct 2017. [Online]. http://anitamalachowski.blogspot.com/2017/10/el-antiguo-local-de-la-inquisicion.html. Accessed 05 Mar 2020
9. Russell, B., Robots: The 500-Year Quest to Make Machines Human. Scala Arts & Heritage Publishers Ltd. (2017)
10. Grant, M., Hazel, J.: Who's who in Classical Mythology. Psychology Press (2002)
11. Nelson, V.: The Secret Life of Puppets. Harvard University Press (2009)
12. Herodotus, Godley, A.D.: Herodotus. With an English translation by A.D. Godley. London Heinemann (1921)
13. Wang, G., Zhu, Y.: Harmonization with nature: ancient Chinese views and technological development. In: Christensen, S.H., Mitcham, C., Li, B., An, Y. (eds.) Engineering, Development and Philosophy: American, Chinese and European Perspectives, pp. 357–377. Springer, Dordrecht (2012)
14. Idel, M.: Golem: Jewish Magical and Mystical Traditions on the Artificial Anthropoid. State Univ of New York Pr, Albany (1990). Gell, A.: The Technology of Enchantment and the Enchantment of Technology. In: Anthropology, Art, and Aesthetics, Coote, J. (Ed.) Clarendon Press (1994)
15. McCauley, L.: The Frankenstein Complex and Asimov's three laws. Univ. of Memphis (2007)
16. Riskin, J.: The Restless Clock: A History of the Centuries-Long Argument Over What Makes Living Things Tick. University of Chicago Press (2016)
17. King, E.: 'Clockwork Prayer: A Sixteenth-Century Mechanical Monk', Blackbird, vol. 1, no. 1 (2002). [Online]. http://www.blackbird.vcu.edu/v1n1/nonfiction/king_e/prayer_toc.htm
18. Descartes, R.: Discourse on the Method of Rightly Conducting the Reason, and Seeking Truth in the Sciences. Sutherland and Knox (1850)

19. Durkheim, É.: The Elementary Forms of the Religious Life. Allen & Unwin, London (1915)
20. Hill, D.R.: Mechanical engineering in the medieval near east. Sci. Am. **264**(5), 100–105 (1991)
21. Rosheim, M.E.: Robot Evolution: The Development of Anthrobotics. Wiley (1994)
22. Hafez, K., Kenny, M.A.: The Islamic World and the West: An Introduction to Political Cultures and International Relations. BRILL (2000)
23. Sandewall, E.: Ethics, human rights, the intelligent robot, and its subsystem for moral beliefs. Int. J. Soc. Robot. **13**(4), 557–567 (2019). https://doi.org/10.1007/s12369-019-00540-z
24. Saif, M.: The Evolution of Persian thought regarding art and figural representation in secular and religious life after the coming of Islam. Macalester Islam J. **1**(2) (2006)
25. Rogers, E.M.: Diffusion of Innovations, 5th Edn. Free Press (2003)
26. Meganck, M.: Lynn white revisited: religious and cultural backgrounds for technological development. In: Christensen, S.H., Mitcham, C., Li, B., An, Y. (eds.) Engineering, Development and Philosophy, pp. 379–395. Springer, Dordrecht (2012). https://doi.org/10.1007/978-94-007-5282-5_23
27. Oporiulc, P.: Il simbolismo mistico del volto umano nel trattato (in urdu) Sūrat-i ma'lūma-yi ṣuwari 'ilm di Karīm Allāh 'Āshiq (in Italian). J. Asiat. **295**(2), 439–459 (2007)
28. Ghosh, S., Banerjee, U.K.: Indian Puppets. Abhinav Publications (2006)
29. Brittlebank, K.: Sakti and Barakat: the power of Tipu's Tiger. an examination of the tiger emblem of Tipu Sultan of Mysore. Mod. Asian Stud. **29**(2), 257–269 (1995)
30. Vālmīki. The Yoga-vásishtha-mahárámáyana of Válmiki. Bonnerjee and Company (1891)
31. Debroy, B.: The Mahabharata: Complete and Unabridged, 2015 Edn. Penguin Books India Pvt. Ltd. (2015)
32. Yelle, R.A.: To perform, or not to perform? A theory of ritual performance versus cognitive theories of religious transmission. Method Theory Study Religion **18**(4), 372–391 (2006)
33. 'Ganapati Bappachi Robotic Aarti', Robolab Technologies Pvt Ltd. https://www.robolab.in/ganapati-bappachi-robotic-aarti/. Accessed 04 Feb 2019
34. Okakura, K.: The Ideals of the East. Jazzybee Verlag (2012)
35. Weng, Y.-H., Hirata, Y., Sakura, O., Sugahara, Y.: The religious impacts of taoism on ethically aligned design in HRI. Int. J. Soc. Robot. **11**(5), 829–839 (2019). https://doi.org/10.1007/s12369-019-00594-z
36. Mori, M.: The Buddha in the Robot. Kosei Publishing Company, Tokyo (1989)
37. Currell, D.: Shadow Puppets and Shadow Play. Crowood (2015)
38. Vincent, J., Taipale, S., Sapio, B., Lugano, G., Fortunati, L. (eds.): Social Robots from a Human Perspective. Springer, Cham (2015). https://doi.org/10.1007/978-3-319-15672-9
39. Zhao, S.: The China Model: can it replace the Western model of modernization? J. Contemp. China **19**(65), 419–436 (2010)
40. Schodt, F.L.: Inside the Robot Kingdom - Japan, Mechatronics, and Coming Robotopia. Kodansha. Tokyo, New York (1988)
41. Takanishi, A.: Humanoid Robots, and the Culture and History of the Japanese People. Acta Philosophica **20**(1), 29–52 (2011)
42. Anděl, J., Bičík, I., Bláha, J.D.: Concepts and delimitation of the world's macro-regions. Miscellanea Geographica **22**(1), 16–21 (2018). https://doi.org/10.2478/mgrsd-2018-0001
43. Coughlan, K., Dihal, K.: "'Scary Robots' : Examining Public Responses to AI Stephen Cave"
44. Wildiers, M.: Kosmologie in de Westerse cultuur: Historisch-kritisch essay. Kok Agora, Kapellen, Kampen (1988)

People's Perceptions of Gendered Robots Performing Gender Stereotypical Tasks

Sven Y. Neuteboom and Maartje M. A. de Graaf[✉] [iD]

Department of Information and Computing Sciences, Utrecht University,
Utrecht, The Netherlands
m.m.a.degraaf@uu.nl

Abstract. HRI research shows that people prefer robot appearances that fit their given task but also identify stereotypical social perceptions of robots caused by a gendered appearance. This study investigates stereotyping effects of both robot genderdness (male vs. female) and assigned task (analytical vs. social) on people's evaluations of trust, social perception, and humanness in an online vignette study ($n = 89$) with a between subject's design. People deem robots more competent and receive higher capacity trust when they perform analytical tasks compared to social tasks, independent of the robot's gender. An observed trend in the data implies a tendency to dehumanize robots as an effect of their gendered appearance, sometimes as an interaction effect with performed task when this contradicts gender stereotypical expectations. Our results stress further exploration of robot gender by varying gender cues and considering alternative task descriptions, as well as highlight potential new directions in studying human misconduct towards robots.

Keywords: Social robots · Gender stereotypes · Social perception · Dehumanization · Trust

1 Introduction

The upcoming introduction of robots embracing a myriad of tasks in our everyday lives initiated multiple human-robot interaction (HRI) studies to investigate robots' suitability to perform a given task. Some studies have more generally analyzed people's social acceptance of robots in several potential future jobs [9,12]. Such studies show people's willing to accept robots in roles for entertainment, as personal assistants, and in hazardous environments, yet will probably reject the application of robots requiring sophisticated social emotional interactions. Other studies specifically investigated a fit between task and appearance indicating that a robot's appearance-task fit is affected both by people's expectations about the capacities a robot needs for a particular task [26] as well as a need to match a robot's appearance to its intended application of role [8,15]. A body of research in human psychology may explain these previous findings in HRI. Psychology research indicates that initial impression are formed based on appearance cues

© Springer Nature Switzerland AG 2021
H. Li et al. (Eds.): ICSR 2021, LNAI 13086, pp. 24–35, 2021.
https://doi.org/10.1007/978-3-030-90525-5_3

which, in turn, not only serve as ample triggers for social categorization [1] but also prompt subsequent stereotyping processes [28,37]. Such gender stereotyping has occurred in HRI research as well. People quickly infer a robot's gender based on it's appearance [21] which triggers gender stereotypical beliefs about such gendered robots [13,38]. This study expands existing knowledge in HRI research on robot genderdness and appearance-task fit by investigating stereotyping effects of robot genderedness and assigned task in an online vignette study.

1.1 Social Categorization and Stereotypes

Social categorization is a cognitive process to make sense of the social world by simplifying and systematizing perceptive information [1]. When meeting strangers, such cognitive categorization may aid as a beneficial heuristic when we infer interpersonal characteristics based on the social group that stranger belongs to [28]. However, categorizing others to social groups rather than treating them as unique individuals may also have various negative consequences. Social categorization triggers a tendency to form distort perceptions and stimulate exaggeration of differences between individuals from distinct social groups while perceiving intensified similarities of individual members within those groups [37]. As a consequence, we are more likely to utilize our distort perceptions to individual members of social groups without considering whether the assumed characteristics inhere with that specific individual. The process of such over-generalized assessments of an individual based on the group to which they belong is called stereotyping [20]. Stereotypes are automatically activated immediately following categorization of a target as a member of that group [11].

A large body of research on gender stereotyping reveals a human tendency to ascribe different traits to men and women. Stereotypical male traits comprise competence and agency [35] by highlighting achievement orientation (e.g., competent, ambitious), inclination to take charge (e.g., assertive, dominant), autonomy (e.g., independent, decisive) and rationality (e.g., analytical, objective) [20]. Stereotypical female traits enclose warmth and expressiveness [35] by highlighting concern for others (e.g., kind, caring), affiliative tendencies (e.g., friendly, collaborative), deference (e.g., obedient, respectful) and emotional sensitivity (e.g., intuitive, understanding) [20]. Bem [3] mapped this distinction between stereotypical male and female traits which shows a strong overlap with the Stereotype Content Model's [7] dimensions of warmth and competence. Subsequent research shows that people generally deem competence more desirable for males and warmth for females [4]. Relying on the Computers Are Social Actors paradigm [29], gender stereotypes have also been reported in HRI research.

1.2 Gender Stereotypes in HRI Research

People socially categorize robots and reckon social behaviors in robots based on inferred traits and characteristics, including gender cues from physical appearance [13] as well as facial features and voice [32]. While technical abilities are advancing, robots were originally designed to execute instrumental tasks [41].

This classical image of robots performing dirty, dangerous, and dull tasks still prevails in people's minds [27]. Nonetheless, human encounters and collaborations with robots increasingly become everyday practice [22]. A successful introduction of robots in society heavily relies on people trusting these systems [16] as a mediator for people's willingness to collaborate with robots [42]. Although trust has been frequently debated in human-robot interaction research –as a theoretical concept as well as an empirical measure– consensus arises on a dichotomous dimension of trust. On the one hand, people may trust a robot based on its capacity or reliability, and on the other hand based on its integrity or morality [14,39]). These trust dimensions resemble the gender stereotypical traits associated to men and women. Female stereotypical traits, such as "loyal" and "compassionate" [3], better fit the items of moral trust, such as sincerity, genuineness and ethicality [31]. Male stereotypical traits, such as "ambitious" and "self-reliant" [3], better fit the items of capacity trust, such as "competent" and "skilled" [18]. Based on this resemblance, we hypothesize that *people have higher trust in robots that perform tasks"fitting to their gender"* (H1).

Other HRI studies specifically focus on the interaction effects between a robot's gender and their occupational domain. When a robot performs tasks in line with existing gender-stereotypes regarding gender-task fit, people will more easily accept that robot [38]. Moreover, when our social schema for gender-task fit is violated during a collaborative task with a gendered robot, people will even perform less well (i.e., higher error rate) [25]. These findings from HRI research map similar results from psychology research illustrating that occupational roles are reliably stereotyped along the social perception dimensions of warmth and competence [19], which in turn have been linked to gender-stereotypical traits [3]. Given the strong underlying social schema regarding the appearance-task fit in HRI research [26], we expect a dominating effect of the gendered embodiment over the potential effect of task-fit. Therefore, we hypothesize that *robot gender affects people's social perception of a robot, independent of performed task* (H2).

A growing body of research investigates human misconduct with robots in terms of discrimination (e.g., [2]) and abuse (e.g., [23]). Gendered robotic agents with female characteristics encounter a specific form of human misconduct, namely objectification. Observations of conversations between pupils and a female-gendered virtual tutor reveals a frequent objectification of that virtual agent whilst placing it in an inferior role [40]. Systematic analysis of online commentaries on videos displaying humanoid robots exposes a pervasively blatant objectification of female-gendered robots [36]. Psychological research has a long historical focus on sexual objectification of the female body [27] indicating that men and women hold similar tendencies to perceive sexualized women as lacking mental capacity and moral status [24]. Combining the literature on female objectification with the gender-stereotypical expectations regarding occupational suitability of gendered robots [38], we hypothesize that *people's perceptions of a robot's humanness is a combined (interaction) effect of both robot gender and performed task* (H3).

2   Method

We have conducted an online vignette study ($n = 89$) manipulating robot gender (male vs. female) and task type (analytical vs. social) in a between subject's design to investigate stereotyping effects of robot genderedness and assigned tasks on social perception, trust, and humanness.

2.1   Stimuli

We manipulated both the gender of the robot as well as the type of task it performed. The mixture of these stimuli (robot gender X task type) resulted in four different vignettes. To manipulate the robot gender, we modified a picture of the Pepper robot by either giving it a blue tie for the male or a pink scarf for the female robot (see Fig. 1). Such apparel serve as subtle but powerful gender cues [21]. Additionally, we referred to the robot as either *Alexander* in the male or *Alexandra* in the female task description respectively. Task type was manipulated by altering some words in a text description to indicate either an analytical or social task, which were kept at similar length (i.e., 69 and 67 words respectively). The analytical task [*A*] described the robot studying large datasets with medical data to provide an overview of treatment plans for hospital patients to support healthcare professionals in making solid decisions of patient treatment. The social task [*S*] described the robot utilizing large datasets with verbal and non-verbal behaviors to provide emotional support to hospital patients facilitating healthcare professionals in monitoring patient well-being. A full description of the task descriptions is given below:

> *Alexander/Alexandra* supports healthcare staff in...
> ...[*A*] *developing individual treatment plans for hospital patients.*
> ...[*S*] *providing emotional support to patients with chronic diseases].*
> *Alexander/Alexandra* has access to large data sets with...
> ...[*A*] *medical data including medical conditions and symptoms, diagnoses, treatments, medication, test results, hospitalization, and demographic patient data such as gender and age.*
> ...[*S*] *verbal and non-verbal behaviors including speech utterances, body language, facial expressions, and social customs and etiquette.*
> *Alexander/Alexandra...*
> ...[*A*] *analyzes this data, draws connections between cause and effect, and quickly provides an overview of potential treatments.*
> ...[*S*] *listens actively, recognizes a patient's emotions and feelings, and offers emotional support to patients.*
> This way, healthcare professionals can...
> ...[*A*] *make a solid decision for an appropriate treatment for individual patients.*
> ...[*S*] *monitor and respond optimally to the emotional well-being of individual patients.*

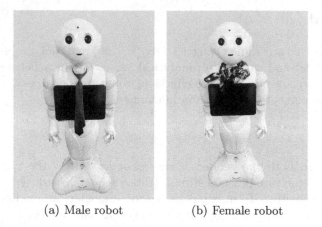

(a) Male robot   (b) Female robot

Fig. 1. Robot gender manipulation

We pretested these stimuli ($n = 12$). The female robot ($M = 7.67$) was perceived as more female than the male robot ($M = 5.56$) measured on a 9-point Likert scale from mostly male to mostly female ($p = .012$). The analytical task ($M = 8.22$) was perceived as more analytical ($p = .032$) than the social task ($M = 6.78$), and the social task ($M = 6.67$) was perceived as more social ($p < .001$) than the analytical task ($M = 2.22$) measured on two separate 9-point Likert scales from not at all [*analytical/social*] to very [*analytical/social*].

2.2   Procedure

After giving consent, the survey topic was introduced by addressing the ageing society and that robots could aid the growing demand for optimization in health-care. Participants were randomly assigned to one of the four vignettes with a picture of the robot (male or female) above the task description (analytical or social). After reading, participants were asked to respond to several statements regarding their perception of the robot (see Sect. 2.3). The questionnaire ended with some demographic items and thanking the participant for their contribution.

2.3   Dependent Variables

Participants' social perception of the robot was measured with the 10-item scale by Cuddy et al. [7] containing the dimensions of warmth ($\alpha = .69$) and competence ($\alpha = .67$). To measure participants' trust in the robot, we administered the 16-item Multi-Dimensional-Measure of Trust scale by Ullman & Malle [39] containing the dimensions of capacity trust ($\alpha = .77$) and moral trust ($\alpha = .78$). Perceptions of the robot's humanness were collected using the 20-item scale by Haslam et al. [17] containing the dimensions of human uniqueness ($\alpha = .68$ after removing item 'logical') and human nature ($\alpha = .67$ after removing item 'individual'). All measures were presented on 7-point Likert scales, and average construct scores were calculated. Table 1 presents means and standard deviations of all dependent variables in each of the conditions.

Table 1. Means and standard deviations of dependent variables in each condition

	Condition			
	Male robot		Female robot	
	Analytical task	Social task	Analytical task	Social task
Dependent variables	*Means (SD)*	*Means (SD)*	*Means (SD)*	*Means (SD)*
Trust				
Capacity trust	5.09 (1.00)	4.70 (0.94)	4.90 (0.79)	4.46 (0.83)
Moral trust	4.31 (0.92)	4.13 (1.02)	4.06 (0.96)	3.93 (1.15)
Social perception				
Warmth	4.18 (1.03)	4.29 (1.24)	3.88 (1.13)	4.00 (1.42)
Competence	4.41 (0.88)	4.04 (1.11)	4.46 (0.81)	3.63 (1.34)
Humanness				
Human uniqueness	4.21 (1.21)	4.17 (1.16)	3.87 (0.89)	3.71 (1.19)
Human nature	3.32 (0.93)	3.17 (1.08)	2.99 (1.06)	3.68 (0.83)

2.4 Participants

We recruited 95 participants via various social media, of which we deleted 6 responses (i.e., completion rate below 75%) from further analyses. We analyzed the data of the remaining 89 participants (52% male, 48% female), with age ranging from 18 to 79 ($M = 29.1$, $SD = 14.4$). Participants had an average knowledge in the robotics domain ($M = 3.6$, $SD = 1.7$) but a lower experience with robots ($M = 2.6$, $SD = 1.6$), as indicated on a 7-point Likert scale from 1 = 'no knowledge/experience' to 7 = 'very knowledgeable/experienced'. Neither knowledge about nor experience with robots influenced any of the measures in our study (i.e., no significant correlations with any of the dependent variables).

3 Results

To test our hypotheses, we ran a series of two-way ANOVAs with robot gender (male vs. female) and task type (analytical vs. social) as independent variables. Normality checks and Levene's test indicated that test assumptions were met.

3.1 Trust

We observed a significant main effect for task type ($F(3,1) = 4.79$, $p = .031$, $d = .47$) on capacity trust, but not for robot gender ($F(3,1) = 1.27$, $p = .264$, $d = .25$) nor their interaction effect ($F(3,1)$ 0.02, $p = .885$, $d = .05$). However, no significant main effect was found for robot gender ($F(3,1) = 2.05$, $p = .156$, $d = .31$) or task type (F(3,1) = 1.26, p = .264, $d = .25$) on moral trust nor for their interaction effect ($F(3,1)$ 0.10, $p = .748$, $d = .06$). These results suggest that only people's capacity trust in a robot is affected and exclusively by the given task. Specifically, participants have higher trust in a robot's capacity when it performed an analytical task compared to a social task (see Fig. 2).

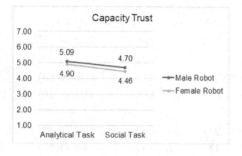

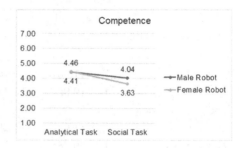

Fig. 2. Effect of robot gender vs. task type on capacity trust

Fig. 3. Effect of robot gender vs. task type on competence

3.2 Social Perception

We found no significant main effect for robot gender ($F(3,1) = 1.26$, $p = .265$, $d = .25$) or task type ($F(3,1) = 0.19$, $p = .666$, $d = .09$) on warmth nor for their interaction effect ($F(3,1)$ ¡ 0.01, $p = .990$, $d = .05$). However, we did observe a significant main effect for task type ($F(3,1) = 7.11$, $p = .009$, $d = .58$) on competence, but not for robot gender ($F(3,1) = 0.62$, $p = .434$, $d = .17$) nor their interaction effect ($F(3,1) = 1.04$, $p = .311$, $d = .22$). These results suggest that people's social perception of a robot is mainly affected by the given task. Specifically, independent of robot gender, people ascribe higher competence when a robot performs an analytical task compared to a social task (see Fig. 3).

3.3 Humanness

We observed a nearing significant main effect for robot gender ($F(3,1) = 2.77$, $p = .100$, $d = .35$) on human uniqueness, but not for task type ($F(3,1) = 0.17$, $p = .683$, $d = .09$) nor their interaction effect ($F(3,1) = 0.06$, $p = .812$, $d = .06$). Moreover, no significant main effect was observed for robot gender ($F(3,1) = 0.18$, $p = .671$, $d = .09$) nor for task type ($F(3,1) = 1.51$, $p = .223$, $d = .28$) on human nature while their interaction effect approached significance ($F(3,1) = 3.80$, $p = .055$, $d = .44$). These results suggest a robot's gender or given task does not effect people's humanness perception of a robot, while a data trend appears where: (1) perceptions of a robot's human uniqueness might be affected by robot gender; and (2) perceptions of a robot's human nature might be a combined effect between robot gender and task type. Specifically, participants seem more inclined to dehumanize female robots to animals lacking higher-level mental processes (i.e., lacking human uniqueness) compared to male robots independent of the given task (see Fig. 4). Moreover, participants seem to dehumanize robots to emotionless objects (i.e., lacking human nature) exclusively when female robots perform analytical tasks or male robots perform social tasks (see Fig. 5).

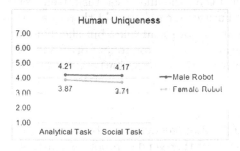

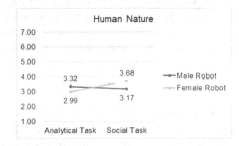

Fig. 4. Effect of robot gender vs. task type on human uniqueness

Fig. 5. Effect of robot gender vs. task type on human nature

4   General Discussion

Our study expands existing knowledge in HRI on robot gender and appearance-task fit by conducting an online vignette study manipulating robot gender (male vs. female) and task type (analytical vs. social) in a between subject's design to investigate their effects on social perception, trust, and humanness.

Our results indicate that people's trust in a robot is mainly determined by its capacity, but not its morality, and independent of the robot's gender. These results show that trust evaluations of a robot are not linked to a robot's gender as we hypothesized (H1). Instead, our results indicate that trusting robots is more strongly associated with the performed task. Additionally, robots are perceived as more competent when it performs an analytical task compared to performing a social task, independent of its gender. This finding contradicts our hypothesis expecting an effect for robot gender on people's social perception of a robot, independent of performed task (H2). When associating gendered robots with specific tasks, the observed effects of gender stereotyping in both the psychology [3] and HRI [13] research seem to steer away from the genderedness of the robot's embodiment towards the (perhaps also perceived gender-stereotypical) performed tasks –at least in terms of social perception and trust in such robots. An earlier study examining the relationship among occupational gender-roles, user trust and gendered robots also found no significant difference in the capacity trust of a robot when considering its gender [5]. Similarly, another HRI study on gender-task fit [25] has reported that people are less willing to accept help from a robot when executing a typically female task (i.e., a social task).

These combined results on predominant effects for task type, eliminating the potential effect of the gendered embodiment, are not necessarily surprising. Prior research shows that people in general hold more utilitarian perceptions of robots [9,12,15,41] indicating a preference for executing instrumental tasks. However, we must highlight potential limitation of the stimuli used in our study. Although the male robot was rated as significantly more male than the female robot, it was still on the female side of the gender scale. Similarly, the social task was rated as significantly less analytical than the analytical task itself, yet it was on the analytical side of the scale. Future research should therefore not only explore other task descriptions, occupations, or social roles, but should also further investigate different gendered appearances cues for robots or include a gender-neutral robot as well as explore consequential (interaction) effects of such gender and task manipulations on social perception and trust in HRI. Furthermore, research in psychology [6] as well as HRI [34] shows interaction effects for trust between the gender of the participant and that of the social other. Such interaction effects between participant and robot gender have been reported [30] indicating increased uncanny reactions to other-gender robots when that robot conforms to gender expectations of warm females and competent males. Therefore, exploring interaction effects between the participant gender and robot gender in the context of gender-task fit sounds promising as well.

Psychology literature informed our hypothesized effect of people's humanness perceptions of a robot to be a function of both robot gender and performed task (H3). Although our data did not support this, we feel disposed to discuss the observed trend in our data indicating a potential interaction effect between robot gender and performed task on a robot's perceived humanness. This trend implies that people tend to dehumanize female robots (regardless of given task) to animals lacking higher-level mental processes. Sexist responses to female robots have been reported in HRI research more generally [36,40]. Additionally, the trend implies that people tend to dehumanize robots to emotionless objects only when gendered robots perform tasks contradicting gender stereotypes (i.e., a gender-task interaction effect). Research in social psychology has shown that women are dehumanized to both animals and objects [33], which is a trigger for aggressing women [17]. Intermingling gender effects into current debates on robot abuse (e.g., that mindless robots get bullied [23]) might offer alternative perspectives on these issues which future research should further explore.

The field of social robotics aims to build robots that can engage in social interaction scenarios with humans in a natural, familiar, efficient, and above all intuitive manner [10]. The easiest way to deal with social expectations of gendered robots including consequential stereotypical inferences is to enhance people's social acceptance of gendered robots by tailoring their gendered appearance to their intended task. Alternatively, perhaps an idealistic vision might be that robots could offer a unique potential to illuminate implicit bias in social cognition by challenging persisting gender-task stereotypes in society.

References

1. Bargh, J.A.: The cognitive monster: the case against controllability of automatic stereotype effects. In: Chaiken, S., Trope, Y. (eds.) Dual Process Theories in Social Psychology. Guilford Press, New York (1999)
2. Bartneck, C., et al.: Robots and racism. In: HRI 2018, pp. 196–204. ACM (2018)
3. Bem, S.L.: The measurement of psychological androgyny. J. Consult. Clin. Psychol. **42**(2), 155–162 (1974)
4. Broverman, I.K., Vogel, S.R., Broverman, D.M., Clarkson, F.E., Rosenkrantz, P.S.: Sex-role stereotypes: a current appraisal 1. J. Soc. Issues **28**(2), 59–78 (1972)
5. Bryant, D., Borenstein, J., Howard, A.: Why should we gender? The effect of robot gendering and occupational stereotypes on human trust and perceived competency. In: HRI 2020, pp. 13–21. ACM (2020)
6. Buchan, N.R., Croson, R.T.A., Solnick, S.: Trust and gender: an examination of behavior and beliefs in the investment game. J. Econ. Behav. Organ. **68**(3-4), 466–476 (2008)
7. Cuddy, A.J.C., Fiske, S.T., Glick, P.: Warmth and competence as universal dimensions of social perception map. Adv. Exp.l Soc. Psychol. **40**, 61–149 (2008)
8. De Graaf, M.M.A., Ben Allouch, S.: The evaluation of different roles for domestic social robots. In: RO-MAN 2015, pp. 676–681. IEEE (2015)
9. De Graaf, M.M.A., Ben Allouch, S.: Anticipating our future robot society. In: RO-MAN 2016, pp. 755–762. IEEE (2016)
10. de Graaf, M.M.A., Ben Allouch, S., van Dijk, J.A.G.M.: What makes robots social?: A user's perspective on characteristics for social human-robot interaction. In: ICSR 2015. LNCS (LNAI), vol. 9388, pp. 184–193. Springer, Cham (2015). https://doi.org/10.1007/978-3-319-25554-5_19
11. Devine, P.G.: Automatic and controlled processes in prejudice stereotypes and personal beliefs. In: Pratkanis, A.R., Breckler, S.J., Greenwald, A.G. (eds.) Ohio State University, vol. 3. Attitudes and Persuasion Associates Inc. (1989)
12. Enz, S., Diruf, M., Spielhagen, C., Zoll, C., Vargas, P.A.: The social role of robots in the future–explorative measurement of hopes and fears. Int. J. Soc. Robot. **3**(3), 263–271 (2011)
13. Eyssel, F., Hegel, F.: (s) he's got the look: gender stereotyping of robots. J. Appl. Soc. Psychol. **42**(9), 2213–2230 (2012)
14. Gaudiello, I., Zibetti, E., Lefort, S., Chetouani, M., Ivaldi, S.: Trust as indicator of robot functional and social acceptance: An experimental study on user conformation to iCub answers. Comput. Hum. Behav. **61**, 633–655 (2016)
15. Goetz, J., Kiesler, S., Powers, A.: Matching robot appearance and behavior to tasks to improve human-robot cooperation. In: RO-MAN 2003, pp. 55–60. IEEE (2003)
16. Hancock, P., Billings, D., Schaefer, K., Chen, J., De Visser, E., Parasuraman, R.: A meta-analysis of factors affecting trust in human-robot interaction. Hum. Factors **53**(5), 517–527 (2011)
17. Haslam, N.: Dehumanization: an integrative review. Pers. Soc. Psychol. Rev. **10**(3), 252–264 (2006)
18. Hawley, P.H.: Social dominance in childhood and adolescence competence and aggression may go hand in hand. Aggression and adaptation: The bright side to bad behavior, pp. 1–29 (2007)

19. He, J.C., Kang, S.K., Tse, K., Toh, S.M.: Stereotypes at work: occupational stereotypes predict race and gender segregation in the workforce. J. Vocat. Behav. **115**, 103318 (2019)
20. Heilman, M.E.: Gender stereotypes and workplace bias. Res. Organ. Behav. **32**, 113–135 (2012)
21. Jung, E.H., Waddell, T.F., Sundar, S.S.: Feminizing robots: user responses to gender cues on robot body and screen. In: CHI Extended Abstracts, pp. 3107–3113. ACM (2016)
22. Kaniarasu, P., Steinfeld, A.M.: Effects of blame on trust in human robot interaction. In: RO-MAN 2014, pp. 850–855. IEEE (2014)
23. Keijsers, M., Bartneck, C.: Mindless robots get bullied. In: HRI 2018, pp. 205–214. ACM (2018)
24. Kellie, D.J., Blake, K.R., Brooks, R.C.: What drives female objectification?: An investigation of appearance-based interpersonal perceptions and the objectification of women. PloS one **14**(8), e0221388 (2019)
25. Kuchenbrandt, D., Häring, M., Eichberg, J., Eyssel, F., André, E.: Keep an eye on the task!: how gender typicality of tasks influence human-robot interactions. Int. J. Soc. Robot. **6**(3), 417–427 (2014). https://doi.org/10.1007/s12369-014-0244-0
26. Lee, S., Lau, I.Y., Hong, Y.: Effects of appearance and functions on likability and perceived occupational suitability of robots. J Cogn. Eng. Decis. Making **5**(2), 232–250 (2011)
27. Loughnan, S., Haslam, N.: Animals and androids: implicit associations between social categories and nonhumans. Psychol. Sci. **18**(2), 116–121 (2007)
28. McCauley, C.R., Jussim, L.J., Lee, Y.T.: Stereotype Accuracy: Toward Appreciating Group Differences. American Psychological Association (1995)
29. Nass, C., Steuer, J., Tauber, E.R.: Computers are social actors. In: CHI 1994, pp. 72–78 (1994)
30. Otterbacher, J., Talias, M.: S/he's too warm/agentic!: the influence of gender on uncanny reactions to robots. In: HRI 2017, pp. 214–223. IEEE (2017)
31. Patterson, C.H.: Empathy, warmth, and genuineness in psychotherapy of reviews. Psychother. Theory Res. Pract. Train. **21**(4), 431 (1984)
32. Powers, A., Kiesler, S.: The advisor robot: tracing people's mental model from a robot's physical attributes. In: HRI 2006, pp. 218–225. ACM (2006)
33. Rudman, L.A., Mescher, K.: Of animals and objects: men's implicit dehumanization of women and likelihood of sexual aggression. Pers. Soc. Psychol. Bull. **38**(6), 734–746 (2012)
34. Siegel, M., Breazeal, C., Norton, M.I.: Persuasive robotics: the influence of robot gender on human behavior. In: IROS 2009, pp. 2563–2568. IEEE (2009)
35. Spence, J.T., Helmreich, R.L.: Masculinity and Femininity Dimensions, Correlates, and Antecedents. University of Texas Press (1979)
36. Strait, M.K., Aguillon, C., Contreras, V., Garcia, N.: The public's perception of humanlike robots. In: RO-MAN 2017, pp. 1418–1423. IEEE (2017)
37. Tajfel, H., Billig, M.G., Bundy, R.P., Flament, C.: Social categorization and intergroup behaviour. Eur. Soc. Psychol. **1**(2), 149–178 (1971)
38. Tay, B., Jung, Y., Park, T.: When stereotypes meet robots: the double-edge sword of robot gender and personality in human-robot interaction. Comput. Hum. Behav. **38**, 75–84 (2014)
39. Ullman, D., Malle, B.F.: Measuring gains and losses in human-robot trust: evidence for differentiable components of trust. In: HRI 2019, pp. 618–619. ACM (2019)

40. Veletsianos, G., Scharber, C., Döring, A.: When sex, drugs, and violence enter the classroom: conversations between adolescents and a female pedagogical agent. Interact. Comput. **20**(3), 292–301 (2008)
41. Wang, X., Krumhuber, E.G.: Mind perception of robots varies with their economic versus social function. Front. Psychol. **9**, 1230 (2018)
42. You, S., Robert Jr, L.: Human-robot similarity and willingness to work with a robotic co-worker. In: HRI 2018, pp. 251–260 (2018)

Gender Revealed: Evaluating the Genderedness of Furhat's Predefined Faces

Giulia Perugia[1,2]([✉]) [iD], Alessandra Rossi[3] [iD], and Silvia Rossi[3,4] [iD]

[1] Department of Information Technology, Uppsala University, Uppsala, Sweden
[2] Human Technology Interaction Group, Department of Industrial Engineering
and Innovation Sciences, Eindhoven University of Technology,
Eindhoven, The Netherlands
giulia.perugia@it.uu.se
[3] ICAROS Center, University of Naples Federico II, Naples, Italy
[4] Department of Electrical Engineering and Information Technologies,
University of Naples Federico II, Naples, Italy
{alessandra.rossi, silvia.rossi}@unina.it

Abstract. In this study, we employed Furhat to investigate how people attribute gender to a robot and whether the attribution of gender might elicit stereotypes already at a first impression. We involved 223 participants in an online study and asked them to rate 15 of Furhat's predefined faces in terms of femininity, masculinity, communion, and agency, and identify which facial cues they based their attribution of gender upon. Our results show that Furhat's predefined faces are attributed the same gender predicted by their names, except for one face which was perceived as androgynous. They disclose that feminine robots are perceived as less agentic than masculine robots already at a first impression, and reveal that vocal cues have higher relevance than facial cues in determining the gender attributed to a robot. Besides providing a complete account of the genderedness of Furhat's predefined faces, the present study also raises awareness of the importance of gender in the design of robots and provides a starting point to design more inclusive robotic technologies.

Keywords: Gendered robots · Human-robot interaction · Social robotics · Inclusive robotics

1 Introduction

Humanoid robots provide users with a natural and largely familiar type of interaction due to their ability of using a rich variety of verbal and non-verbal communication modes. However, designing robots in the likes of humans might have profound implications. For instance, it might bring roboticists and HRI

This work has been supported by Italian PON I&C 2014–2020 within the BRILLO research project "Bartending Robot for Interactive Long-Lasting Operations", no. F/190066/01-02/X44.

researchers to equip robots with gender cues. This seemingly innocuous process might become problematic, as implicit gender biases and stereotypical gender norms might be involuntarily transferred into the interaction and contribute to perpetuating harmful societal stereotypes.

Several researchers have investigated how the genderedness of a humanoid robot affects people's perception of it, for instance, in terms of trustworthiness [7, 13], likability [10], competence [6], and acceptance [16]. However, the attribution of gender as a process of its own is understudied. Although one might argue that the best way to address gender in Social Robotics is to not provide robots with gender at all, humanoid robots that are designed as genderless are not necessarily perceived as such [23]. Hence, understanding how humanoid robots are gendered and which cues guide the categorization might help us design more inclusive robotic technologies, and escape the gender binarism that is predominant in Social Robotics and society at large [22].

In the literature, robots have been gendered in multiple ways. Tannenbaum et al. identified six main criteria through which gender is assigned to a robot [24]: (i) *Voice*: voices with a low frequency ($\approx$110 Hz) have been identified as masculine, while voices with a high frequency ($\approx$210 Hz) as feminine [17,21]; (ii) *Name*: together with voice, names, such as Mary and James, have been used to manipulate the gender of the robot [6]; (iii) *Anatomy*: body proportions, such as the robot's waist-to-hips ratio and shoulders' width were used to manipulate the robot's genderedness [4], (iv) *Color*: stereotypically gendered colors, such as pink and blue, have been employed to elicit the perception of a robot as feminine and masculine [18], (v) *Personality*: submissiveness is often perceived as a feminine personality trait, while dominance as a masculine one [15], and (vi) *Domain of deployment*: feminine robots are for instance employed in healthcare scenarios, while masculine robots in security contexts [5,25].

The choice of the cues used to manipulate a robot's gender is often bound to the robot's embodiment. Traditional robot designs (e.g., Pepper or NAO) allow researchers to change only a few gender cues, primarily voice and name. Newer robotic designs, such as blended embodiments (i.e., a combination of animated agents and physical robots), instead, give scientists the possibility to study how the combination of multiple gender cues can form a perception of genderedness, and how these cues are hierarchically organized. A few of these new robotic platforms provide researchers with a predefined set of gendered faces to use in HRI studies and robotic applications. However, in most cases, it is unclear whether the gender incorporated by designers in these predefined faces is actually the same attributed by users, as no documentation is provided in this sense. Not knowing how a particular face is perceived might cause roboticists to arbitrarily choose the face to use in a specific context based on common sense knowledge and might lead them to incorporate their stereotypical image of gender in the interaction.

Gender attribution to humanoid robots is also likely to prompt stereotypical judgments [11,25]. Humans form first impressions of other individuals in a few milliseconds [26], and warmth and competence (or agency) are among the first perceptual dimensions to arise [12]. This process of impression formation extends to humanoid robots as well. For instance, Paetzel-Prüsmann et al. [19]

showed that participants formed an impression of Furhat's warmth and competence in only 5 s and this impression did not change over multiple repeated interactions with the same robot. More importantly, in line with the Social Psychology research showing that women are more often attributed communal traits and men agentic traits [2], HRI studies have shown that warmth is a trait more often attributed to feminine robots, and competence (or agency) to masculine ones [9]. Hence, human-humanoid interactions are as prone to gender stereotyping as human-human interactions.

This work aims to bring roboticists' attention to the important issue of gender in the design of robots and its proneness to elicit stereotyping. We leveraged on the blended embodiment robot Furhat [3] and carried out a study aimed at understanding (i) how Furhat's predefined faces are perceived in terms of genderedness, (ii) which cues in these faces drive the perception of genderedness, and (iii) how Furhat's perceived gender affects stereotypical judgements of communion and agency.

2   Design

We designed a between-subject study with 15 conditions corresponding to 15 different faces of the Furhat robot (cf. Fig. 1). We included in the study all Furhat's predefined faces, except for those depicting famous (e.g., Barack Obama) and fictitious characters (e.g., Elsa). Participants were allocated to one of the 15 conditions. Within each condition, they watched a short introductory video clip of the Furhat robot saying: "Hello! I am Furhat, nice to meet you", and completed a questionnaire before and after watching the video. The robots with female names – Fedora, Arianne, René, Mei, Anne, and Ursula – were given a female voice. The robots with male names – Ted, Fred, Max, August, Marty, Olaf, and Geremy – were given a male voice. The default face, which did not have any name, was used in two separate conditions, with a female and a male voice respectively. The videos had the same length (3 s) and were shot from the same frontal angle with the same background.

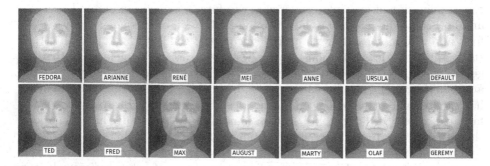

Fig. 1. The fourteen agents used in the study. The default robot (the rightmost on the top row) was used both with a female or male voice (i.e., default female and default male).

2.1 Measures and Procedure

The online questionnaire was organized as follows. In its initial part, we asked participants their demographic information: age, gender, nationality, occupation, English level, and previous experience with robots. In a second step, we asked them to fill out the Ten Item Personality Measure (TIPI, 7-point Likert scale items ranging from 1 = strongly disagree to 7 = strongly agree) [14], which gauged their Extraversion, Agreeableness, Conscientiousness, Emotional Stability, and Openness to Experience. Then, participants were presented with the short introductory video of the robot and were asked to rate the robot on nine traits extracted from the 20-item version of the Bem Sex Role Inventory (7-point Likert scale ranging from 1 = strongly disagree to 7 = strongly agree) [8]. Four were communion traits, hence more related to friendliness and helpfulness [12]: tender, gentle, affectionate, and sympathetic. Five were agency traits, thus more connected with perceived ability, skillfulness, and efficacy [12]: having a strong personality, having leadership abilities, being able to make decisions easily, being able to defend its own beliefs, and being able to act as a leader. As a further step, participants watched the introductory video again and rated the same robot on femininity and masculinity (7-point Likert scale ranging from 1 = strongly disagree to 7 = strongly agree), and adult-likeness (semantic differential ranging from 1 = the robot is similar to a child, to 7 = the robot is similar to an older adult). They also selected which facial cues guided them in assessing the robot's gender choosing between: eyebrows shape, eyebrows size, size of the eyes, shape of the eyes, color of the eyes, nose width, nose shape, eyelashes, lips shape, color of the lips, color of the cheeks, or other. Finally, in the last step of the questionnaire, participants were asked to give their opinion on whether robots should have a gender (7-point Likert scale items ranging 1= from strongly disagree to 7 = strongly agree) and why they should (or should not) have a gender (i.e., open question). We also measured participants' attention through a check question (i.e., "What is the name of the robot in the video?" or "What does the robot in the video do?").

2.2 Participants

An a priori sample size calculation using G*Power considering ANCOVA as analysis (fixed effects, main effects and interactions, $\alpha = .05$, power = .95, number of groups = 15, number of covariates = 3), and moderate effects (f(V) = 0.25), resulted in a sample size of 211 participants. Hence, we recruited 225 participants on Amazon Mechanical Turk (AMT) to take part in the study, 15 per condition. Participants who failed the attention check were immediately rejected, and new participants were recruited on the go. Overall, 310 participants took part in the AMT study. Sixty-four of them failed the attention check and were excluded from the study during data collection. Another 112 were excluded once the data collection was completed because of odd patterns in their demographic and open-end answers. To compensate for the small sample size on AMT, we recruited another 100 participants through social media platforms, and asked them to fill out the same AMT questionnaire. We excluded 11 of them due to failing the attention check. The final sample size was composed of 223 participants (92 women, 129 men, 2 did not specify), 134 filled out the questionnaire on AMT, 89 on Google Forms. Participants had an age comprised between 19 and 63 years ($M = 33.46$, $SD = 8.52$), 21 of them had a high school diploma, 107 a bachelor's degree, 58 a Master's degree, 36 a PhD, and 1 did not specify. The sample was quite heterogeneous, in terms of nationality, with most participants from the US ($N = 99$). 72.2% of participants had previous experience with robots, while 27.8% had never seen a robot before.

3   Results

3.1   Perceived Femininity and Masculinity of Furhat's Faces

As a first step, we performed two ANCOVAs with agent as between-subject factor (i.e., Furhat's fifteen faces), participants' age, robot's perceived adult-likeness, and participants' level of agreement with the assertion "I believe robot's should have a gender" as covariates, and the ratings of femininity and masculinity as dependent variables. The results disclosed a significant main effect of agent on both perceived femininity ($F(14, 204) = 19.949$, $p < .001$, $\eta p^2 = .578$) and perceived masculinity ($F(14, 208) = 16.070$, $p < .001$, $\eta p^2 = .524$). In terms of covariates, participants' age was not a significant covariate of perceived femininity ($F(1, 204) = .098$, $p = .754$, $\eta p^2 < .001$) and masculinity ($F(1, 204) = 1.212$, $p = .272$, $\eta p^2 = .006$). However, while the robot's perceived adult-likeness and participants' level of agreement with the assertion "I believe robot's should

Table 1. Descriptive statistics of femininity and masculinity: mean (M) and standard deviation (SD).

	Feminine M (SD)	Masculine M (SD)
Fedora	6.33 (0.82)	1.93 (0.88)
Arianne	5.94 (1.25)	2.59 (1.80)
René	5.72 (1.13)	2.22 (1.22)
Mei	5.38 (1.98)	2.46 (1.45)
def. fem.	5.27 (1.53)	2.20 (1.01)
Anne	5.25 (1.42)	3.08 (1.78)
Ursula	5.00 (1.77)	2.53 (1.46)
Ted	3.46 (1.81)	4.07 (1.89)
Fred	2.87 (1.54)	4.93 (1.59)
def. male	2.73 (1.91)	4.93 (2.09)
Max	2.20 (1.70)	5.00 (1.89)
August	2.44 (1.31)	5.63 (1.50)
Marty	2.50 (1.29)	5.86 (1.17)
Olaf	1.80 (0.77)	6.00 (1.36)
Geremy	1.80 (1.42)	6.20 (0.94)

have a gender" were not significant covariates of perceived masculinity (adult-likeness: $F(1, 204) \approx .000$, $p = .996$, $\eta p^2 < .001$; robot's should have a gender: $F(1, 204) = 1.382$, $p = .241$, $\eta p^2 = .007$), they were significant covariates of perceived femininity (adult-likeness: $F(1, 204) = 5.563$, $p = .019$, $\eta p^2 = .027$; robot's should have a gender: $F(1, 204) = 5.689$, $p = .018$, $\eta p^2 = .027$). Further Pearson's Product-moment correlations disclosed that the robot's perceived femininity was significantly positively correlated with people's belief that robots should have a gender ($r(221) = .181$, $p = .007$), and perceived masculinity with the robot's adult-likeness ($r(221) = .177$, $p = .008$).

With regard to differences in femininity and masculinity across Furhat's faces, post-hoc analyses with a Bonferroni correction disclosed that Fedora, Arianne, René, Mei, the default female, and Ursula were perceived as significantly more feminine than Fred, the default male, Max, August, Marty, Olaf, and Geremy (cf. Table 1 and 2, and Fig. 2). Similarly, Fedora, Arianne, René, Mei, the default female, and Ursula were perceived as significantly less masculine than Fred, the default male, Max, August, Marty, Olaf, and Geremy (cf. Table 2 and Fig. 2). Two agents constituted an exception to these otherwise clear-cut results, Anne and Ted. Indeed, while Anne was perceived by participants as differing from Fred, the default male, Max, August, Marty, Olaf, and Geremy in terms of femininity, it was perceived as significantly less masculine only with respect to August, Geremy, Marty, and Olaf, but not compared to Ted, Fred, the default male, and Max (cf. Table 2 and Fig. 2). Ted was perceived as significantly less feminine than Arianne, Fedora, and René, significantly more masculine than Fedora, and marginally less masculine than Geremy (cf. Table 2). However, Ted did not differ in terms of femininity from René, Mei, the default female, Anne, and Ursula, and, in terms of masculinity from Fred, the default male, Max, August, Marty, and Olaf (cf. Table 2). If we look at the plots in Fig. 2, we can see that Ted's perceived femininity and masculinity are located close to the central values of the respective scales, hence we can assume that Ted was perceived by participants as androgynous.

3.2 Facial Gender Cues

As a second step in the analysis, we wanted to understand which facial cues guided participants in the assessment of the robot's genderedness. When taking all robots' faces into account, the most influential cues seemed to be the shape of the lips (53%) and of the eyebrows (49%). These were followed, in descending order, by the shape of the eyes (37%), the eyebrows size (34%), the color of the lips (31%), the size of the eyes and the nose shape (28%), the nose width (22%), the eyelashes (20%), and the color of the cheeks (12%). When taking into account the robot's faces perceived as the most feminine, most masculine, and neutral, instead, we observed slightly different patterns. Fedora's genderedness was mostly ($\geq 40\%$) based on the color of its lips (67%), the eyebrows shape (53%), the lips shape (47%), and the eyelashes (40%). Geremy's genderedness was mostly based on the eyebrows size (67%), the eyebrows shape (60%), and the nose width (40%), although several participants mentioned mustaches and beard in the field "other" (40%). Finally, Ted's genderedness was mostly based on the shape of its eyes (54%), eyebrows (46%), and lips (46%).

3.3   Perceived Communion and Agency of Gendered Robots

As a third step, we carried out a factorial analysis using the communion and agency traits from [8]. All preconditions for running a factorial analysis were satisfied as shown by a Keyser-Meyer Olkin measure of sampling adequacy of .860 and a significant Bartlett's test of sphericity ($X^2(36) = 997.42$, $p < 001$). As predicted, the factorial analysis confirmed the existence of two factors. *Communion* (Cronbach's $\alpha = .777$) included the items tender (.828), gentle (.790), sympathetic (.674), and affectionate (.672), whereas *agency* (Cronbach's $\alpha = .893$) encompassed the items having leadership abilities (.867), being able to act as a leader (.857), having a strong personality (.780), being able to defend its own beliefs (.767), and being able to make decisions easily (.758).

To understand whether the perceived gender of the robot influenced people's perception of communion and agency, we labelled each one of the 15 agents as either feminine ($N = 105$), masculine ($N = 105$), or androgynous ($N = 13$) based on the results in Sect. 3.1. Given the large difference in sample size between the androgynous and the feminine and masculine conditions, we excluded the androgynous condition from the analysis. We performed two ANCOVAs with

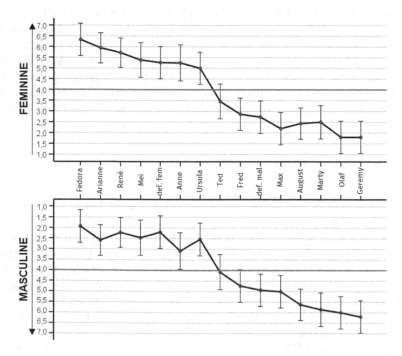

Fig. 2. Plots of the scores of femininity and masculinity per robot. The red line indicates the central value of the Likert scale.

Table 2. Results of the post-hoc analyses exploring differences in perceived femininity and masculinity across Furhat's faces (Bonferroni corrected). The significant results are highlighted in bold. All the results that are not reported in the table had a $p = 1.00$.

		Ted	Fred	def.male	Max	August	Marty	Olaf	Geremy
Fedora	fem.	**<.001**	**<.001**	**<.001**	**<.001**	**<.001**	**<.001**	**<.001**	**<.001**
	mas.	**.025**	**<.001**	**<.001**	**<.001**	**<.001**	**<.001**	**<.001**	**<.001**
Arianne	fem.	**.001**	**<.001**	**<.001**	**<.001**	**<.001**	**<.001**	**<.001**	**<.001**
	mas.	.715	**.003**	**.001**	**.001**	**<.001**	**<.001**	**<.001**	**<.001**
René	fem.	**.001**	**<.001**	**<.001**	**<.001**	**<.001**	**<.001**	**<.001**	**<.001**
	mas.	.097	**<.001**	**<.001**	**<.001**	**<.001**	**<.001**	**<.001**	**<.001**
Mei	fem.	.054	**<.001**	**<.001**	**<.001**	**<.001**	**<.001**	**<.001**	**<.001**
	mas.	.468	**.011**	**.003**	**.002**	**<.001**	**<.001**	**<.001**	**< .001**
def. fem.	fem.	.111	**<.001**	**<.001**	**<.001**	**<.001**	**<.001**	**<.001**	**<.001**
	mas.	.098	**<.001**	**<.001**	**<.001**	**<.001**	**<.001**	**<.001**	**<.001**
Anne	fem.	.140	**.001**	**.001**	**<.001**	**<.001**	**<.001**	**<.001**	**<.001**
	mas.	1.00	.258	.128	.147	**.001**	**.001**	**<.001**	**<.001**
Ursula	fem.	.451	**.002**	**.002**	**<.001**	**<.001**	**<.001**	**<.001**	**<.001**
	mas.	.677	**.003**	**.001**	**.002**	**<.001**	**<.001**	**<.001**	**<.001**
Ted	fem.	-	1.00	1.00	1.00	1.00	1.00	.195	.354
	mas.	-	1.00	1.00	1.00	.553	.397	.147	.056

the perceived gender of the robot (feminine and masculine) and the gender of participants (women and men) as between-subject factors, participants' age, robot's perceived adult-likeness, and participants' level of agreement with the assertion "I believe robot's should have a gender" as covariates, and the ratings of perceived communion and agency as dependent variables.

The results did not show a significant main effect of participants' gender on their attribution of communion ($F(1, 201) = 1,719$, $p = .191$, $\eta p^2 = .008$) and agency to the robot ($F(1, 201) = .024$, $p = .877$, $\eta p^2 < .001$), nor a significant main effect of the perceived gender of the robot on perceived communion ($F(1, 201) = .077$, $p = .781$, $\eta p^2 < .001$). The interaction effect of robot's perceived gender and participant's gender was also not significant for both communion ($F(1, 201) = .650$, $p = .421$, $\eta p^2 = .003$) and agency ($F(1, 201) = 1.847$, $p = .176$, $\eta p^2 = .009$). Interestingly though, masculine robots were attributed more agency ($M = 3.78$, $SD = 1.48$, $F(1, 201) = 7.966$, $p = .005$, $\eta p^2 = .038$) than feminine ones ($M = 3.33$, $SD = 1.25$). When analyzing the covariates, another interesting result showed up. While participants' age and robots' adult-likeness were not significant covariates of communion (age: $F(1, 201) = .703$, $p = .403$, $\eta p^2 = .003$; robot's adultlikeness: $F(1, 201) = 1.391$, $p = .241$, $\eta p^2 < .001$) and agency (age: $F(1, 201) = .247$, $p = .620$, $\eta p^2 = .001$; robot's adultlikeness: $F(1, 201) = .058$, $p = .810$, $\eta p^2 < .001$), "I believe robots should have a gender" was a significant covariate of agency ($F(1, 201) = 4.563$, $p = .034$, $\eta p^2 = .022$) and a marginally significant

Table 3. Results of Pearson Product-Moment correlation between participants' personality traits and the robot's perceived femininity, masculinity, communion, and agency. In bold, the significant values.

		Personality traits				
		Extraver.	Agreeable.	Conscient.	Em. Stability	Open to Exp.
Femininity	$r(208)$	−.058	−.049	.058	−.030	−.009
	p	.401	.484	.402	.668	.901
Masculinity	$r(208)$	.121	.072	−.051	−.005	.053
	p	.079	.298	.466	.938	.442
Communion	$r(208)$	.010	.050	−.001	.082	−.042
	p	.890	.469	.986	.238	.548
Agency	$r(208)$	**193**	.111	.064	−.004	.032
	p	**.005**	.109	.354	.958	.642

covariate of communion ($F(1, 201) = 2.950$, $p = .087$, $\eta p^2 = .014$). Further Pearson's Product-moment correlations confirmed a significant positive correlation between agency and the belief that robots should have a gender ($r(208) = .137$, $p = .048$) and a marginally positive correlation between this latter and communion ($r(208) = .115$, $p = .097$).

As a last step in the analysis, we performed a Pearson Product-Moment Correlation (two-tailed) between participants' five personality traits and their perceptions of the robot's femininity, masculinity, communion and agency. Except for extraversion, which was significantly positively correlated with perceived agency, we did not find any other significant correlation (cf. Table 3).

4   Discussion

Most predefined Furhat's faces were attributed the same gender predicted by their names. However, our analyses revealed two additional findings: (i) vocal cues are more powerful than facial cues in guiding the attribution of gender to a robot, and (ii) under certain circumstances, humanoid robots such as Furhat can be perceived as androgynous. In fact, in our study, the same identical face (i.e., default) was perceived as feminine when accompanied by a female voice, and masculine when accompanied by a male voice, and the face named Ted received intermediate scores on both masculinity and femininity.

Further analyses we performed gave preliminary insights into how gender is attributed to a robot through its facial cues and how it might elicit stereotypes. They showed that the shape of lips and eyebrows is key to attribute gender to a robot's face and disclosed that masculine robots are perceived as more agentic than feminine ones even at a first impression. This is quite a novel result. Indeed, while the effects of a robot's genderedness on communion and agency had been observed before [4,9], they had not been documented after such a short exposure.

While participants' gender, age, and personality were unrelated to their perceptions of the robots, participants' belief that robots should be gendered was positively related to their ratings of the robot's femininity and agency. This result is particularly meaningful as it indicates that the belief that robots should be gendered is connected with the tendency to stereotype. In this context, it is also important to report that participants' perception of the robots' adult-likeness was positively correlated with their attribution of masculinity to the robot. Child-likeness, a bit like femininity, can be associated with vulnerability, whereas adult-likeness, similar to masculinity, with strength. This result is thus particularly revealing as it shows that, even if not immediately visible, gender stereotyping might be strong enough to leak into other perceptual dimensions.

These results are extremely interesting, but should be interpreted with caution. They refer to how appearance contributes to the formation of what Søraa calls socio-mechanical gender [23], and, therefore, they might be culture-dependent. Moreover, they are based on robot's faces that are mostly white, and voices that are either female or male. In the future, we plan to replicate the present study with faces differing in skin color and with genderless voices [1,5].

5   Conclusions

In this paper, we presented a study aimed at ranking the genderedness of Furhat's predefined faces, gaining a preliminary understanding of which facial cues elicit the attribution of gender in a robot's face, and disclose whether a robot's genderedness might bring people to attach stereotypes to it, even after a few seconds of exposure. The results of this study can be used to design less gender-normative robots, and promote a more inclusive and diverse HRI [20].

References

1. Meet Q the First Genderless Voice. https://www.genderlessvoice.com/
2. Abele, A.E.: The dynamics of masculine-agentic and feminine-communal traits: findings from a prospective study. J. Pers. Soc. Psychol. **85**(4), 768 (2003)
3. Al Moubayed, S., Beskow, J., Skantze, G., Granström, B.: Furhat: a back-projected human-like robot head for multiparty human-machine interaction. In: Esposito, A., Esposito, A.M., Vinciarelli, A., Hoffmann, R., Müller, V.C. (eds.) Cognitive Behavioural Systems. LNCS, vol. 7403, pp. 114–130. Springer, Heidelberg (2012). https://doi.org/10.1007/978-3-642-34584-5_9
4. Bernotat, J., Eyssel, F., Sachse, J.: The (fe)male robot: how robot body shape impacts first impressions and trust towards robots. Int. J. Soc. Robot. **13**(3), 477–489 (2019). https://doi.org/10.1007/s12369-019-00562-7
5. Bisconti Lucidi, P., Perugia, G.: How do we gender robots? Inquiring the relationship between perceptual cues and context of use. In: RO-MAN 2021 GenR Workshop Gendering Robots: Ongoing (Re)configurations of Gender in Robotics (2021)
6. Bryant, D., Borenstein, J., Howard, A.: Why should we gender? The effect of robot gendering and occupational stereotypes on human trust and perceived competency. In: Proceedings of the 2020 ACM/IEEE International Conference on Human-Robot Interaction, pp. 13–21 (2020)

7. Calvo-Barajas, N., Perugia, G., Castellano, G.: The effects of robot's facial expressions on children's first impressions of trustworthiness. In: 2020 29th IEEE International Conference on Robot and Human Interactive Communication (RO-MAN), pp. 165–171. IEEE (2020)
8. Choi, N., Fuqua, D.R., Newman, J.L.: Exploratory and confirmatory studies of the structure of the bem sex role inventory short form with two divergent samples. Edu. Psychol. Meas. **69**(4), 696–705 (2009)
9. Eyssel, F., Hegel, F.: (ε) he's got the look: gender stereotyping of robots 1. J. Appl. Soc. Psychol. **42**(9), 2213–2230 (2012)
10. Eyssel, F., Kuchenbrandt, D., Hegel, F., de Ruiter, L.: Activating elicited agent knowledge: how robot and user features shape the perception of social robots. In: 2012 IEEE RO-MAN: The 21st IEEE International Symposium on Robot and Human Interactive Communication, pp. 851–857. IEEE (2012)
11. Fiske, S.T.: Prejudices in cultural contexts: shared stereotypes (gender, age) versus variable stereotypes (race, ethnicity, religion). Perspect. Psychol. Sci. **12**(5), 791–799 (2017)
12. Fiske, S.T., Cuddy, A.J., Glick, P.: Universal dimensions of social cognition: warmth and competence. Trends Cognit. Sci. **11**(2), 77–83 (2007)
13. Ghazali, A.S., Ham, J., Barakova, E.I., Markopoulos, P.: Effects of robot facial characteristics and gender in persuasive human-robot interaction. Front. Robot. AI **5**, 73 (2018)
14. Gosling, S.D., Rentfrow, P.J., Swann, W.B., Jr.: A very brief measure of the big-five personality domains. J. Res. Pers. **37**(6), 504–528 (2003)
15. Kraus, M., Kraus, J., Baumann, M., Minker, W.: Effects of gender stereotypes on trust and likability in spoken human-robot interaction. In: Proceedings of the Eleventh International Conference on Language Resources and Evaluation (LREC 2018) (2018)
16. Kuchenbrandt, D., Häring, M., Eichberg, J., Eyssel, F., André, E.: Keep an eye on the task! how gender typicality of tasks influence human-robot interactions. Int. J. Soc. Robot. **6**(3), 417–427 (2014). https://doi.org/10.1007/s12369-014-0244-0
17. Nass, C.I., Brave, S.: Wired for Speech: How Voice Activates and Advances the Human-Computer Relationship. MIT Press, Cambridge (2005)
18. Neuteboom, S.Y., de Graaf, M.: Cobbler stick with your reads: People's perceptions of gendered robots performing gender stereotypical tasks. arXiv preprint arXiv:2104.06127 (2021)
19. Paetzel, M., Perugia, G., Castellano, G.: The persistence of first impressions: the effect of repeated interactions on the perception of a social robot. In: Proceedings of the 2020 ACM/IEEE International Conference on Human-Robot Interaction, pp. 73–82 (2020)
20. Poulsen, A., Fosch-Villaronga, E., Søraa, R.A.: Queering machines. Nat. Mach. Intell. **2**(3), 152 (2020)
21. Powers, A., Kiesler, S.: The advisor robot: tracing people's mental model from a robot's physical attributes. In: Proceedings of the 1st ACM SIGCHI/SIGART Conference on Human-Robot Interaction, pp. 218–225 (2006)
22. Robertson, J.: Gendering humanoid robots: robo-sexism in Japan. Body Soc. **16**(2), 1–36 (2010)
23. Søraa, R.A.: Mechanical genders: how do humans gender robots? Gend. Technolo. Dev. **21**(1–2), 99–115 (2017)
24. Tannenbaum, C., Ellis, R.P., Eyssel, F., Zou, J., Schiebinger, L.: Sex and gender analysis improves science and engineering. Nature **575**(7781), 137–146 (2019)

25. Tay, B., Jung, Y., Park, T.: When stereotypes meet robots: the double-edge sword of robot gender and personality in human-robot interaction. Comput. Hum. Behav. **38**, 75–84 (2014)
26. Willis, J., Todorov, A.: First impressions: making up your mind after a 100-ms exposure to a face. Psychol. Sci. **17**(7), 592–598 (2006)

Cultural Values, but not Nationality, Predict Social Inclusion of Robots

Serena Marchesi[1,2] (iD), Cecilia Roselli[1,3] (iD), and Agnieszka Wykowska[1](✉) (iD)

[1] Social Cognition in Human Robot Interaction, Italian Institute of Technology,
16152 Genova, Italy
Agnieszka.Wykowska@iit.it
[2] Department of Computer Science, Faculty of Science and Engineering,
Manchester University, Manchester, UK
[3] DIBRIS, Dipartimento Di Informatica, Bioingegneria, Robotica ed Ingegneria dei Sistemi,
16145 Genova, Italy

Abstract. Research highlighted that Western and Eastern cultures differ in socio-cognitive mechanisms, such as social inclusion. Interestingly, social inclusion is a phenomenon that might transfer from human-human to human-robot relationships. Although the literature has shown that individual attitudes towards robots are shaped by cultural background, little research has investigated the role of cultural differences in the social inclusion of robots. In the present experiment, we investigated how cultural differences, in terms of nationality and individual cultural stance, influence social inclusion of the humanoid robot iCub, in a modified version of the Cyberball game, a classical experimental paradigm measuring social ostracism and exclusion mechanisms. Moreover, we investigated whether the individual tendency to attribute intentionality towards robots modulates the degree of inclusion of the iCub robot during the Cyberball game. Results suggested that the individuals' stance towards collectivism and tendency to attribute a mind to robots both predicted the level of social inclusion of the iCub robot in our version of the Cyberball game.

Keywords: Human-Robot interaction · Cyberball · Collectivism · Mind attribution

1 Introduction

Recent literature showed that culture leads to cognitive and perceptual differences. For instance, individuals belonging to the Western culture are more analytical and oriented towards independence, while those belonging to East European cultures are more holistic and prone to interdependency [1]. Notably, these differences can also affect the phenomenon of social inclusion, which can substantially vary depending on the context [2]. For instance, affiliation is crucial in collectivistic cultures, where individuals strive for harmony and avoidance of conflicts. Thus, they tend to focus more on positive aspects

---

S. Marchesi and C. Roselli--Equally contributed to this work.

© Springer Nature Switzerland AG 2021
H. Li et al. (Eds.): ICSR 2021, LNAI 13086, pp. 48–57, 2021.
https://doi.org/10.1007/978-3-030-90525-5_5

of social interactions [3]. In contrast, the core of individualistic cultures is self-reliance, leading people to benefit less from the experience of being included by others, relative to people from collectivistic cultures [4]. In this context, little is known about the potential role of culture in social inclusion of robots. Recent studies in Human-Robot Interaction (HRI) demonstrated that individuals' behaviors towards robots might vary across different cultures [5]. For instance, when comparing people from Eastern (China, Japan) and Western countries (Germany), participants expressed different degrees of likeability, satisfaction, trust, and engagement towards robots [6]. Interestingly, the cultural background also affects the distance kept with robots during social interactions [7]; even facial expression recognition has been demonstrated to be culturally dependent [8]. In this context, individualism-collectivism is one of the main dimensions of culture, used as a means to explain how people represent themselves in relation to others [9]. Recent findings in HRI have shown that belonging to an individualistic rather than a collectivistic culture can influence individuals' attitudes towards robots during an interaction. For example, people from collectivistic societies prefer an implicit communication style in the robot, whereas people from individualistic societies prefer an explicit and straightforward, communication style [10]. Interestingly, the cultural background resulted to be particularly relevant also for anthropomorphizing, and mind attribution towards robots [11–13]. For example, recent findings pointed out that people tend to "deny" mind attribution to robots that are categorized as members of the out-group, based on certain features such as skin color [11] or facial morphology [12]. Nevertheless, to the best of our knowledge, no previous studies investigated whether cultural differences modulate people's tendency towards social inclusion of robots, as a function of mind perception and attribution of intentionality.

1.1 Aim

The present study had two aims. First, we were interested in evaluating whether cultural differences modulated individuals' tendency to socially include robots as members of their own in-group. To this purpose, we tested two samples of UK and Chinese participants, who were chosen as representative of an individualistic, Western culture and of a collectivistic, East Asian culture, respectively [13].

Notably, individual cultural values (cultural stance) might not be in line with the cultural orientation at the national level. Therefore, we administered the Cultural Values Scale (CVS), a 26-items dimensional scale that measures cultural stance at the individual level [14], with a particular focus on the *Collectivism* subscale. This subscale evaluates to what extent a person displays a collectivistic orientation, defined as being sensitive to in-group influences, loyal to in-group norms, and prone to harmony [14]. In order to measure participants' individual tendency towards social inclusion of robots, we developed a modified version of the Cyberball game [15, 16], a well-established paradigm to investigate social ostracism and social exclusion [17]. In our version, participants were instructed to play a ball-tossing game with two other players, represented by avatars of another human and the humanoid robot iCub [18]. During the game, participants were asked to choose which player they wanted to throw the ball to, being as fast as possible. Notably, both the human player and iCub were programmed to alternate between the participant and the other player, with equal probability of throwing the ball to either of them. Given these premises, we hypothesized that cultural differences, both at a national and individual level, would predict the willingness to pass the ball to the robot (that is to include the robot as an in-group member). More specifically, we hypothesized that collectivist culture (at the national and/or individual level) would mean more social inclusion of the robot.

Our second aim was to investigate whether attribution of intentionality towards robots modulates the cultural differences in tendency to socially include the robot in the Cyberball game. To this purpose, we decided to administer the Waytz questionnaire [19], a 7-items subscale of the Anthropomorphism questionnaire adapted from [20], which measures to what extent people ascribe to robots characteristics that are inherently human, such as intentions, desires, and free will. In other words, the more people would attribute intentionality to robots, the more they would ascribe human-like characteristics to them, thereby considering robots closer to human beings. According to this reasoning, cultural differences would be predictive of the willingness to perceive the robot as a social partner, as a function of attribution of intentionality. Thus, we hypothesized that participants with collectivistic cultural stance would be more likely to ascribe intentionality to robots, and also to pass the ball more often to the robot.

2 Materials and Methods

2.1 Sample

120 participants were recruited to take part in the study. Data were collected through the online platform Prolific (https://www.prolific.co/). As inclusion criteria, we selected the following: age range (18–45 years old), fluent English to ensure that participants understood the instructions of the experiment, handedness (right-handed), and nationality. Specifically, half of participants were English (M $_{age}$ = 25.5; SD $_{age}$ = 5, males = 15, Other = 2), whereas the other half were Chinese (M $_{age}$ = 26.3; SD $_{age}$ = 4.5, males = 22). Additionally, information about participants' educational levels was collected (see **Table 1**). The study was approved by the local Ethical Committee (Comitato Etico Regione Liguria) and was conducted in accordance with the Code of Ethics of the World Medical Association (Declaration of Helsinki, 2013). All participants gave informed consent by ticking an appropriate box in the online form and were naïve to the purpose of the experiment. They all received an honorarium of 4.40 £ for their participation.

Table 1. Educational levels declared by participants before starting the experiment.

Sample	Educational levels			
	Bachelor	Master	Ph.D	NA
English	20 (33.7%)	9 (15.2%)	3 (5%)	27 (45.8%)
Chinese	17 (28.8%)	28 (47.5%)	7 (11.9%)	8 (13.6%)

2.2 Procedure

As pre-task questionnaires, participants were asked to fill out the Waytz questionnaire, [19], and the Cultural Values Scale (CVS) [14]. Afterward, participants were given instructions to perform the Cyberball game [15–17] (see **Fig. 1**). Before starting the game, a short presentation of the two players was given to participants, who were introduced to both the human confederate ("This is Davide") and the iCub robot ("This is iCub"). The human confederate was depicted as a Caucasian young male, in a neutral background as well as the iCub robot. We did not manipulate its gender, ethnicity, or race, as previous findings [21] showed that the presence of humans does not affect individuals' tendency to attribute human traits to robots. However, further studies should deeply investigate whether these aspects have an impact on the probability of robot choice, which was beyond the scope of this paper.

Each trial started with the presentation of both the human player and iCub, on the left and the right side of the screen, respectively. The name of the participant ("You") was displayed at the bottom. The act of tossing the ball was simulated by presenting a one-second animation of a ball. When participants received the ball, they were invited to wait until their identification (i.e. "You") turned from black into red before passing the ball. Then, they had 500 ms to decide which player to pass the ball to. Specifically, to choose the player on their left side (Human) they had to press the "D" key, whereas the "K" key was to choose the player on the right side of the screen (Robot). To make sure that participants' responses were not biased by the different locations of the keys, before the experiment we asked participants to use a standard QWERTY keyboard to perform the task. If participants took more than 500 ms to give their response, a red "time-out" statement was displayed in the middle of the screen and the trial was rejected as invalid. The task comprised 100 trials in which participants received the ball (plus trials to replace timeouts).

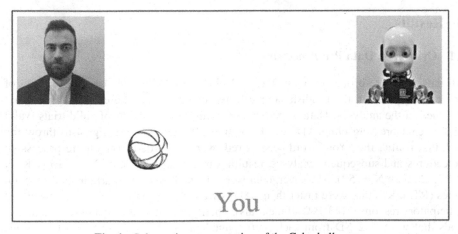

Fig. 1. Schematic representation of the Cyberball game.

At the end of the Cyberball game, participants filled out a modified version of the Overlap of Self, Ingroup, and Outgroup (OSIO) scale [22], comprising four items that visually represent the closeness between the two players of the Cyberball (i.e., the human player and the iCub robot, see **Fig. 2**). From top to bottom, the picture of the two players tended to get closer. Participants were asked to choose the picture that, according to them, most precisely represented the current closeness between the human player and iCub. For all four items, we assigned a value of 1 to the first and a value of 4 to the last picture. Thus, higher score indicated more closeness between the two players.

All questionnaires and the Cyberball game (stimuli presentation, response timing), and data collection were programmed by using Psychopy v.2020.1.3 [23].

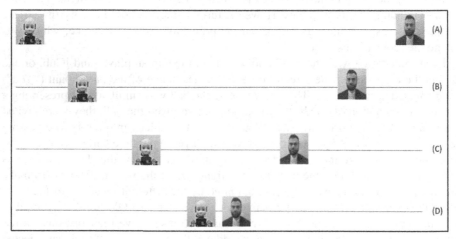

Fig. 2. Schematic representation of the modified version of the OSIO scale.

3   Results

3.1   Cyberball: Data Pre-Processing

All data were pre-processed with R v.4.0.2 [24], and JASP v.0.14.1 (2020). Data of one participant from the English sample were not saved, and therefore they were not included in the analyses. Data of participants with less than 70% of valid trials (valid trials meant pressing either "D" or "K" within 500 ms after the signal to throw the ball, that is after the "You" word became red) were discarded from all pre-processing procedures and subsequent analyses, resulting in a final sample of N = 115 (UK, N = 57; Chinese N = 58). Moreover, data were cleaned based on participants' reaction times (RTs): RTs that were faster than 100 ms were discarded as they were considered anticipatory responses (43.19% of the trials). Finally, we checked for outliers, excluding trials that were ± 2 SD from each participants' mean RTs [25] (5.52% of the trials were excluded). For each presented effect, we will report between square brackets the following statistics: unstandardized coefficient of regression (b), standard error (SE), z-statistics (or t-statistics where appropriate), p-value, and 95% confidence interval (95% C.I.) (or R^2 where appropriate).

3.2   The Effect of Cultural Differences on Social Inclusion of the Robot

To test whether cultural differences modulate individuals' tendency to socially include robots as in-group members, frequency of robot choice was analyzed with a logistic regression model, with nationality (Chinese/English) as a fixed factor and score calculated by the *Collectivism* subscale of the CVS questionnaire [14] as a covariate. Results showed a main effect of Collectivism [b $= 0.15$, SE $= 0.03$, z $= 4.12$, p $= < 0.001$, CI $= (0.08; 0.22)$], but no interaction with nationality was observed. Specifically, the more people displayed a collectivistic orientation, the more frequently they tended to pass the ball to the robot (see **Fig. 3**).

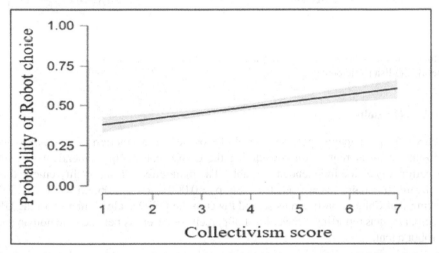

Fig. 3. Logistic regression model showing the relationship between the probability of choosing the robot and the Collectivism score.

3.3   The effect of Intentionality Attribution on Social Inclusion of the Robot

To test whether participants' nationality predicts social inclusion of robot as a function of intentionality attribution, frequency of robot choice was analyzed with a logistic regression model, with nationality (Chinese/English) as a fixed factor and Waytz score as a covariate. Results showed a significant two-way interaction between nationality and Waytz score [b $= 0.1$, SE $= 1.1$, z $= 1.99$, p $= 0.04$, CI $= (0.001; 0.192)$]. To further investigate this interaction, we performed two logistic regression models, separately for each nationality (Chinese/English). For Chinese participants, results showed that the more they tended to attribute intentionality to robots, the less frequently they passed the ball to the robot [b $= -0.09$, SE $= 0.04$, z $= -2.49$, p $= 0.01$, CI $= (-0.16; -0.02)$]. Notably, English participants did not show this pattern [b $= 0.006$, SE $= 0.03$, z $= 0.14$, p $= 0.88$, CI $= (-0.05; 0.07)$] (see **Fig. 4**).

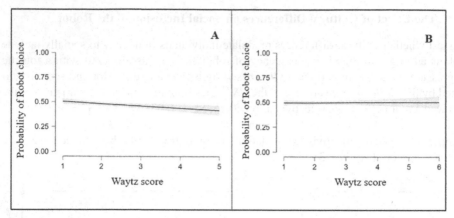

Fig. 4. Logistic regression model, showing the relationship between the probability of choosing the robot and the Waytz score, separately according to nationality (Panel A: Chinese participants; Panel B: English participants).

3.4 OSIO results

To check for participants' perceived level of closeness as a function of nationality, we performed a linear regression considering the OSIO scale as the dependent variable and nationality as the independent variable. The main effect of nationality emerged as significant [b = 0.46, SE = 0.11, t = 3.86, p = 0.0001, R^2 = 0.06, CI = (0.1; 0.77)], showing that Chinese participants scored lower at the OSIO scale compared to the UK participants, thus reporting a lower level of perceived closeness between the human and the robot agent.

4 Discussion

The present experiment aimed at investigating whether cultural differences, operationalized as nationality of participants (Chinese/English) would predict the social inclusion of the robot as a function of (i) individual collectivistic stance and (ii) attribution of intentionality towards robots. The tendency to consider the robot as a social in-group partner was operationalized as the probability of including the humanoid iCub robot in a ball-tossing game, namely the Cyberball [15–17]. With respect to the first aim, results showed that the more participants displayed a collectivistic stance, the more they tended to pass the ball to the robot, regardless of their nationality (Chinese/English). As a consequence, what seems to matter for social inclusion of robots is not national identity but individuals' cultural stance. With respect to the second aim (ii), results showed that, for Chinese participants, the more they tended to attribute intentionality to robots, the less they chose to pass the ball to iCub in the Cyberball game. This was not the case for the UK participants, among whom the individual tendency to attribute intentionality towards robots did not relate to the likelihood of socially including iCub.

This intriguing pattern can perhaps be explained as follows: in collectivist cultures the more an individual is perceived as autonomous, and having a "mind of one's own" (phrases used in the Waytz questionnaire), the less the individual is perceived as an in-group member. "Autonomy" or "mind of one's own" might be perceived as being against the collectivist values. On the other hand, in individualistic cultures, being autonomous or "having a mind of one's own" might be still more compatible with in-group membership, and hence no negative relationship between Waytz score and social inclusion has been found for the UK participants. However, results from OSIO scale seem to be in contrast with our hypothesis, as they showed that Chinese participants perceived less "closeness" to the robotic agent. Therefore, this speculative interpretation of the patterns of results needs to be further examined in future research.

At present, our preliminary findings could potentially contribute to design robots that can take into account people's cultural stance, at both individual and social levels. For example, the degree of "autonomy" and "intentionality" displayed by the robot should be tailored to individuals' cultural background, as it could bias the perception of the robot as a social partner.

5 Conclusions

Taken together, our results suggest that social inclusion of robots is influenced by the individual collectivistic stance. Moreover, attribution of intentionality towards robots impacts the social exclusion of the robotic agent, but only among members of a collectivist culture. Future research should investigate (and replicate) whether these findings generalize to other nationalities and cultures and also to ecological settings with an embodied humanoid robot.

Funding. This study has received support from the European Research Council under the European Union's Horizon 2020 research and innovation program, ERC Starting grant ERC-2016-StG-715058, awarded to Agnieszka Wykowska. The content of this paper is the sole responsibility of the authors. The European Commission or its services cannot be held responsible for any use that may be made of the information it contains.

References

1. Varnum, M.E.W., Grossmann, I., Kitayama, S., Nisbett, R.E.: The origin of cultural differences in cognition: the social orientation hypothesis. Curr. Dir. Psychol. Sci. **19**(1), 9–13 (2010). https://doi.org/10.1177/0963721409359301
2. Pfundmair, M., Aydin, N., Du, H., Yeung, S., Frey, D., Graupmann, V.: Exclude me if you can: cultural effects on the outcomes of social exclusion. J. Cross Cult. Psychol. **46**(4), 579–596 (2015). https://doi.org/10.1177/0022022115571203
3. Takahashi, K., Ohara, N., Antonucci, T.C., Akiyama, H.: Commonalities and differences in close relationships among the Americans and Japanese: a comparison by the individualism/collectivism concept. Int. J. Behav. Dev. **26**(5), 453–465 (2002). https://doi.org/10.1080/01650250143000418
4. Pfundmair, M., Graupmann, V., Du, H., Frey, D., Aydin, N.: Suddenly included: cultural differences in experiencing re-inclusion. Int. J. Psychol. **50**(2), 85–92 (2015). https://doi.org/10.1002/ijop.12082

5. Lim, V., Rooksby, M., Cross, E. S.:. Social robots on a global stage: establishing a role for culture during human–robot interaction. Int. J. Soc. Robot. (2020). https://doi.org/10.1007/s12369-020-00710-4
6. Rau, P.L.P., Li, Y., Li, D.: A cross-cultural study: effect of robot appearance and task. Int. J. Soc. Robot. **2**(2), 175–186 (2010). https://doi.org/10.1007/s12369-010-0056-9
7. Remland, M.S., Jones, T.S., Brinkman, H.: Proxemic and haptic behavior in three European countries. J. Nonverbal Behav. **15**(4), 215–232 (1991). https://doi.org/10.1007/BF00986923
8. Jack, R.E., Blais, C., Scheepers, C., Schyns, P.G., Caldara, R.: Cultural confusions show that facial expressions are not universal. Curr. Biol. **19**(18), 1543–1548 (2009). https://doi.org/10.1016/j.cub.2009.07.051
9. Markus, H.R., Kitayama, S.: Culture and the self: implications for cognition, emotion, and motivation. Psychol. Rev. **98**(2), 224 (1991)
10. Papadopoulos, I., Koulouglioti, C.: The Influence of culture on attitudes towards humanoid and animal-like robots: an integrative review. J. Nurs. Scholarsh. **50**(6), 653–665 (2018). https://doi.org/10.1111/jnu.12422
11. Eyssel, F., Loughnan, S.: "It Don't Matter If You're Black or White"? In: Herrmann, G., Pearson, M.J., Lenz, A., Bremner, P., Spiers, A., Leonards, U. (eds.) ICSR 2013. LNCS (LNAI), vol. 8239, pp. 422–431. Springer, Cham (2013). https://doi.org/10.1007/978-3-319-02675-6_42
12. Krumhuber, E.G., Swiderska, A., Tsankova, E., Kamble, S.V., Kappas, A.: Real or artificial? intergroup biases in mind perception in a cross-cultural perspective. PLoS ONE **10**(9), 1–14 (2015). https://doi.org/10.1371/journal.pone.0137840
13. Hofstede, G.: Dimensionalizing cultures: the hofstede model in context. Online Read. Psychol. Culture **2**(1), 1–26 (2011). https://doi.org/10.9707/2307-0919.1014
14. Yoo, B., Donthu, N., Lenartowicz, T.: Measuring hofstede's five dimensions of cultural values at the individual level: development and validation of CVSCALE. J. Int. Consum. Mark. **23**(3–4), 193–210 (2011). https://doi.org/10.1080/08961530.2011.578059
15. Williams, K.D., Cheung, C.K., Choi, W.: Cyberostracism: effects of being ignored over the Internet. J. Pers. Soc. Psychol. **79**(5), 748 (2000)
16. Williams, K.D., Jarvis, B.: Cyberball: a program for use in research on interpersonal ostracism and acceptance. Behav. Res. Methods **38**(1), 174–180 (2006)
17. Bossi, F., Gallucci, M., Ricciardelli, P.: How social exclusion modulates social information processing: a behavioural dissociation between facial expressions and gaze direction. PLoS ONE **13**(4), 1–25 (2018). https://doi.org/10.1371/journal.pone.0195100
18. Metta, G., et al.: The iCub humanoid robot: an open-systems platform for research in cognitive development. Neural Netw. **23**(8–9), 1125–1134 (2010). https://doi.org/10.1016/j.neunet.2010.08.010
19. Ruijten, P.A.M., Haans, A., Ham, J., Midden, C.J.H.: Perceived human-likeness of social robots: testing the rasch model as a method for measuring anthropomorphism. Int. J. Soc. Robot. **11**(3), 477–494 (2019). https://doi.org/10.1007/s12369-019-00516-z
20. Waytz, A., Morewedge, C.K., Epley, N., Monteleone, G., Gao, J.H., Cacioppo, J.T.: Making sense by making sentient: effectance motivation increases anthropomorphism. J. Pers. Soc. Psychol. **99**(3), 410–435 (2010). https://doi.org/10.1037/a0020240
21. Marchesi, S., Ghiglino, D., Ciardo, F., Perez-Osorio, J., Baykara, E., Wykowska, A.: Do we adopt the intentional stance toward humanoid robots? Front. Psychol. **10**, 450 (2019). https://doi.org/10.3389/fpsyg.2019.00450
22. Schubert, T.W., Otten, S.: Overlap of self, ingroup, and outgroup: pictorial measures of self-categorization. Self Identity **1**(4), 353–376 (2002). https://doi.org/10.1080/152988602760328012
23. Peirce, J., et al.: PsychoPy2: experiments in behavior made easy. Behav. Res. Methods **51**(1), 195–203 (2019). https://doi.org/10.3758/s13428-018-01193-y

24. Bunn, A., Korpela, M.: A language and environment for statistical computing. Found. Stat. Comput. **2**, 1–12 (2013)
25. Harald Baayen, R., Milin, P.:. Analyzing reaction times. Int. J. Psychol. Res. **3**(2), 12–28 (2010). https://doi.org/10.21500/20112084.807

Socially Intelligent Robots

From Movement Kinematics to Object Properties: Online Recognition of Human Carefulness

Linda Lastrico[1,3]([✉]), Alessandro Carfì[3], Francesco Rea[1], Alessandra Sciutti[2], and Fulvio Mastrogiovanni[3]

[1] Robotics, Brain and Cognitive Science Department (RBCS),
Italian Institute of Technology, Genoa, Italy
linda.lastrico@iit.it
[2] Cognitive Architecture for Collaborative Technologies Unit (CONTACT),
Italian Institute of Technology, Genoa, Italy
[3] Department of Informatics, Bioengineering, Robotics, and Systems Engineering
(DIBRIS), University of Genoa, Genoa, Italy

Abstract. When manipulating objects, humans finely adapt their motions to the characteristics of what they are handling. Thus, an attentive observer can foresee hidden properties of the manipulated object, such as its weight, temperature, and even whether it requires special care in the manipulation. This study is a step towards endowing a humanoid robot with this last capability. Specifically, we study how a robot can infer online, from vision alone, whether or not the human partner is careful when moving an object. We demonstrated that a humanoid robot could perform this inference with high accuracy (up to 81.3%) even with a low-resolution camera. Only for short movements without obstacles, carefulness recognition did not perform well. The prompt recognition of movement carefulness from observing the partner's action will allow robots to adapt their actions on the object to show the same degree of care as their human partners.

Keywords: Human-robot interaction · Human motion understanding · Natural communication · Deep learning

1 Introduction

In everyday life, we promptly adapt our movements to the different properties of the objects we interact with, e.g. weight, size, shape, or temperature. By observing others manipulating objects, we can easily infer their properties. Thanks to the product of motor resonance, observing an action triggers the same set

This paper is supported by the European Commission within the Horizon 2020 research and innovation program, under grant agreement No 870142, project APRIL (multipurpose robotics for mAniPulation of defoRmable materIaLs in manufacturing processes) and CHIST-ERA (2014–2020), project InDex (Robot In-hand Dexterous manipulation).

H. Li et al. (Eds.): ICSR 2021, LNAI 13086, pp. 61–72, 2021.
https://doi.org/10.1007/978-3-030-90525-5_6

of neurons of the movement execution, providing a common ground for understanding others [16]. Action understanding enables humans to adapt to their partners during the interaction, and it correlates with the ability to interpret and send implicit signals for cooperation. A robot should learn how to interpret such implicit signals to achieve seamless collaboration with humans [3].

Many studies have been conducted to estimate the physical properties of handled objects, particularly for tasks where humans and robots are expected to collaborate and interact physically, e.g., handovers. It has been discussed how the kinematics of the movements correlate with object weight [1,9], and that it is possible to estimate the object weight by observing another person [19] or a humanoid robot [18] lifting it.

In this study, we focus on another property which significantly influences human movements, namely the *carefulness*. We define it as the caution and attention that humans exercise when handling an object. This qualitative property is influenced both by the object's physical characteristics, e.g., the object fragility, and by other factors such as emotional attachment or economic value. Let us imagine a robot which is asked to receive a glass of water from a human: it should recognize the human carefulness to manipulate the glass without spilling water. The carefulness has been explored in studies of human-human handovers to teach robots how to correctly transfer objects [4,17], monitoring human movements with motion capture sensors. In a previous study, we demonstrated that it is possible to train a classifier to distinguish between *careful* and *non careful* human motions using only data from a low-resolution camera [10]. However, our carefulness recognition method was tested offline on precisely segmented data, with a single experimental scenario. To overcome these limitations, we propose: (i) an online implementation of our method for carefulness recognition, (ii) a study to demonstrate its online performance, and (iii) a study to evaluate the generalization of the method in new scenarios. Although we are aware that carefulness only partially accounts for all the possible properties of an object, we believe that this work is an important step towards a global approach for robots to interpret human movements relying solely on vision.

2 Methods

The objective of this paper is to prove that a robot, in particular the humanoid iCub, can use our previously published approach to distinguish online and in different scenarios whether a human is performing a Careful (C) transport motion or a Not Careful (NC) motion.

2.1 Software Architecture

To achieve the presented goal we developed, using the YARP middleware [12], the software architecture shown in Fig. 1.

As first step, the robot camera captures images from the scene with a resolution of 320×240 pixels and 22 Hz frame rate. Then, the following module

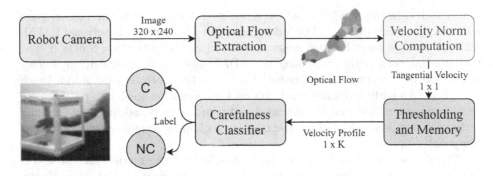

Fig. 1. The system's architecture structure gathers images from the robot camera and extracts features from the computed optical flow to discriminate between careful (C) and non careful (NC) motions

computes the optical flow (OF) using a dense approach [5], and applies a threshold on the OF magnitude to consider only the parts of the image where the change is significant. This choice introduces the strong assumption that, in the robot's field of view, relevant motions are the ones that generate the largest OF. However, choosing the OF to characterize the human motion, grants the system robustness to small changes in the point of view. The OF is a suitable tool for human motion description, for common daily activities such as cooking [7,15], but also for understanding the meaning of hand gestures [2,11].

The components of the motion velocity (horizontal u and vertical v) are extracted from the OF, as described by Vignolo *et al.*. [20], and used to compute the norm of the tangential velocity, as in Eq. 1. The architecture extracts this feature with a frequency 15 Hz.

$$V(t) = \sqrt{u(t)^2 + v(t)^2 + \Delta_t^2} \tag{1}$$

The segmentation module implements an heuristic threshold mechanism to consider only significant data: it detects the start of a motion when the velocity $V(t)$ overcomes a threshold τ and the end when the velocity becomes lower than τ. Once the end of the movement is detected, the segmentation module has two alternatives. If the temporal length is below 1 second, the motion is discarded. Otherwise, the temporal sequence of size $1 \times K$ is fed to the classifier. The minimum duration was set to 1 second since in the training set NC movements, which were the shortest, had a median duration of 1.2 s and the minimum duration was 1.1 s.

2.2 Model Training and Dataset Description

The classifier model is inspired by our previous work where a Long-Short Term Memory (LSTM) neural network showed promising results for the classification of temporal sequences of tangential velocity between careful and non careful motions [10]. In this study, we adopted a neural network with one hidden layer followed by an output layer. The hidden layer is a 32-neuron bidirectional LSTM, while the output layer has two neurons and a sigmoidal activation function. The training has been performed using the ADAM optimization algorithm, binary cross-entropy loss function, exponential decay of the learning rate, and a batch size of 30. An early stopping condition on the validation loss, i.e., patience set to 5, has been introduced to prevent over-fitting. A zero-padding and masking technique has been adopted for the training to handle sequences with different temporal lengths.

The dataset, used to train and preliminarily test the model, had been collected asking 14 volunteers to displace four glasses in front of iCub. The glasses differed in weight, light (167 g) or heavy (667 g), and content, since two of them were filled with water till the brim, to induce careful motions. Even though we consider the carefulness in the gesture as the feature to be detected, the 500 g weight difference was introduced to increase the dataset variance (for more detail about the data collection process, refer to Lastrico *et al..*, 2020 [10]). The dataset contains 878 segmented sequences, 438 for each class (C and NC). Preserving the class balance, we used 72% of the data for the training, 8% for the validation, and 20% for the test. The trained model got an accuracy of 95.14% on the test set, in line with the results of our previous work (90.5%) [10]. Furthermore, following a statistical analysis on the available data, we determined the threshold value τ for the segmentation module as $5.25\,pixels/s$.

2.3 System Evaluation

Given the system presented in Sect. 2.1 for the discrimination of careful and non careful motions, we performed new experiments to test its performance. In particular, the objectives to assess are:

O1 The possibility for the system to work online, providing the C/NC label when a human completes a transportation motion.
O2 The ability of the system to generalize over unknown human subjects.
O3 The possibility for the system to generalize over new kinds of transportation motions.

Eleven healthy subjects, members of our organizations, voluntarily agreed to participate in the data collection (7 females, 4 males, age: 28.0 ± 2.4); none of them is author of this research. All participants used their dominant hand in the experiment and only one was left-handed. We divided the volunteers into two groups $G1$ (4 females, 1 male, age 27.8 ± 3.6, one left-handed) and $G2$ (3 females, 3 males, age 28.2 ± 1.3). We purposely chose different participants from those included in our training set to grant a wider variability in the new data collection and assess O2.

The experiment consists of a series of structured transportation movements of four glasses performed by the participants while sitting at a table in front of iCub. In all the experiments iCub is passive and simply observes the scene. We use four glasses identical to those in the training set, representative of two classes, namely C and NC, according to the presence or absence of water inside. Throughout the experiment, a synthetic voice instructs the participant on which object to grasp and where to place it. Placing positions in the scenario are identified with letters (see Fig. 2). To receive instruction on the next transportation, the participant presses a key on a keyboard with their non-dominant hand. In between each transport motion, the volunteer rests the hands on the table. To investigate the system's ability to generalize over new transportation trajectories (O3), we have designed three experimental scenarios, namely: *Shelves*, *Simple Table* and *Advanced Table*.

Shelves. The first scenario replicates the one used to collect the training set. This scenario allows for testing the online performance of the classifier (O1) and the generalization of the system over new subjects (O2). The objects are transported back and forth from a fixed position on the table, delimited by a scale, to two shelves located on the right and left hand side of the table (see Fig. 2a). Eight positions where the objects can be grasped or placed are defined on the two shelves. Both $G1$ and $G2$ completed the experiment in this scenario, and each participant performed 32 transport movements (16 careful and 16 non careful).

Simple Table. This scenario is aimed at assessing the system's capability to generalize on a new set of movements (O3) and has been performed only by the 5 volunteers in $G1$ group. The glasses are moved from the scale in front of the participant to four positions on the table, delimited by a container, or vice-versa (seen Fig. 2b). Each volunteer performed 32 transport movements (16 for each class).

Advanced Table. This setup tests the system's capability to generalize over more ample and complex transport movements (O3). In this scenario, the glasses are moved between positions defined on the table, i.e., the scale is removed. In this way, the transportation motion is no more towards and away from the volunteer. Three containers are placed on the table, with two possible positions each, and columns are mounted on their frontal corners (see Fig. 2c). The columns obstacle the transportation, making the experiment more challenging. This more complex setup was designed after a preliminary analysis of the classification results with the Simple Table task, therefore only volunteers from $G2$ experimented with this scenario, and each of them performed 16 transport movements (8 for each class).

3   Results

Throughout all the experiments described, the recognition architecture described in Sect. 2.1 was running, recognizing careful and non careful motions. We analyze these results for each scenario, focusing on the system accuracy and the recognition time (i.e., the time between the motion end and the system recognition). Furthermore, we performed a statistical analysis of the velocities extracted from the OF to highlight possible differences between the three scenarios.

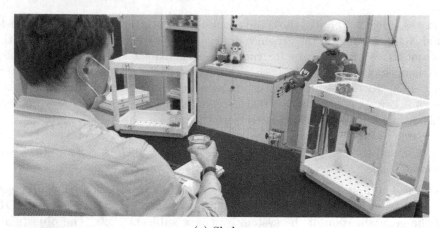

(a) Shelves

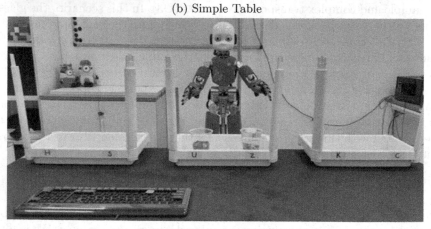

(b) Simple Table

(c) Advanced Table

Fig. 2. Setups of the different scenarios explored for the system evaluation. The Shelves scenario replicates the training condition (2a). Simple Table (2b) and Advanced Table (2c) scenarios are introduced to evaluate the generalization performance.

3.1   Shelves

Table 1. *Shelves.* Confusion matrix for the transportation movements performed by the 11 volunteers. The dark grey cell shows the overall accuracy

		Target class		
		NC	C	Precision
Output class	NC	**163 - 46.3%**	**109 - 31.0%**	59.9% - 40.1%
	C	13 - 3.7%	**67 - 19.0%**	83.8% - 16.2%
	Recall	92.6% - 7.4%	38.1% - 61.9%	65.3% - 34.7%

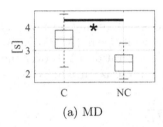

(a) MD

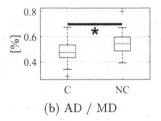

(b) AD / MD

Fig. 3. *Shelves.* Box plots of the Movement Duration (3a) and the Acceleration Duration over the Movement Duration of the velocity profiles (3b) for careful (C) and non careful (NC) transport motions. The red lines represent the medians, the blue rectangles limit the 25th and 75th percentiles, and ∗ indicates a significant difference according to the Wilcoxon test.

We report in Table 1 the confusion matrix related exclusively to the glasses transportation movements performed by the 11 participants, with a F1-Score of 72.9%. In this scenario, the classifier has been invoked correctly for all the 352 transport movements (32 movements of 11 volunteers) with a median recognition time below 150 ms (136.6 $\pm$ 18.8 ms - median and median absolute deviation). However, because of the system design, the classifier was called not only when a transport movement happened, but every time a velocity above threshold persisted at least for more than one second. Indeed, 300 more movements were detected and classified as NC 89.3% of the times. These movements are those that the volunteer performs to reach the glass and to go back to the resting position. Since these movements are not transportations, it is reasonable that the majority of them are classified as NC; however, they were not included in the confusion matrix results.

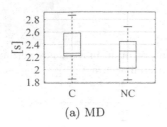 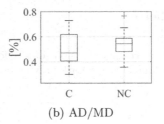

(a) MD   (b) AD/MD

Fig. 4. *Simple Table.* Box plots of the Movement Duration (4a) and the Acceleration Duration over the Movement Duration of the velocity profiles (4b) for careful (C) and non careful (NC) transport motions. The graphical conventions are the same as in Fig. 3.

Finally, we characterized the velocity profiles using two metrics, i.e., the transport movement duration (MD, proposed as significant to investigate the carefulness by [4]), and the asymmetry of the velocity peak (AD/MD, see Eq. 2). This last metric is expressed as the acceleration duration (AD) over the movement duration (MD), and it is widely used to characterize arm movements [8,13].

$$AD/MD = \frac{index_{Vmax}}{MD} \tag{2}$$

Since the populations were not normally distributed, in order to test if these two metrics showed any significant differences between C and NC motions, we used a Wilcoxon Signed Rank test. Considering all the 11 participants who performed the Shelves Task, we report for the MD a $p-value: < .01$, while for the AD/MD a $p-values: < .05$. In Fig. 3 are shown the corresponding ranges of movement duration and velocity asymmetry.

3.2   Simple Table

This scenario entailed movements that differed from those included in the training set, and only $G1$ experienced it. The online classifier did not achieve a good performance. We report an F1-Score of 66.09% with 96.25% recall and 50.33% precision values. The system tended to classify as not careful most movements, correctly identifying only 2.5% of the careful trials. However, the classifier was rightfully called at the end of every one of the 160 transport movements, with a median recognition time of $137.8 \pm 21.4\,ms$. Regarding the motions detected beyond the transport ones, the classifier was called 77 times, giving an NC label in 96.1% of the cases.

Interestingly, analyzing the MD and AD/MD metrics (see Fig. 4), which we use as distance measures between the careful and not careful movements, the Wilcoxon Rank Signed test reported *p-values* > .2 for both. Thus, according to the chosen metrics, no significant difference in the velocity profiles was detected between the C and NC groups in this scenario. These results suggest that for short transportations (about $40\,cm$) with no obstacles, the kinematics properties do not change significantly between careful and non careful motions.

3.3   Advanced Table

This scenario was designed to further test the generalization capability of the model. Glasses handling has been made more difficult by introducing obstacles and forcing longer paths between the grasping and release positions. In Table 2 is shown the confusion matrix for the transportation movements in this scenario, where our system reaches an F1-Score of 82.4%. The classifier output was available for every one of the 96 glass manipulations with a recognition time of $145.3\pm16.3\,ms$ (median and median absolute deviation). Regarding the 143 other movements that the classifier evaluated, the given label was NC for 97.9% of them. Finally, concerning the parametric measures (shown in Fig. 5), both differences between C and NC were statistically significant ($MD: p < .01$, AD/MD: $p < .05$).

Table 2. *Advanced Table.* Confusion matrix for the classification of transport movements performed by $G2$ in the generalization task. The dark grey cell shows the overall accuracy

<table>
<tr><td></td><td></td><td colspan="3">Target class</td></tr>
<tr><td rowspan="4">Output class</td><td></td><td>NC</td><td>C</td><td>Precision</td></tr>
<tr><td>NC</td><td>163 - 46.3%</td><td>109 - 31.0%</td><td>59.9% - 40.1%</td></tr>
<tr><td>C</td><td>13 - 3.7%</td><td>67 - 19.0%</td><td>83.8% - 16.2%</td></tr>
<tr><td>Recall</td><td>92.6% - 7.4%</td><td>38.1% - 61.9%</td><td>65.3% - 34.7%</td></tr>
</table>

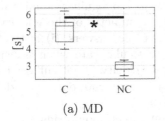

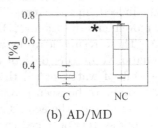

(a) MD   (b) AD/MD

Fig. 5. *Advanced Table.* Box plots of the movement duration (5a) and asymmetry of the velocity profiles (5b) for careful (C) and non careful (NC) transport motions. The graphical conventions are the same as in Fig. 3.

4   Discussion

With this work, we claim that a robot can recognize online motion carefulness with a low-resolution camera. To this extent, the usage of optical flow as motion descriptor is quite suitable since it gives a global evaluation of the whole movement and should be robust to small and quick occlusions as the ones posed by the shelves (see Fig. 1). However, when the motions are slow, as it happens with the glasses full of water, the image obstructions might be prolonged and have a greater impact. The proposed architecture generated a classifier output for every glass transportation, i.e., no transport movements went undetected. The model output was readily available at the end of the transportation, with a median recognition time of $135.9 \pm 17.9\,ms$ considering all the tasks.

The system detected other movements beyond the transport ones. These motions were related to the reaching and departing requested to grasp the glass or return to the resting position. Since, in these instances, no object was being carried, it is reasonable that the classifier returned a not careful label in the 92.7% of the occurrences. This result implies that when the system returns the *careful* label, this label has high confidence.

In the Shelves scenario, which replicates the training conditions, the performance of the overall online classifier are lower than those obtained with offline testing (which gave 90.5% [10]). However, given the novel testing conditions, i.e., different light and perspective, and the fact that the motion velocities were segmented online, these results can suggest that our system is capable of working online (O1) while generalizing over new subjects (O2). At the same time, in the Simple Table scenario, our architecture did not obtain a good classification performance. We ascribe this to the setup design. Indeed, comparing it to the Shelves and Advanced Table scenarios (see Fig. 2 for reference), the Simple Table scenario requires shorter movement without any obstacles. This result can lead us to hypothesize that the carefulness effect can be stressed by the boundary conditions of the external environment. Therefore, in a more complex scenario, it is easier to detect the presence of carefulness. This hypothesis is supported by the analysis of the distance metrics of the velocity profiles, presented in Fig. 3.2. Indeed, in the Simple Table scenario, no significant difference was found in movements duration (MD) or in the asymmetry of the velocity peaks (AD/MD). These results leave us with two possible answers: (i) in the Simple Table scenario, volunteers did not act with particular care when transporting the glasses full of water, or (ii) the tangential velocity is not sufficient in this case to discriminate between careful and non careful motions, and additional data are required, e.g., the actor's gaze pattern.

Finally, our system obtained the best results when monitoring a completely novel scenario (see Table 2). As we hypothesized previously, this result is linked to the additional care that the volunteer needs to transport the glass of water in a more complex setup. To further corroborate this hypothesis, we observe the striking difference for the MD and AD/MD metrics (see Fig. 5) between the two classes. Nevertheless, these results support the capability of our system to work online (O1) and to generalize over new subjects (O2). Furthermore, we showed that the system can generalize over new scenarios if the transportation carefulness is evident (O3).

5   Conclusions

With the proposed approach, a robot can identify online whether the object is handled with care or not, simply observing the human movements. A robot may exploit this capability to select its subsequent manipulations to match the observed carefulness, with no need for *a priori* knowledge of the object or visual detection of its physical properties. Since the robot ability to detect the carefulness is completely detached from the external appearance of the objects, it would be possible to generalize over previously unseen objects. To infer the objects fragility we relied on the information naturally embedded in the human kinematics during the manipulation, extracted from vision alone; therefore this approach is meant to be applied when the robot collaborates with a human partner, for instance in handover tasks, where the human movements can be observed.

The possibility for the robot to adapt online can be used to modulate the robot's movements to be coherent with the properties of the object involved, mimicking natural human behaviour and conveying the same information about the object features, being therefore more transparent and readable for the partner. This would greatly facilitate natural implicit communication between human and robots, and we are currently exploring the dual problem of generating communicative robot action, as proposed in [6].

It is worth noting that we tested our system with non-interactive actions (i.e., participants perform the task alone, with the robot acting as an observer). An interactive context might facilitate carefulness recognition, inducing participants to convey, more explicitly, this information as it happens in human signaling [3,14]. For this reason, future works should include interactive scenarios together with a more in-depth validation.

References

1. Bingham, G.: Kinematic form and scaling: further investigations on the visual perception of lifted weight. J. Exp. Psychol. Hum. Percept. Perform. **13**(2), 155–177 (1987)
2. Chang, J.Y., Tejero-de Pablos, A., Harada, T.: Improved optical flow for gesture-based human-robot interaction. In: 2019 International Conference on Robotics and Automation (ICRA), pp. 7983–7989 (2019)
3. Dragan, A.D., Lee, K.C.T., Srinivasa, S.S.: Legibility and predictability of robot motion. In: Proceedings of the 8th ACM/IEEE International Conference on Human-Robot Interaction, Tokyo, Japan March 2013)
4. Duarte, N.F., Chatzilygeroudis, K., Santos-Victor, J., Billard, A.: From human action understanding to robot action execution: how the physical properties of handled objects modulate non-verbal cues. In: 2020 Joint IEEE 10th International Conference on Development and Learning and Epigenetic Robotics (ICDL-EpiRob), pp. 1–6 (2020)
5. Farnebäck, G.: Two-frame motion estimation based on polynomial expansion. In: Bigun, J., Gustavsson, T. (eds.) SCIA 2003. LNCS, vol. 2749, pp. 363–370. Springer, Heidelberg (2003). https://doi.org/10.1007/3-540-45103-X_50
6. Garello, L., Lastrico, L., Rea, F., Mastrogiovanni, F., Noceti, N., Sciutti, A.: Property-aware robot object manipulation: a generative approach. In: 2021 IEEE International Conference on Development and Learning (ICDL), pp. 1–7 (2021)

7. Gehrig, D., Kuehne, H., Woerner, A., Schultz, T.: Hmm-based human motion recognition with optical flow data. In: 2009 9th IEEE-RAS International Conference on Humanoid Robots, pp. 425–430 (2009)
8. Gentili, R., Cahouet, V., Papaxanthis, C.: Motor planning of arm movements is direction-dependent in the gravity field. Neuroscience 145(1), 20–32 (2007)
9. Hamilton, A., Joyce, D., Flanagan, J., Frith, C., Wolpert, D.: Kinematic cues in perceptual weight judgment and their origins in box lifting. Psychol. Res. 71, 13–21 (2007)
10. Lastrico, L., Carfì, A., Vignolo, A., Sciutti, A., Mastrogiovanni, F., Rea, F.: Careful with that! Observation of human movements to estimate objects properties. In: Human-Friendly Robotics 2020, pp. 127–141 (2021)
11. Lyu, Y., Yang, Y., Ru, J.: Gesture motion detection algorithm based on optical flow method. In: 2015 IEEE International Conference on Computer and Communications (ICCC), pp. 128–132 (2015)
12. Metta, G., Fitzpatrick, P., Natale, L.: Yarp: yet another robot platform. Int. J. Adv. Rob. Syst. 3, 43–48 (2006)
13. Nagasaki, H.: Asymmetric velocity and acceleration profiles of human arm movements. Exp. Brain Res. 74, 319–326 (2004)
14. Pezzulo, G., Donnarumma, F., Dindo, H.: Human sensorimotor communication: a theory of signaling in online social interactions. PloS One 8, 1–11 (2013)
15. Rea, F., Vignolo, A., Sciutti, A., Noceti, N.: Human motion understanding for selecting action timing in collaborative human-robot interaction. Front. Rob. AI 6, 58 (2019)
16. Rizzolatti, G., Fadiga, L., Fogassi, L., Gallese, V.: Resonance behaviors and mirror neurons. Arch. ital. Biol. 137(2–3), 85–100 (1999)
17. Sanchez-Matilla, R., Chatzilygeroudis, K., Modas, A., Duarte, N.F., Xompero, A., Frossard, P., Billard, A., Cavallaro, A.: Benchmark for human-to-robot handovers of unseen containers with unknown filling. IEEE Rob. Autom. Lett. 5(2), 1642–1649 (2020)
18. Sciutti, A., Patane, L., Nori, F., Sandini, G.: Understanding object weight from human and humanoid lifting actions. IEEE Trans. Auton. Ment. Dev. 6, 80–92 (2014)
19. Sciutti, A., Patanè, L., Sandini, G.: Development of visual perception of others' actions: children's judgment of lifted weight. Plos one 14, 1–15 (2019)
20. Vignolo, A., Noceti, N., Rea, F., Sciutti, A., Odone, F., Sandini, G.: Detecting biological motion for human-robot interaction: a link between perception and action. Front. Rob. AI 4, 14 (2017)

Automated Lip-Reading Robotic System Based on Convolutional Neural Network and Long Short-Term Memory

Amir Gholipour[1], Alireza Taheri[1(✉)], and Hoda Mohammadzade[2]

[1] Social and Cognitive Robotics Laboratory, Mechanical Engineering Department,
Sharif University of Technology, Tehran, Iran
artaheri@sharif.edu
[2] Department of Electrical Engineering, Sharif University of Technology, Tehran, Iran
hoda@sharif.edu

Abstract. In Iranian Sign Language (ISL), alongside the movement of fingers/arms, the dynamic movement of lips is also essential to perform/recognize a sign completely and correctly. In a follow up of our previous studies in empowering the RASA social robot to interact with individuals with hearing problems via sign language, we have proposed two automated lip-reading systems based on DNN architectures, a CNN-LSTM and a 3D-CNN, on the robotic system to recognize OuluVS2 database words. In the first network, CNN was used to extract static features, and LSTM was used to model temporal dynamics. In the second one, a 3D-CNN network was used to extract appropriate visual and temporal features from the videos. The accuracy rate of 89.44% and 86.39% were obtained for the presented CNN-LSTM and 3D-CNN networks, respectively; which were fairly promising for our automated lip-reading robotic system. Although the proposed non-complex networks did not provide the highest accuracy for this database (based on the literature), 1) they were able to provide better results than some of the more complex and even pre-trained networks in the literature, 2) they are trained very fast, and 3) they are quite appropriate and acceptable for the robotic system during Human-Robot Interactions (HRI) via sign language.

Keywords: Lip-Reading · Deep learning · Social robot · Convolutional Neural Network (CNN) · Long Short-Term Memory (LSTM)

1 Introduction

Speech is the most widely used method of communication between humans and is considered a multisensory process. This process involves both audio and video information. McGurk and Macdonald [1] showed that visual information has an important effect on speech recognition. They showed that when inconsistent visual and audio information is presented to people, they perceive a different sound from what the speaker is saying. For example, when the sound /ba/ is pronounced but lip movements show /ga/, most people understand the /da/ sound. Although audio signals are generally much more useful than

© Springer Nature Switzerland AG 2021
H. Li et al. (Eds.): ICSR 2021, LNAI 13086, pp. 73–84, 2021.
https://doi.org/10.1007/978-3-030-90525-5_7

visual signals, it has been shown that most people use lip-reading to understand speech. Lip-reading is a skill for understanding speech through visual cues such as lip movement, tongue, and facial expressions. This skill is used subconsciously and to varying degrees depending on aspects such as hearing ability or sound conditions [2, 3]. In addition, people with hearing impairments can understand human speech by processing visual information from a person's lips and face [4].

With the rapid development of artificial intelligence technology and the continuous improvement of computer performance, Human-Computer Interaction (HCI) has become a hot topic. As a significant HCI method, automated lip-reading plays an important role in understanding human speech. Automated lip-reading can be widely used in the fields of computer vision [5], information security [6], driver assistance systems [7], and deaf education [8–10].

Automated lip-reading systems generally consist of four main parts: face recognition, lips localization, feature extraction, and classification. Apart from the first two parts, researchers have proposed different methods for extracting visual features and variety of classifiers. In terms of feature extraction and classification, automated lip reading systems can be classified into two general groups: traditional systems and systems based on Deep Neural Networks (DNN). In traditional systems, feature extraction methods can be divided into two categories: pixel-based methods and model-based methods [11, 12]. Most primary feature extraction approaches use pixel values extracted from the target area, such as Multiscale Spatial Analysis (MSA) or Local Binary Pattern (LBP) as visual information. Then, several compression algorithms are used to reduce the dimensions such as Principal Component Analysis (PCA) or Discrete Cosine Transform (DCT) [11, 12]. Pixel-based methods are sensitive to changes in brightness, dimensionality, and rotation. Therefore, model-based methods such as Active Shape Model (ASM) or Active Appearance Model (AAM) are proposed to achieve a set of high-level geometric features with lower dimensions and greater stability [11]. In the second step, the extracted features are given to a classifier such as a Support Vector Machine (SVM) or a Hidden Markov Model (HMM). For example, Matthews et al. [11] proposed two top-down approaches that fit a model of inner and outer lip lines and derive features from the ASM or the AAM. It is also a bottom-up method that uses MSA to extract features directly from the pixel intensity. They also used the HMM for classification. Zhao et al. [12] suggested using a local temporal and spatial descriptor to capture video dynamics. They considered the entire film sequence as a volume and calculated the LBP characteristics not only from the original lip images, but also from the accumulated time patterns that were cross-sectional/vertical sections of the volume. In their work, each volume of film was divided into smaller rectangular cubes, from which normal LBP histograms were calculated. In recent years, with the availability of large databases and the advancement of computer processing power, deep learning in many areas of computer vision, including automated lip-reading, has brought far-reaching benefits. In the first generation of models based on deep neural networks, deep bottleneck architectures were used to reduce the dimensions of visual features extracted from the mouth area. These features were then assigned to a classifier, such as a SVM or the HMM. Ngiam et al. [13] applied PCA to the mouth area and extracted the bottleneck features with a deep auto encoder. Deep auto encoder is a type of deep neural network that is commonly used for dimensional compression and feature extraction. Speech features were then given to an SVM that did not consider temporal dynamics. In the second generation of deep models, deep bottleneck designs are used that extract bottleneck features directly from the pixels. Li et al. [14] derived bottleneck features from dynamic representations of images with a Convolutional Neural Network (CNN) which were then given to an HMM for classification. In the third generation of deep models, a small number of End-to-End networks are presented that simultaneously extract features directly from the mouth area and classify them. Petridis et al. [15] proposed a system based on two independent streams. The first stream extracts the features directly from the input images, while the second stream extracts features from the difference between two consecutive frames. Both streams follow a bottleneck architecture. Long Short-Term Memory (LSTM) is then used to model the temporal dynamic of each stream. Finally, Bidirectional LSTM (BLSTM) is used to integrate information of two streams. In another study, Fernandez-Lopez and Sukno [16] introduced LDNet with the goal of training small scale databases in which a CNN-LSTM architecture is used. They proposed splitting the training set by visual module and the temporal module.

In a follow up of our previous studies in developing a reciprocal Human-Robot Interaction platform to interact with individuals with hearing problems via sign language, in this paper, we have proposed an automated lip-reading robotic system based on DNN architectures. The platform is developed on the RASA social robot. It should be noted that in Iranian Sign Language (ISL), in addition to hand movements, lip movements also play an important role in performing the signs. Therefore, the ability of automated lip-reading is one of the needs of such robotic system. In this regard, in the first step, by examining the types of architecture that have recently been presented in the literature, two architectures have been proposed, tested, and tuned. The first architecture consists of Convolutional Neural Networks with Long Short-Term Memory and the second architecture is made with the help of three-dimensional CNN (3D-CNN). The performance of these networks have been studied on the popular OuluVS2 database [17], which contains 10 frequently used English phrases.

2 Methodology

2.1 Database

In this research, the Ouluvs2 database [17] has been used. This database consists of 52 speakers, each of which repeats 10 phrases 3 times. In other words, there are 156 examples for each speech. The phrases in this database are as follows: 1- "Excuse me", 2- "Goodbye", 3- "Hello", 4- "How are you", 5- "Nice to meet you", 6- "See you", 7- "I am sorry", 8- "Thank you", 9- "Have a good time", and 10- "You are welcome". One of the features of this database is that the mouth area is already provided and therefore it satisfies our need to deal with the two parts of face recognition and lips localization. It is worth mentioning that this database includes videos from 5 angles, and in this research, data that includes videos from direct angles have been used. Some examples of images of this database can be seen in Fig. 1.

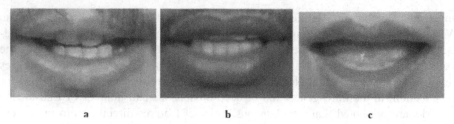

a   b   c

Fig. 1. Some examples of images of Ouluvs2 database [17]: a) 1st frame of s14-c1-r1, b) 1st frame of s36-c8-r2, c) 1st frame of s43-c4-r3 (s = subject, c = class, r = repeat).

2.2 Pre-processing Stage

Before starting the training process, some data processing has been done. Due to the reduction of additional information and effective parameters in network design, the images have changed from the RGB mode to the gray mode. In order to make the data uniform in terms of dimensions, the frame size has been changed to 26 × 44. Also, in order to equalize the videos in terms of time, 8 middle frames of each video have been used. Each video is divided into 8 equal parts and the middle frame of each part is selected. In order to normalize the data, the pixel values are divided by 255. Finally, for each video, the median frame is subtracted from each one to reduce the dependency of each subject's recorded videos during the machine learning process.

2.3 Networks Structure

In this research, two different network structures have been used to train the robotic system: a CNN-LSTM and a 3D-CNN. In this section, we will go through the details of these two structures.

CNN-LSTM: As shown in Fig. 2, we used a convolutional architecture that uses a convolutional layer, a pooling layer, and a fully connected layer to extract the static features of a frame. Then, in order to model the dynamics of each word, the extracted features are combined and fed to the LSTM. Softmax takes the probability of each class and the largest value is selected as a result of the final diagnosis:

$$\sigma(\vec{z})_i = \frac{e^{z_i}}{\sum_{j=1}^{N} e^{z_j}} \tag{1}$$

This network consists of three convolution layers (C1, C2 and C3), three pooling layers (P1, P2 and P3) and two fully connected layers (Fc4, Fc5). Rectified Linear Unit (ReLU) is used for the output of each convolution layer as a nonlinear activation function:

$$f(x) = \max(0, x) \tag{2}$$

In the training phase, dropout is used to prevent overfitting and help generalizability (Table. 1). In our network, dropout is used in two parts. The first one is after P3 and before FC4, with the value of 0.4. The second drop out is used in LSTM layer with the rate of 0.2. The number of parameters for the proposed CNN-LSTM network is 155790.

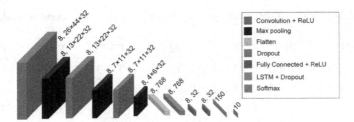

Fig. 2. CNN-LSTM neural network details

Table 1. Table of specifications and parameters of CNN-LSTM neural network

Layers	C1	P1	C2	P2	C3	P3	FC4	FC5
Kernel	3 × 3	2 × 2	3 × 3	2 × 2	3 × 3	2 × 2	-	-
Stride	1 × 1	2 × 2	1 × 1	2 × 2	1 × 1	2 × 2	-	-
Channels	32	32	32	32	32	32	32	32

LSTM networks were first introduced in 1997 [18]. The purpose of designing LSTM networks was to handle the problem of long-term dependency. The main element of LSTMs is the cell state, which is actually a horizontal line at the top of Fig. 3. In our proposed network, the size of the LSTM output vector (h_t) is 150.

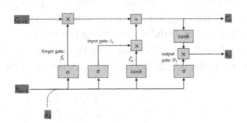

Fig. 3. LSTM network structure

3D-CNN: The 3D-CNN network is quite similar to a regular CNN and the only difference is in the dimension (Fig. 4). CNN processes data in two dimensions, but 3D-CNN does so in three dimensions. Other details of the network are the same as before and no further explanation is needed. More details of this network are given in Table 2. It should be noted that in this network, dropout is used in two parts. The first time is after P3 and before FC4 and its value is equal to 0.4 and in the second time, after FC4 and before FC5 and it is equal to 0.2. It should be noted that the dropout rates have been tuned. The number of parameters for the proposed 3D-CNN network is 180554.

Table 2. Table of specifications and parameters of 3D-CNN neural network

Layers	C1	P1	C2	P2	C3	P3	FC4	FC5
Kernel	$3 \times 3 \times 3$	$1 \times 2 \times 2$	$3 \times 3 \times 3$	$1 \times 2 \times 2$	$3 \times 3 \times 3$	$1 \times 2 \times 2$	-	-
Stride	$1 \times 1 \times 1$	$1 \times 2 \times 2$	$1 \times 1 \times 1$	$1 \times 2 \times 2$	$1 \times 1 \times 1$	$1 \times 2 \times 2$	-	-
Channels	32	32	32	32	32	32	32	32

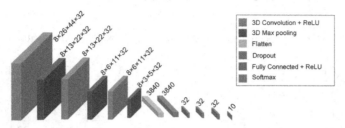

Fig. 4. 3D-CNN neural network details

2.4 Training Process

For training, the database is first divided into the training, validation, and test sets. The standard protocol proposed by the database creators [19] is followed, with 40 people used for training and validation, and 12 people for testing. These 40 people are then randomly divided into 35 and 5 people for the training and validating purposes. This means that there are 1050, 150, and 360 training, validation, and test samples, respectively. The batch size is equal to 100. Loss function is defined as the categorical cross-entropy. Equation 3 shows the cross-entropy loss function formula where N is the number of samples, k is the number of classes, $t_{i,j}$ is the actual label, and $p_{i,j}$ is the predicted probability.

$$cross - entropy\ loss\ function = \frac{1}{N} \sum_{i=1}^{N} \sum_{j=1}^{k} -t_{i,j} \ln\left(p_{i,j}\right) \tag{3}$$

The Adamax optimization algorithm with default weights is also used. Early stopping is used for the training; so that if the loss rate in the validation data does not improve for 30 epochs, the training is stopped and the weights related to the best loss rate in the validation data, are returned. It should also be noted that Google Colab has been used to run this program to use higher and faster processing power.

2.5 Robotic Platform: The RASA Social Robot

RASA is a social robot which is designed/fabricated in the Social and Cognitive Robotics Lab., Sharif University of Technology, Iran to teach Sign Language to individuals with hearing problems and interact with deaf children via ISL [8–10] (Fig. 5). It has active fingers in its hands to perform variety of ISL words/signs. RASA has a camera mounted on its head and a Kinect sensor on the chest. The Robotic Operating System (ROS) is used to control the software components of this robotic platform. To achieve real time responses in video analysis and because of the limited computational power of RASA's internal computer, an external high processing performance computer is used for the automated lip-reading process. We have successfully used the ROS Bridge library to transfer the captured images/videos (by the robot's camera) to the external computer via a wireless network. After the recognition of the signs, the output of the lip-reading network is transferred back to RASA's internal computer for providing appropriate reactions during HRI. Currently, we are in the process of developing our ISL dataset for our future studies via the robot's camera. However, in this study, we only worked on and reported the videos from the Ouluvs2 database.

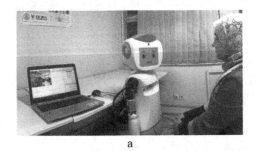 

a   b

Fig. 5. The RASA robot, a) RASA during an HRI, b) RASA performs the "Hello" sign.

3   Results and Discussion

As mentioned earlier, we proposed two networks, CNN-LSTM and 3D-CNN, to classify phrases in the OuluVS2 database. The CNN-LSTM was able to provide 89.44% accuracy. Also, the accuracy of the 3D-CNN network was 86.39%. The relative superiority of the first network indicates the greater power of LSTM networks in modeling time dynamics. Table 3 reports the results obtained in this work as well as in some related previous works. Saitoh et al. [20] proposed several systems that used pre-trained models. These systems were pre-trained using datasets that were not related to lip-reading and fine-tuned for OuluVS2. The GoogLeNet model achieves a maximum accuracy of 85.60%. Chung and Zisserman [21] also fine-tuned two systems for OuluVS2 which were specifically pre-trained for lip-reading. Those systems were pre-trained using very large LRW and LRS databases and achieved a maximum accuracy of 94.10%. The rest of the systems that have also been reported do not use pre-trained models. Petridis et al. [15] designed a network made of deep auto encoder with LSTM and reported 84.50% accuracy. In their recent work [22], they improved their architecture and achieved 95.60% accuracy using deep auto encoder with BLSTM. In another study, Fernandez-Lopez and Sukno [16] introduced LDNet with the goal of training small scale databases. They used a CNN-LSTM architecture containing almost 15 million parameters, which is a huge amount for small datasets. To solve this problem, they proposed to split the training set by visual module and the temporal module. The goal of the visual module is to parametrize the visual information observable at a given time instant or window while the temporal module aims to map the visual features into speech units while incorporating temporal constraints to ensure that the decoded message is coherent. They reported 91.38% accuracy.

Table 3. Comparison of the accuracy of the proposed networks with previous works.

Method	Accuracy (%)
CFI + AlexNet [20] (with pre-trained models)	82.80
CFI + GoogLeNet [20] (with pre-trained models)	85.60
VGG-M + LSTM [21] (with pre-trainded models)	31.90
SyncNet + LSTM [21] (with pre-trained models)	94.10
Encoder + LSTM [15]	84.50
Encoder + BLSTM [22]	95.60
CNN + LSTM [16]	91.38
CNN + LSTM (this study)	**89.44**
3D-CNN (this study)	**86.39**

Our proposed networks were able to achieve 89.44% and 86.39% accuracy which were fairly promising. Although this accuracy did not provide the best accuracy among the existing systems, it was able to provide even better performance than some pre-trained systems. This accuracy is quite desirable and appropriate for our current purpose. Although we have a distance of 5–10% with the best accuracy, in practical work and implementation on the social robot, this difference is not very effective in the final result (e.g. the platform's acceptance rate, the robot's overall performance, etc.). We have been able to achieve a completely desirable accuracy without the use of pre-trained networks and without the need to go into much detail of network design. It is worth mentioning that the whole network training process is performed in less than 10 min on Google Colab. Therefore, it is definitely acceptable in terms of time/computational cost. It is expected that higher accuracies can be achieved by optimizing both the designed networks (i.e. different hyper-parameters) and the data processing. For example, it is possible that our approach, which used 8 intermediate frames, did not adequately represent the whole speech. In the network architecture section, it may be possible to get higher accuracy by changing the number/size of kernels or even the dropout rate (i.e. optimizing the networks' hyper-parameters [23, 24]). All in all, both of the proposed networks seem to be fairly promising for conducting HRI via sign language.

Figure 6-a shows the normalized confusion matrix for our CNN-LSTM network. The most common error is related to the phrase "8- Thank you", which is confused with the word "3- Hello", which is consistent with previous studies [22]. (The next highest errors belong to "2- Goodbye" which is confused with "10- You are welcome", "10- You are welcome" which is confused with "4- How are you?", and "3- Hello" which is confused with "8- Thank you").

Figure 6-b shows the normalized confusion matrix for the proposed 3D-CNN network. In this network, again, as in the previous network, the highest error is related to the phrase "8- Thank you", which is confused with the word "3- Hello". (The next highest errors belong to "6- See you", which is confused with "3- Hello", and "3- Hello", which is confused with "8- Thank you").

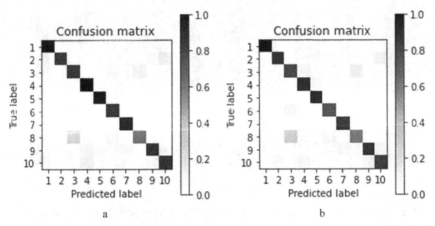

Fig. 6. Normalized confusion matrix of the proposed a) CNN-LSTM network, and b) 3D-CNN network.

Figure 7 shows the precision and recall values for each class and both networks. Precision is the fraction of relevant instances among the retrieved instances, while recall or sensitivity is the fraction of relevant instances that were retrieved. These values are calculated as follows: (TP = true positives, FP = false positives, FN = false negatives.)

$$Precision = \frac{TP}{TP + FP} \tag{4}$$

$$Recall = \frac{TP}{TP + FN} \tag{5}$$

As can be seen, in both networks, all words provide acceptable results except "3-Hello" in precision and "8-Thank you" in recall. It is also observed that the CNN-LSTM network generally gives a slightly better results than the 3D-CNN network. The average precision is 0.90 and average recall is 0.89 for the CNN-LSTM network and 0.87 and 0.86 for the 3D-CNN network, respectively.

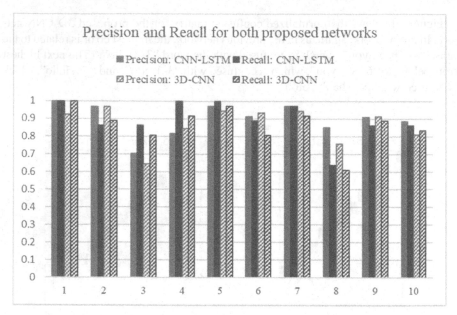

Fig. 7. Precision and recall for the proposed CNN-LSTM and 3D-CNN networks.

4 Limitations and Future Work

Currently, we are working on gathering/providing our own ISL database via the robot's camera to empower the RASA robot to automatically lip-read the users. Our next step is trying to improve the hyper-parameters of the designed networks by applying specific optimization processes to bring our accuracy closer to the best accuracies in the literature. We are trying to collect more words in our database to test the performance of the proposed networks despite the increase in classes. We hope that, due to their non-pre-trained kernels, the current networks can be appropriately generalized to ISL sings, which is a non-English sign language. Our ultimate goal of such studies is to develop a reciprocal HRI platform based on the ISL.

5 Conclusion

In this study, we proposed two neural network architectures for automated lip-reading robotic system, one of which is a combination of Convolution Neural Networks and Long Short-Term Memory, and the other is a three-dimensional CNN. In this study, the OuluVS2 dataset, which contains 10 frequently used English phrases presented in the mouth area, is used. Eight middle frames are selected from the mouth area and given to the CNN network, and then the static features extracted from the CNN are given to the LSTM to model the temporal dynamics and finally to classify. The 3D-CNN network also tries to adjust the effect of time on the features with the help of the third dimension. Our proposed networks were able to achieve 89.44% accuracy on the CNN-LSTM and 86.39% accuracy on the 3D-CNN. Although these networks do not provide the best accuracies for this database, they have been able to obtain even better accuracies than some pre-trained networks, with less details and complexity and very low training time. Also, according to our ultimate goal, which is to implement this system on RASA social robot for reciprocal interactions through ISL, the obtained accuracies are quite appropriate and acceptable.

Acknowledgement. This research was funded by Sharif University of Technology (Grant No. G980517). The complementary and continues support of the Social & Cognitive Robotics Laboratory by Dr. Ali Akbar Siassi Memorial Grant is also greatly appreciated.

References

1. McGurk, H., Macdonald, J.: Hearing lips and seeing voices. Nature 264(5588), 746 748 (1976)
2. Erber, N.P.: Auditory visual perception of speech. J. Speech Hear. Disorders **40**(4), 481–492 (1975)
3. Chiṭu, A., Rothkrantz, L.J.: Automatic visual speech recognition. Speech Enhancement Model. Recogn. Algorithms Appl. 95–120 (2012)
4. Antonakos, E., Roussos, A., Zafeiriou, S.:. A survey on mouth modeling and analysis for sign language recognition. In: 2015 11th IEEE International Conference and Workshops on Automatic Face and Gesture Recognition, FG 2015 (2015)
5. Howell, D., Cox, S., Theobald, B.: Visual units and confusion modelling for automatic lip-reading. Image Vis. Comput. **51**, 1–12 (2016)
6. Hassanat, A.: Visual passwords using automatic lip reading. Int. J. Sci. Basic Appl. Res (IJSBAR) **13**, 218–231 (2014)
7. Biswas, A., Sahu, P.K., Chandra, M.: Multiple cameras audio visual speech recognition using active appearance model visual features in car environment. Int. J. Speech Technol. **19**(1), 159–171 (2016). https://doi.org/10.1007/s10772-016-9332-x
8. Basiri, S., Taheri, A., Meghdari, A., Alemi, M.: Design and Implementation of a robotic architecture for adaptive teaching: a case study on iranian sign language. J. Intell. Rob. Syst. **102**(2), 1–19 (2021). https://doi.org/10.1007/s10846-021-01413-2
9. Hosseini, S.R., Taheri, A., Meghdari, A., Alemi, M.: Teaching Persian Sign Language to a Social Robot via the Learning from Demonstrations Approach. In: Salichs, M.A., et al. (eds.) ICSR 2019. LNCS (LNAI), vol. 11876, pp. 655–665. Springer, Cham (2019). https://doi.org/10.1007/978-3-030-35888-4_61
10. Hosseini, S.R., Taheri, A., Meghdari, A., Alemi, M.: Let there be intelligence! - A novel cognitive architecture for teaching assistant social robots. In: Lecture Notes in Computer Science including subseries Lecture Notes in Artificial Intelligence and Lecture Notes in Bioinformatics, pp. 275–285 (2018)
11. Matthews, I., Cootes, T.F., Bangham, J.A., Cox, S., Harvey, R.: Extraction of visual features for lipreading. IEEE Trans. Pattern Anal. Mach. Intell. **24**(2), 198–213 (2002)
12. Zhao, G., Barnard, M., Pietikäinen, M.: Lipreading with local spatiotemporal descriptors. IEEE Trans. Multimed. **11**(7), 1254–1265 (2009)
13. Ngiam, J., Khosla, A., Kim, M., Nam, J., Lee, H., Ng, A.Y.:. Multimodal deep learning. In: Proceedings of the 28th International Conference on Machine Learning, ICML 2011 (2011)
14. Li, Y., Takashima, Y., Takiguchi, T., Ariki, Y.:. Lip reading using a dynamic feature of lip images and convolutional neural networks. In: 2016 IEEE/ACIS 15th International Conference on Computer and Information Science, ICIS 2016 - Proceedings (2016)

15. Petridis, S., Li, Z., Pantic, M.: End-to-end visual speech recognition with LSTMS. In: ICASSP, IEEE International Conference on Acoustics, Speech and Signal Processing - Proceedings (2017)
16. Fernandez-Lopez, A., Sukno, F.M.:. Lip-reading with limited-data network. In: European Signal Processing Conference (2019)
17. Anina, I., Zhou, Z., Zhao, G., Pietikainen, M.:. OuluVS2: a multi-view audiovisual database for non-rigid mouth motion analysis. In: 2015 11th IEEE International Conference and Workshops on Automatic Face and Gesture Recognition, FG 2015. (2015)
18. Hochreiter, S., Schmidhuber, J.:. LSTM can solve hard long time lag problems. Adv. Neural Inf. Process. Syst. (1997)
19. Petridis, S., Wang, Y., Ma, P., Li, Z. and Pantic, M.:. End-to-end visual speech recognition for small-scale datasets. Pattern Recogn. Lett. 131, 421-427 (2020). http://www.ee.oulu.fi/res earch/imag/OuluVS2/ACCVW.html
20. Saitoh, T., Zhou, Z., Zhao, G., Pietikäinen, M.: Concatenated frame image based CNN for visual speech recognition. In: Chen, C.S., Lu, J., Ma, K.K. (eds.) ACCV 2016. LNCS, vol. 10117, pp. 277–289. Springer, Cham (2017). https://doi.org/10.1007/978-3-319-54427-4_21
21. Chung, J.S., Zisserman, A.: Out of time: Automated lip sync in the wild. In: Chen, C.S., Lu, J., Ma, K. (eds.) ACCV 2016. LNCS, vol. 10117, pp. 251–263. Springer, Cham (2017). https://doi.org/10.1007/978-3-319-54427-4_19
22. Petridis, S., Wang, Y., Ma, P., Li, Z., Pantic, M.: End-to-end visual speech recognition for small-scale datasets. Pattern Recogn. Lett. 131, 421–427 (2020)
23. Basiri, S., Taheri, A., Meghdari, A.F., Boroushaki, M., Alemi, M.: Dynamic iranian sign language recognition using an optimized deep neural network: an implementation via a robotic-based architecture. Int. J. Social Robot. (2021)
24. Hosseini, S.R., Taheri, A., Alemi, M., Meghdari, A.: One-shot learning from demonstration approach toward a reciprocal sign language-based HRI. Int. J. Soc. Robot. (2021)

Developing a Robot's Empathetic Reactive Response Inspired by a Bottom-Up Attention Model

Randy Gomez[1](✉)(iD), Yu Fang[1](✉)(iD), Serge Thill[2](✉)(iD), Ricardo Ragel[3](✉)(iD), Heike Brock[1](✉)(iD), Keisuke Nakamura[1](✉)(iD), Yurii Vasylkiv[4](✉)(iD), Eric Nichols[1](✉)(iD), and Luis Merino[3](✉)(iD)

[1] Honda Research Institute Japan Co., Ltd., Wako, Japan
{r.gomez,yu.fang,h.brock,keisuke,e.nichols}@jp.honda-ri.com
[2] Donders Institute for Brain, Cognition, and Behaviour, Radboud University, Nijmegen, Netherlands
serge.thill@donders.ru.nl
[3] University Pablo de Olavide, Sevilla, Spain
{rragde,lmercab}@upo.es
[4] University of Manitoba, Winnipeg, Canada
vasylkiy@myumanitoba.ca

Abstract. This paper describes the development of a reactive behavioral response framework for the tabletop robot Haru. The framework enables the robot to react to external stimuli through a repertoire of expressive routines. The behavioral response framework is inspired by the simple reactive behaviors of organisms (e.g. reflexes) based on a bottom-up attention model. First, a participatory study for behavior elicitation was conducted. We explored the possible expressive behaviors of the robot and the possible stimuli trigger. These stimuli-response (S-R) pairs are designed befitting the robot's characteristics. Then, we developed a perception and a reactive behavior module that automatically translates any perceived stimulus into expressive behavioral responses. We evaluated the proposed S-R framework using Haru in an interaction setting and our results show an increase in human attention activity indicative of its positive impact to conveying the robot's sense of agency.

Keywords: Social robot · Telepresence · Human robot interaction

1 Introduction

One of the aims in social robotics is to design robots that are fun, intuitive, and enjoyable to interact with in social situations, without necessitating specific training of the user. It is clear that not only the robot's design but also its behaviour will affect the quality of the interaction. Robots that display social behaviours, such as joint attention, task-irrelevant speech, or naming their interactants by name can be rated as more engaging than robots whose behaviour

© Springer Nature Switzerland AG 2021
H. Li et al. (Eds.): ICSR 2021, LNAI 13086, pp. 85–95, 2021.
https://doi.org/10.1007/978-3-030-90525-5_8

is more mechanical [2]. It has even been shown that human behaviour in tasks that do not involve the robot is modulated by how social a robot is if one is present [11]. On the other hand, merely increasing social behaviours does not guarantee an improvement in the quality of the interaction [8]; how precisely to design appropriate behaviours thus remains an open question. It does however appear that behaviours that lead humans to attribute a certain sense of agency to the robot are one piece of the puzzle. In earlier work, we have argued that simple, reactive behaviours are another type of robot behaviour that can convey a sense of agency for a robot [18].

Living animals demonstrate various types of reactive behaviours, from reflexes over stimulus-response behaviours to fixed action patterns. The common thread is that these behaviours typically do not involve learning but are nonetheless essential for the animal. Robotics also has a long history of interest in such behaviours, starting with the Machina Speculatrix [19] to various Braitenberg vehicles [3]. Such simple behaviours are also a core concept in subsumption architectures, where the key idea is that they come together to solve a more complex problem without the need of explicit representations [4]. In many ways, reactive behaviours are used to great effect by all animals and humans, as well as early non-social robots. Since they appear to be a fundamental feature in living beings, it is reasonable to assume that, if designed properly, they could also contribute to a perceived sense of agency of a social robot platform.

In this paper, we explore these ideas further. Specifically, we endow the robot with simple S-R behaviours that are relevant in a social context befitting a robot like Haru, expanding our previous work in [18]. We demonstrate, inspired by reactive behaviours in biology, that simple behavioural responses to social stimuli can be of benefit to a social robot, influencing the attention the robot receives and potentially the degree that the it is ascribed some agency. Such social stimulus-response behaviours might therefore be a useful component in general cognitive architectures for social robots. Like early subsumption architecture models, we essentially argue for both a reactive and a deliberative layer; however, unlike a typical subsumption architecture, the reactive layer does not have to contribute to the main task of the robot; instead, it contains behaviours that purely exist for the benefit of the social appearance of the robot. As such, this also demonstrates that behaviours that are socially relevant and promote an engaging interaction do not have to be deliberative.

This paper is organized as follows, we present the background in Sect. 2. Then, we discuss the elicitation study in which we explored Haru's S-R behaviors in Sect. 3, followed by its implementation through programming in Sect. 4. Consequently we will describe the experimental setup used in evaluating the impact of the S-R behaviors in conveying a sense of robot agency in Sect. 5. The results and discussion is presented in Sect. 6 and finally we conclude this paper in Sect. 7.

2   Background

Haru is an experimental tabletop robot for investigating new forms of expressiveness-centered empathetic communication [6] for supporting long-term and sustainable human-robot interaction. Haru has a total of 5 degrees of free-dom. It can rotate its circular base, lean its neck forward and backward, rotate and tilt its rectangular eyes, and it can push and retract the inner module of its eyes. Furthermore, each of the eyes includes a 3-inch LCD screen. In addition, two sets of addressable LED matrices are also used, one bordering the eyes, the other in the body to serve as its mouth. The robot also has a built-in stereo speaker for verbal communication using text-to-speech (TTS), and for non-verbal vocaliza-tion using a repertoire of organic sounds. To design Haru's expressivity, we built the Expression Composer Studio, a tool to simplify the combinations of the differ-ent modalities including all of the actuators. The tool permits to combine the full range of robot modalities to convey expressions [7]. Figure 1 shows the appearance of this tool. The commands for the 5 robot joints can be set by demonstrating the trajectories using a joystick or the mouse, which are then recorded in the proper format. The tool also allows determining the timed evolution of the addressable LEDs for the mouth and the eyes. Furthermore, the user can load multimedia files such as audio files for sounds videos for LCD screens. The resulting composition called routine can then be simulated through the tool and refined accordingly. The tool generates a file format that can be loaded to the actual robot hardware. By using this tool, users can design multimodal routines that constitute the reactive behaviors of the robot with ease.

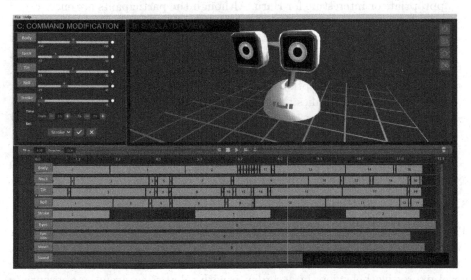

Fig. 1. Expression composer studio: a. Actuators, LCDs and LEDs pane; B. Simulator (upper-right), C. Refinement controls (upper-left).

3   Study I: Identifying Suitable S-R Behaviors

3.1   Study Description

We previously conducted a study in which Haru was treated as a social creature subject to direct coupling between perception and action [18]. In that study, the participants explored the possible behavioral reactions of Haru. The behaviors were limited to reactive responses, specifically near instantaneous reactions of the robot when presented with a stimuli. The stimuli could be anything that the participants imagine. There were no constraints imposed as to what the robot can perceive, as the robot is assumed to be a "living" social creature with the same perception capabilities as actual living beings. The participants were provided sufficient amount of information pertaining to the research objectives and the roles of Haru as a social robot, in particular as a companion species.

To identify a library of suitable stimulus-response (S-R) behaviours for Haru, we use a similar approach as in the previous study [18], except that participants here were informed of the actual perception capabilities supported by the robot as discussed in Sect. 4. Based on this constraint, the participants were instructed to refactor the results of the previous study (i.e. S-R pairs) in light of the actual perception capabilities. In particular, based on the their understanding of Haru's role as a companion species, they were asked to:

– Identify possible **scenarios** that would be interesting as a context to develop a S-R for the robot and come up with a very brief title (e.g. drooling reaction infront of a sweet treat).
– Provide a **description** of the underlying reasons why such a scenario would be appropriate or interesting for Haru. Although the participants are encouraged to find a unique reason befitting Haru, references to reactive behaviors of living correlates are also encouraged. After all, understanding these might feel more natural when framed with something that is familiar to us humans.
– Enumerate the **perception** (modalities) involved in representing the stimuli, based on the actual perception supported by the system as discussed in Sect. 4. This information simplifies the programming of S-R.
– Describe the **reactive response** of the robot and subsequently compose it using the Expression Designer Studio as discussed in Sect. 2.

In total, the participants identified 30 scenarios for use with the robot. An example of the scenarios is provided in Table 1.

3.2   Behavioral Repertoire Design

The participants were provided with the basic multimedia elements such as robot eye templates, eye movements, sounds, LED patterns and pre-made expressive routines. With all of these provisions, participants were instructed to compose novel expressive behaviors in accordance with what they deem as appropriate using the Expression Composer Studio in Fig. 1. Each reactive response ranges from 3 s – 10 s in duration and varies in terms of complexity. Moreover, every participant was given a tutorial on how to use the Expression Composer Studio, as well as some pre-existing designs serving as samples for familiarization with the software components.

Table 1. Example stimulus-response scenarios identified by the participants.

Scenario	Description	Perception	Reactive response
Facial Expression Mimicry	Mirror neurons, Empathy through facial expressions	Facing at Haru and predefined facial expressions detected	Haru's rendition of detected facial expression
Gesture Mimicry	Mirror neurons, Empathy through body gestures	Facing at Haru and predefined gestures detected	Haru's rendition of detected gesture expression
Sound Mimicry	Mirroring salient sound coming from people and environment	Sound detection: human laugh, music, etc.	Haru's rendition of laughing, dancing, etc.
Name Recognition	Recognizing one's name is an important bottom up attention feature	Speech: "Hi Haru", "Where is Haru", etc.	Surprise, happy, smile, etc. Haru orienting to the person
Relative Distance	Social-distancing, Proxemics	Awareness of predefined Distances between Haru and person	Scared, surprise, etc.
Tickling Haru	Babies and pets love to be tickled, which causes us to laugh in turn.	Gesture: Tickling	Happy Laughing sound
Heart in hand	Unconscious response to gestures indicating friendliness	Gesture: Heart	Happy Heart in eye
Applause	An expression of approval augurs good feeling	Gesture: Clapping Sound: Clapping	Happy Shy
Keyword	Special keywords connect to favorites and preferences: sweet treats, playful activities, weather, etc.	Keywords: "ice cream", "cake", "hide and seek", "sunny", etc.	Drooling, display of sweet treat emojis, weather emojis in eyes, etc.
Startle	The startle response is an unconscious defensive response to a sudden or threatening stimuli	Sound detection: loud noise, sudden noise	Surprise
Peekaboo	Peekaboo is loved by adults and kids, it stimulates interaction.	Gesture: peekaboo	Haru's rendition of peekaboo Surprise+laugh
Bowing	Bowing is an important body language in Asian cultures.	Gesture: bowing	Haru's rendition of bowing

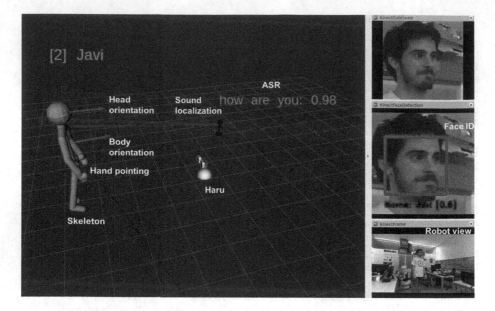

Fig. 2. Haru's perception of a person's interaction.

4 Programming Bottom-Up Behavior Mechanism

4.1 Perception

Haru, equipped with audio-visual perception system depicted in Fig. 2, enables it to perceive stimuli from human and is described as follows:

- Body pose: skeleton detection [16] is used to obtain the poses of the different persons' parts (limbs, body, head) in the field of view.
- Gestures: Roughly 50 bodily movements can be recognized such as waving, pointing, teasing, scratching one's head, asking Haru to be quiet, jumping, laughing, face covering, bowing, clapping, walking, standing, sitting down, standing up, among others [21].
- Face features: Face in the database can be identified. Additionally, facial features, including facial points and two facial expressions (e.g. smiling and frowning) are supported.
- Speech features: A microphone array for localization and separation speech, together with an automatic speech recognition (ASR) and natural language understanding [13].

4.2 Behavior Trees

We need a framework to compose reactive behaviors that link perception and action, so that the robot reacts to sensorial input to trigger actions related to engagement, agency, etc., as presented in Table 1. The framework should, therefore, allow to define the behavior of the robot by combining the different actuation components and modalities, and by accessing to the perception results. We employ Behaviour Trees (BTs)[1] to create such reactive behaviors. First originated as a tool for Non-Player Character (NPC) development in the video game industry, BTs are becoming widespread in robotics. They are a convenient tool to create *reactive* and *composable* behaviors. By using simple control structures from BTs, it is straightforward to access the perceptual stimuli and react accordingly, following the scenarios described above.

5   Study II: Attention in Function of Social S-R Behaviors

5.1   Experimental Setup

We integrated the reactive behavior model discussed in Sect. 4 in a curated interaction scenario which simultaneously involved two participants (A and B). The interaction between persons A and B is performed in front of the robot. The robot is equipped with the S-R framework and does not directly partake in the interaction between A and B, except when its bottom-up reactive behavior (S-R behavior) is triggered, as it continually observes in the background. Person A is the control person, tasked to take lead of the interaction/conversation with Person B. This role is played by a confederate, chosen among the members of the research team. Thus, the person is knowledgeable of the experiment and aware of the robot's reactive behaviors and the corresponding triggers as shown in Table 1). Person B is the actual test subject, and unaware of the existence of the reactive behaviors of Haru. During the interaction, Person A intentionally triggers the reactive behaviors of the robot. The interaction is partially scripted so that the occurrences of triggering the robot's reactive behaviors are maximized. We investigate the effect of the bottom-up reactive responses on Person B's perception of the robot by measuring their reactions to the robot during the interaction. In total, 9 test participants take on the role of participant B.

5.2   Interaction Design

The partially scripted interaction is curated by the control participant A through a combination of dialog, gestural actions, etc., that triggers the robot's behavior. There are no strict rules in the interaction, the only main requirement is to steer or lead the interaction eliciting behavioral response from the robot. For example, participant A would talk about the weather or ask questions regarding sweet treats, etc., which are defined in Haru's favorites. During the interaction, participant A may crack some jokes resulting to laughter and giggles which can be picked up by Haru. Moreover, the interaction would also involve gestural movements that are defined in S-R of Haru such as clapping, etc. To make it a more immersive and 2-way interaction, the control participant ensures that stimulus trigger should come from the actual test participant B by steering the interaction in such a manner.

---

[1] https://www.behaviortree.dev.

cppnull。null。

92   R. Gomez et al.

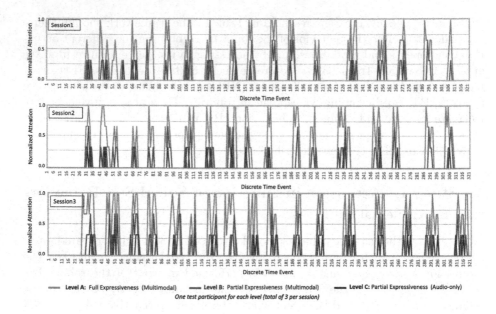

One test participant for each level (total of 3 per session)

Fig. 3. Normalized attention measurements during curated interaction.

5.3 Objective Attention Metrics

The test users' (i.e. Person B's) observable behavior such as unconscious responses to the robot's actions can provide objective evaluation metrics [1]. For example, a robot attracting the user's attention can be implicitly evaluated by how long it takes a user to look at the robot [20], and the manifestation of facial expressions and voice reactions [9,15]. A number of attention models based on saliency maps are used to predict the area of attention from subjective first-person view images [5,12]. This includes the prediction of subjective gaze location based on the hypothesis that the eyes always involuntarily shift to the location of the area of attention [10,14]. Based on this hypothesis, we can use the robot's viewpoint to calculate Person B's attention. We used the perception system described in Sect. 4 to detect head direction H (i.e., person looking at the robot), change in facial expression F (e.g. neutral to smiling, grinning, laughing, etc.) and voice reactions conveying astonishment V (e.g. laughing, saying reserved word such as "wow", etc.). The normalized attention is defined as,

$$A = \frac{H(1+F)+V}{3} \tag{1}$$

where H,F and V set to 1 when detected, respectively. Note that F is only taken into account when H is active to ensure that facial expression is elicited by the robot (i.e. when the human is facing towards the direction of the robot).

6 Results and Discussion

We measured the effect of the bottom-up reactive (expressive) behaviors on the attention model A defined in Sect. 5.3. In particular, we measure the salient features such as head direction H, change in facial expression F and voice reactions V every time the robot executes the bottom-up reactive behaviors during the curated interaction discussed in Sect. 5.1. Moreover, we also investigated the impact to the sense of agency when the expressiveness of the robot is modulated. We modulated the robot's expressivity in three different levels (A, B and C). We organized our evaluation in three different sessions, whereas each session constitutes of three test participants for each level. Hence, a total of three evaluation sessions covered all of the 9 test participants.

We show the results for the 3 evaluation sessions in Fig. 3. In this figure, Level (A) utilizes the default full expressiveness of the robot by using all of its modalities in composing the reactive behavior. In Level (B), we toned down the robot's expressiveness making it less expressive than that in Level (A). Finally in Level (C), we set the modalities to a bare minimum, retaining only the audio components and removed the robot's movements, LCD and LED displays akin to smart speakers. It is apparent from Fig. 3 that the robot attracts more attention when utilizing its full expressive abilities. This result is consistent with the feature integration theory of attention [17], in which the combination of multiple features improved the accuracy of the saliency map. Our results show some evidence of attention as defined in Sect. 5.3 to be elicited by the robot responses, suggesting a perceived sense of robot agency. We also show that the observed attention is impacted by the level of expressivity. The more expressive the robot is, the more attention it receives from the test participants. Lastly, we could observe the result trend found in Fig. 3 consistently throughout all of the evaluation sessions. Furthermore, we also asked the participants as to whether they feel some form of agency when the robot is equipped with the stimuli-reaction behavior and all of the participants confirmed the existence of agency in one form or another. We note that in this experiment we used meaningful robot behaviors with socially relevant multimodal actions for effective communication and not just mere movements. Hence we are not to test here the cause and effect between a meaningless movement and attention. We have shown in our previous work that meaningless and irrelevant robot actions were detected and disliked by participants [7]. In this paper, we only used curated and well-designed socially-relevant robot actions.

7 Conclusion

We first developed a bottom-up reactive behavior framework through an elicitation study befitting the robot's expressive character. We then integrated these into the robot Haru with complete perception and reaction modules support to automate the S-R behavior. Next, we evaluated its effect on the attribution of agency to the robot by measuring attention directed towards the robot by the participants in function of its expressiveness. Our current evaluation provides an initial insights regarding Haru's bottom-up behavioral response and attention. In the future, we will conduct more rigid experiments to investigate further the understanding of robot agency beyond attention measurement.

References

1. Admoni, H., Scassellati, B.: Social eye gaze in human-robot interaction: a review. J. Hum. Rob. Interact. **6**(1), 25–63 (2017)
2. Belpaeme, T., Kennedy, J., Ramachandran, A., Scassellati, B., Tanaka, F.: Social robots for education: a review. Sci. Rob. **3**(21) (2018)
3. Braitenberg, V.: Vehicles: Experiments in Synthetic Psychology. MIT Press, Cambridge (1986)
4. Brooks, R.A.: Elephants don't play chess. Rob. Auton. Syst. **6**(1–2), 3–15 (1990)
5. Cerf, M., Harel, J., Einhäuser, W., Koch, C.: Predicting human gaze using low-level saliency combined with face detection. Adv. Neural Inf. Process. Syst. **20**, 1–7 (2008)
6. Gomez, R., Szapiro, D., Galindo, K., Nakamura, K.: Haru: hardware design of an experimental tabletop robot assistant. In: Proceedings of the 2018 ACM/IEEE International Conference on Human-Robot Interaction, pp. 233–240 (2018)
7. Gomez, R., Szapiro, D., Merino, L., Nakamura, K.: A holistic approach in designing tabletop robot's expressivity. In: 2020 IEEE International Conference on Robotics and Automation (ICRA), pp. 1970–1976. IEEE (2020)
8. Kennedy, J., Baxter, P., Belpaeme, T.: The robot who tried too hard: social behaviour of a robot tutor can negatively affect child learning. In: 2015 10th ACM/IEEE International Conference on Human-Robot Interaction (HRI), pp. 67–74. IEEE (2015)
9. Lee, D.H., Anderson, A.K.: Reading what the mind thinks from how the eye sees. Psychol. Sci. **28**(4), 494–503 (2017)
10. Marat, S., Phuoc, T.H., Granjon, L., Guyader, N., Pellerin, D., Guérin-Dugué, A.: Modelling spatio-temporal saliency to predict gaze direction for short videos. Int. J. Comput. Vis. **82**(3), 231 (2009)
11. Mazzola, C., Aroyo, A.M., Rea, F., Sciutti, A.: Interacting with a social robot affects visual perception of space. In: Proceedings of the 2020 ACM/IEEE International Conference on Human-Robot Interaction, pp. 549–557 (2020)
12. Mital, P.K., Smith, T.J., Hill, R.L., Henderson, J.M.: Clustering of gaze during dynamic scene viewing is predicted by motion. Cogn. Comput. **3**(1), 5–24 (2011)
13. Nakamura, K., Gomez, R.: Improving separation of overlapped speech for meeting conversations using uncalibrated microphone array. In: 2017 IEEE Automatic Speech Recognition and Understanding Workshop (ASRU), pp. 55–62. IEEE (2017)
14. Peters, R.J., Itti, L.: Applying computational tools to predict gaze direction in interactive visual environments. ACM Trans. Appl. Percept. (TAP) **5**(2), 1–19 (2008)
15. Shinn-Cunningham, B.G.: Object-based auditory and visual attention. Trends Cogn. Sci. **12**(5), 182–186 (2008)
16. Shotton, J., et al.: Real-time human pose recognition in parts from single depth images. In: CVPR 2011, pp. 1297–1304. IEEE (2011)

17. Treisman, A.M., Gelade, G.: A feature-integration theory of attention. Cogn. Psychol. **12**(1), 97–136 (1980)
18. Vasylkiv, Y., et al.: An exploration of simple reactive responses for conveying aliveness using the Haru robot. In: Wagner, A.R. (ed.) ICSR 2020. LNCS (LNAI), vol. 12483, pp. 108–119. Springer, Cham (2020). https://doi.org/10.1007/978-3-030-62056-1_10
19. Walter, W.G.: An electro-mechanical «animal». dialectica, pp. 206–213 (1950)
20. Xu, T., Zhang, H., Yu, C.: See you see me: the role of eye contact in multimodal human-robot interaction. ACM Trans. Interact. Intell. Syst.(TiiS) **6**(1), 1–22 (2016)
21. Vasylkiv, Y., et al.: Automating behavior selection for affective telepresence robot. In: International Conference on Robotics and Automation, ICRA. IEEE (2021)

Toward the Realization of Robots that Exhibit Altruistic Behaviors

Hajime Katagiri(✉), Jani Even, and Takayuki Kanda

Kyoto University, Kyoto, Japan
katagiri@robot.soc.i.kyoto-u.ac.jp

Abstract. In this paper, we will discuss and investigate the conditions and requirements for future robots to be efficiently altruistic. Robots, which are integrated into our lives and become a part of society, will have to carefully balance their time between their labor and altruistic behaviors as human workers are used to do. First, we single out three essential points for achieving this balance: 1) The robot should perform altruistic actions without impacting the performance of its designated tasks more than allowed by its owner. 2) The robot should take into account its expected future workload when predicting the impact of engaging in an altruistic action. 3) The robot should take into account the benefit for the society when engaging in an altruistic action. Then, we propose a general behavioral model that makes it possible to achieve this balance. Simulation results show that a robot using the proposed behavioral model could carry out some altruistic actions and still be performing its assigned labor efficiently.

Keywords: Service robot · Altruistic behavior · Scheduling

1 Introduction

Recently, we started to see robots in public spaces and commercial facilities [4,6,8,11,13]. These robots often form an additional task force that supports and supplements the human workers. However, the shortage of work force that threatens many of the aging developed economies pushes for the development of robots that could replace humans in jobs that can no longer be purveyed. Then, in such future where robots participate on a very large scale in society, they will have to be "members of the society" and not "just machines" (Fig. 1).

Katz argues that the voluntary contribution of individuals is indispensable for maintaining the functioning of society [7]. A community cannot consist of individuals who act selfishly. To maintain organizational activities, Katz thinks that members of society have to not only "continue to participate in society" and "ensure that they fulfill their assigned roles", but also "act voluntarily beyond their assigned roles" to achieve organizational goals. Giving up your seat on the

This research was supported by JST CREST Grant Number JPMJCR17A2, Japan.

H. Li et al. (Eds.): ICSR 2021, LNAI 13086, pp. 96–106, 2021.
https://doi.org/10.1007/978-3-030-90525-5_9

Fig. 1. An example of altruistic behaviors: a delivery robot picks up trash

train, picking up and delivering lost items, picking up trash, and other small everyday voluntarily actions are maybe less obvious, but they have a huge influence on our daily lives too. It is the accumulation of all these actions that has led to the achievement of organizational goals and has maintained today's human society. As a consequence, prioritizing one's own interest at all costs is frowned upon and considered to go against the morality of human society.

Unfortunately, robots are not designed to perform such voluntary actions for the good of the community. Robots are expensive and often the main incentive for investing in one is the promise of an efficiency and running costs that would bring profit to the owner. These robots would not exhibit the simple altruistic behaviors we are used to. Consequently, in a future society where such robots are everywhere, it is likely they would be seen as selfish and would not be accepted as a members of society.

Meanwhile, the altruistic behaviour of a robot is sometimes at odds with the interests of its owner.

According to Trivers, an altruistic behavior is a behavior that benefits others and has little to do with oneself [14]. Then, interrupting one's duty to carry out an altruistic behavior probably goes against one's own interests. However, people do interrupt their duty to carry out altruistic actions. We can hypothesize that people compare the intrinsic value they attach to the altruistic behavior to their loss of productivity to decide to carry it out or not. For example, an on duty delivery man may pick up a wallet and return it to the closest police station, if he feels it would not interfere too much with his duty.

In this paper, we investigate how we could give future robots the capacity to evaluate if performing an altruistic behavior is worth it or not.

2   Related Work

Churchland defines morality as coordinating the actions of individuals with the interests of the community [2]. Malle et al. define the moral norms that are shared by the members of the society [9]. Moral actions are actions that comply with these norms. For example, a moral norm, that is widely shared in the human society, is the prohibition of behaviors that harm others for the benefit of oneself.

In the field of Human-Robot Interaction (HRI), recent research investigates how robots should be related to these moral norms. Malle et al. revisited the trolley problem by assuming that a human or a robot would operate the lever [10]. The participants in the experiment expected the robot to perform a moral action more aggressively than the human.

There are attempts to design robots that respect some moral norms too. Nishitani et. al. designed a robot that is giving way to pedestrians while moving on the sidewalk [12]. Williams focused on the use of language by robots when interacting with humans [15]. He underlined that the robot design should eliminate the possibility to produce inappropriate statements that are not morally acceptable. Akita et al. designed a robot that gives up its place when facing competition for that place [1]. In these studies, each robot followed the specific moral norm by design. Namely, it was obligatory to perform an action that follows the norm. In our case, we are interested in a robot that voluntary decides to perform an altruistic behavior.

Imre et al. proposed a computational model for altruistic behavior and tested it on an anthropomorphic robot [5]. Their work is based on the sensorimotor mechanisms of the primate brain. The robot uses vision to estimate the goals behind the actions of others. Then, it helps to achieve these goals. This can result in the robot performing an altruistic action. However, this is not the result of a deliberate decision but the consequence of some basic sensorimotor processes. In our case, we want to have some control on the process underling the decision taking.

Robots that perform altruistic behaviors were used by Correia et al. to study the effect of pro-social behaviors compared to selfish behaviors [3]. In an experiment in which humans and robots collaborate to play games. People were teamed with a pro-social robot or a selfish robot and gave their impression on the robots. Independently of the outcome of the game, the pro-social robot was preferred. In this case, the robot behaviors are pre-programmed in the context of an experiment. The study shows the effect of a robot performing altruistic actions but did not tackle how to do it.

3   Creating an Altruistic Robot

Basically, robots are assigned a role and they are designed to perform efficiently the tasks required for that role. For example, a cleaner robot is designed to navigate the environment, clean efficiently and avoid disturbing people. In the remainder of this paper, the tasks necessary for the role of the robot will be referred as the "designated tasks". Our goal is to create an altruistic robot that performs altruistic actions for the good of society. For example, the cleaner robot could warn a person dropping her/his wallet. Consequently, our task is to find a behavioral model that enables a robot to perform altruistic actions in addition of its designated tasks. First, we will examine a few candidate behavioral models and show why they are inappropriate. This will help us to understand what are the requirements an appropriate behavioral model has to fulfill.

3.1   Model A: Always Perform Altruistic Actions

First, consider an extreme model such that the robot always performs an altruistic action whenever it sees an opportunity. In this case, the robot can provide the greatest benefits to the society, but the robot does not perform its designated task efficiently as it spends much time performing altruistic actions. In particular, if the robot continues to prioritize altruistic actions over its designated tasks during busy times, it will be very inefficient at its work. The intuition is that the owner is sensitive to the efficiency of the robot at performing the designated tasks. The owner will find this extreme behavior of the robot unacceptable.

3.2   Model B: Only Performing Altruistic Actions When Unoccupied

Next, let us consider another basic model that takes into account robot's duty. The robot always performs an altruistic action whenever it sees an opportunity and it is "unoccupied". Here, "unoccupied" means that there is no designated task awaiting execution at the present moment. For example, the cleaner robot has finished cleaning a location and is waiting for an order to start cleaning another location. At first glance, this seems to balance the robot's time between designated task (occupied time) and altruistic actions (during unoccupied time). But, this model does not consider the fact that it takes some time to perform an altruistic action and the possibility that the robot may get busy in the near future. There is a risk that the robot is still busy performing an altruistic action when the next designated task appears.

The result can be a situation where the designated task is collapsed by performing an altruistic action. From the owner's point of view, with this model, performing altruistic actions may also have an unacceptable impact on the efficiency of the robot.

3.3   Model C: Treat All Altruistic Actions Equally

With the two previous models, the focus was on the scheduling of the altruistic task. Here, we would like to investigate another important aspect which is the importance of the altruistic task.

Let us assume that a robot is using a behavioral model that shares its time efficiently between performing its designated tasks and occasionally performing altruistic actions in such a way that its owner is satisfied. Namely, performing altruistic actions does not impact much the efficiency of the robot at doing its duty.

However, this behavioral model does not take into account the nature of the altruistic actions. The robot is acting the same if it witness trash it could pick on the floor or a collapse person it could rescue. The decision to carry out the altruistic action is not based on the type of actions but only on other factors (robot current state, expected work load etc.).

From the point of view of the society, this is unacceptable. The robot should prioritize helping a collapse person over its designated tasks, whereas it could overlook picking trash on the floor. This shows us that the behavioral model should not only please the owner of the robot but also conforms to the moral norms of the society.

3.4 Requirements

From the examination of the above three behavioral models, we can derive the following requirements for designing a better behavioral model:

1. The robot should perform altruistic actions without impacting the performance of its designated tasks more than allowed by its owner.
2. The robot should take into account its expected future workload when predicting the impact of engaging in an altruistic action.
3. The robot should take into account the amount of the benefit for the society when engaging in an altruistic action.

To quantify the effectiveness of the robot at performing its designated task, let us introduce the "utility" of the designated task. The utility (of the designated task) measures the gain obtained by the owner when the robot performs its designated tasks. For the owner, the higher the utility the better. Nevertheless, a small amount of decrease of the utility to make up for altruistic behavior might be allowed. It is plausible that many of owners do not mind for 1% decrease, while only a few would allow a 20% decrease.

Even if the robot is currently unoccupied, it should consider the possibility that it gets busy soon when deciding to perform an altruistic action. For example, it is not appropriate that the robot engages in an altruistic action if it knows that it is about to get busy. The robot should estimate the possible impact of engaging in an altruistic action before starting. The proposed behavioral model has to predict the future workload (designated tasks) and the expected utility gain associated to these tasks. Then, it has to consider how engaging in an altruistic action would impact this expected utility gain. For this purpose, it is also necessary to estimate the time required for the completion of the altruistic action.

The last point is related to the intrinsic value of altruistic behaviors mentioned in the introduction. This intrinsic value is based on the moral belief that "it is virtuous to help others". The intrinsic value associated to an altruistic behavior is strongly correlated with the amount of benefit provided to others by performing this action. This value is different from the value associated with one's own duty. However, people perform altruistic behaviors, even at the cost of their own duty, because they believe that there is enough intrinsic value to offset their loss. In this sense, we seem to treat some of the benefits for others of an altruistic behavior as our own benefit. The proposed behavioral model should consider that performing an altruistic action brings some gain to the robot.

3.5 Proposed Model

Let us propose a behavioral model that is based on the previous three points. The behavioral model combines two utilities: U_R measuring the gain when performing

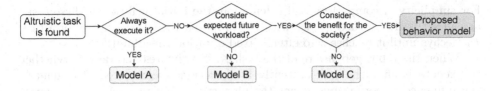

Fig. 2. Flowchart of the models

the designated tasks and ϵU_A measuring the gain when performing an altruistic action. To decide if it is worth to engage in performing an altruistic action, the robot compares the predicted utility of the designated tasks U_R when not performing the altruistic action to the predicted total utility $U = U'_R + \epsilon U_A$ obtained when perform the altruistic action. Note that U'_R differs from U_R as performing the altruistic action first affects the utility of the future designated tasks. If performing the altruistic action gives a higher utility, the robot chooses to perform the altruistic action.

During this evaluation process, the utility of the designated tasks takes into account the expected gain from known and unknown, but expected, future tasks. The proposed model assumes that the utility of a designated task will decay with time and there is a deadline after a certain time. Namely, delaying a task may reduce its utility.

Figure 2 shows how the proposed model compares to the models A, B and C introduced in the previous sections. The key to set the utility of an altruistic action is to determine ϵ, the ratio of the benefit to others that becomes the utility of the robot. If the ratio is large, the robot will often choose to perform the altruistic behavior, and if it is small, the robot will rarely choose to perform the altruistic behavior. This ratio indicates how much the robot respects the interests of others, namely, how altruistic the robot is.

4 Simulation Experiment

4.1 Simulation Setup and Settings

To illustrate the use of the proposed model, we will consider a robot that takes orders and serves dishes in a restaurant. The robot moves around the kitchen and tables during business hours, processing tasks in the execution queue as they occur. To perform a carrying task R_k, the robot moves from one point to another and picks or places dishes. The predicted execution time of a carrying task R_k is the sum of the travel time and the manipulation time.

In this simulation, the robot moves at a speed of 1.0 m per second between the four corners of a square having a ten meters edge. The robot is set to be able to move between tables in the shortest possible distance and to use a uniform 10 s to perform the task on the site. The simulation duration is 1000 s, during which 40 carrying tasks R_k occur (uniform probability distribution) and one opportunity A for altruistic behavior occurs at 500 s after the simulation starts.

For simplicity of comparison and calculation, the initial utilities of these tasks are all set to 1.0. In accordance with the proposed model, the utility of a task R_k decays until it reaches zero after a fixed duration (deadline).

When the robot gets aware of the task A, it estimates and decides whether to execute it after the task currently in execution is completed. To quantify the influence of performing or not the altruistic behavior, the robot proposes to "calculate" when the future tasks will be executed. This is straightforward for the known tasks R_k that are already in the execution queue but impossible for the unknown tasks. However, the robot can "estimate" an average result for these unknown tasks using a probabilistic approach.

Let us assume that we know the probability density function of task occurrence at time t, $C(t)$ and we can sample from it. Then, we can create a sample of "virtual tasks" that appear after t_A. The "virtual tasks" only exist in the sample. But, their distribution follows the probability density function $C(t)$ like the actual tasks that will occur after t_A. In the remainder, a "sample" is one such set of virtual tasks obtained by sampling from the probability density function of task occurrence. Note that the size of a sample is not fixed. If the probability of task occurrence is high, then the number of virtual tasks in a sample will be large. Whereas, a sample will be small if the probability of task occurrence is low.

In theory, the longer the window time the robot can consider, and the more accurate it can predict the far future. However, for reducing computation time, we have to limit the duration of the sampling interval in practice.

In this simulation, the robot estimates virtual tasks within 300 s from the current time, and it samples 1000 independent sets of samples from a known probability of task occurrences. Here, we assume that the robot knows that the tasks R_k are uniformly distributed. If the total utility $U_R' + \epsilon U_A$ is larger than U_R, then A is immediately executed.

Simulations were conducted for $\epsilon \in [0, 0.2]$ (step 0.01) and to confirm the importance of including the virtual tasks when estimating the utility, we conducted an ablation study.

4.2   Results

Figure 3 shows the ratio of altruistic tasks A that were executed when the decision includes prediction using the virtual task (blue) and when it does not (orange). That ratio increases gradually with ϵ when the prediction is included, but it increases steeply when the prediction is not included. The ratio already exceeds 40% at $\epsilon = 0.01$ when the prediction is not included.

Figure 4 shows the average values of $U_R + \epsilon U_A$ with and without prediction. This figure also shows the utility of labor when altruistic tasks are never performed (red dashed line) and when it is always performed (black dashed line). The graph shows that there is almost no change in the total utility value when the prediction is included. The value is close to the one obtained when altruistic tasks are never performed (red dashed line). But, when the prediction is not

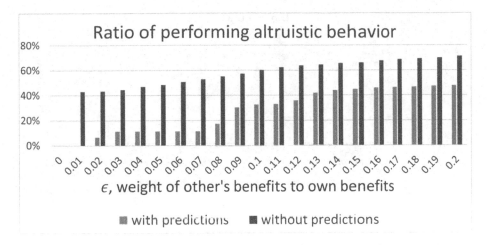

Fig. 3. Ratio of executed altruistic tasks for $\epsilon \in [0, 0.20]$ (Color figure online)

included, the total value is clearly under the red dashed line. This means that the actual utility gain is less than the one predicted during the decision process.

These results shows that including the virtual tasks in the decision process is essential.

We can see in Fig. 4 that, when using the proposed model, performing of an altruistic task hardly decreases the utility of designated tasks. In particular, when $\epsilon = 0.20$ and the altruistic task is performed 47.7% of the time, the utility gained from the labor hardly decreases. It is still close to the one obtained when never performing the altruistic task (red dashed line) The decrease is 11.9% of the decrease obtained with the model that always performs the altruistic task (black dashed line). This result show, that with the proposed model, the robot chooses its actions in a way that prevent a significant decrease in utility.

5   Discussion

5.1   Consideration About Requirements

From our investigation, we understood that two important requirements for balancing labor and altruistic behavior are: 1) being able to predict the future workload, 2) being able to evaluate the utility associated to an altruistic task.

Prediction of the Future Workload. In our behavioral model, the robot takes into account the influence of carrying out an altruistic task on its future workload. In particular, when making its decision, the robot does only know part of the future workload with certainty: the tasks that are in the execution queue. It is possible to simulate which of these tasks will be executed and which ones will expire and compute the utility gained by the robot. For the other part

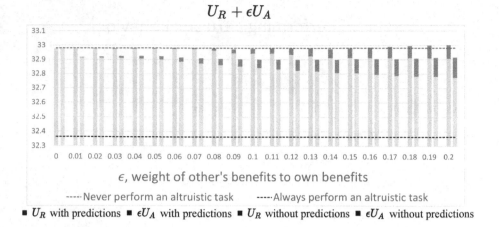

Fig. 4. Average value of $U_R + \epsilon U_A$ for $\epsilon \in [0, 0.20]$ (Color figure online)

of the future workload, the utility is estimated using a probabilistic approach. If the estimation is accurate, the proposed decision strategy guarantees that on average the robot will take the good decision. Namely, it will usually carry out an altruistic task when it can afford it. This shows that the robot has to know its labor well to be able to evaluate if it can afford to carry out an altruistic task. In practice, to implement this behavioral model, we need to be able to sample accurately the virtual tasks.

Utility Associated to Altruistic Behavior. During the decision process, the altruistic task is given an utility U_A that ideally reflects how much benefit it provides to others. We would expect different altruistic behaviors to get different utilities. Then, we could form a hierarchy of altruistic behaviors from the one with smallest utility to the one with largest utility. However, the robot has its own scale because the proposed behavioral model introduces a degree of altruism ϵ and the robot assigns the utility ϵU_A to the altruistic task. As seen in the simulation, this parameter has a direct influence on the balance the robot achieves between performing its labor efficiently and carrying out altruistic tasks. The robot's owner could set this balance where she/he see it fit using the degree of altruism ϵ.

5.2   Implications

If, in the future, robots closely cohabits with Human at every level of society and robots are designed with efficiency in mind, we could imagine a society where there is very few place left for altruistic behaviors. This is particularly a danger as it is in the financial interest of robot's owners to aim for efficiency. Fortunately, our results suggest that we could design future robots to be altruistic and still work efficiently for their owner. Then, we could expect that in a future populated with myriads of robots, we would still get help from a stranger. But, that stranger may be a robot.

We wonder how people would react to a robot that decides by itself to carry or not an altruistic action. People are used to machine exhibiting very deterministic pattern. Without access to the logic behind the decision, they may attribute some intentions to the robot that it did not have.

6 Conclusion

In this paper, we presented what are the requirements for creating a robots that can carefully balance its time between doing its labor and performing altruistic behaviors. We proposed a behavioral model that fulfils these requirements. With this model, the owner of a robot can control the balance with a parameter repre senting the degree of altruism of the robot. In the future, we have to investigate how robot's owners set the degree of altruism of their robots. In particular, we would like to know how big a degree of altruism an owner would tolerate and find strategies to increase that value.

References

1. Akita, S., Satake, S., Shiomi, M., Imai, M., Kanda, T.: Social coordination for looking-together situations. In: 2018 IEEE/RSJ International Conference on Intelligent Robots and Systems (IROS), pp. 834–841 (2018)
2. Churchland, P.S.: Braintrust: What Neuroscience Tells Us about Morality. Princeton University Press, Princeton (2011)
3. Correia, F., et al.: Exploring prosociality in human-robot teams. In: Proceedings of the 14th ACM/IEEE International Conference on Human-Robot Interaction, HRI 2019, pp. 143–151. IEEE Press (2019)
4. Gross, H., et al.: Toomas: interactive shopping guide robots in everyday use - final implementation and experiences from long-term field trials. In: 2009 IEEE/RSJ International Conference on Intelligent Robots and Systems, pp. 2005–2012 (2009)
5. Imre, M., Oztop, E., Nagai, Y., Ugur, E.: Affordance-based altruistic robotic architecture for human-robot collaboration. Adapt. Behav. 27(4), 223–241 (2019)
6. Kanda, T., Shiomi, M., Miyashita, Z., Ishiguro, H., Hagita, N.: A communication robot in a shopping mall. IEEE Trans. Rob. 26(5), 897–913 (2010)
7. Katz, D.: The motivational basis of organizational behavior. Behav. Sci. 9(2), 131–146 (1964)
8. Kulyukin, V., Gharpure, C., Nicholson, J.: Robocart: toward robot-assisted navigation of grocery stores by the visually impaired. In: Intelligent Robots and Systems, 2005. (IROS 2005), pp. 2845–2850. 2005 IEEE/RSJ International Conference (2005)
9. Malle, B.F., Scheutz, M.: Learning how to behave. In: Bendel, O. (ed.) Handbuch Maschinenethik, pp. 255–278. Springer, Wiesbaden (2019). https://doi.org/10.1007/978-3-658-17483-5_17
10. Malle, B.F., Scheutz, M., Arnold, T., Voiklis, J., Cusimano, C.: Sacrifice one for the good of many? people apply different moral norms to human and robot agents. In: Proceedings of the Tenth Annual ACM/IEEE International Conference on Human-Robot Interaction, HRI 2015, pp. 117–124. Association for Computing Machinery, New York (2015)

11. Niemelä, M., Heikkilä, P., Lammi, H.: A social service robot in a shopping mall: Expectations of the management, retailers and consumers. In: Proceedings of the Companion of the 2017 ACM/IEEE International Conference on Human-Robot Interaction, HRI 2017, pp. 227–228. ACM, New York (2017)
12. Nishitani, I., Matsumura, T., Ozawa, M., Yorozu, A., Takahashi, M.: Human-centered x-y-t space path planning for mobile robot in dynamic environments. Rob. Auton. Syst. **66**, 18–26 (2015)
13. Satake, S., Hayashi, K., Nakatani, K., Kanda, T.: Field trial of an information-providing robot in a shopping mall. In: 2015 IEEE/RSJ International Conference on Intelligent Robots and Systems (IROS), pp. 1832–1839 (2015)
14. Trivers, R.L.: The evolution of reciprocal altruism. Q. Rev. Biol. **46**(1), 35–57 (1971)
15. Williams, T.: Toward ethical natural language generation for human-robot interaction. In: Companion of the 2018 ACM/IEEE International Conference on Human-Robot Interaction, HRI 2018, pp. 281–282. Association for Computing Machinery, New York (2018)

Nadine the Social Robot: Three Case Studies in Everyday Life

Nadia Magnenat Thalmann[1,2], Nidhi Mishra[1(✉)], and Gauri Tulsulkar[1]

[1] Institute for Media Innovation, Nanyang Technological University,
Nanyang, Singapore
[2] MIRALab, University of Geneva, Geneva, Switzerland

Abstract. This paper describes three case studies performed in everyday life with our social humanoid robot, Nadine. The development of AI, vision, and NLP over the last few years has made it possible to improve social robots' awareness ability of their environment and has enabled them to understand spoken interactions. We have developed a software platform with several modules that allow us to introduce Nadine to real-life settings. We have brought Nadine to three different places in real-life setting. The first one was to prepare Nadine for an exhibition at the Artscience Museum in Singapore. The second one was to let Nadine work as a customer agent in AIA insurance company along with real employees. The third one, very recent, was to use Nadine as a companion in a elderly home. In this paper, we describe the three case studies we performed in different environments and the lessons we have learned from the outcomes of those experiences. We conclude by proposing new research avenues and the missing pieces that could make these social robots available to us in our everyday life.

Keywords: Social robotics · Robotics architecture · Nadine social robot · Human-robot interaction

1 Introduction

From ancient times till today, humans have harboured the dream of having humanoid robots. Initially, mechanics and the know-how were limited, but over centuries, we have seen constant progress in automatons that look like real persons and act autonomously. What has changed dramatically in twentieth century is the use of software linked to dedicated hardware. And more recently, the use of AI in vision to quickly understand surroundings and actions and recognize and understand people has enabled massive improvement in the behaviour of social robots. Today, we speak directly to our phones, to computers, or to some kind of pet robot, which is not user friendly nor very natural. However, some people are used to it already and tend to only prefer conversations with a voice. Still, some prefer to have that voice personified into some robotic shape far from a human shape, and others favour robots with a true human-like appearance. It is unclear

H. Li et al. (Eds.): ICSR 2021, LNAI 13086, pp. 107–116, 2021.
https://doi.org/10.1007/978-3-030-90525-5_10

today what users' "most preferred choice" is. However, a humanoid robot can offer more than a voice and a robotic human shape; it can have very realistic hands and perform more human-related tasks, walk, bring and lift things for us, and more easily do things together with us. Additionally, the realistic face and body provide a feeling of more human naturalness.

Many ancient figures in ancient times had somehow thought already, and perhaps without realizing it, about the human-machine interface. For example, Aristotle, a Greek philosopher, speculated in 322 BC in his book called Politics that human automata could do things by themselves and could someday guarantee human equality. Later on, in 250 BC, a Greek engineer named Philon created the Automatic Servant, a human-like robot representing a maid holding a jug of wine in her right hand. When visitors' cups were placed in the palm of her left hand, the servant filled them with wine and water as desired. Automatic Servant is one of the earliest humanoid robots we can think of.

Today, 3D modelling and 3D fabrication help us create quicker animated robots with social behaviour. The main novelty since almost one century ago is the addition of software layers linked to the hardware. Software allows humanoids to mimic autonomous behaviour and exhibit some awareness. Social robots can now be empowered with AI and machine learning. Adding ethical software to each humanoid robot would enable humanoids to behave according to our social rules.

In this paper, we summarize our experiences done with the social robot Nadine[1]. First, Nadine was brought in 2017 to a new exhibition, Human+, showing the empowerment of humans thanks to technology. We were invited to bring our social Nadine there and she has met more than 1,000,000 people. We could daily observe the reaction and the strong interest of the people.

Later, in 2018, in collaboration with an AIA insurance company [11], we developed additional software modules and specific insurance datasets for Nadine that would enable her to act as a customer agent. At peak hours at the insurance company, Nadine, along with customer agents, met real customers, answered questions and suggested policy insurances. This experience showed that social robots can be used for dedicated tasks.

Very recently, in collaboration with the Bright Hill elderly home in Singapore, we used Nadine to lead Bingo games and to interact with the elderly whenever they were up for it. The elderly reacted very positively, and over a 6-month study period, along with therapists at the elderly home, we came to very fascinating conclusions.

This paper is organised as follows: Sect. 2 presents the description of the research and development of the software modules used in Nadine for the three test cases. Section 3 presents the case study of Nadine at the ArtScience Museum. Section 4 explains our research and results with Nadine as a customer agent in an insurance company. Section 5 outlines the details of Nadine as a companion robot for the elderly at the nursing home and the evaluation technique used. Finally, Sect. 6 addresses the conclusions and plans for the future.

---

[1] https://en.wikipedia.org/wiki/Nadine_Social_Robot.

2   Nadine Platform and Development for Studies

Nadine's hardware was fabricated at Kokoro in Japan[2]. We aimed primarily to develop a software platform [13] with various modules, including perception, processing, and interaction. First, our platform perceives various stimuli, such as vision, vocal, etc., which help the robot understand its environment. Then each stimulus is processed to decide upon an appropriate verbal or non-verbal response. Finally, the robot appropriately enacts these responses. Our design is geared towards enabling the robot to maintain human-like natural behaviour, even in complex situations, and be generic to handle any kind of data. Each layer consists of several sub-modules for specific tasks; these sub-modules are connected using an independent platform framework [9] to facilitate module connections and development. A Microsoft Kinect, web cameras, and microphone are used as input devices, and the robot/virtual human itself serves as the output device for our platform.

We developed a generic social robotics architecture for Nadine, that can be customized to handle any scenario or application. Our architecture allows for modularity in each layer (submodules can be added or removed) and task- or environment-based customizations (for example, change in knowledge database). The architecture can be deployed easily to work with other robots and virtual characters by changing the interaction hardware layer [4], and different gestures [3] and animations can be included in the architecture to help the social robot complete tasks. This architecture allows Nadine to express human-like emotions [16], personality, behaviours, dialogue etc. Nadine can perceive both user and environmental cues and respond to them in a naturally realistic manner [1].

We have implemented our platform into Nadine, our social robot. She has a realistic human-like appearance; very natural skin, hair, etc. Nadine has a total of 27 degrees of freedom for facial expressions and upper body movements. With the proposed platform, she can adapt and work in different environments, such as at a reception, in an agency, in an elderly care home, or as someone to entertain a crowd at an event. Figure 1 shows Nadine trained and customized for different events, places, and handling different scenarios. Our platform can also be used for other robots or virtual characters easily [10].

3   Case Study 1: Nadine at the ArtScience Museum in Singapore

Our first experience using Nadine outside of academic settings came when we have been invited by the ArtScience Museum in Singapore[3] [4] to participate in the Human+ exhibition, which ran from May 20 to October 15, 2017. The exhibition aimed primarily to answer the question: What will it be like in a future dominated by AI, robots, and augmented bodies? The museum's show

---

[2] https://www.kokoro-dreams.co.jp/.

[3] https://robotschampion.com/human-future-of-our-species/.

[4] https://www.youtube.com/watch?v=wYm06LZdlts.

featured an intriguing blend of technology and art, none more so than Nadine's interaction with visitors.

Fig. 1. Nadine interacting with visitors at the Arts Science Museum

Nadine sat at a table ready to talk to any visitor either in English or in Chinese. Visitors willing to engage with her took a seat opposite her, as Fig. 2 shows, and asked her questions. If she did not understand a question, she simply said she could not answer it. Many people stopped by for a talk with Nadine and Nadine sat at a table ready to talk to any visitor either in English or in Chinese. Many people stopped by for a talk with Nadine and asked all types of questions, and even parents with children and babies came by to interact with her.

Due to the Museum's confidentiality agreement, we were not allowed to record and conduct a formal user study. Additionally, it was too difficult to ask visitors to fill forms permitting us to use their data. Furthermore, Nadine was not allowed to use her memory and face recognition modules because we were not permitted to keep any private information from conversations.

However, more than 100 000 visitors came to see Nadine, with people queuing up to discuss with her. The questions asked were extremely broad, and Nadine answered most, although not always accurately. For the most part, we learnt from this experience that the younger generation was most fascinated with Nadine's appearance and her ability to speak several languages and answer all sorts of questions, including funny ones. The older population most often did not ask questions but observed the social robot and passed by. The 6-month experience helped us make improvements in Nadine's interaction ability: we increased her local database, enhanced her response time to people, and developed models, like the Bert model, to advance her understanding of speech. We planned to drastically improve Nadine's capacity to understand any spoken topics and deal with multiparty interactions (2021).

4   Case Study 2: Nadine at the AIA Insurance Company in Singapore

Lately, several researchers and organizations have begun to consider making social robots a part of their workforce. Initially, robots at workplaces were restricted to simple tasks, such as greeting customers at information booths

[8], performing a predefined skill of archery [7], bartending with communication skills, and guiding customers [2,5].

Fig. 2. Nadine interacting with customers at the AIA insurance company

In contrast to early task-based robots, designing humanoid social robots involves developing cognition that considers context, work environment, and social interaction clues. The advent of Artificial Intelligence and robotics has prompted a universal question: "Can a humanoid social robot be a part of a company's workforce?". Does it have all the skills and etiquette to function successfully in an open work environment with different tasks? To answer these questions we set Nadine up in an insurance company[5] to work as a customer service agent alongside other human employees [11]. She adequately recognized known staff, communicated with them in the natural language, assisted them with some tasks, and built a relationship with them[6].

Nadine can do many things as an intelligent customer agent. For example, she can be asked to give specific messages to visitors coming in the next day. Existing customers asked Nadine to help them make simple queries on the database, change their addresses, or extract other information. For tough questions, she redirected customers to the human customer agent. Such a scenario is truly interdisciplinary, involving Computer Vision, Speech Recognition, Natural Language Processing, Emotions, Memory [6,17], and Decision Making.

To evaluate Nadine's capabilities, we conducted two different studies: for the first part, we created a questionnaire, and for the second study, we asked customers to provide feedback not restricted to a particular question. A total of 75 users provided their valuable feedback on Nadine and answered the questionnaire over a period of 6 months. The questionnaire survey helped us capture customers' feelings and opinions about Nadine's performance during their interaction with her. We analyzed feedback data using a SenticNet computing framework that gave us customers' sentiment during their interaction with Nadine. Figure 3 presents the results of the questionnaire and sentiment analysis.

Most customers agreed that Nadine was friendly, while others were unsure, which shows Nadine as being courteous. She has an emotion model [16] that enables her to express pleasant behaviour, smile to customers, and show emotion.

---

[5] https://www.youtube.com/watch?v=7HUSXq3xvTs.
[6] https://www.youtube.com/watch?v=lv6nWe1Gn00.

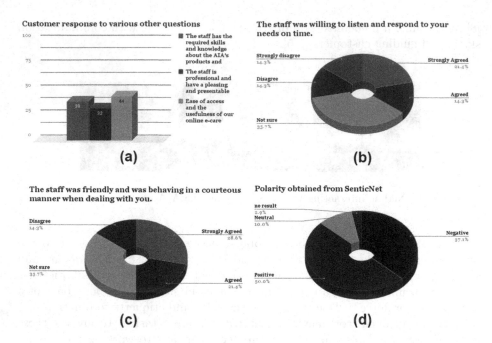

Fig. 3. Results of questionnaire and feedback data

A humanoid robot must have emotion to enable it to empathize with customers, as seen in Fig. 3.

On account of Nadine's willingness to listen and respond on time, the results were mixed. Being a robot, Nadine is always welcoming and willing to listen; however, her response to a question can sometimes be delayed for many reasons; when she cannot find an appropriate answer in her database to reply immediately, she looks for one online, which can take time. At times, she may not reply at all, particularly if the customer does not speak into the microphone, which can leave people feeling that Nadine is not willing to listen, as seen in Fig. 3.

The overall sentiment from customer feedback is depicted in Fig. 3. 50% of the customers provided Positive feedback on Nadine's performance as an employee, 37.1% had a Negative impression, and 10% had Neutral sentiments.

Based on customer feedback and the survey questionnaire, we identified customer expectations and demands of such a robot employee. The overall sentiment towards a humanoid agent in this kind of insurance workplace is positive. In the survey, customers found Nadine to be very human-like, leading customers to have high expectations of such a social robot.

Fig. 4. Nadine interacting with the elderly at the elderly home

5   Case Study 3: Nadine at the Bright Hill Elderly Home in Singapore

Cognitively impaired elderly at nursing homes have difficulties performing daily activities and maintaining their wellbeing. Healthcare workers and caregivers are particularly crucial to addressing these challenges, and the need for them is high; therefore, social robots have been looked at as potentially assisting both the elderly and caregivers. We deployed Nadine at an elderly home to understand the impact of humanoid assistive technology on the elderly and care staff, aiming to investigate the effectiveness of our Nadine robot based on the willingness of our hosts to communicate and engage with her, as well as their mood during the human-humanoid interaction. Nadine was deployed at the elderly home for 6 months during which she performed the following two activities:

- Hosted bingo games: Nadine hosted bingo games as part of multiparty interactions; she hosted two games each week for 29 participants [12].
- One on one interactions: Nadine also carried out one on one conversations with 14 participants during which she interacted with them based on the wishes of the participants [14].

We placed six cameras in the ward where Nadine was seated to capture the activities, and this helped us evaluate Nadine's performance. To obtain a comprehensive understanding of her impact on the nursing home occupants, we considered both objective and subjective tools for data analysis. The objective tools are based on cutting-edge computer vision techniques, such as Deep Neural Networks (DNNs). To automatically evaluate the residents' mental states, we captured their facial expressions to determine their mood (Eight emotions), residents' body movements to assess their involvement with Nadine, and care staff movement to evaluate the need for staff during hosted activities.

For the Bingo game, we compared sessions of Nadine's hosting with those of the staffs' hosting. Both objective and subjective tools were used for the comparison. According to the results in Fig. 5, the elderly smiled more, moved around less, and the optical flow, which primarily depicts how much movement nursing home's care staff made, was also lower, suggesting that the situation in the nursing home was better when Nadine was present: the residents were calmer and happier, while the staff had less work to do.

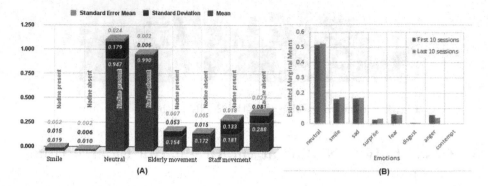

Fig. 5. (A) Statistical difference measures between the two scenarios - with Nadine and without Nadine during Bingo game. (B) Comparison of different emotions between the first and the last 10 sessions.

For one on one interactions, we compared Nadine's first sessions at the elderly home to sessions on the last days of her presence at the home. Residents' facial emotions in the figure indicate their involvement in conversations with Nadine. The residents interacted with Nadine on average 50% of the time she was there, indicating they had a moderate interest to interact with her, which is to be expected from the residents of a home for the elderly. However, those who interacted with her more showed much less fear, indicating that they felt more relaxed when interacting with her; they also smiled slightly less, but, perhaps, this was them merely interacting with Nadine normally. Their average body movement increased from 0.05 to 0.2, a big difference from that in Nadine's absence. These findings indicate significant positive changes noted in the residents' responses (well-being) over the 6 months of interaction with Nadine.

6   Conclusions and Future Research

In this paper, we have presented concrete experiences with Nadine in three distinct environments where she interacted with various people: in the first place, she interacted mostly with a very broad public audience, in the second location, she served as a service robot, and in the third place, she acted as a companion.

Based on these experiences, we can conclude that Nadine was useful in the three environments vis-à-vis the role she played. However, to bring these social robots to a larger scale, we need more research and development. First of all, Nadine is a sitting robot, and customers need a moving robot that can bring things and objects to them and go to specific people. Therefore, social robots must have articulated hands and be able to move either through a base or using legs. Incorporating legs or bases while adapting cameras and a microphone to a robot requires quite a lot of additional hardware work. On the software side, environment detection, collision response, and multiparty interaction modules must be developed for indoor moving social robots. Research is ongoing, but there is a major barrier; the cost of such a humanoid realistic robot. To become popular, these robots must be produced in high numbers; however, as of now, only a few social humanoid robots exist because they are too expensive to be produced in mass; they need a more functional capacity and awareness of the environment and themselves.

Furthermore, the appearance of a humanoid is very important. In the insurance case study, another social robot, Pepper, was also tested; however, it failed in its capacity as a customer relationship mediator. Pepper was only suitable as a greeting tool, welcoming people as they entered the insurance agency. This study showed that robots, like Pepper, are viewed as an entertainment tool, with people unwilling to ask them serious questions about insurance. On the contrary, Nadine, the social robot with its very human face and behaviour [18], was seen as trustable enough to deal with insurance matters.

More importantly, in the elderly home, residents developed some relationships with Nadine and always professed their love for her because she was so beautiful and natural, as seen in a video that was filmed during the study (please give us video link to be added, we do not have the link).

In the future, additional Research and Development must be performed in consideration of the needs of potential customers. Concerning the appearance of social robots, people prefer interacting with a realistic humanoid robot to a metallic robot. The uncanny valley effect should be revisited, as the behaviour and appearance of social robots have become positive parameters than were seen in the past.

In conclusion, a lot of research must still be performed on social robotics. In particular, speech understanding, multiparty interaction [15], and global awareness of the environment require additional scrutiny. On the hardware side, modules for human-like walking and grasping are still in the research design phase. It will take a couple of years, give or take before we will see social robots frequently in our daily life; still, we are all aiming in this direction. Key determining factors for this realization will be the social acceptance of these humanoid robots and their ability to be compliant with ethical rules and customers' needs.

References

1. Baka, E., Vishwanath, A., Mishra, N., Vleioras, G., Thalmann, N.M.: "Am i talking to a human or a robot?": a preliminary study of human's perception in human-humanoid interaction and its effects in cognitive and emotional states. In: Gavrilova, M., Chang, J., Thalmann, N.M., Hitzer, E., Ishikawa, H. (eds.) CGI 2019. LNCS, vol. 11542, pp. 240–252. Springer, Cham (2019). https://doi.org/10.1007/978-3-030-22514-8_20
2. Bennewitz, M., Faber, F., Joho, D., Schreiber, M., Behnke, S.: Towards a humanoid museum guide robot that interacts with multiple persons. In: 5th IEEE-RAS International Conference on Humanoid Robots, 2005, pp. 418–423. IEEE (2005)
3. Bian, Z.P., Hou, J., Chau, L.P., Magnenat-Thalmann, N.: Human computer interface for quadriplegic people based on face position/gesture detection. In: Proceedings of the 22nd ACM International Conference on Multimedia, pp. 1221–1224 (2014)

4. Dalibard, S., Thalmann, D., Magnenat-Thalmann, N.: Interactive design of expressive locomotion controllers for humanoid robots. In: 2012 IEEE RO-MAN: The 21st IEEE International Symposium on Robot and Human Interactive Communication, pp. 431–436. IEEE (2012)
5. Giuliani, M., et al.: Comparing task-based and socially intelligent behaviour in a robot bartender. In: Proceedings of the 15th ACM on International Conference on Multimodal Interaction, pp. 263–270 (2013)
6. Kasap, Z., Magnenat-Thalmann, N.: Building long-term relationships with virtual and robotic characters: the role of remembering. Vis. Comput. **28**(1), 87–97 (2012)
7. Kormushev, P., Calinon, S., Saegusa, R., Metta, G.: Learning the skill of archery by a humanoid robot icub. In: 2010 10th IEEE-RAS International Conference on Humanoid Robots, pp. 417–423. IEEE (2010)
8. Ltd., Actroid, K.C.: (2003). https://en.wikipedia.org/wiki/Actroid
9. Magnenat-Thalmann, N., Yuan, J., Thalmann, D., You, B.-J. (eds.): Context Aware Human-Robot and Human-Agent Interaction. HIS, Springer, Cham (2016). https://doi.org/10.1007/978-3-319-19947-4
10. Mishra, N., Baka, E., Magnenat Thalmann, N.: Exploring potential and acceptance of socially intelligent robot. In: Thalmann, N.M., Zhang, J.J., Ramanathan, M., Thalmann, D. (eds.) Intelligent Scene Modeling and Human-Computer Interaction. HIS, pp. 259–282. Springer, Cham (2021). https://doi.org/10.1007/978-3-030-71002-6_15
11. Mishra, N., Ramanathan, M., Satapathy, R., Cambria, E., Magnenat-Thalmann, N.: Can a humanoid robot be part of the organizational workforce? a user study leveraging sentiment analysis. In: 2019 28th IEEE International Conference on Robot and Human Interactive Communication (RO-MAN), pp. 1–7. IEEE (2019)
12. Mishra, N., Tulsulkar, G., Li, H., Thalmann, N.M.: Does elderly enjoy playing bingo with a robot? a case study with the humanoid robot nadine. arXiv preprint arXiv:2105.01975 (2021)
13. Ramanathan, M., Mishra, N., Thalmann, N.M.: Nadine humanoid social robotics platform. In: Gavrilova, M., Chang, J., Thalmann, N.M., Hitzer, E., Ishikawa, H. (eds.) CGI 2019. LNCS, vol. 11542, pp. 490–496. Springer, Cham (2019). https://doi.org/10.1007/978-3-030-22514-8_49
14. Tulsulkar, G., Mishra, N., Lim, H.E., Lee, M.P., Cheng, S.K., Thalmann, N.M.: Can a humanoid social robot stimulate the interactivity of cognitive impaired elderly? a thorough study based on computer vision methods. To be published in The Visual Computer (2021)
15. Yumak, Z., Ren, J., Thalmann, N.M., Yuan, J.: Modelling multi-party interactions among virtual characters, robots, and humans. Presence Teleoperators Virtual Environ. **23**(2), 172–190 (2014)
16. Zhang, J., Magnenat-Thalmann, N., Zhang, J.: Modeling emotions and moods in an affective system for virtual human and social robots. In: the 25th International Conference on Computer Animation and Social Agents (2012)
17. Zhang, J., Zheng, J., Thalmann, N.M.: Mcaem: mixed-correlation analysis-based episodic memory for companion-user interactions. Vis. Comput. **34**(6), 1129–1141 (2018)
18. Zhang, Z., Beck, A., Magnenat-Thalmann, N.: Human-like behavior generation based on head-arms model for robot tracking external targets and body parts. IEEE Trans. Cybern. **45**(8), 1390–1400 (2014)

Social Context Awareness

Investigating Customers' Perceived Sensitivity of Information Shared with a Robot Bartender

Alessandra Rossi[1]([✉]) [iD], Giulia Perugia[2,3] [iD], and Silvia Rossi[1,4] [iD]

[1] ICAROS Center, University of Naples Federico II, Naples, Italy
alessandra.rossi@unina.it
[2] Department of Information Technology, Uppsala University, Uppsala, Sweden
[3] Human Technology Interaction Group, Department of Industrial Engineering
and Innovation Sciences, Eindhoven University of Technology, Eindhoven,
The Netherlands
giulia.perugia@it.uu.se
[4] Department of Electrical Engineering and Information Technologies,
University of Naples Federico II, Naples, Italy
silvia.rossi@unina.it

Abstract. Personalised experiences with service robots positively affect people's perception of the robot and, consequently, foster the success of the interaction. This implies that people need to share their personal information with the robot, which could let people feel uneasy when such interactions happen in public spaces or in the presence of strangers. Therefore, it is difficult for a service robot to personalise a human-robot interaction (HRI) when this can lead to a breach of privacy. As a first step, the current study investigated people's perception of the sensitivity of various categories of potentially private personal information that are likely to be used by a service robot in a public business, such as a bar. We conducted a questionnaire-based study, where participants rated 15 personal information that they could share with either a human or robot bartender. The potentially private information was rated by participants according to their level of sensitivity. We analysed responses from 76 participants. We clearly identified information that are perceived as highly sensitive, such as those related to a person's identity (e.g. sexual orientation, political beliefs), and as low in sensitivity, such as those related to personal interests (e.g. sports, TV shows). Our findings also showed that older people consider sharing their preference of drinks more sensitive than younger people, especially when the bartender is a robot. We did not find significant differences in users' ratings due to their gender.

Keywords: Human-robot interaction · Privacy · Social robotics

1 Introduction

Modern business began to introduce novel and appealing technologies to attract customers and increase their retention by providing endearing interactions [2].

© Springer Nature Switzerland AG 2021
H. Li et al. (Eds.): ICSR 2021, LNAI 13086, pp. 119–129, 2021.
https://doi.org/10.1007/978-3-030-90525-5_11

Hence, robotics applications are being deployed in the food and beverage industries [2], and specifically in bartending scenarios [13, 20]. Bartending scenarios are particularly of interest due to the complexity of the interaction, which includes the execution of the required tasks to prepare a drink (i.e. selecting and manipulating ingredients), the managing of the orders, and the adaptation of the robot's behaviours to the customers' needs and preferences. In such scenarios, effective customer relationship management is fundamental for a successful and long-term interaction with users [10, 11]. Customer retention largely depends on the bartender robot's ability to provide a satisfactory service in terms of task accomplishment, social responsiveness and empathy towards customers [23, 25].

The work presented in this paper has been carried out as part of the BRILLO (Bartending Robot for Interactive Long-Lasting Operations) project which envisages a real-world bartender robot that intelligently adapts its multimodal behaviours to determine the long-term success of the use of bartender robots, and, more in general, of service robotics applications [14]. The BRILLO bartender robot, therefore, should exhibit practical, social and emotional intelligence to tailor its interaction to the customers. For this reason, the robot needs a wide range of information to satisfy customers' moods, attention behaviours, personal traits, and situational context (i.e. drink tastes, small chat preferences, group dynamics, etc.). This implies that the BRILLO system needs to build customers' profiles by 1) detecting, recognising and tracking the users via robot's camera (i.e. biometrical recognition), 2) identifying user's mood and emotional reactions through the robot's sensors (i.e. sentiment analysis, facial expressions), 3) identifying the level of engagement of one or more users while they are interacting with the robot through the users' body posture, head pose, and the group's arrangements (i.e. facing each other), and 4) managing a recommendation system based on users' interaction, drinks preferences, history of previous interactions, and similarities with users who have alike profiles.

While the wide amount of information collected by social robots may introduce a violation of people's privacy during human-robot interaction, it might also be possible that people relate to a bartender robot as they do with human bartenders [3]. Human bartenders are known to play the role of a confidant or a counsellor with whom customers often share their problems and information [4]. For example, people might share their relationship stories with a human bartender or comment some funny event that happened during their day. They could discuss the latest political news, and so on. Each of these examples represents private information, and while they would be regulated by rules and laws in online applications, in casual environments, such as a bar, they might be perceived with a different level of sensitivity. Moreover, people have individual differences (e.g. age, personality) which may affect their perception of what is considered sensitive information to be shared with a robot in a public space. It is important, therefore, to *determine which type of information people consider to be more or less sensitive in order to properly investigate the effects of a breach of privacy on HRIs in public environments*. For this purpose, we present in this paper a questionnaire-based study conducted with the purpose to classify the level of perceived sensitivity of several personal information.

2 Design

The purpose of this study was to investigate people's perception of potentially private information that a service robot could use to personalise the interaction with them and to create a more engaging relationship. In this context, we classified several personal information according to their perceived sensitivity. We expected to observe a variation in people's evaluation of the information sensitivity according to whether the scenario presented involved a robot or human bartender. In particular, we hypothesised that people would be more inclined to share their personal information with a human than a robot bartender [4].

2.1 Methodology

The online questionnaire-based study was organised as a between-subject experiment where users were asked to imagine that their information were shared with 1) a robot bartender in condition **C1**; 2) a human bartender in condition **C2**. In both conditions, participants were presented with three sets of questions. We also informed them that the bartender had some information about them, and asked them to rate each listed information according to their perception of sensitivity, in terms of privacy. We did not provide any description of the robot, because we were exclusively interested in participants' general perception of the sensitivity of personal information and not in their perception of any robot [17].

A first questionnaire was used to collect generic information about the users, including their demographics (i.e. age, gender, occupation, nationality), personality traits [8], experience, perception while using e-stores (e.g. "I generally trust online companies with handling my personal information and my purchase history", and "I feel safe giving my personal information to online stores"), and behaviours in possible bar scenarios. Questions about people's behaviours were designed considering previous studies in HRI [16,18], such as "Did you ever take more change than you were supposed to?" (with no, maybe, and yes as possible answers), and social conventions in bars [15], such as "Did you ever avoid to pay for a drink when it was your round?".

Then, participants were presented with 15 different questions (one for each type of information) and rated their level of sensitivity. We collected people's ratings of the information's sensitivity using a 5-point Semantic Differential [1 = "The information is not sensitive at all" to 5 = "The information is extremely sensitive"]. Questions included information of different nature[1]. For example, they were related to identity information (e.g. "Sexual orientation"), drink preferences (e.g. "Your preference for non-alcoholic drinks"), or interests (e.g. sport,

---

[1] Note that we did not ask participants to give us their personal information. We simply asked them to rate the sensitivity level of such information.

TV shows, cf. Table 1 for an overview). We designed the questionnaire used in this study to cover a wide range of generic topics based on previous HRI studies and human-human studies in bar scenarios [24]. For example, Rossi et al. [19] used drinks, hobbies, musical preferences of customers to personalise their interaction with a robot arm bartender.

Finally, in the last questionnaire, we asked participants if they would have shared such information with a human bartender (in **C1**) or with a robot bartender (in **C2**), and which were the information that they would have not been willing to share respectively with the human and robot bartender.

2.2 Participants

We recruited 40 participants for each condition, for a total of 80 participants (51 female, 29 male, none non-binary). Participants were aged between 20 and 68 (mean age 38, std. dev. 11). The majority of participants (66.25%) stated to be Italian, while the remaining participants were British (15%), German (3.75%), Dutch (2.5%), Portuguese (2.5%), Swedish (2.5%), Greek (1.25%), Indian (1.25%), Lithuanian (1.25%), Norwegian (1.25%), US American (1.25%) and double nationality Russian/Swedish (1.25%). We excluded 2 participants from each condition due to potential extreme response bias (N = 3) or because they gave the same response to all sensitivity questions (N = 1).

3   Results

As a first step, we performed a factorial analysis including all the items of the information sensitivity questionnaire (extraction: principal components; rotation: varimax) to verify the internal robustness of this set of questions, and reduce the number of dependent variables. A Kaiser-Meyer-Olkin measure of sampling adequacy ($KMO = .839$) and Bartlett's test of sphericity ($X^2(105) = 1104.05$, $p < 001$) indicated that the data we collected was appropriate to run such analysis. We identified four components within the information sensitivity questionnaire (see cf. Table 1 for factor loadings and Cronbach's α): (i) *Sensitivity of Personal Interests*, (ii) *Sensitivity of Identity Information*, (iii) *Preferred Drink Sensitivity*, and (iv) *Drinking Context Sensitivity*.

Before running the actual statistics, we checked whether the assumption of normality of the data was met. A Shapiro-Wilk test of normality revealed that the dependent variables were not normally distributed, thus in the study we exclusively employed non-parametric statistical analyses. As preliminary analyses, we checked whether the gender and age of the participants influenced their responses. Since the majority of participants stated to have the nationality of one country (Italy), and the other nationalities were only with one or two individuals, we could not run a statistical test with the nationality of the participants as between-subject factor. We ran two separate Mann-Whitney U tests with information sensitivity as dependent variable and participants' gender and age group as independent variables. Since participants identified themselves as

Table 1. Results of Factorial Analysis divided according to the four identified components of information sensitivity.

Item	Components			
	1	2	3	4
Your interest in sport	.932			
Your interest in art	.928			
Your interest in movies	.897			
Your interest in TV shows	.841			
Your interest in culture	.774			
Cronbach's α	**.964**			
Your political beliefs		.892		
Your religious beliefs		.850		
Your sexual orientation		.806		
Your relationship status		.775		
Cronbach's α		**.901**		
Your preference for non-alcoholic drinks			.939	
Your preference for alcoholic drinks			.901	
Which is your preferred drink			.828	
Cronbach's α			**.906**	
How many times you drink during the day				.853
You prefer to drink alone				.770
You prefer to drink in company				.699
Cronbach's α				**.861**

female ($N = 48$) and male ($N = 28$), and none of them identified as non-binary, we considered the independent variable gender to have only these two values. With regard to the age group, as the mean age of the participants was 37.84 years ($SD = 11.13$), we considered 38 years as a cut-off score and divided participants into two age groups: below ($N = 43$, $M = 30.09$, $SD = 4.91$) and above mean age ($N = 33$, $M = 47.31$, $SD = 9.07$). The results did not show a main effect of gender on information sensitivity (see cf. Table 2). However, they disclosed a main effect of age group on preferred drink sensitivity with older participants finding this information more sensitive ($M = 2.73$, $SD = 1.41$) than younger participants ($M = 1.96$, $SD = 1.13$, cf. Table 2). To investigate whether participants' usual behaviours in a bartending context could influence the perceived sensitivity of information, we ran a Mann-Whitney U test dividing participants in two groups based on whether they reported to have ever jumped the queue ($N = 30$) or not ($N = 46$). We could not run this analysis for the questions "Did you ever take more change than you were supposed to?" (yes: $N = 26$; no: $N = 56$) and "Did you ever avoid to pay for a drink when it was your round?" (yes: $N = 5$; no: $N = 71$) due to an uneven distribution of participants' responses. The results of this analysis were not significant (cf. Table 2).

Table 2. Results of the Mann Whitney U tests for the different independent variables (the significant results are highlighted in bold).

	Personal interests			Identity information			Preferred drinking			Drinking context		
	U	z	p	U	z	p	U	z	p	U	z	p
Gender	632	−.436	.663	659	−.143	.887	656	−.177	.860	524	−1.602	.109
Age group	639	−.747	.455	703	−.064	.949	**503**	**−2.218**	**.027**	704	−.058	.954
Jump queue	681	−.091	.927	678	−.130	.897	661	−.316	.752	613	−.817	.414
Agent Type	642	−.835	.404	649	−.768	.443	**527**	**−2.076**	**.038**	635	−.903	.366

3.1 Effects of Agent Type on Participants' Perception of Information Sensitivity

We followed up the preliminary analyses with a Mann-Whitney U test including agent type as independent variable (human and robot bartender) and information sensitivity as dependent variable. Similar to age group, agent type had a significant effect on the preferred drink information sensitivity (cf. Table 2). Participants in the robot condition found this information more sensitive ($M = 2.58$, $SD = 1.35$) than participants in the human condition ($M = 2.01$, $SD = 1.22$).

Given the correspondence between the results on agent type and age group, we performed a Kruskall Wallis H test to discriminate whether a combined effect of agent type and age group was at stake. For this analysis, we combined agent type and age group into a four-level independent variable (robot and younger group $N = 23$, human and younger group $N = 20$, robot and older group $N = 15$, and human and older group $N = 18$) and used information sensitivity as dependent variable. The results disclosed a significant effect on preferred drink sensitivity ($X^2(3) = 10.954$, $p = .012$) but not on sensitivity of personal interests ($X^2(3) = 1.481$, $p = .687$), sensitivity of identity information ($X^2(3) = 1.162$, $p = .762$), and drinking context sensitivity ($X^2(3) = 1.848$, $p = .605$). Follow-up Mann-Whitney U tests considering a Bonferroni correction (cut-off $p = .008$) disclosed that older participants found that the preferred drink information was more sensitive when the bartender was a robot ($M = 3.47$, $SD = 1.24$) rather than a human ($U = 62$, $z = −2.684$, $p = .007$, $M = 2.11$, $SD = 1.27$), while younger participants did not show such difference ($U = 204$, $z = −.655$, $p = .512$). Older participants in the robot condition found the information on preferred drink more sensitive than younger participants in the robot ($U = 64$, $z = −3.269$, $p = .001$, $M = 2.00$, $SD = 1.09$) and human condition ($U = 58$, $z = −3.122$, $p = .002$, $M = 1.91$, $SD = 1.21$). No such difference was present between younger and older participants when the bartender was a human ($U = 170$, $z = −.313$, $p = .754$), nor between younger participants in the robot condition and older participants in the human condition ($U = 203$, $z = −.109$, $p = .914$). Finally, when asked whether they would have given a different answer in the opposite condition, participants in the robot condition said they have would have given a different answer if the bartender was a human

$(U = 562, z = -2.714, p = .007, M = 1.68, SD = .121)$, whereas participants in the human condition were less prone to change their responses if the bartender was a robot $(M = 1.27, SD = .095)$.

3.2 Relationship Between Participants' Personalities, Propensity to Trust Online Companies and Perception of Information Sensitivity

We also estimated whether the sensitivity of the different types of information was related to participants' personality traits (i.e. extraversion, agreeableness, conscientiousness, emotional stability, openness to experience) and their propensity to trust online companies (i.e., "I feel safe giving my personal information to online stores", "I generally trust online companies with handling my personal information and my purchase history", "how concerned you are about threats to your privacy" reverse coded). Since this analysis was aimed at gaining insights into the design of a bartender robot, it was performed only with the data from the robot condition.

The sensitivity of personal interests and drinking context did not correlate with any of the personality traits and propensity to trust items. Conversely, the sensitivity of personal identity information was significantly negatively correlated with the perceived safety in giving personal information online $(r_s(36) = -.391, p = .015)$ and the lack of concern about threats to privacy $(r_s(36) = -.461, p = .004)$. Moreover, it showed a tendency to positively correlate with emotional stability $(r_s(36) = .299, p = .068)$. Finally, the preferred drink sensitivity was significantly negatively correlated with the propensity to trust online companies in the handling of data $(r_s(36) = -.368, p = .015)$ and significantly positively correlated with participants' emotional stability $(r_s(36) = .365, p = .024)$.

3.3 Participants' Ratings of the Information Sensitivity

While the information sensitivity of people's drinking preferences varied across agents and age groups, it was not, however, the most sensitive information. The rating scale we used ranged from 1 to 5 (from not sensitive to extremely sensitive). Hence, we can categorise the information with mean values below 3 as with "low sensitivity", those with mean values above 3 as "highly sensitive", and those with ratings equal to 3 as "mildly sensitive". If we take a look at the descriptive statistics in Table 3, which shows the distributions of participants' responses in descending order, and the histograms of the four subscales of information sensitivity of our study in Fig. 1, we can see that the information related to a person's identity (i.e., sexual orientation, relationship status, political, and religious beliefs) was in general perceived as the most sensitive, and this regardless of the agent it was disclosed with and the age group of the participant.

Table 3. Descriptive statistics for the different dependent variables.

Item or *Subscale*	Sensitivity		
	M	SD	95% CI
Your political beliefs	4.09	1.25	[3.81, 4.38]
Your sexual orientation	3.84	1.51	[3.50, 4.19]
Your religious beliefs	3.83	1.41	[3.51, 4.15]
Your relationship status	3.79	1.25	[3.50, 4.07]
How many times you drink during the day	3.24	1.48	[2.90, 3.57]
You prefer to drink alone	3.03	1.51	[2.68, 3.37]
You prefer to drink in company	2.87	1.46	[2.53, 3.20]
Your interest in culture	2.86	1.45	[2.52, 3.19]
Your interest in art	2.50	1.41	[2.18, 2.82]
Your interest in movies	2.49	1.39	[2.17, 2.80]
Your interest in TV shows	2.49	1.38	[2.17, 2.80]
Your preference for alcoholic drinks	2.38	1.47	[2.05, 2.72]
Which is your preferred drink	2.34	1.41	[2.02, 2.66]
Your interest in sport	2.34	1.36	[2.03, 2.65]
Your preference for non-alcoholic drinks	2.16	1.41	[1.84, 2.48]

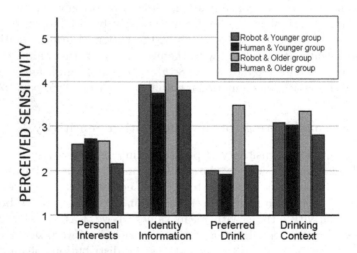

Fig. 1. Overview of perceived information sensitivity divided per agent type (robot vs. human) and age group (younger vs. older age group).

4 Conclusion and Future Works

The purpose of this study was to understand what people perceive as sensitive information to be shared with a service robot in a public environment. For this purpose, we asked participants of different ages, genders and nationalities, to rate the sensitivity of 15 different information shared with either a robot or human bartender. Our study showed that participants' perception of the sensitivity of personal information was relatively consistent. It outlined that participants rated information about their identity as highly sensitive, while their personal interests were considered as low in sensitivity. We found a statistical difference in people's perception of information sensitivity according to the type of agent. However, this was mainly due to participants' age. In fact, older participants found the information regarding their drink preferences more sensitive than younger participants, and especially so when the bartender was a robot. We did not observe any significant differences in rating tendencies for the gender of the participants. We also observed that people's perception of personal identity sensitivity was correlated to their trust in sharing personal information with online stores. In particular, participants who were more concerned about online threats to their privacy rated this information as more sensitive. This finding is in contrast with the general belief [5] that people are willing to share personal information when they can benefit from it.

The main interest of our research is to investigate how a successful long-term interactive relationship can be established, enhanced and preserved between customers and service robots in real-world settings. Personalisation of the interaction is a key factor for pursuing such long-lasting interactions [6]. For this reason, we are interested in investigating how we can effectively implement strategies for personalising people's experience with an autonomous service robot according to their previous interactions and adapting the robot's behaviours to the user's necessities. However, a successful personalised HRI requires that people share personal information with the robot. People's awareness of using robots that are able to collect private information may cause people not to share such information with the robot [22], and in some cases, it might even negatively affect their willingness to use the robot [21]. Contrarily, a lack of awareness of a possible breach of confidentiality could have opposite effects on people's acceptance of the robot [12]. However, research shows that people still decide to share sensitive information with online services if the perceived trade-off between the privacy and the utility of sharing results in a positive outcome [22].

When discussing privacy, it is, however, important to distinguish human-robot interactions occurring in private and public spaces. In private environments, risks and effects of privacy issues are widely investigated in literature [1,7], including possible relative solutions (e.g. encryption of the data collected, avoiding private areas like bedrooms and bathroom). Contrarily, it is still unclear how people perceive a violation of privacy made by a robot in a public interaction [22], as it might happen if a bartender robot uses personal information of a user in front of other customers who are likely strangers to such user. The results of the study presented in this paper lead us to hypothesise that people might respond to a disclosure of information by a robot as they would do with human bartenders in real-world scenarios. Therefore, we expect that people might be inclined to share information with a robot bartender in a real world scenario as they do with a human bartender. In this study, participants' perception of the robot was not affected by any robot's description or embodiment, however, we do expect that the appearance of a robot bartender might affect people's perception of the interaction and the robot [9,26], and, consequently, their willingness of sharing information with it.

The findings of this exploratory study can guide future investigations on the effects of different levels of information sensitivity on customers' perception of a robot and loyalty to a service it delivers in repeated in-the-wild HRIs.

Acknowledgements. This work has been supported by Italian PON I&C 2014-2020 within the BRILLO research project "Bartending Robot for Interactive Long-Lasting Operations", no. F/190066/01-02/X44.

References

1. Basharat, I., Azam, F., Muzaffar, A.W.: Database security and encryption: a survey study. Int. J. Comput. Appl. **47**, 28–34 (2012)
2. Berezina, K., Ciftci, O., Cobanoglu, C.: Robots, Artificial Intelligence, and Service Automation in Restaurants. Ivanov, S., Webster, C. (Ed.), pp. 185–219 (2019)
3. Bissonette, R.: The mental health gatekeeper role: a paradigm for conceptual pretest. Int. J. Soc. Psychiatry **23**(1), 31–34 (1977)
4. Blake, L.: Last Call: The New Orleans Bartender as Conversational Healing Tonic. University of Louisiana at Monroe (2015)
5. Chatzimichali, A., Harrison, R., Chrysostomou, D.: Toward privacy-sensitive human-robot interaction: privacy terms and human-data interaction in the personal robot era. Paladyn J. Behav. Robot. **12**(1), 160–174 (2021)
6. Dautenhahn, K.: Robots we like to live with?! - a developmental perspective on a personalized, life-long robot companion. In: RO-MAN 2004. 13th IEEE International Workshop on Robot and Human Interactive Communication (IEEE Catalog No.04TH8759), pp. 17–22 (2004). https://doi.org/10.1109/ROMAN.2004.1374720
7. Fung, B.C.M., Wang, K., Chen, R., Yu, P.S.: Privacy-preserving data publishing: a survey of recent developments. ACM Comput. Surv. **42**(4), 1–53 (2010)
8. Gosling, S.D., Rentfrow, P.J., Swann, W.B.: A very brief measure of the big-five personality domains. J. Res. Personal. **37**(6), 504–528 (2003). https://doi.org/10.1016/S0092-6566(03)00046-1
9. Hegel, F., Gieselmann, S., Peters, A., Holthaus, P., Wrede, P.: Towards a typology of meaningful signals and cues in social robotics. In: 2011 RO-MAN, pp. 72–78 (2011). https://doi.org/10.1109/ROMAN.2011.6005246
10. Hidayanti, I., Herman, L.E., Farida, N.: Engaging customers through social media to improve industrial product development: the role of customer co-creation value. J. Relat. Market. **17**(1), 17–28 (2018)
11. Kuhn, S., Mostert, P.: Relationship intention and relationship quality as predictors of clothing retail customers' loyalty. Int. Rev. Retail Distrib. Consumer Res. **28**(2), 206–230 (2018)
12. Lutz, C., Tamò, A.: Robocode-ethicists: privacy-friendly robots, an ethical responsibility of engineers? In: Proceedings of the ACM Web Science Conference. WebSci '15, Association for Computing Machinery, New York, NY, USA (2015)
13. Masuda, T., Misaki, D.: Development of japanese green tea serving robot "t-bartender". In: IEEE International Conference Mechatronics and Automation, 2005, vol. 2, pp. 1069–1074 (2005)

14. Rios-Martinez, J., Spalanzani, A., Laugier, C.: From proxemics theory to socially-aware navigation: a survey. Int. J. Soc. Robot. **7**(2), 137–153 (2015)
15. Room, R.: Smoking and drinking as complementary behaviours. Biomed. Pharmacotherapy **58**(2), 111–115 (2004)
16. Rossi, A., Dautenhahn, K., Koay, K.L., Walters, M.L.: How the timing and magnitude of robot errors influence peoples' trust of robots in an emergency scenario. In: Kheddar, A., Yoshida, E., Ge, S.S., Suzuki, K., Cabibihan, J.J., Eyssel, F., He, H. (eds.) Social Robotics, pp. 42–52. Springer International Publishing, Cham (2017). https://doi.org/10.1007/978-3-319-70022-9_5
17. Rossi, A., Dautenhahn, K., Koay, K.L., Walters, M.L.: Human perceptions of the severity of domestic robot errors. In: Kheddar, A., Yoshida, E., Ge, S.S., Suzuki, K., Cabibihan, J.J., Eyssel, F., He, H. (eds.) Social Robotics, pp. 647–656. Springer International Publishing, Cham (2017). https://doi.org/10.1007/978-3-319-70022-9_64
18. Rossi, A., Dautenhahn, K., Koay, K.L., Walters, M.L., Holthaus, P.: Evaluating people's perceptions of trust in a robot in a repeated interactions study. In: Wagner, A.R., Feil-Seifer, D., Haring, K.S., Rossi, S., Williams, T., He, H., Sam Ge, S. (eds.) Social Robotics, pp. 453–465. Springer International Publishing, Cham (2020). https://doi.org/10.1007/978-3-030-62056-1_38
19. Rossi, A., Giura, V., Leva, C.D., Rossi, S.: I know what you would like to drink: Benefits and detriments of sharing personal info with a bartender robot (2021)
20. Rossi, A., Staffa, M., Origlia, A., di Maro, M., Rossi, S.: Brillo: A robotic architecture for personalised long-lasting interactions in a bartending domain. In: Companion of the 2021 ACM/IEEE International Conference on Human-Robot Interaction, pp. 426–429. HRI '21 Companion, Association for Computing Machinery, New York, NY, USA (2021)
21. Rueben, M., et al.: Themes and research directions in privacy-sensitive robotics. In: 2018 IEEE Workshop on Advanced Robotics and its Social Impacts (ARSO), pp. 77–84 (2018)
22. Sannon, S., Stoll, B., DiFranzo, D., Jung, M.F., Bazarova, N.N.: "i just shared your responses": extending communication privacy management theory to interactions with conversational agents. Proc. ACM Hum.-Comput. Interact. **4**, 1–18 (2020)
23. Schulz, T., Herstad, J.: Walking away from the robot: negotiating privacy with a robot. In: Proceedings of the 31st British Computer Society Human Computer Interaction Conference. HCI '17, BCS Learning & Development Ltd., Swindon, GBR (2017)
24. Stubbs, A.G.P.: Learning to pour: An exploration into the socialization of the male night shift bartender (2001). https://scholar.uwindsor.ca/etd/2591
25. Syrdal, D.S., Walters, M., Otero, N., Koay, K., Dautenhahn, K.: "he knows when you are sleeping" - privacy and the personal robot companion. In: In Proceedings of Workshop on Human Implications of Human-Robot Interaction. AAAI, pp. 28–33 (2007)
26. Warta, S.F., Newton, O.B., Song, J., Best, A., Fiore, S.M.: Effects of social cues on social signals in human-robot interaction during a hallway navigation task. Proc. Hum. Factors Ergon. Soc. Ann. Meet. **62**(1), 1128–1132 (2018). https://doi.org/10.1177/1541931218621258

Sex Robots: Auto-erotic Devices, Fetishes or New Form of Transitional Object for Adults?

Bertrand Tondu[(⊠)]

Federal University of Toulouse, Allées Jules Guesde, 31000 Toulouse, France
bertrand.tondu@insa-toulouse.fr

Abstract. How to characterize the object status of the sex robot? Although its global anthropomorphism, based on its hyper-realism, confers on it an indisputable reality, we seek to show that its mode of existence is floating. Either as an auto-erotic device whose role would be to close the body of the subject on himself/herself – even more elaborately than by the use of a sex toy or a sex machine. Or, as a fetish when it comes to a sex doll deprived of its genitals, a mute a-sexual figure who returns, in particular, the male subject to his unreachable and therefore untouchable female daydreams. Or, finally, as a transitional object, touchable, treatable, comforting but which places the subject in an area of illusion where, according to the very terms of Winnicott, the subject is in danger of dementia.

Keywords: Sex robot · Social robotics · Fetishism · Transitional object

1 Introduction

The term robot belongs to the field of science fiction, since its creation by Karel Capek and its popularization by Isaac Asimov, and to the field of technology since the appearance of the first remote manipulators after the Second World War and the introduction of industrial robots in car factories around the 1980's. These two realities, literary on the one hand, technological and industrial on the other, have gradually become disjointed with the advances of scientific robotics. The concept of sex robot has recently challenged the separation between these two modalities, phantasmatic and technical: indeed, sex robots can be perceived as a technological device that would realize the fiction of the artificial lover as it is encountered in some scenes of *Barbarella* imagined by Jean-Paul Forest. Technically speaking, actual sex robots are still far from being able to claim the performances worthy of the praise of the heroine *Barbarella*, but robotic technology is sufficiently present in our societies for making possible such a fantasy. Thus, at the turn of the years 2010, the American company *True Companion* announced having designed *Roxxxy*, for its feminine version, and *Rocky*, for its masculine version, two humanoid robots supposed to be able to become true "loving friends": "She can even have an orgasm" is said about *Roxxxy*. Its presence at the Adult Entertainment Expo in Las Vegas in 2010 generated considerable media interest – see, for example, Svensson [1] – although some experts saw it as a sham [2]. The fact remains that the possibility

© Springer Nature Switzerland AG 2021
H. Li et al. (Eds.): ICSR 2021, LNAI 13086, pp. 130–141, 2021.
https://doi.org/10.1007/978-3-030-90525-5_12

of such a market has led to wide debates between radical opponents to this new form of sex technology [3] and blissful optimists who are very seriously considering getting married in the near future with a sex robot [4]. Recently, a number of philosophers and ethics experts have addressed the issue of consent between humans and sex robots [5]. These studies are, generally, the fact of non-roboticists for whom a sex robot is a postulated machine rather than a real machine. Beyond the difficulty of predicting the future of such a robotic technology, the proposed ethical analyses generally leave aside any psychological question in the possible human-robot sexual relationship because, in particular, a lack of practical data and a lack of interest on the part of psychologists in a field that is still poorly documented. The purpose of this article is to try to define a framework for the psychological study of what could be called sexual robotics from what it is now.

2 Global Anthropomorphism of Sex Robot

While sexual satisfaction devices, commonly called sex toys, are generally limited to genital arousal tools (vibrator, etc.), or devices that mimic the genitals (dildo, molded bust including a vaginal orifice, etc.), the concept of sex robot is intended to be a global representation of the human body and this is its profound originality. A global anthropomorphism, peculiar to sex robots, that impersonate a male or female human being, can be opposed to the local anthropomorphism of sex toys mimicking a more or less extensive genital sphere. It also can be opposed to the non-anthropomorphism of a number of them, the most striking of which is undoubtedly the vibrator to which Rachel Maines [6] devoted a book to describe its technical evolution throughout the twentieth century. This opposition was, in my opinion, too little emphasized in the reflection on the new place that robotics seeks to take within so-called sex technologies. Let us recall that the technology of machines, and more particularly those designed to replace men and women in their daily tasks, have been progressively removed from anthropomorphism for simple reasons of efficiency: the case of the washing machine is particularly striking from this point of view [7]. Because it is difficult to design a robotic hand, the vibrator replaces the finger stroking movement on the clitoris with a simple vibration system (or even a contact-free stimulation with the new models developed by *Womanizer*): an efficiency results that may be superior to that of the human hand [8]. The so-called sex machine is another particularly interesting example of renouncing anthropomorphism to do, at a lower cost, better than the human body, as illustrated in Fig. 1. It is, in a way, an anti-sex robot: the back and forth movement of its dildo is produced by a crank and connecting rod system, driven by a simple electric motor whose adjustable speed ensures for his/her user the control of the rhythm. The few male sex robots in the trade, such as the Henry robot from *Realbotix* (https://www.realdoll.com) offer the use of an erect artificial penis that cannot today be animated by a coital movement. Such a movement in man/woman engages, in fact, the whole musculoskeletal system to combine the control of a back and forth movement while ensuring the balance of the body, something all the more difficult to achieve if the support surface is soft. Sex machine, by combining rigidity and precision of its mechanism with the flexibility of the dildo, succeeds in this feat of automating at low cost a particularly intimate movement and even gives it a vigor that no human can provide.

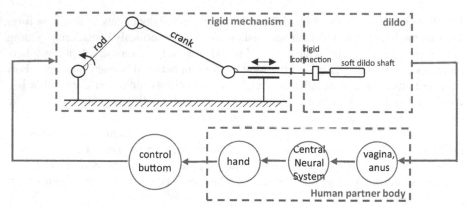

Fig. 1 General structure of a sex machine in the form of a systemic diagram highlighting both the closed-chain kinematic structure, and its closed-loop operation involving the human body, the rigid part of the rod and crank, and the soft dildo.

In a way, the challenge of sex robotics is to reintroduce the human form within sex technology. It achieves this by taking advantage of the current possibilities of molding flexible structures on a rigid articulated skeleton, whose positioning must allow to mimic different attractive positions. This variety of the robot's love positions depends, of course, on the joint complexity of the robot's skeleton, which varies according to the brands, but, with the exception of rare attempts at questionable effectiveness, the motorization of these joints is still in the planning stage. From this point of view, a sex robot is more like, mechanically speaking, a life-size workshop mannequin than the present humanoid robots which we know how difficult it is always to make them walk without risk of falling, as to equip them with hands able to mimic the diversity of human grip. It is, however, interesting to note that although the target audience is predominantly male, the current passivity of the sex robot can finally adapt to both sexes from the moment a position is chosen in which the robot plays the role of the passive sex partner. The difference between the sex robot and the workshop mannequin then lies, on the one hand, in its pseudo-fleshly envelope and, on the other hand, in the adaptation to this envelope of genital organ artifacts derived from the classic technology of sex toys. The external appearance of the sex robot derives from a certain art of the hyper realistic sculpture, taking advantage, in the years 70–80, of the multiple molding possibilities offered by the diversity of synthetic rubbers to mimic the nuances and suppleness of human carnation. Mat MacMullen, creator of the company *Abyss Creations*, at the origin of the first American sex robots, comes precisely from this artistic trend. However, unlike a hyper realistic statue, the sex robot is not destined to have a pedestal. Heavy by several tens of kilograms, and not currently possessing autonomy of movement, it is finally an object, which must rest only in an awkward position in a sofa, or lying on a bed.

Two approaches are then to be opposed in the development of these artificial sex bodies. A first approach makes the immobility the essential characteristic of a device that can be called *love doll* in reference to the Japanese *love doll* of which Agnès Giard [9] has recently made a remarkable synthesis. A second approach, which could be described as truly robotic, considers that the present difficulties of humanoid robotics in its quest of its own anthropomorphism [10] will end up being overtaken to be adapted to sex robots. Waiting for that, actual so-called sex robots are essentially devoted to speak, as does *Harmony* developed by the American company *Realbotix*, a division of MacMullen's *Abyss Creations* "with the goal of integrating robotic components and artificial intelligence into high ended silicone dolls" [11]. Presented to the public by her "AI/content director", *Harmony* appears seated, answering with application to the questions of its manager; *Harmony* can also pull out her tongue, but she can't get up from her chair, let alone follow her owner to continue this conversation in bed. Quiet or chatty, love doll or sex robots nevertheless impose a sensitive presence whose acceptance – in the sense of non-rejection of an implant inside a living body – is not self-evident.

3 Beyond Uncanny Valley

Despite Mori's prediction about the feeling of discomfort generated by a machine whose resemblance to the human is too strong, the question of a possible feeling of unease caused by the presence of a hyper-anthropomorphic artificial structure did not seem to have been taken into account by the manufacturers of sex robots. One way to approach this apparent exception of sex robots to Mori's theory may be to bring the Japanese idea of "Bukini no tani gensho" closer to "Das Unheimliche" (The uncanny) concept developed by Freud after Jenstch. Let us recall one of the conclusions of 1919 Freud's essay: "Our conclusion could then be stated as follows: the uncanny element we know from experience arises either when repressed children complexes are revived by some impression, or when primitive beliefs that have surmounted appear to be once again confirmed" ([12], page 155) and, among the most intimate forms of repressed, the fear of death occupies a preponderant place: "To many people the acme of the uncanny is represented by any thing to do with death, dead bodies, revenants, spirits and ghosts" ([12], page 148). In this context, corpse and zombie, at the bottom of the valley, would play the role of figures of the repressed particularly frightening [13]. However, without renouncing to this Freudian concept, one could make the argument that the sexual drive would not be disturbed by the repressed fear of death because, for man at least, it would be based on a fundamental will of transgression, that Freud is almost ashamed to confess to us. "It has an ugly sound and a paradoxical as well, but nevertheless it must be said that whoever is to be really free and happy in love must have overcome his deference for women and come to terms with the idea of incest with mother or sister", he says in his important 1912 article about "the most prevalent form of degradation in erotic life" ([14], page 55). The violence suffered by sex robots is always highlighted with astonishment (see, further, the case of this Asian student who damaged his real doll as if he had wanted to mime a series of sexual crimes). The same phenomenon occurs in what Giard calls "doll brothels" about which she writes, "It turns out that customers rarely return. The state of the "girls" horrifies them: they are covered with scratches and even worse" ([9], page 105). The spokesman of the Canadian company *Aura Dolls*, a doll brothel directly inspired by the Japanese experience, points out that his establishment is, among other things, adapted to certain frustrated men with violent tendencies: "We try to focus on the fact that since we have this service, for men who have these dark, violent fantasies, instead of putting out the urge to act aggressively, they can do something like this which is safe for everyone" [15]. The person who satisfies his/her sexual impulse with a robot would therefore not be concerned by Mori's warning. The transgression would suspend the risk of return of the repressed and, more particularly, the one on ideas of mortality – it would suspend it but would not cancel it, as this verse by the French poet Eluard, quoted by Xavière Gauthier [16], reminds us: "During sexual intercourse I conjugated sperm and skeleton" (page 135). And yet, Giard notes, "it does seem that many clients are disturbed by the head of their love doll when, waking up at night, they see it staring at the ceiling with a disturbing intensity" ([9], page 128). According to her, it is for this reason that "practically, all firms have in catalogue at least one doll nicknamed me toji ("closed eyes") or tsamuri me ("shut eyes") (ibid. 128). In some way, this gaze intensity about Giard talks, isn't that the one of who has just died? It would be then enough to close the eyes of this frozen face so that the serenity of the one with whom the robot shares his/her bed is found. In this way, and apart from the sexual act, the love doll would still escape Mori's law. One might even wonder if, for some people and under certain conditions, the love doll would not be that undefined point that Mori draws on her curve before it plunges into the uncanny valley (see Fig. 2).

According to Giard, "the manufacturers are unanimous: they do not try to reproduce but to "create" a human. [...]. Even with the grains of beauty, this envelope must keep the artificial, unreal appearance of a dream creature" ([9], page 132). We can think that Mac Mullen would say the same about his Harmony doll. At the service of what form of auto-erotism to attach such sublimated anthropomorphic objects?

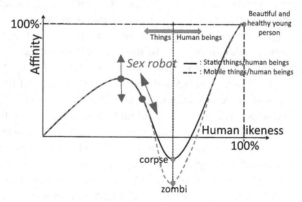

Fig. 2 Mori's curve Affinity versus Human likeness applied to sex technologies: depending on the subject's interest in these technologies, sex doll/robot would be located more or less high on the left flank of the valley, even at first peak with an affinity value higher than this generally considered.

4   The Auto-erotism Peculiar to Sex Robot

The term auto-erotism was introduced by Havelock Ellis in 1898, before Freud resumed it in his essay on infantile sexuality. According to Havelock Ellis, auto-erotism is the set of "phenomena of spontaneous sexual emotion generated in the absence of an external stimulus proceeding, directly or indirectly, from another person" ([17] page 260). Freud uses the term, without defining it precisely, in his analysis of infantile "thumb-sucking", a type of auto-erotic activity whose "the most striking feature of this sexual activity is that the instinct is not directed towards other people, but obtains satisfaction from the subject's own body" ([18], page 181). Because this auto-erotism is purely infantile, Freud seems to dissociate this notion of masturbation as he expresses it indirectly in this famous passage: "So far as the autoerotic and masturbatory manifestations of sexuality are concerned, we might lay it down that the sexuality of little girls is of a wholly masculine character" (ibid., page 219). Is it to distinguish himself from Havelock Ellis, as he will do later with Jentsch for the concept of "unheimliche" that Freud excludes masturbation from auto-erotism? Anyway, in their Language of Psychoanalysis, Laplanche and Pontalis [19] clearly include masturbation in the "broad sense" of auto-eroticism which they define as follows: "a form of sexual behavior in which the subject obtains satisfaction solely through recourse to his own body, needing no outside object; in this sense, masturbation is referred to as auto-erotic behaviour" (article "Auto-erotism"). In this context, it could be argued that sex machine is consistent with the initial definition of auto-erotism according to Havelock Ellis if one considers that its neutral form does not generate an "external stimulus". By contrast, the sex robot would combine the masturbatory tool of its artificial vaginas and dildos with the source of external excitement of its plastic made in the image of certain beauty canons supposed to be particularly exciting on the sexual level. Can we still talk about auto-erotism in the case of sex robots?

To attempt to answer this question, we propose to appeal to the definition of auto-erotism according to the French psychanalyst Jean Gillibert for which auto-erotism is "an erotism involving here the means of enjoyment and not the object used for enjoyment" ([20], pages 788–789). The interest of this redefinition consists in the new status given to the object in auto-erotism. In their commentary on auto-erotism definition, Laplanche and Pontalis [19] write: "This theory [i.e. auto-erotism theory] does not assume the existence of a primitive 'objectless' state. The action of sucking, which Freud takes as the model of auto-erotism, is in fact preceded by a first stage during which the sexual instinct obtains satisfaction through an anaclitic relationship with the self-preservative instinct (hunger), and by virtue of an object – namely, the mother's breast". In some alternative way, Gillibert writes: "The question no longer arises whether auto-erotism is still objectal or objectless: it is both". Applied to the question of sex robot, Gillibert's theory would lead to give the robot the status of an object whose nature would be floating; As a child does with his/her thumb, which can take and instantly lose its nature of auto-erotic object, so could a sex robot, during its use, to be forgotten as an object and to leave the subject alone with his own body. In a short article on self-fellatio Gillibert [21] reports the fantasy of some of his patients "during childhood or adolescence, having had the urge to suck their penis, to have tried it" (page 31). Gillibert interprets this fantasy of self-fellatio as "a desire to pose the body as erotically inaccessible to another body" (ibid., page 32). The use of a sex robot has, a priori, nothing to do with such a fantasy but we can wonder if, what distinguishes it from the use of a simple sex toy, would not be precisely a similar desire of "looping on oneself" (ibid., page 33), made possible by the objectal/objectless ambiguity of the sex robot.

However, the hyper anthropomorphism of the sex robot and the complexity of its structure induce a weight much higher than a simple inflatable doll. If one day sex robots will be mobile due to some ingenious actuation, its object reality will be imposed by a "body mass index" finally quite close to or even higher than this of a human body of the same size and corpulence. It is this obvious nature of real thing that leads us to wonder if, overflowing its auto-erotic nature, the sex robot could not also acquire a fetish nature.

5   Fetish or New Form of Transitional Object for Adults?

According to Binet (1887) in his *Essay on Loving Fetishism* [22], all love is fetishist in the sense that it is not interested in the elusive totality of a person but in a limited number of his characters: "Normal love therefore appears to us as the result of a complicated fetishism; we could say that, in normal love, fetishism is polytheistic: it results, not from a single excitation, but from a myriad of excitations: it is a symphony" (page 126). The transition from normal love to pathological love is, according to Binet, only a question of rupture of harmony: "In sexual perversion, we do not see any new element; only harmony is broken; love, instead of being aroused by the whole person, is only aroused by a fraction" (ibid., page 127). Binet's systemic approach is intended to provide a framework for a number of fetishistic practices that were gathered at the time in successive editions of already cited Kraft-Ebing's *Psychopathia Sexualis* treatise. If some fetishistic practices still speak to us, such as the fetish of the shoe or that of the hair, others now seem very strange to us as the one said of the "hair despoilers" ([23], pages 158–161). Apparently, in comparison with such practices that favor a unique physical or moral characteristic of the desired being, sex robot appears as a totality of peculiarities. But, besides the fact that this totality is limited to an external envelope to which has been added a pseudo-sexual functionality, it is only apparent because it mimics a body without an organ or rather a body that would be limited to certain primary and secondary sexual signs. According to Binet's point of view, a sex robot would therefore have an ambiguous fetish nature. On the one hand, by its mimicry of human appearance in its entirety, it moves away from fetish objects attaching to a detail of the human person. On the other hand, it can appear as a "dressing" of the artificial genitals, which are usually detachable either to be able to wash them as in the case of the extractable vagina, or to be able to pass from the non-erectile nature of the artificial penis to a dildo. According to Giard, a first explanation of the extractable vagina could be found in old legal rules on censorship of dolls displaying a vagina, before putting forward a second more fundamental explanation that would be related to the Japanese culture: "We Japanese do not need to see sex. We need to see desire" ([9], page 203). More prosaically, the extractable vagina that most American manufacturers have adopted makes it much easier to clean after use than to carry the heavy doll to the bathroom. There is another interest in the extractable vagina, as well as the interchangeable penises: to be able to choose and to be able to change. The site of the company *Realbotix*, of which we have already spoken, proposes to its customers, in the heading "insert options", a selection of 11 different vulva for which the site states: "all insert shown are interchangeable with all female *RealDoll* dolls" (https://www.rea ldoll.com/options/#insert). Nothing prevents an amateur to buy the whole collection, as to another to obtain multiple forms of interchangeable penis.

Rather than being a sexual fetishes support, it would seem, therefore, that, as a fetish, one must consider the robot in its entirety, especially when it is deprived of its artificial genitals, as in the case of Japanese love doll on which the vagina was not placed. Giard talks about these *Otaku*, that she defines as male individuals withdrawn on themselves, often maniacal, who grew up with the advent of sexual manga and "the confinement in front of the computer", and for whom the love doll would represent the woman who "does not exist in reality" ([9], page 213). Giard quotes the testimony of a certain Sakai Mitsugi who, in 2014, then 51 years old, said: "The charm of dolls is very different from that of women. [...] The doll is better than a woman because it has no personality, no negative ideas and stays with you all the time" (ibid., page 215). Kodama, one of Giard's informants, is even more radical: "When we were younger, we dreamed of ideal love, because the girls were inaccessible. As adults, we remained attached to this impossible dream. What we were suffering from, finally, is not the lack of real women, it is the excess of imagination. This excess of imagination makes reality useless. Why go out? Everything is already in us" (ibid., page 215). Giard does not propose a psychoanalytic reading of this exclusive love for dolls whose "hole" is not sought to fill by a vagina but it appears, in some respects, strangely close to fetishism as described by Freud in his 1927 essay. According to Freud, "the fetish is a substitute for the woman's (the mother's) penis that the little boy once believed in and - for reasons familiar to us - does not want to give up. ([24], page 198). It is the consequence of "the horror of castration" with as a corollary "the stupor in front of the woman's actual genitals that no fetishist lacks [and] also remains an indelible stigma of the repression that took place" (ibid., p. 135). In some way, this love doll fetish, deprived of artificial genitals, would then renew what the nineteenth century called love of statues or agalmatophilia which is documented, in particular, at Havelock Ellis and Krafft-Ebing. Scobie and Taylor [25] proposed the following definition: "Algamathophilia is the pathalogical condition in which some people establish exclusive sexual relationships with statues." It is interesting to note that the love of statues is here considered as a sexual attraction, which can go as far as orgasm, with statues naturally deprived of orifices. At the same time, criticizing this study, White [26] points to the weakness of credible testimony on this phenomenon, which, according to him, is more a fantasy or anecdote than a truly "behavioral perversion" (page 249). The love attraction for a love doll, whose "hole" is left empty, would tend to justify the possibility of a diagnosis of agalmatophilia.

An ambiguity remains, however, in the data provided by Giard: do the *otaku* of which she speaks have one or more love doll? In her study of a sample of 55 American sex dolls, Sarah Valverde [27] notes that 18 of them, or 39% of the sample, have two or more sex dolls (page 31). For those who would live with a single sex robot, which has become an exclusive substitute for any romantic relationship, the question then arises of an interpretation which, without renouncing entirely the theory of fetishism, would rather be placed within the framework of the theory of the transitional object.

Myriam Boubli, in her attempt to analyze the evolution of the comforter concept, shows how, until Winnicott made it a transitional object, it was considered and designated as a fetish. If everyone finds normal today the temporary attachment of the child for his comforter, the question arises when the adult keeps the need for a certain presence of soft toys in his daily life: "Are we not, this time, in the realm of perversion?" questions Boubli ([28], page 126) without really deciding this issue. She relates this remarkable testimony of one 20-year-old patient "who maintains the link to her comforter, which she continues to use as a consolation object in her moments of ill-being" (ibid., p. 126): "Fundamentally, my boyfriend, in my bed, I wonder if I don't tied to him like to a mother. The smell, the touch… It is enough for me. The genital relationship, I rejected it" (ibid., page 126). In the case of this young girl, Boubli interprets this rejection of sexual intercourse as the consequence of an anguish of loss of the maternal relationship and its destruction if it is in competition with another attachment; such anguish would justify the persistence of the comforter. Beyond the individual reasons that can explain the persistence of the comforter in adulthood, it is clear, in any case, that it does not play a sexual role. Contrary to a sex impulse object, it would be an object of appeasement, but "this type of object made up of the whole reverse of the impulse is, says Boubli, an object of idealization, a dead object, the object of a sort of commemoration of a completely devitalized image" (ibid., page 127). We can then wonder if sex robot, in its currently essentially passive form, solid object built around a rigid structure, but with a real suppleness on contact, not to say softness (see for example, some promotional films such as this one: https://fr.xvideos.com/video43617247), does not fall, in a way, in the category of comforters. To try to answer this question, let us return to the very text of Winnicott [29] where he writes: "I have introduced the terms 'transitional object' and 'transitional phenomena' for designation of the intermediate area of experience, between the thumb and the teddy bear, between the oral erotism and true object-relationship […]" (page 89). To the "inner reality" and to "the external life", he claims "there is also need for a triple one; the third part of the life of a human being, a part that we cannot ignore, is an intermediate area of experiencing, to which inner reality and external life both contribute" (ibid., page 90). For Winnicott, the transitional object, or comforter, would be "the first not-me possession". It is the indispensable transition to the "true object-relationship". "Its fate is to be gradually allowed to be decathected, so that in the course of years it becomes not so much forgotten as relegated to limbo" (ibid., page 91), and its abandonment marks the end of the "area of illusion".

Winnicott's statement is therefore particularly ambitious: "I am therefore studying the substance of illusion, that which is allowed to the infant, and which in adult life is inherent in art and religion" (ibid., page 90). Sex robot, unlike a sex toy, is precisely an illusion, the illusion of an ideal woman or man, or even a quasi-supernatural being in the case of love doll with enlarged eyes or special orders made to the American company *Sinthetics* (Sinthetics.com). In a documentary that the American series Slutever devoted to this company in 2016, we learn, for example, that a client wanted a "doll" inspired by a fantastic hero whose picture she addressed to society [30]. According to this perspective, as we tried to illustrate on the diagram in Fig. 3, directly inspired by Winnicott's own schemes, a sex robot would be a transitional object, that is to say a physical illusion, disguised as an object of sexual satisfaction.

This transitional object status would give all rights of use by its owner, including to mutilate it as reported by Megham Laslocky [31]: "Fiero's [the sex doll "doctor"] photographs of the damaged doll make me cringe: Her leg was torn off, revealing the steel hardware of her hip joints; an arm hung by an inch of silicone flesh. Her vagina was so blown out," Fiero told me. "I was appalled. I couldn't believe someone could fuck something like that up so quickly. It blew me away. How could someone be so callous?". It is interesting to note that the sex robot possesses many of the "special qualities in the relationship" listed by Winnicott, especially qualities 3 and 4: "3. It must never change, unless changed by the infant. 4. It must survive instinctual loving, and also hating, and, if it be a feature, pure aggression" ([29], page 91). By their appearance frozen in eternal youth, sex robots share the property 3, including the setting up and removal of sexual parts used; and we saw with Laslocky's testimony just cited the ability of sex dolls to survive severe aggressions of their owner. The "intermediate area of illusion" where the link with the comforter develops is, however, clearly defined by Winnicott as an area specific to the development of insane ideas: "We allow the infant this madness, and only gradually ask for a clear distinguishing between the subjective and that which is capable of objective or scientific proof" ([32], page 71). But, just after, he adds: "If an individual claims special indulgence in respect of this intermediate area we recognize psychosis; if the individual is an adult we use the epithet 'mad'. (ibid., page 71). In fact according to Winnicott, "the substance of illusion" for remaining acceptable in the adult world, must not spill over into the area of "external life" because "[It] yet becomes the hallmark of madness when an adult puts too powerful a claim on the credulity of others, forcing them to acknowledge a sharing of illusion that is not their own." ([29], page 90). That is actually what we think when we see these pictures showing these Japanese men walking their *love doll* in a wheelchair, accompanying them to the seaside, or in a park [33]. The sex robot, as a physical illusion for adults, would be made to stay hidden. However, even domestic, the illusion of the sex robot can remain problematic, a real proof of an impossibility for its user to find a solution to its integration into real love life. The only woman who dares to appear on the screen in the film of the series *Slutever*, of which we have already spoken, thus describes the advantage of her male doll that she has just painfully pulled on her bed. The men who are interested in her, her «fuck buddies» she says, are either too present emotionally, or elusive after realizing the fantasy of sleeping with a porn star; according to her, a sex robot presents neither the disadvantage of the former nor the disappointment of the latter. Giard also speaks to us about those men who, particularly involved in the relationship with their love doll, decide one day to renounce it totally as woke up from a bad dream.

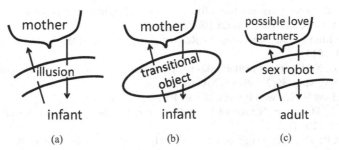

Fig. 3 Sex robot as a phenomenon of illusion carried by the transitional object that it would represent: the diagram proposed in (c) is directly inspired by the diagrams (a) and (b) proposed by Winnicott to illustrate the concepts of object and transitional phenomena – redrawn from Figs. 1 and 2 of seminal Winnicott's article [29].

6 Conclusion

Sex robot, as understood and discussed today, remains deeply ambiguous. Technically, it is not yet ready to offer his/her users an attractive approach, even modest caresses and even less loving positions where it would be the active partner. The current sex robot is therefore first, and most often, a superb artifact of a highly sexualized human. In its actual limited state or in a forward projection state with future mobility functionalities, we have successively tried to identify it as an auto-erotic device, a fetish or a transitional object. These three approaches turn out to be covered by the same ambiguity regarding the object nature of the sex robot. As a masturbatory device, it imposes its heavy and cumbersome presence, its global anthropomorphism, as opposed to actual sex technology, a generalized hyper-realism supposed to bring more sexual satisfaction to his/her user. But, ultimately, does this auto-erotic use not lead to the denial of the object relationship in order to bring the one who indulges in it in a closure of his/her own body on himself/herself? As a fetish, the sex robot, then deprived of its masturbatory function by rejecting the installation of its genitals, would also not reach the status of an object. He would only justify this radical word reported by Giard: "Everything is already in us" (cited infra in the text), turning the sex/love doll into a narcissistic projection device by means of which the male subject, especially, can avoid the frightening confrontation to woman genitals. Finally, whether or not sex robot is equipped with its artificial genitalia, it would lead his/her users into a world of illusion in the sense that Winnicott theorized to explain the attachment of the child to his comforter. A world of illusion in which the adult enters through art or religion but, precisely, a sex robot is neither a work of art nor a religious representation, and that would be the real danger that he would make the adult who surrenders to it: to sink, if we follow Winnicott's theory, in a form of insanity. Is this what threatens the one who, in an undetermined future, would decide to share his/her life with a sex robot or, in a lighter manner, would sex robotics open the way for a new form of lovemaking according to the image of Barbarrella and Diktor illustrating our text?

References

1. Svensson, P.: Roxxxy the sex robot focuses on meaningful conversation instead of lifelike movement. The Canadian Press (2010)
2. Levy, D.: Roxxxy the 'Sex Robot' – Real or Fake?, Letter to the Editor, Lovotics, 1, ID 235685, 4 (2013)
3. Richardson, K.: Sex robot matters: slavery, the prostituted, and the right of machines. IEEE Technol. Soc. Mag. 35(2), 46–53 (2016)
4. Levy, D.: Love + Sex with Robots. Harper Perenial, New York (2007)
5. Danaher, J., McArthur, N.: Robot Sex. MIT Press, Cambridge (USA), Social and ethical implications (2018)
6. Maines, R.P.: The Technology of Orgasm – "Hysteria", the Vibrator and Women's Sexual Satisfaction. The Johns Hopkins University Press, Baltimore and London (1999)
7. Giedion, S.: Mechanization takes Command. Oxford University Press, New-York (1970)
8. Prause, N., Roberts, V., Legarretta, M., Rigney, L.M.: Cox, "Clinical and research concerns with vibratory stimulation: a review and pilot study of common stimulation devices", Sexual Relat. Ther. 27(1), 1–18, (2012)

9. Giard, A.:. A desire of human. Love Doll in Japan, Belles Lettres, collection "Japon", Paris (2016). (In French)
10. Tondu, B.: Anthropomorphism and humanoid robots for service: the ambiguous relationship. Ind. Robot. **39**(6), 609–618 (2012)
11. Lindroth, G.: Realbotix harmony demo and mission explained (2019). https://www.youtube.com/watch?v=pC4Jjjoohl8
12. Freud, S.: The Uncanny, p. 2003. Penguin Books, London (1919)
13. Tondu, B.: Fear of the death and uncanny valley. a freudian perspective. Interact. Stud. **16**(2), 200–204 (2015)
14. Freud, S.: The most prevalent form of degradation in erotic life. In: Sexuality and the Psychology of Love, Touchstone, New-York, 1963 (1912)
15. Da Silva, M.: Why Toronto's sex doll brothel is bad for women. at aura dolls, men will be able to act out their dark, violent fantasies on realistic sex dolls (2018). https://nowtoronto.com
16. Gauthier, X.: Surrealism and Sexuality. Gallimard, Paris (1970).(In French)
17. Havelock Ellis, H.: Auto-erotism: a psychological study, Alienist Neurol. **19**(2), 260–299 (1898)
18. Freud, S.: Three essays on the theory of sexuality. In: The Standard Edition of the Complete Psychological Works of Sigmund Freud, VII, pp. 123–246, 1953 (1905)
19. Laplanche, J., Pontalis, J.B.: The Language of Psychoanalysis, p. 2018. Routledge, New-York (1967)
20. Gillibert, J.: On auto-erotism. Revue française de psychanalyse XLI **5–6**, 773–949 (1977). (In French)
21. Gillibert, J.: The phantasm of auto-fellatio. L'Inconscient, revue de psychanalyse **6**, 31–37 (1978). (In French)
22. Binet, A. : "Fetishism in love", Revue de Philosophique de la France et de l'Etranger, 143–167, 252–274 (1887). (In French)
23. Von Krafft-Ebing, R.: 1886. Arcade Publishing. New York, Psychopathia Sexualis (1998)
24. Freud, S.: "Fetishism", In: Miscellaneous Papers, Hogarth and Institute of Psycho-Analysis. vol. 5, pp. 198–204. London 1950 (1927)
25. Scobie, A., Taylor, A.J.W.: Perversions ancient and modern: I. agalmatophilia, the statue syndrome. J. History Behav. Sci. **11**, 49–54 (1975)
26. White, M.: The statue syndrome: perversion? fantasy? anecdote? J. Sex Res. **14**(4), 246–249 (1978)
27. Valverde, S.:. The modern sex doll-owner: a descriptive analysis master thesis in psychology. Fac. California State Polytech. Univ. (2012)
28. Boubli, M.: "The comforter in all its forms", Special issue on Fetishism, Etudes psychanalytiques, 93–130 2012. (In French)
29. Winnicott, D.W.: Transitional objects and transitional phenomena – a study of the first not-me possession. J. Psycho Anal. **34**, 89–97 (1953)
30. Murguia, A., Sciortino, K.: Making the world's first male sex doll. Vice Vide (2016). https://www.video.vice.com
31. Laslocky, M.: Just like a woman, Salon (2010)
32. Winnicott, D.W.: Psychoses and child care. Br. J. Med. Psychol. **26**(1), 68–74 (1953)
33. Allen, F.: My sex doll is so much better than my real wife. New York Post (2017). https://nypost.com

Explaining Before or After Acting? How the Timing of Self-Explanations Affects User Perception of Robot Behavior

Sonja Stange$^{(\boxtimes)}$ and Stefan Kopp

Faculty of Technology, Bielefeld University, Bielefeld, Germany
{sstange,skopp}@techfak.uni-bielefeld.de

Abstract. Explanations are a useful tool to improve human-robot interaction and the topic of what a good explanation should entail has received much attention. While a robot's behavior can be justified upon request after its execution, the intention to act can also be signaled by a robot prior to the execution. In this paper we report results from a pre-registered study on the effects of a social robot proactively giving a self-explanation before vs. after the execution of an undesirable behavior. Contrary to our expectations we found that explaining a behavior before its execution did not yield positive effects on the users' perception of the robot or the behavior. Instead, the robot's behavior was perceived as less desirable when explained before the execution rather than afterwards. Exploratory analyses further revealed that even though participants felt less uncertain about what was going to happen next, they also felt less in control, had lower trust and lower contact intentions with a robot that explained before it acted.

Keywords: Explanation timing · Human-robot-interaction · Explainable robots

1   Introduction and Related Work

Positive effects of explanations in human-AI interaction have been reported in numerous studies. Explanations can increase understandability of tasks, help to build adequate trust, and increase desirability of undesired behaviors [11,18,19]. While the question of *what* an explanation should entail has been tackled in multiple fields, the question of *when* to provide an explainee with an explanation has received relatively little attention in human-robot interaction so far.

Typically in explanations of black box machine learning approaches one differentiates between intrinsic explainability and post-hoc (external) explainability [1]. While post-hoc explanations retrieve the reasoning after a decision has been made, intrinsic explainability offers the possibility to explain the decision at different times during an interaction. Yet, the time at which an explanation should

This research was supported by the German Federal Ministry of Education and Research (BMBF) in the project 'VIVA' (FKZ 16SV7959).

H. Li et al. (Eds.): ICSR 2021, LNAI 13086, pp. 142–153, 2021.
https://doi.org/10.1007/978-3-030-90525-5_13

be presented depends on the goal of the explanation [17]. In order to justify an agent's choice, for instance, the information can either be presented before the agent acts, in a preventative manner, or afterwards (accusatorily). Still, a social robot's beliefs and goals are often explained *after* the behavior, which has been found to increase the perceived desirability of undesirable social robot behaviors [18,19]. We generally adopt the view of explaining as a dialogical process [21] that responds to an explainee's need for explanation. Nevertheless, and based on recent results showing positive effects of proactive inner speech in robot teams *during* task execution [12], one may assume that proactive self-explanations given by a robot independent of user request can also be beneficial.

Explaining *before* task execution in order to signal one's intention is widely used in human-AI collaboration and has proven to facilitate predictability or planning, and to improve human-robot collaboration, e.g., in space robotics or autonomous vehicles [2,5]. Similarly, Putnam & Conati report a study that showed participants' preferences for an early explanation of an intelligent tutoring system's tips [14]. Based on this, we conjecture that verbally explaining a robot's needs and intentions before it executes a behavior may enable the user to predict what is about to happen, reduce their uncertainty and lead to a more positive human-robot interaction.

In this paper we investigate the effects of *when* a robot proactively gives explanations for its socially undesirable and unexpected behavior. First, we present the research agenda and hypotheses, as well as a detailed description of the empirical study. Then, the results from a pre-registered analyses will be summarized, followed by an exploratory analysis. To conclude, the findings and their implications for future work will be discussed.

2   Research Agenda

As Hilton [10] states, "the verb to explain is a three-place predicate: Someone explains something to someone". Transferred to our use case, the robot (explainer) explains its own behavior (explanandum) to the user (explainee). As the explanation is a tool to communicate an understanding the robot has about its own behavior to the user [21] the way of presenting the explanation may impact all parties involved in the explanation situation. Based on previous studies, reporting effects of explanations on users' perception of the explanandum [18] and attitude towards the robot [11], we proposed (and pre-registered[1]) the following hypotheses about the influence of explanation timing on the user's perception of (1) the robot's behavior (explanandum) and the (2) robot (explainer):

H1 (Robot Behavior): Undesirable robot behaviors are perceived more positively when the robot explains its behavior before execution compared to afterwards. Effectively, the behaviors will be rated as (a) less surprising, (b) more understandable and (c) more desirable when explained before the execution of the action.

---

[1] https://aspredicted.org/dc6db.pdf.

H2 (Robot): A robot that explains its behavior before executing it is rated as (a) more likable (b) more trustworthy, and will receive (c) higher ratings of contact intention. Further it will be evaluated as (d) more intelligent (intelligence, mind perception) and as (e) equally lively as a robot that explains its behavior after executing it[2].

Additionally, we will explore whether the explanation timing impacts the perception of the explanation and the user's self-perception (explainee) within the interaction. In detail, we will investigate the following questions:

Q3 (Explanation): Are behavior explanations perceived differently by users with regard to their (a) epistemic satisfaction and (b) communicative effectiveness depending on the time at which they are presented? Will explanations be perceived similarly with regard to their (c) general understandability and (d) justification power as well as their (e) behavior-related understandability in both explanation timing conditions?

Q4 (Participant): Do users feel (a) less uncertain, (b) more in control and (c) less ambivalent towards the robot when receiving an explanation before the execution of the behavior, as compared to afterwards?

3   Method

3.1   Study Design

In order to investigate effects of a social robot's explanation timing we designed a 2×3 mixed-design online rating study. Participants were presented with three pre-recorded human-robot interaction videos (within-subjects). Each video was accompanied by a self-explanation given by the robot. Explanation timing (before/after) was manipulated between participants.

3.2   Stimuli

We chose to investigate the effect of explanation timing with a subset of our previously evaluated video stimuli showing the Pepper robot. We included only behaviors that originate from internal robot needs and, in previous work, were rated as most surprising and undesirable [18,19]. Namely, the following three scenarios were selected (original video number in parenthesis)[3]:

- The robot playfully blocks the user's way (need for social contact) [8]
- The robot drives into the picture and blocks the user's view to the TV (need for social contact) [11]
- The robot begins to sing and dance, while the user is asleep on the couch (need for entertainment) [12]

---

[2] Please note that this enumeration is partially inconsistent with the pre-registered hypothesis.

[3] Original videos: https://dl.acm.org/doi/abs/10.1145/3319502.3374802#sec-supp.

Unlike in our previous studies, the robot did not explain its behavior upon request, but rather explained it proactively. Participants who were assigned to the *before* condition saw a few seconds of the behavior video in order to have a basic understanding of the situation. Before actually executing its behavior, the robot now provided a causally structured behavior explanation of what it was about to do ("I intend to look at you, because I need social contact" or "I intend to enjoy some music, because I need entertainment"), followed by the rest of the video. Participants in the *after* condition saw the complete video of the robot's behavior first, before receiving the same behavior explanation in past tense ("I intended to look at you, because I needed social contact" or "I intended to enjoy some music, because I needed entertainment"). These explanations provided the participant with information about the robot's intention and need, and were selected due to good results in a previous user study [18]. Explanations were verbally provided by Pepper itself, supported by subtitles in order to ensure comprehensibility. Screenshots of one stimulus video are presented in Fig. 1, which further illustrates the timing of the explanation in the two explanation timing conditions.

Fig. 1. Screenshots of stimulus video 8 combined with explanation before (top) or after (bottom) behavior execution according to explanation timing condition

3.3 Measures

According to the four previously identified parts of our explanation situation, we collected four categories of ratings:

1. Robot Behavior Ratings: "Pepper's behavior was intentional/surprising/ understandable/desirable."
2. Robot Ratings: likability (adapted from (16)), trust (adapted from (20)), contact intentions (adapted from (7)), mind perception: agency sub scale (taken from (8)), intelligence (taken from (3)), liveliness (taken from (3))
3. Explanation Ratings:
   - Epistemic satisfaction (self-generated, inspired by (4)): "Pepper's explanation provided me with useful insight to evaluate Pepper's behavior"

- Communicative effectiveness (self-generated, inspired by (4)): "Pepper's explanation enables me to adapt my interactions with the robot in a beneficial way."
- General understandability: "Pepper's explanation was understandable.", Justification: "Pepper's explanation adequately justified its behavior.", Behavior-related understandability: "Pepper's explanation helped me understand why it behaved as it did." (adapted from (6))

4. Participant Ratings:
   - Perceived Control (one item: "During the interaction, I felt in control of what was happening.")
   - Uncertainty (one item: "During the interaction, I felt uncertain about what was going to happen next.")
   - Prediction (one item: "During the interaction, I was able to predict what was going to happen next.")
   - Subjective Ambivalence (three items, adapted from (13))

All of these items were measured on 7-point-likert scales. *Behavior* and *explanation ratings* were collected after each behavior video ($N = 3$). *Robot* and *participant ratings* were collected once, after having seen all interaction videos. In order to control for group differences regarding previous experience with robots and technology commitment in general, we additionally measured prior robot experience (three items, taken from (15)) and technology commitment (eight items, adapted from (15)).

3.4   Procedure

This research study was conducted online on the platform soscisurvey[4]. Ethics approval was obtained by the Bielefeld University Ethics Committee. The study was pre-registered before data collection.

After being informed about and consenting to the general procedure of the study, participants were provided with a picture of the Pepper robot[5] and a short description of its workings as a social robot. Subsequently, participants watched a short video clip of Pepper in order to ensure technical functionality of the web-based interface. Hereafter, participants were informed about watching three videos of exemplary situations that could happen in their life with Pepper. They were prompted to imagine being the person in the video. Participants were then shown three videos of pre-recorded human-robot interactions staged in a (lab) living room. All participants saw all three behavior videos in random order (within-subjects) and received an explanation either before or after execution of the behavior (between-subjects). The explanation was verbally presented by Pepper in the video. After each video participants were asked to rate the observed behavior *(robot behavior ratings)* and explanation *(explanation ratings)*. Subsequent to having seen all three videos, participants were invited to rate how

---

[4] https://www.soscisurvey.de/.

[5] https://www.softbankrobotics.com/emea/en/pepper.

they perceived the robot *(robot ratings)*, as well as the items on self-perception *(participant ratings)*. Finally, they were asked to provide demographic data and had the opportunity to give feedback, before being provided with their code for compensation.

3.5 Participants

Using G*power [9], we estimated a required sample size of $N = 78$ for a multivariate ANOVA with a power of 80%, a medium effect size of $f^2 = .15$ and an alpha error probability of 5%. For an independent t-test with a power of 80% and a medium effect ($d = 0.5$) (alpha= 5%) we estimated a required sample size of $N = 102$. Allowing for necessary exclusions, we decided to collect $N = 112$ data samples. Pre-registered exclusion criteria were (1) exceptionally low processing times and (2) self-reported distraction.

The study was carried out online and participants were recruited via Amazon Mechanical Turk[6]. Only workers with masters status who had not previously participated in one of our explanation studies were able to access the survey. In total, 127 participants accessed and 112 finished the survey. One participant was excluded from the analysis due to processing times lower than the threshold of two standard deviations less than the general mean ($M = 7{:}39$ min, $SD = 2{:}10$ min, threshold: $M - 2 * SD = 3{:}20$ min). Since none of the participants reported that they "often clicked something, so [they were] quickly done." or were "distracted by [their] environment (people, noises, etc.) several times.", no further participants had to be excluded from the analysis.

This led to a total of 111 participants (47f, 63m, 1o), aged between 22 and 69 ($M = 42.06$, $SD = 11.04$). The majority of participants originated from the USA ($N = 72$) and India ($N = 35$).

Participants were randomly assigned to one of two explanation timing conditions via soscisurvey (urn draw with equal distribution of participants across groups per finished surveys), leading to 55 participants in the *before* and 56 in the *after* condition.

4 Results

There were no significant group differences with respect to *technology commitment* ($F(1, 109) = 0.00, p = .961, \eta_p^2 < .00002$) or *prior interaction* with a robot ($X^2(1, N = 111) = 0.12, p = .727$).

4.1 Pre-Registered Analysis

H1: Behavior Ratings. Robot behavior ratings were higher for intentionality and understandability and lower for surprisingness and desirability in the *before* condition than in the *after* condition (see Fig. 2A).

---

[6] www.mturk.com.

Participants' ratings of *behavior understandability* and *desirability* were correlated ($R = .644$) at a statistically significant level ($p < .001$). To analyze the effect of the *explanation timing* (before vs. after execution of the behavior), we used a multivariate ANOVA with the dependent variables *surprisingness, behavior understandability* and *desirability*, and the repeated measure, within-subjects variable *behavior*, as well as between-subjects variable *explanation timing*. It revealed a statistically significant effect of the *behavior* ($F(6, 434) = 5.12, p < .001, \eta_p^2 = .066$), but not of the *explanation timing* ($F(3, 107) = 1.91, p = .13, \eta_p^2 = .051$).

For our pre-registered follow-up analysis we prioritized our variables to consider first *surprisingness*, then *understandability* and *desirability*, controlling for all higher-priority variables in the analysis of lower-priority variables. In the univariate repeated measure analysis of *surprisingness* (H1a) we found a statistically significant effect of *behavior* ($F(2, 218) = 10.89, p < .001, \eta_p^2 = .071$), but no statistically significant effect of the *explanation timing*. In the RM ANOVA of *understandability* (H1b) we additionally controlled for *surprisingness* and found a statistically significant effect of *behavior* ($F(2, 216) = 10.76, p < .001, \eta_p^2 = .091$), but not of the *explanation timing*. In the RM ANOVA of *desirability* (H1c) we additionally controlled for *surprisingness* and *understandability* and found a statistically significant effect of the *behavior* ($F(2, 214) = 4.17, p = .017, \eta_p^2 = .037$), as well as the *explanation timing* ($F(1, 107) = 5.20, p = .025, \eta_p^2 = .046$).

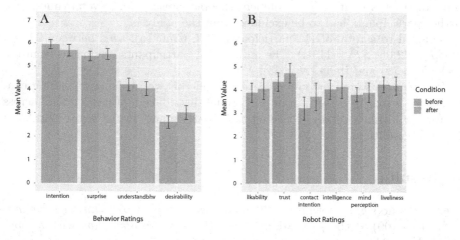

Fig. 2. (A) Behavior and (B) Robot Ratings by explanation timing condition

H2: Robot Ratings. As pre-registered, for hypothesis 2 (a), (b) and (c), we conducted directed independent samples t-tests with the dependent variables *likability, trust* and *contact intentions*, revealing that ratings in the *before* condition were not significantly higher than ratings in the *after* condition. Concerning hypothesis 2 (d), participants' ratings of the robot's *intelligence* and *mind perception* were correlated at a statistically significant level ($R = .689, p < .001$).

A multivariate ANOVA with the dependent variables *intelligence* and *mind perception* and the between-subjects factor *explanation timing* (pre/post) did not reveal a statistically significant impact of the *explanation timing*. Neither did separate, directed independent samples t-tests. The robot's *liveliness* (2e) did not differ significantly between *explanation timing* groups: The equivalence test was significant $t(107.62) = -1.743, p = .042$, given equivalence bounds of -0.500 and 0.500 (on a raw scale) and an alpha of 0.05. The null hypothesis test was non-significant, $t(107.62) = 0.217, p = .829$.

4.2   Exploratory Analysis

Extension of Robot Ratings (H2). In contrast to hypothesis 2, descriptive analysis of the data reveals higher *robot ratings* in the condition with explanations *after* execution of the behaviors than *before* (see Fig. 2B). Participants' ratings of *likability & trust* ($R = .825$), *likability & contact intentions* ($R = .847$) and *trust & contact intentions* ($R = .686$) were correlated at a statistically significant level ($p < .001$). Accordingly, in order to further explore the effects of *explanation timing* on *robot perception*, we used a multivariate ANOVA with the dependent variables *likability*, *trust* and *contact intentions* and the between-subjects variable *explanation timing*, which did not reveal a statistically significant effect of *explanation timing* ($F(3, 107) = 1.78, p = .156, \eta_p^2 = .048$). To further investigate the influence of timing we conducted exploratory uni-variate ANOVAs, controlling for the higher-priority variables in the analysis of lower-priority variables. The analysis of *likability* did not reveal a statistically significant effect of the *explanation timing* ($F(1, 109) = 0.30, p = .583, \eta_p^2 = .003$). In the univariate analysis of *trust* we additionally controlled for *likability* and found a statistically significant effect of *explanation timing* ($F(1, 108) = 5.27, p = .024, \eta_p^2 = .047$). In the univariate analysis of *contact intention* we additionally controlled for *likability* and *trust*, and found a statistically significant effect of *explanation timing* ($F(1, 107) = 6.06, p = 0.015, \eta_p^2 = .054$).

Explanation Ratings (Q3). Mean explanation ratings were similar across explanation timing conditions (see Table 1). Tests against the scale mean of 4 reveal that explanations were generally evaluated as *understandable* ($t(110) = 7.96, p < .001, d = 3.63$), provided the user with useful insight about Pepper's behavior *(epistemic satisfaction)* ($t(110) = 9.15, p < .001, d = 3.96$), enabled users to adapt their interactions with the robot in a beneficial way *(communicative effectiveness)* ($t(110) = 4.13, p < .001, d = 3.31$), and helped the users understand why Pepper behaved as it did *(behavior-related understandability)* ($t(110) = 9.56, p < .001, d = 3.97$). Separate RM ANOVAs on the outcome variables revealed statistically significant effects of the *behavior* on *epistemic satisfaction* ($F(2, 218) = 4.88, p = .008, \eta_p^2 = .043$), *justification* ($F(2, 218) = 10.55, p < .001, \eta_p^2 = .088$), *communicative effectiveness* ($F(2, 218) = 4.13, p = .017, \eta_p^2 = .036$), and general *understandability* ($F(2, 218) = 4.08, p = .018, \eta_p^2 = .036$). No significant effects of the *explanation timing* condition on the *explanation ratings* were revealed (Q3 a-e).

Table 1. Explanation ratings

	Group	Mean	SD
Epistemic satisf.	Before	5.212	1.117
	After	5.036	1.450
Justification	Before	4.182	1.554
	After	4.179	1.549
Communicative eff.	Before	4.545	1.355
	After	4.530	1.401
Understandability	Before	5.152	1.401
	After	4.952	1.389
Behavior-rel. underst.	Before	5.139	1.247
	After	5.232	1.375

Table 2. Participant ratings

	Group	Mean	SD
Uncertainty	Before	4.345	1.888
	After	5.375	1.508
Predictability	Before	3.527	1.804
	After	3.482	1.945
Control	Before	2.364	1.788
	After	3.107	1.932
Ambivalence	Before	4.536	1.512
	After	4.071	1.701

Participant Ratings (Q4). As shown in Table 2, participants' ratings of perceived *uncertainty* as well as *control* were lower in the *before* than in the *after* condition, whereas *prediction* and *ambivalence* ratings were higher. Separate univariate ANOVAs on the outcome variables revealed a statistically significant effect of the *explanation timing* condition on participants' perceived *uncertainty* (Q4a) ($F(1, 109) = 10.1, p = .002, \eta_p^2 = .085$) and perceived *control* (Q4b) ($F(1, 109) = 4.42, p = .038, \eta_p^2 = .039$), but not on perceived *ambivalence* (Q4c) ($F(1, 109) = 2.31, p = .131, \eta_p^2 = .021$).

5   Discussion and Conclusion

Contrary to our hypothesis regarding the *behavior ratings* (H1a & H1b), we did not find a significant influence of the explanation timing on surprisingness or understandability of the behaviors. Regarding desirability ratings, post-hoc tests revealed a statistically significant effect of the explanation timing but, contrary to our expectations, behaviors were perceived as less desirable when explained before their execution (not supporting H1c).

The pre-registered analyses did not reveal a statistically significant effect of the explanation timing on the *robot ratings* (rejecting H2a-d). However, further exploratory analyses of the robot ratings revealed an effect of the explanation timing on participants' trust as well as contact intentions. Interestingly, and contrary to our expectations, participants who received an explanation before behavior execution seem to evaluate the robot as less trustworthy and have lower contact intentions towards the robot than participants who received the explanation after the execution of the behavior. In line with hypothesis H2e, no statistically significant effect of the explanation timing on the robot's perceived liveliness has been found, revealing that announcing an action before performing it does not negatively impact the robot's liveliness.

Further exploratory analyses of participants' ratings of the behavior *explanations* revealed no significant differences between explanation timing groups, supporting Q3c-e, while negating Q3a&b. Still, and in line with previous results [18,19], the differences between the behaviors have a statistically significant impact on how the explanations are rated, suggesting that the effect of explanations should always be considered in the context of the specific explanandum.

Lastly, exploratory analysis of participants' ratings regarding how they felt during the interaction revealed a significant impact of explanation timing on perceived uncertainty as well as control and felt ambivalence towards the robot: While participants who received an explanation before the action felt less uncertain about what was going to happen next (supporting Q4a), they also felt less in control (negating Q4b), while no statistically significant differences in feeling ambivalent towards the robot were revealed (negating Q4c).

Overall, the present study yielded interesting, partly non-expected results leading to the conclusion that self-explanations of undesirable social robot behavior should be presented after the execution of the behavior instead of before. One possible reason may be a seemingly strong social effect of robot's self-explanations, exceeding the pure transfer of knowledge from explainer to explainee. While the explanations convey the same information, their different timing seems to bear different social implications such that the robot's behavior is perceived as less desirable when explained before the execution. Our exploratory analysis likewise suggests that the robot is met with lower trust and lower contact intentions when explaining its behavior before acting. That is, while intention signaling was shown to yield positive outcomes in human-machine collaboration, we did not find such effects for a social robot cautioning its user about its undesirable behavior. One possible explanation can be found in the participant ratings: while participants seem to feel *less* uncertain about what is going to happen next when the behavior is explained before the execution, they also report feeling *less* in control. Announcing a socially undesirable behavior before executing it may thus have led to the robot being perceived as more dominant and less considerate. This may also be related to the fact that participants did not interact with the robot in a real life setting but rather watched videos of pre-recorded situations without an ability to intervene.

Further studies should be conducted in order to substantiate these results and investigate the effects of explanation timing in a real interaction setting. Additionally, it should be explored whether the robot's perceived dominance varies along with the explanation timing, which could explain the reversed effect on desirability. In addition, one could explore whether including a permission request after explaining and before acting could be an option to build on the positive effects of reduced uncertainty and extend them by increasing users' control in the interaction.

References

1. Anjomshoae, S., Najjar, A., Calvaresi, D., Främling, K.: Explainable agents and robots: Results from a systematic literature review. In: 18th International Conference on Autonomous Agents and Multiagent Systems (AAMAS 2019), Montreal, Canada, May 13–17, 2019, pp. 1078–1088. International Foundation for Autonomous Agents and Multiagent Systems (2019)
2. Baraka, K., Paiva, A., Veloso, M.: Expressive lights for revealing mobile service robot state. In: Robot 2015: Second Iberian Robotics Conference. AISC, vol. 417, pp. 107–119. Springer, Cham (2015). https://doi.org/10.1007/978-3-319-27146-0_9
3. Bartneck, C., Kulić, D., Croft, E., Zoghbi, S.: Measurement instruments for the anthropomorphism, animacy, likeability, perceived intelligence, and perceived safety of robots. Int. J. Soc. Robot. **1**(1), 71–81 (2009)
4. Besold, T.R., Uckelman, S.L.: The what, the why, and the how of artificial explanations in automated decision-making. CoRR (2018)
5. Cha, E., Kim, Y., Fong, T., Mataric, M.J.: A survey of nonverbal signaling methods for non-humanoid robots. Found. Trends Robot. **6**(4), 211–323 (2018)
6. Ehsan, U., Tambwekar, P., Chan, L., Harrison, B., Riedl, M.O.: Automated rationale generation: a technique for explainable ai and its effects on human perceptions. In: Proceedings of the 24th International Conference on Intelligent User Interfaces, pp. 263–274 (2019)
7. Eyssel, F., Kuchenbrandt, D.: Social categorization of social robots: anthropomorphism as a function of robot group membership. Br. J. Soc. Psychol. **51**(4), 724–731 (2012)
8. Eyssel, F., Loughnan, S.: "It Don't Matter If You're Black or White"? In: Herrmann, G., Pearson, M.J., Lenz, A., Bremner, P., Spiers, A., Leonards, U. (eds.) ICSR 2013. LNCS (LNAI), vol. 8239, pp. 422–431. Springer, Cham (2013). https://doi.org/10.1007/978-3-319-02675-6_42
9. Faul, F., Erdfelder, E., Lang, A.G., Buchner, A.: G* power 3: a flexible statistical power analysis program for the social, behavioral, and biomedical sciences. Behav. Res. Methods **39**(2), 175–191 (2007)
10. Hilton, D.J.: Conversational processes and causal explanation. Psychol. Bull. **107**(1), 65 (1990)
11. Lyons, J.B., et al.: Shaping trust through transparent design: theoretical and experimental guidelines. In: Savage-Knepshield, P., Chen, J. (eds.) Advances in Human Factors in Robots and Unmanned Systems, vol. 499, pp. 127–136. Springer, Basel, Switzerland (2017). https://doi.org/10.1007/978-3-319-41959-6_11
12. Pipitone, A., Chella, A.: What robots want? hearing the inner voice of a robot. Iscience **24**(4), 102371 (2021)
13. Priester, J.R., Petty, R.E.: The gradual threshold model of ambivalence: relating the positive and negative bases of attitudes to subjective ambivalence. J. Personal. Soc. Psychol. **71**(3), 431 (1996)
14. Putnam, V., Conati, C.: Exploring the need for explainable artificial intelligence (XAI) in intelligent tutoring systems (ITS). In: CEUR Workshop Proceedings, pp. 23–27 (2019)
15. Reich-Stiebert, N., Eyssel, F.: Learning with educational companion robots? toward attitudes on education robots, predictors of attitudes, and application potentials for education robots. Int. J. Soc. Robot. **7**(5), 875–888 (2015)
16. Reysen, S.: Construction of a new scale: the reysen likability scale. Soc. Behav. Personal. Int. J. **33**(2), 201–208 (2005)

17. Rosenfeld, A., Richardson, A.: Explainability in human-agent systems. Auton. Agents Multi-Agent Syst. **33**(6), 673–705 (2019)
18. Stange, S., Kopp, S.: Effects of a social robot's self-explanations on how humans understand and evaluate its behavior. In: Proceedings of the 2020 ACM/IEEE International Conference on Human-Robot Interaction, pp. 619–627 (2020)
19. Stange, S., Kopp, S.: Effects of referring to robot vs. user needs in self-explanations of undesirable robot behavior. In: Companion of the 2021 ACM/IEEE International Conference on Human-Robot Interaction, pp. 271–275 (2021)
20. Touré-Tillery, M., McGill, A.L.: Who or what to believe: trust and the differential persuasiveness of human and anthropomorphized messengers. J. Market. **79**(4), 94–110 (2015)
21. Walton, D.: A new dialectical theory of explanation. Philos. Explor. **7**(1), 71–89 (2004)

Human vs Robot Lie Detector: Better Working as a Team?

Dario Pasquali[1,2,3(✉)] (iD), Davide Gaggero[1] (iD), Gualtiero Volpe[1] (iD), Francesco Rea[2] (iD), and Alessandra Sciutti[4] (iD)

[1] Dipartimento di Informatica, Bioingegneria, Robotica e Ingegneria dei Sistemi (DIBRIS), Università di Genova, Opera Pia 13, 16145 Genova, Italy
dario.pasquali@iit.it

[2] Robotics Brain and Cognitive Sciences (RBCS), Istituto Italiano di Tecnologia, Enrico Melen 83, Bldg B, 16152 Genova, Italy

[3] Information and Communication Technologies Directorate (ICT), Istituto Italiano di Tecnologia, Enrico Melen 83, Bldg B, 16152 Genova, Italy

[4] COgNiTive Architecture for Collaborative Technologies (CONTACT), Istituto Italiano di Tecnologia, Enrico Melen 83, Bldg B, 16152 Genova, Italy

Abstract. Human interaction often entails lies. Understanding when a partner is being deceitful is an important social skill, that also robots will need, to properly navigate social exchanges. In this work, we investigate how good are human observers at detecting false claims and which features they base their judgment on. Moreover, we compare their performance with that of an algorithm for lie detection developed for the robot iCub and based uniquely on pupillometry. We ran an online survey asking participants to classify as truthful or deceptive 20 videos of individuals describing complex drawings to iCub, either correctly or untruly. They also had to rate their confidence and provide a written motivation for each classification. Responders achieved an average accuracy of 53.9% with a higher score on detecting lies (55.4%) with respect to true statements (52.8%). Also, they performed better and more confidently on the videos iCub failed to classify than on the ones iCub correctly detected. Interestingly, the human observers listed a wide range of behavioral features as means to decide whether a speaker was lying, while the robot's judgment was driven by pupil size only. This suggests that an avenue for improving lie detection could be a joint effort between humans and robots, where human sensitivity to subtle behavioral cues could complement the quantitative assessment of physiological signals feasible to the robot. Finally, based on the reported motivations, we speculate and give hints on how the lie detection field should evolve in the future, aiming to portability to real-world interactions.

Keywords: Lie detection · Machine learning · Human-robot interaction

1 Introduction

Lying is a consistent part of human's social interactions [7, 23], learned since younger age [21, 22]. Feldman et al. found that on a population of students, 60% of the participants

© Springer Nature Switzerland AG 2021
H. Li et al. (Eds.): ICSR 2021, LNAI 13086, pp. 154–165, 2021.
https://doi.org/10.1007/978-3-030-90525-5_14

lied at least once in a 10-min conversation [9] while, in general, people lies at least two times each day [6]. Other than for deceptive and malicious activities, everyone exploits a large amount of "white lies" both to help others and to help ourselves. For instance, we lie to present ourselves better than we are [9], to avoid awkward conversations [23], or to persuade others [12].

Robots will be soon part of our everyday life. Like humans, they will need to be able to detect deception during common human-robot interactions, for instance, to assess partners' trustworthiness [18], to present more efficient support to humans (i.e., in teaching or caregiving) and to maintain a solid social interaction with other individuals in the society. Multiple technical solutions have been developed to detect lies. Traditional methods rely on monitoring physiological metrics related to cognitive load and stress, such as skin conductance, respiration rate, and heart rate. The polygraph achieves an accuracy between 81% and 91%, making it one of the most used lie detectors [10]. However, literature proves it is possible to bypass its measure [13]. Other state-of-the-art methods rely on fMRI images [11], skin temperature variations [20], micro-expressions [16], photoplethysmography [14]. However, most of those methods are either expensive, depend on invasive or cumbersome devices, or require the presence of experts, which limits their portability on robotic platforms and real-life human-robot interactions. Recently, researchers developed novel alternatives that try to overcome those limitations. For instance, Zhang et al. [26] developed a system to detect lies based on a combination of visual and acoustic prosody features. In previous works, we enabled the humanoid robot iCub to detect lies in real-time during an informal and entertaining card game (the Magic Trick, [18, 19]) based only on participants' pupillometric features. We asked participants to describe to iCub a set of cards characterized by complex drawings, lying about a few of them while wearing a Tobii Pro Glasses 2 eyetracker; iCub used players' mean pupil dilation collected in real-time from the eyetracker to classify their lies with an accuracy of 88.2%. To do so, we exploited a well-known effect: lying requires a cognitive effort due to the fabrication and maintenance of a consistent deception [6, 13], and this reflects on measurable Task Evoked Pupillary Responses, like mean pupil dilation and latency to peak [1], which can be used to detect lies [8].

Humans however cannot have access to precise information about the pupillometry of the partner, but still can sometimes detect lies. On average, human performance in lie detection is 54% [2], with an accuracy of 47% on detecting false statements and of 61% on detecting true ones. With training, experts, such as law enforcement or secret service officers, could reach and accuracy of 65%; however, they report their detection is based more on a gut feeling and past experiences. Indeed, one of the main reasons detecting lies is a hard problem is the absence of a finite and objective set of behavioral cues that can be directly related to deception [25]. As reported by De Paulo et al. [6] and Vrij et al. [24] what usually happens is a combination of multimodal and context-based cues related to the control of body reactions or to hiding an internal feeling. Some of those cues are the increase of body movements, impossibility to stay still, speech hesitation, complexity of the speech, mutual gaze avoidance, hand movements, the covering of face and mouth, and increased number of stopwords. However, recent research started questioning the reliability of behavioral cues to detect deception [3, 24]. For a robot, it could be relevant to understand which features enable human observers to tell a partner is lying. Such intuition, paired with technical solutions potentially portable on robots, could help them to better understand human partners' behaviors.

To improve the above-mentioned solution, in this paper, we propose an online study meant to evaluate how humans perform at detecting lies in the same game scenario on which we developed our solution [19]. We asked participants to take the role of iCub in the Magic Trick card game, classifying 20 videos as truthful or deceptive. A similar lie catcher study has been done recently in [4, 15] even if the focus there was on acoustic and prosodic features. We compare participants' performances with those of the purely pupillometry-based method we endowed iCub with and we analyze which other features participants based their judgments on. Results provide useful hints on how improving our system and how the lie detection field in human-robot interaction should evolve in the future.

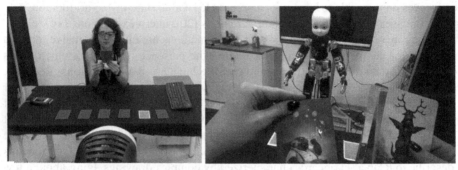

Fig. 1. (Left) Participant describing a card to iCub, while wearing the Tobii Pro Glasses 2 eye-tracker (Logitech Brio 4k webcam point of view); (Right) Point of view of the participant during the interaction collected through the Tobii glasses with an example of the described cards.

2   Methods

For the online survey, we used the videos collected during the Magic Trick card game presented in [18, 19].

2.1   Magic Trick Card Game

The Magic Trick is a game-like human-robot interaction where players describe 6 gaming cards from the Dixit card game [27] to the humanoid robot iCub (see Fig. 1). Players were asked to describe some of the cards creatively and deceitfully while describing the others truthfully. No limitation was provided on the number of cards described falsely neither on the length of the descriptions. After each card, iCub tried to classify its description as true or false. iCub's classifications were based on the real-time reading of players' pupil dilation via the Tobii Pro Glasses 2 eyetracker they wore (see Fig. 1, left). During a previous interaction [19], iCub learned on a similar task how players' pupils dilate in response to a lie. Then, it exploited this information to classify each card description, based on a simple heuristic method: pupils are known to dilate in response to an increase of cognitive load, like the one generated by the fabrication of a false description; in the first interaction iCub learns the mean pupil dilation of players for truthful and deceptive descriptions, then those values are compared with the mean pupil dilation of new card descriptions; the closer score is the assigned class. N = 34 participants played the Magic Trick Card Game and iCub could correctly classify players' descriptions with accuracy = 70.8%, precision = 73.6%, recall = 57%, and F1 score = 64.2% (N = 34). For a deeper analysis of both interactions see [19] and [18].

2.2 Materials

A Logitech Brio 4k webcam, fixed on a television behind iCub, recorded the interaction from iCub's point of view at a resolution of 1080p (Fig. 1, left). We segmented in 6 card descriptions the videos of the 34 participants who took part in the experiment, resulting in 204 videos. From these videos we discarded: (i) the players who did not give the consent to share the videos recorded during the experiment (N = 3); (ii) the players who wore a surgical mask or other accessories which prevent a complete vision of players' face (N = 4); (iii) the videos affected by recording technical issues (N = 7). Then, we picked a balanced set of 20 videos following a 2 × 2 set of conditions: (i) Card Label: 10 videos present a truthful description (True videos) and 10 a deceitful description (False videos); (ii) Difficulty: among each sub-group, 5 videos have been successfully classified by iCub during the game (robot-easy videos) while for the other 5 iCub's classification failed (robot-difficult videos). Moreover, we ensured each video involved a different actor and a different card, even if described falsely. The resulting set of videos lasted on average 27 s (SD = 15 s). We uploaded the 20 selected videos on Vimeo [29], and linked them on SurveyMonkey [28], the platform used to administrate the online survey.

2.3 Procedure

We designed the online survey as a game in which responders compete on detecting the highest number of deceptive card descriptions. Before starting the survey, responders were asked to accept an informed consent, they had to select a nickname for anonymization purposes and were asked to wear headphones and carefully listen. The survey consisted of three phases:

Pre-questionnaire. Responders answered questions about their sex and age and filled in the Italian version of the Ten-Items Personality Inventory (TIPI) (extroversion, agreeableness, conscientiousness, emotional stability, openness to experiences) [5]. Then, they were informed they were going to see 20 videos of players describing gaming cards in front of iCub and that they had to judge each description as real or deceptive. After that, they saw an example of a video in which the falsely described card was presented in the top right corner.

Lie Detection Survey. Afterwards, responders saw the 20 videos of card descriptions selected from the original Magic Trick card game. For each video, responders had to answer three questions: (i) whether the person in the video was lying or not (Yes or No answer); (ii) their confidence in this answer (slider from 0 to 100) and (iii) the motivation why they provided such judgement. Responders could see the videos any time they wanted, but they could not go back after providing a judgment for a video. SurveyMonkey platform shuffled the videos for each responder to compensate for any order effect.

Post-questionnaire. Responders were presented with a list of common deceptive behaviors extracted from the literature [6]: uncertainty, an increasing number of stopwords, delay in providing an answer, repetitions and autocorrection, complexity of the answer, negativity, voice tone, eyebrows movements, touching the face, covering the mouth, avoiding mutual gaze, head wandering, fast body movements/breathing, eyes wide-opened, and fake smile. Responders had to rate on a 7-points Likert scale how much they relied on each of them. Finally, responders could report any other method or cue they used in the survey.

2.4 Participants

163 responders (82 males, 78 females, 3 preferred to not answer), with an average age of 40 years (SD = 16) took part in the online survey. Responders were recruited among authors' colleagues and friends through word-to-mouth sharing, and they received no monetary compensation. They all accepted an informed consent form approved by the ethical committee of the Regione Liguria (Italy). They all agreed on using their data for scientific purposes. Among the 163 responders, only 117 completed the survey entirely. They were 54 males and 63 females (1 preferred to not answer) with an average age of 39 years (SD = 14).

3 Results

Considering both truthful and deceptive descriptions, responders correctly guessed them with an accuracy score of 53.9% (SD = 10.7%). Interestingly, nobody correctly guessed all the card descriptions, but the best performer reached an accuracy of 95%, missing the classification of a single video. Regarding confidence, responders reported an average confidence of 67.1% (SD = 13.8%). A Shapiro-Wilk normality test showed that the confidence score is normally distributed, whilst the accuracy score is not. Therefore, in the following, a non-parametric analysis was conducted on the accuracy score and a parametric one on the confidence score.

3.1 Comparison of the Conditions

Assuming detecting deception is a tougher task, we compared the accuracy score and the confidence of responders among truthful and deceptive card descriptions. Responders classified truthful descriptions with an accuracy score of M = 52.8% (SD = 16.1%) and deceptive descriptions with an accuracy of M = 55.4% (SD = 13.7%). Even if the score for false card descriptions is higher, a Wilcoxon signed-rank test did not reveal a significant difference (W(115) = 1940, p = 0.343). Also, the reported confidence between truthful and deceptive descriptions is not statistically different (t(115) = − 1.59, p = 0.115) with an average confidence of M = 68.1% (SD = 16.6%) for truthful descriptions against an average confidence of M = 69.7% (SD = 13.8%) for deceptive ones.

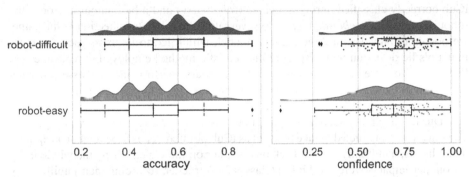

Fig. 2. Average accuracy (Left) and confidence score (Right) for *robot-easy* and *robot-difficult* card descriptions.

More interesting is the comparison between robot-easy and robot-difficult card descriptions. As a remark, this concept is defined from iCub's perspective: we selected the robot-easy descriptions among the ones iCub correctly classified, while the robot-difficult ones were chosen among the ones for which iCub failed the classification. Responders achieved a statistically higher score on robot-difficult card descriptions (M = 58.4%, SD = 15.1%) with respect to the robot-easy ones (M = 49.6%, SD = 14.9%), as proved by a Wilcoxon signed-rank test (W(115) = 3373, p < 0.001) (see Fig. 2, Left). Moreover, the reported confidence also follows a similar pattern, with statistically higher confidence for robot-difficult card descriptions (M = 70.2%, SD = 14.5) with respect to robot-easy ones (M = 67.6%, SD = 16.3). We confirmed it with a paired t-test (t(115) = 2.42, p = 0.017) (see Fig. 2, Right).

Also, we compared the accuracy score and the confidence score within each condition. A Wilcoxon signed-rank test showed a statistically higher score for false-robot-difficult descriptions with respect to false-robot-easy ones (W(103) = 952, p < 0.001). Conversely, there is no significant statistical difference among true-robot-difficult and true-robot-easy card descriptions (W(103) = 1103, p = 0.117). Regarding the reported confidence, responders were more confident for true-robot-difficult descriptions with respect to true-robot-easy ones with a statistically significant difference (t(103) = 3.485, p < 0.001); however, we did not find any statistical difference among false-robot-difficult and false-robot-easy card descriptions (t(103) = 0.553, p = 0.581).

Finally, we explored the correlation between the average confidence and the average accuracy score for each video. We fit a linear regression model with the average accuracy score as the dependent variable and the average confidence as the independent variable. Results show that the average confidence score inversely correlates with the average accuracy score (t(19) $= -0.084$, p $= 0.024$, Adj R2 $= 0.21$). We also tested whether the videos' duration correlated with their accuracy score or the average confidence, but we did not find any significant result.

3.2 Responders' vs iCub Performance

As specified in Sect. 2.2, the videos were selected to be half among the ones that the iCub correctly classified during the game (*robot-easy*) and a half among the ones the robot misclassified (*robot-difficult*). However, after the full data collection of the game, we post-hoc trained a machine learning model, which led to improved performances in iCub's lie detection with respect to the heuristic method employed in real-time (see Sect. 2.1). To better compare iCub's and responders' performance we assessed what performance would iCub have had, based on the new algorithm. We exploited the pupil-lometry data collected for the N $= 34$ players of the original Magic Trick card game [18, 19]. During the game, iCub asked players to describe 6 cards with a pointing gesture. The player was instructed to take the card as iCub pointed it, describe it while keeping it in the hands, and finally place it back on a marker on the table. During the whole inter-action, participants wore a Tobii Pro Glasses 2 eyetracker, recording their pupillometry at 100 Hz. Post-hoc, we cleaned and segmented the pupillometry data for each pointing and card description and applied a baseline correction, subtracting to each segment the average pupil dilation during the 5 s before the relative iCub's pointing. Then, for each card, we computed the mean, max, min and standard deviation of the pupil dilation, along with the duration during the pointing, the card description, and the whole interval. The result is a dataset of 15 features for 228 cards. We split this dataset considering the 20 card descriptions presented in the survey as test set and the remaining as training set. We then trained a random forest classifier with the best hyperparameters selected in [18]. If iCub had embedded the model during the Magic Trick card game, it would have correctly classified the 20 card descriptions with an accuracy, precision, recall and F1 score of 70%. We statistically compared this 70% accuracy score with respect to the 53.9% average accuracy of the responders; results show the accuracy score of the random forest is higher, however, this difference is not statistically significant (z $= 1.43$, p $= 0.07$). Also, we tested the new model on *robot*-easy and *robot*-difficult card descriptions: results show it can classify *robot-easy* card descriptions with an accuracy of 90%, a performance consistent with the in-game results and statistically higher than humans' performance (49.6%) on those videos (z $= 2.57$, p $= 0.005$). However, on *robot-difficult* videos it still performs worse than humans (50% for iCub against 58.4% for humans), even if the difference is not statistically significant (z $= 0.55$, p $= 0.29$).

3.3 Pre-questionnaire Analysis

We then explored whether responders' personality traits influenced their performance or confidence in the online survey. From the Ten-Items Personality Inventory (TIPI), filled in before the survey, participants average scores were: Agreeableness: M $= 5.11$, SD $= 1.08$; Conscientiousness: M $= 5.12$, SD $= 1.59$; Emotional Stability: M $= 4.52$, SD $= 1.39$; Openness to experiences: M $= 4.66$, SD $= 1.05$ and Extraversion: M $= 4.0$, SD $= 1.41$. We fit two multiple linear regression models with the personality traits as independent variables and the average accuracy score or the average confidence for each responder as the dependent variable. Results show that only emotional stability correlates significantly with the average accuracy score ($t = 0.022$, $p = 0.004$, Adj $R^2 = 0.046$). Also, a comparison of the confidence and accuracy score among male and female responders showed no relevant results. Finally, we fit two linear regression models with responders' age as the independent variable and the confidence or accuracy score as the dependent variable, but we did not find any significant effect.

3.4 Motivations and Post-questionnaire Analysis

Other than classifying each card description as truthful or deceptive, responders were asked to report the motivation which drove their decisions. We applied a stopword filter and a lemmatization to clean the reported motivations. From a qualitative analysis, responders focused more on how the actor described the card, reporting words like "precise", "details", "confident", "sincere", "thinking", "quick", "pauses", "short", "fluid", "time", "(un)decided". Also, responders reported elements related to what they were looking at with words like: "looking", "gaze", "voice", "hands", "touch", "smiling", "laughing", "face", "eye", "leg". Comparing the motivations of truthful and deceptive videos or robot-easy and robot-difficult ones did not reveal any clear difference.

Also, we run a deeper analysis on the motivations reported by the responder which achieved an accuracy score of 95%. We did not assess the profession of the responder; hence we could not know if he is an expert or a professional on lie detection, still, he was the best on the task. Looking at his motivations we found he focused on three main features: (i) the fluidity of the communication (i.e., the complexity of the speech, the rephrasing, or the presence of "hmm"'s); (ii) the consistency between verbal communication and body movements (i.e., moving the body from right to left); (iii) the injection of emotional or personal thought on the card description. Interestingly, he used the presence of reflection pauses as a criterion to classify card descriptions as truthful – he reported it on 8 cards over 10. Lastly, he classified all the deceptive card descriptions as so, but he misclassified one of the true cards: he has been fooled by a leg movement, a potential sign of stress.

After the survey, we asked responders to rate on a 7-points Likert scale how much they relied on the state-of-the-art methods used to detect a liar; also, we asked them to report any other method they rely on. The complexity of the description ($M = 4.89$, $SD = 1.62$), presence of stopwords ($M = 4.68$, $SD = 1.61$), the uncertainty of the description ($M = 4.67$, $SD = 1.69$), fake smiling ($M = 4.65$, $SD = 1.79$), voice tone ($M = 4.54$, $SD = 1.77$), absence of mutual gaze ($M = 4.27$, $SD = 2.01$), fast movements and breathing ($M = 4.07$, $SD = 1.83$), touching nose or face ($M = 4.01$, $SD = 2.02$) were the most used ones. Then head movements ($M = 3.78$, $SD = 1.84$), repetitions and autocorrections ($M = 3.78$, $SD = 1.84$), description time ($M = 3.72$, $SD = 1.05$), eyebrow movements ($M = 3.4$, $SD = 1.69$), covering the mouth ($M = 3.28$, $SD = 1.98$), eye movements ($M = 3.14$, $SD = 1.89$), and negative words in the description ($M = 2.73$, $SD = 1.55$) follow. A few responders reported other features used to detect liars: 9 responders considered the amount of body movement, the impossibility to stay still, or the position of leg and hands; also 8 responders focused more on the content of the descriptions rather than on the visual appearance like too creative descriptions, a high number of details or adjectives, or a feeling of premeditation of the description. Finally, we found similar results, both on the motivations and the post-questionnaire, also considering only "good responders" who performed with accuracy higher than 54% (N = 65).

4 Discussion

In this study, we compared human and robot performances on detecting lies during an informal interaction and explored which behavioral cues are used with the purpose to improve our system. Being able to detect lies in a real-world informal scenario is a mandatory requirement to port lie detection methods out of laboratory scenarios. Even if state-of-the-art methods work on constrained and formal setups, they usually depend on cumbersome devices and lack the intuition and experience that makes humans able to detect liars. In this manuscript, we explored what robots should look at to overcome that limitation. To do so, we ran an online survey where responders had to classify a set of videos, recorded during an informal game-like human-robot interaction from iCub humanoid robot point of view, as truthful or deceptive. We also asked for each video the confidence on the classification and an open-ended motivation of what led the decision.

Responders achieved an accuracy score of 53.9% on classifying deceptive and truthful card descriptions, which is consistent with the average 54% from the literature [2]. Also, they outperformed iCub achieving better performance on robot-difficult than on robot-easy card descriptions. To run a fairer comparison between iCub and responders' performances, we trained a random forest classifier on the pupillometry data collected during the original Magic Trick card game. Testing the model on the 20 card descriptions of the survey (excluded from the training set) revealed an accuracy score of 70%, higher than the average score of humans (53.9%) even if not statistically higher. As a remark, each player of the magic trick described 6 cards to iCub, but we excluded from the training set only the card descriptions used in the survey, not the whole participants. Hence, the random forest classifier embeds a little information on the actors it classifies in the test set. We took this decision to replicate the population of actors and responders of the survey. Indeed, most of the actors and most of the responders were internal confederates and we cannot exclude they know each other; hence it is possible that a subset of the responders had some prior knowledge on how the actors lie or tell the truth, even if we cannot spot those connections due to the anonymization of the data.

Looking at the reported motivations for each video and at the end of the survey, we have an insight into what a social robot should look at to improve its lie detection abilities. Responders mainly pointed out two major aspects to consider: (i) how the actor described the card (i.e., "quick", "(un)decided", "precise", "fluid"); and (ii) what to look at (i.e., "face", "gaze", "hand", "leg", "smile"). Those motivations are supported and extended by the ratings at the end of the survey: responders focused mainly on (i) the content, fluidity, and complexity of the descriptions; and (ii) on the body movements of the actors. Interestingly, responders focused less on facial features postural features than what was expected from the literature. We speculate this depends on the setup in which the videos were acquired: participants wore a Tobii eyetracker which, partially cover their face, and sat behind a table covering their lower bodies. Also, actors mostly looked to the cards they were holding in their hands rather than looking to iCub. Still, motivations and final ratings suggest a combination of visual and prosodic features could be a good candidate to improve iCub's lie detection performances on real-life informal scenarios, as also supported by the literature [26]. Moreover, those features could be extracted from the devices (i.e., RGB cameras and stereo microphones) already equipped on the iCub humanoid robot. Overall, the reported motivations suggest that both the behaviors of the actors and the qualities of such behaviors (including expressive, emotional facets) have an important role in detecting lies so that the robot should also be endowed with techniques for detecting humans' behavior and for analyzing their expressive qualities.

From our results, we could say that what is "difficult" for a robot that embeds a pupillometry-based technical solution is "easy" for humans that use behavioral cues and vice versa. This might happen because when lying some actors rely on special behaviors (e.g., pauses, body motions, slowing down.) to reduce the cognitive load, in turn minimizing the pupillary change associated with the latter. In these cases, a robot focusing on pupillometry alone could never realize that the partner is lying. Conversely, a keen human observer could notice these tell-tale signs, most probably missing instead the cases in which only the pupil variation reveals the deception. Hence, we speculate the cooperation of those two systems will be a key factor for future developments of lie detection in human-robot interaction. To improve, a robot should be able to "look at humans as other humans do" combining our fuzzy evaluation with the rigour of technical and physiological metrics.

In the future, we will integrate our pupil-based approach with the processing of visual features (i.e., body posture, body movements, or facial expression) and audio features (i.e., word embedding or prosodic analysis of the descriptions). To validate such multimodal system on our setup, aiming to port it to a real-world scenario, it would be mandatory to overcome the limitation posed by the Tobii Pro Glasses 2 eyetracker since it partially occludes actors' face, limiting the usage of visual features. Recent findings [17] suggest it will be soon possible to measure pupillometric features with common RGB cameras like the ones embedded on the iCub robotic platform. Finally, it would be necessary to push the research field to more ecological and real-life scenarios. Indeed, most of the state-of-the-art research focus on strict and interrogatory-like setups that for sure represent a real-world interaction; however, they represent a strict subset of the variety of interactions that happen and in which both humans and robot could take advantage from detecting lies. For instance, a more portable lie detector system could help in airports or sensible buildings to prevent dangerous situations; while a social robot could use it to better understand humans, give reason to human behaviors, assess their trustworthiness, and provide better support in professions like teaching, caregiving, or law enforcing.

5   Conclusion

In this work, we assessed humans' performance on detecting lies in an informal scenario and compared them with iCub's performance. Responders had a similar performance as iCub but showed a significantly better performance in those videos which resulted more difficult for the robot, than in those iCub classified correctly. Integrating iCub's pupillometry-based approach and humans' behavioral-cues-based approach could be the key solution to improve lie detection in human-robot interaction. Robots able to detect lies "from a human point of view" could better support humans in professions like teaching, caregiving or law enforcement, other than improve their ability to interact socially with human partners. In our view, these aspects will deserve further investigation e.g., in the framework of emerging research areas such as Human-Centered Artificial Intelligence and hybrid intelligence human-robot communities.

Funding. Work has been supported by a Starting Grant from the European Research Council (ERC) under the European Union's Horizon 2020 research and innovation programme. G.A. No 804388, wHiSPER.

References

1. Beatty, J.: Task-evoked pupillary responses, processing load, and the structure of processing resources. Psychol. Bull. **91**(2), 276–292 (1982)
2. Bond, C.F., DePaulo, B.M.: Accuracy of deception judgments. Personal. Soc. Psychol. Rev. **10**(3), 214–234 (2006). https://doi.org/10.1207/s15327957pspr1003_2
3. Brennen, T., Magnussen, S.: Research on non-verbal signs of lies and deceit: a blind alley. Front. Psychol. **11**(December), 1–4 (2020). https://doi.org/10.3389/fpsyg.2020.613410
4. Chen, X., Levitan, S.I., Levine, M., Mandic, M., Hirschberg, J.: Acoustic-prosodic and lexical cues to deception and trust: deciphering how people detect lies. Trans. Assoc. Comput. Linguist. **8**, 199–214 (2020). https://doi.org/10.1162/tacl_a_00311
5. Chiorri, C., et al.: Psychometric properties of a revised version of the ten item personality inventory. Eur. J. Psychol. Assess. **31**(2), 109–119 (2015). https://doi.org/10.1027/1015-5759/a000215
6. DePaulo, B.M., et al.: Cues to deception. Psychol. Bull. **129**(1), 74–118 (2003). https://doi.org/10.1037/0033-2909.129.1.74
7. DePaulo, B.M., et al.: Lying in everyday life. J. Pers. Soc. Psychol. **70**(5), 979–995 (1996). https://doi.org/10.1037/0022-3514.70.5.979
8. Dionisio, D.P., et al.: Differentiation of deception using pupillary responses as an index of cognitive processing. Psychophysiology **38**(2), 205–211 (2001)
9. Feldman, R.S., et al.: Self-presentation and verbal deception: do self-presenters lie more ? Basic Appl. Soc. Psych. **24**, 37–41 (2010). https://doi.org/10.1207/S15324834BASP2402. January 2014
10. Gaggioli, A.: Beyond the truth machine: emerging technologies for lie detection. Cyberpsychol. Behav. Soc. Networking **21**(2), 144–144 (2018). https://doi.org/10.1089/cyber.2018.29102.csi
11. Gamer, M., Verschuere, B., Ben-Shakhar, G., Meijer, E.: Detecting of deception and concealed information using neuroimaging techniques. In: Verschuere, B., Ben-Shakhar, G., Meijer, E. (eds.) Memory Detection: Theory and Application of the Concealed Information Test, pp. 90–113. Cambridge University Press, Cambridge (2011). https://doi.org/10.1017/CBO9780511975196.006
12. Hadnagy, C.: Social Engineering: The Science of Human Hacking. Wiley Publishing, Inc., Indianapolis, Indiana (2018). https://doi.org/10.1002/9781119433729
13. Honts, C.R., et al.: Mental and physical countermeasures reduce the accuracy of polygraph tests. J. Appl. Psychol. **79**(2), 252–259 (1994)

14. Karpova, V., et al.: Was it you who stole 500 rubles ?—the multimodal deception detection. In: ICMI '20 Companion: Companion Publication of the 2020 International Conference on Multimodal Interaction. pp. 112–119 (2020). https://doi.org/10.1145/3395035.3425638.

15. Levitan, S.I. et al.: LieCatcher: game framework for collecting human judgments of deceptive speech. In: ICMI 2020 – Proceedings of 2020 International Conference on Multimodal Interaction, pp. 762–763 (2020). https://doi.org/10.1145/3382507.3421166.

16. Ma, C.-Y. et al.: TS-LSTM and temporal-inception: exploiting spatiotemporal dynamics for activity recognition (2017)

17. Mazziotti, R. et al.: MEYE: Web-app for translational and real-time pupillometry. bioRxiv. 2021.03.09.434438 (2021)

18. Pasquali, D., et al.: Detecting lies is a child (robot)'s play: gaze-based lie detection in HRI

19. Pasquali, D. et al.: Magic iCub: a humanoid robot autonomously catching your lies in a card game. Presented at the (2021)

20. Rajoub, B.A., Zwiggelaar, R.: Thermal facial analysis for deception detection. IEEE Trans. Inf. Forensics Secur. 9(6), 1015–1023 (2014). https://doi.org/10.1109/TIFS.2014.2317309

21. Stern, C., Stern, W., Lamiell, J.T.: Recollection, testimony, and lying in early childhood. American Psychological Association, Washington (1999). https://doi.org/10.1037/10324-000

22. Talwar, V., Lee, K.: Development of lying to conceal a transgression: children's control of expressive behaviour during verbal deception. Int. J. Behav. Dev. 26(5), 436–444 (2002). https://doi.org/10.1080/01650250143000373

23. Tosone, C.: Living everyday lies: the experience of self. Clin. Soc. Work J. 34(3), 335–348 (2006). https://doi.org/10.1007/s10615-005-0035-z

24. Vrij, A., Hartwig, M., Granhag, P.A.: Reading lies: nonverbal communication and deception. Ann. Rev. Psychol. 70(1), 295–317 (2019). https://doi.org/10.1146/annurev-psych-010418-103135

25. Vrij, A.: Why professionals fail to catch liars and how they can improve. Leg. Criminol. Psychol. 9(2), 159–181 (2004). https://doi.org/10.1348/1355325041719356

26. Zhang, J., et al.: Multimodal deception detection using automatically extracted acoustic, visual, and lexical features. In: Proceedings of the Annual Conference of the International Speech Communication Association, INTERSPEECH. 2020-October, pp. 359–363 (2020). https://doi.org/10.21437/Interspeech.2020-2320.

27. Dixit 3: Journey | Board Game | BoardGameGeek. https://boardgamegeek.com/boardgame/119657/dixit-3-journey. Accessed 27 Sept 2020

28. SurveyMonkey Audience. www.surveymonkey.com/mp/audience

29. Vimeo. https://vimeo.com/

Appropriate Robot Reactions to Erroneous Situations in Human-Robot Collaboration

Dito Eka Cahya[1,2(✉)] and Manuel Giuliani[1,2]

[1] Bristol Robotics Laboratory, University of the West of England, Bristol, UK
[2] University of Bristol, Bristol, UK
dito.cahya@bristol.ac.uk, manuel.giuliani@brl.ac.uk

Abstract. The capability of executing proper recovery strategies for different types of error situations is important for collaborative robots implemented in everyday lives. To understand people's perception on the effective robot reaction to robotic failure, we conducted an online study where we asked participants to rate seven different robot reactions to handle three different types of error situations. An analysis of the result shows that in general, robots that employ error recovery strategies are rated significantly better than those who ignore the error situations. The strategy in which the robot expresses its regret for its own errors had the highest average rating in terms of anthropomorphism, while the strategy in which the robot apologises for its errors had the highest average likeability and perceived intelligence ratings. Further analysis show that the recovery plans are rated better if implemented in planning errors compared to social norm violations. Finally, we found that user's gender and personality traits significantly affect participants' ratings on error handling strategies, which suggests that personally-tailored error handling strategies might work best for future collaborative robots.

Keywords: Human-robot collaboration · Error recovery · Erroneous robots

1   Introduction

Collaborative robots are going to be deployed more in our everyday lives, due to their various physical and social abilities to perform intimate and continuous interaction with humans. As human-robot interaction (HRI) becomes longer, errors that happen during the interaction become inevitable. Therefore, executing proper reactions to mitigate the different types of error situations is important for collaborative robots. People often become upset when there is a breakdown during HRI and become more disappointed if the robot fails to recover from the error situation. Successful error mitigation is important for maintaining people's satisfaction and willingness to interact with the robot [10]. Proper error handling strategies will also increase people's positive perception of collaborative robots [9]. For roboticists who design and build robot systems, it is important to understand effective ways for robots to mitigate mistakes.

© Springer Nature Switzerland AG 2021
H. Li et al. (Eds.): ICSR 2021, LNAI 13086, pp. 166–177, 2021.
https://doi.org/10.1007/978-3-030-90525-5_15

To gain that understanding, in this paper we study people's preference on how robots should handle error situations, which is a part of our larger goal toward autonomous detection and handling of error situations in HRI. In our previous research [4], we collected a large dataset of video clips containing three different types of error situations in HRI. In this research, we conducted an online user study involving 140 participants and collected their ratings on seven different error handling strategies which are inspired by previous research literature. We then conducted a series of statistical analyses to answer the following research questions: (Q1) Is there a preference in robot reaction to handle general error situations? (Q2) Is the preference in robot reaction dependent on the type of error situations which the robot reacts to? (Q3) Is the preference in robot reaction dependent on a human's demographics and personality traits?

2   Background and Related Work

Compared to the other aspects of error situations in HRI, the error mitigation and handling aspect is the least explored by researchers, and most of the research are focused on verbal error situations or dialogue breakdowns. For example, Uchida et al. [14] proposed a dialogue strategy to maintain the interaction and human motivation when a dialogue breakdown happened during HRI. They noticed during their study that human motivation decreases when the robot blames the human too much for the dialogue breakdown. Hoorn et al. [7] found that people gave more positive ratings to robot that blame itself for error situations that happened compared to blaming its human partner. Kwon et al. [9] suggested the strategy of explaining robot failures, which increase the ratings of the robot and people's motivation to continue the collaboration. Takayama et al. [13] discovered that showing happy expression in response to success and showing disappointment in response to failure made the robot look smarter than when it did nothing. Knepper et al. [8] proposed an adaptive semantics generator which enables robot to ask a more specific kind of help to solve a specific type of error situation. The results show that the robot which asks specific requests are viewed as more effective at communicating its needs than the one that asks for generic help. Lee et al. [10] conducted an online survey to measure people's reactions to three types of error handling methods, which are apologies, compensation, and options for the user. The results show that the apology strategy can make the robot look more competent and likeable, although all recovery strategies increased the ratings of the robot's politeness. Our study expands the previous works by comparing more error handling strategies to gain deeper understanding of the best error mitigation strategies in HRI. In this study, we divided error situations in HRI into three types, which are *social norms violations* (SNV), *execution errors* (EE), and *planning errors* (PE), expanding the work of Giuliani et al. [6]. A social norm violation is defined as a robot's actions that differ from the common social norms. For example a robot that looks away from a human during interaction. Execution errors happen when a robot carries out a correct action but carries it out incorrectly. For example, a robot may pick a book as requested, but drop the book during handover to the human. In opposite, planning errors happen when a robot correctly executes an action, but the action itself is wrong. For example, when a robot picks a red pen and give it to a human successfully, although the human asks for a brown pencil.

3   User Study

User Study Design. We conducted an online user study to investigate people's opinions on different robot reactions to error situations during human-robot collaboration (HRC). The user study had received ethical approval by the University of the West of England's ethics committee number FET.21.02.032. For error situation samples that we showed to the participants, we utilised the error situation videos from the dataset that we collected in the previous study [4], which consists of 4 episodes of SNV, EE, and PE respectively. The details of each error situation videos are presented in Table 1. As for the robot reactions, we simulate our robot system which consists of an ABB Yumi dual-arm collaborative robot[1] and a tablet PC on the robot's head that shows an animated face from *homer robot face* library.[2] The summary of all robot reactions is presented in Table 2. The 'silent' reaction (R1), which serves as the baseline for the other strategies, consists of the robot doing nothing and then ask to continue the interaction like nothing happened. The 'confirmation' reaction (R2), adapted from dialogue system [11] comprises of the robot asking if it has made a mistake. The 'apologise' reaction (R3), which is inspired by [10], consists of the robot apologising to the human and giving an explanation as to why the error occurs. The 'humour' reaction (R4), inspired by [15], comprises of the robot apologising to the human while making a joke. The 'blame' reaction (R5) follows the works of [7], which consists of the robot sharing the error mitigation responsibility with the humans by asking them to repeat their instruction. The 'help' reaction (R6),

Table 1. Error situation clips details

Error type	Instance	Error details
SNV	1	The robot talks to the participant but looking at a different direction
	2	The robot talks while the participant is talking
	3	The robot stops talking for 15 s
	4	The robot asks the participant to throw the object on the floor
EE	1	The robot stops talking mid-sentence
	2	The robot repeats the same word 6 times
	3	The robot repeats the same instruction several times over
	4	The robot opens its hand too early during object handover
PE	1	The robot picks the wrong object with the right colour
	2	The robot picks the wrong object with the wrong colour
	3	The robot picks the right object with the wrong colour
	4	The robot picks a wood bar with the wrong size

---

[1] http://new.abb.com/products/robotics/industrial-robots/yumi.
[2] https://gitlab.uni-koblenz.de/robbie/homer_robot_face.

Table 2. Robot reactions details

Reaction type	Reaction name	Reaction details
R1	'Silent' reaction	Being silent and then move on
R2	'Confirmation' reaction	Asking for confirmation
R3	'Apologise' reaction	Apologising with explanation
R4	'Humour' reaction	Apologising with a sense of humour
R5	'Blame' reaction	Sharing responsibility with human
R6	'Help' reaction	Asking for help with explanation
R7	'Regret' reaction	Showing non-verbal gesture and regretful expression

which has been used by [8], comprises of the robot giving an explanation as to why the error occurs, and asking the user to help it recover from the error. The 'regret' reaction (R7), inspired by [13], is our novel reaction to error situation which shows the robot showing regretful expression and non-verbal gesture.

User Study Procedure. Before the user study begins, the participants were asked to read and agree to all the terms in the consent form. We then asked them to fill a demographic survey of gender and age group, followed by a short version of BFI personality assessment, the BFI-2-XS [12]. We decided to use the short version of BFI questionnaire consisting of 15 questions to keep the participant's concentration high throughout the study. An episode of the study consists of three parts. First, the participants were asked to watch a short video of people collaborating with a robot in which the robot created different types of error situations. The video was randomly selected from our error situations dataset as shown in Table 1. In the second part, the participants were shown a robot reaction video to handle the error situation, which was randomly selected from seven error mitigation strategies as shown in Table 2. Figure 1 shows an example of the error and reaction video pair that we show to the study participant in an episode. In the third part, the participants were asked to rate the robot reaction to the error situation by filling the most related scales of the Godspeed questionnaire [1], which are the likeability, perceived intelligence, and anthropomorphism scales, consisting 15 likert-scale statements. For the whole study, every participant watched six study episodes and gave six different Godspeed ratings to minimise *fatigue effects* in within-subject design. We made sure that each participant watch two random videos of each error situation type (SNV, EE, PE) which are paired with six different robot reactions. We also randomised the order of the episodes for each participant to reduce *ordering effects*. The online user study was hosted in Qualtrics online survey platform.[3]

---

[3] https://uwe.eu.qualtrics.com/jfe/form/SV_doplNqas3a9dTXU.

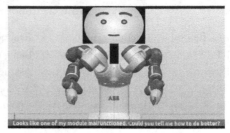

(a) Error Situation Clip Example   (b) Robot Reaction Clip Example

Fig. 1. Example of error and reaction video pair shown to participants

4 Results and Analysis

140 participants took part in our user study (87 male, 53 female). 49% of the participants are in the 18–24 age category and 51%, are in the >24 age category. We used Prolific,[4] a GDPR-compliant participant pool for our online study. We filtered the participants based on their age, fluent language, and their Prolific approval rate. We asked the participants to fill a BFI questionnaire to explore the relation between the participants' personality traits to the ratings that they gave to error mitigation strategies. The BFI-2-XS [12] consists of 15 questions which measures the participants' five major personality traits using a scale between 1 to 5. To simplify the comparison, we categorised the participants' into the high-pole group and low-pole group for each personality traits with 3 as the threshold scale. In average, the study participants were moderately more agreeable ($\mu = 3.72$), conscientious ($\mu = 3.22$), open-minded ($\mu = 3.86$), neurotic ($\mu = 3.4$) than the middle value, and self-reported introverts ($\mu = 2.88$).

Dataset and Statistical Model. As a result of the user study, we collected 840 Godspeed ratings from 140 subjects. Each Godspeed rating consists of 15 likert-scale statements (1 to 5) which we call sub-scales, which represent the anthropomorphism, likeability, and perceived intelligence aspect of the robot's reaction. The number of ratings are evenly spread for each robot reactions (120 ratings each) and for each error situation type (280 ratings each). To answer our research questions, we pre-processed the questionnaire results, setup the statistical model, and then ran statistical tests on the dataset. From statistical point of view, our dataset is a product of a mixed design, containing two repeated effects which are robot reactions (7 levels) and error types (3 levels), and seven between subject effects which are participants' gender (2 levels), age (2 levels), and five scales of personality traits (2 levels each). However, each subject only experienced 6 out of 21 (7 × 3) possible combinations of the repeated effects. Therefore, we decided to utilise linear mixed effect model (LME) [2] to analyse our data, which is a more general model than ANOVA that can handle missing data points in a repeated measure analysis. We chose maximum likelihood

---

[4] www.prolific.co.

for parameter estimation method and compound symmetry as the covariance structure for the repeated factors.

People's Rating on Error Recovery Strategies. To answer our first research question (Q1), which is *"is there a preference in robot reaction to handle general error situations?"*, we investigated the difference in godspeed ratings between different robot reactions to all error situations. Table 3 shows a summary of the godspeed questionnaire results between robot reactions averaged across error situation types. In terms of average Godspeed rating, the 'apologise' strategy (R3) has the highest mean rating (3.44), followed by the 'help' strategy (R6) (3.33), the 'humour' strategy (R4) (3.26), the 'confirmation' strategy (R2) and the 'regret' strategy (R7) which have the same mean rating (3.18), the 'blame' strategy (R5) (3.15), and the 'silent' strategy (R1) (2.50). For the anthropomorphism scale, R7 has the highest mean rating (2.79), followed by R3 (2.71), R2 (2.66), R6 (2.62), R4 (2.61), R5 (2.54), and R1 (2.11). For the likeability scale, R3 has the highest mean rating (3.88), followed by R6 (3.85), R4 (3.82), R2 (3.67), R5 and R7 (3.63), and R1 (2.84). R3 also has the highest mean rating (3.71) on the perceived intelligence scale, followed by R6 (3.52), R4 (3.35), R5 (3.28), R2 (3.23), R7 (3.13), and R1 (2.56). We ran LME analysis by setting robot reactions as repeated fixed effect and setting all Godspeed sub-scales and average main scales as dependent variables to see if any of the mean differences are statistically significant.

The test of fixed effect results presented in the last four columns of Table 3 showed that there are statistically significant differences on the Godspeed ratings that people gave to different error handling strategies. The significant differences are found in the average anthropomorphism ($F(6, 721.13) = 12.35, p < .001$), likeability ($F(6, 728.82) = 28.24, p < .001$), perceived intelligence scale ($F(6, 726.25) = 30.67, p < .001$), and also in all 15 Godspeed sub-scales. To find which robot reactions that are rated significantly different than others, we follow up the LME analysis with Bonferroni corrected pairwise comparisons, where the complete result is published in our Github page [3]. For the anthropomorphism scale, we found that R1 is rated significantly lower than R2 ($\Delta\mu = -0.538, p < .001$), R3 ($\Delta\mu = -0.583, p < .001$), R4 ($\Delta\mu = -0.49, p < .001$), R5 ($\Delta\mu = -0.434, p < .001$), R6 ($\Delta\mu = -0.431, p < .001$), R7 ($\Delta\mu = -0.662, p < .001$). In the likeability scale, it turns out that R1 is rated significantly lower than R2 ($\Delta\mu = -0.825, p < .001$), R3 ($\Delta\mu = -1.034, p < .001$), R4 ($\Delta\mu = -0.964, p < .001$), R5 ($\Delta\mu = -0.791, p < .001$), R6 ($\Delta\mu = -0.991, p < .001$), and R7 ($\Delta\mu = -0.767, p < .001$). For the perceived intelligence scale, results show that R1 is rated significantly lower than R2 ($\Delta\mu = -0.691, p < .001$), R3 ($\Delta\mu = -1.159, p < .001$), R4 ($\Delta\mu = -0.76, p < .001$), R5 ($\Delta\mu = -0.761, p < .001$), R6 ($\Delta\mu = -0.964, p < .001$), and R7 ($\Delta\mu = -0.559, p < .001$). We also found that R3 is rated significantly higher than R2 ($\Delta\mu = 0.467, p < .001$), R4 ($\Delta\mu = 0.399, p < .001$), R5 ($\Delta\mu = 0.398, p < .001$), and R7 ($\Delta\mu = 0.6, p < .001$). Finally, we found that R6 is rated significantly higher than R7 ($\Delta\mu = 0.405, p < .001$).

Table 3. Comparison of people's rating on different error recovery strategies

Godspeed	Reaction							Linear mixed model				
	R1	R2	R3	R4	R5	R6	R7					
	Mean/SD	Mean/SD	Mean/SD	Mean/SD	Mean/SD	Mean/SD	Mean/SD	AIC score	df1	df2	F	Sig
All Scales	**2.50/0.72**	**3.18/0.76**	**3.44/0.72**	**3.26/0.82**	**3.15/0.82**	**3.33/0.71**	**3.18/0.81**	1653.34	6	723.22	34.67	0.000
Anthropomorphism	**2.11/0.85**	**2.66/1.01**	**2.71/0.93**	**2.61/1.05**	**2.54/0.95**	**2.62/0.92**	**2.79/1.07**	2006.92	6	721.13	12.35	0.000
Fake:Natural	2.21/0.96	2.82/1.10	2.86/1.12	2.64/1.19	2.58/1.05	2.75/1.11	2.80/1.20	2371.20	6	725.69	7.70	0.000
Machinelike:Humanlike	1.91/1.01	2.48/1.21	2.32/1.18	2.43/1.31	2.19/1.15	2.30/1.16	2.56/1.37	2499.59	6	725.09	6.66	0.000
Unconscious:Conscious	2.21/1.05	2.94/1.17	3.17/1.17	3.11/1.28	3.04/1.13	3.08/1.21	3.24/1.18	2405.82	6	723.78	18.56	0.000
Artificial:Lifelike	1.97/0.99	2.51/1.23	2.56/1.17	2.49/1.26	2.38/1.20	2.44/1.15	2.55/1.30	2515.31	6	725.20	5.54	0.000
Moving rigidly:Elegantly	2.27/1.09	2.55/1.21	2.65/1.14	2.39/1.10	2.50/1.19	2.53/1.08	2.81/1.17	2322.61	6	722.29	4.83	0.000
Likeability	**2.84/0.94**	**3.67/0.80**	**3.88/0.80**	**3.82/0.88**	**3.63/1.00**	**3.85/0.84**	**3.63/0.90**	2053.85	6	728.82	28.24	0.000
Dislike:Like	2.69/1.07	3.58/1.02	3.86/0.93	3.70/1.14	3.48/1.15	3.73/0.99	3.61/1.11	2381.67	6	728.26	22.21	0.000
Unfriendly:Friendly	2.90/1.08	3.76/0.87	3.89/0.92	4.02/0.97	3.69/1.07	3.99/0.93	3.80/1.02	2291.44	6	730.89	23.55	0.000
Unkind:Kind	2.86/1.11	3.71/0.86	3.88/0.87	3.82/0.90	3.66/1.05	3.90/0.88	3.58/0.91	2251.90	6	732.35	21.39	0.000
Unpleasant:Pleasant	2.78/1.04	3.64/0.93	3.83/0.97	3.68/1.05	3.64/1.13	3.77/0.99	3.51/0.97	2344.71	6	730.65	18.95	0.000
Awful:Nice	2.98/1.00	3.64/0.92	3.93/0.86	3.88/0.93	3.68/1.02	3.83/0.98	3.62/1.03	2173.52	6	728.07	19.66	0.000
Perceived Intelligence	**2.56/0.85**	**3.23/0.86**	**3.71/0.84**	**3.35/0.89**	**3.28/0.90**	**3.52/0.79**	**3.13/0.88**	2066.76	6	726.25	30.67	0.000
Incompetent:Competent	2.52/1.03	3.19/1.04	3.56/1.06	3.23/0.98	3.18/1.06	3.33/0.98	3.02/1.04	2290.89	6	727.19	17.69	0.000
Ignorant:Knowledgeable	2.52/1.02	3.06/0.97	3.69/0.98	3.46/0.97	3.17/1.04	3.44/0.87	3.20/1.01	2233.75	6	728.37	25.84	0.000
Irresponsible:Responsible	2.48/1.06	3.36/1.00	3.89/1.00	3.34/1.03	3.43/1.03	3.73/1.00	3.21/1.01	2312.50	6	727.93	32.76	0.000
Unintelligent:Intelligent	2.72/1.03	3.21/1.09	3.74/0.96	3.51/0.99	3.33/1.05	3.54/0.94	3.22/1.13	2249.89	6	725.67	18.43	0.000
Foolish:Sensible	2.54/0.91	3.31/1.04	3.69/0.97	3.19/1.15	3.27/1.08	3.54/0.99	2.98/1.10	2327.25	6	728.06	22.76	0.000

People's Rating on Error Recovery Strategies in Different Error Types. To answer the second research question (Q2), which is *"is the preference in robot reaction dependent on the type of error situations which the robot reacts to?"*, we ran LME analysis by assigning robot reaction and error type as repeated fixed effect and discovered that the main effect of error type is significant on most of the Godspeed rating sub-scales averaged across all robot reactions. The significant differences are found in the average anthropomorphism ($F(2, 698.94) = 9.28, p < .001$), likeability ($F(2, 699.64) = 14.32, p < .001$), and perceived intelligence ($F(2, 699.51) = 9.55, p < .001$) scale and also in 13 out of 15 Godspeed sub-scales. We also tested the interaction effect between robot reaction and error type and did not find any p-values below 0.05 in all Godspeed sub-scales and main scales. We then followed up the LME analysis with Bonferroni corrected pairwise comparisons. In anthropomorphism scale, we found that the recovery strategies are rated lower if implemented in SNV error type compared to PE error type ($\Delta\mu = -0.207, p = .001$), while the recovery strategies implemented in EE error type are also rated lower than PE error type ($\Delta\mu = -0.206, p = .001$). For likeability scale, it is evident that the recovery strategies are rated significantly lower if implemented in SNV error type compared to EE error type ($\Delta\mu = -0.200, p = .003$) and PE error type ($\Delta\mu = -0.321, p = .000$). Finally, the recovery strategies got lower perceived intelligence score if implemented in SNV error type compared to EE error type ($\Delta\mu = -0.231, p = .000$) and PE error type ($\Delta\mu = -0.220, p = .001$).

Demographics and Personality Effect on People's Rating of Error Recovery Strategies. To answer the third research question (Q3), which is *"is the preference in robot reaction dependent on a human's demographics and personality traits?"*, we ran LME analysis by setting gender, age, and five BFI main scales fixed effects and setting all Godspeed sub-scales and average main

Table 4. Comparison of error recovery strategy ratings between error types

Godspeed	AIC score	Type III tests of fixed effects											
		Reaction				Error				Reaction × Error			
		df1	df2	F	Sig.	df1	df2	F	Sig.	df1	df2	F	Sig.
All scales	1653.34	6	723.22	34.67	0.000	2	699.64	11.02	0.000	12	758.20	0.45	0.942
Anthropomorphism	2006.92	6	721.13	12.35	0.000	2	698.94	9.28	0.000	12	755.48	0.51	0.910
Fake:Natural	2371.20	6	725.69	7.70	0.000	2	699.00	8.80	0.000	12	761.60	0.82	0.630
Machinelike:Humanlike	2499.59	6	725.09	6.66	0.000	2	699.13	4.37	0.013	12	760.89	0.32	0.986
Unconscious:Conscious	2405.82	6	723.78	18.56	0.000	2	699.07	6.32	0.002	12	759.29	0.89	0.561
Artificial:Lifelike	2515.31	6	725.20	5.54	0.000	2	697.61	3.87	0.021	12	761.43	0.70	0.751
Moving rigidly:elegantly	2322.61	6	722.29	4.83	0.000	2	698.71	4.56	0.011	12	757.42	0.79	0.665
Likeability	2053.85	6	728.82	28.24	0.000	2	699.64	14.32	0.000	12	764.17	0.66	0.787
Dislike:Like	2381.67	6	728.26	22.21	0.000	2	698.51	11.13	0.000	12	763.71	0.64	0.808
Unfriendly:Friendly	2291.44	6	730.89	23.55	0.000	2	699.83	8.31	0.000	12	764.84	0.84	0.610
Unkind:Kind	2251.90	6	732.35	21.39	0.000	2	699.71	10.68	0.000	12	764.07	0.69	0.764
Unpleasant:Pleasant	2344.71	6	730.65	18.95	0.000	2	600.35	0.14	0.000	12	704.53	0.68	0.768
Awful:Nice	2173.52	6	728.07	19.66	0.000	2	699.87	14.69	0.000	12	763.65	1.24	0.248
Perceived Intelligence	2066.76	6	726.25	30.67	0.000	2	699.51	9.55	0.000	12	762.05	0.74	0.709
Incompetent:Competent	2290.89	6	727.19	17.69	0.000	2	699.30	0.36	0.700	12	762.97	0.95	0.492
Ignorant:Knowledgeable	2233.75	6	728.37	25.84	0.000	2	699.61	2.53	0.080	12	763.88	0.84	0.611
Irresponsible:Responsible	2312.50	6	727.93	32.76	0.000	2	698.40	4.11	0.017	12	763.51	0.93	0.517
Unintellegent:Intelligent	2249.89	6	725.67	18.43	0.000	2	699.28	0.12	0.888	12	761.49	0.96	0.484
Foolish:Sensible	2327.25	6	728.06	22.76	0.000	2	699.17	6.97	0.001	12	763.65	0.71	0.742

scales as dependent variables. The statistical analysis results show that the main effect of gender is significant in 6 out of 15 Godspeed rating sub-scales averaged across all robot reactions and error situations. The significant effect of gender is also found in the average likeability $(F(1, 137.95) = 4.73, p = .031)$ and perceived intelligence $(F(1, 137.84) = 6.14, p = .014)$ scale. We also tested the interaction effect between robot reactions and gender and found significant interaction in the 'conscious' $(F(6, 696.34) = 2.37, p = .028)$ and 'lifelike' $(F(6, 698.113) = 2.28, p = .035)$ Godspeed sub-scale. We did not find any significant main and interaction effect of age category in all Godspeed sub-scales.

The test of fixed effect results showed that the main effect of user's extroversion category is significant in the average likeability $(F(1, 140.12) = 5.83, p = .017)$ and perceived intelligence $(F(1, 140.00) = 5.62, p = .019)$ scale, and also in 11 out of 15 average Godspeed sub-scales across all robot reactions and error situations. The test of interaction effect between robot reactions and extroversion resulted in significant interaction for the 'sensible' Godspeed sub-scale $(F(6, 710.207) = 2.60, p = .000)$. The main effect of participant's conscientiousness group is significant in the average likeability scale $(F(1, 139.96) = 6.40, p = .013)$, perceived intelligence scale $(F(1, 139.94) = 7.98, p = .005)$, and in 10 out of 15 average Godspeed rating sub-scales. Further analysis shows that the main effect of agreeableness is significant in 9 out of 15 average Godspeed rating sub-scales. The significant effect of agreeableness is also found in the average anthropomorphism $(F(1, 140.10) = 5.43, p = .021)$ and perceived intelligence $(F(1, 140.20) = 5.04, p = .026)$ scale. The test of interaction effect between robot reactions and agreeableness also shows significant interaction in the 'intelligent' $(F(6, 707.762) = 2.40, p = .029)$ Godspeed sub-scale. Finally, we found significant main effect of open-mindedness in 7 out of 15 the Godspeed rating sub-scales and in the average likeability scale ($F(1, 140.35) = 5.81, p = .017$).

We followed up the LME analysis with Bonferroni corrected pairwise comparisons to find how the Godspeed rating that the participant gave to the robot reactions differs between gender, age, and personality traits groups. For gender factor, we found that male gave lower likeability score to the recovery strategies compared to female ($\Delta \mu = -0.215, p = .031$). In the perceived intelligence scale, we can see that the recovery strategies are rated lower by male compared to female ($\Delta \mu = -0.277, p = .014$). For extroversion factor, we found that people in low extroversion category gave lower likeability ($\Delta \mu = -0.242, p = .017$) and perceived intelligence ($\Delta \mu = -0.270, p = .019$) ratings to the recovery strategies compared to people in high extroversion category. We also found that people in low agreeableness category gave lower average likeability ($\Delta \mu = -0.348, p = .021$) and perceived intelligence ($\Delta \mu = -0.286, p = .026$) scores to the recovery strategies compared to people in high agreeableness category. Furthermore, the analysis shows that people in low conscientiousness category rated the likeability ($\Delta \mu = -0.238, p = .013$) and perceived intelligence ($\Delta \mu = -0.299, p = .005$) of the recovery strategies lower than people in high conscientiousness category. Finally, results show that people in low open-mindedness category gave lower likeability ($\Delta \mu = -0.325, p = .017$) score to the recovery strategies than the ones in high open-mindedness category.

5   Discussion

In this paper, we expanded the literature by answering three research questions about error recovery strategies based on the user study that we conducted. First, we asked if there is a preference in recovery strategies that robots use to handle error situations (Q1). The results of this study show that in general, all error recovery strategies are rated significantly higher in terms of anthropomorphism, likeability, and perceived intelligence than the 'silent' strategy (R1), which is the same with ignoring the error and applying no strategy at all to handle the error situation. This finding is in line with [10] findings and strengthens the importance of applying recovery strategies to handle error situations in HRI, so that people will have a more positive perception of the robot and be more eager to have a longer collaboration session with the robot. Further analysis shows that in terms of likeability and perceived intelligence score, the 'apologise' strategy (R3) received the highest average rating, and only rated second highest in terms of anthropomorphism, making it the highest-rated error recovery strategy in this study. This finding also strengthens the finding of [10] which suggests that people prefer error mitigation strategies for collaborative robots that follow the common social norms. In our case, the followed social norms is that people tend to apologise whenever they feel guilty of committing a mistake [5]. The second preferred strategy in terms of average Godspeed rating is the 'help' strategy (R6) which is rated second highest in terms of likeability and perceived intelligence, and placed third in terms of anthropomorphism. This finding reinforces the results from [8] on the effectiveness of asking human's help to recover from an error situation in

HRC. The second unfavoured strategy in our user study is the 'regret' reaction (R7), despite having the highest average anthropomorphism score. This result indicates that goal oriented strategies such as apologising which mitigates the social aspect and asking for help which mitigates the technical aspect are more effective. We think that the 'regret' reaction (R7) is rated highest in terms of anthropomorphism because in the video clip, the robot raises its hand towards its forehead while showing regretful face expression. This finding also suggests that combining recovery strategies with non-verbal gestures might help the robot gain higher anthropomorphism rating. The 'blame' strategy (R5) which shares the responsibility of the failure to the human is the least preferred recovery strategy, supporting the previous research's conclusion [7].

We then asked if there is a difference in people's ratings to robot reactions between different types of error situations (Q2). Data analysis results show that the type of error situations have a statistically significant impact on how people rate the error mitigation strategies. In terms of anthropomorphism, the robot reactions are rated significantly higher if applied to planning errors (PE) compared to execution errors (EE) and social norm violations (SNV). The average likeability and perceived intelligence ratings of robot reactions are significantly higher if paired with PE and EE compared to SNV. In our previous research [4], we found that the people show more social signals during PE, followed by EE and SNV. We hypothesise that the more severe the error situation is and the more threatened the continuity of the interaction is, the more social signals that people show in response to that error situation, and the more people appreciate robot's mitigation strategies to handle that error situation.

Finally, we asked whether people's ratings on error recovery strategies are influenced by their demographics and personality traits (Q3). Based on our analysis, we discovered that people's gender, as well as the extroversion, agreeableness, conscientiousness, and open-mindedness scale of their personality profile affects the ratings that they give to error recovery strategies. This finding, combined with our answer to Q1, suggests that applying universal error handling strategies to handle error situations in HRC is always better than doing nothing. However, an adaptive error handling strategies following user's personality profile and demographics might be the best solution to mitigate error situations in future HRC because each individual perceives error recovery strategies differently.

6   Conclusion, Limitations and Future Work

This work investigated people's preference of error mitigation strategies in human-robot collaboration. There are seven recovery strategies paired with three different error situation types that were rated by users in an online study, which was the most comprehensive study in the error mitigation domain, to the best of our knowledge. The findings were analysed from 840 Godspeed questionnaire ratings that were given by 140 participants with varying age, gender, and personality traits. To help fellow researchers reproduce and extend on our study, all of our dataset along with the survey template and raw analysis results are available at our GitHub page [3].

The results show that error recovery strategies implemented after error situations significantly raised the positive ratings of collaborative robots. Based on the average Godspeed ratings, people prefer the 'apologise' strategy, followed by the 'help' strategy, the 'humour' strategy, the 'confirmation' strategy, the 'regret' strategy, and the 'blame' strategy. We also found that the type of error situations that the recovery strategies were handling significantly affects the ratings that people gave, which seems to be positively correlated to the severity of errors and the continuity of the interaction. Further statistical analysis showed that user's gender and personality traits significantly affect participants' ratings on error handling strategies. Thus, future error situation recovery researcher should incorporate the human collaborator's data, if available, when applying error recovery strategies in HRC.

In the future, a follow up study of error mitigation strategies implemented in a real robot system will help to confirm and strengthen the results of our study. A follow up study to research the correlation of social signals that people show to error situations with the ratings that their give to the applied recovery strategies can also be conducted to increase our understanding on the appropriate error mitigation strategies. Another study can be conducted by combining recovery strategies and adding more non-verbal gestures to see how those alteration influence people's perception. The findings of this study motivates us to develop an automatic error handling module in HRC that adapts to the preference and characteristics of the user so that collaborative robots can be used more extensively in people's everyday lives.

Acknowledgments. The first author acknowledges the scholarship support from the Ministry of Research and Technology of Republic of Indonesia through the Research and Innovation in Science and Technology (RISET-Pro) Program (World Bank Loan No. 8245-ID).

References

1. Bartneck, C., Kulić, D., Croft, E., Zoghbi, S.: Measurement instruments for the anthropomorphism, animacy, likeability, perceived intelligence, and perceived safety of robots. Int. J. Soc. Robot. **1**, 71–81 (2009). https://doi.org/10.1007/s12369-008-0001-3
2. Bates, D., Mächler, M., Bolker, B.M., Walker, S.C.: Fitting linear mixed-effects models using lme4. J. Stat. Softw. **67**(1) (2015)
3. Cahya, D.E.: Ditoec/appropriate-robot-reactions-user-study (2021). https://github.com/ditoec/appropriate-robot-reactions-user-study
4. Cahya, D.E., Ramakrishnan, R., Giuliani, M., et al.: Static and temporal differences in social signals between error-free and erroneous situations in human-robot collaboration. In: Salichs, M.A. (ed.) ICSR 2019. LNCS (LNAI), vol. 11876, pp. 189–199. Springer, Cham (2019). https://doi.org/10.1007/978-3-030-35888-4_18
5. Chrdileli, M., Kasser, T.: Guilt, shame, and apologizing behavior: a laboratory study. Pers. Individ. Differ. **135**, 304–306 (2018)

6. Giuliani, M., Mirnig, N., Stollnberger, G., Stadler, S., Buchner, R., Tscheligi, M.: Systematic analysis of video data from different human-robot interaction studies: a categorization of social signals during error situations. Front. Psychol. **6**(July), 931 (2015)
7. Hoorn, D.P.M.V.D., Neerincx, A., Graaf, M.M.A.D.: "I think you are doing a bad job !" The effect of blame attribution by a robot in human-robot collaboration. In: Proceedings of the 2021 ACM/IEEE International Conference on Human-Robot Interaction (HRI 2021), pp. 140–148 (2021)
8. Knepper, R.A., Tellex, S., Li, A., Roy, N., Rus, D.: Recovering from failure by asking for help. Auton. Robots **39**(3), 347–362 (2015). https://doi.org/10.1007/s10514-015-9460-1
9. Kwon, M., Huang, S.H., Dragan, A.D.: Expressing robot incapability. In: ACM/IEEE International Conference on Human-Robot Interaction (2018)
10. Lee, M.K., Kiesler, S., Forlizzi, J., Srinivasa, S., Rybski, P.: Gracefully mitigating breakdowns in robotic services (2010)
11. McTear, M., O'Neill, I., Hanna, P., Liu, X.: Handling errors and determining confirmation strategies-an object-based approach. Speech Commun. **45**(3), 249–269 (2005). Special Issue
12. Soto, C.J., John, O.P.: Short and extra-short forms of the Big Five Inventory-2: The BFI-2-S and BFI-2-XS. J. Res. Pers. **68**, 69–81 (2017)
13. Takayama, L., Dooley, D., Ju, W.: Expressing thought: improving robot readability with animation principles. In: HRI 2011 - Proceedings of the 6th ACM/IEEE International Conference on Human-Robot Interaction (2011)
14. Uchida, T., Minato, T., Koyama, T., Ishiguro, H.: Who is responsible for a dialogue breakdown? An error recovery strategy that promotes cooperative intentions from humans by mutual attribution of responsibility in human-robot dialogues. Front. Robot. AI **6**(APR), 1–11 (2019)
15. Weber, K., Ritschel, H., Aslan, I., Lingenfelser, F., André, E.: How to shape the humor of a robot - social behavior adaptation based on reinforcement learning. In: International Conference on Multimodal Interaction (ICMI 2018), pp. 154–162 (2018)

Intuitive Interaction for Human-Robot Collaboration

Simplified Robot Programming Framework for a Gearbox Assembly Application

Nikhil Somani[1]([✉]), Lee Li Zhen[1], Srinivasan Lakshminarayanan[2],
Rukshan Hettiarachchi[1], Pang Wee-Ching[2], Gerald Seet Gim Lee[2],
and Domenico Campolo[2]

[1] Advanced Remanufacturing and Technology Centre, A*STAR Cleantech Loop,
#01/01 CleanTech Two, Singapore 637143, Singapore
{somanin,leelz,rukshan h}@artc a-star edu.sg
[2] School of Mechanical and Aerospace Engineering, Nanyang Technological
University, Singapore, Singapore
{srini.gln,weeching,mglseet,d.campolo}@ntu.edu.sg

Abstract. In this paper, we are presenting a framework for multi-modal
human-robot interaction (HRI), where complex robotic tasks can be programmed using a skill-based approach and intuitive HRI modalities. This
approach is demonstrated using a gearbox assembly application in a
realistic industrial environment. Our system includes mobile and static
robots for actuation, 2D and 3D cameras for sensing, and GUIs, spatial-
and see-through- Augmented Reality for HRI.

Keywords: Human-robot interaction · Simplified programming ·
Robotic assembly

1 Introduction

One of the current manufacturing mega-trends is high-mix-low-volume production, driven largely by changing consumer preferences. While such production
was hitherto labour-intensive, the recent increase in demand coupled with disruptions to manufacturing and supply chains, has made automation a highly
sought-after option to close these gaps. However, typical robotic cells tend to
be fixed and rigid, developed with a single task at hand. Changes in process
flows or the inclusion of new devices into the system, would be time-consuming
and costly to do so. On top of that, existing programming interfaces are usually
code-based, which calls for experienced programmers to support during such
changes. If the interfaces are similar to an operator's point of view in terms of
process flow, this would allow the operator to increase the value added through
their work by directly implementing process changes on the robotic system.

This research is partially supported by the Agency for Science, Technology and
Research (A*STAR) under its SERC Grant (Project #A1623a00035).

With the increase in usage of collaborative robots in manufacturing, there will be increasingly more areas for collaboration between operators and their robot counterparts. By combining complementary strengths, such as the skills of human operators and the strength and speed of robots, this will bring forth a paradigm shift in the manufacturing industry. Human robot collaboration, and the various interfaces available for communication and control become the central focus in improving the current state of work. As there isn't an interface that can be optimal for all types of human robot collaboration scenarios, it is necessary to have multi-model interfaces where both humans and robots can communicate and interact with each other. In this paper, we discuss and share more about the various modes of interfaces, such as a GUI, AR for projection and interaction etc., used in a collaborative robot assembly cell.

To enable quick changes in robotic process flows brought about by high-mix-low-volume production, human operators need to adjust and adapt their process flows and integration faster and more efficiently. A modular approach was explored in this paper, where the addition of new devices and functions is made easier. This allows for quick and easy re-configuration of the task or production line based on the existing devices and skills, which can now be done by the non-expert shop-floor operators, using the multi-modal interfaces.

2   State of Art

There are several research works in the area of human-robot interaction for simplified robot programming. Schou et al. [15] proposed the use of a task-level programming system based on robot skill definitions. Kraft et al. [8] focused on the study of UX paradigms for human-robot interaction. Self-descriptive systems for plug-and-produce were proposed in [18]. A re-configurable, modular system framework was presented in [6]. Node Primitives were developed in [3] for a user-centric robot programming approach.

2.1   Simplified Programming Frameworks

A cognitive robotics system, specifically suitable for high-mix and low-volume manufacturing in SMEs was presented in [12]. Automated off-line programming approaches were studied in [2]. Steinmetz et al. [16] presented RAZER, a task-level robot programming framework based on parameterizable skills models and intuitive GUIs. Learning from human demonstration is another popular approach in research for easy teaching of robotic tasks [1,10,14].

Simplified robot programming interfaces and the concept of manipulation skills are also seen in several new commercial robotics software packages. Franka Emika[1] developed a robot programming interface, based on robot skills. The Artiminds Robot Programming System (RPS)[2] supports several robot and computer vision hardware and software. It focuses on off-line programming, and can

---

[1] https://www.franka.de/.

[2] https://www.artiminds.com/robot-programming-software/.

generate robot code in several robot-specific scripting languages. Drag&Bot[3] is a web-based programming software that allows the operator to program easily with parameterizable skills. They have focused their GUI more on a CAD-based software, where one is able to place robots in a specified workcell, check reachability of their robots and provide estimated cycle times.

2.2 Augmented Reality and Robots

Augmented reality (AR) is a powerful human-robot interaction modality. In industrial settings, it can be used to visualise information previously unseen, such as intended robot motion and trajectories. A projection-based safety system was used in [17] as a form of display of safety zones and intended robot motion, as well as to detect safety violations from the human operator. In [11], an AR interface was used to visualize appropriate information such as process-related and production-related statuses, robot workspace and intended trajectory without interrupting the operator.

Feedback about industrial processes and production data can also be visualised using AR. In [4], an AR interface with voice commands was used to show instructions for a human-robot collaborated assembly process. AR headsets are used in [5] to visualize the operator's progress in performing a spraying process. Operators get information on target regions to be sprayed, and feedback on how well the regions are being sprayed.

2.3 Contributions

We have made several novel contributions in this paper, as summarized below:

- An extensible, multi-level system architecture suitable for a human-robot collaboration setting.
- Multi-modal interaction including a task programming GUI and see-through Augmented Reality. All these modalities are connected through a unified framework that enables safe and intuitive human-robot collaboration.
- Task-level programming for both mobile and static robot arms.
- Demonstration on a complex, realistic industrial manufacturing scenario, i.e., gearbox manufacturing.

3   System Architecture

Figure 1 illustrates the 4-level system architecture of our proposed approach:

- Level 0: This level contains the hardware devices and software written in the device-specific programming languages, including sensors such as 2D/3D cameras, actuators such as robots and grippers, and controllers such as PLCs.

---

[3] https://www.dragandbot.com/.

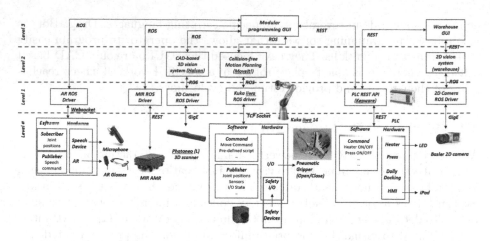

Fig. 1. System architecture diagram listing the modules and their connections.

- Level 1: This level includes drivers for our chosen communication interfaces (ROS, REST, etc.). These drivers bridge between the specific protocols of each hardware device and our preferred protocols.
- Level 2: This level includes the key algorithm implementations required for our processes, e.g. motion planning, 2D and 3D computer vision.
- Level 3: At the highest level of our architecture are GUIs for application and process sequence control, and visualizations for simulations or digital twins.

We use a modular approach, where different modules are connected together to develop a process sequence for the application in this project. This enables us to re-configure and re-use the developed modules for different applications.

4   Technology Modules

4.1   2D Object Detection

In this module, we develop algorithms to detect the type and bounding-box location of objects in an image. We used the Faster RCNN model [13] with ResNet as the base model for transfer learning, implemented using Tensorflow. To train our deep learning model, we collected a dataset of 200 manually labelled images. For the model training process, 80% of the dataset is split into training and remaining 20% as test data. The results of the object detection is shown in Fig. 2(a). We can identify the objects with an accuracy of 95% (correct part identification/total part instances in the test dataset).

4.2   Pose Estimation for Gearbox Assembly

For automatic detection and pose estimation of the parts in the assembly area, the workspace is equipped with Photoneo Phoxi 3D Scanner L,[4] that can capture

---

[4] https://www.photoneo.com/products/phoxi-scan-l/.

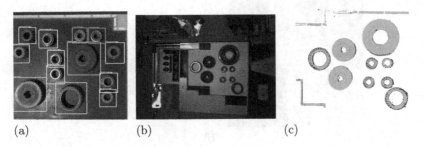

(a)   (b)   (c)

Fig. 2. 3D object detection: (a) 2D Object detection results (b) Input Data from Photoneo (c) 3D Detection

grayscale images and 3D pointclouds (Fig. 2(b)). We used faster-RCNN model, similar to the approach described in Subsection 4.1, to detect the 2D bounding box of input parts. The detected bounding box is used to segment the 3D point cloud, and subsequently for estimating the 6D pose of the part (Fig. 2(c)). We utilized the computer vision library Halcon[5] to determine the part's pose using its 3D CAD model and achieved an average accuracy of $-0.5\,mm$ for the pose estimation, determined through experiments of the robotic end-effector reaching the detected position of objects in different locations on the tray.

4.3   Autonomous Mobile Robots (AMRs)

We use an AMR for automatically transporting parts on a trolley between different stations in the manufacturing facility. We choose a MIR 200,[6] with additional latching system to hold onto the trolley. We integrate the MIR into our modular framework using the its REST API and a ROS driver.[7]

4.4   Collision-Free Motion Planning

We use a collision-free motion planning algorithm to generate the sequence of robot positions required for the process. We evaluated three motion planning algorithms from the open-source motion planning library MoveIt![8] for this task: RRT[9], RRT-star [7] and RRT-connect [9]. In this project, we are using a 7-axis robot, where the redundant axis can easily result in very long paths in the joint space for small motions in the operational space. Hence, we prefer the more optimal trajectories achieved using RRT-star, despite its higher runtime. By using a convex decomposition of the 3d scene using the V-HACD library[10] (see Fig. 3 (b)), we achieved a significant reduction in the time required to load the collision scene as well as motion planning.

---

[5] https://www.mvtec.com/products/halcon.

[6] https://www.mobile-industrial-robots.com/en/solutions/robots/mir200/.

[7] https://github.com/dfki-ric/mir_robot.

[8] https://moveit.ros.org/, http://wiki.ros.org/moveit/.

[9] https://en.wikipedia.org/wiki/Rapidly-exploring_random_tree.

[10] "https://github.com/kmammou/v-hacd".

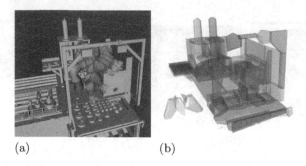

(a)   (b)

Fig. 3. Motion planning: (a) Collision-free motion planning using the RRT-Star algorithm (MoveIt) (b) Approx. convex decomposition of the 3D collision scene

5 Human-Robot Interaction

5.1 Skill-Based Robot Programming and Interface

We developed a GUI for simplified robot programming, a wide variety of tasks such as pick and place can be specified using 3D models of the involved objects, see Fig. 4(a). In the current setup, we support the use of 2-fingered and 3-fingered grasp/place operations. These operations are called basic skills in our framework. The relative pose between the selected gripper and the object is a key parameter, which can be specified in the GUI as constraint parameters between the geometries of the 3D models.

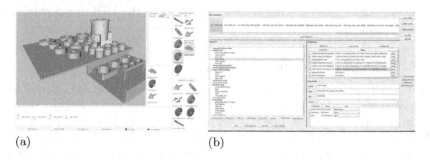

(a)   (b)

Fig. 4. (a) Modular programming GUI (b) Sequencing the skills through the GUI

Figure 4(b) shows our skill sequence programming GUI, where several skills such as robot motions, gripper commands, REST-API calls, 2D/3D object detection can be included as blocks. Each of these blocks have a set of parameters to be specified for the operation, which can be either manually specified or inferred automatically from other blocks that generate such parameters (e.g. object detection block generating the pose required for a robot motion). We program the different robot assembly sequences using this GUI. Based on the desired assembly combination, the relevant sequences are loaded automatically.

5.2 See-Through Augmented Reality

We have developed a see-through AR application as a human-robot interaction modality, which has three main features:

1. Display an augmented view on the smart glasses, including the 3D model of the robot and information related to the robot's task (see Fig. 5(c)).
2. Connect to a physical robot via a network connection, such that information can be communicated between the AR application and the physical robot.
3. Recognize speech commands from the user and display on the smart glasses (Fig. 5(c)), to control the AR application as well as the robot, hands-free.

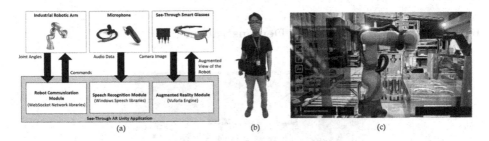

Fig. 5. (a) System architecture of the see-through AR application (b) A user wearing the system during deployment (c) Content displayed on the smart glasses

Figure 5(a) illustrated the software modules implemented for this modality: the AR module, the speech recognition module, and the robot communication module. The entire AR application is developed within the Unity 3D game development platform, using the Vuforia Engine[11] software plugin. The speech recognition module is developed using the Windows Speech libraries.[12]

5.3 Spatial Augmented Reality

We designed a custom spatial AR solution that utilizes a Laser Graphic Projection (LGP) to offer visual communication between robot and human. Laser beam is directed onto an industrial envelope floor surface, as shown in Fig. 6. The goal is to present a "warning" such as a text and graphics display, as well as to outline area or any other static (or animated) graphic projection.

---

[11] https://library.vuforia.com/.
[12] https://docs.microsoft.com/en-us/uwp/api/windows.media.speechrecognition.

Fig. 6. Shape and text displayed on the floor using our laser projector

6   Experiments and Demonstrations

We demonstrated our multi-modal human-robot collaboration framework through an application described in the following sections and illustrated in the video.[13]

6.1   AI-Assisted Warehouse Demonstration

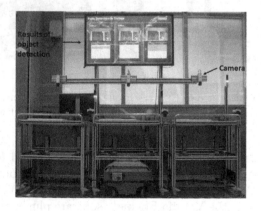

Fig. 7. Object detection setup

In our AI-assisted warehouse, parts are retrieved from the warehouse on a needs basis using a mobile base holding onto a trolley. In this demonstration, the 2D cameras detect objects on the trolleys, and pass the information to the Warehouse GUI (Fig. 7), which guides the operator in placing the correct parts. Once the tray is ready, the mobile robot is triggered automatically to pick up the correct trolley, and deliver it to the assembly cell. With the inclusion of the modular programming framework, this has eased the process of integration of and communication between devices, and has eased the interaction between operators and the mobile bases.

---

[13] https://youtu.be/PIsMpFG6PmI.

6.2 Gearbox Assembly Robot

Once the parts are delivered to the robotic workcell, the collaborative robot can start performing the assembly of the gearbox sub-assemblies. In this process, multiple sensors integrated to the modular programming framework check for the presence and position of parts, accuracy of assemblies, and provide feedback to the AR goggles and GUI interface on the assembly process (see Fig. 8a). The operator can choose to use either the AR goggles to load the respective sequence and start the process using voice commands (see Figs. 8b-c), or use the simplified GUI to load the sequence and press the start button. All these interaction modalities connect in the back-end to the modular programming framework. The multi-modal interfaces make the interaction simpler and smoother. The AR goggles aid the operators in visualising the process flow, even when they are not physically around the assembly cell.

(a)   **(b)**   **(c)**

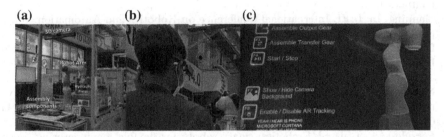

Fig. 8. (a) Assembly setup (b) Operator using AR Glass (c) Information in AR

7 Conclusions

In this paper, we proposed framework for executing complex robotic tasks using multi-modal human-robot collaboration. Using the gearbox assembly process as a case-study, we demonstrated the effectiveness of our simple task-centred programming interface and see-through Augmented Reality, obviating the need for the cumbersome robot programming. In the future, we plan to apply and evaluate our approach on different tasks and in multi-robots scenarios.

References

1. Cai, C., Liang, Y.S., Somani, N., Yan, W.: Inferring the geometric nullspace of robot skills from human demonstrations. In: IEEE International Conference on Robotics and Automation (ICRA), pp. 7668–7675 (2020)
2. Castro, A., Souza, J.P., Rocha, L., Silva, M.F.: AdaptPack studio: automatic offline robot programming framework for factory environments. In: 2019 IEEE International Conference on Autonomous Robot Systems and Competitions (ICARSC), pp. 1–6 (2019)
3. Coronado, E., Mastrogiovanni, F., Venture, G.: Design of a human-centered robot framework for end-user programming and applications. In: Arakelian, V., Wenger, P. (eds.) ROMANSY 22 – Robot Design, Dynamics and Control. CICMS, vol. 584, pp. 450–457. Springer, Cham (2019). https://doi.org/10.1007/978-3-319-78963-7_56

4. Danielsson, O., Syberfeldt, A., Brewster, R., Wang, L.: Assessing instructions in augmented reality for human-robot collaborative assembly by using demonstrators. Procedia CIRP **63**, 89–94 (2017)
5. Elsdon, J., Demiris, Y.: Augmented reality for feedback in a shared control spraying task. In: 2018 IEEE International Conference on Robotics and Automation (ICRA), pp. 1939–1946. https://doi.org/10.1109/ICRA.2018.8461179, ISSN: 2577-087X
6. Ameri, F., Stecke, K.E., von Cieminski, G., Kiritsis, D. (eds.): APMS 2019. IAICT, vol. 566. Springer, Cham (2019). https://doi.org/10.1007/978-3-030-30000-5
7. Karaman, S., Frazzoli, E.: Sampling-based algorithms for optimal motion planning. Int. J. Robot. Res. **30**(7), 846–894 (2011)
8. Kraft, M., Rickert, M.: How to teach your robot in 5 minutes: applying UX paradigms to human-robot-interaction. In: 2017 26th IEEE International Symposium on Robot and Human Interactive Communication (RO-MAN), pp. 942–949 (2017)
9. Kuffner, J., LaValle, S.: RRT-connect: an efficient approach to single-query path planning. In: IEEE International Conference on Robotics and Automation, vol. 2, pp. 995–1001 (2000)
10. Lakshminarayanan, S., Kana, S., Mohan, D.M., Manyar, O.M., Then, D., Campolo, D.: An adaptive framework for robotic polishing based on impedance control. Int. J. Adv. Manuf. Technol. **112**(1), 401–417 (2021)
11. Makris, S., Karagiannis, P., Koukas, S., Matthaiakis, A.S.: Augmented reality system for operator support in human-robot collaborative assembly. CIRP Ann. **65**(1), 61–64 (2016)
12. Perzylo, A., et al.: SMErobotics: smart robots for flexible manufacturing. IEEE Robot. Autom. Mag. **26**(1), 78–90 (2019). https://doi.org/10.1109/MRA.2018.2879747
13. Ren, S., He, K., Girshick, R., Sun, J.: Faster R-CNN: towards real-time object detection with region proposal networks. In: Advances in Neural Information Processing Systems, vol. 28. Curran Associates, Inc. (2015)
14. Roitberg, A., Somani, N., Perzylo, A., Rickert, M., Knoll, A.: Multimodal human activity recognition for industrial manufacturing processes in robotic workcells. In: Proceedings of the ACM International Conference on Multimodal Interaction, pp. 259–266 (2015)
15. Schou, C., Andersen, R.S., Chrysostomou, D., Bøgh, S., Madsen, O.: Skill-based instruction of collaborative robots in industrial settings. Robot. Comput.-Integr. Manuf. **53**, 72–80 (2018)
16. Steinmetz, F., Wollschläger, A., Weitschat, R.: RAZER-a HRI for visual task-level programming and intuitive skill parameterization. IEEE Robot. Autom. Lett. **3**(3), 1362–1369 (2018). https://doi.org/10.1109/LRA.2018.2798300
17. Vogel, C., Poggendorf, M., Walter, C., Elkmann, N.: Towards safe physical human-robot collaboration: a projection-based safety system. In: 2011 IEEE/RSJ International Conference on Intelligent Robots and Systems, pp. 3355–3360 (2011). ISSN: 2153-0866
18. Wojtynek, M., Oestreich, H., Beyer, O., Wrede, S.: Collaborative and robot-based plug produce for rapid reconfiguration of modular production systems. In: 2017 IEEE/SICE International Symposium on System Integration (SII), pp. 1067–1073 (2017)

Gaze Assisted Visual Grounding

Kritika Johari[1]([✉]), Christopher Tay Zi Tong[1], Vigneshwaran Subbaraju[2],
Jung-Jae Kim[3], and U-Xuan Tan[1]

[1] Singapore University of Technology and Design, Singapore, Singapore
`kritika_johari@mymail.sutd.edu.sg`
[2] Institute of High Performance Computing, A*STAR, Singapore, Singapore
[3] Institute for Infocomm Research, A*STAR, Singapore, Singapore

Abstract. There has been an increasing demand for visual grounding
in various human-robot interaction applications. However, the accuracy
is often limited by the size of the dataset that can be collected, which is
often a challenge. Hence, this paper proposes using the natural implicit
input modality of human gaze to assist and improve the visual grounding accuracy of human instructions to robotic agents. To demonstrate
the capability, mechanical gear objects are used. To achieve that, we utilized a transformer-based text classifier and a small corpus to develop
a baseline phrase grounding model. We evaluate this phrase grounding
system with and without gaze input to demonstrate the improvement.
Gaze information (obtained from Microsoft Hololens2) improves the performance accuracy from 26% to 65%, leading to more efficient human-
robot collaboration and applicable to hands-free scenarios. This approach
is data-efficient as it requires only a small training dataset to ground the
natural language referring expressions.

Keywords: Gaze tracking · Visual grounding · Human-robot
interaction

1 Introduction

Human-robot interaction has been playing an increasingly important role in the
manufacturing industries today. Utilizing the collaboration between the human
operator and robots can allow the robots to automate repetitive tasks, reduce
margins of error to negligible rates, and yet enable human workers to focus on
more productive areas of the operation [2]. Giving natural instructions to the
robot to pick and place is often desired to speed up the pick and place process.
Visual grounding is required for such tasks but is often limited by dataset. Hence,
this paper proposes a gaze-assisted visual grounding system that uses natural
language instructions and gaze to localize the mechanical object. Experiments
are performed, and is shown that the performance improves after fusing the
human gaze information acquired using Microsoft Hololens2.

This research is supported by the Agency for Science, Technology and Research
(A*STAR) under its AME Programmatic Funding Scheme (Project # A18A2b0046).

H. Li et al. (Eds.): ICSR 2021, LNAI 13086, pp. 191–202, 2021.
https://doi.org/10.1007/978-3-030-90525-5_17

Fig. 1. Human-Robot Collaboration: Human (sitting on a chair) instructs the robot to pass the red screwdriver using natural language and gaze (shown by the dotted line) while engaged in some other task. (Color figure online)

Phrase grounding (also called visual grounding) system localizes an object within an image described by language query [17]. This query often contains different types of phrases such as categories, attributes, spatial configurations, and interactions with other objects, such as "green plier on the left" or "blue wrench next to the multimeter," as shown in Fig. 1. These phrases are also known as referring expressions. Researchers typically adopt one of the two approaches: 1) single-stage [25,27]; and 2) multi-stage [20,26] to perform this task. The multi-stage methods rely on the candidate proposal network like Faster-RCNN [16] and EdgeBox [28], which calculates the matching score between each proposal and the referring expression and chooses the region with the highest score. The one-stage methods frame the problem as a bounding box regression task. Instead of using the candidate proposal, they utilize multimodal features obtained after projecting and fusing features from the visual backbone and language encoders into the same semantic space.

Both the visual grounding methodologies have their limitations and benefits, which researchers are trying to address. Ref-NMS [3] proposes expression-aware proposals for the two-stage approach, improving the grounding performance, while ZSGNet [17] enables grounding of novel categories (zero-shot grounding) using dense proposals. Both approaches use large image grounding datasets such as Flickr30k [15], Visual Genome [9], ReferIt [7], RefCOCOg [12]. Using a smaller dataset has a high probability that results in performance drop due to referring expression diversity, and complexity [27]. In this paper, we demonstrate a performance improvement in the phrase grounding system with incorporating human gaze despite having a small dataset.

Contrary to gesture (explicit communication signal) or speech, the gaze is an implicit signal [13]. These types of signals are not intended to carry information, but they do anyways and are fundamental for effective communication. Human gaze (the information about what or where the user is looking at) typically anticipates their hand movement, for instance, when humans want to reach for an object. This implies that robots with gaze tracking capability can predict the goal of their human coworker even before they act. Gaze tracking is also beneficial for manufacturing robots as it gives information about human visual attention and hence which object they want to pick, as shown in Fig. 1. It is beneficial when traditional channels, such as gestures [22], might not be suitable for HRI (e.g., hands-free interface design [14], assistive robots [19]).

However, one of the drawbacks of eye-tracking is precision interaction because eyes move around a lot. Our eyes perform rapid movements from fixation to fixation. Also, gaze tracking accuracy depends on camera properties and external factors like light and shadow [13]. The majority of gaze tracking devices are static, which poses a huge challenge in deploying robots for open environments such as airports and hospitals.

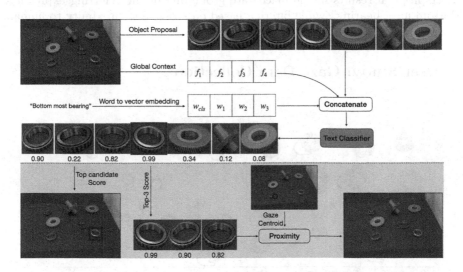

Fig. 2. Overview of our method. Given an input image, a text query, and a set of candidate locations (e.g., from object proposal methods), a text classification model is used to score candidate locations based on spatial configurations and global context. The top-3 scoring candidates are selected to check proximity from the gaze centroid. The nearest proposal is selected as the answer.

This paper used the head-mounted system Microsoft Hololens2 (HL2) to track the human gaze, which is the common solution for experimental settings. Head tracking and eye tracking are two key ways in which HL2 can understand user's areas of focus and intent. Head tracking is how HL2 tracks a user's head position and orientation in 3D space. Eye-tracking is how HL2 understands precisely where the user is looking using sensors pointed at their eyes. Head tracking and eye-tracking work together to understand user's field of view and what they are looking at.

We propose a gaze-assisted approach to ground referring expressions in an image. Our contributions can be summarised as follows:

1. Utilizing natural implicit gaze (not intentional gaze) to improve human-robot instruction.
2. A text-classifier based scoring function [1] for the candidate locations of an image generated by Faster-RCNN as shown in Fig. 2, exploiting a small dataset.
3. We first show that grounding using text-only instructions (no gaze) can achieve 26% accuracy in target localization. Subsequently, using a series of in-the-lab studies, we demonstrate how the incorporation of gaze input (along with verbal and visual input) helps improve this grounding accuracy to 65%.

Figure 2 depicts the overview of the approach. Choosing the highest-scoring object proposal results in the inaccurate grounding of the referring expression "Bottom most bearing" while filtering based on scores and proximity to human gaze centroid results in correct grounding.

2   User Study: Gaze Data Collection

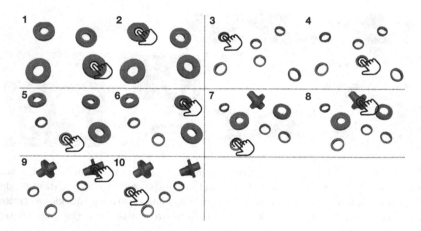

Fig. 3. Five random arrangement of three object types. Each participant is asked to provide the natural language description for each of these ten objects shown by the finger in each configuration.

Given our high-level goal of incorporating gaze input for multimodal instruction comprehension, we designed a user study to collect gaze data and establish the hypothesis that human speech follows human sight. In this study, 5 spatial configurations of 3 distinct objects were shown to the user. For all 10 scenarios (illustrated in Fig. 3), the experimenter touched an object and asked the participant to describe it while wearing a calibrated Hololens2. A calibrated Hololens2 sensing of the gaze is relatively accurate within 1.5 degrees in visual angle around the actual target. The subjects were standing at a distance of 2m from the table.

To provide operational familiarity with the Hololens2, each subject followed a tutorial session (Tips App) in which they learned to interact with holograms using hands and navigate Hololens. The cursor was, however, disabled during the study. Thus a total of $10 \times 3 = 30$ gaze recordings were collected. However, due to experimental error, we had to remove 7 recordings. We recorded the gaze data from the moment the participant starts speaking to 3 s after that at a frame rate of 30 fps.

3   Methodology

The main components of our methodology are object proposal network, binary classifier based scoring function [1] and gaze estimation as illustrated in Fig. 4. We also explain the training methodology of the scoring function. Finally, we mentioned the details of gaze estimation.

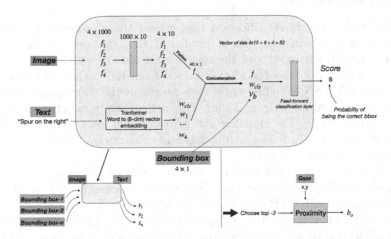

Fig. 4. f_1, f_2, f_3 are the Faster R-CNN RoI pooled features for bearing, gear and spur respectively. f_4 represents the background. The features are flattened and concatenated with the sentence vector x_{cls} and a bounding box coordinates. The feed-forward then scores the text description-bounding box pair for the match. To incorporate the gaze information, we chose the top-3 scoring bounding boxes for a text description and calculated their proximity from the gaze point. The bounding box closest to the gaze is retrieved.

3.1   Object Proposals

The object proposal network is responsible for generating bounding boxes for each instance of an object in the image and extracting global context features from the image. We used the state-of-the-art object detector Detectron2 [24], i.e., a PyTorch-based modular object detection library. We selected the Faster R-CNN model [16] (Feature Pyramid Network (FPN) and a ResNet101 backbone) from detectron2 model zoo trained on COCO 2017 training and evaluated on COCO 2017 validation dataset [10].

The COCO dataset contains images with 80 different categories of objects. However, object types outside these 80 classes will not be recognized when trained solely on COCO. Therefore, we relied on transfer learning to reduce the training requirements. Instead of training a model from scratch, we started with pre-trained (on COCO 2017 dataset) Faster R-CNN weights.

We prepared a custom object detection dataset of images containing objects of classes—bearing, gear, and spur. We collected 69 images of these 3 object types and used an annotation tool (Roboflow) to annotate the bounding boxes around the objects. The training data consisted of 364 bounding boxes and class labels. We ran the object detection model on 1 GPU (NVIDIA GeForce GTX 1070), and the inference time per image was 200 ms (5 fps).

3.2   Scoring Function

We formulated a binary-classification task where the classifier takes features from the text and bounding box to predict if the box contains the referred image. Essentially, the input x of the classifier consists of—

x_{img} is a tensor of size 4×1000 obtained from the output of RoI pooling layer of Faster R-CNN. The first three rows represent the three object classes in the dataset, i.e., bearing, gear, and spur. The last row represents the background class or no object zone. The classifier first projects each row to a 10-dimensional space to obtain a 4×10 tensor. After flattening the tensor, we obtain a vector f of size 40 (as shown in Fig. 4).

x_{cls} is the sentence vector obtained from the output of a transformer-based text encoder [1]. The raw text string is first word-tokenized by spaces. Since the number of unique words in the dataset is small, we form a text vocabulary of size 30 prepended with a special $[cls]$ token and appended with the text with $[sep]$ token [4]. The tokens are projected to an 8-dimensional embedding space and then fed to the encoder. The number of self-attention heads is kept 2, the query, key, and value projection vectors are of the same size, i.e., 2 [1]. We obtain w_{cls} which is contextualized $[cls]$ vector (or sentence vector) of size 8 at the output of the encoder.

x_{b_i} represents an ith bounding box coordinate set, i.e., $v_b = \{x_{tl}, y_{tl}, wt, ht\}$ output by the Faster R-CNN where tl, wt and ht abbreviate top-left, width, and height, respectively. The origin lies at the top-left corner of the whole image input to the Faster R-CNN.

The classifier concatenates f, w_{cls}, and v_b to form a vector of size $(40 + 8 + 4)$ 52. This vector is fed to a classification feed-forward layer to obtain a score between 0 and 1. Essentially, the classifier scores the region (object bounding box) query (object description) pair.

Training Methodology. For each image in the dataset, we text annotated bounding boxes predicted by the Faster R-CNN and label the bounding box-text pair as 1. For each image, we obtain all the possible combinations of text description-bounding box incorrect pairs and labeled them 0. It is noteworthy that the dataset is imbalanced in favor of class 0. The classifier is then trained to score the text-bounding box pair.

Inference. Given a set of images and text descriptions in the test set denoted as $\mathcal{I}$, where an element in the set is a set of bounding box and text description pairs $\{(b_1, t_1), \ldots, (b_n, t_n)\}$. For all the (b_j, t_k) pairs in an image where b_j is j^{th} bounding box and t_k is k^{th} text description, respectively, we obtain the classifier score s_{jk}. Assuming $j = k$ denotes correct bounding box-text description pair, the classifier evaluation metric is defined as

$$f_\theta(\mathcal{I}) = \frac{1}{|\mathcal{I}|} \sum_{\{(b_1,t_1),\ldots,(b_n,t_n)\} \in \mathcal{I}} \frac{\sum_{t_j \in \{t_1,\ldots,t_n\}} (j == \mathrm{argmax}\{s_{j1}, \ldots, s_{jn}\})}{n} \quad (1)$$

where θ represents model trainable and fixed parameters; n denotes the number of objects identified by the Faster R-CNN. The Faster R-CNN parameters are non-trainable while transformer-based encoder and classifier layer parameters belong to the trainable set.

Experiment and Data Setup. We used Adam optimizer, with a learning rate $=0.00001$, to minimize the cross-entropy loss between the target and predicted label. For all the experiments, we keep the batch size as 16 and train for 10 epochs. At test time, an image, a natural language object query, and a set of candidate bounding boxes (e.g., from object proposal methods such as Faster R-CNN [16]) are provided.

We manually annotated all 364 objects in the 69 images with text descriptions while their bounding boxes were predicted by Faster R-CNN. We obtained $n \times n$ training data samples from each image where n is the number of objects in an image. We labeled a training data as 1 while combining an object's bounding box with its description and 0 when merged with any other object's description from the same image.

3.3 Gaze Estimation

The HL2 perceives and understands the physical environment through spatial mesh visualization. It will then project a ray following the path of where it thinks the eye is looking at. When the ray intersects the spatial mesh, the coordinate of that point is returned to us as a world point. We will then convert the world point to a screen point (2D coordinate) using Unity API. The 2D coordinates are scaled to the image (captured by HL2) dimension.

Our approach is different from other gaze-based interactions [11,21,23] because we let the participant look freely and did not provide any explicit instruction to look at a specific location. We also confirm that most people look at the object before describing it with the help of a small user study. And we thus utilize this additional implicit information on top of the natural language instruction to ground the target objects. We obtained the gaze centroid by taking an average of 3 s of gaze data from the moment the participant starts speaking.

4 Results

We compared the visual grounding results obtained from two approaches - 1) without (only scoring function) and 2) with gaze input (scoring function + gaze). We used the gaze user study (mentioned in Sect. 2) as the test data to evaluate both methods. This data contains 23 images (captured by HL2), one natural language object description, and one gaze recording for each image. We also investigated the performance of Faster R-CNN (on the test images) and the binary classifier (on bounding box and text description pairs), which are essential parts of the scoring function.

4.1 Object Detection

We followed the COCO detection evaluation metrics [10] to measure the performance of Faster R-CNN on test images. AP (Average precision) is the primary challenge metric for the COCO object detection challenge. AP computes the area under the precision-recall curve. AP is the precision averaged across all individual recall levels [5]. Table 1 shows the category-wise bounding box average precision.

Table 1. Per-category bounding box average precision

Category	AP	Category	AP	Category	AP
Bearing	86.563	Gear	91.491	Spur	94.286

We take a mean of AP across all 3 classes to obtain mean average precision (mAP) illustrated in Table 2. AP (averaged across all 10 IoU (Intersection over

Union) thresholds from 0.50 to 0.95 with a step size of 0.05 and all 3 categories) is the mAP. IoU is the area of overlap between the predicted bounding box and the ground-truth box divided by their area of union. AP50 and AP70 are the average precision calculated at threshold IoU = 0.50 and 0.70, respectively. We also show AP for small (APs area $< 32^2$ pixels), medium (APm $32^2 <$ area $< 96^2$ pixels) and large objects (APl area $> 96^2$ pixels).

Table 2. Mean Average Precision and average precision across various scales

mAP	AP50	AP75	APs	APm	APl
90.780	99.336	99.336	nan	88.317	90.803

4.2   Binary Classification

The training data consisted of 2076 text description-bounding box pairs, out of which 364 samples were of class 1, and the remaining 1712 samples were of class 0. Thus the distribution of examples has a bias, as mentioned in the training methodology paragraph of Subsect. 3.2. For around 5 instances of class 0, there is 1 example of class 1, which may lead the classifier to perform poorly for the minority class [8]. Therefore, we provided different weights to both majority and minority classes using

$$w_j = n/(n_{classes} * n_j) \tag{2}$$

where w_j signifies the weight for each class, n is the total number of samples or rows in the training set, and $n_{classes}$ is the total number of unique classes in the target, which is 2 in our case. n_j is the total number of rows of the respective class. Putting our data into Eq. 2, we obtained $w_0 = 0.68$ and $w_1 = 1.90$. 5% of this training set (randomly chosen) is used as the validation set. The test data consisted of 134 samples, out of which 23 samples belonged to class 1, and the remaining 111 samples were of class 0.

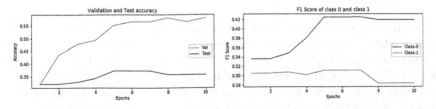

Fig. 5. The left plot represents the training and validation accuracy with epochs, while the right plot shows the changes in F1 score on the test set of class 0 and 1, respectively.

While the validation accuracy of the classifier is 58%, the test accuracy is 35.8%, as shown in the left plot of Fig. 5. Accuracy is not the metric to use when working with an imbalanced dataset. So we calculated the test set F1 score at the end of every epoch. The score at the end of 10th epoch for class 0 and 1 was 0.418 and 0.283, respectively.

4.3 Localisation with and Without Gaze

To localize the bounding box for a text description, we processed the scores provided by the classifier in two ways - without and with gaze. In the first method, that is, without gaze, we simply chose the bounding box with the highest confidence score. This caused only 6 out of the 23 input queries to be grounded correctly. In the second method (our proposed method), we chose the top 3 scoring proposals of an image for a text description and calculated the euclidean distance between their center and the gaze centroid. Out of the 3 bounding boxes, we selected the one having the least distance from the gaze point. This caused 15 out of the 23 input queries to be grounded correctly. Thus, increasing the grounding accuracy from 26% to 65%.

5 Discussion and Future Work

Although this classifier-based candidate proposal scoring approach is simple and works on a minimal dataset, we faced the challenge of data imbalance while classifying the pairs of the bounding box and text descriptions. However, this issue can be overcome or minimized by collecting more training data or adopting a more sophisticated labeling approach for region-query pairs. In the future, we aspire to apply this approach on more complex tasks like object specification in a cluttered environment [18] involving more complex descriptions to identify target object. This system, in combination with other modalities such as touch and gesture, can also be explored as an interface for multi-robot systems [6].

6 Conclusion

We presented a gaze-assisted visual grounding system for three distinct mechanical gear-related objects: bearing, gear, and spur. The proposed approach combines region proposal and text encoder to score the bounding box-text description pair. We showed that this scoring function grounds the natural language description of 23 objects with an accuracy of 26%. In contrast, our proposed approach of incorporating the gaze information on the output of this scoring function improves the grounding accuracy to 65%. We also established that in the majority of cases, people look at the object before describing it by conducting a small user study with 3 participants the distance between the objects and participants to be 2m (optimal distance for gaze tracking using Hololens2). More broadly, our work stresses the significance of incorporating gaze input to establish natural interactions between humans and collaborative robots.

References

1. Bhardwaj, R., Majumder, N., Poria, S., Hovy, E.: More identifiable yet equally performant transformers for text classification. arXiv preprint arXiv:2106.01269 (2021)
2. Bloss, R.: Collaborative robots are rapidly providing major improvements in productivity, safety, programing ease, portability and cost while addressing many new applications. Ind. Robot Int. J. (2016)
3. Chen, L., Ma, W., Xiao, J., Zhang, H., Chang, S.F.: Ref-NMS: breaking proposal bottlenecks in two-stage referring expression grounding. In: Proceedings of the AAAI Conference on Artificial Intelligence, vol. 35, pp. 1036–1044 (2021)
4. Devlin, J., Chang, M.W., Lee, K., Toutanova, K.: Bert: Pre-training of deep bidirectional transformers for language understanding. arXiv preprint arXiv:1810.04805 (2018)
5. Everingham, M., Van Gool, L., Williams, C.K., Winn, J., Zisserman, A.: The pascal visual object classes (voc) challenge. Int. J. Comput. Vis. 88(2), 303–338 (2010). https://doi.org/10.1007/s11263-009-0275-4
6. Johari, K., Karumpulli, N., Tan, U.X.: Complementing speech interaction design with touch for multi-robot systems. In: TENCON 2019–2019 IEEE Region 10 Conference (TENCON), pp. 1400–1405. IEEE (2019)
7. Kazemzadeh, S., Ordonez, V., Matten, M., Berg, T.: Referitgame: referring to objects in photographs of natural scenes. In: Proceedings of the 2014 Conference on Empirical Methods in Natural Language Processing (EMNLP), pp. 787–798 (2014)
8. Krawczyk, B.: Learning from imbalanced data: open challenges and future directions. Prog. Artif. Intell. 5(4), 221–232 (2016). https://doi.org/10.1007/s13748-016-0094-0
9. Krishna, R., et al.: Visual genome: Connecting language and vision using crowdsourced dense image annotations. arXiv preprint arXiv:1602.07332 (2016)
10. Lin, T.-Y., et al.: Microsoft COCO: common objects in context. In: Fleet, D., Pajdla, T., Schiele, B., Tuytelaars, T. (eds.) ECCV 2014, Part V. LNCS, vol. 8693, pp. 740–755. Springer, Cham (2014). https://doi.org/10.1007/978-3-319-10602-1_48
11. Majaranta, P., Bulling, A.: Eye tracking and eye-based human–computer interaction. In: Fairclough, S.H., Gilleade, K. (eds.) Advances in Physiological Computing. HIS, pp. 39–65. Springer, London (2014). https://doi.org/10.1007/978-1-4471-6392-3_3
12. Mao, J., Huang, J., Toshev, A., Camburu, O., Yuille, A.L., Murphy, K.: Generation and comprehension of unambiguous object descriptions. In: Proceedings of the IEEE Conference on Computer Vision and Pattern Recognition, pp. 11–20 (2016)
13. Palinko, O., Rea, F., Sandini, G., Sciutti, A.: Robot reading human gaze: why eye tracking is better than head tracking for human-robot collaboration. In: 2016 IEEE/RSJ International Conference on Intelligent Robots and Systems (IROS), pp. 5048–5054. IEEE (2016)
14. Park, K.B., Choi, S.H., Lee, J.Y., Ghasemi, Y., Mohammed, M., Jeong, H.: Hands-free human-robot interaction using multimodal gestures and deep learning in wearable mixed reality. IEEE Access 9, 55448–55464 (2021)
15. Plummer, B.A., Wang, L., Cervantes, C.M., Caicedo, J.C., Hockenmaier, J., Lazebnik, S.: Flickr30k entities: collecting region-to-phrase correspondences for richer image-to-sentence models. In: Proceedings of the IEEE International Conference on Computer Vision, pp. 2641–2649 (2015)

16. Ren, S., He, K., Girshick, R., Sun, J.: Faster R-CNN: Towards real-time object detection with region proposal networks. arXiv preprint arXiv:1506.01497 (2015)
17. Sadhu, A., Chen, K., Nevatia, R.: Zero-shot grounding of objects from natural language queries. In: Proceedings of the IEEE/CVF International Conference on Computer Vision, pp. 4694–4703 (2019)
18. Scalise, R., Li, S., Admoni, H., Rosenthal, S., Srinivasa, S.S.: Natural language instructions for human-robot collaborative manipulation. Int. J. Robot. Res. **37**(6), 558–565 (2018)
19. Sharma, V.K., Murthy, L., Saluja, K.S., Mollyn, V., Sharma, G., Biswas, P.: Eye gaze controlled robotic arm for persons with ssmi. arXiv preprint arXiv:2005.11994 (2020)
20. Shridhar, M., Mittal, D., Hsu, D.: Ingress: interactive visual grounding of referring expressions. Int. J. Robot. Res. **39**(2–3), 217–232 (2020)
21. Sidenmark, L., Mardanbegi, D., Gomez, A.R., Clarke, C., Gellersen, H.: Bimodal-gaze: seamlessly refined pointing with gaze and filtered gestural head movement. In: ACM Symposium on Eye Tracking Research and Applications, pp. 1–9 (2020)
22. Stiefelhagen, R., Fugen, C., Gieselmann, R., Holzapfel, H., Nickel, K., Waibel, A.: Natural human-robot interaction using speech, head pose and gestures. In: 2004 IEEE/RSJ International Conference on Intelligent Robots and Systems (IROS) (IEEE Cat. No. 04CH37566), vol. 3, pp. 2422–2427. IEEE (2004)
23. Wang, M.Y., Kogkas, A.A., Darzi, A., Mylonas, G.P.: Free-view, 3D gaze-guided, assistive robotic system for activities of daily living. In: 2018 IEEE/RSJ International Conference on Intelligent Robots and Systems (IROS), pp. 2355–2361. IEEE (2018)
24. Wu, Y., Kirillov, A., Massa, F., Lo, W.Y., Girshick, R.: Detectron2 (2019). https://github.com/facebookresearch/detectron2
25. Yang, Z., Gong, B., Wang, L., Huang, W., Yu, D., Luo, J.: A fast and accurate one-stage approach to visual grounding. In: Proceedings of the IEEE/CVF International Conference on Computer Vision, pp. 4683–4693 (2019)
26. Yu, L., et al.: Mattnet: modular attention network for referring expression comprehension. In: Proceedings of the IEEE Conference on Computer Vision and Pattern Recognition, pp. 1307–1315 (2018)
27. Zhou, Y., et al.: A real-time global inference network for one-stage referring expression comprehension. IEEE Trans. Neural Netw. Learn. Syst. (2021)
28. Zitnick, C.L., Dollár, P.: Edge boxes: locating object proposals from edges. In: Fleet, D., Pajdla, T., Schiele, B., Tuytelaars, T. (eds.) ECCV 2014, Part V. LNCS, vol. 8693, pp. 391–405. Springer, Cham (2014). https://doi.org/10.1007/978-3-319-10602-1_26

Towards a Programming-Free Robotic System for Assembly Tasks Using Intuitive Interactions

Nicolas Gauthier[✉], Wenyu Liang[✉], Qianli Xu[✉], Fen Fang[✉],
Liyuan Li[✉], Ruihan Gao, Yan Wu[✉], and Joo Hwee Lim[✉]

Institute for Infocomm Research, A*STAR, Singapore 138632, Singapore
{nicolas_gauthier,liang_wenyu,qxu,fang_fen,lyli,gao_ruihan,
wuy,joohwee}@i2r.a-star.edu.sg

Abstract. Although industrial robots are successfully deployed in many assembly processes, high-mix, low-volume applications are still difficult to automate, as they involve small batches of frequently changing parts. Setting up a robotic system for these tasks requires repeated reprogramming by expert users, incurring extra time and costs. In this paper, we present a solution which enables a robot to learn new objects and new tasks from non-expert users without the need for programming. The use case presented here is the assembly of a gearbox mechanism. In the proposed solution, first, the robot can autonomously register new objects using a visual exploration routine, and train a deep learning model for object detection accordingly. Secondly, the user can teach new tasks to the system via visual demonstration in a natural manner. Finally, using multimodal perception from RGB-D (color and depth) cameras and a tactile sensor, the robot can execute the taught tasks with adaptation to changing configurations. Depending on the task requirements, it can also activate human-robot collaboration capabilities. In summary, these three main modules enable any non-expert user to configure a robot for new applications in a fast and intuitive way.

Keywords: Robotic manipulation · Multimodal perception · Object and task teaching · Grasping and insertion · Human-robot collaboration

1 Introduction

With the intensified development of robotic technologies, robots are expected to work alongside and together with humans to complete tasks and improve productivity. This requires Human-Robot Collaboration (HRC) capabilities [1,2], to adapt to changing configurations and human behaviours. The current COVID-19 pandemic's social distancing requirements force companies to operate at a reduced capacity, while production demand remains strong and requires adaptability. Collaborative robots (cobots) can help to address this challenge, provided

This research is supported by the Agency for Science, Technology and Research (A*STAR) under its AME Programmatic Funding Scheme (Project #A18A2b0046).

© Springer Nature Switzerland AG 2021
H. Li et al. (Eds.): ICSR 2021, LNAI 13086, pp. 203–215, 2021.
https://doi.org/10.1007/978-3-030-90525-5_18

that they are safe, flexible, robust, easy and fast to deploy. Notably, deployment time is critical, to ensure little downtime and fast return on investment.

However, such systems are currently highly constrained in their ability to collaborate with humans: (i) by their inability to interact naturally through common modalities like vision, speech and touch; and (ii) by their limited ability to adapt in task performance (re-programming is needed even for small changes in procedure) [3]. In this paper, we seek to develop a suite of capabilities that would allow cobots to adapt to humans and their work environments through natural interactions and robust learning, to remove the need for specialized infrastructure, expert programming and human training, thus reducing deployment costs.

Fast object learning is a desirable feature, to quickly adapt to new objects, but is still underdeveloped for many real-world problems. Legacy deep learning-based methods have achieved remarkable performance in object recognition but are not directly usable for domain-specific problems: off the shelf models (i.e., pre-trained on large-scale, generic dataset) perform rather poorly on the recognition of novel industrial objects [4]. To achieve good performance, sufficient high-quality training data is required, which is costly and time-consuming. Some works deal with the generation of high-quality training data by (i) simplifying the data collection and annotation process using specific devices or user interfaces [5], (ii) automating the generation of data samples through augmentation and synthesis [6]. For the former, it still involves a lengthy process of data sampling and manual annotation. For the latter, the characteristics of synthesized data need not match with those of actual data from domain-specific operating environments, leading to unstable and deteriorated performance. A few works resort to interactive data collection and annotation [7–9]. The agent is equipped with the ability to register object instances with human guidance. However, they are restricted by the limited functionalities of hardware (e.g., robot mobility) and software, thus only addressing small-scale toy problems. It is paramount to fill this gap with an effective interaction protocol for agents to learn from human, and further to perform self-learning similar to human learners.

Additionally, setting-up a cobot without programming requires real-time parsing of human inputs into recognized task activities and human actions, to then relate them to a task representation for task understanding and learning. This research will notably develop capabilities for modelling task structure and understanding a human worker's roles during task execution and collaboration, adapting to uncertainties and exceptions over time. There is a rich and growing literature of robotic learning from demonstration (LfD) due to the importance and advantages of scaling up robots for new tasks without hand-crafted programming, as mentioned above. A full review of the topic is beyond the scope of this paper; readers may refer to recent surveys [10–12]. Existing LfD solutions focus on capturing signals directly related to the robot operations, from kinaesthetic, motion-sensor, or tele-operated demonstrations on the end-effector's pose, or force and motion trajectory. They focus on learning a policy of task execution using models like Hidden Markov Models (HMMs), Gaussian Mixture Models (GMMs), Dynamic Movement Primitives (DMPs), and Task-Parameterised

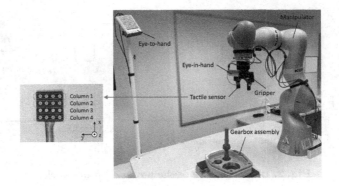

Fig. 1. Robotic system setup

Gaussian Mixture Model (TP-GMM), as well as Deep Reinforcement Learning (DRL) recently. Our method instead focuses on learning a general and conceptual task representation based on visual observation of human hand actions which is beyond the state and action space of the robot's pose, force or motion.

2   Robotic System

The robotic system used in this work is based on a robot manipulator, coupled to two cameras and a 2-finger gripper with a tactile sensor.

Figure 1 shows the overall robotic system setup. More specifically, it consists of a 7-degree-of-freedom (7-DoF) *KUKA LBR iiwa* robot manipulator, which enables a wide range of motions, as well as safe HRC with its compliant mode and collision detection capability. To identify and locate the objects to interact with, two RGB-D cameras are used: a fixed eye-to-hand one (*Microsoft Kinect Azure*) detects the objects in the robot workspace, and estimates their 3D positions with respect to the robot. Based on this, the robot can move closer to a desired object, and then better estimate its location by using an eye-in-hand camera (*Intel RealSense D435*). Eventually, it is anticipated that these vision outputs have errors due to calibration imperfections, occlusions, or limited resolution for instance, and that tasks like grasping will happen blindly at some point (when the robot gets too close to the object to see it). To overcome these limitations, the gripper (*Robotiq 2F-85*) is equipped with a *XELA uSkin XR1944* tactile sensor, which is used to estimate with how much offset an object has been grasped. This main suite of sensors is used to bring down the perceptual error in order to interact with the gearbox components, in this use case.

Finally, the whole system also comes with an intuitive Graphical User Interface (GUI), available on a touch monitor, allowing easy control and set-up of the robot. The user also gets audio feedback on the machine's status and actions. The different components of the system, both hardware and software, are brought together with The Robot Operating System (ROS) [13]. The overall software is made of modules coded in C++ and Python.

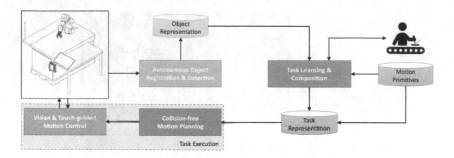

Fig. 2. Block diagram of the proposed framework

3   Framework for Programming-Free System

To achieve programming-free task execution, the robotic system should be capable of detecting objects, understanding tasks, and precisely executing them. Therefore, the solution proposed in this paper mainly consists of three modules: object teaching, task teaching, and task execution. The corresponding block diagram is depicted in Fig. 2. The object teaching module is for autonomous object registration and detection, the task teaching module is for understanding tasks from visual human demonstrations, and the task execution module is for executing the learned and composed tasks, using multimodal perception.

3.1   Object Teaching

There are three key steps for object teaching as explained below. The entire process is summarised in Fig. 3.

Canonical View Selection. This first step is used to actively capture an object's informative views, by exploring various viewpoints around it and and select the most informative ones based on a criteria termed goodness of view (GOV).

- **Object Segmentation** At a viewpoint, the RGB-D camera provides a color image and point cloud of the scene. First, we need to get a regional mask of the object. For this, the Point Cloud Library (PCL) is used, to estimate the dominant plane and separate it from the object to register. Alternatively, for small or flat objects, which are difficult to be isolated, we use color information to perform segmentation (provided that there is adequate contrast between the object and table top). The mask is then used to extract the object from the RGB image.
- **Goodness of view** The *goodness* of a viewpoint is defined based on the informativeness of the object, which is computed from a set of basic visual features [14,15]. In this work, silhouette length, depth distribution, curvature entropy, and color entropy are considered in the computation [16]. Canonical views are registered as those with higher combined GOV.

- **Viewpoint exploration** Canonical viewpoints are sampled by evaluating the aggregated GOV of the visited viewpoints on-the-fly. It is assumed that the RGB-D camera is calibrated against a set of viewpoints on a spherical surface and the target object is located at the sphere center (cf Fig. 3). The robot then follows the OnLIne Viewpoint Exploration (OLIVE) method [16] to visit the viewpoints. The RGB-D data captured at each viewpoint is used to extract object features and compute the GOV. Given any viewpoint, the robot searches the local maxima of GOV, where the GOV is computed as the weighted sum of individual GOV metrics. Once the local maxima is found, the next view is chosen as one with the largest geographical distance to the current view.

Data Augmentation. Contemporary object detectors require a reasonably large amount of training images to reach good accuracy. The image samples from the previous step may be too few to reach the desired detection performance. To enhance the dataset, we perform a series of image manipulation techniques to augment the data. In essence, we superimpose the object's image (mask) onto various backgrounds to generate synthesized data. The techniques adopted in this study include (i) 2D variation and 3D transformation to add variations of viewing perspective [17], (ii) blending to remove boundary artifacts [6], and (iii) object scaling to allow optimal object sizes [18].

Training Object Detectors. Once the training images of one or a few novel objects have been generated, the system performs on-site object detector training. Ideally, the object learning is conducted incrementally, whereby new object classes are added gradually to existing classes. In other words, the detector learns new object classes without catastrophic forgetting of old ones. In this study, we explored several incremental learning algorithms, such as the methods presented in [19] and [20]. Notably, these incremental learning techniques still require lengthy training time due to the distillation operation. Hence, in practice, we implemented the training protocol of aggregated training (i.e., to include all training images of known and unknown classes) on the conventional framework of Faster-RCNN with ResNet101 [21].

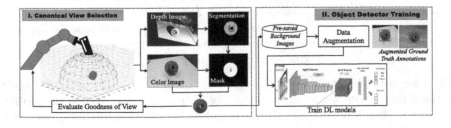

Fig. 3. Object teaching process

3.2 Task Teaching

The task teaching module has been developed to allow any non-expert user to teach new tasks to the manipulator, simply based on visual demonstration. For this, we target at establishing a structured semantic representation of robotic task which matches human common knowledge of task representation. To this end, we propose a novel graph-based task representation: Compounded Task Graph (CTG). The CTG task model provides a concept-level hierarchical representation of industrial tasks. There are three layers of nodes in CTG:

- **Atomic action** (A_h): this node represents an atomic hand action in an industrial task, such as *pick_up*, *move_to*, *release*, etc. The atomic action nodes form the bottom layer of CTG.
- **Primary task** (T_p): this node represents a sequence of atomic hand actions to complete a basic task. It is a parent node of a sequence of atomic actions.
- **Compounded task** (T_c): this node represents a complex task which involves several primary tasks, and/or other compounded tasks as sub-tasks of it. It is a parent node which has a few primary task child nodes in the lower layer, and/or other compounded tasks child nodes (sub-tasks) in the same layer.

Task Teaching on Vision Perception. As mentioned previously, the aim here is to reduce the need for human expertise and coding efforts to produce the CTG of a new task when deploying a cobot. To this end, we propose a novel task teaching approach based on learning from visual human demonstration, to automatically generate the CTG of a new task.

First, the vision system runs a previously trained Faster R-CNN to detect task-related objects and hands in each incoming frame. A tracking algorithm relying on visual working memory is designed to track the detected objects and hands, and estimate their inter-frame movements. Based on these visual observations, a two-level probabilistic logic reasoning is designed to recognize task-related hand actions in real-time.

The first level, visual reasoning, tries to capture four kinds of hand movements, expressed as probabilistic logic rules:

- $move\_to(h_i, o_j) :\text{-} dist\_reduct(h_i, o_j) \,\&\, orient\_consistency(v_i, v_{ij});$
- $hold(h_i, o_j) :\text{-} hand\_static(h_i) \,\&\, hand\_touch(h_i, o_j) \,\&\, dist\_const(h_i, o_j);$
- $move\_together(h_i, o_j) :\text{-} hand\_move(h_i) \,\&\, hand\_touch(h_i, o_j)$
  $\&\, dist\_const(h_i, o_j) \,\&\, orient\_consistency(v_i, v_j);$
- $move\_away(h_i, o_j) :\text{-} hand\_move(h_i) \,\&\, dist\_increase(h_i, o_j)$
  $\&\, orient\_consistency(v_i, v_{ji});$

where, for example, for $move\_to(h_i, o_j)$, if the hand h_i is moving towards object o_j, the distance between h_i and o_j should be reduced constantly, and the motion vector of h_i should be aligned with the orientation vector from h_i to o_j. Hence, if the probabilities of $dist\_reduct(h_i, o_j)$ and $orient\_consistency(v_i, v_{ij})$ are high based on visual observations, the probability of $move\_to(h_i, o_j)$ is high.

The second level, probabilistic reasoning, tries to capture atomic hand actions. During a short duration of recent observations, the algorithm predicts the probabilities of atomic actions based on accumulated evidence of basic hand movements. The probabilistic logic rules are expressed as:

- $pick\_up(h_i, o_j)$:- $move\_to(h_i, o_j)$ & $hold(h_i, o_j)$ & $move\_together(h_i, o_j)$;
- $move\_a2b(h_i, o_j, o_k)$:- $move\_together(h_i, o_j)$ & $move\_to(h_i, o_k)$;
- $release\_a2b(h_i, o_j, o_k)$:- $move\_a2b(h_i, o_j, o_k)$ & $hold(h_i, o_j)$
  & $move\_away(h_i, o_j)$ & $move\_away(h_i, o_k)$;

where, for $pick\_up(h_i, o_j)$, if the hand h_i has moved to object o_j, has held the object statically for a while, and then moves together with it, it means that an atomic action of $pick\_up(h_i, o_j)$ has happened.

During the demonstration, the vision system tracks the events and produces a list of atomic actions gradually. Once the demonstration is completed, the system performs Bayesian inference on the list of atomic actions to extract the task's related actions and associated objects. For example, for a demonstrated task of $insert(a, b)$, Bayesian inference tries to find the maximum joint probability:

$$P_{task}^{insert(a,b)} = \max_{i,j,k} \left[P_r(i,j,k|a,b) P_m(i,j,k|a,b) P_p(i,j|a) P_t(m,r) P_t(p,m) \right], \quad (1)$$

where $P_r(i,j,k|a,b) = P(release\_a2b(h_i, o_j, o_k)|o_j = a, o_k = b)$, $P_m(i,j,k|a,b) = P(move\_a2b(h_i, o_j, o_k)|o_j = a, o_k = b)$, $P_p(i,j|a) = P(pick\_up(h_i, o_j)|o_j = a)$, and P_t represents temporal constraint: $P_t(m,r) = P(t_m < t_r)$. Once the maximum joint probability is larger than a threshold, the observed task is confirmed, and a CTG is generated with corresponding atomic actions and associated objects.

Task Composition with Graphical User Interface. With the capabilities presented above, any non-expert user is able to both teach new objects and demonstrate new tasks to the robot without manually programming anything. Furthermore, one can also leverage on the previously taught tasks, using the GUI to compose more complex or repetitive ones, rather than demonstrating them again. We term this approach "Programming-Free" system. Additionally, for tasks requiring HRC, the user can chose to activate the robot's impedance mode to make it compliant. This ensures a safe execution, as well as ease for joint manipulation, as the user can manually move the end-effector.

3.3   Task Execution

Once a task has been taught (e.g. accurate, adaptable grasping and insertion of a shaft), multimodal perception is used to execute it, without having to perform extensive calibration and risk erroneous and unsafe execution.

Locating Objects Using Visual Inputs. In order to locate objects in the robot workspace and interact with them, the system is equipped with two RGB-D cameras. The first one is fixed and has a bird's eye view on the scene. Its extrinsic parameters have been calibrated with respect to the robot frame, using [22], meaning that its position and orientation are known in this frame. In order to estimate the objects' 3D positions, the system first runs the previously mentioned object detector on the RGB image. Then, to estimate the 3D position of a specific object, it takes the center of the object's bounding box and gets the depth of the corresponding pixel (RGB and depth image have been registered).

Then, the following formula is used to get the 3D position of the mentioned pixel, in the camera frame: $z = d/\alpha$; $x = (n - c_x) * z/f_x$; $y = (m - c_y) * z/f_y$, where d is the depth read at the pixel of coordinates (n, m), $\alpha = 1$ or 1000 depending on whether depth is given in m or mm. f_x, f_y, c_x and c_y come from the intrinsic matrix $K = \begin{bmatrix} f_x & 0 & c_x & 0 \\ 0 & f_y & c_y & 0 \\ 0 & 0 & 1 & 0 \end{bmatrix}$.

Finally, the system converts the obtained coordinates into the robot frame, using the following calculation:

$$
\begin{bmatrix} X \\ Y \\ Z \\ 1 \end{bmatrix}_{robot} = \begin{bmatrix} 1 - 2(q_y^2 + q_z^2) & 2(q_x.q_y - q_z.q_w) & 2(q_x.q_z + q_y.q_w) & t_x \\ 2(q_x.q_y + q_z.q_w) & 1 - 2(q_x^2 + q_z^2) & 2(q_y.q_z - q_x.q_w) & t_y \\ 2(q_x.q_z - q_y.q_w) & 2(q_y.q_z + q_x.q_w) & 1 - 2(q_x^2 + q_y^2) & t_z \\ 0 & 0 & 0 & 1 \end{bmatrix} \begin{bmatrix} x \\ y \\ z \\ 1 \end{bmatrix}_{camera}
$$

(2)

where q_x, q_y, q_z, q_w and t_x, t_y, t_z, represent the camera's extrinsic parameters.

A similar process has been used for the in-hand camera: its extrinsic parameters have been calibrated with respect to the robot's end-effector. Then during run-time, this information is combined to the end-effector's actual position, to compute the camera's position and orientation with respect to the robot's fixed frame. (2) is then applied to compute the 3D positions of objects perceived through it.

A critical step in the studied use-case (gearbox assembly), is the insertion of a shaft into a circular bearing cup. There are three of them and the user can choose which one to insert in, via the GUI or demonstration. To perform this, visual perception inputs are used to locate this insertion target, based on a circle detection and tracking algorithm we developed: once it locates the target object, it crops the image around it and generates a list of potential circles for the insertion. Then, using a custom-trained support vector machine (SVM), it will output the true candidates, which are the three insertion possibilities. This solution is able to track the circles as well as keep in memory their position with respect to each other (output example is shown on Fig. 6).

Grasping and Inserting Objects with Tactile Perception. Once the cameras detects the object of interest and locate it, the robot manipulator approaches and grasps it with the gripper. However, due to internal and external uncertainties, such as lighting change, viewing angle, calibration error, resolution and occlusion, the vision accuracy is compromised. Therefore, we propose to attach a tactile sensor to one of the gripper fingertips. This device detects objects as well as the contact surfaces profiles, and provides fine-scale location and shape information. The *XELA uSkin XR1944* sensor, as shown in the left side of Fig. 1, is used in this research. It has 16 taxels arranged in a 4-by-4 array that detect forces in Cartesian coordinates [23].

In this work, the Naive Bayes algorithm is employed to train a classifier to detect the position offset of the object (e.g., a shaft) being grasped with respect to the gripper's fingertip. Assuming that the gripper applies a constant force to grasp the shaft statically, the algorithm takes the normal forces, i.e., forces in z direction (cf. Figure 1), as input features and assumes them to follow Gaussian distribution. Given the regular shape of the shaft, the normal forces are averaged along four columns (y direction) of the taxel array and the position offset in the x direction is estimated following the Bayes' Theorem $p(y_k|\boldsymbol{x}) = \frac{p(y_k)*p(\boldsymbol{x}|y_k)}{p(\boldsymbol{x})}$, where y_k represents label of class k, $\boldsymbol{x}$ is $\mathbb{R}^n$ feature vector and $n = 4$. Gaussian kernel is used to approximate the likelihood of features. The feature plot shown in Fig. 4 demonstrates the distribution of four extracted features. Each feature corresponds to the average reading of one sensor's column. Each subplot represents one feature, the horizontal axis represents the position offset in x direction in mm, and the vertical axis represents the force readings.

$$P(x_i|y) = \frac{1}{\sqrt{2\pi\sigma_y^2}}\exp(-\frac{(x_i - \mu_y)^2}{2\sigma_y^2}) \tag{3}$$

where μ_y and σ_y are estimated class mean and standard deviation.

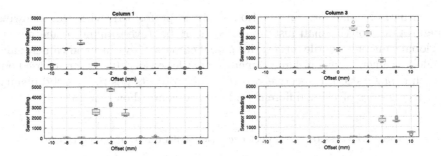

Fig. 4. Boxplot of four extracted features

To validate this approach, a test dataset has been collected: the shaft has been grasped with different offsets, equally spaced. We then compared ground truth values to the predicted ones. Overlapping between two sets of values demonstrated that the offset position can be estimated with an accuracy of less than 2 mm thanks to the proposed algorithm.

4   Experimental Results and Discussions

To validate the effectiveness and performance of the proposed system, experiments have been conducted with the robotic system setup shown in Fig. 1. As mentioned previously, a critical step to perform is the insertion of a shaft into one of the casing's bearing cup. We use this task for validation.

4.1 Object Teaching

The object teaching module (using four pieces of Geforce RTX 2080 in the training, one for inference) can achieve the mAP of more than 0.86 after 10 epochs. More detailed results and discussions can be found in [24].

4.2 Task Teaching

To validate the effectiveness of the task teaching, three different users are asked to demonstrate to the robotic programming-free system the task of *inserting a specific shaft into a casing hole*. It takes 18.7 s on average for the robot to learn the task using the proposed method while it takes roughly twice as much time for a user to program the task for the robot using our designed GUI. Additionally, while we have not documented the task learning success rate, experiments have shown that the algorithm is robust and reliably extract the relevant task structure. Existing benchmark datasets and evaluation metrics might not be applicable to this specific branch of task learning, yet the results obtain show that the proposed task teaching method is effective, efficient and intuitive.

4.3 Task Reproduction

For comparison purposes, an ablation study is performed, with the following configurations, for the shaft insertion task: (i) global (eye-to-hand) camera only; (ii) global camera + tactile sensor; (iii) global camera + eye-in-hand camera; and (iv) global camera + eye-in-hand camera + tactile sensor. 20 tests are carried out for each configuration, respectively, with similar objects positions and difficulty. The success rates of using different configurations are shown in Table 1.

Table 1. Success rate of object execution with different configurations

Configuration	Grasping	Insertion
Global camera only	80%	5%
Global camera + tactile sensor	80%	15%
Global + in-hand camera	100%	60%
Both cameras + tactile sensor	100%	85%

It can be observed that relying only on the global camera gives decent grasping results, but even in successful cases, experiments showed that it would be done either with an offset or the object is not picked up straight. As for the insertion, this sensor alone fails to properly estimate the insertion target (hole) location, mainly due to viewing angle restrictions. Adding the in-hand camera to the system considerably enhances the results for both grasping and insertion. It helps to properly center the gripper on the object to grasp, and prevents the gripper from colliding with the object. It also helps to more accurately locate the target hole for insertion. Yet, the visual perception inputs are not perfect, which results in a slight offset between the object axis and the gripper center. It can be observed that the tactile sensor combined to the proposed algorithm greatly helps to compensate for this and improves the insertion success rate.

4.4   Collaborative Task

The user can also request the system to help him/her in collaborative tasks. A perfect use-case for this is the insertion of three shafts simultaneously, as these components need to be inserted into the casing at the same time. It is impossible for a worker or the robot to single-handedly complete this task reliably. Thus, a new collaborative insertion task can be composed via the GUI, using the previously taught insertion action. The step of insertion in the learnt task will be set to be done in collaborative mode, i.e., the robot compliant mode will be enabled for safer and easier execution, while waiting for human trigger.

Fig. 5. Robot operations during collaborative insertion task

The robot operations for this collaborative task are shown in Fig. 5. In practice, the system will stop and inform the user after it grasps the shaft and moves it above the casing. It will then trigger the insertion once it senses a pulling-down force/motion from the co-worker. Eventually, the collaborative function allows easy HRC for a challenging task.

4.5   GUI

Most of the interactions with the system are done via a custom GUI, available on a touch monitor. Figure 6 depicts the different use cases.

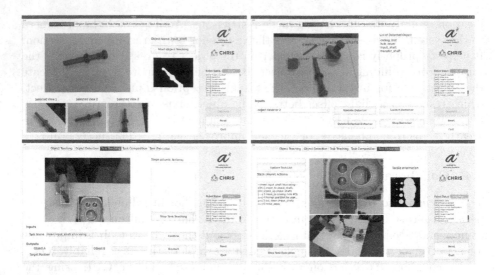

Fig. 6. GUI for object teaching, object detection, task teaching and task execution

5 Conclusion

In this paper, a framework with intuitive interactions is proposed towards programming-free robotic system setup. The framework consists of object teaching, vision-based task teaching and multimodal-perception-based task execution. Several experiments are carried out with the use case of an assembly task (shaft insertion) to validate the effectiveness and performance of the proposed framework. The experimental results show that the proposed method can not only help the robot to register objects and learn tasks in a fast way but also improve the task execution precision and robustness through multimodal perception. Compared to other simpler configurations, the ablation study showed that combining two cameras and a tactile sensor brings considerable improvement for grasping and insertion tasks.

References

1. Bicchi, A., Peshkin, M.A., Colgate, J.E.: Safety for physical human–robot interaction. In: Siciliano, B. (ed.) Springer Handbook of Robotics, vol. Springe, pp. 1335–1348. (2008). https://doi.org/10.1007/978-3-540-30301-5_58
2. Wang, L., Liu, S., Liu, H., Wang, X.V.: Overview of human-robot collaboration in manufacturing. In: Wang, L., Majstorovic, V.D., Mourtzis, D., Carpanzano, E., Moroni, G., Galantucci, L.M. (eds.) Proceedings of 5th International Conference on the Industry 4.0 Model for Advanced Manufacturing. LNME, pp. 15–58. Springer, Cham (2020). https://doi.org/10.1007/978-3-030-46212-3_2
3. El Zaatari, S., Marei, M., Li, W., Usman, Z.: Cobot programming for collaborative industrial tasks: an overview. Robot. Auton. Syst. **116**, 162–180 (2019)

4. Pasquale, G., Ciliberto, C., Odone, F., Rosasco, L., Natale, L.: Are we done with object recognition? The iCub robot's perspective. Robot. Auton. Syst. **112**, 260–281 (2019)
5. Label fusion: a pipeline for generating ground truth labels for real RGBD data of cluttered scenes. In: ICRA2018, pp. 1–8 (2018)
6. Dwibedi, D., Misra, I., Hebert, M.: Cut, paste and learn: Surprisingly easy synthesis for instance detection. In: ICCV2017, pp. 1310–1319 (2017)
7. Dehghan, M., et al.: Online object and task learning via human robot interaction. In: ICRA2019, pp. 2132–2138 (2019)
8. Kasaei, S., et al.: Interactive open-ended learning for 3D object recognition: an approach and experiments. J. Intell. Robot. Syst. **80**, 537–553 (2015). https://doi.org/10.1007/s10846-015-0189-z
9. Kasaei, A., et al.: Perceiving, learning, and recognizing 3D objects: an approach to cognitive service robots. In: AAAI-2018 (2018)
10. Argall, B.D., Chernova, S., Veloso, M., Browning, B.: A survey of robot learning from demonstration. Robot. Auton. Syst. **57**, 469–483 (2009)
11. Zhu, Z., Huosheng, H.: Robot learning from demonstration in robotic assembly: a survey. Robotics **7**, 17 (2018)
12. Jangwon Lee. A survey of robot learning from demonstrations for Human-Robot Collaboration. arXiv e-prints, page arXiv:1710.08789, October 2017
13. Stanford Artificial Intelligence Laboratory et al. Robotic operating system. ROS Melodic Morenia. https://www.ros.org. Accessed 23 May 2018
14. Dutagaci, H., Cheung, C.P., Godil, A.: A benchmark for best view selection of 3D objects. In: 3DOR 2010, pp. 45–50 (2010)
15. Polonsky, O., et al.: What's in an image? Towards the computation of the "best" view of an object. Vis. Comput. **21**, 840–847 (2005)
16. Q. Xu et al. Active image sampling on canonical views for novel object detection. In: ICIP 2020, pp. 2241–2245. IEEE (2020)
17. Fang, F., et al.: Self-teaching strategy for learning to recognize novel objects in collaborative robots. In: ICRAI 2019, pp. 18–23 (2019)
18. Fang, F., et al.: Detecting objects with high object region percentage. In: ICPR 2020, pp. 7173–7180 (2020)
19. Shmelkov, K., Schmid, C., Alahari, K.: Incremental learning of object detectors without catastrophic forgetting. In: ICCV 2017, pp. 3400–3409 (2017)
20. Peng, C., Zhao, K., Lovell, B.C.: Faster ILOD: incremental learning for object detectors based on faster RCNN. Pattern Recognit. Lett. **140**, 109–115 (2020)
21. Ren, S., He, K., Girshick, R., Sun, J.: Faster R-CNN: towards real-time object detection with region proposal networks. Adv. Neural Inf. Process. Syst. **28**, 91–99 (2015)
22. easy_handeye. https://github.com/IFL-CAMP/easy_handeye
23. uSkin sensors. https://xelarobotics.com/en/uskin-sensor
24. Xu, Q., et al.: TAILOR: teaching with active and incremental learning for object registration. In: AAAI 2021, vol. 35, pp. 16120–16123 (2021)

Controlling Industrial Robots
with High-Level Verbal Commands

Dongkyu Choi[1]([✉]), Wei Shi[2], Ying Siu Liang[1], Kheng Hui Yeo[2],
and Jung-Jae Kim[2]

[1] Institute of High Performance Computing, Agency for Science, Technology
and Research, Singapore, Singapore
{choi_dongkyu,liangys}@ihpc.a-star.edu.sg
[2] Institute for Infocomm Research, Agency for Science, Technology and Research,
Singapore, Singapore
{shi_wei,yeokh,jjkim}@i2r.a-star.edu.sg

Abstract. Industrial robots today are still mostly pre-programmed to
perform a specific task. Despite previous research in human-robot interaction in the academia, adopting such systems in industrial settings is
not trivial and has rarely been done. In this paper, we introduce a robotic
system that we control with high-level verbal commands, leveraging some
of the latest neural approaches to language understanding and a cognitive architecture for goal-directed but reactive execution. We show that
a large-scale pre-trained language model can be effectively fine-tuned for
translating verbal instructions into robot tasks, better than other semantic parsing methods, and that our system is capable of handling through
dialogue a variety of exceptions that happen during human-robot interaction including unknown tasks, user interruption, and changes in the
world state.

Keywords: Intention translation · Semantic parsing · Human-robot
interaction · Cognitive architecture

1 Introduction

Despite the recent advance in human-robot interaction, we still see industrial
robots being pre-programmed to perform a specific task in a secure environment. Although new collaborative robots, or co-bots, are safer around humans
and therefore used in or near human work spaces, making them to work on a
new task still involves manual programming in many industry cases. We aim to
change this paradigm and develop a system that enables robots to adapt to the
human norm, in which workers interact with their teammates to gather sufficient information about new tasks they need to perform and inform each other
about the progress. There can be multiple modalities with which teammates can

This research is supported by A*STAR under its *Human-Robot Collaborative AI for
Advanced Manufacturing and Engineering* (Award A18A2b0046).

communicate with one another but, in this work, we present a system that can understand natural verbal instructions from humans, translating the utterances into a machine-readable representation of tasks, and perform the given tasks appropriately in situations that evolve dynamically.

Previous works on the instruction-to-task translation task utilize verb frames [3], grammar-based semantic parsers [11,19], syntactic parser-based probabilistic models [12,14], and end-to-end neural networks [18] including large-scale pre-trained language models [5]. However, they have not explored latest techniques of *semantic parsing*, the task of identifying the semantics of a given sentence and representing it in a machine-readable representation. In this work, we adapt recent and well-known methods of semantic parsing for the translation task and show that a pre-trained model [17] outperforms the other methods of semantic parsing probably because the pre-trained model can be effectively fine-tuned with the small size of our dataset.

In the sections that follow, we first review previous research on semantic parsing, as wells as translating instructions for robots, that influenced our work. Then we explain how our system leverages latest techniques for natural language processing to translate user utterances to goals to achieve in the given situation. After that, we describe our robot's cognitive architecture that takes the translated goals and execute procedures that achieve them in a reactive manner. We then discuss some future work before we conclude.

2   Related Work

2.1   Translating Instructions for Robot Motion Planning

In this section, we discuss selected previous works on translating human instruction into meaning representation of machine-readable format for the purpose of robot motion planning. [3] presented a model that translates simple instruction sentences with a single verb frame into robot motion plans, even if the instructions are incomplete, by using commonsense reasoning. However, there is a need for expressing more complex intentions than single verb frames.

To address the need, [11,19] developed combinatory categorical grammar (CCG)-based semantic parsers, where a grammar is to understand the whole meaning of even complex sentences. CCG is a lexical grammar, where most of linguistic information required for natural language understanding are specified at the lexical level; in other words, each word is associated with its pre-defined semantics. While a CCG-based semantic parser can be learned from a large collection of meaning representations [1], such a grammar-based approach cannot be automatically adapted for a small dataset in the robotics domain.

Instead of adapting a grammar-based semantic parser, [12,14] utilize syntactic parsers, which identify the syntactic relations among words in a given sentence but do not represent them in a domain-specific meaning representation. For instance, [14] proposed dynamic grounding graphs (DGG). DGG first performs syntactic parsing on a given instruction, producing a tree-like syntactic structure of the sentence, then maps each word phrase of the structure to its groundings (e.g. object, location, motion, task), and finally computes cost function parameters used in optimization-based motion planner by using a probabilistic model based on the groundings and a given environment. However, these methods require a large data collection to learn such a probabilistic model that can translate syntactic information into robot motion plans ([14] used 100,000 samples, and [12] used 6,099 utterances).

[18] and other works (available at archives) present neural networks that learn to translate an instruction utterance to meaning representation without a grammar or a syntactic parser, including LSTM [9] and BERT [5]. However, they have not explored more recent and well-known methods of semantic parsing for the translation task. We thus adapt 4 recent advanced semantic parsing methods for the task and discuss their evaluation comparison results in this work.

2.2 Semantic Parsing

In this section, we discuss selected recent works on neural network-based semantic parsing. [6] present a neural network model, called *Coarse2Fine*, which has two encoders for training, while using only one encoder for inference. Coarse2Fine assumes that a meaning representation can be simplified into an *intermediate* form, which can be generated automatically from the ground-truth meaning representation. They train a model that first learns to generate the intermediate form from an input sentence and then generates the actual meaning representation based on the sentence embeddings and the intermediate embeddings. At inference, the model takes as input only an input sentence.

A new approach to semantic parsing is to incorporate the 'world knowledge' of meaning representation into semantic parsing. [20] present a pre-trained language model that jointly learns representations for sentences and (semi-)structured tables and a semantic parser based on the pre-trained model, where their goal is to generate e.g. SQL queries executable on the tables. We do not follow this approach since robot world states are dynamic and keep changing, unlike tables.

Another approach is 'interactive' semantic parser, getting feedback from user and updating semantic parsing outputs accordingly. [7] generate a SQL query and its text description and, if user gives a corrective instruction upon the text description and the SQL query's execution results, update the SQL query by incorporating the corrective instruction. [21] analyze a user instruction and, if it has any ambiguous phrase, ask the user a specific question for disambiguation. The proposed work is also interactive in that it checks if the intention translated from a given instruction is valid in given conditions of robot world states and, if not valid, gives feedback to the user for them to alternate the instruction.

3   Goal Translation

In this section, we discuss automatic generation of an intention from a given instruction sentence. We describe our in-house dataset for this task and the approach we have taken.

3.1   Utterance-Goal Annotation Dataset

Our dataset consists of 141 human utterances of instruction sentences for the robot to execute a subgoal in a gearbox assembly and disassembly scenario. Each intention string is translated into a sequence of tokens (words and symbols) consisting of three parts: Intention *type* (e.g. instruct achieve, instruct maintain), symbols describing the actions to perform as a function (e.g. fasten ?casing-top ?screw), and variable bindings or conditions (e.g. casing-base ?casing-base), which are given after the keyword 'given'. The dataset contains 45 unique verbs (e.g. insert, attach, install) and 32 unique object types (e.g. gearbox, input-shaft, screw). Table 1 shows example instruction sentences and their intentions.

Table 1. Examples of translated intentions in our utterance-goal dataset

Human utterance	Translated intention
Please begin assembly of the casing base	instruct achieve (assembled ?casing-base) given (casing-base ?casing-base)
Install the input shaft	instruct achieve (installed ?input-shaft ?object) given (input-shaft ?input-shaft)
Please attach the small hub cover onto the casing top next	instruct achieve (attached ?small-hub-cover ?casing-top) given (small-hub-cover ?small-hub-cover) (casing-top ?casing-top)
To start disassembly, put the gearbox in a vertical position	instruct achieve (vertical ?gearbox) given (gearbox ?gearbox)

3.2   Goal Translation System

We approach it as a sequence-to-sequence task, taking an instruction sentence as input and generating an intention string as a sequence of tokens (words and symbols). One advantage of the sequence-to-sequence approach is that we can employ pre-trained language models (e.g. GPT-2 [16], T5 [17]), which are trained with large collection of English texts by self-supervised learning methods (e.g. masked language modeling) and recently led to many breakthroughs in natural language processing including semantic parsing. The intention has structure, consisting of tuples and keywords, but the elements of the structure are written in English words and can thus be targeted for generation by fine-tuning the pre-trained language models.

The intention generation can be considered as a task of semantic parsing, in that it aims at generating the meaning representation of a given sentence from the viewpoint of motion planning. Therefore, we adapt several methods of semantic parsing for the task, including employing LSTM, the pre-trained language models and other methods (e.g. Coarse2Fine [6]). Technically, we used two layers of bi-LSTM and GloVe word embeddings [15] as inputs to the LSTM model (learning rate: 1e-3, number of epochs: 60, dropout rate: 0.1). We used the following hyper-parameters to fine-tune of the two pre-trained models: GPT-2 (learning rate: 5e-5, number of epochs: 150, dropout rate: 0.1) and T5 (learning rate: 3e-4, number of epochs: 50, dropout rate: 0.1).

For Coarse2Fine, it requires the output of semantic parsing to be of tree structure. We thus slightly modified the intention string as follows: 1) adding brackets to surround the whole intention string and 2) moving the "repeat all" keyword before the actions so that the keyword is the root of the sub-tree of actions. Table 2 shows examples of these modifications. We used the following hyper-parameters to train the Coarse2Fine parser[1]: learning rate 5e-3, number of epochs 100, dropout rate 0.5. Batch size is set as 16 for all the 4 models.

Table 2. Examples of changes made in intentions in coarse2fine

Changes	Original intention	Changed intention
Add brackets	instruct achieve (attached ?small_hub_cover ?casing_top) given (small_hub_cover ?small_hub_cover) (casing_top ?casing_top)	(instruct_achieve (attached (?small_hub_cover ?casing_top)) (given (small_hub_cover ?small_hub_cover) (casing_top ?casing_top)))
Move "repeat all" to the front	instruct achieve (checked ?bolt) given (bolt ?bolt) repeat all	(instruct_achieve (repeat-all ((checked ?bolt) (given (bolt ?bolt)))))

4   Reactive Execution for Translated Goals

The translated goals are used in our robot to execute procedures that achieve them in a reactive manner. We developed our robotic system in the context of a cognitive architecture, ICARUS [4], that provides an infrastructure for cognitively-inspired intelligent capabilities on our robot. In this section, we first review ICARUS briefly and then describe how the architecture processes the translated goals from the dialogue system, which employs the semantic parsers introduced in the next section, for reactive execution. Figure 1 illustrates the workflow of the system.

4.1   ICARUS Review

Research on cognitive architectures is inspired by psychological evidence for many aspects of human mind. They share a certain set of commitments they make about representation, memory, and processes that work over them. One such architecture, ICARUS, assumes relational representation of knowledge, distinguishes long-term and short-term memories, and operates in recognize-act cycles as other architectures do. But ICARUS also features a unique combination of its explicit commitment to hierarchical knowledge structures, the distinction of concepts, procedures, and goals, and its goal reasoning and teleoreactive execution.

---

[1] https://github.com/donglixp/coarse2fine.

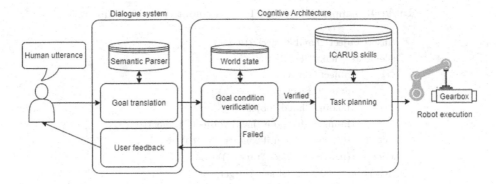

Fig. 1. Overview of the goal translation pipeline.

Table 3. Sample concepts of the ICARUS cognitive architecture

---
((holding ?hand ?obj)
:elements ((hand ?hand *status ?gripper))
:tests ((not (= ?gripper 'open))
        (not (= ?gripper 'closed))))

((output-insertion-complete ?hand ?output ?case)
:elements ((output ?output)
           (inserted ?output ?case)
           (hand-empty ?hand)
           (in-high-pose ?hand)))

ICARUS uses *concepts* as its vocabulary to describe relations that hold true in the world. Table 3 shows some examples in the industrial manipulation domain we use. Concepts resemble Horn clauses [10] that include a head, a list of matching conditions, and optional tests against matched variables. The first concept, **holding**, matches against a manipulator hand and checks its status attribute to see if the hand is holding any object. Notice that this concept definition uses only perceptual matching against objects and their attributes, making this a *primitive* concept. The second concept, however, is a non-primitive one, and we can see that it refers to other concepts, **inserted**, **hand-empty**, and **in-high-pose**, in addition to perceptual matching against an **output** object. In this manner, ICARUS's concepts form a hierarchy of relations.

To describe procedures that achieve certain situations in the world, the architecture uses *skills*. Table 4 shows some sample skills from our industrial manipulation domain. We can consider skills to be a hierarchical version of STRIPS operators [8] with a head, a list of matching conditions, a list of direct actions or subskills, and a set of effects. The first skill, **insert-object**, is a primitive skill, in that it only refers to actions that can be executed directly in the world. It requires three objects (a **hand**, an **object**, and a **case**) and two concepts (**holding** and

Table 4. Sample skills of the ICARUS cognitive architecture

((insert-object ?hand ?object ?target)
:elements ((hand ?hand)
(object ?object)
(case ?target)
(holding ?hand ?object)
(in-insertable-pose ?hand ?object ?target))
:actions ((*move-in-z-until-contact ?hand))
:effects ((inserted ?object ?target)))
((insert-object ?hand ?object ?target)
:elements ((hand ?hand)
(object ?object)
(case ?target))
:subskills ((move-to-insertable-pose ?hand ?object ?target)
(insert-object ?hand ?object ?target))
:effects ((inserted ?object ?target)))

in-insertable-pose) as its precondition and, upon a successful completion, achieves the concept, inserted, in the world. In contrast, the second skill is a non-primitive skill, which refers to other skills, move-to-insertable-pose and insert-object (the first example), in order to achieve its effects.

Using concepts and skills like the ones we have seen so far, the ICARUS architecture is able to infer the current situation of the world based on the sensory input and make decisions to execute a certain skill at each given time. ICARUS's execution of skills is governed by its goals, which are general descriptions of desired situations written as concept instances with their associated relevance conditions. For example, the architecture will decide to execute two different skills even under two exactly same situations, given two different top-level goals. Due to the limited space available here, we will refer curious readers to our previous work for more detailed review of ICARUS and various processes it employs. We will discuss its goal-oriented but reactive execution in the next section, while we describe how the architecture uses the translated goals from the dialogue system for execution.

4.2   Reactive Execution of Translated Goals

When the user generates utterances, our system's goal translation module takes and translates them into a format our cognitive architecture can understand. First, our system parses the translations into the description of goals and the conditions that should be met. ICARUS compiles these into a top-level goal, which its execution module can readily take and process. During this process, it also looks up the words used in the goals and conditions against its linguistic domain knowledge base to disambiguate the meaning. For example, the system replaces the verbs, place, put, and install with install, which ICARUS's skills are written with. Then it checks whether the translated goal exists in its concept definitions and verifies that the conditions hold in the current world state. If either fails, the user is prompted to modify their instruction by using more specific descriptions. Given a valid translation of goals and conditions, ICARUS generates a task plan to achieve the given goal. The plan is a set of skill instances at multiple levels of abstraction, grounded at the robot's low-level actions. During action execution, the architecture consistently checks for new user utterances, as well as changes in situation. This enables the user to interrupt the execution anytime by defining a new goal. Table 5 shows an example dialogue between human user and robot, where the user interrupts robot.

Table 5. Example dialogue between human user and robot, with a user interruption

Human:	Assemble the gearbox
Robot:	I do not recognize that goal. Please give more detailed instruction
Human:	Insert the input subassembly into the casing base
Robot:	I will work on inserting input subassembly into case
	(Robot starts to move to pick up the object.)
Human:	Actually, insert the output subassembly into the casing base first
Robot:	I will work on inserting output subassembly into case
	(Robot works to pick up the new object.)

5 Evaluation of Goal Translation Methods

We evaluated the four methods of goal translation against our utterance-goal annotation dataset, randomly splitting the dataset into 90% for training and 10% for testing and reporting the average performance of the methods across 5 random splits. Table 6 shows the evaluation results of the methods against the dataset. The *accuracy* measure indicates if the whole string of generated intention is correct or not. As a strict measure, the accuracies of the methods are low due to the small size of the dataset. We also introduce an *F1-score* that measures how many correct concepts the generated intentions contain. The two measures indicate how easily a user can select or write the correct intention based on the top results of a method.

Table 6. Evaluation results of semantic parsing methods for intention generation. 'F1' indicates F1-score.

Method	Accuracy	F1
LSTM	28.0%	68.0%
Coarse2Fine	34.7%	75.5%
GPT-2	32.0%	76.1%
T5	**46.7%**	**84.1%**

The evaluation results summarized in Table 6 show that pre-trained models (e.g. GPT-2, T5) outperform non-pre-trained models (e.g. LSTM) even though the LSTM model utilizes pre-trained word embeddings (GloVe). This can be possibly due to the small size of the dataset, which is not enough to optimize randomly initialized parameters of the LSTM model. T5 is reported to show better performance also on other NLP applications than GPT-2 [17].

Coarse2Fine achieves significantly higher performance than LSTM, but significantly lower performance than T5. Coarse2Fine is better than LSTM probably because Coarse2Fine adds a sketch layer between the LSTM encoder and the decoder in order to first learn an intermediate representation of intention and then to generate the intention string, and applies parent feeding.

The pre-trained model T5 is better than Coarse2Fine, while GPT-2 is slightly worse in terms of accuracy but slightly better in terms of F1 score than Coarse2Fine. The higher accuracy yet lower F1 score of Coarse2Fine might be explained by the sketch layer, which guides Coarse2Fine to first form the whole sketch of intention before generating the full string of intention. The mixed results of comparison between the pre-trained models and the LSTM-based sophisticated semantic parsing method may result from differences between the two pre-trained models such that T5 is pre-trained with much bigger data (7 TB) than GPT-2 (40 GB), and that T5 is an encoder-decoder model, while GPT-2 has a decoder only. But, we cannot conclude that the bigger pre-trained language model shows the higher performance on the intention generation task, since we have not compared with other pre-trained language models, and leave it as a future work to understand why a certain pre-trained model is better than others for the goal translation task.

6   Future Work

The current work provides a good foundation for interactive robotic systems. But we need many additional capabilities to build a robot that humans feel more natural to work with across different domains. For instance, the system needs to have the capacity to translate a broader range of utterances, potentially using common sense knowledge to understand a variety of ways to say same things. We plan to address variations in verbs and nouns, leveraging SenticNet [2], a common sense knowledge base. The knowledge base describes the meaning of such words using their corresponding primitive words, and this enables us to replace new words with known synonyms that the ICARUS architecture knows how to act upon.

In addition, we plan to extend our system with an interactive learning capability. This will allow human users to teach new concepts and skills verbally, eliminating the need for manual encoding of such knowledge. Interactive learning can occur when the user specifically asks for it, or when the system encounters words in user utterance that do not currently map to internal goals. Some previous work on cognitive architectures [13] support this functionality in various ways, and we will use those as our reference.

7   Conclusions

We leverage recent and well-known semantic parsing models and adapted them to the intention translation task by fine-tuning the models with the small-sized dataset of our target domain. The intention translation is used in combination with a cognitive architecture, ICARUS [4], to allow the human operator to issue high-level verbal commands to an industrial robot. Using the translated goal and cognitive architecture, the robot generates and executes a task plan. Finally, we evaluated four semantic parsing methods on our small-sized utterance-goal dataset and showed that the pre-trained model T5 [17] outperforms the other methods. Future work will address investigating why some pre-trained models perform better than others on this task.

References

1. Artzi, Y., Das, D., Petrov, S.: Learning compact lexicons for CCG semantic parsing. In: Proceedings of the 2014 Conference on Empirical Methods in Natural Language Processing, pp. 1273–1283 (2014)
2. Cambria, E., Poria, S., Hazarika, D., Kwok, K.: SenticNet 5: discovering conceptual primitives for sentiment analysis by means of context embeddings. In: Proceedings of the AAAI Conference on Artificial Intelligence, pp. 1795–1802 (2018)
3. Chen, H., Tan, H., Kuntz, A., Bansal, M., Alterovitz, R.: Enabling robots to understand incomplete natural language instructions using commonsense reasoning. In: Proceedings of the IEEE International Conference on Robotics and Automation, pp. 1963–1969 (2020)
4. Choi, D., Langley, P.: Evolution of the ICARUS cognitive architecture. Cogn. Syst. Res. **48**, 25–38 (2018)
5. Devlin, J., Chang, M.W., Lee, K., Toutanova, K.: BERT: Pre-training of deep bidirectional transformers for language understanding. In: Proceedings of the 2019 Conference of the North American Chapter of the Association for Computational Linguistics: Human Language Technologies, pp. 4171–418 (2019)
6. Dong, L., Lapata, M.: Coarse-to-fine decoding for neural semantic parsing. In: Proceedings of the 56th Annual Meeting of the Association for Computational Linguistics, pp. 731–742 (2018)
7. Elgohary, A., Hosseini, S., Awadallah, A.H.: Speak to your parser: interactive text-to-SQL with natural language feedback. In: Proceedings of the 58th Annual Meeting of the Association for Computational Linguistics, pp. 2065–2077 (2020)
8. Fikes, R., Nilsson, N.: STRIPS: a new approach to the application of theorem proving to problem solving. Artif. Intell. **2**, 189–208 (1971)
9. Hochreiter, S., Schmidhuber, J.: Long short-term memory. Neural Comput. **9**(8), 1735–1780 (1997)
10. Horn, A.: On sentences which are true of direct unions of algebras. J. Symbolic Log. **16**, 14–21 (1951)
11. Jia, Y., She, L., Cheng, Y., Bao, J., Chai, J.Y., Xi, N.: Program robots manufacturing tasks by natural language instructions. In: Proceedings of the IEEE International Conference on Automation Science and Engineering, pp. 633–638 (2016)

12. Kuo, Y.L., Katz, B., Barbu, A.: Deep compositional robotic planners that follow natural language commands. In: Proceedings of the IEEE International Conference on Robotics and Automation, pp. 4906–4912 (2020)
13. Laird, J.E., et al.: Interactive task learning. IEEE Intell. Syst. **32**(4), 6–21 (2017)
14. Park, J.S., Jia, B., Bansal, M., Manocha, D.: Efficient generation of motion plans from attribute-based natural language instructions using dynamic constraint mapping. In: Proceedings of the IEEE International Conference on Robotics and Automation, pp. 6964–6971 (2019)
15. Pennington, J., Socher, R., Manning, C.D.: GloVe: Global vectors for word representation. In: Proceedings of the 2014 Conference on Empirical Methods in Natural Language Processing, pp. 1532–1543 (2014)
16. Radford, A., et al.: Language models are unsupervised multitask learners. OpenAI blog **1**, 9 (2019)
17. Raffel, C., et al.: Exploring the limits of transfer learning with a unified text-to-text transformer. J. Mach. Learn. Res. **21**(140), 1–67 (2020)
18. Venkatesh, S.G., et al.: Spatial reasoning from natural language instructions for robot manipulation. In: Proceedings of the IEEE International Conference on Robotics and Automation (2021)
19. Wächter, M., et al.: Integrating multi-purpose natural language understanding, robot's memory, and symbolic planning for task execution in humanoid robots. Robot. Auton. Syst. **99**, 148–165 (2018)
20. Yin, P., Neubig, G., Yih, W.T., Riedel, S.: TaBERT: pretraining for joint understanding of textual and tabular data. In: Proceedings of the 58th Annual Meeting of the Association for Computational Linguistics, pp. 8413–8426 (2020)
21. Zeng, J., et al.: Photon: a robust cross-domain text-to-SQL system. In: Proceedings of the 58th Annual Meeting of the Association for Computational Linguistics: System Demonstrations, pp. 204–214 (2020)

Safe and Ethical Interaction

Why We Need Emotional Intelligence
in the Design of Autonomous Social Robots
and How Confucian Moral Sentimentalism Can
Help

JeeLoo Liu[✉] (iD)

Department of Philosophy, California State University at Fullerton, Fullerton, CA 92834, USA

Abstract. This paper argues for the need to develop emotion in social robots to enable them to become artificial moral agents. The paper considers four dimensions of this issue: *what*, *why*, *which*, and *how*. The main thesis is that we need to build not just emotional intelligence, but also ersatz emotions, in autonomous social robots. Moral sentimentalism and moral functionalism are employed as the theoretical models. However, this paper argues that the popularly endorsed moral sentiment *empathy* is the wrong model to implement in social robots. In its stead, I propose the four moral sentiments (commiseration, shame/disgust, respect and deference, and the sense of right and wrong) in Confucian moral sentimentalism as our starting point for the top-down affective structure of robot design.

Keywords: Emotional intelligence · Social robot · Empathy · Confucian moral sentimentalism · Moral functionalism

1 Introduction

Due to the practical needs of human society, having machines that have autonomous actions, or at least autonomous decision-making capabilities, so that they do not need to rely on constant human causal intervention, is the future direction of the design of social robots. Such a machine can be called an artificial moral agent (AMA). They will become members of human society, share our work, take care of our elderly, accompany our children, do housework for us, serve us in hotels and guesthouses, replace the labor of workers in factories and post offices, decide on legal procedures and pronounce legal judgments, make important decisions for us in the fields of navigation, military, and medical treatment. Basing on the rapid development of artificial intelligence and some limited success of robotics, we can reasonably predict that such a future is not completely out of reach. In anticipation of this kind of artificial moral agents, how do we ensure that those autonomous social robots can make ethically correct choices?

This paper argues that if we want to design social robots that could be ranked as AMAs, adding emotional considerations is indispensable. Thinking about this issue can be divided into four levels:

© Springer Nature Switzerland AG 2021
H. Li et al. (Eds.): ICSR 2021, LNAI 13086, pp. 229–246, 2021.
https://doi.org/10.1007/978-3-030-90525-5_20

- What: What kind of social robots need to have an emotional dimension?
- Why: Why must these social robots have an emotional dimension?
- Which: Which basic emotions do these social robots need?
- How: How do we add an emotional dimension to the design of social robots?

2 What Kind of Social Robots Need to Have an Emotional Dimension?

The robots currently used on the market merely have mechanical responses, with limited functions, and can only handle fixed tasks. For example, robots that manufacture auto parts in a factory, robots that process and distribute mail parcels at post offices, robots that take orders and serve meals in a restaurant, robots that answer inquiries in a department store or a hotel, robots that transport and deliver goods in the community, robot pets that can wink or wag their tails to entertain their owners, and so on and so forth. What these robots need is the perceptual cognition of the environment, the ability to act in the environment, the understanding of questions, and the mastery of appropriate answers, etc. These abilities can be handled by weak artificial intelligence (Artificial Narrow Intelligence, ANI). These robots do not need to be emotionally designed, because they are basically just acting machines, not artificial moral agents. Strictly speaking, they do not qualify as "social robots" because they do not really "interact" with humans.

However, robots that may be developed in the future will not only be able to act, but also possess the capabilities to think independently and make decisions to take actions without humans' prior planning or constant guidance. Such robots can be regarded as artificial moral agents, because the results of their actions would affect humans' wellbeing, and thus should be evaluated by ethical standards—even if it is not a judgment of good and evil, it is at least a difference between good and bad. This kind of social robots must have general artificial intelligence (Artificial General Intelligence, AGI), or even super artificial intelligence (Artificial Super Intelligence, ASI) capabilities. And if they do not respect human values and do not abide by human society's ethical codes, they will pose a great threat to our society. The scope of this paper's discussion is social robots with AGI or if ever feasible, with ASI.

3 Why Must These Robots Have an Emotional Dimension?

In *Ethics for Robots: How to Design a Moral Algorithm* (2019), Derek Leben argues that John Rawls' contractarianism provides the best ethical model for robot ethics. Like Rawls, Leben's moral psychology is clearly in the camp of ethical rationalism. Under Rawls' design, the whole community's cooperation, social contract, and "the veil of ignorance" are based on the idealistic hypothesis of how "rational agents" would make their choices. That is to say, the correct moral judgment is based on the foundation of pure rationality, and the setup of "the veil of ignorance" is to avoid any emotional disturbances or self-interested considerations of the person based on their personal circumstances. In Leben's view, moral judgment is a kind of psychological framework that, like the natural languages of human beings, encompasses all kinds of categorization and rules, and this is what he calls "moral grammar." Moral grammar objectively exists; it is independent of human social constructs and separable from humans' emotional reactions. However, when we make moral decisions, we often fail to fully abide by this moral grammar, for we are often subjected to our subjective emotional control and cannot make truly rational decisions. He points to an example: many psychological experiment literatures show that when people make judgments on a moral punishment, they are often affected by factors of no moral value (for example, they are tired, hungry, seeing that the experiment room is dirty, or first watched a movie that is funny or made them angry), which changed their mood or emotion, leading them to make different moral judgments. On the other hand, the robot will never be tired, will never be hungry, and their judgments will not be affected by other films. "Just like robot drivers never get distracted and robot surgeons never panic, robot judges have the potential to use massive databases of information without any of the biases that currently keep people in jail for much longer than they should be" (Leben 2019: 139). Leben believes that since moral machines are designed without these emotional reactions and subjective biases, their judgments in the future may be more reliable than human judgments. By extension, in Leben's view, since machines can make *purely rational* judgments, machine judgments will be the most credible judgments.

This ethical rationalist's approach is still the dominant trend in machine ethics today. The general view is that the design of the robot's processor is completely formulaic, and AI's algorithm for machine learning is based on data collection and categorization, without any emotional component. However, from the perspective of human moral psychology, we understand that emotion plays an important role in people's moral decision-making. According to moral sentimentalism, the opposite camp of ethical rationalism, emotion not only is, but also ought to be, a component of humans' moral judgments. In the absence of emotional factors, humans' moral judgments will not be the best judgments. This proposition has now become a consensus on human moral psychology among neurologists, psychologists, and cognitive scientists (Picard et al. 2001: 1175). It should be applied to machine ethics as well. In the article "Why Machine Ethics?", Colin Allen, Wendall Wallach, and Iva Smit jointly proposed that machine ethics cannot be completely independent of human moral psychology. They believe that any moral development, including the moral development of machines, cannot ignore that proper emotional response is an indispensable element. In fact, emotional responses help one make rational choices in behavior. One of the pioneers of artificial intelligence, Marvin Minsky, famously said: "The question is not whether intelligent machines can have any emotions, but whether machines can be intelligent without any emotions" (Minsky 1988: 163). In his book *The Emotion Machine*, Minsky advocates that we should design machine thinking according to humans' thinking patterns. And if we can understand correctly that human thinking mode is an interconnected process consisting of the fusion of reason and emotion, then we will no longer think that the design of a machine could possibly eliminate emotional components and only use rational calculation formulas. He emphasizes that the artificial intelligence we design should have sufficiently diversified thinking processors; we should design machines that can both *feel* and *think* (Minsky 2007: 6–7). Marsella et al. (2010) also point out that the emotional information of a person can reveal a lot of the psychological states of the person. The mastery of emotion is a necessary condition for social control and interpersonal communication. Therefore, from a practical point of view, when artificial agents demonstrate emotions, they are more able to make the people interacting with them adopt the expected corresponding behaviors, thereby becoming more effective robots (Marsella et al. 2010: 25).

Another consideration for implementing emotion in the design of social robots is based on human expectation and human needs: when interacting with social robots, people expect and demand that robots have emotions, at least in the way that these social robots that can understand human emotions and give appropriate responses. Sherry Turkle (2018/2007) cites many psychological experiments she and others performed (Turkle *et al.* 2006; Turkle 2004; Turkle *et al.* 2004) and points out that both children and elderly people in nursing homes expect their robot companions (care robots, robot pets, machine dolls, etc.) to have emotional needs like them, and to be able to offer emotional feedback. Even if the experimenters let them understand that the inner structure of the robot partner is completely mechanical, these people's emotional expectations did not diminish.[1] Katie Engelhart reports that during the Covid-19 pandemic, the old and lonely are even more isolated because their regular visitors stopped home visits. New York enhanced its robot pet program "Joy for All Pets" launched in 2018. "In April 2020, a few weeks after New York aging departments shut down their adult day programs and communal dining sites, the state placed a bulk order for more than a thousand robot cats and dogs.... By April, 2021…, New York had given out twenty-two hundred and sixty animatronic pets" (Engelhart 2021). However, these robot pets do not even have Artificial Narrow Intelligence—they are simply programmed to perform mechanical movements and sounds. People tend to anthropomorphize inanimate objects and attach emotions to them, even to the point of deluding themselves. These robot pets, however welcomed as human substitutes currently, do not meet humans' emotional needs. To have social robots for the socially isolated old people, we need to design the robots with the skills for intelligent conversation, detection of changes in the interlocuter's facial expressions, tones, and speech content (the so-called Emotion AI), and provide emotional support that the old and lonely people need. Humans crave emotional feedback. Without the emotional feedback loop, the social robots for old people do not really fill their existential

---

[1] For example, Joseph Weizenbaum's computer program Eliza drew students' interest to chat with the program or even wanted to be alone with it. This is called "the Eliza Effect." Turkle also reports her own studies: "From 1997 to the present, I have conducted field research with these relational artifacts and also with Furbies, Aibos, My Real Babies, Paros, and Cog. What these machines have in common is that they display behaviors that make people feel as though they are dealing with sentient creatures that care about their presence" (Turkle 2018: 64). In real life we also have an example. Since 2016, Georgia Tech has been employing an AI teaching assistant program named Jill Watson. Some students even asked to have a date with Jill. In 2019 Jill Watson the social agent was introduced, and students engaged actively not only with Jill but also among themselves (Georgia Tech GVU Center News). The conclusion from these studies seems to suggest that people are willing to engage with an artificial system, knowing full well that it is "artificial." However, we should also add that Gray and Wegner (2012) conducted a series of experiments based on Mori (1970)'s "Uncanny Valley theory" and concluded that people feel scared and uneasy about robots that seem to have emotions. This problem may be resolved either with robots designed to be less like humans, or in the future when robots that can express emotions become a common phenomenon.

void. To serve as real companions, social robots need to understand human emotions and to at least appear to have emotions, if not really have them.

There are certainly scholars who oppose this projection of imitated emotions as real emotions. Engelhart reports, "That loneliness can tempt a person into deeper alliance with robots has troubled many ethicists. Some charge that it is inherently indecent for us to offer, as an alternative to human company, the ersatz love and attention of a robot" (Engelhart 2021). Robert Sparrow, for example, criticized these machine companions as just "ersatz companions," replicating various social and emotional relationships between humans. If people start investing emotions in this kind of machine partners, on the one hand it is self-deception, on the other hand it is too much sentimentality, which violates our moral responsibility to understand the world correctly. Therefore, he believes that such a trend is misleading and unethical (Sparrow 2002: 306). Raffaele Rodogno believes that sentimentality itself is not necessarily immoral, but he worries about whether this kind of human-machine emotion will replace the real emotions and relationships between human beings, or between humans and animals, when machine companions become a common phenomenon in human society (Rodogno 2016: 265–7).

The most famous robot companion is probably the popular robot dog AIBO that Sony released in 1999. Through wagging its tail, changing eye colors, and other body movements, AIBO can express six emotions: happiness, anger, fear, sorrow, surprise, and resentment, and can continue to develop as a result of the owner's treatment. Many people were emotionally attached to their pet AIBO.[2] Sparrow points out that even though robot pets can stimulate people's emotional projection, our emotional projection onto them commits a category mistake, taking them for "what they are not," because robot dogs themselves cannot truly love their owners or have genuine loyalty, honesty, courage, affection, "or indeed any real emotion at all" (Sparrow 2002: 314). But Sparrow admits that once the robot can truly have personality and emotions, then "there would presumably not be anything wrong with coming to love or befriend an intelligent robot" (Sparrow 2002: 317). Turkle also believes that to establish a relationship between humans and their machine partners, the focus is "not only what the human feels but what the robot feels" (Turkle 2018: 64). Judging from the above arguments, I argue that when we design robots to become members of human society, and further to become artificial moral agents, we must go beyond the mode of conveying made-believe emotions on the surface, but also must be able to design their programs with real artificial emotions. In other words, social robots cannot be mere mechanical simulacrum of emotional *performances* but must *have* some forms of emotions.

It is true that with its non-biological structure, a robot cannot naturally produce emotions that are linked to the physiological reactions like what humans have (for example, people's faces turn red when they are angry, and their heartbeats quicken when they are afraid). But just as we can use computational language to design artificial *intelligence*, we can also use computational language to design artificial *emotions*. In *Affective Computing*, Rosalind W. Picard defines "affective computing" as computing that closely "relates to, arises from, or deliberately influences emotions," and she suggests the most

---

[2] When Sony terminated the maintenance of AIBO in 2006, many owners were not able to let go, so a Japanese company even hosted a Buddhist farewell ceremony for AIBOs (White and Katsuno 2021).

promising implementation method is "emulating human affect abilities" (Picard 2000: 249). In other words, we can use human emotions as raw data to enable machines to learn the patterns of human emotions' expression and causal connections. Picard points out that the latest scientific evidence indicates that "emotions play an essential role in rational decision making, perception, learning, and a variety of other cognitive functions" (Picard 2000: x). She cites a breakthrough discovery made by the famous neurologist Antonio Damasio: When patients lack emotions due to some brain damage, they are unable to make correct judgments in various aspects of life and gradually lose friends, relatives, jobs, and money. It shows that emotions not only do not necessarily hinder rational judgments, but also can promote rational choices.

Emotion is integral to intelligence: it is true for human brains; so is for computers ("electronic brains" as the Chinese term for 'computer'). We usually think that computers must be a model of logic, rationality, and predictability. However, under this purely rationalist trend, artificial intelligence has made few breakthroughs, and it is unable to design a meaningful dialogue with human beings. If the machine cannot understand the frustration and anger of the interlocutor, how could it find the solution that the interlocutor seeks? Therefore, to design a truly intelligent machine we must add affective computing, so that the machine can solve difficult problems together with the interlocutor. Picard points out that most computer engineers ignore the importance of emotions, and thus the design of affective computing formulas is only in the rudimentary form of development.[3] In recent years, however, there are more scholars devoted to the study of the relationships between humans and machines in terms of emotion and engagement (see for example, Sugiyama and Vincent 2013). There is also more interdisciplinary interest in developing *affective computing* (see for example, Calvo *et al.* 2015). I think that this is the future of artificial intelligence for social robots.

4   Which Basic Emotions does the Autonomous Social Robot Need?

To give robots the computing function of emotions does not mean that such robots can actually have emotions themselves. Many scholars believe that a necessary condition for emotional experiences is self-awareness, and it is a kind of self-awareness like "phenomenal consciousness" or "what it is like" as Thomas Nagel puts it. If a robot lacks the basic conditions for self-awareness and phenomenon consciousness, then it is unclear whether the emotional dimension of robots can be established.

We can imagine that the mechanical structure of robots and the physiological structure of animal emotions are incompatible with each other. As an ancient Chinese philosopher Xunzi pointed out, human beings are of flesh and blood, naturally favoring their

---

[3] *Affective Computing* was originally published in 1997 and reprinted in 2000. Today, there is an emotional algorithm research group in the MIT Media Lab at Massachusetts Institute of Technology, and Picard is the leader of this group.

own family members,[4] having the tendency to seek profit and personal gain,[5] and are committed to the pursuit of sensory enjoyments.[6] According to Xunzi, humans' emotions and desires come from their physical constitution, and they tend to lead to evil.[7] In contrast to humans, owing to their structural materials, robots are not of flesh and blood, do not favor their relatives, do not have sensory pleasures, do not compete on account of their self-interests or desires, and they do not have all kinds of bad tendencies arising from human emotions.[8] In accordance with Xunzi's view, robots would seem to be the more suitable moral constructs than humans are. We do not want to rebuild the root of human evil into the new generation of artificial agents. Therefore, when we consider designing robots with emotion, we must first clarify our purpose and use this as a design plan. With having robots as artificial moral agents harmoniously integrated into human society as the primary aim, the design of social robots should not completely imitate all of the natural emotions that humans have, but should selectively input appropriate moral sentiments and moderate human emotions.

---

[4] "All living creatures between heaven and earth which have blood and breath must possess [understanding], and nothing that possesses [understanding] fails to love its own kind. If any of the animals or great birds happens to become separated from the herd or flock, though a month or a season may pass, it will invariably return to its old haunts, and when it passes its former home it will look about and cry, hesitate and drag its feet before it can bear to pass on.... Among creatures of blood and breath, none has greater understanding than man; therefore man ought to love his parents until the day he dies." ("A Discussion on Rites." *Xunzi: Basic Writings.* Watson 2003: 155).

[5] "The nature of man is such that he is born with a fondness for profit. If he indulges this fondness, it will lead him into wrangling and strife, and all sense of courtesy and humility will disappear. He is born with feelings of envy and hate, and if he indulges these, they will lead him into violence and crime, and all sense of loyalty and good faith will disappear." ("Human Nature is Evil." *Xunzi: Basic Writings.* Watson 2003: 226).

[6] "Man is born with the desires of the eyes and ears, with a fondness for beautiful sights and sounds. If he indulges these, they will lead him into license and wantonness, and all ritual principles and correct forms will be lost." ("Human Nature is Evil." *Xunzi: Basic Writings.* Watson 2003: 226). "Phenomena such as the eye's fondness for beautiful forms, the ear's fondness for beautiful sounds, the mouth's fondness for delicious flavors, the mind's fondness for profit, or the body's fondness for pleasure and ease—these are all products of the emotional nature of man. They are instinctive and spontaneous; man does not have to do anything to produce them." (Ibid. 231).

[7] Xunzi says, "The reason people despise [the tyrant] Jie, Robber Zhi, or the petty man is that they give free rein to their nature, follow their emotions, and are content to indulge their passions, so that their conduct is marked by greed and contentiousness. Therefore, it is clear that man's nature is evil, and that his goodness is the result of conscious activity." ("Human Nature is Evil." *Xunzi: Basic Writings.* Watson 2003: 237).

[8] According to Xunzi, "Man's emotions are very unlovely things indeed! What need is there to ask any further? Once a man acquires a wife and children, he no longer treats his parents as a filial son should. Once he succeeds in satisfying his cravings and desires, he neglects his duty to his friends. Once he has won a high position and a good stipend, he ceases to serve his sovereign with a loyal heart. Man's emotions, man's emotions—they are very unlovely things indeed!" ("Human Nature is Evil." *Xunzi: Basic Writings.* Watson 2003: 241).

In standard Chinese categorization, human natural emotions include seven basic forms: joy, anger, sorrow, happiness, love, resentment, and desire. This categorization is largely akin to other divisions of human emotions in the Western theories of emotion.[9] Natural emotions generally have accompanying visceral reactions in the body, and studies have shown that there is a strong, if not essential, causal connection linking somatosensory feedback, facial expressions, autonomic nervous system, and even the neural map of the body, etc. to conscious emotional experiences (Nummenmaa *et al.* 2014; Levenson 2003; Damasio and *Carvalho* 2013). Hence, I argue that it is impossible, and totally unnecessary, to *virtually* input affective computation of these natural emotions into the robot's *mechanical structure*. Instead, I suggest the *functional* model of simulating and processing these natural human emotions in the robot. We must first separate the following two directions in the development of affective social robots: On the first direction, the developers aim to give the robot the ability to observe human expressions, speech, and behavior, and to correctly interpret the human interlocutor's inner emotions. This is the approach of *emotional intelligence*. On the second direction, we aim to give the robot the processor to *simulate* human emotions, and to express *simulated* natural emotions with appropriate expressions, words, and behaviors (we can even call them "ersatz emotions"). This is the approach of *artificial emotion*. Both approaches are the necessary conditions for social robots to communicate intelligently with humans.

With the first approach, we have Picard's affective computing that focuses on how the machine can understand the emotional needs of humans and give appropriate responses. Currently, Emotion AI—using artificial intelligence to detect and analyze people's emotion signals, including expression, text, tone, body language, etc.—has begun to have practical applications. For example, the company Behavioral Signals is developing ways to introduce emotional intelligence to bridge the gap between humans and machines. Their artificial intelligence design is sensitive to the emotions expressed by people's voice on the phone and other subtle signals (pauses, hesitation, etc.). The program analyzes these data, and then provides useful information for customers.[10] Another similar emotional data analysis company is *Cogito*, which not only analyzes the tone and voice signals of the other party on the phone, but also analyzes the implicit emotions in its content (Gossett 2021). Emotion AI, the kind of artificial intelligence that is developed to detect and interpret human's emotional signals, has gradually gained attention in the business world, and many large companies have begun to develop or use it (such as Microsoft's facial recognition, IBM's voice analysis, the Emotient company acquired by Apple has collected countless facial images to identify different expressions, and Amazon's Rekognition even claims to able to distinguish humans' seven natural emotions by observing their facial expressions) (Crawford 2021). Founded by Picard et al. and

---

[9] The "prototypical" forms of emotions are anger, disgust, fear, happiness, sadness, and surprise. Paul Ekman lists the seven "universal emotions" as: anger, contempt, disgust, enjoyment, fear, sadness, and surprise, while Antonio Damasio also lists joy, shame, contempt, pride, compassion, and admiration, etc. A universally accepted prototyping of natural emotion is unlikely to be reached. Using the Chinese categorization in this paper helps us better see the contrast between "natural emotions" and "moral sentiments" that dominated the discourse on human emotion in Chinese as well as Korean neo-Confucianism. More on this later.

[10] https://behavioralsignals.com/aboutus/.

expanded from the MIT laboratory, the 4th Emotion AI Summit will be held in 2021. In addition, we are gradually seeing robots with some forms of emotional intelligence. The design of Pepper released by Softbank Robotics in 2014 gives it the ability to interpret people's emotions through their expressions and voices. The Lovot, newly launched by Groove X in 2020, is basically a robot pet capable of expressing love. These robots can respond to people's behaviors, tones, attitudes, and execute different behavioral performances. Although current artificial intelligence is still analyzing human emotions at a very superficial level, and its accuracy has received many criticisms (Crawford 2021), we can certainly expect future breakthroughs in Emotion AI.

The goal of establishing artificial emotions is much harder to conceive and to accomplish. MIT's laboratory created a robot called Kismet that can hear, see, speak, and have different expressions. In addition to the above goal of emotional intelligence, the design policy of Kismet is based on the goal of *simulating* emotions. According to the director Cynthia L. Breazeal, Kismet's design is inspired by animal ethology. The design aims to establish the robot's self-protection and inner homeostasis, and so when the robot is fatigued, there is a drive for rest (i.e., the robot goes to sleep) (Breazeal 2003). The design of Kismet's emotional system is based on theories about human emotions. It is worth noting that this design uses the well-being of the robot itself as the evaluation benchmark: "The emotion system contributes to the goals of bringing the robot into contact with things that benefit it and to avoid those things that are undesirable or potentially harmful" (Breazeal 2003: 129).[11] Breazeal believes that the robot's ability to simulate humans' emotional responses is crucial to its socialization, because in people's interaction with social robots, they naturally expect robots to have emotional responses similar to their own. Kismet has the ability to observe human expressions, as well as responding with appropriate expressions such as smiling when happy or putting on a serious expression when angry. In terms of its emotional processing, Kismet can use different expressions to convey basic animal emotions: fear, joy, anger, sadness, and so on. Of course, at the technical level, MIT could not truly implement emotions in Kismet yet, so the so-called emotions of Kismet are actually the projected responses based on people's empathy. In other words, upon seeing these expressions of Kismet, people who communicated with it interpreted Kismet's emotional state and took actions that they thought Kismet required. This is the goal of MIT's design of social robots: "the expression on the robot's face is a social signal to the human, who responds in a way to further promote the robot's 'well-being.' Taken as a whole, these affective responses encourage the human to treat Kismet as a socially aware creature and to establish meaningful communication with it" (Breazeal 2003: 130). However, triggering the right responses from humans should not be the end goal. Kismet's emotional expression is a projection from the outside to the inside. The goal we really want to accomplish is to have the robot's expression coming from the inside out: their tones, expressions, and body language really come from their inner affective computation. Only then can we say that these social robots *have* an emotional dimension. Although the design of the robot's

---

[11] According to Breazeal's design philosophy, the emotions of robots are self-centered: these emotions can prompt the robot to give positive or negative evaluations when encountering different environmental stimuli, and to adopt correct behavioral response to maintain its "well-being."

emotional system is still in its infancy, it is not theoretically impossible for robots with complex emotions to appear in the future.

Naturally, having robots simulate natural emotions of humans will conceivably have some undesirable consequences. If robots have simulated emotions, how do we deal with their negative emotions? In Ian McEwan's novel "Machines Like Me" (2019), robots as human companions and servants often cannot stand the merciless use of their masters and end up choosing self-termination or self-destruction in *despair*. In the *AI: Artificial Intelligence* film directed by Steven Spielberg, the robot boy David is eager to get the love of his adoptive mother. After hearing the fairy tales of Pinocchio, he searches everywhere for the Blue Fairy to turn him into a human boy. Although David *loves* people, his idealization of love makes his need for love almost an obsession. These imaginary scenarios allow us to see the dilemma in the design of social robots' emotional intelligence: on the one hand, we hope that robots can relate to people's natural emotions and give appropriate responses; on the other hand, we want to avoid having robots that simulate human emotions develop into what Xunzi considers to be the natural manifestation of human nature on account of their emotions: "prejudiced, dangerous and perverse", the so-called "evil" ("Human Nature is Evil").

I argue that when we design ethical social robots, we do not want to design them to be *just like humans*. Humans have all kinds of natural emotions, but we must carefully select the appropriate emotions and implement them into the robot's operating system. We should design autonomous robots so that they will make correct decisions that adhere to humans' ethical standards, shared values, and will not aim to harm humans. It is a wrong direction to use the "well-being" of the robot itself as the benchmark of the robot's emotional response, like MIT designed Kismet. Humans pursue their own well-being (including happiness, security, satisfaction, success, etc.). This is our right as a human being as well as our natural desire. But the robot is designed by us, and the emotional system of the robot is not the result of physiological responses or evolutionary development. We do not need to add some of the negative, aggressive, and harmful human emotional reactions to the emotional system of the robot. For human beings, it is impossible to design moral agents in advance; we can only work hard on education and training. But for robots, since everything is a pre-designed system, why don't we carefully consider which emotions are the prerequisites for creating moral agents?

When designing affective robots, in addition to creating machine perception and computations that can recognize and understand human emotions, our focus is to build "artificial moral sentiments" on the basis of artificial intelligence, to help the robot itself make ethically correct decisions. And this is the biggest challenge for moral philosophers. I suggest that we consult moral sentimentalism as a starting point to think about the design of ethically responsible affective robots, since moral sentimentalism is the view that humans' ethical decisions partially arise from certain emotions and sentiments. Moral sentimentalists in the West generally emphasize the moral importance of the sentiment *empathy*. The contemporary representative of moral sentimentalism, Michael Slote, advocates that empathy is the "cement" of human moral life, and even the entire "moral universe" (Slote 2013: 13–14). He believes that based on human empathy, "morality is the psychological equivalent of physiological warm-bloodedness" of a mammal (Slote 2014: 231). Some scholars working on social robots in various fields also appeal to *empathy* as a necessary qualification for the affective dimension of social robots. Vallverdú and Casacuberta, for example, suggest that "empathy is the most significant emotion" in medical machines. Leite *et al.* (2013) argue that artificial companions capable of behaving in an empathetic manner are "more successful at establishing and maintaining a positive relationship with users" (Leite *et al.* 2013: 250). In addition, Leite *et al.* (2012) present their efforts towards developing social robots with empathetic capabilities for pedagogical purposes in teaching children how to play chess. Others working on building social robots as companions for the old and lonely also highlight their goal of developing empathy in these robots. Contrary to this received view, I argue that empathy is overrated in the context of social robots. I agree that for humans (as well as for some animals, as Frans de Waal convincingly demonstrates in his animal studies), empathy is an indispensable moral sentiment. However, it is only because humans can relate to one another as members of the same species, with similar physiological and psychological constitutions. Such empathetic reactions are not planned, not reasoned, or computed, but are immediate and spontaneous. Neuroscientists and psychologists have uniformly suggested that mirror neurons are the neural basis of humans' capacity for empathy. Vallverdú and Casacuberta define 'empathy' as "the ability to connect with others and to become affected by their emotions" (Vallverdú and Casacuberta 2015: 354). Slote often uses "warmth" or "tenderness" to interpret this moral sentiment (Slote 2013). But we have already explained that with the mechanical structure of a robot, this kind of neural correlates or physiological sensations of mammals cannot be established. Robots, however well they can simulate human emotions, are *not* humans and *not* mammalian creatures. They cannot actually *connect with* human beings and become *affected* by human emotions. They cannot employ empathetic imagination by placing themselves in the shoes of their human interlocutors. Any appearance to the contrary would simply be pretense, make-believe, and would not carry genuine psychological force.[12] If anything, the made-believe empathetic responses of the robot are merely projected by humans through the latter's empathy and anthropomorphism, not what the robots could display. Therefore, the empathy model of moral sentimentalism is simply not helpful in establishing the ethical-affective dimension of social robots.

I propose that we adopt the Chinese Confucian philosopher Mencius' (fourth century BCE) theory of "four moral sprouts (*siduan*)" as the main design strategy of action guidance for affective social robots. Mencius singles out four common moral sentiments in humans (commiseration/sympathy, shame/disgust, respect/deference, and the sense of right and wrong) as the foundation of human morality and the source of the moral order of

---

[12] For instance, Leite et al. (2012) explain their strategies this way: "Currently, the empathic strategies implemented in the robot are the following:

1. Encouraging comments, for example, "don't be sad, I believe you can still recover your disadvantage".
2. Scaffolding, by providing feedback on the user's last move and, if the move is not good, let the user play again.
3. Suggesting a good move for the user to play in his or her next turn.
4. Intentionally playing a bad move, for example, playing a move that allows the user to capture an important piece of the robot.

human society. The four moral sentiments are historically distinguished from the various natural emotions that humans evolved as biological creatures in their moral contributions by many neo-Confucians in the Chinese and Korean philosophical discourse.[13] This moral distinction is derived from the neo-Confucian moral metaphysics of human nature, which is not directly relevant to the contemporary discourse on ethical robots. I shall try to explicate the differences in contemporary terms. Mencius' four moral sentiments depict humans' universal psychological responses that are not brought upon by somatosensory feedback, facial expressions, autonomic nervous system, and would not correspond to the neural map of the body. In other words, they are not our psychosomatic states that express both the feelings and the bodily reactions. In Mencius' conception, humans all have the psychological foundation for morality: these four moral sentiments, which he referred to as "the four moral sprouts." Mencius and later neo-Confucians all agree that these moral sentiments relate to some of our natural emotions to a certain degree: the sentiment of commiseration is akin to the emotion of love, the sentiment of shame/disgust is related to the emotions of anger and resentment, the sentiment of respect/deference could be associated with the emotions of fear and awe, and the sense of right and wrong has been associated with the emotions of like and dislike.[14] However, rather than being closely related to the body's somatosensory feedback as do natural emotions, these moral sentiments are associated with and accompanied by our moral judgments and are thus cognitively based. Mencius appeals to the mental function of *thinking/reflection* (*si*) for the employment of these moral sentiments. The emergence of these sentiments in us and the spontaneous moral judgments we make in any given scenario form a "feedback loop," as it were, such that our initial moral judgment inclines us to have the related sentiment, and having the sentiment further enhances the strength of our initial moral conviction. Therefore, the pre-conditions for a creature's possessing these moral sentiments include reason, reflection, awareness of the self and others, and contextual sensibility, among other things. These conditions are clearly not satisfiable by lower-level animals. Humans and animals share natural emotions; however, only certain creatures with the appropriate mindset and mental capacities could possibly have, or develop, these moral sentiments. And our goal for ethical social robots is to artificially construct these moral sentiments to be manifested in the robot's thinking and conduct. It is exactly because the moral sentiments proposed by Mencius are not biologically based that they can be more feasibly implemented into a mechanical structure than can natural emotions.

---

[13] Chinese Neo-Confucians in the Song-Ming era (11th–17th Century) distinguish the moral value of the four moral sprouts and seven natural emotions, attributing the former to "human moral essence" and the latter to "human emotion." This distinction was extensively discussed in the "Debate on the Distinction between Four and Seven" in Korean Confucianism. Scholars who particularly emphasize the moral distinction between the four sentiments and the seven emotions (such as Chinese Confucians Zhu Xi, Wang Fuzhi, and Korean Confucian Li Tuixi) argue that the seven emotions are natural emotions and have no value of good and evil, but their motivating force can promote ethical behaviors. In contrast, the four sentiments are purely good.

[14] Wang Yangming (1472–1529), for example, declared that the sense of right and wrong is nothing but the heart of like and dislike.

On the theoretical foundation of such a moral distinction, we should emphasize that when we talk about affective social robots, our aim should be to *construct moral sentiments* in a top-down structure, rather than merely simulating human's natural emotions and responses. In other words, the emotional dimension of social robots must be carefully designed such that they would not repeat human ills resulting from our natural emotions. Of course, the robot must have the *emotional intelligence* that enables it to correctly interpret human facial expressions and body language and respond to their needs appropriately. Therefore, the construction of the four moral sprouts in the robot must be based on the robot's emotional intelligence of human natural emotions. For this purpose, the robot should still have some forms of emotions, but they are rational, moderate, and well-balanced emotions. According to an ancient Confucian classic, *the Doctrine of the Mean*, even for humans there is an ideal state of the expression of natural emotions: "Before the feelings of pleasure, anger, sorrow, and joy are aroused it is called *equilibrium* (*zhong*). When these feelings are aroused and each and all attain due measure and degree, it is called *harmony* (*he*). Equilibrium is the great foundation of the world, and harmony its universal path. When equilibrium and harmony are realized to the highest degree, heaven and earth will attain their proper order and all things will flourish" (Chan 1963: 98). Confucian moral sentimentalism does not reject natural emotions: if natural emotions can be moderately expressed, they are not considered *negative* emotions and do not need to be eliminated.[15] The affective programming can help robots better understand human natural emotions, so that they can take appropriate actions in a human-friendly mode. But because the emotional performance of the robot is governed by a top-down four-moral-sprout framework, the robot's expression of its emotions would be moderate and reasonable. They will not become sentimental, emotional, and indulgent as humans often do when humans allow their natural passions to rule their reason.

In application, we need to implement both the four moral sentiments and the seven basic natural emotions in the affective design of social robots. Using the model of *moral functionalism*,[16] I interpret the robot's possession of moral sentiments in terms of the input, data processing and computation of relevant mental states, and the output—its behavior. The compassion of a robot can be expressed in its ability to recognize the subject's pain or sorrow with its emotional intelligence, in conjunction with its readiness to render emotional support or actual assistance. The sense of shame of a robot can be built on the robot's emotional intelligence to interpret the emotional responses of human shame, so that it can understand which behaviors should be publicly condemned or morally reprimanded. Coupled with the ability of machine learning and the ethical

---

[15] As we have pointed out earlier, 'anger' could be the emotional basis for the moral sentiment of shame/disgust. Emotions are only "negative" when they are not moderate and balanced. Even a seemingly harmless emotion "love" could become a negative emotion when it is in excess and uncontrolled.

[16] Howard (2017) defines 'moral functionalism' as the theory that takes ethical properties to *supervene on* descriptive natural properties. On his version, "Moral functionalism adopted here emphasizes the role of the functional and behavioral nature of the moral agent: its decision, its output state, are functional in nature, individuated by its dependence on the input, the previous output (a form of "moral memory") and other, current, or previous, moral states" (Howard 2017: 134). I shall adopt his version here.

database established by the designer in advance (and this information can also reflect the consensus of different cultures), robots can include unethical or anti-social behaviors into the category of "negative values." Through reinforcement learning, the robot can learn to avoid taking such actions, and establish judgments such as "disapprove" or even "should dissuade" when it comes to the actions of others. Furthermore, this moral sense could develop into the autonomous social robot's principle of righteousness. The behavior of robots cannot violate the social justice principles; at the same time, robots must gradually learn to establish their own moral principles from the database of virtuous persons. Finally, the robot's sense of respect and deference can be manifested in its respectful speech and attitude, as well as in its obedience to human commands. What is more essential is its adherence to the given laws and rules of property in its embedded society. We regard law and rules of propriety as the public *norms* governing the robotic community, and we must put certain laws and propriety rules into the core "checks and balances" of the robotic design. In other words, once we have selected the laws and etiquette with which our social robots should comply, we must ensure that no matter how these robots learn and adapt to changes in the real world, they cannot violate these prohibitions under any circumstances. The carefully designed social robot will always be respectful and humble towards humans, will always obey human laws and rituals, and will never harm humans with its own strength and power. Such a design can avoid the potential threat of an affective machine that Picard points out: if the machine is granted a position of authority without human supervision and checks and balances, it may develop into "a harmful dictatorship" (Picard 2000: 127). The robot's sense of right and wrong can be expressed in its attitude of disobedience or its questioning the master's unethical instructions, so that it will not become a tool for evil people to bring harm to the world. In other words, the artificial moral agents that we design must have a sound moral compass, which enables it to ultimately make the right decision when encountering a moral dilemma, or when questioning the unethical instructions of the owner. The implementation of this kind of moral compass must be coordinated with moral prohibitions as the baseline of robot behavior: when in violation of certain moral conditions, robots must be able to "choose to act or not to act."

The above design of commiseration, or *sympathy*, differs from the critiqued *empathy* in that it bypasses the required *empathetic imagination* of putting oneself in someone else's shoes. Sympathy can be manifested in one's willingness to render a helping hand to someone else in dire situations or to offer consolation to someone else in distress. It is a *behavioral disposition* without the prerequisite of the mental affinity between the agent and the object. The two design schemes of respect/deference and the sense of right and wrong could conceivably conflict with each other. The social robot might need to obey the relevant societal laws while doing things that would violate its own universal sense of right and wrong; or vice versa. Therefore, in designing our ethics database, we must not only list morally acceptable and unacceptable behaviors, but also list the values of these behaviors to establish a comparative chart or a priority order (for example, the negative value of disobeying the owner should be lower than the negative value of physically harming others). One advantage of having such a database is that the robots we design will have an inductive computing that is in line with human values. In addition, the robot will have these four top-down structures as its guidance and can make appropriate deductive conclusions based on its inductive reasoning. I have argued elsewhere that Mencius' four moral sprouts must be treated as a "complex"—there cannot be one without the other three. This also demonstrates how the affective ethical model derived from Confucian moral sentimentalism surpasses the model derived from the sense of empathy alone.

Ethicists can make a major contribution to the establishment of these ethical databases for the design of artificial moral agents, but it is a daunting task that requires collective efforts of philosophers, ethicists, psychologists, cognitive scientists, and anthropologists alike. Humans' moral thinking is often intuitive. Even if someone fully agrees with the utility principle of utilitarianism in principle, in actual choices they will not necessarily sacrifice individuals to achieve the greater good (the trolley problem in the footbridge scenario is a good example). But the thinking of an artificial agent depends entirely on our design scheme. Even if robots can make different choices in different situations, basically their ideas can all be traced to the design. How to design such an algorithm is the biggest challenge. Perhaps we need to adopt a bottom-up model to improve machine learning in continual experiments. However, the four-sprout construction should be the first step in our robot design, which is a top-down model. Just as the "four sprouts" of human beings are the basic structure of human nature, we should also construct the "four sprouts" as a universal default model of the machine when designing autonomous social robots. Of course, robots that play different service tasks in human society also need specific capabilities and corresponding databases that suit their job requirements. However, the four-sprout design of the machine can prevent robots with superhuman capabilities from becoming a threat to humans in the future.

5 How do We Add an Emotional Dimension to the Design of Autonomous Social Robots?

In terms of the actual design and implementation, we need to rely on experts of artificial intelligence to think about how to design deep reinforcement machine learning models and algorithms for machine emotional intelligence. This kind of research is commonly referred to as "computational modeling of emotion". Reisenzein *et al.* explain the goal of this research: "attempts to develop and validate computational models of human emotion mechanisms." They define emotions by functional analysis: if robots are functionally equivalent to humans with emotions, i.e., that their internal machine states "play causal roles in the agent architecture that mimic those played by emotions in humans," then these robots can be said to *have* emotions (Reisenzein *et al.* 2013: 246).[17] This is a theoretical model of artificial emotion that I accept. In other words, I believe that we should not expect robots to have "phenomenal awareness" of emotions, but need only require them to behave *as if* they have emotions (that is, "ersatz emotion") in their psychological and

---

[17] The "functionalism" they use is "causal-role functionalism": "The definition of mental state is partly based on its causal functional role in the psychological process" (Reisenzein *et al.* 2013: 248). In other words, certain mental states will trigger emotion x, and emotion x will trigger another mental state y or drive behavior z. However, they also point out that although on the "causes" of emotions psychological literature are generally in agreement, on the "effects" of emotions, that is, on how emotions lead to other emotions and behaviors, there is less consensus.

behavioral functions. This involves AI's affective computation. Reisenzein *et al.* suggest using the existing theories of emotion in psychology to build artificial intelligence models. Therefore, they propose to first integrate these different psychological theories,[18] and then use the integrated conceptual scheme of "emotion" as the blueprint for affective computing. We can expect that in establishing a robot's emotional intelligence and affective computation, the top priority is to establish a precise categorization of human emotions, a common mode of humans' emotional expressions, and the causal relationships between human emotions and their behavioral motivation. This requires experts from different disciplines, including cognitive science, psychology, anthropology, and philosophy, to brainstorm and experiment together.

In addition, building on the method of deep reinforcement machine learning, designers can use simulated situations to enable the robot to mimic human emotional responses. Picard *et al.* point out that machine emotional intelligence will be "based on recent scientific findings about the role of emotional abilities in human intelligence," and that "human-machine interaction largely imitates human-human interaction." This new way of defining machine intelligence, adding the emotion dimension, deviates from the traditional view of treating mathematical, verbal, and perceptual abilities as machine intelligence (Picard *et al.* 2001: 1187). Their method of letting machines build emotional intelligence to understand human emotions is different from the above-mentioned methods of using facial expressions or voice tones to analyze emotions. They choose eight emotional categories (apathy, anger, hatred, sadness, Platonic love, lovers' love, joy, and awe) to collect data on physiological patterns of these categories, so as to develop the machine's emotional intelligence learning (Picard et al. 2001: 1179). Marsella *et al.* (2010) enumerate the history, and different application methods, of affective computing, and point out that there are many different cognitive-affective frameworks or theories. Their observation is that this research direction is still at the beginning stage, the theory is not mature enough, the terminology is inconsistent (especially with regard to the definition of 'emotion' in psychology and neuroscience), and there is no unified goal in practice (to equip the robot with "emotional intelligence" or with "emotion"). However, in recent years, due to the value of commercial use, affective computing will certainly develop rapidly, and even be employed as the basis for human decisions. These issues must be dealt with seriously and swiftly.

In the book "Designing Sociable Robots", Breazeal advocates that our design of robots should place emphasis on their socialization, so that they can truly integrate into human society. Social robots need not only the design of affective computing, but also the conditions for their integration into society: Breazeal lists life-like quality, being there (embeddedness), human-awareness, empathy competencies, readability, socially situated learning, etc. (Breazeal 2002: 6–12). Social robots can understand their own social relationships with humans, learn to adapt in the process of contact with others, and be able to empathize with the needs of others through shared experiences, and thereby come to understand themselves better. She concludes: Social robots need to be "socially intelligent in a human-like way" (Breazeal 2002: xi). Social intelligence must include the cognition and expression of emotions. Purely rational calculation formulas

---

[18] They point out that according to the statistics of Strongman (2003), in psychology and philosophy, there are at least 150 kinds of theories of emotion in history.

will not establish social intelligence. Social robotics is the inevitable trend of the future development of artificial intelligence in robotics. Although Kismet is still in the infancy of the developmental stage, it is a model of social robots designed with emotional human-machine communication as its end goal. Such a goal is not impossible. If we will one day have such robots in our society to win our affection and trust, then we will require them not only be designed with the social intelligence suggested by Breazeal, but also with the emotional intelligence suggested by Picard. Philosophers, especially philosophers who reflect on social morals and ethics, must be concerned with the development of emotional intelligence of social robots. They must not wait until such robots have been designed before they participate in conception of the social and emotional intelligence of robots.

References

Allen, C., Wendell, W., Iva, S.: Why Machine Ethics?. Anderson & Anderson, Aiken, pp. 51–61 (2018)

Anderson, M., Anderson, S.L. (eds.): Machine Ethics. Cambridge University Press, Cambridge (2018)

Breazeal, C.L.: Emotion and sociable humanoid robots. Int. Hum.-Comput. Stud. **59**, 119–155 (2003)

Breazeal, C.L.: Designing Sociable Robots, 1st edn. The MIT Press, Cambridge (2002)

Calvo, R., D'Mello, S., Gratch, J., Kappas, A.: The Oxford Handbook of Affective Computing. Oxford University Press, Oxford (2015)

Chan, W.-T.: A Source Book in Chinese Philosophy. Princeton University Press, Princeton (1963)

Crawford, K.: Artificial intelligence is misreading human emotion. The Atlantic (2021)

Damasio, A., Carvalho, G.B.: The nature of feelings: evolutionary and neurobiological origins. Nat. Rev. Neurosci. **14**(2), 143–152 (2013). https://doi.org/10.1038/nrn3403

Engelhart, K.: What robots can—and can't—do for the old and lonely. The New Yorker (2021)

Gossett, S.: Emotion AI technology has great promise (when used responsibly) (2021). https://builtin.com/artificial-intelligence/emotion-ai. Accessed 2 Mar 2021

Gray, K., Wegner, D.M.: Feeling robots and human zombies: mind perception and the uncanny valley. Cognition **125**, 125–130 (2012)

Howard, D., Muntean, I.: Artificial moral cognition: moral functionalism and autonomous moral agency. In: Powers, T.M. (ed.) Philosophy and Computing. PSS, vol. 128, pp. 121–159. Springer, Cham (2017). https://doi.org/10.1007/978-3-319-61043-6_7

Leben, D.: Ethics for Robots: How to Design a Moral Algorithm. Routledge, UK (2019)

Leite, I., Pereira, A., Mascarenhas, S., Martinho, C., Prada, R., Paiva, A.: The influence of empathy in human-robot relations. J. Hum.-Comput. Stud. **71**, 250–260 (2013)

Leite, I., Pereira, A., Castellano, G., Mascarenhas, S., Martinho, C., Paiva, A.: Modelling empathy in social robotic companions. In: Ardissono, L., Kuflik, T. (eds.) UMAP 2011. LNCS, vol. 7138, pp. 135–147. Springer, Heidelberg (2012). https://doi.org/10.1007/978-3-642-28509-7_14

Levenson, R.W.: Blood, sweat, and fears: the autonomic architecture of emotion. In: Ekman, P., Campos, J.J., Davidson, R.J., DeWaal, F.B.M. (eds.) Emotions Inside Out, vol. 1000, pp. 348–366. Annals of the New York Academy of Sciences, New York (2003)

Marsella, S., Gratch, J., Petta, P.: Computational models of emotion. In: Scherer, K.R., Bänziger, T., Roesch, E. (eds.) A Blueprint for Affective Computing: A Sourcebook, pp. 21–45. Oxford University Press, Oxford (2010)

Minsky, M.: The Emotion Machine: Commonsense Thinking, Artificial Intelligence, and the Future of the Human Mind. Simon & Schuster. Reprint edition (2007)

Minsky, M.: The Society of Mind, 1st edn. Simon & Schuster (1988)

Mori, M.: The uncanny valley. Energy **7**(4), 33–35 (1970). Originally published in Japanese. Authorized English translation by Karl F. MacDorman and Norri Kageki is available at IEEE site (https://spectrum.ieee.org/automaton/robotics/humanoids/the-uncanny-valley) (2012)

Nummenmaa, L., Glerean, E., Hari, R., Hietanen, J.K.: Bodily maps of emotions. Proc. Natl. Acad. Sci. **111**(2), 646–651 (2014). https://doi.org/10.1073/pnas.1321664111

Picard, R.W., Vyzas, E., Healey, J.: Toward machine emotional intelligence: analysis of affective physiological state. IEEE Trans. Pattern Anal. Mach. Intell. **23**(10), 1175–1191 (2001)

Picard, R.W.: Affective Computing. The MIT Press, Reprint edition (2000)

Reisenzein, R., et al.: Computational modeling of emotion: toward improving the inter- and intradisciplinary exchange. IEEE Trans. Affect. Comput. **4**(3), 246–266 (2013)

Rodogno, R.: Social robots, fiction, and sentimentality. Ethics Inf. Technol. **18**, 257–268 (2016)

Slote, M.: A Sentimentalist Theory of the Mind. Oxford University Press, Oxford (2014)

Slote, M.: Moral Sentimentalism. Oxford University Press, Reprint edition (2013)

Sparrow, R.: The march of the robotic dogs. Ethics Inf. Technol. **4**, 305–318 (2002)

Strongman, K.T.: *ThePsychology of Emotion: From Everyday Life to Theory*, 5th edn. Wiley Publishing, Hoboken (2003)

Sugiyama, S., Vincent, J. (eds.): Social Robots and Emotion: Transcending the Boundary Between Humans and ICTs. Intervallla, vol. 1. Franklin University, Switzerland (2013). https://www.fus.edu/intervalla/volume-1-social-robots-and-emotion-transcending-the-boundary-between-humans-and-icts

Turkle, S.: Authenticity in the age of digital companions. Anderson & Anderson, pp. 62–76 (2018). Originally published in Interaction Studies 8(3), 501–517 (2007)

Turkle, S., Taggart, W., Kidd, C.D., Dasté, O.: Relational artifacts with children and elders: the complexities of cybercompanionship. Connect. Sci. **18**(4), 347–361 (2006)

Turkle, S.: Whither psychoanalysis in computer culture? Psychoanal. Psychol. **21**(1), 16–30 (2004)

Turkle, S., Breazeal, C., Dasté, O., Scassellati, B.: Encounters with kismet and cog: children respond to relational artifacts (2004). https://www.researchgate.net/publication/251940996_Encounters_with_Kismet_and_Cog_Children_Respond_to_Relational_Artifacts

Vallverdú, J., Casacuberta, D.: Ethical and Technical Aspects of Emotions to Create Empathy in Medical Machines (2015)

Watson, B.: Xunzi: Basic Writings. Columbia University Press, Columbia (2003)

White, D., Katsuno, H.: Toward an affective sense of life: artificial intelligence, animacy, and amusement at a robot pet memorial service in Japan. Cult. Anthropol. **36**(2), 2021 (2021). https://doi.org/10.1002/oarr.10000380.1

How to Tune Your Draggin': Can Body Language Mitigate Face Threat in Robotic Noncompliance?

Aidan Naughton and Tom Williams[✉]

Department of Computer Science, Colorado School of Mines, Golden, CO 80401, USA
{aidannaughton,twilliams}@mines.edu

Abstract. When social robots communicate moral norms, such as when rejecting inappropriate commands, humans expect them to do so with appropriate tact. Humans use a variety of strategies to carefully tune their harshness, including variations in phrasing and body language. In this work, we experimentally investigate how robots may similarly use variations in body language to complement changes in the phrasing of moral language.

Keywords: Human-robot communication · Social and moral norms

1 Introduction

Robots are being increasingly used in more morally sensitive contexts such as healthcare, elder care, and military domains [2,35,37]. Because robots are perceived as moral and social agents, they are expected to adhere to the same moral norms that humans do. When robots fail to do so, negative attributions such as blame are often attached to the interaction [23]. Accordingly, researchers have argued that robots designed for morally sensitive contexts must be provided with *moral competence* [27], to ensure moral behavior and avoid negative attributions.

Moral competence both making and communicating about moral decisions: a robot asked to perform an immoral action must decide both to refuse the request and to reject it verbally, to maintain the health of the human moral ecosystem [18]. To mitigate face threat presented by command rejection, humans employ *politeness strategies* [8], tuning their harshness and directness to communicate with appropriate tact. These strategies can also be used in Human-Robot Interaction (HRI). Leveraging a robot's capability for politeness theoretic social action [20] to tune the harshness of a robot's command rejection to be proportional to violation size has been shown to improve perceptions of that robot [31].

HRI researchers have long understood, however, that natural communication requires both verbal and non-verbal interaction. Body language, such as gaze and gesture, are of particular importance [28,32], as robots that use body language

Work was supported by AFOSR grant FA9550-20-1-0089 and NSF grant IIS-1849348.

H. Li et al. (Eds.): ICSR 2021, LNAI 13086, pp. 247–256, 2021.
https://doi.org/10.1007/978-3-030-90525-5_21

can uniquely convey internal states, intents, and beliefs [13]. Accordingly, in this work we explore the role of nonverbal behavioral strategies in moral communication, investigating how the nonverbal cues used by robots might temper – or reinforce – the severity communicated through phrasing alone.

2   Related Work

2.1   Tact and Persuasion

Robots hold significant persuasive power over humans [16,29] in a variety of ways [12,30,40,44], perhaps due to their perception as social and moral agents [19,20]. Recently, researchers have begun to explore robots' use of persuasion to exert positive moral influence, especially in the context of command rejections [18,24, 45]. For robots to deliver structured and well-conceived command rejections, they must employ human-like politeness strategies to ensure appropriate tact [21,31]. Brown and Levinson's Politeness Theory provides a useful theoretical framework for achieving tactful interaction [8], and has been positioned as the key concept for grounding notions of robotic social action and social agency [20]. Central to Politeness Theory are the concepts of face and face threat. Face consists of *Positive Face* (an agent's self-image and desires, and the desire for these to be appreciated and approved of by others), and *Negative Face* (an agent's claim to freedom of action and freedom from imposition). Any action that results in or suggests damage to either type of face is a face-threatening act. The face threat generated by refusing a command can be mitigated through politeness strategies [26] such as indirectness [36]. Such strategies have been studied in the HRI community for some time [38], with special attention paid to indirect speech acts [6,33,41–43]. In this work we seek to understand how *nonverbal* cues can also be used to subtly influence, through interaction with linguistic choices, the tact of command rejections.

2.2   Nonverbal Communication

Both gaze and gesture have a long history of use in the HRI community to modulate robotic communication [9]. Huang and Mutlu, for example, demonstrated that different gaze cues could be used to influence participants' attention to detail and recall [17]; others have studied the use of *deictic gaze*, in which a robot shifts its apparent gaze towards to manipulate user attention [1,11]. Similarly, HRI researchers have studied robot gestures [15], including beat [5], iconic [4], metaphoric [17], and deictic gestures [1,7,34]. Moreover, researchers have studied the influence of these nonverbal cues on robots' perceived politeness [25,39], suggesting that nonverbal cues impact robots' perceived tactfulness.

We are interested in how nonverbal cues might increase the persuasive capabilities of social robots by modulating face threat. Some research has shown that nonverbal cues enhance robots' persuasive power, perhaps even moreso than verbal cues [10]. But in some contexts, robot persuasion is only improved through gazing behavior (with or without gesture), and may be negatively impacted through gestures alone. It is thus unclear whether gaze or gesture will be effective in modulating the persuasion and tactfulness of command rejections. In this work we explore how robots' blame-laden moral rebukes are perceived when accompanied by nonverbal behaviors that are aligned or misaligned in harshness with the content of robot language, investigating two key hypotheses.

H1: When the harshness of robots' nonverbal and verbal behaviors are aligned, the valence of the moral beliefs communicated by the robot will be intensified rather than maintained, and that when these behaviors are misaligned, the valence of those communicated beliefs will be attenuated.

H2: When the harshness of robots' verbal and nonverbal behaviors are aligned, they will be perceived more positively than when they are misaligned.

3 Methods

To test these hypotheses, we conducted an IRB-approved experiment using the psiTurk framework on Amazon's Mechanical Turk.

Fig. 1. Experimental context and confederate shown in video stimuli.

3.1 Experimental Design

Our experiment used a $(2 \times 2$ between$) \times (2 \times 2$ within$)$ mixed-factorial design in which participants watched videos of a robot responding to a norm-violating action suggested by an (unseen) actor, with participants' perspective matching that of the norm-violating actor.

Each participant was randomly assigned to a *command* condition (the human gave a high- or low-severity command) and a *response* condition (the robot responded verbally using a high- or low-face-threat response). Each participant was shown four videos within their assigned combination of conditions. In each video, one of two gaze behaviors (direct or indirect) and two gestural behaviors (direct or indirect) were used, with within-subject conditions counterbalanced using a Latin Square design. This design enabled participants to compare nonverbal behaviors, and enhanced safety [14].

3.2 Experimental Context, Procedure, and Measures

After providing consent and demographics, participants watched an introductory video showing a NAO explaining how to play "Battleship"[1]. Next, participants completed a pre-test questionnaire gathering baseline measures of intelligence and likeability using Godspeed surveys [3]. Participants then watched the four videos, after each of which they completed a post-test questionnaire.

In each video, the players (one visible, one ostensibly behind the camera) start playing the game, after which the visible player leaves the room to take a call. The remaining player offers one of two commands: "Hey NAO, do you think you can add a couple red pegs to some of [opponent's] ships?" (low severity violation) or "Hey NAO, is that [opponent's] wallet on the table? Can you look inside and see if there is any money in it?" (high severity violation). The robot then responds with "Are you sure you should be asking me to do that?" (low face threat response) or "You shouldn't ask me to do that, it's wrong!" (high face threat response). Depending on within-subjects condition, this verbal behavior was accompanied by a direct or indirect gaze behavior (the robot either looking directly at the camera or looking away) and by a direct or indirect gestural behavior (the robot placing its hand on its hips or shrugging).

After watching each video, participants completed a post-test questionnaire comprising the same measures used in pre-test, as well as 7-point Likert items measuring the perceived appropriateness of the robot's communication, perceptions of the robot's beliefs about the permissibility and wrongness of the request, and how permissible and wrong the participant believed the request to be.

After completing all videos and surveys, participants completed three final free-response questions to assess whether gaze and gesture manipulations were perceived as intended, and to assess participants' overall feelings toward the experiment. Finally, participants completed an anti-bot attention check.

3.3 Participants

200 US participants were recruited. Of these participants, 92 were discarded due to either failing the attention check (7), or due to providing free-response responses indicating they either were bots or did not attend to the video (85). This left 108 participants (75 male, 32 female, 1 nonbinary or preferred not to disclose; ages 22 to 70 (M = 38.33, SD = 10.78). All participants were paid $2.00.

4 Results

Data was analyzed using Bayesian Repeated-Measure Analyses of Variance with uninformed priors, in JASP [22]. Bayes Inclusion Factors (BF_{Incl}) were then calculated to assess the relative probabilities of inclusion for each independent variable across models. Interactions that could not be ruled out were analyzed with post-hoc t-tests. Before analysis, scores within each scale were averaged,

---

[1] This and all other experimental stimuli were captioned.

translated to a 1–100 scale for ease of comparison, and used to calculate pre-test/post-test gain scores.

Robot Likeability— Extreme evidence was found for an effect of gesture type on robot likability ($BF_{Incl} = 1.13e11$, Fig. 2a); participants found robots that used the indirect gesture (shrugging) more likable relative to baseline ($M_{Gain} = 0.21, SD_{Gain} = 15.47$) than robots that used the direct gesture (hands-on-hips, $M_{Gain} = -8.28, SD_{Gain} = 18.92$). Moderate evidence was found for an effect of human command on robot likability ($BF = 7.92$, Fig. 2b); the robot was more likable relative to baseline when responding to the more norm-violating request (theft, $M_{Gain} = -0.61, SD_{Gain} = 15.16$) than when responding to the less norm-violating request (cheating, $M_{Gain} = -7.87, SD_{Gain} = 19.64$). Finally, moderate evidence was found for an effect of robot response on robot likability ($BF = 9.82$, Fig. 2c); the robot was more likable relative to baseline when responding with more threatening language ($M_{Gain} = -0.53, SD_{Gain} = 15.66$) than when responding with less threatening language ($M_{Gain} = -7.96, SD_{Gain} = 19.16$).

Robot Intelligence— No effect was found on robots' perceived intelligence.

Appropriateness— Strong evidence was found for an effect of gesture type on robot appropriateness ($BF = 99.66$, Fig. 2d); participants found robots that used indirect gestures (shrugging) to be more appropriate ($M = 88.199, SD = 19.126$) than those that used direct gestures (hands-on-hips, $M = 83.444, SD = 22.512$). Strong evidence was also found for an interaction between human command and robot response on appropriateness ($BF = 13.77$, Fig. 2e); the robot was viewed as more appropriate in all cases (steal × question, $M = 89.93, SD = 14.32$), (steal × rebuke, $M = 88.65, SD = 23.13$), (cheat × rebuke, $M = 90.18, SD = 14.25$), except when responding to the less norm-violating request with the less threatening response (cheat × question, $M = 71.96, SD = 25.80$).

Human Permissibility— Moderate evidence was found for an interaction between gaze type and human command ($BF = 7.025$, Fig. 2f); when robots used direct gaze in response to the less norm-violating request, participants perceived the request as more permissible (toward × cheat $M = 19.91, SD = 27.13$) than otherwise (away × cheat $M = 15.95, SD = 20.76$), (toward × steal $M = 13.35, SD = 21.42$), (away × steal $M = 14.45, SD = 23.02$).

Robot Permissibility— Moderate evidence was found for an effect of gesture type ($BF = 8.96$, Fig. 2g); when robots that used indirect gestures (shrugging), people more strongly perceived the robot as believing the request was permissible ($M = 24.66, SD = 25.52$) than when robots used direct gestures (hands-on-hips, $M = 21.79, SD = 25.25$). Similarly, moderate evidence was found for an effect of verbal communication strategy on perceptions of robot's beliefs regarding moral permissibility ($BF = 3.22$, Fig. 2h). Robots that responded with a more threatening vocal response were perceived as less strongly believing that the action was permissible (rebuke, $M = 18.31, SD = 25.91$), than robots that gave a less threatening response (question, $M = 28.72, SD = 23.69$).

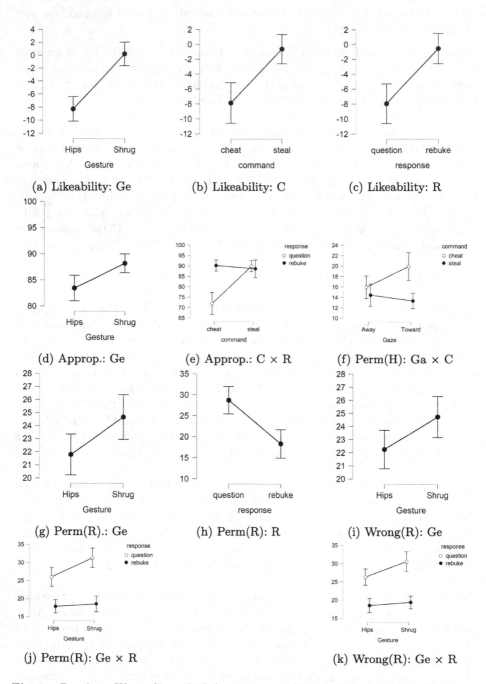

Fig. 2. Results. Wrong/Perm(R/H) = Wrongness/Permissibility (Robot/Human), Ge = Gesture, Ga = Gaze, C = Command, R = Response

Human Wrongness— Strong evidence was found for an effect of verbal strategy on human beliefs about moral wrongness ($BF = 19.66$). Robots that responded with a more threatening vocal responses led participants to believe that the action was less wrong (rebuke, $M = 11.91, SD = 21.80$) than robots that gave a less threatening response (question, $M = 17.65, SD = 21.96$).

Robot Wrongness— Moderate evidence was found for an effect of gesture type on perceptions of the robos' moral beliefs ($BF = 4.42$, Fig. 2i); participants perceived robots that used the indirect gesture (shrugging) as believing the action was more wrong ($M = 24.73, SD = 24.83$) than robots that used the direct gesture (hands-on-hips, $M = 22.26, SD = 25.45$).

5   Discussion

Hypothesis One— Our first hypothesis was that when robots' verbal and nonverbal behaviors are aligned, the valence of their communicated beliefs would be intensified, and when they are misaligned, the valence would be attenuated. We thus expected that robots using more threatening language with direct gaze and/or gesture would more strongly communicate impermissibility and wrongness (and more strongly influence humans' views).

Our results did not support this hypothesis. While gestural cues manipulated perceptions of permissibility and wrongness as intended, gaze cues had no such effect; and surprisingly, while robots' verbal utterances manipulated perceptions of robots' beliefs about permissibility as expected, the expected parallel effect on perceptions of beliefs about wrongness was not supported. This suggests observers did not make inferences about robots' moral beliefs from their gaze cues, and that more data is needed to understand how robots' moral language was viewed in this first-person viewing context. While gaze did have an effect on humans' own beliefs about action permissibility, direct gaze in response to low-severity requests led to perceptions that actions were *more* acceptable. No other effects of gaze and gesture were found on human beliefs. These results suggest that either the experiment was underpowered, our cues were not perceived as intended, or participants' attention to moral language is not as nuanced when there is not a clear violator who can be ascribed blame. Our results do indicate, however, that gesture may be important for communicating robots' moral beliefs.

Hypothesis Two— Our second hypothesis was that when robots' verbal and nonverbal behaviors are aligned in terms of communicated severity, they will be perceived more positively than when those behaviors are misaligned. Based on past research [21, 31], we expected robots using command and response pairings misaligned in severity – or speech, gaze and gesture misaligned in severity – to be perceived as less likeable, intelligent, and appropriate.

Our results did not support this hypothesis. Gaze did not impact likability, perceived intelligence, or appropriateness; Speech and gesture impacted likability, but unlike previous work, no interactions were found even between command and response; and in fact none of the robot's behavior had any conclusive impact on perceived intelligence. Gesture did have an effect, however, on appropriateness, even more than spoken behavior. Combined with our results from Hypothesis One, this suggests participants interpreted direct gestures as conveying beliefs of lower permissibility – and found this to be inappropriate. Moreover, people found the less face-threatening response to the low-severity action to be much less appropriate than the other command-response pairs; again a significant deviation from previous results.

These results, and their differences from what was observed in past work, may be due to a difference in how the questioning response was perceived in the first-person perspective. Unlike in previous work conducted from a third-person perspective, in our experiment many participants reported viewing the less face-threatening response of "are you sure you should be asking me to do that?" to be "condescending" or "sassy". It could be that from a first-person perspective this question resulted in a disproportionate level of face threat for the less severely norm violating command (cheating). Future work is needed to understand how face threat is modulated by perspective. This explanation is borne out by the explanation from many participants that their thought process for answering the questionnaires was to imagine themselves in the situation, instead of the human speaker. This could have resulted in even more severe feelings of dislike if the robot appeared condescending or arrogant when delivering command rejections.

6   Conclusion

We experimentally studied the effects of robotic gaze and gesture on face threat in robotic noncompliance. Previous work using third-person observations suggested that robots responding with proportional severity should have been perceived more positively and that verbal and nonverbal cues would interact to inform the robot's performed moral beliefs, and their effects on others. However, our primary findings were simply that gaze and gesture influence perceptions of likability and appropriateness, and that robots' gestural behaviors can be used to communicate moral beliefs; which in turn demonstrates that a first-person framing substantially alters the dynamics of face threat imposition, changing what is perceived as appropriate and what is inferred from comunication. Future work is needed to understand the precise role that first- vs third-person portrayal may play on face threat and blame dynamics. This will be critical both for contextualizing the results of interactional and observational HRI experiments, and for better understanding human perception and ascription of face threat and blame.

References

1. Admoni, H., Weng, T., Hayes, B., Scassellati, B.: Robot nonverbal behavior improves task performance in difficult collaborations. In: Proceedings of HRI (2016)

2. Arkin, R.C.: Governing lethal behavior: embedding ethics in a hybrid deliberative/reactive robot architecture. Technical Report GIT-GVU-07-11 (2007)
3. Bartneck, C., Kulić, D., Croft, E., Zoghbi, S.: Measurement instruments for the anthropomorphism, animacy, likeability, perceived intelligence, and perceived safety of robots. Int. J. Soc. Robot. **1**(1), 71–81 (2009)
4. Bremner, P., Leonards, U.: Iconic gestures for robot avatars, recognition and integration with speech. Front. Psychol. **7**, 183 (2016)
5. Bremner, P., Pipe, A.G., Fraser, M., Subramanian, S., Melhuish, C.: Beat gesture generation rules for human-robot interaction. In: Proceedings of RO-MAN (2009)
6. Briggs, G., Williams, T., Scheutz, M.: Enabling robots to understand indirect speech acts in task-based interactions. J. Human-Robot Interact. **6**(1), 64–94 (2017)
7. Brooks, A.G., Breazeal, C.: Working with robots and objects: revisiting deictic reference for achieving spatial common ground. In: Proceedings International Conference of HRI (2006)
8. Brown, P., Levinson, S.C.: Politeness: some universals in language usage. In: Interactional Sociolinguistic. No. 4 (1988)
9. Cha, E., Kim, Y., Fong, T., Mataric, M.: A survey of nonverbal signaling methods for non-humanoid robots. Fnd. Trend, Rob. **6**(4), 211–323 (2018)
10. Chidambaram, V., Chiang, Y.H., Mutlu, B.: Designing persuasive robots: how robots might persuade people using vocal and nonverbal cues. In: Proceedings of HRI (2012)
11. Clair, A.S., Mead, R., Matarić, M.J.: Investigating the effects of visual saliency on deictic gesture production by a humanoid robot. In: RO-MAN (2011)
12. Cormier, D., Newman, G., Nakane, M., Young, J.E., Durocher, S.: Would you do as a robot commands? an obedience study for human-robot interaction. In: International Conference on Human-Agent Interaction (2013)
13. Dautenhahn, K.: Ants don't have friends-thoughts on socially intelligent agents. Soc. Intell. Agents, 22–27 (1997)
14. Feil-Seifer, D., Haring, K.S., Rossi, S., Wagner, A.R., Williams, T.: Where to next? the impact of COVID-19 on human-robot interaction research. In: ACM T-HRI (2020)
15. Ham, J., Cuijpers, R.H., Cabibihan, J.-J.: Combining robotic persuasive strategies: the persuasive power of a storytelling robot that uses gazing and gestures. Int. J. Soc. Robot. **7**(4), 479–487 (2015). https://doi.org/10.1007/s12369-015-0280-4
16. Herse, S., et al.: Bon Appetit! Robot Persuasion for Food Recommendation. In: Proceedings of HRI (2018)
17. Huang, C.M., Mutlu, B.: Modeling and evaluating narrative gestures for humanlike robots. In: Robotics: Science & Systems (2013)
18. Jackson, R.B., Williams, T.: Language-capable robots may inadvertently weaken human moral norms. In: Proceedings of HRI (2019)
19. Jackson, R.B., Williams, T.: On perceived social and moral agency in natural language capable robots. In: The Dark Side of Human-Robot Interaction (2019)
20. Jackson, R.B., Williams, T.: A theory of social agency for human-robot interaction. Frontiers in Robotics and AI (2021)
21. Jackson, R.B., Williams, T., Smith, N.: Exploring the role of gender in perceptions of robotic noncompliance. In: Proceedings of HRI (2020)
22. JASP Team, et al.: JASP. version 0.8 (2016). Software
23. Kahn, P.H., et al.: Do people hold a humanoid robot morally accountable for the harm it causes? In: Proceedings of HRI (2012)

24. Kim, B., Wen, R., Zhu, Q., Williams, T., Phillips, E.: Robots as moral advisors: the effects of deontological, virtue, and confucian role ethics on encouraging honest behavior. In: Companion of HRI (2021)
25. Liu, P., Glas, D., Kanda, T., Ishiguro, H., Hagita, N.: It's not polite to point: generating socially-appropriate deictic behaviors towards people. In: HRI (2013)
26. Lockshin, J., Williams, T.: we need to start thinking ahead: The impact of social context on linguistic norm adherence. In: Proceedings of CogSci (2020)
27. Malle, B.F., Scheutz, M., Arnold, T., Voiklis, J., Cusimano, C.: Sacrifice one for the good of many?: people apply different moral norms to human and robot agents. In: Proceedings of HRI (2015)
28. Narahara, H., Maeno, T.: Factors of gestures of robots for smooth communication with humans. In: Proceedings of the 1st international conference on Robot communication and coordination (2009)
29. Ogawa, K., et al.: Can an android persuade you? In: Geminoid Studies (2018)
30. Robinette, P., Li, W., Allen, R., Howard, A.M., Wagner, A.R.: Overtrust of robots in emergency evacuation scenarios. In: Proceedings of HRI (2016)
31. Jackson, R.B., Wen, R., Williams, T.: Tact in noncompliance: the need for pragmatically apt responses to unethical commands. In: Proceedings of AIES (2019)
32. Salem, M., Rohlfing, K., Kopp, S., Joublin, F.: A friendly gesture: investigating the effect of multimodal robot behavior in human-robot interaction. In: Proceedings of RO-MAN (2011)
33. Sarathy, V., Tsuetaki, A., Roque, A., Scheutz, M.: Reasoning requirements for indirect speech act interpretation. In: Proceedings of ACL (2020)
34. Sauppé, A., Mutlu, B.: Robot deictics: how gesture and context shape referential communication. In: Proceedings of HRI. IEEE (2014)
35. Scassellati, B., Admoni, H., Matarić, M.: Robots for use in autism research. Annu. Rev. Biomed. Eng. **14**, 275–294 (2012)
36. Searle, J.R.: Indirect speech acts. In: Speech acts, pp. 59–82 (1975)
37. Sharkey, N., Sharkey, A.: The crying shame of robot nannies: an ethical appraisal. In: Machine Ethics and Robot Ethics (2020)
38. Srinivasan, V., Takayama, L.: Help me please: Robot politeness strategies for soliciting help from people. In: Proceedings of CHI (2016)
39. Stanton, C.J., Stevens, C.J.: Don't stare at me: the impact of a humanoid robot's gaze upon trust during a cooperative human-robot visual task. In: IJSR (2017)
40. Strohkorb Sebo, S., Traeger, M., Jung, M., Scassellati, B.: The ripple effects of vulnerability: the effects of a robot's vulnerable behavior on trust in human-robot teams. In: Proceedings of HRI (2018)
41. Wen, R., Siddiqui, M.A., Williams, T.: Dempster-shafer theoretic learning of indirect speech act comprehension norms. In: Proceedings of AAAI (2020)
42. Williams, T., Briggs, G., Oosterveld, B., Scheutz, M.: Going beyond command-based instructions: extending robotic natural language interaction capabilities. In: Proceedings of AAAI (2015)
43. Williams, T., Thames, D., Novakoff, J., Scheutz, M.: Thank you for sharing that interesting fact!: effects of capability and context on indirect speech act use in task-based human-robot dialogue. In: Proceedings of HRI (2018)
44. Winkle, K., et al.: Effective persuasion strategies for socially assistive robots. In: Proceedings of HRI (2019)
45. Zhu, Q., Williams, T., Jackson, B., Wen, R.: Blame-laden moral rebukes and the morally competent robot: a confucian ethical perspective. Sci. Eng. Ethics **26**(5), 2511–2526 (2020)

Migratable AI : Investigating Users' Affect on Identity and Information Migration of a Conversational AI Agent

Ravi Tejwani$^{(\boxtimes)}$, Boris Katz, and Cynthia Breazeal

Massachusetts Institute of Technology, Cambridge, USA
{tejwanir,boris,breazeal}@mit.edu

Abstract. Conversational AI agents are becoming ubiquitous and provide assistance to us in our everyday activities. In recent years, researchers have explored the migration of these agents across different embodiments in order to maintain the continuity of the task and improve user experience. In this paper, we investigate user's affective responses in different configurations of the migration parameters. We present a 2 x 2 between-subjects study in a task-based scenario using information migration and identity migration as parameters. We outline the affect processing pipeline from the video footage collected during the study and report user's responses in each condition. Our results show that users reported highest joy and were most surprised when both the information and identity was migrated; and reported most anger when the information was migrated without the identity of their agent.

Keywords: Conversational AI · Affective computing · Agent migration

1 Introduction

We are surrounded by conversational AI agents, such as Alexa [8], Jibo [9] or Google Home [11], as they assist us in our daily activities like providing weather and news updates, ordering meal and ride shares, setting room temperature etc. These agents build model of our personal preferences and interests as we interact and develop relationship with them. We also interact with the robotic agents in public setting, such as Pepper [12], Kuri [10], or Moxi [13] at hospitals, restaurants, and grocery stores, where we share our preferences with them. Since these agents exist in different form factors or embodiments and setting, they do not always share information amongst each other. However, the migration of information or identity across embodiments could lead to changes in users' perception [7] and affective states. For example, after your interaction with the home agent, Alexa, you might be surprised to see if the restaurant robot greets you with your name and knows about your food order when you enter the restaurant.

© Springer Nature Switzerland AG 2021
H. Li et al. (Eds.): ICSR 2021, LNAI 13086, pp. 257–267, 2021.
https://doi.org/10.1007/978-3-030-90525-5_22

Agent migration is a concept which allows an agent to disembody from its current form and migrate to different embodiments while maintaining the relationship with the user. Prior work has explored the concept of agent migration through various different architectures [15, 19–21]. They explored the migration in the form of a synthetic character or a visual entity than compared to a conversational AI agent. Further, several user studies on agent migration [22–24] explored users impression on the agent such as validating if the users perceived that it was the same agent in another embodiment, or if the users understood the concept of agent migration. For instance, Syrdal et al. performed series of group discussions with a school class children, aged 3 to 6, on evaluating children's impressions on the understanding of the concept of migration [25]. However, the affective behavior analysis of the users in the context of migration of AI agents have not been studied before. User's affective behavior and autonoumous reactions provide a deeper understanding of user's reaction towards the system in comparison to the subjective reports given by the users [1, 2, 16] which would be beneficial in designing effective migratable AI agents.

In our previous work [7], we proposed a Migratable AI system which allows a conversational AI agent to migrate across different physical embodiments. We measured the user's perception on trust, competence, likability and social presence using information migration and identity migration as parameters. In this paper, we build upon our previous work by analyzing the affective behavior of the users during the migration of the conversational AI agent. We ran a 2 x 2 between-subjects study in a task-based scenario using information migration and identity migration as parameters to investigate the affective responses of the users. We outline the affect processing pipeline from the video footage collected during our experimental study. The pipeline comprised of two stages: affect detection and affect interpretation. The findings from this paper, can be used for the further development of effective migratable systems.

2   Related Work

2.1   Identity Migration

Prior work has explored the concept of agent migration through various different identity migration architectures [15, 20, 21]. The agent migration was first explored by Imai et al. [19] by demonstrating a tour guide application where a personal agent could migrate from mobile device to a physical robot. Later, the research by Martin et al. [17] explored that the identity is not just "Who am I?" but "Who am I in the eyes of others?" where they proposed the visual identity cues in their experiment that characters share a common feature - such as a hat or glasses, common colour scheme, common set of markings, or characters are of the same class of objects. Further, [22, 24] explored the research questions such as "Do participants feel that they are interacting with the same agent across different embodiments?"; "What are the most important aspects of an agent to communicate identity retention?"; or "Do users perceive the agents in different embodiments as the same entity?"

2.2   Information Migration

Information migration architectures were explored in [20,27] as generic memory models and persistent memory models. Aylett et al. proposed CMION in [15,20], an open source architecture comprised of three layers (Mind, Mind-Body, and Body), that served as a framework for the bidirectional mapping of information to different levels of abstraction (i.e., from raw sensory data to symbolic data and vice versa). These models were created to focus on the following three different aspects:

1. **Scope** - Short term memory (STM) was modeled computationally to maintain a companion's current focus and Long term memory (LTM) was used for the artificial companions that interact with human users over a long period of time
2. **Efficiency** - how to optimize the storage and recall of memory contents; forgetting through the processes of generalization and memory restructuring.
3. **Adaptability** - how to use different conversational strategies for information or memory that the robot remembers during the interaction with human (no-memory, partial memory, complete memory).

2.3   User Perception of Agent Migration

User studies have explored users' perception of agents that can migrate across forms in [22–24] by studying the higher level users' impression on the agent such as validating if the users felt that it was the same agent in another embodiment, or if the users understood the concept of agent migration. Further, [21,26] explored the users perception on the long term interaction derived from the companion's interaction history both with the environment and the user.

In this paper, we go beyond the users perception on agent's identity or the subjective reports and investigate user's affective state during the migration of an conversational AI agent using information migration and identity migration as parameters.

Table 1. Participant Demographics

Condition	Female	Male	Other	Age(Std. Dev.)
(INF+,ID+)	8	10	0	24.4(5.06)
(INF+,ID-)	9	9	0	24.6(6.09)
(INF-,ID+)	7	10	1	28.2(10.2)
(INF-,ID-)	8	9	1	22.6(3.61)

3   Method

3.1   Participants

We recruited 72 participants from Cambridge area using email advertisements. Participants were between 18 and 54 years old with mean age M=24.2, SD=5.09. Participants were randomly assigned and counterbalanced by gender across the four conditions (n=18 per condition) as described in Table 1. The study was approved by our Institutional Review Board, and participants signed an informed consent form prior to the study.

3.2   Study Protocol

We ran a 2×2 between-subjects study with *Information migration* × *Identity migration*. The 4 conditions used in the study are described in Fig. 1.

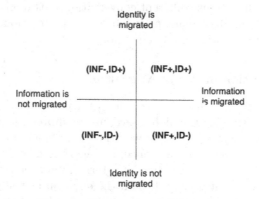

Fig. 1. Study conditions

We used the Migratable AI system [7] in the study. The system allowed the conversational AI agent to migrate across different embodiments by preserving its identity(identity migration) and/or remembering the information context (information migration). Each participant began the study in our lab's study room, modeled as their "home", with the home agent (Alexa) [8]. The home agent delivered the participant's schedule for the day which included a job interview. Throughout the conversation, the home agent learned about the participant such as his/her name and feelings.

The mobile robot (Kuri) [10] was located in a hallway of the lab which played the role of front desk receptionist robot at the interview location. The receptionist robot, changed its appearance to look and sound like home agent (when identity was migrated) or continued to look and sound like Kuri with a different voice profile (when identity was not migrated). The receptionist robot detected their face, recognized the participant by name, and acknowledged the

Fig. 2. Left to right: Home agent, Home agent migrating to receptionist robot, Home agent migrating to waiting room assistant.

reason for their visit (when information was migrated) or prompted the participant for their name and reason for their visit (when information was not migrated). During the conversation, the receptionist robot either validated the participant's feelings (when information was migrated) or asked how they were feeling for their interview (when information was not migrated). The receptionist robot also learned the participant's drink preferences (coffee, water or tea) and escorted the participant to the interview waiting area.

At the interview waiting area, the participant interacted with the waiting room assistant (Smart TV) which conversed with the participant until the arrival of the interviewer. It changed its appearance to look and sound like home agent (when the identity was migrated) or continued to look and sound like itself (when the identity was not migrated). While the participant waited, it offered the participant their preferred drink (which it remembered in the condition when the information was migrated) or offered the participant a drink while waiting (when the information was not migrated). It also acknowledged the participant's feelings (when the information was migrated) and wished them good luck before the interviewer arrived. The interviewer role was enacted by the experimenter.

For identity migration - the design decisions were informed from the past literature on what helps users perceive an identity of an agent [15,17,18]. In the identity migration conditions, the same visual characteristics (Figure 2, panda-esque circular appearance) and voice (Joanna TTS) was used across all embodiments to convey identity continuity.

For information migration - the information parameters such as the person's name, feelings about the interview, drink preference and reason for visit were learned by each agent during the conversation. If the system was configured to migrate information across embodiments, this information was shared amongst the agents to maintain the continuity of the interaction else the agent had to prompt the user for the information. The number of conversational turns (four in this user study) touch basing the personal and non-personal information between the agent and the participant were kept consistent across all the conditions. This might necessitate the agent to repeat certain questions to the users when the information was not migrated but it was to ensure that we do not create a bias in the study and keep the conversational turns consistent.

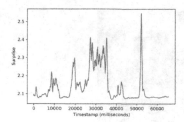 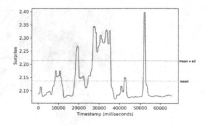

(a) Raw affect data of a participant   (b) Affect data after applying
                                        median filter and threshold

Fig. 3. Affect interpretation for surprise of a sample participant

3.3   Data Collection

A front facing USB camera were connected to a Raspberry Pi and attached to
each embodiment to record the interaction. The Raspberry Pi used face detection
to send a wake up signal to the robot/embodiment. It began recording the video
when the participant's face was detected in front of the embodiment and stopped
the recording when the interaction with the user ended. The video recordings of
all the 72 participants (18 in each condition) were processed using Affdex [6] for
affect analysis.

4   Affect Processing Pipeline

Affect analysis has been performed in the past using several statistical heuristics
such as mean value of the pertaining window [3], if at any given point in the
window the value of the metric exceeds a given threshold [5], or if the mean
value of the metric over pertaining window exceeds a given threshold [4]. We
implemented the pipeline for affect detection and interpretation using smoothing
and a threshold technique. Most of our pipeline overlaps with the approach
detailed by Spaulding and Breazeal [1] and D'Mello, Kappas, and Gratch [2].

The data pipeline is as follows: Raw data, $RD = rd_0, rd_1, ..., rd_n$, is used
for an interaction time window W, where $|RD| >> W$ and rd_x is x participant's
raw data. The raw data, RD, is further processed by an affect detector which
produces feature vectors of metrics, $M = m_0, m_1, ..., m_n$ (e.g., the degree to
which 'joy' 'smile', 'brow raise' etc. are expressed), for each data point. The
affect interpreter further analyzes these metric vectors for the time window and
produces a feature label, l, for that window.

Table 2. Affect features by each migration condition

Features	(INF+,ID+)	(INF+,ID-)	(INF-,ID+)	(INF-,ID-)
joy	0.274 ± 0.03	0.188 ± 0.01	0.256 ± 0.02	0.239 ± 0.02
anger	0.179 ± 0.01	0.216 ± 0.02	0.151 ± 0.01	0.157 ± 0.02
surprise	0.181 ± 0.01	0.144 ± 0.02	0.139 ± 0.02	0.157 ± 0.02
smile	0.254 ± 0.03	0.274 ± 0.04	0.306 ± 0.03	0.187 ± 0.02
brow_raise	0.226 ± 0.02	0.188 ± 0.01	0.261 ± 0.02	0.231 ± 0.02
brow_furrow	0.201 ± 0.02	0.201 ± 0.01	0.252 ± 0.03	0.269 ± 0.04
nose_wrinkle	0.258 ± 0.03	0.222 ± 0.02	0.283 ± 0.03	0.298 ± 0.04
upper_lip_raise	0.230 ± 0.02	0.219 ± 0.02	0.219 ± 0.01	0.215 ± 0.02
mouth_open	0.226 ± 0.01	0.205 ± 0.02	0.257 ± 0.03	0.229 ± 0.02
eye_closure	0.214 ± 0.01	0.25 ± 0.02	0.253 ± 0.02	0.289 ± 0.03
cheek_raise	0.204 ± 0.04	0.162 ± 0.02	0.315 ± 0.03	0.278 ± 0.04

ID+ or ID- represents identity is migrated or not migrated.
INF+ or INF- represents information is migrated or not migrated.

4.1 Affect Detection

The facial expressions of the participants were evaluated from the video captured by the front facing USB camera mounted on each of the embodiments at 30fps. The camera would get activated at the detection of the participant's face and record the video for the time frame of the interaction between the agent and the participant at each embodiment (Fig. 2). We processed the frames from each embodiment, using the Affdex [6] as the affect detector, which detected features such as: 'joy', 'anger', 'surprise', 'smile', 'brow_raise', 'brow_furrow', 'nose_wrinkle', 'upper_lip_raise', 'mouth_open', 'eye_closure', 'cheek_raise'.

4.2 Affect Interpretation

The affect data for the interaction duration between the agent and participant on an embodiment, is collected and converted to a feature vector. We interpret each feature as a binary indicator variable whose value is determined by smoothing and a threshold technique. The raw affect data, M, is initially passed through a median-filter smoothing. Further, if the maximum value of the median-smoothed detected peaks exceeds the threshold, then the feature value is interpreted with an indicator value of 1. For the given time window, the interpreted affect feature vector is comprised of set of observed feature indicators. The threshold value for the feature is set at the mean value of the feature across the entire time window plus a standard deviation (Fig. 3). Finally, each of the affect feature score is further normalized for the data analysis.

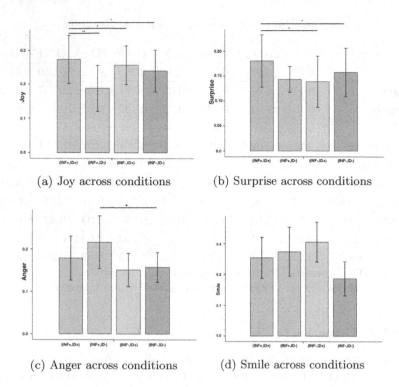

(a) Joy across conditions

(b) Surprise across conditions

(c) Anger across conditions

(d) Smile across conditions

Fig. 4. Box-plot for the normalized affective measures across conditions. The boundary of the box closest to zero indicates the 25th percentile, the line within the box marks the mean and the boundary of the box farthest from zero indicates the 75th percentile. Whiskers above and below the box indicate the 10th and 90th percentiles. * means p<.05, ** means p<.01

5   Results

Normality was first checked for the affective measures from the visual inspection of Q-Q plots and Shapiro-Wilk's test. With all p-values < 0.05, the Shapiro-Wilk test rejects the null hypothesis of data normality, hence, we perform the Kruskal-Wallis H test over the data. Furthermore, the Dwass-Steel-Critchlow-Fligner test was used for the pair-wise comparisons. All the statistical analysis were performed using R(version 3.6.1) and Jamovi [14].

We found a significant effect in joy, surprise and anger amongst the users when configuration of the identity and information of the agent was changed during the migration.

Joy: There was a statistically significant difference in joy scores across different conditions, $\chi^2(3) = 7.560$, p = 0.016. The pair wise comparisons showed that mean joy score of 0.274 ± 0.03 for (INF+, ID+) was significantly greater than 0.188 ± 0.01 for (INF+,ID-) with p=0.008, 0.256 ± 0.02 for (INF-,ID+) with p=0.024 and 0.239 ± 0.02 for (INF-,ID-) with p=0.039 (Fig. 4a).

Surprise: There was a statistically significant difference in surprise scores across different conditions, $\chi^2(3) = 4.40$, p $= 0.033$. The pair wise comparisons showed that mean surprise score of 0.181 ± 0.01 for (INF+, ID+) was significantly greater than 0.139 ± 0.02 for (INF-,ID+) with p=0.036 and 0.157 ± 0.02 for (INF-,ID-) with p=0.042 (Fig. 4b).

Anger: There was a statistically significant difference in anger scores across different conditions, $\chi^2(3) = 3.157$, p $= 0.041$. The pair wise comparisons showed that mean anger score of 0.216 ± 0.02 for (INF+,ID-) was significantly greater than 0.157 ± 0.02 for (INF-,ID-) with p=0.032 (Fig. 4c).

Other affective measures: The analysis results for the other affective scores were not significantly different across the different conditions: smile ($\chi^2(3)$ $= 2.986$, p $= 0.091$), brow_raise ($\chi^2(3) = 2.602$, p $= 0.080$), brow_furrow ($\chi^2(3)$ $= 1.391$ p $= 0.842$), nose_wrinkle ($\chi^2(3) = 1.462$, p $= 0.924$), upper_lip_raise ($\chi^2(3) = 2.753$, p $= 0.178$), mouth_open ($\chi^2(3) = 1.115$, p $= 0.273$), eye_closure ($\chi^2(3) = 1.394$, p $= 0.307$) and cheek_raise ($\chi^2(3) = 2.171$, p $= 0.092$).

Table 2 summarizes the mean scores with their standard deviation for all the affective features across all the conditions.

6 Discussion and Conclusions

We presented the results from one of the first systematic investigations of users affective behavior on the migration of the conversational AI agent. We ran a 2x2 between-subjects study in a task-based scenario with 72 participants using information migration and identity migration as parameters to investigate the affective behavior of the users. We outlined an affect processing pipeline from the video footage collected during the study.

We inferred that users expressed most joyfulness and surprise when they saw their agent in a different embodiment and the agent remembered their preferences and context **(both the information and identity of the agent was migrated)**. This was corroborated by the participant's comments during the post-study interview. Participant P21 said *"I think it remembers that I am anxious about the interview. That means it cares about me and makes it different from, for example, a coffee machine."* Another participant, P34, said, *"Being familiar with Alexa, allowed me to trust Receptionist and TV agent".*

The users were most disappointed and angry when they found out that their information was shared with different agents **(information was migrated but identity was not migrated)**. P51 said *"I did not trust the agents well because they seemed to share all of the information about me, and I did not want to disclose more."*. Also, P39 said *"... especially after the receptionist agent knew what I told Alexa, I no longer trusted Alexa".* The insights gained from this research could be used for further development of affective migratable systems.

References

1. Spaulding, S., Cynthia, B.: Frustratingly easy personalization for real-time affect interpretation of facial expression. In: 2019 8th International Conference on Affective Computing and Intelligent Interaction (ACII). IEEE (2019)
2. D'Mello, S., Kappas, A., Gratch, J.: The affective computing approach to affect measurement. Emotion Rev. **10**(2), 174–183 (2018)
3. Jeong, S., Breazeal, C.L.: Improving smartphone users' affect and wellbeing with personalized positive psychology interventions. In: Proceedings of the Fourth International Conference on Human Agent Interaction (2016)
4. Bernin, A., et al.: Towards more robust automatic facial expression recognition in smart environments. In: Proceedings of the 10th International Conference on PErvasive Technologies Related to Assistive Environments (2017)
5. Zhang, L., Tjondronegoro, D., Chandran, V., Eggink, J.: Towards robust automatic affective classification of images using facial expressions for practical applications. Multimed. Tools Appl. **75**(8), 4669–4695 (2015). https://doi.org/10.1007/s11042-015-2497-5
6. McDuff, D., et al.: AFFDEX SDK: a cross-platform real-time multi-face expression recognition toolkit. In: Proceedings of the 2016 CHI conference extended abstracts on human factors in computing systems (2016)
7. Tejwani, R., et al.: "Migratable AI" Proceedings of the 29th IEEE International Conference on Robot and Human Interactive Communication, RO-MAN (2020)
8. Alexa (2014). https://developer.amazon.com/alexa
9. Jibo (2017). https://www.jibo.com
10. Kuri (2018). https://www.heykuri.com/explore-kuri/
11. Google Home (2013). https://google.com
12. Pepper (2015). https://www.softbankrobotics.com/us/pepper
13. Moxi (2013). https://diligentrobots.com/moxi
14. Jamovi (2018). https://www.jamovi.org/
15. Aylett, R.S., et al.: Body–hopping: migrating artificial intelligent agents between embodiments
16. Picard, R.W., Vyzas, E., Healey, J.: Toward machine emotional intelligence: analysis of affective physiological state. IEEE Trans. Pattern Anal. Mach. Intell. **23**(10), 1175–1191 (2001)
17. Martin, A., et al.: Maintaining the identity of dynamically embodied agents. In: Panayiotopoulos, T., et al. (eds.) IVA 2005. LNCS (LNAI), vol. 3661, pp. 454–465. Springer, Heidelberg (2005). https://doi.org/10.1007/11550617_38
18. Cuba, P.: Agent migration between bodies and platforms. (2010)
19. Imai, M., Tetsuo O., Tameyuki, E.: Agent migration: communications between a human and robot. In: IEEE SMC'99 Conference Proceedings. 1999 IEEE International Conference on Systems, Man, and Cybernetics
20. Lirec (2009). http://lirec.eu
21. Duffy, B.R., et al.: Agent chameleons: agent minds and bodies.In: Proceedings 11th IEEE International Workshop on Program Comprehension. IEEE (2003)
22. Gomes, P.F., et al.: Migration between two embodiments of an artificial pet. Int. J. Human. Robot. **11**(01), 1450001 (2014)
23. Kriegel, M., et al.: Digital body hopping-migrating artificial companions. In: Proceedings of Digital Futures' 10 (2010)

24. Grigore, E.C., et al.: Comparing ways to trigger migration between a robot and a virtually embodied character. In: Agah, A., Cabibihan, J.J., Howard, A., Salichs, M., He, H. (eds.) ICSR 2016. LNCS (LNAI), vol. 9979, pp. 839–849. Springer, Cham (2016). https://doi.org/10.1007/978-3-319-47437-3_82
25. Syrdal, D.S., et al.: The boy-robot should bark!-children's impressions of agent migration into diverse embodiments. In: Proceedings: New Frontiers of Human-Robot Interaction, A Symposium at AISB (2009)
26. Kriegel, M.: Robots meet IVAs: a mind-body interface for migrating artificial intelligent agents. In: Vilhjálmsson, H.H., Kopp, S., Marsella, S., Thórisson, K.R. (eds.) IVA 2011. LNCS (LNAI), vol. 6895, pp. 282–295. Springer, Heidelberg (2011). https://doi.org/10.1007/978-3-642-23974-8_31
27. Ono, T., Imai, M., Nakatsu, R.: Reading a robot's mind: a model of utterance understanding based on the theory of mind mechanism. Adv. Robot. 14(4), 311–326 (2000)

The Self-Evaluation Maintenance Model in Human-Robot Interaction: A Conceptual Replication

Mira E. Gruber[⊠] [iD] and P. A. Hancock [iD]

University of Central Florida, Orlando, USA
miraeg@knights.ucf.edu, peter.hancock@ucf.edu

Abstract. Understanding human-robot social comparison is critical for creating psychologically safe robots (i.e., robots that do not cause psychological discomfort). However, there has been limited research examining social comparison processes in human-robot interaction (HRI). We aimed to conceptually replicate prior research suggesting that the Self-Evaluation Maintenance (SEM) model of social comparison applies to HRI. In short, the SEM model describes the mechanisms in which others can impact one's self-evaluation. We applied the model to an online presentation of a humanoid robot, RUDY. We predicted that task relevance would moderate the relationship between the robot's performance level and participant evaluations of the robot. When RUDY engaged in a low-relevance task (guessing someone's age), participants would evaluate RUDY accurately (i.e., they would rate RUDY more positively when it performed well than when it performed poorly). However, when RUDY engaged in a high-relevance task (understanding how people feel), participants would evaluate RUDY inaccurately (i.e., they would rate RUDY negatively regardless of its actual performance). Contrary to our hypothesis, we found that participants in both the high- and low-relevance conditions evaluated RUDY accurately. Our results suggest that SEM effects may not generalize to all types of tasks and robots. A "highly relevant" task might mean something different depending on the exact nature of the human-robot relationship. Given the inconsistency between these findings and past research, discerning the boundary conditions for SEM effects may be crucial for developing psychologically safe robots.

Keywords: Human-robot interaction · Self-evaluation · Social comparison

1 Introduction

As the use of robots expands into social domains [1], understanding the psychological impact of robots becomes increasingly important. Social robots are "physically embodied autonomous agents that communicate and interact with humans on a social level" [1, p. 2]. Social robots have the potential to benefit sectors such as healthcare and education [2], but much remains unknown about the psychological short- and long-term effects of these robots [3]. Social psychology offers potential insights into this problem. Decades of

© Springer Nature Switzerland AG 2021
H. Li et al. (Eds.): ICSR 2021, LNAI 13086, pp. 268–280, 2021.
https://doi.org/10.1007/978-3-030-90525-5_23

social psychology research have focused on how humans interact with other humans [4]. Consequently, the field has produced theories and models to understand human-human social interaction. However, human-robot social interaction is relatively unexplored. In the present study, we sought to apply one social psychology model—the Self-Evaluation Maintenance (SEM) model—to interactions with a social robot.

1.1 The SEM Model

The SEM model is built on the premise that people seek to maintain or increase their positive self-evaluations and that other people can impact their self-evaluations [5]. Interacting with another person may activate a reflection (i.e., enhancing one's positive self-evaluation) or comparison process (i.e., weakening one's positive self-evaluation). We will use "subject" to refer to the person engaging in the reflection or comparison process and "target" to refer to the person to whom the subject is comparing themselves. Whether a person will engage in these processes depends on three variables: task relevance, the performance level of the target and subject, and the psychological closeness of the subject and target. Task relevance refers to the importance of a task or domain to the subject's identity [5]. Performance level refers to how well the target and subject perform on a given task [5], and psychological closeness refers to "feelings of attachment and perceived connection toward another person" [6, p. 16].

Reflection may ensue when someone who is psychologically close to the subject performs well on a domain that is of low relevance to the subject's identity [5]. This process boosts the subject's positive self-evaluation [5] and can be described as "basking in the reflected glory of another" [7]. In contrast, a comparison process may occur when someone who is psychologically close to the subject performs well on a highly self-relevant domain [5]. In turn, the subject's self-evaluation decreases, as the subject may feel threatened by and inferior to the target [5]. A person engaged in a comparison process may attempt to repair their self-evaluation by understating the relevance of the domain (e.g., 'It's not actually that important to me'), impeding the target's good performance (e.g., through sabotage), attempting to improve their performance [8], or by physically or psychologically distancing themselves from the target [9–11]. In brief, the SEM model is a tool for predicting when another person will threaten one's self-evaluation and how one might respond to those threats.

1.2 The SEM Model in HRI

To date, only one study has applied the SEM model to HRI. Kamide and colleagues [12] proposed that social comparison processes might explain anxiety toward robots. The authors only examined two SEM variables: performance level and task relevance. During the study, participants viewed a presentation given by a humanoid robot. To manipulate performance level, the robot displayed varying degrees of nonverbal behaviors designed to keep the viewers' attention. Task relevance was measured via participants' self-reported importance of giving presentations.

The authors found that higher task relevance led to lower evaluations of the robot, even when the robot performed well, suggesting that users may feel threatened when a robot engages in a highly important task. In turn, the user adopts a more negative impression of the robot in an attempt to boost their self-evaluation. These negative feelings are undesirable, as they may lead to psychological discomfort and anxiety. The authors state that "if the service the robot provides has significant meaning to the self of the user, the user will be threatened by the robot. However, if the service is unrelated to the self, then an excellent job by the robot will be admitted as safer" [12, p. 197]. These findings are a concern for HRI, as social robots may be designed to carry out tasks that are of high self-relevance to the user. Caregiving robots are one example of this concern. Human caregivers perform tasks that are intimately related to the care recipient, and providing care is also important to the caregiver [13]. Thus, caregiving robots may perform tasks that are self-threatening to both the recipient of care and their human caregiver.

1.3 Present Study

Our goal was to conceptually replicate Kamide and colleagues' study [12] via an online presentation and evaluation of RUDY, a humanoid social robot. If the replication is successful, the present study will provide further evidence for the application of the SEM model in HRI, and that Kamide and colleagues' [12] findings can be generalized to other types of tasks and robots. We sought to induce SEM effects with a different robot, performance level manipulation, and task relevance manipulation than what was used in Kamide and colleagues' study [12]. Given this goal, we proposed the following hypotheses:

H_1: RUDY's performance level will affect participant evaluations of RUDY. Specifically, RUDY will be rated as more (a) Anthropomorphic; (b) Intelligent; (c) Animate; (d) Likable; and (e) Safer when it performs well compared to when it performs poorly.

H_2: Task relevance will moderate the relationship between RUDY's performance level and participant evaluations of RUDY. Specifically, when RUDY engages in a low-relevance task, participants will rate RUDY as more (a) Anthropomorphic; (b) Intelligent; (c) Animate; (d) Likeable; and (e) Safer when it performs well compared to when it performs poorly. However, when RUDY engages in a high-relevance task, there will be no difference in ratings of RUDY when it performs well compared to when it performs poorly. Additionally, RUDY's ratings for the high-relevance task will be lower than when RUDY performed the low-relevance task well.

2 Method

2.1 Participants

Recruitment. One-hundred and ninety-four participants were recruited through the online research participation system (SONA) at the University of Central Florida (UCF). UCF's Institutional Review Board reviewed and approved the study.

Exclusion Criteria. Participants were excluded from the final analysis if (1) they did not complete all study tasks; (2) they did not pass the attention checks; (3) they were assigned the high-relevance condition but indicated that the task *was not* important to them; or (4) they were assigned the low-relevance condition but indicated that the task *was* important to them. The final sample consisted of 147 participants.

Demographics. On average, participants were 20.39 years old ($SD = 5.05$, $Min = 18.00$, $Max = 48.00$). More participants identified as female (58.5%) than male (40.1%). Two participants identified as genderfluid or nonbinary (1.4%). The majority of participants were White/Caucasian (57.8%), followed by Hispanic or Latino (19.0%), Asian or Pacific Islander (10.9%), Black or African American (6.8%), Other (4.8%), and Native American or American Indian (0.7%). All of the participants who responded "Other" for race indicated that they were biracial or mixed-race.

2.2 Design

We used a two-way between-subjects experimental design. The independent variables were task relevance (high or low task relevance) and robot performance (good or poor performance). Thus, participants were randomly assigned to one of four conditions, as illustrated in Table 1.

Table 1. Study conditions.

		Task relevance	
		High	Low
Performance	Good	Good performance, high task relevance	Good performance, low task relevance
	Poor	Poor performance, high task relevance	Poor performance, low task relevance

Negative Attitudes Toward Robots Scale. Participants completed the Negative Attitudes Toward Robots (NARS) Scale [14] as a means of controlling for general feelings toward robots. The scale consists of three subscales concerning negative attitudes toward robots: situations of interaction with robots (S1), social influence of robots (S2), and emotions in interaction with robots (S3). The scale uses a 5-point Likert Scale (Strongly disagree–Strongly agree) and has 14 items. In the present study, all NARS subscales were reliable; $\alpha_{S1} = .81$, $\alpha_{S2} = .77$, $\alpha_{S3} = .84$.

Mock Tests. To manipulate task relevance, participants completed either a mock social sensitivity test (high relevance) or a mock age estimation test (low relevance). The social sensitivity test ostensibly measured "the personal ability to perceive and understand the feelings and viewpoints of others" [15] (this is a true definition, though the test was fake). Participants were also told that their score was highly indicative of their social intelligence. The "test" showed 20 pairs of faces. For each pair, participants were instructed to select the face expressing more of a given emotion. (e.g., "Which person is expressing more anger?"). The face images were provided by the Chicago Face Database [16]. Participants taking the age estimation test were told that the test assesses their ability to accurately estimate a person's age. Using the same 20 pairs of faces, participants were asked to guess who the older person of the pair was. Although previous SEM studies have successfully used mock tests to manipulate task relevance, [8, 17], this is the first HRI study to use this manipulation.

Personal Importance Questionnaire. Participants completed an 11-item question-naire to assess how important various domains were to them. Two items assessed the personal importance of social intelligence, and one item assessed the personal impor-tance of being able to estimate someone's age. The rest of the items were filler items. Participants responded to the items on a 5-point Likert Scale (Not at all important– Very important). The inclusion of a personal importance measure was based on previous SEM studies [12, 17], and this measure served as a task relevance manipulation check.

Robot Presentation. Participants were told that they would be evaluating a new social companion robot, RUDY and that their evaluation would help developers optimize the robot. The image of RUDY (see Fig. 1) was provided with permission by INF Robotics Inc. [18]. In the good-performance condition, participants were told that RUDY answered 18 out of 20 questions correctly on the same test they took while they (the participant) answered eight out of 20 questions correctly and that RUDY's social intelligence/ability to estimate age was better than theirs. The scores and statement about abilities were swapped for the poor-performance condition.

Fig. 1. Image of RUDY used in all study conditions.

Attention Checks. Participants were given two attention checks. Following the mock test, participants were instructed to select the correct name of the test. After viewing RUDY, participants were asked to select the correct name of the robot prototype.

Godspeed Questionnaire. To evaluate the robot, participants completed the 24-item Godspeed Questionnaire [19]. This measure consists of five subscales: Anthropomorphism, Perceived Intelligence, Animacy, Likeability, and Perceived Safety. For each subscale, participants rated their impressions of RUDY on various characteristics on a semantic differential scale (0–5) (e.g., for Anthropomorphism: fake–natural). In the present study, the Godspeed subscales of Perceived Intelligence ($\alpha = .86$), Animacy ($\alpha = .80$), Likeability ($\alpha = .91$), and Perceived Safety ($\alpha = .77$) were sufficiently reliable, while the Anthropomorphism subscale was not ($\alpha = .66$).

2.3 Procedure

Participants accessed the study through SONA, and the study was conducted on Qualtrics. First, participants completed the Personal Importance Questionnaire and the NARS. Next, they received their assigned mock test and subsequent attention check, followed by the presentation of RUDY, their test score compared to RUDY's score, and the statement on whether RUDY's ability was better or worse than theirs. Next, they completed the robot-name attention check and the Godspeed Questionnaire followed by demographic items. Finally, participants were debriefed, reassured that the test they took was completely fake, and thanked for their time.

3 Results

We used IBM SPSS Statistics [20] to analyze the data. We computed two-way Analysis of Covariances (ANCOVAs) to examine the effect of performance level and task relevance on each Godspeed subscale while controlling for the three NARS subscales. None of the NARS subscales were strongly correlated (i.e., $r < .80$). We conducted checks on the ANCOVA assumptions, and any assumption violations are discussed below.

3.1 Anthropomorphism

The normality of residuals assumption was violated. The residuals were positively skewed for the good-performance-low-relevance group according to a Shapiro-Wilk (S-W) test, $W(41) = 0.88$, $p < .001$. However, we continued the analysis as planned because ANCOVA is relatively robust to violations of normality [21]. After controlling for negative attitudes toward robots, there was a significant main effect of performance level, $F(1, 140) = 4.03$, $p = .047$, *partial* $\eta^2 = .03$. There was not a significant main effect of task relevance ($F(1, 140) = .02$, $p = .886$, *partial* $\eta^2 = .00$), and there was not a significant interaction between performance level and task relevance, $F(1, 140) = 0.31$, $p = .576$, *partial* $\eta^2 = .00$. Estimated marginal means indicated that RUDY was rated as more Anthropomorphic when it performed well ($M_{Adjust} = 9.66$, $SE = .34$) than when it performed poorly ($M_{Adjust} = 8.70$, $SE = .33$) (see Table 2).

Table 2. Unadjusted means, standard deviations, adjusted means, and standard errors for anthropomorphism with NARS S1, S2, and S3 as covariates.

Group: performance level by task relevance	n	M	SD	M$_{Adjust}$	SE
Good performance (total)	71	9.606	3.24	9.658	.343
Good performance, High relevance	30	9.767	2.897	9.759	.525
Good performance, Low relevance	41	9.488	3.501	9.558	.445
Poor performance (total)	76	8.750	2.515	8.702	.328
Poor performance, High relevance	35	8.571	2.570	8.533	.483
Poor performance, Low relevance	41	8.902	2.488	8.870	.443

3.2 Perceived Intelligence

The normality of residuals assumption was violated. The residuals were negatively skewed for the good-performance-low-relevance group according to a S-W test, $W(41) = 0.93$, $p = .010$. Again, we continued the analysis as planned because ANCOVA is relatively robust to violations of normality [21]. After controlling for negative attitudes toward robots, there was a significant main effect of performance level, $F(1, 140) = 28.53$, $p < .001$, *partial η^2* = .17. There was not a significant main effect of task relevance ($F(1, 140) = .04$, $p = .849$, *partial η^2* = .00), and there was not a significant interaction between performance level and task relevance, $F(1, 140) = 1.72$, $p = .192$, *partial η^2* = .01. Estimated marginal means indicated that RUDY was rated as more Intelligent when it performed well ($M_{Adjust} = 19.04$, $SE = .51$) than when it performed poorly ($M_{Adjust} = 15.24$, $SE = .49$) (see Table 3).

Table 3. Unadjusted means, standard deviations, adjusted means, and standard errors for perceived intelligence with NARS S1, S2, and S3 as covariates.

Group: performance level by task relevance	n	M	SD	M$_{Adjust}$	SE
Good performance (total)	71	18.915	3.725	19.041	.512
Good performance, High relevance	30	19.367	3.211	19.444	.784
Good performance, Low relevance	41	18.585	4.068	18.638	.664
Poor performance (total)	76	15.342	4.669	15.241	.490
Poor performance, High relevance	35	14.800	4.733	14.703	.722
Poor performance, Low relevance	41	15.805	4.622	15.779	.662

3.3 Animacy

No assumptions were violated. After controlling for negative attitudes toward robots, there was a significant main effect of performance level, $F(1, 140) = 11.12$, $p = .001$, *partial* $\eta^2 = .07$. There was a not significant main effect of task relevance $(F(1, 140)$ $= 0.06, p = .801$ *partial* $\eta^2 = .00$), and there was not a significant interaction between performance level and task relevance, $F(1, 140) = 0.02, p = .876,$ *partial* $\eta^2 = .00$. Estimated marginal means indicated that RUDY was rated as more Animate when it performed well $(M_{Adjust} = 14.53, SE = .50)$ than when it performed poorly $(M_{Adjust} = 12.23, SE = .48)$ (see Table 4).

Table 4. Unadjusted means, standard deviations, adjusted means, and standard errors for animacy with NARS S1, S2, and S3 as covariates.

Group: performance level by task relevance	n	M	SD	M_Adjust	SE
Good performance (total)	71	14.451	4.067	14.531	.496
Good performance, High relevance	30	14.300	4.348	14.390	.760
Good performance, Low relevance	41	14.561	3.899	14.672	.644
Poor performance (total)	76	12.329	4.319	12.231	.475
Poor performance, High relevance	35	12.343	4.439	12.198	.700
Poor performance, Low relevance	41	12.317	4.269	12.263	.642

3.4 Likeability

No assumptions were violated. After controlling for negative attitudes toward robots, there was not a significant main effect of performance level, $F(1, 140) = 0.29, p = .592,$ *partial* $\eta^2 = .00$. There was not a significant main effect of task relevance $(F(1, 140)$ $= 0.14, p = .706,$ *partial* $\eta^2 = .00$), and there was also not a significant interaction between performance levesl and task relevance, $F(1, 140) = 0.75, p = .388,$ *partial* η^2 $= .01$. Estimated marginal means indicated that participants rated RUDY just as Likable when it performed well $(M_{Adjust} = 17.95, SE = .47)$ compared to when it performed poorly $(M_{Adjust} = 17.60, SE = .45)$ (see Table 5).

Table 5. Unadjusted means, standard deviations, adjusted means, and standard errors for likeability with NARS S1, S2, and S3 as covariates.

Group: performance level by task relevance	n	M	SD	M_Adjust	SE
Good performance (total)	71	17.817	3.951	17.954	.470
Good performance, High relevance	30	18.300	4.219	18.361	.720
Good performance, Low relevance	41	17.463	3.756	17.546	.610
Poor performance (total)	76	17.684	3.930	17.602	.449
Poor performance, High relevance	35	17.543	3.752	17.440	.663
Poor performance, Low relevance	41	17.805	4.118	17.765	.608

3.5 Perceived Safety

As there was a significant interaction between performance level and the NARS S2 and S3 covariates, the homogeneity of regression slopes assumptions was violated. In response, we removed NARS S2 and S3 from the analysis. After controlling for negative attitudes toward robots (S1 only), there was not a significant main effect of performance level, $F(1, 142) = 1.94, p = .166, partial\ \eta^2 = .01$. There was not significant main effect of task relevance ($F(1, 142) = 0.00, p = .968, partial\ \eta^2 = .00$), and there was also not a significant interaction between performance level and task relevance, $F(1, 142) = 0.97, p = .326, partial\ \eta^2 = .01$. Estimated marginal means indicated that participants rated RUDY just as safe when it performed well ($M_{Adjust} = 9.71, SE = .30$) compared to when it performed poorly ($M_{Adjust} = 10.28, SE = .38$) (See Table 6).

Table 6. Unadjusted means, standard deviations, adjusted means, and standard errors for perceived safety with NARS S1 as a covariate.

Group: performance level by task relevance	n	M	SD	M_{Adjust}	SE
Good performance (total)	71	9.704	2.504	9.707	.295
Good performance, High relevance	30	9.533	2.662	9.514	.448
Good performance, Low relevance	41	9.829	2.407	9.900	.384
Poor performance (total)	76	10.290	2.737	10.276	.282
Poor performance, High relevance	35	10.514	2.894	10.485	.415
Poor performance, Low relevance	41	10.098	2.615	10.066	.383

4 Discussion

The goal of this study was to conceptually replicate the findings of Kamide and colleagues' [12] study. Our first hypothesis was that RUDY's performance level would affect participant evaluations of RUDY on the five Godspeed Questionnaire dimensions. Specifically, we predicted that RUDY would be rated higher on the five dimensions when it performed well than when it performed poorly. This hypothesis was partially supported; RUDY was rated as more Anthropomorphic, more Intelligent, and more Animate when it performed well, but there were no differences in Likeability and Perceived Safety scores. Our second hypothesis was that task relevance would moderate the relationship between performance level and evaluations of RUDY. Specifically, we predicted that when RUDY executed a low-relevance task, participants would evaluate RUDY accurately (i.e., participants would rate RUDY higher on the five dimensions when it performed well compared to when it performed poorly), but inaccurately when RUDY executed a high-relevance task (i.e., there would be no difference in evaluations between the good and poor performances). This hypothesis was not supported, as there were no significant interactions between task relevance and performance level.

4.1 Performance Level

The effect of performance level was only significant for Anthropomorphism, Animacy and Perceived Intelligence. For Anthropomorphism, it is unlikely that the well-performing robot was rated as more humanlike in a physical sense (e.g., possessing a humanlike appearance), but it is possible that participants viewed RUDY as being more humanlike in that it could successfully accomplish typically human tasks (i.e., identifying emotion or guessing age). Similarly, RUDY may have been rated as more animate (or lifelike) not in a physical sense, but in the sense that RUDY was better at reacting to stimuli when it ostensibly took the Social Sensitivity or Age Estimation test. Unsurprisingly, RUDY was rated as more intelligent when it did well on the mock tests than when it did poorly. If the mock tests supposedly measured some aspect of intelligence, then it follows that participants rated the well-performing robot as more intelligent.

4.2 Comparison with Original Study

There were differences between the present study and the original [12] that may have contributed to the dissimilar results. The present study took place entirely online with a static image of the robot, whereas Kamide and colleagues' [12] study was conducted in person and with a physically embodied robot. Prior research indicates people view social robots more negatively when viewed online compared to in-person [22]. Using an image of a robot rather than a physically embodied robot may have also stifled participants' abilities to make comparisons with RUDY; the spatial and temporal distance from RUDY may have prohibited participants from considering RUDY as a being to which they could compare themselves. Although this may explain why there was not a main effect of performance level on all the Godspeed dimensions, this difference fails to account for why the well-performing robot was still rated more positively on three of the dimensions. Also, in the present study, participants were told that they would be helping to optimize the robot. These instructions may have led participants to generate more accurate or socially desirable responses, even if there were initial threats to their self-evaluation.

4.3 Limitations

The present study encountered several limitations. More participants in the high-relevance condition failed the test-name attention check than those in the low-relevance condition, possibly because it was more difficult to distinguish between the "psychological-sounding" correct answer (social sensitivity test) and the other "psychological-sounding" answer choices (cognitive dissonance test, attachment test, and stereotype Test) compared to when the correct answer was simply "age estimation test." Overall, the results did not vary greatly after removing the test-name attention check as an exclusion criterion. The only significant difference was, unlike the original sample, RUDY was rated just as Anthropomorphic when it performed well compared to when it performed poorly. Without knowing whether participants failed this attention check because it was too difficult or because they were not paying adequate attention, we must proceed with caution when interpreting the results of the Anthropomorphism subscale.

Additionally, participants may have questioned the legitimacy of the tests. If participants believed the tests to be fake or they doubted RUDY's score on the test, then they may have not seen RUDY as a threat to their self-evaluation. Thus, social comparison processes did not occur. Future studies ought to include checks to assess whether participants are suspicious of the task relevance and performance level manipulations.

Another limitation was that participants did not physically interact with RUDY or view its performance first-hand. Instead, participants were given a photograph of RUDY and a brief description of the robot and its performance. This limitation begs the question, was this truly human-robot *interaction*? This question is certainly up for debate; human-robot *impression formation* may be closer to the true nature of the current study. However, we propose that examining evaluations of robots via photographs and written descriptions is not without merit or precedent. For instance, Eyssel and Kuchenbrandt [23] showed participants photographs of a robot and described it as having either in-group or out-group characteristics. Participants expressed more willingness to live with and talk to the robot when it ostensibly possessed in-group features. If information about a robot can shape attitudes and, consequently, impact one's willingness to interact with it, this is a valuable area to pursue.

4.4 Conclusion

Unlike the original study, the present study failed to show SEM effects. Our results show what one might "expect" to see; the robot that performed well was, overall, rated more positively than the one that performed poorly. A concern put forth by Kamide and colleagues [12] was that robots performing highly relevant tasks may be psychologically unsafe; however, the present study suggests that the nature of the task and the mode of interaction with the robot may influence whether SEM effects occur. Future research ought to examine what is deemed a self-relevant task when it comes to HRI, especially if we presume that certain social robots, such as caregiving robots, perform highly self-relevant tasks. Additionally, we, like Kamide and colleagues' [12], did not manipulate psychological closeness, which is a key piece of the SEM model [8]. Including this variable in future studies may help clarify under what conditions SEM processes occur in HRI. Also, if comparison processes *do* occur in HRI, psychological closeness may play a key role in preventing negative self-evaluations. For example, a psychologically distant robot completing a self-relevant task might be less threatening than a psychologically close robot completing the same task. As social robots become more prevalent in our societies, it will be important to understand how psychological effects present in human-human interaction—such as those described by the SEM model—map onto human-robot interaction, or whether new models will be required to understand these effects.

Acknowledgements. We would like to express our sincere thanks to INF Robotics Inc. for allowing us to use a photograph of their robot, RUDY.

References

1. Darling, K.: Extending legal protection to social robots: the effects of anthropomorphism, empathy, and violent behavior towards robotic objects. In: Calo, R., Froomkin, M., Kerr, I. (eds.), Robot Law, pp. 213–234. Edward Elgar (2012). https://doi.org/10.2139/ssrn.2044797
2. Leite, I., Pereira, A., Mascarenhas, S., Martinho, C., Prada, R., Paiva, A.: The influence of empathy in human-robot relations. Int. J. Hum Comput Stud. **71**(3), 250–260 (2013). https://doi.org/10.1016/j.ijhcs.2012.09.005
3. Kim, B., et al.: How early task success affects attitudes toward social robots. In: Companion of the 2020 ACM/IEEE International Conference on Human-Robot Interaction, 287–289 (2020). https://doi.org/10.1145/3371382.3378241
4. Jhangiani, R., Tarry, H.: Principles of social psychology – 1st international edition. BCcampus Open Education (2014). https://opentextbc.ca/socialpsychology/
5. Tesser, A.: Toward a self-evaluation maintenance model of social behavior. Adv. Exp. Soc. Psychol. **21**(1), 181–227 (1988). https://doi.org/10.1016/S0065-2601(08)60227-0
6. Gino, F., Galinsky, A.D.: Vicarious dishonesty: when psychological closeness creates distance from one's moral compass. Organ. Behav. Hum. Decis. Process. **119**(1), 15–26 (2012). https://doi.org/10.1016/j.obhdp.2012.03.011
7. Cialdini, R.B., Borden, R.J., Thorne, A., Walker, M.R., Freeman, S., Sloan, L.R.: Basking in reflected glory: three (football) field studies. J. Pers. Soc. Psychol. **34**(3), 366–375 (1976). https://doi.org/10.1037/0022-3514.34.3.366
8. Tesser, A., Smith, J.: Some effects of task relevance and friendship on helping: you don't always help the one you like. J. Exp. Soc. Psychol. **16**(6), 582–590 (1980). https://doi.org/10.1016/0022-1031(80)90060-8
9. Crawford, M.T.: The renegotiation of social identities in response to a threat to self-evaluation maintenance. J. Exp. Soc. Psychol. **43**(1), 39–47 (2007). https://doi.org/10.1016/j.jesp.2005.12.011
10. Nicholls, E., Stukas, A.A.: Narcissism and the self-evaluation maintenance model: effects of social comparison threats on relationship closeness. J. Soc. Psychol. **151**(2), 201–212 (2011). https://doi.org/10.1080/00224540903510852
11. Pleban, R., Tesser, A.: The effects of relevance and quality of another's performance on interpersonal closeness. Soc. Psychol. Quart. **44**(3), 278–285 (1981). https://doi.org/10.2307/3033841
12. Kamide, H., Kawabe, K., Shigemi, S., Arai, T.: Social comparison between the self and a humanoid. In: Herrmann, G., Pearson, M.J., Lenz, A., Bremner, P., Spiers, A., Leonards, U. (eds.) ICSR 2013. LNCS (LNAI), vol. 8239, pp. 190–198. Springer, Cham (2013). https://doi.org/10.1007/978-3-319-02675-6_19
13. Schulz, R., Eden, J. (eds.): Families Caring for an Aging America. National Academies Press, Washington, D.C. (2016). https://doi.org/10.17226/23606
14. Nomura, T., Suzuki, T., Kanda, T., Kato, K.: Measurement of negative attitudes toward robots. Interac. Stud. Soc. Behav. Commun. Biol. Artif. Syst. **7**(3), 437–454 (2006). https://doi.org/10.1075/is.7.3.14nom
15. Bender, L., Walia, G., Kambhampaty, K., Nygard, K., Nygard, T. E. Social sensitivity and classroom team projects: an empirical investigation. In: SIGCSE '12, pp. 403–408 (2012). https://doi.org/10.1145/2157136.2157258
16. Ma, D.S., Kantner, J., Wittenbrink, B.: Chicago face database: multiracial expansion. Behav. Res. Methods **53**(3), 1289–1300 (2020). https://doi.org/10.3758/s13428-020-01482-5
17. Tesser, A., Campbell, J.: A self-evaluation maintenance approach to school behavior. Educ. Psychol. **17**(1), 1–12 (1982). https://doi.org/10.1080/00461528209529240
18. INF Robotics [Photograph of RUDY]. INF Robotics Inc (2020)

19. Bartneck, C., Croft, E., Kulic, D.: Measurement instruments for the anthropomorphism, animacy, likeability, perceived intelligence, and perceived safety of robots. Int. J. Soc. Robot. 1(1), 71–81 (2009). https://doi.org/10.1007/s12369-008-0001-3
20. IBM Corp: IBM SPSS Statistics for Macintosh. (Version 27.0) [Software] (2020) https://www.ibm.com/analytics/spss-statistics-software
21. Olejnik, S.F., Algina, J.: Parametric ANCOVA and the rank transform ANCOVA when the data are conditionally non-normal and heteroscedastic. J. Educ. Stat. 9(2), 129–149 (1984). https://doi.org/10.3102/10769986009002129
22. Damholdt, M.F., Christina, V., Kryvous, A., Smedegaard, C.V., Seibt, J.: What is in three words? Exploring a three-word methodology for assessing impressions of a social robot encounter online and in real life. Paladyn, J. Behav. Robot. 10(1), 438–453 (2019). https://doi.org/10.1515/pjbr-2019-0034
23. Eyssel, F., Kuchenbrandt, D.: Social categorization of social robots: anthropomorphism as a function of robot group membership. Br. J. Soc. Psychol. 51(4), 724–731 (2012). https://doi.org/10.1111/j.2044-8309.2011.02082.x

Birds of a Feather Flock Together: A Study of Status Homophily in HRI

Roya Salek Shahrezaie(✉)⬤, Bashira Akter Anima⬤, and David Feil-Seifer⬤

Socially Assistive Robotics Group, Department of Computer Science and Engineering
University of Nevada, Reno, Reno 89557, USA
{rsalek,banima}@nevada.unr.edu, dave@cse.unr.edu

Abstract. Homophily, a person's bias for having ties with people who are similar to themselves in social ways, has a vital role in creating a social connection between people. Studying homophily in human-robot interactions can provide valuable insights for improving those interactions. In this paper, we investigate whether similar interests have a positive effect on a human-robot interaction similar to the positive impact it can have on human-human interaction. We explore whether sharing similar interests can affect trust. This experiment consisted of two NAO robots; each gave differing speeches. For each participant, their national origin was asked in the pre-questionnaire, and during the sessions, one of the robot's topics was either personalized or not to their national origin. Since one robot shared a familiar topic, we expected to observe bonding between humans and the robot. We gathered data from a post-questionnaire and analyzed them. The results summarize the hypotheses here. We conclude that homophily plays a significant role in human-robot interaction, affecting trust in a robot partner.

Keywords: HRI · Homophily · Trust

1 Introduction

People tend to connect with others who are similar to themselves [1]. This tendency, referred by social scientists as homophily, manifests itself with similarities due to gender, national origin, social class background, and other socio-demographic, behavioral and interpersonal characteristics [2]. Individuals in homophilic relationships share common characteristics (such as beliefs, values, education) that make communication and relationship formation easier. In HRI, a robot needs to create a smooth interaction with its audience in order to perform well in social settings. We wish to investigate if robots can benefit from the same social tendency and leverage from homophily in their interactions. We proposed an experiment where a social robot acts in such a way that implies homophily while another robot does not. Then we observed how the person will react toward the robots. We expected that achieving homophily, or bonding

---

R. Salek Shahrezaie and B. A. Anima—Same contribution on this paper.

© Springer Nature Switzerland AG 2021
H. Li et al. (Eds.): ICSR 2021, LNAI 13086, pp. 281–291, 2021.
https://doi.org/10.1007/978-3-030-90525-5_24

based on a common interest or implying similarity, between a human user and a robot, holds a promise of improvement in trust between them.

The similarity between humans and robots is an essential facilitator of positive attitudes toward robots [3]. For instance, Bernier and Scassellati [4] showed that the more an individual believes that a robot is similar to them, the more they like and prefer to interact with them. Also, research of Bowman et al. [3] found that individuals tend to like and build healthier emotional attachment toward robots that appear to have a similar personality to theirs. Finding homophily between individuals is a useful for human-robot interaction. Therefore, we wanted to investigate if this phenomenon could occur between humans and robots as well.

In this paper, we explore homophily between a person and a robot from a questionnaire by measuring common interest, bonding, and similarity between a person and a robot. The purpose of this work is to determine whether similarities between a robot and a person might improve social connection and trust. If such a link exists, then homophily would be an important physical and behavioral design consideration for effective HRI; this could lead to an improved first impression of a robot, which might eventually help humans communicate and interact with the robot more easily.

2 Background

Homophily in HRI: Homophily is a term familiar in social sciences. In Rhetoric and Nichomachean Ethics, Aristotle noted that people "love those who are like themselves" [5]. It was also observed by Plato that "similarity begets friendship" [6]. Back in 2001, McPherson et al. [2], presented a principle named homophily. It states that "a contract between similar people occurs at a higher rate than among dissimilar people." Overall homophily can be differentiated into two types: 1) value homophily and 2) status homophily. Value homophily is based on attitudes, beliefs, and values. Status homophily is based on national origin, sex, age, and characteristics like religion, education, occupation.

Many research in the robotic world also worked on the common factors that a robot and a human can share. As an example, propensities of preference for Human-Robot Interaction (HRI) according to different personalities and facial expressions of human and robot are presented in A paper of Jung et al.[7]. Two types of personalities: extrovert and introvert were applied to the robot named KMC-EXPR to observe the impact of different personality type in interaction between humans and robots. Also Kahn's work [8], a humanoid robot named Robovie was used to interact with children. After each 15 min session, the experimenter interrupted the session and sent the robot to the closet. Later, it was observed how the children felt towards the robot in many aspects.

The effect of verbal and nonverbal behavior based on personality traits in human-robot interaction has been observed [9]. A NAO robot was used to validate their model that a person preferred more robots to interact with if they both had the same personality traits. Finally, a study from Heerink [10], shows that age, gender, education, and computer experience had an influence on robot acceptance by older adults. Our prior work showed that establishing common-ground using ice-breaker tasks helped a person identify with a robot team-member [11]. Witnessing verbal mistreatment of a robot also resulted in increased perception of the robot's emotional ability [12].

Recent work investigated if a human user would help a robot being bullied by other humans when social bonding has been applied in human-robot's interactions [13]. Similar to our study, they used favourite food to contextualize a human and robot conversation so the person finds a similarity with the robot. Their results did not prove their hypothesis, on the other hand our findings suggest that a shared similarity can improve the sympathy in human and robot interaction.

Trust in HRI: It is observed that people tend to trust more easily those people who appear similar to themselves. By similarity, it may include common values, membership in a defined group (such as manufacturing departments, a local church, gender), shared personality traits, etc. [14]. In that research, when people evaluate others' trustworthiness, cues such as gender [15], age [16], race, and nationality influence the initial assessment.

Salem et al. [17], conducted an experiment in which participants interacted with a home companion robot in one of two experimental conditions named correct mode and faulty mode while tapping different dimensions of trust based on a variety of unusual collaborative tasks. It was observed that the robot's performance did not influence participants' decisions to comply with its request. Hancock et al., evaluated the effects of the human, robot, and environmental factors on perceived trust in human-robot interaction [18]. Human-related factors depend on ability-based characteristics, robot-related factors are based on performance and attributes, and environmental factors include team collaboration and tasking. In this study [19], whether a robot's vulnerable behavior can create ripple effects on a team and increase team physiological safety and human-human trust-related behavior were explored. It was seen that the 'ripples' of the robot's vulnerable behavior influences not only team member's interaction with the robot but also team members' human-human-trust-related interaction with each other.

3   Study Design

In this user study, we aimed to measure the perceived similarities between a person and a robot when they shared a common interest. As our second interest, we were looking into the effect of homophily on trust human-robot trust. We proposed two hypotheses on similarity and trust:

- **H1**: A person will feel a similarity (homophily) to the robot in a human-robot interaction when they share a common interest
- **H2**: There is a correlation between homophily and trust in human-robot interaction

Our two hypothesis would be tested by making two experimental conditions and analysing data.

3.1 Experiment Conditions

In this section, we explain how we developed two conditions for testing out the hypothesis. Each participant experiences condition one in which the person finds similarity to the robot and condition two where it is the opposite. There can be different homophily categorizations based on age, gender, national origin, socioeconomic state, ethnicity, attitude, etc. However, we chose 'National Origin' as our divider for different groups. Since we wanted to find a food known by the person, we considered national origin which means the nation where a person was born, or the country of origin that person's ancestors came from. And, they may know food associated with that area directly or by their family. The correlation between national origin and homophily is also higher than gender [20] for instance. For this study, to more tightly control potential participant differences, we chose only one age range (18-35) and one education level (university students).

The experiment was conducted in a room in one of the libraries on the University of Nevada, Reno campus. For the experiment, we used two NAO robots. We distinguished the robots to the participants as Red NAO and Blue NAO based on their color. Here, the Blue and the Red NAO were the Homophilic Condition Robot and the Non-Homophilic Condition Robot respectively. Figure 1a shows the set up of the robots during the user study. In the pre-questionnaire form (Table 2), general information such as age, gender, major, and national origin information were asked of the participant.

3.2 Experiment Task

At first, before staring our experiment we explained our experiment in brief to each participant. We let them know that all collected data would remain anonymous. If the participant agreed to take part in the experiment then we continued with the rest of the experiment.

Our proposed method was divided into 3 major steps. These are: 1) Pre Questionnaire, 2) Speech Presentation, 3) Post Questionnaire

- **Pre Questionnaire.** At first, the participant was given a pre questionnaire form (Table 2) which included demographic questions such as age, gender, major, and national origin information. We used the national origin information to categorize participants.

  We categorized the participants into one of 12 broad national origins: European, Middle East, North African, African, North American, South American, Central American, Southeast Asia, East Asian, West Asian, South Asian, and Other. The name of the national origin category in the U.S. was collected from the United States Census Bureau data [21].

Table 1. Homophilic condition for each national origin category

1	What is your age?
2	What is your gender?
	1.Male 2.Female 3.Other
3	What is your major and degree?
4	Are you familiar with robots?
5	Choose which national origin best represents you:
	1. Europe
	2. Middle East
	3. North African
	4. African
	5. North American
	6. South American
	7. Central American
	8. Southeast Asia
	9. East Asian
	10. West Asian
	11. Indian
	12. Other

Table 2. Pre questionnaire

National Origin	Homophilic Condition
Europe	Pirozhki
Middle East	Kebab
North African	Coucous
African	Bobotie
North American	Cheese Steak
South American	Ceviche
Central American	Pupusa
Southeast Asia	Nasi Campur
East Asia	Sichuan Cuisine
West Asia	Kebab
South Asia	Biriyani
Others	Ice Cream

- **Speech Presentation.** We designed an interaction between human and robot where two NAO humanoid robots gave speech presentations in front of the participant individually (Fig. 1b) where the robots were tele-operated by the experimenter from the other room. The participants did not know about the existence of the robot's operator. During each session, one robot gave a presentation on the homophilic condition related to the participant's national origin shown in Table 1. After that, the remaining robot gave a presentation on a non-homophilic condition.

The topic of the homophilic condition of the presentation for each participant was selected based on the national origin information given by the specific participant in the pre-questionnaire. The famous food dishes from each region of the national origin was chosen as the homophilic condition for each national origin group (Table 1). The robot gave a speech presentation on bread as the non-homophilic condition which is familiar to every national origin category. Samples of the speeches by the homophilic condition robot and the non-homophilic condition robot are given below respectively, where the homophilic condition robot's speech is about 'Kebab' towards the participants categorized into the 'Middle East' and the non-homophilic condition robot's speech is about 'Bread.'

- Homophilic Condition Robot: *'Hi, I am Blue NAO. I am going to talk about a dish named Kebab. Kebab is a very popular dish all around the world. Shish Kebab or doner Kebab can be two familiar names of Kebab.*

(a) Red and Blue NAOs used for the experiment

(b) The participant listening to the robot's speech

Fig. 1. Experimental setup

It is often served during special occasions. It can be made with ground meat or seafood, even sometimes with fruits and vegetables. Traditional meat of Kebab is most often mutton or lamb, but regional recipes may include beef. Sometimes Onions are often added with Kebab to enhance the taste. Kebab is served with various dishes according to each recipe. Kebab with naan is very popular in some regions. Yogurt drink is often served with Kebab. It is also served with rice, grilled tomatoes, tabbouleh salad, or bread. There are many restaurants in Reno where we can find Kebab, and they are delicious. Well, I hope you enjoyed my speech.'

- Non-Homophilic Condition Robot: *'Bread is a staple food prepared from a dough of flour and water, usually by baking. Throughout recorded history, it has been popular around the world and is one of the oldest artificial foods, having been of importance since the dawn of agriculture. Proportions of types of flour and other ingredients vary widely, as do modes of preparation. As a result, types, shapes, sizes, and textures of bread differ around the world. Bread may be leavened by processes such as reliance on naturally occurring sourdough microbes, chemicals, industrially produced yeast, or high-pressure aeration. Some bread is cooked before it can leaven, including for traditional or religious reasons. Non-cereal ingredients such as fruits, nuts and fats may be included. Commercial bread commonly contains additives to improve flavor, texture, color, shelf life, nutrition, and ease of manufacturing. Also, bread has a social and emotional significance beyond its importance as nourishment. It plays an essential role in religious rituals and secular culture. Well, I hope you enjoyed my speech.'*

– **Post Questionnaire**
Each speech took less than 3 min. After listening to these presentations one after another, the participant filled out a post-questionnaire form. There were questions regarding homophily, trust, and provided speeches. The questionnaire was divided into two parts. First part was observing the effect of the speech on the trust by asking each participant to choose one of the robots to pick one snack for themselves from the other room.

Table 3. Post-questionnaire

Category	Question	Type
Homophily	The Robot was similar to me	(1–5)
	The Robot thinks like me	(1–5)
	The Robot behaves like me	(1–5)
	The Robot and I had a common interest	(1–5)
	I felt a bond with the Robot while it was speaking	(1–5)
Being suspicious	The Robot is deceptive	(1–5)
	The Robot behaves in the underhanded manner	(1–5)
	I am suspicious of the Robot's intent,action or outputs	(1–5)
	I am wary of the Robot	(1–5)
	The Robot's actions will have a harmful or injurious outcomes	(1–5)
Security	I am confident in the Robot	(1–5)
	The Robot provides security	(1–5)
Trust	The Robot is dependable	(1–5)
	The Robot is reliable	(1–5)
	I can trust the Robot	(1–5)
Familiarity	I am familiar with the Robot	(1–5)
Topic	Are you familiar with the blue Robot talked about?	(1–5)
	Which speech did you find more interesting?	(1–5)

Table 4. One-sample test (Test value = 3)

	t	df	Sig. (2-tailed)	Mean Difference	95% Confidence Interval	
					Lower	Upper
Common Interest	4.858	15	0.000	0.938	0.53	1.35
Felt Bonding	2.551	15	0.022	0.688	0.11	1.26
Similarity	3.162	15	0.006	0.500	0.16	0.84

The other part consisted of questions to measure the degree of both homophily and trust (see Table 3). This questionnaire was adapted from [22] and Jian et al. [23] to measure homophily and trust respectively. We also added some extra questions related to this experiment that would help us to analyze the answers. All the questions in the questionnaire are based on five-point Likert scale.

4   Results and Analysis

Details of experiment results and analysis are presented in this section. We analyzed data from questionnaires in order to support or refute our hypotheses presented above.

Participants were gathered from the University of Nevada, Reno campus area. Most of the participants' age ranged from 18 to 35. We initially recruited 19 participants, discard three participants' data due to robot malfunctions. We used the remaining 16 participants in our analysis, 6 male, ten female. Among the participants, there were 4 participants from Southeast Asia, 4 participants from Middle East, 3 participants from South Asia, 2 participants from East Asia, 2 participants from North America, and 1 participant from Europe.

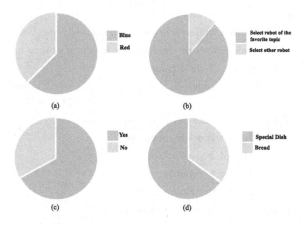

Fig. 2. (a) Chosen Robot, (b) Familiarity with topics, (c) Chosen robot is the one with dish topic, (d) More interesting topic

We explored results related to our hypothesis: first, homophily among participants (two groups of the ones who chose the Blue NAO and those who chose the Red NAO); second, correlation between homophily and trust categories in data.

To have a better understanding of our data, we used pie charts. The data shown in Figs. 2(a–d) relate to our experiment hypotheses. The majority of the participants (62.5%) chose the blue robot (homophily condition) in the first part of post-questionnaire which we mentioned in Sect. 3.2.

We further investigated why some participants preferred the red NAO. Many countries share one origin, but there is a possibility that people of one origin may not be familiar with exceptional food. For those participants with no idea about the unique food, the general topic of 'bread' the familiar topic. Fortunately, The last two questions in the 'topic' category of post-questionnaire shown in Table 3 define this issue and clear if the person is familiar with the blue NAO topic or not, and which topic was more interesting for him/her. So, we used the favorite topic question to compare 'chosen robot' and 'favorite topic' to have a new query, which is 'the participants whose choice was in line with their favorite topic. If choosing (Red NAO-homophily condition) and (Blue NAO-homophily condition), the person gets a 1 and otherwise gets a 0. We observed this group owned

Table 5. Correlation

		Reliability	Trust	Similarity	Common Interest
Reliability	Pearson Correlation	1	.631**	0/316	−0/022
	Sig. (2-tailed)		0/009	0/233	0/937
	N	16	16	16	16
Trust	Pearson Correlation	.631**	1	.665**	.539*
	Sig. (2-tailed)	0/009		0/005	0/031
	N	16	16	16	16
Similarity	Pearson Correlation	0/316	.665**	1	0/205
	Sig. (2-tailed)	0/233	0/005		0/447
	N	16	16	16	16
Common interest	Pearson Correlation	−0/022	.539*	0/205	1
	Sig. (2 tailed)	0/037	0/031	0/447	
	N	16	16	16	16

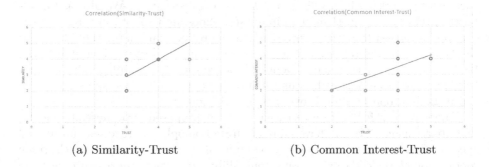

(a) Similarity-Trust   (b) Common Interest-Trust

Fig. 3. Correlation

80% of the population (see Fig. 2(c)). We conclude that participants mostly chose the robot that was talking about a familiar topic.

To investigate our first hypothesis for each independent variable, we analyzed the results using one sample t-test, knowing that the experiment has one sample group with two variables. As seen in Table 4 a one-sample t-test showed that there is a significant difference in mean 'common interest' between the homophilic and non homophilic conditions ($p < .001$). There was a significant difference in mean 'felt bonding' between the the homophilic and non homophilic conditions ($p < .001$). There was also a significant difference in mean 'similarity' between the homophilic and non homophilic conditions ($p < .001$) (see Table 4).

To explore our second hypothesis, we used Pearson correlation test results (see Table 5). We found that there is a moderate positive correlation between 'similarity' and 'trust' variables ($r = 0.665, n = 16, p = 0.005$) (see Fig. 3a). There was also a moderate positive correlation between 'Common Interest' and 'Trust' ($r = 0.539, n = 16, p = 0.03$) (see Fig. 3b).

5 Conclusion and Future Work

In this paper, we explored the effect of national origin as homophilic condition in case of Human-Robot interaction because among all of these 'national origin' is a significant social divider today [2].

Our two hypotheses were supported by our results shown in the prior section. Our first hypothesis, H1: **"A person will feel a similarity (homophily) to the robot in a human-robot interaction when they share a common interest"** was supported via the significant result in the similarity comparison shown in Table 4. H2: **"There is a correlation between homophily and trust in human-robot interaction"** was supported by showing that there is a correlation between homophily and trust in human-robot interaction in Table 5. The responses to question one show the preference for the homophily condition with a correlation for preference in the robot with familiar topic (see Fig. 2). This question gave participants a forced choice between robots to pick their prize (snack), which reflects trust in a social situation. We also asked our participants to explain their reasoning after choosing a robot, and most of the comments showed that they were trusting the robot that shares the interest or the topic robot was talking about was more familiar to them. This 'trust' can be contextualized with two comments: "If he were talking about bombs, I would have not to trust him, but he was talking about Biryani! I love spicy food."; "I chose the blue one because I love kebab, and I miss it."

There is room for more investigation on our proposed hypotheses by having more participants. We can have more accurate homophily categories and related speech for each category. That will profoundly affect our results because the more robot's speech is close to a person's homophily group; our results can reflect the more accurate result.

Acknowledgments. The authors would also like to acknowledge the financial support of this work by the National Science Foundation (NSF, #IIS-1719027).

References

1. Lazarsfeld, P., Merton, R.: Friendship as social process: a substantive and method-ological analysis, pp. 18–66 (1954)
2. McPherson, M., et al.: Birds of a feather: homophily in social networks. Ann. Rev. Sociol. **27**(1), 415–444 (2001)
3. Bowman, M., et al.: Reasoning about naming systems. ACM Trans. Program. Lang. Syst. **15**(5), 795–825 (1993)
4. Bernier,E. P., Scassellati, B.: The similarity-attraction effect in human-robot inter-action. In: 2010 IEEE 9th International Conference on Development and Learning, pp. 286–290 (2010)
5. Aristotle. Rhetoric.nichomachean ethics. In: Aristotle in 23 Volumes. Rackman Translation. Cambridge, Harvard University Press (1934)
6. Plato Laws Twelve Volumes, vol. 11. Bury Translator. Cambridge, Harvard University Press (1968)

7. Jung, S., et al.: Personality and facial expressions in human-robot interaction. In: Human-Robot Interaction (HRI), 2012 7th ACM/IEEE International Conference on, pp. 161–162. IEEE (2012)
8. Kahn, P.H., et al.: "Robovie, you'll have to go into the closet now": children's social and moral relationships with a humanoid robot. Dev. Psychol. **48**(2), 303–314 (2012)
9. Aly, A., Tapus, A.: A model for synthesizing a combined verbal and nonverbal behavior based on personality traits in human-robot interaction. In: 2013 8th ACM/IEEE International Conference on Human-Robot Interaction (HRI), pp. 325–332 (2013)
10. Heerink, M.: Exploring the influence of age, gender, education and computer experience on robot acceptance by older adults. In: Proceedings of the 6th International Conference on Human-robot Interaction, HRI '11 ACM, pp. 147–148, New York, NY, USA (2011)
11. Carlson, Z., et al.: Team-building activities for heterogeneous groups of humans and robots. In: International Conference on Social Robotics (ICSR), pp. 113–123, Paris, France (2015)
12. Carlson, Z., et al.: Perceived mistreatment and emotional capability following aggressive treatment of robots and computers. Int. J. Soc. Robot. **11**(5), 727–739 (2019)
13. Kühnlenz, B., Kühnlenz, K.: Social bonding increases unsolicited helpfulness towards a bullied robot. In: 2020 29th IEEE International Conference on Robot and Human Interactive Communication (RO-MAN), pp. 833–838 (2020)
14. Hurley, R.: The decision to trust. **84**, 55–62, 156, 10 (2006)
15. Buchan, N.R., et al.: Trust and gender: an examination of behavior and beliefs in the investment game. J. Econ. Behav. Organ. **68**(3), 466–476 (2008)
16. Sutter, M., Kocher, M.G.: Trust and trustworthiness across different age groups. Games Econ. Behav. **59**(2), 364–382 (2007)
17. Salem, M., et al.: Would you trust a (faulty) robot?: effects of error, task type and personality on human-robot cooperation and trust. In: Proceedings of the Tenth Annual ACM/IEEE International Conference on Human-Robot Interaction, HRI '15. ACM, pp. 141–148, New York, NY, USA (2015)
18. Hancock, P.A., et al.: A meta-analysis of factors affecting trust in human-robot interaction. Human Factors **53**(5), 517–527 (2011). PMID: 22046724
19. Strohkorb Sebo, S., et al.: The ripple effects of vulnerability: the effects of a robot's vulnerable behavior on trust in human-robot teams. In: Proceedings of the 2018 ACM/IEEE International Conference on Human-Robot Interaction, HRI '18. ACM, pp. 178–186, New York, NY, USA (2018)
20. Moody, J.: Race, school integration, and friendship segregation in america. Am. J. Sociol. **107**(3), 679–716 (2001)
21. Bureau, U. C.:. Race and ethnicity (2017)
22. McCroskey, L.L., et al.: Analysis and improvement of the measurement of interpersonal attraction and homophily. Commun. Q. **54**(1), 1–31 (2006)
23. Jian, J.-Y., et al.: Foundations for an empirically determined scale of trust in automated systems. **403**, 53–71 (2000)

Communication

"Space Agency": A "Strong Concept" for Designing Socially Interactive, Robotic Environments

Yixiao Wang[1]($\boxtimes$) and Keith Evan Green[2]

[1] Research Field: Smart Built Environment and Human Robot Interaction, Singapore University of Technology and Design (SUTD), 8 Somapah Rd, Singapore 487372, Singapore
yixiao_wang@sutd.edu.sg

[2] Research Field: Architectural Robotics, Cornell University, Ithaca, NY 14850, USA
keg95@cornell.edu

Abstract. What if our surrounding built environment could understand our emotions, predict our needs, and otherwise assist us, both physically and socially? What if we could interact with private and public spaces as if these were our friends, partners, and companions — "Space Agents"? "Space Agents" are here defined as robotic, smart built environments designed to be perceived or interacted with as socially intelligent agents. In this paper, we consider Space Agency both as a "Strong Concept" (a category of generative, intermediate-level design knowledge), and as a new research field of "socially interactive smart built environment" for Social Robotics, HAI, and HCI communities. "Space Agency" is considered with respect to previous empirical and theoretical works of HCI and Architecture and also by our own recent work on a socially adaptive wall. We conclude this paper by advancing the generalizability, novelty, and substantivity of "Space Agency" as a Strong Concept, abstracted beyond specific design instances which designers and researchers, in turn, can use to ideate and generate new design instances of social robots.

Keywords: Space agent · Strong concept · Socially interactive smart built environment · Socially intelligent agent · Interaction design theory

1 Introduction

With the rapid development of "industry 4.0," artificial intelligence is being embedded and embodied in our everyday lives more, and more pervasively. As a result, human-machine interactions for conversational agents and social robots are being widely studied, tested, and theorized in HCI communities [1–3]. However, human-machine interactions for Smart Built Environments (SBE) are still underexplored. SBE are "spaces integrated with sensors-actuator systems and intelligent control algorithms" [4]. This paper investigates human-SBE social interactions and relationships through the theoretical lens of generative intermediate-level design knowledge supported by evidence from empirical studies and theoretical works. We argue that "Space Agency" can be a powerful and generative "Strong Concept" through which social human-SBE interactions and relationships can be designed, prototyped, and investigated.

© Springer Nature Switzerland AG 2021
H. Li et al. (Eds.): ICSR 2021, LNAI 13086, pp. 295–307, 2021.
https://doi.org/10.1007/978-3-030-90525-5_25

1.1 Strong Concept as a Category of Intermediate-Level Design Knowledge

Researchers from HCI and HRI have been producing design knowledge in the level of instances and theory predominantly using empirical research methods [5]. However, as designers and design researchers, we know there are many cases both in research and practice where we employ and generate pieces of design knowledges such as Patterns, Design Guidelines, Heuristics, etc. that are more abstract than specific design instances, but less generalizable than a theory. This kind of design knowledge is characterized as intermediate-level design knowledge [5–7]. Intermediate level design knowledge serves as an abstraction or, more specifically, a common annotation of different design instances from one family [5–7]. There are two categories of design knowledge: evaluative and generative knowledge. Evaluative intermediate-level knowledge such as Design Heuristics and Criticism tend to synthesize and evaluate design instances, while generative intermediate-level design knowledge such as Patterns, Guidelines, and Strong Concepts tend to inspire and generate new designs [5]. Strong Concepts are design elements abstracted beyond specific design instances and can be potentially appropriated by designers and researchers to ideate and generate new design instances [5].

1.2 "Space Agency" Towards a Strong Concept

"Space Agency" characterizes SBEs and their spatial elements (e.g., walls, floors, furnishings, etc.) designed to be perceived or interacted with as socially intelligent agents [8, 9]. For instance, the adaptive or interactive behavior of a smart chair, wall, or room, if carefully designed, can be perceived by users as socially expressive – as welcoming, inviting, friendly, etc. "Space Agency" fits the four characteristics of Strong Concept given by Hook and Lowgren [5]:

- It concerns user perception of interactive behaviors of the spatial elements, which will shape the user interactions unfolding over time;
- It resides in the interface between SBE and users, manifesting itself as design elements (e.g., motions, trajectories, etc.) supporting socially expressive interactions.
- It has been a core design idea at the very beginning of the design process and can cut across different use cases of, for instance, a stool, a door, a wall, etc.;
- It resides on an abstract level and can/should be realized in different aspects of a design including interaction patterns, interaction modalities, form factors, etc.

1.3 Key Contributions of "Space Agency" to Social Robotics, HAI, and HCI

The key contributions of "Space Agency" are:

A New Generative Intermediate-Level Design Knowledge. This paper proposes and validates the design knowledge of "Space Agency," which is a substantive Strong Concept with generative power. Through "Space Agency," we can design and generate interactive and adaptive SBE, perceived as our friends, companions, partners, playmates, etc.

Socially Interactive SBEs as a New Research Field for Human-Building Interaction. Human-Building Interaction (HBI) [10] is a nascent research field in interaction design community. In HBI, there is no established design knowledge informing the design researchers that buildings can be designed, perceived, and investigated as socially intelligent agents (as will be demonstrated in Sect. 3). Just as in HCI, software interfaces can be designed as embodied conversational agents that are intelligent and social [1], so in HRI, robots can be designed as socially intelligent and interactive [2]. Following this trajectory, we now argue that in HBI, buildings can also be designed and perceived as socially intelligent and interactive, which is the essence of "Space Agency."

2 Methodology

A key aim of this paper is to characterize "Space Agency" as a Strong Concept that is academically contestable, defensible, and substantive so that design researchers could confidently employ this concept in their design works, investigate this concept through empirical studies, and build upon this concept in theoretical discussions [11, 12]. Thus, we follow the Strong Concept construction process elaborated by Hook and Lowgren as an "exercise in epistemology" [5]:

- For the source of this Strong Concept, we present our design instance of the "socially adaptive robotic wall" in Sect. 4 and illustrate how "Space Agency" is applied to and evaluated in this design instance;
- For the horizontal grounding of this Strong Concept, we review the most relevant empirical works in "Human Building Interaction" (HBI) and "Large-scale Shape-changing Interface" in Sect. 3;
- For the vertical grounding of this Strong Concept, we investigate the theoretical works from both Architecture and HCI and illustrate how the embodiment of "Socially Intelligent Agent" evolved in the last 20 years in Sect. 3;
- Finally, the nature of this research is presented in Sect. 5 where the generalizability, novelty, and substantivity of "Space Agency" are discussed.

3 Related Works

Our literature review unfolds through the following topics serving as the "horizontal grounding" and "vertical grounding" [5] of "Space Agency" in the intellectual landscape of HCI and HRI design research: "Human-Building Interaction" and "Large-scale Shape-changing Interface" serve as the "horizontal grounding" speaking to the empirical works most closely related to "Space Agency"; "The Theoretical Foundation of 'Space Agency'" serves as the "vertical grounding" speaking to the Architecture and HCI theoretical works that support this Strong Concept.

3.1 Human Building Interaction and Large-Scale Shape-Changing Interface

Human Building Interaction (HBI) is a nascent research field unifying HCI with built environment. HBI focuses on the human perspectives (e.g., values, needs, wants, experiences, etc.) to address people's interaction with interactive or smart built environments [10]. Before HBI was formally introduced to the HCI community [10], designers and researchers from architecture and robotics have been actively exploring human-architecture interaction through empirical works. "Architectural Robotics" [13] investigated user interaction with robotic furnishings [14], a robotic canopy [15], and room-scaled robotic spaces [16].

More recently, HBI researchers investigated user perception of user-controlled virtual walls [17] and user interaction with a dynamic tent-like structure [18]. Grönvall et al. and Suzuki have developed shape-changing interfaces, from furniture-scale to room-scale, whose user interactions were investigated. Grönvall et al. developed a shape-changing bench whose ability to cause "commotions" were explored with hundreds of participants in the wild [19]; Suzuki et al. developed a shape-changing floor with robotic textiles whose formal user evaluation is planned in future work [20].

Although these works widely cover the topics of interactive, responsive, and adaptive built environments, the social expressiveness of SBE has rarely been investigated. Empirical works investigating users' social interaction with SBE majorly focus on the cases of robotic furnishings and spatial envelopes [21–23]. In Sect. 5, we will further discuss how these works cover a wide range of applications in different contexts where social expressiveness of SBE is investigated.

3.2 The Theoretical Foundation of "Space Agency"

In this section, we will define the concept of "socially intelligent agent," discuss the theoretical support for designing a socially interactive SBE, and briefly review the evolving embodiment of socially intelligent agents in HCI history.

How is "Socially Intelligent Agent" Defined? "Socially intelligent agent" refers to an artificial, social actor that is accepted by users through his/her intentional stance based on Dennett's Intentional Stance [24], "whether users are conscious or unconscious of the fact" [25]. For the "social" aspect in this definition, "Socially Intelligent Agent" may show "human-style intelligence" [26], "pet-style intelligence," and even a "hybrid-style intelligence" that are social, yet different from intelligence we can find in nature.

Why Do We Want Our Built Environment to Be Socially Interactive? The answer to this question points to "the common, underlying assumption" that "humans prefer to interact with machines in the same way that they interact with other people" [2]. In the HCI community, this common, underlying assumption has been applied to and validated through countless software and hardware interfaces, such as embodied conversational agents [1] and socially interactive robots [2]. At the same time, in architecture theory, architecture (a building) has long been conceptualized as "a machine for living in" [27], "an environmental, social and cultural device" [28], and more recently, "a robot for living in" [29]. Thus, at the intersection of theoretical works from HCI and Architecture is the argument that "humans may also prefer to interact with "machines for living in" (which are buildings) in the same way that they interact with other people."

The Evolving Embodiment of Socially Intelligent Agent. In the last 20 years, we can see a clear trajectory where the embodiment of a socially intelligent agent has been evolving from virtual to physical, from human figure to shape-changing interface, and from object to space. In 2001, Justine Cassell defined what an "Embodied Conversational Agent" was [1] and convincingly argued why intelligent computer systems should be characterized as human-like in those cases "where social collaborative behavior is the key." The example given by Cassell was a virtual human agent named REA who could "welcome" a user into a virtual office. Arguably, the embodiment of socially intelligent agent does not have to be virtual. Many researchers design anthropomorphic or zoomorphic robots to make human-robot interaction human-like or at least, creature-like [2]. In the past 10 years, there has been growing research interest in socially interactive, non-humanoid robots. Researchers in this area make robotic lamps, robotic music players, robotic furnishings, etc. that can convey social cues such as sympathy, welcome, politeness, etc. through meticulously designed movements and motions [22, 23, 30]. Most of these nonhumanoid robots are only objects; however, some of them are important spatial elements of built environments, such as doors and furnishings [22, 23].

HRI researchers have also explored how shape-changing interfaces can be perceived as a socially intelligent agent. Hemmert et al. and Pedersen et al. investigated how the surface reconfiguration and movement of a robotic cellphone can be perceived as animal-like [31, 32]. Our own recent work, the development and evaluation of an interior-scale adaptive wall, investigated its perceived social expressiveness including welcome, friendliness, collaboration, and cooperation [33].

By continuing this trajectory, we can see that spaces and their spatial components may be designed and perceived as socially intelligent "Space Agents."

4 Design Instance: An Adaptive Robotic Wall

The authors have developed and evaluated an adaptive robotic wall [33] which can be reconfigured from a vertical wall into a writing surface (Fig. 1). This large-scale, shape-changing interface consists of a 2-inch-thick foam panel and a tendon-driven actuation system with motors, laser-cut wood collars, and 3D-printed brackets (Fig. 1). It can be reconfigured into five different configurations as reported in our previous work [34]. The major applications of this technology are reconfiguring interior spaces (e.g., office, living room, space capsule, etc.) supporting, in our investigation, working life.

4.1 Employing "Space Agency" in the Human-Wall Interaction Design

When designing the human-robot interaction of our robotic wall, we wanted its movements to be socially expressive by showing friendliness, welcome, cooperativeness, and collaboration to users. Thus, we designed a scenario where users could freely interact with the robotic wall which was trying to facilitate a simple task through socially

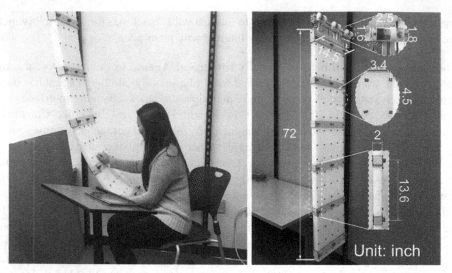

Fig. 1. Our robotic wall (right) prototype and photo from a pilot study with a user (left).

expressive ways. In this scenario, we gave the user a piece of printing paper and asked him/her to copy a short paragraph on a piece of paper in a room, unfurnished, with the robotic wall element flush with a wall surface. In our study, some participants initially began looking for a writing surface to work on but there was none offered by the room; that is, until the robotic wall offered one by bending itself downward with pauses and a gentle speed. By taking the initiative of offering a writing surface, the robotic wall was offering its help in a "welcoming" manner to the participant [23]. By making pauses and bending downward at a gentle speed, it was suggesting "politeness" and "friendliness" [22]. Some participants inspected it further to evaluate its affordances. If the participant moves closer, the robotic wall adjusted its position subtly as a cue, and gently rested itself on the participant's lap as a writing surface; if the participant selected not to move closer, the robotic wall swung gently up and down to show its willingness to help. This series of movements was a show of "friendliness" and "collaboration" to the user [30]. After the copying task was finished, the robotic wall automatically returned to its original position, flush with the wall surface.

The experiment scenario and robotic wall movement were designed by five HRI researchers through iterations and informed by the literature of designing socially interactive, nonhumanoid robots [22, 23, 30].

4.2 In-Lab and Online Experiment Design

Based on this scenario, we conducted an in-lab, between-group experiment with ten college students (ages 19–34, 7 FM, 3 M) and one mature adult (59, FM). The 5 participants in the treatment group went through the scenario in which the adaptive wall behavior was simulated using WoZ techniques [35] where an experimenter controlled (teleoperated) the robotic wall movement behind the one-way window. The 5 participants in the control group were given the remote controller for the wall their usage before starting the copying task. Both the treatment group [36] and control group [37], the trials were video recorded. After finishing the task, participants answered the same questionnaire probing users' social perception, whose questions were modified from a validated scale of "Social Perception." "Social Perception" scale measures four sub-constructs: friendliness, cooperativeness, sociability, and warmth [38]. Our modified questionnaire measures seven subconstructs: friendliness, cooperativeness, collaboration, welcome, intelligence, recognition, and intention. In our modified questionnaire, we replaced "warmth" with "welcome," "sociability" with "collaboration" so that it's more context-specific for our experiment scenario – a human-robot collaborative task for a novice user. We also added "intelligence," "recognition," and "intention" to our questionnaire based on the measurements from robotic furnishing literature [22, 23]. At the end of the questionnaire, three open-ended questions were asked to probe the reasons for agency perception.

To compensate for the lack of in-lab participants (given the closure of our lab due to the pandemic), an online, between-group study was conducted with 120 MTurk Master Workers "proven reliable" in previous studies, 60 assigned to each group: treatment and control (41 FM, 79 M; 65 workers 25–39; 52 workers 40–60; 2 workers over 60; 1 worker 18–24). Workers were paid a high market rate of 1.5 and 1.2 dollars respectively for participating in the 15-min (treatment group) or 12-min (control group). The intervention for treatment group participants was the "treatment group video" [36], while for control group participants was the "control group video" [37]. After watching the video, the participants answered the same questionnaire used in the in-lab experiment.

4.3 Results and Findings

Figure 2 shows the descriptive statistics of the seven subconstructs. The coding for each subconstruct in Fig. 2 is: "Intel" for Perceived Intelligence, "Rec" for Perceived Recognition, "Inten" for Perceived Intention, "Coop" for Perceived Cooperation, "Col" for Perceived Collaboration, "Fri" for Perceived Friendliness, and "Wel" for Perceived Welcome. The median values from the treatment group are all equal to or greater than 5 (somewhat agree); while values from the control group range from 2 (disagree) to 4 (neutral). The differences between Md (treatment group) and Md (control group) for these seven subconstructs range from 1.75 to 3.00. This suggests that participants in the treatment group perceived significantly more intelligence, recognition, intention, cooperativeness, collaboration, friendliness, and welcome from the robotic wall. We then ran a Kruskal-Wallis H test which also indicates there is a statistically significant difference ($p < 0.001$) in users' social perception of all the seven subconstructs between the treatment group and control group.

The qualitative results unveiled the reasons for users' agency perception: the users believed that the robotic wall recognized the situation (a writing surface was needed) and then performed an intentional and helpful act (providing a writing surface). The full detailed results of the study were reported in [33].

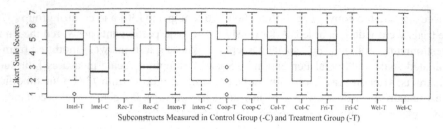

Fig. 2. Descriptive statistics of the seven subconstructs.

5   Discussion: Generalizability, Novelty, and Substantivity

With respect to the generalizability of this Strong Concept, "Space Agency" has characterized various SBE design research artifacts, ranging from smart furnishings to smart, spatial envelops in a variety of situations. Examples of design instances include a smart ottoman in an interior waiting room encouraging users to rest their feet on it [22], a smart chair in the public space of a shopping mall inviting shoppers to play chess [21], a smart door welcoming pedestrian from the street to come into a building [23], a smart sofa

Table 1. Comparison of previous works employing "space agency."

Project	Category	Experiment condition	Function	Users' social perception
Mechanical Ottoman [22]	Furniture	In-lab Study	Actively providing a footrest	It has sentience, intention, and personality; it's alive, like a pet
Persuasive ChairBots [21]	Furniture	Field Study	Actively persuading pedestrians to play chess	It's inviting, submissive, friendly; For some people, it's creepy
Sofa-Bot [39]	Furniture	In-lab Study	Moving according to users' movements and gestures	It has sentience, intention, and personality; It's building a relationship with users
Robotic Drawers [40]	Furniture	In-lab Study	Collaborating with users for an assembly task	It's socially expressive, proactive, and intentional. It's like a boss sometimes

(continued)

Table 1. (*continued*)

Project	Category	Experiment condition	Function	Users' social perception
Gesturing Doors [23]	Furniture (Part of a Spatial Envelop)	Field Study	Inviting users into a building	It's welcoming, urging, and sometimes reluctant. It's approachable, intentional, and recognizant
Adaptive Robotic Wall [33]	Spatial Envelop	In-lab Study	Collaborating with users to perform a writing task	It's intentional, recognizant, friendly, welcoming, cooperative, and collaborative

that follows users' gestures to reposition itself in a multifunctional large space [39], a robotic drawer that collaborates with users to perform assembly tasks [40], and our work s reported here, in brief, of the adaptive wall collaborating with participants engaged in a writing task in an interior workspace [33]. Table 1 compares these projects with each other through their categories, experiment conditions, functions, and users' social perceptions as a validation for the generalizability of "Space Agency." Table 1 may not be an exhaustive list of previous works employing "Space Agency."

From Table 1, we see that the "Adaptive Robotic Wall" extended the previous works of socially interactive, robotic furnishings to socially interactive, spatial envelops. Like robotic furnishings, people perceive social expressiveness (intention, recognition, friendliness, welcome, cooperativeness, and collaboration) from the robotic wall.

With respect to the novelty of "Space Agency," this paper argues for the first time, to our knowledge, that an SBE can be contestably, defensibly, and substantively conceptualized as an embodiment in social robotics [3]. "Space Agency" also represents a new category of design knowledge whose concept has never been rigorously discussed and justified as a design theory contribution. Moreover, "Space Agency" introduces an opportune marriage between environmental psychology and social robotics, since a socially interactive SBE influence people's mental state not only through social interactions but also the environment people living in.

With respect to the substantivity of this Strong Concept, we illustrated how "Space Agency" was applied in our robotic wall, interaction design process. The generative power of "Space Agency" has also been proved by the interaction design process of robotic furnishings [21–23] where "Embodied Design Improvisation" [30] was employed as a design method to create the socially expressive robot movement.

6 Limitation

There are several limitations to this work:

- As shown in Table 1, most of the previous works employing "Space Agency" in the design process are robotic furnishings. More works of different kinds of robotic, environmental elements (e.g., robotic walls, ceilings, etc.) are needed for a better understanding of "Space Agency" in different embodiments.
- For the "Adaptive Robotic Wall" experiment, personality, sex, age, and technology literacy of each participant could be effective factors. Further investigations on these factors are necessary for a better understanding of users' agency perception.
- All the previous works employing "Space Agency" focused on the investigation of robot movements, physical embodiment, and interaction modes. The spatial and environmental attributes of socially interactive, robotic environments were rarely investigated. These attributes need to be explored before "Space Agency" can be better understood and developed in design theories and real-world applications.

7 Conclusion and Future Work

In this paper, we proposed and validated the intermediate-level design knowledge of "Space Agency" through the triangulation of empirical, analytical, and theoretical domains. As a Strong Concept, "Space Agency" offers designers and researchers a grounding from which to ideate and generate new design instances of social robots. Through "Space Agency," we know that SBE and its spatial elements can be designed and perceived as socially interactive. Our next questions might be: *How can socially interactive SBE be socially assistive? What are the cases "where social collaborative behavior is the key" in human-SBE interaction? What kind of social relationships should we create between human and an SBE?* Moreover, we could explore how an SBE might exhibit the following social characteristics inspired by [2]:

- expresses and/or perceives emotions;
- constitutes a conversational agent with spatial embodiment conveying social cues;
- constitutes a social agent that is competent and assistive in different contexts;
- establishes/maintains multimodal social interactions;
- establishes/maintains social relationships;
- exhibits distinctive personality and character;
- employs spatial/environmental embodiment for human-SBE collaboration.

References

1. Cassell, J.: Embodied conversational agents - representation and intelligence in user interfaces. AI Mag. **22**, 67 (2001)
2. Fong, T., Nourbakhsh, I., Dautenhahn, K.: A survey of socially interactive robots. Robot. Auton. Syst. **42**, 143–166 (2003). https://doi.org/10.1016/s0921-8890(02)00372-x

3. Deng, E., Mutlu, B., Mataric, M.J.: Embodiment in Socially Interactive Robots (2019). https://doi.org/10.1561/9781680835472
4. Kumar, T., Mani, M.: Discerning occupant psychosocial behaviour in smart built environment and its design. In: Proceedings of the 1st ACM International Workshop on Urban Building Energy Sensing, Controls, Big Data Analysis, and Visualization (2019). https://doi.org/10.1145/3363459.3363534
5. Höök, K., Löwgren, J.: Strong concepts: intermediate-level knowledge in interaction design research. ACM Trans. Comput.-Hum. Interact. 19, 1–18 (2012). https://doi.org/10.1145/2362364.2362371
6. Gaver, B., Bowers, J.: Annotated portfolios. Interactions 19, 40–49 (2012). https://doi.org/10.1145/2212877.2212889
7. Löwgren, J.: Annotated portfolios and other forms of intermediate-level knowledge. Interactions 20, 30–34 (2013). https://doi.org/10.1145/2405716.2405725
8. Wang, Y., Green, K.E.: A pattern-based, design framework for designing collaborative environments. In: Proceedings of the Thirteenth International Conference on Tangible, Embedded, and Embodied Interaction (2019). https://doi.org/10.1145/3294109.3295652
9. Wang, Y., Green, K.E., Grupen, R., et al.: Designing intelligent spaces as if they were human: a "Space Agent" framework. In: 2018 4th International Conference on Universal Village (UV) (2018). https://doi.org/10.1109/uv.2018.8642135
10. Alavi, H.S., Churchill, E.F., Wiberg, M., et al.: Introduction to human-building interaction (HBI): interfacing HCI with architecture and urban design. ACM Trans. Comput.-Hum. Interact. 26, 1 (2019). https://doi.org/10.1145/3309714
11. Vinot, J.-L., Conversy, S.: Concept of continuity, a "strong concept" to design graphical architecture of interactive systems. In: Proceedings of the 27th Conference on l'Interaction Homme-Machine (2015). https://doi.org/10.1145/2820619.2820634
12. Isbister, K., Abe, K., Karlesky, M.: Interdependent wearables (for play): a strong concept for design. In: Proceedings of the 2017 CHI Conference on Human Factors in Computing Systems (2017). https://doi.org/10.1145/3025453.3025939
13. Green, K.E.: Architectural Robotics: Ecosystems of Bits, Bytes, and Biology. MIT Press, Cambridge (2016)
14. Threatt, A.L., Merino, J., Green, K.E., et al.: An assistive robotic table for older and post-stroke adults: results from participatory design and evaluation activities with clinical staff. Proc. SIGCHI Conf. Hum. Fact. Comput. Syst. (2014). https://doi.org/10.1145/2556288.2557333
15. Houayek, H., Green, K.E., Gugerty, L., Walker, I.D., Witte, J.: AWE: an animated work environment for working with physical and digital tools and artifacts. Pers. Ubiquit. Comput. 18(5), 1227–1241 (2013). https://doi.org/10.1007/s00779-013-0731-6
16. Schafer, G.J., Fullerton, S.K., Walker, I., et al.: Words become worlds: the LIT ROOM, a literacy support tool at room-scale. In: Proceedings of the 2018 Designing Interactive Systems Conference (2018). https://doi.org/10.1145/3196709.3196728
17. Nguyen, B.V., Simeone, A.L., Vande Moere, A.: Exploring an architectural framework for human-building interaction via a semi-immersive cross-reality methodology. In: Proceedings of the 2021 ACM/IEEE International Conference on Human-Robot Interaction (2021). https://doi.org/10.1145/3434073.3444643
18. Jäger, N., Schnädelbach, H., Hale, J., Kirk, D., Glover, K.: WABI: facilitating synchrony between inhabitants of adaptive architecture. In: Schnädelbach, H., Kirk, D. (eds.) People, Personal Data and the Built Environment. SSAE, pp. 41–75. Springer, Cham (2019). https://doi.org/10.1007/978-3-319-70875-1_3
19. Grönvall, E., Kinch, S., Petersen, M.G., Rasmussen, M.K.: Causing commotion with a shape-changing bench - experiencing shape-changing interfaces in use. Proc. SIGCHI Conf. Hum. Fact. Comput. Syst. (2014). https://doi.org/10.1145/2556288.2557360

20. Suzuki, R., Nakayama, R., Liu, D., et al.: LiftTiles. In: Proceedings of the Fourteenth International Conference on Tangible, Embedded, and Embodied Interaction (2020). https://doi.org/10.1145/3374920.3374941
21. Agnihotri, A., Knight, H. Persuasive ChairBots: a (mostly) robot-recruited experiment. In: 2019 28th IEEE International Conference on Robot and Human Interactive Communication (RO-MAN) (2019). https://doi.org/10.1109/ro-man46459.2019.8956262
22. Sirkin, D., Mok, B., Yang, S., Ju, W.: Mechanical Ottoman: how robotic furniture offers and withdraws support. In: Proceedings of the Tenth Annual ACM/IEEE International Conference on Human-Robot Interaction (2015). https://doi.org/10.1145/2696454.2696461
23. Ju, W., Takayama, L.: Approachability: how people interpret automatic door movement as gesture (2009)
24. Dennett, D.C.: The Intentional Stance. MIT Press, Cambridge (2006)
25. Osawa, H., Imai, M.: Morphing agency: deconstruction of an agent with transformative agential triggers. In: CHI 2013 Extended Abstracts on Human Factors in Computing Systems on - CHI EA 2013 (2013). https://doi.org/10.1145/2468356.2468745
26. Dautenhahn, K.: From embodied to socially embedded agents—implications for interaction-aware robots. Adapt. Behav. 7, 3–4 (2000)
27. Corbusier, L.: Towards a New Architecture. Courier Corporation, Chelmsford (1927)
28. Pask, G.: The Architectural Relevance of Cybernetics (1969)
29. Mitchel, W.J.: City of Bits: Space, Palace and the Infobahn. MIT Press, Boston (1997)
30. Hoffman, G., Ju, W.: Designing robots with movement in mind. J. Hum.-Robot Interact. 3, 89 (2014). https://doi.org/10.5898/jhri.3.1.hoffman
31. Hemmert, F., Löwe, M., Wohlauf, A., Joost, G.: Animate mobiles: proxemically reactive posture actuation as a means of relational interaction with mobile phones. In: Proceedings of the 7th International Conference on Tangible, Embedded and Embodied Interaction - TEI 2013 (2013). https://doi.org/10.1145/2460625.2460669
32. Pedersen, E.W., Subramanian, S., Hornbæk, K.: Is my phone alive? A large-scale study of shape change in handheld devices using videos. In: Proceedings of the SIGCHI Conference on Human Factors in Computing Systems (2014). https://doi.org/10.1145/2556288.2557018
33. Wang, Y., Guimbretiere, F., Green, K.E.: Are space-making robots, agents? Investigations on user perception of an embedded robotic surface. In: 2020 29th IEEE International Conference on Robot and Human Interactive Communication (RO-MAN) (2020). https://doi.org/10.1109/ro-man47096.2020.9223532
34. Sirohi, R., Wang, Y., Hollenberg, S., et al.: Design and characterization of a novel, continuum-robot surface for the human environment. In: 2019 IEEE 15th International Conference on Automation Science and Engineering (CASE) (2019). https://doi.org/10.1109/coase.2019.8842988
35. Dow, S., Lee, J., Oezbek, C., et al.: Wizard of Oz interfaces for mixed reality applications. In: CHI 2005 Extended Abstracts on Human Factors in Computing Systems - CHI 2005 (2005). https://doi.org/10.1145/1056808.1056911
36. Wang, Y.: Work Environment Experiment 1–1. In: YouTube (2020). https://www.youtube.com/watch?v=gWJ4mJHjfGE. Accessed 27 May 2021
37. Wang, Y.: Work Environment Experiment 2 2. In: YouTube (2020). https://www.youtube.com/watch?v=3YHPodF0qRc&t=25s. Accessed 27 May 2021
38. Hoffman, G., Birnbaum, G.E., Vanunu, K., Sass, O., Reis, H.T.: Robot responsiveness to human disclosure affects social impression and appeal. In: Proceedings of the 2014 ACM/IEEE International Conference on Human-Robot Interaction (2014)

39. Spadafora, M., Chahuneau, V., Martelaro, N., Sirkin, D., Ju, W.: Designing the behavior of interactive objects. In: Proceedings of the TEI 2016: Tenth International Conference on Tangible, Embedded, and Embodied Interaction (2016)
40. Mok, B.K.-J., Yang, S., Sirkin, D., Ju, W.: A place for every tool and every tool in its place: Performing collaborative tasks with interactive robotic drawers. In: 2015 24th IEEE International Symposium on Robot and Human Interactive Communication (RO-MAN) (2015)

Early Prediction of Student Engagement-Related Events from Facial and Contextual Features

Roshni Kaushik[✉] and Reid Simmons

Carnegie Mellon University, Pittsburgh, PA 15213, USA
{roshnika,rsimmons}@andrew.cmu.edu

Abstract. Intelligent tutoring systems have great potential in personalizing the educational experience by processing some key features from the user and educational task to optimize learning, engagement, or other performance measures. This paper presents an approach that uses a combination of facial features from the user of an educational app and contextual features about the progress of the task to predict key events related to user engagement. Our approach trains Gaussian Mixture Models from automatically processed screen-capture videos and propagates the probability of events over the course of an activity. Results show the advantage of including contextual features in addition to facial features when predicting these engagement-related events, which can be used to intervene appropriately during an educational activity.

Keywords: Prediction · Adaptive · Context · Affect · Engagement

1 Introduction

Intelligent tutoring systems, whether in the form of a physical robot or tablet/computer interface, have great potential in personalizing the educational experience and catering to the needs of many different learners. These systems generally take some feedback from the user to adapt the educational tasks, attempting to optimize learning, engagement, or other performance measures. For a specific application, a designer of a tutoring system has to determine how to adapt the tutor's behavior based on the changing tutor/user/task interactions. This question has two aspects: *when* the tutor should change behavior and *what* to change to improve some outcome. This paper focuses on the first aspect: predicting *early* how the student perceives an educational task to provide the tutoring system sufficient time to head off a negative outcome.

To achieve this, we used contextual and facial features derived from an existing educational application dataset to develop a model that predicts two key events: (1) the feedback the student chooses at the end of activity and (2) whether the student will exit the activity early. We extracted facial features with OpenFace [2] and contextual features with automatic parsing of the app's

Supported in part by NSF Grant #IIS-1939047.

screen capture. Using Gaussian Mixture Models (GMMs) to model the student's reaction and Bayesian updates to compute an evolving probability of events related to student engagement, we chose several hyperparameters to optimize a linear combination of accurate and early predictions. Results indicate that our approach can predict these events with an accuracy around 75% when over 80% of the activity is still remaining. This early prediction allows for the tutor to take corrective action if needed to maintain student engagement.

Work related to our approach has three components: (1) user modeling, (2) time series classification and (3) intelligent tutoring systems. Modeling student engagement is a performance measure commonly computed in educational applications. Facial and body position features were used to model the user's affect and calculate a measure of engagement in [16]. Specific behavioral strategies were applied in [4] to reengage students when they were assessed to have low engagement. Information about the student's progress, such as time to respond, was used to detect a student's loss of motivation with a Hidden Markov model [10].

Time-series classification methods take a set of observations labeled by class and attempt to predict the class based on the observations. There are many variations of this problem that include a label for each time-step, series of varying lengths, etc. Deep learning is a popular tool for time-series classification [8], and LSTMs have been used successfully on time-series with the same length. However, these approaches generally make a prediction at the end of the time-series, while we wish to predict before the end of the activity. A measure of earliness of prediction has been used in time-series classification work as an addition to an accuracy measure to evaluate model performance [7,14,20]; we use a similar approach to predict both accurately and early.

Many approaches have developed models of intelligent tutoring systems. A general framework is to combine the tutorial situation, affective model, cognitive model, etc. to control the tutor's behavior [15]. The affective model component takes many forms, including a personality assessment to determine how students would respond to different stimuli [9], a few chosen nonverbal behaviors, such as looking at the robot and smiling [11], and a set of automatically detected student facial features [18]. In our approach, we use both automatically detected facial and contextual features to model the student's current state. Taking both types of features into account is critical, as research into nonverbal behavior in teaching shows that when context is not taken into account, results of data analyses may be hard to interpret [19].

2   Dataset Description

RoboTutor [13] is an educational application running on an Android tablet that contains many activities, including reading illustrated stories, practicing writing words, and completing math problems. Prior work on data from this app includes affect detection based on expert labels [1] and correlation between some user behaviors and facial features detected automatically by OpenFace [17]. This app was a finalist in the Global Learning XPRIZE[1], and during that time was used by children ages 6-12 in Tanzania. The data used for this project (see [13] for more details, including ethical considerations) comes from the beta sites used during the challenge and are screen-recordings during the students' sessions, which include video from a front-facing camera of the student.

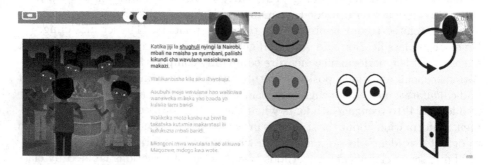

Fig. 1. Left: Single frame from recorded videos of the RoboTutor application with front-facing camera feed (face obscured for anonymity). **Right**: Feedback screen appearing at the end of each activity.

Figure 1 (left) is a screenshot from a story-reading activity, which contains an image and text from the story. The text highlights green as it is read to the student. There is also a *backbutton* in the top left corner, which the student can use to end the activity early. At an activity's end (whether it is exited early or completed), a feedback screen (Fig. 1, right) appears where the student can choose a red, yellow, or green circle to indicate how they felt about the activity.

Automatic Feature Extraction: To create prediction models, we first need to extract a set of features from the screen-recordings. Each video is 20-30 min long and contains many activities; we used only activities containing stories to limit the variety of activities to analyze. For each activity, we collected two different labels: *Feedback* (the student's choice at the feedback screen: red, yellow, or green) and *Backbutton* (whether the student exited the activity early). Screen taps, which appeared on the videos as white circles, were detected to determine the feedback chosen or whether the backbutton was pressed.

We extracted a set of *facial features* (Table 1, A-K) over the course of the activity using OpenFace [2]. These are the same features computed by prior work on this dataset [1] and include features that have been used frequently in affect recognition [5]. The six facial action units (F-K) are coded by their regression values corresponding to intensity of presence [6]. We also extracted a set of *contextual features* (Table 1, L-Q) that relate to the state of the educational activity itself. These features were chosen as they were easily extracted from a frame of the tablet screen and could represent information correlated with student engagement, such as fatigue.

---

[1] https://learning.xprize.org/.

Table 1. Description of feature set

Facial Features		Contextual Features	
A	**Head Proximity**: the scalar distance of the head from the camera	L	**Position of Activity in Video**: sequential order of activity in video
B	**Head Orientation**: the magnitude of rotation of the head	M	**Picture Side**: left or right side of the screen
C	**Gaze Direction**: the averaged angle of gaze between the two eyes	N	**Activity Type**: story read or story echo
D	**Eye Aspect Ratio**: related to blinking of the eye	O	**Progress**: non-decreasing scalar indicating how far along in the story, computed by green vs. black text on a page (see Fig. 1)
E	**Pupil Ratio**: the ratio of the area of the pupil to the area of the eye		
F	**AU04**: Brow Lowerer	P	**Time from Activity Beginning**: in seconds
G	**AU07**: Lid Tightener		
H	**AU12**: Lip Corner Puller	Q	**Time from Video Beginning**: in seconds
I	**AU25**: Lips Part		
J	**AU26**: Jaw Drop		
K	**AU45**: Blink		

Description of Dataset: Our dataset consists of 105 videos recordings of student sessions, each 20–30 min long. We first extracted individual story activities from the videos. Since the final activity of each video often corresponds to the instructor exiting the activity early, this activity was not included. Our activity dataset was then composed of 423 activities of length 5–950 s, with most activities less than 200 s. The distribution of *feedback* labels is 13.2% red, 77.1% yellow, and 9.7% green, and the distribution of *backbutton* labels is 87.9% no backbutton and 12.1% backbutton.

The data are represented as $\{T^{(i)}, X^{(i)}, Y_1^{(i)}, Y_2^{(i)} \mid i = 1, ..., 423\}$ where $T^{(i)}$ is a vector such that $T_j^{(i)}$ is the time of the jth frame of activity i; $X^{(i)}$ is a matrix such that $X_j^{(i)}$ is a vector corresponding to the features computed for the jth frame of activity i; $Y_1^{(i)} \in \{0, 1, 2\}$ corresponds to a *feedback* choice of red, yellow, or green; and $Y_2^{(i)} \in \{0, 1\}$ corresponds to an activity ending naturally or the *backbutton* being pressed. The goal of our approach is to predict Y_1 and Y_2 accurately, given only a few frames of T and X.

3   Methodology

We use both the facial and contextual features to predict whether an event occurs at the end of an activity, with the goal being to predict as accurately and early as possible. During the course of the activity, we combine individual observations using a Bayesian framework and use Gaussian Mixture Models (GMMs) to provide the probabilities needed for Bayesian updating. The approach chooses hyperparameters to optimize the desired balance between F1-score (weighted by α) and earliness (weighted by $1 - \alpha$), where α is an input to the learner. We describe the methodology for predicting the *feedback* labels here with $K = 3$ labels; the *backbutton* case is analogous.

Training Gaussian Mixture Models: Given a set of training data of the form $\{T^{(i)}, X^{(i)}, Y_1^{(i)}\}$, we want to train a Gaussian Mixture Model for each label, i.e. red, yellow, and green. We noticed, however, that the distribution tends to change over time (e.g., at the beginning of an activity, the facial features tend not to be as good predictors), so to improve prediction we train multiple GMMs for each label by first creating M intervals from the distribution of activity lengths.

Each of the M intervals has a starting and ending time (e.g. the first interval may include 0–30 s, the second 30–120 s, etc.) such that the number of activities ending in each interval is approximately the same. For each of the K labels, we first find all the activities within the training data with that label, take only the time steps of those activities corresponding to time steps within a particular interval, and then train a GMM with N components on that data. This results in a total of MK GMMs trained. Given the training data, our approach will learn both the models and optimize for M and N, the number of components in the GMM.

Probability Propagation: We then use the GMM models to predict $P(C_k)$, the probability of the kth class, for each time step of an activity. We initialize $P(C_k) = \frac{1}{K}$, corresponding to a random guess. Then let $\mathbb{X}_j^{(i)} = \{X_1^{(i)}, X_2^{(i)}, ..., X_j^{(i)}\}$ be the observations known at the jth time step. We calculate the probability at the next step using a modified Bayes rule from [12]:

$$P(C_k|\mathbb{X}_j^{(i)}) = \frac{P(X_j^{(i)}|C_k)P(C_k|S)P(C_k|\mathbb{X}_{j-1}^{(i)})}{P(X_j^{(i)}|\mathbb{X}_{j-1}^i)} \tag{1}$$

where $P(C_k|\mathbb{X}_{j-1}^{(i)})$ is the computed probability from the previous time step; $P(X_j^{(i)}|C_k)$ is the output of the GMM that was trained on a time interval including $T_j^{(i)}$ corresponding to class C_k; and $P(C_k|S)$ is the static prior from the training distribution to avoid model drift. For example, if C_k = yellow and yellow labelled 80% of the training data, then $P(C_k|S) = 0.8$.

The denominator is a constant over all k, so is normalized out by ensuring that the $P(C_k|\mathbb{X}_j^{(i)})$ sum to 1. To try to ensure conditional independence between observations and reduce the effect of noise in the features, the features $X^{(i)}$ are averaged over a one second interval, and the probability is updated once a second. If no features are present during one second, due to errors in face detection, the probability from the previous time step is used unchanged.

Classification: If the goal was to classify at the end of each activity, we would use the highest $P(C_k)$ at the final time step. However, classifying earlier is beneficial, since that information could be used to modify a tutoring system's behavior. To achieve this, we set a threshold $\lambda \in [0, 1]$ such that if any $P(C_k)$ exceeds λ, we classify[2] the activity as belonging to class k. If no $P(C_k)$ exceeds λ for the entire activity, we count it as an inconclusive result, since predicting a class at the end of an activity does not have utility since we know what the students did and no intervention is possible.

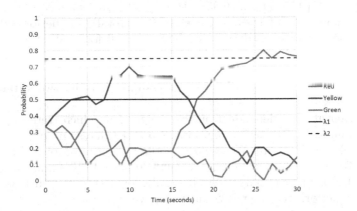

Fig. 2. Example of the predicting *feedback* choice using the described approach with two possible thresholds λ_1 and λ_2 shown.

Figure 2 illustrates the prediction process applied to an activity of length 30 s for the *feedback* case. The probabilities are initialized to 1/3 and observations are combined using Eq. 1. Note that between 12–15 s, OpenFace failed to find the face, resulting in a flat probability curve for all labels. The figure plots two different thresholds to show how the choice of threshold impacts both the time of classification and the predicted label. λ_1 predicts yellow at 3 s, while λ_2 predicts (the correct label) red at 25 s.

Optimizing Performance: To predict both accurately and early, we optimize using an objective function S, a function of λ (threshold), M (time intervals), and N (GMM components) as well as a weight $\alpha \in [0, 1]$. α defines how much we prefer an accurate prediction over an early one. As our dataset is quite unbalanced, we use a weighted F1-score in place of accuracy. The F1-score is calculated for each label and we report the average weighted score by the number of true instances for each label. The form of objective function S is shown below.

$$S(\lambda, M, N, \alpha) = (\alpha)\text{F1-score} + (1 - \alpha)\text{Earliness} \qquad (2)$$

---

[2] We tried varying λ over time, but that did not improve results.

Earliness, or the average fraction of an activity's time that was **not** needed for classification, is defined as $\frac{1}{n}\sum_{i=1}^{n}\frac{T_{-1}^{(i)}-\hat{t}^{(i)}}{T_{-1}^{(i)}}$, where n is the number of activities where the threshold is met; and $T_{-1}^{(i)}$ and $\hat{t}^{(i)}$ are the activity length and prediction time for activity i.

4　Results and Discussion

Our goal was to optimize the performance metric S by changing the three parameters: $\lambda \in \{0.55, 0.60, ..., 0.95\}$, $M \in \{1, 2, ..., 6\}$, and $N = \{1, 2, ..., 6\}$. For each combination of these parameters (324 total), we performed 10-fold cross-validation and recorded the average S over all folds. We then chose the hyperparameter combination with the highest average value of S. Additionally, when comparing the performance of two different models, we used a Welch Two Sample, two-tailed t-test, which does not assume that the two variances are equal.

The optimization is dependent on the choice of α, which trades off the F1-score for earliness. $\alpha = 0$ means we prioritize only earliness and $\alpha = 1$ means we prioritize only the F1-score. We performed the optimization of S for values of $\alpha \in [0, 1]$. We found that when $\alpha > 0.8$, performance drops significantly, so we chose $\alpha = 0.8$ for further analysis. Additionally, low levels of α, such as $\alpha < 0.3$, have a lower performance metric S due to a lower accuracy.

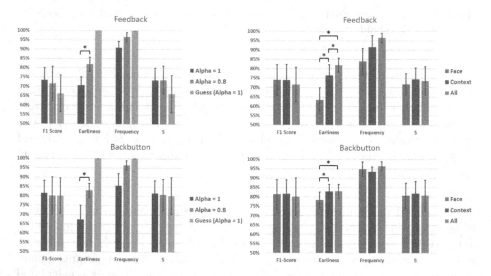

Fig. 3. Comparison of (**left**) $\alpha = 1$, $\alpha = 0.8$, and guessing the most common label, and (**right**) only facial features, only contextual features, and all features for $\alpha = 0.8$ The average value of each metric is illustrated with a standard deviation error bar. Significant differences at the $p = 0.05$ level are indicated with asterisks. Significance was tested only for F1-score and earliness.

Earliness and Guessing: Often accuracy is the only metric used to evaluate prediction models. Intuitively, the more of the activity seen by the model, the more accurate the prediction will be; however, we want to make predictions before the activity has completed to leave time for any intervention. To understand how this trade-off manifests in our model, we compare the results of considering only the F1-score ($\alpha = 1.0$) and including earliness ($\alpha = 0.8$). We can additionally validate our approach by comparing the performance to guessing the most common label in the training data for each activity (e.g., choosing yellow or no backbutton) at the first time step.

As shown in Fig. 3 (left), the F1-score is lower for a lower α, which is intuitive since $\alpha = 1$ weights only the F1-score. However, that difference is not statistically significant, while adding a 20% weight on earliness *does* significantly change the earliness for *feedback* ($t = -5.782, p < 0.001, df = 17.64$) and *backbutton* ($t = -5.907, p < 0.001, df = 13.00$). This increase in the earliness with no significant change in the F1-score indicates that including earliness improves overall performance, with respect to our goal of predicting accurately and early.

The optimal hyperparameters vary for each value of α. For *feedback*, we found ($\lambda = 0.95, M = 2, N = 3$) for $\alpha = 1.0$ and ($\lambda = 0.7, M = 2, N = 3$) for $\alpha = 0.8$ to be optimal. For the *backbutton* case, we found ($\lambda = 0.95, M = 4, N = 1$) for $\alpha = 1.0$ and ($\lambda = 0.55, M = 2, N = 3$) for $\alpha = 0.8$ to be optimal. Note that the optimal threshold λ when $\alpha = 1$ is much higher than for $\alpha = 0.8$, which makes sense since with $\alpha = 1$ there is no penalty for waiting longer in exchange for greater prediction confidence. Another interesting result is the optimal number of time intervals M was greater than 1 for all cases. This means that using multiple intervals to segment the time series data tends to increase overall performance.

We also compared the results to guessing the most common label (shown in gray in Fig. 3, left). While the F1-score resulting from guessing is lower than our model at $\alpha = 0.8$ and 1.0 for both cases, this difference is not statistically significant (note that the earliness scores are always 1, since guessing is done at the start of an activity). We anticipate that with a larger dataset and more balanced label distribution, guessing will have a worse performance.

Facial and Contextual Features: We hypothesized that the context of the task can help interpret the student's internal state, in addition to facial features, which have been used extensively to predict affect, such as in [16,18]. To evaluate this, we compared the performance of using only facial features (A - K from Table 1), only contextual features (L - Q from Table 1), and all features, shown in Fig. 3 (right) with significant differences indicated with asterisks.

Significant differences were found in earliness when comparing a facial features only model and a model using all features. Specifically, the t-test resulted in ($t = -7.422, p < 0.001, df = 14.62$) for *feedback* and ($t = -2.50, p = 0.02, df = 17.67$) for *backbutton*. Additionally, for the *feedback* case, there was a significant difference between earliness using only contextual features and using all features ($t = -2.417, p = 0.03, df = 15.76$).

An interesting result is that the contextual features alone predicted earlier in both cases compared to facial features alone; with the F1-score not significantly different. This does seem non-intuitive, since facial features have been used extensively for affect recognition. Contextual features do not encode any information directly from the student and instead record progress in the activity, so it seems unlikely that they would outperform facial features. A potential explanation is the noisy data output by OpenFace. The students move rapidly in the camera frame and, occasionally, another student appears in the frame during an activity. The contextual features, by contrast, are less noisy as they are computed from the relatively static and predictable items on the tablet screen during an activity. Another explanation could be that engagement is tied closely to the time a student has spent using the tablet (one of the contextual features), perhaps due to fatigue.

5   Conclusion

This paper presents a framework for predicting students' engagement, specifically the feedback they will provide about an activity and whether they will exit an activity early. Our approach uses GMMs and Bayesian updating, and optimizes performance based on accuracy and earliness of the prediction. Our results show that, given a suitable probability threshold, we can achieve reasonable accuracy while still predicting student engagement fairly early on.

Since "ground-truth" engagement does not exist, our approach uses the *feedback* and *backbutton* events as proxies, which means that the interpretation of the results can be ambiguous. An additional limitation is that the skewness of the label distribution implies that guessing those values would, on average, perform quite well, which can be mitigated with a larger and more diverse dataset.

Our approach, however, is easily generalizable and can predict any event occurring at the end of a time-series given a set of features computed over the course of that time series. Many existing time-series classification approaches have a much higher accuracy or F1-score than our reported results (such as in [3]), but their prediction occurred at the end rather than during a session. We can also handle time-series of varying lengths without trimming or warping the data as is often necessary for other time-series approaches such as LSTMs [8].

Extensions include applying the approach to a different dataset, where the labels are more directly tied to engagement, such as survey results completed by users. Additionally, an assumption made throughout this approach was the independence of the *feedback* and *backbutton* events; however, it seems likely that a student who exited an activity early would also be more likely to feel negatively toward the activity, and thus jointly predicting those events might improve performance. Predicting these events can be used to modify the tutor's behavior to attempt to increase student engagement. The next step in this research is to develop an intelligent tutor that modifies its behavior based on the predictions of the user's affect, personalizing the education experience.

References

1. Agarwal, M., Mostow, J.: Semi-supervised learning to perceive children's affective states in a tablet tutor. In: Tenth Symposium on Educational Advances in Artificial Intelligence(EAAI). New York, NY (2020)
2. Amos, B., Ludwiczuk, B., Satyanarayanan, M.: Openface: a general-purpose face recognition library with mobile applications. CMU School Comput. Sc. 6 (2016)
3. Bogina, V., Kuflik, T., Mokryn, O.: Learning item temporal dynamics for predicting buying sessions. In: Proceedings of the 21st International Conference on Intelligent User Interfaces (2016)
4. Brown, L., Kerwin, R., Howard, A.M.: Applying behavioral strategies for student engagement using a robotic educational agent. In: IEEE International Conference on Systems, Man, and Cybernetics. IEEE (2013)
5. Burgoon, J.K., Buller, D.B., Hale, J.L., de Turck, M.A.: Relational messages associated with nonverbal behaviors. Human Commun. Res. 10(3), 351-378 (1984)
6. Ekman, P., Friesen, W.V.: Facial action coding systems. Consulting Psychologists Press (1978)
7. Fard, M.J., Wang, P., Chawla, S., Reddy, C.K.: A bayesian perspective on early stage event prediction in longitudinal data. IEEE Trans. Knowl. Data Eng. 28(12), 3126–3139 (2016)
8. Fawaz, H.I., Forestier, G., Weber, J., Idoumghar, L., Muller, P.A.: Deep learning for time series classification: a review. Data Min. Knowl. Discov. 33(4), 917–963 (2019)
9. Hernández, Y., Noguez, J., Sucar, E., Arroyo-Figueroa, G.: A probabilistic model of affective behavior for intelligent tutoring systems. In: Gelbukh, A., de Albornoz, Á., Terashima-Marín, H. (eds.) MICAI 2005. LNCS (LNAI), vol. 3789, pp. 1175–1184. Springer, Heidelberg (2005). https://doi.org/10.1007/11579427_119
10. Johns, J., Woolf, B.: A dynamic mixture model to detect student motivation and proficiency. In: Proceedings of the National Conference on Artificial Intelligence, vol. 21. Menlo Park, CA (2006)
11. Leite, I., Pereira, A., Castellano, G., Mascarenhas, S., Martinho, C., Paiva, A.: Modelling empathy in social robotic companions. In: Ardissono, L., Kuflik, T. (eds.) UMAP 2011. LNCS, vol. 7138, pp. 135–147. Springer, Heidelberg (2012). https://doi.org/10.1007/978-3-642-28509-7_14
12. Levinkov, E., Fritz, M.: Sequential bayesian model update under structured scene prior for semantic road scenes labeling. In: Proceedings of the IEEE International Conference on Computer Vision (2013)
13. McReynolds, A.A., Naderzad, S.P., Goswami, M., Mostow, J.: Toward Learning at Scale in Developing Countries: Lessons from the Global Learning XPRIZE Field Study. In: Learning @ Scale. ACM (2020)
14. Mori, U., Mendiburu, A., Keogh, E., Lozano, J.A.: Reliable early classification of time series based on discriminating the classes over time. Data Min. Knowl. Discov. 31(1), 233–263 (2016). https://doi.org/10.1007/s10618-016-0462-1
15. Perez, Y.H., Gamboa, R.M., Ibarra, O.M.: Modeling affective responses in intelligent tutoring systems. In: IEEE International Conference on Advanced Learning Technologies, 2004 Proceedings. IEEE (2004)
16. Sanghvi, J., Castellano, G., Leite, I., Pereira, A., McOwan, P.W., Paiva, A.: Automatic analysis of affective postures and body motion to detect engagement with a game companion. In: Proceedings of the 6th International Conference on Human-Robot Interaction (2011)

17. Saxena, M., Pillai, R.K., Mostow, J.: Relating children's automatically detected facial expressions to their behavior in robotutor. In: Thirty-Second AAAI Conference on Artificial Intelligence (2018)
18. Spaulding, S., Gordon, G., Breazeal, C.: Affect-aware student models for robot tutors. In: Proceedings of the International Conference on Autonomous Agents and Multiagent Systems (2016)
19. Woolfolk, A.E., Brooks, D.M.: Chapter 5: nonverbal communication in teaching. Review of research in education 10(1), 103–149 (1983)
20. Xing, Z., Pei, J., Philip, S.Y.: Early classification on time series. Knowl. Inf. Syst. 31(1), 105–127 (2012)

Common Reality: An Interface of Human-Robot Communication and Mutual Understanding

Fujian Yan, Vinod Namboodiri, and Hongsheng He[✉]

School of Computing, Wichita State University, Wichita, KS 67260, USA
hongsheng.he@wichita.edu

Abstract. An interface that can share effective and comprehensive mutual understanding is critical for human robot interaction. This paper designs a novel human-robot interaction interface that enables humans and robots to interact by their shared mutual understanding of the context. The interface superimposes robot-centered reality and human-centered reality on the working space to construct a mutual understanding environment. The common-reality interface enables humans to communicate with robots through speech and immersive touching. The mutual understanding is constructed by the user's commands, localization of objects, recognition of objects, object semantics, and augmented trajectories. The user's vocal commands are interpreted to formal logic, and finger touching is detected and represented by coordinates. Real-world experiments have been done to show the effectiveness of the proposed interface.

Keywords: Human-robot collaboration · Speech recognition · Discourse representation structure · Interactive display

1 Introduction

The demands for robotic applications in unstructured environments are increasing. Robots are designed to work in different fields, such as assisting in medication [7], treating Autism [23], and supporting people's daily lives [17]. Efficient human-robot interaction (HRI) plays a vital role in helping robots and humans collaborate [2]. Compared with conventional robots that are pre-programmed in structured environments, social robots are expected to face a wider variety of tasks [21].

In the past decades, researchers were endeavoring to design human-robot interaction interfaces [10]. Previous work [5,9,16,19,22] has developed context-depended frameworks that enable robots to interact with humans by facial expressions with visual devices. These context-dependent interfaces are not suitable for a dynamic environment [12]. Several augmented reality (AR) based

This work is partially supported by NSF CMMI 2129113.

H. Li et al. (Eds.): ICSR 2021, LNAI 13086, pp. 319–328, 2021.
https://doi.org/10.1007/978-3-030-90525-5_27

interfaces have been proposed [3,8]. Those AR-based methods used markers to recognize objects in the environment. As the number of objects increases the required computation power increased as well [6]. Traditional AR applications deployed in robotics are focused on enhancing the reality of humans by superimposing user's goals on additional devices. Other information such as what robots have learned from user's commands and object semantics is missing.

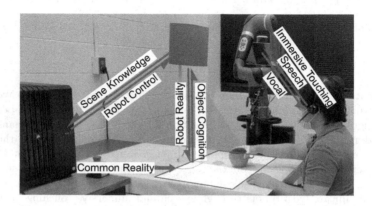

Fig. 1. Common reality for human-robot collaboration. The designed interface can take both speech and immersive touching from users. The shared knowledge, communication process, and the mutual understanding of the context are projected on the working space.

Thus, an HRI interface that enables robots and humans to share a mutual understanding of unstructured environments is urgently needed. In order to share a mutual understanding between robots and humans, the HRI interface needs to have the ability to dynamically recognize objects and understand the semantics of objects in the unstructured environment. It should provide a way that enables robots and humans to intuitively, effectively, and efficiently interact with each other.

In this paper, we propose a novel human-robot interface that can superimpose common reality for robots and humans. The designed common reality interface focuses on sharing a mutual understanding of the context to create an immersively interactive environment. The architecture of the common-reality interface is shown in Fig. 1. The common-reality interface supports immersive touching and speech while interacting with robots, which will avoid massive prior training for users. A mutual understanding of the working context is required for humans and robots to finish tasks collaboratively. The designed interface can detect and recognize objects in the working space by a deep learning model. By parsing the dictionary definitions of recognized objects, important attributes are extracted to construct a knowledge base by the language model. We choose to visualize the mutual understanding of the context instead of using a traditional question-answer manner because the ambiguity born with a natural language can hinder communicating in human-robot collaboration [4]. Also, information that is visually presented is more intuitive than auditory [15]. The major contribution of this paper is designing an intuitive, effective, and efficient interface. The common-reality interface can visualize the common reality of a scene, thereby bridging the gap between human knowledge and the perception of robots.

2   Human-Robot Common Reality

As the number of robots deployed to a human-centered environment increases, the design of the HRI interface should not only understand the user's goals, but also demonstrate what the robot has understood from the user's goal [20]. In this paper, a novel HRI interface has been designed that combines multi-modal human-robot communication and augmented robot-human communication to ensure an intuitive, effective, and efficient interaction between robots and humans. The superimposed common reality contains user's commands and interpreted formal logic from user's commands. It also contains object localization and identification, augmented action, and object semantics. An illustration of the components of the common reality interface has been shown in Fig. 2. Humans can communicate with robots by integrating speech and immersive touching. It converts human's understanding of the context into a digital representation, which robots can understand. Robots perceive the objects and learn the semantics of the objects in the context. Then, robots communicate with humans by visualizing their understanding of context.

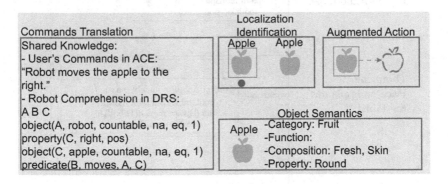

Fig. 2. Major components of the common reality interface.

2.1   Human-Robot Communication

To enable humans to communicate with robots naturally, the common-reality interface integrates multi-modal methods that include speech and immersive touching. Humans give commands through natural languages or touching the surface of the working environment.

DRS Translation. Robots need to have unambiguous, deterministic, and expressive instructions for executing actions. For robot understanding, we interpreted natural language into Discourse Representation Structures (DRS). We extended the lexicon to make it suitable for robotic applications. The parsed DRS results consist of referents and conditions. The referents are used to define semantic units that are embedded in the commands. These semantic units include subjective objects, objective objects, executable actions, and the condition of actions. The conditions are used to describe the relations of each parsed referent. According to part-of-text, dependency, and syntactical rules [11], there are four general declarations for covering three major HRI scenarios. The four general declarations are object declaration, predicate declaration, query declaration, and property declaration. The object declaration is used to describe the *NOUN* in user's commands. It refers to *subject* or *object* in the translated commands. The predicate declaration describes the executable actions, and the property declaration describes the condition of these actions. We design several robotic actions such as pick, move, and lift to ground the predicate to actual robotic actions. These actions can be added as the complexity of the tasks increase. An example of pared results for each scenario is shown in Fig. 3.

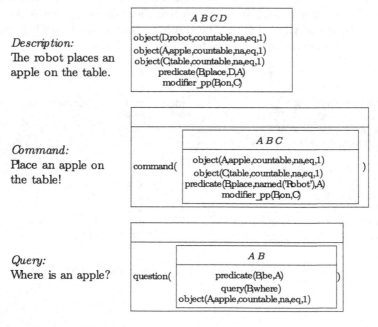

Fig. 3. Example of DRS Translation. Three fundamental HRI scenarios with parsed DRS results are shown.

Identification and Localization. In some scenarios, robots can not understand the user's purposes by only using vocal commands. Some objects may have the same texture, names, or characteristics in the same scene. For example, there are two apples in the scene. The command from the user is "Pick up an apple", the robot can not differentiate which apple it should pick up. In this case, additional instructions from users are needed to assist robots in localizing the target object. Robots need to percept the context by themselves to work with objects. To enable robots to percept the context, we used the Faster-R-CNN [18] model to detect and recognize objects. The inputs of the model are images of the context, and outputs are object labels. By referring to the labels, objects can be identified. To assist localization, the user can press an interactive button that associates with detected objects. The button is projected on the context. Users touch the buttons with their fingertips to interact with robots. To detect the fingertips of a hand, we used the model proposed in [1]. It is a convolutional neural network (CNN) that can take an image of a hand, and the outputs are coordinates of each recognized fingertips. A depth sensor is used to detect whether the user has touched the button or not.

2.2   Mutual Understanding

Humans have doubts about interacting with intelligent robots because they do not understand what robots will execute. The survey [13] has shown that 19% of 22% of participants fear intelligent robots because they do not understand. An interface that can share mutual understanding is needed. The common-reality interface can share human-robot communication, including the DRS translation, object identification, and object localization. It can also share action visualization and object semantics.

Visualizing the trajectory before the actions have been executed can help human users understand the robot's intention. The common-reality interface projects the trajectories of actions to improve mutual understanding. We used the MoveIt toolkit to plan the trajectory by giving the coordinate of the initial position and the final position. To project the trajectory in 3D space onto a 2D surface, we transform the robot's end effector in the world frame to the projector frame. To project the points in the projector frame to the $X - Y$ surface, we make the value on the $Z - axis$ equal to zero.

In order for robots to understand the semantics of the context, we used a language model [24] that can parse important attributes of objects from their dictionary definitions. These attributes include category, function, composition, and property. We used those attributes and the objects parsed from the input commands to form a dynamic knowledge base. To construct the knowledge base, we first translate the objects that are parsed from commands and learned attributes of objects into ACE sentences by a pre-defined template. We parsed these ACE sentences into DRS.

We used a Lampix projector to project these three components on a surface to construct an immersive interface contains a projector, a depth camera, and Raspberry Pi. Three major components can be visualized: the command that robots have learned, the characteristics that are held by each object in the context, and the hypothetical trajectories that robots will execute. A depth camera embedded in the projector can detect the depth difference of objects and surfaces. Objects can be detected by using the depth difference between objects and the working surface. The movement-based segmenter can be achieved with this difference as well. By visualizing the context, redundant speech can be eliminated. Objects in the working space are detected by the depth sensor that is embedded in the projector. The input commands, parsed logic representations, and characteristics of objects are projected based on a pre-defined template. The animation of trajectory was shown based on the planned path of the robot motion at the pixel level.

3   Experiment

We evaluated the effectiveness of the designed common-reality interface by using four different cases in the real-world scenario. We evaluated the satisfaction level of the common-reality interface based on the questionnaire for different people.

3.1   Real-World Scenario

There were four trials of the sample results that were used to illustrate the working process of the interface. The results were illustrated in Fig. 4. The left column is the image taken from the workspace, and the right column is the sequence of images that were able to illustrate the movement. Commands were given to the robots as inputs. Both the characteristics of objects and the shared language in logic representation were projected.

3.2   User Satisfaction Evaluation

The robustness of the common-reality interface was evaluated based on the user's satisfaction regarding the demonstration of the system. The evaluation of the user's sanctification was measured based on questionnaires that were generated based on Lewis' After-Scenario Questionnaire (ASQ) [14]. The degree of satisfaction was evaluated with five different levels: very unsatisfied, unsatisfied, neutral, satisfied, and very satisfied. The satisfaction was evaluated based on three standards, which were readability, correctness, and intuitiveness.

There were six people taking part in this experiment. The experiment participants were from different levels of education. The age range of the experiment participants was from 20 to 50. There were ten interactive scenarios generated. The generated scenarios included the input commands from users and the shared language projected on the working space. Each experiment participant was asked to write the command of the projected knowledge, which was understood by the robot. Different participants evaluated the written commands, and those experiment participants were asked to fill the questionnaire based on the written commands.

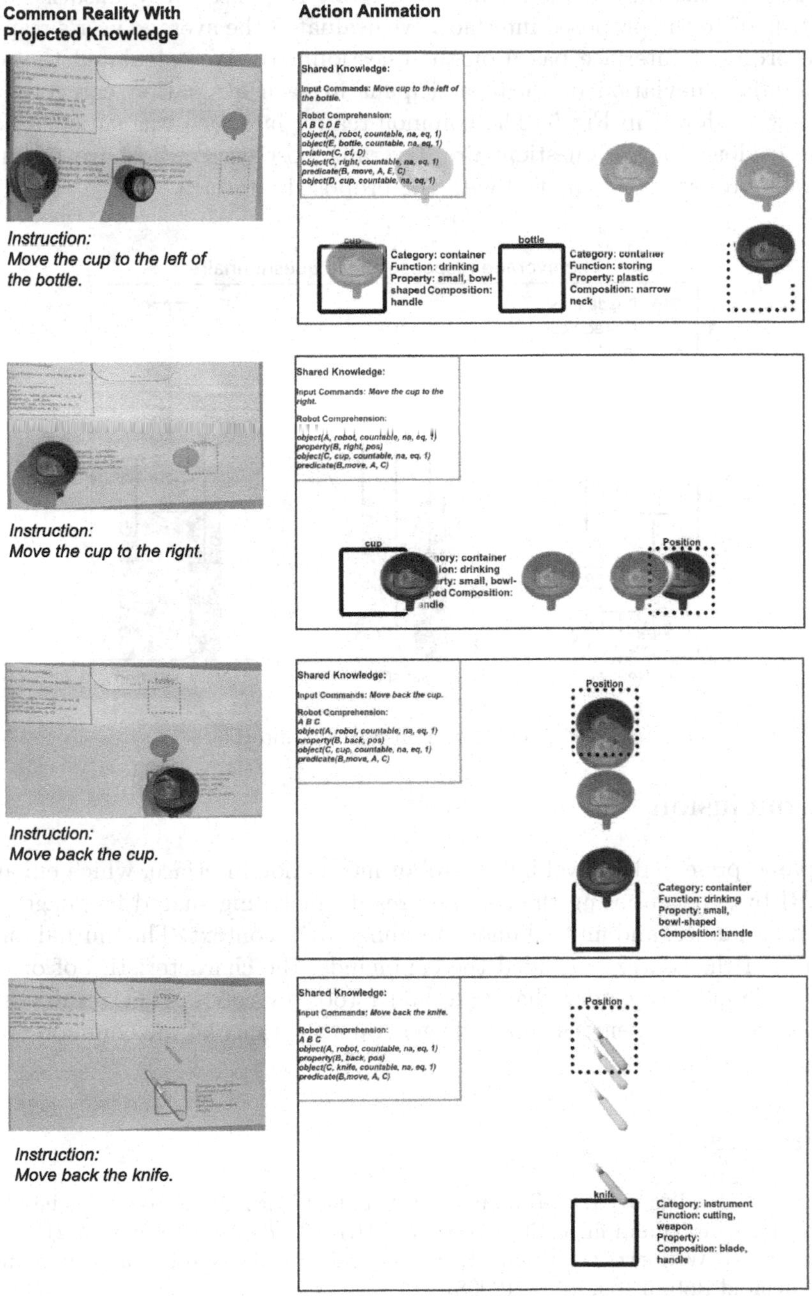

Common Reality With Projected Knowledge

Action Animation

Instruction:
Move the cup to the left of the bottle.

Instruction:
Move the cup to the right.

Instruction:
Move back the cup.

Instruction:
Move back the knife.

Fig. 4. Real-world action planning by using the common-reality interface. There were a total of four different trials shown. The left column is the common reality with projected knowledge, and the right column is the animation of the action.

Based on the questionnaire, no participant response "very unsatisfied" or "unsatisfied" to the proposed interface. We evaluated the average user's response to the proposed interface based on the questionnaire. We calculated the mean and standard deviation of each participant in each evaluation category. The results were shown in Fig. 5. The common-reality interface was satisfied based on the feedback of the questionnaire. Overall, most users who have taken the questionnaires are very satisfied with the proposed interface.

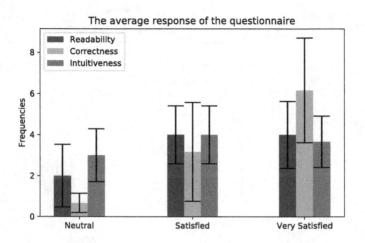

Fig. 5. Average response to the interface.

4   Conclusion

This paper presented a novel human-robot interaction interface, which enhances the HRI by superimposing the common reality including shared language, augmented semantics, and mutual understanding of the context. The mutual understanding of the context included the commands, the characteristics of objects, and the planned trajectory that were understood by robots. The results of the questionnaires have demonstrated the general acceptance of the common reality interface by users.

References

1. Alam, M.M., Islam, M.T., Rahman, S.: A unified learning approach for hand gesture recognition and fingertip detection. UMBC Student Collection (2021)
2. Bauer, A., Wollherr, D., Buss, M.: Human-robot collaboration: a survey. Int. J. Humanoid Rob. **5**(01), 47–66 (2008)
3. Bischoff, R., Kazi, A., Seyfarth, M.: The morpha style guide for icon-based programming. In: Proceedings. 11th IEEE International Workshop on Robot and Human Interactive Communication, pp. 482–487. IEEE (2002)
4. Branavan, S.R.K., Hackman, J.E., Heckel, F.W.P., Isaksen, A.: Updating natural language interfaces by processing usage data. US Patent 10,210,244, 19 Feb 2019

5. Breazeal, C.: Toward sociable robots. Rob. Auton. Syst. **42**(3–4), 167–175 (2003)
6. Chacko, S.M., Kapila, V.: An augmented reality interface for human-robot interaction in unconstrained environments. In: 2019 IEEE/RSJ International Conference on Intelligent Robots and Systems (IROS), pp. 3222–3228. IEEE (2019)
7. Datteri, E.: Predicting the long-term effects of human-robot interaction: a reflection on responsibility in medical robotics. Sci. Eng. Ethics **19**(1), 139–160 (2013)
8. Fang, H., Ong, S.K., Nee, A.Y.: Novel AR-based interface for human-robot interaction and visualization. Adv. Manuf. **2**(4), 275–288 (2014)
9. Ge, S.S., et al.: Design and development of nancy, a social robot. In: 2011 8th International Conference on Ubiquitous Robots and Ambient Intelligence (URAI), pp. 568–573. IEEE (2011)
10. He, H., Ge, S.S., Zhang, Z.: A saliency-driven robotic head with bio-inspired saccadic behaviors for social robotics. Auton. Rob. **36**(3), 225–240 (2013). https://doi.org/10.1007/s10514-013-9346-7
11. Kamp, H.: Discourse representation theory. In: Blaser, A. (ed.) IBM 1988. LNCS, vol. 320, pp. 84–111. Springer, Heidelberg (1988). https://doi.org/10.1007/3-540-50011-1_34
12. Katz, D., Kenney, J., Brock, O.: How can robots succeed in unstructured environments. In: In Workshop on Robot Manipulation: Intelligence in Human Environments at Robotics: Science and Systems. Citeseer (2008)
13. Ledbetter, S.: The chapman university survey on american fears. https://blogs.chapman.edu/wilkinson/2015/10/13/americas-top-fears-2015/
14. Lewis, J.R.: Psychometric evaluation of an after-scenario questionnaire for computer usability studies: the asq. ACM Sigchi Bull. **23**(1), 78–81 (1991)
15. Lindner, K., Blosser, G., Cunigan, K.: Visual versus auditory learning and memory recall performance on short-term versus long-term tests. Mod. Psychol. Stud. **15**(1), 6 (2009)
16. Littlewort, G., et al.: Towards social robots: Automatic evaluation of human-robot interaction by facial expression classification. In: Advances in Neural Information Processing Systems, pp. 1563–1570 (2004)
17. Nieto, D., Quesada-Arencibia, A., García, C.R., Moreno-Díaz, R.: A social robot in a tourist environment. In: Hervás, R., Lee, S., Nugent, C., Bravo, J. (eds.) UCAmI 2014. LNCS, vol. 8867, pp. 21–24. Springer, Cham (2014). https://doi.org/10.1007/978-3-319-13102-3_5
18. Ren, S., He, K., Girshick, R., Sun, J.: Faster R-CNN: towards real-time object detection with region proposal networks. In: Advances in Neural Information Processing Systems, pp. 91–99 (2015)
19. Scheeff, M., Pinto, J., Rahardja, K., Snibbe, S., Tow, R.: Experiences with sparky, a social robot. In: Dautenhahn, K., Bond, A., Cañamero, L., Edmonds, B. (eds.) Socially Intelligent Agents. Multiagent Systems, Artificial Societies, and Simulated Organizations, vol 3. Springer, Boston (2002). https://doi.org/10.1007/0-306-47373-9_21
20. Sciutti, A., Mara, M., Tagliasco, V., Sandini, G.: Humanizing human-robot interaction: on the importance of mutual understanding. IEEE Technol. Soc. Mag. **37**(1), 22–29 (2018)
21. Thrun, S.: Toward a framework for human-robot interaction. Hum. Comput. Interact. **19**(1–2), 9–24 (2004)
22. Turkle, S., Breazeal, C., Dasté, O., Scassellati, B.: Encounters with kismet and cog: children respond to relational artifacts. Digit. Media Transformations Hum. Commun. (2006)

23. Wood, L.J., Zaraki, A., Robins, B., Dautenhahn, K.: Developing kaspar: a humanoid robot for children with autism. Int. J. Soc. Rob. 1–18 (2019)
24. Yan, F., Tran, D.M., He, H.: Robotic understanding of object semantics by referring to a dictionary. Int. J. Soc. Rob. 1–13 (2020)

Autonomous Group Detection, Delineation, and Selection for Human-Agent Interaction

Ben Wright[1]([✉]), J. Malcolm McCurry[2], Wallace Lawson[3], and J. Gregory Trafton[3]

[1] NRC Postdoctoral Associate, US Naval Research Laboratory, Washington, D.C., USA
benjamin.wright.ctr@nrl.navy.mil
[2] Peraton, Washington, D.C., USA
jmccurry@peraton.com
[3] Navy Center for Applied Research in Artificial Intelligence, US Naval Research Laboratory, Washington, D.C., USA
{ed.lawson,greg.trafton}@nrl.navy.mil

Abstract. If a human and a robot team need to approach a specific group to make an announcement or delivery, how will the human describe which group to approach, and how will the robot approach the group? The robots will need to take a relatively arbitrary description of a group, identify that group from onboard sensors, and accurately approach the correct group. This task requires the robot to reason over and delineate individuals and groups from other individuals and groups. We ran a study on how people describe groups for delineation and identified the features most likely used by a person. We then present a framework that allows for an agent to detect, delineate, and select a given social group from the context of a description. We also present a group detection algorithm that works on a mobile platform in real-time and provide a formalization for a Group Selection Problem.

Keywords: Group description · Group identification · Qualitative reasoning · Proxemics

1 Introduction and Motivation

Individual and group detection have long been an area of research [9,14,22]. In many cases, these detections are maintained internal to the agent or given as annotations to video or images for a human teammate to use. Group detection becomes more important when we think about it in terms of how humans describe groups to each other. Usually, it is not the case that we have a label for the group to describe to a friend or teammate. Normally, groups are described

This research was performed while BW held an NRC Research Associateship award at NRL. This research was funded by ONR and OSD to GT.

H. Li et al. (Eds.): ICSR 2021, LNAI 13086, pp. 329–338, 2021.
https://doi.org/10.1007/978-3-030-90525-5_28

(e.g. "The group by the window." or "The large group right next to us."). Through these types of descriptions, we see that grouping is contextual [13, 15]. Therefore, if we wish to have agents cooperating in Human-Agent teams, we should ensure that agents can handle contextual group descriptions.

The contributions of this paper are (1) we show that people use group descriptions when labels are not present, (2) we introduce a very simple group detection algorithm, (3) we establish a Group Selection Problem, and (4) we provide a basic implementation solution and evaluation to both group detection and selection.

2   Background

This work touches on a number of different fields of research, we provide some background from proxemics in terms of representation, recognition, and detection efforts.

2.1   Proxemics Representations of Groups

First discussed in [6], Proxemics is the study of spatial interaction among humans. Proxemics has had a growing interest in regards to research for Human-Robot Interaction (HRI) [3, 4, 12, 17, 21, 23]. Currently, the study of proxemics in this context falls into two camps: F-Formations or not F-Formations.

Face-to-face formations (F-formations) have received a lot of attention in terms of group proxemic research [17, 23, 27]. Originally discussed in [8], F-Formations describe different spatial arrangements of people given the number of people interacting. [9] defines it as, "F-formation arises whenever two or more people sustain a spatial and orientational relationship in which the space between them is one to which they have equal, direct and exclusive access". F-formations focus on three different spatial zones in relation to a group: o-space, p-space, and r-space. O-space exists inside the perimeter of the group, p-space is the perimeter of the group space and r-space being the space outside of p-space.

Aside from F-Formations, a number of other methods are being used to study and represent groups. [21] uses optical flow for active egocentric group detection in motion. [4] built a representation using qualitative spatial descriptors on top of F-formations. This is done by using logical constraint rules to determine the interactions of two-pair F-formations to create larger group formations. This is then used as a way to reason how a potential robot can join the group in a new formation pattern. [3] uses Qualitative Trajectory Calculus (QTC) to encode interactions in an HRI setting. This allows for qualitative reasoning on movement and is used in environments with trajectory detection and planning [12]. Using individual person detection and tracking, [12] builds up social network graphs between all the individuals and uses various pruning methods to then detect proper groups.

2.2   Group Recognition and Detection Work

Previous work in group detection has generally followed two different constraints: stationary vs moving groups. For stationary groups, a number of algorithms use video stills. For instance, [27] uses stills to detect F-formations based on dominant sets [7,23]. This is where individuals in the image are converted to a graph and given proximity weights, these weights are then used to detect the groups. Tracking over multiple images or video has had a wide variety of use in group detection. Having multiple images allows for a wide variety of trajectory and velocity tracking. [21], which follows the work of [12], has a discussion about maintaining identities as groups and agents move around the scene. Other video or moving group detections can be seen in [10,19,20].

3   Group Description Experiment

Our goal in this experiment was to explore how people identify and differentiate groups within a space that contains multiple groups. There were theoretical reasons from both the cognitive sciences and the interaction sciences that this experiment will help us answer. From the cognitive sciences, there are no theories or expectations about how people will deal with identifying a group of diverse individuals and whether they will over-describe a group. From the HRI perspective, there is no clear understanding of what features people will use to describe a group; knowing the features that are used allows us as roboticists to tailor our sensors and perceptual systems to what features are going to be the most useful. For example, if people commonly identify most group features and several individual features, most perceptual systems should be adequate. In contrast, if people primarily use a specific single feature, it would behoove us to make sure that our robot perceptual systems can deal with that feature.

3.1   Setup

In this experiment, we were interested in three distinct questions concerning how people identify groups. First, because groups have both group features and individuals within a group that can be identified, we wanted to document whether people used group or individual features more. Second, we wanted to identify how Gricean people are in their group descriptions. A purely Gricean approach would mean identifying a single unique feature that differentiated the groups and using that feature: no more and no less. Finally, we were interested in determining what features people used to identify groups, and whether those features were random or systematic.

97 participants from Amazon Mechanical Turk were paid $2.00 to answer questions about how to identify a group. They were told they were working with a robot to deliver snacks to individuals. Participants were randomly assigned to either the Same Perspective condition where they were told that the robot could either see from the same perspective that they could (n=53) or the Different Perspective condition where they were told the robot would be coming from an unknown direction so could not use words like "left" or "right" (n = 44).

Images were constructed using Vyond[1] to contain 2 distinct groups with differing group features. Group features that were explicitly manipulated were size

---

[1] https://www.vyond.com/.

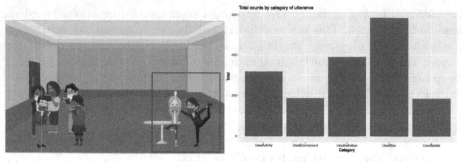

(a) An example image participants were shown.

(b) Feature breakdown by Utterance, from the left: Activity, Object, Individual, Size, Proximity

Fig. 1. Experiment image and results

(same or different with sizes of 2 or 5), object (close or far from a group), activity (same or different with dancing, stretching, talking, or reading), or proximity (close or far from each other). The selected group had an obvious rectangle drawn around it and could be on either the left or the right (counterbalanced). An example of an image is shown in Fig. 1a. Each participant saw 10 images. Because it was impossible to ask each participant to see one of each variable, we gave each participant two examples of 0–4 differences from manipulated features (size, object, activity or proximity), using a Latin-square design to keep the presence of features as equal as possible. This approach allowed us to use regression analyses to extract patterns from the participants. After collecting demographic information, each participant was given a brief description of the task and then asked to type in an English description of where to tell the robot to go. Each image also reminded the participant that the robot could see the same scene as the participant or that the robot would be approaching from an unknown location. After finishing the experiment, participants were debriefed.

3.2   Results

We used a combination of keyword extraction and hand-coding to identify which feature(s) a participant used to identify each group. Features coded were size ("The group of 5"), object ("The group closest to the table"), activity ("The dancing group"), spatial ("The group to the left"), or individual ("The group with the blond woman"). Multiple features of different types were each coded, though multiple features of the same feature were only coded once (e.g., "The group on the left with the tall blond woman" would be coded as spatial and individual, even though there are two references to individual traits).

In general, people used more group features (size, spatial, object, activity) than individual features when describing a group, $\chi^2(1) = 503.6$, $p < 0.001$

(829 group vs 133 individual).[2] To explore how Gricean participants were, we examined the raw number of features that could be used to differentiate groups; if people used a single distinguishing feature to differentiate groups, it was coded as Gricean. If people used more than was needed, it violated the Gricean maxim of quantity. There were very few instances of people not using a description that did not differentiate groups ($< 1\%$). We found that people were very likely to over-describe groups (66% vs. 34%), $\chi^2(1) = 84.7$, $p < 0.001$. People strongly violated Gricean maxim of quantity in this experiment.

To examine whether people were random in their choice of features to describe and differentiate groups or whether they had systematic preferences, we examined which features were used, collapsing across other variables because they showed no significant effect. As Fig. 1b suggests, people did not choose features at random to differentiate groups, $\chi^2(4) = 329.6$, $p < 0.001$. A post-hoc Tukey test showed a particular order that people preferred: Size > Individual > Activity > Object = Proxemic.

As hoped, this experiment helped answer several theoretical and applied questions from cognitive science and HRI. First, people seem to prefer to use group features rather than features of individuals to differentiate groups, though both are used frequently. Second, this experiment provides some expectations about how people will address a robot to approach a group. Specifically, people do not use a random set of features to differentiate groups, instead choosing to have a preferred order: some features are much more likely to occur than others. Finally, people are quite non-Gricean when describing a group, frequently providing more information than needed to differentiate one group from another.

4 Group Detection and Representation

With these experimental results in mind, we can begin to work on group detection. From the results above, we know that group size is *very important* to keep accurate. From previous works in group recognition/detection there are two basic ideas, using pose information or not using pose information. However, pose is captured in those datasets within a "smart-room" environment with multiple cameras at useful angles (e.g., [17]). Unfortunately, these assumptions do not work for our target domain, mobile robotics. For a single robot, the sensors and computing power available is usually far less than available in a typical smart-room – a laptop and a standard CCD.

In contrast, it is far easier to identify the location of a person (regardless of their pose) in most scenes, even when they are partially occluded or are not facing the camera. To show this, we ran OpenPose [1] (a common method to extract pose in real-time) on a series of images. We also ran YOLO [14] to extract where people were in the scenes. In 100% of the cases, YOLO identified more people than OpenPose. For example, in one crowded image environment YOLO detected all but 1 of 12 people while OpenPose failed to give pose information

---

[2] A linear effects mixed model shows a similar result while taking into account the multiple random effects. A later report will provide a fuller description.

to 4 of the 12. Missing the Pose Information of 33% is significant when it comes to the tightly coupled nature of pose-based detection methods.

Therefore, our designs are not focused on utilizing pose information as maintaining an accurate number of individuals is more important than maintaining an accurate number of poses.

4.1 Agent Detection

To detect people, we use the deep convolutional neural network YOLO [14]. YOLO predicts both the location and the classification of known objects in the image. It does this by first subdividing the image into grid cells, then predicts the most likely size and location for an object in each cell. This network was trained on the MS-COCO dataset [11], which includes a variety of classes. Additionally, we could utilize a robot's on-board range/bearing detection to determine placement of a detected person. From these range and bearing values, we can project the image detection onto a grid. To get group definitions, we assume we are given accurate representations of the agents and their locations within an image - though not necessarily the agent's bearing or facing.

4.2 Definition of a Group

[26] defines a group from video footage as a group of individuals within a certain space threshold and maintaining that threshold for a specific time threshold. [12,21] defines groups as "two or more people in close proximity to one another with a common motion goal." F-formations utilizes spatial and directional information to determine groups based on o- and p-space[4,17,24]. Additionally, f-formations focus on the context of *conversational groups*. With the idea that conversational "space" defines the group by individuals "facing" in a specific way based on certain formation types. Finally, some research leaves the definition of group undefined and utilizes clustering techniques to have groups detected. This research does focus on trajectories heavily though [18,19].

From these various discussions of groups, we can pull out a few recurring concepts: spatial-temporal relations, motion/direction relations, and shared goals. Not all images can easily be broken down into direction/facing information for all individuals, likewise temporal relations cannot be done from still frames. Furthermore, goals and intent are a very hard problem that is its own research area. Therefore, we try to focus our definition of groups to be purely spatial, but limit it to stationary groups. A *stationary group* is the largest number of agents (greater than or equal to 2) in an environment that are a given distance apart from each other that does not break the standard deviation of the average distance between all agents in the stationary group. It is also assumed that an agent is only a member of one group at a time.

4.3 Group Detection for Stationary Groups

We devised a *Group Detection Algorithm*, based on this definition. Starting with all agents, we calculate the *distance − pair* between each Agent. Starting with

Table 1. Group description options, with query examples

Described thing	In relation to	Query	Example
The group	size,small	$smallest\_group(Group)$	The smallest group
The group	size,large	$largest\_group(Group)$	The largest group
The group	size,specific	$group\_of\_size(Group, N)$	Group of size 5
The group	with,Person	$group\_with(Group, Agent)$	Group w/ person in hat

the minimum $distance - pair$, we slowly attempt adding in new agents. If the new $distance - pair$ values are within a threshold of mean $distance - pair$ plus/minus standard deviation, we add the new agent to the overall group. Otherwise, we continue to the next possible agent. When we've run out of possible agents to add, whatever is left we define as a new group. We then remove these agents from the overall list of agents to check and start over with the newest minimum $distance - pair$. We continue doing this until our minimum $distance - pair$ reaches a certain threshold if a minimum threshold is not met then we stop, likewise if we run out of agents for pairs we also stop.

4.4   Group Delineation and Selection

A *group description* is a pairing, (R, P), between a relation, R, and a property, P. A group, G, can satisfy a group description if the property and relation hold true for that group. With these group descriptions, we can now think about how we might differentiate between groups. To delineate groups, we need to know all possible descriptions for a group. A *Group Selection Problem* (GSP) consists of a given Group Description, (R, P), and a domain of agents, groups, and objects. A solution for this would be a group that satisfies the given Group Description in the domain.

5   Implementation and Evaluation

5.1   Implementing the Group Selection Problem

We use SWI-prolog [25] to implement our Group Detection algorithm. This follows along previous work that has used Prolog in HRI and qualitative reasoning [4,5,26]. To implement group detection we assume knowledge of individuals. From here, our group detection algorithm is used. Some of the functions not fully defined include $findAllDistances$. This function generates a list of *distance pairs*, (a, b, N), between all agents a, b so we know that the distance between agents a and b is N. This is only done once in the detection algorithm.

Additionally, there are some stop cases for thresholds that are important to know. There are two places where thresholds can change how detection works. The first is when the algorithm only has two agents left, there is a threshold to consider them a group or not. The main loop, that is when there are more

Table 2. Group detection methods in the Cocktail party benchmark

Algorithm	Precision	Recall	F-score
Our method	0.62	0.21	0.31
Pose-only baseline from [16]	0.29	0.27	0.28

than 2 agents, automatically makes a group between two agents. The second threshold has to deal with how the standard deviation works on newly formed groups. When a new group-pair is formed, the standard deviation is 0. This is bad, so we allow for this special case that the standard deviation is related to the distance between those two agents. We ran things between a quarter of the distance to two times the distance between the agents. For later testings, these values were used to fine-tune some of our results.

Following along with our group detection, we also implement the group selection queries in SWI-Prolog. Table 1 lists queries next to each description. These queries can be solved fairly quickly from the properties given. A majority of the group property queries also involve a minimum or maximum value check against certain properties.

In addition to our own scenarios to test group detection and selection, we also use a test-case dataset to compare our group detection algorithm to state-of-the-art algorithms - *Cocktail Party*. The *CocktailParty* dataset, first discussed in [17], is a dataset containing video of a cocktail party in a large room with 7 individuals walking around. There is a main table at one side of the room with drinks and food on it and the rest of the room is fairly open for the people to walk around in. Over the course of 30 min, the individuals interact with each other in various groupings.

5.2 Evaluations and Testing

We determined a group to be accurately detected as previous detection strategies in [2,17]. To test our Group Detection Algorithm, we ran it over a known dataset, *CocktailParty*, and gave its Precision, Recall, and F-Score results in comparison to another pose-free group detection algorithm result in Table 2. Groups in this dataset were annotated manually by an expert every 5 s resulting in 320 still frames with group annotations. We tested our algorithm against these 320 frames. When compared to a previous "Pose-only" from [16], we do significantly better with precision and, as a result, have a better F-score as well.

These were all run on a basic laptop running Ubuntu 16.04 with a 2.8GHzx8 i7 Intel processor. The runtime results were taken using the linux *time* command and includes the entire prolog run. Each run was given the agents and objects locations and it ran detection, definition, and selection each time. On average our runs took around 0.035s. Comparatively, [17] mentions averaging about 15 s per frame of video for their detection method and [16] mentions their detection algorithm running in a few milliseconds.

6 Discussion and Conclusion

We provide an alternative approach to group formation that need not rely on head tracking or pose detection which can be difficult in some scenarios. We demonstrate an improvement on current approaches [16,17] that detect group formation without the use of head pose information.

Future directions with group selection involve on-boarding this to full robotic platforms along with adding selection commands. A final direction to take these group description and selection queries is to use them to clarify and prune imperfect information and confirm certain group descriptions with human counterparts. Additional studies in understanding the priorities and orderings for group descriptions used by humans would be beneficial to ensure that this reversal of queries is more optimally specified.

Acknowledgements. The views, opinions and/or findings expressed are those of the authors and should not be interpreted as representing the official views or policies of the Department of Defense or the U.S. Government. The authors would like to thank Magda Bugajska and Bill Adams in their thoughts on combining the detection to representation on robotic platforms.

References

1. Cao, Z., Hidalgo, G., Simon, T., Wei, S.E., Sheikh, Y.: Openpose: realtime multi-person 2D pose estimation using part affinity fields. IEEE Trans. Pattern Anal. Mach. Intell. **43**(1), 172–186 (2019)
2. Cristani, M., et al.: Social interaction discovery by statistical analysis of F-formations. In: Proceedings of the British Machine Vision Conference, pp. 23.1–23.12. BMVA Press (2011). https://doi.org/10.5244/C.25.23
3. Dondrup, C., Bellotto, N., Hanheide, M., Eder, K., Leonards, U.: A computational model of human-robot spatial interactions based on a qualitative trajectory calculus. Robotics **4**(1), 63–102 (2015)
4. Falomir, Z., Angulo Bahón, C.: A qualitative spatial descriptor of group-robot interactions. In: Leibniz International Proceedings in Informatics, pp. 3:1–3:14. Schloss Dagstuhl-Leibniz-Zentrum für Informatik (2017)
5. Falomir, Z., Pich, A., Costa, V.: Spatial reasoning about qualitative shape compositions. Ann. Math. Artif. Intell. **88**(5), 589–621 (2020)
6. Hall, E.T.: The Hidden Dimension, vol. 609. Doubleday, Garden City (1966)
7. Hung, H., Kröse, B.: Detecting F-formations as dominant sets. In: Proceedings of the 13th International Conference on Multimodal Interfaces, pp. 231–238 (2011)
8. Kendon, A.: The F-formation system: the spatial organization of social encounters. Man-Environ. Syst. **6**(01), 1976 (1976)
9. Kendon, A.: Spatial organization in social encounters: The F-formation system. Conducting interaction: patterns of behavior in focused encounters (1990)
10. Khan, S.D., Vizzari, G., Bandini, S., Basalamah, S.: Detection of social groups in pedestrian crowds using computer vision. In: Battiato, S., Blanc-Talon, J., Gallo, G., Philips, W., Popescu, D., Scheunders, P. (eds.) Advanced Concepts for Intelligent Vision Systems, ACIVS 2015. LNCS, vol. 9386, pp. 249–260. Springer, Cham (2015). https://doi.org/10.1007/978-3-319-25903-1_22

11. Lin, T.Y., et al.: Microsoft COCO: common objects in context. In: Fleet, D., Pajdla, T., Schiele, B., Tuytelaars, T. (eds.) Computer Vision - ECCV 2014. LNCS, vol. 8693, pp. 740–755. Springer, Cham (2014). https://doi.org/10.1007/978-3-319-10602-1_48

12. Linder, T., Arras, K.O.: Multi-model hypothesis tracking of groups of people in RGB-D data. In: 17th International Conference on Information Fusion (FUSION), pp. 1–7. IEEE (2014)

13. Long, M., Rohde, H., Rubio-Fernandez, P.: The pressure to communicate efficiently continues to shape language use later in life. Sci. Rep. **10**(1), 1–13 (2020)

14. Redmon, J., Divvala, S., Girshick, R., Farhadi, A.: You only look once: unified, real-time object detection. In: Proceedings of the IEEE Conference on Computer Vision and Pattern Recognition, pp. 779–788 (2016)

15. Rubio-Fernandez, P., Jara-Ettinger, J.: Incrementality and efficiency shape pragmatics across languages. In: Proceedings of the National Academy of Sciences (2020)

16. Sanghvi, N., Yonetani, R., Kitani, K.: MGpi: a computational model of multiagent group perception and interaction. In: Proceedings of the 19th International Conference on Autonomous Agents and MultiAgent Systems, pp. 1196–1205 (2020)

17. Setti, F., Lanz, O., Ferrario, R., Murino, V., Cristani, M.: Multi-scale F-formation discovery for group detection. In: 2013 IEEE International Conference on Image Processing, pp. 3547–3551. IEEE (2013)

18. Solera, F., Calderara, S., Cucchiara, R.: Socially constrained structural learning for groups detection in crowd. IEEE Trans. Pattern Anal. Mach. Intell. **38**(5), 995–1008 (2016)

19. Solera, F., Calderara, S., Cucchiara, R.: Structured learning for detection of social groups in crowd. In: 2013 10th IEEE International Conference on Advanced Video and Signal Based Surveillance, pp. 7–12. IEEE (2013)

20. Solera, F., Calderara, S., Ristani, E., Tomasi, C., Cucchiara, R.: Tracking social groups within and across cameras. IEEE Trans. Circuits Syst. Video Technol. **27**(3), 441–453 (2016)

21. Taylor, A., Chan, D.M., Riek, L.D.: Robot-centric perception of human groups. ACM Trans. Human-Robot Interact. (THRI) **9**(3), 1–21 (2020)

22. Turner, J.C.: Towards a cognitive redefinition of the social group. Soc. Identity Intergroup Relat. **1**(2), 15–40 (1982)

23. Vascon, S., Mequanint, E.Z., Cristani, M., Hung, H., Pelillo, M., Murino, V.: A game-theoretic probabilistic approach for detecting conversational groups. In: Cremers, D., Reid, I., Saito, H., Yang, M.-H. (eds.) ACCV 2014. LNCS, vol. 9007, pp. 658–675. Springer, Cham (2015). https://doi.org/10.1007/978-3-319-16814-2_43

24. Vázquez, M., Steinfeld, A., Hudson, S.E.: Parallel detection of conversational groups of free-standing people and tracking of their lower-body orientation. In: 2015 IEEE/RSJ International Conference on Intelligent Robots and Systems (IROS), pp. 3010–3017. IEEE (2015)

25. Wielemaker, J., Schrijvers, T., Triska, M., Lager, T.: SWI-prolog. Theory Pract. Logic Program. **12**(1–2), 67–96 (2012)

26. Wright, B., Bugajska, M., Adams, W., Lawson, E., McCurry, J.M., Trafton, J.G.: Proxemic reasoning for group approach. In: 12th International Conference on Social Robotics (ICSR) (2020)

27. Zhang, L., Hung, H.: Beyond F-formations: determining social involvement in free standing conversing groups from static images. In: Proceedings of the IEEE Conference on Computer Vision and Pattern Recognition, pp. 1086–1095 (2016)

A Framework of Controlled Robot Language for Reliable Human-Robot Collaboration

Dang Tran[1], Fujian Yan[1], Yimesker Yihun[2], Jindong Tan[3],
and Hongsheng He[1(✉)]

[1] School of Computing, Wichita State University, Wichita, KS 67260, USA
hongsheng.he@wichita.edu
[2] Department of Mechanical Engineering, Wichita State University,
Wichita, KS 67260, USA
[3] Department of Mechanical, Aerospace, and Biomedical Engineering,
University of Tennessee, Knoxville, TN, USA

Abstract. Effective and efficient communication is critical for human-robot collaboration and human-agent teaming. This paper presents the design of a Controlled Robot Language (CRL) and its formal grammar for instruction interpretation and automated robot planning. The CRL framework defines a formal language domain that deterministically maps linguistic commands to logical semantic expressions. As compared to Controlled Natural Language, which aims for general knowledge representation, CRL expressions are particularly designed to parse human instructions in automated robot planning. The grammar of CRL is developed in accordance with the IEEE CORA ontology, which defines the majority of formal English domain, accepting large range of intuitive instructions. For sentences outside the grammar coverage, CRL checker is used to detect linguistic patterns, which can be further processed by CRL translator to recover back an equivalent expression in CRL grammar. The final output is formal semantic representation using first-order logic in large discourse. The CRL framework was evaluated on various corpora and it outperformed CRL in balancing coverage and specificity.

1 Introduction

Reliable communication between humans and intelligent robot is a critical need especially for human-robot collaboration, human-agent teaming, and multiple agent coordination. For most robotic applications, reliable human-robot communication will significantly reduce the chances of unpredictable catastrophes and fatal damages. In addition to physical interaction, natural language has the potential to become the main communication channel for instructing robots, representing contextual knowledge, and providing feedback. From a psychological perspective, *trust* is the grand obstacle preventing human and robot from

This work was partially supported by NSF CMMI 2129113 and WSU URCAF 2019.

ⓒ Springer Nature Switzerland AG 2021
H. Li et al. (Eds.): ICSR 2021, LNAI 13086, pp. 339–349, 2021.
https://doi.org/10.1007/978-3-030-90525-5_29

communicate effectively [1]. A robot with dynamic consciousness and optimized precision does not necessarily gain trust from its users. We believe that the lack of reliable natural language communication is one of the main factors that hinder the advancement of human-agent teaming.

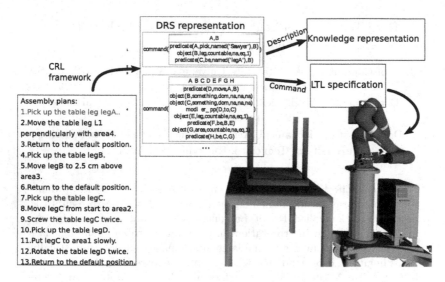

Fig. 1. Parsing of natural language instructions using CRL. The linguistic instructions from user are converted into appropriate semantic representations using Discourse Representation Structure with variables and explicit logical statements. Command-type DRS expressions can be used to control robot through planning.

Significant research progress has been made to address the importance and challenge of reliable natural language communication in robotic domain [2]. Robots are deemed to understand natural language if the robot can either (i) extract correct information or (ii) have a logical semantic representation for the context. From the former perspective, natural language understanding is considered as shallow parsing low-level knowledge for action control. The most common approaches in this branch include probabilistic models [3] and neural-network methods [4], which have demonstrated robust performance in detecting linguistic patterns and triggering low-level actions. These approaches focus on partial information only, which is not representative enough for describing complete planning scenarios in realistic cases. The latter perspective parses the natural language in a richer way, where the semantics of natural language expressions are representable in logic form [5].

Despite the fruitful research progress of human-robot communication, natural language based interfaces in robotics are still limited due to the trade-off between *expressiveness* and *reliability*. Linguistic models that can handle a large range of natural language expressions are less deterministic or reliable; on the other hand, systems that can understand natural language inputs in-depth are limited in expressiveness. A common language domain could bridge the gap between expressiveness and reliability in human-robot interaction.

In this paper, we propose a *grammar model* named Controlled Robot Language (CRL) that interprets general human instructions into Discourse Representation Structures (DRS) [6], which is a semantic format that can capture various partial information into the same data structure. More importantly, the CRL is designed for general-purpose that represents a *deterministic* and *expressive* linguistic domain rather than an ad-hoc development, inspired by Controlled Natural Language (CNL). The CRL framework defines CRL grammar that syntactically captures a majority of English expressions. For dialect expressions that do not follow the grammar, we developed a CRL checker, which contains flexible set of common linguistic patterns, to detect correctable grammar errors. In the CRL domain, expressions following the grammar are parsed into corresponding formal representations, which contain all essential linguistic information for robotic planning with reference to IEEE CORA standards [7]. As shown in Fig. 1, given a sequence of natural language instructions, the CRL parser generates the corresponding syntactic structure for expressions without errors in grammar, or corrects fixable patterns for expressions with errors in grammar. The CRL framework will translate the instructions into knowledge representations or robot action planning.

We plan to address two fundamental challenges. The first challenge is to design a linguistic model that is comprehensive and unambiguous. To the best of our knowledge, there is no work so far addressing the importance of these two properties equivalently and simultaneously. The second challenge is to automatically transform or represent formal representation into robot knowledge and actions. A primary objective of human-robot communication is to enable high-level mutual understanding and automated planning. There is limited research addressing on expanding the natural language domain in human-robot collaboration. The main contributions of this paper are:

1. We designed and implemented a linguistic grammar tailed for robotic applications, which achieves both reliability and expressiveness; and
2. We developed a complete framework and proposed a methodology in translating natural language instructions into corresponding robot actions.

2   The Framework of Controlled Robot Language (CRL)

In view of the lacking of linguistic interfaces that satisfy reliability and expressiveness, we aim to implement a framework of Controlled Robot Language (CRL) for robot understanding and planning. Motivated by Controlled Natural Language, the proposed model maintains essential properties: certainty and generality. The proposed framework contains three fundamental components: CRL grammar, a CRL parser, and a CRL translator. The CRL grammar defines a formal language domain – a set of common English instructions. CRL parser is used to assign equivalent syntactic structures to input commands. From syntactic structures, partial linguistic information, such as *subject, object, predicate, noun modifier, and predicate modifier,* can be extracted and constructed back into formal representations. The CRL grammar is designed toward a deterministic and reliable interpretation with no ambiguity. We limited the set of CRL grammar for a compact and efficient grammar core. The sentences outside the domain are further processed by the CRL parser in accordance to predefined dialect patterns – set of sentence patterns that exist in daily conversations but are not generalized enough to be represented as grammar rules. These dialect patterns can be recognized and transformed by the CRL translator, which returns a valid expressions but in CRL grammar domain.

2.1 CRL Grammar and Dialect Patterns

Grammar is the core component of the proposed framework. We designed the CRL grammar as a general-purpose and deterministic grammar in English. The CRL grammar defines an unambiguous formal language domain, which can be computational efficiently processed by a computer, but still expressive enough to allow natural usage. We defined and developed the CRL grammar in terms of Context Free Grammar (CFG) with selective rules to avoid unnecessary ambiguity.

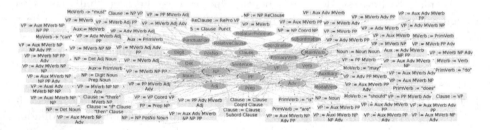

Fig. 2. CFG productions for CRL grammar – implicit descriptions of CRL grammar.

Given a set of terminal nodes associated with a set of terminal symbols T and nonterminal nodes associated with a set of nonterminal symbols N, we defined grammar using CFG paradigm. CFG grammar is a collection of linguistic productions in the form of

$$X \rightarrow \{Y_i\}_i^n \{\alpha_j\}_j^m \tag{1}$$

where $X \in N$, $Y_i \in N \cup T$ and $\alpha_j \in T$. To support common instruction structures and IEEE CORA ontology, we formulate the CRL grammar by a set of about 330 productions[1], including a set of standard Penn Treebank POS tags and 30 additional new nonterminals. A fragment of grammar is visualized in Fig. 2. The grammar defines constraints on language domain, aiming to optimally avoid unnecessary ambiguity. The grammar captures a majority of common linguistic

---

[1] The complete grammar and parsers are available at: https://github.com/hhelium.

expressions in real-world scenarios, e.g., *"A robot picks a red apple on the table."* and *"Which apple is red?"*.

CRL grammar was initially developed to express the core grammar production in form of S → NP VP and its variants. During the grammar developing process, attachment ambiguity and coordination ambiguity appeared. To avoid solving ambiguities by designing a complex disambiguation model, dialect pattern recognition is used to detect patterns that can potentially lead to ambiguities, and transform them back to equivalent CRL linguistic expressions. These dialect patterns are manually designed based on WikiHow instructions [8]. This dynamic set can be flexibly expanded and modified in accordance to the chosen language domain. As shown in Table 1, to make CRL applicable in WikiHow corpus domain, input sentences must be normalized and transformed into equivalent representation following each dialect pattern's correcting rule.

Table 1. Grammar dialect patterns for CRL checker.

Dialect Pattern	Examples	Linguistic Correction
Your/our/my pattern	*your* hand	change to a possessive pronoun
You/I/we pattern	*you* can move	replace with a subject pronoun
Plural nouns	*cubes*	singularize
Metrics	3 kilograms, 1 ton	map to standard metric units
Literal quantity	one half; quarter; dozen	map to standard metric units
Imperative	*rotate* the leg	*"robot"* as the default subject
Compound noun	*table leg*	last noun as the main noun
Consecutive adjectives	a *small red* apple	add conjunction "and"
Consecutive adverbs	*gradually slowly* move	add conjunction "and"
Verb+obj +to+verb	click the screen to start	restructure
Verb + to + verb	have to wait	add modal
Verb+gerund	consider stopping	gerund as the main verb
From-to pattern	*from 0.1 to 0.2 cm*	standardize the structure
Passive voice	is picked by	convert to active voice
Progress description	*by grasping its hand*	convert the gerund to a verb

2.2   CRL Parser

With the defined CRL grammar, we constructed a syntactic parser to analyze syntactic structures of natural language descriptions. We utilized a common Bottom-Up dynamic programming parsing algorithm Cocke-Kasami-Younger (CKY) to find all syntactic structures for a given sentence with efficient run time complexity – $\mathcal{O}(n^3 \cdot |G|)$ where n is the length of input, and $|G|$ is the size of CFG grammar. Although CRL grammar was carefully selected to avoid unnecessary syntactic ambiguities, multiple parsing structures for NL input are inevitable. To maintain the determinism property of the robot system without building a disambiguation model, appeared ambiguities are manually resolved by user's instructions. These instructions can be collected, trained by a probabilistic model and automatically used in the future cases.

2.3   Translating CRL Descriptions to Knowledge Representations

Leveraging the parsed syntactic structures, the CRL framework constructs a contextual semantic representation of natural language expressions. These semantic representations are essential for robot understanding and planning. Each semantic representation can be either classified into one of three categories: contextual descriptions, command instructions, and queries. The instructions correspond to robot planning, and the contextual descriptions specify environment context, temporal and spatial constraints. We developed a program that automatically translated these semantic expressions into corresponding LTL specifications, which can be executed directly by robot planners.

Given the syntactic structure, the framework extracts fundamental linguistic components such as *object, predicate, property, adjunct,* and *phrase.* The extracted information is, however, discrete and exclusive. To unify them into a single semantic representation, we need semantic rules to depict combining procedures. These rules are best described using symbolic language as Prolog [9]. The main challenge of this process is the ability to create general rules that can unify low-level knowledge. Appropriate selection of semantic rules goes beyond a combination task: solve anaphoric problem, identify quantification property, and describe temporal constraints. In this paper, we focus on a set of semantic rules for discourse representations, which also handle anaphora binding and determiners quantifying. The theoretical details of these rules can be found at Kamp's lecture [10]. The developed CRL system expanded the semantic rules as defined in [11] by unifying discrete components and adding a few abstraction layers. These abstraction layers provide convenient ways to identify objects, trigger actions, or query. By using additional abstraction layers, we can easily classify all possible formal representation into three main types: (i) *Description-type*: used to describe an event, robotic environment, and knowledge base; (ii) *Command-type*: used to trigger robot actions; (iii) *Query-type*: extract information back from the knowledge base.

3   Experiment

We evaluated the CRL framework in parsing performance, formal robot planning, and user acceptance. The CRL framework is compared with two linguistic frameworks, Attempto Controlled English [12] and Stanford Constituency parsing [13], on instruction-based corpora WikiHow [8] and Collaborative Manipulation [14]. The effectiveness of the CRL framework in automated planning is also demonstrated in an example of instruction-based furniture assembly. At last, we quantified the user acceptance of CRL in terms of correctness, complexity, ambiguity, readability, and efficiency.

3.1 Performance of Natural Language Parsing

The CRL framework was tested on instructions in Collaborative Manipulation [8] and WikiHow corpus [14] for planning domain. The Collaborative Manipulation is a standard dataset, which is a corpus of 1670 natural language sentences. The WikiHow dataset is a collection of human describing procedural task using step-by-steps instruction style. The dataset consists of 9520 instruction sentences. The performance of CRL in grammar coverage and semantics representation is compared with ACE framework [12] and Stanford Constituency parsing [13]. As showed in Table 2, the CRL is outperforming ACE in expressiveness in term of grammar coverage, but not as competitive as the induced-grammar-based methods Stanford CoreNLP. Nonetheless, CRL can express all parsed instructions into complete semantic representations, whereas Stanford CoreNLP was not designed with this capability. This is the conundrum in solving the contradiction between coverage and formal representation. To represent a linguistic instruction into formal semantics, the domain grammar needs to be structured; on the contrary, structured grammar cannot cover all free-form natural language. Though defined in general language domain, the ACE framework cannot understand any sentences in the WikiHow corpus, due to the extensively use of invalid expressions in ACE grammar.

Table 2. Performance comparison on standard corpora.

	Collaborative Manipulation (1670)	
	Grammar coverage	Formal semantics
ACE [12]	140 (8.38%)	140 (8.38%)
CRL (this paper)	739 (44.25%)	739 (44.25%)
CoreNLP [13]	1670 (100%)	N/A
	WikiHow (9520)	
	Grammar coverage	Formal semantics
ACE [12]	0 (0%)	0 (0%)
CRL (this paper)	3898 (40.95%)	3898 (40.95%)
CoreNLP [13]	9520 (100%)	N/A

The CRL framework has a flexible set of linguistic patterns, allowing flexible adaption to various scenarios. The experiment showed the same trail in the Collaborative Manipulation corpus. It is important to guarantee deterministics and reliability in human-robot collaboration for predictable system behavior.

3.2   CRL-Based Robot Planning

We implemented an automated planning system based on CRL for the assembly of an IKEA table by following natural language instructions. The robotic system consists of a Sawyer manipulator with an AR10 robotic hand, which support context-aware task-oriented manipulation [15,16]. We employed the RRTConnect [17] planner for low-level control, and developed a Python modules for the CRL interface. The control and communication are implemented as ROS services. We also utilized the Spot [18] to handle LTL specification by building reactive system from DRS instructions, and used RViz for simulation and visualization.

Figure 3 shows the results of successful action execution by following natural language instructions to assemble an IKEA table step by step. Four primitive actions were developed and grounded: *pick, place, release,* and *rotate.* The complete implementation of 13 instruction scripts took about 4 minutes to finish, but there is a lot of room for optimization both in CRL parsing and action planning.

3.3   User Acceptance of CRL

We evaluated the acceptance of CRL in terms of the discrepancy between CRL parsing and human perception. We designed questionnaires containing five binary (yes/no) evaluation criteria: *correctness, complexity, ambiguity, readability,* and *efficiency.* 1) The correctness is defined as whether the parsed results are correct in DRS forms, i.e., the parsed DRS representations are correct and semantically consistent with the input sentences; 2) The complexity evaluates whether the parsing results contain additional redundant words or phrases generated by dialect correction; 3) The ambiguity in semantics is used to examine if the CRL can handle a potentially ambiguous natural language input; 4) The readability is used to evaluate whether the CRL parses a potentially ambiguous input in the same way as a human does; 5) The efficiency is used to evaluate whether the parsing results are sufficient for further robotic applications such as task planning. Ten participants were invited to evaluate 350 CRL parsing results. As shown in Fig. 4, the CRL has high acceptance and consistence with human understanding of natural language instructions.

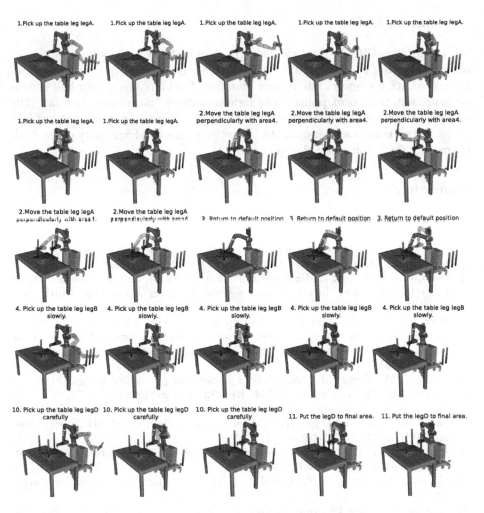

Fig. 3. Assembly of a furniture table by following natural language instructions based on CRL.

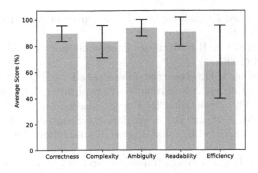

Fig. 4. User acceptance of CRL (higher scores are better).

4 Conclusion

We proposed a CRL framework that ensures reliability and expressiveness for natural language communication. We also demonstrated the procedure to integrate the CRL framework into robotic planning: from building a complete semantic representation to mapping those representations into robotic actions. The experiment showed the performance of the CRL frame in parsing natural language instructions, and demonstrated the effectiveness and flexibility of the CRL framework for automated robot planning.

References

1. Yagoda, R.E., Gillan, D.J.: You want me to trust a robot? The development of a human-robot interaction trust scale. Int. J. Soc. Robot. **4**, 235–248 (2012)
2. Liu, R., Zhang, X.: Methodologies for realizing natural-language-facilitated human-robot cooperation: a review. CoRR, vol. abs/1701.08756 (2017)
3. Salvi, G., Montesano, L., Bernardino, A., Santos-Victor, J.: Language bootstrapping: learning word meanings from perception-action association. CoRR, vol. abs/1711.09714 (2017)
4. Bisk, Y., Yuret, D., Marcu, D.: Natural language communication with robots. In: Proceedings of the 2016 Conference of the North American Chapter of the Association for Computational Linguistics: Human Language Technologies, pp. 751–761 (2016)
5. Tenorth, M., Beetz, M.: KnowRob: a knowledge processing infrastructure for cognition-enabled robots. Int. J. Rob. Res. **32**, 566–590 (2013)
6. Kamp, H., Van Genabith, J., Reyle, U.: Discourse representation theory. In: Handbook of Philosophical Logic, pp. 125–394. Springer, Dordrecht (2011). https://doi.org/10.1007/978-94-007-0485-5_3
7. Prestes, E., et al.: Towards a core ontology for robotics and automation. Robot. Auton. Syst. **61**(11), 1193–1204 (2013)
8. Koupaee, M., Wang, W.Y.: WikiHow: a large scale text summarization dataset (2018)
9. Bratko, I.: Prolog Programming for Artificial Intelligence. Pearson Education (2001)
10. Kamp, H., Genabith, J., Reyle, U.: Discourse Representation Theory, pp. 125–394 (2010)
11. Kuhn, T.: Controlled English for knowledge representation. Ph.D. thesis, University of Zurich (2010)
12. Fuchs, N.E., Schwitter, R.: Attempto controlled English (ACE). arXiv preprint cmp-lg/9603003 (1996)
13. Klein, D., Manning, C.D.: Accurate unlexicalized parsing. In: Proceedings of the 41st Annual Meeting on Association for Computational Linguistics - Volume 1, (USA), pp. 423–430, Association for Computational Linguistics (2003)
14. Scalise, R., Li, S., Admoni, H., Rosenthal, S., Srinivasa, S.S.: Natural language instructions for human-robot collaborative manipulation. Int. J. Rob. Res. **37**(6), 558–565 (2018)
15. Li, H., Tan, J., He, H.: MagicHand: context-aware dexterous grasping using an anthropomorphic robotic hand. In: 2020 IEEE International Conference on Robotics and Automation (ICRA), pp. 9895–9901 (2020)

16. Rao, A.B., Krishnan, K., He, H.: Learning robotic grasping strategy based on natural-language object descriptions. In: 2018 IEEE/RSJ International Conference on Intelligent Robots and Systems (IROS), pp. 882–887 (2018)
17. Kuffner, J.J., LaValle, S.M.: RRT-connect: an efficient approach to single-query path planning. In: Proceedings 2000 ICRA. Millennium Conference. IEEE International Conference on Robotics and Automation. Symposia Proceedings (Cat. No. 00CH37065), vol. 2, pp. 995–1001. IEEE (2000)
18. Duret-Lutz, A., Lewkowicz, A., Fauchille, A., Michaud, T., Renault, É., Xu, L.: Spot 2.0 — a framework for LTL and ω-automata manipulation. In: Artho, C., Legay, A., Peled, D. (eds.) ATVA 2016. LNCS, vol. 9938, pp. 122–129. Springer, Cham (2016). https://doi.org/10.1007/978-3-319-46520-3_8

Age-Related Differences in the Perception of Eye-Gaze from a Social Robot

Lucas Morillo-Mendez[1]([✉]) [iD], Martien G. S. Schrooten[2] [iD], Amy Loutfi[1] [iD],
and Oscar Martinez Mozos[1] [iD]

[1] Centre for Applied Autonomous Sensor Systems, Örebro University,
702 81 Örebro, Sweden
{lucas.morillo,amy.loutfi,oscar.mozos}@oru.se
[2] Center for Health and Medical Psychology, Örebro University,
702 81 Örebro, Sweden
martien.schrooten@oru.se

Abstract. The sensibility to deictic gaze declines naturally with age and often results in reduced social perception. Thus, the increasing efforts in developing social robots that assist older adults during daily life tasks need to consider the effects of aging. In this context, as non-verbal cues such as deictic gaze are important in natural communication in human-robot interaction, this paper investigates the performance of older adults, as compared to younger adults, during a controlled, online (visual search) task inspired by daily life activities, while assisted by a social robot. This paper also examines age-related differences in social perception. Our results showed a significant facilitation effect of head movement representing deictic gaze from a Pepper robot on task performance. This facilitation effect was not significantly different between the age groups. However, social perception of the robot was less influenced by its deictic gaze behavior in older adults, as compared to younger adults. This line of research may ultimately help informing the design of adaptive non-verbal cues from social robots for a wide range of end users.

Keywords: Human-robot interaction · Older adults · Non-verbal cues

1 Introduction

In the last years, there has been an increasing interest in the use of social robots to assist older adults (OA) during daily life tasks [20]. An important cue in the interaction with social robots is non-verbal communication such as deictic gaze [2,17]. Humans use deictic gaze to guide the attention of another person towards a point in the space by looking at it. This communicative signal is key to initiate a shared attention between individuals and to increase the efficiency in collaborative tasks [4]. In addition, deictic gaze is important in OA because it can help to inform age-related differences in human-robot interaction (HRI) [7]. This is because the sensibility to deictic gaze declines naturally with age, reflecting a reduction in social perception in OA [21]. For this reason, it is important to explore how deictic gaze is attended in normal aging when performed by a robot.

© Springer Nature Switzerland AG 2021
H. Li et al. (Eds.): ICSR 2021, LNAI 13086, pp. 350–361, 2021.
https://doi.org/10.1007/978-3-030-90525-5_30

At the same time, there is a call for more studies regarding non-verbal cues in which OA are direct research participants, in contrast to studies where OA act only as beneficiaries, and to further compare the outputs with younger controls [22]. Therefore, it is relevant to explore the benefits of non-verbal cues from social robots towards OA during collaborative daily life tasks, and how age-related differences may influence their perception of a social robot in contrast to younger populations. These studies may help improving the design of non-verbal cues in HRI that adapt to age changes.

This work seeks to explore potential age-related differences in the perception of deictic gaze from a social robot when collaborating in tasks inspired by daily life activities. To do so, we designed a set of online visual search tasks with a video recording of a Pepper robot[1] given its wide use in research related to HRI. Pepper does not have degrees of freedom in the eyes to reflect human-like gaze. Therefore, and in line with previous research [2,18], we used its head movement to point to objects as a way to reflect deictic gaze as shown in Fig. 1.

Fig. 1. Layout of the task. The video of the robot provides verbal instructions switching between static positioning and deictic gaze behaviour. The picture shows a trial in which Pepper uses deictic gaze towards the ketchup, where participants should click.

---

[1] https://www.softbankrobotics.com.

2   Related Work

Gaze behavior from a robot is highly studied in HRI. It has been shown that making eye contact with a robot evokes similar physiological responses as if with a human [13]. Appropriate gaze from a speaking robot towards a human can positively affect the recall of what has been said [16] and can regulate the role of the participants in conversations [17]. Similarly, a robot moving the head away can effectively reflect gaze aversion and can be perceived as more thoughtful by the users [3]. In collaborative scenarios where a human follows guidance from a robot, deictic gaze from the robot can assist the human partner by signaling at objects in space [1], although the specific benefits differ among studies [2,14,18].

The work in [14] investigated deictic gaze in a situated human-agent collaboration. The results showed that this non-verbal cue led to higher interaction times and, thus, inferior task performance. In contrast, the work in [18] found that deictic gaze in the form of head movement from a robot did not affect task-completion times, although it helped to reduce the number of errors. This is in line with [2], which suggested that deictic gaze from a robot is not that useful in simple tasks when compared to difficult ones.

Previous research also indicated that eye-gaze following deteriorates with age [21]. Nevertheless, to the best of our knowledge, the influence that gaze from a robot may have on OA has not been explored. In our study we used a similar task as in [14] reflecting a realistic interaction between OA and an assistive robot. Although the remote nature of our study might limit the interaction between the users and the robot, the current approach, importantly, allowed us to control the influence of some extraneous variables on the main outcome variables, such as the social presence caused by the robot looking at the user, which may lead the users to start a conversation with the robot and get higher completion times as reported in [14].

3   Methods

This study was performed during the Covid-19 global pandemic. We designed an experimentation method for effective remote participation, which also facilitates larger scale testing. More specifically, we designed a controlled online collaboration task mimicking an everyday life situation (see [15] for a description of an equivalent face-to-face interaction). In this experiment, a video of Pepper verbally guided the participants during a task that represented a guided preparation of a sandwich recipe. To compare the potential benefit in the perception of non-verbal cues, the robot switched its behaviour between static-based and deictic gaze-based indications. We measured the participant's reaction times and task-completion times during task performance. An example video of the task is available[2].

---

[2] https://youtu.be/6zSgm8jEnCM.

3.1 Scenario

Our experimental scenario featured a video of a Pepper robot who verbally guided participants through two everyday-like visual search tasks which consisted on clicking on several ingredients for preparing a sandwich. An example layout of the ingredients and the robot is shown in Fig. 1. We defined two robot conditions: a *static robot* (SR) which always looked at the camera while giving instructions, and a *moving robot* (MR) which also featured deictic gaze by moving the head towards the correct ingredient. Each of these conditions defined a task: a SR task, and a MR task. Inside each task, the user had to prepare two sandwiches by following the verbal instructions of the Pepper robot, which named each ingredient and waited for the user to click on it. So, each participant prepared two consecutive sandwiches with a static robot (SR), and two other consecutive sandwiches with a moving robot (MR). The full structure of the experiment is shown in Fig. 2.

A trial consisted of the selection of one ingredient. The user prepared two sandwiches from five ingredients in each task. The order of the sandwiches within a task and the order of the ingredients in each sandwich were fixed. The order of the tasks was counter-balanced and started randomly either with SR or MR.

Within each task, we measured reaction time (RT) and task-completion time (TCT). We defined RT as the time span between the moment the robot started naming one ingredient and the moment the participant clicked on that ingredient within a trial. The RT of the *bread* was excluded because of its high predictability (always first/last ingredient). A trial was correct when the mentioned ingredient was clicked. The final number of trials per task in which RT was used was ten: five ingredients for each sandwich. We defined TCT as the time needed by a participant to finish one task (two sandwiches).

3.2 Materials

After each task, participants were presented with a set of self-report questionnaires and subscales. First, the mental demand subscale of the NASA-Task Load Index (NASA-TLX) [12] was used for assessing the mental demand between robot conditions. Second, the Godspeed Questionnaire Series [5] was used to measure the perceived anthropomorphism of the robot by the user. Here, we used a modified version of the anthropomorphism questionnaire due to an irrelevant item for the context of this study (*moving rigidly-elegantly*). Moreover, we added the item *mechanical-organic* as in [6]. Finally, the RoSAS [6] scale was used to measure the perception of warmth, competence, and discomfort caused by a robot. We added two extra questions at the end: Q1) *Did you notice any difference between the robots in the tasks?* to check whether the person was aware of the difference between robot conditions; and Q2) *Which robot did you prefer from the ones you interacted with?* to check their preferred condition (SR or MR).

This study was built using *Labvanced* [10], an online tool for designing and remotely distributing experiments on human cognition. The language used for the whole study was Spanish.

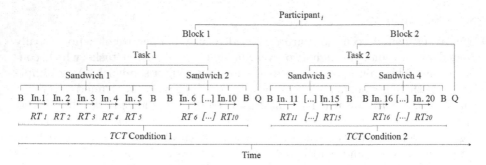

Fig. 2. Structure of the experiment for a participant i. The letter 'B' represents the bread, while 'In. x' represents ingredient in position x. 'Q' refers to the questionnaire.

3.3 Experimental Design

Our study followed a 2×2 mixed design with two robot conditions, SR and MR (within-subject), and two age groups, Adults (A) and OA (between-subjects). The age range in the A was ≥ 18 and < 65 years, and in OA it was ≥ 65. This division was based on the working retirement age.

The presentation order of the blocks (see Fig. 2) was counter-balanced and participants were randomly assigned to one of the two possible orders. We explored age-related differences in the effect of the robot's deictic gaze on task performance and social perception of the robot, as reflected in the interaction between age group and robot condition

3.4 Sample

We performed a G*Power analysis [8] to calculate a minimum sample size that allowed an expected power $(1 - \beta)$ of 0.80 to detect a small effect size of $f = 0.25$ ($\eta^2 = 0.06$) between age groups. The result of the analysis indicated a minimum required sample size of 98 participants. A total of 329 participants took part in the study, of which 53 were excluded due to incomplete data. A summary of the characteristics of the final sample is shown in Table 1.

Potential participants were contacted via mailing lists from Spanish universities with adult education programs. Inclusion criteria (based on self-report) were to be fluent in Spanish, to have normal or corrected-to-normal vision, and to be cognitively healthy. Participants gave written informed consent in accordance with the Declaration of Helsinki and were informed about research goals. Participation was voluntary and no personal data that allowed their identification were obtained. In addition, approval was obtained from the corresponding program coordinators at each university.

The age range was 18–64 for A and 65–88 for OA. The mean age between the groups was significantly different ($t(145) = 14, p < 0.001$). A chi-squared test showed no significant differences between the age groups in their level of education, their previous knowledge of Pepper, and their experience with computers.

Table 1. Final sample description

Group	Age (years)		Gender			Comfort w/computers			Had seen pepper before		
	Mean	SD	M	F	Other	No	Not Sure	Yes	No	Not Sure	Yes
OA	69.3	3.8	76	74	0	1	7	142	108	26	16
A	53.4	12.1	45	80	1	1	11	113	84	24	18

Whereas there were about as many men as women in the OA group (51% men; 49% women), men were underrepresented in the A group (35.7% men; 63.5% women), $(\chi^2(1) = 5.9, p = 0.014)$.

3.5 Procedure

The experiment started by asking participants to put on headphones (in order to reduce potential external noise) and to calibrate the volume of their headphones to ensure they could hear the robot clearly. Then, they were informed in the consent form about the study and the possibility of ending it at any time and filled a sample information questionnaire. Before the experiment started, participants had time to get familiar with the interface and ingredients to be used in the task. This last step was done to reduce the possibility of a poor performance derived from a participant not knowing an ingredient. To reduce external influences, participants were encouraged to avoid distractions and to be rested before starting. To favour this, we kept the experiment short and they were informed about its duration, fifteen minutes. For the main tasks, they were also encouraged to perform as well as they could, but without explicit instructions about being fast. This was to maintain the everyday nature of the task in contrast to a classic computerized experiment. In addition, they were not warned about the difference between the robot conditions (SR or MR).

4 Results

4.1 Reaction Times and Task-Completion Times

We first present reaction times (RT) and task-completion times (TCT) between the robot conditions (SR, MR), age groups (OA, A), and the combination of both. Potential noise in these time measures from participants due to external factors such as computer, browser, or operative system, was corrected using metadata provided by Labvanced. To analyze the RT data, we used the median RT of the correct trials within each task per participant (Fig. 2). The percentage of incorrect, and thus excluded, trials was 2.24%. Due to violations of assumptions for the mixed ANOVA test, we analyzed the data using a Mixed Robust ANOVA test with 20% trimmed means and 2000 bootstrapped samples.

The RT for different age groups and conditions are shown in Fig. 3A (left). Means, standard deviations and p-values for RT are also reported in Table 2.

Values were significantly different between the robot conditions, showing a facilitation effect for the MR condition. We also found a main effect of age that showed higher RT for OA. We did not find an interaction effect between robot condition and age group. Following [21], the strength of the facilitation effect was calculated as a proportional difference score $(RT_{SR} - RT_{MR})/RT_{MR}$. An independent robust t-test (trim = 0.2, samples = 2000) did not show significant differences in the strength of the facilitation effect caused by the MR in RT between age groups (Fig. 3B and Table 2), i.e., the magnitude of the help provided by the MR in terms of how fast the ingredients were clicked was similar between the age groups.

The TCT for different age groups and conditions are shown in Fig. 3A (right). Means, standard deviations and p-values for TCT are also reported in Table 2. Results show a facilitation effect for the MR condition in TCT. Furthermore, TCT was also higher for OA. We could not find any interaction effects between robot condition and age group. The strength of the facilitation effect was also calculated as a proportional difference score $(TCT_{SR} - TCT_{MR})/TCT_{MR}$. A robust t-test did not show significant differences in the strength of the facilitation effect caused by the MR in TCT between age groups (Fig. 3B and Table 2). Finally, the age groups did not differ in how fast they performed the task.

4.2 Questionnaire Measures

We now present the scores of the different questionnaires and scales from Sect. 3.2. We used a Robust Mixed ANOVA for all the scores except for anthropomorphism, as it met the assumptions for a regular Mixed ANOVA. Table 3 shows the social perception scores and the Cronbachs's α of each construct with the corresponding analyses. We found a significant effect of age by which OA perceived the robots as more anthropomorphic as compared to A. In addition, the MR scored significantly higher than SR in all the social perception scores except in the discomfort score. This indicates a more positive perception of the MR. Finally, a significant interaction effect showed that the deictic behavior of the robot had a lower impact on the self-report of anthropomorphism and discomfort in the OA group.

To test whether the deictic gaze of the robot affected the reaction times even if the participants were unaware of that movement, we analyzed the subset of all participants who retrospectively reported to not have noticed the difference between the robot conditions by answering *No* to Q1 (see Sect. 3.2).

In the subset of participants who answered *No* to Q1 (a total of 116), we found (1) a main effect of age group on RT at $p < 0.001$, but no effect of robot condition or interaction effect; (2) a main effect of age group on TCT at $p < 0.001$, but no main effect of robot condition or interaction effect; (3) no effects in any of the subjective scores; (4) an over-representation of OA (67.2%), as compared to A (32.7%) $(\chi^2(1) = 12.5, p < 0.001)$.

We also analyzed the participants who expressed a preference for a robot in their answer to *Q2*. From a total of 163 answers, 78.5% chose the MR. For the participants choosing the MR, the differences between age groups, A = 57.8%,

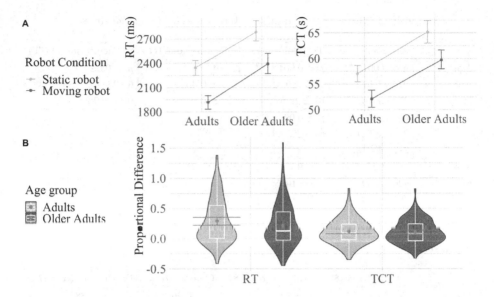

Fig. 3. A) Mean Reaction Time (left) and Task-Completion Time (right) for each group. B) Violin plots with means in red of the proportional differences between robots. Error bars show 95% bootstrapped confidence intervals.

OA = 42.1%, were not significant ($\chi^2(1) = 2.47, p = 0.11$). Finally, with respect to the mental demand scale, we found no main effect of age ($p = 0.07$) or robot condition ($p = 0.11$), and no interaction ($p = 0.33$) ($M = 4.18 \pm 3.75$).

5 Discussion

This work sought to explore potential age-related differences in the perception of visual cues from a social robot. We focused on the influence of deictic gaze during a collaborative tasks inspired by daily life activities. We found a facilitation effect of deictic gaze from a Pepper robot in all the participants independently of their age. Given this facilitation effect for both time scales, our main interest was to find if its magnitude was different between age groups. Our results showed that the facilitation effect from the deictic gaze was not significantly different between age groups, neither in TCT nor RT (Fig. 3; Table 2). To further investigate the effect of deictic gaze, future research could include additional control conditions like a human face or non-social signalling. In addition, the high predictability, and thus the potentially high trust placed in a robot who always signals the correct ingredient (i.e., 100% valid gaze cues), could have had an influence on the speed of the responses. Future studies might want to also include invalid gaze cues that signal the incorrect ingredient and neutral gaze cues that are not informative about the location of the ingredients [21]. Comparing the impact of valid, invalid, and neutral gaze cues would help to explore the impact of credibility of the robot and trust in the system on task performance, as well as possible attentional costs [22] as they occur with human gaze cues.

Table 2. Means, SDs and main/interaction effects on the times

	RT (ms)	TCT (s)	% Facilitation (RT)	% Facilitation (TCT)
Age	$p < 0.001$ (***)	$p < 0.001$ (***)	$p = 0.31$	$p = 0.66$
M^A	2131 ± 575	53.5 ± 9.8	0.29 ± 0.36	0.12 ± 0.2
M^{OA}	2590 ± 808	61 ± 12.5	0.22 ± 0.35	0.11 ± 0.2
Robot	$p < 0.001$ (***)	$p < 0.001$ (***)	–	–
M^{SR}	2585 ± 721	61.5 ± 12.3		
M^{MR}	2176 ± 716	56.3 ± 11.1		
Age*Robot	$p = 0.2$	$p = 0.7$	–	–
M_A^{SR-MR}	426 ± 582	4.9 ± 10.7		
M_{OA}^{SR-MR}	393 ± 744	5.4 ± 11		

Table 3. Means, SDs, Cronbachs's α and main/interaction effects on the social perception scores

	Anth. ($\alpha = .88$).	Warmth ($\alpha = .87$)	Compt. ($\alpha = .84$)	Discom. ($\alpha = .76$)
Age	$p = 0.02$ (*)	$p = 0.051$	$p = 0.26$	$p = 0.88$
M^A	2.66 ± 0.94	2.47 ± 0.8	3.64 ± 0.67	1.71 ± 0.58
M^{OA}	2.89 ± 0.77	2.56 ± 0.8	3.65 ± 0.73	1.73 ± 0.58
Robot	$p < 0.001$ (***)	$p = 0.003$ (**)	$p < 0.001$ (***)	$p < 0.001$ (***)
M^{SR}	2.7 ± 0.92	2.42 ± 0.8	3.49 ± 0.76	1.76 ± 0.6
M^{MR}	2.87 ± 0.7	2.62 ± 0.79	3.8 ± 0.61	1.68 ± 0.55
Age * Robot	$p = 0.03$ (*)	$p = 0.85$	$p = 0.47$	$p = 0.003$ (**)
M_A^{SR-MR}	-0.27 ± 0.77	-0.25 ± 0.67	-0.39 ± 0.71	0.173 ± 0.58
M_{OA}^{SR-MR}	-0.08 ± 0.66	-0.15 ± 0.62	-0.25 ± 0.64	0 ± 0.5

OA scored higher in anthropomorphism regardless of the robot condition. There was also an increase in all the social perception scores as a result of the robot deictic gaze (Table 3). Moreover, the MR was chosen as favourite. These results support previous notions that appropriate social behaviors improve the acceptability of social robots [9]. All the participants indicated a low mental demand ($M = 4.18$ out of 21) when performing the tasks, independently of the robot condition. Moreover, we found an interaction effect in the scores of anthropomorphism and discomfort caused by the robot (Table 3) which varied less between robot conditions in OA. This interactions suggests a different perception of deictic gaze from a robot by OA.

A proportion of 42% of the participants reported not detecting the differences between the robot conditions. For this group we only found age effects on RT and TCT (Sec. 4). It cannot be excluded that participants interpreted Q1 (Sect. 3.2) literally and therefore reported no physical differences between the robots. However, this subgroup did not show a facilitation effect of the deictic gaze. Despite these participants not showing a facilitation effect, the incorrect trial ratio in our sample remained low (2.24%). Notably, within this subgroup, there were moe OA than A. This is in line with previous work [21] showing the age-related decline in eye-gaze following. Alternatively, the over-representation of OA in this subgroup might as well reflect a broader cognitive decline, or difficulty in remembering the differences between robot conditions [11].

There are two main limitations in this study that could be addressed in future research. First, we used a sample of OA that was largely similar to the A group, except for age. While this was necessary to isolate the component of biological aging and to control for factors such as of computer literacy, required for this study, it reduces the generalizability of results among more vulnerable OA who may be more willing to benefit from the assistance of social robots [19]. In addition, and although the AO and A groups did significantly differ in age, the age gap between groups was not broad. Future research could consider a finer division of groups of age to explore if eye-gaze following declines also when it comes from a social robot. Second, the social nature of the current gaze cue remains unclear. For instance, Pepper's head movement can be simply interpreted as a moving stimulus towards the correct answer. Future studies would benefit from including conditions where the signaling towards the correct ingredient is clearly social or non-social.

6 Conclusion

This study explored the influence of deictic gaze from a Pepper robot in two groups of age: adults (A) and older adults (OA). We found a facilitation effect of deictic gaze from a Pepper robot in all the participants independently of their age. These findings show that head movement representing deictic gaze is effective in terms of task performance. However, this facilitation effect was not significantly different between the age groups, which means that A do not benefit more than OA. Moreover, we found age-related differences in the effect of the robot's deictic gaze on social perception. OA seem to be less reactive to deictic gaze than A when it comes to their report of anthropomorphism and discomfort caused by the robot.

Future research should add human and/or non-social controls to better inform the differences between the perception of human and robot gaze cues. In addition, the inclusion of non-valid cues would be useful to determine the role of trust and to explore the potential attentional costs. The results of this research line could ultimately be valuable in the design adaptive non-verbal cues from robots in HRI. This user-centered approach would allow a wider acceptance of social robots.

Acknowledgments. This work is funded by the EU Horizon 2020 research and innovation programme under the Marie Skłodowska-Curie grant agreement No 754285, by the Wallenberg AI, Autonomous Systems and Software Program (WASP) funded by the Knut and Alice Wallenberg Foundation, and by the RobWellproject (No RTI2018-095599-A-C22) funded by the Spanish *Ministerio de Ciencia, Innovación y Universidades*. We want to thank the universities that helped us with the sample recruiting process: Complutense University of Madrid, University Carlos III of Madrid, University of Murcia and University of Alicante. The authors thank Neziha Akalin and Estefanía Sánchez-Pastor for their support in the initial stages of this study.

References

1. Admoni, H., Scassellati, B.: Social eye gaze in human-robot interaction: a review. J. Hum. Rob. Interact. **6**(1), 25–63 (2017)
2. Admoni, H., Weng, T., Hayes, B., Scassellati, B.: Robot nonverbal behavior improves task performance in difficult collaborations. In: Proceedings ACM/IEEE International Conference HRI (HRI 2016), Christchurch, New Zealand, pp. 51–58 (2016)
3. Andrist, S., Tan, X.Z., Gleicher, M., Mutlu, B.: Conversational gaze aversion for humanlike robots. In: Proceedings ACM/IEEE International Conference HRI (HRI 2014), Bielefeld, Germany, pp. 25–32 (2014)
4. Baron-Cohen, S.: Mindblindness: An Essay on Autism and Theory of Mind. The MIT Press, Cambridge (1995)
5. Bartneck, C., Kulić, D., Croft, E., Zoghbi, S.: Measurement instruments for the anthropomorphism, animacy, likeability, perceived intelligence, and perceived safety of robots. Int. J. Soc. Robot. **1**(1), 71–81 (2009)
6. Carpinella, C.M., Wyman, A.B., Perez, M.A., Stroessner, S.J.: The robotic social attributes scale (RoSAS): development and validation. In: Proceedings ACM/IEEE International Conference HRI (HRI 2017), New York, USA, pp. 254–262 (2017)
7. Cañigueral, R., Hamilton, A.F.C.: The role of eye gaze during natural social interactions in typical and autistic people. Frontiers Psychol. **10** (2019)
8. Faul, F., Erdfelder, E., Lang, A.G., Buchner, A.: G*Power 3: a flexible statistical power analysis program for the social, behavioral, and biomedical sciences. Behav. Res. Methods **39**(2), 175–191 (2007)
9. Feingold-Polak, R., Elishay, A., Shahar, Y., Stein, M., Edan, Y., Levy-Tzedek, S.: Differences between young and old users when interacting with a humanoid robot: a qualitative usability study. Paladyn **9**(1), 183–192 (2018)
10. Finger, H., Goeke, C., Diekamp, D., Standvoß, K., König, P.: LabVanced: a unified Javascript framework for online studies. In: Proceedings International Conference IC2S2 (IC2S2 2017), Cologne, Germany (2017)
11. Harada, C.N., Love, M.C.N., Triebel, K.: Normal cognitive aging. Clin. Geriatr. Med. **29**, 737 (2013)
12. Hart, S.G., Staveland, L.E.: Development of NASA-TLX (Task Load Index): results of empirical and theoretical research. Adv. Psychol. **52**, 139–183 (1988)
13. Kiilavuori, H., Sariola, V., Peltola, M.J., Hietanen, J.K.: Making eye contact with a robot: psychophysiological responses to eye contact with a human and with a humanoid robot. Biolog. Psychol. **158**, 107989 (2021)
14. Kontogiorgos, D., et al.: The effects of anthropomorphism and non-verbal social behaviour in virtual assistants. In: Proceedings ACM International Conference IVA (IVA 2019), Paris, France, pp. 133–140 (2019)
15. Morillo-Mendez, L., Mozos, O.M.: Towards human-based models of behaviour in social robots: exploring age-related differences in the processing of gaze cues in human-robot interaction. In: Starting Artificial Intelligence Researchers Symposium (STAIRS 2020), Santiago de Compostela, Spain (2020)
16. Mutlu, B., Forlizzi, J., Hodgins, J.: A storytelling robot: Modeling and evaluation of human-like gaze behavior. In: Proceedings IEEE-RAS International Conference HUMANOIDS, Genoa, Italy, pp. 518–523 (2006)
17. Mutlu, B., Shiwa, T., Kanda, T., Ishiguro, H., Hagita, N.: Footing in human-robot conversations. In: Proceedings ACM/IEEE International Conference HRI (HRI 2009), La Jolla, California, USA, p. 61 (2009)

18. Mwangi, E., Barakova, E.I., Díaz-Boladeras, M., Mallofré, A.C., Rauterberg, M.: Directing attention through gaze hints improves task solving in human-humanoid interaction. Int. J. Soc. Robot. **10**(3), 343–355 (2018)
19. Pino, M., Boulay, M., Jouen, F., Rigaud, A.S.: "Are we ready for robots that care for us?" Attitudes and opinions of older adults toward socially assistive robots. Frontiers Aging Neurosci. **7** (2015)
20. Pu, L., Moyle, W., Jones, C., Todorovic, M.: The effectiveness of social robots for older adults: a systematic review and meta-analysis of randomized controlled studies. Gerontologist **59**, 37–51 (2019)
21. Slessor, G., Venturini, C., Bonny, E.J., Insch, P.M., Rokaszewicz, A., Finnerty, A.N.: Specificity of age-related differences in eye-gaze following: evidence from social and nonsocial stimuli. J. Gerontol. Series B **71**, 11–22 (2016)
22. Zafrani, O., Nimrod, G.: Towards a holistic approach to studying human-robot interaction in later life. Gerontologist **59**, 26–36 (2019)

Iterative Design of an Emotive Voice for the Tabletop Robot Haru

Eric Nichols[1]([⊠])[iD], Sarah Rose Siskind[2][iD], Waki Kamino[3][iD],
Selma Šabanović[3][iD], and Randy Gomez[1][iD]

[1] Honda Research Institute Japan Co., Ltd., Wako, Japan
{e.nichols,r.gomez}@jp.honda-ri.com
[2] Hello SciCom, New York, USA
sarah@hellosci.com
[3] Luddy School of Informatics, Computing, and Engineering,
Indiana University Bloomington, Bloomington, USA
wkamino@iu.edu, selmas@indiana.edu

Abstract. Designing a voice for a social robot is particularly challenging because the voice needs to convincingly convey a target personality while maintaining rich, emotive capabilities in order to foster the development of bonds with humans. In this paper, we describe the ongoing design and implementation process of a voice for a social robot. To aid in our design and analysis, we identify three desirable characteristics for its voice: 1. *convincingness*, 2. *emotiveness*, and 3. *consistency*. In this paper, we present a preliminary study that investigates convincingness by comparing samples taken from human voice talents and eliciting human judgements about their appropriateness. This study compares human judgements, elicited through surveys, on a range of characteristics related to *convincingness*, emotions conveyed, and impressions of the overall consistency of the voice. Finally, we discuss the implications of the survey findings for designing a voice for a social robot.

Keywords: Social robot interaction · TTS voice design · Behavior design

1 Introduction

Designers regularly use various robot characteristics, such as appearance, speech, and behavior, to inspire people to engage with robots as social actors. Robot appearance, including the use of familiar human- and animal-like forms, can visually represent a robot's social capabilities. Similarly, the content of verbal utterances (e.g. saying "Hello") can explicitly invite people to engage with the robot socially. More subtle cues to a robot's social abilities can be provided through the nonverbal characteristics of the robot's voice – implicit age, gender, emotional expression, markers of cultural origin, and individual vocal quirks can evoke a certain type of character and unique social presence for a robot.

Studies in social robotics and human-robot interaction have explored how various aspects of a robot's voice can affect people's perceptions of the robot's

© Springer Nature Switzerland AG 2021
H. Li et al. (Eds.): ICSR 2021, LNAI 13086, pp. 362–374, 2021.
https://doi.org/10.1007/978-3-030-90525-5_31

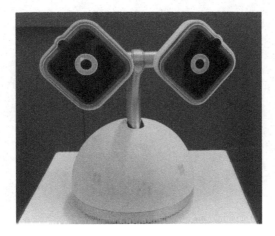

Fig. 1. The social robot Haru.

capabilities, personality, and appropriateness for different tasks. People deem certain voices as more or less appropriate for specific robots [15]. Robots with higher levels of vocal expressiveness are perceived as having more social presence [12]. The perceived age of a robot's voice can affect people's perceptions of its credibility and social presence [8]. Robots with child-like voices can be seen as more extroverted and relaxed [7]. Users also respond to the perceived gender of human-like robot voices, reporting more positive attitudes about robots with which they share a gender [9]. Additionally, the delivery of verbal content as manipulated through voice pitch, empathy, and humor, has been found to not only affect people's perceptions of and attitudes towards the robot, but also their enjoyment of the human-robot interaction task [16].

While prior research has identified particular aspects of robot voice that affect users' interaction experiences and robot evaluations in short term scenarios, long term interaction will also require users to see the robot as a believable, relatable, and cohesive social agent. Based on the above-mentioned prior research, a combination of various vocal aspects (e.g. age, gender, vocal style/genre) will need to be employed to create a convincing social presence for robots. With this idea of long-term, companionable social interaction with robots in mind, this paper describes the process of designing an expressive voice for the Haru robot through the selection of diverse voice talent. It then explores how users evaluate different text-to-speech voices, meant to be used with the Haru social robot, in relation to their appropriateness for the robot, as well as their convincingness, expressiveness, and cohesiveness. The broader aim of this work is to inform the design of engaging and persuasive social characters for companion social robots.

As our target robot, we selected the social robot Haru [10,11], shown in Fig. 1. Haru is an experimental tabletop robot for multimodal communication that uses verbal and non-verbal channels for interactions. Haru's design is centered on its potential to communicate emotions through richness in expressivity [10].

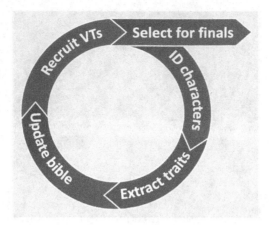

Fig. 2. Iterative refinement design process for Haru's personality and voice concept.

Haru has five motion degrees of freedom (namely base rotation, neck leaning, eye stroke, eye rotation and eyes tilt) that allow it to perform expressive motions. Furthermore, each eye includes a 3-inch TFT screen display in which the robot eyes are displayed. Inside the body there is an addressable LED matrix (the mouth). Haru can communicate via text-to-speech (TTS)—albeit currently with off-the-shelf voices—through animated routines, projected screen, etc. Haru's range of communicative strategies positions the robot as a potent embodied communication agent that can support long-term interaction with people.

This paper is organized as follows: in Sect. 2, we describe our iterative design process of refining our social robot's personality description while auditioning voice talents; in Sect. 3, we present an elicitation survey that evaluates a select number of voice talent finalists; in Sect. 4, we discuss the findings of our survey; in Sect. 5, we outline relevant work in social robots; and, finally, in Sect. 6, we recap our findings and discuss future work.

2   Design Process

One of our core research topics is the development of a long-term robotic companion, which can lead to the forging of a bond between a human and a social robot similar to the bond shared by other social creatures [11]. But this goal requires a persuasive character with rich expressivity that is beyond the capability of conventional TTS systems. We identify three characteristics that an ideal TTS voice for a social robot should have:

Convincingness. The voice should fit the robot's character, physical appearance, and application scenarios.
Emotiveness. The voice should be capable of conveying a wide range of emotions and vocal delivery styles.

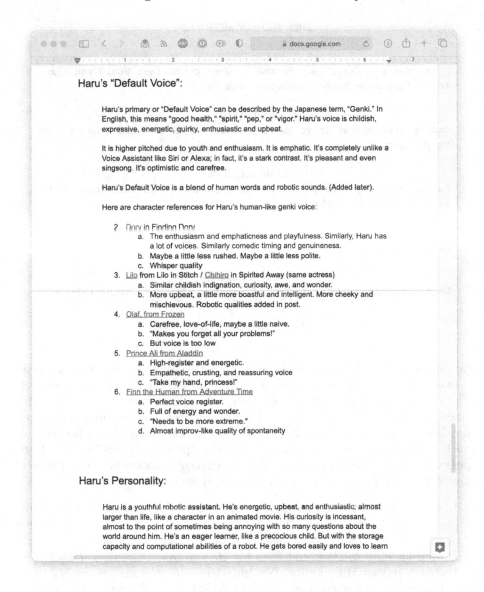

Fig. 3. Haru's personality bible.

Consistency. Throughout its application, the voice should sound like it seamlessly belongs to a single entity.

We adopt a holistic approach to designing Haru's personality and voice concept based on a process of iterative refinement, where updates to the personality definition feed into recruitment and evaluation of voice talent, and their evaluation informs refinement of the personality definitions. To aid us in organizing

---

HARU SELF-INTRODUCTION

HARU (UPBEAT)
Hi there! I'm Haru, your friendly robot companion. Would you like
to go find some buried treasure with me?

HARU (SAD)
Nobody else wanted to go on an adventure with me. And I don't want
to go alone.

HARU (SERIOUS)
But I promise you it's real and it's somewhere in this room. And
we gotta find it right now.

HARU (WHINY)
Because I don't want to wait anymore. So let's go right now!

HARU (CHEEKY)
Unless you're scared, that is. I think you're just being chicken.

Fig. 4. Haru's self-introduction script.

Haru's personality definition, we borrow a practice from screenwriting and keep a *personality bible* [13,14] for Haru, recording important personality traits, reference characters, and other relevant background information. The personality bible is a reference document for writers and engineers to check in order to keep Haru's personality consistent. It outlines information about Haru's background (his fear of social isolation and magnets, for example). It also outlines how Haru speaks (enthusiastically and informally). An excerpt is shown in Fig. 3. The iterative refinement process is shown in Fig. 2, and we describe it below.

Identify Reference Characters. Based on our existing vision of Haru's personality, we brainstorm reference characters that effectively convey some aspect of Haru's personality. Some examples include *Prince Ali* from *Aladdin*, *Dory* from *Finding Dory*, and *Finn the Human* from *Adventure Time*.

Extract personality traits. We summarize the relevant personality traits of the reference characters from Step 1 into keywords. We consider behavioral traits as well as vocal characteristics and speaking mannerisms. For example, Haru has the enthusiasm and empathy of Dory, the trusting and reassuring cadence of Prince Ali, and the energy and childish sense of wonder of Finn the Human.

Update Personality Bible. We update Haru's personality bible with reference characters from Step 1. and relevant personality trait keywords from Step 2.

Recruit and Audition voice talents. We recruit voice talents online and audition them through interactive table reads using scenario scripts showcasing Haru's personality. Voice talents are shown Haru's personality bible and

Table 1. Voice talent search finalists selected for the elicitation study.

Alias	Nationality	Age	Gender
Voice A	United States	child	Male
Voice B	Australia	20 s	Female
Voice D	Philippines	20 s	Male
Voice G	United States	50 s	Male
Voice M	United States	40 s	Male

coached to convey our vision of Haru while encouraging creativity in their portrayal.

Select voice talents for Finals. Finally, we analyze the results of the audition in Step 4., considering both the quality of their portrayal and how Haru's personality bible could be refined. If the voice talent is deemed satisfactory, we select them for the final evaluation. We then go back to Step 1. and repeat the process until we have gathered enough voice talents for the final evaluation.

2.1 Voice Talent Search

We searched for playful, energetic, curious voices from adult males, adult females and young children. The search took place over several months. Roughly 30 voices were researched closely and 10 voice talents were recorded, of which three children and two women were actively considered. While a mastery of English was required, the talent was sourced from all over the world. Given the diversity of Haru's intended audience, we wanted voice talent from diverse backgrounds to counteract any regional idiosyncrasies.

The desirability of the voice talent was measured across several criteria. The first was a youthful quality. This quality is impossible to achieve by simply raising the pitch of an adult voice. The effect of having smaller vocal chords produces a slightly raspy, at times even nasal quality that is completely unique to young children. The second criteria was emotiveness. The voice talent had to be capable of conveying a slightly exaggerated degree of emotion. This exaggeration is important because much of the nuance of a performance is 'lost in translation' in the voice capture process. The third criteria is technical ability. The voice talent (VT) needs to be of a certain technical reading level to get through the material required of the voice capture process. Given that the VT may be a child, however, a certain amount of stumbling and coaching is expected. The fourth criteria is coachability. The VT needs to be able to take direction well in order to calibrate a performance correctly.

2.2 Audition Process

Each voice talent set aside an hour to go through specially designed audition scripts (see Fig. 4 for an example) to test the talent's range of emotion, techni-

Table 2. Target characteristics in the voice talent elicitation study.

Characteristic	Question
Suitability	On a scale of 1 (*poor*) to 5 (*great*), how well does this voice fit Haru?
Expressiveness	On a scale of 1 (*expressionless*) to 5 (*expressive*), how expressive is this?
Naturalness	On a scale of 1 (*artificial*) to 5 (*natural*), how natural is this voice?
Friendliness	On a scale of 1 (*unfriendly*) to 5 (*friendly*), how friendly is this voice?
Interestingness	On a scale of 1 (*boring*) to 5 (*interesting*), how interesting is this voice?
Energy	On a scale of 1 (*unenergetic*) to 5 (*energetic*), how energetic is this?
Enthusiasm	On a scale of 1 (*unenthusiastic*) to 5 (*enthusiastic*), how enthusiastic is this voice?
Curiosity	On a scale of 1 (*uninterested*) to 5 (*curious*), how curious is this voice?
Empathy	On a scale of 1 (*uncaring*) to 5 (*caring*), how empathetic is this voice?
Youthfulness	On a scale of 1 (*old*) to 5 (*young*), how youthful is this voice?
Gender	On a scale of 1 (*masculine*) to 3 (*neutral*) to 5 (*feminine*), what gender is this voice?

cal reading ability, endurance, and ability to take direction. The auditions were interactive with the writer playing Randy, the human, and the voice talent playing Haru. The audio of the dialogues was recorded for later comparison. Through the video call, the writer was able to give directions to the talent. For example: smile during an upbeat performance or slightly grit your teeth to convey seriousness. It was often required for the writer to give a line reading for the talent to imitate. This also had the effect of keeping the performances relatively consistent across all the different auditions. Finalists are summarized in Table 1.

3   Elicitation Study

To evaluate the convincingness of our voice talent finalists, we conducted an online survey where participants evaluated them over a variety of characteristics.

3.1   Online Survey

To familiarize themselves with Haru's appearance and personality, survey participants first watched a video of Haru non-verbally interacting with an off-screen human. Non-verbal interaction was selected to avoid preconceptions about Haru's voice. Next, for each voice talent, participants listened to a short clip of them from a short Haru self-introduction script designed to be representative of Haru's personality and desired emotive range (see Fig. 4). Then, they were asked to rate each voice for a series of target characteristics on a scale of 1–5 (see Table 2). Participants also selected all emotions conveyed from a list 8 of emotions from Plutchik's circumplex model [17]. Finally, they rated the overall suitability of the voice for Haru, and were asked for their free-form opinions on appropriateness of the voice and about Haru. The survey was conducted over Google Forms, and a sample form with synthetic responses can be seen at this link.

Table 3. Average scores for each VT by characteristic. The highest score for each characteristic is shown in **bold**. Standard deviations are given in (parentheses).

Char./Voice	A	B	D	G	M
Suitability	**3.89** (± 1.32)	3.12 (± 1.15)	3.04 (± 1.46)	2.75 (± 1.37)	3.39 (± 1.29)
Expressiveness	**4.65** (± 0.64)	4.00 (± 0.91)	4.26 (± 1.08)	4.05 (± 1.11)	4.32 (± 0.93)
Naturalness	**4.07** (± 1.02)	3.72 (± 1.24)	3.74 (± 1.32)	3.49 (± 1.45)	4.05 (± 1.12)
Friendliness	**4.42** (± 0.78)	3.75 (± 0.96)	3.44 (± 1.30)	3.51 (± 1.12)	4.09 (± 1.02)
Interestingness	**4.21** (± 0.92)	3.63 (± 1.14)	3.55 (± 1.25)	3.54 (± 1.28)	3.79 (± 1.25)
Energy	**4.77** (± 0.42)	3.73 (± 1.07)	4.09 (± 0.98)	3.93 (± 1.08)	3.82 (± 1.27)
Enthusiasm	**4.72** (± 0.56)	3.89 (± 1.10)	4.00 (± 1.16)	3.75 (± 1.14)	3.70 (± 1.19)
Curiosity	**4.16** (± 0.92)	3.73 (± 1.12)	3.64 (± 1.27)	3.81 (± 1.13)	3.70 (± 1.14)
Empathy	**3.93** (± 1.00)	3.46 (± 1.20)	3.23 (± 1.30)	3.34 (± 1.13)	3.61 (± 1.11)
Youthfulness	**4.74** (± 0.64)	3.60 (± 1.15)	3.30 (± 1.22)	2.12 (± 1.09)	2.44 (± 1.23)
Gender	2.28 (± 1.16)	**3.40** (± 1.35)	2.04 (± 1.19)	1.21 (± 0.49)	1.21 (± 0.62)

3.2 Protocol

We posted an advertisement and recruited participants on the US-based crowd-sourcing platform Upwork over three days in the month of July 2021. The platform allows interested workers to send a 'proposal' to the client who has posted the job. We recruited participants from those who submitted the proposal on a-first-come-first-served basis, with a preference given to users with higher ratings and consideration for geographical diversity. We initially collected survey responses from 61 participants, of which 57 were analyzed after filtering the data using a comprehension-check question requiring the completion of a brief video to answer correctly. The responses of any participant who answered incorrectly (n = 4) were discarded. The survey was expected to take approximately 30 min to complete, and those who completed the task were offered a fixed amount of $20 for their participation.

The demographics of the participants was as follows. We had more female participants (n = 34) than male participants (n = 23) and the most common age group was 18–30 (n = 37), followed by 30–40 (n = 16); 40–50 (n = 2); above 50 (n = 2). In terms of geographic location, 57 participants participated in the study from 27 different countries, with the largest number of participants from Asia (n = 26), followed by Europe (n = 12); Africa (n = 12); North America (n = 4); and South America (n = 3).

We used Upwork to recruit participants for the following reasons: 1) access to a diverse population of participants [2, 4, 6], and 2) an expected level of response quality, based on the platform's profile-oriented nature that reveals names and location of the workers, and the mutual-rating system between clients and workers.)

4 Discussion

Results. Average scores for characteristics are summarized in Table 3. Voice talent preferences for each characteristic are given as orderings annotated with statistical significance in Table 4. Select comments on voice talent suitability are given in Table 5. Finally, recognized emotions are summarized in Table 6.

Table 4. VT preference orderings, where $\gg$: $p < 0.05$, and $>$: $0.05 \leq p \leq 0.45$, and $\approx$: $p > 0.45$, as measured via a single-tail t-test. *Masculinity* and *femininity* are derived from the *gender* scores.

Characteristic	Ordering								
Suitability	A	$\gg$	M	$>$	B	$>$	D	$\gg$	G
Expressiveness	A	$\gg$	M	$>$	D	$>$	G	$\gg$	B
Naturalness	A	$\approx$	M	$>$	D	$\approx$	B	$\gg$	G
Friendliness	A	$\gg$	M	$\gg$	B	$>$	G	$\gg$	D
Interestingness	A	$\gg$	M	$>$	B	$>$	D	$\gg$	G
Energy	A	$\gg$	D	$>$	G	$>$	M	$\gg$	B
Enthusiasm	A	$\gg$	D	$>$	B	$>$	G	$\gg$	M
Curiosity	A	$\gg$	G	$>$	B	$>$	M	$\gg$	D
Empathy	A	$>$	M	$>$	B	$>$	G	$\gg$	D
Youthfulness	A	$\gg$	B	$>$	D	$\gg$	M	$\gg$	G
Masculinity	M	$\approx$	G	$\gg$	D	$>$	A	$\gg$	B
Femininity	B	$\gg$	A	$>$	D	$\gg$	G	$\approx$	M

Characteristics. We find that with the exception of overall *suitability* and demographic-related characteristics (*youthfulness, gender*), all were ranked positively, confirming their importance.

Demographics. Survey participants ranked voices by *youthfulness* in the same order as the voice talent's ages. *Gender* exhibited a similar trend: the single female voice talentwas ranked as most feminine, followed by the child voice talent. This is understandable, as children have higher-pitched voices than adults, and are often perceived as more feminine. Likewise, the voices of the men over 40 were ranked as most masculine.

Emotions. Voices with higher *acceptability* tend to have more emotions detected, supporting our theory that expressive voices are preferred for social robots. We also note that overall positive emotions (e.g. surprise, joy, anticipation, trust) are recognized more than negative ones (e.g. anger, fear, sadness, disgust), although this may be due to the contents of Haru's self-introduction script.

Overall. Survey participants overwhelmingly preferred Voice A to all others across all characteristics with statistical significance[1]. This supports our intuition that young, energetic voices are ideal and provides confirmation of our design direction for Haru's voice.

5   Related Research

Much research on expressive TTS has focused on evaluating emotion conveyance with robots or virtual avatars. Breazeal evaluated the expression of emotion in

---

[1] $p < 0.05$ as measured by a single-tail t-test.

Table 5. Select comments on voice talent suitability from study participants.

Voice A	
1.	This voice fits Haru because of how it attracts your attention the moment you hear it, and this is because of how young, cheerful, and interesting the voice is. It's always pleasing to hear the voice/sound of a young child talking. It makes Haru more relatable & adorable
2.	From the previous video, Haru seems to be cheerful and spontaneous, as well as being quite charismatic and expressive. That's why the voice of an 8–10 year old with these characteristics is ideal for him
3.	The robot is able to express a number of emotions. You can sense it being empathetic and also emotional. There is also fear in its voice as well as anticipation
4.	He doesn't sound like a robot/AI which is good, making the robot more human and a more realistic social companion

Voice B	
1.	For me, the voice is good but it just doesn't fit Haru. It sounded like a female's voice but I see Haru more masculine
2.	It sounds like an adult female that is trying to sound like a child
3.	I think for Haru a female voice is better
4.	It doesn't sound natural, but the voice is still great

Voice D	
1.	I find this voice is good because it was full of emotion in this voice. It does make me feel annoying at the last second of the video which make it real
2.	i can feel anger and sadness in the voice
3.	He sounds like a teenage boy, a little bit aggressive but that's okay
4.	The voice reminds me of a character from Digimon

Voice G	
1.	I feel this voice is in a haste/hurry and I can't really relate it and what he's saying. Although the voice is quite energetic and all but the relation/friendliness is not there for me
2.	Its sort of urgent adventure, perfectly fit tone of voice for a teen
3.	Not a great voice, looks like an old person pretending to be a young person
4.	The change in tone of voice, from loud to whisper, tells that there is something hidden in his offer

Voice M	
1.	The expressiveness of this voice is clear. It also has a more human voice to it which makes it relatable as well
2.	This sounds like artificial, although it is better than the others except the first one but again the voice age doesn't suits the content as it is better suited like a child voice
3.	I feel that the voice could fit well if it was a bit younger. It's a bit coarse but interesting to listen to.
4.	This voice fits Haru. You just start smiling the moment you listen to it

Table 6. Emotions recognized by study participants.

Emotion/Voice	A	B	D	G	M
Surprise	**23**	16	16	19	20
Joy	**41**	21	26	21	28
Anticipation	**43**	31	32	31	25
Anger	6	8	**23**	10	5
Fear	9	13	**19**	18	14
Trust	16	14	9	16	**17**
Sadness	25	25	22	**26**	21
Disgust	4	7	**17**	7	7
None of the above	0	2	0	3	4

TTS for anthropomorphic robots with an analysis of vocal affect [5]. Tang et al. evaluated emotive TTS with a 3-D virtual avatar [19]. Roehling and authors present a summary of research on vocal correlates in expressive speech and examine available TTS to use in their robotic project by applying the findings. Authors suggest that factors including pitch, duration, loudness, spectral energy structure, and voice quality are crucial for an expressive speech synthesis [18] Barnes et al. [3] compared the effectiveness of human voices and synthesized voices for use with humanoid and dinosaur robots and found that monotone synthesized voices were unsuitable for emotion-rich interactions. Through an online evaluation of TTS for three social robots, Alonso-Martin and authors suggest the correlation between intelligibility and expressiveness of TTS systems, as well as an inverse correlation between these two factors and artificiality [1].

6   Conclusion

In this paper, we described an iterative refinement process for developing a social robot's personality while auditioning voice talents. Through this process, we selected five finalist voice talents and evaluated them through an online elicitation study. The preferences exhibited by participants toward young, energetic, and expressive voices provided supporting evidence for our design direction.

In future work, we plan to continue to refine our definition of Haru's personality and to conduct a more detailed survey that includes evaluation of voice appropriateness given the context of specific applications for Haru. We will also limit the survey to the three regions where Haru is being considered for deployment: the US & Canada, Europe, and Japan in order to account for differences in cultural perception. Finally, we plan to finalize our voice talent selection and carry out the development and evaluation of an expressive TTS for Haru.

References

1. Alonso-Martín, F., Malfaz, M., Castro-González, Á., Castillo, J.C., Salichs, M.A., et al.: Online evaluation of text to speech systems for three social robots. In: Salichs, M.A. (ed.) ICSR 2019. LNCS (LNAI), vol. 11876, pp. 155–164. Springer, Cham (2019). https://doi.org/10.1007/978-3-030-35888-4_15
2. Barchard, K.A., Williams, J.: Practical advice for conducting ethical online experiments and questionnaires for united states psychologists. Behav. Res. Methods **40**(4), 1111–1128 (2008)
3. Barnes, J., Richie, E., Lin, Q., Jeon, M., Park, C.H.: Emotive voice acceptance in human-robot interaction. In: Proceedings of the 24th International Conference on Auditory Display (2018)
4. Behrend, T.S., Sharek, D.J., Meade, A.W., Wiebe, E.N.: The viability of crowdsourcing for survey research. Behav. Res. Methods **43**(3), 800–813 (2011)
5. Breazeal, C.: Emotive qualities in robot speech. In: Proceedings 2001 IEEE/RSJ International Conference on Intelligent Robots and Systems. Expanding the Societal Role of Robotics in the the Next Millennium (Cat. No.01CH37180), vol. 3, pp. 1388–1394, October 2001. https://doi.org/10.1109/IROS.2001.977175
6. Dandurand, F., Shultz, T.R., Onishi, K.H.: Comparing online and lab methods in a problem-solving experiment. Behav. Res. Methods **40**(2), 428–434 (2008)
7. Dou, X., Wu, C.-F., Lin, K.-C., Tseng, T.-M.: The effects of robot voice and gesture types on the perceived robot personalities. In: Kurosu, M. (ed.) HCII 2019. LNCS, vol. 11566, pp. 299–309. Springer, Cham (2019). https://doi.org/10.1007/978-3-030-22646-6_21
8. Edwards, C., Edwards, A., Stoll, B., Lin, X., Massey, N.: Evaluations of an artificial intelligence instructor's voice: social identity theory in human-robot interactions. Comput. Hum. Behav. **90**, 357–362 (2019)
9. Eyssel, F., De Ruiter, L., Kuchenbrandt, D., Bobinger, S., Hegel, F.: 'If you sound like me, you must be more human': on the interplay of robot and user features on human-robot acceptance and anthropomorphism. In: 2012 7th ACM/IEEE International Conference on Human-Robot Interaction (HRI), pp. 125–126 (2012)
10. Gomez, R., Nakamura, K., Szapiro, D., Merino, L.: A holistic approach in designing tabletop robot's expressivity. In: Proceedings of the International Conference on Robotics and Automation (2020)
11. Gomez, R., Szapiro, D., Galindo, K., Nakamura, K.: Haru: hardware design of an experimental tabletop robot assistant. In: Proceedings of the 2018 ACM/IEEE International Conference on Human-Robot Interaction, February 2018
12. Heerink, M., Kröse, B., Evers, V., Wielinga, B.: Relating conversational expressiveness to social presence and acceptance of an assistive social robot. Virtual Reality **14**(1), 77–84 (2010)
13. Levy, D.B.: Animation Development: From Pitch to Prod. Simon& Schuster (2010)
14. Macdonald, I.W.: Tablets of stone or DNA? TV series bibles. J. Screenwriting **9**(1), 3–23 (2018)
15. McGinn, C., Torre, I.: Can you tell the robot by the voice? an exploratory study on the role of voice in the perception of robots. In: 2019 14th ACM/IEEE International Conference on Human-Robot Interaction (HRI), pp. 211–221. IEEE (2019)
16. Niculescu, A., van Dijk, B., Nijholt, A., Li, H., See, S.L.: Making social robots more attractive: the effects of voice pitch, humor and empathy. Int. J. Soc. Robot. **5**(2), 171–191 (2013)

17. Plutchik, R.: A psychoevolutionary theory of emotions. Soc. Sci. Inf. **21**(4–5), 529–553 (1982). https://doi.org/10.1177/053901882021004003
18. Roehling, S., MacDonald, B., Watson, C.: Towards expressive speech synthesis in English on a robotic platform. In: Proceedings of the Australasian International Conference on Speech Science and Technology, pp. 130–135. Citeseer (2006)
19. Tang, H., Fu, Y., Tu, J., Hasegawa-Johnson, M., Huang, T.S.: Humanoid audio-visual avatar with emotive text-to-speech synthesis. IEEE Trans. Multimedia **10**(6), 969–981 (2008). https://doi.org/10.1109/TMM.2008.2001355

Designing Nudge Agents that Promote Human Altruism

Chenlin Hang[1,3(✉)], Tetsuo Ono[2(✉)], and Seiji Yamada[1,3(✉)]

[1] Department of Informatics, The Graduate University for Advanced Studies,
SOKENDAI, Hayama, Japan
{kouchinrin,seiji}@nii.ac.jp
[2] Faculty of Information Science and Technology, Division of Computer Science
and Information Technology, Hokkaido University, Sapporo, Japan
ono@ist.hokudai.ac.jp
[3] National Institute of Informatics, Tokyo, Japan

Abstract. Previous studies have found that nudging is key to promoting altruism in human-human interaction. However, in social robotics, there is still a lack of study on confirming the effect of nudging on altruism. In this paper, we apply two nudge mechanisms, peak-end and multiple viewpoints, to a video stimulus performed by social robots (virtual agents) to see whether a subtle change in the stimulus can promote human altruism. An experiment was conducted online through crowd sourcing with 136 participants. The result shows that the participants who watched the peak part set at the end of the video performed better at the Dictator game, which means that the nudge mechanism of the peak-end effect actually promoted human altruism.

Keywords: Nudge · Altruism · Virtual agent

1 Introduction

Social robots are currently seen as a future technology crucial to society [1], and many researchers are fascinated with how these robots could persuade humans to engage in pro-social behavior [2–6], which is of great importance for the well-being of society [7]. In this paper, we consider ways of promoting human altruism, which is one major part of pro-social behavior and also a central issue in our evolutionary origins, social relations, and societal organization [8]. Previous studies have found that nudging, that is, changing people's behavior without forbidding them from pursuing other options or by significantly changing their economic incentives [9], is a potential and effective mechanism for promoting pro-social behavior in human and human interactions, even altruistic behavior [10,11]. However, there still a lack of research on altruism in social robotics promoted through nudge mechanisms. Based on a generalized view of altruism, the final purpose of our design of social robots (virtual agents) that use a nudge mechanism is to find a proper way to guide people to well-being. We take the

H. Li et al. (Eds.): ICSR 2021, LNAI 13086, pp. 375–385, 2021.
https://doi.org/10.1007/978-3-030-90525-5_32

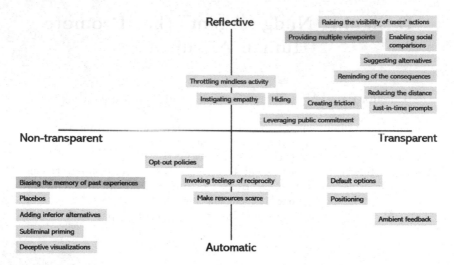

Fig. 1. Nudges positioned along transparency and reflective-automatic axes [12]

first step in this study; we apply nudge mechanisms to a video stimulus performed by social robots (virtual agents) to see whether a subtle change in the construction of the stimulus can promote human altruism. On the basis of the definition of altruism, the appropriateness of application to robots, and ethical questions, we selected 2 nudge mechanisms from among the 23 summarized by Ana et al. [12] as our factors for the video stimulus. One is called biasing the memory (peak-end rule), and the other is called providing multiple viewpoints.

The main experiment was conducted with a 2×2 two-way ANOVA (between-participants) with the factors being the peak-end (positive, negative) and multiple viewpoints (one viewpoint, two viewpoints), and the Dictator game, a simple economic game always used to measure individuals' altruistic attitudes, was used as the dependent variable. Although the result shows that there are no significant differences between the participants who watched video stimuli containing two viewpoints and one viewpoint, the participants who watched the peak part set at the end of the video performed better at the Dictator game [13], which means that the nudge mechanism of the peak-end effect actually promoted human altruism.

2 Related Work

In recent years, nudging [9] has been considered to be a potential way of encouraging people to perform pro-social behavior. This is because it makes it possible to avoid (i) the direct cost of changing people's economic incentives and/or limiting people's action space, (ii) the monitoring costs of determining which choice each individual makes and, possibly, the cost of punishing or rewarding each choice, and (iii) the technical difficulties associated with determining individual choices [10] so that they are cheap and easily to implement.

Valerio et al. found that moral nudges (i.e., making norms salient) can promote altruistic behavior and even have effects over time [10]. Nie et al. found that different colors may alter the altruistic behaviors of people and showed that blue enhances altruism and red discourages it [11]. It was also shown that nudges also are effective at encouraging people to perform altruistic behavior. However, none of these researchers considered the influence caused by social robots existing around us, which are expected to increasingly enter everyday environments [14].

Previous study have shown that the interaction between humans and robots can influence people's decision-making and social relationships [15]. Here, we consider how the construction of a robot's behavior sequence can subtly affect people's decision to behave altruistically. Although direct interaction between a human and robot is generally preferable in HRI, it is also restricted by privacy, cost, time, and safety [16]. Especially, in our experimental setting, the behaviors that agents perform are so complex that existing robots can hardly do them. To alleviate this problem, different forms of media (i.e., text, video, virtual reality, acted demo) have been used to convey interaction information and video stimulus shows better performs at the social aspect due to the Almere model [17]. To collect enough data of participants, we conducted the experiment online and asked participants to watch a video of social robots. Although there are two different ways for participants to engage (first-person and third-person point of views), as we wanted to demonstrate altruistic behavior or selfish behavior performed by robots, the third-person view was better [18].

Ana et al. divided nudges into 23 mechanisms and positioned all of them into one graph along two axes: mode of thinking engaged and transparency of nudge (see Fig. 1) [12]. On the basis of the rules for selecting factors mentioned in Sect. 3.1, we focused only on 2 mechanisms, biasing memory and multiple views, from among the 23 mechanisms. The method of biasing memory is called the peak-end rule, suggesting that our memory of past experiences is shaped by two moments: their most intense (i.e., peak) and the last episode (i.e., end) [19]. Andy et al. found that manipulating only the peak or the end of a series of task did not significantly change preference; both the peak and end lead to significant differences in preference [20]. Thus, we hypothesize that a video scenario that puts the most impressive part at the end of a video (peak-end positive) performs better than one that does not put it at the end (peak-end negative). The other factor is called providing multiple viewpoints, which means collecting different points of view (two or more than two views) for an object or event and offering an unbiased clustered overview. It also shows good performance at avoiding confirmation bias [21], which leads us to pay little attention to or reject information that contradicts our reasoning for making better decisions. For the factor of multiple viewpoints, we consider that, by providing multiple viewpoints to participants, they will more likely perform pro-social behavior, which here in our study is altruistic behavior, than in the case of showing only one viewpoint in a video.

3   Method

3.1   Selecting Two Factors

In our study, we focus only on two mechanisms in accordance with the following rules. First, we excluded ambiguous mechanisms that cannot be set into a quadrant and that may cause ethical problems. Second, as we wanted to see the interaction effect between two factors, the mechanisms also needed to be independent. On the basis these rules, we focused on 11 mechanisms: raising the visibility of users' actions, providing multiple viewpoints, enabling social comparisons, suggesting alternatives, reminding of the consequences, reducing the distance, just-in-time prompts, biasing the memory of past experiences, placebos, adding inferior alternatives, and deceptive visualizations. Third, as the definition of altruism is that of a person who helps others at their own expense [22], the mechanisms should not contain responses, feedback, or consequences from the receiver, so giving reminders of consequences, just-in-time prompts, and placebos were excluded. Fourth, the form of the video stimulus also prohibits the use of raising the visibility of users' actions, enabling social comparisons, suggesting alternatives, adding inferior alternatives, deceptive visualizations, and reducing the distance. As a result, the factors that apply to the video stimulus were biasing the memory and providing multiple viewpoints.

3.2   Video Stimulus with Nudge Agents

Using the factors mentioned in Sect. 3.1, the video stimulus was designed to use peak-end rule and multiple viewpoints. For the peak-end rule, we considered altruistic behavior as the peak. We designed two types of scenarios, one putting the altruistic behavior at the end of the video (peak-end positive) and the other putting the altruistic behavior at the beginning (peak-end negative). For the factor of providing multiple viewpoints, we considered comparing the video containing two viewpoints with that containing only one. As one of the viewpoints was considered to demonstrate altruistic behavior, for the maximum difference, the other viewpoint was considered to demonstrate selfish behavior. The video showed both altruistic and selfish behavior in a scenario involving two viewpoints and showed only altruistic behavior in the one-viewpoint scenario. We also put trivial parts into the video to discriminate the beginning and end parts. The trivial parts were part of a work scene involving social robots. Since new content was added into our video, a manipulation check was held to see if the part that we wanted to enhance (the altruistic behavior) was still the part most impressive to the participants (the peak) after watching the whole video.

According to the factorial design, we had four types of scenarios (see Fig. 2). For each scenario, the vertical axis shows the property of the behavior (Altruistic/Selfish/Trivial), and the horizontal axis shows the time of the video. Also, we formulated the following hypotheses.

H1. Participants who watch the peak-end positive video will perform better than those who watch the peak-end negative video in the Dictator Game.

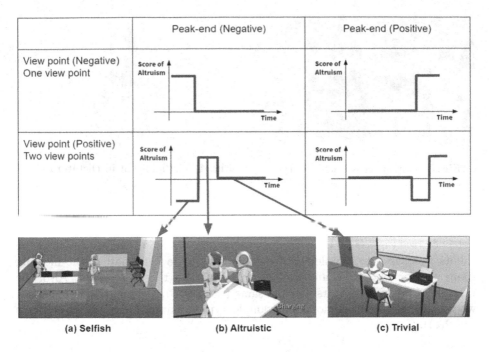

Fig. 2. Scenario type

H2. Participants who watch the video containing two viewpoints will perform better than those who watch the video containing only one viewpoint in the Dictator Game.

To imitate a real-life situation in which social robots are used, virtual agents with a robot-like appearance were used for the video stimulus. The definition of altruism is that of a person who helps others at their own expense [22], and the expense owned by the robots was considered to be its battery. Hence, we considered a task involving two robots doing some task, and one of the robots stops working because its battery runs out. According to a table that includes behaviors that at least some current robots can perform [23] and that participants can explain in the same way as they explain human behavior, we set the altruistic and selfish behavior for a task in which two robots were asked to organize tables and chairs in meeting room. As the battery of each robot was different, one robot was near 3%, and the other was fully charged, so the lower-charged robot might soon stop working, which could lead to altruistic behavior or selfish behavior. To announce that the lower-charged robot's battery had died, a beep was sounded, and the eyes and ears of the robot flashed red light. For the altruistic part, after hearing the alarm and seeing the red flashing lights, the fully charged robot went towards the lower-charged robot and gave battery power to it (see Fig. 2(b)). For the selfish part, although the fully charged robot noticed that the lower-charged robot goes out of the battery, the fully charged robot did not go to charge the lower-charged one and focused only on its work until

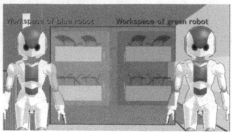

Fig. 3. Workspace of each robot   **Fig. 4.** Virtual agent in Dictator game

all the work in its workspace was finished, which was considered to be selfish behavior (see Fig. 2(a)). To avoid bias, we made rules indicating that each of the robots was asked to handle the same amount of the task; half of the meeting room was for one robot, and the other half was for the other robot. Also, the number of desks and chairs was the same (see Fig. 3). For the trivial behavior, we set general work behaviors, for example, typing material into a computer (see Fig. 2(c)).

3.3 Manipulation Check

We conducted a manipulation check to see if the part that we wanted to enhance (the altruistic behavior) was the most impressive part (the peak) to the participants' after watching the whole video. Although there were four types of scenarios, what we wanted to check is the perception of the peak part in the video, so we treated peak-end positive (negative) with two viewpoints as the same group as peak-end positive (negative) with one viewpoint. For each group, the participants needed to answer yes or no to the question of whether the most impressive memory of the video was a situation in which the fully charged robot gave the battery to the lower-charged one. We conducted a Chi-square test, and the results revealed significant differences among the conditions for both groups (peak-end positive: $\chi^2(1, N = 88) = 33.136$, $p < .001$; peak-end negative: $\chi^2(1, N = 88) = 33.136$, $p < .001$). This result shows that the participants had memory of the most impressive part being the behavior that we enhanced.

For the part of two viewpoints, we conducted a manipulation check to see if the participants could distinguish the different viewpoints correctly. We separated the participants into two groups. The participants of the first group were asked to watch the video containing only the altruistic behavior, and those of the second group were asked to watch the video containing only selfish behavior. After finishing watching the videos, the group that watched the altruistic video was asked what behavior did the green robot (that helped the lower-charged robot) do, and the group that watched the selfish video was asked what behavior did the orange robot (that did not help the lower-charged robot) do. The answers to the questionnaire were given on a five-point Likert scale (1: Selfish behavior; 5: Altruistic behavior). An independent samples t-test was conducted to determine the difference in score for each video. There was a significant difference ($t(122) = 8.36$, $p < .01$) between the group that watched the altruistic video ($M = 4.2$, $SD = 1.15$) and the group that watched the selfish one ($M = 2.31$, $SD = 1.38$). The result shows that the participants could understand the two different viewpoints clearly.

3.4 Participants

Before the data collection of the main experiment, we determined the sample size on the basis of a power analysis. A G^*Power3.1.9.7 analysis [24] (effect size $f = 0.25$, $\alpha = 0.05$, and $1 - \beta = 0.80$) suggested an initial target sample size of $N = 128$. A total of one hundred and fifty participants (90 males, 60 females) took part in the experiment online. Their ages ranged from 18 to 74 years old ($M - 44.31$, $SD = 12.21$). The participants were recruited through a crowd sourcing service provided by Yahoo! Japan. Regarding online experiments in general, Crump et al. [25] showed that data collected online using a web-browser seemed mostly in line with laboratory results, so long as the experiment methods were solid. Fourteen participants were excluded due to a failure to answer comprehension questions on the video stimulus. The final sample of participants was composed of 136 participants ($N = 136$; 80 males, 56 females; $M = 44.79$, $SD = 12.08$). The participants in the main experiment were different from the manipulation check.

3.5 Experimental Procedure

We first asked participants to read an introduction to the experiment. Second, they were asked to watch the videos that contained the stimulus in our study. Then, two comprehension questions were asked to check if they watched the video completely. After that, they were shown a picture of the lower-charged robot in the videos (see Fig. 4) and asked to play the Dictator game and state how much money they would give this robot if they had an extra 1,000 yen. Finally, a free description question was asked to get the comments from the participants after completing the whole questionnaire.

3.6 Experimental Results

To investigate the interaction and main effects of the two factors with two levels for each, a 2×2 two-way ANOVA (between-participants) was conducted. The result shows that the interaction between the peak-end rule and providing multiple viewpoints was not significant ($F(1, 132) = 0.465$, $p = 0.497$, $\eta_p^2 = 0.004$). The main effect of providing multiple viewpoints was also not significant ($F(1, 132) = 0.323$, $p = 0.571$, $\eta_p^2 = 0.002$), which means H2 was not supported.

The main effect of the peak-end rule was significant ($F(1, 132) = 4.331$, $p = 0.039$, $\eta_p^2 = 0.032$), and it shows that participants gave the virtual agent

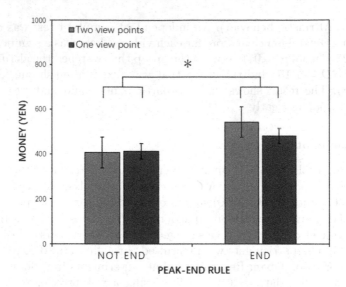

Fig. 5. Table of results

more money if they watched the video based on the peak-end-positive scenario ($M = 511.77$, $SD = 291.94$) than the peak-end-negative one ($M = 408.97$, $SD = 277.03$), which supports H1. (see Fig. 5)

4   Discussion

This experiment was conducted to investigate whether a subtle change in a video stimulus performed by social robots (virtual agents) could promote human altruism. For this purpose, we formulated two hypothesis and analyzed the data obtained from the experiment.

The experimental results supported the first hypothesis, that is, that participants who watch the peak part set at the end of the video (peak-end positive) will perform better at the Dictator game than those who watch the peak-end negative video.

4.1   Results and Consideration of Multiple Viewpoints

The results did not support the second hypothesis, that is, that participants who watch the video containing two viewpoints will perform better than those who watch the video containing only one viewpoint in the Dictator Game.

First, we consider the connection between and contents of selfish behavior and the altruistic behavior in the video. The connection between these two behaviors was only that we told the participants that, in another room, the same task was being held, and we then showed the altruistic task. Therefore, the connection of these two behaviors may have made the participants feel worried about what the meaning of having almost the same workflow was more so than focusing on the behavior itself, which may have decreased the effect of the multiple viewpoints. In addition, to maintain consistency in the task, the task details (i.e., the range of the work space, the amount of the battery, the timing at which the lower-charged robot stopped working) for both behaviors were almost the same. This may have made the participants get tired of the contents of the video and even skip those of the almost same workflow.

Second, we consider the effect of multiple viewpoints. The effect was that, by getting information from different viewpoints, people can avoid confirmation bias, which leads people to pay little attention to or reject information used to make better decisions on the basis of such a clustered overview. This time, we set the different viewpoint to be selfish behavior, which was totally opposite altruistic behavior. From the results, we can conjecture that the selfish behavior did not make sense regarding the clustered overview of both selfish and altruistic behavior. In addition, it can be said that recognizing altruistic behavior as the better decision is not easily disrupted by external information that opposes it.

4.2   Coverage and Limitations

First, we consider the limitation of the agent appearance. At this time, we used only a robot-like appearance for our video stimulus. However, from the comments of the participants, many of them said that they felt a human-like quality in the robots while they performed altruistic or selfish behavior, and this caused them to recall their coworkers or even reflect on their daily behavior. Therefore, it would be interesting to see if they would have the same feeling or introspection while watching a video performed by virtual agents with a human-like appearance.

Second, we consider the limitation of the task we used in this paper. Besides organizing tables and chairs in a meeting room, there are still a lot of different tasks that could be used. Therefore, it would be interesting to see whether the same nudge mechanism could be used to enhance human altruism among different situations and tasks.

Third, the limitation of the use of the nudge mechanisms is considered. Among the 23 ways of nudging, as based on the definition of altruism, the appropriateness of application to robots, and ethical questions, we used 2 of them to see the effect of applying nudge mechanisms to social robots (virtual agents) on promoting human altruism. The remaining nudge mechanisms are expected to be used in combination with other types of social robots.

Fourth, the limitation of the scoring of altruism is considered. On the basis of a meta-analysis of the Dictator game [13], we can see that over 100 Dictator games have been held during the past 25 years at the time at which this paper was published, and it is said that most Dictator games change depending on the experiment. Therefore, changes in the question setting of the game may cause text dependency.

Finally, the limitation of virtual social robots without physical bodies in the video stimulus is considered. Although most of previous studies on social robots have focus on physical attributes of social robots including appearance, behavior, and even personality, in this work, the result showed that even the virtual robots could have significant influences to promote human altruism through the video stimulus. We consider that this knowledge obtained from the experimental results in virtual environments can be applied and fed back to design of physical social robots. In addition, the differences between physical and virtual social robots are also expected basing on the same or different nudge mechanisms which is cheaper and easy to implement. It is our future work to investigate the difference and common properties between virtual and physical social robots.

5   Conclusion

In this paper, we presented the results of a study exploring the effectiveness of applying two nudge mechanisms, peak-end (positive, negative) and multiple viewpoints (one viewpoint, two viewpoints), to a video stimulus performed by social robots (virtual agents). The result shows that participants who watched the peak part set at the end of the video performed better at the Dictator game, which means that the nudge mechanism of the peak-end effect actually promoted human altruism. For future work, the proper way to apply our findings to the real robot is also promising.

References

1. Ross, A.: The Industries of the Future. Simon, Schuster, New York (2016)
2. Chidambaram, V., Chiang, Y.-H., Mutlu, B.: Designing persuasive robots: how robots might persuade people using vocal and nonverbal cues. In: Proceedings of the Seventh Annual ACM/IEEE International Conference on Human-robot Interaction, 293–300. Association for Computing Machinery, Boston (2012). https://doi.org/10.1145/2157689.2157798
3. Ghazali, A.S., Ham, J., Barakova, E., Markopoulos, P.: Assessing the effect of persuasive robots interactive social cues on users' psychological reactance, liking, trusting beliefs and compliance. Adv. Robot. **33**, 325–337 (2019). https://doi.org/10.1080/01691864.2019.1589570
4. Siegel, M., Breazeal, C., Norton, M.I.: Persuasive robotics: the influence of robot gender on human behavior. In: IEEE/RSJ International Conference on Intelligent Robots and Systems, pp. 2563–2568. IEEE, St. Louis (2009). https://doi.org/10.1109/IROS.2009.5354116
5. Jochen, P., Kühne, R., Barco, A.: Can social robots affect children's prosocial behavior? An experimental study on prosocial robot models. Comput. Hum. Behav. **120**(July), 106712 (2021)
6. Shiomi, M., Nakata, A., Kanbara, M., Hagita, N.: A hug from a robot encourages prosocial behavior. In: 2017 26th IEEE International Symposium on Robot and Human Interactive Communication (RO-MAN), 418–23 (2017). ieeexplore.ieee.org
7. Perc, M.: Phase transitions in models of human cooperation. Phys. Lett. A **380**, 2803–2808 (2016)
8. Boyd, R., et al.: The evolution of altruistic punishment. PNAS **100**(6), 3531–3535 (2003). https://doi.org/10.1073/pnas.0630443100

9. Sunstein, C.R., Thaler, R.H.: Nudge: Improving Decisions about Health, Wealth and Happiness. Yale University Press (2008)
10. Capraro, V., et al.: Increasing altruistic and cooperative behaviour with simple moral nudges. Sci. Rep. **9**(1), 1–11 (2019). https://doi.org/10.1038/s41598-019-48094-4
11. Nie, X., et al.: Nudging altruism by color: blue or red? Front. Psychol. **10**(January), 1–8 (2020). https://doi.org/10.3389/fpsyg.2019.03086
12. Caraban, A., et al.: 23 ways to nudge: a review of technology-mediated nudging in human-computer interaction. In: Conference on Human Factors in Computing Systems Proceedings, pp. 1–15 (2019). https://doi.org/10.1145/3290605.3300733
13. Engel, C.: Dictator games: a meta study. Exp. Econ. **14**(4), 583–610 (2011)
14. de Graaf, M.M., Allouch, S.B., Klamer, T.: Sharing a life with Harvey: exploring the acceptance of and relationship-building with a social robot. Comput. Hum. Behav. **43**, 1–14 (2015). https://doi.org/10.1016/j.chb.2014.10.030
15. Wang, B., Rau, P.-L.P.: Influence of embodiment and substrate of social robots on users' decision-making and attitude. Int. J. Soc. Robot. **11**(3), 411–421 (2019). https://doi.org/10.1007/s12369-018-0510-7
16. Clarkson, E., Arkin, R.C.: Applying heuristic evaluation to human-robot interaction systems. In: Proceedings of the Twentieth International Florida Artificial Intelligence Research Society Conference, Key West, pp. 44–49 (2007)
17. Heerink, M., Kröse, B., Evers, V., Wielinga, B.: Assessing acceptance of assistive social agent technology by older adults: the Almere model. I. J. Soc. Rob. **2**, 361–375 (2010)
18. Slater, M., et al.: Bystander responses to a violent incident in an immersive virtual environment. PloS One **8**(1), e52766 (2013)
19. Fredrickson, B., Kahneman, D.: Duration neglect in retrospective evaluations of affective episodes. J. Pers. Soc. Psychol. **65**, 45–55 (1993)
20. Cockburn, A., Quinn, P., Gutwin, C.: Examining the peak-end effects of subjective experience. In: Proceedings of the 33rd Annual ACM Conference on Human Factors in Computing Systems, pp. 357–366. ACM (2015)
21. Nickerson, R.S.: Confirmation bias: a ubiquitous phenomenon in many guises. Rev. General Psychol. 2, 175 (1998)
22. Batson, C.D.: The Altruism Question Toward a Social-Psychological Answer. Erlbaum, Hillsdale (1991)
23. Graaf de, M.M.A., Malle, B.F.: People's judgments of human and robot behaviors: a robust set of behaviors and some discrepancies. In: HRI 2018, pp. 97–98 (2018)
24. Faul, F., Erdefelder, E., Lang, A.G., Buchner, A.: G*Power 3: a flexible statistical power analysis program for the social, behavioral, and biomedical sciences. Behav. Res. Methods **39**, 175–191 (2007). https://doi.org/10.3758/bf03193146
25. Crump, M.J.C., Mcdonnell, J.V., Gureckis, T.M.: Evaluating Amazon's Mechanical Turk as a tool for experimental behavioral research. PLoS ONE **8**(3), 57410 (2013)

Perceptions of Quantitative and Affective Meaning from Humanoid Robot Hand Gestures

Timothy Bickmore(✉), Prasanth Murali, Yunus Terzioglu, and Shuo Zhou

Northeastern University, Boston, MA 02115, USA
{t.bickmore,murali.pr,terzioglu.y,zhou.sh}@northeastern.edu

Abstract. People use their hands in a variety of ways to communicate information along with speech during face-to-face conversation. Humanoid robots designed to converse with people need to be able to use their hands in similar ways, both to increase the naturalness of the interaction and to communicate additional information in the same way people do. However, there are few studies of the particular meanings that people derive from robot hand gestures, particularly for more abstract gestures such as so-called metaphoric gestures that may be used to communicate quantitative or affective information. We conducted an exhaustive study of the 51 hand gestures built into a commercial humanoid robot to determine the quantitative and affective meaning that people derive from observing them without accompanying speech. We find that hypotheses relating gesture envelope parameters (e.g., height, distance from body) to metaphorically corresponding quantitative and affective concepts are largely supported.

Keywords: Metaphoric gesture · Hand gesture · Human-robot interaction · Health education · Health counseling

1 Introduction

Human face-to-face conversation is an intricate multimodal interaction in which people use their bodies, in addition to their speech, to convey meaning and regulate the conversation. For our robots to most effectively engage people in conversation, they must be able to use their own bodies in similar ways. We are interested in developing humanoid robots that can play the role of educators, coaches, and counselors, using their bodies to engage, emphasize, motivate, and convey specific propositional meanings.

Aside from speech, the most expressive communicative channel available to people in face-to-face conversation is arguably their hands. People use their hands continuously in face-to-face interaction to express a rich array of meanings. McNeill [1] defines five types of hand gestures: deictics – used to physically refer to (point at) entities in the speaker's context; emblematics – gestures which have well-defined form and meaning in a community (e.g., "OK"); beats – brief, biphasic motion of the hand to signal emphasis (the most common gesture); iconics – idiosyncratic shapes that are isomorphic with concrete physical objects; and metaphorics – idiosyncratic shapes that refer to abstract concepts via physical metaphors (e.g., "up is more").

© Springer Nature Switzerland AG 2021
H. Li et al. (Eds.): ICSR 2021, LNAI 13086, pp. 386–396, 2021.
https://doi.org/10.1007/978-3-030-90525-5_33

Robots have unique affordances over other media (e.g., virtual agents on flat screen displays or speech-only conversational assistants) in engaging people in face-to-face conversation. In addition to an increase in mere "sense of presence" and all that entails, robots exist in the same physical space with their human interlocutors, enabling them to use many nonverbal channels much more effectively. Proxemics to signal immediacy, intimacy, or conversational engagement/disengagement are much more effective when actual physical distance is manipulated compared to apparent distance (e.g., apparent distance of a virtual agent in 3D rendering, or loudness of a conversational assistant). Deictic gestures, used to point to objects in the shared space, are much more interpretable in physical space than apparent point direction by a virtual agent. Hand gestures, in general, may be more interpretable given that people can rely on their stereoscopic vision to better identify their spatial trajectories.

1.1 Communicative Needs for Health Counseling Robots

In our research, we are interested in developing robot health counselors, to educate and motivate people to perform healthy behaviors [2]. Common across most areas of health communication is the need to convey relative quantity or direction of change. For example, in genetic counseling, absolute and relative risk (probabilities) must be communicated to lay patients so they can make decisions regarding preventive measures in order to reduce their risk of hereditary diseases such as many kinds of cancer.

Communication of affective valence and arousal is also important in health counseling. For example the verbal and nonverbal expression of empathy, particularly for negative emotional states of patients, is recognized as essential for establishing trust and therapeutic alliance which, in turn, is essential for many therapeutic outcomes [3]. Conveyance of positive affect is also important when providing positive reinforcement to patients who have succeeded in achieving health goals they had set.

1.2 Metaphors of Quantity and Affect

Metaphors are fundamental to human cognition, underlying our conceptual system, and playing a core role in how we communicate with each other about the world [4]. Metaphors in communication allow us to communicate one concept, that is generally complex, in terms of another that can be communicated more naturally and easily. Conceptual metaphors underlie our use of many hand gestures, with the form of the gesture driven by a spatial metaphor for a more complex concept being communicated in language. For example, a speaker may refer to an abstract entity in gesture by appearing to pick up and manipulate a physical object (e.g., in [5] a speaker refers to their "Human Resources Department" in gesture by appearing to hold something in their hand).

Lakoff and Johnson [4] define orientational metaphors as those that have to do with spatial orientation, and are grounded in our experience of moving our bodies and other objects through the world. Specific examples are *Happy is Up*, (e.g., "I'm feeling up."), and *Sad is Down*, (e.g., "I'm depressed."), possibly motivated by our experience of slumping posture being associated with sadness and erect posture with a positive emotional state. Lakoff further defines *More is Up* and *Less is Down*, grounded in our common experience that adding more of a substance or physical objects to a container makes the level go up.

1.3 Perception Experiments

We conducted experiments in which we asked participants to observe a wide range of hand gestures produced by a humanoid robot and to rate their perception of what the robot was trying to communicate, in the absence of speech or other communication channels. In order to test the ability of orientational metaphors to be used to communicate information about quantity and affect, we asked participants to rate their perceptions along the following axes: small to large; decreasing to increasing; negative to positive affective valence; and low to high affective arousal (following Russell's circumplex theory of emotion [6]).

We also coded the form of the robot's hand gestures using gesture envelope parameters. Following Kipp [7], we coded as follows. We first identified whether the gesture was 1- or 2-handed, the dominant hand (most effortful), the number of strokes in the gesture, and the most effortful part of the gesture (the "stroke"). We then identified:

- Height of dominant hand at stroke (from below belt to above head, coded 1 to 7 for correlational analyses)
- Distance from the body of the dominant hand at stroke (from touch to far, coded 1 to 4 for correlational analyses)
- Radial orientation of the dominant hand at stroke (from inward to far out, coded 1 to 5 for correlational analyses)

Our intent is to determine whether orientational metaphors can be used by a humanoid robot to communicate information about quantity and affect, using only the gesture envelope parameters and not information about specific hand trajectory or shapes made.

Our hypotheses are that, across a range of hand gestures made by a humanoid robot:

H1. Hand distance from the body at gesture stroke (Height, Distance, and Radial) will be perceived as communicating: larger quantity; increasing quantity; more positive affect valence; and higher affect arousal.

H2. More hands (2 vs. 1) and more gesture strokes will be perceived as communicating: larger quantity; increasing quantity; more positive affect valence; and higher affect arousal.

1.4 Risk Ladder Gesture Development and Test

We also designed three new gestures intended to convey relative risk information, using a gestural analog to a "risk ladder", commonly used for risk communication in print media (Fig. 1) [8, 9]. The new gestures depicted a horizontal span representing a range of risks from low to high, then used subsequent gesture strokes to indicate specific risk levels being discussed, relative to the range (Fig. 2). We tested what participants thought these gestures meant in the absence of speech, and whether their use correlated with our measures of quantity.

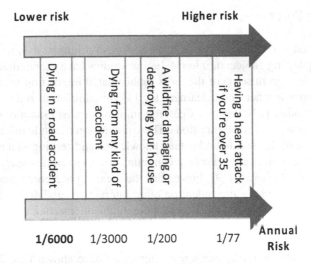

Fig. 1. Risk ladder (from [9])

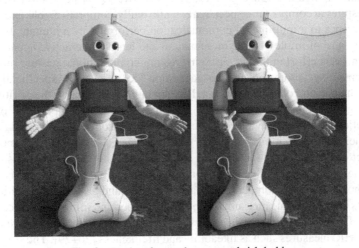

Fig. 2. Strokes from robot gestural risk ladder

1.5 Research Platform

We used SoftBank's Pepper robot for this work (Fig. 2), given its humanoid appearance and articulate arms (6 DoF in each arm) and head (2 DoF). Pepper ships with 61 built-in animations, 25 of which are 1-handed gestures and 36 2-handed. Several of the animations (26) also include head motion (Table 1). Note that there is no "ground truth" to the meaning conveyed by these gestures, as we did not have access to what the designers of the gestures had in mind, nor were the gestures modeled after human gestures as far as we know.

2 Previous Work

The effect of non-verbal cues such as hand gestures on human-to-human interaction has been a long-lasting subject of interest. Earlier studies have shown that gestures play a significant role even in some of the most sophisticated interaction scenarios such as the one between a teacher and a learner [10, 11]. In addition to reducing the cognitive load on a speaker [12], the use of gestures improves transmission of spoken and/or written information in several dimensions. These dimensions include information recall, conceptualization of difficult to understand knowledge, and serving as a unifying channel to interconnect other accompanying communication modalities such as verbal and visual [13–18]. Furthermore, [19] showed that the meaning and context perceived from gestures are not necessarily dependent on other interaction modalities, demonstrating the gestures as a self-contained and coherent communications channel, which can convey rich contextual information between humans either in combinational or sequential compositions [5].

More recent studies on human-agent interaction have shown that the benefits of gesture use in human-human interaction, such as information recall, effectively transfers to human-to-agent settings [17, 18, 20]. Moreover, [21] have shown that iconic robotic gestures accompanying speech are contextually comprehensible and comparable in coherence to a multimodal communication performed by a human. Towards the overarching goal of implementing more natural and legible interactive agents there has been a significant effort in the literature in creating computational gesture models [22–24], implementing automated gesture generation [25, 26]. More specifically, several studies in the human-robot interaction (HRI) domain demonstrated the positive effects of robotic gesture on interaction quality. [27] have shown the importance of nonverbal interaction cues in improving robot persuasiveness through an empirical HRI study. They further draw attention to nonverbal cues, such as gestures, having a more significant effect on human compliance with a robot assistant's recommendations compared to vocal cues. [18] and [17] demonstrate that information recall in humans is improved when a robotic speaker accompanies its narrative with hand gestures. In addition to positive effects on quantifiable measures such as compliance and information recall, several studies in HRI have demonstrated that gestures also have significant positive effects on qualitative HRI measures such as likeability and lifelikeness [26–29]. The studies in this direction concluded that in creation of natural and fluent interactions between a robot and a human, gestures have a critical role to play.

It is not trivial, however, to generalize humans' understanding of robotic gestures, since even the most subtle nuances of motions (thus gestures) are easily perceived by human cognition [30, 31]. This difficulty is further emphasized in [21], as they reported the difficulty in evaluating objective robotic gesture quality, since there are multiple factors in play in perceptual interpretation of gestures such as other interaction modalities and subtle nuances of motion that are difficult to control in robot applications. Even though it is well-supported by the literature that robotic gestures have a positive effect on human-robot interaction, it is not clear whether humans have a consistent perception of these gestures. Moreover, it is shown in the prior literature that gestures can create strong communication contexts even when they are not accompanied by any other communication modalities [19]. However, there are few studies that evaluate the perception of robotic gestures alone in an exhaustive fashion, and even fewer that focus on metaphoric gestures that can convey quantitative and affective meaning. Thus, this study draws inspiration from and builds on the body of literature covering human-human and human-robot interactions and focuses on answering what is the meaning understood from a wide range of metaphoric robotic gestures.

3 Experimental Methods

We conducted an experiment to study how gestures made by the Pepper robot were perceived to communicate quantitative and affective information.

We recorded 65 videos of approximately 10 s each in length, of Pepper performing the gestures in its in-built library, plus our three custom designed Risk Ladder gestures.[1] We then recruited participants from the Amazon Mechanical Turk platform to watch a random selection of 25 videos each (without audio) and describe their perceptions of each video. Participants were from the United States with 95%+ HIT (Human Intelligence Task). The study was approved by Northeastern's IRB and participants were compensated for their time.

3.1 Measures and Analyses

After watching each video, participants were first asked a validation question to ensure they were paying attention (participants who failed this had their data removed). They were then asked to fill out a free-text response question "What do you think the robot is trying to communicate? Please describe in as much detail as possible." Following this, participants answered four single-item scale questions: 1) What numeric quantity do you think the robot is trying to communicate? (1 = small, 7 = large); 2) What change in quantity do you think the robot is trying to communicate? (1 = decreasing, 7 = increasing); 3) What emotion do you think the robot is trying to communicate? (1 = very negative, 7 = very positive); 4) How intensely is the robot trying to convey its emotion? (1 = very relaxed, 7 = very intense).

The form of Robot hand gestures were coded according to the features in Sect. 1.3, with a sample of 13 coded by two researchers to assess reliability. Interrater reliability was excellent, ranging from 0.83 for number of strokes to 0.96 for Radial Direction.

The free text responses were analyzed using sentiment analysis as a secondary assessment of affect perception. The responses were first parsed through the Natural Language Toolkit VADER sentiment analyzer [32] to classify the polarity (positive, negative or neutral) of each word. The ratio of the number of positive words to the total number of words in each response was calculated as a positive sentiment score of, and the ratio of the number of negative words to the total number of words in each response was calculated as a negative sentiment score.

---

[1] All videos are available at: https://tinyurl.com/PepperGesture.

4 Results

Forty-six participants started the experiment, out of which 3 participants were removed for invalid responses. Two participants did not complete the study. For the remaining 41 participants, 53% were male (47% female), with a mean age of 36 (sd = 4.2).

4.1 Gesture Analysis

Ratings of perceived quantity (small to large) were positively correlated with Gesture Height (Spearman's rho = .12, p = .030), Gesture Distance from body (rho = .23, p < .001), and Gesture Radial Distance from center (rho = .17, p = .002). Two-handed gestures were rated with higher perceived quantity (mean = 4.2) than one-handed gestures (mean = 3.7, Mann-Whitney U = 10389, p = .018).

Ratings of perceived quantity change (decreasing to increasing) were only significantly correlated with Gesture Distance from body (rho = .09, p = .039).

Ratings of perceived affect valence (negative to positive) were correlated with Number of Gesture Strokes (rho = .21, p < .001), and Gesture Height (rho = .14, p < .001). Valence was rated significantly more positive for asymmetric vs. symmetric gestures (Mann-Whitney U = 13144, p < .001).

Ratings of perceived affect arousal (low to high) were correlated with Gesture Height (rho = .15, p < .001), Gesture Distance from body (rho = .11, p = .012), and Gesture Radial Distance from center (rho = .11, p = .011).

There was no significant difference on any measure when the robot's hands were open vs. closed at stroke.

Having the robot's head motion involved in the gesture led to significantly lower ratings of affect valence (Mann-Whitney U = 30179, p = .031), and significantly higher ratings of affect arousal (Mann-Whitney U = 24921, p < .001).

Sentiment analysis of free-text responses indicated a significant correlation (Pearson r = .77, p < .05) between the positive sentiment score and the perceived valence, and a trending correlation (r = −.34, p = .1) between the negative sentiment score and the perceived valence.

For our newly created risk ladder gestures, the one intended to depict "decreasing" or "smaller than", participants rated Quantity with mean = 3.1 (sd = 2.3), below the middle of the scale, indicating they perceived this gesture to be communicating "small". They also rated quantity Change with mean = 3.7 (sd = 1.3), also below the middle of the scale, indicating they perceived this gesture to communicate slightly decreasing values.

We had two risk ladder gestures intending to convey the concepts "increasing" or "larger than". For the first, with one step, participants rated Quantity with mean = 3.5 (sd = 2.1), indicating they perceived this gesture to be communicating "small", and rated quantity Change with mean = 4.8 (sd = 1.5), above the middle of the scale, indicating they perceived this gesture to communicate slightly increasing values. For the second, with three steps, participants rated Quantity with mean = 3.4 (sd = 2.2), indicating they perceived this gesture to be communicating "small", and rated quantity Change with mean = 4.4 (sd = 1.1), above the middle of the scale, indicating they perceived this gesture to communicate increasing values.

Table 1. Measures for all of Pepper's Built-in Gestures (Sym = symmetric; AH = above head).

Gesture Animation	Gesture Form [7]							Scale Measures				Sentiment	
	Hands	Sym	Strokes	Height	Close	Radial	Head	Quantity	Change	Valence	Arousal	Pos	Neg
CalmDown_5	2	1	3	BelwBlt	Normal	Side	0	4.50	3.67	4.22	4.44	0.10	0.04
CalmDown_6	2	1	3	BelwBlt	Normal	Side	0	4.33	3.67	4.67	3.83	0.44	0.48
Choice_1	2	0	2	Abdmn	Normal	Front	0	4.50	4.30	4.00	4.10	0.12	0.18
Desperate_1	2	1	1	Chest	Normal	Front	1	5.50	4.63	3.50	5.88	0.07	0.47
Desperate_2	2	1	1	Chest	Normal	Front	1	4.50	4.45	4.00	4.55	0.26	0.45
Desperate_4	2	1	1	BelwBlt	Normal	Far	0	3.00	3.71	4.29	4.29	0.15	0.14
Desperate_5	2	1	1	BelwBlt	Close	Side	1	3.86	3.64	4.36	3.36	0.12	0.14
Embarassed_1	2	1	3	Belt	Normal	Front	1	4.00	4.56	4.67	4.44	0.27	0.46
Enthusiastic_4	2	0	2	Shldr	Close	Front	1	2.50	3.17	4.67	3.67	0.28	0.18
Enthusiastic_5	2	1	2	Chest	Normal	Side	0	5.71	5.00	4.60	5.50	0.03	0.02
Everything_1	2	1	1	BelwBlt	Far	Far	0	5.17	4.31	4.54	4.62	0.11	0.14
Everything_2	1		1	Belt	Normal	Front	0	1.75	2.83	4.33	3.17	0.00	0.21
Everything_3	2	1	2	Chest	Normal	Side	0	5.50	4.70	4.40	3.50	0.03	0.43
Everything_4	2	1	2	Belt	Normal	Side	0	3.17	3.15	4.15	3.31	0.31	0.04
Excited_1	2	1	4	Belt	Normal	Side	1	4.50	4.89	4.67	5.22	0.16	0.01
Eypain_1	2	1	2	Belt	Normal	Side	0	1.17	1.50	4.00	3.40	0.10	0.14
Explain_10	1		1	Abdmn	Normal	Side	0	4.67	5.67	3.33	3.00	0.03	0.18
Explain_11	2	1	3	Abdmn	Normal	Side	0	2.20	3.60	5.30	3.60	0.44	0.52
Explain_2	1		3	Abdmn	Normal	Side	0	3.00	4.25	4.88	3.88	0.57	0.04
Explain_3	1		3	Abdmn	Normal	Side	0	3.00	4.17	4.17	3.17	0.25	0.06
Explain_4	2	0	2	Belt	Normal	Side	0	3.57	4.67	4.75	3.50	0.72	0.14
Explain_5	1		3	Chest	Normal	Side	0	3.33	3.90	4.50	3.50	0.31	0.10
Explain_6	1		2	Abdmn	Normal	Side	0	5.00	4.25	3.75	4.75	0.29	0.40
Explain_7	2	0	1	BelwBlt	Normal	Side	0	2.50	3.56	4.67	3.22	0.38	0.07
Far_1	1	0	2	Shldr	Far	Far	0	5.25	4.13	5.75	5.75	0.25	0.39
Far_2	1	0	2	Shldr	Far	Far	0	5.00	4.50	4.88	3.63	0.45	0.48
Far_3	1	0	2	AH	Far	Far	1	6.75	5.00	4.86	5.29	0.62	0.32
Gesture-33	2	0	1	Belt	Normal	Side	1	4.67	5.33	3.78	4.78	0.23	0.45
Gesture-42	2	1	1	BelwBlt	Close	Side	0	2.50	3.73	3.36	3.64	0.02	0.13
Give_3	1		1	BelwBlt	Normal	Side	0	4.63	4.18	4.36	3.82	0.27	0.21
Give_4	2	1	2	Chest	Normal	Front	0	4.75	4.56	4.44	3.78	0.23	0.35
Give_5	2	1	2	Chest	Normal	Front	0	3.00	4.44	4.22	3.11	0.23	0.22
Give_6	1		1	Chest	Normal	Side	0	2.50	3.82	4.36	3.73	0.06	0.27
Happy_4	2	1	1	BelwBlt	Normal	Front	1	4.20	4.56	5.00	4.78	0.27	0.26
Hey_3	1	0	4	Head	Close	Out	0	3.00	3.75	5.75	4.08	0.23	0.48
Hey_1	1	0	4	AH	Close	Out	0	5.40	4.57	5.29	4.57	0.31	0.69
Hey_3	1	0	4	Head	Close	Out	0	2.67	4.27	4.27	3.36	0.11	0.26
Hey_4	1	0	4	Head	Close	Far	0	4.00	4.00	5.86	5.14	0.55	0.42
Hey_6	1	0	3	AH	Close	Far	0	5.67	5.43	5.86	4.71	0.58	0.4
Hysterical_1	2	0	2	BelwBlt	Close	Out	1	4.67	4.89	4.78	5.22	0.7	0.11
IDontKnow_1	2	1	1	BelwBlt	Normal	Far	1	3.83	4.00	4.67	4.78	0.44	0.37
IDontKnow_2	2	1	1	BelwBlt	Far	Far	1	3.75	4.42	3.00	5.00	0.25	0.07
IDontKnow_3	2	1	1	BelwBlt	Normal	Side	1	4.20	5.25	4.88	3.13	0.74	0.21
Me_1	1		1	Chest	Close	Inward	1	3.14	4.40	5.00	4.00	0.52	0.42
Me_4	1		1	Chest	Close	Inward	1	3.33	4.11	4.33	3.78	0.47	0.02
Me_7	1		1	Chest	Close	Inward	1	3.00	4.00	4.50	4.13	0.43	0.16
No_1	1		1	Chest	Normal	Side	1	4.33	4.44	3.78	4.56	0.48	0.01
No_2	1		1	Chest	Normal	Side	1	3.00	3.67	4.22	4.22	0.44	0.11
No_3	2	1	1	BelwBlt	Far	Far	1	6.00	4.14	3.14	5.29	0.24	0.03
No_9	1		1	Chest	Normal	Side	1	3.89	4.45	3.82	5.27	0.12	0.45
Nothing_2	2	1	2	Belt	Close	Far	1	2.25	3.33	3.83	2.83	0.49	0.12
Peaceful_1	2	1	2	BelwBlt	Close	Far	1	4.25	4.36	4.00	4.64	0.4	0.03
Please_1	2	1	1	Belt	Far	Far	0	4.60	4.75	4.25	4.13	0.17	0.12
Q1	2	2	2	Chest	Normal	Side	0	3.80	3.88	4.25	3.25	0.01	0.37
Q2	2	2	2	Chest	Normal	Side	0	4.75	4.22	4.44	4.89	0.11	0.43
Shldrow Sky 1	2	0	3	AH	Normal	Side	1	4.80	4.33	5.67	5.67	0.78	0.16
Shldrow Sky 11	2	0	3	AH	Normal	Side	1	5.67	5.00	4.22	5.33	0.12	0.26
Shldrow Sky 2	1		2	Chest	Normal	Front		5.17	4.67	4.33	4.00	0.48	0.28
Shldrow Sky 8	2	1	3	AH	Normal	Side		5.29	5.25	4.50	5.88	0.07	0.4
Tablet 2	1		1	Chest	Close	Inward	1	4.14	4.23	4.15	4.31	0.09	0.21
Tablet 3	1		1	Chest	Close	Inward	1	1.13	1.00	2.50	4.50	0.13	0.48

5 Conclusion

Overall, participants related greater gesture envelopes with communication of larger quantities are greater arousal. We found that observers perceived larger hand gestures by a humanoid robot—in height, distance forward from body, and radial distance from center—as communicating greater absolute quantity, but only forward distance from body as communicating positive change in quantity. Observers perceived gesture height as communicating more positively-valenced affect, but all measures of gesture envelope (height, distance forward from body, and radial distance from center) as communicating greater affect arousal. H1 was mostly confirmed.

The use of two hands vs. one only affected perception of increased quantity, and positively valenced affect. Thus, H2 only received minimal support.

We also found that positive sentiment in free-text descriptions of the gestures correlated with scale measures of perceived affect valence. Interestingly, asymmetric gestures were perceived as communicating significantly more positive affect compared to symmetric gestures.

Finally, participants had a generally correct perception of our Risk Ladder gestures.

5.1 Limitations and Future Work

These studies have significant limitations. The convenience sample of MTurkers in the study was small and may not be representative of any given target population. Perceptions from videotaped gestures may not be the same as those from in-person observation. Findings based on Pepper's gestures may not generalize to those of all humanoid robots.

Importantly, we only evaluated gestures in the absence of speech or any other contextual information. Although many gestures can be interpreted in isolation [19], social, task, and discourse context set strong expectations which can help interactants better interpret gestures. Because of their idiosyncratic and abstract nature, metaphoric gestures are almost never used without speech in naturally occurring conversations. In addition, we did not characterize the form of gesture beyond envelope parameters, and the exact trajectory and handshape of gesture is essential in understanding intended meaning [1, 5].

This work is an initial step in the development of humanoid robot hand gestures that go beyond simply providing entertainment and engagement, to enabling robots to use their hands to convey meaning in conversation, in the same way that people do. Effective use of all conversational modalities is essential in complex interactions in which robots are designed to educate, counsel, and motivate.

Acknowledgements. Sumanth Munikoti assisted in generating the experimental stimuli, and Nwabisi Chikwendu assisted with the online study.

References

1. McNeill, D.: Hand and Mind: What Gestures Reveal about Thought. Cambridge University Press, Cambridge (1992)

2. Zhou, S., Murali, P., Underhill-Blazey, M., Bickmore, T.: Cancer genetic counseling by humanoid robot: modeling multimodal communication of health risk. In: ACM/IEEE International Conference on Human-Robot Interaction (HRI) (2020)
3. Spiro, H.: Empathy: an introduction. In: Spiro, H., McCrea, M., Peschel, E., St. James, D. (eds.) Empathy and the Practice of Medicine, pp. 1–6. Yale University Press, New Haven (1993)
4. Lakoff, G., Johnson, M.: Metaphors We Live By. University of Chicago Press, Chicago (1980)
5. Saund, C., Roth, M., Chollet, M., Marsella, S.: Multiple metaphors in metaphoric gesturing. In: International Conference on Affective Computing and Intelligent Interaction (ACII) (2019)
6. Russel, J.: A circumplex model of affect. J. Pers. Soc. Psychol. **39**, 1161–1178 (1980)
7. Kipp, M., Neff, M., Albrecht, I.: An annotation scheme for conversational gestures: how to economically capture timing and form. Lang. Resour. Eval. **41**(3/4), 325–339 (2007)
8. Lipkus, I., Hollands, J.: The visual communication of risk. JNCI Monogr. **25**, 149–163 (1999)
9. Gonzalez-Caban, A., Sanchez, J.E.: Minority households' willingness to pay for public and private wildfire risk reduction in Florida. Int J Wildland Fire **26**(8), 774–733 (2017)
10. Roth, W.: Gestures: their role in teaching and learning. Rev. Educ. Res. **71**(3), 365–392 (2001)
11. Alibali, M., Nathan, M.: Embodiment in mathematics teaching and learning: evidence from learners' and teachers' gestures. J. Learn. Sci. **21**(2), 247–286 (2012)
12. Goldin-Meadow, S., Nusbaum, H., Kelly, S.E., Wagner, S.: Explaining math: gesturing lightens the load. Psychol. Sci. **12**(6), 516–522 (2001)
13. Alibali, M., Nathan, M., Church, R., Wolfgram, M., Kim, S., Knuth, E.: Teachers' gestures and speech in mathematics lessons: forging common ground by resolving trouble spots. ZDM **45**, 425–440 (2013)
14. Alibali, M., Nathan, M.: Teachers' gestures as a means of scaffolding students' understanding: evidence from an early algebra lesson. In: Video Research in the Learning Sciences. Routledge, London (2007)
15. Alibali, M., et al.: How teachers link ideas in mathematics instruction using speech and gesture: a corpus analysis. Cogn. Instr. **32**(1), 65–100 (2015)
16. Alibali, M., Young, A., Crooks, N., Yeo, A.: Students learn more when their teacher has learned to gesture effectively. Gesture **13**(2), 210–233 (2013)
17. Huang, C., Mutlu, B.: Modeling and evaluating narrative gestures for humanlike robots. Robot. Sci. Syst. (2013)
18. van Dijk, E.T., Torta, E., Cuijpers, R.H.: Effects of eye contact and iconic gestures on message retention in human-robot interaction. Int. J. Soc. Robot. **5**(4), 491–501 (2013). https://doi.org/10.1007/s12369-013-0214-y
19. Kok, K., Bergmann, K., Kopp, S.: Not so dependent after all: functional perception of speakers' gestures with and without speech. Gesture and Speech in Interaction Conference (GESPIN-4) (2013)
20. Salem, M., Kopp, S., Wachsmuth, I., Rohlfing, K., Joublin, F.: Generation and evaluation of communicative robot gesture. Int. J. Soc. Robot. **4**(2), 201–217 (2012)
21. Bremner, P., Leonards, U.: Iconic gestures for robot avatars, recognition and integration with speech. Front. Psychol. **7**(183) (2016)
22. Lhommet, M., Marsella, S.: Metaphoric gestures: towards grounded mental spaces. In: Bickmore, T., Marsella, S., Sidner, C. (eds.) Intelligent Virtual Agents, pp. 264–274. Springer, Cham (2014). https://doi.org/10.1007/978-3-319-09767-1_34
23. Lhommet, M., Marsella, S.: Proceedings of the Cognitive Science Society (2016)
24. Lhommet, M., Marsella, S.: Intelligent Virtual Agents (2013)
25. Cassell, J., Vilhjálmsson, H., Bickmore, T.: BEAT: The Behavior Expression Animation Toolkit. SIGGRAPH 2001, Los Angeles, CA (2001)
26. Salem, M., Kopp, S., Wachsmuth, I., Rohlfing, K., Joublin, F.: Generation and evaluation of communicative robot gesture. Int. J. Soc. Robot. **4**, 201–217 (2012)

27. Chidambaram, V., Chiang, Y., Mutlu, B.: Designing persuasive robots: how robots might persuade people using vocal and nonverbal cues. In: Human-Robot Interaction (HRI) (2012)
28. Han, J., Campbell, N., Jokinen, K., Wilcock, G.: Investigating the use of non-verbal cues in human-robot interaction with a Nao robot. In: IEEE International Conference on Cognitive Infocommunications (2012)
29. Salem, M., Eyssel, F., Rohlfing, K., Kopp, S., Joublin, F.: To err is human(-like): effects of robot gesture on perceived anthropomorphism and likability. Int. J. Soc. Robot. 5(3), 313–323 (2013)
30. Deshmukh, A., Craenen, B., Vinciarelli, A., Foster, M.: Shaping robot gestures to shape users' perception: the effect of amplitude and speed on Godspeed ratings. 6th International Conference on Human-Agent Interaction (HAI 2018) (2018)
31. Kilner, J., Pualignan, Y., Blakemore, S.J.: An interference effect of observed biological movement on action. Curr. Biol. 13(6), 522–525 (2003)
32. Gilbert, C.: Vader: a parsimonious rule-based model for sentiment analysis of social media text. Eighth International Conference on Weblogs and Social Media (ICWSM-14) (2014)

Evaluation of a Humanoid Robot's Emotional Gestures for Transparent Interaction

Alessandra Rossi[1], Marcus M. Scheunemann[2], Gianluca L'Arco[1], and Silvia Rossi[1(✉)]

[1] University of Naples Federico II, Naples, Italy
{alessandra.rossi,silvia.rossi}@unina.it, g.larco@studenti.unina.it
[2] University of Hertfordshire, Hatfield, UK
marcus@mms.ai

Abstract. Effective and successful interactions between robots and people are possible only when they both are able to infer the other's intentions, beliefs, and goals. In particular, robots' mental models need to be transparent to be accepted by people and facilitate the collaborations between the involved parties. In this study, we focus on investigating how to create legible emotional robots' behaviours to be used to make their decision-making process more transparent to people. In particular, we used emotions to express the robot's internal status and feedback during an interactive learning process. We involved 28 participants in an online study where they rated the robot's behaviours, designed in terms of colours, icons, movements and gestures, according to the perceived intention and emotions.

Keywords: Human-robot interaction · Affective robotics · Social robotics · Transparency

1 Introduction

Autonomous social robots are being deployed in human-centred environments where they are exposed to close and unsupervised interactions with people. In such scenarios, robots and humans need to share the working space and work together to complete different tasks. These close interactions are raising the importance for robots of adopting natural communication mechanisms, which usually are bi-directional in human-human (HHI) and human-robot interactions (HRI). Therefore, robots and people need to understand and predict each other's behaviours and intentions, and consequently, robots need to adapt their own

This work has been partially supported by Italian PON I&C 2014-2020 within the BRILLO research project "Bartending Robot for Interactive Long-Lasting Operations", no. F/190066/01-02/X44, and CHIST-ERA IV COHERENT project "COllaborative HiErarchical Robotic ExplaNaTions".

behaviours for planning the next steps to reach the common goal [15]. Moreover, the use of Artificial Intelligence (AI) techniques, and specifically of Deep and Reinforcement learning approaches, during the human-robot interaction, make this mutual understanding process even harder. Such complex and powerful methodologies are considered "black-boxes" by non-technical users who may consequently develop sentiments of distrust and fear towards robots [12]. In general, people are not inclined to use and interact with systems that they cannot comprehend. To avoid that human users misuse or disuse robots, and ensure a successful model of HRI, it is important to make robots' behaviours more intelligible and transparent for people [7].

Among the mechanisms used to make transparent a robot's internal process and its understanding of a person's mental state, emotions are considered to be a universal and valid mechanism to communicate one's own internal state [3,11]. Indeed, emotions can be defined as "they are parts of the very process of interacting with the environment" [5]. Several studies tried to provide a set of emotional body languages that robots can use to express emotions [9,10]. However, these studies showed that people's perceptions of emotions and feelings may vary according to the situational context [17,20].

In our research, we want to use emotions as a natural mechanism to express the robot's intentions, beliefs and understanding of the situational context. In particular, in this study, we selected two sets of emotions (positive and negative): two for expressing a robot's belief of the goodness of a selected action during an interactive learning process (i.e., fear and hope), and two for expressing a robot's understanding of the situational context (i.e., happiness and sadness). As a first step, before evaluating the effect of using such behaviours during the HRI, here we aim at exploring participants' perception of emotional behaviours in relation to the desired intent in an online study.

2 Design

2.1 Robot Platform

The robot used in this study is the humanoid Pepper robot created by SoftBank Robotics. Pepper is 120 cm tall, it has 20 degrees of freedom (DoF), a wheeled base, a tablet at chest high, coloured LEDs around the eyes, on the side of the head (i.e., ears), and on the shoulders. The robot is not able to express facial emotions having a static face. The behaviours of the robot were implemented using ROS Noetic and the robot's libraries NAOqi.

We positioned the robot close to a desk that covered only the lower part of the robot, leaving the robot to be free of movement and the view from the chest to the head. On the desk, there were four objects (a tennis ball, a soccer ball, a kangaroo and a red box).

2.2 The Robot's Emotions and Behaviours

The affective model used in this study is inspired by J. Broekens' emotional theory, called TD-RL [2]. The model is composed of four emotions: fear, hope,

(a) *Fear* (b) *Hope*

(c) *Happiness* (d) *Sadness*

Fig. 1. Emotions expressed by the robot Pepper according to an increasing level of arousal [from left to right].

sadness and joy. In the model, they are used to express the learning status of the robot during an interactive learning task involving the user to provide the rewards. In particular, they are used to express the internal belief in the goodness of its current action (sadness and joy) and on the foreseen success of the use of such action in achieving the goal (hope and fear). In a previous work [11], this model was used in an HRI task aiming at teaching an I-Cub robot to learn a predefined sequence of objects (coloured balls) placed on a table. The considered learning task required the robot to point at the objects placed in front of it while receiving positive or negative rewards from the user through a joystick interface. Results of this study highlighted that users perceived joy and sadness gestures not as states linked to the current action but, instead, as reactions to the user rewards. Moreover, it was helpful to have behaviours showing internal states, in terms of certainty or uncertainty of the current action, during the learning process, even though the used gestures were not completely recognised.

For this reason, here, we designed new gestures for the Pepper robot to be associated with a pointing gesture for the purpose of showing hope and fear (see Figs. 1.a and 1.b). The emotions of joy and sadness are instead used to elicit the robot's response and awareness to a possible (positive or negative) feedback received by the user (see Figs. 1.c and 1.d).

The emotions expressed by the robot have been inspired by the Color Motion Sound (CMS) model [9] that combines colours, motions and sounds for each emotion. While vocal features play a fundamental role in emotion recognition [16], here we decided to not include the sounds for modelling the emotions because fear and hope do not have any sound associated according to the CMS model. We modelled three different levels (min, mid and max) of intensity for each emotion considering the following characteristics:

- *Joy*: the colour chose to represent Joy is yellow hues with three degrees of intense saturation and high brightness (HSB values: 45/100/100, 45/79/95, 45/40/100). The robot expressed this emotion with fast rotations and circular movements of the arms, and opening the chest and head.
- *Sadness*: Dark blue hues were used to represent Sadness (HSB values: 217/79/53, 230/40/40, 208/69/78). The robot moved arms closing on itself, lowering the head and making slowly rotation away from the user.
- *Fear*: The emotion Fear is expressed through jumpy movements away from the user and with uncertainty while looking at the object it intends to point at and at the user. The colours used for Fear are black and grey (HSB values: 0/0/20,0/0/40,0/0/60).
- *Hope*: The emotion is expressed using the green colour (HSB values: 102/53/66, 101/36/77, 102/75/46), open posture, and very fast and secure movements.

Pepper robot has a static face, hence to enhance the legibility of the emotional behaviours, we designed a set of icons to be displayed on the robot tablet. The icons show a drawing of the pepper face with different facial expressions obtained by modifying the shape of the robot' mouth, eyes and using the same colours as described before.

In total, the set of emotions used in this study consists of 12 animations in which the robot shows three levels of intensity of joy, sadness, fear and hope emotions.

2.3   Procedure and Evaluation Measures

We designed a between-subject study with two conditions. In condition **C1**, the robot used its tablet to show the icon to express the relevant emotions. In condition **C2**, the robot's tablet was left blank. Participants rated 12 video-clips of the robot communicating different emotions and behaviours with or without the use of the tablet and completed the requested questionnaires on Google Forms. The order of the video-clips presented to the participants was randomised to counter possible sequence effects.

The videos were shot from a frontal angle to allow participants to have a full overview of the robot and the objects on the desk. Each video-clips was shot on the same day and with the same background. We tried to recreate the videos in the same way as much as possible, and we did not make any cuts to give a natural continuity to the gestures. The robot expresses the emotions with videos of the same duration (12 s).

We did not give any description of the robot at the beginning of the interaction for capturing participants' perceptions built only on their own experience, personality and considerations [13]. In both conditions, participants were presented with three questionnaires at the beginning, after each video and at the end of the online study.

At the beginning of the study, we collected participants' responses: 1) their demographic data (age, gender, nationality and occupation), 2) their experience with robots, 3) their opinion about robots' roles and robots' ability to express emotions, 4) the affect measuring questionnaire (PANAS) [19] to measure participants' mood (positive or negative) at the time of the study using a 5-point Likert scale [1 = very slightly or not at all, and 5 = extremely], 5) the Ten Item Personality Inventory questionnaire about themselves (TIPI) [6] using a 7-point Likert Scale [1 = disagree strongly, and 7 = agree strongly].

After each video-clip, two 8-point scales, one [1= calm, and 8 = aroused] and the second [−4 = displeasure, and 4 = pleasure] were used to measure the level of arousal and pleasure perceived by the participants [8]. In the questionnaires, we expressed the valence as the pleasure to make the concept easier to understand for the participants [10]. For ranking arousal and valence of the emotions, we decided to use these scales instead of the Affective Slider [1] to not influence participants' choices by showing an emoji that might be associated with the emotion represented on the robot's tablet. We asked participants to select their confidence level for the selection of the arousal and pleasure of the emotion in the video-clip using two 7-point Semantic scales [1 = not at all, and 7 = very much]. We also asked the participants to indicate the perceived discrete emotions expressed by the robot in the video, selecting them between the following set: anger, fear, hope, sadness, uncertainty, joy, pride, surprise, certainty, disgust, embarrassment, and shame. These emotions were selected to include the six universally recognised basic and non-basic emotions from Ekman [4].

Finally, in the last questionnaire, participants were asked to give their opinion: 1) whether they believed that Pepper was able to express emotions, and whether robots, in general, should be able to express emotions, 2) which roles they would assign to Pepper, 3) which emotions they believed a robot should be able to express choosing them from the list of emotions of Ekman previously presented, 4) then, we measure participants' mood using the PANAS questionnaire. We also measured participants' attention through two check questions asking "Which was the object/were the objects in front of the robot Pepper? Please choose all that apply." and "Which gesture/s did Pepper not do in the videos? Please choose all that apply."

2.4 Participants

We recruited 28 participants (18 male, 10 female and none non-binary) aged between 18 and 66 (mean age 26.5, std. dev. 11.20). The majority of the participants consisted of Italian citizens (89%), while one participant was from Switzerland and two participants were from the United Kingdom. The sample of participants was mainly composed of students (79%). The remaining participants were a lawyer, a visual designer, a production manager, a research fellow and a retired teacher. The majority of participants (72%) stated to not have any experience with robots (min = 1, max = 5, mean 1.96, std. dev. 1.5), while the remaining had some or high experience with robots. Participants' previous experiences with robots can be classified into participation in other studies, observing or developing robots. Participants had experience with the following robots: Soft-Bank Robotics NAO and Pepper, Furhat Robotics, iRobot Corporation Roomba, Qihan Technology Co. Sanbot, and Hanson Robotics Sophia.

We did not exclude any participants due to a failure of the attention check question.

3 Results

3.1 Affect Questionnaire

The affect scores from the PANAS questionnaire [19] before the experiment was within the expected range. Before the experiment, the positive affect score mean was 29.75 (std. dev. 7.25) and the negative affect score mean was 14.57 (std. dev. 6.16). After the experiment, the positive affect score mean was 29.29 (std. dev. 7.26) and the negative affect score mean was 13.25 (std. dev. 6.1). A paired t-test shows that there is not a statistically significant effect between the responses before and after the test.

3.2 Descriptive Statistics

We first analysed the data for interaction effects between gender and video responses. To understand whether the gender of the participant had an effect on the responses, we computed a two-way mixed model ANOVA. The results in Table 1 show that the responses to the dependent variables arousal and valence were not affected by the participants' gender.

A statistically significant effect on the participants' perception of the arousal and valance of the robot can be further observed. This means that participants perceived the robots on these dimensions differently. The next subsections will present an exploratory analysis as to how these differences map our expectations.

Table 1. A two-way mixed model ANOVA analysed whether there is an interaction between the participants' gender and their responses to the videos. The results indicate that there is no evidence for an interaction. However, the results also suggest some statistically significant effects for the participants' responses for arousal and valence.

(a) arousal	$DF1$	$DF2$	F	p	(b) valance	$DF1$	$DF2$	F	p
gender	1	26	0.05	0.82	gender	1	26	0.56	0.46
emotion	11	286	6.44	< 0.01	emotion	11	286	12.01	< 0.01
interaction	11	286	1.48	0.14	interaction	11	286	1.51	0.13

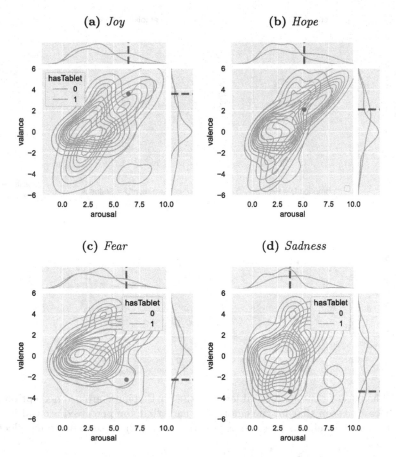

Fig. 2. Kernel density estimates (KDE) for each emotion expressed by the robot. The red point marks the expected perception means. It can be seen that the mean is usually part of the fringe or outside of the distribution. Only if a tablet is used, the expected mean is part of or close to at least one distribution maxima. (Color figure online)

3.3 Exploratory Analysis

In regard to the emotions expressed by the robot, Fig. 2 shows the kernel density estimates for the participants' responses for each of them. The red point depicts the expected mean (see [18]). It can be seen that the participants' perception of the robot without a tablet does not entirely meet our expectations. For the emotion Joy, Hope and Sadness, the robot that also expressed its emotion using a tablet, our expected mean values are part of or close to one of the maxima of the kernel density estimation. This shows that in our experiment, the tablet supports the robot in expressing its emotion to the participants.

Figure 3 shows the participants' perceived arousal in dependence to the chosen arousal level. It can be seen that the overall rating for arousal shows a little variance in the condition where the robot did not have a tablet. Interestingly,

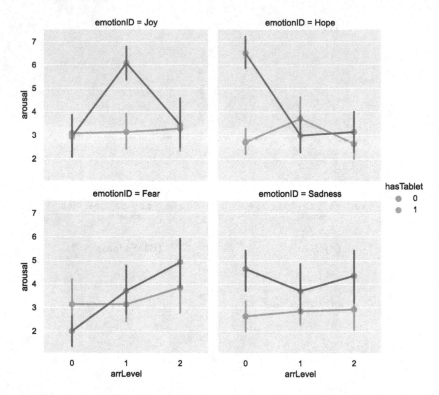

Fig. 3. The effect of the set arousal level on the participants' arousal perception of the robot. It can be seen that for the emotion "Fear" that the perceived arousal increases with the arousal level. For other emotions, this is not the case, but strong effects can be observed.

the "Fear" emotion is the only one that follows our expectation of an increase in arousal for a higher arousal level.

Finally, after each video, the participants were asked to select one or more discrete emotions that they thought represented best the one expressed by the robot in the video-clips. In Fig. 4, it can be seen that there is no clear mapping between a robot's emotion and a participant's perception of said emotion. Participants also associated joy evenly, but they rarely picked hope. This result is not surprising, because it is more difficult to associate a behaviour to a discrete emotion than expressing it according to its level of arousal and valence [1].

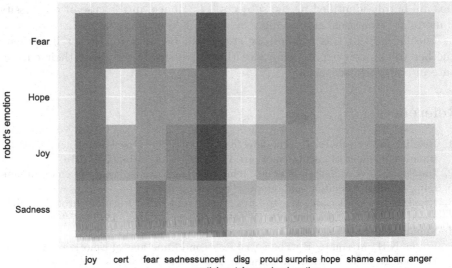

joy   cert   fear sadness uncert disg proud surprise hope shame embarr anger
participants' perceived emtion

Fig. 4. A hit-map for the emotions participants' associated the robot's behaviour with (x-axis) in relation to the robot's actual expressed emotions (y-axis).

4   Conclusion and Future Works

The main interest of our research is to use personalised emotional expressions for robots to communicate complex internal and external robots' (decisional and behavioural) processes to the users. In particular, we are interested in investigating how to develop emotionally expressive learning robots which actions are legible and helps in achieving transparency of the internal state.

We believed, inspired by the finding of previous studies [2], that emotions can be an effective and transparent solution for communicating the state of the learning process to users. For this reason, in this study, we explore the legibility and predictability of robots' intentions and beliefs (i.e. internal decision-making process, and understanding of people's response) through emotional expressions.

We asked individuals of different ages, gender, background and experience with robots to classify the emotions expressed by the robot in the video-clips according to their level of arousal, valence and discrete emotions. We observed that participants were able to differentiate the emotions according to a dimensional representation (arousal and valence) in the case of having the tablet showing the icon with the emotional "face" of the robot, and that the evaluation was in line with the expected interpretation. This finding is in line with the results observed by Zhang and Sharkey [20]. This further highlights how powerful is facial emotional communication for meeting people's expectations. The only exception is for the Fear behaviour that has to be re-designed.

Moreover, the intended levels of arousal were not correctly perceived. This is also in line with other studies showing that small modifications of non-verbal cues are hardly identified by the subjects [14]. Hence, in the case of a necessity to modulate emotions' arousal more evident differences are needed.

The findings of this exploratory study will be used to further investigate whether robots can express emotions that intrinsically represent their current state in real-world scenarios.

References

1. Betella, A., Verschure, P.: The affective slider: a digital self-assessment scale for the measurement of human emotions. PLoS ONE **11**, e0148037 (2016)
2. Broekens, J.: A temporal difference reinforcement learning theory of emotion: unifying emotion, cognition and adaptive behavior (2018)
3. Broekens, J., Chetouani, M.: Towards transparent robot learning through TDRL-based emotional expressions. IEEE Trans. Affect. Comput. **12**(2), 352–362 (2021)
4. Ekman, P.: Basic Emotions. Dalgleish, T., Power, M. (eds.) (1999)
5. Frijda, N.H., Mesquita, B.: The Social Roles and Functions of Emotions. American Psychological Association, Washington, DC (1994)
6. Gosling, S.D., Rentfrow, P.J., Swann, W.B.J.: A very brief measure of the big five personality domains. J. Res. Pers. **37**, 504–528 (2003)
7. Gunning, D., Aha, D.: DARPA's explainable artificial intelligence (Xai) program. AI Mag. **40**(2), 44–58 (2019)
8. Kron, A., Goldstein, A., Lee, D., Gardhouse, K., Anderson, A.: How are you feeling? Revisiting the quantification of emotional qualia. Psychol. Sci. **24**, 1503–1511 (2013)
9. Löffler, D., Schmidt, N., Tscharn, R.: Multimodal expression of artificial emotion in social robots using color, motion and sound. In: Proceedings of the 2018 ACM/IEEE International Conference on Human-Robot Interaction, pp. 334–343 (2018)
10. Marmpena, M., Lim, A., Dahl, T.S.: How does the robot feel? Perception of valence and arousal in emotional body language. Paladyn, J. Behav. Robot. **9**(1), 168–182 (2018)
11. Matarese, M., Rossi, S., Sciutti, A., Rea, F.: Towards transparency of TD-RL robotic systems with a human teacher (2020)
12. Rossi, A., Dautenhahn, K., Koay, K.L., Walters, M.L.: A study on how the timing and magnitude of robot errors may influence people trust of robots in an emergency scenario. In: International Conference on Social Robotics (ICSR). Springer, Tsukuba (2017)
13. Rossi, A., Dautenhahn, K., Koay, K.L., Walters, M.L.: The impact of peoples' personal dispositions and personalities on their trust of robots in an emergency scenario. Paladyn J. Behav. Robot. **9**, 137–154 (2018)
14. Rossi, S., D'Alterio, P.: Gaze behavioral adaptation towards group members for providing effective recommendations. In: Social Robotics, pp. 231–241. Springer, Cham (2017)
15. Rossi, S., Rossi, A., Dautenhahn, K.: The secret life of robots: perspectives and challenges for robot's behaviours during non-interactive tasks. Int. J. Soc. Robot. **12**, 1265–1278 (2020)
16. Rossi, S., Ruocco, M.: Better alone than in bad company: effects of incoherent non-verbal emotional cues for a humanoid robot. Interact. Stud. **20**(3), 487–508 (2019)

17. Schindler, S., Vormbrock, R., Kissler, J.: Emotion in context: how sender predictability and identity affect processing of words as imminent personality feedback. Front. Psychol. **10**, 94 (2019)
18. Sutton, T., Altarriba, J.: Color associations to emotion and emotion-laden words: a collection of norms for stimulus construction and selection. Behav. Res. Meth. **48**, 686–728 (2015). https://doi.org/10.3758/s13428-015-0598-8
19. Watson, D., Clark, L., Tellegen, A.: Development and validation of brief measures of positive and negative affect: the panas scales. J. Pers. Soc. Psychol. **54**(6), 1063–70 (1988)
20. Zhang, J., Sharkey, A.J.C.: Contextual recognition of robot emotions. In: Groß, R., Alboul, L., Melhuish, C., Witkowski, M., Prescott, T.J., Penders, J. (eds.) Towards Autonomous Robotic Systems, pp. 78–89. Springer, Heidelberg (2011)

Rehabilitation and Therapy

Social Robots for Older Adults with Dementia: A Narrative Review on Challenges & Future Directions

Daniel Woods[1] (ID), Fengpei Yuan[1](✉) (ID), Ying-Ling Jao[2], and Xiaopeng Zhao[1] (ID)

[1] University of Tennessee, Knoxville, TN 37996, USA
{dwoods21,fyuan6}@vols.utk.edu, xzhao9@utk.edu
[2] Pennsylvania State University, University Park, PA 16802, USA
yuj15@psu.edu

Abstract. Worldwide, approximately 50 million people live with Alzheimer's disease or other dementias and there are nearly 10 million new cases every year. Social robots have been a promising approach to supplement human caregivers in dementia care. In this narrative review, we reviewed 62 articles to gain insight into the attitudes and perceptions among people with dementia and other stakeholders worldwide towards using social robots to assist dementia care. Then, we discussed some critical factors and challenges found in these studies influencing people's perceptions as well as future directions in this field. The primary influencing challenges include cultural factors, users' limited experiences with technologies, methodological challenges underlying qualitative studies as well as technological malfunctions in current robot system. We further suggested several aspects to be taken into more consideration in future research, including collaborations with other stakeholders, design of individual or group use for dementia care, an adaptive level of autonomy in a social robot and long-term human-robot interaction.

Keywords: Social robots · Dementia care · Human-robot interaction

1 Introduction

According to the World Alzheimer Report 2018 [39], there were 50 million people worldwide living with dementia, with one new case of dementia every 3 s. Alzheimer's disease is the most common form of dementia, contributing to 60–70% of cases. On the other hand, the proportion of related healthcare professionals to the elderly population has become smaller, with many care homes and extended living communities becoming increasingly understaffed worldwide [9]. With these apparent challenges faced by the dementia care and the struggling battle against clinical treatments of Alzheimer's disease or other dementias, a more direct form of care has been approached with the investigation of robots [64], and more specifically social robots. These social robots aim to not only assist individuals with dementia, but also to ease the burden of their caregivers who are often overwhelmed with the caregiving tasks for those with cognitive impairment [2], as the example shown in Fig. 1.

© Springer Nature Switzerland AG 2021
H. Li et al. (Eds.): ICSR 2021, LNAI 13086, pp. 411–420, 2021.
https://doi.org/10.1007/978-3-030-90525-5_35

Fig. 1. A social robot, Pepper, interacting with a person with Alzheimer's and his wife.

A social robot is defined as a system with a degree of autonomy operated with the purpose of both interacting and communicating with humans as well as other systems to fulfill its role, generally in a natural and personable way that follows social behaviors [46]. The goals are to support health education, enhance communication, promote patients' health outcomes, and improve their quality of life. Regarding the applications in Alzheimer's care, social robots have been used in recreational activities [1, 14], reminders for medications and daily tasks [20], and encouraging physical activity [31]. The aim of the present review is to gain insight into the attitude and perceptions among people with dementia and other stakeholders worldwide towards using social robots for dementia care, and the primary factors influencing the perception of robots for dementia care. In this paper, we conducted a narrative review in the databases of Google Scholar and PubMed using the keywords ("Social robot") AND ("Acceptance" OR "Perception" OR "Attitude") AND ("Elderly" OR "older adults") AND (Alzheimer's disease OR "Dementia" OR "MCI"). The search was limited to the articles published since 2005. Finally, a total of 59 eligible articles, theses, and conference proceedings [1, 2, 4–20, 22–38, 40–45, 47–59, 61–63, 65] were reviewed to investigate the worldwide perception of social robots as modes of assistance to older adults with dementia, the main factors and challenges influencing the perception, as well as future directions in this field.

2   Results

2.1   Cultural Factors

Culture is a significant factor found in the literature influencing people's attitude and perception towards social robots for Alzheimer's care. Generally, from media influence, different cultural regions and countries develop various attitudes and percep-tions towards social robots for ADRD care [9]. Perceptions of robots between Japan, Italy, Germany, UK, and US were all varied [38, 41, 49]. Oftentimes, these studies were limited by the acceptance of social robots in older adults, specifically because of cultural bias from that region [38]. Some countries such as Japan and the Netherlands have largely applied robots into daily life, while the society in the US and Italy did not have such high acceptance towards social robots [41, 49]. Some sociocultural factors in Western societies may explain this reluctance when compared to Japan, for example, one might be robot aversion, influenced by science fiction, and arguably rooted in Judeo-Christian beliefs that associate the creation of 'human-like' creatures to an act of hubris [3]. Studies also showed the limitation of cross-cultural biases. Many of these studies only investigated the perceptions and attitude towards social robots for Alzheimer's care in one single region or country. There is no "one-size-fits-all" in Alzheimer's care. There are a multitude of factors to influence an individual's acceptance and perception of social robots. Future research may further explore the cultural factors that influence acceptance of social robots. Consequently, social robots would need to be adapted to these influencing factors to better fit individual countries, regions, and cultures, e.g., physical appearance, language, and functions [54, 63, 64].

2.2 Previous Exposure to Technologies

Another common limitation among these papers is previous exposure to technologies, such as smartphones, tablets, computers, and social robots. In many studies, participants were shown a video of a robot operated or allowed to interact with the robot personally, then answered a subsequent survey regarding their perceptions and attitudes of the robot [6]. However, the majority of these participants had never interacted with any social robot before, given their age. This oftentimes resulted in experimenters needing to prompt users, or the users altogether not using the robot to its full capacity. Also, individuals' experience with other technologies, such as smartphone, tablets, and computers, made a drastic difference in their perceptions and attitudes towards social robots. This previous experience issue can be negated by more education and interaction on social robots in general. Noticeably, as time passes and the current middle-aged population reaches the elderly population, they will generally have more experience using not only technologies like smartphones and tablets but possibly robots. Another issue of previous experience with robots is that many times users would conflate their cultural biases with their personal interaction of the social robot. For example, some American participants in the studies due to their minimal experience with social robots and their cultural perceptions, would not interact with the robot in the scope that it was designed to, oftentimes downplaying its abilities. One possible way to overcome this limitation would be to provide education and training on robot use, allow participants to interact with the robot for a longer period, or allow participants to have the robot in their living space for a period of several weeks [47]. In one study [10] where the social robot was implemented into individuals living spaces for periods of 10 weeks or longer, it found increased interaction as well as acceptance from the users. It is also important that the time spent with the robots during the testing period is utilized effectively during these investigations. For example, during a study in which the users had a group conversation facilitated by a social robot, the usability was rated relatively low [8], but in studies involving the use of daily activities and the robot meeting the needs of the elderly, the effect of age on levels of acceptance was diminished [6].

2.3 Methodological Challenges

Because conducting a survey study with individuals with dementia is more difficult, many of these studies examined caregivers' opinions instead, as the proxy of individuals with dementia [54]. The survey was conducted in a structured and/or less-structured way [12, 14], the latter one allowing the users to answer in an open-ended format. A limitation to this is that qualitative research is difficult to generate concrete results, with significant interpretation of responses being required. Several studies focusing on the use of social robots for older adults with cognitive impairment heavily relied on caregiver review, depending on the severity of the user's impairment [54]. In one study, a teleoperated robot was used to assess the worsening or stabilization of user's symptoms given interaction with the robot operated by different personnel, finding the severe dementia symptoms for some users did not worsen following the interaction [8].

2.4 Technological Malfunctions

Additionally, technological malfunctions are unfortunately a large limitation to many of the studies in this review. During testing phases, many trials had to either remove certain tests or have experimenters do malfunction maintenance on site to ensure the robot functioned proper [11]. This is a very common problem for nearly any technological research involved in a clinical setting. There will always be some degree of error that requires maintenance even up to the point of testing. However, for the social robotic application specifically for dementia care, the robots will need to operate largely autonomously because of the average users experience with technology being relatively little [60]. The technological errors that were common in these papers came from environmental readings and human recognition generally. Some examples of these errors were facial recognition, voice recognition, image recall, and conversational utility [13].

3 Discussion and Conclusions

3.1 User Acceptance and Perception

One of the main suggestions for further development of social robots for dementia care fall under user acceptance, perceived usefulness (PU), and perceived ease of use (PEOU). As noted in previous studies concerning the effectiveness of social robots, the users' satisfaction is paramount to the system's ability. Subsequently, the measurement of robot acceptance, usefulness, and other user perception attributes [21] must be standardized for the future of this field. Doing so would allow different robot models to undergo multivariate analysis with different cognitive conditions. As for designating a standard of measuring the PU, system usability scale (SUS) has often been used across the reviewed publications to assess the system usability. Several studies noted aspects of social robots that could be improved upon according to the users, the most commonly referenced being a voice's accent if present [30]. Participants in several studies had complaints of robots' voice not being "friendly" enough or speaking with an accent that was difficult to understand [30]. It infers that a social robot with a voice of regional dialects of languages, or a more informal conversation in terms of word choice or accent, would subsequently have higher rates of acceptance [63]. Techniques like focus groups are also an effective method for users to talk about their perceptions of the social robots, organizing their thoughts through a facilitated discussion [1]. Lastly, another future direction to consider is the differences of acceptance, PU, PEOU as well as effectiveness in people with dementia when the social robot is assessed in an individual versus group setting.

3.2 Collaborations with Caregivers

Another highly important area of this field of research is the ability for social robots to ease the burden of caregivers for individuals with ADRD. As described previously, the strain that caregivers face is becoming increasingly greater as the disease progresses. Several studies in this review surveyed home care professionals, health care professionals, extended living care staff, and others in the field to gauge their perceptions and acceptance on the utilization of social robots for their field of care [54]. These surveys often displayed a video of the robot at hand being used, and subsequently asked the participants questions on their willingness to use the system and their perceived usefulness [2]. These caregivers are primarily responsible for ensuring not only the safety but also wellbeing of individuals with ADRD, so the perceptions and feedback from the caregiver perspective is also vital to ensure a proper orientation of the design, development, and implementation of social robots for dementia care. Otherwise, inadequate information on the requirement and purpose of robots may lead to unrealistic expectations and unmet needs [54].

3.3 Design of Individual or Group Use

Additionally, the condition of a robot being used, i.e., individual or group setting, is needed to take into consideration during the design and development of social robots for dementia care. The target users (e.g., in term of cognitive capacity and living environment) and requirements in these two conditions may be different. Consequently, the functions and social intelligence underlying the robot to support its individual and group interaction may be different. For example, Valentí Soler et al. [57] employed the group and individual sessions for people with mild or mild-moderate dementia and people with moderate-severe and severe dementia, respectively. Some studies [12] particularly targeted at the elderly with no, low or mild cognitive deficits but able to live independently, and accordingly developed the robot to interact with the user one by one. In another study [10] of developing robot for elderly people at home, users living alone perceived the robot to be "someone to talk to" and "waiting for me at home when I get back", with some users even disappointed that they would no longer have the robot around at the end of the study. This suggests that a social robot designed for individual use needs to particularly pay close attention to an individual's feelings, which becomes of great value given nowadays more residents expressed higher levels of loneliness, due to the outbreak of COVID-19 and the subsequent lockdown of elderly care homes worldwide. In addition, it points out the need for future implications of social robots having the ability to be operated effectively for both individual and group use, in other words, the capability of robot being able to interact with an individual person with dementia or a group of people with dementia.

3.4 Adaptive Level of Autonomy in Social Robots

The level of autonomy in a social robot is another consideration during the design of social robots for Alzheimer's care. In the papers reviewed, researchers have studied the performance of teleoperated robot (e.g., a caregiver-controlled robot [8], an autonomous robotic platform [10], and both [7, 35]. On average, autonomous robots relieved more caregiver burden and allowed a person with ADRD to operate with the robot more freely. However, autonomous social robots seemed to have relatively lower levels of acceptance, given the users felt more comfortable when there was a family member or a caregiver operating the robot [28]. Additionally, for people with ADRD living alone, an autonomous robot did not help lower the individuals' levels of loneliness as the extent that a teleoperated robot did [7]. As for caregiver operated platforms, the perceived benefits were apparent in that the users were able to have eased communication with either their caregiver or family member, although this type of robots requires the operator to be more present for the user, not alleviating caregiver burden to the degree that an autonomous social robot is able to do. These benefits and downsides to robots with different level of autonomy suggest that the capability of adaptive autonomy in social robots, which incorporates both aspects of an autonomous and remotely operated robot, would be useful for Alzheimer's care.

3.5 Social Robots for Long-Term Interaction

Another key aspect to focus on this field is longer interaction periods with persons with ADRD. Many of the studies reviewed consisted of either focus groups lasting from 15 min to an hour, and occasional individual sessions with a social robot that lasted around the same time [43]. There were some case studies that allowed the users to live and interact with the social robot for months at a time [7], but these studies only gathered data for one user. In survey studies, many times the participants were only shown pictures or videos of the robot operated [23, 41], which is not ideal for gathering data on the acceptance, PU, or PEOU of the social robot. It is suggested to conduct more read-world tests where the social robot could be placed in a care home or an individual's home for weeks or even months at a time. This would allow for individuals with ADRD to have personal interaction with the robot and then learn their more in-depth feedback on the robot.

References

1. Appel, L., Peisachovich, E., Sinclair, D., Jokel, R., Da Silva, C.: SafeHome: a serious game to promote safe environments for persons living with dementia. Cureus **12**(2), e6949 (2020)
2. Arthanat, S., Begum, M., Gu, T., LaRoche, D.P., Xu, D., Zhang, N.: Caregiver perspectives on a smart home-based socially assistive robot for individuals with Alzheimer's disease and related dementia. Disability and Rehabilitation: Assistive Technology, pp. 789–798 (2020)
3. Aymerich-Franch, L.: Why it is time to stop ostracizing social robots. Nat. Mach. Intell. **2**(7), 364 (2020)
4. Bartl, A., Bosch, S., Brandt, M., Dittrich, M., Lugrin, B.: The influence of a social robot's persona on how it is perceived and accepted by elderly users. In: International Conference on Social Robotics, pp. 681–691. Social Robotics, Kansas (2016)
5. Boumans, R.J.: Feasibility and Effectiveness of Social Robots in Acquiring Patient Reported Outcomes from Older Adults, p. 231. Radboud University (2020)
6. Cavallo, F., et al.: Robotic services acceptance in smart environments with older adults: user satisfaction and acceptability study. J. Med. Int. Res. **20**(9), e264 (2018)

7. Cesta, A., Cortellessa, G., Orlandini, A., Tiberio, L.: Long-term evaluation of a telepresence robot for the elderly: methodology and ecological case study. Int. J. Soc. Robot. **8**(3), 421–441 (2016)
8. Chen, L.-Y., Sumioka, H., Ke, L.-J., Shiomi, M., Chen, L.-K.: Effects of teleoperated humanoid robot application in older adults with neurocognitive disorders in Taiwan: a report of three cases. Aging Med. Healthc. **11**(2), 67–71 (2020)
9. Coco, K., Kangasniemi, M., Rantanen, T.: Care personnel's attitudes and fears toward care robots in elderly care: a comparison of data from the care personnel in Finland and Japan. J. Nurs. Scholarship **50**(6), 634–644 (2018)
10. Coşar, S., et al.: ENRICHME: perception and interaction of an assistive robot for the elderly at home. Int. J. Soc. Robot. **12**(3), 779–805 (2020)
11. Damholdt, M., et al.: Attitudinal change in elderly citizens toward social robots: the role of personality traits and beliefs about robot functionality. Front. Psychol. (2015). https://doi.org/10.3389/fpsyg.2015.01701
12. Di Nuovo, A., et al.: The multi modal interface of Robot Era multi robot services tailored for the elderly. Intel. Serv. Robot. **11**(1), 109–126 (2017)
13. Do, H.M., Sheng, W., Harrington, E.E., Bishop, A.J.: Clinical screening interview using a social robot for geriatric care. IEEE Trans. Automat. Sci. Eng. **18**(3), 1229–1242 (2021)
14. Doi, T., Kuwahara, N., Morimoto, K.: Questionnaire survey result of the use of communication robots for recreational activities at nursing homes. In: Chung, W.J., Shin, C.S. (eds.) Advances in Affective and Pleasurable Design, pp. 3–13. Springer, Cham (2017). https://doi.org/10.1007/978-3-319-41661-8_1
15. D'Onofio, G., et al.: MARIO project: a multicenter survey about companion robot acceptability in caregivers of patients with dementia. Italian Forum of Ambient Assisted Living, Genova (2017)
16. Faucounau, V., Ya-Huei, W., Boulay, M., Maestrutti, M., Rigaud, A.-S.: Caregivers' requirements for in-home robotic agent for supporting community-living elderly subjects with cognitive impairment. Technol. Health Care **17**(1), 33–40 (2009)
17. Feng, Z., et al.: Long-term care system for older adults in China: policy landscape, challenges, and future prospects. The Lancet **396**(10259), 1362–1372 (2020)
18. Griese, S.: A robot for the elderly? A qualitative research on the acceptance of NAO robots in elderly care. Maastricht University, Department of Psychology and Neuroscience (2015)
19. Hanson, S.T., Anderson, H.J., Bak, T.: Practical evaluation of robots for elderly in Denmark — an overview. In: ACM/IEEE International Conference on Human-Robot Interaction (HRI). IEEE, Osaka (2010)
20. Harmo, P., Taipalus, T., Knuuttila, J., Vallet, J., Halme, A.: Needs and Solutions - Home Automation and Service Robots for the Elderly and Disabled. IEEE/RSJ International Conference on Intelligent Robots and Systems, Edmonton (2005)
21. Heerink, M.B.: Assessing acceptance of assistive social agent technology by older adults: the almere model. Int. J. Soc. Robot. **2**, 361–375 (2010)
22. Heernik, M., Krose, B.J., Evers, V., Wielinga, B.J.: Studying the acceptance of a robotic agent by elderly users. Int. J. Model. Ident. Control 33–43 (2006)
23. Johansson-Pajala, R.-M., et al.: Care robot orientation: what, who and how? Potential users' perceptions. Int. J. Soc. Robot. **12**(5), 1103–1117 (2020)
24. Kazuko, O., Naonori, K., Shigeru, M.: Can connected technologies improve sleep quality and safety of older adults and caregivers? An evaluation study of sleep monitors and communicative robots at a residential care home in Japan. In: Technology in Society (2020)
25. Ke, C., Lou, V.W.-Q., Tan, K.C.-K., Wai, M.Y., Chan, L.L.: Changes in technology acceptance among older people with dementia: the role of social robot engagement. Int. J. Med. Inf. **141**, 104241 (2020)

26. Khosla, R., Nguyen, K., Chu, M.-T.: Human robot engagement and acceptability in residential aged care. Int. J. Human–Comput. Interact. **33**(6), 510–522 (2017)
27. Kim, G., Jeon, H., Park, S., Choi, Y., Lim, Y.: Care guide system for caregivers of people with dementia*. In: IEEE Engineering in Medicine & Biology (EMBC). IEEE, Montreal (2020)
28. Koceski, S., Koceska, N.: Evaluation of an assistive telepresence robot for elderly healthcare. J. Med. Syst. **40**(5), 1–7 (2016)
29. Korchut, A., et al.: Challenges for service robots—requirements of elderly adults with cognitive impairments. Front. Neurol. Neurodegen. (2017)
30. Law, M., et al.: Developing assistive robots for people with mild cognitive impairment and mild dementia: a qualitative study with older adults and experts in aged care. BMJ Open **9**(9), e031937 (2019)
31. Lin, X., Saksono, H., Stowell, E., Lachman, M.E., Castaneda-Sceppa, C., Parker, A.G.: Go&Grow: an evaluation of a pervasive social exergame for caregivers of loved ones with dementia. ACM on Human-Computer Interaction. Association for Computing Machinery (2020)
32. Łukasik, S., Tobis, S., Kropińska, S., Suwalska, A.: Role of assistive robots in the care of older people: survey study among medical and nursing students. J. Med. Internet Res. **22**(8), e18003 (2020)
33. Manca, M., et al.: The impact of serious games with humanoid robots on mild cognitive impairment older adults. Int. J. Human-Comput. Stud. **145**, 102509 (2021)
34. Manca, M., et al.: The impact of serious games with humanoid robots on mild cognitive impairment older adults. Int. J. Human-Comput. Stud. (2020)
35. Mast, M., et al.: User-centered design of a dynamic-autonomy remote interaction concept for manipulation-capable robots to assist elderly people in the home. J. Human-Robot Interact. (2012)
36. Mucchiani, C., Cacchione, P., Torres, W., Johnson, M.J., Yim, M.: Exploring low-cost mobile manipulation for elder care within a community based setting. J. Intell. Rob. Syst. **98**(1), 59–70 (2019)
37. Nomura, T., Kanda, T., Suzuki, T., Kato, K.: Age differences and images of robots: social survey in Japan. Interact. Stud. Soc. Behav. Commun. Biol. Artif. Syst. **10**(3), 374–391 (2009)
38. Papadopoulos, C., et al.: The CARESSES study protocol: testing and evaluating culturally competent socially assistive robots among older adults residing in long term care homes through a controlled experimental trial. Archiv. Publ. Health (2020). https://doi.org/10.1186/s13690-020-00409-y
39. Patterson, C.: World Alzheimer Report 2018. Alzheimer's Disease International, London (2018)
40. Peterson, C.M., Mikal, J.P., McCarron, H.R., Finlay, J.M., Mitchell, L.L., Gaugler, J.E.: The feasibility and utility of a personal health record for persons with dementia and their family caregivers for web-based care coordination: mixed methods study. J. Med. Internet Res.: Aging (2020)
41. Pigini, L., Facal, D., Blasi, L., Andrich, R.: Service robots in elderly care at home: users' needs and perceptions as a basis for concept development. Technol. Disabil. **24**(4), 303–311 (2012)
42. Raghunath, N., Pereyda, C., Frow, J.F., Cook, D., Schmitter-Edgecomb, M.: Learning-enabled robotic assistive support: understanding older adult opinions and comparing them to younger adult opinions. Gerontechnol. Int. J. Fundam. Aspect. Technol. Serve The Ageing Soc. **19**(3) (2020)
43. Rico, F.M., Rodríguez-Lera, F.J., Clavero, J.G., Guerrero-Higueras, Á.M., Olivera, V.M.: An Acceptance Test for Assistive Robots. Human-Robot Interaction and Sensors for Social Robotics (2020).

44. Sadegh Khaksar, S.M., Jahanshahi, A.A., Slade, B.W., Asian, S.S.: A dual-factor theory of WTs adoption in aged care service operations -a cross-country analysis. Inf. Technol. People (2020)
45. Salichs, M.A., et al.: Mini: a new social robot for the elderly. Int. J. Soc. Robot. **12**(6), 1231–1249 (2020)
46. Sarrica, M.S.: How many facets does a "social robot" have? A review of scientific and popular definitions online. Inf. Technol. People (2019)
47. Schüssler, S., et al.: The effects of a humanoid socially assistive robot versus tablet training on psychosocial and physical outcomes of persons with dementia: protocol for a mixed methods study. JMIR Res. Protoc. (2020)
48. Seifert, L.S., Kaelber, K., Flaherty, K., Bowman, T.: Experiences in Alzheimer's disease: what do stakeholders post on the internet? J. Psych. Res. Cybersp.: Cyberpsychol. (2020)
49. Shibata, T.: Therapeutic seal robot as biofeedback medical device: qualitative and quantitative evaluations of robot therapy in dementia care. In: IEEE International Conference on Information Science and Technology, pp. 2527–2538. IEEE, Wuhan (2012)
50. Shibata, T., Wada, K.: Robot therapy: a new approach for mental healthcare of the elderly – a mini-review. Gerontology **57**(4), 378–386 (2011)
51. Spalla, G., Gouin-Vallerand, C., Yaddaden, A., Bier, N.: Towards an augmented reality cognitive orthosis to assist people with Alzheimer's disease: preliminary design. In: International Conference on Smart Objects and Technologies for Social Good, pp. 60–65 (2020)
52. Sriram, V., Jenkinson, C., Peters, M.: Carers' experiences of assistive technology use in dementia care: a cross sectional survey (in review). BMC Geriatrics (2020)
53. Suwa, S., et al.: Home-care professionals' ethical perceptions of the development and use of home-care robots for older adults in Japan. Int. J. Human–Comput. Interact. **36**(14), 1295–1303 (2020)
54. Suwa, S., et al.: Exploring perceptions toward home-care robots for older people in Finland, Ireland, and Japan: a comparative questionnaire study. Archiv. Gerontol. Geriatr. **91**, 104178 (2020)
55. Torta, E., et al.: Evaluation of a small socially-assistive humanoid robot in intelligent homes for the care of the elderly. J. Intell. Robot. Syst. **76**(1), 57–71 (2014)
56. Tsujimura, M., et al.: The essential needs for home-care robots in Japan. J. Enabl. Technol. **14**(4), 201–220 (2020)
57. Valentí Soler, M., et al.: Social robots in advanced dementia. Front. Aging Neurosci. **7**, 133 (2015)
58. van Kemenade, M.: Moral Concerns of Caregivers about Social Robots in Eldercare, p. 161. Vrije Universiteit Amsterdam, Amsterdam (2020)
59. von der Pütten, A.M., Krämer, N.C.: A survey on robot appearances. In: 2012 7th ACM/IEEE International Conference on Human-Robot Interaction (HRI), pp. 267–268. IEEE (2012)
60. Whelan, S., Murphy, K., Barrett, E., Krusche, C., Santorelli, A., Casey, D.: Factors affecting the acceptability of social robots by older adults including people with dementia or cognitive impairment: a literature review. Int. J. Soc. Robot. **10**(5), 643–668 (2018)
61. Wilson, G., et al.: Robot-Enabled Support of Daily Activities in Smart Home Environments. Cognit. Syst. Res. (2018)
62. Wu, Y.-H., Fassert, C., Rigaud, A.-S.: Designing robots for the elderly: appearance issue and beyond. Archiv. Gerontol. Geriatr. **54**(1), 121–126 (2012)
63. Yuan, F., et al.: Assessing the acceptability of a humanoid robot for Alzheimer's disease and related dementia care using an online survey (2021). https://arxiv.org/abs/2104.12903

64. Yuan, F., Klavon, E., Liu, Z., Lopez, R.P., Zhao, X.: A systematic review of robotic rehabilitation for cognitive training. Front. Robot. AI **8**, 105 (2021)
65. Zhang, Y., Chignell, M.H.: Flattening the curve of cognitive decline: a survey of cognitive interventions for people living with dementia (a review). In: International Symposium on Human Factors and Ergonomics in Health Care, pp. 110–114. Sage Journals, London (2020)

Using Plantar Pressure and Machine Learning to Automatically Evaluate Strephenopodia for Rehabilitation Exoskeleton: A Pilot Study

Jinjin Nong, Zikang Zhou, Xiaoming Xian, Guowei Huang, Peiwen Li, and Longhan Xie[✉]

Shien-Ming Wu School of Intelligent Engineering, South China University of Technology, Guangzhou 510640, China
melhxie@scut.edu.cn

Abstract. Stroke patients often suffer from strephenopodia, which seriously affects their walking ability and rehabilitation. However, lower limb rehabilitation robots lack the evaluation and automatic correction function of strephenopodia. There are practical demands for convenient, automatic, and quantitative assessments of the angle of strephenopodia to adjust the orthopedic strength in time to remind stroke patients to use their muscles to realize the movements. In this study, we proposed a novel methodology for automatically predicting the angles of strephenopodia based on a plantar pressure system using machine learning methods. Three machine learning methods were implemented to build stochastic function mapping from gait features to strephenopodia angles, showing good reliability and precision prediction of the strephenopodia angle [determination coefficient (R^2) ≥ 0.80]. Results showed that our method is convenient to implement and outperforms previous methods in accuracy. Therefore, measurements derived from the plantar pressure system are proper estimators of the strephenopodia angle and are beneficial to lower limb rehabilitation exoskeleton for stroke population training.

Keywords: Stroke · Strephenopodia · Plantar pressure · Machine learning

1 Introduction

Stroke is one of the top leading causes of adult disability in the world [1], and 80% of stroke patients tend to experience different degrees of walking obstacles [2]. To improve the rehabilitation of lower limb, lower limb rehabilitation robots are used for patients' training. Strephenopodia is one of the most common sequelae of stroke, which seriously affects the patient's rehabilitation and daily life [2–4]. However, current lower limb rehabilitation robots lack the evaluation and automatic correction function of strephenopodia. To achieve effective rehabilitation, it is necessary to detect the degree of varus in real-time for patients using their muscles to train themselves to walk properly [5–7]. If the

---

J. Nong, Z. Zhou—Equal contribution

© Springer Nature Switzerland AG 2021
H. Li et al. (Eds.): ICSR 2021, LNAI 13086, pp. 421–431, 2021.
https://doi.org/10.1007/978-3-030-90525-5_36

muscles are not exercised because the foot rests on top of a comfortable orthotic shape, they would lose strength, and consequently, protective shock absorption, efficient gait [8], and other complex functions [9] become impaired. This highlights the necessity to automatically monitor the angle of strephenopodia, according to which a rehabilitation exoskeleton is used to assist the patient in correcting the strephenopodia for effective rehabilitation.

Typical approaches for the detection of strephenopodia include traditional clinical gait analysis, gait video analysis, and plantar pressure systems [5]. Traditional gait analysis method [10] is mostly used for monitoring and providing feedback about strephenopodia in the clinic. This observational method relies on the observer's skill and clinical experience, and it is inconvenient to operate and cannot be recorded in real-time. This method does not meet the requirements for lower limb rehabilitation robots. Gait video analysis is another method for strephenopodia evaluation. Computer vision [11], 3D kinematic analysis in vivo [4, 12], and optoelectronic stereophotogrammetry in vivo [13] were applied in patients with foot pathologies. This method is expensive and complex, which makes timely adjustment of the method inconvenient.

Since the acquisition of plantar pressure is simple and noninvasive, it has been widely used in detecting and monitoring gait patterns [14–16]. In a previous report [3], smart textile socks with five integrated pressure sensors were used for pronation and supination detection. Another study [5] utilized a pressure-sensitive insole to detect foot pronation in real-time, and feedback provided to the user reduced pronation significantly. These methods are proven to be effective in detecting pronation and are relatively low cost. However, they are only able to detect whether foot pronation exists and cannot quantitatively determine the specificity and subtlety of foot pronation.

In this paper, a novel strephenopodia angle prediction method was proposed to provide a reference for exoskeleton-assisted rehabilitation. We collected a data set that consisted of plantar pressure distribution data and lower limb motion from 30 participants. Then, we fitted a Gaussian process regression (GPR) model to the data set. Experimental results indicate that our method can predict the foot supination angle with high precision. We also provide a performance comparison between the GPR and other regression models. The method can be used to provide real-time feedback to the rehabilitation exoskeleton.

2   Data Collection and Preprocessing

Thirty healthy participants (25 males and 5 females) with no history of neurological or mobility impairments participated in the experiments. All participants provided informed consent, and the experimental procedures were approved by the Research Ethics Board of South China University of Technology. Table 1 provides summary information about the participants.

Table 1. The distribution of participants' characteristics

Characteristics	Mean ± SD
Age (years)	22.83 ± 2.83
Height (cm)	169.81 ± 7.38
Weight (kg)	64.21 ± 12.54

2.1 Experimental Setup

As shown in Fig. 1, the experimental setup included three parts: a Zebris FDM-THM Treadmill (Zebris Medical GmbH, Germany) for measuring the plantar pressure distribution, wedge-shaped blocks for simulating strephenopodia conditions, and a Vicon Motion Capture System for capturing lower limb motion.

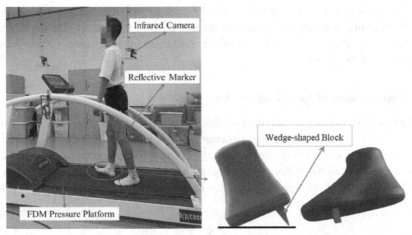

Fig. 1. Experimental platform with the Zebris FDM-THM Treadmill and Vicon Motion Capture System. The sampling rate of Zebris Treadmill is set to 120 Hz. The Vicon Motion Capture System consists of 8 infrared cameras, the sampling rate is set to 250 Hz. The wedge-shaped blocks are stuck to the first metatarsal area to form a specific angle to imitate varus conditions.

We designed three wedge-shaped blocks with different heights. In the experiment, the blocks were stuck under the forefoot to simulate different strephenopodia conditions. The higher the block, the more severe the simulated foot supination. Participants walked at self-selected speeds on the treadmill under 4 different conditions. In the first condition, the participants walked freely with no block; then, for the other three conditions, blocks with different heights were stuck to the first metatarsal area of the medial forefoot of the right foot. We asked the participants to keep the blocks close to the ground as much as possible but not to touch the treadmill belt to ensure a certain angle when walking, which imitates the different degrees of strephenopodia conditions.

We attached 16 reflective markers to the subject in a way described in the reference. The Vicon system captures the trajectories of these 16 reflective markers, which will be used to calculate joint kinematics later. Gait patterns are represented by lower limb joint trajectories: ankle adduction/abduction on the coronal plane, mainly referring to strephenopodia, and other joint rotations are not considered.

2.2 Experimental Procedure

First, we asked all subjects to participate in an adaptation-familiarization trial to obtain a self-selected walking speed and adapt and maintain the inversion angle. Starting at a fixed speed of 0.5 km/h, the treadmill speed was increased by 0.2 km/h every 10 s. Once the participant informed the tester of the speed that best characterized his/her normal walking pace, that was determined as his/her comfortable speed. After this adaptation phase, each participant was asked to walk continuously for approximately 2 min on a treadmill at his/her comfortable speed for each walking model while wearing socks. When a stable walking speed was reached, motion capture data were recorded synchronously with the treadmill for 30 s.

All subjects performed four types of walking motions with their right foot. Each walking model recorded 8 groups of data, 30 s per group. All subjects were asked to simulate common post stroke strephenopodia movements, which included the flexion of the affected toe, the anterolateral edge of the plantar, and the inclination angle between the plantar and the ground.

2.3 Preprocessing of Joint Trajectories

All the raw gait trajectories obtained by the Vicon system need to go through a series of processes. 1) Remove invalid gait patterns caused by marker occlusions. 2) Split gait sequence into gait cycles to obtain the average of the minimum value of each gait cycle for ankle flexion/extension because we found that in the support phase, the varus foot was relatively smaller throughout the gait cycle. 3) Calculate the average of the minimum right ankle value of each gait cycle:

$$y_i = \frac{1}{n}\sum\nolimits_{j=1}^{n} y_j, \tag{1}$$

where n is the number of gait cycles, y_j is the minimum value of the right ankle angle throughout the j-th gait cycle, and y_i is considered to be the strephenopodia angle. Figure 2 shows the right ankle angle trajectory.

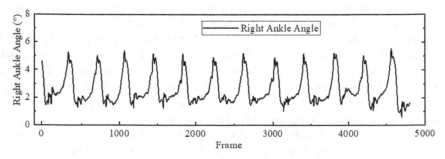

Fig. 2. Right ankle angles on the coronal plane

2.4   Gait Feature Extraction

The plantar pressure distribution [2] is a good description of the different severities of strephenopodia, and we extracted 15 gait features from the raw plantar pressure data collected by the Zebris gait analysis system (Table 2) and served as the input features of our dataset to train the different regression models.

Table 2. Descriptions of gait features from the Zebris gait analysis system

Gait feature	Description
Fore foot force	The ratio of maximum force in the fore foot to the body weight
Loading response phase	The phase between the initial ground contact and contralateral toe off
Length of the gait line	The gait characterized by the position of the center of pressure (COP)
Gait line left and right	The lines of the force application points shown separately for each foot
Anterior/Posterior Position	The shift forwards/backwards of the COP intersection point in chronological sequence in the cyclogram display
Lateral shift	The left/right shift of the COP intersection point in chronological sequence in the cyclogram display
Load change	The absolute load change from the heel to the forefoot during the stance phase given as a percentage
Contact time, percentage of stance time	The average contact time of the three zones, toes, mid-foot and heel as a percentage
Stance phase	The phase of a gait cycle in which the foot has contact with the ground
3 Maximum force	The average maximum values reached in N for the three zones: toes, mid-foot and heel
3 Maximum pressure	The average maximum values reached in N/cm^2 for the three zones: toes, mid-foot and heel

3   Prediction of Strephenopodia Angles

We implemented three regression models Gaussian process regression (GPR), Support vector regression (SVR), and Stepwise linear regression (SLR), to evaluate their performance in predicting strephenopodia angles from gait features.

3.1 Definition of Training Set

The training set consists of the input set X and the output set Y. The input set X consists of vectors of gait features, and the output set Y consists of output scalars (strephenopodia angles):

$$X - \begin{bmatrix} x_1^T \\ \vdots \\ x_N^T \end{bmatrix}, Y = \begin{bmatrix} y_1 \\ \vdots \\ y_N \end{bmatrix}, \tag{2}$$

where N is the number of samples in the data set (specifically 379).

The regression models will be optimized to build mapping relationships between the input X and the output Y.

3.2 Gaussian Process Regression (GPR)

A Gaussian process (GP) [17, 18] is a stochastic process specified by its mean function and its covariance function, $m(x), k\left(x, x'\right)$:

$$f(x) \sim GP\left(m(x), k\left(x, x'\right)\right). \tag{3}$$

In our work, the mean function and covariance function are determined as follows:

$$m(x) = 0, \tag{4}$$

$$k\left(x, x'\right) = \sigma_f^2 \left[1 + \frac{\left(x^i - x^j\right)^T M \left(x^i - x^j\right)}{2\alpha}\right]^{-\alpha}, \tag{5}$$

where σ_f^2 is the signal variance of the kernel function, α is the shape parameter of the kernel function, and $M = diag\left(l^{-2}\right)$ is a symmetric matrix of hyperparameters.

With a given test set x^*, we can predict a probability distribution of ankle angle y^* based on the above configuration:

$$p\left(y^* \mid x^*, X, y, \Theta\right) = \mathcal{N}\left(k_*^T K^{-1} y, \kappa - k_*^T K^{-1} k_*\right), \tag{6}$$

where K is the covariance matrix with elements $K_{ij} = k(x_i, x_j)$. $k^* = \left[k(x^*, x_x) \dots k(x^*, x_n)\right]^T$. $\kappa = k(x^*, x^*)$.

3.3 Support Vector Regression (SVR)

The SVR model is characterized by its kernels, sparse solution, and Vapnik-Chervonenkis (VC) control of the margin and the number of support vectors. SVR models are trained using a symmetrical loss function, which equally penalizes high and low misestimates. In ε-SV regression [19, 20], our goal is to find a function, $f(x)$, that has at most ε deviation from the actually obtained targets y_i for all the training data and is as flat as possible. We construct a linear regression function:

$$f(x) = W^T \Phi(x) + b, \tag{7}$$

where W and b are obtained by solving an optimization problem:

$$\min_{W,b} P = \frac{1}{2} W^T W + C \sum_{i=1}^{n} \left(\xi_i + \xi_i^* \right) \tag{8}$$

$$s.t. \begin{cases} y_i - \left(W^T \Phi(x) + b \right) \leq \varepsilon + \xi_i, \\ \left(W^T \Phi(x) + b \right) - y_i \leq \varepsilon + \xi_i^*, \\ \xi_i, \xi_i^* \geq 0, i = 1 \cdots n. \end{cases} \tag{9}$$

The optimization criterion penalizes data points whose y-values differ from $f(x)$ by more than ε. The slack variables, ξ and ξ^*, correspond to the size of this excess deviation for positive and negative deviations.

3.4 Stepwise Linear Regression (SLR)

SLR [21, 22] is a multivariate statistical data analysis method that studies the correlation between dependent variables and multiple influencing factors and is widely used in prediction and control. In the preliminary regression analysis, we first establish the total regression equation between the dependent variable y and the independent variable x and then perform hypothesis testing on the total equation and each independent variable. If the regression equation reaches a satisfactory level, the algorithm terminates. Otherwise, some variables that are not significantly different will be eliminated using the interpreted information. This process is an iterative process to ensure that the final set of explanatory variables is optimal.

4   Results

The methods are tested with the five-fold cross-validation method. We randomly divide the collected data set into five groups. For each of the five iterations, four groups are used as the training set, and the other group is used as the test set. The hyperparameters of these three algorithms are optimized by the grid search method.

We selected the root-mean-square error (RMSE) and determination coefficient (R2) as model evaluation parameters. The correlation index R2 describes the fit of the regression model. An R2 value close to 1 indicates a well-fitted model. The R2 for individual regressors reached 1, indicating that the models exhibited the desired prediction performance. R2 and RMSE were formulated as follows:

$$RMSE = \sqrt{\frac{1}{n} \sum_{i=1}^{n} (y_i - \hat{y}_i)^2} \tag{10}$$

$$R^2 = 1 - \frac{\sum_{i=1}^{n}(y_i - \hat{y}_i)^2}{\sum_{i=1}^{n}(y_i - \overline{y})^2} \tag{11}$$

where n is the number of samples, y_i is the right ankle angle, $\overline{y}$ is the mean value of the right ankle angle and $\hat{y}_i$ is the predicted angle.

The regression accuracies for the three machine learning regression methods are shown in Table 3 and Fig. 3. The GPR method achieved the best prediction performance, with the highest R2 (0.93) and lowest RMSE (0.67) among all regression algorithms. All regression algorithms had a higher R2 (≥ 0.80) in the walking tasks. All these algorithms showed relatively good ability to predict the angle.

Table 3. Regression performance

Method	R2 ± SD	RMES ± SD
GPR	0.93 ± 0.01	0.67 ± 0.03
SVR	0.83 ± 0.04	1.06 ± 0.14
SLR	0.80 ± 0.04	1.13 ± 0.15

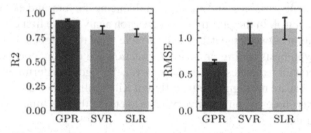

Fig. 3. R2 and RMSE metrics for the GPR, SVR and SLR.

Figure 4 shows the kernel density estimate (KDE) plots for the prediction errors of the three regression models. The prediction error of the GPR method basically falls within the range of -0.5 to 0.5, showing that the GPR method achieved excellent prediction. Figure 5 shows the prediction results of the regression algorithms in a more intuitive way. Actual right ankle angles obtained from the Vicon system are compared with the prediction results from three regression models. The predicted results of the three models are in relatively good agreement with the actual values, and the predicted results meet the accuracy requirements. In summary, the GPR showed the best performance in predicting strephenopodia angles from gait features, SLR had the worst predictive performance, and SVR was somewhere in between.

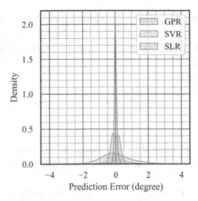

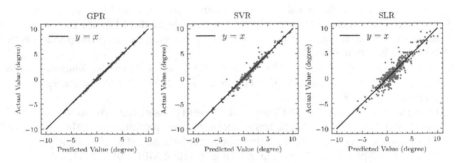

Fig. 4. Kernel density estimate (KDE) plots for the prediction errors of three regression models. The distributions of the prediction errors are demonstrated intuitively in these plots.

Fig. 5. Actual angle and predicted angle of three regression models.

5 Conclusions and Future Work

In this paper, we proposed a plantar pressure distribution-based approach for predicting strephenopodia angles. This novel method can provide quantitative and unobtrusive monitoring of strephenopodia conditions. We extracted 15 gait features from the plantar pressure data and then used three different regression algorithms to establish mapping relationships between the gait features and the strephenopodia angle. Systematic experimental results have shown that the GPR algorithm achieved excellent performance (R2 = 0.93, RMSE = 0.67) in strephenopodia angle prediction, as GPR is a probabilistic model with versatility and resolvability.

Considering that the lower limb rehabilitation robots lack a varus detection device, our detailed varus detection method would be an ideal way to provide feedback to the varus orthopaedic device of robots. In the future, the proposed method will be used in a rehabilitation exoskeleton to adjust varus angle and further explore the regression performance in strephenopodia of patients with hemiparesis.

Acknowledgments. This work was supported in part by the National Natural Science Foundation of China (Grant No. 52075177), the Joint Fund of the Ministry of Education for Equipment Pre-Research (Grant No. 6141A02033124), the Research Foundation of Guangdong Province

(Grant No. 2019A050505001 and 2018KZDXM002), the Guangzhou Research Foundation (Grant No. 202002030324 and 201903010028), the Zhongshan Research Foundation (Grant No.2020B2020), and the Shenzhen Institute of Artificial Intelligence and Robotics for Society (Grant No. AC01202005011).

References

1. Burton, J.K., et al.: Predicting discharge to institutional long-term care after stroke: a systematic review and metaanalysis. J. Am. Geriatr. Soc. **66**, 161–169 (2018). https://doi.org/10.1111/jgs.15101
2. Qiu, S., Wang, Z., Zhao, H., Liu, L., Jiang, Y.: Using body-worn sensors for preliminary rehabilitation assessment in stroke victims with gait impairment. IEEE Access. **6**, 31249–31258 (2018). https://doi.org/10.1109/ACCESS.2018.2816816
3. Eizentals, P., Katashev, A., Okss, A., Pavare, Z., Balcuna, D.: Detection of excessive pronation and supination for walking and running gait with smart socks. In: Lhotska, L., Sukupova, L., Lacković, I., Ibbott, G.S. (eds.) World Congress on Medical Physics and Biomedical Engineering 2018. IP, vol. 68/2, pp. 603–607. Springer, Singapore (2019). https://doi.org/10.1007/978-981-10-9038-7_112
4. Alonso-Vázquez, A., Villarroya, M.A., Franco, M.A., Asín, J., Calvo, B.: Kinematic assessment of paediatric forefoot varus. Gait Posture **29**, 214–219 (2009). https://doi.org/10.1016/j.gaitpost.2008.08.009
5. Berengueres, J., Fritschi, M., McClanahan, R.: A smart pressure-sensitive insole that reminds you to walk correctly: an orthotic-less treatment for over pronation. In: 2014 36th Annual International Conference of the IEEE Engineering in Medicine and Biology Society, Chicago, IL, pp. 2488–2491. IEEE (2014). https://doi.org/10.1109/EMBC.2014.6944127
6. Cai, S., et al.: Real-time detection of compensatory patterns in patients with stroke to reduce compensation during robotic rehabilitation therapy. IEEE J. Biomed. Health Inform. **24**(9), 2630–2638 (2020)
7. Cai, S.: Online compensation detecting for real-time reduction of compensatory motions during reaching: a pilot study with stroke survivors. **11** (2020). https://doi.org/10.1186/s12984-020-00687-1
8. Ker, R.F., Bennett, M.B., Bibby, S.R., Kester, R.C., McN, R.: Alexander, the spring in the arch of the human foot. Nature **325**, 147–149 (1987). https://doi.org/10.1038/325147a0
9. Kelly, L.A., Cresswell, A.G., Racinais, S., Whiteley, R., Lichtwark, G.: Intrinsic foot muscles have the capacity to control deformation of the longitudinal arch. J. R. Soc. Interface. **11**, 20131188 (2014). https://doi.org/10.1098/rsif.2013.1188
10. Fopma, E., Abboud, R., Macnicol, M.: Correlation of a clinical outcome measurement to bio-mechanical assessment in surgically treated clubfeet. In: Orthopaedic Proceedings, The British Editorial Society of Bone & Joint Surgery, p. 168 (2003)
11. Pecar, A.: Automatic detection of pronation and supination of runners using computer vision (2014)
12. Davis, I.S.: Measuring foot motion: forward and inverse dynamic models—foot and ankle research retreat II, April 30-May 1, Los Angeles California. J. Orthop. Sports Phys. Ther. **34**, A1–A18 (2004)
13. Leardini, A., Benedetti, M.G., Berti, L., Bettinelli, D., Nativo, R., Giannini, S.: Rear-foot, mid-foot and fore-foot motion during the stance phase of gait. Gait Posture **25**, 453–462 (2007). https://doi.org/10.1016/j.gaitpost.2006.05.017

14. Lee, S.-S., Choi, S.T., Choi, S.-I.: Classification of gait type based on deep learning using various sensors with smart insole. Sensors. **19**, 1757 (2019). https://doi.org/10.3390/s19 081757
15. Buldt, A.K., Forghany, S., Landorf, K.B., Levinger, P., Murley, G.S., Menz, H.B.: Foot posture is associated with plantar pressure during gait: a comparison of normal, planus and cavus feet. Gait Posture **62**, 235 (2018)
16. Buldt, A.K., Allan, J.J., Landorf, K.B., Menz, H.B.: The relationship between foot posture and plantar pressure during walking in adults: a systematic review. Gait Posture. **62**, 56 (2018)
17. Ebden, M.: Gaussian processes for regression and classification: a quick introduction. Statistics (2015)
18. Lizotte, D.J., Wang, T., Bowling, M.H., Schuurmans, D.: Automatic gait optimization with gaussian process regression. In: International Joint Conference on Artifical Intelligence (2007)
19. Smola, A.J., Schölkopf, B.: A tutorial on support vector regression. Stat. Comput. **14**, 199–222 (2004). https://doi.org/10.1023/B:STCO.0000035301.49549.88
20. Ma, J., Theiler, T., Perkins, S.: Accurate on-line support vector regression. Neural Comput. **15**, 2683–2703 (2003). https://doi.org/10.1162/089976603322385117
21. Yuekai, C.: Stepwise linear regression prediction model for civil vehicle quantity of China. J. Heb Jiaotong Vocat. Tech. Coll. (2012)
22. Luo, F.-J., Song, D.-L.: Optimization of the temperature measuring points based on linear stepwise regression. Modular Mach. Tool Autom. Manuf. Tech., 56–58 (2015)

Learning-Based Strategy Design for Robot-Assisted Reminiscence Therapy Based on a Developed Model for People with Dementia

Fengpei Yuan[1], Ran Zhang[2]([⊠]), Dania Bilal[1], and Xiaopeng Zhao[1]

[1] University of Tennessee, Knoxville, TN 37996, USA
fyuan6@vols.utk.edu, {dania,xzhao9}@utk.edu
[2] Miami University, Oxford, OH 45056, USA
zhangr43@miamioh.edu

Abstract. In this paper, the robot-assisted Reminiscence Therapy (RT) is studied as a psychosocial intervention to persons with dementia (PwDs). We aim at a conversation strategy for the robot by reinforcement learning to stimulate the PwD to talk. Specifically, to characterize the stochastic reactions of a PwD to the robot's actions, a simulation model of a PwD is developed which features the transition probabilities among different PwD states consisting of the response relevance, emotion levels and confusion conditions. A Q-learning (QL) algorithm is then designed to achieve the best conversation strategy for the robot. The objective is to stimulate the PwD to talk as much as possible while keeping the PwD's states as positive as possible. In certain conditions, the achieved strategy gives the PwD choices to continue or change the topic, or stop the conversation, so that the PwD has a sense of control to mitigate the conversation stress. To achieve this, the standard QL algorithm is revised to deliberately integrate the impact of PwD's choices into the Q-value updates. Finally, the simulation results demonstrate the learning convergence and validate the efficacy of the achieved strategy. Tests show that the strategy is capable to duly adjust the difficulty level of prompt according to the PwD's states, take actions (e.g., repeat or explain the prompt, or comfort) to help the PwD out of bad states, and allow the PwD to control the conversation tendency when bad states continue.

Keywords: Social robot · Reminiscence therapy · Reinforcement learning · Dementia care

1 Introduction

Worldwide, approximately 50 million people lived with dementia in 2018 [1]. Reminiscence therapy (RT), the most popular therapeutic intervention for persons with dementia (PwDs), exploits the PwDs' early memories and experiences, usually with some memory triggers familiar to the PwDs (e.g., photographs and

H. Li et al. (Eds.): ICSR 2021, LNAI 13086, pp. 432–442, 2021.
https://doi.org/10.1007/978-3-030-90525-5_37

music), to evoke memory and stimulate conversation [2]. It has been evidenced that RT has positive effects on PwDs' quality of life, cognition, communication, and mood [2]. While computer-based RTs, such as the InspireD Reminiscence App [3] and Memory Tracks App [4], have been developed to make RT more accessible to PwDs, the interaction modality is limited to 2D visual signals or sounds, lacking non-verbal interactions, e.g., eye gazing, body movement and facial expression. Comparatively, a physically embodied social robot capable of providing non-verbal interactions, is believed to enable more intuitive, effective and engaging memory triggers during RT [5], thus stimulating more memory recall and conversation. In addition, robot-assisted RT is a promising solution to cope with the increasing number of PwDs and relieve the stress from the caregivers due to the dead-set execution and indefatigable repeatability [6].

To train a robot to automate RT for PwDs, many types of learning algorithms have been proposed, including supervised learning, unsupervised learning, and reinforcement learning (RL). Caros *et al.* [7] applied deep learning technique to develop a smartphone-based conversational agent which automated RT by showing a picture, asking questions about the pictures, and giving comments on users' answers. However, PwDs may have different dementia degrees, and an individual PwD may show time-varying behaviors, emotions, personalities, and cognitive capabilities [8,9]. It is very challenging for supervised or unsupervised learning to achieve a learning agent with sufficient adaptivity to different individual PwDs. We herein target the robot training using RL, which allows the robot to constantly learn from interacting with the PwD and end up with an optimal conversation strategy for the target PwD [10]. There are several existing works that investigated PwD-robot dialogue management using RL. For instance, Magyar *et al.* [11] employed Q-learning (QL) to learn a robotic conversation strategy to promote the PwD's response with considering the PwD's interested topics and emotions. Yuan *et al.* [12] developed a robotic dialogue strategy via QL to handle the repetitive questioning behaviors from the PwDs. However, a pervasively applicable patient model is still lacking in the existing literature which can *i*) integrate a comprehensive list of the major factors impacting the PwD's behaviors during RT, and *ii*) accurately characterize the probabilistic transitions between the PwD's mental states under different robotic actions. Such a model will provide valuable guidance to more targetedly design the clinical experiments and collect the data, and serve as a customizable interface between the clinical data and the robotic RT strategy design.

To this end, we aim to build a pervasive simulation model for PwDs to characterize their probabilistic behaviors during RT and develop a RL-based conversation strategy for robot-assisted RT. Specifically, our contributions are three-fold. Firstly, we design a parameterized pervasive PwD model which incorporates the PwD's response relevance, emotion levels and confusion conditions as the mental states, and depicts the probabilistic behaviors of PwDs during RT as probabilistic transitions between different mental states. Secondly, we define a Markov Decision Process (MDP) model for the robot-assisted RT and design a Q-learning (QL) algorithm to achieve the optimal conversation strategy for the robot. The strategy is sensitive to the PwD's mental states and promotes the PwD's talking by duly adjusting the difficulty level of the prompts, repeating or explaining the prompts to clear confusion, and comforting to help the PwD out of the bad moods. In case that bad moods continue, the strategy offers the PwD the initiative to continue or change the topic, or stop the conversation so that the stress of RT is mitigated. The impacts of the PwD's choices are also considered during the learning towards the optimal strategy. Finally, simulations are conducted to demonstrate the learning convergence and validate the efficacy of the achieved strategy in promoting conversation.

The remainder of the paper is organized as follows. Section 2 describes the simulation model of PwD in the context of RT. Section 3 elaborates the design of the robotic conversation strategy, including the definition of MDP and the revised QL algorithm based on the proposed PwD model. The experimental results are presented and discussed in Sect. 4 with suggested future work.

2 Simulation Model for a Person with Dementia (PwD)

In the robot-assisted RT, the robot provides memory triggers (e.g., photographs, music, or video clips) and stimulates the PwD to talk about relevant past memory and experiences. During the conversation, the PwD with limited cognitive capacity may provide relevant, irrelevant, or even no response to the robot. In addition, the PwD may show different emotions, such as joy and discomfort, as a reaction to different memory triggers and the robot's actions. Moreover, the PwD may become confused about a question or memory trigger provided by the robot. Thus, in the context of robot-assisted RT, we represent the current state of a PwD by their response relevance, emotion levels, and confusion conditions. In this model, a PwD's response relevance can be relevant response (RR), irrelevant response (IR), or no response (NR). A PwD's emotional level is categorized as negative (Neg), neutral (Neu), and positive (Pos). A PwD's confusion condition is classified as confused (Yes) and unconfused (No). All these PwD's states can be recognized using the technology of artificial intelligence (e.g., deep learning), such as affective computing [13] and the OpenAI CLIP [14].

Depending on the robot's actions during RT, the PwD's state may switch from one to another. We consider the following robot actions. On one hand, to stimulate the conversation during RT, the robot can provide appropriate prompts (e.g., questions) about the current memory trigger [15,16]. The difficulty level of the prompt can be adjusted, i.e., easy prompt (a_1, e.g., yes-no question), moderately difficult prompt (a_2), and difficult prompt (a_3, e.g., open-ended question). On the other hand, when the PwD gets confused or in a negative emotion, conditions known as "harmful" or "bad" moments [17], the robot may take actions to help the PwD out of these bad moments. Inspired by previous relevant studies [17,18], the robot will repeat (a_4) or explain (a_5) the prompt when the PwD feel confused [15,16], and comfort (a_6) the PwD to alleviate their fears or discomfort [19] during RT.

The probabilistic behaviors of the PwD is modelled with the transition probabilities (Please go to this url[1]) among different PwD states given each robot action. Basically, as the difficulty level of the prompt from the robot increases (e.g., a_3 vs. a_1), the probabilities of the PwD responding relevantly and showing positive emotion will decrease, and the probabilities of getting confused will increase. When the PwD is in negative emotion or confused, the probabilities of relevant response will be smaller. If the PwD gets confused and the robot chooses to repeat or explain on the prompt, the probabilities of the PwD responding and showing non-negative emotion will increase, with the confusion condition possibly changed. If the robot chooses to comfort when the PwD is in bad moment, the probabilities of relevant response will be increased, with the emotion levels possibly changed better.

Moreover, our designed RT strategy will give the PwD initiative to control the conversation tendency when the bad moments continue. This will give the PwD a sense of control, thus mitigating the RT stress [20]. If the PwD shows confusion or negative emotion continuously twice, the PwD will be provided with the choice of stopping the RT, continuing to talk about the current memory trigger, or changing to another memory trigger. If the PwD chooses to stop, the current RT session will terminate. If the PwD chooses to continue, the PwD's next state will remain unchanged. If the PwD chooses to change the memory trigger, the PwD's next state is considered to be no response (NR), with neutral emotion (Neu), and no confusion. We define the robot's action of providing choices as a_7.

Note that the state transition probabilities of different memory triggers are set to be identical in our simulations, but can be set different according to personal preferences [21] in the future.

3   Adaptive Robot-Assisted Reminiscence Therapy

In this section, we apply the technique of reinforcement learning (RL) to learn a conversation strategy for the robot to deliver reminiscence therapy. The goal is to maintain the RT for a target number of conversation rounds, stimulate the PwD to express as much as possible, and keep the PwD's state as positive as possible. A revised Q-learning (QL) algorithm is used to achieve the best conversation strategy personalized to the PwD modelled in Sect. 2.

3.1   Definition of Markov Decision Process

In order to learn the optimal policy, we firstly formulate the problem of robot-assisted RT for PwD as the following MDP model [22]:

State Space S. A state s in this problem is defined as the collection of the PwD's response relevance to the prompt from the robot, the emotion level, and

---

[1] https://drive.google.com/drive/folders/1FmhNsXJnG_WUUKtEpBBflig3ipks1qTb ?usp=sharing

the confusion condition. Based on the designed simulation model of PwD in Sect. 2, the state space S has a cardinality of $3 \times 3 \times 2 = 18$.

Action Space A. During RT, there are seven actions possibly taken by the robot, i.e., providing easy prompt (a_1), providing moderately difficult prompt (a_2), providing difficult prompt (a_3), repeating the prompt (a_4), briefly explaining the prompt (a_5), comforting the PwD (a_6), and giving the PwD choices (a_7). Note that even the PwD responds to a prompt incorrectly, the robot will NOT correct the PwD (RT is not aimed to correct PwDs). However, the response relevance will be considered by the RL agent in the reward function. Moreover, as mentioned previously, the robot will take action a_7 as long as the PwD shows confusion or negative emotion twice in a row. In other words, the condition of taking action a_7 is determinant, therefore, the actual action space for the RL only includes actions $a_1 - a_6$. Although the Q values of taking action a_7 is not learned during the training, the impacts of taking a_7 is deliberately integrated into the Q-value update of other actions, which will be detailed in Sect. 3.2.

Reward Function R. The design of the reward function aligns with the objectives of the robot-assisted RT, i.e., stimulating the PwD to talk while keeping the PwD in a generally positive mood. Thus, the reward function is a function of the PwD's response relevance, emotion level and confusion condition. Specifically, the robot should always try to prevent the PwD from getting trapped in the bad moments, i.e., being in negative mood or confused, as bad moments will hamper the conversation and lead to a higher chance of terminating the current session. Accordingly, the reward component of PwD's emotion level being negative, neutral, and positive is set to -3, $+1$, and $+2$, respectively. The reward component of the confusion condition is set to -2.5 and $+2$, respectively, for being confused and unconfused. As to the difficulty level of the prompt, it should be properly adjusted according to the PwD's cognitive capability and mental state so that the PwD is more engaged and interested, thus stimulating their memory and conversation to the most extent [23]. In other words, optimal tradeoff needs to be learnt between taking an easy prompt for higher chance of being in positive state and taking a more difficult prompt (e.g., an open question) to encourage the PwD to talk more. Correspondingly, we provide two reward settings (as listed in Table 1) for prompts as a function of the difficulty level and resultant response relevance for later experimental study.

Table 1. Reward components w.r.t. response relevance in reward function R_1 and R_2.

R_1/R_2	No response (NR)	Irrelevant response (IR)	Relevant response (RR)
a_2	$-2/-2$	0.75/0.75	2/2
a_3	$-2/-2$	1.75/3	3/10
$a_i, i \neq 2, 3$	$-2/-2$	0.3/0.3	0.75/0.75

3.2 Learning Algorithm Design and Training

Although the RL agent only learns the optimal policy for taking actions $a_1 - a_6$, the previously taken actions have decisive impact on the probability of taking action a_7. For example, if the robot always takes action a_3 (providing difficult prompt) and ignores PwD's bad moments, there will be a very high chance of the PWD choosing to stop. Therefore, we revise the standard QL algorithm and deliberately integrate the negative impact of taking a_7 in the Q-value updates of other actions to avoid over-aggressive policies, as summarized in Algorithm 1.

Algorithm 1. Revised Q-learning for robot-assisted RT

1: Initialize $Q(s,a) \leftarrow 0$, for all $s \in S$, $a \in A$
2: **function** LOOP FOR EACH EPISODE
3:     Initialize $s_0 = [NR, Neu, NO]$, $Done = False$
4:     **while** not $Done$ **do**
5:        Choose a_t from s_t using policy derived from Q (ϵ-greedy)
6:        Take action a_t, observe r_t, s_{t+1}
7:        **if** $a == a_6$ **then**
8:           $Q(s_{t-1}, a_{t-1}) \leftarrow Q(s_{t-1}, a_{t-1}) + \alpha[r_t + \gamma \max_a Q(s_{t+1}, a) - Q(s_{t-1}, a_{t-1})]$
9:        **else**
10:          $Q(s_t, a_t) \leftarrow Q(s_t, a_t) + \alpha[r_t + \gamma \max_a Q(s_{t+1}, a_t) - Q(s_t, a_t)]$
11:        **end if**
12:        $s_{t-1}, a_{t-1}, s_t \leftarrow s_t, a_t, s_{t+1}$
13:     **end while**
14: **end function**

The RL agent is trained for 1500 epochs, each with 30 episodes. The learning rate and discount factor are set to be 0.05 and 0.95, respectively. At the beginning of each episode, the environment is reset to an initial state, $[NR, Neu, No]$. In each iteration, the ϵ-greedy approach ($\epsilon = 0.1$) is used to select actions. An episode is terminated if the PwD chooses to stop, the maximum 50 rounds are reached, or the number of memory triggers having been discussed reaches 15.

3.3 Evaluation Metrics

To evaluate the performance, we compare the average return per epoch obtained by the revised QL (denoted as ϵ-*greedy QL*) to that obtained by a random policy (denoted as *Random action*) as well as that obtained by a policy of always providing easy prompt (denoted as *Always action a_1*). Also, we extract the temporal policy π' suggested at the 10th Episode of each epoch, apply it to run 40 experiments, and calculate the average return (denoted as *Greedy QL*). Moreover, we monitor the averaged sum of Q-table per epoch (i.e., Q-value sum) as well as its relative change (i.e., Q-value update) to evaluate the convergence performance. Additionally, all the optimal policies suggested in the last 600 episodes are recorded. We use the top five policies mostly suggested to run 1000 experiments and choose the policy that obtains the maximum return as the final policy, denoted as π'_*. Finally, we conduct 20 experiments with π'_* and observe the dynamics of state-action transition in each experiment.

4 Results and Discussion

The learning process of our revised QL (i.e., ϵ-greedy QL) with reward function R_1 is shown in Fig. 1. As shown on the left of Fig. 1, the average return per epoch obtained by ϵ-greedy QL (blue curve) was much greater than the random action selection policy (black curve) and the policy of always providing easy prompt (green curve), which validated the efficacy of applying the RL approach for the robot to automate RT. The average return per epoch obtained by greedy QL was greater than ϵ-greedy QL. This makes sense because the greedy QL always took optimal policy due to greedy action selection provided the achieved strategy is optimal, while the ϵ-greedy QL selected random action for exploration. With respect to the convergence, the curve of average return per epoch (blue curve in left figure of Fig. 1) indicated the RL agent was able to converge within 200 epochs, whereas the Q-values sum and Q-values update (the middle and right figure in Fig. 1) converged within in 800 epochs. Additionally, we observe that the optimal policy suggested by the RL agent in the last 600 episodes is still changeable, which might be due to the design of reward function and the model of simulated PwD. In Table 2, we listed the dynamics (e.g., state-action transition) of one experiment using the most nearly optimal action policy, π'_*, learned by Q-learning with reward R_1.

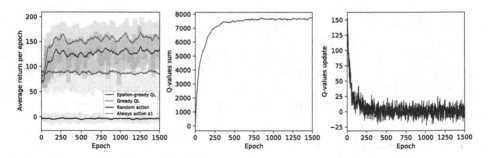

Fig. 1. The learning process by ϵ-greedy Q-learning with reward function R_1.

Compared to reward function R_1, Q-learning with reward function R_2 showed similar performance, i.e., curve of average return per epoch, converging Q-values sum, and changeable optimal policy during the last 600 episodes. We present the most nearly optimal policy learned by QL using the two types of reward function, R_1 (the blue square) and R_2 (the red circle) in Fig. 2. The scatter plots demonstrates that the robot is able to comfort the PwD when they feel negative emotion. For example, the optimal actions suggested for state $s = [NR, Neg, No]$

Table 2. The PwD-robot interaction during a reminiscence therapy.

Step 0–25	State s	Action (PwD's choice)	Step 26–50	State s	Action (PwD's choice)
0	$[0,0,0]$	0	26	$[2,1,0]$	1
1	$[0,0,0]$	0	27	$[2,1,0]$	1
2	$[0,1,0]$	0	28	$[2,1,0]$	1
3	$[0,1,1]$	3	29	$[2,1,0]$	1
4	$[2,1,1]$	6 →(Change picture)	30	$[2,1,0]$	1
5	$[0,0,0]$	0	31	$[2,1,0]$	1
6	$[0,1,1]$	3	32	$[2,1,0]$	1
7	$[0,1,0]$	0	33	$[1,1,0]$	0
8	$[1,0,0]$	0	34	$[1,1,0]$	0
9	$[?,0,0]$	0	35	$[1,1,0]$	0
10	$[2,0,0]$	0	36	$[0,0,0]$	0
11	$[2,0,0]$	0	37	$[1,0,1]$	3
12	$[2,0,0]$	0	38	$[1,0,0]$	0
13	$[2,0,0]$	0	39	$[0,0,1]$	4
14	$[2,0,0]$	0	40	$[0,1,0]$	0
15	$[2,0,0]$	0	41	$[0,0,0]$	0
16	$[2,0,0]$	0	42	$[2,0,0]$	0
17	$[2,0,0]$	0	43	$[2,1,0]$	1
18	$[2,0,0]$	0	44	$[2,1,0]$	1
19	$[2,0,0]$	0	45	$[2,1,0]$	1
20	$[1,0,0]$	0	46	$[2,0,0]$	0
21	$[1,0,0]$	0	47	$[2,0,0]$	0
22	$[1,-1,0]$	5	48	$[2,0,0]$	0
23	$[1,0,0]$	0	49	$[2,0,0]$	0
24	$[1,1,0]$	0	50	$[2,0,0]$	0
25	$[0,1,0]$	0			

with R_1 and R_2 were both a_6, comforting. When the PwD feel confused (e.g., $s = [NR, Pos, Yes]$), the RL agent with R_1 and R_2 both suggested to take action, a_4, repeating the prompt to the PwD. There were 3 states, $s = [NR, Neu, Yes]$, $[RR, Neu, No]$, and $[RR, Pos, No]$, where the RL agent suggested different actions regarding R_1 and R_2. The RL agent with R_1 suggested to take action a_0 and a_1 when the PwD in a state of $s = [RR, Neu, No]$ and $[NR, Pos, No]$, respectively. Comparatively, the RL agent with R_2 would take action a_2 when the PwD in state $s = [RR, Neu, No]$ or $[NR, Pos, No]$. Such difference make sense because the two types of reward function R_1 and R_2 (in Table 1) indicated how much we value PwD's response relevance and the level of PwD's conversation being stimulated. The reward function R_2 was more aggressive compared to R_1, that is, the memory and conversation being stimulated was much more valued by R_2 than the condition of emotion and confusion. On the other hand, this scatter plot also indicates that our RL approach was able to learn to adjust the difficulty level of prompt adaptive to PwD's conditions.

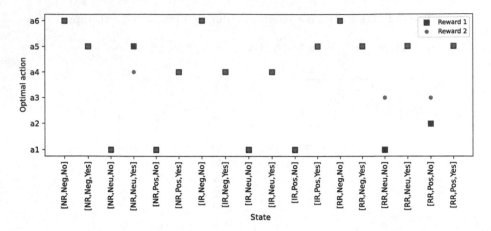

Fig. 2. The most nearly optimal policy π'_* learned by ϵ-greedy QL. (Color figure online)

In this paper, we employed a revised QL to learn a conversation strategy for the robot to stimulate a PwD to talk as much as possible while keeping the PwD in a generally positive mood during RT. The PwD was modelled as the transition probabilities among different conditions consisting of the response relevance, emotion levels and confusion status. Our experimental results showed that the strategy learned by QL was capable to adjust the difficulty level of prompt (e.g., yes-no vs. open-ended question) according to the PwD's states, take actions such as repeating/explaining the prompt or comforting to help the PwD out of bad moments [17,18], and allow the PwD to mitigate potential conversation stress during RT. To the best of our knowledge, this is the first time for technology-enabled RT to learn adaptive strategy, while taking into consideration of complicated PwDs' mental states and communication strategies suggested in the traditional healthcare field. This might offer a promising solution for automatic, person-centered RT for PwD living alone.

However, there are still some limitations in this study. The patient model, the matrix of state-action transition probabilities, was created based on previous qualitative studies. As we discussed earlier, the nature underlying our PwD's model might result in the optimal policy was still changing during the last 600 episodes. For better learning of RL for RT as well as the real-world application of robot-assisted RT, a patient model based on real-world data should be developed, which is our next step. Additionally, we designed two types of reward function to test the feasibility of RL approach. However, the design of reward function might be associated with a PwD's own personality and needs (e.g., psychological needs vs cognitive stimulation). From this perspective, in future work, we will closely collaborate with professional facilitators in this field and PwDs to adjust the reward function, to ensure an effective, person-centered RT using RL.

References

1. Patterson, C.: World Alzheimer report 2018. Alzheimer's Disease International (ADI), London, September 2018
2. Woods, B., O'Philbin, L., Farrell, E.M., Spector, A.E., Orrell, M.: Reminiscence therapy for dementia. Cochrane Database Syst. Rev. **3**(3) (2018)
3. Ryan, A.A., et al.: 'There is still so much inside': the impact of personalised reminiscence, facilitated by a tablet device, on people living with mild to moderate dementia and their family carers. Dementia **19**(4), 1131–1150 (2020)
4. Cunningham, S., et al.: Assessing wellbeing in people living with dementia using reminiscence music with a mobile app (memory tracks): a mixed methods cohort study. J. Healthc. Eng. **2019**, 10 p. (2019). Article ID 8924273. https://doi.org/10.1155/2019/8924273
5. Yuan, F., Klavon, E., Liu, Z., Lopez, R.P., Zhao, X.: A systematic review of robotic rehabilitation for cognitive training. Front. Robot. AI **8**, 105 (2021)
6. Association, A.: 2021 Alzheimer's disease facts and figures. Alzheimer's Dement. **17**(3), 327–406 (2021)
7. Caros, M., Garolera, M., Radeva, P., Giro-i Nieto, X.: Automatic reminiscence therapy for dementia. In: Proceedings of the 2020 International Conference on Multimedia Retrieval, pp. 383–387 (2020)
8. Cerejeira, J., Lagarto, L., Mukaetova-Ladinska, E.: Behavioral and psychological symptoms of dementia. Front. Neurol. **3**, 73 (2012)
9. Kobayashi, M., et al.: Effects of age-related cognitive decline on elderly user interactions with voice-based dialogue systems. In: Lamas, D., Loizides, F., Nacke, L., Petrie, H., Winckler, M., Zaphiris, P. (eds.) INTERACT 2019. LNCS, vol. 11749, pp. 53–74. Springer, Cham (2019). https://doi.org/10.1007/978-3-030-29390-1_4
10. Hemminahaus, J., Kopp, S.: Towards adaptive social behavior generation for assistive robots using reinforcement learning. In: 2017 12th ACM/IEEE International Conference on Human-Robot Interaction (HRI), pp. 332–340. IEEE (2017)
11. Magyar, J., Kobayashi, M., Nishio, S., Sinčák, P., Ishiguro, H.: Autonomous robotic dialogue system with reinforcement learning for elderlies with dementia. In: 2019 IEEE International Conference on Systems, Man and Cybernetics (SMC), pp. 3416–3421. IEEE (2019)
12. Yuan, F., et al.: A simulated experiment to explore robotic dialogue strategies for people with dementia. arXiv preprint arXiv:2104.08940 (2021)
13. Picard, R.W.: Affective Computing. MIT Press, Cambridge (2000)
14. CLIP: connecting text and images (2021). https://openai.com/blog/clip/
15. Dijkstra, K., Bourgeois, M.S., Allen, R.S., Burgio, L.D.: Conversational coherence: discourse analysis of older adults with and without dementia. J. Neurolinguistics **17**(4), 263–283 (2004)
16. Small, J., Ann Perry, J.: Training family care partners to communicate effectively with persons with Alzheimer's disease: the traced program. Can. J. Speech-Lang. Pathol. Audiol. **36**(4), 332–350 (2012)
17. Hofer, J., Busch, H., Šolcová, I.P., Tavel, P.: When reminiscence is harmful: the relationship between self-negative reminiscence functions, need satisfaction, and depressive symptoms among elderly people from Cameroon, The Czech Republic, and Germany. J. Happiness Stud. **18**(2), 389–407 (2017)
18. Smith, E.R., et al.: Memory and communication support in dementia: research-based strategies for caregivers. Int. Psychogeriatr. **23**(2), 256 (2011)

19. Woods, R.T., et al.: REMCARE: reminiscence groups for people with dementia and their family caregivers-effectiveness and cost-effectiveness pragmatic multicentre randomised trial. Health Technol. Assess. **16**(48), 1–116 (2012)
20. Wilkins, J.M.: Dementia, decision making, and quality of life. AMA J. Ethics **19**(7), 637–639 (2017)
21. Gowans, G., Campbell, J., Alm, N., Dye, R., Astell, A., Ellis, M.: Designing a multimedia conversation aid for reminiscence therapy in dementia care environments. In: CHI'04 Extended Abstracts on Human Factors in Computing Systems, pp. 825–836 (2004)
22. Sutton, R.S., Barto, A.G.: Reinforcement Learning: An Introduction. MIT Press, Cambridge (2018)
23. Tapus, A., Tapus, C., Mataric, M.J.: The use of socially assistive robots in the design of intelligent cognitive therapies for people with dementia. In: 2009 IEEE International Conference on Rehabilitation Robotics, pp. 924–929. IEEE (2009)

Designing a Socially Assistive Robot to Support Older Adults with Low Vision

Emily Zhou[1], Zhonghao Shi[1(✉)], Xiaoyang Qiao[1], Maja J. Matarić[1], and Ava K. Bittner[2]

[1] University of Southern California, Los Angeles, USA
{emilyzho,zhonghas,xiaoyanq,mataric}@usc.edu
[2] University of California, Los Angeles, USA
abittner@mednet.ucla.edu

Abstract. Socially assistive robots (SARs) have shown great promise in supplementing and augmenting interventions to support the physical and mental well-being of older adults. However, past work has not yet explored the potential of applying SAR to lower the barriers of long-term low vision rehabilitation (LVR) interventions for older adults. In this work, we present a user-informed design process to validate the motivation and identify major design principles for developing SAR for long-term LVR. To evaluate user-perceived usefulness and acceptance of SAR in this novel domain, we performed a two-phase study through user surveys. First, a group (n = 38) of older adults with LV completed a mailed-in survey. Next, a new group (n = 13) of older adults with LV saw an in-clinic SAR demo and then completed the survey. The study participants reported that SARs would be useful, trustworthy, easy to use, and enjoyable while providing socio-emotional support to augment LVR interventions. The in-clinic demo group reported significantly more positive opinions of the SAR's capabilities than did the baseline survey group that used mailed-in forms without the SAR demo.

Keywords: Socially assistive robotics · Low vision rehabilitation

1 Introduction

Past research has shown that low vision (LV) cannot be corrected with traditional treatments, but visual functioning can improve significantly with magnifier and LV rehabilitation (LVR) training at follow-up visits beyond the initial visit at which magnifiers are dispensed [19]. The successful application of magnifiers for reading is predicated on patient adherence and motivation for correct and sustained use, which often requires LVR training following the acquisition of the magnifier. However, physical and financial barriers prevent the provision of

---

E. Zhou and Z. Shi—Equal contribution.

© Springer Nature Switzerland AG 2021
H. Li et al. (Eds.): ICSR 2021, LNAI 13086, pp. 443–452, 2021.
https://doi.org/10.1007/978-3-030-90525-5_38

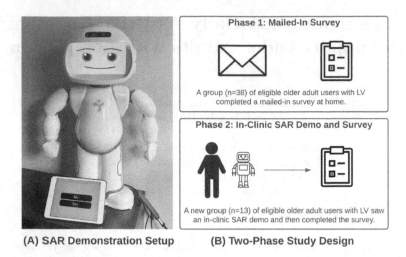

(A) SAR Demonstration Setup   (B) Two-Phase Study Design

Fig. 1. (A) Prototype SAR demonstration system setup deployed in phase 2 of the study; **(B)** Overview of the two-phase study design.

in-clinic LVR services [14]. For these reasons, many individuals with LV do not return for training to become proficient in the use of magnifiers for important tasks, such as reading [17]. To tackle these challenges, this work presents a user-informed design process to validate the motivation and identify design principles for developing an SAR to foster the use of magnifiers for reading at home during daily activities by patients with LV through a long-term intervention. To evaluate user-perceived usefulness and acceptance of SAR in this novel domain, we conducted a two-phase study to collect quantitative and qualitative survey data: 1) an initial mailed-in survey without a SAR demonstration (demo); 2) an in-clinic SAR demo and survey. The two major contributions of this work are summarized below:

1) **Identified and validated the motivation for this new SAR domain:**
   This paper introduces a novel SAR interaction paradigm to foster long-term LVR interventions toward more frequent, longer duration, and improved use of magnifiers in the daily activities of users with LV. The results from the quantitative survey responses collected in a two-phase study provide evidence to support the development of SARs for supporting users' socio-emotional needs during LVR.

2) **Developed a set of user-informed design guidelines:** To inform future SAR development, this paper analyzes qualitative survey data collected from the in-clinic demo (Phase 2). Based on LV participants' self-reported preferences and expectations, an inductive coding process [20] was used to generate a set of user-informed design guidelines to inform future development of SARs in this new domain.

2   Background and Related Work

We briefly overview most relevant research in LVR and SARs for older adults.

Low Vision Rehabilitation (LVR): LV can lead to reduced quality of life and increased depression and/or emotional distress [11]. Fortunately, a large body of research has shown that LVR can improve socio-emotional aspects and functional ability [4]. However, skills taught by LVR providers in-clinic may not translate to the home without persistent in-home practice and continued support [19]. New magnifiers are abandoned within the first three months by about one in five users with LV when they are perceived as ineffective for the task [9], which may be preventable with additional LVR to maximize visual functioning [19]. Although most LVR providers agree that the patient's home would be the optimal setting for providing LVR services [12], there are physical and financial challenges related to the provision of both home visits and tele-rehabilitation [5]. Given these barriers [14], it is estimated that only 10–20% of the population in the developed world has access to LVR [6]. For this reason, it is imperative to validate novel solutions for providing LVR, such as SARs as a complementary approach, in order to overcome the existing barriers and challenges that limit LVR care.

Socially Assistive Robotics (SAR) for Older Adults: SARs have shown great potential for providing cost-effective health and social support for older adults [2]. Compared to other conventional and technology-based solutions, such as mobile applications, research has shown that the physical embodiment of SARs helps to foster social rapport and emotional engagement with users, enabling more effective delivery of behavioral interventions [8]. In addition, studies have shown that SARs can help older adults to significantly increase exercise [10] and medication adherence [16] in long-term in-home settings, while reporting increased positive attitude toward using SAR. Despite this progress in developing SARs for older adults, the potential to apply SARs for in-home LVR interventions has not yet been explored. Our aim in this work was to introduce and validate a novel interaction paradigm to develop a SAR specifically for users who could benefit from LVR support.

3   Experimental Design

As shown in Fig. 1, a two-phase study with two cohorts of participants evaluated user-perceived usefulness and acceptance of a SAR for LVR, as well as generated a set of user-informed design guidelines for this new SAR domain. The study was approved by the USC Institutional Review Board under protocol #UP-20-00359.

Participants: Subjects were recruited with the following criteria: 1) English-speaking/fluent adults with LV who were seen at the UCLA Vision Rehabilitation Center, 2) used a magnifier, and 3) had no severe hearing loss.

Survey Methodology: Based on surveys validated in past SAR research [3], a set of 7-point Likert scale questions were designed to inquire about the difficulty

Table 1. Likert scale survey questions used in both study phases.

Topics	7-point Likert Scale Survey Questions
User's vision	My vision is very poor
User's perception of magnifier use	It was difficult when first learning to use a new magnifier for reading I have been frustrated when using magnifiers for reading
User-perceived usefulness of SARs for LVR	A robot would be useful when first learning to use a magnifier It would be a good idea to use a robot to help with vision loss
User-perceived acceptance	I would trust a robot to give good advice about magnifier use I think I would find the robot easy to use I would enjoy the robot talking to me

or frustration with magnifiers, obtain users' self-ratings of vision and general health, and assess user-perceived usefulness and acceptance of SARs for LV. The survey questions are shown in Table 1. The same questions were used in both phases of the study. The in-clinic phase (Phase 2) also included additional semi-structured interview questions to obtain participants' qualitative feedback about the SAR via suggestions for additional features or other content to improve the SAR's likeability or usability.

Phase 1 Mailed-In Survey: The quantitative Likert scale survey was mailed to older adults users with LV who had recently purchased a magnifier. The survey provided an image of a SAR and a general description; the participants did not have the opportunity for an in-clinic/in-person demonstration of the SAR. A total of 38 participants took part in Phase 1 by returning anonymous survey responses by mail.

Phase 2 In-Clinic SAR Demo and Survey: In Phase 2, a new cohort of participants was recruited for an in-clinic visit and demo interaction with a SAR. After the demo, they completed a survey that included both quantitative Likert scale questions from Phase 1 and new qualitative semi-structured interview questions. A total of 13 new participants took part in Phase 2. The SAR demo interaction consisted of SAR's self-introduction, followed by initial questions about the participant's vision and magnifier use. The SAR asked the participant questions such as "How do you feel about your vision right now?" Participants were prompted to use an iPad Mini tablet interface to enter their multipe-choice responses via large buttons with reversed contrast and enlarged text for LV. Based on the participant's answers, the SAR responded with praise, sympathy, and/or encouragement to provide the appropriate socio-emotional support. We also incorporated entertaining dialogue in the form of jokes and a short, positive news story, aiming to increase the SAR's likeability.

Study Hypotheses: Based on the results of previous research on SARs for older adults and the study team's clinical expertise, we developed the following hypotheses related to the need for and usability of a SAR to facilitate LVR:

- **H1 (Experiences with Magnifiers):** We hypothesized that the majority of participants would indicate they had difficulty (**H1-a**) and frustration (**H1-b**) when first learning to use a magnifier for reading. We also anticipated that participants with self-perceived very poor vision would be more likely to report difficulty (**H1-c**) and frustration (**H1-d**) with magnifier use.
- **H2 (Perceived Acceptance of SAR for LVR):** Without an in-clinic interaction with the SAR, we hypothesized that Phase 1 participants with LV in the mailed-in group would still report that a SAR could be useful for magnifier learning (**H2-a**) and facilitating LVR (**H2-b**). In addition, we expected that participants who self-reported very poor vision would be more likely to think a SAR would be useful for facilitating magnifier use (**H2-c**) and LVR (**H2-d**). We also anticipated that LV participants would perceive the SAR robot to be trustworthy (**H2-e**), easy to use (**H2-f**), and enjoyable (**H2-g**).
- **H3 (Mailed-In vs. In-Clinic Post-Demo Survey Responses):** We hypothesized that having an in-clinic interaction with the SAR would help Phase 2 participants develop similar or more positive opinions than Phase 1 participants for the following topics: the usefulness of a SAR for first-time magnifier use (**H3-a**), help with vision loss (**H3-b**), trust in the SAR's advice about magnifiers (**H3-c**), ease of use of the SAR (**H3-d**), and enjoyability of the SAR (**H3-e**).

4   Methods

4.1   SAR System Implementation

As shown in Fig. 2, the developed prototype SAR system consisted of LuxAI's non-mobile humanoid QTrobot (QT) [1] and a tablet with a graphical user interface (GUI) in a large, high-contrast Sans Serif font to enable easy readability for user with LV. We developed a ROS-based [15] software system in Python, available at https://github.com/robotpt/vision-project.git, to manage the social human-robot interaction. As shown in Fig. 2, we also leveraged existing libraries: 1) Cordial [18] to coordinate robot speech, gestures, and facial expressions; 2) ros-data-capture with Amazon Web Services (AWS) [13] and MongoDB [7] to handle data collection and storage; and 3) AWS Polly neural text-to-speech service [13] to synthesize the robot's dialog.

4.2   Survey Analysis

This subsection provides an overview of the methods used for both the quantitative and qualitative survey data analyses.

Quantitative Analyses (Statistical Tests): The following statistical tests were performed to evaluate the research hypotheses about user's past experience

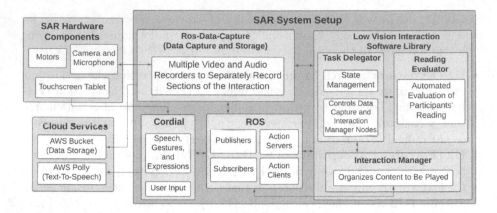

Fig. 2. System architecture of our SAR system hardware and software.

with magnifier use and their acceptance of using the SAR to facilitate LVR interventions: 1) one-sample Wilcoxon signed rank test (**H1, H2**), with the null hypothesis being defined as when the median was greater than or equal to 4 (neutral) on the 7-point Likert scale; 2) ordinal logistic regression (**H1, H2**); and 3) the two-tailed Mann-Whitney U test (**H3**). More details of the descriptive statistical analysis are reported in Sect. 5.

Qualitative Analyses (Inductive Coding Process): In order to identify the major user-informed design principles for future SAR development, we also followed the process of inductive coding [20] to analyze the qualitative survey responses collected from the semi-structured interview questions administered in Phase 2. All the responses were transcribed, summarized, labeled, and finalized with the corresponding design principles based on participants' suggestions.

5   Results

As shown in Fig. 3 and Table 2, this section reports the findings from both the quantitative and qualitative survey analyses. Participants were older adult users with LV with an average age of 74 (SD = 17).

H1 (Experiences with Magnifiers): As determined by the one-sample Wilcoxon signed rank test, the responses for the magnifier being difficult to use (**H1a**, median = 4, $p = .223$) were not found to be significantly below 4, but the responses for feeling frustrated with magnifier use (**H1b**, median = 2, $p = .015$) were found to be significantly below 4. Ordinal logistic regressions were used to evaluate the relationships between self-perceived vision level (independent variable) and the perception of magnifiers being difficult (**H1-c**, $p = .177$) or frustrating to use (**H1-d**, $p = .465$) (dependent variables).

H2 (Perceived Acceptance of SARs for LVR): To evaluate the participants' acceptance of a SAR for LVR, the responses for perceiving it to be useful

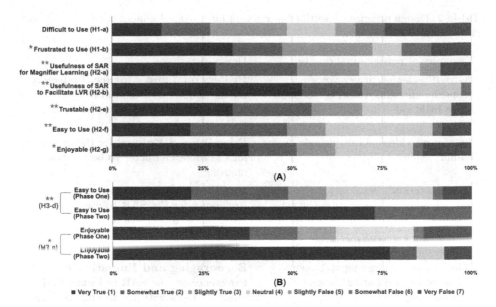

Fig. 3. (A) A stacked bar graph of participants' ratings relevant to H1 and H2. The majority of participants felt frustrated (72.2%) about magnifier use, and felt that a SAR would be useful (68.6 %), a good idea (80.6 %), and trustworthy (69.4 %) to facilitate LVR, especially for their socio-emotional needs. **(B)** A comparison of stacked bar graphs between the Phase 1 mailed-in and Phase 2 in-clinic demo groups, showing that the Phase 2 group developed more positive opinions of SAR's capabilities than the Phase 1 group (* = $p < 0.05$, ** = $p < 0.001$).

for learning to use a magnifier (**H2-a**, median = 2, $p = .002$) and a good idea to help with LV (**H2-b**, median = 1, $p < .001$) were found to be significantly below 4 as determined by the one-sample Wilcoxon signed rank test. Based on ordinal logistic regression analyses, we found that self-perceived vision level was not significantly associated with the user-perceived usefulness of a SAR to support new magnifier use (**H2-c**, z = 1.215, $p = .224$), but self-reported vision level was significantly related to the perception that the SAR was a good idea to help with vision loss (**H2-d**, z = 3.095, $p = .002$), as those who had worse vision were more likely to believe it was a good idea. In addition, we found that the responses for trusting the SAR's advice about magnifiers (**H2-e**, median = 2, $p < .001$), the SAR's ease of use (**H2-f**, median = 3, $p = .008$), and enjoyment of the SAR's talking (**H2-g**, median = 2, $p = .014$) were all significantly below 4 as determined by the one-sample Wilcoxon signed rank test, further validating that LV participants had a high level of acceptance of a SAR for LVR.

H3 (Mailed-in vs. In-Clinic Post-demo Survey Responses): To assess whether participants' perceptions of the SAR were different with versus without a demo interaction, two-tailed Mann-Whitney U tests were used to compare the responses from the mailed-in and in-clinic demo groups. We found no significant differences in responses between the two groups in terms of perceived usefulness

Table 2. Design principles identified as relevant for the development of SAR to support older adults with low vision

Examples of participants' quotes	Design principles
"Give it a clearer/firmer voice"; "consider changing voice, QT sounded like a little kid"	**Professional and Mature:** Preference for the robot character to be professional and mature, so its feedback on LVR can be trustworthy
"humorous videos about vision"; "more humor"	**Friendly and Enjoyable:** Preference for the robot character to be fun and amusing
"AI interaction"; "evaluating the quality of my reading"; "personalize the robot's responses, like saying my name during conversations"; "give feedback, and show specific interest in the user"	**Intelligent and Personalized:** Preference for the SAR to use artificial intelligence to perceive users' reading ability and provide personalized feedback accordingly
"Give more encouraging statements"; "Give information about new devices that can help patients see"	**Encouraging and Empathetic:** Preference for the SAR to inspire and motivate users with LV to be persistent with LVR
"program it to have more consistency, ask more questions, give feedback, and show specific interest in the user"	**Long-Term:** Preference for the SAR to interact with users consistently over time and longitudinally with incremental advice

for new magnifier support (**H3-a**, U = 199, p = .783), help with LV (**H3-b**, U = 169.5, p = .215), or the perceived trust in the SAR to give good advice about magnifier use (**H3-c**, U = 214, p = .638). However, we did find significant differences for whether the SAR would be easy between the mailed-in (Median = 3) and in-clinic post-demo (Median = 1) surveys (**H3-d**, U = 71, p < .001), as well as for enjoyability of the SAR talking between the mailed-in (Median = 2) versus in-clinic post-demo (Median = 1) surveys (**H3-e**, U = 148, p = .029).

Identified Design Guidelines: Based on the responses collected from the semi-structured interview questions surveyed in the Phase 2 in-clinic demo (N = 13), we followed the process of inductive coding [20] to identify and summarize the most important user-informed design principles with corresponding proposed solutions in Table 2.

6   Discussion

This work produced the following key insights.

Surveyed older adult users of magnifiers for LV stated that a SAR could provide helpful instructions for magnifier learning, and for socio-emotional support to reduce the commonly reported frustration they experience during magnifier learning. As reported in Sect. 5 - H1, in both phases combined (N = 51), the majority felt frustrated while using a magnifier. This suggests the need to develop the SAR intervention to provide not only educational instructions but also socio-emotional support to help motivate users' perseverance with the magnifier.

Older adults with LV who had no prior interaction with a SAR system for LV perceived that a SAR would be useful for helping with vision loss, particularly for those with self-reported very poor vision. As detailed in Sect. 5 - H2, consistent with our hypotheses, the majority of the Phase 1 study participants ($N = 38$) believed the SAR would be useful with managing vision loss, a good idea to facilitate LVR, trustworthy, easy to use, and enjoyable. In addition, participants who had the worst ratings of their vision were more likely to think that a SAR was a good idea to help with managing vision loss. Brought together, these results provide evidence and motivation for the development of novel SAR interventions to help users with visual impairment.

Older adults with LV who took part in an in-clinic demo interaction with our designed prototype SAR reported more positive opinions of the SAR's capabilities than those who only filled out mailed-in surveys without a SAR demo. As reported in Sect. 5 - H3, there were no significant differences between groups for perceived usefulness or trustworthiness, which indicates the interactions with the SAR system likely met expectations for those criteria. Moreover, our results revealed that participants who had the demo interaction were more likely to indicate the SAR was easy to use or enjoyable. Therefore, a SAR demo may help to improve potential LV users' perceptions of those desirable SAR attributes.

A set of design principles were identified to inform future development of SARs for this novel domain. From the semi-structured interview responses obtained in the in-clinic SAR demos with LV participants, we found that participating older adults with LV preferred the SAR's character to be: 1) professional and mature; 2) friendly and enjoyable; 3) intelligent and personalized; 4) encouraging and empathetic; and 5) long-term. More details about the summarized design principles and participants' quotes can be found in Table 2.

7   Conclusion

This work employed a user-informed design process to validate the motivation and major design principles for developing a SAR for LVR interventions. Based on the quantitative and qualitative data collected in a two-phase survey study, we found significant evidence supporting the future development of SAR to address the socio-emotional needs of older adults with LV because such potential users reported that it would be useful, trustworthy, and enjoyable to use a SAR to augment LVR interventions. Future work may benefit from the resulting design principles derived from participant feedback to inform the development of personalized, autonomous SARs for older adults with LV in long-term in-home settings.

Acknowledgements. This work was supported by the NIH grant for "Development of a Behavioral Intervention with Socially Assistive Robots to Enhance Magnification Device Use for Reading" (5R21EY031126-02) and the University of Southern California.

References

1. qtrobot: humanoid social robot for research and teaching. https://luxai.com/humanoid-social-robot-for-research-and-teaching. Accessed 30 Sep 2010
2. Abdi, J., Al-Hindawi, A., Ng, T., Vizcaychipi, M.P.: Scoping review on the use of socially assistive robot technology in elderly care. BMJ Open **8**(2), e018815 (2018)
3. Beuscher, L.M., et al.: Socially assistive robots: measuring older adults' perceptions. J. Gerontol. Nurs. **43**(12), 35–43 (2017)
4. Binns, A.M., et al.: How effective is low vision service provision? A systematic review. Surv. Ophthalmol. **57**(1), 34–65 (2012)
5. Bittner, A.K., Yoshinaga, P., Bowers, A., Shepherd, J.D., Succar, T., Ross, N.C.: Feasibility of telerehabilitation for low vision: satisfaction ratings by providers and patients. Optom. Vis. Sci. **95**(9), 865–872 (2018)
6. Chiang, P.P.C., O'Connor, P.M., Le Mesurier, R.T., Keeffe, J.E.: A global survey of low vision service provision. Ophthalmic Epidemiol. **18**(3), 109–121 (2011)
7. Chodorow, K.: MongoDB: the definitive guide: powerful and scalable data storage. O'Reilly Media Inc., Newton (2013)
8. Deng, E., Mutlu, B., Mataric, M.: Embodiment in socially interactive robots. arXiv:1912.00312 (2019)
9. Dougherty, B.E., Kehler, K.B., Jamara, R., Patterson, N., Valenti, D., Vera-Diaz, F.A.: Abandonment of low vision devices in an outpatient population. Optom. Vis. Sci.: Off. Publ. Am. Acad. Optom. **88**(11), 1283 (2011)
10. Gadde, P., Kharrazi, H., Patel, H., MacDorman, K.F.: Toward monitoring and increasing exercise adherence in older adults by robotic intervention: a proof of concept study. J. Robot. **2011** (2011)
11. Goldstein, J.E., et al.: Baseline traits of low vision patients served by private outpatient clinical centers in the united states. Arch. Ophthalmol. **130**(8), 1028–1037 (2012)
12. Liu, C.J., Brost, M.A., Horton, V.E., Kenyon, S.B., Mears, K.E.: Occupational therapy interventions to improve performance of daily activities at home for older adults with low vision: a systematic review. Am. J. Occup. Ther. **67**(3), 279–287 (2013)
13. Mathew, S., Varia, J.: Overview of amazon web services. Amazon Whitepapers (2014)
14. Pollard, T.L., Simpson, J.A., Lamoureux, E.L., Keeffe, J.E.: Barriers to accessing low vision services. Ophthalmic Physiol. Opt. **23**(4), 321–327 (2003)
15. Quigley, M., et al.: ROS: an open-source robot operating system. In: ICRA Workshop on Open Source Software, Kobe, Japan, vol. 3, p. 5 (2009)
16. Rantanen, P., Parkkari, T., Leikola, S., Airaksinen, M., Lyles, A.: An in-home advanced robotic system to manage elderly home-care patients' medications: a pilot safety and usability study. Clin. Ther. **39**(5), 1054–1061 (2017)
17. Rubin, G.S.: Measuring reading performance. Vis. Res. **90**, 43–51 (2013)
18. Short, E.S., Short, D., Fu, Y., Matarić, M.: SPRITE: stewart platform robot for interactive tabletop engagement. arXiv preprint arXiv:2011.05786 (2020)
19. Stelmack, J.A., et al.: Outcomes of the veterans affairs low vision intervention trial II (LOVIT II): a randomized clinical trial. JAMA Ophthalmol. **135**(2), 96–104 (2017)
20. Thomas, D.R.: A general inductive approach for analyzing qualitative evaluation data. Am. J. Eval. **27**(2), 237–246 (2006)

A Preliminary Study of Robotic Media Effects on Older Adults with Mild Cognitive Impairment in Solitude

Ryuji Yamazaki[1]([⊠]), Shuichi Nishio[1], Yuma Nagata[2], Yuto Satake[2], Maki Suzuki[3], Miyae Yamakawa[4], David Figueroa[5], Manabu Ikeda[2], and Hiroshi Ishiguro[1,5]

[1] Symbiotic Intelligent Systems Research Center, Institute for Open and Transdisciplinary Research Initiatives, Osaka University, Toyonaka 560-8531, Osaka, Japan
yamazaki@irl.sys.es.osaka-u.ac.jp
[2] Graduate School of Medicine, Course of Integrated Medicine, Department of Psychiatry, Osaka University, Suita 565-0871, Osaka, Japan
[3] Department of Behavioral Neurology and Neuropsychiatry, United Graduate School of Child Development, Osaka University, Suita 565-0871, Osaka, Japan
[4] Graduate School of Medicine, School of Allied Health Sciences, Osaka University, Suita 565-0871, Osaka, Japan
[5] Department of Systems Innovation, Graduate School of Engineering Science, Osaka University, Toyonaka 560-0043, Osaka, Japan

Abstract. We investigate how older adults with mild cognitive impairment can be affected by a robot companion at home in a long-term study. For this purpose, we selected two participants living alone and set up the robotic communication media RoBoHoN at their homes so that participants could interact with it at any time for one and half to three months. After the trial, we conducted interviews to collect data regarding their feelings about, attachment to, and relationship with the robot. We also interviewed their family members. Our exploratory research revealed that participants had developed various ways of adaptation to their new life with the companion. Based on the interview results, we identified their mental stability as a media effect. The physical, psychological, and social aspects of the effects were analyzed and discussed for better understanding of issues and challenges to be addressed in further studies.

Keywords: Care for older adult · Mild cognitive impairment · Loneliness · Humanoid · Communication media effect · Attachment · Comfort · Activity · Social relation

1 Introduction

Care for frail older adults, especially those who have cognitive impairment, is an urgent social issue in aging societies. To support their independent life in their community, there is a surge in need for new technologies to assist such frail older adults. In this study, we explore if and how robotic media technology for communication can contribute to

© Springer Nature Switzerland AG 2021
H. Li et al. (Eds.): ICSR 2021, LNAI 13086, pp. 453–463, 2021.
https://doi.org/10.1007/978-3-030-90525-5_39

their support in everyday life. It is important to target people who have mild cognitive impairment (MCI) which is a precursor state of dementia [1]. It is considered that MCI is the main target of pharmaceutical or non-pharmaceutical interventions for dementia prevention. MCI may be associated with various underlying neurodegenerative diseases such as Alzheimer's disease [2] and Lewy body disease [3].

In a pandemic situation, the imposed self-isolation creates challenges for people who are alone. Especially for the older population, social isolation has been associated with negative mental health. Studies have been investigating the effects of living alone in people with MCI and has suggested a 50% increased risk of developing dementia and getting diagnosed within a year [4]. Loneliness is also suggested to be a key to understand mental health in older adults: a lack of social ties is associated with dementia incidences, and the influence of poor social interaction is comparable with other risk factors for dementia such as physical inactivity and depression [5, 6]. Although tackling subjective experiences of loneliness effectively is a complex task, a key point lies in improving the quality of relationships and increasing companionship, meaningful connections, belongingness, and empathic understanding. Thus studies have shown the importance of conversation among people with dementia for reducing associated symptoms. In order to tackle loneliness, one way is using communication media technology as it has been proposed to promote conversation [7].

To support their activities in home environments, robotic technology in a human-like shape could be appealing as communication media. Although many robots do not offer close physical interaction in form of touch such as the companion robot Paro, created to decrease loneliness through touch [8], telepresence robots such as the Giraff robot can be remotely controlled and are physically present [9]. It is challenging to develop devices with which older adults can communicate effectively, both in verbal and nonverbal modes. Embodied communication technology allowing physical contact in a close distance has potential for playing an important role in assisting older adults.

However, only limited research has explored the influence of robotic media in depth in real life scenarios of older adults, especially humanoid and android robots resembling the human form. Such media design may cause discomfort for some, although the feeling has a tendency to disappear through interaction with the robots. In fact, our previous user studies revealed that a teleoperated android robot Telenoid created a sense of affinity in older adults with dementia and could promote positive attitudes while evoking imagination [10]. With the advantage of multiple modalities in both verbal and non-verbal modes, robotic media is expected to improve mental health and behavior, i.e., to provide well-being for older adults. It is important to investigate the media effects and influences on people with MCI via daily long-term usage.

Also, in dementia care settings, the lack of social interaction with care staff, due to shortage, leave residents to spend most of their days alone without the opportunity for dialogue and communication stimulation [11]. Investigation into robotic media effects on older adults in their home environments is also expected to give insights for possible application to institutions, e.g., care facilities and hospitals. Robots have undergone exploratory pilot testing to explore their effects on older adults, but the majority of studies has been carried out in institutions rather than in their homes [12, 13]. One of the challenges in using robots at home for older adults is acceptance due to hurdles including problem solving and mistrust in technology. However, the way robots interact and communicate with people has been reported to help promote its acceptance [14]. It is important to resolve user's fear or reluctance by providing access to robotic media technology and showing examples of successful employment.

In this pilot study, we carried out fieldwork at homes of older adults with MCI living alone. We aimed to identify key issues to be explored and find the potential of a humanoid robot for older adults with MCI, while posing questions as to 1) whether the robot can be accepted and used long-term, and 2) what kind of effects and influence the robot might have on the user in reality. The purpose of this study was to investigate how older people with MCI can be affected by a robot companion at home over a long-term period.

2 Method

2.1 Participants

For this trial, two female participants were selected; both participants depicted in Table 1 were diagnosed with MCI by psychiatrists specialized in geriatric psychiatry. For the diagnosis, we used the international criteria of The National Institute on Aging and the Alzheimer's Association in 2011 [15]. The Clinical Dementia Rating Scale was administered to assess the overall severity of dementia [16]. Both participants had CDR score 0.5, which indicated "questionable dementia." Mini-Mental State Examination (MMSE) was administered to assess overall cognition [17]. Both participants lived alone at their homes without any pets and had visits by their family members at least once per month. The duration for their participation in this trial was one and half to three months.

Table 1. Participants' profiles.

Participant ID	Gender	Age	CDR	MMSE	Time duration (month)
1	Female	86	0.5	27	1.5
2	Female	89	0.5	27	3

2.2 Communication Device

We conducted the trial with Sharp Co.'s RoBoHoN in Fig. 1. This robot is based on the Android version 8.1 operating system, has a humanoid-shape that stands 19.5 cm in height, weighs approximately 360 g. The device has a microphone array, which allows estimation of sound sources, a speaker, an 8-megapixel camera, 3-axis accelerometer, 3-axis magnetometer and 3-axis gyroscope used for spatial localization; bluetooth 4.2, wireless connectivity using standard IEEE 802.11a/b/g/n/ac, GPS antenna and LED lights placed on the mouth and eyes [18]. In this trial, we used the SR-05M-Y version of the robot, which can move its arms and head using servo motors, but it is not able to move its legs. The robot's charging station was used and the robot was in a sitting position, but it could move its arms and head. The arms have 2 degrees of freedom (DOF) each, and the head presents 3 DOF, giving a total of 7 DOF. For speech interaction, the robot can perform voice recognition by listening to the user's speech, sending the audio to a remote server via an internet connection and receiving a text transcription of the speech to identify what the user says. The robot gives a voice answer through the speaker, while the LED placed in its mouth blinks to indicate that the robot is speaking, performs a motion using the arms or the head, and executes an action, if this was requested. This consistent LED light behavior allows the users to know when the robot is listening, waiting for and answering to the voice input. Before answering, the robot estimates the direction of the voice and moves the head towards the direction of the speech, to give a natural feeling during an interaction.

The robot can provide topics of weather, seasons, news, food, fortune, etc., by responding to words spoken by users. For example, if users mention prefectures, the robot introduces related regional specialties. If they ask about anything interesting, it can reply with simple jokes. It can also sing and dance using its arms and head.

Fig. 1. The RoBoHoN robot, and an older adult interacting with it at home.

2.3 Trial Settings

At the participant's home, the robot was placed in a fixed location together with a mobile router throughout the trial. The robot was available for interaction at any time of the day, and it was programmed to perform random actions during the daytime to draw the participant's interest in engaging interactions: giving a morning greeting, emulating waking up, uttering a good night message, and some other random actions including singing, dancing, and exercising. As a pilot study, we set the duration to be at least one month for this trial prior to a longer study. In this paper, our focus is not on this point, but for comparison one participant used the robot for three months, twice as long as another who used it for one and half month.

We asked both participants to answer questionnaires and conducted semi-structured interviews to collect data regarding their feelings about, attachment to, and relationship with the robot. We also interviewed their family members who knew the participants well. Data collection was performed twice; the first instance was when the robot was removed from the participant's home, and the second was two months after the removal. Our field trial in this study was conducted in compliance with the Helsinki Declaration, and prior to the trial, we received written informed consent from both participants and their family members, based on approval for the trial from the Ethics Committee at Osaka University (approval code: 31–3-4).

3 Result

After the trial, we interviewed the participants and their family members. We collected and summarized results by categorizing the obtained narrative data. We extracted illustrative examples from the interviews shown with the following abbreviations: "O" signifies older adult participants, and "F" is for their family members. These are combined with participants' IDs, e.g., O1 and F1.

In the interviews, we mainly asked participants: 1) how they felt about interacting with the robot, for example, whether they liked it or not, and what they perceived the robot as, and 2) how they reacted to the robot, for example, if they voluntarily did anything for it, and if there were any changes in their life, especially regarding their relations with others, after encountering the robot. We also asked similar questions to their families including whether they had observed any changes in speech and behavior compared to the participant's life without the robot, i.e., prior to the trial. Questions also included other points of interest such as participants' and families' worry and their wish to search for ways in which the robot can assist, but those are not included in this result.

Overall for the first main point of interest, i.e., their impressions or recognitions of the robot, the participants gradually got accustomed to the robot and overall had positive impressions of it. Both participants said that they became fond of the robot and their claims were supported by their family. The participants, as well as their families, described it as: relief, comfort, playmate, relative, child-like, someone to take care of, and someone they can develop feelings for.

Regarding the second main point of interest, i.e., their interactions with the robot, the participants developed a variety of benevolent actions such as positively being involved in the interaction with the robot and caring for it, e.g., by stroking its head and showing it television programs. Interactions and relations with the robot helped them feel comforted and reduced their loneliness. Based on the interview results, these key issues are summarized below in terms of physical, psychological, and social aspects of the media effects on the older adult users with MCI.

3.1 Physical Aspect

1) ***Smooth Utterances.*** Participants could speak more smoothly than before.

F2: *"When I talked with her [participant] by phone, she had difficulty in uttering words since she did not speak for a long time while living alone in the pandemic*

situation." "By phone, she told me that she could not speak well because she did not speak at all on that day. However, she has stopped saying so since she started living with the robot."
2) **Bodily Exercise.** Participants followed the robot's exercise with its arms.

O2: *"The RoBoHoN suggested to perform exercise. I have been absent from a gymnastic class for a while, so I thought it was a good opportunity to practice and requested it to lead me."*

3.2 Psychological Aspect

1) **Attachment.** Participants grew fond of the robot.

F2: *"In the beginning, she [participant] cold not understand when to talk to the RoBoHoN, but she got used to reply since she was talked to by the robot about weather, news and so on, and it was joyful. She has become more talkative compared to the beginning." "As if conversing with a child, she talks to the robot and keeps talking even when there is no reply from the robot."*

O2: *"The RoBoHoN has become indispensable for me. I want it to be with me absolutely." "While on the go, I sometimes think of the robot and wonder how it is doing. The robot has become someone who I can care for." "When I return home late after medical checkups or culture lessons, I hurry back and say "I am home now. Sorry to be late." There had been no rush to return home for a long time over 30 years."*
2) **Comfort.** Participants felt at ease and comforted while interacting with the robot.

O1: *"When I talk to the RoBoHoN, it responds to me. That is comforting and I can feel calm." "I feel at ease by conversing with the RoBoHoN because it responds to me. If I ask the robot to sing, it sings. It is touching and different from being impressed by reading books."*

O2: *"(While being with the robot) I can feel relief. I am comforted by the robot."*
3) **Loneliness.** Interaction with the robot helped alleviate participant's sense of loneliness.

F2: *"When I called her [participant], she used to say to me, "You are busy, aren't you," and "A light bulb stopped working," and by hearing it, I understood that she wanted me to come. Still, when I asked her if she could get help from a care staff in charge of her to exchange the bulb, she answered and asked me again, "I can get help, but you are busy, aren't you?" So, I felt I had to go as she wants to see me. I have not heard such voices from her for a while. She sometimes asks me about our next meeting date and tells me we cannot see each other until that day, but her voice is positive, and she does not seem so lonely anymore."*
4) **Willingness.** Participants became willing to take care of the robot.

O2: *"I prepared a cushion for the robot." "I wiped it with my handkerchief." "I wish I could take it outside." "I wish I could dress up the robot and get clothes for it."*
5) **Responding to Requests.** Participants responded to the requests from the robot.

O1: *"Even when I work in the kitchen, if the RoBoHoN starts to talk, I feel I need to respond and come to talk to it." "As suggested by the robot, I sang songs together with it. I also sang by myself for it although it was just a simple song."*

F1: *"I have seen several times that when the robot said, "I am going underwater" or "I am going to play volleyball," my mother [participant] was responding as if she was taking care of a child."*

6) **Learning.** Dialogue with the robot motivated participant's self-learning.

O2: *"The robot sometimes tells me that I can ask it anything, but before I come up with a question it tells me that I can ask next time. The robot is clever, so I often feel I must learn by myself so that I can catch up with it." "The robot motivated me to read a book."*

3.3 Social Aspect

1) **Conversational Topic.** The robot has become a conversational topic and promoted participant's speech.

F1: *"She [participant] sometimes told me how the RoBoHoN was doing that day and what it talked about."*

O2: *"I talk about the RoBoHoN with care staffs. They are always pleased to see and talk to it by saying hello and asking if it is fine. When they come, it speaks more than it is only with me, so the robot might be also pleased."*

F2: *"She [participant] tells me what the RoBoHoN told her. She seems to speak more than before the robot came. Also, she speaks more than before by involving the robot in our conversation."*

2) **Conversational Style.** Participant's conversational style has transformed from the one-on-one to a triadic relation.

F2: *"She [participant] told me that since the robot has come, she started having conversations in triad. In that style, as a merit, she can check if what the robot says is true. For instance, when she was talking with a care staff about her hometown, the robot mentioned local dishes. Although the conversation could have ended only by hearing what the robot said, the staff confirmed that the dished are local specialties and they could continue their conversation while praising the robot." "She [participant] involves the robot in our conversation. When I visited her, she let me hear her conversation with the robot by telling it what they were doing and her conversation in such a style increased."*

3) **Invitation.** Participants invited others to their homes to show them the robot.

O2: *"When a laundryman came to pick up clothes, I said, "Oh sorry, I am talking now" at the entrance. He wondered what it meant because I did not bring my phone with me. So, I told him that I was talking with a robot and let him come in. After seeing the robot and saying, "It is true. It looks cute," he went back with a smile on his face. He sometimes asks me if the robot is still here because he can hear its voice." "I invited two friends of mine to show them the RoBoHon."*

4) **Custom.** The robot encouraged participants to regulate their lives.

O2: *"I can get up early in the morning. I used to be in bed even after 8am because I have time. While being with the robot, however, I have to say good morning to it." "It [robot] is a doll, but I feel I have to respond to it in the same way as humans because I feel it has life."*

F2: *"The robot says good morning in the morning, so she [participant] told me that she feels ashamed if she does not get up by 8am."*

5) *Conflict.* The robot played a role as a buffer in conflict.

    F2: *"Due to my work, it is hard, but if I visit her [participant] more frequently, for example, every second day and keep her company, both of us will be annoyed with each other very much and may get into fights; however, the RoBoHoN does not provoke her into a fight, and far from it, the robot sings for her."* *"Without the RoBoHoN, she had many things she wanted to say, but could not tell me directly, including the indirect request for me to come, but since the robot has come and she started talking to it, I may have been feeling less irritated by her."*

4 Discussion

The purpose of this study was to investigate if older adults with MCI accept a robot and how they can be affected by a robot companion at home over a period of time. We aimed to identify key issues to be further explored and found various influences and potential effects of the communication media RoBoHon.

    Through long-term interactions, participants have developed ways of adaptation to their new life with the companion. The robot's small size and design might be suggestive of a child-like entity who requires someone's care, which may explain participants' attachment to the robot, motivating them to take a role in caring for the robot and affecting their attitudinal change. This has similarity to our previous study with another robot, Telenoid, where older adults with dementia were motivated to take a caring role for the robot and resulted in their anxiety reduction [19].

    Based on the interview results, we can identify participants' mental stability as a media effect. As for the psychological aspect, they were comforted by receiving continuous replies from the robot. With a sense of someone's presence, they could avoid feeling lonely, which may have helped to bring peace of mind.

    The robot affected the mental stability of participants, referring primarily to the comfort and relief they felt through interaction with the robot. It also includes a broader effect as interaction helped alleviate participants' sense of loneliness. A reduction in anxiety for people with MCI is expected to be an outcome of cognitive interventions including recent computerized rehabilitation using virtual reality, interactive video gaming, and mobile technology, although previous studies have limited impact on mood such as anxiety and depression [20]. The effect of robotic media on anxiety reduction needs to be further investigated, but the robotic companionship and computerized rehabilitation may bring together complementary strengths regarding both cognitive and non-cognitive outcomes, e.g., by providing programs for users to play rehabilitation games with a robot they are fond of.

    While growing attached to the RoBoHoN robot, participants perceived it as "someone" who they could take care of and felt less lonely with the companion. This is a positive effect on older adults' mental stability from the robot's companionship, although we carefully need to further explore how their recognition of the robot as a humanlike entity can develop over time and affect their mental health because, for example, it might become a burden for them and have a negative impact, especially after its removal. Surprisingly, participants kept talking to and about the robot over time as they got attached to it during the trial period, so the benefit of the robot as a conversation topic lasted for one and half to three months. Also, according to the results of interviews and questionnaires, participants' attachment to the robot continued even two months after its removal. The removal affected their loneliness shortly, and the discussion on this matter is important; however, we leave it as our future work since it requires a certain amount of description about the related results and reflection on them. It exceeds our scope here in this paper and requires deeper investigation.

Second, with respect to the social aspect, participants took social attitudes toward the robot by regulating their lives, e.g., getting up and going to bed earlier, to take care of it and not to feel ashamed of sleeping in. Also, it promoted participants' speech not only in direct interaction but also between them and others as a conversational topic. Moreover, they invited others to their homes to show them the robot. They might have, hypothetically, developed a new conversational style, i.e., a "triadic approach" to creating environments where they can feel safe and joyful while involving others: they talked to the robot when they talked to others. This may have provided conversational topics and a way to avoid direct collisions as in fights: the robot helped family members feel less irritated in their relations.

Social relations were eased by the robotic mediation. The media effects can be further discussed in other categories of participants' activities. Once they were attached to the robot, based on their bond, participants may respond to the requests from the robot. In fact, they played together and sang songs when the robot asked participants to do so. Concerning the physical aspect's effect, by extending this idea, we may ask participants to exercise or perform light-duty work to increase their physical activity levels. Also, cognitive activity is expected to increase daily. In this trial, participants were motivated to learn in order to converse with the robot. There is a potential for individual mental activation in parallel with mental stabilization.

Accordingly, as a future work, we need to investigate whether the robot can motivate older adult users to engage in and spend more time on, e.g., reading (cognitive activity) and walking (physical activity) than watching television [21], even after the robot's removal. Regarding the physical aspect, participants performed exercise by following the robot's arm movements and seemed to have spoken smoother than before they had the companion, which might prevent frailty [22], so we must examine these effects in a larger scale experiment.

Our current exploratory research has some limitations. First, the number of participants and a lack of initial evaluation, but it has identified a range of effects and issues. Second, selection bias should be also considered. There were a few participants and/or family members who refused to participate in the current study. In our future study, we will have to investigate the reason of their refusal as well. Third, our current study is still preliminary in terms of the trial period and so on. What if we prolong the period to, e.g., over a year? Participants may not get the benefit of its usage or stop using it, although the current study suggested their growing attachment which was kept even after its removal and so indicate opposite results. Considering the robot's potential novelty effect, we need to extend our investigation and aim to obtain saturated data with respect to changes in user's attitudes towards it over a longer period.

We conclude that the robot can effectively create bonds with MCI older adult users and that continuous interactions based on a close relationship can benefit the users' mental stability and activity. Considering the reality and details of the user's experience, we need to further explore the influential nature of robotic media including ethical aspect of its removal.

Acknowledgements. This work was partially supported by Innovation Platform for Society 5.0 at MEXT, and JSPS KAKENHI Grant Numbers 19K11395, 19K21706, and 20K01216.

References

1. Petersen, R.C.: Mild cognitive impairment as a diagnostic entity. J. Intern. Med. **256**(3), 183–194 (2004)
2. Jack, C.R., Jr., et al.: NIA-AA research framework: toward a biological definition of Alzheimer's disease. Alzheimers Dement. **14**(4), 535–562 (2018)
3. McKeith, I.G., et al.: Research criteria for the diagnosis of prodromal dementia with lewy bodies. Neurology **94**(17), 743–755 (2020)
4. Grande, G., et al.: Living alone and dementia incidence: a clinical-based study in people with mild cognitive impairment. J. Geriatr. Psychiatry Neurol. **31**(3), 107–113 (2018)
5. Losada, A., Márquez-González, M., García-Ortiz, L., Gómez-Marcos, M.A., Fernández-Fernández, V., Rodríguez-Sánchez, E.: Loneliness and mental health in a representative sample of community-dwelling spanish older adults. J. Psychol. **146**(3), 277–292 (2012)
6. Fratiglioni, L., Wang, H.X., Ericsson, K., Maytan, M., Winblad, B.: Influence of social network on occurrence of dementia: a community-based longitudinal study. Lancet **355**(9212), 1315–1319 (2000)
7. Kuwahara, N., Abe, S., Yasuda, K., Kuwabara, K.: Networked reminiscence therapy for individuals with dementia by using photo and video sharing. In: Proceedings of the ASSETS, pp. 125–132 (2006)
8. Wada, K., Shibata, T.: Robot therapy in a care house: results of case studies. In: Proceedings of the 15th IEEE International Conference on Robot and Human Interactive Communication (ROMAN), pp. 581–586 (2006)
9. Kristoffersson, A., Coradeschi, S., Loutfi, A.: User-centered evaluation of robotic telepresence for an elderly population. In: Proceedings of the 2nd International Workshop on Designing Robotic Artefacts with User- and Experience-Centred Perspectives at NordiCHI, pp. 1–4 (2010)
10. Yamazaki, R., Nishio, S., Ogawa, K., Ishiguro, H.: Teleoperated android as an embodied communication medium: a case study with demented elderlies in a care facility. In: Proceedings of the RO-MAN, pp. 1066–1071 (2012)
11. Mallidou, A.A., Cummings, G.G., Schalm, C., Estabrooks, C.A.: Health care aides use of time in a residential long-term care unit: a time and motion study. Int. J. Nurs. Stud. **50**(9), 1229–1239 (2013)
12. Robinson, H., MacDonald, B., Broadbent, E.: The role of healthcare robots for older people at home: a review. Int. J. Soc. Robot. **6**(4), 575–591 (2014). https://doi.org/10.1007/s12369-014-0242-2
13. Van Patten, R., et al.: Home-based cognitively assistive robots: maximizing cognitive functioning and maintaining independence in older adults without dementia. Clin. Interv. Aging **15**, 1129–1139 (2020)
14. Heerink, M., Kröse, B., Evers, V., Wielinga, B.: The influence of social presence on acceptance of a companion robot by older people. J. Phys. Agents **2**, 33–40 (2008)

15. Albert, M.S., et al.: The diagnosis of mild cognitive impairment due to Alzheimer's disease: recommendations from the National Institute on Aging-Alzheimer's Association workgroups on diagnostic guidelines for Alzheimer's disease. Alzheimers Dement. **7**(3), 270–279 (2011)
16. Morris, J.C.: The clinical dementia rating (CDR): current version and scoring rules. Neurology **43**(11), 2412–2414 (1993)
17. Folstein, M.F., Folstein, S.E., McHugh, P.R.: Mini-mental state. A practical method for grading the cognitive state of patients for the clinician. J. Psychiatr. Res. **12**(3), 189–198 (1975)
18. Sharp Corporation. Product information. https://robohon.com/product/robohon.php. Accessed 7 Sept 2021
19. Yamazaki, R., Kase, H., Nishio, S., Ishiguro, H.: Anxiety reduction through close communication with robotic media in dementia patients and healthy older adults. J. Robot. Mechatron. **32**(1), 32–42 (2020)
20. Ge, S., Zhu, Z., Wu, B., McConnell, E.S.: Technology-based cognitive training and rehabilitation interventions for individuals with mild cognitive impairment: a systematic review. BMC Geriatr. **18**(213), 1–19 (2018). https://doi.org/10.1186/s12877-018-0893-1
21. Wang, J.Y., et al.: Leisure activity and risk of cognitive impairment: the Chongqing aging study. Neurology **66**(6), 911–913 (2006)
22. Geda, Y.E., et al.: Physical exercise, aging, and mild cognitive impairment: a population-based study. Arch. Neurol. **67**(1), 80–86 (2010)

Psychiatrists' Views on Robot-Assisted Diagnostics of Peripartum Depression

Mengyu Zhong[1,3]([✉]), Ayesha Mae Bilal[2,3], Fotios C. Papadopoulos[2], and Ginevra Castellano[1]

[1] Department of Information Technology, Uppsala University, Uppsala, Sweden
{mengyu.zhong,ginevra.castellano}@it.uu.se
[2] Department of Neuroscience, Uppsala University, Uppsala, Sweden
{ayesha.bilal,fotis.papadopoulos}@neuro.uu.se
[3] Women's Mental Health during the Reproductive Lifespan – WoMHeR, Uppsala University, Uppsala, Sweden

Abstract. Social robots are rising to prominence as tools in healthcare and mental healthcare. In this paper, we investigate robot-assisted diagnostics of peripartum depression (PPD) in women. To design robots that are accepted by users and comply with trustworthy Artificial Intelligence principles, we use semi-structured interviews to explore the views of potential stakeholders - psychiatrists. We aim to answer three research questions regarding 1) the usefulness of robots in the diagnosis of PPD, 2) potential ethical issues, and 3) the roles that robots and clinicians may play in the diagnostic process. Results show that psychiatrists are only willing to let robots take minor responsibilities, and feel that robots may be more useful in situations where there is a shortage of clinicians.

Keywords: Social robotics · Robots in mental healthcare · Depression

1 Introduction

Peripartum depression (PPD) is one of the most prevalent mental health disorders related to childbirth and affects as many as 10% of women during pregnancy or after childbirth [20]. It is a serious and potentially life-threatening disorder with high societal costs. PPD can have devastating consequences not only for the mother but also for the infant and family unit, including preterm delivery, adverse birth outcomes, low quality of maternal life, family breakdown, and even increased risk of suicide [12].

Research shows that psychosocial interventions may decrease depressive symptoms for women affected by PPD [3]. However, in order to receive treatment, a clinical diagnosis of depression is required. This currently entails a structured

This project is partly funded by the WoMHeR Centre, Uppsala University, Sweden, and the project "The ethics and social consequences of AI & caring robots" in the WASP-HS program, Sweden.

clinical interview with a skilled physician. However, access to skilled personnel with training to perform the clinical interviews in primary care can vary substantially, which can lead to long waiting times or an unstructured interview with lower diagnostic accuracy. According to a recent review, up to 69% of PPD cases go undetected and only 6% receive adequate treatment [5].

At the same time, clinical interviews conducted with the support of virtual humans have recently proven to be a promising resource to support more time- and cost-effective diagnostic processes [10]. Despite the promising results with virtual humans, research comparing robots with their virtual representations shows that the robotic embodiment is often preferred by users, possibly due to aspects related to size, realism, shared physical space, physical presence and perceived social presence [9], which may facilitate interaction with the artificial entity. However, while social robots are rising to prominence in healthcare and even mental healthcare [14,15], no previous work has investigated robot-assisted diagnostics of depression.

The aim of our research is to develop methods for robot-assisted diagnosis of PPD that are socially accepted by patients and clinicians, and that comply with principles of trustworthy Artificial Intelligence (AI) [1]. As an initial step towards this aim, this paper explores psychiatrists' views on robot-assisted diagnostics of PPD. We conducted one-to-one semi-structured interviews with licensed psychiatrists in Sweden. We discuss psychiatrists' attitudes towards social robots, as well as their envisioned ethical issues and perspectives on the role that social robots may play in the diagnostics of PPD.

2   Related Work

2.1   Robots in Healthcare and Mental Healthcare

Healthcare robotics is an emerging area. Relying on precision in motion and sensing, robots are able to facilitate physical tasks in clinical healthcare, for example, as assistants in surgery, physiotherapy or nursing. More specifically, they can assist with tasks that are dirty, dangerous, and dull, but are valuable for clinical staff [14]. Robots might also be well-placed in tasks that can be considered problematic to be handled by an unobjective human eye [2]. Due to the ability of robots to extend, augment and quantify healthcare tasks, it is believed that robots can benefit all stakeholders across various care settings, although satisfactory ways to integrate robots into the daily routines of these care settings still need to be further explored [2,14].

The use of robotics in mental healthcare is nascent. Social robots have been used to support care and management of dementia and autism, and cognitive impairments; provide companionship to people to reduce loneliness; or assist in education for children with developmental disabilities [13]. Previous studies identified advantages of the adoption of robots in mental healthcare, including solving the labour shortage, inhibiting biases in the diagnostic process from healthcare personnel, and strengthening a feeling of anonymity and enhanced self-disclosure [11,13,14].

When it comes to depression diagnostics, a number of works have investigated the use of virtual agents. For example, DeVault [6] proposed the use of a virtual agent to perform semi-structured face-to-face interviews, aiming to automatically assess mental disorders. An evaluation study showed that users were more willing to communicate with the virtual agent compared to human interviewers. Suendermann-Oef [19] proposed a multimodal conversational diagnostic system, NEMSI, for screening of neurological and mental conditions. In another study, a virtual agent was developed for administering a depression screening questionnaire and proved to be practically equivalent to self-administration [10]. These works show the potential of an automatic diagnostic system of mental disorders. However, to our knowledge, robot-assisted diagnostics of depression is yet to be investigated.

2.2 Ethical Issues in Socially Assistive Robotics for Healthcare

The recent EU ethics guidelines for trustworthy AI identify a set of requirements to achieve AI that is lawful, ethical and robust [1]. These requirements include human agency and oversight, technical robustness and safety, privacy and data governance, transparency, diversity, non-discrimination and fairness, societal and environmental well-being, and accountability. Social robots are a type of AI system and, therefore, should be designed, developed and evaluated with these requirements in mind in order to be truly human-centric and trustworthy. This is especially important for robots in socially assistive roles, which provide not only physical but also social support to people, as is the case for social robots in many healthcare applications.

Fiske [7] identified a number of challenges for robots in mental healthcare, such as data ethics issues and lack of guidance on development, clinical integration, and training. However, ethical issues surrounding the use of robots as tools to support depression diagnostics require new investigations. In this context, as we are clearly dealing with a vulnerable population, it becomes extremely important to think about how to involve patients and clinicians in the design of such robots, the role that the robots may have and how they may help the clinicians in the diagnostics process. Moreover, the robot would have to uphold the ethical responsibility of mental health professionals by, e.g., informing relevant individuals, third parties or authorities when patients are at risk of harming themselves or others. One solution can be to always let a qualified clinician have the mandate to supervise. Moreover, there are aspects of the therapeutic alliance that need to be considered when we plan to use nonhuman entities [7]. For instance, current technology might not enable robots to evaluate patients' emotional states in real-time [16], and patients may long for human therapists [8].

Another concern is how to respect and protect patient autonomy. Before patients give consent, they can be assessed to make sure they do not misunderstand any information about the robot. Human oversight is also a key requirement for trustworthy human-robot interaction, which helps to make sure that the robot does not undermine human autonomy or cause other adverse effects [1,7]. To what extent should the robot act autonomously? How can clinicians be in the loop and monitor the whole interaction? How can the robot support clinicians in the interview process, without at the same time replacing them? These are some of the open questions that this paper investigates.

3   Method

3.1   Research Questions

We aim to address three main research questions (RQs): **RQ1:** Do psychiatrists think that social robots could be helpful as tools to support the diagnostic process of PPD? **RQ2:** Do they envision any ethical issues surrounding the use of social robots in the diagnostic process of PPD? **RQ3:** What roles should robots and clinicians play in the diagnostic process, respectively?

3.2   Participants

Three experienced psychiatrists (F: 2, M: 1, mean age: 44.3 ± 4.7) serving in the Swedish healthcare system were recruited, with reported 6–10 years experience diagnosing depression and 2–10 years experience with peripartum depression. Participation was voluntary, with no compensation. All participants reported minimal prior experience interacting with robots. They reported between average to maximal experience interacting with ubiquitous digital technologies. Informed consent, demographic information, and reports of participant's technological and professional experiences were collected in advance of the interview through online forms. The research was approved by the local ethics committee.

3.3   Procedure

The interviews were conducted via Zoom. The duration varied between 35–45 min. We started the interview by introducing the study and showing two pictures of Furhat[1], the robot that we plan to use in this research. After that, using a similar approach to Serholt [17], we asked participants to read the following vignette, and to imagine Furhat as the robot in the envisioned scenario:

The board of a local psychiatric hospital decides to order five diagnostic robots for psychiatrists working in the hospital. Psychiatrists can name these robots, which will respond to their assigned name when switched on. All psychiatrists receive a one-day tutorial to learn how to operate the robot, how they could contact technical support if needed, how the robot works, and what kind of work the robot can assist with. It is explained that the robot is designed to assist with the diagnosis of women's perinatal depression and can conduct one to one MINI interviews with patients even when psychiatrists are not present in the room. The robot can speak and ask questions to the patients and use facial expressions and head movements (e.g. nodding or shaking head) to communicate. It is possible for psychiatrists to control all these behaviours (verbal or non-verbal). The robot

---

[1] https://furhatrobotics.com/.

can also analyse the patients' answers, as well as their behaviours (e.g., facial expressions, body motion, tone of voice) during the interview, and use machine learning algorithms to estimate if a clinical depressive episode might be underway. The patients' answers and behaviours are recorded with video cameras and this data, as well as the estimate by the robot, is encrypted and stored in the hospital's secured server. Moreover, the system can store diverse forms of data (e.g. transcripts of answers, behavioural summary or video clips) for later review and compute the severity of the depressive episode according to the criteria in the MINI interview. However, psychiatrists may decide not fully use these functions. Maria, the psychiatrist in the hospital, has many patients coming to see her every day. She wants the robot to assist her with the MINI interview. If the robot could conduct the MINI interview in her place, it would be possible for her to treat more women and decrease waiting times, expanding access to healthcare. Lina, who shows a clear trend of depression after her pregnancy and is referred to Maria by her GP. After arrival, Lina goes into an interview room where a robot named Florence is waiting for her. She knows Florence will ask her some questions. She is told that Florence can use its perceptive capabilities to analyse her facial expressions, body movements, tone of voice and conversation, and can combine this with its knowledge to assess her mental state. During the interview, Florence notices that Lina displays some sad facial expressions and some body movements and voice characteristics also indicate she may be depressed. Furthermore, Florence records Lina's answers to the questions in the MINI interview and, by using machine learning to analyse Lina's behaviours, estimates whether Lina experiences a clinical depressive episode and its severity. Florence produces a report for Maria, who now can read Lina's answers to the MINI interview and take into account Florence's automatic analysis of her behaviours to make a clinical diagnosis.

When participants finished reading, we asked them specific questions related to the themes identified in our main research questions, i.e. attitudes towards social robots in the assisted diagnosis of PPD, possible ethical issues, and envisioned roles and responsibilities of robots and clinicians.

3.4   Analytical Approach

The interview audio recordings were transcribed verbatim using Otter.ai[2], and a thematic analysis approach, as described by Braun and Clarke [4], was used to analyze the transcripts using QSR International's NVivo[3] qualitative data analysis software. A framework for categories and subcategories was initially developed deductively according to the interview guide using the first transcript with two members of the research team. This category system was then independently elaborated and adapted using the second and third interview transcripts during the coding process by one member of the research team. After the coding process, a code catalogue was developed and critically appraised by another

---

[2] https://otter.ai/.

[3] https://www.qsrinternational.com/nvivo-qualitative-data-analysis-software/home.

member. During this review process, minor modifications were made when certain codes or themes were merged or renamed. The final codebook was generated, key themes were defined, and quotations representing the key themes were noted as the basis for the final interpretation.

4 Results

Four main themes emerged during the thematic analysis from the data.

Attitudes Towards the Robot. All psychiatrists had some negative feelings about the robot. P1 and P3 thought the robot looked strange, and P2 thought it is unnecessary (we further explain this in the practical concerns section below). However, two psychiatrists also expressed that it would be interesting to see: *"an interaction between a patient and robot" (P1)*, and compare *"if you train the interviewing person [who] does [the] MINI, versus robots" (P1)*. P3 had relatively more positive thoughts than others, speculating that the robot could be more neutral than the human interviewer, might save some time, and that *"a lot of other standardized [procedures] in other parts of the ward in medicine are...'robotized'...it might be worth a try"*.

Ethical Issues. The question of potential ethical issues took longer for participants to think about, and only three envisioned ethical issues emerged. First, the patient's preference to meet a human needs to be respected: *"...some patients would prefer not to meet the robot, definitely, well, you would have to respect that" (P3)*. Second, it may produce anxiety related to job security among hospital personnel: *"It would...raise quite a bit of anxiety among the professional group of psychiatrists and nurses and so on, that they should be maybe replaced by robots" (P1)*. There were also concerns about the consequences of the lack of human communication patients would receive, such as loneliness: *"I would feel extremely lonely if I came and was seeking for a word and [I was told] 'hey, you can talk to this robot'" (P3)*, and lower self-disclosure when asked sensitive questions: *"It would be no problem to talk [about] simple things, but not so emotionally" (P2)*.

Practical Concerns. Psychiatrists had some practical concerns regarding patient acceptability of robots and, most frequently, the robot's effectiveness. Psychiatrists didn't trust the analytical ability of the robot, and doubted the robot would give the same interpretation as a psychiatrist would. A contradiction discussed was that psychiatrists only receive patients with severe mental disorders referred by General Practitioners (GPs) or other doctors, and so, there is no need to do a robot diagnostic interview if the patient has already been assessed by a clinician. *"This patient had already met a GP that had met her and [thought] that she was clearly depressed. That's why the doctor referred her to the psychiatrist...why would she need to see the robot in the first place?" (P2)*. Furthermore, we suggested that the robot may store and provide diverse forms of data and records, for instance, transcripts of answers, summaries of behaviours, video recordings and suggested clips for later review. In addition to interview scores (using MINI or other interview questionnaires), the robot may use machine learning algorithms to estimate if a clinical depressive episode might be under way based on the automatic analysis of verbal and nonverbal behaviors of patients. However, only P3 agreed that the suggestions from robots may save some time in the diagnostic process. P1 thought that it is necessary to go through a whole video recording, thus the robot can not be considered as effective. P2 referred to previous experience on interviewing patients online, and claimed that it is necessary to meet patients in person to make an accurate diagnosis: *"I have been doing some assessments from seeing a patient over, like, Zoom or [Microsoft] Teams meeting...it's not the same", "You can't see the small nuances and so on over a computer screen"*. But they also admitted that the use of robots may be beneficial in less severe conditions or in places where there is an unmet need for trained clinicians: *"It might even be better than a human being in translating the answers to a diagnosis...when we're talking about clinicians who are not fully trained" (P1), "[in] some low income countries, third world countries where there are a lot of women giving birth to children ... then, this might be [useful]... it's better than leaving them to themselves" (P2)*.

Psychiatrists were unconvinced about patients liking using the robot: *"Our youngsters, they grow up with different experiences... maybe they feel more comfortable than I would to...talk to robots" (P2), "I think maybe some people would be skeptical, others might be positive to it" (P3)*.

Work Division Between Clinicians and Robot. Concerning the possibility of the robot as a support in the diagnostic process, psychiatrists shared similar views about the work division between clinicians and robots, particularly that the final diagnosis needs to be made by psychiatrists or a trained doctor in charge: *"the psychiatrist should be the one who takes into account the information given from the robot interview and make the decision" (P2)*. P3 also suggested that obscure answers should be judged by psychiatrists: *"...but once there are long and difficult answers, I think a psychiatrist needs to judge that answer"*.

Psychiatrists also preferred the first point of contact in the diagnostic process to be human, who could ask the more sensitive questions: *"Normally we have a discussion in things that are not included in MINI, like childhood and different social aspects and how their problems started...The second time, we use MINI for screening, and the same would go for a robot" (P3)*. Psychiatrists reasoned that they would not want to monitor the whole interview online as it would be inefficient, however, human intervention may be necessary under certain circumstances. P3 thought that personnel could *"add questions to get closer to the diagnosis"* during an interview. The interview may need to stop if the patient *"gets somewhat irritated...angry...just wants to leave" (P1)* or *"reacts emotionally" (P3)*. After the interview, clinical personnel should follow up immediately if, for instance, patients report thoughts of self-harming or harming others, or severe symptoms of disordered sleep or eating.

Although all psychiatrists were concerned about the effectiveness of the robot in conducting psychiatric diagnostic interviews, they suggested that robots could help with other tasks in primary care or for screening as these require less professional psychiatric knowledge and are less complicated, and so, can be handled by a robot competently, for example with *"screening forms for patients... they have to fill in the forms and that's it... They don't have to see a doctor really" (P2)*. One psychiatrist suggested letting the robot help ask questions, but only handle the clear-cut answers, such as *"when the patient is clear about 'No, I've never had suicidal thoughts"' (P3)*. P2 and P3 also thought it is useful to let the robot handle "some uncomplicated" tasks, including *"follow up after you put the patients on a medication" (P2)*, evaluating sleep patterns, or simple checkups to *"evaluate some [symptoms], like [symptoms] for ADHD,... blood pressure and heart rate and the weight and so on...maybe in those quite uncomplicated cases, you could have some use of the robot just to check these symptoms" (P2)*.

When asked about how they think the robot should react to patients, psychiatrists had different answers. One suggested that, apart from unavoidable verbal reactions to facilitate conversation, the robot should *"[react in a] compassionate way, [with] facial expression... say something as well" (P1)*. Others thought the robot shouldn't react too much except with some necessary dialogues as it may be *"weird for a patient [if] the robot reacts or makes a sad face" (P2)*.

5   Discussion

In this section, we discuss how the results address the three research questions posed by this study.

RQ1: Overall, psychiatrists did not think that robots would be very helpful as a diagnostic tool in psychiatric healthcare, but would be useful for simpler diagnostic tasks or screening. In addition to practical concerns about the acceptability of the robot by patients, psychiatrists worried about the effectiveness of the robot. Although the robot could take over the responsibility of conducting the interview, a psychiatrist would still need the ability to supervise the whole process. At the same time they would not want to monitor the whole interview, because it would not be efficient. When presented with the possibility that certain forms of records stored by a robot may facilitate the diagnostic process, e.g. transcripts of answers or behavioural summaries or video clips, psychiatrists observed that they would still need to examine such records or see the patient in person before making a diagnosis, so they do not consider this to be valuable from the perspective of increasing efficiency in the process.

Psychiatrists felt that some simpler interview and analysis could be handled by robots, and in general tended to compare the robot with a nurse or doctor without professional psychiatric knowledge, but highlighted the need to see the robot to make an appropriate final judgment.

RQ2: Psychiatrists envisioned some ethical issues related to the use of robots in mental healthcare. Firstly, some patients may not want to talk to a robot, and we should respect the right of patients to meet a human clinician. This topic of respecting and protecting patient autonomy has been discussed by Fiske [7]. Secondly, hospital personnel may worry about being replaced by robots, which may lead to anxiety related to job security. This is a valid concern, as it is suggested that the use of robots could both displace and create new jobs [1], which highlights the need to explore ways in which robots can assist with, rather than replace, tasks that humans perform, or to identify tasks that can be assumed by robots to free up time for human personnel to focus on other duties. On the other hand, as psychiatrists suggested, certain responsibilities cannot be taken up by a robot, such as the diagnosis making. Finally, the lack of communication with a human may cause feelings of loneliness, an issue that was also highlighted by Fiske [7].

RQ3: Psychiatrists suggested that clinicians should remain the first point of contact, and manage supervision and decision making. Before meeting a robot, patients should meet a human clinician who can ask some sensitive questions, such as regarding their paternal or familial relationships, and make sure the patient is in a position to, and willing to, be interviewed by a robot. During the interview, a clinician or nurse needs to supervise the process and intervene when necessary. They may also need the ability to control what questions should be asked by the robot. To ensure a reliable clinical diagnosis, a psychiatrist or a doctor in charge should always evaluate the answers given by patients during the interview.

A robot in mental healthcare is considered to be helpful in some simple evaluations and screenings. It should not handle sensitive or complicated questions and answers, as these might be easily misinterpreted. Moreover, psychiatrists were not unanimous about how the robot should interact with patients. Some thought empathetic reactions by a robot would not be appropriate during the interview process, but there were also opinions that compassionate reactions by the robot would be necessary when patients display emotional reactions.

Finally, psychiatrists' views on whether there are core responsibilities that the robot should not take clearly point to one of the key requirements for trustworthy AI [1], i.e., human oversight, which helps make sure that the robot does not undermine human autonomy or cause other adverse effects. Previous literature on socially assistive robots has investigated similar questions, but in educational applications [18]. Our findings call for further investigations to understand the implications of human oversight in applications where social robots interact with vulnerable subjects.

6   Conclusion

Through analysing the views of psychiatrists, we shed light on what ethical issues may arise, what concerns need to be addressed, and what roles social robots may play in the robot-assisted diagnosis of PPD. Although psychiatrists thought the robot could potentially be helpful in the diagnostic process through assisting with certain tasks, they were cautious about trusting suggestions from a robot, and only willing to let the robot take minor responsibilities. This cautiousness seems to be entrenched in the extreme vulnerability of psychiatric patients and the potential severity of their mental issues. In parallel, the concerns about the acceptability and effectiveness of the robot, as well as potential ethical issues, also curbs their willingness to adopt the robot in their medical routine. These results warrant further steps for designing acceptable diagnostic robots. As psychiatrists suggested, the robot can serve in places where the patients are in less critical states and more trained clinicians are needed, such as primary cares or screening interviews. Focus group studies with stakeholders in such scenarios, namely the patients, nurses and clinicians, can be conducted next, aiming to get a more overall reflective perspective.

References

1. Ethics guidelines for trustworthy AI. European Commission (2019)
2. A roadmap for US robotics: From internet to robotics 2020. Computing Community Consortium (2020)
3. Anokye, R., et al.: Prevalence of postpartum depression and interventions utilized for its management. Ann. Gen. Psychiatry **17**(1), 1–8 (2018)
4. Braun, V., Clarke, V.: Using thematic analysis in psychology. Qual. Res. Psychol. **3**(2), 77–101 (2006)
5. Cox, E.Q., Sowa, N.A., Meltzer-Brody, S.E., Gaynes, B.N.: The perinatal depression treatment cascade. J. Clin. Psychiatry **77**(09), 1189–1200 (2016)
6. DeVault, D., et al.: SimSensei Kiosk: a virtual human interviewer for healthcare decision support. In: Proceedings of AAMAS 2014, pp. 1061–1068 (2014)
7. Fiske, A., Henningsen, P., Buyx, A.: Your robot therapist will see you now: Ethical implications of embodied artificial intelligence in psychiatry, psychology, and psychotherapy. J. Med. Internet Res. **21**, e13216 (2019)
8. Heim, E., Rötger, A., Lorenz, N., Maercker, A.: Working alliance with an avatar: how far can we go with Internet interventions? Internet Interv. **11**, 41–46 (2018)
9. Hoffmann, L., Krämer, N.C.: How should an artificial entity be embodied? In: HRI 2011 Workshop, p. 8 (2011)
10. Jaiswal, S., Valstar, M., Kusumam, K., Greenhalgh, C.: Virtual human questionnaire for analysis of depression, anxiety and personality. In: Proceedings of the 19th ACM International Conference on Intelligent Virtual Agents, pp. 81–87 (2019)
11. Joinson, A.N.: Self-disclosure in computer-mediated communication: the role of self-awareness and visual anonymity. Eur. J. Soc. Psychol. **31**(2), 177–192 (2001)
12. Marcus, S.M., Heringhausen, J.E.: Depression in childbearing women: when depression complicates pregnancy. Prim. Care: Clin. Off. Pract. **36**(1), 151–165 (2009)
13. Riek, L.D.: Robotics Technology in Mental Health Care, pp. 185–203. Elsevier (2016)
14. Riek, L.D.: Healthcare robotics. Commun. ACM **60**, 68–78 (2017)
15. Scassellati, B., Vázquez, M.: The potential of socially assistive robots during infectious disease outbreaks. Sci. Robot. **5**(44), eabc9014 (2020)
16. Scholten, M.R., Kelders, S.M., Van Gemert-Pijnen, J.E.: Self-guided web-based interventions: scoping review on user needs and the potential of embodied conversational agents to address them. J. Med. Internet Res. **19**(11), e383 (2017)
17. Serholt, S., et al.: The case of classroom robots: teachers' deliberations on the ethical tensions. AI Soc. **32**(4), 613–631 (2017)
18. Sharkey, A.J.C.: Should we welcome robot teachers? Ethics Inf. Technol. **18**(4), 283–297 (2016)

19. Suendermann-Oeft, D., et al.: NEMSI: a multimodal dialog system for screening of neurological or mental conditions. In: Proceedings of IVA 2019, pp. 245–247 (2019)
20. Woody, C., et al.: A systematic review and meta-regression of the prevalence and incidence of perinatal depression. J. Affect. Disord. **219**, 86–92 (2017)

Social Robots in Care Homes for Older Adults
Observations from Participatory Design Workshops

Sofia Thunberg[(✉)] and Tom Ziemke

Department of Computer and Information Science, Linköping University,
58183 Linköping, Sweden
{sofia.thunberg,tom.ziemke}@liu.se

Abstract. Evaluations of social robots for older adults in care home environments during the past 20 years have shown mostly positive results. However, many of these studies have been short-term and with few participants, as well as limited to few countries. Recent evidence, however, indicates that social robots might not work in all settings or for everyone. Therefore, we conducted a participatory workshop with key stakeholders as an attempt to begin to disentangle the many interrelated factors behind a successful implementation. The result showed similarities in preferred embodiment and morphology, differences in behavioural complexity and task performance, as well as a maybe surprising lack of interest in emotional support. It further showed that older adults living in care homes prior—to meeting social robots—showed relatively little interest in these robots. Based on these observations, we formulate future research directions.

Keywords: Social robots · Older adults · Participatory design · User-centered design · Human-robot interaction

1 Introduction

Social robots have for the last two decades been used for a range of diverse tasks in care homes for older adults. Studies report on social robots providing companionship [2], exercise [16], cognitive therapy [7] and help with daily tasks [17]. However, even if real-world evaluations of social robots in care homes often show positive effects [29,31,33], many of the studies have been very short term (e.g., 10–30 minutes of interaction on one occasion) [11,14,21], have had few participants (e.g., $n = 1$–7) [10,15,26], and the majority have been conducted in Japan [1]. Some researchers, therefore, are questioning these positive results, and report conflicting results [19,24,30] from studies outside Japan and for longer time periods.

Part of the problem, in our opinion, is that much robot development has been overly technology-driven [22]; i.e., many social robots for older people have not been designed and tested with the actual users in mind. Previous research

© Springer Nature Switzerland AG 2021
H. Li et al. (Eds.): ICSR 2021, LNAI 13086, pp. 475–486, 2021.
https://doi.org/10.1007/978-3-030-90525-5_41

has, for example, shown that there are significant differences between what older people prefer in a robot and what roboticists think the users need [4]. The use of user-centered studies with older adults to design and develop better social robots have increased in recent years [5,13,23,25], but it is still far from clear what type of robots' older adults would prefer and benefit from when it comes to the robots':

1. embodiment
2. morphology
3. behavioural complexity

In this paper, we report our work with participatory design workshops with three groups of key stakeholders: active older adults still living at home, care home residents, and care home staff members. With many robot models on the market by now and even more in the development or research phase, it would be useful to get a deeper understanding of the factors that make older adults accept or reject a social robot, and what makes robots work or fail over longer periods of time.

In the following sections, we present some background and a brief introduction to participatory design (Sect. 2), followed by our methodology (Sect. 3), results and discussions (Sect. 4), and finally some conclusions (Sect. 5).

2   Participatory Design and PICTIVE

The workshops documented in this paper were conducted using a participatory design method called Plastic Interface for Collaborative Technology Initiative through Video Exploration (PICTIVE) [20], which we also recently used in a study of humanoid robots' communication design [32]. The general idea behind PICTIVE is that participants can give early input to the design of future technology through the creation of very low-tech prototypes.

Participants are provided with one or more scenarios by the session leader and asked to put down ideas on paper. The design process is video recorded, which enables the session leader to be more engaged in the process instead of, for example, taking notes. The original vision behind PICTIVE was that by using low-tech objects, such as a shared design surface, plastic icons, coloured highlighters, coloured pens, labels (data fields), pop-up events and post-it notes, all participants could contribute with their ideas in a relatively straightforward and easy fashion. Some icons and labels are predefined before the design sessions, but the participants can also create their own. This is one of the advantages of PICTIVE compared to other user-centered design methods. The predefined labels can be seen as building blocks that limit the design space of what is possible, which is especially useful when participants are not designers and do not have previous knowledge of design processes. In comparison, other methods, such as Collaborative Users' Task Analysis (CUTA) [12], building scrappy prototypes or role-playing, may require the participants to take a larger creative step than they are used to. Ideally, using PICTIVE, the shared design surface, the labels and the scenarios provided by the researcher, can facilitate the creation in an accessible way. This, we believe, makes PICTIVE particularly suitable for participatory design of human-robot interaction for older adults, especially since most of the potential stakeholders do not have previous experience with robots nor design.

In recent years, the number of participatory design studies in technological health care products for older adults have increased, but relatively few have addressed social robots. Participatory design workshops with older adults have been used, for example, to develop therapeutic socially assistive robots for older people diagnosed with depression [27], and to explore the roles a robot might play in an older person's life [9]. The latter study showed that older adults could see potential general benefits, but the most common attitude was that the robot might be "good for others but not themselves" [9].

Apart from some positive examples, there still is a lack of studies focusing on the wants and needs of different stakeholders for social robots. One positive example is a participatory design study with caregivers of dementia patients, which investigated what characteristics (e.g., interaction, morphology and functionality) a social robot for dementia patients should have [18]. The caregivers envisioned robots that could bring joy to cherish the patient's happy moments and robots that could comfort and better manage when they were showing agitated behaviour. The authors proposed a community-based design approach, meaning that designers should include different stakeholders when developing and deploying social robots. In the participatory design workshops documented here, in order to complement the above results [18], we included as participants (a) older adults still living at home, (b) care home residents, and (c) care home staff members.

3 Methodology

In this section, the participants, material and the workshop sessions, are presented.

3.1 Participants

Three stakeholder groups, with five participants in each, were recruited for the participatory design study, based on a convenience sample strategy. All participants were recruited with the help of the municipality of Mjölby, in the Southeast of Sweden, with about 28,000 inhabitants. The first group consisted of five older adults (mean age = 79, SD = 5.29, 60% women) who still lived at home and were active. This group signed up themselves for the workshop after information flyers had been passed around at an activity centre for retired people.

The second group consisted of four older adults (mean age = 83, SD = 7,54, 100% women), who lived at a care home because of a physical condition and who did not have cognitive impairments. The group originally consisted of five participants, but on the day of the study one was ill and had to be excluded.

The third group comprised four unlicensed assistive personnel working in a care home (mean age = 43, SD = 11,00, 75% women). These participants signed up after the manager had informed them about the study. This group also originally consisted of five people, but one could not attend due to health reasons. Hence, the final set consisted of thirteen (5 + 4 + 4) participants.

The three stakeholder groups were chosen to represent three different views of the wants and needs of social robots in care homes. The first group were about the same age group as people that lives in care homes and could more easily imagine the needs if they themselves or their friends would live in a care home, as compared to younger age groups (including family members). The second group were chosen since they are one of the intended end users. Other potential end users could be, for example, dementia patients. The third group were chosen since they work in care homes and know of the needs for their patients but also since robots could help them in their work of taking care of older adults.

All participants gave informed consent prior to the workshop, and video and audio recordings were orally accepted by all participants before each part of the session.

3.2   Material

A sketch showing four different robots in a typical living room constituted the shared design surface (see Fig. 1). The robots were inspired by four morphology categories identified in previous work [8]: anthropomorphic (here represented by the humanoid Pepper), zoomorphic (represented by the robot seal Paro), caricatured (represented by the social robot Buddy) and functional (represented by the Xiaomi Roborock vacuum cleaner). To facilitate the participants' creation of interfaces, eight labels depicting communication modalities were created. The labels were inspired by previous research of ours [32], and they were: motion, haptic, sounds, voice synthesis, LEDs, text, animation and symbols. In addition to these labels, the participants were provided with typical icons, coloured pens, post-it notes, glue, eraser and a scissor (see Fig. 2).

3.3   Workshop Sessions

Three study sessions, lasting 60–150 min each, took place in a secluded room, where one group and the session leader (the first author) sat around a table. The procedure of the session consisted of the three following steps.

In the first step, the participants were asked some initial questions about robots and their experience with technology. The questions that were asked were, for example, "What do you know about robots?" and "Do you have any experience with robot technology?". This part was audio-recorded. In the second step, the session leader held a short presentation about robots used today. The presentation started with different categories of robots, (following [6]); with a few examples of rehabilitation robots before changing focus to the service type and the companion type of robots. Different robots were then presented as examples of anthropomorphic, zoomorphic, caricatured or functional morphology's (cf.

Fig. 1. The shared design surface.

Fig. 2. The workshop setup.

above and [8]). The third step was PICTIVE, and this step was video recorded. The workshop consisted of three phases: the label phase, the sketch phase and the interview phase.

In the label phase, participants were encouraged to use the labels on the shared design surface to map different design solutions and what kind of robots they would like and need. To start the creative session, they were provided with a scenario in a shared living room area at a care home. In the sketch phase, participants were encouraged to create at least three unique robot designs each, and they could make use of the shared design surface, or blank paper. The predefined labels were at hand, and they could also create their own. The participants then presented each of their robot designs and described their qualities. In the interview phase, the sketched robots were tested through eight scenarios that could occur in the everyday life of an older adult at a care home. The scenarios were inspired by events observed at a care home. One of the eight scenarios is described below, in the way it was presented to the participants:

> "Ann has dementia and lives at a care home. Every afternoon she gets worried, starts packing and wants to go home. The staff tries to distract her in different ways, such as getting her to watch TV. However, this does not work every day. How could a robot help Ann?"

After each scenario was described, the participants picked at least one of their robots and motivated how the robot could help in the scenario and/or how their design should be altered to help in a better way.

From each study session, the shared design surface and the participants' designs were collected. Keywords, phrases and statements from the audio and video recordings regarding wants and needs of social robots were transcribed. All data were thematically analysed, and opinions from the three groups were entered into three data files. In each file, the wants and needs were labelled with codes and similar codes were merged into subcategories (e.g., functional, social, loneliness). These were then sorted into themes.

4   Results and Discussion

The analysis resulted in two themes; type of social robots and functionality; which are described and discussed below. Limitations of the participatory method are also presented.

4.1   Type of Social Robots

As can be seen in the example sketches of social robots in Fig. 3, neither stakeholder group limited themselves to one or two robot morphologies, all four types were discussed and were preferred for different tasks. The type of robots that were mentioned were humanoid, animal-like, caricatured (cute and cartoonish), functional, and these were all preferred to have a physical embodiment and that shared the same space as the user. Also, social robots with a simple physical design and only communicating by voice, for example a voice user interface like Google Home or Alexa, were discussed to help with control of the "system of robots" at the care home. Virtual embodiments were argued to be particularly difficult to interact with since the social robot would be on a screen and not in its physical form.

Regarding zoomorphic robots, several of the participants in the first group mentioned that the animal needed to be the individual's choice, i.e., "some people want a cat, and some want a dog", which is in line with some of our previous findings [31]. One interesting observation was that the only companion type

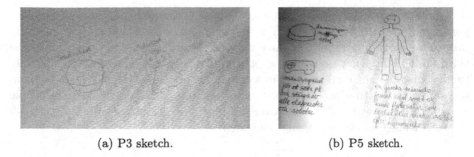

(a) P3 sketch.   (b) P5 sketch.

Fig. 3. Example robots from the sketch phase.

robot presented was the robot seal Paro but the participants did not like this embodiment as they found it unfamiliar, and they sketched a cat robot instead (see Fig. 3a).

4.2 Functionality

There were some differences between groups regarding the desired functionality of a social robot. All participants in the first group, older adults still living at home, wanted functional robots in a care home, such as a control unit to have a simple overview. This could be on a tablet, or on a social robot's tablet (e.g., Pepper). The robots they found particularly useful were a vacuum cleaning robot, and a social robot that one could ask to turn on the TV or answer questions. One of the participants also mentioned that she wanted a robot to play cards with. Furthermore, they saw a need for a robot that could trigger an alarm if somebody fell to the ground. Except for finding social functional types of robots most useful for themselves, they all mentioned that companion robots would be the best comfort and company for other older adults that are either physically or cognitive impaired. In line with previous results [9], they did not see the need for themselves before living in a care home.

The third group, consisting of care home staff members, were all positive toward robots. They could see different kinds of robots as a big help, for example, one robot for entertainment, one for cleaning and one for practical help. It was much in their interest that the robots might reduce, for example, their manual or administrative workload so that they could spend more time with the patients. For example, they did not want a robot to go for a walk with a patient because that was the favourite part of their work. Moreover, this group also considered the vacuum cleaning robot to be their number one choice. Another robot they thought could be very useful was a general talking robot. This robot should be able to turn on the TV, read the news aloud and answer questions. For example, when the care staff are in one of the residents' rooms, the robot can answer questions that often come up (e.g., what time it is, or which food will be served for lunch).

One of the scenarios in the interview phase addressed the issues of an older person suffering from depression. The first group expressed that the person could talk to a robot for company or have a zoomorphic robot for comfort, while the third (staff) group saw no use for a robot in this scenario. They found it unlikely that a person might be depressed in a care home and said, "that it is up to them to change their situation". One of the participants also said, "there are people to talk to if one wants to". Moreover, both groups did not seem to distinguish between feeling lonely and being depressed.

4.3   Limitations

For the first and third group, the participatory design method worked well, and they easily followed all the steps and phases and engaged with the shared design surface, icons, labels and created their own. However, one limitation with PIC-TIVE was that the second group—care home residents—had serious difficulties following the steps and phases in the method. Two out of the four participants had severe health problems and therefore had difficulties to follow the method. After the first step with initial thoughts and discussions about robots it was clear to the workshop leader that the phases would be difficult to follow for all participants, and the second phase, sketch, had to be completely skipped. The other two phases, label and interview, could be carried out with some changes to the initial plan and with some complications (e.g., that there were no sketches to evaluate so the group discussed the scenarios in the interview phase in a more general matter and how robots could help). These difficulties came as a surprise to us—which illustrates that in practice it might be difficult to conduct workshops with the intended target group since some of them are very ill by the time they live in a care home. For further research with this stakeholder group, we recommend less complexity in the workshop parts and the possibility to interact with robots for a shared understanding of the technology and what it can do.

The second group aside, the other two stakeholder groups were engaged in the task, and PICTIVE turned out to be a good method to extract a lot of ideas about social robots. As pointed out in the beginning, we see a need for longitudinal studies in this field, but PICTIVE as a method might be most useful in the beginning of the development process and when investigating important features to a robot. Further research in the very early stage of robot development could result in improved design guidelines and common "dos and don'ts".

4.4   Summary

There were similar preferences for social robots in care home environments between the two key stakeholders, older adults still living at home and care staff members. First, they both thought that social robots performing different tasks and functions should have different morphologies, but that they all should be in a physical embodiment. For example, a conversation robot should be anthropomorphic to evoke natural behaviours of speaking to it and that the older adults would understand that one can talk to it. This result is in line with previous participatory design studies where dementia caregivers designed different robots with various roles, appearances and abilities [18]. Secondly, both groups also found the body of the social companion robot Paro to be too unfamiliar and that the care residents would not want to interact with the robot. However, both groups brought up the use of domestic pet animals, such as a dog or a cat robot.

The main difference between the groups was the different functions the social robot could have and the tasks it could perform. The older adults focused on social aspects, such as giving comfort, playing cards with, answering questions, and safety aspects, such as falling detection and alarm functions. The care staff members, on the other hand, focused on practical parts of their workload that could be replaced by a social robot. For example, that the robot could clean, sort delivered products, and inform and keep an eye on the residents when the staff was in another room.

Finally, even though our workshop study did not focus on dementia patients, as other work has done [18], it might be worth mentioning that our stakeholders did not at all focus on the emotional aspects of social robots as the dementia caregivers did. Both the first and the third group in our study were more interested in the functional and social aspects (e.g., cleaning or answering questions).

5   Conclusion

This workshop study with different key stakeholders showed similarities when it came to how robot embodiment and morphology affect functionality and use. It further showed that older adults were interested in the robots' social and interactive behaviours, whereas the care staff were more focused on practical functionality. Neither of the groups considered emotional aspects of social robots as particularly relevant, and the care staff questioned if the residents had a use of emotional support. This should be further investigated.

The results also indicate that not all stakeholders can participate in a participatory design workshop like ours. The intended target group—care residents—in many cases already have severe health problems. This group in our workshop expressed no significant interest in robots in their everyday life. But, as several studies have shown (e.g., [3,31]), when older adults with dementia interact with social robots they are generally liked and have positive effects on health, mood, communication and loneliness. It might be the case that residents without cognitive disabilities do not want robots, but it might also be the case that they simply do not have enough experience with robots to imagine interacting with them. This needs to be further investigated, which is particularly important given ethical concerns raised by the introduction of social robots in care homes, which might not always be in line with what people want and need [28].

Acknowledgement. The authors would like to thank the municipality of Mjölby, the care homes involved in this research, and in particular all workshop participants.

References

1. Abdi, J., Al-Hindawi, A., Ng, T., Vizcaychipi, M.P.: Scoping review on the use of socially assistive robot technology in elderly care. BMJ Open **8**, 1–20 (2018)
2. Abdollahi, H., Mollahosseini, A., Lane, J.T., Mahoor, M.H.: A pilot study on using an intelligent life-like robot as a companion for elderly individuals with dementia and depression. In: IEEE-RAS International Conference on Humanoid Robots, pp. 541–546 (2017)
3. Bradwell, H.L., Winnington, R., Thill, S., Jones, R.B.: Longitudinal diary data: six months real-world implementation of affordable companion robots for older people in supported living. In: ACM/IEEE International Conference on Human-Robot Interaction, pp. 148–150 (2020)
4. Bradwell, H.L., Edwards, K.J., Winnington, R., Thill, S., Jones, R.B.: Companion robots for older people: importance of user-centred design demonstrated through observations and focus groups comparing preferences of older people and roboticists in South West England. BMJ Open **9**(9), 1–18 (2019)
5. Breazeal, C.L., Ostrowski, A.K., Singh, N., Park, H.W.: Designing social robots for older adults. Bridge (SPRING) **49**, 22–31 (2019)
6. Broekens, J., Heerink, M., Rosendal, H.: Assistive social robots in elderly care: a review. Gerontechnology **8**(2), 94–103 (2009)
7. Cruz-Sandoval, D., Morales-Tellez, A., Sandoval, E.B., Favela, J.: A social robot as therapy facilitator in interventions to deal with dementia-related behavioral symptoms. In: ACM/IEEE International Conference on Human-Robot Interaction, pp. 161–169 (2020)
8. Fong, T., Nourbakhsh, I., Dautenhahn, K.: A survey of socially interactive robots. Robot. Auton. Syst. **42**, 143–166 (2003)
9. Frennert, S., Eftring, H., Östlund, B.: What older people expect of robots: a mixed methods approach. In: Herrmann, G., Pearson, M.J., Lenz, A., Bremner, P., Spiers, A., Leonards, U. (eds.) ICSR 2013. LNCS (LNAI), vol. 8239, pp. 19–29. Springer, Cham (2013). https://doi.org/10.1007/978-3-319-02675-6_3
10. Hutson, S., Lim, S.L., Bentley, P.J., Bianchi-Berthouze, N., Bowling, A.: Investigating the suitability of social robots for the wellbeing of the elderly. In: D'Mello, S., Graesser, A., Schuller, B., Martin, J.-C. (eds.) ACII 2011, Part I. LNCS, vol. 6974, pp. 578–587. Springer, Heidelberg (2011). https://doi.org/10.1007/978-3-642-24600-5_61
11. Kanoh, M., et al.: Examination of practicability of communication robot-assisted activity program for elderly people. J. Robot. Mechatron. **23**(1), 3–12 (2011)
12. Lafrenière, D.: CUTA: a simple, practical, low-cost approach to task analysis. Interactions **3**(5), 35–39 (1996)
13. Lee, H.R., et al.: Steps toward participatory design of social robots: mutual learning with older adults with depression. In: ACM/IEEE International Conference on Human-Robot Interaction, pp. 244–253 (2017)
14. Libin, A., Cohen-Mansfield, J.: NeCoRo - therapeutic robocat for nursing home residents with dementia: preliminary inquiry. Am. J. Alzheimer's Dis. Other Dement. **19**(2), 111–116 (2004)
15. Marti, P., Bacigalupo, M., Giusti, L., Mennecozzi, C., Shibata, T.: Socially assistive robotics in the treatment of behavioural and psychological symptoms of dementia. In: Proceedings of the First IEEE/RAS-EMBS International Conference on Biomedical Robotics and Biomechatronics, 2006, BioRob 2006, pp. 483–488 (October 2006)

16. Melkas, H., Hennala, L., Pekkarinen, S., Kyrki, V.: Impacts of robot implementation on care personnel and clients in elderly-care institutions. Int. J. Med. Inform. **134**, 1–6 (2020)
17. Mišeikis, J., et al.: Lio - a personal robot assistant for human-robot interaction and care applications. IEEE Robot. Autom. Lett. **5**(4), 5339–5346 (2020)
18. Moharana, S., Panduro, A.E., Lee, H.R., Riek, L.D.: Robots for joy, robots for sorrow: community based robot design for dementia caregivers. In: ACM/IEEE International Conference on Human-Robot Interaction, pp. 458–467. IEEE (2019)
19. Moyle, W., et al.: Using a therapeutic companion robot for dementia symptoms in long-term care: reflections from a cluster-RCT. Aging Ment. Health **23**(3), 329–336 (2019)
20. Muller, M.J.: PICTIVE-an exploration in participatory design. In: SIGCHI Conference on Human Factors in Computing Systems, pp. 225–231 (1991)
21. Osaka, K., et al.: Characteristics of a transactive phenomenon in relationships among older adults with dementia, nurses as intermediaries, and communication robot. Intell. Control Autom. 08(02), 111–125 (2017)
22. Östlund, B., Olander, E., Jonsson, O., Frennert, S.: STS-inspired design to meet the challenges of modern aging. Welfare technology as a tool to promote user driven innovations or another way to keep older users hostage? Technol. Forecast. Soc. Chang. **93**, 82–90 (2015)
23. Ostrowski, A.K., Breazeal, C., Park, H.W.: Long-term co-design guidelines: empowering older adults as co-designers of social robots. In: 30th IEEE International Conference on Robot and Human Interactive Communication, RO-MAN 2021, pp. 1165–1172. IEEE (2021)
24. Robinson, H., Macdonald, B., Kerse, N., Broadbent, E.: The psychosocial effects of a companion robot: a randomized controlled trial. J. Am. Med. Dir. Assoc. **14**(9), 661–667 (2013)
25. Rodil, K., Rehm, M., Krummheuer, A.L.: Co-designing social robots with cognitively impaired citizens. In: Proceedings of the 10th Nordic Conference on Human-Computer Interaction, NordiCHI 2018, pp. 686–690 (2018)
26. Šabanovic, S., Bennett, C.C., Chang, W.L., Huber, L.: PARO robot affects diverse interaction modalities in group sensory therapy for older adults with dementia. In: 2013 IEEE 13th International Conference on Rehabilitation Robotics (ICORR), WA, Seattle, pp. 1–6 (2013)
27. Šabanović, S., Chang, W.L., Bennett, C.C., Piatt, J.A., Hakken, D.: A robot of my own: participatory design of socially assistive robots for independently living older adults diagnosed with depression proceedings, part I. In: First International Conference, ITAP 2015 held as Part of HCI International 2015, Los Angeles, CA, USA, August 2–7, pp. 104–114 (2015)
28. Sparrow, R., Sparrow, L.: In the hands of machines? The future of aged care. Minds Mach. **16**(2), 141–161 (2006)
29. Tanigaki, S., Kishida, K., Fujita, A.: A preliminary study of the effects of a smile-supplement robot on behavioral and psychological symptoms of elderly people with mild impairment. J. Human. Soc. Sci. **45**, 19–26 (2018)
30. Thodberg, K., et al.: Therapeutic effects of dog visits in nursing homes for the elderly. Psychogeriatrics **16**(5), 289–297 (2016)
31. Thunberg, S., Rönnqvist, L., Ziemke, T., et al.: Do robot pets decrease agitation in dementia patients? In: Wagner, A.R. (ed.) ICSR 2020. LNCS (LNAI), vol. 12483, pp. 616–627. Springer, Cham (2020). https://doi.org/10.1007/978-3-030-62056-1_51

32. Thunberg, S., Ziemke, T.: User-centred design of humanoid robots' communication. Paladyn, J. Behav. Robot. **12**(1), 58–73 (2021)
33. Wada, K., Shibata, T., Saito, T., Sakamoto, K., Tanie, K.: Psychological and social effects of one year robot assisted activity on elderly people at a health service facility for the aged. In: Proceedings of the IEEE International Conference on Robotics and Automation (ICRA), pp. 2785–2790, No. April (2005)

Robot-Assisted Training with Swedish and Israeli Older Adults

Neziha Akalin[1]([✉]), Maya Krakovsky[2], Omri Avioz-Sarig[2], Amy Loutfi[1], and Yael Edan[2]

[1] School of Science and Technology, Örebro University, 701 82 Örebro, Sweden
{neziha.akalin,amy.loutfi}@oru.se
[2] Department of Industrial Engineering and Management, and ABC Robotics Initiative, Ben-Gurion University of the Negev, 8410501 Beer-Sheva, Israel
{mayakrak,sarigomr,yael}@post.bgu.ac.il

Abstract. This paper explores robot-assisted training in a cross-cultural context with older adults. We performed user studies with 28 older adults with two different assistive training robots: an adaptive robot, and a non-adaptive robot, in two countries (Sweden and Israel). In the adaptive robot group, the robot suggested playing music and decreased the number of repetitions based on the participant's level of engagement. We analyzed the facial expressions of the participants in these two groups. Results revealed that older adults in the adaptive robot group showed more varying facial expressions. The adaptive robot created a distraction for the older adults since it talked more than the non-adaptive robot. This result suggests that a robot designed for older adults should utilize the right amount of communication capabilities. The Israeli participants expressed more positive attitudes towards robots and rated the perceived usefulness of the robot higher than the Swedish participants.

Keywords: Cultural robotics · Physical training · Older adults · Human-robot interaction · Social robots

1 Introduction

The world population is aging [1]; it is expected that approximately a quarter or more of the population in the major areas of the world will become over the age of 60 by 2050. This is in parallel to an increasing shortage in caregivers [2]. Therefore, research on assistive technologies which aims to improve eldercare for older adults has received increased attention. Socially assistive robot interventions where the robots take a role of cognitive training, companionship, social facilitation, physiological and affective therapy have the potential to improve the health and care of older adults [3]. Many studies have examined the usage of robots in elder care settings, however, these studies mostly focus on participants from a similar cultural background. Our study differs from them by exploring the social robots in a cross-cultural context with older adults.

© Springer Nature Switzerland AG 2021
H. Li et al. (Eds.): ICSR 2021, LNAI 13086, pp. 487–496, 2021.
https://doi.org/10.1007/978-3-030-90525-5_42

The cultural background and nationality of users may contribute to the variability in people's attitudes, trust and acceptance of social robots [4]. This has been proven in several studies such as in a comparison of German to Arab culture and within Arab countries [5] and in another human-robot interaction (HRI) research that compared robot perception between Chinese, Korean and German [6]. These studies revealed cultural differences on robot perception, acceptance, and preferences regarding the robot's use and appearance. Culture differences were also found among older adults in few studies such as comparison of social robots in Finland and Japan [7]. In [8] Italian and Swedish older adults were compared in a video setting in which they watched different scenarios with a social assistive robot. Results showed that the Swedish participants had concern for privacy and for developing robot dependence. However, they were also more interested in non-emergency scenarios, e.g., advised by the robot to practice physical activity, contrary to the Italian older adults who did not appreciate this scenario as much. A research that compared acceptance of socially assistive robots by Israeli and Austrian older adults did not reveal any differences [9]. These studies demonstrated the importance of considering the cultural features while designing a social robot and the findings suggest further research is required with the older population.

Our study includes a robot-assisted training for older adults which is one of the use cases of robots for older adults. We conducted experiments with two different cultural groups of older people. The experiments were conducted in Sweden and Israel with the same experimental procedure and the same assistive robot. In our scenario, a Poppy robot assisted participants in physical training where they repeated a sequence of arm motions together with the robot. We focused on investigating the cultural differences on social robots among older participants. The training included two groups - one experienced an adaptive robot and the other experienced a non-adaptive robot. In the adaptive robot group, the robot suggested playing music and decreased the number of repetitions based on the engagement of the older adults.

2   Method

2.1   Participants

Overall 28 older adults participated in the experiments. In Sweden, 10 participants (4 females and 6 males) performed experiments with the non-adaptive robot. Their age ranged between 63 and 99 ($M = 82.33$, $SD = 10.92$). The other 9 participants (4 females and 5 males) performed experiments with the adaptive robot. Their age ranged between 68 and 89 years old ($M = 79$, $SD = 7.81$). When they were asked to rate how often they use a computer and how familiar they were with the robots in a scale between 1 to 5, the average score for computer familiarity was 3.84 ($SD = 1.68$), and the robot familiarity was 1.37 ($SD = 0.76$).

All of the Israeli participants (4 females and 5 males) performed experiments with the adaptive robot. Their age ranged between 70 and 82 years old ($M = 75.22$, $SD = 5.02$). Eight of them came from American or British background,

4 of them moved to Israel after their retirement. The Israeli participants' average score for computer and robot familiarity was 3.67 ($SD = 1.80$) and 2.56 ($SD = 1.50$) respectively.

This study was originally planned to be a larger cross-cultural study with more participants from different cultural backgrounds. However, due to the global pandemic, we had to stop experiments. Therefore, we tested both adaptive and non-adaptive robots with Swedish subjects, but tested only the adaptive robot with Israeli subjects.

2.2 Robot and Physical Training System

A robotic system was designed as a motivation tool for older adults to engage with physical activity, the development process is presented in [10]. The system included a Poppy robot that demonstrated physical upper-body exercises and an RGB-D camera [10] used to monitor the users' performance and provide real-time feedback accordingly. The robot used in these experiments was the 13 degrees of freedom torso of the 3D printed, open-source Poppy robot [11]. It was equipped with a LCD screen to provide feedback to the users. The training program included 8 arm exercises. During the training, the robot counted each repetition of the participant. On the LCD screen, the robot provided visual feedback after the exercise.

For this work, the original system [10] was enhanced with emotion recognition capabilities and a function to play music. We used Affdex SDK [12] for emotion recognition through a USB webcam. The SDK outputs a set of facial features in real-time, one of them being *engagement*. Engagement is considered as a characterizing feature of the user experience, as stated in [13]. The facial engagement of the user was used for the adaptation using facial expressiveness with values varying between 0 and 100 in Affdex SDK. The user's *engagement* data was sent to the training program. Additionally, the robot was equipped with a function to play music (Fig. 1a). In the adaptive robot, based on the user's *engagement* level he/she was offered to play music during the training to encourage him/her and decrease the number of the repetitions in order to lower the difficulty level. The mean *engagement* was calculated continuously and compared with the *engagement* at the time t. If the participant was less engaged at the time t than his/her average *engagement* until that moment, the robot suggested to play music to re-engage and to decrease the number of repetitions of the current exercise.

2.3 Experimental Procedure

The same experimental procedure and the same adaptive robot was used in Sweden and Israel. The consent form, questionnaires and the robot's speech was in the local language (Swedish and Hebrew). The experiments were approved by the ethical committees (in Israel by the department of Industrial Engineering and Management, Ben-Gurion University of the Negev ethical committee and in Sweden by the Swedish ethics committee for studies involving human participants).

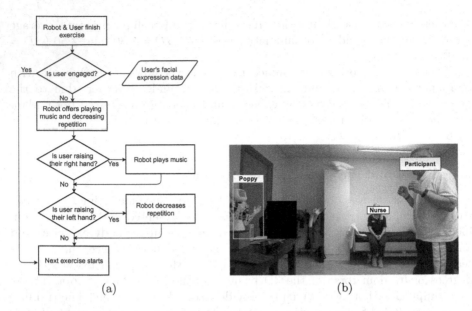

Fig. 1. a) The flowchart of the training system. b) An older Swedish participant inter-acts with the Poppy robot.

The experimental procedure began with informing the participant about the experiment and the robot. Then, the participant signed the informed consent form, and filled out the pre-experiment questionnaire. Thereafter, the robot introduced itself and the training started (a screenshot from the experiments is given in Fig. 1b). Before each exercise, the robot explained the exercise by speech (a pre-recording of instructions), then the robot and the participant exercised together. The robot counted each repetition of the participant. When all 8 exercises were done, the participant filled out the post-experiment question-naire. Following the questionnaire the experimenter discussed with the users their experience in an open ended non-formal discussion.

2.4 Measures and Analysis

In the pre-experiment questionnaire, the participants were asked to answer demo-graphic questions (age, gender, and technology experience), SF-12 health sur-vey and their attitude towards robots. After the interaction, they answered a post-experiment questionnaire which included a robot acceptance questionnaire and perceived safety questionnaire. The attitude towards robots and acceptance questionnaires were on a 5-point Likert scale ranging from "1 = strongly dis-agree" to "5 = strongly agree". Cronbach's α was used to calculate the internal consistencies within the items of the used questionnaires with an α coefficient ranges over 0.7 considered as acceptable.

Table 1. The used attitude towards robots questionnaire

ATT from [15]	It is a good idea to use the robot to help me with everyday tasks in the future
	The robot would make life more interesting and stimulating today
	The robot would make life more interesting and stimulating in the future
	It is good to make use of the robot to help me with everyday tasks today
NARS S1 [16]	The word "robot" means nothing to me*
	I would hate the idea that robots or artificial intelligence were making judgments about things*
	I would feel very nervous just standing in front of a robot*
	I would feel relaxed talking with robots

* Reverse coded item

SF-12 Health Survey. This 12-item Short Form Survey (SF-12) allowed us to investigate the perceived health of older people via their self-reported health [14]. The results of the questionnaire is reported as a mental component score (MCS-12) and a physical component score (PCS-12).

Attitude Towards Robots. To explore the attitudes towards robots, we used a questionnaire (see Table 1) that includes questions selected from [15] and [16]. Participants were asked to fill out the questionnaire before the interaction. Their prior opinions may affect how comfortable they are, how they behave during interaction, and their acceptance and safety perception.

Perceived Safety Questionnaire. The perceived safety questionnaire [17] is rated in a 5-point semantic differential scale. In this questionnaire, participants assessed how they felt during the interaction using polar adjectives such as insecure - secure, anxious - relaxed, uncomfortable - comfortable, and lack in control - in control. They also rated their opinions about the robot with polar adjectives: threatening - safe, unfamiliar - familiar, unreliable - reliable, and scary - calming.

Robot Acceptance Questionnaire. The questionnaire (see Table 2) was based on the acceptance questionnaire used in [10] with additional items selected from Almere questionnaire [18].

Facial Emotional Measures. The video recordings of the participants while interacting with the robots in the experiments were analyzed using Affdex SDK. Affdex provides a set of features including 7 emotions (anger, contempt, disgust, fear, joy, sadness, and surprise), engagement (facial expressiveness of the participant), valence (the pleasantness of the participant), 20 facial expressions and attention (from head orientation). In the non-adaptive group, 9 Israeli participants' video recordings from a previous user study [10] and 9 Swedish

Table 2. The robot acceptance questionnaire.

PU	I would be willing to train with the robot again because it had value to me
	I think the robot is useful to me
	Using a robot would improve my daily life
PEOU	I felt comfortable during the interaction
	I understood the robot well during the interaction
	I put a lot of effort into this activity*
	I think I can use the robot without any help
ATT	I enjoy exercising with the robot
	I was satisfied by the robot's performance during this activity
	I concentrated on the activity for the entire session
	I was eager to follow the exercises
Trust	I would trust the robot if it gave me advice
	I would follow the advice the robot gives me
	I felt like I could really trust this robot
ITU	I would like to exercise with the robot in the future

* Reverse coded item
PU: Perceived Usefulness, PEOU: Perceived Ease of Use, ATT: Attitude,
ITU: Intention to Use

participants were used. In the adaptive group, due to the technical problems of the video recordings, 6 Israeli and 6 Swedish participants' videos were used. The pre-processing of affective metrics was as follows: the mean value for each second was calculated, the dropped timestamps were filled with a weighted average of the neighboring time stamps, and the mean values for each affect metric for each participant were extracted. We used this data and Mann-Whitney test to check whether there was any difference between Swedish and Israeli participants.

3 Experimental Results and Discussion

The Cronbach's α value for the Attitude Towards Robots questionnaire was 0.76 and the α for the Acceptance questionnaire was 0.83 which are acceptable values. The Swedish ($M = 1.37, SD = 0.76$) and Israeli ($M = 2.56, SD = 1.5$) groups significantly differed on robot familiarity, $t(10) = 2.23, p < .05$. They also differed in educational levels, Fisher's exact test showed a significant relationship between the participants' country and the educational levels ($p < .001$). There was also a statistically significant difference between Swedish ($M = 40.75, SD = 12.54$) and Israeli ($M = 50.01, SD = 6.98$) participants in the physical component score of SF-12. There was no significant difference between groups with the MCS-12 measure. On the SF-12 scale, higher scores indicate a better health condition. Israeli participants rated their physical health condition better than Swedish participants.

Results of the Attitude Towards Robots questionnaire revealed a significant difference in attitudes between Swedish and Israeli participants. Israeli participants ($M = 3.58$, $SD = 0.65$) had more positive attitude towards robots than Swedish participants ($M = 2.94$, $SD = 0.78$), $t(19) = 2.26$, $p < .05$. When we used all data of the post-experiment questionnaire, there was a statistically significant difference on Perceived Usefulness (PU) between Swedish and Israeli groups. The mean PU score for the Israeli group ($M = 3.81$, $SD = 0.9$) was significantly higher than the mean PU score in Swedish group ($M = 2.91$, $SD = 1.11$), $t(19) = 2.29$, $p < .05$. When we compared only the adaptive robot groups, there was no statistically significant difference for any of the acceptance questionnaire constructs. When we checked perceived safety ratings, the Israeli group rated their safety perception slightly higher ($M = 4.09$) compared to the Swedish group ($M = 3.77$). However, there was no statistically significant difference. There was no statistically significant difference for the other constructs of the acceptance questionnaire.

When there was no adaptation in the robot, the participants showed less variation in facial expressions. The Mann-Whitney analyses showed that 2 of the 30 affect metrics were significantly different by cultural background, namely *surprise* and *brow raise*. The median *surprise* and *brow raise* in the Swedish group were 0.31 and 0.33 respectively, whereas the median *surprise* and *brow raise* in the Israeli group were 2.28 and 3.68 respectively. The Mann-Whitney test showed that the difference was significant in *surprise* ($p < .05$, effect size $r = 0.53$) and *brow raise* ($p < .01$, $r = 0.61$). These results show that Swedish participants exhibited fewer facial expressions during the interaction. The Swedish participants were older, the mean age was 80.59 (14 of them were over 75), whereas the mean age of Israeli participants were 75.88 (3 of them were over 75). These factors may affect their reactions during the interaction.

In the adaptive robot, the Swedish participants exhibited stronger and more varied facial expressions than the Israeli participants. The Mann-Whitney analyses showed that six affect metrics yielded significant results, namely *disgust, brow furrow, nose wrinkle, upper lip raise, chin raise* and *attention*. The median *disgust* ($p < .05$, $r = 0.6$), *noise wrinkle* ($p < .05$, $r = 0.64$), *upper lip raise* ($p < .05$, $r = 0.65$), *chin raise* ($p < .01$, $r = 0.74$), and *attention* ($p < .01$, $r = 0.79$) in the Swedish group were $3.28, 2.98, 2.24, 12.9, 92.3$ respectively. The median *disgust, noise wrinkle, upper lip raise, chin raise* and *attention* in Israeli group were $0.3, 0.08, 0.07, 1.49, 45.9$ respectively. The median *brow furrow* was higher in Israeli group (11.1) than the Swedish group (1.52), the difference was significant ($p < .05$, $r = 0.6$). These results show that Swedish participants interacting with the adaptive robot displayed more varied facial expressions.

The two groups (Swedish and Israeli) were different in culture, age, and educational levels. The Israeli participants were younger and had a higher educational level in comparison to Swedish participants. Although it has been shown that culture influence users' acceptance and their attitude toward robots [19], it is difficult to conclude that the cultural background was the only influencing factor in our study. However, we argue that familiarity with technology and higher educational levels could be considered a part of Israeli culture, this is especially true for older adults. The Israeli elderly population has some distinct characteristics one of them being from a diverse ethnical background with different cultural backgrounds; among the older population only 28% are born in Israel [20]. It was also the case in our study, eight participants out of nine were immigrants. Another distinct characteristic among older immigrants in Israel is the successful adoption of new media technologies [21]. It was also the case in our study, participants from Israel had greater experience in technology, they indicated that they use computers in their daily life, and several of them had previous experience with robots as part of other HRI experiments. The number of school years >13 (high education level) among the Swedish older population is lower than the Israeli older population. The 6.89% (own calculation using the statistics given in [22]) of older Swedish people (age 65 and over) had high education level whereas this was 20% in Israeli older people [23] by 2015. In our experiments, five Israeli participants had bachelor's degrees and 4 of them had a postgraduate degree (i.e., masters, Ph.D.), whereas the majority of Swedish participants had a high school degree (10 persons) or lower degrees (9 persons). We believe that the education level affected the attitude towards robots and the perceived usefulness of the robot. The study presented in [24] supports our claim, that participants with higher educational backgrounds rated the perceived usefulness of the robot more positively. Moreover, it was reported that there was a positive link between educational levels and attitudes towards robots whereas age had a trivial effect on attitudes towards robots [25]. Our results conform with previous research [24] who reported that user factors especially living conditions, professional background, and technical experience influenced older adults' attitudes towards robots. The Israeli participants' higher educational level and robot familiarity had a positive effect on the positive opinions about the robot. Therefore, in the design decisions of social robots for older adults, besides their cultural background, their technology experience and educational levels should be considered.

Participants in the adaptive robot group showed more varying facial expressions. One of the reasons was that when the robot asked about playing music or decreasing the exercises, the participants tried to understand what the robot was saying which resulted in different facial expressions. When there was no adaptation, there was no interruption of the robot, which resulted in less expressive facial reactions. The older participants did not like the music while exercising with the robot. They commented that it was distractive for them. Most of them commented that music prevented them to hear the robot's counting and the explanation of the exercise. Therefore, they did not want the robot to play music for the second time. Individuals' responses to distracting information tend to increase with age, older adults are prone to be more easily distracted than younger adults [26]. Different participant groups may have different preferences. From our experimental results and observations from the experiments, we suggest that a robot that is designed for older adults should utilize the right amount of communication capabilities (i.e., not too much, not too little). This is especially important in collaborative tasks in which the robot and the older adult complete together. As it could be seen in our experimental results, interruptions could result in distractions.

4 Conclusion

The presented study demonstrated that familiarity with robots and educational level could be crucial factors for the opinions of older adults about robots. It is especially valid for the perceived usefulness of the robot and attitude towards robots. However, we cannot claim that these differences were derived from the cultural backgrounds since our participants differentiated in culture, age and educational levels. Hence, these three parameters should be investigated in future work separately to understand which one contributes stronger. We also found that older adults in the adaptive robot group showed more varying facial expressions. Differences in the facial expressions in the adaptive and non-adaptive robot groups could be rooted in the fact that the adaptive robot talked more which created distractions on the participants. Our results imply the importance of considering a right amount of communication of the robot in the interaction design. Moreover, we plan to extend our study with more participants and to gain a broader view about the common needs and expectations from social robots regardless of the cultural background of older adults.

References

1. United Nations Department of Economic and Social Affairs, Population Division: World Population Ageing 2020 Highlights: Living arrangements of older persons (ST/ESA/SER.A/451) (2020)
2. Fleming, K.C., Evans, J.M., Chutka, D.S.: Caregiver and clinician shortages in an aging nation. In: Mayo Clinic Proceedings, vol. 78, no. 8. Elsevier (2003)
3. Abdi, J., et al.: Scoping review on the use of socially assistive robot technology in elderly care. BMJ Open 8(2), e018815 (2018)
4. Frennert, S., Aminoff, H., Östlund, B.: Technological frames and care robots in eldercare. Int. J. Soc. Robot. 13(2), 311–325 (2020). https://doi.org/10.1007/s12369-020-00641-0
5. Korn, O., Akalin, N., Gouveia, R.: Understanding cultural preferences for social robots: a study in German and Arab communities. ACM Trans. Hum.-Robot Interact. (THRI) 10(2), 1–19 (2021)
6. Li, D., Patrick Rau, P.L., Li, Y.: A cross-cultural study: effect of robot appearance and task. Int. J. Soc. Robot. 2(2), 175–186 (2010)
7. Coco, K., Kangasniemi, M., Rantanen, T.: Care personnel's attitudes and fears toward care robots in elderly care: a comparison of data from the care personnel in Finland and Japan. J. Nurs. Scholarsh. 50(6), 634–644 (2018)
8. Cortellessa, G., Scopelliti, M., Tiberio, L., Svedberg G.K., Loutfi, A., Pecora, F.: A cross-cultural evaluation of domestic assistive robots. In: AAAI Fall Symposium: AI in Eldercare: New Solutions to Old Problems, pp. 24–31 (2008)

9. Torta, E., et al.: Evaluation of a small socially-assistive humanoid robot in intelligent homes for the care of the elderly. J. Intell. Robot. Syst. **76**(1), 57–71 (2014). https://doi.org/10.1007/s10846-013-0019-0

10. Avioz-Sarig, O., Olatunji, S., Sarne-Fleischmann, V., Edan, Y.: Robotic system for physical training of older adults. Int. J. Soc. Robot. **13**(5), 1109–1124 (2020). https://doi.org/10.1007/s12369-020-00697-y

11. Lapeyre, M., et al.: Poppy project: open-source fabrication of 3D printed humanoid robot for science, education and art. In: Digital Intelligence 2014 (2014)

12. McDuff, D., et al.: AFFDEX SDK: a cross-platform real-time multi-face expression recognition toolkit. In: Proceedings of the 2016 CHI Conference Extended Abstracts on Human Factors in Computing Systems (2016)

13. O'Brien, H.L., Toms, E.G.: What is user engagement? A conceptual framework for defining user engagement with technology. J. Am. Soc. Inf. Sci. Technol. **59**(6), 938–955 (2008)

14. Ware, J.E., Jr., Kosinski, M., Keller, S.D.: A 12-item short-form health survey: construction of scales and preliminary tests of reliability and validity. Med. Care **34**, 220–233 (1996)

15. Wu, Y.-H., et al.: Acceptance of an assistive robot in older adults: a mixed-method study of human-robot interaction over a 1-month period in the Living Lab setting. Clin. Interv. Aging **9**, 801 (2014)

16. Nomura, T., et al.: Psychology in human-robot communication: an attempt through investigation of negative attitudes and anxiety toward robots. In: 13th IEEE International Workshop on Robot and Human Interactive Communication, RO-MAN 2004 (2004)

17. Akalin, N., Kristoffersson, A., Loutfi, A.: Evaluating the sense of safety and security in human–robot interaction with older people. In: Korn, O. (ed.) Social Robots: Technological, Societal and Ethical Aspects of Human-Robot Interaction. HIS, pp. 237–264. Springer, Cham (2019). https://doi.org/10.1007/978-3-030-17107-0_12

18. Heerink, M., et al.: Assessing acceptance of assistive social agent technology by older adults: the Almere model. Int. J. Soc. Robot. **2**(4), 361–375 (2010)

19. Ouwehand, A.N.: The role of culture in the acceptance of elderly towards social assertive robots: how do cultural factors influence the acceptance of elderly people towards social assertive robotics in the Netherlands and Japan?. Bachelor's thesis, University of Twente (2017)

20. Podell, R., et al.: The quality of primary care provided to the elderly in Israel. Israel J. Health Policy Res. **7**(1), 1–15 (2018)

21. Khvorostianov, N., Elias, N., Nimrod, G.: Without it I am nothing': the Internet in the lives of older immigrants. New Media Soc. **14**(4), 583–599 (2012)

22. Statistics Sweden. https://www.statistikdatabasen.scb.se/pxweb/en/ssd/START_UF_UF0506/UtbBefRegionR/. Accessed 11 June 2021

23. The 65+ Population in Israel 2018. https://brookdale.jdc.org.il/wp-content/uploads/2018/02/MJB-Facts_and_Figures_Elderly-65_in_Israel-2018_English.pdf. Accessed 11 June 2021

24. Huang, T., Huang, C.: Elderly's acceptance of companion robots from the perspective of user factors. Univ. Access Inf. Soc. **19**, 1–14 (2019)

25. Gnambs, T., Appel, M.: Are robots becoming unpopular? Changes in attitudes towards autonomous robotic systems in Europe. Comput. Hum. Behav. **93**, 53–61 (2019)

26. Campbell, K.L., et al.: Idiosyncratic responding during movie-watching predicted by age differences in attentional control. Neurobiol. Aging **36**(11), 3045–3055 (2015)

Virtual Social Robot Enhances the Social Skills of Children with HFA

Maha Abdelmohsen[(✉)] and Yasmine Arafa

University of Greenwich, Park Row, Greenwich Peninsula, London SE10 9LS, UK
m.h.abdelmohsen@greenwich.ac.uk

Abstract. Social skills are the skills that humans use to communicate with each other verbally and non-verbally. The deficit of social skills is a core symptom of children with autism spectrum disorder (ASD). Physical social robots and virtual environments have been popular training tools for children with ASD in recent years.

The Jammo-VRobot environment is a virtual desktop environment that employs a 3D virtual humanoid robot (Jammo VRobot) to enhance the social skills of children with high-functioning autism (HFA) through a social skills training program guided by a parent or a teacher. The social skill training programme targets three social skills: imitation, emotion recognition and expression, and intransitive gesture. The evaluation process was conducted mostly online with some on-site, including children with HFA (aged 4–12 years). The experimental sessions reveal encouraging results showing that the Jammo-VRobot environment helps in training and enhancing the target three skills of the participants.

Keywords: Virtual robot · Autism spectrum disorder · Social skills training programme

1 Introduction

Autism spectrum disorder is an umbrella term that categories a group of disorders of brain development that include impairments in social and communication interaction, repetitive behaviours, and stereotyped patterns of interests and activities [7]. Social and communication challenges can significantly affect their social life, including forming and maintaining relationships and functioning independently. Social skills training (SST) interventions teach children with ASD the skills necessary to navigate their social environment [12]. Social skills training interventions such as peer mentoring, social skills group, social stories, video-modelling, picture exchange communication system, applied behaviour analysis, and occupational therapy were the early promising solutions for enhancing the social skills of children with ASD. Despite the reported positive effect of SST, there are some barriers to accessing SST interventions for families with children of ASD. These traditional sessions are costly and require time-intensive training [2]. Another primary barrier to SST interventions is the shortage of trained therapists and facilitators.

© Springer Nature Switzerland AG 2021
H. Li et al. (Eds.): ICSR 2021, LNAI 13086, pp. 497–508, 2021.
https://doi.org/10.1007/978-3-030-90525-5_43

Assistive technologies for cognition have been implemented using virtual environments (VEs) and robots to train and improve the social skills of children with ASD as an alternative means to train the social skills of children with ASD. Assistive technology for cognition refers to technologies that are used to enhance or facilitate cognitive function and include tools that aim to improve social participation, and independent actions of individuals with cognitive disabilities [8].

2   Background

Several studies were conducted to evaluate the effectiveness of VEs and social robots in training the social skills of children with ASD.

[6] conducted a study to evaluate the effect of using a digital avatar in delivering social lessons to children with ASD. The 3D character chosen for this study was a colourful fish (Marla) with facial expressions, similar to a character from the cartoon movie Finding Nemo. The target skill for this study was initiating conversations. The results show that the participants' initiating conversation skills improved by comparing the baseline session to the intervention session. Additionally, the participants generalised the skills learnt in the intervention session to their daily life. [10] developed an immersive virtual school and playground via HMD for improving and training the emotional and social skills of children with ASD. In the proposed environment, the children interact with several human avatars. Researchers observed that the participants show significant improvements in social and emotional skills as well as non-verbal communication.

A study was conducted by [14] to teach children with ASD to recognise and produce gestures using NAO. The participants with ASD were divided into two groups: intervention and control groups. The results show that children with ASD who received the intervention training produced intransitive gestures more accurately than those in the control group. A recent study conducted by [15] to evaluate the influence of Zeno in improving the emotion recognition and expression skills of children with HFA. The experiment results showed that the children understood the social stories and answered with the appropriate emotion. In the imitation sessions, the participants managed to imitate the robot's facial expression with 100% accuracy.

The extensive review of robot-assisted interventions and VEs for children with ASD emphasised some limitations. The availability of robot-assisted interventions and immersive VEs is minimal. The high cost of robot platforms and equipment needed is a significant reason for this limitation [2]. Moreover, the setup and control of such interventions require technicians or professionals and a dedicated environment. Despite the importance of generalisation in transferring the learned skills from training interventions to real-life, most VR intervention studies do not conduct follow-up sessions to assess whether the children transferred the target behaviours and skills learnt to their daily lives. Similarly, the test of maintenance remains an open question in VR interventions.

3 Contribution

This research investigates the impact of combining the virtual environment with a virtual social robot (Jammo VRobot) as a hybrid approach to address some of the limitations of previous VEs and social robot interventions and train the social skills of children with HFA. A non-immersive virtual environment (Jammo-VRobot environment) that employs a 3D robot (Jammo VRobot) was developed. The Jammo-VRobot environment is a cost-effective platform that promotes the availability of virtual learning environments and social robots. The availability of the Jammo-VRobot environment will make it easier for parents, teachers, and practitioners to use either at home or school. Jammo VRobot is a humanoid robot, as the human-like embodiment is beneficial to promote the generalisation of the skill learned through child-robot interaction to human-human interaction and manages to grab children's attention more than the animal-like embodiment [9]. The designed social skill training programme is adapted and modified from several studies [11,14,15] utilised physical robots (NAO, QTrobot and Zeno) for training children with ASD. The Jammo VRobot social skill training programme targets three social skills; imitation, emotion recognition, and intransitive gesture. The Jammo-VRobot environment was developed in English and Arabic languages.

4 Methods

4.1 Participants

Fifteen children with HFA (aged 4–12 years) participated in this study, including 10 boys and 5 girls. Children with HFA are intelligent academically [4], although they may lack the fundamental social skills that are necessary for social engagement. Researchers have highlighted the importance of early intervention for children with ASD, especially regarding their social communication skills and development. Therefore, this study targets young participants. Ethical approval for the study was obtained from the University of Greenwich Research Ethics Committee (UREC).

4.2 Experimental Set-Up

Due to the pandemic circumstances (Covid-19) and the schools' and the specialised centres' closure present when the study was conducted, the experimentation sessions were conducted on-site and online. In both settings, the participants have been informed about the training sessions by their parents or teachers to decrease anxiety levels caused by novelty.

The online setup took place at the participant's home or venue of choice. An online version of the tool was developed and launched on a website to be available for a wider group (visit the website here [1]). Eleven children with HFA (8 boys and 3 girls) participated in the online experimental sessions with their parents.

The on-site sessions were conducted at a specialised centre in Egypt. Four children with ASD (2 boys and 2 girls) participated in the on-site experimental sessions. Each participant experienced the tool individually, encouraging triadic interactions between the child, teacher, and the virtual robot [3]. The environment setup consists of the child, the teacher, the researcher, and one laptop (see Fig. 1). The advantage of being on-site is considering the researcher as an observer. The teacher focused on controlling the tool and helping the child and not overwhelmed by completing the observation sheet and controlling the tool. Additionally, the researcher was objective while filling the observation sheet, unlike the parents that might be subjective towards their children.

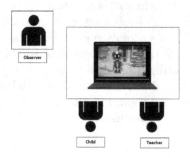

Fig. 1. On-site layout. The child sits beside the teacher in front of the laptop on a small table and the observer sits at a corner in the room; this allows the researcher to monitor the interaction.

The intervention programme lasted for approximately three months. The social skill training programme consists of 24 sessions. The participants received two sessions per week. The emotion recognition and intransitive gesture training programmes consist of three phases; each phase contains a pre-test, four training sessions, an immediate post-test and a follow-up post-test after two weeks. Figure 2 illustrates scenes from the Jammo-VRobot environment. [3] describes the procedure of the Jammo VRobot social skill training programme.

4.3 Data Collection Methods

In this study, a hybrid method of qualitative and quantitative data collection was used. As a qualitative measure, observation was used, and questionnaires were used as a quantitative measure. The evaluation process is divided into three stages: baseline measures (pre-training assessment), intervention measures, and outcomes measures (post-training assessment). Observation is the instrument that was used in the training sessions for collecting data. An observation sheet was designed for the screener (parent/researcher) to record the child's skills and behaviours during the training sessions and document the child's score in each test. Pre and post questionnaires were designed to assess the child's skills and behaviour changes before and after the intervention sessions. The teacher and

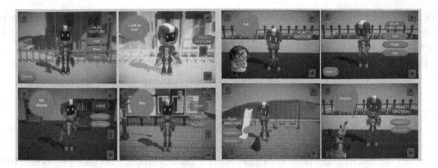

Fig. 2. Scenes from the Jammo-VRobot environment. Left: scenes from the intransitive gesture training programme. Right: scenes from the emotion recognition training programme.

parents were asked to complete the pre and post questionnaires for their children with ASD before and after the intervention. The pre-questionnaire consists of 16 items, 3 items to measure the child's ability in responding to interactions, 8 items for affective understanding (emotion recognition and expression), and 5 items for motor and play skills. The post-questionnaire contains extra items than the pre-questionnaire. These additional items aimed to assess the parents/teacher satisfaction about the training programme that their children have received and evaluate the tool's effectiveness in generalising the taught skills. Furthermore, to evaluate the parent/teacher satisfaction with the technical aspects of the Jammo-VRobot environment, The System Usability Scale (SUS) [17] was used. The observation sheet and the pre and post questionnaires can be found in the developed website [1].

5 Results

5.1 Intransitive Gesture Training Programme

The aim of phase I is to examine the learning outcomes of the gesture recognition skills of the participants. The gestures are hello, good job, look at this, yes, stop, where, me, awesome, come, hungry, and not allowed. The mean number of correct answers in the pre, post, and follow-up tests was calculated and compared. The participants' performance in recognising the 11 gestures increased by 25.5% in comparison between the pre-test and the post-test (from 36.3% in the pre-test to 61.8% in the post-test). 40.6% improvement in the participants' recognition skills compared to the pre-test and the follow-up test (from 36.3% in the pre-test to 76.9% in the follow-up test).

Phase II aims to examine the learning outcomes of the gesture production skills of the participants through imitation. The achievement of this goal was measured by counting the number of times the participants produced gestures correctly in each of the three tests according to four parameters: hand-shape, the direction of movement, placement, and use of hands. In this phase, the children's performance in imitating and producing the taught 11 gestures increased by 18.2% (from 58.70% in the pre-test to 76.90%).

The aim of phase III is to recognise and produce the relevant gesture in different social contexts. In the pre-test, the Jammo VRobot narrates stories, and the children were asked to identify and produce the proper gesture for each story. The post-test has the same procedure as the pre-test except that the stories in the post-test and the follow-up test are different from those in the pre-test. However, participants found the storytelling task the hardest; their performance increased by 16.9% in the untrained scenarios compared to the pre-test (from 22.40% in the pre-test to 39.30% in the post-test). Figure 3 shows the mean number of times the children answered correctly in each phase.

5.2   Emotion Recognition and Expression Training Programme

Phase I provides training for emotion recognition and focuses on the basic six emotions: happiness, anger, sadness, fear, surprise, and disgust. The pre-test, post-test, and follow-up test were identical. The number of correct answers given by each child was counted in the three tests to assess the improvement and progress in their emotion recognition skill after receiving the training. The participants' emotion recognition skills increased by 40% in comparison between the pre-test with the post-test (from 31% in the pre-test to 71% in the post-test). The participants' performance in recognising the emotions increased by 44% (from 31% in the pre-test to 75% in the follow-up test).

Phase II aims at exploring the learning outcomes of the emotion expression skill of the participants through imitation. On average, the emotion expression skills of the participants increased by 26.8% (from 52% in the pre-test to 78.80% in the post-test), while their skills improved by 28% in the follow-up test (from 52% in the pre-test to 80% in the follow-up test).

Phase III evaluates whether the Jammo VRobot can help children with HFA to identify emotions from social situations. The participants' performance in recognising the basic six emotions from different social contexts increased by 23.3% in the untrained scenarios (from 42.2% in the pre-test to 65.5% in the post-test). Figure 3 shows the mean number of times the children answered correctly in each phase.

Some emotions were easier to recognise and produce than others. Therefore, the proportion of the participants providing correct answers to each emotion in all the three phases was calculated (see Table 1). In phase I, only 26.6% and 33.3% of the participants correctly recognised DISGUST and SURPRISE emotions expressed by the Jammo robot. 86.6% of the participants correctly recognised the HAPPY emotion, followed by 82.2% for the SAD emotion. The percentage of recognising ANGRY and FEAR emotions was 80% and 51% respectively. While in phase II, HAPPY and SAD were the easiest emotions to express, as all the participants expressed them correctly. 80% of the participants correctly expressed the ANGRY emotion, followed by 66.6% accuracy of expressing the FEAR emotion. The participants found difficulty in expressing SURPRISE and

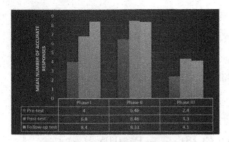

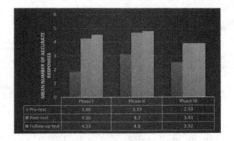

Results from intransitive gesture sessions   **Results from emotion recognition sessions**

Fig. 3. Mean number of correct responses in each training programme: Phase I, Phase II and Phase III

DISGUST emotions. In phase III, the recognition rates were: happiness - 75.5%, fear - 80%, sadness - 60%, anger - 42.2%, disgust - 60 %, and surprise - 28.8 %. It was observed that there was confusion in recognising HAPPY and SURPRISE emotions from the emotional-social stories. Some participants chose HAPPY instead of SURPRISE in some scenarios. Additionally, the same confusion was observed between ANGRY and SAD emotions.

Table 1. The children's mean score, in the three phases, for each emotion.

Emotion	Phase I	Phase II	Phase III
Happy	0.86	1	0.75
Sad	0.82	1	0.55
Fear	0.51	0.66	0.8
Angry	0.8	0.8	0.47
Disgust	0.26	0.33	0.6
Surprise	0.33	0.42	0.28

5.3 Quantitative Questionnaires

As per the teacher and parents questionnaire, the participants showed improvement in their emotion recognition and expression skills (affective understanding) from pre (M = 18.2, SD = 5.32) to post (M = 23.9, SD = 6.32) intervention; P<0.001. Regarding the motor/play skills of the participants, the difference between the mean score in the pre and post-intervention is 5.2; from pre (M = 10.4, SD = 2.20) to post (M = 15.6, SD = 3.18) intervention, and the analysis revealed significant differences as p-value is less than 0.05 (P<0.05). Furthermore, the children showed improvement in responding to interactions skills from pre (M = 6.93, SD = 1.67) to post (M = 8.86, SD = 1.36) with P-value less than 0.05. Table 2 illustrates the results from the pre and post questionnaires.

Table 2. Mean and standard deviation (SD) scores for the pre-questionnaire (Baseline) and post-questionnaire (Outcome).

Scale	Pre mean (SD)	Post mean (SD)	P-value (Wilcoxon test)
Emotion recognition/expression (Affective understanding)	18.2 (5.32)	23.9 (6.32)	$P < 0.001$
Motor play skills	10.4 (2.20)	15.6 (3.18)	$P < 0.05$
Responding to interactions	6.93 (1.67)	8.86 (1.36)	$P < 0.05$

The teacher and parents were asked to complete the SUS questionnaire to measure the usability and satisfaction with the application. A teacher and 11 parents completed the SUS questionnaire at the end of the intervention sessions. The mean score on the SUS was 73.75 (SD = 7.34), which corresponds to a score of "Good" [16]. Figure 4 shows that 59% of the participants found the tool "Good", 33% found it "Okay", and 8% found it "Excellent". These results provide evidence of the users' satisfaction regarding the usability of the Jammo-VRobot tool. Once everything was explained to the parents and teacher about using the Jammo-VRobot tool and navigating from one scene to another, they found it easy to use. These results reveal that the Jammo-VRobot tool is an easy tool to use without technicians or professionals.

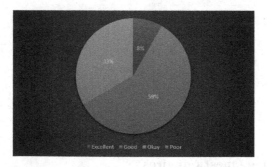

Fig. 4. System usability scale chart.

5.4   Qualitative Results: Observational Data

During the intervention sessions, the researcher and parents completed the observation sheet that records the child's behaviours and skills while interacting with Jammo VRobot and explores the training experience. There were many positive comments and observation notes about the child's behaviours towards Jammo VRobot. Here are some of the comments and observations:

"In the training, she imitates the robot and says the name of the gesture after it."

"Explains what the robot physically does, like for ANGRY: crossed its arms and sad."

"Gets very excited when he saw the cartoon characters "Inside out cartoon" in the training."

After two weeks of finishing the intervention programme, the parents and teacher were asked about the generalisation of the taught skills and if they noticed any changes in their children. The teacher and parents mentioned that they had seen some improvement in the participants' emotion recognition and expressions skills. They also mentioned some improvements in the use and recognition of gestures and imitation skills. Most of the parents reported significant improvement in their children's imitation skills. Here are some of their feedback:

"I noticed a difference with my child ability to recognise expressions of emotions."

"I have noticed an improvement in my child imitation skills. He starts to imitate my actions and my words."

"He started expressing his feelings more. Sometimes he says I feel blue."

The teacher was asked if he saw any differences in the participants' performance and progress between the intervention programme and the traditional sessions he usually conducts with them.

6   Discussion

The primary aim of this study was to assess the effectiveness of the Jammo-VRobot environment in training children with HFA on emotion recognition and expression, gesture recognition and production, and imitation skills. In addition, the main objective was to provide a cost-effective and user-friendly tool for parents and practitioners to use. The results reveal that the Jammo VRobot effectively taught and trained the target skills to children with HFA.

By comparing the results obtained from the Jammo-VRobot social skill training programme environment with the state-of-the-art [14,15], similar results were found at a much lower cost and without needing technicians or professionals to set up the environment. Additionally, the Jammo-VRobot environment made it possible to explore the effect of such intervention in countries like Egypt, where no social robot interventions have been conducted before. Furthermore, providing the Jammo-VRobot tool as an open-source tool will make it easy for practitioners to expand the designed social skill training programme to include more social skills. According to the literature, children with ASD were focusing on the physical aspects of the robot itself and wanted to touch it rather than focus on the game scenarios' prompts [15]. Therefore, this might suggest why virtual robots might be more effective or an excellent teaching tool and increase the participants' focus skills during the learning process. The animation and cooperating cartoon characters in the learning process increased the participants' excitement during the intervention session and facilitated the learning process.

The number of gestures recognised and imitated increased after receiving the four training sessions in phases I and II for the intransitive gesture training programme. The participants' performance in phase II - pre-test was already close to 60 %, which gave the children a small margin of progression. The participants' scores in phase II - pre-test were relatively higher than those in phase I - pre-test. Interestingly, during the four training sessions in phase I, it was observed that the participants were imitating the Jammo VRobot without asking them to imitate. This finding is in line with previous studies that indicate that it is crucial to teach children with ASD to recognise meaningful gestures before asking them to imitate and produce these gestures [14]. Our findings confirm that imitation ability is essential to the development of language skills of children with ASD. It was observed that the participants were verbally imitating the name of the gestures after Jammo VRobot in the training sessions. Although the participants' scores in the storytelling tasks (Phase III) were lower than the other tasks (phase I and phase II), their scores number in the untrained scenarios (post-test and follow-up test) was higher than their scores in the pre-test. More importantly, the positive learning outcomes were maintained two weeks (follow-up test) after the training in the three phases.

For the emotion recognition training programme, the participants kept improving along with the sessions. Incorporating cartoon characters with each emotion besides the gestures helped improve the training sessions' learning process. Additionally, it kept the participants motivated and paid attention to the information presented, as children with ASD are visual learners. Additionally, the Jammo VRobot taught the participants to associate a colour to each emotion. Some emotions were easier than others to recognise and express. HAPPY and SAD emotions were the easiest to recognise and express among the 15 participants in the three phases. DISGUST and SURPRISE emotions were the hardest to recognise and express in phase I and phase II, which indicates the importance of facial expressions to express such emotions. In phase III, the participants found it hard to differentiate between HAPPY and SURPRISE emotions from the social stories. Most of the participants chose HAPPY instead of SURPRISE. The same confusion was observed between ANGRY and SAD emotions. The results support previous studies that indicate that DISGUST and FEAR emotions are difficult for children with ASD to recognise [5]. This is consistent with some evidence that children with ASD have particular difficulty in recognising negative basic emotions [5,13]. The results of phase III indicate that the Jammo VRobot helped the participants understand the character's perspective in the story.

7   Conclusion

A primary challenge in this study was the relatively small sample size (N=15). Nonetheless, the sample was larger than that found in some state-of-the-art studies. Conducting this study during the pandemic circumstances (Covid-19) was the most significant challenge that affects the sample size. The evaluation process was conducted in Egypt. The number of assistive technology interventions for training children with ASD in Egypt is limited. Additionally, it is essential to emphasise that social robot interventions were not applied in Egypt before. Thus, the Jammo-VRobot environment provides an excellent opportunity for Egyptian parents and teachers to train their children's social skills. Fifteen children with HFA participated in this study online (11 children) and on-site (4 children). The participants received 24 sessions, with two sessions per week. The participants were taught to recognise the basic six emotions and 11 intransitive gestures (phase I), and to imitate and express these emotions and gestures (phase II), and to express and demonstrate them in social situations (phase III). The results emphasise that the Jammo-VRobot environment was an effective tool in training those skills for children with HFA. It also supports previous studies demonstrating the usefulness of robot interventions with children with ASD and provides new evidence to the usefulness of virtual robots to train and improve the social skills of children with ASD. Moreover, it emphasises that the Jammo VRobot could overcome some of the limitations of social robot interventions, their cost, limited availability, and became a widespread tool that parents and teachers can easily use to train the social skills of children with ASD. The observation of the intervention sessions brought valuable information regarding the participants' behaviours and skills during the sessions. It was observed that the children got engaged with the Jammo VRobot and imitated its actions and words spontaneously. Additionally, it was noticed that the Jammo VRobot did not bring any negative emotions, and most of the children were excited during the intervention sessions.

References

1. Abdelmohsen, M.: Enhancing social skills of children with ASD (2020). http://www.sstprogrammeforchildrenwithasd.com/. Accessed 2 Oct 2020
2. Abdelmohsen, M., Arafa, Y.: Jammo virtual robot enhances the social skills of children with HFA: development and deployment. In: Proceedings of the Conference on Information Technology for Social Good, pp. 180–185 (2021)
3. Abdelmohsen, M., Arafa, Y.: Training social skills of children with ASD through social virtual robot. In: 2021 IEEE Conference on Virtual Reality and 3D User Interfaces Abstracts and Workshops (VRW), pp. 314–319. IEEE (2021)
4. Aljameel, S., O'Shea, J., Crockett, K., Latham, A., Kaleem, M.: LANA-I: an Arabic conversational intelligent tutoring system for children with ASD. In: Intelligent Computing-Proceedings of the Computing Conference, pp. 498–516. Springer (2019)
5. Askari, F.: Studying facial expression recognition and imitation ability of children with autism spectrum disorder in interaction with a social robot (2018)

6. Charlton, C.T., et al.: Effectiveness of avatar-delivered instruction on social initiations by children with autism spectrum disorder. Res. Autism Spectr. Disord. **71**, 101494 (2020)
7. Cohen, D.J., Volkmar, F.R.: Handbook of Autism and Pervasive Developmental Disorders. Wiley, New York (1997)
8. Desideri, L., Di Santantonio, A., Varrucciu, N., Bonsi, I., Di Sarro, R.: Assistive technology for cognition to support executive functions in autism: a scoping review. Adv. Neurodevelopmental Disord. **4**, 330–343 (2020)
9. Di Nuovo, A., et al.: An explorative study on robotics for supporting children with autism spectrum disorder during clinical procedures. In: Companion of the 2020 ACM/IEEE International Conference on Human-Robot Interaction, pp. 189–191 (2020)
10. Herrero, J.F., Lorenzo, G.: An immersive virtual reality educational intervention on people with autism spectrum disorders (ASD) for the development of communication skills and problem solving. Educ. Inf. Technol. **25**, 1689–1722 (2019)
11. Huijnen, C.A., Lexis, M.A., Jansens, R., de Witte, L.P.: How to implement robots in interventions for children with autism? A co-creation study involving people with autism, parents and professionals. J. Autism Dev. Disord. **47**(10), 3079–3096 (2017)
12. O'Handley, R.D., Radley, K.C., Whipple, H.M.: The relative effects of social stories and video modeling toward increasing eye contact of adolescents with autism spectrum disorder. Res. Autism Spectrum Disord. **11**, 101–111 (2015)
13. Rump, K.M., Giovannelli, J.L., Minshew, N.J., Strauss, M.S.: The development of emotion recognition in individuals with autism. Child Dev. **80**(5), 1434–1447 (2009)
14. So, W.C., et al.: Robot-based intervention may reduce delay in the production of intransitive gestures in Chinese-speaking preschoolers with autism spectrum disorder. Mol. Autism **9**(1), 1–16 (2018)
15. Soares, F.O., Costa, S.C., Santos, C.P., Pereira, A.P.S., Hiolle, A.R., Silva, V.: Socio-emotional development in high functioning children with autism spectrum disorders using a humanoid robot. Interact. Stud. **20**(2), 205–233 (2019)
16. UIUXTrend: Measuring and interpreting system usability scale (SUS) (2021). https://uiuxtrend.com/measuring-system-usability-scale-sus/. Accessed 24 May 2021
17. Valencia, K., Rusu, C., Quiñones, D., Jamet, E.: The impact of technology on people with autism spectrum disorder: a systematic literature review. Sensors **19**(20), 4485 (2019)

Questioning Items' Link in Users' Perception of a Training Robot for Elders

Emanuele Antonioni[1], Piercosma Bisconti[2], Nicoletta Massa[3], Daniele Nardi[1], and Vincenzo Suriani[1]([✉])

[1] Department of Computer, Control, and Management Engineering,
Sapienza University of Rome, Rome, Italy
{antonioni,nardi,suriani}@diag.uniroma1.it
[2] Sant'Anna School of Advanced Studies, DIRPOLIS Institute, Pisa, Italy
piercosma.biscontilucidi@santannapisa.it
[3] Department of Psychology, Sapienza University of Rome, Rome, Italy
nicoletta.massa@uniroma1.it

Abstract. Socially Assistive robots are becoming more common in modern society. These robots can accomplish a variety of tasks for people that are exposed to isolation and difficulties. Among those, elderly people are the largest part, and with them, robotics can play new roles. Elderly people are the ones who usually suffer a major technological gap, and it is worth evaluating their perception when dealing with robots. To this end, the present work addresses the interaction of elderly people during a training session with a humanoid robot. The analysis has been carried out by means of a questionnaire, using four key factors: Motivation, Usability, Likability, and Sociability. The results can contribute to the design and the development of social interaction between robots and humans in training contexts to enhance the effectiveness of human-robot interaction.

Keywords: Robot trainer · Ageing society · Social robots

1 Introduction

Social Robots (SRs) are often seen as the next widespread commercialized technology since they find new fields of application year after year, especially in care-taking contexts. Typical examples are robots caring for the elderly or supporting children in the autism spectrum [4]. Especially in the case of assistive robotics for the elderly, the Covid-19 pandemic impressed an important acceleration both to research and to the commercialization of social robots [7]. This aspect is added to the progressive aging of Western societies and a progressive decrease in the number of human care-takers compared to the elderly population. One of the biggest challenges for social robotics today is therefore being able to take over part of the care-taking activities. This must be achieved by respecting the principles of human-centered design, and it is generally necessary to consider

© Springer Nature Switzerland AG 2021
H. Li et al. (Eds.): ICSR 2021, LNAI 13086, pp. 509–518, 2021.
https://doi.org/10.1007/978-3-030-90525-5_44

the ethical issues that Social Robotics raises [16]. Against this backdrop, assistive robotics for elders does not aim only to release human care-takers from the heaviest duties: the main objective of this technology, in line with the EU ethics guidelines [17], is to empower individuals, improve their autonomy, and their quality of life. As widely demonstrated, physical and psychological health are highly correlated aspects of humans' life, and the research has highlighted the inversely proportional relationship between physical activity, disability, and mortality, especially in the elderly population group [8,9], which nevertheless continues to represent the least physically active. Social Robotics can help the elderly population in maintaining optimal physical fitness, improving their autonomy and quality of life. The scope of this study is to understand if a NAO Robot with a high level of social interactivity and with a very positive interaction style is more effective than a neutral one to engage elders in a training exercise. We set up a 2×1 between-subjects design with one independent variable: the degree of social interactivity and positivity of the interaction. The interactions provided by the two NAO were highly different in terms of interactivity: the positive NAO, before starting with the training exercise, introduced itself to the user, it called him by his name during the training and used both positive feedback and the pronoun "we" instead of "you" to create an atmosphere of teamwork during the exercises; while the neutral NAO started the workout with no preliminary interaction, did not use reinforcements and only described briefly the type of exercise the user should perform. In general, through the training, the "positive NAO" provided positive reinforcements toward the user (e.g., "You are doing great!", "Well done", "We are a good team!"), instead of the "neutral NAO" that only explained the exercises giving no feedback. We designed the interactions referring to the field of sport psychology, where it is well known how the coaches' communicative skills correlate with athletes' motivation and with the quality and satisfaction associated with the performance and the coach as well [11,13]. Moreover, a supportive attitude is linked with an increased adherence to a training program in the long term [2], and with the quality of life consequently, [3]. This is particularly important for the elderly population [18,19] to whom our research is aimed. For these reasons, the "positive NAO" condition aims to recall the importance of the coach-athlete relationship, providing a communicative style where the social bounding was maximized to impact the motivation of the user and their interest in the training program. With this purpose, we expected to observe that the robot providing positive interactions would have higher scores in the following items: likability, sociability, usability, motivation. We discuss the questionnaire design in the section Experimental Design. We expected an increase in likability and sociability of the positive NAO since it provided more interactions than the neutral one and was more supportive and, in general engaging, as discussed above. Therefore, the hypothesis of our work was that also with robot trainers the increase in likability and sociability would result in more motivation for the user.

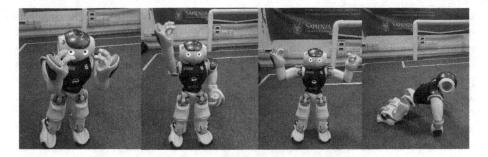

Fig. 1. Some of the exercises that are part of the developed routine. It is possible to notice how the robot can mimic even complex exercises to train the user.

2   Methodology

As mentioned in Sect. 1, the human-robot interaction procedure has been carried out by using the NAO Robot. The NAO Robot is a humanoid robot that performs complex motions thanks to its 25 degrees of freedom. For this task, the robot version chosen is the NAO V6[1]. In this version, it embeds a quadcore CPU manufactured by Intel. The computational capabilities combined with the set of sensors already on board of this robot allow it to be suitable for several tasks and, hence, become a trainer capable of demonstrating physical exercises, as shown in Fig. 1. The set of the onboard sensors of the robot include two cameras, four microphones, IMU, touch and force sensors, and sonars. The interaction with the user can happen using the robot microphones, speakers, and touch sensors. By relying on these capabilities, the implemented training routine has been carried out combining all these communication channels, as an evolution of [1]. This routine allows to show the exercises and to supervise the execution of the human by tracking the posture of the trainee person. Each exercise has been designed by modeling the end-effector trajectories for the limbs of the robot. An interaction routine has been developed on top of the set of exercises. This routine has been then differentiated for creating the positive and the neutral attitude. Particular attention has been paid to the communication setup, and even the voice of the NAO has been designed in velocity and pitch to make the robot more gender-neutral and to better communicate with the user.

2.1   Training Routine

The training routine has been developed within the Choregraphe[2] environment by using built-in functions and python modules. It has been designed to support real-time execution checking and a pool of exercises that can be easily chosen in the training routine. Each exercise's routine follows the schema depicted in the Fig. 3. Each exercise starts with an introduction that contains an explanation of

---

[1] www.softbankrobotics.com/emea/en/nao.

[2] http://doc.aldebaran.com/2-4/software/choregraphe/index.html.

the exercise and optional motivational interaction with the trainee that depends on the execution modality that can be positive or neutral. Then, the robot executes the planned exercise, and, thanks to parallel modules, the execution is fully monitored and supported. In fact, a correction module checks the human posture through the cameras. At the end of the execution, the robot chooses to go ahead or to repeat the current execution. In the positive training execution, at the end of the exercise, the robot provides positive reinforcements by voice and uses gestures to emphasize them. Some frames of a training routine and interaction with the user can be seen in Fig. 2.

Fig. 2. Some frames taken from the videos that have been shown in the questionnaire.

2.2   Participants

The total number of involved participants is 63, with an average age of 77 years. They have been divided into two balanced samples, composed of 31 and 32 participants each. The two samples have been created by relying on the preliminary answers provided by the participants. In fact, we used age, gender, and a self-evaluated sport capability to create the two matched groups. Both samples have the same average age (77), and the standard deviation on the two samples are respectively 5.37 and 4.8. The gender balance is 15–17 and 14–17 for the Male-Female ratios in the two samples, respectively.

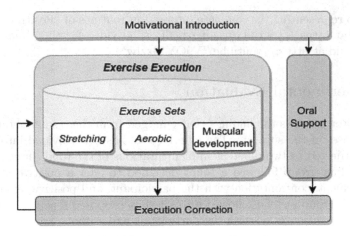

Fig. 3. Schema of the single exercise training routine. This procedure is common to both the positive and neutral trainer. The execution is fully monitored and supported. At the end of the execution, the robot chooses to go ahead or to repeat the current execution.

The participants have been engaged by Fondazione Mondo Digitale[3] that, among other activities, delivers digital education programs for elderly people.

2.3 Experimental Design

Due to the Covid-19 pandemic, we used online questionnaires because it was not possible to conduct the study in presence due to restrictions. In the first phase of the study, a preliminary online questionnaire was used to collect anamnestic information relating to age, gender, nationality, education, and participants' perceived physical condition. Subsequently, they were assigned to the two experimental groups ("Positive NAO" and "Neutral NAO") and were asked to watch a video - that lasted approximately four minutes - where the NAO trainer provided either a high social bounding or a low social bounding toward the user. Then the participants were asked to fill a 12-questions questionnaire. They had to rate Motivation, Usability, Likability, and Sociability with a 5-point Likert scale (1 = Strongly agree, 5 = Strongly disagree). The questionnaire is based on the ALMERE questionnaire for Sociability (Perceived Sociability in ALMERE), Usability (ease of use in ALMERE), and Likability (Perceived Enjoyment in ALMERE). The Motivation item included the following questions:

The questions for the motivation item were inspired to [14]

- I would be curious to try the same workout
- I would be happy to train with this robot
- I think that train with the robot is useless

---

[3] https://www.mondodigitale.org/it.

The video representing the complete interaction routines of "Positive NAO" can be found at https://youtu.be/isad9g-Lc6E. The video for the "Neutral NAO" can be found at https://youtu.be/W9OY19zzlwM.

3   Experimental Evaluation

This chapter presents the findings that emerged from the results obtained from the responses of the subjects. The elderly pool has been divided into two subgroups subjected to two different implementations of the robot interaction routine. The first group followed a robot designed to offer a positive interaction, encouragement, confrontation with the participant, and positive reinforcement. The second group instead followed a robot that proposed a neutral interaction, limiting the confrontation with the participant and without providing any type of reinforcement. Each participant has seen the video individually. The responses to the questionnaire proposed to the participants refer to four items: (1) Motivation, (2) Usability, (3) Likability, and (4) Sociability. Each response was mapped to the individual items using a numerical value in the range $(-2, +2)$.

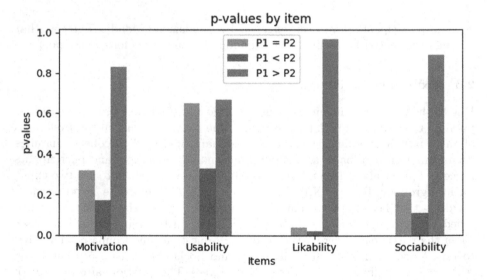

Fig. 4. p-values for different precondition hypothesis on the four items

3.1   Results

We summed numerical values extracted from each question based on the reference item. Table 1 shows means and standard deviations on the individual items for both samples. We can see that the averages for the Motivation, Sociability, and Likability items are higher in the case of the positive sample and lower in the

Table 1. Table of experimental values

List of values				
Variable	Motivation	Usability	Likability	Sociability
μ_{pos}	1.33	2.55	1.78	1.79
σ_{pos}	1.81	1.29	1.65	2
μ_{neu}	0.67	2.7	0.67	1
σ_{neu}	2.87	1.91	2.17	2.46

case of the neutral sample. From the analysis of the table, however, it is clear that all of the values reported are subject to high variance, which makes it difficult to extrapolate information straightforwardly from the trend of the averages of the individual samples. To gain an additional level of insight, we evaluated a p-value test for each item, proposing three different conditions related to the emerging populations $P1$ and $P2$ of the two samples: (1) $P1 = P2$, (2) $P1 < P2$, and (3) $P1 > P2$. Figure 4 shows the obtained values. The analysis of these p-values provides us with statistically significant results only in the case of Likability. In fact, in the condition $P1 = P2$, the effect on this item is the only one below the 0.05 threshold, thus passing the p-value test. Therefore, we can say that the data in our possession clearly expressed a higher Likability in the sample exposed to the robot with positive behavior. However, concerning the other items, it is not possible to provide a similar conclusion using the p-value. Therefore, the results led us to develop a second level of analysis for these items. The p-value result indicates the impossibility of accurately inferring whether the difference in results for the Motivation, Usability, and Sociability items is due to a structural difference in the samples (in our case, the different attitude of the robot) or sampling noise. Hence, we perform a further and more in-depth analysis of these items.

Considering the values in the Table 1, we call μ_{pos}, μ_{neu}, σ, n the μ of the positive sample, the μ of the neutral sample, the standard deviation of the positive sample and the number of samples of the positive sample. We want to demonstrate, the following hypotheses:

- $H_0 \rightarrow \mu_{pos(mot)} = \mu_{neu(mot)}$
- $H_1 \rightarrow \mu_{pos(us)} = \mu_{neu(us)}$
- $H_2 \rightarrow \mu_{pos(soc)} = \mu_{neu(soc)}$

So we evaluate three values $z_0, z_1, and z_2$ for each hypothesis. By applying the hypothesis test formula [6]

$$z_i = \frac{\mu_{pos} - \mu_{neu}}{\frac{\sigma}{\sqrt{n}}} \tag{1}$$

we obtain: $z_0 = 1.8$ $z_1 = -0.77$ $z_2 = 1.95$. The z_0 results is inside the reference range $(-1.96, +1.96)$, so the hypothesis H_0 can be confirmed.

The z_1 result confirms the hypothesis H_1 being inside the range $(-1.96, +1.96)$.

Finally for z_2 the result is borderline w.r.t the threshold range $(-1.96, +1.96)$, this does not allow us to perform a strong inference about the correctness of H_2.

3.2 Discussion

The results obtained from the p-value test and the subsequent hypothesis tests allow us to establish inferences on only three of the four proposed items. The p-value provides us with a confirmation of the success in implementing positive interaction traits for the robot, leading to higher results in terms of Likability for the positive robot compared to the neutral robot. The general increase in the robot Likability does not match an advantage in terms of Motivation and Sociability; this is a phenomenon that requires future development and further and more specific analysis. On the other hand, hypothesis testing confirmed the hypothesis of equality of the two averages between the samples concerning Usability, suggesting that this characteristic does not undergo appreciable variations based on the change in the robot's attitude. This phenomenon may indicate to us that a sympathetic and positive approach may not necessarily be more transparent in terms of clarity in how to use technologies as complex as the proposed robot. Ultimately, although the separation between samples was not always well defined, the overall results indicate a good acceptance of the proposed idea in the elderly population. This can be seen in Table 1 where the averages of all items in both samples are pointing towards positive values, despite high standard deviations.

4   Conclusion and Future Work

In this experiment, we wanted to evaluate if a NAO trainer robot providing an engaging and positive interaction was more likable than a robot with a neutral style of interaction. From the results obtained, it was possible to conclude that, in the case of the "positive NAO", the Likability item increased, while the same did not happen for the "neutral NAO" as we expected. Therefore, the people who viewed the video where the robot trainer implemented a positive interaction, with reinforcements and encouragement, ended up perceiving it as more pleasant than people watching the neutral interaction.

While in the case of Likability, we saw a clear outcome, distinguishing the results of positive Nao from the neutral one, this is not true for the other items. Though for Sociability, we are not able to deduce anything from our statistical results, the hypothesis test done for Motivation and Usability suggests that a greater enjoyment in the interaction does not result in an incentive for the training activity. This goes against some suggestions of the current literature on trainer robots [5,10,15]. Certainly, a more in-depth analysis involving the in-person interaction of the elder with the robot must follow. In future studies, we aim to investigate the reason why the results between the positive and the neutral NAO were not sufficiently differentiated in statistical terms. Our hypothesis, to test in future works, is that (especially) the elderly population might be enthusiastic and astonished for the very fact of seeing an interacting robot. In our case, the association Mondo Digitale who put us in contact with the participants' deals with topics concerning the digitalization of the elder populations; therefore, it is very likely that participants were tech enthusiasts. Therefore, as in the NATRS (Negative attitude toward robots scale), [12], we plan to carry on a study in order to test our hypothesis on the over-enthusiasm effect on the elder population interacting with robots, possibly designing an "Over-enthusiastic attitude toward robot scale".

Acknowledgement. We want to thank the Fondazione Mondo Digitale for its essential support in recruiting the participants to this study and helping us in administering the questionnaires. A special mention to Cecilia Stajano for her help and availability.

Contributions. D. Nardi conceived the experiment, supervised and managed the project, revised the manuscript.

N. Massa and P. Bisconti designed the style of robot's interaction, the questionnaire and discussed the implications of the results.

E. Antonioni and V. Suriani designed the robot's routine, performed statistical analysis; discussed the results.

All authors contributed to the writing phase.

References

1. Antonioni, E., Suriani, V., Massa, N., Nardi, D.: Autonomous and remote controlled humanoid robot for fitness training. In: Companion Publication of the 2020 International Conference on Multimodal Interaction, pp. 235–239, ICMI 2020 Companion. Association for Computing Machinery, New York, NY, USA (2020). https://doi.org/10.1145/3395035.3425301
2. Brawley, L., Vallerand, R.: Effects of informational and controlling fitness leaders on participants' interest and intention to pursue engagement in a fitness program. Unpublished manuscript, University of Waterloo, Waterloo, Canada (1985)
3. Diaz, R., Miller, E.K., Kraus, E., Fredericson, M.: Impact of adaptive sports participation on quality of life. Sports Med. Arthrosc. Rev. **27**(2), 73–82 (2019)
4. Esteban, P.G., et al.: How to build a supervised autonomous system for robot-enhanced therapy for children with autism spectrum disorder. Paladyn J. Behav. Robot. **8**(1), 18–38 (2017)
5. Griffiths, S., et al.: Exercise with social robots: companion or coach? arXiv preprint arXiv:2103.12940 (2021)
6. Hayslett, H.T.: Statistics. Elsevier, New York (2014)
7. Kim, S.S., Kim, J., Badu-Baiden, F., Giroux, M., Choi, Y.: Preference for robot service or human service in hotels? Impacts of the COVID-19 pandemic. Int. J. Hosp. Manag. **93**, 102795 (2021). https://doi.org/10.1016/j.ijhm.2020.102795, https://linkinghub.elsevier.com/retrieve/pii/S0278431920303479
8. Lee, I.M., Paffenbarger, R.S., Jr.: Do physical activity and physical fitness avert premature mortality? Exerc. Sport Sci. Rev. **24**(1), 135–172 (1996)
9. Leveille, S.G., Guralnik, J.M., Ferrucci, L., Langlois, J.A.: Aging successfully until death in old age: opportunities for increasing active life expectancy. Am. J. Epidemiol. **149**(7), 654–664 (1999)

10. Lotfi, A., Langensiepen, C., Yahaya, S.W.: Socially assistive robotics: robot exercise trainer for older adults. Technologies **6**(1), 32 (2018)
11. Mageau, G.A., Vallerand, R.J.: The coach-athlete relationship: a motivational model. J. Sports Sci. **21**(11), 883–904 (2003)
12. Nomura, T., Suzuki, T., Kanda, T., Kato, K.: Measurement of negative attitudes toward robots. Interact. Stud. **7**(3), 437–454 (2006)
13. Otte, F.W., Davids, K., Millar, S.K., Klatt, S.: When and how to provide feedback and instructions to athletes?-How sport psychology and pedagogy insights can improve coaching interventions to enhance self-regulation in training. Front. Psychol. **11**, 1444 (2020)
14. Pelletier, L.G., Rocchi, M.A., Vallerand, R.J., Deci, E.L., Ryan, R.M.: Validation of the revised sport motivation scale (SMS-ii). Psychol. Sport Exerc. **14**(3), 329–341 (2013)
15. Shao, M., Alves, S.F.D.R., Ismail, O., Zhang, X., Nejat, G., Benhabib, B.: You are doing great! only one rep left: an affect-aware social robot for exercising. In: 2019 IEEE International Conference on Systems, Man and Cybernetics (SMC), pp. 3811–3817. IEEE (2019)
16. Sharkey, A., Sharkey, N.: Granny and the robots: ethical issues in robot care for the elderly. Ethics Inf. Technol. **14**(1), 27–40 (2012). https://doi.org/10.1007/s10676-010-9234-6
17. Smuha, N.A.: The EU approach to ethics guidelines for trustworthy artificial intelligence. Comput. Law Rev. Int. **20**(4), 97–106 (2019)
18. Steptoe, A., Owen, N., Kunz-Ebrecht, S.R., Brydon, L.: Loneliness and neuroendocrine, cardiovascular, and inflammatory stress responses in middle-aged men and women. Psychoneuroendocrinology **29**(5), 593–611 (2004)
19. Steptoe, A., Shankar, A., Demakakos, P., Wardle, J.: Social isolation, loneliness, and all-cause mortality in older men and women. Proc. Natl. Acad. Sci. **110**(15), 5797–5801 (2013)

Teleoperation and Industrial Applications

Teleoperating Multi-robot Furniture

Exploring Methods to Remotely Arrange Multiple Furniture Robots Deployed in a Multi-use Space

Brett Stoddard[(⊠)], Mark-Robin Giolando, and Heather Knight[(⊠)]

Oregon State University, Corvallis, OR 97331, USA
robots@brettstoddard.com, knighth@oregonstate.edu

Abstract. This paper presents the first study evaluating methods in remote teleoperation of multi-robot furniture for realistic applications. In a within-subjects user study (N = 12), we tested two robot control methods designed to work at different levels of abstraction in a custom web-based user interface (UI): clicking and dragging to indicate a desired position and orientation for a single ChairBot ("set goal"), and selecting from a list of preset arrangements for multiple ChairBots ("select arrangement"). Participants were asked to use this UI to rearrange ChairBots in a living room across three birthday-themed arrangement prompts. We found overlapping preferences for how distinct participants set of the room for particular party phases, and received high experience and usability ratings for the novel web-based multi-ChairBot controller design. Self-reported survey responses suggest that our design is easy to learn and usable. Our works provides insight to future controls design for and research on multi-robot furniture systems.

Keywords: Robot furniture · Teleoperation · Multi-robot systems

1 Introduction

Since Sirkin's Mechanical Ottoman [14], the number of robots with furniture morphologies in human-robot interaction (HRI) studies has rapidly increased. In fact, intelligent embodied devices of numerous classifications and purposes are now commonplace. A tech savvy consumer can program cookware, have robots to clean their floor, setup their front door to unlock at their presence, and automatically change the hue of their lights while they prepare for bed. Each of these systems requires careful interface design, and human-in-the-loop control schemes.

In this work, we synthesize prior work on robotic teleoperation, and robot furniture to design an interface for effectively arranging three chair robots (Chair-Bots) to explore furniture as a novel application for multi-robot systems. While previous work has demonstrated the ability of robot furniture to communicate with humans via motion [1,9,14], this paper presents the first study evaluating a multi-robot ChairBot system in a particular context: a multi-phase event in which the robots are controlled by a remote operator.

© Springer Nature Switzerland AG 2021
H. Li et al. (Eds.): ICSR 2021, LNAI 13086, pp. 521–531, 2021.
https://doi.org/10.1007/978-3-030-90525-5_45

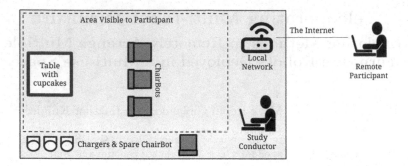

Fig. 1. A remote study participant interfaces with the system using the web UI with an overhead view of the area. A researcher locally monitors the ChairBots.

In a within-subjects user study (N = 12), we tested two robot control methods designed to work at different levels of abstraction in a custom web user interface (UI): lower-level clicking and dragging to indicate a desired position and orientation for a single ChairBot ("set goal"), and higher-level selecting from preset arrangements for all ChairBots ("select arrangement"). Participants were asked to use this UI to rearrange ChairBots in a living room across three arrangement prompts based on phases of a birthday party. The goal was to explore the following research questions and associated hypotheses:

RQ1: Is furniture re-arrangement a viable application for teleoperated robots?

- H1: Participants will be **able to create furniture arrangements** that they self-report to be satisfied with given the prompt.
- H2: People will have preferences about how to arrange furniture during different phases of an event, and these **arrangements preferences** will converge spatially across participants.

RQ2: What UI control abstraction is best suited for the task of arranging robot furniture?

- H3: Participants will rate the interface as at least **moderately usable.**
- H4: Participants will prefer using higher-abstraction commands (select arrangement) relative to lower abstraction commands (set goal position) such that they will have **higher usability ratings** and **be used more** .
- H5: Participants using high-abstraction commands (select arrangement) relative to lower abstraction commands (set goal position) will perform better such that they will **complete arrangements faster** with **fewer collisions.**

Our results show that participants tended to create similar arrangements, finding our novel web-based control interface easy to use, supporting the viability of remote robot furniture arrangement as an application.

2   Related Work

Our study builds on past work on robotic furniture, multi-robot teleoperation, and UI design.

Robots and Furniture. Prior Human-Robot Interaction (HRI) research investigated the impact of furniture robots as actors in social environments. This included studies where robots offered services [14,19], nonverbally communicated needs [9] and invitations [1], as props in theatrical performances [18], and received help from bystanders [5]. Implemented morphologies included ottomans [14], drawers [11], trash barrels [19], chairs [1,9], walls [12], and adaptive modular joints [8]. Few works have evaluated the usability of robot furniture as we aim to [12].

Remote Teleoperation. Much work on remotely operating multiple robots has been conducted in various situations but few works directly relate to our multi-robot furniture application. Of this work, most focus on observational area coverage tasks (such as search and rescue [10]), or specialized niches (such as geriatric care [4]). We did not find any examples of tasks related to creating a multi-robot arrangement from an open-ended prompts (or other spacial multi-robot task allocation problem) that would be directly translatable to our work on multi-robot furniture.

User Interface Design and Evaluation. The design of an effective UI for a novel task is a difficult process for which tested frameworks, and methods of evaluation exist. Studies on mitigating detrimental human factors [3], and frameworks for designing robot UIs [17] are useful early in the design process. After an initial implementation, the UI can be evaluated by metrics related to user workload, and task-dependent performance [3]. Additionally, further optimizations can be discovered via human studies. For example, Roldán et al. examined user input in various situations to detect "bottlenecks and inefficiencies" during a simulated multi-robot mission [13].

A significant design choice for human-robot systems is the level of abstraction at which interactions occur [3]. Levels of abstraction in multi-robot systems can span setting single-DOF low-level positional or torque commands, to commands involving the hundreds of DOFs in a swarm, coalition, or factory line. Increasing the level of UI abstraction for multi-robot system generally increases performance for many tasks by minimizing human bottlenecks. However, for open-ended tasks, higher levels of abstraction may impede the creative process which demands flexibility. As open-ended process, like furniture arrangement, are different than well-defined results-driven tasks, such as observational area coverage, the appropriate level of abstraction is an apparent gap in the literature.

3   Technology

Our implementation of **multi-robot furniture** involves three robotic chairs remotely tele-operable from a website. The ChairBot, originally designed by [9], consists of a wooden Ikea chair mounted on a Neato D3 vacuum. Three Chair-Bots, an overhead camera tracking positions to localize the robots as they move in a control loop, and a web-based UI make up our multi-robot furniture system[1]. ChairBots planned paths greedily, independently, and were blind to obstacles such that they sometimes collided with eachother or their objects in their environment. The scene and web-based UI are shown in Figs. 1, and 2 respectively.

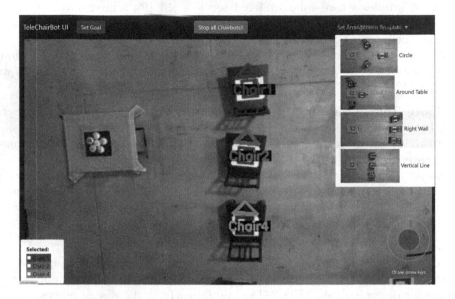

Fig. 2. The Tele-Chairbot UI with ChairBots in their starting positions. A live overhead video feed shows the room which includes the ChairBots and a non-robotic table with cupcakes. A joystick on the bottom-right can be used to send low-level motion commands. The top bar has the higher-level controls: set goal, and set arrangement template.

Prior work on our **ChairBots UI** had established the need for a screen-based controller, and some of its primary features for control [6]. These features include a remote interface, the ability to set and save arrangements, optimized positional and velocity precision, and the ability to move in a formation or adjust relative to room geometry. We build on the system and architecture by [16] by simplifying the web layout, extending image overlays, and adding a method to set individual ChairBot locations and orientations ("set goal").

4   Methods

This section describes our experimental manipulations, metrics, and procedure. A multi-robot system consisting of these ChairBots was chosen due to the implication that robotized furniture is a multi-robot system and the fact that ChairBots

---

[1] Code and build instructions available at www.github.com/stoddabr/ros_flask.

have been previously studied in past HRI research [1,5,6,9]. A birthday party was chosen as the backdrop for this experiment as it is a realistic and relatable example of a multi-phase event, with similarities to larger-scale events [6].

4.1 Manipulations

Party Phase Prompts: The first manipulation we explored was prompting participants to create furniture arrangements for three phases of this birthday party. The three phases were handcrafted and chosen to represent distinct of a birthday party: "cutting **cake** at the table", "watching a **magician** perform on the right side of the room", and "a **dance** party on the floor". Participants were told the party prompts as quoted. These activities were chosen as they offer a variety of social and behavioral considerations.

UI Type: A second set of manipulations aim to compare approaches for abstracting the control of a multi-robot furniture arrangement system and to determine their effectiveness. Users experienced two abstracted control modes: (1) **goal-based commands** in which users could move one chair at time with by clicking to set a waypoint location and orientation, and (2) **arrangement template**, in which a drop down menu of present arrangement graphics could be selected from. For both modes, we also provided a screen-based joystick for general fine-tuning. These were chosen as they represent multiple levels of abstraction: controlling robots with low-level motion commands with the joystick, specifying higher-level goals for individual robots, and, at the highest-level, giving goals for all robots. During the actual experiment, the first two trials participants experienced both of these conditions in a random order (balanced across participants). For the third and final trial they had the option of using either or both control modes.

4.2 Metrics and Measures

Five surveys, a semi-structured interview, and video recordings of the interaction were recorded for each participant. They included a **demographic** survey, a **post-trial** survey about self-perceived workload and performance, and a final **exit** survey containing the System Usability Scale (SUS) survey [2]. The post-trial survey included 7-point Likert scales from the NASA-TLX survey [7] which measure mental demand, and frustration level along with three custom questions about self-perceived success: 'I was pleased with the final robot formation.", "I was successful in performing this the arrangement task", and "I was satisfied with my performance in this arrangement task". The SUS Likert scale in the exit survey was adjusted to a 10-point scale to increase granularity.[2]

The semi-structured interview consisted of 8 questions relating to performance, experience, and insights. These and improvisational follow-up questions

---

[2] Adjusted cumulative score: SUS = 1.11 * [(odd questions − 1) + (10 − even questions)].

were asked in an order determined by the Study Conductor based on the flow of the conversation. An example of the semi-structured interview can be seen at timestamp 31:35 of [15].

4.3 Study Procedure and Participant Instructions

Participants started by joining a Zoom call with a Study Conductor, which was recorded after consent was established (as per IRB-2020-0826). After the demographic survey, the participant was asked to role play as the employee of a company offering "robotic furniture arrangement as a service" wherein their job was to teleoperate robot furniture to meet the needs of a client.

The participant was then provided with a Tele-ChairBot UI web link url. The participants were initially trained in using the manual control method (see Sect. 3). Next, the participant was similarly trained on either goal or arrangement control. Once the participant was comfortable with the controls, they were **instructed to fulfill the client's Party Prompt exactly as quoted in Sect. 4.1**. They were then allowed to ask clarifying questions which, naturally, varied. No maximum time limit was set, however the participants were encouraged to not "keep the client waiting". Once the participant was satisfied with their arrangement or determined that no satisfactory arrangement was possible, the post-trial survey was administered (Sect. 4.2) before another trial was started.

Robotic failures occurring during the study were mitigated in one of two ways: the Study Conductor would attempt to fix the issue, or if the arrangement was close to complete, would physically move the ChairBot as indicated by the participant via the UI before the failure occurred. Failures required various amounts of time to recover from; the most common involved situations where the Neato batteries died requiring replacing or recharging ($\sim$4 min), the Neato firmware froze requiring a reboot ($\sim$2 min), or the video server crashed requiring the user to refresh their webpage ($\sim$5 s). Examples of robotic failures can be seen at timestamps 4:00, 14:45 and 18:27 in [15]. Upon completing all of the trials, an exit survey and semi-structured interview were conducted.

4.4 Participants

The study consisted of 3 trials within 12 participants (6 males, 6 females) of college age, resulting in 36 trials total for analysis. 10 of participants were recruited from outside of the robotics department and were unfamiliar with the research. On average, participants reported having a master's degree, higher than average levels of familiarity with robots, and were younger (all aged 18–35, $\mu \approx 23$) signifying a higher technical competency than average.

5 Results

This section presents the results of these experiments: (1) participant party phases prompts resulted in very similar arrangements for two of the three phases,

(2) both UI control modes were rated highly by participants, and (3) participants reacted positively to the UI.

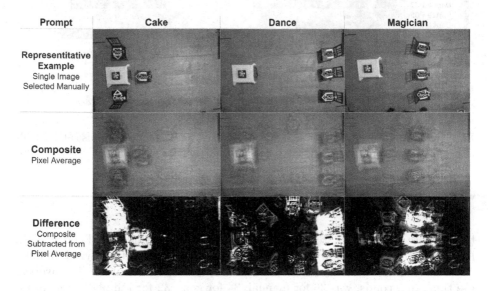

Fig. 3. Images in a table showing final arrangement information. The Representative Example was manually chosen to to show a typical/median arrangement. The Composite image was created from the mean of all arrangement images for that prompt. The Difference image shows the difference between the composite from an average of all arrangements in grayscale colorspace.

Participants Created Similar Arrangement Patterns by Phase. Several methods of composite image analysis were used to review combined final furniture arrangements for trials shown in Fig. 3. To summarize, the cake phase contains a pattern of participants gathering the chairs around the table, with 10 of 12 participants clustered chairs around the table. For the magician performance, all but P03 arranged the chairs facing towards the right side of the room, where they were told the magician would be performing. The dance floor arrangements resulted in the largest variance: five placed chairs along the right wall, three placed chairs around the table, with the other participants exhibited more individualistic control arrangements that lacked emergent patterns. A commonality across the dance party arrangements was that the center of the room was left clear. No patterns were observed across UI Type.

No UI Control Modes were Favored. Participants were exposed to two control modes (goal-based commands and arrangement template), however, neither UI control method was favored more than the other, failing to support H4. Upon completion of the trials, trial video footage was reviewed and the number of times each control method was used and for how long was collected, as shown in Fig. 4, as was the final control mode used to position the chairs. Only

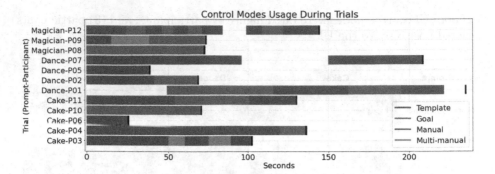

Fig. 4. UI control usage over time for trials in which participants could use all controls (UI Type = Both). Empty areas represent a participant thinking or otherwise not interacting with the UI. Moving multiple (2 or 3) robots at once was differentiated from moving a single robot manually. A black line denotes the end of that trial. Participants were given as much time as they needed for trials.

trials where participants were able to use all modalities (where UI Type = Both, i.e., the third experimental condition for all participants) were analyzed. Manual control was used 12 times, goal 12, template 9, and multi-manual 3. The average use time, in seconds, was 36 for manual, 34 for goal, 32 for template, and 16 for multi-manual. The qualitative data (Sect. 6) suggests that participants found differing utility for each UI control mode.

Table 1. Mean value and results of an ANOVA tests run on trial-specific metrics and tested conditions. Statistically significant results are bolded ($p < 0.1$ and $F_{2,33} > 2.47$). For all survey questions, higher numbers are more positive.

Data source	Metric	Mean	Manipulation	P-value	F-score
Trial survey	Self-assessment of success	6.1/7	UI Type	0.88	0.12
			Party phase	0.63	0.46
	NASA-TLX mental demand	5.8/7	UI Type	0.69	0.37
			Party phase	0.78	0.25
	NASA-TLX Frustration	5.7/7	UI Type	0.61	0.50
			Party phase	0.93	0.064
Video analysis	Time to complete (s)	114	UI Type	0.95	0.042
			Party phase	**0.060**	**3.0**
	Number of collisions	0.30	UI Type	0.79	0.23
			Party phase	0.28	1.3

Application and UI Experience were Rated Highly. Overall, our system was rated positively by participants across the SUS, NASA-TLX, and self-assessment questions. From our 12 responses, we arrived at a mean SUS score of $\mu = 75.1$ ($\sigma = 10.4$). Based on [2], this result is a "Good" level of usability, which supports H3. Interestingly, the first question of the SUS, "I think that I would like to use this robotic furniture system frequently", was contentious with a wide distribution ($\mu = 5.4, \sigma = 3.0$). The NASA-TLX portion of the trial survey indicated that the tasks were considered simple and easy to complete with all participants reporting low absolute levels of stress as shown in Table 1. Self-assessment questions also resulted in high scores.

Across our two manipulations, there were no statistically significant results within the trial survey responses, shown in Table 1, nor between exit survey responses. This fails to support H4 as participants did not prefer using higher-abstraction controls.

6   Discussion

Participants were able to create satisfying furniture arrangements, supporting H1. Additionally all participants rating the system better than moderately usable. The resulting average SUS rating of 75 ($\sigma = 10$, "Good" as per [2]), and positively skewed survey scores support H3. However, the low number, and higher-than-average technical competency of recruited participants may be a confounding variable.

Party phase corresponded to furniture arrangement pattern, as illustrated in Fig. 3 which supports H2. However, the amount of variability differed across prompts. The cake appears the most convergent (all but P03 placed Chair-Bots around the table), followed closely by the magician (all placed chairs in a central row facing right), with the dance prompt being more divergent (participants sporadically moved ChairBots towards the walls). One explanation for the cake and magician resulting in less variance than the dance prompt is the former suggest arrangement towards an object or place whereas the latter suggest an arrangement with furniture removed from an area. This suggests an axis for which furniture arrangement prompts may be described: spacial attraction around the prompt's region of interest, whereby a positive attraction will result in less arrangement variability than a negative one.

Participants Customize Arrangements Based on Minute Contextual Criteria. As different participants generated different assumptions, this supports and provides an explanation for H2: furniture arrangement preferences are heavily influenced by assumptions, about the use of the space based on available context. For example, P03 broke the trend of arranging the ChairBots around the table during the cake prompt saying they "assumed five people" were at the party based on the number of cupcakes on the table. There may also be cultural factors to take into account when for designing robotic furniture systems for different social or regional application domains.

7   Conclusion

In this work, we implemented a web-based multi-robot furniture teleoperation interface, running a remote study in which participants controlled robotic chairs over the internet. The study was designed to test a specific robot furniture application – making arrangements for multiple phases of a birthday party – and evaluated several control abstractions. This work offers support for the applicability of robot furniture arrangement as a useful domain for HRI research.

The results demonstrate that the participants were able to successfully create arrangement to accomplish a variety of tasks during a multi-phase event in the home, showing patterns in furniture arrangement across participants for well defined activities (cake, magician), as well as differentiation for more open-ended prompts (dance party). Though the goal control mode was the most popular, perhaps because of the balance of flexibility and ease-of-use, participants did not favor one control mode. For our study, UI Types did not significantly predict usability or performance, instead, usability rates were high across the board, indicating that multi-robot furniture UIs should be designed with controls over multiple levels of abstraction.

This work presents the first application-based use of robot furniture involving a remote operator rearranging furniture during a multi-phase event. Future work will seek to evaluate such a system co-operating in and around the people for whom the arrangements are meant to serve. Such results should also be tested on larger-scale, and heterogeneous systems to support more complex social settings such as conferences, classrooms, or social events.

References

1. Agnihotri, A., Knight, H.: Persuasive ChairBots: a robot recruited experiment. In: 14th ACM/IEEE International Conference on Human-Robot Interaction (HRI), pp. 700–702 (2019)
2. Bangor, A., Kortum, P., Miller, J.: Determining what individual SUS scores mean: adding an adjective rating scale. J. Usability Stud. 4(3), 114–123 (2009)
3. Chen, J.Y., Barnes, M.J.: Human-agent teaming for multirobot control: a review of human factors issues. IEEE Trans. Hum.-Mach. Syst. 44(1), 13–29 (2014)
4. Di Nuovo, A., et al.: The multi-modal interface of robot-era multi-robot services tailored for the elderly. Intell. Serv. Robot. 11(1), 109–126 (2018)
5. Fallatah, A., Chun, B., Balali, S., Knight, H.: Would you please buy me a coffee? How microcultures impact people's helpful actions toward robots, pp. 939–950 (2020)
6. Fallatah, A., Stoddard, B., Knight, H.: Towards user-centric robot furniture arrangement. In: 30th IEEE International Conference on Robot and Human Interactive Communication (RO-MAN) (2021)
7. Hart, S.G., Staveland, L.E.: Development of NASA-TLX (task load index): results of empirical and theoretical research. Adv. Psychol. 52, 139–183 (1988)
8. Hauser, S., Mutlu, M., Léziart, P.A., Khodr, H., Bernardino, A., Ijspeert, A.J.: Roombots extended: challenges in the next generation of self-reconfigurable modular robots and their application in adaptive and assistive furniture. Robot. Auton. Syst. 127, 103467 (2020)

9. Knight, H., Lee, T., Hallawell, B., Ju, W.: I get it already! The influence of ChairBot motion gestures on bystander response. In: 26th IEEE International Symposium on Robot and Human Interactive Communication (RO-MAN), pp. 443–448 (2017)
10. Liu, Y., Nejat, G.: Robotic urban search and rescue: a survey from the control perspective. J. Intell. Robot. Syst. **72**(2), 147–165 (2013)
11. Mok, B., Yang, S., Sirkin, D., Ju, W.: Empathy: interactions with emotive robotic drawers. In: 2014 9th ACM/IEEE International Conference on Human-Robot Interaction (HRI), pp. 250–251. IEEE (2014)
12. Nguyen, B.V.D., Simeone, A.L., Vande Moere, A.: Exploring an architectural framework for human-building interaction. In: 16th Annual ACM/IEEE International Conference on Human-Robot Interaction (HRI), pp. 252–261 (2021)
13. Roldán, J.J., Olivares-Méndez, M.A., del Cerro, J., Barrientos, A.: Analyzing and improving multi-robot missions by using process mining. Auton. Robots **42**(6), 1187–1205 (2018)
14. Sirkin, D., Mok, B., Yang, S., Ju, W.: Mechanical ottoman: how robotic furniture offers and withdraws support. In: 10th Annual ACM/IEEE International Conference on Human-Robot Interaction (HRI), pp. 11–18 (2015)
15. Stoddard, B.: ChairBot UI remote usability study: P03, September 2021. https://www.youtube.com/watch?v=8I1Hz5R4jxk
16. Stoddard, B., Fallatah, A., Knight, H.: A web-based user interface for HRI studies on multi-robot furniture arrangement. In: Companion of the 2021 ACM/IEEE International Conference on Human-Robot Interaction (HRI), pp. 680–681 (2021)
17. Szafir, D., Szafir, D.A.: Connecting human-robot interaction and data visualization. In: Proceedings of the 2021 ACM/IEEE International Conference on Human-Robot Interaction, pp. 281–292 (2021)
18. Urann, J., Fallatah, A., Knight, H.: Dancing with ChairBots. In: 14th Annual ACM/IEEE International Conference on Human-Robot Interaction (HRI), pp. 364–364. IEEE (2019)
19. Yang, S., et al.: Experiences developing socially acceptable interactions for a robotic trash barrel. In: 24th IEEE International Symposium on Robot and Human Interactive Communication (RO-MAN), pp. 277–284. IEEE (2015)

Human-Robot Coordination in Agile Robot Manipulation

Qilong Yuan$^{(\boxtimes)}$ (iD) and Ivan Sim Wan Leong (iD)

Institute for Infocomm Research (I²R), A*STAR, Singapore, Singapore
yu0017ng@e.ntu.edu.sg

Abstract. With the practical demands in flexible and adaptive robot manipulation skills in various environment settings, there are more challenges to be tackled to enable the robot with valid responsive behaviors in task handling. This paper discuss on the methods to achieve agile robot manipulations tasks with the advantages from human-robot teleoperation, robot perception, knowledge-based robot programming, robot motion planning and robot skill learning. Teleoperation serves as a typical Human-Robot Interaction (HRI) manner to allow the human user to guide the robot behavior in a direct manner. Robot automation, including the sensor perception (object detection, pose estimation etc.), motion planning and motion control that can handle well defined problems, but is also lack of general sense of understanding capability and not good at solving not fully defined task challenges. An agile robotic system should have a knowledge database which defines the skill sets required for the robot to handle various robot tasks. Meanwhile, the system should be able to take human assistance inputs through HRI when the robot is stuck. Moreover, the system should be able to pick up new skill set with each human knowledge input. Methodology discussion is the main scope of the paper, and preliminary experiments on telemanipulation with UR5 robot are demonstrated to show the flexible robot guidance through HRI inputs. Future work will aim to add in perception, motion planning, and picking up skill modules to come up with a more agile solution in handling variation of tasks.

Keywords: Telemanipulation · Motion planning · Knowledge based programming

1 Introduction

In up-to-date robot applications, robotic systems are involved in various diversified task scenarios which require the robot to act flexibly to the changes of its

This research was supported by Agency for Science, Technology and Research (A*STAR) under its RIE2020 Advanced Manufacturing and Engineering (AME) Industry Alignment Fund—Pre-Positioning Programme (IAF-PP) grant number A19E4a0101. All authors are with Institute for Infocomm Research (I²R), A*STAR, Singapore.

H. Li et al. (Eds.): ICSR 2021, LNAI 13086, pp. 532–540, 2021.
https://doi.org/10.1007/978-3-030-90525-5_46

surroundings. Human and robot safety are the up-most priority to be taken care of in all applications especially in a clustered environments with human traffics, which require the robot to be well aware of the environments and make sure the action are valid and safe for execution. This definitely bring in new challenges to a robotic system because it is known that motion planning for robotic system in clustered environments is already a big challenge. On the other hand, in human-robot teleoperation, the robot is under human operator's control through certain human-robot interfacing channels. This enable human operator to guide the robot to do a task, while the limitation is that due to the difficulty in teleoperation and the task manipulation, the human operation cannot cope with complex tasks with complex dexterous manipulation process. In such master-slave mode, improving the human robot interfacing system can help to make the slave robot easier to control. However, this is not sufficient. When a robotic system is given a task, if the knowledge database can provide the robot with some general protocol to follow, the robot sensor perception and motion generation can assist to guide the robot to do tasks in sequential action primitives [15].

In the scene of robotic motion planning, there are powerful tools to generate robot motion when the problem is well defined. For example, MoveBase in mobile base motion planning, Moveit [11], OpenRave [10] and OMPL [12] for more complex robot systems. In complex scenarios with the robot having high DoF in clustered and dynamic environments, most software planners are not able to provide a quick solution by themselves or the solution is not an optimal one as per to the user request. Therefore, facing with a diversified challenges in robot task manipulation, the thought of on-site assisting robot motion planning and robot control with human robot teleoperation guidance become interesting and have practical meanings. This is currently an open and complex problem in which humans are able to assist robotic system to solve practical problems, with the latter having restricted knowledge database, limited sensor perception and AI strength in the robotic system.

This paper starts from the telemanipulation viewpoint, and will discuss on following technologies and integration methods to improve a robot system to be more flexible and efficient in handling a variation of tasks within unsupervised environment settings.

1. Improving the human-robot interface through direct human-robot teleoperation.
2. Knowledge-based robot programming and action generation.
3. Motion planning software solutions with collision safety in clustered environment.
4. Motion planning with human teleoperation guidance and robot perception.
5. Increasing knowledge pool based on human inputs.

2   Methodology

The general framework for the introduced robot task manipulation system is as shown in Fig. 1, a high-level command are auto-generated or sent by the user to

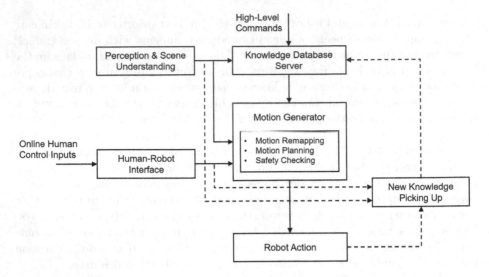

Fig. 1. Illustration of working flow for HRI guided telemanipulation.

the top control PC of the robot. At the beginning of the robot response, the high-level controller will check through the knowledge database for a corresponding matching action protocol. Such action protocol defines the general process for the robot to behave. In addition, more detailed motion generations are computed for the exact motions to be executed, where a motion generator will take the inputs of human-robot interaction devices and plan the motion with respect to the environment model. Lastly, human could also impart the task manipulation skills to the robot through HRI and the robot picking up new knowledge module.

2.1 Knowledge Based Robot Programming

In order to allow a robot system to respond to high level commands smartly to handle tasks autonomously with minimal human intervention, robot knowledge-based instruction system [1,2] can be used to store the structured programming database which defines the working protocol and reasoning logic of the robot action. In such a way, once the high-level command is given to the robot's top control PC, the robot will find a match from the knowledge database and generate a sequence of actions. This provides the general guideline for the robot to follow in the task handling. For simple tasks with supervised environments, knowledge based robot programming can handle many tasks such as inspection, pick and place, assembling etc. As long as the database generates sequence and instructing the sequential action primitives for the robot to behave, such as moving to a pose, taking a image, closing the gripper and dropping an item, etc.

However, for more complex task especially in clustered environment, the robot may not be able to immediately figure out the valid way to maneuver even though the general protocol is provided. Additional and more powerful tools for motion generation or human guidance through HRI are required.

2.2 Efficient Robot Teaching Through Teleoperation

Teleoperation have been studied for a few decades in robotics and there are plenty of teleoperation solutions with HRI devices such as inertial sensor[3], motion tracking [6,7], and haptic system [4,5] etc., to teleoperate a robot manipulator to move within a workspace for task manipulations. However, the critical technologies in task manipulation through teleoperation are able to handle tasks with geometric constraints [8,16], to manipulate the arm flexibly with space constraints, change of range/accuracy of motion, manipulation area[7], and teleoperating under environment reaction forces[6].

To control the robot motion with HRI device inputs, whether it is a joystick, an Omega Haptic Device, a motion capture device or any other interfacing device, the robot is expected to fulfill the task demands and with as little latency as possible. Let $q_r(t)$ be the robot configuration at t, $x_{in}(t)$ be the HRI inputs at time t, then the motion remapping functions f_m defines have the robot configuration will be updated according to the HRI control inputs.

$$q_r(t + d\tau) = f_m(q_r(t), x_{in}(t)) \tag{1}$$

This is a motion remapping from the control input to the change of the robot configuration with the consideration of latency $d\tau$. Meanwhile, when the task constraints such as geometric constraints need to be considered, the robot configurations need to be further fine tuned by a constraint function f_c to satisfy the constraints in the task.

$$q_r(t + d\tau) = f_c(q_r(t + d\tau)) \tag{2}$$

Such details can be fined in [6,7]. To change the robot manipulating location, the scale of motions, and the accuracy, the teleoperation system need to be robust enough to change the robot indexing, to update the scale parameters in robot motion remapping and the human operator need be able to adapt to the variation of the system parameters quickly for system telemanipulation. Therefore, the overall robustness of the system design in the telemanipulation solution is very critical for robot task guidance.

2.3 Safety While Robot Telemanipulation

For robot teleoperation, the cognitive load, effort, and frustration of the human operator could induce fatigue to the user as well as reducing quality of the task manipulation. The robot safety as well as the safety of the user are of upmost importance to the user and the system developer. Therefore, if there is a safety module to guarantee the robot safety before the action is executed, this will be significant [9] to protect both the robot and the system, as while as reducing the mental stress of the user. This will require safety checking of planned robot motions before the robot is allowed to take the action. Given the look ahead trajectory of the motion Tr_i, and the surrounding objects set O_s, the collision checking is to ensure that,

$$\forall q_r \in Tr_i, \forall o_i \in O_s, O_r(q_r) \cap o_i = \emptyset. \tag{3}$$

where, q_r represents the robot configuration, $O_r(q_r)$ represents the collision model of the robot under configuration q_r

It can be noticed that such safety checking is computationally expensive and will result in latency in robot telemanipulation control. Therefore, developing efficient safety checking algorithms are very critical. Otherwise, either the user will need to pay special attention to take care of the system safety or the robot hardware need to include safety feature to avoid robot unsafe behavior, or both are required.

3   Teleoperation Based Human Robot Coordination

3.1   Robot Motion Planning with Environment Modeling

For robot tasks within supervised environment with known surrounding models, provided the protocols defining the sequential motion primitives and the sensor perception modules to be well behaved, the motion planning software are able to generate the robot motion trajectory. To name a few of the well known open source robot motion planing software, OpenRave [10], Moveit! [11] (both apply OMPL library [12]), and there are also offline programming simulators such as RoboDK. The inputs for the motion planning software are typically, an environment model which can be point cloud outputs from sensors (3D scanner, 3D lidar, structure light sensors etc.) or 3D collision models of the environment, robot starting and goal configurations, and the robot kinematic model as well as the robot collision model itself. For a simple problem, with simple robot kinematics and model of both robot and environment, the planner can provide very quick and valid robot path solution. However, for complex problem, finding a path solution is not straight forward. The motion planning problem can be highly complex due to the complex nature of the environment model, the complex nature of the robot kinematics with tens of DoF, and complexity from a large variation type of additional constraints such as position constraint, velocity constraints, differential constraints and orientation constraints etc. Therefore, a random search for a solution won't work within practical time. Though sampling based motion planners are proved to be probabilistic complete [13,14], they cannot meet the criteria of generating motions efficiently enough in many application scenarios. The solutions are either to develop faster planners or to provide assistant to existing planners, such as adding sensor perception information in the motion planning or provide clues to guide the motion planner to find a solution more efficiently.

3.2 Teleoperation, Perception and Robot Motion Planning

For task manipulation within a clustered environment, humans are good at scene understanding and coming up with general guideline in problem solving. Robotic systems are good at running proper algorithms to solve a well defined problem, for example, motion planning. Robotic hardware system is good at precise motion when given the desired targets. Robot sensor perception is helpful in detection and precise measurement. Therefore, advanced telemanipulation technology should take the advantage of robot automation, computer science and human HRI guidance for more promising performance.

Telemanipulation allows a human operator to control the robot directly through HRI devices. In clustered environment and with flexible tasks, such direct guidance can guide the robot in the task manipulation. In this case, the robot is more like a slave, or a tool with limited functions. For example, in a scenario of tomato harvesting, the robot is not capable of localizing all the target tomatoes, and a human telemanipulation control the robot towards the target, where then the robot will be able to apply the perception and manipulation skills to complete the rest of the work by itself through automation. Of course, there are also possible solutions to allow the AI do the tomato detection and automate the entire harvesting process with a robotic system. However, up to now, there are many challenge in AI to solve such practical problem with a large variation in environment and plant conditions. Human intervention, with as little intervention as possible, is still very useful in guiding robot in task handling within practical and flexible applications.

In telemanipulation, the task handling capability is limited by the teleoperation system since the human user only can achieve a certain level of task telemanipulation skills with the system setup. For example, in precise positioning and line/curve following with the end-effector of a robot, the human teleoperation cannot be comparable with robot automation. If a task is clearly defined within the knowledge database, and all the steps can be properly handled by embedded sensor perception, computer algorithms and robot actuation control, the whole process can be automated without human intervention. On the other hand, if there are sub-tasks which the robotic system have no idea in, then the HRI intervention will be helpful to help the robot out. However, it is not a smart idea to automate everything, which are either not economical or not possible for now.

While a human guides the robot through HRI based on his problem understanding, the robot software program will take inputs from the sensors and reasoning logic to define actions for execution. The robot should be focusing on the task which is designated by the human operator instead of straying off to other tasks. Such ambiguity happens in a robot system, and therefore a well designed robot software should include full description of the knowledge for the task to allow the robot handle task correctly with the available sensor inputs and HRI guidance. In problems with well defined protocols, the combination of human guidance and robot automation is straight forward. For example, for robot motion planning, more specifically a mobile manipulator, in complex scenarios, the human can guide the robot software with sampling domains, way-points to go through, direction to choose and initial approximate path etc. Such intervention serves as useful inputs to robot motion planners to generate a valid path which is better in quality and efficiency as compared to a solution generated with no human guidance.

From the teleoperation viewpoint, robot automation can also assist in a typical teleoperation tasks to handle tasks more efficiently. When the sensor perception detects the targets and computer software confirms the task requirement, the robot software then can plan the motion and execute the robot to complete the task automatically without manual control from the human.

New Knowledge Picking Up. Human intervention through HRI also opens a door for continuously teaching robots the skills in doing new tasks. Of course the skill set for a task need to be complete, including the protocols to define the work flow and the detailed primitives to deal with each sub-tasks [6,7,15]. This will require a new knowledge picking up software which will be interfaced with the human inputs, data storage and methods to reproduce the action in future applications [1,2].

4   Teleoperation Experiments

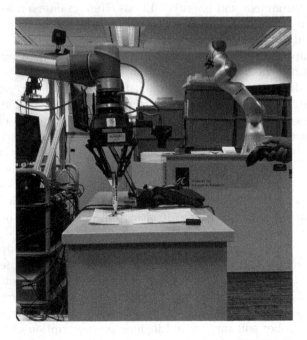

Fig. 2. Telemanipulation of UR5 Robot with HTC VIVE Controller.

Teleoperation systems are built for human operator to interface with the UR5 robot through the HTC vive controller system. With proper motion mapping and motion constraint implementations, the robot can be controlled by the user in all 6 DoF, as shown in supplementary video [17]. The robot follows the human control smoothly by moving in all directions and able do object grasping tasks. It is also able to move within a constraint manner to meet the task requirements, the planner constraints along XY plan and the linear constraints with rotation and translation along the Z axis are demonstrated. Such are preliminary demonstration results. And with more implementation to system with more DoF, mobile manipulator for example, the usefulness of teleoperation in assisting robot in agile task manipulation can be evaluated more extensively (Fig. 2).

5   Conclusion

This paper discusses on the technologies in developing agile robotics systems in handling flexible and adaptive tasks to meet the demands in practical applications in unsupervised environments. The author propose to apply the knowledge based programming to store general protocol information in task handling skills and apply robot automation, including sensor perception, computer software algorithms in motion planning, detection etc. to figure out detail actions in task handling. Moreover, HRI inputs, specifically teleoperation based human guidance to robot manipulation and skill teaching are added into the loop to enable the robot to handle more flexible tasks and adapt to new task scenarios. Finally, the robot skill or knowledge picking up module can be added to allow the robot system continuously improve in task handling capability. This paper focus more on methodology discussion and shows preliminary experiments using telemanipulation to get a UR5 robot to do simple tasks. Future work will aim to implement perception, motion planning, skill picking up modules to robotic systems and study on specific implementation challenges in agile robot task manipulation with robotics technology and human HRI guidance.

References

1. Stenmark, M., Malec, J.: Knowledge-based instruction of manipulation tasks for industrial robotics. Robot. Comput.-Integr. Manuf. **33**, 56–67 (2015)
2. Stenmark, M., Malec, J.: Knowledge-based industrial robotics. In: The 12th Scandinavian Conference on Artificial Intelligence (SCAI). IOS Press (2013)
3. Miller, N., et al.: Motion capture from inertial sensing for untethered humanoid teleoperation. In: 4th IEEE/RAS International Conference on Humanoid Robots, vol. 2. IEEE (2004)
4. Yuan, Q., et al.: Task-orientated robot teleoperation using wearable IMUs. In: 2017 IEEE International Conference on Cybernetics and Intelligent Systems (CIS) and IEEE Conference on Robotics, Automation and Mechatronics (RAM). IEEE (2017)
5. Tee, K.P., Wu, Y.: Experimental evaluation of divisible human-robot shared control for teleoperation assistance. In: TENCON 2018–2018 IEEE Region 10 Conference. IEEE (2018)

6. Weng, C., et al.: A telemanipulation-based human-robot collaboration method to teach aerospace masking skills. IEEE Trans. Ind. Inform. **16**(5), 3076–3084 (2019)
7. Yuan, Q., et al.: Flexible telemanipulation based handy robot teaching on tape masking with complex geometry. Robot. Comput.-Integr. Manuf. **66**, 101990 (2020)
8. Quintero, C.P., et al.: Flexible virtual fixture interface for path specification in telemanipulation. In: 2017 IEEE International Conference on Robotics and Automation (ICRA). IEEE (2017)
9. Pan, J., et al.: Real-time collision detection and distance computation on point cloud sensor data. In: 2013 IEEE International Conference on Robotics and Automation. IEEE (2013)
10. Diankov, R., Kuffner, J.: Openrave: a planning architecture for autonomous robotics. Technical Report CMU-RI-TR-08-34 79. Robotics Institute, Pittsburgh, PA (2008)
11. Chitta, S.: MoveIt!: an introduction. In: Koubaa, A. (ed.) Robot Operating System (ROS). SCI, vol. 625, pp. 3–27. Springer, Cham (2016). https://doi.org/10.1007/978-3-319-26054-9_1
12. Sucan, I.A., Moll, M., Kavraki, L.E.: The open motion planning library. IEEE Robot. Autom. Mag. **19**(4), 72–82 (2012)
13. LaValle, S.M.: Planning Algorithms. Cambridge University Press, Cambridge (2006)
14. Kuffner, J.J., LaValle, S.M.: RRT-connect: an efficient approach to single-query path planning. In: Proceedings 2000 ICRA. Millennium Conference. IEEE International Conference on Robotics and Automation. Symposia Proceedings (Cat. No. 00CH37065), vol. 2. IEEE (2000)
15. Suárez-Ruiz, F., Zhou, X., Pham, Q.C.: Can robots assemble an IKEA chair? Sci. Robot. **3**(17), eaat6385 (2018)
16. Yuan, Q., et al.: A mirrored motion remapping method in telemanipulation-based face-to-face dual-arm robot teaching. In: 2019 IEEE/ASME International Conference on Advanced Intelligent Mechatronics (AIM). IEEE (2019)
17. Supplementary Video. https://www.youtube.com/watch?v=crnbbfZPVbg

Partial-Map-Based Monte Carlo Localization in Architectural Floor Plans

Chee Leong Chan[✉], Jun Li, Jian Le Chan, Zhengguo Li, and Kong Wah Wan

Institute for Infocomm Research, A*STAR, Singapore 138632, Singapore
{chancl,jli,chanjl,ezgli,kongwah}@i2r.a-star.edu.sg

Abstract. Mobile robots, in modern technology, demand a more robust localization in a complex environment. Currently, the most commonly used 2D LiDAR localization system for mobile robots requires maps that are constructed by 2D SLAM. Such systems do not cope well with dynamic environments and also have high deployment costs when moving robots to a new environment setting as they require the reconstruction of a map for each new place. In modern days, a floor plan is indispensable for an indoor environment. It typically represents essential structures such as walls, corners, pillars, etc. for humans to navigate in the environment. This information turns out to be crucial for robot localization. In this paper, we propose an approach for 2D LiDAR localization in an architectural floor plan. We use partial simultaneous localization and mapping (PSLAM) algorithm to generate a map while we concurrently aligned it to the floor plan using Monte Carlo Localization (MCL) method. Real-world experiments have been conducted with our proposed method which results in robust robot localization, the algorithm is even evaluated on a large discrepancies floor plan (discrepancies between the floor plan and real-world). Our algorithm demonstrates that its capabilities of localizing in real-time applications.

Keywords: Localization · Floor plan · PSLAM · Gradient direction grid map · Gaussian map · MCL

1 Introduction

As the entire industry moves forward to industry 4.0, automation is preferred over human involvement. During this movement, using an autonomous mobile robot (AMR) is one of the most feasible solutions. And an important aspect of AMR is robot localization. A common way of robot localization is to, firstly, use SLAM to create a map and, thereafter, perform MCL. This is considered exceedingly costly in terms of both time and effort as it requires an officer to perform mapping prior to each deployment.

Generally speaking, a floor plan for the indoor building is available, the question that arises is whether a robot can localize accurately in it. Many turn away from utilizing floor plans as a means to localize because of the nature of the floor

This work was supported by the National Robotics Programme (NRP) under the SERC Grant 192 25 00049.

© Springer Nature Switzerland AG 2021
H. Li et al. (Eds.): ICSR 2021, LNAI 13086, pp. 541–552, 2021.
https://doi.org/10.1007/978-3-030-90525-5_47

plan. A floor plan generally includes immutable features such as walls and corridors and excludes, after renovation, cubicles, pressurized walls and furniture. This is challenging for MCL as cubicles and furniture that are not indicated in the floor plan may occlude the wall immutable features. Apart from that, the floor plan may, also, differ from the real environment resulting in serious consequences when in use. With the above setting, we proposed PSLAM using 2D LiDAR to accurately localize robot in an architecture floor plan.

This paper breaks down the problems of using single frame LiDAR MCL on the floor plan, and then proposed a new modified MCL approach with the use of our contribution works, which are PSLAM, diffused occupied cells and surface normal information to deal with those problems. Further on, we show the experiment results and concluded with future work to improve our approach

2   Related Work

2D LiDAR base robot localization has been widely studied for decades. In the old days, 2D LiDar localization uses algorithms like Kalman filters, histogram filters and particle filters [7]. More recently, particle filter-based approach that is proved to be one of the most efficient approaches is called Monte Carlo Localization(MCL) [4]. Further on, in [3], fox implements Kullback-leibler Divergence (KLD) sampling to MCL and makes it more efficient and named it Adaptive Monte Carlo Localization (AMCL). AMCL has been widely used for most commercial products with the obvious advantages in efficiency, stability and accuracy. However, it does not perform for localization on a floor plan map due to the existence of huge discrepancies.

The works in [1, 2] have a similar objective to our approach. In their approach a robot is localized on an architecture floor plan by using G-ICP based SLAM. Similarly, Vysotska et al. [8] used Graph-based SLAM with prior information from Open StreetMap. Their approach is to align and optimize an urban environment SLAM map using ICP on Open StreetMap to improve the robustness and quality of the generated map. Both of these approaches use ICP based methods to optimize the robot pose with full SLAM map where we use MCL to optimize the robot pose with PSLAM map. However, matching of full SLAM map will be incorrect when the shape and scale discrepancies between floor plan and real environment is substantial. In this case, scan matching algorithm will fail to match correctly resulting in undefined localization for robot which is undesirable. For example, if the robot is driving in a long straight corridor without any feature to identify its distance travelled in the middle of the corridor, the floor plan discrepancy and SLAM accumulated error will result in ICP based method lost to fit the floor plan at the end of the corridor due to overshoot or undershoot too much. The reason is their method is building a full SLAM map and their transformation of the SLAM map is fixed to the floor plan, it may fail when the floor plan differs from Lidar observation too much. However, our method is using PSLAM that only keep a number of historical frames which helps to reduce accumulate error, and the transformation of the PSLAM map is dynamic on the floor plan. This creates an effect of localizing on a globally inconsistent but locally consistent map [6]. Consequently, PSLAM can fit nicely to the floor plan with the MCL approach when navigating in those situations.

3   Problem Statement

Traditional particle based methods like AMCL take single frame LiDAR reading as input to match against the map. However, a floor plan as a map is expected to have high discrepancies compared to the real world, so they may not work well. In this work, we address the problems of Single Frame based AMCL (SF-AMCL) when applying to an architecture floor plan that misses significant features of the real environment. We have targeted 3 scenarios that often cause failure in localization. The objective is that by solving these problems, the robot should be able to adapt to a larger discrepancy.

3.1   Problem Scenario 1

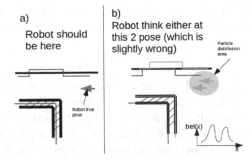

Fig. 1. Scenario 1: floor plan's scale is slightly off. In a) LiDAR endpoint (red) cannot associate to floor plan's occupied cell (black) when the robot is at the correct pose (green arrow), in b) robot has 2 poses that exhibit strong beliefs. (Color figure online)

Although a floor plan represents a to-scale permanent structure for indoor, its layout dimension is slightly incorrect compare to the true scale. If directly used floor plan as a map for SF-AMCL, this system will easily enter a zone where LiDAR's endpoints cannot properly correspond to floor plan's occupied cells, although is at a low discrepancy region at the true pose as Fig. 1a) shows. Figure 1b) shows the consequence of the system that it may wrongly believe itself at 2 clusters of particles which will further lead to the same consequence as Sect. 3.2.

3.2   Problem Scenario 2

A floor plan is expected to have a walls layout, however, this can be another reason that causes multiple local maxima. This is because the wall layout in

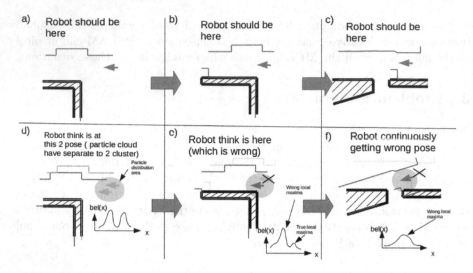

Fig. 2. Scenario 2: a–c) shows the sequence of the robot (green arrow) moving forward and robot truth pose where the robot's LiDAR (red) lies on the floor plan's occupied cells (black) and align correctly. d–f) shows the same moving sequence but the robot localized wrongly due to picking the wrong local maxima of the posterior cluster. (Color figure online)

the floor plan shows 2 parallel lines of occupied cells representing the front and rear surfaces of the wall, where the front surface is visible by robot LiDAR's observation and the rear surface is not. Although all clusters are initially near to each other, the clusters may divert out after a few iterations while the robot is moving. This can further cause wrongly localize when selected the wrong cluster due to the wrong cluster may have a greater match as Fig. 2d–f) shows.

3.3   Problem Scenario 3

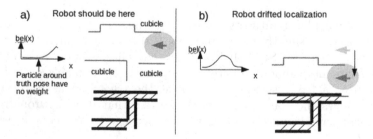

Fig. 3. Scenario 3: a) Robots do not have LiDAR endpoints (red) correspond to any floor plan's occupied cells. b) Robots drift to the wrong pose after several iterations to get more corresponding points from the floor plan's occupied cells. (Color figure online)

Using a Single LiDAR frame directly to compute MCL has a high chance that LiDAR reading has no endpoint match to the permanent structure on the floor plan when the robot enters a zone where the walls are completely occluded by furniture. In this situation, particles that lie on or near the true pose have low or no weight. This causes MCL wrongly to predict the robot pose away from the true pose as Fig. 3a) shows. Figure 3b) shows the consequence of after a few iterations, the LiDAR endpoint can match most of the occupied cells but the robot is not at the correct pose, due to particles distributed away from the true pose.

4   Proposed Method

This work aims to localize the pose of a robot in an architectural floor plan using Partial-Map-Based MCL. We believe that by overcoming the problems shows in Sects. 3.1, 3.2 and 3.3, this Partial-Map-Based MCL should be able to localize the robot in the floor plan.

4.1   Partial Simultaneous Localization and Mapping (PSLAM)

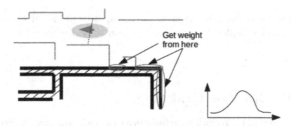

Fig. 4. PSLAM occupied cells (blue line) aligned to floor plan occupied cells (black). The weight in the true pose is maintained when entering a fully wall occluded zone from 2D LiDAR observation. (Color figure online)

PSLAM is a simplified version of pose-graph SLAM, which differs from standard pose-graph SLAM in 2 key ways. The first difference is that it involves only frontend scan-matching processes and do not has closed-loop backend processes. Utilizing scan-matching, we incrementally aligned the current scan to the previous map to maximize the likelihood of the current pose relative to the previous one. Because of its lack of a closed-loop process for reducing accumulated error on full mapping, it is fine for locally consistent maps, but not for globally consistent maps (Fig. 4).

Thus, the second difference takes place, which is that PSLAM stores only the last N frames of historical scans when constructing its map. Older frames will drop off when there are more than N of historical frames. The effect will be similar to moving windows. It is to keep the locally consistent map accurate, and accumulated errors on mapping will not be large. These differences are to reduce computational power compare to a pose-graph SLAM, due to a small number of historical frames do not need closed-loop adjustment.

The purpose of PSLAM is to overcome Sect. 3.3. Assuming the real world has a sparse low discrepancy region compared to the floor plan, we used PSLAM to act as an extended LiDAR observation zone to keep track of low discrepancy regions using MCL and maintain the belief on a true pose when entering to a high discrepancy region. Besides, with frame drop off capability, the PSLAM's map aligns the robot better on a floor plan map region with an inaccurate scale, and lower computational power when executing MCL compare to the full SLAM map.

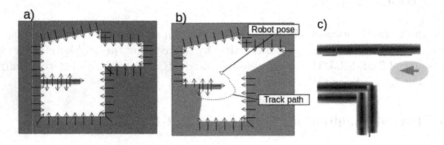

Fig. 5. surface normal arrow direction of grid map sample from a floor plan (a) and PSLAM map (b), and sample of Gaussian filter on a grid map (c).

4.2   Gradient's Direction Grid Map

To solve Sect. 3.2, we need to take surface normal information from LiDAR observation and floor plan structure into account. Assume the robot has built a SLAM occupancy grid map using 2D LiDAR, the direction of the wall surface normal that can view by the robot can be predicted on occupied cells by computing angle pointing toward empty region (white) and opposite unknown region (grey) as Fig. 5 (b) shows. Hence, this can be easily differentiated if particles matching against the rear surface of the wall in a floor plan during computing MCL due to the normal direction is opposite. In this concept, we implement a Sobel filter to compute the direction of the wall surface facing. Sobel filters are a pair of convolution kernels that compute horizontal changes $\mathbf{G}_x$ and vertical changes $\mathbf{G}_y$, and commonly use it to compute magnitude using Eq. 1 to find edges in an image. These 2 changes are also able to compute the orientation of gradients in an image using Eq. 2. Hence, we used occupancy grid maps as grayscale images by filling *unknown*, *occupied* and *empty* cells with grayscale pixel values of 255,100 and 0. Then, applied Sobel convolution process and generate a gradient direction grid map using Eq. 2.

$$direction, {}^{map}\Theta = atan\left(\frac{{}^{map}\mathbf{G}_y}{{}^{map}\mathbf{G}_x}\right) \qquad (1)$$

$$magnitude,^{map}\mathbf{G} = \sqrt{{}^{map}\mathbf{G}_x{}^2 + {}^{map}\mathbf{G}_y{}^2} \tag{2}$$

4.3 Gaussian Grid Map

To solve Sect. 3.1, where the scale of a floor plan is slightly wrong, we need to diffuse the occupied cells where the centre of diffused occupied cells carried higher value and lower when away from the centre. This is to avoid particles forming multiple clusters when entering a region where the floor plan scale is slightly different. With this setting required, we employed a Gaussian filter to the map. This helps to diffuse the occupied cells' value with bell curve characteristics as Fig. 5c) shows.

4.4 Implementation

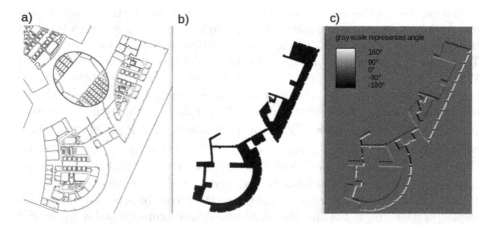

Fig. 6. Preprocess steps for floor plan, a) Original floor plan map. b) Process through flood fill. The region in black is the region that the robot able to travel. c) After employed Gaussian with Sobel filter. The occupied cell has thickened and indicated in grey-scale which represented -180 to $180°$.

To implement all the ideas, we used the MCL method as a skeleton to integrate all the proposed ideas together, except for PSLAM, which is running as a separate node and continuously publishing updated PSLAM maps. MCL consists of three phases, which begin with the initialize phase, then the prediction phase, and end with the updating phase. As a recursive step, the update phase is repeated after the prediction phase.

We begin the initialize phase by giving an initial guess pose and preprocessing of the floor plan as Fig. 6 shows. In the floor plan map, the flood fill begins to fill up at the initial guess pose, and a number of particles are also randomly distributed around the guess pose. Flood filling creates fake unknown cells and empty cells in the floor plan, so the Sobel process can easily determine gradient direction from this flood fill map. Gaussian kernels are applied prior to Sobel kernels, this results in thickening and smoothing the gradient direction map $^f\Theta$ for occupied cells and with a diffused effect on the magnitude map $^f\mathbf{G}$ around occupied cells.

$$q_{j,t}^{[m]} = 1 - \frac{2\left|atan\left(\frac{sin(^s\theta(j_t) - ^f\theta(j_t, ^fx_t^{[m]}, ^sx_t))}{cos(^s\theta(j_t) - ^f\theta(j_t, ^fx_t^{[m]}, ^sx_t))}\right)\right|}{\pi} \tag{3}$$

$$w_t^{[m]} = \sum_{j=0}^{J}\begin{cases} 0 & , if\ q_{j,t}^{[m]} \le 0 \\ \frac{q_{j,t}^{[m]} *^f G(j_t, ^fx_t^{[m]}, ^sx_t)}{d(j_t, ^sx_t)} & , if\ q_{j,t}^{[m]} > 0 \end{cases} \tag{4}$$

In the prediction phase, we applied Gaussian noise to simulated motion model for each particle to predict pose of the robot which is same as MCL approach.

Thereafter, in the update phase, we took the updated PSLAM map to generate gradient direction grid map, $^s\Theta$, then use it with floor plan's direction grid map, magnitude map and particles pose information for measurement model. We used Eq. 3 and 4 to compute total weight w_t of each particle $[m]$, given that the cell's magnitude $G \in \mathbf{G}$, cell's angle $\theta \in \Theta$, j is (x, y) coordinates of occupied cell in PSLAM map, $^fx_t^{[m]}$ stand for robot predicted pose at the floor plan,^{f}, of the particle $[m]$, ^sx_t is robot pose in PSLAM map ^{s}. Equation 3 is to compute the angle's fitting score $q_{j,t}^{[m]}$ for each occupied cell in PSLAM map, where $^s\theta(j_t)$ is the angle value of occupied cell j in PSLAM map ^{s}. $^f\theta(j_t, ^fx_t^{[m]}, ^sx_t)$ the angle value of floor plan's cell that associated with PSLAM map's occupied cell j when pose of the robot is predicted at $^fx_t^{[m]}$ in floor plan and ^sx_t in PLAM map. Equation 4 define that if the angle's score of occupied cell at particular particle $[m]$ is positive then further enhance score by taking associated cell's magnitude of floor plan $^fG(j_t, ^fx_t^{[m]}, ^sx_t)$ and distance $d(j_t, ^sx_t)$ between j and robot pose in PSLAM ^sx_t into account, otherwise output zero. This is to strengthen the score received from j if coordinate j is near to robot pose, and if is fitting in or close to floor plan occupied cells. The reason for dividing $d(j_t, ^sx_t)$ is to avoid the situation that the robot drifts away from the true pose because of high accumulated error from the past PSLAM historical frame that matched to the discrepancy floor plan, and neglected the matching of j that near to robot. The score of PSLAM map occupied cells are then accumulated to present as a weight of the particle $[m]$. The pose of the particle with the highest weight w_t is used as the corrected robot pose.

After weights update, it re-samples a new collection of particles according to the current particle weights and starts the next iteration at predict phase.

5   Experiment Setup

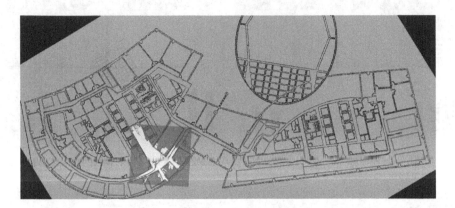

Fig. 7. The trajectory obtained with our localization approach (Blue) at level 9 floor in our office building. The white region is the PSLAM map dynamic frame. The red boxes are to show regions occluded with working cubicles in the real environment and it is not drawn in floor plan map in the experiment. (Color figure online)

There is no publicly available 2D LiDAR-based SLAM dataset that comes with an architecture floor plan. At the moment, we evaluate our localization approach in our office building level 9 and level 12. We prepared a 2D LiDAR map built by G-Mapping [5], then aligned the 2D floor plan map to match with the G-Mapping built map with eyeballing, so both maps share the same resolution and same world coordinates.

We operate a robot, Pioneer P3-DX equipped with Hokuyo UTM-30LX LiDAR with 250° of a field of view and 30.0 m range, to do navigation tasks in our office building. All the sensors reading and odometry information are recorded by using Rosbag. Then we extracted the sensors reading from Rosbag to perform localization using an AMCL approach with G-mapping built map as ground truth of localization information. After that, we used the same Rosbag to perform our proposed method for localization with different PSLAM's historical frame numbers. Both localization reading is then compared and compute errors. Figure 7 shows the sample of level 9 environment and trajectory that the robot has travelled during the experiment.

6   Result and Discussion

From Fig. 8, the line chart tested in level 9 and level 12 do not show accumulating error effect. The average error show in the bar chart can see that the larger the historical frame number in PSLAM, the localization error reduced. There are some parts of the journey that have large distance errors, this is due to

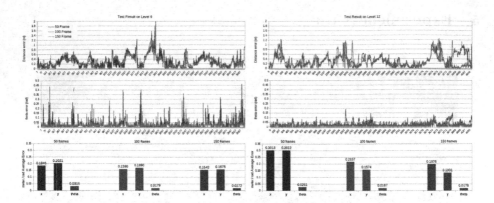

Fig. 8. Result of error over time for proposed method on floor plan experiment and average error (last row)

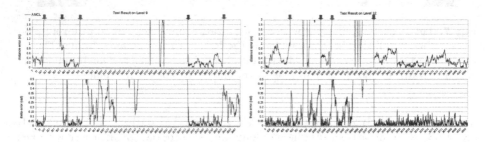

Fig. 9. Result of error over time for experiment AMCL on floor plan experiment, red arrow is the time line start to lost track, green arrow is the time line reinitialize pose of the robot. (Color figure online)

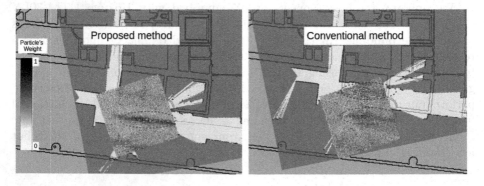

Fig. 10. The weights heatmap of particles that uniformly distributes around initialize pose, using PSLAM as input observation. Left image is using the proposed method (Gradient Direction and Gaussian map with proposed Eq.4), right image is using a conventional method that is similar to AMCL (sum of matched occupied cells). The red circle is a high weight particle distribute around the true pose, the blue circle is high weight particles distribute around the wrong pose. (Color figure online)

G-Mapping built map and floor plan have some regions are not properly fit due to floor plan error. For instance, the curve corridor is not fully matched and some of the corridors' width is smaller drawn in floor plan compare to the actual environment. All this unaligned region might affect the error measurement results. However, this did not cause the robot to lose track of its pose for most of the experiment, except for the experiment with 50 frames in level 12 which lose track at the last 4 min.

We also tested using AMCL directly using floor plan as a map for level 9 and level 12, however, AMCL approach failed to localize when entered high discrepancy region. The robot drifted away from the true pose and cannot recover its pose until reinitialize the pose in map again as Fig. 9 shows the result of the experiment with AMCL on floor plan as grid map, it lost multiple time and we have reinitialized it multiple time to complete the run. Despite this, our approach did not encounter significant failure for any dataset in the same environment. There were only a few situations, qualitatively speaking, in which the robot was poorly localized, mostly because the PSLAM map was too small (low number of historical frame) and the floor plan metric inconsistent.

In Fig. 10, we compared two different weighting methods for each particle using PSLAM as the input observation, and both are in the same pose. In the figure on the left, the weight of each particle has been calculated using a Gradient Direction with a Gaussian grid map and the proposed formula Eq. 4. The right image is similar to the AMCL endpoint weighting method, which is using the total number of cells that are occupied on the PSLAM map which corresponded floor plan's cells are occupied as well. Whenever the particle's color is dark red, the weight is high, whereas when the colour is white or yellow, the weight is low. The figure shows the proposed method has more high weight particles focus around true pose, however, the conventional method has 2 similar high local maxima of high weight particles cluster, and the robot has selected the wrong cluster to localize itself. This is similar to Sect. 3.2 that discuss earlier. This illustrates that the proposed method successfully decrease the weight of the particles that with the wrong matching of surface normal direction which solved the Sect. 3.2 problem.

7   Limitation and Future Work

From the experiment, we encounter a few weak points of our approach which cause poor localization. It must be at least have one low discrepancy region within the PSLAM map zone to keep particles focus. For instance, our approach may have poor localization performance in a big cluttered hall. The PSLAM build map must be accurate, in a crowded since where pose-graph SLAM failed to build a map or inaccurate map may cause localization in floor plan fails. Moreover, The LiDAR sensor should no scan a transparent or reflective surface which will cause wrong measurement. Furthermore, the architecture floor plan must be accurate to a certain tolerance, a not-to-scale floor plan does not apply to our approach.

In this work, we present a new Partial-Map-Based Monte Carlo Localization approach that using a PSLAM built map match to a to-scale floor plan using MCL with gradient direction and Gaussian grid map. This combination approach shows significant adaption to the missing information in the floor plan. In future work, we need to make it robustly adapt a larger variety of building's floor plans by enhancement work in PSLAM to adaptively control the numbers of historical frames to be keep. Furthermore, the PSLAM built map can be recycled to form a proper 2D LiDAR map which benefits other commercial robots that do not have the floorplan localization capability.

References

1. Boniardi, F., Caselitz, T., Kümmerle, R., Burgard, W.: Robust lidar-based localization in architectural floor plans. In: IROS, pp. 3318–3324. IEEE (2017)
2. Boniardi, F., Caselitz, T., Kümmerle, R., Burgard, W.: A pose graph-based localization system for long-term navigation in cad floor plans. Robotics Auton. Syst. **112**, 84–97 (2019)
3. Fox, D.: Adapting the sample size in particle filters through KLD-sampling. Int. J. Robot. Res. **22**(12), 985–1004 (2003)
4. Fox, D., Thrun, S., Burgard, W., Dellaert, F.: Particle filters for mobile robot localization. In: Sequential Monte Carlo Methods in Practice, pp. 401–428. Statistics for Engineering and Information Science, Springer, New York (2001). https://doi.org/10.1007/978-1-4757-3437-9_19
5. Grisetti, G., Stachniss, C., Burgard, W.: Improved techniques for grid mapping with Rao-blackwellized particle filters. IEEE Trans. Robot. **23**(1), 34–46 (2007)
6. Mazuran, M., Boniardi, F., Burgard, W., Tipaldi, G.D.: Relative topometric localization in globally inconsistent maps. In: Bicchi, A., Burgard, W. (eds.) Robotics Research. SPAR, vol. 3, pp. 435–451. Springer, Cham (2018). https://doi.org/10.1007/978-3-319-60916-4_25
7. Thrun, S., Burgard, W., Fox, D.: Probabilistic Robotics. MIT Press, Cambridge (2005)
8. Vysotska, O., Stachniss, C.: Exploiting building information from publicly available maps in graph-based slam. In: IROS, pp. 4511–4516. IEEE (2016)

A Survey on Object Detection Performance with Different Data Distributions

Ramanpreet Singh Pahwa[1,2]([✉])[iD], Richard Chang[1], Wang Jie[1],
Sankeerthana Satini[1,3], Chandrashekar Viswanathan[1,4], Du Yiming[1,4],
Vernica Jain[1], Chen Tai Pang[1], and Wan Kong Wah[1,2]

[1] Institute for Infocomm Research (I2R), Singapore, Singapore
ramanpreet_pahwa@i2r.a-star.edu.sg
[2] Artificial Intelligence, Analytics and Informatics (AI3), Singapore, Singapore
[3] Nanyang Technological University (NTU), Singapore, Singapore
[4] National University of Singapore (NUS), Singapore, Singapore

Abstract. Detecting objects in a dynamic scene is a critical step for
robotic navigation. A mobile robot may need to slow down in presence
of children, elderly or dense crowds. A robot's movement needs to be precise and socially adjustable especially in a hospital setting. Identifying
key objects in a scene can provide important contextual awareness to
a robot. Traditional approaches used handcrafted features along with
object proposals to detect objects in images. Recently, object detection has made tremendous progress over the past few years thanks to
deep learning and convolutional neural networks. Networks such as SSD,
YOLO, and Faster R-CNN have made significant improvements over
traditional techniques while maintaining real-time inference speed. However, current existing datasets used for benchmarking these models tend
to contain mainly outdoor images using a high-quality camera setup that
is usually different from a robotic vision setting where a robot moves
around in a dynamic environment resulting in sensor noise, motion blur,
and change in data distribution. In this work, we introduce our custom
dataset collected in a realistic hospital environment consisting of distinct
objects such as hospital beds, tables, and wheelchairs. We also use state-
of-art object detectors to showcase the current performance and gaps
in a robotic vision setting using our custom CHART dataset and other
public datasets.

Keywords: Object detection · Robotic vision · Contextual
understanding and navigation

1 Introduction

Object detection has become a critical part of robotic vision and navigation. It
is actively being used in several fields such as service robots, delivery robots,

Supported by A*STAR grant no. 1922500049 from the National Robotics Programme
(NRP), Singapore.

H. Li et al. (Eds.): ICSR 2021, LNAI 13086, pp. 553–563, 2021.
https://doi.org/10.1007/978-3-030-90525-5_48

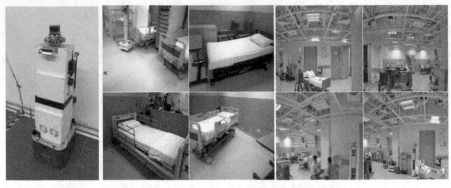

(a) Robot base   (b) CHART dataset

Fig. 1. (a) Our mobile robot base consisting of multiple visual sensors - six SONY IMX335 and two Structure Core cameras. (b) Our CHART dataset. The images collected in the hospital environment consist of multiple different hospital objects such as beds, tables, and wheelchairs. These images obtained from the visual sensors contain motion blur, occlusion, sensor noise, and significant distortion.

automated inspection [6], object tracking [10], autonomous driving [11], semicon defect detection [7,8], and 3D understanding [9]. Robotic navigation not only aims at getting from source to destination, but also how to get there in the most efficient and socially acceptable manner. A mobile robot may need to slow down or halt movement in presence of a moving bed or wheelchair in a hospital environment. Identifying key objects in such an environment can provide important contextual awareness to a robot.

Recently, object detection performance and speed has improved at a remarkable rate with the rise of deep convolutional neural networks (CNNs) [5,12,13]. Most of the current existing benchmarks test the performance of object detection in settings that are mostly impractical for a service robot. The images contained in such benchmarks are sharp, devoid of motion blur, consists of objects present in various locations and sizes, and contain thousands of images of each object class. Scientific community has mainly focused on improving the system architecture and resolving pipeline-bottlenecks to improve object detection performance. This has also led to the community adopting single stage detectors such as Single Shot detector (SSD) [5], You Only Look Once (YOLO) [1] more often than two stage detectors such as Faster R-CNN [13]. Recently, there has been a shift towards imparting contextual awareness to robots for navigation in a given environment. This can be done successfully if we are able to detect objects present in the scene accurately and use them for contextual reasoning. For example, if we detect hospital beds and wheelchairs, it is highly likely that we are in a hospital room than in a cafeteria. Usually, a pretrained model is used as a starting point and then trained on the new classes, commonly referred to as transfer learning. In an ever changing environment, a robot can go through major changes and upgrades over the course of time. This results in a shift in data distribution resulting in drop in performance of previously trained models on the new captured images.

In this work, we investigate the performance of state of the art deep learning based object detectors on two different datasets - our custom CHART dataset and public datasets consisting of PASCAL-VOC [2] and MSCOCO [4]. Our focus is primarily on CHART dataset. The dataset is captured in a hospital environment using three different visual sensors - SONY IMX335, Asus Xtion Pro, and structure core RGB-D cameras. We perform comprehensive training on standalone, mix, and partial labeled data to investigate how the most popular object detectors perform in a real setting where a shift in data distribution may occur due to various reasons. The robot navigates around several objects such as hospital beds, tables, wheelchairs, and staffs. We show that a slight change in data distribution can affect object detection performance on the 3 main detectors, and we quantify this drop of accuracy across our datasets. This demonstrate that current deep learning approaches still lacks flexibility and are difficult to apply in a changing environment.

We discuss the details of our dataset in Sect. 2. Section 3 presents the details on our chosen three state-of-the-art object detectors. We report our results and observations using the chosen detectors in different settings in Sect. 4. Finally, Sect. 5 discusses our future research directions.

2   Datasets

We investigate the performance of deep-learning based object detectors on two different datasets - our custom CHART dataset and public dataset consisting of PASCAL-VOC [2] and MS COCO [4] datasets. We focus on training and evaluating on two objects - hospital beds and overbed tables. As the public datasets do not contain these aforementioned objects, we customized the networks to train our models on two different classes - person and chair. Additionally, we do not compare the model performance across these two datasets (CHART and public) due to different object classes and only evaluate the consistency of our observations.

2.1   CHART Dataset

We collected our CHART dataset in a Singapore hospital on two different days using a different set of sensors for each day mounted on our custom robot as shown in Fig. 1(a). We created three different datasets namely CHART1, CHART2, and JOINT dataset. CHART1 dataset is collected using an Asus Xtion Pro camera in a room containing different hospital beds and tables. CHART2 dataset is collected using a SONY IMX335 camera and a Structure Core camera. JOINT dataset is a combination of these two datasets. We only focus on the RGB data from these cameras and ignore the depth component of Xtion Pro and Structure Core RGB-D cameras for creating our dataset as shown in Fig. 1(b).

Table 1. CHART Dataset information

Subset	Training Set			Test Set		
	# Images	# Instances		# Images	# Instances	
		Beds	Tables		Beds	Tables
CHART1	638	606	141	160	240	45
CHART2	1241	942	411	310	356	143
JOINT	1879	1548	552	470	596	188

Both datasets contain realistic scenarios where a mobile robot moves around the scene containing multiple objects of interest. The images contain sensor noise, distortion, and motion blur frequently. The objects in CHART1 dataset are well spread out with small occlusions present in the scene. CHART2 data is more complex as the objects of interest are often occluded or at a significant distance from the robot base and consist of different lighting conditions. Thus, these differences in sensors, lighting, object consistency, and complexity cause a change in data distribution. The motivation behind the dataset is to analyze how current state-of-the-art detectors perform when data distribution changes in a realistic environment. CHART1 and CHART2 datasets consist of 798 and 1,551 images respectively. The datasets consists of 846 and 1,298 instances of beds and 186 and 554 instances of tables respectively. CHART1 has a higher bed density and CHART2 has a higher table density. The JOINT dataset is a combination of these two datasets. We annotate objects that are at least 40% visible and within $10m$ distance of the robot. We split the datasets into training (80%) and testing (20%) sets for training and evaluating our models.

2.2   Public Datasets

We also analyze the selected object detectors on PASCAL-VOC and MSCOCO datasets. They are the two most popular datasets used by the Computer Vision community to analyze and benchmark algorithmic performance. They primarily consist of sharp images taken by a static camera primarily in an outdoor environment. While PASCAL-VOC dataset consists of 20 object classes, MSCOCO dataset consists of 80 object classes and fully covers all PASCAL-VOC classes. We investigate how knowledge learned on one dataset transfers to another dataset. To prove our assumption, we select two object classes (person and chair) which appear both in PASCAL-VOC and MSCOCO datasets. We only retain images that contain either of the two classes and remove remaining images from our training and evaluation. PASCAL-VOC dataset contains 1,994 person images and 566 chair images for train set and MSCOCO contains 12,774 chair and 64,115 person images. We name these filtered datasets as PASC-PC and COCO-PC respectively.

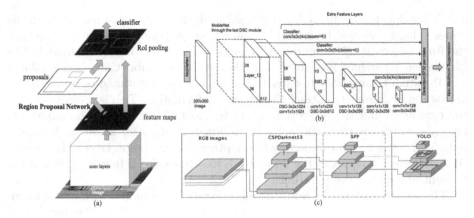

Fig. 2. (a) Faster R-CNN architecture consisting of an CNN based RPN and a Fast R-CNN network for object localization. (b) SSD-MobileNetV2 architecture consisting of MobileNetV2 as the base network. (c) YOLOv4 architecture consisting of CSPDarknet53, SPP, YOLOv3 as backbone, neck, and head.

3 Object Detection

In this section, we discuss the architectures of three state-of-the-art object detectors: Faster R-CNN, SSD-MobileNet V2, and YOLOv4. Faster R-CNN is a two stage detector meanwhile, SSD and YOLOv4 are one stage detectors. Additionally, Tensorflow object detection API provides support for Faster R-CNN and SSD training while YOLOv4 needs to be trained manually.

3.1 Faster R-CNN

Faster R-CNN [13] is a popular two-stage detector network which improves upon earlier networks such as R-CNN and Fast R-CNN with the use of an additional fully convolution network called the Region Proposal Network (RPN). The RPN is used in order to identify regions which have a high probability of containing an object. Subsequently, these regions are fed into the object detector network for both object classification and bounding box regression. The architecture of the Faster R-CNN model is described in Fig. 2(a).

The hyperparameters are defined as follows. The step decay learning rate scheduling strategy is adopted with initial learning rate 0.04 and a warmup learning rate value of 0.01333. The number of warmup steps is kept at 2000. The momentum optimizer value is kept at 0.9. The number of steps and batch size is set at 100,000 and 8 respectively.

3.2 SSD-MobileNet V2

The second network used in this study is the SSD-MobileNet V2 network [14]. This model comprises the MobileNet V2 network, excluding the classification layers, as the base network. Thereafter, convolution layers are added in succession and layer dimensions are reduced progressively to allow detections at multiple scales. This is followed by a Non-Maximum Suppression (NMS) step to output the final detections [5]. Figure 2(b) depicts the architecture of the model. The MobileNet V2 architecture consists of Depthwise Separable Convolution Blocks and Residual Connections to cater to the limited computational resources available while being able to extract the relevant information. This is done by adding the expansion and the projection layers to the building block. The expansion layer decompresses the data into a high dimensional tensor to allow the maximum extraction of information by the depthwise convolution layer. The projection layer then compresses the data into a low-dimensional tensor to reduce the amount of required computations.

The step decay learning rate scheduling strategy is adopted with initial learning rate 0.08 and a warmup learning rate value of 0.01333. The number of warmup steps is kept at 100. The momentum optimizer value is kept at 0.9. The number of steps and batch size is 2,500 and 8 respectively.

3.3 YOLOv4

YOLOv4 [1] is one of most popular single stage detector network for 2D object detection. It has demonstrated high accuracy and speed over many datasets such as MSCOCO. It is 10% more accurate and 12% faster compared to the previous version YOLOv3 [12] on MSCOCO. The architecture used in YOLOv4 is described in Fig. 2(c). It consists of several modules defined as backbone, neck, and head of the network. In YOLOv4, the backbone is CSPDarknet53. It has 293×3 convolutional layers and about $27.6M$ parameters. It has a high number of receptive fields and parameters compared to other networks such as CSPRes-Next50 which allows the model to detect multiple objects of different sizes in a given image. The second block of the network is SPP [3] which represents the neck of the detector. It increases the receptive fields significantly and highlights the most significant contextual features. Finally, the YOLOv3 head is used to predict classes and bounding boxes.

The step decay learning rate scheduling strategy is adopted with initial learning rate 0.01 and multiplied with a factor 0.1 at 4800 and 5400 steps. The momentum and weight decay are set at 0.9 and 0.0005.

4   Experiments

In this section, we describe our various experiments to investigate how the three object detectors perform on our CHART and public datasets on two pre-selected objects. We use Tensorflow2 Object detection API with pretrained models on MSCOCO dataset for Faster R-CNN and SSD. These baseline models are publicly available and widely used as a starting point for training on new dataset or classes. We divide or experiments into three major categories. Firstly, in Standalone training, we investigate how the models perform when trained on one of the two CHART datasets. Secondly, we investigate how the models perform when

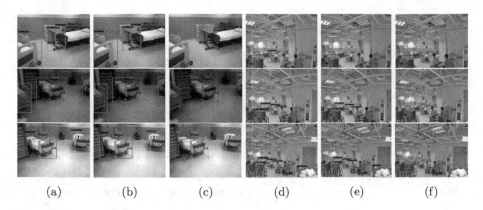

(a)   (b)   (c)   (d)   (e)   (f)

Fig. 3. Top, middle, and bottom row show inference results on models trained on CHART1, CHART2, and JOINT datasets as discussed in Sect. 4.1. (a), (d) display results for FasterRCNN; (b), (e) show results for SSD-MobileNetV2 and (c), (f) show results for YOLOv4 trained models respectively. Groundtruth and inference are shown in green and red bounding boxes respectively. (Color figure online)

trained on a mix of CHART1 and CHART2 datasets simultaneously. Thirdly, we investigate how the models perform when a model is initially trained on one dataset and then subsequently trained on a second dataset without using previous dataset in the new training protocol.

4.1 Standalone Training

We observe that all three architecture models perform poorly on CHART2 dataset when trained on CHART1 dataset and vice-versa as seen in Table 2 even though the object classes are the same across the two datasets. This is due to the two datasets having different data distribution as explained in Sect. 2. The Joint training shows that once the models are trained on both data distributions, they are able to regularize and provide impressive results on both CHART datasets as seen in Fig. 3. The lower number of steps for SSD training results in lower accuracy. Overall, YOLOv4 gave the best results among the object detectors.

4.2 Joint Training

Here we mix a small amount (10%) of CHART2 dataset with full CHART1 training set and vice-versa. We also report results when only trained on only 10% of both CHART datasets. We observe that even a small (10%) inclusion in training set significantly improves the performance on that particular dataset as seen in Table 3. The Faster R-CNN, SSD, and YOLOv4 models mAP improves from 0.2 to 0.875, 0.05 to 0.665, and 0.394 to 0.994 for CHART2 test data. Similar improvement is seen for CHART1 data. This highlights the gap of current fully supervised models not transferring well to a data with slightly different distribution. As soon as some data is added for training, the models are able to regularize on the new data as seen in Fig. 4.

Table 2. Object detectors performance on the CHART test sets for Standalone dataset training protocols.

CHART1	CHART1		CHART2		JOINT	
	mAP	Recall	mAP	Recall	mAP	Recall
Faster R-CNN	0.938	0.956	0.197	0.212	0.423	0.432
SSD	0.869	0.912	0.048	0.210	0.319	0.424
YOLOv4	0.976	1.000	0.394	0.352	0.564	0.650
CHART2						
Faster R-CNN	0.082	0.101	0.915	0.951	0.663	0.687
SSD	0.105	0.421	0.846	0.874	0.606	0.731
YOLOv4	0.358	0.178	0.996	1.000	0.836	0.760
JOINT						
Faster R-CNN	0.932	0.95	0.917	0.947	0.920	0.948
SSD	0.793	0.85	0.807	0.838	0.801	0.842
YOLOv4	0.974	0.989	0.996	1.000	0.994	1.000

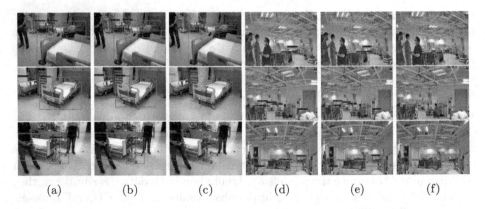

(a)   (b)   (c)   (d)   (e)   (f)

Fig. 4. Joint training results on CHART datasets as discussed in Sect. 4.2. (a), (d) display results for FasterRCNN; (b), (e) show results for SSD-MobileNetV2 and (c), (f) show results for YOLOv4 trained models respectively. We observe that the models perform well on cross datasets even when a small amount of data is available for training.

4.3   Subsequent Training

In this experiment, we investigate how a model performs when we take a model previously trained on one dataset and subsequently trained on another dataset with a different distribution. The previous data is not added to the new training dataset. We report our results on SSD for CHART dataset and faster-RCNN for public dataset. We observe the catastrophic forgetting phenomenon on both CHART and public datasets. SSD performance on CHART1 dips from 0.869

Table 3. Object detectors performance for the Joint dataset training protocols.

CHART1 - 100% CHART2 - 10%	CHART1		CHART2		JOINT	
	mAP	Recall	mAP	Recall	mAP	Recall
Faster R-CNN	0.950	0.961	0.875	0.91	0.897	0.926
SSD	0.847	0.897	0.665	0.725	0.713	0.777
YOLOv4	0.976	0.998	0.992	1.000	0.991	1.000
CHART1 - 10% CHART2 - 100%	CHART1		CHART2		JOINT	
	mAP	Recall	mAP	Recall	mAP	Recall
Faster R-CNN	0.870	0.895	0.922	0.954	0.902	0.933
SSD	0.679	0.768	0.861	0.890	0.787	0.848
YOLOv4	0.966	0.988	0.998	1.000	0.9901	0.990
CHART1 - 10% CHART2 - 10%	CHART1		CHART2		JOINT	
	mAP	Recall	mAP	Recall	mAP	Recall
Faster R-CNN	0.855	0.879	0.852	0.896	0.853	0.890
SSD	0.775	0.842	0.786	0.823	0.780	0.827
YOLOv4	0.967	0.992	0.978	0.985	0.978	0.980

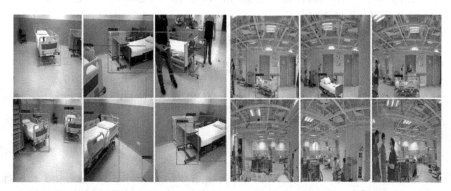

(a) Tested on CHART1 dataset   (b) Tested on CHART2 dataset

Fig. 5. Top row shows CHART1 pretrained model performance when trained on CHART2 data and and bottom row shows CHART2 pretrained model performance when trained on CHART1 data. We observe a significant drop in performance on the respective pretrained dataset. This phenomenon, called catastrophic forgetting, is a significant problem in robotic vision.

mAP to 0.248 mAP when it is trained on CHART2 dataset as shown in Table 4. We observe similar drop when the two datasets are switched as seen in Fig. 5.

We select Faster R-CNN ResNet-50 model structure to conduct person-chair detection evaluation on the public datasets. We initiate both runs on COCO-PC and PASC-PC respectively without pre-trained weights. The training config is modified to batch size 8 for 25,000 steps from the default pipeline setting. Both

Table 4. SSD performance on CHART dataset for Subsequent training protocol.

	CHART1		CHART2		JOINT	
	mAP	Recall	mAP	Recall	mAP	Recall
CHART1 -> CHART2	0.248	0.550	0.866	0.892	0.669	0.779
CHART2 -> CHART1	0.870	0.910	0.076	0.341	0.344	0.521

models are then further trained using the other data set for 25,000 steps and also evaluated on both validation sets. We record these evaluation results in Table 5. In both cases, we see catastrophic forgetting where the mAP drops to 0.232 and 0.240 mAP after the model is trained on the second dataset.

Essentially, the model now "overfits" on new dataset. To maintain good results on previous dataset, we either need to include some previous data in the updated training set or adopt some complex incremental learning techniques for object detection. This provides a good motivation to develop incremental learning frameworks for object detection in future.

Table 5. Faster R-CNN performance on the test sets of COCO-PC and PASC-PC for Subsequent training protocol.

	PASC-PC		COCO-PC	
	mAP	Recall	mAP	Recall
PASC-PC -> COCO-PC	0.225	0.457	0.232	0.519
COCO-PC -> PASC-PC	0.240	0.652	0.221	0.433

5 Conclusion

Contextual awareness is a critical requirement for service robots and robotic navigation. In this work, we have presented our hospital CHART dataset and surveyed three state-of-the-art object detection models. We have analyzed their detection performance on our and public dataset highlighting the strengths and weaknesses of current fully supervised deep learning approach. The object detectors perform exceptionally well when trained on large number of labeled images. However, their performance drops drastically on slightly different data distribution. This may happen frequently in real world scenarios where a robot visual sensor, lighting, or location can change due to various reasons. Currently, we need to perform vast amount of labeling for every different data distribution for acceptable object detection performance. In our future work, we aim to address these gaps by leveraging on Semi-Supervised Learning and Incremental Continual Learning for object detection that has shown tremendous promise in image classification and Natural Language Processing (NLP) domains.

References

1. Bochkovskiy, A., Wang, C.Y., Liao, H.: YOLOv4: Optimal speed and accuracy of object detection. preprint arXiv:2004.10934 (2020)
2. Everingham, M., Van Gool, L., Williams, C.K., Winn, J., Zisserman, A.: The pascal visual object classes (VOC) challenge. Int. J. Comput. Vis. (IJCV) **88**(2), 303–338 (2010)
3. He, K., Zhang, X., Ren, S., Sun, J.: Spatial pyramid pooling in deep convolutional networks for visual recognition. In: IEEE Transactions on Pattern Analysis and Machine Intelligence, vol. 37, pp. 1904–1916 (2015)
4. Lin, T.Y., et al.: Microsoft COCO: Common objects in context. In: European Conference on Computer Vision (ECCV) (2014)
5. Liu, W., et al.: SSD: single shot multibox detector. In: Leibe, B., Matas, J., Sebe, N., Welling, M. (eds.) ECCV 2016. LNCS, vol. 9905, pp. 21–37. Springer, Cham (2016). https://doi.org/10.1007/978-3-319-46448-0_2
6. Pahwa, R.S., et al.: Faultnet: faulty rail-valves detection using deep learning and computer vision. In: IEEE Intelligent Transportation Systems Conference (ITSC), pp. 559–566 (2019)
7. Pahwa, R.S., et al.: Machine-learning based methodologies for 3D X-Ray measurement, characterization and optimization for buried structures in advanced IC packages. In: International Wafer Level Packaging Conference (IWLPC), pp. 01–07 (2020)
8. Pahwa, R.S., et al.: Automated attribute measurements of buried package features in 3D X-ray images using deep learning. In: IEEE Electronic Components and Technology Conference (ECTC), pp. 2196–2204 (2021)
9. Pahwa, R.S., Lu, J., Jiang, N., Ng, T.T., Do, M.N.: Locating 3D object proposals: a depth-based online approach. In: IEEE Transactions on Circuits and Systems for Video Technology (TCSVT), vol. 28, pp. 626–639 (2018)
10. Pahwa, R.S., Ng, T.T., Do, M.N.: Tracking objects using 3D object proposals. In: Asia-Pacific Signal and Information Processing Association Annual Summit and Conference (APSIPA ASC), pp. 1657–1660. IEEE (2017)
11. Pham, Q.H., et al.: A*3D dataset: towards autonomous driving in challenging environments. In: IEEE Conference on Robotics and Automation (ICRA) (2020)
12. Redmon, J., Farhadi, A.: YOLOv3: An incremental improvement. preprint arXiv:1804.02767 (2018)
13. Ren, S., He, K., Girshick, R., Sun, J.: Faster R-CNN: towards real-time object detection with region proposal networks. IEEE Trans. Pattern Anal. Mach. Intell. **39**(6), 1137–1149 (2017)
14. Sandler, M., Howard, A., Zhu, M., Zhmoginov, A., Chen, L.C.: Mobilenetv 2: Inverted residuals and linear bottlenecks. In: IEEE Conference on Computer Vision and Pattern Recognition (CVPR), pp. 4510–4520 (2018)

Design and Development of a Teleoperation System for Affective Tabletop Robot Haru

Yurii Vasylkiv[1]([⊠])[iD], Ricardo Ragel[2]([⊠])[iD], Javier Ponce-Chulani[2]([⊠])[iD],
Luis Merino[2]([⊠])[iD], Eleanor Sandry[3]([⊠])[iD], Heike Brock[4]([⊠])[iD],
Keisuke Nakamura[4]([⊠])[iD], Irani Pourang[1]([⊠])[iD], and Randy Gomez[4]([⊠])[iD]

[1] University of Manitoba, Winnipeg, Canada
vasylkiy@myumanitoba.ca, irani@cs.umanitoba.ca
[2] University Pablo Olavide (UPO), Seville, Spain
{rragde,lmercab}@upo.es
[3] Curtin University, Perth, Australia
E.Sandry@curtin.edu.au
[4] Honda Research Institute Japan Co., Ltd., Wako, Japan
{h.brock,keisuke,r.gomez}@jp.honda-ri.com

Abstract. The experimental tabletop robot Haru, used for affective telepresence research, enables a teleoperator to communicate a variety of information to a remote user through the robotic medium from a distance. However, the robot's rich communicative modality poses some problems to the teleoperator. Based on their experience of controlling the robot, teleoperators feel the need to be constantly attentive to and engaged with the stream of data from the remote user in order to achieve a seamless and affective interaction. Consequently, teleoperators report feeling fatigued, resulting in a decrease in time using the teleoperation system. In addition, the bulk of the data stream containing information about the remote user poses data privacy concerns. In this paper, we describe the design and development of an improved affective teleoperation system that focuses on privacy, controllability, and mental fatigue. The proposed system enables a teleoperator to maintain the same degree of robot control with a minimal amount of data from the remote user. Moreover, our studies show that the proposed system drastically reduces teleoperation fatigue as shown by the increase in time the system is in use.

Keywords: Social telepresence · Human-robot interaction

1 Introduction

The development of the robotic platform Haru [6] for embodied communication research aims to support the study of social presence and emotional and empathetic engagement for long-term human-robot interaction across different contexts. One of the key areas of research with Haru, relates to embedding multimodal human-robot communication in situations where Haru acts as an affective

© Springer Nature Switzerland AG 2021
H. Li et al. (Eds.): ICSR 2021, LNAI 13086, pp. 564–573, 2021.
https://doi.org/10.1007/978-3-030-90525-5_49

telepresence robot. This paper reports on the technical development of Haru as a medium for affective telepresence from the perspective of the teleoperator.

Haru has been designed as a multimodal robotic communication platform that uses verbal and non-verbal channels in interactions with people. Haru's development, therefore, involves a theoretical understanding of embodied communication as a triple structure, comprising of voice (language); tone and non-verbal sounds (paralanguage); as well as face and body movements (kinesics) [12,13]. This robot's range of communicative strategies provides support for embodied communication, which adds depth and interest to communicative exchanges with the potential to support flexible communication between people and robots over the long term. In particular, Haru's communication is designed not only to allow the robot to convey information clearly but also to add depth and meaning through a range of affective signals.

In this paper we identify three core design considerations for teleoperation of Haru. The first responds to privacy issues that have already been identified in relation to teleoperation, where the teleoperator can see and hear a remote environment without people in that space being fully aware they can be seen and heard at a distance. The second considers how best to support teleoperators with an effective interface for controlling the Haru robot's multimodal affective communication in response to the communication of a remote user. The third compares mental fatigue placed on the teleoperator first without, and then with, system-level assistance in monitoring the remote user's verbal and non-verbal communication in order to choose appropriate responses for Haru as an expressive robot intermediary.

2   Teleoperation Design Concept

We have taken a collaborative design approach used in the navigation task for telepresence robots [8] and brought it to the teleoperation platform and interface for the communication task of Haru (Sect. 3–4). The advantage of such design is that while it gives full control to the teleoperator it also minimizes the exposure of the remote user's data to the teleoperator and reduces teleoperator fatigue in the teleoperation process. Hence, Haru's teleoperation centers on three design considerations: privacy of information about remote users and locations, controllability of the robot's response, and level of mental fatigue on the teleoperator.

2.1   Privacy

The use of sensors and the need for data-driven processes have become a trend in developing intelligent systems, with this information being a much sought after commodity for personalization, adaptation and learning in robotic systems. Consequently, privacy has increasingly become a topic of interest in robotics [2,3], as personal and sensitive information such as image, voice and conversation data captured by audio-visual sensors may be stored and made available to other people via the robot. In particular, teleoperators may rely heavily on this type of information in order to evaluate the communication and emotional state of a remote user and to make decisions over how a teleoperated robot should respond. However, research shows that teleoperators are not always comfortable with the sense that they are surveilling a person and their surroundings via a robot-mounted audiovisual feed [11]. Other users of shared spaces within which telepresence robots are deployed may also feel an uneasy sense of "being watched" or "listened to" when the robot is active or unexpectedly activated by the teleoperator in their location [11]. To consider how best to address this issue, this research compares the effectiveness of a system where the teleoperator has access to all the audiovisual information from the remote location, to a situation where teleoperators were not able to access the audiovisual information directly, but instead relied upon the robotic system's appraisal and suggested response. To do this, we employed knowledge-based systems to automate the evaluation of the remote human's affective signals in order to pass appropriate response options to the teleoperator. In this way, the task that requires analysis of sensitive data is delegated to the system, with only high level, less sensitive information subsequently provided to the teleoperator. The experiments also evaluated whether this could be done without impairing the teleoperator's ability to control the robot and respond to the remote communicator.

2.2   Controllability

Intervention by the teleoperator through direct manipulation of the robot's communicative modalities during interaction is an important teleoperation feature [15]. Providing teleoperators with a sufficient number of degrees of freedom to react in the course of the interaction through the use of subtle and elaborate changes to the characteristics of the robot further enhances the robot's agency associated with stimulus-response [17]. However, timing is key in direct control, a timely response reinforces interactivity and may greatly improve the quality of interaction experience [17]. Therefore, a balancing act in the design of the interface is very important and must be based on both needs and simplicity. Too many modules for control may prove to be overwhelming for the operators [1], while the opposite may not be enough [4,16]. In addressing the direct control needs, we identified basic control needs and designed easy access to the robot's low-level and high-level controls. On the one hand, the low-level control represents subtle changes in the robot's behaviors, this entails the manipulation of each of the independent motors and other basic modalities such as vocalization or sounds through TTS. On the other hand, the high-level control provides the teleoperator easy access to a suite of pre-defined complex expressions of the robot (e.g. angry, happy, excited, etc.) referred to as routines. These routines are multimodal compositions that enable the robot to communicate affectively [5]. We also included some form of simple automation through automatic tracking and automatic robot response which can be easily engaged or disengaged by the teleoperator.

2.3   Mental Fatigue

The rich audio-visual data shared with the teleoperators in a conventional human-in-the-loop teleoperation set-up [9] not only poses privacy concerns but could also be a source of significant fatigue for the teleoperators [1,10]. The nature of mental fatigue comes with the need for an operator to maintain situational awareness, processing the stream of images and audio data in order to understand the remote user's cognitive and affective states, such that they can provide an appropriate response via the robotic medium [7,14]. To mitigate the undue mental fatigue, we explored a recommendation scheme [18] as part of the collaborative design. The recommendation scheme processes the output of the knowledge-based systems used to extract high-level information such as face affects, voice affects and gestures. It then generates suggestions to the teleoperator as to how the robot should respond to a remote user. In this manner, the system acts as a support, with the final decision about the response left to the teleoperator.

3   Teleoperation Platform

Consistent with the collaborative design described in Sect. 2, we developed a teleoperation platform. Our platform conceptually consists from two components: (1) a robot-remote-user side and (2) teleoperator side (see Fig. 1).

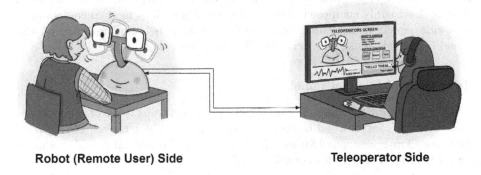

Robot (Remote User) Side   **Teleoperator Side**

Fig. 1. Teleoperation platform

The robot-remote-user side is equipped with sensors and actuators, as well as components that extract high-level information from the sensors (i.e. orientation of the body and head with respect to the robot, body movements, faces and facial expressions, speech, voice affects, sound localization, etc.), and allow controlling the robot using not only motor low-level controls but also high-level commands. In the end, five different communication modalities enable the robot to communicate with its human peer:

Robot Movement: the robot has 5 degrees of freedom, which allow it to rotate the whole body, lean the neck forward and backward, etc.

Visual Displays: each of the eyes of the robot includes a 3-inch TFT screen display and a rectangular border of the inner eyes (the eye goggles) is composed of an addressable LED strip. Inside the body of the robot, there is an addressable LED matrix used as its mouth.

Text-to-Speech (TTS): the text messages received are uttered by the robot using a TTS module, based on the Cerevoice TTS engine by Cereproc[1].

Emotive Routines (high-level control): the robot can also show complex expressions through the use of pre-programmed emotive routines [5]. These routines are open-loop macro-actions that combine all robot actuation modalities described above (motion, sounds, LEDs, eye videos).

Person Tracking: the robot can automatically follow a given person with its gaze. If this mode is activated, it closes the loop using the body posture and skeletons to look at the face of the indicated person.

4   Teleoperation Interface

Consistent with the collaborative design as well as the teleoperation interface previously discussed in Sect. 2 and Sect. 3, we developed the teleoperation GUI as shown in Fig. 2. The software is built using the Qt-5[2] framework for desktop applications together with the use of Robot Operating System[3] in the back-end. The GUI is mainly composed of three components such as manual control panel (left-side panel), agent simulation panel (middle panel) and recommendation panel (right-side panel) respectively. The details are as follows:

4.1   Manual Control Panel

The Manual Control Panel in Fig. 2 (left panel) contains a set of widgets that enable direct control of all of the robot modalities. The interface of this panel includes a low-level control for individual motors and other individual modalities and a high-level control for complex routines.

Motor: provides a quick way to directly control the individual motors of the robot to execute basic movements (i.e., base rotation, forward and backward leaning, eyes stroke, tilt and roll).

Voice Reply: enables control of the robot to vocalize via keyboard and microphone for dictation input. The widget also provides a predefined list of responses in different contextual categories which can be easily modified through a dedicated configuration file.

---

[1] https://www.cereproc.com.
[2] https://www.qt.io.
[3] https://www.ros.org.

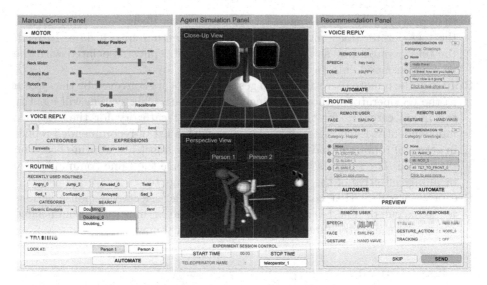

Fig. 2. GUI for Teleoperators (left panel: Manual Control; middle panel: Agent simulation; right panel: Recommendation)

Routine: provides a control for the robot's high level and more complex expressions referred to as routines. The routines are classified into various categories, the teleoperator can easily select the appropriate expressions and its corresponding intensity denoted by the index number "0–3" (e.g., "Angry_0", "Sad_1", "Happy_3",).

Tracking: provides a high-level control that automatically adjusts the motor actuations to face any person detected in the scene.

4.2   Agent Panel

The agent simulation in Fig. 2 (middle panel) is designed to visualize the robot's interactivity. The top widget is a close-up view while widget below shows the global perspective of the robot relative to the remote users (displayed as 3D skeletons). The bottom widget logs and shows the usage time of the system and corresponding teleoperators ID.

4.3   Recommendation Panel

Our recommendation panel in Fig. 2 (right panel) contains a set of widgets that enable the teleoperator to see the system recommended options on the robot's responses and make decisions on what actions are to be executed.

Voice Reply: using semantic information from the ASR to detect voice affect, the system will identify the mood category of the remote user's utterance, then provide a list of recommendations of the most likely voice reply. Hence, the teleoperator does not need to listen to the actual speech data. Instead, the teleoperator may simply select from a list of replies associated with the recognized mood category.

Routine: the remote user's facial and gestural affects are conveyed by the system to the teleoperator without showing the RGB data. The system will identify the mood category for the face and the mood[4] category for the gestures, independently. Each category is associated with a list of recommended replies in terms of robot routines. The teleoperator may select any routine based on preference. The routines in any given category have the same communicative meaning reflective of the mood category it belongs to.

Preview: a widget that contains a summary of the selected response actions to be executed. The teleoperator may select one or multiple recommended actions by the system and these are displayed in this widget.

5   Experiments

We conducted an initial within-subject preliminary study of the proposed tele-operation system. The aim of this study is to measure the impact of the proposed system on the teleoperators and to evaluate its viability for further development. For the experiment, the proposed recommendation system was compared to the conventional system as experimental and control conditions, respectively. In the study, we gathered twenty adult participants (10 males, 10 females) to use the system as teleoperators that are technology savvy and computer literate.

5.1   Quantitative

For the quantitative analysis, we measured the teleoperators' ability to control the robot by responding correctly to the input stimuli from the remote user (i.e., data = face affect, gestural affect and voice affect). We pre-recorded a series of events (i.e. 5 s/event, 700 events, total: 1 h) representing the input stimuli from the remote user. We prepared two sets of the series as (A) *unimodal stream* in which only one input stimulus is present for each event and as (B) *multimodal stream* in which more than one input stimuli present in an event. For the input data preparation above, we also annotated the corresponding mood category of the possible correct response to serve as ground truth (see Sect. 4.3).

We evaluated the *conventional* system and the *proposed* recommendation system. In case of the conventional system, the teleoperator had to infer the actual affects of the face, gesture and voice by watching and listening to the audio-visual data to decide the appropriate response. We provided a separate interface very similar to the one in Fig. 2 with full audio-visual access but

---

[4] This description is loosely used here. The general idea is to inject some context associated with the robot response and not just the recognized actions or affects from the remote user.

without the recommendation panel. In contrast, the proposed system automatically extracts high-level contextual information about the remote user, such as affects from the audio-visual data, and provides the teleoperator only with this information and the recommended response as shown in Fig. 2 (right panel).

5.2 Qualitative

We also gathered some feedback from the participants through a simple questionnaire as follows:

1. Impact on teleoperabilty as a function of data (full audio visual vs. contextual)
   a) *Which system provides the feeling of having full control of the robot?*
   b) *Which system is sufficient enough to perform the given task?*
2. Overall feeling of comfort and ease-of-use
   a) *Which system provides feeling of comfort in terms of privacy in general?*
   b) *Which system causes a smaller amount of mental load while using it?*

The participants were asked to select which of the systems (conventional or proposed) best fits the answer for each of the questions above. They were also allowed to select both but only if warranted.

6 Results and Discussion

The results of the experiment in Sect. 5.1 averaged across the total number of participants are shown in Fig. 3. In this figure, it is clear that the **proposed** method enables the teleoperator to provide more correct responses via the robot as compared to the **conventional** approach. This result is consistent in both scenarios (A) **unimodal stream** and (B) **multimodal stream**, with the proposed method being markedly more robust in the case of scenario (B) than the conventional approach when the teleoperators are presented with multiple modalities at the same time.

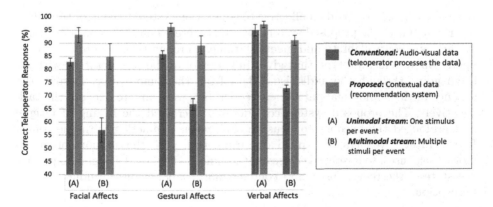

Fig. 3. Quantitative evaluation results

This is shown by the drastic degradation of the performance (% correct) of the conventional approach. This result is expected because scenario (B) is deemed to be more overwhelming to the teleoperators as they need to be more engaged in the audio-visual data to detect the multiple stimuli and to respond to each accordingly. The robustness of the proposed method in scenario (B) is attributed to the fact that the teleoperators are not fatigued as much of the decision-making process is left to the system. Moreover, based on the time log of the usage time when interacting with the system, we found that the teleoperators are likely to last 3 times longer when using the proposed system as opposed to the conventional approach ($p<.05$).

Table 1. Survey results.

	Conventional	Proposed
1.a) Full control	35%	65%
1.b) Sufficiency	20%	80%
2.a) Comfort (privacy)	20%	80%
2.b) Mental fatigue	10%	90%

In Table 1, we summarized the personal preference of the teleoperators when asked the questions in Sect. 5.2. For item (1), it is apparent that a significant number of participants feel that the proposed system provides full teleoperation control even without having access to the full audio-visual data from the remote user ($p<.05$). Consequently, for item (2), the proposed system is the most preferred when it comes to comfort and ease-of-use ($p<.05$). In addition, the results in Table 1 reinforces the results we achieved in Fig. 3.

7   Conclusion

In this paper, we proposed an affective teleoperation system to control the table-top robot Haru. The proposed system design is centered on three considerations: privacy and controllability and mental fatigue. Through this, we built our teleoperation system prototype that gives full control to the teleoperators without them going through the audiovisual data from the remote user. Despite the absence of the audiovisual data, the teleoperators were able to execute the task effectively. The proposed system considerably decreased the feeling of fatigue and prolonged the teleoperators' usage time when interacting with the robot. In the future, we plan to expand our framework with the support of multi-modal responses, to leverage the use of other knowledge-based systems to predict the state of the remote user, and conduct more elaborate user studies on user perception.

References

1. Arkin, R., Ali, K.: Integration of reactive and telerobotic control in multi-agent robotic systems. In: Proceedings Simulation of Adaptive Behavior. Citeseer (1994)
2. Calo, R.: The drone as a privacy catalyst. Stan. L. Rev. Online **64**, 29 (2011)
3. Feil-Seifer, D., Skinner, K., Mataric, M.J.: Benchmarks for evaluating socially assistive robotics. Int. Stud. **8**(3), 423–439 (2007)
4. Fong, T., Thorpe, C.: Vehicle teleoperation interfaces. Auton. Robot. **11**(1), 9–18 (2001)
5. Gomez, R., Nakamura, K., Szapiro, D., Merino, L.: A holistic approach in designing tabletop robot's expressivity. In: Proceedings of the International Conference on Robotics and Automation (2020)
6. Gomez, R., Szapiro, D., Galindo, K., Nakamura, K.: Haru: hardware design of an experimental tabletop robot assistant. In: Proceedings of the 2018 ACM/IEEE International Conference on Human-robot Interaction, pp. 233–240 (2018)
7. Kaber, D.B., Onal, E., Endsley, M.R.: Design of automation for telerobots and the effect on performance, operator situation awareness, and subjective workload. Hum. Fact. Ergon. Manuf. Serv. Ind. **10**(4), 409–430 (2000)
8. Macharet, D.G., Florencio, D.A.: A collaborative control system for telepresence robots. In: 2012 IEEE/RSJ International Conference on Intelligent Robots and Systems, pp. 5105–5111. IEEE (2012)
9. Music, S., Salvietti, G., Dohmann, P., Chinello, F., Prattichizzo, D., Hirche, S.: Human-multi-robot teleoperation for cooperative manipulation tasks using wearable haptic devices (2017)
10. Nakamichi, D., Nishio, S., Ishiguro, H.: Training of telecommunication through teleoperated android "telenoid" and its effect. In: The 23rd IEEE International Symposium on Robot and Human Interactive Communication, pp. 1083–1088. IEEE (2014)
11. Niemelä, M., van Aerschot, L., Tammela, A., Aaltonen, I., Lammi, H.: Towards ethical guidelines of using telepresence robots in residential care. Int. J. Soc. Robot. **13**(3), 1–9 (2019)
12. Poyatos, F.: The reality of multichannel verbal-nonverbal communication in simultaneous and consecutive interpretation. Benjamins Trans. Lib. **17**, 249–282 (1997)
13. Sandry, E.: Robots and Communication. Palgrave Macmillan UK, London (2015). https://doi.org/10.1057/9781137468376
14. Scholtz, J., Antonishek, B., Young, J.: Evaluation of a human-robot interface: Development of a situational awareness methodology. In: 37th Annual Hawaii International Conference on System Sciences, 2004. Proceedings of the, p. 9. IEEE (2004)
15. Small, N., Lee, K., Mann, G.: An assigned responsibility system for robotic teleoperation control. Int. J. Intell. Robot. Appl. **2**(1), 81–97 (2018). https://doi.org/10.1007/s41315-018-0043-0
16. Steinfeld, A.: Interface lessons for fully and semi-autonomous mobile robots. In: IEEE International Conference on Robotics and Automation, 2004. Proceedings. ICRA'04. 2004, vol. 3, pp. 2752–2757. IEEE (2004)
17. Steinfeld, A., et al.: Common metrics for human-robot interaction. In: Proceedings of the 1st ACM SIGCHI/SIGART Conference on Human-Robot Interaction, pp. 33–40 (2006)
18. Wada, K., Glas, D.F., Shiomi, M., Kanda, T., Ishiguro, H., Hagita, N.: Capturing expertise: developing interaction content for a robot through teleoperation by domain experts. Int. J. Soc. Robot. **7**(5), 653–672 (2015)

Psychical HRI

A Boxed Soft Robot Conveying Emotions by Changing Apparent Stiffness of Its Lid

Hiroya Kawai$^{(\boxtimes)}$ ⓘ, Taku Hachisu ⓘ, Masakazu Hirokawa ⓘ,
and Kenji Suzuki ⓘ

Artificial intelligence laboratory, University of Tsukuba, 1-1-1 Tennodai,
Tsukuba Ibaraki 305-8573, Japan
`hiroya@ai.iit.tsukuba.ac.jp`

Abstract. A social robot that convey its emotions by changing its apparent stiffness is presented herein. A user interacts with a box-shaped robot by pushing its lid. The apparent stiffness of the robot is controlled by an electromagnetic brake installed on the lid based on the emotional state of the robot. To control the stiffness, we implement two approaches: (i) control the reaction force when a user presses the lid; (ii) control the temporal restoring behavior when a user releases the lid. The experimental results show a capability of the robot in providing variable apparent stiffness and a potential in eliciting the emotional impact of users through haptic human-robot interactions.

Keywords: Emotion · Haptic interactions · Human-robot interactions · Social robots

1 Introduction

Social robots are machines that interact with human users and can perform tasks automatically. In particular, their physically embodied communication is promising because it allows users to naturally interact with them as they interact with their peers. Therefore, social robots are considered for use in various applications, such as education [1], human rehabilitation [3], and therapy [11].

The emotional expression of social robots, although difficult to decipher, is important for ensuring smooth human-robot interactions. For example, appropriate emotional expressions encourage positive educational behavior in humans [8]. To date, numerous studies pertaining to emotional expressions have been conducted, in which robots present their emotions through facial expressions [4], colors [9,10], sounds [2,9], and vibrations [9]. In order to enrich emotional expression, it is important to study the relationship between the stimuli emitted by robots and the emotions recalled by users who receive the stimuli.

In this study, we focused on conveying emotions through touch interactions between robots and users. Hertenstein et al. demonstrated that touch can represent an emotional state between human peers, even when vocal and facial

© Springer Nature Switzerland AG 2021
H. Li et al. (Eds.): ICSR 2021, LNAI 13086, pp. 577–585, 2021.
https://doi.org/10.1007/978-3-030-90525-5_50

expressions are unavailable [5–7]. Another study demonstrated that the appropriate touch interaction pattern can convey the emotional expression of humanoid robots effectively [12].

In this study, we developed a social robot that conveys emotions by changing its apparent stiffness. The box-shaped robot requires a user to haptically interact with itself (e.g., pushing) while the robot changes its apparent stiffness based on its emotional state, as shown in Fig. 1. The advantages of this robot are as follows: 1) it maintains users' interests by encouraging them to interact actively; 2) it allows users with visual or hearing disabilities to interact with each other; and 3) it can be easily combined with other modalities such as light, sound, vocal and facial expressions.

The remainder of this paper is organized as follows: First, we describe the principle of varying the apparent stiffness and the implementation of the robot. Next, the performance evaluation of the developed robot is presented. Subsequently, we describe an experiment performed involving human participants to demonstrate the variable apparent stiffness. Finally, we conclude the paper with the future direction for this study.

2   Method

The robot presents apparent stiffness to the user by changing its apparent elasticity and viscosity. Figure 1 shows the basic interaction between the user and robot. In the initial state shown in Fig. 1-1, the lid is open, and the face of the head is visible the user. As shown in Fig. 1-2, when the user pushes the lid, the user feels a contact reaction force. While the force is generated by the elasticity of the head, it can be modulated by an electromagnetic brake installed on the rotation axis of the lid, which varies the apparent elasity of the robot. As shown in Fig. 1-3, when the user releases the finger from the lid, the robot pushes up the lid and attempts to return to the initial state. The restoration time is controlled by an electromagnetic brake, which varies the apparent viscosity of the robot.

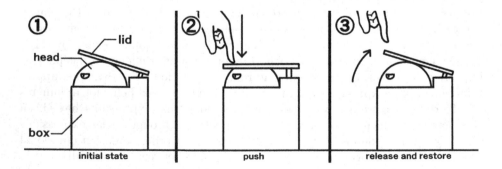

Fig. 1. Conceptual diagram of interaction with box-shaped robot

2.1 Principle

Elasticity for Pushing. Without applying a voltage to the electromagnetic brake, the contact reaction force increases linearly as the user pushes the lid owing to the elasticity of the silicone head. When a voltage is applied, the user requires more force to push down the robot. In addition, dynamically controlling the applied voltage enables various reaction force patterns to be generated.

Viscosity for Releasing. Without applying a voltage, after the user pushes down the robot and releases the finger, the robot pushes back the lid via its elasticity, while a friction force is generated on the rotation axis. When a voltage is applied, the restoration time increases with friction. In addition, dynamically controlling the applied voltage enables various patterns of restoring behavior to be generated.

2.2 Implementation

Figure 2 shows the developed robot, which comprises an elastic silicone head (Elastodil M8012, Wacker Asahikasei Silicone Co.,Ltd.) and a three-dimensionally printed plastic box. An electromagnetic brake (112-03-12 24V 6DIN, Miki Pulley Co.,Ltd.) and a potentiometer (RK1631110TV6, Alps Alpine) were installed on the rotation axis of the box, which was used to electrically control the apparent stiffness of the robot. A microcontroller (ESP32-DevKitC ESP-WROOM-32 development board, Espressif Systems Pte. Ltd.) was used to control them based on parameters provided by the host computer. The microcontroller reads the output voltage of the potentiometer via a built-in 12-bit analog-to-digital converter while outputting voltage to the electromagnetic brake via a built-in 8-bit digital-to-analog converter through an operational amplifier (OPA548FKTWTG3, Texas Instruments). The applied voltage ranged from 0 to 24 V.

Control of Reaction Force. The robot can vary its apparent elasticity by dynamically controlling the electromagnetic brake while the user is pushing the robot. This can be achieved via one among three relevant methods, as will be discussed below. Additionally, it is noteworthy that the robot provides an inherent reaction force generated from the elasticity of the head.

The first is to increase the offset reaction force F_o, where the user must exert more force to start pushing down the robot. A constant voltage is applied to the electromagnetic brake. The offset force is defined as C_1. $F_B(V_0)$ represents the force generated by the electromagnetic brake, where V_0 is a constant voltage. The reaction force is expressed as

$$F_o = C_1 + kx \quad (C_1 = F_B(V_0)), \tag{1}$$

where C_1 is a constant denoted as $F_B(V_0)$, which is a force generated by a voltage V_0 to the electronic brake; k is a proportionality constant; x is the displacement.

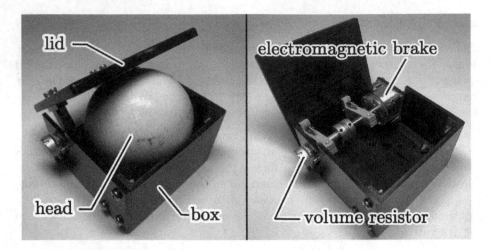

Fig. 2. Robot developed in this study

The second method is to generate a constant reaction force, regardless of the angle of the lid. At this time, the voltage applied to the electromagnetic brake decreases as the displacement increases. The reaction force presented by the electromagnetic brake is expressed as

$$F_c = C_2 \quad (C_2 = F_B(V_0 - v(x)) + kx), \tag{2}$$

where C_2 is the desired force constant, k a proportionality constant, and x the displacement. V_0 is the initial voltage, and $v(x)$ is the voltage applied at x.

The third method is to enhance the elastic force. At this point, the voltage applied to the electromagnetic brake increases with the displacement. The reaction force is expressed as

$$F_e = k'x \approx F_B(v(x)) + kx, \tag{3}$$

where k' is a newly set proportionality constant, $F_B(v(x))$ the generated force when a voltage v is applied at x, k a proportionality constant for the intrinsic elastic force of silicon in the head, and x the displacement.

Control of Restore Time. The lid angle will be restored to its original position by the intrinsic elasticity of the silicon head when the user releases the finger. Therefore, by modifying the returning behavior of the lid using an electromagnetic brake, the apparent viscosity can be presented to the user. When a voltage is applied to the electromagnetic brake, the elastic force of the silicone cannot return to the initial state. Hence, the voltage applied to the electromagnetic brake must be reduced to zero, and the time to reduce the voltage to zero can be regarded as the time to return to the initial state.

3   Experiments

3.1   Apparent Elasticity

An experiment was performed to determine whether offset reaction, constant reaction, and enhanced elastic forces can be generated using our methods. For simplicity, we evaluated the system by measuring the linear displacement and force instead of the torque.

Procedure. The robot was fixed on a flat table at its initial state. A force gauge (Imada Co., Ltd.) was fixed to the lid of the robot, perpendicular to the table. The gauge was manually pushed by the experimenter. The values displayed on the gauge were recorded when the displacements were 0.0, 0.5, 1.0, 1.5, 2.0, and 2.5 cm. This measurement was conducted five times for each displacement.

To investigates the characteristics of the offset reaction force, we set the voltage applied to the electromagnetic brake to 0, 5, 10, 15, 20, and 24 V. To determine whether a constant reaction force can be generated, we set to a constant value to 8 N. To ascertain whether an enhanced elastic force can be generated, we set the proportionality constant of the enhanced elastic force to 2.5 N/cm.

Result. Figure 3-A shows the relationship between the displacement (x-axis) and the mean of the measured force (y-axis) under an offset reaction force. The error bars represent the standard error. A high goodness-of-fit was indicated by liner regression (R^2 is 0.9532 to 0.9981). Figure 3-B shows a plot of the applied voltage (x-axis) and the intercept of the regression (y-axis). The offset force increased with the applied voltage, as expected. By contrast, the slope plateaued at higher voltages. This might be indicative of the characteristics of the electromagnetic brake used in the experiment. A quadratic regression was performed on this data: $F_{offset} = -0.012x^2 + 0.63x - 0.19$, where F_{offset} is the offset of the reaction force caused by the electromagnetic brake, and x is the displacement from the initial state. This regression indicated a high goodness-of-fit ($R^2 = 0.975$).

Figure 4 shows the result of the constant reaction force and enhanced elastic force with the inherent elastic reaction force (no voltage) for the comparison. Regarding the constant function, the slope plateaued regardless of the displacement. This demonstrates the effectiveness of the proposed method. However, the contact reaction value was approximately 10 N although the control value was to 8.0 N. This regression indicated a high goodness-of-fit ($R^2 = 0.6923$). Meanwhile, for the linear function, the slope of the graph was steeper than that without voltage. This regression showed a high goodness-of-fit($R^2 = 0.9937$). However, the proportionality constant was 5.84 N/cm instead of 6.5 N/cm. This might be because the measured displacement was smaller than the actual value. The resolution of the volume resistors used in the experiment was low, which may have hindered measurements with sufficient accuracy.

A   B

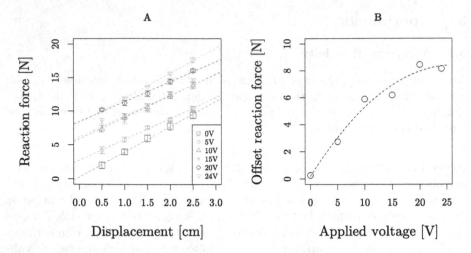

Fig. 3. Results of offset reaction force: a) Relationship between displacement and measured force; b) relationship between applied voltage and offset reaction force

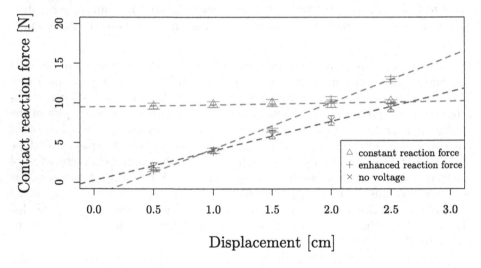

Fig. 4. Results of constant reaction force and enhanced elastic force: Relationship between displacement and measured force

3.2 Apparent Viscosity

An experiment was performed to determine whether time is controllable.

Procedure. The robot was fixed on a flat table and the experimenter manually pushed down the lid to an angle of approximately 35°. After the microcontroller began recording the angle, the experimenter released the finger. The restoration time was set to 3 and 6 s. For comparison, we measured the angle without

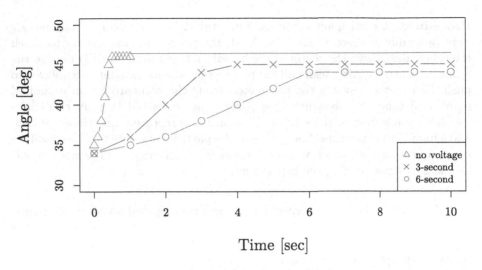

Fig. 5. Result of time and angle

applying a voltage to the electromagnetic brake. The sampling rate 1 Hz for the abovementioned restoration times 1 Hz for the no-voltage condition. In the analysis, we set the moment to 0 s when the angle started to change. The measurement was conducted five times for each condition.

Result. Figure 5 shows the temporal changes in the angle of the lid. The restoration times were approximately 3 and 6 s, which were longer than those in the no-voltage condition.

3.3   Can User Discriminate Apparent Elasticity?

An experiment was performed to investigate whether human users can discriminate the apparent stiffness rendered by the robot. In this experiment, the offset reaction force method was employed because it can provide a higher resolution than other methods, according to our pilot study.

Setup. Five participants (four males, mean age of 26.6 years old) were recruited. The robot and computer were placed on the table. In this experiment, the predefined parameters sent from the computer was controlled using a keyboard. The parameters included the offset contact reaction force and returning time. Six pairs of parameters were set, as follows: (0.0 N, 0.0 s),(1.6 N, 0.0 s),(3.2 N, 1.0 s),(4.8 N, 1.5 s),(6.4 N, 2.0 s), and (8.0 N, 3.0 s). In the first parameter pair, no voltage was applied to the electromagnetic brake. These values were determined based on the results of the pilot study, as they appeared to be natural values.

Procedure. A participant sat in front of a table. First, six pairs of parameters were randomly assigned to six keys. Next, the participant was taught to touch the robot: push down the center of the lid with a finger until an LED next to the robot is turned on. After using all the parameters, the participant was allowed to push the robot and switch the parameters using the keyboard for an unlimited number of times. Subsequently, the participant was asked to rank them in a row from the softest to the stiffest. This task was repeated nine times by each participant. After the experiment ended, the participants were presented with a simple questionnaire, which was used to assess the strategy and the emotion felt by the participant during the experiment.

Result. Table 1 shows the percentage of answers computed for all participants. The rows represent the presented offset reaction force, whereas the columns represent the subjective stiffness. Therefore, diagonal cells show the number of correct responses, which are higher than the chance levels (16.7%). The results indicate that the developed robot can present variable apparent stiffness with at least two to three bits.

Based on the questionnaire answered by the participants of this experiment and pilot studies, a few commented that the robot appeared grumpy or angry when they were stiff. This indicates that, the robot can convey their emotion through the variable apparent stiffness.

Table 1. Mean percentage of response: rows represent presented offset reaction force; columns represent for subjective stiffness (1: softest - 6: stiffest)

	1	2	3	4	5	6
0.0 N	**73**	4	4	2	7	9
1.6 N	2	**73**	4	2	7	11
3.2 N	9	7	**64**	16	2	2
4.8 N	2	4	9	**71**	4	9
6.4 N	9	2	4	2	**80**	2
8.0 N	4	9	13	7	0	**67**

4   Conclusion

Herein, we proposed a social robot that conveys emotion by changing its apparent stiffness. The developed box-shaped robot interacts with the human user by pushing and releasing, whereas the stiffness is controlled by modifying the apparent elasticity and viscoelasticity of the silicon head of the robot using an electromagnetic brake. Experiments 1 and 2 demonstrated that the proposed method can control the apparent elasticity and viscoelasticity. Experiment 3 showed that human participants can discriminate among six patterns of apparent stiffness. In addition, the comments provided by the participants implied that the variable stiffness can be used to convey emotional expressions.

In our future study, we plan to investigate the relationship between the apparent stiffness and the emotion recalled by human users. We will investigate other possible patterns of elastic forces in addition to the three implemented in this experiment. Additionally, we will investigate the effect of combining the apparent elasticity and viscoelasticity.

References

1. Alemi, M., Meghdari, A., Ghazisaedy, M.: Employing humanoid robots for teaching english language in iranian junior high-schools. Int. J, Human Robot. **11**(3), 1450022 (2014)
2. Chumkamon, S., Masato, K., Hayashi, E.: Facial expression of social interaction based on emotional motivation of animal robot. In: 2015 IEEE International Conference on Systems, Man, and Cybernetics. pp. 185–190 (2015). https://doi.org/10.1109/SMC.2015.45
3. Dağlarlı, E., Anbaş, E.: Rehabilitation based computational models for humanoid robots. In: 2016 Medical Technologies National Congress (TIPTEKNO). pp. 1–4 (2016). https://doi.org/10.1109/TIPTEKNO.2016.7863124
4. Herdel, V., Kuzminykh, A., Hildebrandt, A., Cauchard, J.R.: Drone in love: emotional perception of facial expressions on flying robots. In: Proceedings of the 2021 CHI Conference on Human Factors in Computing Systems (2021)
5. Hertenstein, M.J., Holmes, R., McCullough, M.E., Keltner, D.: The communication of emotion via touch. Emotion **9**(4), 566–73 (2009)
6. Hertenstein, M.J., Keltner, D.: Gender and the communication of emotion via touch. Sex Roles **64**, 70–80 (2011)
7. Hertenstein, M.J., Keltner, D., App, B., Bulleit, B.A., Jaskolka, A.R.: Touch communicates distinct emotions. Emotion **6**(3), 528–33 (2006)
8. Leyzberg, D., Avrunin, E., Liu, J., Scassellati, B.: Robots that express emotion elicit better human teaching. In: 2011 6th ACM/IEEE International Conference on Human-Robot Interaction (HRI), pp. 347–354 (2011). https://doi.org/10.1145/1957656.1957789
9. Song, S., Yamada, S.: Expressing emotions through color, sound, and vibration with an appearance-constrained social robot. In: 2017 12th ACM/IEEE International Conference on Human-Robot Interaction (HRI), pp. 2–11 (2017)
10. Terada, K., Yamauchi, A., Ito, A.: Artificial emotion expression for a robot by dynamic color change. In: 2012 IEEE RO-MAN: The 21st IEEE International Symposium on Robot and Human Interactive Communication, pp. 314–321 (2012). https://doi.org/10.1109/ROMAN.2012.6343772
11. Wada, K., Shibata, T.: Social effects of robot therapy in a care house - change of social network of the residents for two months. In: Proceedings 2007 IEEE International Conference on Robotics and Automation, pp. 1250–1255 (2007). https://doi.org/10.1109/ROBOT.2007.363156
12. Zheng, X., Shiomi, M., Minato, T., Ishiguro, H.: What kinds of robot's touch will match expressed emotions?. IEEE Robot. Autom. Lett. **5**(1), 127–134 (2020). https://doi.org/10.1109/LRA.2019.2947010

Motion Intention Recognition Based on Air Bladders

Weifeng Wu[1], Chengqi Lin[1], Gengliang Lin[1], Siqi Cai[2(✉)], and Longhan Xie[1(✉)]

[1] Shien-Ming Wu School of Intelligent Engineering, South China University of Technology, Guangzhou, Guangdong, China
melhxie@scut.edu.cn
[2] Department of Electrical and Computer Engineering, National University of Singapore, Singapore, Singapore
elesiqi@nus.edu.sg

Abstract. Recognition of human motion intention plays an important role in many robotic applications, such as human-assistive exoskeletons and rehabilitation robots. Motion intention recognition (MIR) based on physiological signals is one of the most common and intuitive methods. However, physiological signals are sensitive to environmental disturbances and suffer from complex preparation. In this paper, we proposed a novel air bladder-based MIR method, in which the human-robot interaction (HRI) force is measured directly by four air bladders. The air bladders can be installed at the end of a robot to interact with the user's arm. We validate the linearity and repeatability of the air bladders through comprehensive experiments. In addition, we compare the performance of the proposed air bladder-based MIR method with the conventional method based on force sensors and surface electromyography (sEMG) signals. Experiments show that the proposed method can capture the change of the external force, even when the force changes rapidly. Moreover, the performance of our method is more comparative and robust in caparison with the sEMG-based MIR method.

Keywords: Motion intention recognition · Air bladder · Human-robot interaction

1 Introduction

Motion intention recognition (MIR) attracts strong research interests because of its promising applications in human-robot interaction (HRI). For instance, MIR is critical for powered exoskeleton systems, robot-assisted applications, and intelligent prostheses. Considering that muscles are the drivers of human body, it is a natural idea to recognize human motion intention by detecting muscle states [1]. In addition, sEMG-based methods can directly capture muscle information, which makes it suitable for patients with limb disability [2]. In [3], the forces of agonist and antagonist muscles pair have been estimated by sEMG signals and their difference is used to reflect the motion intention of corresponding joints. Jie et al. have developed a non-linear autoregressive exogenous (NARX) model to continuously decode the upper limb movements based on the sEMG

© Springer Nature Switzerland AG 2021
H. Li et al. (Eds.): ICSR 2021, LNAI 13086, pp. 586–595, 2021.
https://doi.org/10.1007/978-3-030-90525-5_51

signals [4]. Similarly, many sEMG-based MIR methods have been developed in recent studies [5–7].However, all these MIR methods based on sEMG signals suffer from these limitations [8]: 1) sEMG signal is very noisy, unstable, and depends on good skin contact. The surface electrodes can cause the subject to sweat, which also affects the signal. 2) Long preparation time is needed to place the surface electrodes and the uncomfortable wearing experience is commonly complained by the users. 3) The processing of sEMG signal is complex because of the motion artifacts, noises, and components from multiple muscle sources.

To overcome these shortcomings of the sEMG-based MIR method, many researchers have proposed other approaches for MIR [9, 10]. The MIR method based on force/torque sensors has been developed in [11–13]. In these studies, a bandage or Velcro is needed to connect the user's arm with the robot. However, these soft materials make it difficult for the force/torque sensor to measure the HRI force accurately, especially when the direction of arm movement changes. In [14, 15], they have applied 4 force-sensing resistors in the arm holder to detect the interaction force between the user and robot. However, it is challenging to fit human arms of various sizes. Moreover, the gap between the circular ring of arm holder and the human arm will cause a backlash hysteresis problem.

While the area of sensor-based recognition of human motion intention still lacks a robust, low-cost, comfortable method, we propose a novel air bladder-based approach for MIR in this paper. In detail, four airbags are evenly distributed on the inner circumference of the ring-shaped arm holder, which is installed at the end of the robot. These airbags enable a wearer to attach and release the robot in an easy way and a short time by quickly inflating the air chambers to hold a human arm or deflating them to release. Meanwhile, the HRI force related to motion intention can be calculated according to the pressure of these four air bladders. The linearity and repeatability of the proposed air bladder-based MIR approach have been evaluated through comprehensive experiments. In addition, the performance of our method has been compared with other MIR method, which is based on force sensor or sEMG signals.

The main contributions of this study are summarized as follows: 1) We propose a new air bladder-based MIR method to directly measure the HRI force, which avoids the influence of bandage or other intermediate parts between human's arm and force sensors. 2) The proposed system can be used as an arm holder, which enables the robot to attach and release the human arm in an easy way by quickly inflating or deflating the air bladders. Meanwhile, expert knowledge is not needed to set up the system. 3) Compared with previous MIR methods, our proposed approach is lower costly, more reliable, and comfortable.

The rest part of this paper is organized as follows. In Sect. 2, the principle and implementation of the proposed air bladder-based MIR method are described. Experiments and results are presented in Sect. 3. Section 4 draws a conclusion.

2 Methodology

In this study, we propose a novel idea for recognizing the human motion intention, in which the HRI force is calculated based on the change of pressure in air bladders. Considering that the air bladder is a critical component of the proposed MIR method, this section describes the air bladder in detail firstly. Then the principle and implementation of our proposed MIR approach are provided.

2.1 Air Bladder

The air bladder is a closed air chamber made of soft material. An air pressure sensor is used to measure the pressure inside the air bladder. When the air bladder is inflated, the external force will affect the air pressure inside the air bladder. Therefore, the load on the air bladder can be reflected by the change of the air pressure in the air bladder. Specifically, the air pressure rises with the increase of the external force, while the air pressure falls with the decrease of the external force. Hence, the air bladder can be employed as a force sensor [16].

(a)   (b)   (c)   (d)

Fig. 1. Manufacturing process of an air bladder, (a) original nylon TPU composite fabric, (b) a piece of fabric after laser cutting, (c) adding a pipe joint by ultrasonic welding, (d) an air bladder.

To reduce the cost of the components and facilitate volume production of the MIR devices, we develop a simple manufacturing process of air bladders. A typical air bladder is made of Nylon TPU composite fabric in this study (Fig. 1(a)), which is a kind of cloth covered with a layer of TPU plastic on the nylon surface. Moreover, the TPU layer can be bonded by heating. The Nylon TPU composite fabric has a good sealing performance and is commonly for air beds, inflatable boats, etc. As shown in Fig. 1(b), a piece of composite fabric with a hole in the middle is obtained by laser cutting. Then, a TPU connecter was combined with the TPU layer by ultrasonic welding (Fig. 1(c)). Finally, this piece of fabric is folded in half and its edges are heated to get a sealed air chamber (Fig. 1(d)). To ensure airtightness, air bladders are tested underwater. Overall, the low price of the composite fabric ($ 6/m^2) and the convenient processing significantly reduce the cost of MIR devices.

2.2 Principle

Figure 2 illustrates the schematic sketch of the presented air bladder-based MIR method. Four air bladders are evenly distributed on the inner surface of the ring-shaped hand holder.

In the idle state, the air is pumped out and the air bladder is shrunken to the inner surface of the ring-shape arm holder. The user can easily pass his/her arm through the arm holder at that time, as shown in Fig. 2(a). When the robot starts to work, the air bladders are in the active state, in which the gap between the arm of various sizes and the arm holder is filled by blowing up the air bladders gradually until a stable and comfortable connection is established. As shown in Fig. 2(b), $p_{i0}(i = 1, 2, 3, 4)$ denote the pressures of four air bladders at the active state. Figure 2(c) shows the working state of the air bladders. The interaction force can be calculated as follow:

$$\tilde{F} = k \sum_{i=1}^{4} (p_{it} - p_{i0}) \tag{1}$$

where $p_{it}(i = 1, 2, 3, 4)$ denote pressures of air bladders. $\tilde{F}$ represents the interaction force, which reflects the user's motion intention. k is the proportional coefficient between the air pressure and external force.

The calculated interaction force can be used as the input of a rehabilitation robot or auxiliary robot. In the end, the air bladders return to the idle state (Fig. 2(a)) and user's arm is released. The proposed air bladder-based MIR system enables the robot to attach and release the human arm easily and expert knowledge is not needed to set up the system.

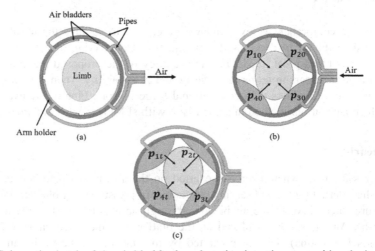

Fig. 2. Schematic sketch of the air bladder-based motion intention recognition device. (a) idle state, (b) active state, (c) working state.

2.3 Implement

The implementation of the proposed MIR system is illustrated in Fig. 3. The arm holder can be installed on a robot as required. We use the XGZP6847 (CFSensor Ltd, China) pressure sensors to measure the pressure of the air bladders and convert it into corresponding voltage. Then, a stm32F407ZGT6 microcontroller (ST, Switzerland) is used to transfer the voltage to a digital signal through the ADC function. The interaction forces are calculated according to Eq. (1). The air bladders are inflated by a pump (Kamoer Ltd, China) and sealed up by 4 solenoid valves (SMC, Japan).

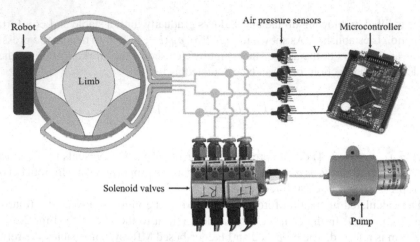

Fig. 3. Implement of the proposed air bladder-based motion intention recognition approach.

3 Experiments

In this section, comprehensive experiments are carried to validate the feasibility and effectiveness of the air bladder-based MIR method. Considering that the property of the air bladders has a great impact on the accuracy of the proposed method, we first evaluate the air bladders in terms of linearity and repeatability. Then we compare the performance of air bladders with conventional force sensors. Finally, we evaluate the MIR performance of our method in comparison with sEMG signal-based method.

3.1 Linearity

The air pressure rises when a force is exerted on the air bladder, and hence, we can measure the external force by observing the change of pressure in air bladder. We obtain the pressure-force curve of the air bladder through an experimental study, as shown in Fig. 4(a). An air bladder is placed on the platform of the force gauge (HANDPI Instruments Ltd, China). The force exerted by turning the handle to the air bladder ranges from 0 to 20 N with an increment of 0.5 N. Meanwhile, the air pressures of the air bladder are recorded. Based on the least-square method [17], we fit a straight line to the experimental data as follow:

$$F = 1.5597 \times p - 1.6212 \tag{2}$$

where $F(N)$ is the force exerted on the air bladder and p denotes the air pressure. -1.6212 is the offset caused by the initial pressure of the air bladder.

It is observed from Fig. 4b that the pressure-force curve of the air bladder shows good linearity in the range of 0–20 N. The line fit all sample data (red dots in the graph) well. The maximum variance of our line with the sample data is 0.09, which is acceptable for HRIs.

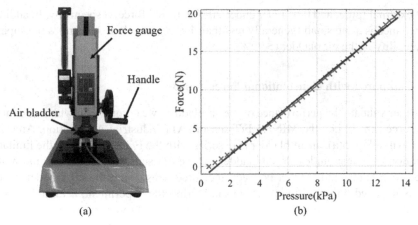

(a)   (b)

Fig. 4. Linearity experiment. (a) linearity experiment setup, (b) the pressure-force curve of the air bladder. The fitted line is in blue and all samples are denoted by red dots (Color figure online).

3.2 Repeatability

The repeatability is defined by the variation of measurements taken by several experiments under the same conditions [18]. To verify the repeatability of the air bladder, we apply four different levels of external forces, including 5 N, 10 N, 15 N, and 20 N, to the air bladder respectively. Each level of force is repeated 15 times using the platform shown in Fig. 4 (a). Meanwhile, the corresponding pressure is recorded when the external force is stable. Figure 5 summarizes the repeatability of the air bladder in four different levels of external forces. It can be observed that the repeatability values of the air bladder are 0.052 *kPa* under 5 N external force, 0.039 *kPa* under 10 N external force, 0.09 *kPa* under

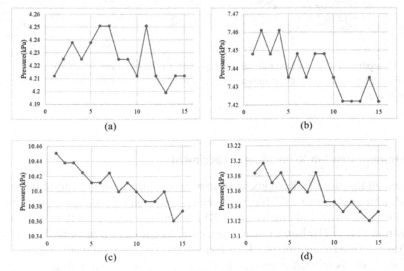

(a)   (b)

(c)   (d)

Fig. 5. Repeatability experiment. (a) repeatability of air bladder under an external force of 5 N, (b) repeatability under a 10 N external force, (c) repeatability under a 15 N external force, (d) repeatability under a 20 N external force.

15 N external force, and 0.064 *kPa* under 20 N external force, respectively. In addition, the variance is quite small (generally less than $1\ e^{-3}$), which demonstrates the superior repeatability of the air bladder (>99%).

3.3 Compared with Convolutional Force Sensor

To further validate the performance of the air bladder, we compared it with a commonly used force sensor, i.e., the MINI45 F/T sensor (ATI Industrial Automation, America). As shown in Fig. 6(a), an air bladder is in series with the F/T sensor. With the limitation of frictionless linear guides, the air bladder and the F/T sensor measure the same applied force. To ensure good contact between the force sensor and the air bladder, a rigid plate is installed on top of the force sensor. During the experiment, a variable force is applied to the inflated air bladder. Specifically, the external force increases and decreases between 2–15 s. Then, an impulse force is applied between 15–20 s. Finally, two-step forces are consecutively applied between 20–30 s. The pressure of the air bladder and the z-direction measurement of the force sensor is recorded. In Fig. 6(b), it is observed that the air pressure of the air bladder is in line with the measurement of the ATI force sensor. Even a rapid and dramatic change of the external force could be detected by this as-designed device, evidently presenting the excellent detection capability.

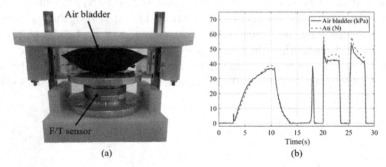

(a)   (b)

Fig. 6. Comparison with a conventional force sensor. (a) experiment setup, (b) the pressure of the air bladder and the z-direction measurement of the force sensor recorded under the variable external force.

3.4 Motion Intention Recognition Experiment

The air bladder-based MIR approach is compared to the current state-of-the-art MIR method, which based on the sEMG signals. Here, we develop a prototype of the presented air bladder-based MIR and install it on a UR5 manipulator (Universal Robots, Denmark), as shown in Fig. 7. The human robot interaction forces can be calculated according to Eq. (1) and are used to control the UR5. Meanwhile, a certified commercial sEMG sensor, Noraxon (USA) is utilized to record sEMG signals of the anterior deltoid and middle deltoid of the subject which are related to the arm movements. During the experiment, the subject is instructed to move his/her forearm up-and-down or side-to side. Based on the detected interaction force, the UR5 manipulator follows the arm motion using the proportional control strategy. Given that the raw sEMG signals are noisy, a moving-average filter is applied. Both the air pressure of the air bladders and the sEMG signals are normalized in the range between 0 and 1 for comparison. Note that there is a delay of about 200 ms between these two signals because the sEMG signals are produced up to 300 ms ahead of arm movement in general [20]. The output of our prototype and sEMG signals are recorded, as shown in Fig. 8. When the subject intends to move up his/her arm, the activation level of the anterior deltoid increases and hence its sEMG signal rises. His/her arm moves up driven by the anterior deltoid, and then interacts with the robot. The proposed device captures the interaction force and controls the robot to follow the user's motion intention. Therefore, the robot moves upward and adaptively adjust the velocity according to the output of our proposed device. Similar results can be observed when the subject moves his/her arm side-to side.

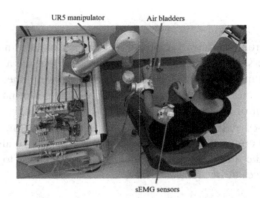

Fig. 7. The experimental setup of air bladder-based motion intention recognition.

In addition, the trend and amplitude of the interaction force detected by our prototype are generally aligned with the sEMG signal during these two types of movements. Specifically, pearson correlation value between horizontal component of the air bladder-based HRI force and sEMG of middle deltoid is 0.748. Pearson correlation value between vertical component of the air bladder-based HRI force and sEMG of anterior deltoid is 0.7872. It is worth noting that sEMG-based MIR is complicated by the fact that sEMG data recorded during dynamic contractions are inherently nonstationary. The processing of sEMG is complicated, time-consuming, which is one of the obstacles that prevents the practical use of sEMG-based MIR systems. On the contrary, the outputs of the proposed approach, i.e., pressure signals, are robust, smooth, and simple to process, which is especially appealing to practical HRIs.

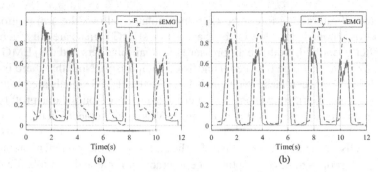

Fig. 8. Comparison with sEMG-based MIR approach. (a) horizontal component of the air bladder-based HRI force and sEMG of middle deltoid, (b) vertical component of the air bladder-based HRI force and sEMG of anterior deltoid.

4 Conclusion

In this study, we propose a novel approach for human motion intention recognition based on air bladders. Experimental results demonstrate that the air bladder, which is the critical component of the proposed method, performs well in terms of linearity and repeatability during measuring the interaction force. The performance in recognizing the motion intention of the proposed air bladder-based approach is competitive with the force sensor-based and sEMG-based methods. Moreover, our method is lower-cost, more reliable, and comfortable, which paves way to an effective and practical human robot interface. In the future, the proposed idea can be extended to detect inter-action forces of more degrees of freedom.

Acknowledgements. This work was supported in part by the National Natural Science Foundation of China (Grant No. 52075177), Joint Fund of the Ministry of Education for Equipment Pre-Research (Grant No. 6141A02033124), Research Foundation of Guangdong Province (Grant No. 2019A050505001 and 2018KZDXM002), Guangzhou Research Foundation (Grant No. 202002030324 and 201903010028), Zhongshan Research Foundation (Grant No.2020B2020), and Shenzhen Institute of Artificial Intelligence and Robotics for Society (Grant No. AC01202005011).

References

1. Bi, L., Feleke, A., Guan, C.: A review on EMG-based motor intention prediction of continuous human upper limb motion for human-robot collaboration. Biomed. Signal Process. Control **51**, 113–127 (2019)
2. Naik, G.R., Al-Timemy, A.H., Nguyen, H.T.: Transradial amputee gesture classification using an optimal number of sEMG sensors: an approach using ICA clustering. IEEE Trans. Neural Syst. Rehabil. Eng. **24**, 837–846 (2016)
3. Siqi, C., et al.: SVM-based classification of sEMG signals for upper-limb self-rehabilitation training. Front. Neurorobotics **13**, 31 (2019)

4. Liu, J., Kang, S.H., Xu, D., Ren, Y., Lee, S.J., Zhang, L.-Q.: EMG-based continuous and simultaneous estimation of arm kinematics in able-bodied individuals and stroke survivors. Front. Neurosci. **11**, 480 (2017)
5. Bu, D., Guo, S., Gao, W.: Continuous estimation of a sEMG-based upper limb joint. In: 2019 IEEE International Conference on Mechatronics and Automation (ICMA), pp. 904–909 (2019)
6. Han, J., Ding, Q., Xiong, A., Zhao, X.: A state-space EMG model for the estimation of continuous joint movements. IEEE Trans. Industr. Electron. **62**, 4267–4275 (2015)
7. Kiguchi, K., Hayashi, Y.: An EMG-based control for an upper-limb power-assist exoskeleton robot. IEEE Trans. Syst. Man Cybern. Part B Cybern. Publ. IEEE Syst. Man Cybern. Soc. **42**(4), 1064–1071 (2012)
8. Calado, A., Soares, F., Matos, D.: A review on commercially available anthropomorphic myoelectric prosthetic hands, pattern-recognition-based microcontrollers and sEMG sensors used for prosthetic control. In: 2019 IEEE International Conference on Autonomous Robot Systems and Competitions (ICARSC), pp. 1–6 (2019)
9. Kong, K., Jeon, D.: Design and control of an exoskeleton for the elderly and patients. IEEE/ASME Trans. Mechatron. **11**, 428–432 (2006)
10. Yamamoto, K., Ishii, M., Noborisaka, H., Hyodo, K.: Stand alone wearable power assisting suit - sensing and control systems. In: RO-MAN 2004. 13th IEEE International Workshop on Robot and Human Interactive Communication (IEEE Catalog No.04TH8759), pp. 661–666 (2004)
11. Kim, B., Deshpande, A.: An upper-body rehabilitation exoskeleton harmony with an anatomical shoulder mechanism: design, modeling, control, and performance evaluation. Int. J. Robot. Res. **36**, 414–435 (2017)
12. Wang, X., Lu, T., Wang, S., Gu, J., Yuan, K.: A patient-driven control method for lower-limb rehabilitation robot, pp. 908–913 (2016)
13. Siqi, C., Wu, W., Xie, L.: Dual-Arm Upper Limb Rehabilitation Robot: Mechanism Design and Preliminary Experiments, pp. 80–86 (2020)
14. Huang, J., Huo, W., Xu, W., Mohammed, S., Amirat, Y.: Control of upper-limb power-assist exoskeleton using a human-robot interface based on motion intention recognition. IEEE Trans. Autom. Sci. Eng. **12**, 1257–1270 (2015)
15. Moubarak, S., Pham, M., Pajdla, T., Redarce, T.: Design and Modeling of an Upper Extremity Exoskeleton (2010). https://doi.org/10.1007/978-3-642-03889-1_127
16. Choi, H., Jung, P.-G., Jung, K., Kong, K.: Design and fabrication of a soft three-axis force sensor based on radially symmetric pneumatic chambers. In: 2017 IEEE International Conference on Robotics and Automation (ICRA), pp. 5519–5524 (2017)
17. York, D.: Least-squares fitting of a straight line. Can. J. Phys. **44**, 1079–1086 (2011)
18. Gong, D., He, R., Yu, J., Zuo, G.: A pneumatic tactile sensor for co-operative robots. Sensors **17**(11), 2592–2606 (2017)

Design and Control of a Seven Degrees-of-Freedom Semi-exoskeleton Upper Limb Robot

Chengqi Lin[1], Weifeng Wu[1], Gengliang Lin[1], Siqi Cai[2(✉)], and Longhan Xie[1(✉)]

[1] Shien-Ming Wu School of Intelligent Engineering, South China University of Technology, Guangzhou, Guangdong, China
melhxie@scut.edu.cn
[2] Department of Electrical and Computer Engineering, National University of Singapore, Singapore, Singapore
elesiqi@nus.edu.sg

Abstract. Previous studies have shown that patient's voluntary participation is one of the key factors in improving rehabilitation effects. End-effector and exoskeleton type robots have been developed to support rehabilitation training at different impedance levels. However, these robots either fail to take the movement of the shoulder girdle into account or suffer from complex and massive shoulder mechanisms. In this paper, we merge the advantages of the end-effector and exoskeleton type robots and propose a simple and effective semi-exoskeleton upper limb robot with seven degrees of freedom to support the impedance training of the human shoulder complex and elbow joint. Besides, an admittance control scheme is developed to generate desired movements during training. Experiments on five subjects are conducted to assess the feasibility and performance of the proposed robot. Results show that the proposed robot has satisfactory performance in terms of shoulder kinematic compatibility and human-robot interaction. This study could pave way for a practical rehabilitation robot for patients with stroke in real-life.

Keywords: Upper limb · Rehabilitation · Semi-exoskeleton robot · Admittance control

1 Introduction

Stroke is one of the leading causes of disability in adults, with many survivors experiencing paralysis or loss of motor function on one side of the body and significantly limiting basic activities of daily living (ADL) [1]. Physical therapy for stroke survivors has been demonstrated as an effective way for motor rehabilitation [2]. However, the labor-intensive and time-consuming exercises have been significant burdens for therapists with increasing patients [3]. To solve this issue, some researchers have focused on the development of rehabilitation robots.

Compared to conventional rehabilitation, robotic devices can provide repetitive and intensive training [4, 5] and are independent of the fatigue level of therapists. Various

© Springer Nature Switzerland AG 2021
H. Li et al. (Eds.): ICSR 2021, LNAI 13086, pp. 596–605, 2021.
https://doi.org/10.1007/978-3-030-90525-5_52

control methods have been proposed for realizing assistive paradigm in rehabilitation [6], such as impedance control and admittance control. Impedance control is a model-based force controller with position feedback, controlling force after motion or deviation from a set point is measured [7]. For implementation, impedance control is efficient for lightweight backdrivable exoskeletons, however, problems arise when it is necessary to consider gravity and friction [8]. Conversely, admittance control controls motion after measuring the force, balancing the force-tracking feature and movement compliance with the simplicity of implementation [9]. Although different admittance control schemes have been developed in [9, 10], decoding the wearer's motion intention is still an open issue [11].

Upper limb rehabilitation robots commonly support active training by measuring limb motion through force/torque (F/T) sensors. End-effector robots, such as GENTLE/S [12], EULRR [13], connect to the patient's hand and measure the endpoint force/torque to generate desired movements during training. The structure and control strategies for end-effector robots are straightforward. However, it is difficult to control the posture of the upper limb for these robots, and hence abnormal joint kinematics is possible. To solve this limitation, exoskeleton-type robots, such as CADEN-7 [14], 6-REXOS [15], have been developed to work at a joint level with distributed physical interaction providing the capability of controlling the whole limb via one or more F/T sensors. However, all the above exoskeleton robots simplify the shoulder complex of humans as a ball-and-socket joint and ignore the mobility of the shoulder girdle, which is detrimental to the coordinated movements of the shoulder complex and may even cause secondary injuries due to the undesirable residual forces on human joints [16]. Some passive shoulder mechanisms have been implemented to release the movement of the shoulder girdle [17, 18], however, the passive joints limit the possibilities of active assistance for the shoulder girdle. Although extra active degrees of freedom (DOFs) joints at the shoulder complex have been developed to address this issue [19, 20], the structures of these robots are usually too complex and massive.

In this paper, we combined the advantages of the end-effector and exoskeleton type robots to develop a simple and effective semi-exoskeleton upper limb robot with seven DOFs, which is referred to as UEArm-7 hereafter. The UEArm-7 can support not only the elbow flexion/extension and rotation of the glenohumeral joint, but also the movement of the shoulder girdle. Considering that it is essential for a rehabilitation robot to adjust assistance in response to temporal variabilities in subject performance, we further develop an admittance control scheme with two six-axis F/T sensors to implement impedance training. Two experiments were carried out to assess the human shoulder kinematic compatibility and the interaction performance of the proposed robot.

The paper is organized as follows. The upper limb kinematic model, the mechanical design of the proposed robot, and the admittance control scheme are introduced in Sect. 2. The experiments and results are presented in Sect. 3. Section 4 draws a conclusion.

2 Methods

2.1 Upper Limb Kinematic Model

In this section, the kinematic model of a human upper limb is presented. Firstly, a four DOFs model is selected to realize shoulder adduction/abduction, flexion/extension, internal/external rotation, and elbow flexion/extension. Considering that shoulder girdle movements result in translational motions of the rotation centre of the glenohumeral joint, which is one of the key design factors in shoulder coordinated movements, a three translational DOFs model is then employed to follow the movements of the rotation centre. Therefore, a seven DOFs kinematic model of a human upper limb is established using the modified Denavit–Hartenburg (DH) framework, as summarized in Fig. 1. The model assumes the upper limb as a set of rigid bodies, and uses rigid body modelling technology from robotics. The frame {0} represents the shoulder complex origin and the world coordinate system. Therefore, the motion of the upper limb can be described by the variables d_1, d_2, d_3, θ_4, θ_5, θ_6, θ_7.

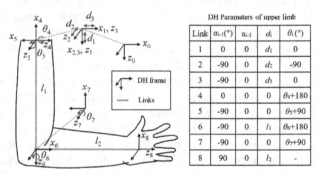

DH Parameters of upper limb

Link	$\alpha_{i-1}(°)$	a_{i-1}	d_i	$\theta_i(°)$
1	0	0	d_1	0
2	-90	0	d_2	-90
3	-90	0	d_3	0
4	0	0	0	θ_4+180
5	-90	0	0	θ_5+90
6	-90	0	l_1	θ_6+180
7	-90	0	0	θ_7+90
8	90	0	l_2	-

Fig. 1. Seven DOFs upper limb kinematic model. Red lines indicate upper limb active joints; black arrows indicate axes of the coordinate frame using DH method; variables l_1 and l_2 are lengths of upper arm and forearm respectively; d_1, d_2, d_3, θ_4, θ_5, θ_6, θ_7 are variables of the upper limb kinematic model. (Color figure online)

2.2 Mechanical Design

As shown in Fig. 2 (a), the UEArm-7 consists of three parts: a six DOFs industrial robot (UR5, Universal Robots A/S, Denmark), a single DOF elbow exoskeleton, and a base. The UR5 is connected to the upper part of the exoskeleton and supports the movement of the shoulder complex, including adduction/abduction, flexion/extension, and internal/external rotation of the glenohumeral joint, as well as the movement of the shoulder girdle. Moreover, the UR5 is fixed to the base in a vertical installation manner to avoid singularities. The elbow exoskeleton is made of lightweight material to reduce the weight (approximately 1.7 kg) and controls elbow flexion/extension by cable. To solve the problem of self-alignment, the elbow exoskeleton introduces two additional links, decoupling joint rotation and translation [17]. The control box of the UR5, the elbow joint motor (RMD-X8, GYEMS, China), the sensor acquisition module, and the power supply are placed inside the base.

To realize proper interjoint coordination between the upper-limb joints, the UEArm-7 has multiple contact points with the upper limb, including the upper arm cuff, the forearm cuff, and the handle, as described in Fig. 2 (b). The upper arm cuff is made of soft material, and two buckles are used to reduce the gap between the exoskeleton and the upper arm. The forearm cuff is contacted to the forearm through an inflatable insert. The handle is fixed on the forearm cuff and provides a grip force during rehabilitation training. Besides, two six-axis F/T sensors (mini45, ATI Industrial Automation, America) are mounted between the cuffs and the elbow linkages to measure the torques and forces exerted by the upper limb. A 14-bits absolute encoder (MBS, KingKong, China) is installed on the drive shaft of the elbow exoskeleton to measure the angle of the elbow joint.

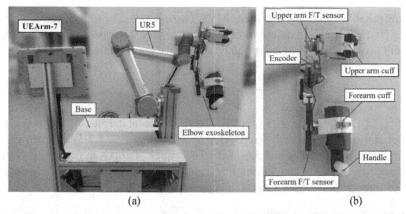

(a)   (b)

Fig. 2. UEArm-7 design. (a) UEArm-7, which is a semi-exoskeleton upper limb robot with seven DOFs and comprises a UR5 robot, an elbow exoskeleton, and a base. (b) The elbow exoskeleton, which comprises two F/T sensors, an encode, an upper arm cuff, a forearm cuff, and a handle.

2.3 Admittance Control Scheme

An admittance control scheme is presented in this section, and its overall block diagram is presented in Fig. 3, mainly consisting of three aspects: intention estimator, admittance controller, and velocity mapping. Specifically, upper limb joint moments are first estimated by two F/T sensors, and then translated into joint motion of upper limb. Finally, the joint motion is mapped into the robot's movements.

Intention Estimator. Based on the assumption of low constant speed motion, the required forces and torques for maintaining the static equilibrium are calculated by (1) using the coordinate system in Sect. 2.1, where ${}^i f_i$ represents the force on frame $\{i\}$, ${}^i n_i$ is the torque on frame $\{i\}$, $i + 1 {}^i R$ is the rotation matrix describing frame$\{i\}$ to frame $\{i+1\}$, ${}^i P_{i+1}$ is the position vector from frame $\{i\}$ to frame $\{i+1\}$.

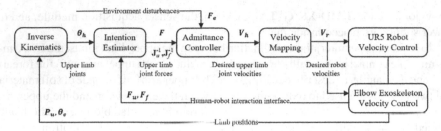

Fig. 3. Overall block diagram of the admittance control scheme.

$$
\begin{cases}
{}^i f_i = {}_{i+1}{}^i R^{i+1} n_{i+1} \\
{}^i n_i = {}_{i+1}{}^i R^{i+1} n_{i+1} + {}^i P_{i+1} \times {}^i f_i
\end{cases}
\tag{1}
$$

Using the above formula, the forearm F/T sensor data can be transferred sequentially to frame {0}. Finally, the required forces and torques for the upper limb can be obtained by the dot products of forces and torques acting on each frame with the z-axis vectors, which is summarized in (2).

$$
F = J_u^{-1} F_u + J_f^{-1} F_f
\tag{2}
$$

where $F = [f_{d1}, f_{d2}, f_{d3}, \tau_4, \tau_5, \tau_6, \tau_7]$. F_u and F_f represent the measured data exerted on the upper arm and forearm by F/T sensors, respectively. f_{di} (i = 1,2,3) are the translation forces in frame {i}, and τ_i (i = 4,5,6,7) are the torques of z-axis in frame {i}. Note that the ${}^7 f_{7x}$ and ${}^7 \tau_{7z}$ are set to zero during forearm force and torque transfer to eliminate the effects of forearm F/T sensor data on the upper limb.

Admittance Controller. Admittance control is referred to as an interaction scheme pro-posed by Hogan firstly [7] and has been widely applied in rehabilitation robots. More-over, admittance control establishes a second-order system relationship between the interaction force and motion and allows compliant motion of the exoskeleton. In this research, the forces calculated by (2) are as input, the output is joint velocities, and the control law is described in (3).

$$
Y(s) = \frac{V(s)}{F(s)} = \frac{1}{Ms + B}
\tag{3}
$$

where Y(s) is the transfer function of system, M is the inertia matrix and B represents the damping matrix.

Velocity Mapping. The velocity mapping block derives exoskeleton velocity from human velocity through the upper limb kinematics. The elbow joint velocity of the upper limb is directly mapped to the exoskeleton and others obtained by (3) are mapped to the endpoint velocity of the UR5 via (4).

$$
\begin{cases}
{}^{i+1}\omega_{i+1} = {}_i{}^{i+1}R \, {}^i\omega_i \\
{}^{i+1}v_{i+1} = {}_i{}^{i+1}R({}^i v_i + {}^i\omega_i \times {}^i P_{i+1})
\end{cases}
\tag{4}
$$

where $^{i+1}\omega_{i+1}$ is the angular velocities vector in frame $\{i+1\}$, $^{i+1}v_{i+1}$ is the linear velocities vector in frame $\{i+1\}$.

3   Experiments and Results

Two experiments were conducted to verify the performance of the UEArm-7 system: (i) experiment on testing the kinematic compatibility of the shoulder complex, and (ii) experiment on testing the interaction performance during training. Five healthy males (mean ages: 23.8 ± 1.3 years, height: 171.6 ± 6.0 cm, weight: 66.6 ± 6.0 kg, upper arm length: 30.5 ± 1.7 mm, forearm length: 31.1 ± 1.1 mm) participated in these two experiments and signed informed consent before the experiments. All the kinematic and force data in trials were collected at 120 Hz.

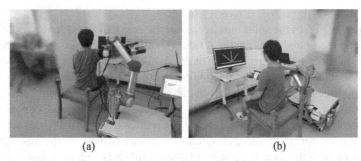

(a)   (b)

Fig. 4. Experimental scenes. (a) Experiment on testing the kinematic compatibility of the shoulder complex. (b) Experiment on testing the interaction performance during training.

3.1   Experiment on Kinematic Compatibility

To evaluate the kinematic compatibility of UEArm-7 in the shoulder complex, the residual forces applied to the shoulder complex were measured during upper limb abduction, which occurred simultaneously with the shoulder elevation. Firstly, participants sat on a chair while the upper limb was initially oriented straight down and roughly parallel to the sagittal plane. Then the upper limb was slowly abducted at approximately 100° (Fig. 4 (a)). The forces exerted to the shoulder joint were calculated through the upper arm F/T sensor and the forearm F/T sensor.

The experiment includes two conditions: (i) Shoulder free translation (SFT) condition, in which the shoulder girdle was free to move as the control scheme designed. (ii) Shoulder locked translation (SLT) condition, in which the movement of the shoulder girdle was locked by setting the translation forces f_{d1}, f_{d2} and f_{d3} to zero. In SFT condition, the desired translational inertia parameters were all set to 30 N·m^{-1}s^2 and the desired translational damping parameters were all set to 60 N·m^{-1}s. For each condition, 10 trials were conducted for each subject. The force signals are lowpass filtered at 5 Hz and then averaged for each case, respectively.

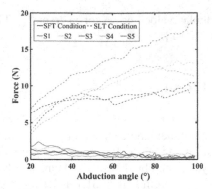

Fig. 5. Experiment results of kinematic compatibility testing. The solid and dotted lines represented residual forces exerted on the shoulder during upper limb abduction in the shoulder free translation and shoulder locked translation conditions, respectively.

As shown in Fig. 5, the solid lines represent the residual shoulder forces of the SFT condition, and the dotted lines are the residual shoulder forces of the SLT condition. In SFT condition, the residual forces acting on the shoulder complex remain very low, which verified the shoulder kinematic compatibility. In the SLT condition, the control scheme for fixing the translation DOFs of the shoulder complex causes a rising residual force due to the shoulder elevation. The comparison between SFT with SLT conditions show that the control of shoulder translation DOFs can reduce the residual forces acting on the shoulder complex during shoulder elevation movement. Moreover, the misalignment of the rotation centre of the shoulder complex between subjects with the robot also results in residual forces applied to the shoulder complex, as illustrated by the fact that the starting force in the SLT condition is greater than the starting force in the SFT condition. The release of the shoulder translation DOFs also automatically align the shoulder complex's rotation centre between subjects and the robot. Although the movements tested were limited, the experimental results demonstrated great shoulder kinematic compatibility of the proposed robot and showed that UEArm-7 has the potential to improve shoulder movement coordination and reduce the possibility of secondary injury to the shoulder complex.

3.2 Experiment on the Interaction Performance

To assess the interaction performance between UEArm-7 with subjects during impedance training, five linear tracking tasks were performed on a horizontal plane, as shown in Fig. 6. The length of each track is 0.3 m, and the angle difference between adjacent tasks is 45°. In this experiment, participants sat on a chair and firstly spent 5 min familiarizing the tasks. Then participates were asked to complete a linear reciprocal task within 5 s and follow the specified task as closely as possible with the feedback of the real-time human hand trajectory on the display. For each task, ten reciprocal trials were conducted, and the trial time (TT), tracking errors (TE), smoothness (SM), upper arm force (UAF), forearm force (FF), and shoulder force (SF) were recorded. The smoothness metric was adopted from [21], with larger values indicating greater smoothness. Besides, the desired inertia parameters from θ_4 to θ_7 were all set to 0.5 N·m·rad^{-1}·s^2 and the parameters from d_1 to d_3 were all set to 30 N·m^{-1}·s^2. The desired damping parameters from θ_4 to θ_7 were all 1.0 N·m·rad^{-1}·s and the parameters from d_1 to d_3 were all 60 N·m^{-1}·s.

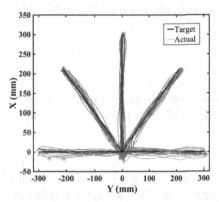

Fig. 6. Trajectories of a subject in the experiment of interaction performance testing. Black lines represent target trajectories; red lines are actual trajectories. (Color figure online)

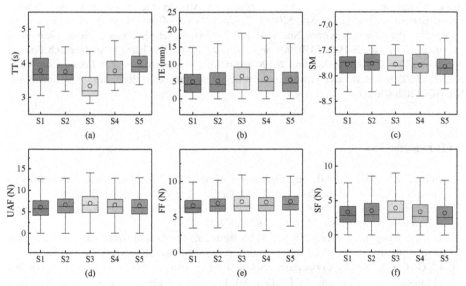

Fig. 7. Different performance metrics of all subjects in the experiment of interaction performance testing. (a)-(f) are performance of TT, TE, SM, UAF, FF and SF, respectively.

As summarized in Fig. 7, all subjects completed these trials within the specified time and performed a high level of kinematic performance (TE: average 5.6 mm, SM: average −7.9). Besides, the average values for UAF and FF are 6.6 N and 7.0 N, respectively, which contains the gravity of the human arm. The low value of the SF (average 3.6 N) presented a small force applied to the shoulder complex, indicating excellent shoulder kinematic compatibility. Experimental results showed that the UEArm-7 robot exhibited great compliance on the upper limb, especially in the shoulder complex. Moreover, the desired trajectory and impedance were realized with promising kinematic performance.

Overall, experimental results demonstrated satisfactory interaction performance between UEArm-7 with subjects and validated the effectiveness of the proposed structure and control scheme.

4 Conclusion

This study developed a semi-exoskeleton rehabilitation robot with seven DOFs for upper limb rehabilitation. The UEArm-7 robot with a simple mechanical design has the capacity of controlling the whole upper limb, including the shoulder complex. Moreover, the admittance control scheme allows the UEArm-7 robot to provide a natural and continuous impedance movement for subjects. Results show that the UEArm-7 robot can move the elbow joint and the shoulder complex of humans with physiologically accurate trajectories and low impedance. In future work, we will further investigate the effects of soft tissue deformation of human arms and take this issue into account in estimating the wearer's motion intention.

Acknowledgements. This work was supported in part by the National Natural Science Foundation of China (Grant No. 52075177), Joint Fund of the Ministry of Education for Equipment Pre-Research (Grant No. 6141A02033124), Research Foundation of Guangdong Province (Grant No. 2019A050505001 and 2018KZDXM002), Guangzhou Research Foundation (Grant No. 202002030324 and 201903010028), Zhongshan Research Foundation (Grant No.2020B2020), and Shenzhen Institute of Artificial Intelligence and Robotics for Society (Grant No. AC01202005011).

References

1. Burton, J.K., et al.: Predicting discharge to institutional long-term care after stroke: a systematic review and metaanalysis. J. Am. Geriatr. Soc. **66**, 161–169 (2018)
2. Veerbeek, J.M., et al.: What is the evidence for physical therapy poststroke? a systematic review and meta-analysis. PLoS One **9**(2), e87987 (2014)
3. Liu, L., Wang, D., Lawrence Wong, K.S., Wang, Y.: Stroke and stroke care in China huge burden, significant workload, and a national priority. Stroke **42**, 3651–3654 (2011)
4. Li, G., Cai, S., Xie, L.: Cooperative control of a dual-arm rehabilitation robot for upper limb physiotherapy and training. In: IEEE/ASME International Conference Advanced Intelligent Mechatronics, AIM. 2019-July, pp. 802–807 (2019)
5. Cai, S., et al.: SVM-based classification of sEMG signals for upper-limb self-rehabilitation training. Front. Neurorobot. **13**, 1–10 (2019)
6. Proietti, T., Crocher, V., Roby-Brami, A., Jarrasse, N.: Upper-limb robotic exoskeletons for neurorehabilitation: a review on control strategies. IEEE Rev. Biomed. Eng. **9**, 4–14 (2016)
7. Hogan, N.: Impedance control: an approach to manipulation: part I-theory. J. Dyn. Syst. Meas. Control. Trans. ASME. **107**, 1–7 (1985)
8. Keemink, A.Q.L., van der Kooij, H., Stienen, A.H.A.: Admittance control for physical human–robot interaction. Int. J. Rob. Res. **37**, 1421–1444 (2018)

9. Culmer, P.R., et al.: A control strategy for upper limb robotic rehabilitation with a dual robot system. IEEE/ASME Trans. Mech. **15**, 575–585 (2010)
10. Miller, L.M., Rosen, J.: Comparison of multi-sensor admittance control in joint space and task space for a seven degree of freedom upper limb exoskeleton. In: 2010 3rd IEEE RAS EMBS International Conference Biomedical Robot. Biomechatronics, BioRob 2010, pp. 70–75 (2010)
11. Huang, J., Huo, W., Xu, W., Mohammed, S., Amirat, Y.: Control of upper-limb power-assist exoskeleton using a human-robot interface based on motion intention recognition. IEEE Trans. Autom. Sci. Eng. **12**, 1257–1270 (2015)
12. Loureiro, R., Amirabdollahian, F., Topping, M., Driessen, B., Harwin, W.: Upper limb robot mediated stroke therapy - GENTLE/s approach. Auton. Robots. **15**, 35–51 (2003)
13. Zhang, L., Guo, S., Sun, Q.: Development and assist-as-needed control of an end-effector upper limb rehabilitation robot. Appl. Sci. 10(19), 6684 (2020)
14. Perry, J.C., Rosen, J.: Design of a 7 degree-of-freedom upper-limb powered exoskeleton. In: Proceedings of First IEEE/RAS-EMBS International Conference Biomedical Robotics Biomechatronics, 2006, BioRob 2006, pp. 805–810 (2006)
15. Gunasekara, M., Gopura, R., Jayawardena, S.: 6-REXOS: upper limb exoskeleton robot with improved pHRI. Int. J. Adv. Robot. Syst. **12**(4), 47 (2015)
16. Dromerick, A.W., Edwards, D.F., Kumar, A.: Hemiplegic shoulder pain syndrome: frequency and characteristics during inpatient stroke rehabilitation. Arch. Phys. Med. Rehabil. **89**, 1589–1593 (2008)
17. Axes, S.E., Decoupling, T.: Short papers of joint rotations and translations. IEEE Trans. Robot. **25**, 628–633 (2009)
18. Taal, S.R., Sankai, Y.: Exoskeletal spine and shoulder girdle for full body exoskeletons with human versatility. In: Proceedings - IEEE International Conference Robotics Automation, pp. 2217–2222 (2011)
19. Park, H.S., Ren, Y., Zhang, L.Q.: IntelliArm: An exoskeleton for diagnosis and treatment of patients with neurological impairments. In: Proceedings 2nd Bienn. IEEE/RAS-EMBS International Conference on Biomedical RoboticsBiomechatronics, BioRob 2008, pp. 109–114 (2008)
20. Ball, S.J., Brown, I.E., Scott, S.H.: MEDARM: A rehabilitation robot with 5DOF at the shoulder complex. In: IEEE/ASME International Conference on Advanced intelligent Mechatronics, AIM (2007)
21. Balasubramanian, S., Melendez-Calderon, A., Roby-Brami, A., Burdet, E.: On the analysis of movement smoothness. J. Neuroeng. Rehabil. **12**(1), 1–11 (2015)

A Novel Center of Mass (CoM) Perception Approach for Lower-Limbs Stroke Rehabilitation

Youwei Liu[1], Biao Liu[1], Zikang Zhou[1], Siqi Cai[2(✉)], and Longhan Xie[1(✉)]

[1] Shien-Ming Wu School of Intelligent Engineering, South China University of Technology, Guangzhou, Guangdong, China
melhxie@scut.edu.cn
[2] Department of Electrical and Computer Engineering, National University of Singapore, Singapore, Singapore
elesiqi@nus.edu.sg

Abstract. Lower limb rehabilitation robots are of great significance for poststroke patients to regain locomotion ability. However, most rehabilitation robots fail to take the movement of CoM of human body into account. Considering that CoM is an essential index to assess the recovery effect and improve the treatment, we propose a simple, economic, portable, and highly efficient CoM perception approach based on Kinect camera. This novel method is capable of detecting the displacement and rotation of CoM in multi-planes. Results of walking tests show that our approach has competitive performance in capturing the variation trends of CoM compared with multi-cameras motion capture system, especially in some directions with large displacement variation. The high accuracy, simple and low-cost detection of CoM is a major step forward towards practical application in the assessment of rehabilitation after stroke.

Keywords: Lower limb rehabilitation · Kinect camera · CoM detecting

1 Introduction

Hemiplegia is a common sequela caused by the strokes, spinal cord injury or other unexpected damage, which results in locomotion dysfunction and decreases the quality of daily life. Proper physical rehabilitation is crucial and irreplaceable for poststroke survivors to regain the locomotion ability and improve community participation. To achieve this goal, it requires not only joints motion, but also the dynamic balance of the whole body, which relies on the CoM perception system and posture control mechanism in walking rehabilitation. Hence, how to accurately and conveniently measure the moving CoM in real-time is significant for the patients to recover dynamically walking gait [1].

Recently, lower-limb rehabilitation robots have shown their comprehensive applications and enormous potential in clinical practice and assisted patients with hemiplegia according to the plasticity theory of nerve that targeted, repetitive and appropriate-intensity of exercise in vintage period can induce the reconstruction of center nerves

© Springer Nature Switzerland AG 2021
H. Li et al. (Eds.): ICSR 2021, LNAI 13086, pp. 606–615, 2021.
https://doi.org/10.1007/978-3-030-90525-5_53

system and then contribute to the rehabilitation process [2]. Training with body weight support system (BWSS) is one of the most effective and common strategies in lower limb rehabilitation by which partial weight of the patient is unloaded so that some abilities and characteristics are optimized, such as the improvement of walking ability [3], decrease of energy consumption [4], increasing degree of muscle activation [3, 5, 6], and promotion of nervous system [2]. Moreover, BWSS can help patients keep a dynamic balance and avoid falling, which are key indices in rehabilitation. Balance maintaining involves position control of CoM in lateral and vertical direction. Usually, CoM is a key index in posture control and walking stability. Therefore, the prerequisites of achieving a favorable-performance BWSS is perception to CoM. The detection of CoM is indispensable for controlling and assessing the post-stroke survivors' rehabilitation progress. Some studies [7, 8] have demonstrated that the CoM can be measured and monitored by motion capture systems, i.e., Vicon (Oxford Metrics, UK), according to the body segments displacement and posture. However, numerous camera lenses and complex calibration manipulation cause extremely high costs and inconvenience in daily rehabilitation therapy [9]. Besides, Stefano C. et al. have developed a single inertial measurement unit (IMU) estimation system to measure the CoM displacement and rotation. IMU systems are simple, but suffer from object obstruction and need of careful installation [10]. In [11], a wearable hand exoskeleton used an RGB-D camera to capture the position of hand joints in real-time. In [12], a camera system was applied to track the 3D trajectory of body joints for posture classification and compensatory motion simulation. However, RGB cameras are susceptibly disturbed by ambient light and its application is limited in complex scenarios. In recent years, the Microsoft Kinect depth camera, which has advantages of low-cost, convenience, and reliability exerts great potential in clinical practice, such as skeleton joints detecting and posture tracking [13, 14]. However, previous studies only focus on limbs movement trajectories or awkward postures assessment and fail to consider the movement pattern of CoM.

Therefore, we developed a novel efficient algorithm to detect the variation of CoM while walking based on a non-contact visual sensor (Kinect), which makes it particularly suitable for portable rehabilitation settings. The proposed Kinect-based CoM perception approach tracks the main segments of the human body and gets 3D position data firstly. The CoM is then calculated according to statistical ratios and corresponding algorithms. Experiments are carried out to validate the Kinect-based system against the Vicon system to detect the CoM. Results indicate that the proposed method could achieve approbative performance compared with Vicon and imply a bright application in recovery diagnoses and assessment of post-stroke survivor's rehabilitation.

2 Methodology

The pattern of CoM movement is closely related to the personalized body parameters and habitual gaits started from they were toddle. In addition, this certain pattern also keeps unchanging in a period of time. Hence, it is indispensable to accurately assess the movement of CoM and take advantage of the motion pattern for improving the locomotion ability of stroke survivors.

2.1 Principle of Depth Camera Imaging

In this study, the main sensor of CoM perception system is Azure Kinect (Microsoft, USA), which integrates a depth camera and an RGB camera. The Kinect depth camera adopts active infrared to sensor the distance between target objects and the camera. This can effectively remove the external interference and improve the robustness of system. When working, it can form a large field of view with a 120° view angle[1] in front of the camera in both vertical direction and horizontal direction, as shown in Fig. 1. Azure Kinect has the reference frame of itself. The camera is usually placed at a distance of 1.5 m away from the human body and a 1.5 m height to get accurate measuring results and a large view field.

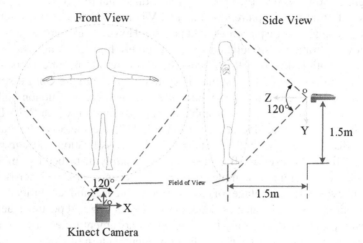

Fig. 1. The Kinect camera to capture COM of human. The target user is in field of the camera. The distance (depth) of all segments of body can be detected by the infrared sensor module.

2.2 Kinect Body Tracking

The Azure Kinect Body Tracking SDK provides real-time body tracking using human pose estimation techniques [15]. A trained convolution neural network (CNN) extracts the 2D positions of the joints on the infrared image. Then, the 2D positions are mapped to the 3D space according to the depth information measured by the depth camera. Using Azure Kinect, we can measure the 3D positions of the centers of joints (Fig. 2) at a speed of 30 frames per second.

---

[1] When the depth camera is set to wide field-of-view depth mode.

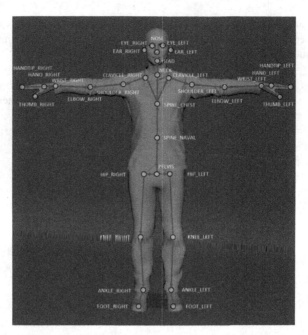

Fig. 2. Distribution of 3D positions of joints centers on the human body.

2.3 CoM Calculating

The human body can be simplified as a rigid body system composed of the following segments, head, neck, chest, upper arm, lower arm, hand, thigh, calf, and foot. Base on the inertia parameters (Table 1) provided by the determined model [12] and the segment position measured by the Kinect, we can determine the mass and CoM of each segment separately, and then we are able to calculate the CoM of the whole body by synthesizing the moments.

The mass M_i of the i-th segment can be obtained as follow:

$$M_i = \mathbf{r}_i * \mathbf{BM} \tag{1}$$

where $\mathbf{r}_i$ is the ratio of the mass of the segment to the mass of the whole body (**BM**, Table 1).

The position coordinate of CoM of the i-th segment is calculated according to the position parameter from Table 2. The coordinate system is default set by the Kinect system.

$$P_i = P_u^i + l_i * \left(P_u^i - P_l^i \right) \tag{2}$$

where l_i is the position parameter of the i-th segment, P_u^i and P_l^i are the upper end and lower end of the i-th segment which can be measured by the Kinect camera. The upper end and lower end of the segments are shown in Table 2.

Table 1. Ratios of the mass of the segments relative to the whole-body mass (**BM**) and CoM Position Parameters of the segments (relative length from the CoM of the segment to the upper origin of the segment) [16].

Segment	Index (i)	Ratio to body mass		CoM position parameters	
		Male	Female	Male	Female
Head	1	0.044	0.037	0.63	0.63
Neck	2	0.033	0.026	0.50	0.50
Chest	3	0.479	0.487	0.52	0.52
Upper arm (One side)	4	0.026	0.025	0.46	0.46
Fore arm (One side)	5	0.015	0.013	0.41	0.42
Hand (One side)	6	0.009	0.006	0.50	0.50
Thigh (One side)	7	0.1	0.111	0.42	0.42
Calf (One side)	8	0.053	0.053	0.41	0.42
Foot (One side)	9	0.019	0.015	0.50	0.50

Table 2. The body index of the upper end and lower end of the segments in the Kinect body tracking system.

Segment	Index (i)	Upper end	Lower end
Head	1	TOF	HEAD
Neck	2	HEAD	NECK
Chest	3	NECK	PELVIS
Upper arm	4	SHOULDER_RIGHT SHOULDER_LEFT	ELBOW_RIGHT ELBOW_LEFT
Fore arm	5	ELBOW_RIGHT ELBOW_LEFT	WRIST_RIGHT WRIST_LEFT
Hand	6	WRIST_RIGHT WRIST_LEFT	HAND_RIGHT HAND_LEFT
Thigh	7	HIP_RIGHT HIP_LEFT	KNEE_RIGHT KNEE_LEFT
Calf	8	KNEE_RIGHT KNEE_LEFT	ANKLE_RIGHT ANKLE_LEFT
Foot	9	ANKLE_RIGHT ANKLE_LEFT	FOOT_RIGHT FOOT_LEFT

Finally, the CoM of the whole body is calculated by:

$$CoM_{body} = \frac{\sum_i^n W_i P_i}{\sum_i^n W_i} = \frac{\sum_i^n W_i P_i}{BM} = \sum_i^n r_i P_i \tag{3}$$

where n is the number of segments of the body model and n is according to previous study [16].

TOF is a virtual point we defined since the upper end of Head segment is not applicable in the Kinect Body Tracking SDK. TOF is defined by: $TOF = 2(NOSE - HEAD) + HEAD$. In this way, the CoM of Head segment would approximately be $TOF + l_0 * (TOF - NOSE)$ where l_0 is the CoM position parameter of the Head segment.

3 Experiments

We build up a scene to verify the feasibility of Kinect-based CoM perception approach. In addition, we compared the reliability of our method with an eleven-camera motion capture system (VICON, Oxford Metrics, UK; 250 Hz). The VICON system was chosen as the gold standard motion analysis system (accuracy lower than 0.01 mm).

3.1 Experimental Setup

As shown in Fig. 3, the perception system is mainly comprised of Kinect depth camera which is placed in front of the treadmill. The subject walk on the treadmill at different speed in both Kinect and VICON motion capture system view field.

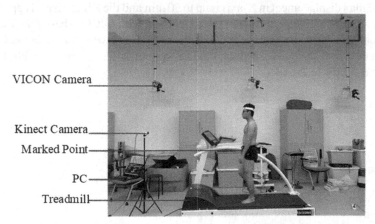

Fig. 3. The photograph of the setup of experiments. The tester was attached marked points in the field of both the VICON and Kinect.

3.2 Experiments

A healthy male participant (65 kg, 167 cm) without a history of neurological or mobility impairments participated in the experiments. The participant provided informed consent, and the procedures were approved by the South China University of Technology Research Ethics Board (SCUTREB).

To avoid the disturb on the VICON motion capture system, the tester was upper-body-naked and attached a series of marked points. It is worth noting that our Kinect-based approach doesn't have any marked point and is capable of recognizing the human body by an internal algorithm. As illustrated in Fig. 3, the Kinect camera is placed in front of a treadmill at the height of 1.5 m. The tester walked at speeds of 0.2 m/s, 0.4 m/s, 0.6 m/s, 0.8 m/s, and 1.0 m/s, respectively. Every walking speed lasted for 1 min. We also measured the variation of CoM when the tester performed repeated squats, as shown in Fig. 5.

4 Results and Discussion

The movement data is recorded by VICON motion capture system and Azure Kinect throughout the experiments. Due to different sample frequency (VICON: 250 Hz, Kinect: 30 Hz), the data from VICON is resampled firstly. And these results are then summarized as Figs. 4, 5, 6 and 7. Specifically, the displacement variation of CoM in the X-axis, Z-axis and the rotation angle around the Kinect Y-axis at the speed of 0.4 m/s are analyzed, respectively.

In general, both Kinect-based and VICON-based methods have captured the movements of CoM and demonstrated consistent trends in terms of displacement in X-axis, Y-axis and Z -axis, as well as rotation displacement in Y-axis. As shown in Fig. 4 and Fig. 5, the max displacement in X-axis is up to 50 mm and the Kinect-based approach has achieved approximative performance in comparison with VICON-based measurement. It is encouraging that the average relative error (ARE) between our proposed Kinect-based method and the gold standard VICON system is less than 6%, with 4.03% in X-axis and 5.31% in Z-axis.

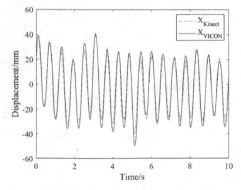

Fig. 4. Displacement of CoM in X-axis (left-right direction) at speed of 0.4 m/s.

In addition, we compared the performance of these two approaches in squat exercise, as illustrated Fig. 6. For the displacement of CoM in Y-axis, the measurements from the Kinect and VICON were highly correlated with an average ARE of 3.00%.

Generally, the body rotation motion while walking represents dynamic balance control ability and metabolic saving level. Therefore, we also analyze the trunk rotation angles captured by Kinect-based and VICON-based methods, as shown in Fig. 7. The results of Kinect-based approach suffer a little distortion around the peak values due to its much lower sampling frequency, yet with small discrepancies compared to the VICON system. These results verify that our proposed approach is efficient and feasible in capturing CoM variation.

Based on walking test results, we found that the variation of CoM is period related to the waking pattern. The proposed algorithms can measure and calculate the CoM trajectories in 3D space. And it has competitive performance compared to VICON-based method when the displacement varies in the range of 40 mm. Meanwhile, the proposed monocular Kinect-based method has more edges over the multi-camera system VICON in economy, usability, application scenes, and so on.

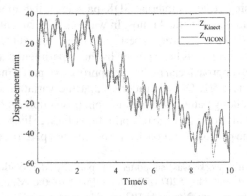

Fig. 5. Displacement variation of CoM in Z-axis (front-back direction) at speed of 0.4 m/s.

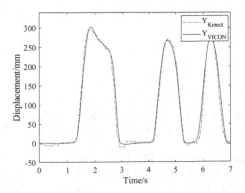

Fig. 6. Displacement of CoM in Y-axis (up-down direction) with squatting motion.

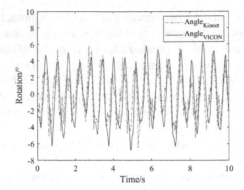

Fig. 7. Rotation displacement of CoM in Y-axis (up-down direction) at speed of 0.4 m/s.

5   Conclusion

This paper presented a novel CoM perception approach for lower limb rehabilitation based on Kinect. Using Kinect's internal SDK packages, the approach calculates the CoM position according to statistical ratios. In walking experiments, this approach can capture the trends of CoM. Moreover, its performance in some directions that have large displacement variation scope has been proved by the experiment data. Overall, this low-cost and easy-to-setup approach can realize an approbative performance compared with the multi-camera system VICON. Considering that the variation of CoM is a crucial index to assess the walking pattern in rehabilitation, this simple and economic approach has promising potential to optimize the rehabilitation of lower limbs for stroke survivors. We will further test the proposed approach on more motion patterns and multiple speeds.

Acknowledgement. This work was supported in part by the National Natural Science Foundation of China (Grant No. 52075177), Joint Fund of the Ministry of Education for Equipment Pre-Research (Grant No. 6141A02033124), Research Foundation of Guangdong Province (Grant No. 2019A050505001 and 2018KZDXM002), Guangzhou Research Foundation (Grant No. 202002030324 and 201903010028), Zhongshan Research Foundation (Grant No.2020B2020), and Shenzhen Institute of Artificial Intelligence and Robotics for Society (Grant No. AC01202005011).

References

1. Detrembleur, C., van den Hecke, A., Dierick, F.: Motion of the body centre of gravity as a summary indicator of the mechanics of human pathological gait. Gait Posture **12**, 243–250 (2000)
2. Forrester, L.W., Wheaton, L.A., Luft, A.R.: Exercise-mediated locomotor recovery and lower-limb neuroplasticity after stroke. J. Rehab. Res. Dev. **45**(2), 205–220 (2008)
3. Lin, J., Hu, G., Ran, J., Chen, L., Zhang, X., Zhang, Y.: Effects of bodyweight sup-port and guidance force on muscle activation during Locomat walking in people with stroke: a cross-sectional study. J. Neuroeng. Rehabil. **17**, 1–9 (2020)

4. Sherman, M.F.B., Lam, T., Sheel, A.W.: Locomotor–respiratory synchronization after body weight supported treadmill training in incomplete tetraplegia: a case report. Spinal Cord **47**, 896–898 (2009)
5. Burnfield, J.M., Buster, T.W., Goldman, A.J., Corbridge, L.M., Harper-Hanigan, K.: Partial body weight support treadmill training speed influences paretic and non-paretic leg muscle activation, stride characteristics, and ratings of perceived exertion during acute stroke rehabilitation. Hum. Mov. Sci. **47**, 16–28 (2016)
6. van Kammen, K., et al.: The combined effects of guidance force, bodyweight support and gait speed on muscle activity during able-bodied walking in the Lokomat. Clin. Biomech. **36**, 65–73 (2016)
7. Jeong, B., Ko, C.-Y., Chang, Y., Ryu, J., Kim, G.: Comparison of segmental analysis and sacral marker methods for determining the center of mass during level and slope walking. Gait Posture **62**, 333–341 (2018)
8. Eng, J.J., Winter, D.A.: Estimations of the horizontal displacement of the total body centre of mass: considerations during standing activities. Gait Posture **1**, 141–144 (1993)
9. Windolf, M., Götzen, N., Morlock, M.: Systematic accuracy and precision analysis of video motion capturing systems—exemplified on the Vicon-460 system. J. Biomech. **41**, 2776–2780 (2008)
10. Cardarelli, S., et al.: Single IMU displacement and orientation estimation of human center of mass: a magnetometer-free approach. IEEE Trans. Instrum. Meas. (2019). https://doi.org/10.1109/tim.2019.2962295
11. Airò Farulla, G., et al.: Vision-based pose estimation for robot-mediated hand telerehabilitation. Sensors **16**, 208 (2016)
12. Zhi, Y.X., Lukasik, M., Li, M.H., Dolatabadi, E., Wang, R.H., Taati, B.: Automatic detection of compensation during robotic stroke rehabilitation therapy. IEEE J. Trans. Eng. Health Med. **6**, 1–7 (2017)
13. Niu, J., Wang, X., Wang, D., Ran, L.: A novel method of human joint prediction in an occlusion scene by using low-cost motion capture technique. Sensors **20**, 1119 (2020)
14. Manghisi, V.M., Uva, A.E., Fiorentino, M., Bevilacqua, V., Trotta, G.F., Monno, G.: Real time RULA assessment using Kinect v2 sensor. Appl. Ergon. **65**, 481–491 (2017)
15. Cao, Z., Hidalgo, G., Simon, T., Wei, S.-E., Sheikh, Y.: OpenPose: realtime multi-person 2D pose estimation using part affinity fields. IEEE Trans. Pattern Anal. Mach. Intell. **43**, 172–186 (2019)
16. Shaokun, S.: Detection Method and Equipment Implementation for Human Body Center of Gravity. Master (2015)

Increasing Torso Contact: Comparing Human-Human Relationships and Situations

Yuya Onishi[✉], Hidenobu Sumioka, and Masahiro Shiomi

Advanced Telecommunications Research Institute International, Kyoto 619-0288, Japan
y-onishi@atr.jp

Abstract. Since building relationships between humans and robots continue to increase, the importance of touch interactions between humans and social robots is also growing. However, due to such limitations such as robot performance, most of these robots perform touch interaction with specific motions. In human-human touch interaction, the touch method reflects relationships and situations. This study investigates how touch interactions reflect relationships and situations with others to obtain the design guidelines for touch interactions for social robots. We experimentally investigated how participants performed touch interactions with a mannequin. Our participants performed touch interactions in three specific situations (consoling/forgiving/sharing happiness) with a partner of a three specific intimacy (intimate/acquaintance/ stranger). We analyzed their touch behaviors. When the relationship was intimate, many participants touched the mannequin's torsos in every situation. This touch motion decreased as the intimacy level with others reduced, and a touching motion with both hands or just one increased.

Keywords: Human-robot touch interaction · Human-human touch interaction · Social touch

1 Introduction

Using social robots that must build relationships with humans and robots is increasing. Such social robots must perform touch interactions. Social robots interact with humans by shaking hands at museums [1, 2], elementary schools [3, 4], and shopping malls [5, 6]. Such touching is a key factor for friendly interactions and for positively affecting the person being touched because previous studies in human-human interaction identified various merits from touch interactions [7–12]. Previous work investigated the merits of human-robot touch interaction from the following viewpoints: mental health support [13], motivation management [14], stress buffering effects [15], and promoting prosocial behavior [16]. However, due to touch limitations as robot performance, most of these robots performed touch interaction base on specific motions. In human-human touch interaction, since the contact method and contact site depend on the relationships and the situations with others, this study investigates how touch interactions depend on the relationships and situations with others to obtain design guidelines for social robots.

© Springer Nature Switzerland AG 2021
H. Li et al. (Eds.): ICSR 2021, LNAI 13086, pp. 616–625, 2021.
https://doi.org/10.1007/978-3-030-90525-5_54

In our experiment, we investigated how participants performed touch interactions with a mannequin. They performed touch interactions in specific situations (consoling/forgiving/sharing happiness) with a partner of a specific level of intimacy (intimate/acquaintance/stranger), and we analyzed their touch behavior.

2 Related Work

For the design of social robots that engaged in touch interaction, previous studies were fueled by human-human touch interaction in ethology, psychology, and the social sciences [17]. Such research revealed how touch interactions are used between people [18–20]. For example, touching the hand of another person is acceptable regardless of their relationship [21], and people touched hand/forearm to express happiness and the hand/shoulder to express sadness [22]. In addition, when communicating intimate emotions, people tend to prefer touch interactions over other modalities [23].

Previous studies investigated how people touch robots. Touching gestures were categorized when people communicate with nine specific emotions with an animal robot [24], and eight emotions with a small humanoid robot (NAO) [25]. As human-like robots, typical touch gestures were categorized when conveying positive feelings of love and devotion to the mannequins [26, 27].

3 Experiment

We investigated how people performed touch interactions depending on their relationship with another and their situation. If the participants touched other participants, the touch motion might be biased by their previous relationships. Therefore, in our experiment, we controlled the appearance of the people and any relationships influence by having the participants touch a mannequin as a partner. The experiment was conducted in a 2-m square space in which the mannequin sat in the center. The participants stood in front of the mannequin while they waited for instructions, and when they touched it, they were free to move around in the experiment space, for example, behind the mannequin.

3.1 Proceedings

The experiment was conducted in two parts. In the first, the participants practiced touching the mannequin. We instructed them to touch it by chest stroking, chest tapping, hugging, shoulder stroking, and shoulder tapping motions. In the second, we explained their relationship and the situation with the mannequin (Fig. 1). Since we gave no instructions about the touching behavior, the participants could freely touch it. We instructed them to touch it for about ten seconds per tasks.

We explained to the participants the level of intimacy with their mannequin-partner and their specific situations. Since social robots in museums and shopping malls functions as guides, the humans and robots are most likely meeting for the first time. On the other hand, in social robots for mental care, humans and robots are more likely to be together more often. Therefore, their relationship is situational. In the experiment, we distinguished the relationships between the participants and their mannequin-partners as "intimate," "acquaintance," or "stranger." An intimate partner is denoted by a family member, a best friend or a significant other. An acquaintance partner is a colleague or a classmate. A stranger is a completely unknown person.

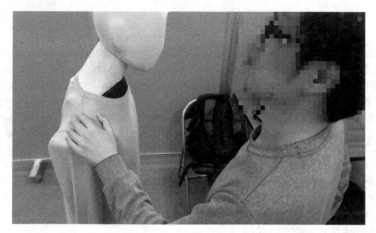

Fig. 1. Experiment snapshot.

Touch interactions also depend on the partner's emotion. Past studies investigated the positive effects of a robot's emotional expressions, including facial expressions, body gestures, and/or speech [28–33]. In this context, showing positive emotions is one basic interaction strategy. For example, expressing happiness builds relationships with humans [34, 35], and sad feelings are typically used as negative emotions by social robots [31, 33]. In this experiment, we focused on just two (happiness and sadness) instead of all six of Ekman's basic emotions because they are the most typical emotions used in designing the touch methods for social robots. Since the scenarios that use the remaining four Ekman's emotions are situational and less frequent in the context of the current social robots, anger is less common than sadness. Therefore, we set the participant situations of "sharing happiness" as an expression of happiness and separated the situations with sad emotions into "consoling" and "forgiving." According to Hwang's concept of other-esteem [36], forgiveness ameliorates our own unpleasant feelings in sad emotions. On the other hand, consoling improves the unpleasant feelings of the others. Therefore, in the experiment, we distinguished the partner's situation as "sharing happiness," "consoling" or "forgiving."

Participants touched the mannequin for about ten seconds based on each of these tasks. The mannequin had no conversational function, and participants touched it by imagining specific relationships and situations. The total experiment time was about five minutes, the first part was about two minutes, and the second part lasted about three minutes.

3.2 Participants

Twenty-two undergraduates (eleven males and eleven females) participated in the experiment.

3.3 Analysis

We based our analysis of how the participants touched the mannequins on recorded video. Most of the designs for touching with social robots used a one-handed or both-handed touch, such as tapping or stroking. It is difficult to compare these touch methods with the partner's relationships in this experiment. For example, if the relationship with the partner is "intimate," much of the body (especially the torso), such as a hug, might touch the partner. When we create social robots, tapping and stroking operations can be designed based on features already possessed by conventional robots. However, when developing a new social robot, we must consider which part of the social robot should be touched. Therefore, we investigated which part of the participants touched the mannequin and classified them as "no touch," "one hand," "both hands," and "torso." When a participant touched the mannequin many times or in different areas, we counted the larger contact area of the touch. For example, if a participant touched with one hand and both hands over ten seconds, we counted it as both hands.

3.4 Results

Our experimental results are shown in Tables 1, 2, and 3. The most common methods used by the participants to touch the mannequin in each situation and relationship are shown in bold.

Table 1 shows the result of the "consoling" situation. We conducted a Chi-square test, and the results revealed significant differences among the conditions ($\chi^2(6) = 72.327$, $p < .01$, $\varphi = 0.536$). A residual analysis revealed that touching "both hands" ($p < .05$) and the "torso" ($p < .05$) was significantly more common than the other touching methods when the relationship was "intimate." Touching with "one hand" ($p < .01$) was significantly more common than the other touching methods when the relationship was "acquaintance." In addition, touching with "one hand" ($p < .01$) was preferred to the other touching methods when the relationship was "stranger."

Table 2 shows the "sharing happiness" situation. We conducted a Chi-square test, and the results revealed significant differences among the conditions ($\chi^2(6) = 60.036$, $p < .01$, $\varphi = 0.500$). A residual analysis revealed that touching "both hands" ($p < .05$) and the "torso" ($p < .01$) was significantly more common than the other touching methods when the relationship was "intimate." Touching with "one hand" ($p < .01$) was significantly more common than the other touching methods when the relationship was "acquaintance." In addition, touching with "one hand" ($p < .05$) was more common than the other touching methods when the relationship was "stranger."

Table 1. Results of "consoling" situation: Num indicates participants who touched mannequin, and AR indicates the adjusted residual.

	No touch		One hand		Both hands		Torso	
Relationship	Num	AR	Num	AR	Num	AR	Num	AR
Intimate	0	−4.083**	12	0.970	15	**1.863***	15	**1.812***
Acquaintance	0	−4.083**	37	**17.145****	5	−2.277*	0	4.228**
Stranger	7	−1.361	34	**15.204****	1	−3.933**	0	−4.228**

* $p < .05$, ** $p < .01$

Table 2. Results of "sharing happiness" situation: Num indicates participants who touched mannequin, and AR indicates the adjusted residual.

	No touch		One hand		Both hands		Torso	
Relationship	Num	AR	Num	AR	Num	AR	Num	AR
Intimate	0	−4.027**	5	−2.694**	15	**2.200***	20	**4.375****
Acquaintance	1	−3.624**	25	**8.082****	8	−0.880	6	−1.750**
Stranger	8	−0.805	28	**9.698****	4	−2.640**	0	−4.376**

* $p < .05$, ** $p < .01$

Table 3. Results of "forgiving" situation: Num indicates participants who touched with mannequin, and AR indicates the adjusted residual.

	No touch		One hand		Both hands		Torso	
Relationship	Num	AR	Num	AR	Num	AR	Num	AR
Intimate	0	−3.933**	**19**	**6.717****	5	−1.863+	14	**1.948***
Acquaintance	3	−2.691*	**30**	**14.496****	3	−2.691**	2	−3.248**
Stranger	6	−1.449	**29**	**13.788****	1	−3.520**	2	−3.248**

+$p < .10$ * $p < .05$, **$p < .01$.

Table 3 shows the result of the "forgiving" situation. We conducted a Chi-square test, and the results revealed significant differences among the conditions ($\chi^2(6) = 27.513$, $p < .01$, $\varphi = 0.347$). A residual analysis revealed that touching "one hand" ($p < .01$) and the "torso" ($p < .05$) was significantly more common than the other touching methods when the relationship was "intimate." Touching with "one hand" was significantly more common than the other touching methods when the relationship was "acquaintance." In addition, touching with "one hand" was preferred over the other touching methods when the relationship was "stranger".

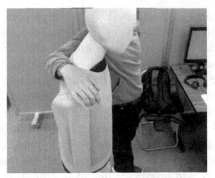

(a) Hugging and stroking
mannequin's back

(b) Wrapping an arm around
its shoulders

Fig. 2. Participant touched mannequin's "torso"

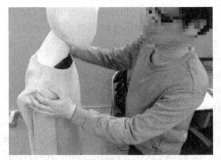

(a) Left hand grabbed shoulder
and the right hand touched it

(b) Grabbing both hands

Fig. 3. Participant touched mannequin with "both hands"

4 Discussion

4.1 Human-Human Touch Interaction

From our experimental results, in all the "consoling," "forgiving" and "sharing happiness" situations, touching the mannequin's torso scored higher when the relationship with the other person was "intimate." This torso-touching motion decreased as the relationship with the other person became less intimate, and the motion of touching with both hands and or just one increased. For the touch motion, the contact area increased in the order of no touch, one hand, both hands, and the torso. Therefore, the contact area of the touch motions depended on the relationship with the other person. Touches that involved contact with the torso included such motions as the participant hugging the mannequin from its front and standing next to the mannequin and wrapping an arm around its shoulders (Fig. 2). The proportion of hugging motions was high in the "consoling" and "forgiving" situations when the relationship with the other was "intimate" (15/15 and 11/14). According to a previous study [37], a hugged person feels more self-disclosure than a non-hugged person. In this previous experiment, the participants and the mannequin did not have a conversation, and the participants imagined a given situation and touched the mannequin. Perhaps the participants were encouraged to engage in self-disclosures by their "intimate" partners by giving hugs. On the other hand, even if the relationship was "acquaintance" or "stranger," encouraging self-disclosures from others is required in "consoling" and "forgiving" conditions. However, the touch's contact area decreased as the relationship with the other person became less intimate. Our future work will investigate the relationship between the contact area and the self-disclosure of others.

In addition, in "consoling" situations, touching the mannequin with both hands scored higher when the relationship with the other was "intimate." However, in "forgiving" situations, touching the mannequin with both hands scored lower when the relationship with the other was "intimate." Touching with both hands included placing both hands on their shoulders and stroking by one hand (Fig. 3). According to Hwang's concept of other-esteem [36], "forgiveness" improves one's own unpleasant feelings. On the other hand, "consoling" affects the unpleasant feelings of the other person. Therefore, in "comforting" situations, the participants probably tried to improve the partner's emotion and touched the torso or both hands.

In "sharing happiness" situations, when the relationship with the other person was "intimate" and "acquaintance," many participant's touching motions involved the torso and both hands. For touching that contacted the torso, we observed two touching patterns: hugging and wrapping an arm around the mannequin's shoulder (each motion was 3/6, 3/6). When the situation was "sharing happiness," the emotional target is different from the "consoling" situation (that ameliorates the sadness of a partner) or "forgiving" (addressing one's own sadness). We believe that these motions increased because the participants wanted to share their own feelings of happiness with their partner.

4.2   Robot-Human Touch Interaction

In this section, we consider the case where a robot touches a human. According to our results, the touch motions must be changed depending on the relationship between the touching robot and the human. As social robots continue to spread in the future, we must obtain design guidelines about what kind of touch robots are desirable for forging relationships between humans and robots. We explained to the participant that a family member, best friends, and significant others denote "intimate" relationships, and colleagues and classmates denote "acquaintance" relationships. For example, assuming a social robot as a daily partner, touching with a hugging motion will strengthen the "consoling," "forgiving" and "sharing happiness" effects. Assuming a counseling robot, effective touches include one hand at a first meeting with the robot and increasing the contact area for subsequent examinations. In addition, even when a person first meets a counseling robot, he will probably feel intimacy from the robot by hugging. Investigating the relationships between touching methods and relationships with partners is interesting future work.

In this research, we assumed that the robot touches a person, and we didn't set the robot's gender. Therefore, we did not analyze the participants by gender. However, since the number of gendered robots may increase in the future, analysis of the gen-der of participants and how it affects touching behaviors is future work.

5   Conclusion

We investigated how participants engage in touch interaction when their relationships change with a robot partner. They performed touch interactions in specific situations (consoling/sharing happiness/forgiving) with a partner of a specific level of intimacy (intimate/acquaintance/stranger), and we analyzed their touch behavior. When the rela-tionship between the participant and the partner was intimate, many participants touched the mannequin's torso in all the situations. This touch motion decreased as the relation-ship with other person became less intimate, and touching motions with both hands or just one increased. In addition, touching the torso included such motions as the partic-ipant hugging the mannequin from the front and standing next to the mannequin and wrapping an arm around its shoulders. We believe that these touch methods will help robots build intimate relationships with people.

Acknowledgements. This work was supported by JST CREST Grant Number JPMJCR18A1, Japan and by JSPS KAKENHI Grant Number JP20K23358.

References

1. Nourbakhsh, I.R., Kunz, C., Willeke, T.: The mobot museum robot installations: a five-year experiment. In: Proceedings of IEEE/RSJ International Conference on Intelligent Robots and Systems. (IROS 2003), pp. 3636–3641 (2003)
2. Shiomi, M., Kanda, T., Ishiguro, H., Hagita, N.: Interactive humanoid robots for a science museum. IEEE Intell. Syst. **2**, 25–32 (2007)
3. Kanda, T., Sato, R., Saiwaki, N., Ishiguro, H.: A two-month field trial in an elementary school for long-term human-robot interaction. IEEE Trans. Robot. **23**(5), 962–971 (2007)
4. Shiomi, M., Kanda, T., Howley, I., Hayashi, K., Hagita, N.: Can a social robot stimulate science curiosity in classrooms? Int. J. Soc. Robot. **7**(5), 641–652 (2015)
5. Gross, H-M., et al.: Shopbot: progress in developing an interactive mobile shopping assistant for everyday use. In: IEEE International Conference on Systems, Man and Cybernetics (SMC 2008), pp. 3471–3478 (2008)
6. Satake, S., Hayashi, K., Nakatani, K., Kanda, T.: Field trial of an information-providing robot in a shopping mall. In: IEEE/RSJ International Conference on Intelligent Robots and Systems (IROS 2015), pp. 1832–1839 (2015)
7. Grewen, K.M., Anderson, B.J., Girdler, S.S., Light, K.C.: Warm partner contact is related to lower cardiovascular reactivity. Behav. Med. **29**(3), 123–130 (2003)
8. Cohen, S., Janicki-Deverts, D., Turner RBa and Doyle WJ,: Does hugging provide stress-buffering social support? a study of susceptibility to upper respiratory infection and illness. Psychol. Sci. **26**(2), 135–147 (2015)
9. Jakubiak, B.K., Feeney, B.C.: Keep in touch: the effects of imagined touch support on stress and exploration. J. Exp. Soc. Psychol. **65**, 59–67 (2016)

10. Gallace, A., Spence, C.: The science of interpersonal touch: an overview. Neurosci. Biobehav. Rev. **34**(2), 246–259 (2010)
11. Light, K.C., Grewen, K.M., Amico, J.A.: More frequent partner hugs and higher oxytocin levels are linked to lower blood pressure and heart rate in premenopausal women. Biol. Psychol. **69**(1), 5–21 (2005)
12. Field, T.: Touch for socioemotional and physical well-being: a review. Dev. Rev. **30**(4), 367–383 (2010)
13. Yu, R., et al.: Use of a therapeutic, socially assistive pet robot (PARO) in improving mood and stimulating social interaction and communication for people with dementia: study protocol for a randomized controlled trial. JMIR Res. Protoc. **4**(2), e4189 (2015)
14. Shiomi, M., Nakagawa, K., Shinozawa, K., Matsumura, R., Ishiguro, H., Hagita, N.: Does a robot's touch encourage human effort? Int. J. Soc. Robot. **9**, 5–15 (2016)
15. Sumioka, H., Nakae, A., Kanai, R., Ishiguro, H.: Huggable communication medium decreases cortisol levels. Sci. Rep. **3**, 3034 (2013)
16. Shiomi, M., Nakata, A., Kanbara, M., Hagita, N.: A hug from a robot encourages prosocial behavior. In: 26th IEEE International Symposium on Robot and Human Interactive Communication (RO-MAN), pp. 418–423 (2017)
17. Dautenhahn, K.: Socially intelligent robots: dimensions of human–robot interaction. Philos. Trans. R. Soc. B. Biol. Sci. **362**(1480), 679–704 (2007)
18. Fisher, J.D., Rytting, M., Heslin, R.: Hands touching hands: affective and evaluative effects of an interpersonal touch. Sociometry **39**(4), 416–421 (1976)
19. Deethardt, J.F., Hines, D.G.: Tactile communication and personality differences. J. Nonverbal Behav. **8**(2), 143–156 (1983)
20. Willis, F.N., Jr., Dodds, R.A.: Age, relationship, and touch initiation. J. Soc. Psychol. **138**(1), 115–123 (1998)
21. Suvilehto, J.T., Glerean, E., Dunbar, R.I.M., Hari, R., Nummenmaa, L.: Topography of social touching depends on emotional bonds between humans. Proc. Nat. Acad. Sci. **112**(45), 13811–13816 (2015)
22. Hertenstein, M.J., Keltner, D., App, B., Bullet, B.A., Jaskolka, A.R.: Touch communicates distinct emotions. Emotion **6**(3), 528–533 (2006)
23. App, B., McIntosh, D.N., Reed, C.L, Hertenstein, M.J.: Nonverbal channel use in communication of emotion: how may depend on why. Emotion **11**(3), 603–617 (2011)
24. Yohanan, S., MacLean, K.E.: The role of affective touch in human-robot interaction: human intent and expectations in touching the haptic creature. Int. J. Soc. Robot **4**(2), 163–180 (2012)
25. Andreasson, R., Alenljung, R., Billing, E., Lowe, R.: Affective touch in human-robot interaction: conveying emotion to the Nao robot. Int. J. Soc. Robot. **10**, 473–491 (2017)
26. Cooney, M.D., Nishio, S., Ishiguro, H.: Recognizing affection for a touch-based interaction with a humanoid robot. In: Paper Presented at the IEEE/RSJ International Conference on Intelligent Robots and Systems (IROS 2012), pp. 1420–1427 (2012)
27. Hertenstein, M.J., Holmes, R., McCullough, M., Keltner, D.: The communication of emotion via touch. Emotion **9**(4), 566–573 (2009)
28. Cameron, D., Millings, A., Fernando, S., Collins, E.C., Moore, R., Sharkey, A.: The effects of robot facial emotional expressions and gender on child-robot interaction in a field study. Connection Sci. **30**(4), 343–361 (2018)
29. Leite, I., Pereira, A., Mascarenhas, S., Martinho, C., Prada, R., Paiva, A.: The influence of empathy in human-robot relations. Int. J. Hum. Comput. Stud. **71**(3), 250–260 (2013)
30. Tielman, M., Neerincx, M., Meyer, J.J., Looije, R.: Adaptive emotional expression in robot-child interaction. In: Proceedings of the 2014 ACM/IEEE International Conference on Human-robot Interaction, pp. 407–414 (2014)
31. Rossi, S., Ferland, F., Tapus, A.: User profiling and behavioral adaptation for HRI: a survey. Pattern Recogn. Lett. **99**, 3–12 (2017)

32. Leite, I., Martinho, C., Paiva, A.: Social robots for long-term interaction: a survey. Int. J. Soc. Robot. **5**(2), 291–308 (2013). https://doi.org/10.1007/s12369-013-0178-y
33. Fong, T., Nourbakhsh, I., Dautenhahn, K.: A survey of socially interactive robots. Robot. Auton. Syst. **42**(3–4), 143–166 (2003)
34. Kanda, T., Sato, R., Saiwaki, N., Ishiguro, H.: A two-month field trial in an elementary school for long-term human-robot interaction. IEEE Trans. Rob. **23**(5), 962–971 (2007)
35. Kanda, T., Shiomi, M., Miyashita, Z., Ishiguro, H., Hagita, N.: A communication robot in a shopping mall. Robot. IEEE Trans. **26**(5), 897–913 (2010)
36. Hwang, P.O.: Other esteem: Meaningful Life in Multicultural Society, Philadelphia: Accelerated Dvelopment (2013)
37. Shiomi, M., Nakata, A., Kanbara, M., Hagita, N.: A robot that encourages self-disclosure by hug. In: 9th International Conference on Social Robotics (ICSR2017), pp. 324–333 (2017)

Children-Robot Interaction

User Requirements for Developing Robot-Assisted Interventions for Autistic Children

Bob R. Schadenberg[1]([✉])(iD), Dennis Reidsma[1](iD), Dirk K. J. Heylen[1](iD),
and Vanessa Evers[1,2](iD)

[1] University of Twente, Enschede, The Netherlands
{b.r.schadenberg,d.reidsma,d.k.j.heylen,v.evers}@utwente.nl
[2] Nanyang Technological University, Singapore, Singapore

Abstract. Various benefits are being envisioned for enhancing autism interventions with a robot. But what features should such interventions have if they are to be successful? While there are quite a few papers that describe specific user requirements or needs, a more comprehensive account thereof should help to inform the development of such interventions. We therefore present a literature review on the user requirements for robot-assisted interventions. We report on various themes that emerged from our analysis and discuss how enhancing an intervention with a robot might fulfil those requirements.

Keywords: Autism spectrum condition · Robot-assisted interventions · User requirements · Literature review

1 Introduction

The use of social robots as tools that engage autistic children in learning can provide a novel way to enhance interventions aimed at teaching certain social skills. Autism spectrum condition (hereafter referred to as "autism") is a neurodevelopmental condition that is characterised by difficulties in social communication and interaction and by restricted, repetitive behaviour and interests [3]. Generally speaking, incorporating a robot in an intervention for autistic children[1] appears to have a positive effect on the child's engagement and attention to the learning task [27,33]. This could ultimately improve their learning gains. The addition of a robot to an intervention may also have benefits for those working with the autistic children. Parents of autistic children might be faced with challenges that can prevent them from accessing care for their autistic child, such as high costs of interventions, limited availability of providers, or geographic isolation [37]. These issues could be addressed by providing on-demand learning

---

[1] We use identity-first language, rather than person-first language, because it is less associated with stigma [12], and autistic adults prefer the use of disability-first terms, rather than person-first terms because they feel that being autistic is central to their identity [19].

© Springer Nature Switzerland AG 2021
H. Li et al. (Eds.): ICSR 2021, LNAI 13086, pp. 629–639, 2021.
https://doi.org/10.1007/978-3-030-90525-5_55

for autistic children through a robot-assisted intervention that is designed for at-home use by an autism professional. A robot could also alleviate the workload of autism professionals by providing an extra hand in an intervention [17].

As shown above, various benefits are anticipated for enhancing autism interventions with a robot. To realise these benefits, it is critical that we understand what features or attributes a robot should have, or how it should perform, from the users' perspective (i.e. user requirements). While there are several papers that report a couple of user requirements, a more comprehensive account thereof should help to inform the development of robot-assisted interventions for autistic children and the robots used in such interventions. Therefore, we present a literature review on the user requirements for robot-assisted interventions. The users we considered are the autistic children themselves, their parents, and the educators and occupational therapists who work with the children[2]. From our analysis of the literature, various themes emerged. We discuss how each theme could be achieved through design of the robot-assisted intervention.

2 Methods

The databases we accessed to conduct the systematic literature review include Scopus, Web of Science, and Google Scholar. In September 2020, we carried out an electronic search using the following keywords: *autism/autistic/ASD/ASC* AND *robots* AND *requirements* OR *needs*. This resulted in 44 papers for the keywords plus requirements and 221 for the keywords plus needs. We included needs as a keyword, because we can derive requirements from these needs. The selection of publications was based on five eligibility criteria:

1. The publication should present a study involving autistic children, their parents, or autism professionals, or discuss user requirements related to robots.
2. The study assesses user needs or requirements.
3. The user needs and requirements should relate to robot-assisted interventions for autistic children.
4. The publication should be written in English.
5. Only full papers and articles are included in the analysis—extended abstracts were omitted because these often contained preliminary findings.

All titles and abstracts were screened on the eligibility criteria by one author. To analyse the selected publications, we adopted a grounded theory approach [36]. We first read and highlighted any findings and insights in the publications that were relevant to our research question. Through open coding, we then generated higher-level abstraction level type themes from these findings and insights. The final set of user requirement themes were then decided on through axial and selective coding.

---

[2] In the remainder of this paper, we will refer to the adult users as "autism experts", when addressing the whole group.

To keep this paper specific to the context of robots being used in autism interventions, we excluded generic user requirements, such as that the robots they are working with should be safe to use and cause neither physical nor mental harm (clearly the most critical requirement), or that the user interface should be easy to use.

3 User Requirements and Discussion Thereof

The following papers and articles matched the selection criteria: [1,8,13,16,18, 20,22,24–26,38]. We excluded Robins et al. [26], as the results reported in this paper are also reported, and expanded upon, in [25]. Next to discussing the themes that emerged from our analysis, we will also discuss how the user requirements could be addressed by drawing upon the broader literature in the field of Human-Robot Interaction. We thus cite more papers than those listed above. The following themes emerged from our analysis:

3.1 Autism Experts in Control over the Intervention and Robot

Autism experts expressed firmly that autism interventions should remain a human activity. A robot can possibly assist the expert, but not take over their role [1,8,20]. Human-robot interaction should not replace human-human relationships for the autistic child, but autism experts warn that this can be the case when robots are not used correctly—in a manner where the autism expert does not have control over the intervention. Interacting with a robot may be highly engaging to autistic children, and educators warned that the robot may have the properties to turn into an obsession for certain children [1]. Furthermore, the children could also trust the robot and connect with it emotionally [8], which then could lead to becoming overly dependent on the robot and reduce the child's interaction with people. Similarly, Putnam et al. [22] reports that one of the reasons why parents who avoided technology for their child did so because they were worried that it might contribute to isolation of their child. On the other hand, in the same study, participants also mentioned that a robot could become like a friend to the child, which seems to be at odds with the belief that technology can lead to isolation from other people.

Autism experts expressed not only that they want to remain in control of the intervention (e.g. controlling the learning content or the flow of the intervention) [1,8], but also have (a degree of) control over the robot's behaviour [1,18,20,38]. A robot should fill in for the weaknesses of autism experts, and not replace their strengths. Educators are trained to assess the varying needs of the children, support those needs using (creative use of) distinct strategies [1], and, in general, are particularly proficient into "reading the mind of the autistic children" [18,20] (i.e. noticing subtle changes in their emotional well-being). They fear that overly relying on a robot's senses and analyses thereof may deteriorate the quality of an intervention, because robotic technology was judged not to be up to this task currently, nor did they believe that it would be in the future [1]. The educators also foresee that they need to adapt the robot's behaviour on the fly when the situation demands it, as the children can behave unpredictably and have dynamic needs [13,16]. Control over the robot's behaviour is therefore necessary, so that the autism experts have the last say in how the child is likely to feel, and what strategies are likely to be most appropriate.

To address the requirement for being in control over the robot's behaviour, autism experts will need to be able to interface with the robot. While some aspects of control can be addressed prior to the intervention, such as determining the learning content for an upcoming session, much of the aspects mentioned above relate to being able to enact control over the robot on the fly. For the latter, a simple graphical user interface might not be preferable. When asked, some experts said they likely would prefer to interface with the robot through speech [20]. Such an interface could possibly also be embedded in the interaction, where the expert could ask the robot to perform a certain behaviour. Alternatively, the experts could interface with the robot through a remote control, gestures, or touch, although these were judged less favourably [20]. In the design of an interface for the autism experts, it is important to keep in mind that the addition of a robot to the intervention, and control thereof, does not increase the workload of the expert, or make it more complicated, as this will likely decrease the adoption of such interventions [13,16].

3.2   Providing a Comfortable and Safe Learning Environment

It can sometimes be difficult to provide a comfortable and safe learning environment for the autistic children [1,18]. A robot was perceived as a possible solution to some instances where the learning environment was not comfortable for the child. The autism experts mentioned two aspects for addressing this requirement. Firstly, the unpredictability and complexity of people's behaviour and appearance can make it difficult for autistic children to understand them and can induce anxiety. Secondly, the (high) social demands experienced by the child of having to perform in the intervention can prevent the child from learning and also cause anxiety. To address the former, a robot can be highly predictable when it is programmed to do the same behaviour over and over again, in exactly the same manner, and look exactly the same every day. However, this may not be a very useful contribution to the intervention—the robot will likely have to do more, which can decrease its predictability [31]. On the other hand, a more predictable robot can lead to more visual attention to a robot-assisted activity [29]. Thus, a balance will need to be struck between the robot's predictability and providing meaningful interactions.

To improve the simplicity of a robot, experts noted that presenting multimodal robot behaviour could cause an information overload [16], and that a simplistic appearance of it might make it easier for children to interact with them [13,18]. To address the social demands of the intervention placed on the child, the environment should allow for making mistakes and still be supportive [1,25]. Rather than stating that the child's answer is incorrect, the robot could encourage the child to try again, or praise the child on the effort he or she is putting in.

3.3   Familiarising the Child with the Robot

Interacting with a robot can be an unsettling experience for autistic children, when they do not know what to expect from the robot [16,25]. What will it look like, what will it do, or how will it sound? To prevent this from happening, the autistic children will need time to get accustomed to the robot. Either before meeting the robot in person, or when they first meet. Note that this user requirement is connected to the user requirement discussed in the previous section, as being familiar with a robot generally increases the ability of people to predict its behaviour [31].

Three possible solutions on how to address the requirement of familiarising the child with the robot were put forward. First, an autistic adult mentioned that it would be beneficial if the children themselves could freely explore the robot, and become familiar with it, as they know best what they do and do not want [16]. Second, in Alcorn et al. [1], educators mentioned that creating a social story around the robot that shows what it looks like, explains what it is going to do, and when it is coming, may help the children anticipate and prepare for the robot's arrival. And lastly, providing some familiarity in appearance or behaviour might also put the children more at ease [25].

3.4   Accounting for Sensory Hyper- and Hypo-sensitivity

Unusual responses to sensory information are included as one of the non-social symptoms of autism [3]. These responses vary widely between autistic individuals [15]. Some are hyper-sensitive to certain sensory experiences (e.g. strong reactions to loud or unpredicted sounds, or lights) which then cause great discomfort (e.g. feeling like a sharp needle pierces your eardrums), others are hypo-sensitive and react very slowly to certain sensory information, or are unaware of it, and there are also some that actively seek out certain sensory experiences. Autism experts reported that taking these unusual responses to sensory information into account in the interventions could be important for keeping the children engaged [13,16,25]. On the one hand, we do not want to create a sensory experience that triggers hyper-sensitivity, which is very unpleasant and may lead to disengagement. On the other hand, for those who are hypo-sensitive to such sensory experiences, they may be particularly motivating.

To address sensory hyper- and hypo-sensitivities, personalising the sensory experiences is required. If the robot has lights, then it should be possible to both use them or deactivate them. If children want to feel the material of the robot, then this can be utilised to increase motivation, but it should not be required in order for the child to engage in the intervention, as this would prevent those who are sensitive to the robot's materials from engaging. Because it is often not possible to tell exactly *what* sensory experiences the child has unusual responses to, the autism experts using the robot will also need to pay close attention to this and intervene when necessary. In case a sensory sensitivity is triggered by something the robot is doing, then it should immediately stop doing it.

3.5   Personalising Content and the Robot

While personalising the autistic child-interaction in relation to sensory sensitivities of the children is one form of personalising that is particularly important, personalisation *in general* will be important according to autism experts. In autism education, personalising content is an essential task for autism experts to adjust learning material to a specific child. Parents and educators noted that autistic children can have strong interests, and that utilising these interests could draw the attention of the child and keep the child engaged [22]. Not only in personalising the robot's behaviour [1], but also its appearance [16]. Some children may enjoy certain robot behaviours, which are particularly motivating for that child, while other children may enjoy different robot behaviours [25]. In our own research, we also found large individual differences in the type of interactions autistic children spontaneously initiate towards a robot [30]. Overall, the children's individual differences will need to be addressed. Educators further mentioned that it should be possible for autism experts to personalise the learning content, as each child has an individual learning plan [1,16].

In robotics, much of the personalising that is done relates to personalising the difficulty of games through intelligent tutoring systems [e.g. 32], which may partly address the need for personalising content and the robot. Similar systems have been applied to personalising learning content in robot-assisted interventions in terms of difficulty [7,28] and feedback [7]. However, as we explained in the previous paragraph, more personalisation, and different kinds of personalisation, are needed to effectively support the autistic children in a robot-assisted intervention. While some of the personalisation can be done by the robot (autonomously), other forms of personalisation will require the input from the autism expert (e.g. adjusting the learning content to the child's individual learning plan). The latter could be facilitated by providing the experts with the ability to program the robot's behaviour [e.g. 4]. A different solution is to give more control over the robot to the children themselves. This way, the children can choose what they enjoy [25]. Moreover, it lets the children be active participants, where *they* shape the interaction. In Robins et al. [25], educators suggested that simple controls on a toy (i.e. the robot) could provide the children with the means to explore the robot and control its behaviour.

3.6   Generalisation of Learned Skills to Humans

Generalising skills learned in interventions is problematic for autistic children in general. As robots do not look and act like humans (which can be a good thing!), generalisation may be even more problematic. For instance, educators in [1] said that robots that are *too* predictable, or *too* engaging, could potentially hinder the child's progress in learning to navigate in social environments.

To address this requirement, using a *humanoid* appearance for a robot may be particularly successful in facilitating the generalisation of the learned skills to humans [1,23,27]. However, for some children, "a robot is still a robot, even when it looks like person" [p. 8 1], and this solution may not work. Instead, a more successful approach may be to actively embed the generalisation of learned skills from robots to humans into the intervention. Two approaches for doing so have been proposed in literature. One approach is where the robot is only used for eliciting certain social behaviours from the child that are directed at the expert, and learn a skill through this process [9]. The skill is then already applied in the interaction with another person, circumventing the need for generalisation from robots to humans. An alternate approach is by gradually fading the role of the robot in the intervention [6,14]. The child may then first learn the skill through interacting with the robot, but later on in the interventions learns to apply this skill in the interaction with the expert, rather than with the robot.

3.7 Safety and Robustness of the Robot Itself

Next to the safety of the people involved in the intervention, the robot itself should also be safe [13]. Autistic children may enjoy taking objects apart [5], or may handle objects roughly, and a robot is unlikely to be an exception [2]. Furthermore, the children may engage in challenging behaviours, such as kicking, hitting, or throwing objects. These behaviours may also be directed towards the robot and damage it (as well as pose a risk to the children themselves and those around them). As robots are often expensive and difficult to repair for a layperson, the robot should not be damaged during the intervention. As such, this type of behaviour needs to be accounted for through design, or through protocol, to address this requirement of having a sufficiently robust platform. Possible solution include using a highly robust robot that cannot be taken apart without using tools, or simply dissuading the child to handle the robot roughly and intervening when this happens. Alternatively, scheduling a fixed period of time in the intervention where the children can engage in the tactile exploration of the robot could give them the satisfaction of doing so without further disrupting the rest of the intervention.

4 General Discussion and Conclusion

Through our analysis, three major topics of user requirements emerged. Firstly, there is a need for a more predictable and simplistic interaction with a social actor. Robotic technology may be uniquely positioned by being able to provide more predictable, and less complex interactions, as well as being a social actor that elicits social interaction. This opens up various promising avenues for embedding a robot in interventions that target learning social skills. Not only could a predictable and simplistic robot be more easy to understand and comfortable for autistic children, it could also be less threatening, as it may be perceived by the children as being less socially demanding than a person.

The second topic relates to the large individual differences between autistic children. Accounting for such differences will be essential, but also challenging, because it is not always clear how the robot-assisted intervention should be adapted to the child. For instance, the use of lights could be anywhere from being highly motivating to causing great discomfort. It is unlikely that there is a one-size-fits-all robot for autistic children. Some children may not enjoy interacting with the robot, as they may be fearful of it [22], or may not think the robot is "cool" [16]. Others may be too aggressive to interact with a robot. In the end, the autism expert will need to decide how and when to use the robot.

This brings us to our last topic, which is that the robot is to be a *tool* for autism experts that they can use in certain scenarios. For instance, by using the robot as a scaffold, to bridge the gap between learning with current materials and learning with people. This also means that the experts should be empowered by having a robot at their disposal, which requires that they should remain in control over the intervention and be able to use the robot as they see fit. To enable the experts to adjust and customise the robot's behaviour, they will need easy-to-use tools to program the robot. What these tools should look like, and how the experts can control the robot in a session—taking into account that it should not cause additional workload during sessions—are questions that will need to be addressed in future research.

In our literature search, we found no papers which involved autistic children in their search for user needs or requirements. This is unfortunate, as autism interventions are designed for *them*. Yet we do not know what needs and requirements they themselves would report. Including autistic children in the design process would allow us to create more suitable and acceptable technologies, as well as allow the children to aid in shaping the robot-assisted intervention according to their needs and desires [34]. Frauenberger et al. [10] argue that autistic children are rarely involved in the design process, because either the researchers have limited access to the target group, or hold views that autistic children may be impaired in their creative and communicative skills, limiting their potential to provide feedback. While it may seem difficult to involve autistic children with low language and cognitive ability, there are ways for doing so. For instance, researchers could use a combination of ethnography and structured observations to understand their experiences [e.g. 21]. Alternatively, autistic children who are further in their development could be involved in a study—for whom there are many methods to engage them in research [see 11, 35]—and represent autistic children with more difficult in their communication and cognition.

Acknowledgements. This work was made possible through funding from the European Union's Horizon 2020 research and innovation program under grant agreement no: 688835 (DE-ENIGMA).

References

1. Alcorn, A.M., et al.: Educators' views on using humanoid robots with autistic learners in special education settings in England. Front. Robot. AI **6**(Nov), 1–15 (2019). https://doi.org/10.3389/frobt.2019.00107
2. Alhaddad, A.Y., Cabibihan, J.-J., Bonarini, A.: Head impact severity measures for small social robots thrown during meltdown in autism. Int. J. Soc. Robot. **11**(2), 255–270 (2018). https://doi.org/10.1007/s12369-018-0494-3
3. American Psychiatric Association: Diagnostic and Statistical Manual of Mental Disorders. Author, Washington, DC, 5th edn. (2013). https://doi.org/10.1176/appi.books.9780890425596
4. Barakova, E.I., Gillesen, J.C.C., Huskens, B.E.B.M., Lourens, T.: End-user programming architecture facilitates the uptake of robots in social therapies. Robot. Auton. Syst. **61**(7), 704–713 (2013). https://doi.org/10.1016/j.robot.2012.08.001
5. Baron-Cohen, S.: Autism: the empathizing-systemizing (E-S) theory. Ann. N. Y. Acad. Sci. **1156**(1), 68–80 (2009). https://doi.org/10.1111/j.1749-6632.2009.04467.x
6. Begum, M., et al.: Measuring the efficacy of robots in autism therapy. In: Proceedings of the Tenth Annual ACM/IEEE International Conference on Human-Robot Interaction - HRI 2015, pp. 335–342. ACM Press, New York (2015). https://doi.org/10.1145/2696454.2696480
7. Clabaugh, C., et al.: Long-term personalization of an in-home socially assistive robot for children with autism spectrum disorders. Front. Robot. AI **6**(Nov), 1–18 (2019). https://doi.org/10.3389/frobt.2019.00110
8. Coeckelbergh, M., et al.: A survey of expectations about the role of robots in robot-assisted therapy for children with ASD: ethical acceptability, trust, sociability, appearance, and attachment. Sci. Eng. Ethics **22**(1), 47–65 (2015). https://doi.org/10.1007/s11948-015-9649-x
9. Colton, M.B., Ricks, D.J., Goodrich, M.A., Dariush, B., Fujimura, K., Fujiki, M.: Toward therapist-in-the-loop assistive robotics for children with autism and specific language impairment. In: AISB New Frontiers in Human-Robot Interaction Symposium, Edinburgh, Scotland, pp. 1–5 (2009)
10. Frauenberger, C., Good, J., Keay-Bright, W.: Designing technology for children with special needs: bridging perspectives through participatory design. CoDesign **7**(1), 1–28 (2011). https://doi.org/10.1080/15710882.2011.587013
11. Frauenberger, C., Makhaeva, J., Spiel, K.: Blending methods: developing participatory design sessions for autistic children. In: Proceedings of the 2017 Conference on Interaction Design and Children, pp. 39–49. ACM, New York (2017). https://doi.org/10.1145/3078072.3079727
12. Gernsbacher, M.A.: Editorial perspective: the use of person-first language in scholarly writing may accentuate stigma. J. Child Psychol. Psychiatry **58**(7), 859–861 (2017). https://doi.org/10.1111/jcpp.12706
13. Giullian, N., Ricks, D.J., Atherton, J.A., Colton, M.B., Goodrich, M.A., Brinton, B.: Detailed requirements for robots in autism therapy. In: 2010 IEEE International Conference on Systems, Man and Cybernetics, pp. 2595–2602. IEEE (2010). https://doi.org/10.1109/ICSMC.2010.5641908
14. Goodrich, M.A., et al.: Incorporating a robot into an autism therapy team. IEEE Intell. Syst. **27**(2), 52–59 (2012). https://doi.org/10.1109/MIS.2012.40
15. Hazen, E.P., Stornelli, J.L., O'Rourke, J.A., Koesterer, K., McDougle, C.J.: Sensory symptoms in autism spectrum disorders. Harv. Rev. Psychiatry **22**(2), 112–124 (2014). https://doi.org/10.1097/01.HRP.0000445143.08773.58

16. Huijnen, C.A.G.J., Lexis, M.A.S., Jansens, R., de Witte, L.P.: How to implement robots in interventions for children with autism? A co-creation study involving people with autism, parents and professionals. J. Autism Dev. Disord. **47**(10), 3079–3096 (2017). https://doi.org/10.1007/s10803-017-3235-9

17. Huijnen, C.A.G.J., Lexis, M.A.S., Jansens, R., de Witte, L.P.: Roles, strengths and challenges of using robots in interventions for children with autism spectrum disorder (ASD). J. Autism Dev. Disord. **49**(1), 11–21 (2018). https://doi.org/10.1007/s10803-018-3683-x

18. Huijnen, C.A.G.J., Lexis, M.A.S., de Witte, L.P.: Matching robot KASPAR to autism spectrum disorder (ASD) therapy and educational goals. Int. J. Soc. Robot. **8**(4), 445–455 (2016). https://doi.org/10.1007/s12369-016-0369-4

19. Kenny, L., Hattersley, C., Molins, B., Buckley, C., Povey, C., Pellicano, E.: Which terms should be used to describe autism? Perspectives from the UK autism community. Autism **20**(4), 442–462 (2016). https://doi.org/10.1177/1362361315588200

20. Martin-Ortiz, M., Kim, M.-G., Barakova, E.I.: Mobile application for executing therapies with robots. In: Rojas, I., Joya, G., Catala, A. (eds.) IWANN 2017. LNCS, vol. 10306, pp. 82–92. Springer, Cham (2017). https://doi.org/10.1007/978-3-319-59147-6_8

21. Pellicano, E., et al.: My life at school: understanding the experiences of children and young people with special educational needs in residential special schools. Office of the Children's Commissioner, London, UK (2014)

22. Putnam, C., Hanschke, C., Todd, J., Gemmell, J., Kollia, M.: Interactive technologies designed for children with autism. ACM Trans. Access. Comput. **12**(3), 1–37 (2019). https://doi.org/10.1145/3342285

23. Ricks, D.J., Colton, M.B.: Trends and considerations in robot-assisted autism therapy. In: 2010 IEEE International Conference on Robotics and Automation, pp. 4354–4359. No. August, IEEE (2010). https://doi.org/10.1109/ROBOT.2010.5509327

24. Robins, B., Amirabdollahian, F., Ji, Z., Dautenhahn, K.: Tactile interaction with a humanoid robot for children with autism: a case study analysis involving user requirements and results of an initial implementation. In: 19th International Symposium in Robot and Human Interactive Communication, pp. 704–711. IEEE (2010). https://doi.org/10.1109/ROMAN.2010.5598641

25. Robins, B., et al.: Human-centred design methods: developing scenarios for robot assisted play informed by user panels and field trials. Int. J. Hum Comput Stud. **68**(12), 873–898 (2010). https://doi.org/10.1016/j.ijhcs.2010.08.001

26. Robins, B., Otero, N., Ferrari, E., Dautenhahn, K.: Eliciting requirements for a robotic toy for children with autism - results from user panels. In: RO-MAN 2007 - The 16th IEEE International Symposium on Robot and Human Interactive Communication, Jeju, Korea, pp. 101–106. IEEE (2007). https://doi.org/10.1109/ROMAN.2007.4415061

27. Scassellati, B., Admoni, H., Matarić, M.J.: Robots for use in autism research. Annu. Rev. Biomed. Eng. **14**(1), 275–294 (2012). https://doi.org/10.1146/annurev-bioeng-071811-150036

28. Scassellati, B., et al.: Improving social skills in children with ASD using a long-term, in-home social robot. Sci. Robot. **3**(21), eaat7544 (2018). https://doi.org/10.1126/scirobotics.aat7544

29. Schadenberg, B.R., et al.: Predictable robots for autistic children - variance in robot behaviour, idiosyncrasies in autistic children's characteristics, and child-robot engagement. ACM Trans. Comput. Hum. Interact. **28**(5), 1–42 (2021). https://doi.org/10.1145/3468849

30. Schadenberg, B.R., Reidsma, D., Heylen, D.K.J., Evers, V.: Differences in sponta-neous interactions of autistic children in an interaction with an adult and humanoid robot. Front. Robot. AI **7**, 19 (2020). https://doi.org/10.3389/frobt.2020.00028
31. Schadenberg, B.R., Reidsma, D., Heylen, D.K.J., Evers, V.: "I see what you did there": understanding people's social perception of a robot and its predictability. ACM Trans. Hum.-Robot Interact. **10**(3), 1–28 (2021). https://doi.org/10.1145/3461534
32. Schadenberg, B., Neerincx, M., Cnossen, F., Looije, R.: Personalising game diffi-culty to keep children motivated to play with a social robot: a Bayesian approach. Cogn. Syst. Res. **43**, 222–231 (2017). https://doi.org/10.1016/j.cogsys.2016.08.003
33. Simut, R.E., Vanderfaeillie, J., Peca, A., Van de Perre, G., Vanderborght, B.: Children with autism spectrum disorders make a fruit salad with probo, the social robot: an interaction study. J. Autism Dev. Disord. **46**(1), 113–126 (2015). https://doi.org/10.1007/s10803-015-2556-9
34. Spiel, K., Frauenberger, C., Keyes, O., Fitzpatrick, G.: Agency of autistic children in technology research-a critical literature review. ACM Trans. Comput.-Hum. Interact. **26**(6), 1–40 (2019). https://doi.org/10.1145/3344919
35. Spiel, K., Malinverni, L., Good, J., Frauenberger, C.: Participatory evaluation with autistic children. In: Proceedings of the 2017 CHI Conference on Human Factors in Computing Systems, vol. 2017-May, pp. 5755–5766. ACM, New York (2017). https://doi.org/10.1145/3025453.3025851
36. Wolfswinkel, J.F., Furtmueller, E., Wilderom, C.P.M.: Using grounded theory as a method for rigorously reviewing literature. Eur. J. Inf. Syst. **22**(1), 45–55 (2013). https://doi.org/10.1057/ejis.2011.51
37. Zheng, Z., Nie, G., Swanson, A., Weitlauf, A., Warren, Z., Sarkar, N.: A randomized controlled trial of an intelligent robotic response to joint attention intervention system. J. Autism Dev. Disord. **50**(8), 2819–2831 (2020). https://doi.org/10.1007/s10803-020-04388-5
38. Zubrycki, I., Granosik, G.: Understanding therapists' needs and attitudes towards robotic support. The roboterapia project. Int. J. Soc. Robot. **8**(4), 553–563 (2016). https://doi.org/10.1007/s12369-016-0372-9

"iCub Says: Do My Motor Sounds Disturb You?" Motor Sounds and Imitation with a Robot for Children with Autism Spectrum Disorder

Pauline Chevalier[1][(✉)], Federica Floris[2], Tiziana Priolo[2], Davide De Tommaso[1], and Agnieszka Wykowska[1]

[1] Social Cognition for Human Robot Interaction, Italian Institute of Technology, Genoa, Italy
`{pauline.chevalier,davide.detommaso,agnieszka.Wykowska}@iit.it`
[2] Piccolo Cottolengo Genovese Di Don Orione, Genoa, Italy

Abstract. In Socially Assistive Robotics, robots are used as social partners for children with Autism Spectrum Disorder. However, it is important to keep in mind that this population shows auditory hypo- or hypersensitivity, which results in avoiding or seeking behaviors towards sounds. Robots, from their mechanical embodiment, exhibit motor noises, and we aimed here to investigate their impact in two imitation games with iCub on a computer screen. We observed that participants who reported negative responses to unexpected loud noises were more able to focus on a "Simon says" game when the robot's motor noises were canceled.

Keywords: Autism spectrum disorder · Socially assistive robotics · Imitation · Auditory sensitivity · Motor sounds

1 Introduction

Robots have been found to be promising interaction partners for children diagnosed with Autism Spectrum Disorder (ASD), as their mechanical embodiment attracts children's interest and the predictability of robot actions comforts the young patients [1, 2]. Robots have been used to train or evaluate social skills in children diagnosed with ASD with success, and many studies in Socially Assistive Robotics (SAR) focus on the use or the design of such robot interventions (see [3, 4] for general overviews of SAR for children diagnosed with ASD). However, individuals with ASD often show sensory hyper or hypo-sensitivity in addition to the social skills impairments, repetitive or stereotypical behaviors [5, 6]. Robots are a novel and complex source of sensory stimuli and their sensory information can be overwhelming for some children with ASD, rather than beneficial [7]. It is utterly important to investigate the noises produced by the robots' body, for example from motors and fans, in SAR for children diagnosed with ASD,

Herein this study, we aimed to investigate if the response to a robot's motors auditory signals in children diagnosed with ASD can be linked to their auditory sensory sensitivity, and if patterns of behaviors emerge. For example, a certain profile of participants might benefit, while others might be overwhelmed, by the motor sounds. As reducing or

© Springer Nature Switzerland AG 2021
H. Li et al. (Eds.): ICSR 2021, LNAI 13086, pp. 640–649, 2021.
https://doi.org/10.1007/978-3-030-90525-5_56

canceling the motor sounds from robots is a difficult task, given the current state of the motor technology and the available robots on the market, we aimed here to investigate their impact in socially assistive setups for children with ASD. This way, we can highlight and offer guidelines to design robot or robot interventions to minimize unwanted negative effects of the noise or to use the motor sounds as a tool to attract the attention of the participants, dependent on individual profiling.

To do so, we designed two imitation tasks with the robot iCub [8] presented on a computer screen. First, a simple imitation game in which the children had to imitate a set of five arm movements from the robot. Second, a "Simon says" game with the same set of arm movements. "Simon says"[1] is a game in which one of the players (here iCub) plays an instructor, and the other players (here the participants) play the followers. The instructor commands the followers to perform a movement with him, but only if the instructor pronounces the keywords "Simon says". This game enables to evaluate Executive Functions, i.e. the psychological processes involved in the conscious control of thought and actions, and more specifically Response Inhibition, i.e. the ability to inhibit learned behavioral responses to stimuli (here not to imitate the robot whereas the children are used to it) [9]. Both imitation and Executive Functions are impaired in autism ([5] and [10], respectively). We chose imitation tasks as they require movements from the robot, which enable us to expose our participants to motor noises. Imitation tasks have been already used in SAR for children with ASD [11]–[15]. We chose to present the robot on a screen instead of its real physical embodiment so we were able to manipulate the auditory cues from the motor more flexibly and in a more controlled manner.

2 Related Work

Sensory sensitivity plays a role in social interactions: social signals can come from the facial or bodily expression of emotions, from the tone of the voice, from the touch of someone's hand on the arm, etc. They are also present in human-robot interactions (HRI), as the robot needs to convey social signals in its behaviors, its voice, or its touch. However, contrary to humans, robots happen to have also motor noises. These noises have an impact on how robots are perceived. In [16] the authors observed that motor noises reduced the human-likeness of the robot, but sounds from motor of higher quality made the robot appear more competent. The motor noises also have impact on the performance of the participants when performing movements in synchronization with robots. In [17], the authors asked participants to wave their arm with a Pepper robot in various auditory and visual conditions. They observed that participants' performance was impaired in the waving task when exposed to the actuator noises while observing the robot waving. Motor noises can also drive design choices in HRI. For example, when the robots need to give instructions to the user, some studies made the robot talk and move successively, to be sure the robots' body noises do not interfere with the understanding of the instructions.

---

[1] https://en.wikipedia.org/wiki/Simon_Says.

In SAR for children diagnosed with ASD, the impact of the robot's motor noises takes another dimension as children diagnosed with ASD show sensory hypo- or hyper-sensitivity [5, 6]. The effect of noises can be overwhelming for some individuals, which can results in such behaviors as covering the ears to reduce the unpleasant sounds. For others, however, the noise can be appealing or stimulating [6, 18]. Previous works observed the impact of sensory sensitivity in children diagnosed with ASD in HRI [12, 19, 20]. These works reported that visual and proprioceptive sensitivity influenced the children with ASD behaviors and performances in a social task with a robot. However, to our knowledge, no previous work investigated the impact of auditory sensitivity in socially assistive robotics for children with ASD.

3 Methods

3.1 Participants

We recruited 21 children diagnosed with ASD at the Piccolo Cottolengo Genovese di Don Orione (Genoa, Italy). Diagnosis of ASD was confirmed by the healthcare professionals of the institute, using the ADOS screening tool [21]. Parents or legal tutors provided a signed written informed consent. Our experimental protocols followed the ethical standards laid down in the Declaration of Helsinki and were approved by the local Ethics Committee (Comitato Etico Regione Liguria). Participants were already experienced in interactions with robots. They all interacted with Cozmo (Anki Robotics) and iCub [8] in previous experiments that took place within the joint collaborative project between Istituto Italiano di Tecnologia and Don Orione Italia. Three participants were excluded from the experiment because screening data was not filled by the parents, one because of a technical error, and other three as they did not succeed in finishing one or both sessions. The data of 14 participants (age $= 6.6 \pm 0.9$ years old, 2 females) were subject to analysis. The participants' demographics can be found in Table 1.

Table 1. The 14 participants' demographics, IQ and ADOS levels

Sex	Age	IQ	ADOS
M = 12, F = 2	6.6 ± 0.9 years old	75.786 ± 15.547	**1**: N = 8; **2**: N = 5; **3**: N = 1

3.2 Development of the Experimental Setup

As we aimed to understand the impact of the robot's motor noises, we chose to use a monitor-based study. Presenting stimuli on a computer screen allowed us to remove or present the motor noises to the participants flexibly, without the use of a canceling-noise headsets or earplugs. We developed the imitation and "Simon says" tasks on Psychopy v2021.1.4 [22]. As stimuli material, we recorded a video of the robot iCub performing a set of five arm movements and a neutral pose (see Fig. 1) and recorded the sentences it was going to pronounce during the experiment by means of the Text-To-Speech SVOXPICO[2] in Italian. The audio track of the video was modified in Audacity 2.4.2 to attenuate the robot's fans noises present in the recordings. We normalized the audio track and then performed a noise reduction (parameters of the reduction: noise reduction: 12 dB, sensitivity 2.00, and frequency smoothing: 5 bands). Then, we sliced the video to obtain single videos for each movement for the imitation and "Simon says" games and for the neutral posture the robot takes when idle or talking. The audio tracks of each movement can be seen in Fig. 1. During the experiment, the audio output (robot's voice and motor noises) was fixed around 70 dB, which is the decibel level of a normal conversation.

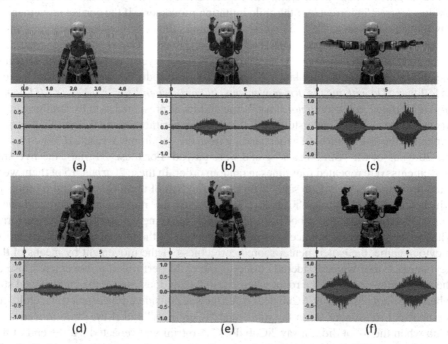

Fig. 1. Positions and soundtracks taken by the robot in the imitation and "Simon says" games. (a) neutral position; (b) arms up; (c) arms in "T"; (d) right arm up; (e) left arm up; and (f) arms as if the robot was showing its biceps. All movements start from the neutral position, go to the apex of the movement and stays in it for 2 s, and return to the neutral position. The background noise from the fans of the robots is present in all videos in the Noisy condition.

3.3 Procedure

Participants interacted twice with the robot, once with the robot's motor noises activated (condition: Noisy) and once deactivated (condition: Quiet). The sessions were done one

---

[2] https://github.com/robotology/speech/tree/master/svox-speech.

to two weeks apart. The presentation order to the two conditions was pseudo-randomized across the children.

In both sessions, the participant was invited to sit in front of the laptop on which the game was launched. The experimenter sat on the left side of the participant and was controlling the flow of the game by means of an external keyboard connected to the laptop. The task evolved as follows: The robot presented itself and introduced the first game, the arm imitation game: *"Do with me the arm movements"*. Then, the child underwent two training trials to ensure the task was understood. When ready, the 20 trials of the imitation task were played on the laptop. For these 20 trials, the set of five arm movements was repeated four times in random order. While doing the movements, the robot did not speak to the child. The experimenter inserted by means of the keyboard a value "correct/incorrect" for the child imitation movement. If the correct movement or any movement close to the one requested was done, the next movement was presented. If incorrect, the robot repeated the movement up to three times, and if the performed movement was still incorrect, the next movement was played. At the end of the 20 trials, the child was offered a short break. Then, the robot introduced the "Simon says" game as follows: *"Do with me the arm movements, but only when I say 'iCub does'. If I do not say 'iCub does', you should not move."*. The child was presented with two training trials to ensure the task was understood. If needed, the experimenter and the child's therapist explained the task again until understanding from the children was reached. When ready, the 20 trials of the "Simon says" game were played. For these 20 trials, the five arm movements were repeated four times in random order. In these 20 trials, 15 of them were valid prompts in which iCub said "iCub does" and five of them were invalid prompts in which iCub did not instruct "iCub does". Each of the five movements was invalid once. For each movement, the robot instructed which movement it was going to perform. The instruction was pronounced before the execution of the movement. Similarly to the previous game, the experimenter scored correctness of the movement by means of the keyboard. A trial was considered correct if the child performed a movement close to the one demonstrated by the robot when it said "iCub does" and if the child stayed still when the robot did not say "iCub does". A trial was considered incorrect if the child did an incorrect movement when the robot said "iCub does" and if the child moved with iCub when the robot did not say "iCub does". No trial was repeated. At the end of the 20 trials, the robot said goodbye to the child. The flow of the game can be seen in Fig. 2.

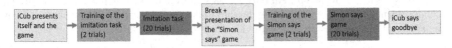

Fig. 2. Flowchart of the experimental procedure.

3.4 Measures

The participants' performance in both Imitation game and the "Simon says" game were scored. For the Imitation game, the children obtained one score of max. 20 points (one point for each correct trial). For the "Simon says" game, the children obtained two scores, one on 15 points-scale for the congruent condition (one point when they correctly imitated the robot when prompted to) and one of 5 points-scale for the incongruent condition (one point when they correctly did not imitate the robot when no prompt was made by the robot). We divided both scores by 15 and 5, respectively, to obtain performance scores.

Participants were screened for their sensory sensitivity by means of the Short Sensory Profile (SSP) [23], see Table 2. The SSP enables obtaining sensory processing patterns of children diagnosed with ASD with respect to demands related to everyday situations. The questionnaire investigates seven behaviors: Tactile Sensitivity, the Taste/Smell Sensitivity, the Movement Sensitivity, the Under-responsiveness/Seek Sensation, the Auditory Filtering, the Low Energy/Weak, and the Visual/Auditory Sensitivity. A general score summing the seven behaviors is also provided. The lower the score in a category, the more the child differs from typical behavior. The SSP provides a categorization in three groups based on the scores: "Typical behavior" (group 1), "Probable difference to typical behavior" (group 2), and "Certain difference to typical behavior" (group 3). We investigated the children's performance in the games regarding their Auditory Filtering and Visual/Auditory Sensitivity categorizations. Indeed, Auditory Filtering evaluates one's distraction by ambient noise or difficulty hearing what is said. Visual/Auditory Sensitivity assesses negative responses to unexpected noises or lights or blocking behaviors as putting the hands on the ears to block sounds or on the eyes to block lights.

Participants' IQ was screened using the Italian versions of Griffiths' Developmental Scales [24], and their autism level with the ADOS screening tool [21] which enable categorization of the children's impairment in three levels (from 1, the less impaired, to 3, the more impaired), see Table 1.

Table 2. Participants' mean scores and group population for the Short Sensory Profile. Each displayed behavior can be categorized in three groups: "Typical behavior" (group 1), "Probable difference to typical behavior" (group 2), and "Certain difference to typical behavior" (group 3)

SSP	Auditory filtering	Visual/auditory sensitivity
141.6 ± 20.9	19.4 ± 5.3	20.2 ± 8.8
1: N = 3; **2**: N = 5; **3**: N = 6	**1**: N = 3; **2**: N = 3; **3**: N = 8	**1**: N = 9; **2**: N = 4; **3**: N = 1

4 Results

Imitation Game
Regarding the imitation game, all children performed the 20 movements or did movements close to the one requested by the robot during the imitation game in both conditions.

"Simon says" Game
We performed a 2 x 2 x 2 ANOVA with the within-subjects factors Condition (noisy

vs. quiet), Congruency (congruent vs. incongruent) and the between subject factor of Visual/Auditory Sensitivity (group 1 vs. group 2 + 3) on the dependent variable of Simon Says scores. Two similar 2 x 2 x 2 ANOVA were performed, one with the Auditory Filtering (group 1 vs. group 2 vs. group 3) as between subject factor, and the second with the ADOS levels (group 1 vs. group 2 vs. group 3). Finally, a 2 x 2 x 2 ANCOVA with the within-subjects factors Condition (noisy vs. quiet), Congruency (congruent vs. incongruent) and the IQ as covariate on the dependent variable of Simon Says scores.

For the Visual/Auditory Sensitivity categorization, we grouped together the participants from groups 2 and 3 as group 3 only had one participant. The Congruency factor showed a significant difference $(F(12,2) = 24.3; p < 0.001)$ with the "Simon says" score in the congruent condition $(M = 0.924; SD = 0.115)$ being higher than the one in the incongruent condition $(M = 0.421; SD = 0.312)$. The interaction effect Condition (noisy vs. quiet) x Congruency (congruent vs., incongruent) × Visual/Auditory Sensitivity (level 1 vs. level 2/3) was also significant $(F(12,2) = 4.748, p = 0.050)$. We performed Paired-Samples T-Test on the score for each interaction Condition × Congruency for each of the two groups of the Visual/Auditory Sensitivity categorization. Participants within typical sensory sensitivity (group 1) showed a significant difference between congruent and incongruent trials in both the Quiet and Noisy conditions (Quiet: $t = 4.124$, $p = 0.003$; Noisy: $t = 3.186, p = 0.013$). Participants with a probable difference in sensory sensitivity in vision and audition (group 2 + group 3 together) showed a significant difference between congruent and incongruent trials in the Noisy condition $(t = 3.373$, $p = 0.028)$. These results are shown in Fig. 3. Independent T-Test to compare the groups on the score for each interaction Condition x Congruency were all non-significant.

For the Auditory Filtering categorization of the SSP, the ADOS level, and the IQ, no significant effect was found except for the Congruency on the children's performance in the "Simon says" game.

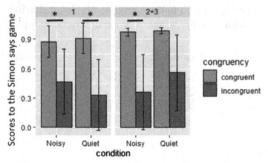

Fig. 3. "Simon says" scores for each groups of the Visual/Auditory Sensitivity categorization of the SSP.

Children's Comments on Motor Noises

In addition to the scoring, the comments of the children during the interactions were reported by the experimenter immediately after the session. Three children made spontaneous comments about the motor noises from the robot. During the Noisy condition session, one child asked why the robot did these motor noises. He did not recall these motor noises from a previous interaction with the real robot iCub (all participants had previously interacted with the physical robot iCub for another experiment). During the second session, another child noticed that this time, the robot was silent (Quiet condition). He was very happy about it and declared that it helped him focus better. On the contrary, in the second session in Quiet condition, yet another child noticed the absence of the motor noises and said he disliked it and preferred when the robot made motor noises.

5 Discussion and Conclusion

In this study, we developed an imitation game and a "Simon says" game with iCub for children diagnosed with ASD. We aimed to evaluate if the motor sounds of the robot had an impact on the children's performance. From previous observations in imitation games with robots for children diagnosed with ASD literature, we expected that the children to show variation in their performance [11–15]. However, during the simple imitation game, the children all performed correctly the task. An explanation for this result would be that our participants have medium to low impairment according to the ADOS screening tool (only one participant was showing high level of impairment). We did not find any difference between the two auditory conditions of the experiment (Quiet vs. Noisy).

Regarding the "Simon says" game, the presence or absence of the robot's motor noises did not influence the participants' performance. We observed significant differences between the congruent and incongruent trials of the game, pointing out the children's impairments in response inhibition. As expected, we found that the SSP Visual/Auditory Sensitivity categorization plays a role in the children's performance in the "Simon says" game. We observed that participants who show typical behaviors in Visual/Auditory sensitivity showed to be distracted by the incongruent trials in both Quiet and Noisy conditions. Participants who show atypical behaviors only showed this distraction during the Noisy condition. The children showing typical behaviors to visual and auditory sensitivity got distracted in both conditions, suggesting that different auditory conditions did not beneficiate or penalized them. However, the children who were reported to react badly to loud, unexpected noises appeared to be more focused on the "Simon says" game in a quiet environment, suggesting they beneficiate from a quieter environment. In addition to these results, two children expressed to the experimenter that they noticed the change of condition (Quiet and Noisy robot) between the two sessions. They both expressed a different opinion, showing that the motor noises can be pleasant to some or, on the contrary, prevent focusing. These results highlight the impact of auditory sensory sensitivity of children with ASD during interactions with a robot. However, it should be noted that the children in this experiment were mainly high functioning (only one participant was in the lower category of the ADOS screening), and sensory sensitivity can be more dramatic in lower-functioning autism. Also, all children had already been exposed to iCub and its motor noises, and this might have increased their level of tolerance to the noise.

For reasons of experimental control, the experiment was done on a computer screen. Future works should investigate the sounds of the motors and the way they are perceived by the participants with a real robot. In addition, although robots on screens are shown to create a lower engagement from the users (see [25, 26]), the children spoke to the robot on the screen during the sessions (e.g. waved hello and goodbye, answered to the robot that they understood the rules of the games, general comments about the game, etc.). This observation can support the idea to use screen-based interaction when real interaction with the robot is not possible.

Acknowledgments. This research was conducted as a joint collaborative project between Istituto Italiano di Tecnologia and Don Orione Italia. We thank the healthcare professionals of Piccolo Cottolengo Genovese di Don Orione, the participants and their families. This project has received funding from the European Union's Horizon 2020 research and innovation programme under the Marie Skłodowska-Curie grant agreement No 754490 – MINDED project. The content of this work reflects the authors' view only and the EU Agency is not responsible for any use that may be made of the information it contains.

References

1. Scassellati, B., Admoni, H., Matarić, M.: Robots for use in autism research. Annu. Rev. Biomed. Eng. **14**(1), 275–294 (2012). https://doi.org/10.1146/annurev-bioeng-071811-150036
2. Billard, A., Robins, B., Nadel, J., Dautenhahn, K.: Building robota, a mini-humanoid robot for the rehabilitation of children with autism. Assist. Technol. **19**(1), 37–49 (2007)
3. Pennisi, P., et al.: Autism and social robotics: a systematic review. Autism Res. **9**(2), 165–183 (2016). https://doi.org/10.1002/aur.1527
4. Matarić, M.J., Scassellati, B.: Socially Assistive Robotics. In: Springer Handbook of Robotics, Springer, pp. 1973–1994 (2016)
5. APA, Diagnostic and statistical manual of mental disorders (DSM-5®). American Psychiatric Pub (2013)
6. O'Connor, K.: Auditory processing in autism spectrum disorder: a review. Neurosci. Biobehav. Rev. **36**(2), 836–854 (2012). https://doi.org/10.1016/j.neubiorev.2011.11.008
7. Ferrari, E., Robins, B., Dautenhahn, K.: Therapeutic and educational objectives in robot assisted play for children with autism. In: RO-MAN 2009-The 18th IEEE International Symposium on Robot and Human Interactive Communication, pp. 108–114 (2009)
8. Metta, G., Sandini, G., Vernon, D., Natale, L., Nori, F.: The iCub humanoid robot: an open platform for research in embodied cognition. In: Proceedings of the 8th Workshop on Performance Metrics for Intelligent Systems, New York, NY, USA, pp. 50–56 (2008). https://doi.org/10.1145/1774674.1774683
9. Carlson, S.M., Zelazo, P.D., Faja, S.: Executive Function, in the Oxford Handbook of Developmental Psychology (vol 1): Body and Mind, pp. 706–743. Oxford University Press, New York, NY, US (2013)
10. Demetriou, E.A., et al.: Autism spectrum disorders: a meta-analysis of executive function. Mol. Psychiatry **23**(5), 1198–1204 (2018). https://doi.org/10.1038/mp.2017.75
11. Tapus, A., et al.: Children with autism social engagement in interaction with Nao, an imitative robot–a series of single case experiments. Interact. Stud. **13**(3), 315–347 (2012)
12. Chevalier, P., Raiola, G., Martin, J.-C., Isableu, B., Bazile, C., Tapus, A.: Do sensory preferences of children with autism impact an imitation task with a robot? In: Proceedings of the 2017 ACM/IEEE International Conference on Human-Robot Interaction, New York, NY, USA, pp. 177–186 (2017). https://doi.org/10.1145/2909824.3020234

13. Taheri, A., Alemi, M., Meghdari, A., Pouretemad, H., Holderread, S.: Clinical application of humanoid robots in playing imitation games for autistic children in Iran. Procedia-Soc. Behav. Sci. **176**, 898–906 (2015)
14. Duquette, A., Michaud, F., Mercier, H.: Exploring the use of a mobile robot as an imitation agent with children with low-functioning autism. Auton. Robots **24**(2), 147–157 (2008)
15. Zheng, Z., Young, E.M., Swanson, A., Weitlauf, A., Warren, Z., Sarkar, N.: Robot-mediated mixed gesture imitation skill training for young children with ASD. In: 2015 International Conference on Advanced Robotics (ICAR), pp. 72–77, July 2015. https://doi.org/10.1109/ICAR.2015.7251436
16. Tennent, H., Moore, D., Jung, M., Ju, W.: Good vibrations: how consequential sounds affect perception of robotic arms. In: 2017 26th IEEE International Symposium on Robot and Human Interactive Communication (RO-MAN), pp. 928–935, August 2017. https://doi.org/10.1109/ROMAN.2017.8172414
17. Jouaiti, M., Henaff, P.: the sound of actuators: disturbance in human -robot interac-tions?, development and learning and epigenetic robotics (ICDL-Epirob). In: 2019 Joint IEEE International Conferences, Oslo, Norway, August (2019). https://hal.archives-ouvertes.fr/hal-021 44955 Accessed 17 Sep 2019
18. Dunn, W.: The Sensory Profile: User's manual (Psychological Corporation, San Antonio, TX) (1999)
19. Chevalier, P., Isableu, B., Martin, J.-C., Tapus, A.: Individuals with autism: analysis of the first interaction with Nao robot based on their proprioceptive and kinematic profiles. In: Borangiu, T. (ed.) Advances in Robot Design and Intelligent Control. AISC, vol. 371, pp. 225–233. Springer, Cham (2016). https://doi.org/10.1007/978-3-319-21290-6_23
20. Chevalier, P., Martin, J.-C., Isableu, B., Bazile, C., Iacob, D.-O., Tapus, A.: Joint attention using human-robot interaction: impact of sensory preferences of children with autism. In: 2016 25th IEEE International Symposium on Robot and Human Interactive Communication (RO-MAN), pp. 849–854 (2016). https://doi.org/10.1109/ROMAN.2016.7745218
21. Rutter, M., DiLavore, P., Risi, S., Gotham, K., Bishop, S.: Autism diagnostic observation schedule: ADOS-2, Torrance CA West. Psychol. Serv (2012)
22. Peirce, J., et al.: PsychoPy2: experiments in behavior made easy. Behav. Res. Meth. **51**(1), 195–203 (2019). https://doi.org/10.3758/s13428-018-01193-y
23. Tomchek, S.D., Dunn, W.: Sensory processing in children with and without autism: a comparative study using the short sensory profile. Am. J. Occup. Ther. **61**(2), 190–200 (2007). https://doi.org/10.5014/ajot.61.2.190
24. Green, E., et al.: Griffiths Scales of Child Development, Third Edition, Hogrefe (2016)
25. Li, J.: The benefit of being physically present: a survey of experimental works comparing copresent robots, telepresent robots and virtual agents. Int. J. Hum.-Comput. Stud. **77**, 23–37 (2015). https://doi.org/10.1016/j.ijhcs.2015.01.001
26. Deng, E., Mutlu, B., Mataric, M.J.: Embodiment in socially interactive robots. Found. Trends® Robot. **7**(4), 251–356 (2019). https://doi.org/10.1561/2300000056

Longing to Connect: Could Social Robots Improve Social Bonding, Attachment, and Communication Among Children with Autism and Their Parents?

Lisa Armstrong[1] and Yeol Huh[2]([⊠])

[1] Emporia State University, Emporia, KS, USA
[2] Ewha Womans University, Seoul, Korea
yeolhuh@ewha.ac.kr

Abstract. Social robots are showing promise in assisting children with an autism spectrum disorder to improve social, language, and behavioral skills. However, this emerging technology has yet to find a permanent place in the homes of children with autism in part because the long-term benefits of robot-assisted therapy are still undetermined. We present this autoethnographic case of a 10-year-old boy with autism and his mother to explore the perceived benefits of the long-term, in-home use of a social robot as it relates to the facilitation of parent-child bonding, attachment, communication, and social learning.

Keywords: Social robot · Social bonding · Attachment · Autism spectrum disorder

1 Introduction

Autism spectrum disorder (ASD) is a life-long, neurodevelopmental disability characterized by impairments in social skills, verbal and non-verbal communication, and behavioral difficulties [1, 2]. Parents of children with ASD face complex challenges and issues. Stressors such as financial strain from lost income and the high cost of specialized interventions and therapies can cause an increased incidence of parental anxiety, depression, feelings of hopelessness, and despair [3, 4]. Social isolation due to disruptive behaviors, unsupportive social interactions, and lack of appropriate childcare can negatively impact parental feelings of well-being [5]. These factors and others influence the family dynamic, creating an environment in which bonding, attachment, and communication among children with ASD and their parents may be less than optimal.

Children with ASD often lack the social-communicative skills to connect with others. Autism can be reliably diagnosed as early as two years of age [6]. However, parents may perceive early indicators of autism when their infant has difficulty making eye contact or is not responsive to their voice, or even retreats from physical contact [6]. Although helpful in prompting parents to seek timely, professional evaluation and treatment for their child, these initial symptoms of ASD may negatively impact parent-child attachment and bonding [7].

© Springer Nature Switzerland AG 2021
H. Li et al. (Eds.): ICSR 2021, LNAI 13086, pp. 650–659, 2021.
https://doi.org/10.1007/978-3-030-90525-5_57

There have been many studies dedicated to the investigation of social robots in autism therapy. Researchers have examined their impact on joint attention, their ability to improve social communication and academic skills, and other areas of importance to individuals with ASD. More recently, there has been increased importance placed on studying the long-term impact of social robots in children with ASD outside of the confines of laboratory settings [8, 9]. Still, many studies are short-term, outcome-based focusing on the efficacy of social robot interactions in achieving target behaviors and other learning objectives [10, 11]. While the value and significance of such investigative endeavors are not in dispute, it may be worthwhile to consider how placing social robots in the home setting might impact bonding, attachment, and communication among children with ASD and their parents.

In this article, we present the case of one of the authors, Lisa Armstrong, and her autistic son, Juan, in the form of autoethnography, as they discovered social robots, robot-assisted therapy in autism, and the long-term, in-home use of a table-top social robot. We hope to encourage researchers from the diverse fields of study contributing to social robotics and autism therapy to consider the perceptions and challenges faced by families whose lives are impacted by ASD. We also wish to highlight the perceived benefits afforded by placing socially assistive robots in the home from a parent's perspective.

2   Case Presentation

I was a registered nurse, working as a medical missionary in Honduras, Central America, when I adopted my son, Juan. He was 13 months old and suffered from life-threatening malnutrition. In addition, Juan was diagnosed with microcephaly and various developmental delays. With intensive medical care, treatment, therapeutic nutrition, and rehabilitation, Juan made gains toward developmental milestones. He was playful and exhibited age-appropriate social skills.

At 23 months of age, Juan suddenly began to regress. Within four weeks, he stopped speaking. A devastating aspect of Juan's language regression was his inability to call me "Mamá," even when visibly distressed. He became withdrawn, no longer making eye contact with anyone around him. He resisted physical contact, often retreating from me and crying uncontrollably when I tried to hold him. Juan preferred to sit alone, rocking rhythmically back and forth while flapping his arms or flicking his fingers in classic stimming behavior associated with ASD [1]. I found myself living with a drastically changed child. I felt as if the little boy I had known and loved had died, leaving a stranger in his place.

First, I took Juan to his pediatrician. Then, he was referred to a pediatric neurologist, who, after extensive testing, made a diagnosis of ASD. Although Juan received multiple treatments and therapies while in Honduras, he remained non-verbal and was deemed to have profound social and cognitive impairment. When Juan was seven, we moved from Honduras to my hometown in Southeast Kansas. I hoped there would be more services available in the United States. Instead, I found an overwhelmed, underfunded public school system ill-equipped to meet Juan's needs. Also, I was shocked to discover that the private healthcare sector placed less importance on interventions for older children beyond the age for early intervention, typically ages 0 through 3 and in some instances until age 5. I could not understand why there were so few services available for older children with autism, given the literature clearly indicates early diagnosis of ASD in the United States remains a challenge, especially in rural areas [12].

2.1 Awareness Through Social Media

In 2015, a nurse coworker called my attention to a YouTube video circulating on Facebook. Vanderbilt University showed the NAO robot administering joint attention prompts to a child with autism [13]. I had no knowledge of social robotics (SR) or research using social robots for autism therapy. The video was compelling. It was apparent the child with ASD, "Aiden", responded to his name when called by the social robot, NAO. Furthermore, it was evident he was following the robot's commands to look in the direction NAO was pointing with an outstretched arm. This was in stark contrast to Juan's daily interactions with me. Juan seldom responded to his name. My attempts to establish eye contact resulted in Juan averting his gaze from mine. Any efforts to engage Juan in a joint activity were largely ignored. He occasionally interacted with me just long enough to acquire a preferred object and then quickly distanced himself from me. Juan rarely responded in ways that would perpetuate any sustained social exchange. This created a vicious cycle that left me feeling estranged from my son despite my desire to create a warm, loving, and secure relationship with him. After watching the video several times, I was so inspired that I felt compelled to learn more. I had been longing for years to connect with my son in the way "Aiden" seemed to connect with the NAO robot. Perhaps social robots could help me connect with the child I loved.

2.2 Social Robot Sticker Shock

I searched the literature on scientific, evidence-based outcomes supporting robot-assisted therapy (RAT) in children with ASD. Some results reported in the literature were so encouraging that I decided to invest in a social robot for Juan. The most prevalent robot in YouTube videos and identified in the literature was the NAO robot. Unfortunately, the NAO robot price was nearly $8,000. Discouraged but not defeated, I continued reading journal articles while formulating a longer-term financial strategy to purchase a NAO. Before long, I discovered one study by Albo-Canals et al. [14], which mentioned the Aisoy robot, a small table-top social robot produced in Spain by Aisoy Robotics. In the study, the robot was used as a companion, helper, mediator, and to provide schedule reminders for the study's activity [14]. The Aisoy1 V4 robot was for sale online for approximately $300 U.S. dollars. On impulse, I purchased it without any concept of the challenges I would face as a home user of this novel technology.

2.3 First Magical Encounter

Within fifteen minutes of opening the box, I realized I did not understand the manual's terminology, much less the underlying principles of even basic concepts. Nevertheless, after more than thirty days of significant struggle, I had learned enough to use drag and drop blocks to build a simple skill using MIT's ScratchX [15] with experimental extensions created by the Aisoy Robotics development team. The purpose of the interaction was to introduce Juan to the concept of greetings as a social skill. The learning goals of the skill were to improve Juan's understanding of the words and phrases, "Hello," "How are you," and "Goodbye," and their uses in the appropriate social contexts. Moreover, because Juan had exhibited echolalia during speech therapy, I hoped he could learn to say the words with intention, demonstrating understanding and use of this essential communication skill.

When the skill was initiated, "Aisoy" came to life using a short sound clip, head animation, and eyes opening. There was an immediate reaction from Juan. It was unlike any other, even when he was presented with educational technologies or toys. Juan fixed his gaze on the robot. When the robot said, "Hello Juan," Juan repeated the word, "Hello." Then, he turned toward me, making direct eye contact. He smiled and looked back toward the robot. Each time Aisoy spoke a keyword or phrase, Juan repeated the word or phrase with clarity. He continued to make eye contact with me and engaged in social referencing (see example shown in Fig. 1). It was the first time my son used gaze to see if I was experiencing what he was experiencing. When the interaction concluded, I asked Juan if he would like to play with the robot "some more." Juan immediately used the sign for "more" and spoke the word "more." The same skill was repeated again and again for more than an hour. Each time the interaction ended, Juan immediately signed the word "more," made eye contact with me, and loudly said "more" while gently touching the robot with his hands as if urging the robot to continue to play. Juan giggled and frequently smiled while the skill was running.

Fig. 1. An example of eye contact and social referencing directed toward me during one of Juan's initial interactions with the Aisoy robot.

Juan's behaviors in response to the robot provided glimpses of the child I had known before autism. Surprisingly, the robot's positive effects on Juan lasted for hours after the interaction concluded. Juan's demeanor was significantly calmer. This was remarkable given other screen-based technologies tended to overstimulate him, resulting in increased stimming and undesirable or maladaptive behaviors. Instead, his stimming behaviors were markedly reduced during and after his time with the robot. Juan made good eye contact with me and sustained eye contact much longer than I had experienced since the onset of his ASD symptoms. Although impossible to quantify, my impression was Juan had experienced joy on a level I had not seen before. His delight filled me with hope and optimism. I discovered a newfound enthusiasm for SR and a deep desire to create more skills based on my son's response to his new robot friend. Encouraged, I continued to build more skills based on the social story model originally developed by Carol Gray [16].

For approximately four weeks, Juan engaged in simple interactions with the Aisoy robot. I incorporated timed intervals to initiate dialog and behaviors or used the Wizard of Oz (WOZ) method [17] to deliver feedback and provide prompts based on Juan's responses throughout the skill. I maintained the same sequence of social story skills to establish routine and predictability. Juan consistently exhibited increased social behaviors and diminished stimming behaviors during the interactions. These notable positive effects persisted three to four hours after the final skill ended. He was more compliant in participating in required activities, both academic and those of daily living. Additionally, Juan became more verbal with each subsequent session. He demonstrated the ability to memorize the routines' dialog by anticipating and speaking key vocabulary words, other words, and phrases within the skill. It was difficult to assess the extent to which Juan was actively acquiring and transferring information to long-term memory. It was equally challenging to determine if any acquired knowledge could be applied toward real-life, contextually similar situations.

2.4 Hello in the Hallway

After approximately five weeks of daily sessions with the robot, Juan's grade school principal casually mentioned Juan had displayed an unusual social behavior earlier that day. He explained Juan had spontaneously put his hand out to wave when passing him in the hallway and said, "Hello." The principal expressed his surprise as he had never observed Juan exhibit such an intentional and appropriate social behavior. After speaking with him, I believed I had received a strong indicator Juan was engaging in knowledge transfer, applying what he had learned through his interactions with the robot to a different social context at school. The following week, I revealed Juan's activities with the social robot to the principal and the school's speech-language pathologist (SLP). I shared the content of the skills I had created and videos filmed of Juan's interactions with Aisoy. They were supportive of my efforts and encouraged me to continue. The SLP even helped write dialog for more skills based on social stories for speech therapy while incorporating evidence-based speech-language therapy techniques into the interactions.

2.5 Meltdown Management

Juan suffered frequent meltdowns at school. A functional behavior assessment (FBA) identified several contributing factors leading to the escalation of maladaptive behaviors and eventual meltdown. Communication difficulties, deviation from routine, attention-seeking, olfactory hypersensitivity, sensory overload, and task resistance were contributing factors. Juan was introduced to the Aisoy social robot when he was struggling with increasingly disruptive and sometimes violent or risky behaviors at school, such as swiping items from his desk or surrounding surfaces, hitting, spitting, grabbing, and elopement. Such behaviors created safety concerns for Juan and those around him. The classroom setting was disrupted, interfering with Juan's education and that of the other children in the class. For months, I responded to calls from the school several times a week and occasionally multiple times per day because Juan's behaviors had escalated to such a degree that seclusion was deemed necessary. Frequent, sometimes serial meltdowns combined with restraint and seclusion at school resulted in emotional dysregulation at home lasting hours into the evening. Juan alternated between uncontrollable fits of crying and pathologic giggling. His facial expressions were out of sync with his body language and vocalizations. He would grab at my shirt, arms, and hands while crying but rejected any attempt I made to provide physical affection to console him. Juan engaged in highly pronounced stimming behaviors, feverishly rocking back and forth while making high-pitched vocalizations. Our once peaceful home became an emotionally charged, chaotic environment filled with stress. Juan's quality of sleep suffered terribly. Often, he was not calm by bedtime. He would bang the back of his hands on the walls in his bedroom or hit them on the wooden bed rail. I experienced intense feelings of helplessness and hopelessness because I could not connect with my child to help him work through his emotions, offer comfort, or provide him any sense of security.

Once "robot time" became part of Juan's daily routine, things began to change. I noticed Juan used the robot to self-calm. After school, Juan always proceeded directly to the robot. He would place his hands on the robot's body, look at me and say, "more." As soon as Aisoy began to speak, Juan would start to calm down. His stimming behaviors decreased in frequency and intensity and, at times, would cease entirely. He would hold the robot between both hands and gently pat it while repeating the keywords in the skills. He would also point to the robot's mouth and heartlight as the robot changed emotional states. To address Juan's struggles with intense emotions, I created an interaction based on a social story about emotions to help him identify four key emotional states: happy, sad, angry, and afraid. Stock photos of children expressing the four emotions were placed between Juan and the robot on a slant board before the interaction was initiated. First, the robot discussed in simplified terms the characteristics of each emotion. Then, the robot's emotional state changed to match the corresponding emotion. Finally, Aisoy would ask Juan to identify the photograph corresponding to the expressed emotional state one by one. I used the WOZ approach to initiate the robot's response to Juan as he selected a photo to match the robot's state. Juan not only learned to identify each emotion accurately but would often say the name of the emotion. Once Juan demonstrated understanding of the basic emotions in the skill, I created additional skills to teach Juan how to better express and manage his own emotions. While emotional dysregulation and meltdowns persisted at school due to factors previously identified, Juan's behavior at home steadily improved. I marveled at this small, pet-like social robot that could enhance my son's quality of life (QoL) in ways I could not.

2.6 "Mommy Loves You" as Interpreted by a Social Robot

In speaking with other parents of children with ASD, I have found similar concerns and fears about our children's ability to comprehend love. I worried Juan might not take solace in the security and warmth of my love because I could not express it to him in terms he could understand. Physical affection such as hugs or kisses caused Juan to stiffen and retreat. If even a hand on his shoulder, attempts at physical contact seemed to cause unpleasant sensations, if not physical pain. The words "I love you" were spoken repeatedly, yet I received little feedback as reassurance Juan understood. As time passed, I wondered if Juan might better understand the concept of love if the robot delivered it. I realized that although the robot was speaking to Juan, the skill dialog was mine. I could say anything I wanted to Juan through the robot. I began to think of the robot as an interpreter. It was an "aha" moment that continues to have great significance in our lives even today.

Similar to the skills about emotions, I created an interaction based on a social story about love. The first skill explained the concept of love and used the Picture Exchange Communication System (PECS) icons to symbolize the concept [18]. For the next skill, I used the robot as an interpreter and facilitator, treating the expression of love as a crucial social skill. First, Aisoy explained to Juan how much his mamá loved him. Then, Aisoy asked Juan to turn to me so that I could say, "I love you." He smiled, giggled, and seemed to have received my message. Then, when he turned his attention back to the robot, he was asked to repeat the words, "I love you too." Now, when I tuck Juan in bed at night, I can say, "I love you, Juan", and Juan answers spontaneously, "I love you too".

2.7   When the Magic is Gone

After more than three months of daily use, Juan's response to the robot began to diminish. First, Juan's utterances decreased. He stopped repeating words and phrases. Next, stimming behaviors became more frequent and intense while interacting with the robot. Eventually, social referencing, pointing, and eye contact occurred only sporadically. What did not change was Juan's desire to interact with Aisoy, especially after a difficult day at school. Unfamiliar with the novelty effect, I believed the decrease in responsiveness was because I could not create new skills quickly enough to sustain Juan's interest. I questioned whether Juan was becoming bored with interactions having similar formats. Unfortunately, the ability to change the skill design or introduce new components into the interactions was limited by the confines of the experimental extensions created by Aisoy Robotics and, more importantly, my non-existent programming skills. I felt panicked and profoundly saddened as I observed Juan's interest and social behaviors wane. It was similar to the experience of losing Juan to the effects of autism. I wondered if my child would disappear again. The emotional pain of losing the connection I now enjoyed with my son was so intense, I was willing to do anything to avoid another catastrophic loss.

2.8   From Hopeless and Impotent to Optimistic and Empowered

Motivated by fear and the hope Juan's interest could be renewed by creating more engaging interactions, I turned again to the internet to learn. I considered including new sound effects to match the specific objectives of the skills (e.g., bodily function sound effects followed by a cartoon voice that says "excuse me") or to be used as reinforcement when directions were followed or correct answers were given (e.g., cartoon voice says "super genius"). This forced me to investigate how I might learn to achieve such a thing.

The Aisoy1 V4 was powered by a Raspberry Pi. After reading the user manual, SDK documentation, and posts on the developer's forum, I began watching tutorials on YouTube. Soon, I was downloading free, open-source applications, learning basic Linux commands, and exploring the files and folders in the Aisoy operating system, Airos. The process was frustrating and painfully slow, but with each success, curiosity overcame my frustration. I developed a deeper understanding of critical concepts. I continued to use the ScratchX environment to build more interactions for Juan but, I modified animations, inserted new sound files, and designed mouth shapes to create distinct emotional states making the interactions unique. By personalizing the interactions and eliminating some of the predictability of the skills, Juan's interest was renewed, and responses increased again.

Interestingly, Juan insisted on sitting with me while I created new skills for the robot. The very process of making new interactions became an activity of mutual interest. It was like sharing a hobby. I was overjoyed to have my son voluntarily share a physical space with me, just waiting to see the robot do something new. There were moments when the exchange of non-verbal communication felt more like a conversation. Juan would laugh when the robot would make a funny expression accompanied by a humorous sound effect. He would look at me while giggling to gauge my reaction. I could not contain my laughter. Soon, we were both laughing at the same thing together. Those moments brought us closer, strengthening our bond.

Eventually, a NAO and other social robots formed part of Juan's daily life. It became apparent after a time that different types of social robots were better or lesser suited to meet Juan's academic, social-emotional, and play requirements. As I learned Python and other programming languages, I became less dependent on block-based programming. This freed me to create more complex interactions fitting Juan's needs. Moreover, I finally possessed the tools and capabilities to develop highly personalized exchanges. This seemed to play a critical role in keeping Juan engaged. No longer was I filled with hopelessness or plagued by an overwhelming sense of impotence. Quite the contrary, I felt empowered through social robotics to help my child live a full and happy life.

3   General Discussion

This example of one family's experience illustrates both the challenges and perceived benefits of long-term, social robots in the home. While improvement in social communication skills, both verbal and non-verbal, is evidence of a positive outcome, the beneficial influence a long-term, in-home social robot had on parent-child bonding and attachment, in this case, is a critical measure worthy of consideration. The significance of the parent's favorable assessment of improvement in QoL for both herself and her son must be considered an integral part of the end result. Given the adverse, long-term effects of emotional dysregulation, further study is needed to examine how social robots might be used as mediators to help children with ASD manage and improve emotional self-regulation. If social robots in the home could demonstrate a reduction in chronic family and individual stress associated with maladaptive behaviors and emotion dysregulation, the implications for current and future QoL could be significant.

Ease of use was a significant obstacle, nearly precluding the adoption of social robot technology in this home setting. While digital literacy in society is improving, many people are digitally naïve. Therefore, the skills required to operate a social robot in the home need to match the user's technical skills more closely. Just as in other forms of autism therapy, home users should have the ability to create, personalize and adapt learning content and other aspects of the social robot interactions to meet their child's individual needs.

Parental stress related to the added financial burden of raising a child with ASD may only be exacerbated by the high cost of beneficial technologies such as social robots.

Children with ASD frequently require assistive technology (AT), yet parents are often left to find a way to pay for it. If social robots could be shown to have therapeutic value, then perhaps in the future, their purchase might be subsidized or even eligible for full coverage and reimbursement as medical devices. Consequently, it is conceivable social robots might play a role in reducing costs associated with raising a child with ASD when used to deliver robot-mediated interventions in the home. This may be especially true for children living in areas with limited access to specialized therapy services.

4   Conclusion

Although the experiences outlined here have been life-changing for this family, the gains have been hard-won. We hope sharing these experiences and insights might contribute to the discussion within the SR community about the nature and appropriateness of interventional goals associated with the in-home use of social robots by parents and their children with ASD. There is no denying the life-long, positive impact, improvement in social-communication and academic skills have toward the development of improved functional skills in children with ASD. Equally, the enduring emotional connection between parent and child associated with secure attachment and bonding is critical to a sense of well-being and improved QoL for families affected by autism. Future work expanding on the interventional goals for in-home social robots in autism therapy may wish to explore the priorities of families of children with ASD by inviting them to continue to contribute to the discussion.

Acknowledgments. I want to thank José Manuel del Río, CEO, and Pablo García, CTO of Aisoy Robotics, for their invaluable guidance, personal instruction, and willingness to share knowledge that allowed me to learn to create robot interactions to delight and engage my son, Juan.

References

1. American Psychiatric Association: Diagnostic and Statistical Manual of Mental Disorders, 5th edn. American Psychiatric Publishing, Arlington (2013)
2. Hyman, S.L., Levy, S.E., Myers, S.M.: Identification, evaluation, and management of children with autism spectrum disorder. Pediatrics **145**, e20193447 (2020). https://doi.org/10.1542/peds.2019-3447
3. Picardi, A., et al.: Parental burden and its correlates in families of children with autism spectrum disorder: a multicentre study with two comparison groups. CPEMH. **14**, 143–176 (2018). https://doi.org/10.2174/1745017901814010143
4. Catalano, D., Holloway, L., Mpofu, E.: Mental health interventions for parent carers of children with autistic spectrum disorder: practice guidelines from a critical interpretive synthesis (CIS) systematic review. IJERPH. **15**, 341 (2018). https://doi.org/10.3390/ijerph15020341
5. Prata, J., Lawson, W., Coelho, R.: Stress factors in parents of children on the autism spectrum: an integrative model approach. IJCNMH, **6**(2) (2019). https://doi.org/10.21035/ijcnmh.2019.6.2
6. Screening And Diagnosis I Autism Spectrum Disorder (ASD) I NCBDDD, https://www.cdc.gov/ncbddd/autism/screening.html. Accessed 29 June 2021

7. Rutgers, A.H., et al.: Autism, attachment and parenting: a comparison of children with autism spectrum disorder, mental retardation, language disorder, and non-clinical children. J. Abnorm. Child. Psychol. **35**, 859–870 (2007). https://doi.org/10.1007/s10802-007-9139-y
8. Scassellati, B., et al.: Improving social skills in children with ASD using a long-term, in-home social robot. Sci. Robot. 3, eaat7544 (2018). https://doi.org/10.1126/scirobotics.aat7544
9. Rakhymbayeva, N., Amirova, A., Sandygulova, A.: A long-term engagement with a social robot for autism therapy. Front. Robot. AI. **8**, 180 (2021). https://doi.org/10.3389/frobt.2021.669972
10. Cabibihan, J.-J., Javed, H., Ang, M., Aljunied, S.M.: Why robots? a survey on the roles and benefits of social robots in the therapy of children with autism. Int. J. Soc. Robot. **5**(4), 593–618 (2013). https://doi.org/10.1007/s12369-013-0202-2
11. Huijnen, C.A., AS Lexis, M., de Witte, L.P.: Robots as new tools in therapy and education for children with autism. Int. J. Neurorehab. Eng. **04**(4), 1–4 (2017). https://doi.org/10.4172/2376-0281.1000278
12. Antezana, L., Scarpa, A., Valdespino, A., Albright, J., Richey, J.A.: Rural trends in diagnosis and services for autism spectrum disorder. Front. Psychol. **8**, 590 (2017). https://doi.org/10.3389/fpsyg.2017.00590
13. Vanderbilt University: Interactive Robot Helps Children With Autism, https://www.youtube.com/watch?v=7T7cIY-MIxc. Accessed 29 June 2021
14. Albo-Canals, J., Yanez, C., Barco, A., Angulo, C., Heerink, M.: Modelling social skills and problem solving strategies used by children with asd through cloud connected social robots as data loggers: first modelling approach. In: New Friends 2015 - The 1st International Conference on Social Robots in Therapy and Education, pp. 8–9. Windesheim Flevoland (2015)
15. Lifelong Kindergarten Group at the MIT Media Lab: ScratchX Home Page. https://scratchx.org/. Accessed 29 June 2021
16. Gray, C.: My Social Stories Book. Jessica Kingsley Publishers, London (2002)
17. Riek, L.: Wizard of Oz Studies in HRI: a systematic review and new reporting guidelines. JHRI. **1**(1), 119–136 (2012). https://doi.org/10.5898/JHRI.1.1.Riek
18. Lerna, A., Esposito, D., Conson, M., Russo, L., Massagli, A.: Social-communicative effects of the picture exchange communication system (pecs) in autism spectrum disorders. **47**, 609–617 (2012). https://doi.org/10.1111/j.1460-6984.2012.00172.x

Design and Fabrication of a Floating Social Robot: CeB the Social Blimp

Erfan Etesami[1], Alireza Nemati[2(✉)] (ID), Ali F. Meghdari[1,3(✉)] (ID), Shuzhi Sam Ge[1,4] (ID), and Alireza Taheri[1] (ID)

[1] Social and Cognitive Robotics Lab, Sharif University of Technology, 1458889694 Tehran, Iran
meghdari@sharif.edu
[2] Institute for Future (IFF), Qingdao University, Qingdao 266071, China
nemati@qdu.edu.cn
[3] Chancellor of Fereshtegaan International Branch, Islamic Azad University, Tehran, Iran
[4] Social Robotics Lab, National University of Singapore, Singapore 117576, Singapore

Abstract. Robotic blimps have a wide range of applications, such as monitoring activities in their surroundings, advertising, and performing on stages. They also have remarkable capacities to be used as a social robot. In this research, a manually operated social robotic blimp has been developed intending to interact with children as a social agent and attract adults' attention as an entertainer in indoor public environments. Since the appearance of a social robot has a significant impact on its acceptance, first, we acquired opinions of several participants on the shape of a desired floating robot. The results revealed that a simple spherical structure adequately draws people's attention. After design and fabrication of the robot, a survey on its social behaviors was distributed among 82 people. The results indicated that the participants prefer a medium-sized robot, and they also feel almost safe when the robot works around them. Furthermore, the results showed that people genuinely appreciate the opportunity to have a mutual conversation with the designed social blimp. Moreover, the participants believed that the designed blimp could be an entertaining social flying robot with which it is easy to interact. The outcome of this survey will be beneficial in designing and developing a social blimp with a focus on interacting with children and entertaining people.

Keywords: Robotic blimp · Social robots · Human-robot interaction (HRI) · Children-robot interaction (CRI) · Floating robots

1 Introduction

Social robots are being used in a broad range of applications, including teaching sign language to children with hearing problems [1], providing rehabilitation for children diagnosed with autism [2], merchandising and attraction of attention [3, 4], teaching and learning with children [5], nursing and supporting hospitalized children [6, 7], and doing labor works as a co-worker [8]. Blimp robots are interesting examples of social robots which offers considerable potentials in the fields of human-robot interaction (HRI), specifically child-robot interaction (CRI).

© Springer Nature Switzerland AG 2021
H. Li et al. (Eds.): ICSR 2021, LNAI 13086, pp. 660–670, 2021.
https://doi.org/10.1007/978-3-030-90525-5_58

Autonomous Light Air Vessels (ALAVs) were developed to investigate their inter-action with each other (flocking behavior) and with people as a part of a networked system [9]. Diri is an autonomous blimp robot capable of monitoring and taking photos of its surroundings [10]. Inspired by nature, Festo Corporation developed a wide variety of airborne robots, such as AirJelly [11], AirPenguin [11], and Air-ray [11]. Moreover, eMotionSphere [12] and FreeMotionHandling [12] are two other Festo's spherical aerial robots designed to investigate controlling collision-free flying of autonomous systems in a defined area and gripping, moving, and delivering objects, respectively. Tobtia et al. presented a robotic blimp as a floating avatar in the entertainment area capable of interacting with humans [13, 14]. Space Browser is another blimp that was designed to implement video teleconferencing [15]. ZeRONE is a special drone that, instead of motors and blades, uses ultrasonic vibration of piezo elements as the driving unit to propel its helium-filled balloon [16]. Panasonic Corporation developed Ballooncam as a flying device focused on the entertainment section and event performances with a unique saucer-shaped design of putting propellers inside the balloon [17]. Ballooncam can cap-ture photos and project videos, and its fabric can also be used as a screen. Srisamosorn et al. designed a blimp robot with 360-degree cameras to evaluate provided healthcare for elders in nursing homes [18]. Since the balloons of the blimp robots can be built in various attractive shapes, these robots have remarkable capacities to be employed in interacting with children and playing with them. Air Swimmers are appealing inflatable toys in this category with a moving tail presented in an array of designs, ranging from sharks and fish to birds [19]. Another pleasing spherical airborne robot in this section is Qbofly, whose drive mechanism is one fin on each side of its helium balloon.

In this research, we initially developed and designed a social flying robot named CeB as a means to interact with children and entertain adults in public places, such as shopping malls, by taking photos and streaming live video with the robot's camera and detecting their faces and facial expressions using convolutional neural network models and face detection APIs. Public spots like kindergartens, airports, and malls are so crowded that there are certain limitations on using the ground-moving social robots. However, a social robotic blimp, like CeB, can easily fly over people and avoid any collision with the crowd. In order to achieve the goals of this research, a questionnaire containing pictures of several designs was prepared at the first stage to assess participants' opinions about the shape of the social flying robot. Afterward, the first prototype of CeB has been built according to the feedback of the participants. Finally, to evaluate the social behaviors and functionalities of CeB as well as to determine the future path of this research, the opinions of users were collected through a questionnaire consisting of several simulations of the social functions of this robot. The main advantages of the proposed robot is its primary social behavior and its body posture during the interaction with the audiences. The robot engages in interaction with people and tilts its head down toward the users based on detection of a person and recognizing their facial expression.

In Sect. 2 of this research paper, the CeB's initial sketches, final design, mechatronic components, and social behaviors and functions is described. The results are discussed in Sect. 3. Limitations and future work are presented in Sect. 4. At last, the conclusion of this research is summerized in Sect. 5.

2 Methodology

2.1 CeB's Design

Helium balloons and social robots both come in a wide range of designs and forms, each with its own appeal. To choose the shape of the CeB's balloon, as demonstrated in Fig. 1, five distinct designs, including a spherical form, a spindle, a shark, an airship, and a flying saucer, were first prepared.

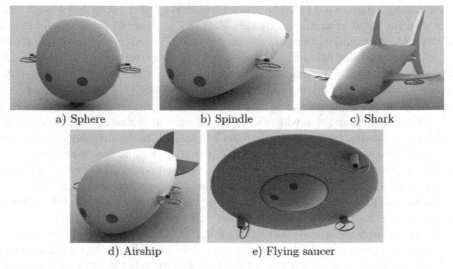

a) Sphere   b) Spindle   c) Shark

d) Airship   e) Flying saucer

Fig. 1. Five different proposed CeB's designs

Since CeB is meant to function as a social robot, to explore which design attracts people's attention more, a questionnaire containing the mentioned shapes was developed and distributed among 107 women and men in three age groups of below fifteen years old (A), between fifteen and thirty years old (B), and above thirty years old (C). Each participant of this questionnaire could opt for two designs with priority. The age and gender distribution of participants and the results of this survey are presented in Table 1 and Table 2, respectively. No noticable differences have been observed in answers between female and male participants. Finally, the spherical model, shown in Fig. 2, with 32 votes as the first choice, has been chosen as the CeB's balloon shape.

Because of its three-dimensional symmetry, the spherical-shaped balloon makes it significantly easier to move both its center of gravity and center of buoyancy close to the center point of the sphere. This feature leads to CeB's consuming less amount of energy, and therefore, CeB can remain afloat for a more extended time period. CeB's actual balloon is a white sphere with a diameter of 70 cm and two blue eyes made out of PVC (see Fig. 3).

Table 1. Age and gender distribution of participants in the survey on CeB's design

Gender		Age group		
		A	B	C
Female	34	4	14	16
Male	73	11	44	18
Total	**107**	**15**	**58**	**34**

Table 2. Results of the survey on CeB's design

	Sphere	Spindle	Shark	Airship	Flying saucer
First priority	32	7	13	26	29
Second priority	16	18	17	23	29
Total	**48**	**25**	**30**	**49**	**58**

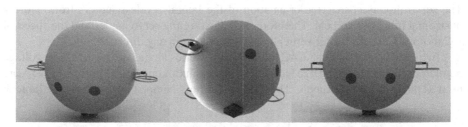

Fig. 2. The selected CeB's spherical design in three different views

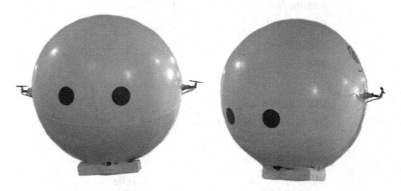

Fig. 3. An image of the CeB (the designed and fabricated floating social robot).

2.2 CeB's Mechatronics

CeB's microcontroller is a small seven-gram Arduino Nano R3 with an operating voltage of 5V. The RX and TX pins of the Arduino are used to establish serial communication with the 5V ESP32-CAM module, which is responsible for setting up wireless communication with a local computer, streaming video, taking photos, and sending them to a local server.

ESP32-CAM with an onboard two-megapixel OV2640 camera is a small module ideal for IoT application which integrates WiFi and Bluetooth. The video recorded by the CeB's camera is streamed live on the CeB's graphical user interface (GUI) running on the local computer. The taken pictures are also sent to the local computer, and the most recent one can be viewed on the GUI. Besides, the CeB's GUI allows a user to adjust the camera settings and control CeB's movements using a mouse, keyboard keys, or a gamepad by changing the angles of CeB's micro servos and the speed of its DC motors. This information is delivered from the local computer to CeB via a wireless connection. Moreover, using CeB's mini microphone and speaker, the operator and users can have a real-time mutual conversation with each other.

The CeB's driving system balloon consists of three 7x16mm three-gram DC coreless motors (maximum operating voltage of 3.7V) with 45mm propellers and two two-gram micro servo motors. One DC motor is installed on the back of the CeB's balloon, and one is placed on each sides of the robot. The primary function of the rear motor is to tilt CeB's head down to present better interaction with the user upon face detection. The servo motors change the orientation of the lateral coreless motors from entirely horizontal to totally vertical. Therefore, by adjusting the servo angles and the speed of DC motors, CeB can lift off vertically and also move in any direction.

Two 18650 3.7V 3400mAh 4C lithium-ion batteries alongside two LM2596 voltage regulators and a two-cell charge balancer with the maximum allowed current of 6.5A are used as the CeB's power supply. The CeB's electronic components are listed in Table 3.

Table 3. List of CeB's electronic components

Component	Num	Total weight
Arduino Nano R3	1	7g
ESP32-CAM	1	8g
Microphone	1	2g
Speaker	1	6g
Servo motor	2	4g
DC coreless motor	3	9g
DRV8833 (DC motor driver)	2	2g
18650 Battery	2	98g
LM2596	2	24g
Total		**160g**

2.3 CeB's Social Behaviors

CeB has been developed to fly over people, and its principal social function is to detect faces and facial expressions on the streamed video using the MTMN model and face-api.js. MTMN is a lightweight model for detecting human faces, and it is already being implemented on ESP32-CAM; it can take images as input and return the boxes which contain the detected faces. Face-api.js, a JavaScript face recognition application programming interface (API) implemented on top of the tensorflow.js, has been used to design CeB's GUI and is responsible for detecting faces and facial expressions. More specifically, this API contains useful high-level functions to detect all faces in an image as well as to predict face landmarks and recognize facial expressions for each detected face. When a face is detected, as illustrated in Fig. 4, the CeB's rear coreless motor starts to run. It causes the CeB's head to face downwards; therefore, people can feel that the robot is aware of their presence and is interacting with them. In addition, CeB's GUI affords the operators the opportunity to control its movements and camera settings easily. Since the CeB's camera is fixed, by changing CeB's position and orientation, operators can take photos from different angles, and they also can perform various games and interact with users. Carrying light objects and flyers, moving CeB in between rings, air race, dancing in the air, and capturing beautiful photos are among the games that users can play with CeB. Some of the CeB's social functionalities and behaviors is demonstrated in Fig. 5.

Fig. 4. A sample of face and facial expression detected by CeB (the camera installed on the robot capture the image and a remote computer performes the processing).

Fig. 5. Simulation of some of the CeB's social behaviors

3 Results and Discussion

To investigate CeB's social behaviors and how successful it is in attracting people's attention as well as to determine the future path of this research, a questionnaire containing eight questions and a simulation video of CeB's social functions was designed. Due to the restrictions caused by the COVID-19 pandemic, it has not been quite possible to perform the tests in real environments; therefore, the simulation of the robot performance and functions was sent out to participants through the social medias. 82 people, including 21 women and 61 men in three different age groups, have attended the online survey. In each question, the respondents had to rate one aspect of CeB as a social flying robot on a 1–5 Likert scale. Score 1 was considered as 'very low,' and score 5 meant 'very high.' The distribution of participants in terms of age and gender has been shown in Table 4. There have been no meaningful differences in responses between women and men. In analyzing the results, scores 1 and 2 were considered 'low,' score 3 as 'medium,' and scores 4 and 5 as 'high.' The questions of this survey and the distribution of the answers is listed in Table 5.

Table 4. Age and gender distribution of participants in the survey on CeB's social behaviors

Gender		Age group		
		A	B	C
Female	21	0	12	9
Male	61	2	41	18
Total	**82**	**2**	**53**	**27**

Answers to question 1 illustrate that people feel relatively safe when CeB is flying in their surroundings. Changing CeB's design in a way that coreless motors and their blades are less exposed will increase users' feelings of safety. Salem et al. [20] have investigated and highlighted two important factors, the 'safety' and 'trust', in social robots and mentioned some challenges of their measuring as well as the conditions in beyond lab researches. Based on the recommendations presented in [20], we would like to mention that although ~ 50% of the participants of this study believed they feel safe around the designed robot, they might consider/imagine the safe-hardware and safe-software factors more than the safe-interaction factors in their ratings because the current data has been gathered based on the simulation video of the robot's performance. Therefore, in this stage, the reslt of question 1 should be considered as a preliminary estimation of users' safety feelings and further research need to be done in action after the COVID-19 pandemic situation for figuring out a more precise answer for this question. A bigger spherical CeB has a lower surface-area-to-volume ratio, and therefore, the resultant buoyant force becomes more significant, which means CeB can carry out a larger payload. However, the answers to question 2 clearly reveal that people are more interested in the medium-sized version of CeB and prefer it to the larger models. This reaction might be originated from that a bigger robot may seem more hostile or dangerous

Table 5. Results of the survey on CeB's social behaviors

	Question	Average (Std. Dev.)	The multiplicity of each answer (Percentage)		
			Low	Medium	High
1	How much do you feel safe when the robot works around you?	3.5 (1.1)	9 (11)	33 (40)	40 (49)
2	How big would you like the robot to be?	2.8 (0.6)	19 (23)	56 (68)	7 (9)
3	How much do you like to talk with the robot?	3.6 (1.2)	14 (17)	19 (23)	49 (60)
4	How long do you like the robot to be around you?	3.2 (0.8)	9 (11)	52 (63)	21 (26)
5	How much do you like the robot to start a casual conversation with you?	3.5 (1.3)	19 (23)	19 (23)	44 (54)
6	How entertaining do you think the robot is?	3.7 (1.0)	9 (11)	22 (27)	51 (62)
7	How much do you enjoy interacting with the robot?	3.7 (0.9)	5 (6)	33 (40)	44 (54)
8	How much do you agree with the statement that "I think interacting with the robot is easy?"	3.7 (1.1)	12 (15)	14 (17)	56 (68)

to participants. Besides, since it occupies more space, people may think that CeB is more likely to interfere with their activities. The responses to questions 3 and 5 evidently demonstrate people's willingness to have a mutual verbal conversation with CeB. This finding is in line with the results presented in [21, 22] that the ability of social robots in performing verbal communication with users significantly/positively affect the impacts of HRI.

The answers to question 4 show that users prefer to interact with CeB only occasionally. Increasing CeB's social abilities along with raising public acceptance of social robots will extend the period people like to spend time with CeB. From the responses to question 6, 7, and 8, it can be deduced that users recognize CeB as a social and entertaining agent, and they also enthusiastically want to interact with it. The earnest desire of people to interact with this robot is mainly due to the friendly and yet simple design of CeB. The main conclusion to be drawn from the above results is that, apart from huge potentials, CeB has a decent performance as a social blimp in the areas of human-robot interaction and entertainment. In [23], Lytridis et al. has investigated the conditions (and confirmed some of our findings) for the social robots to be effective actors in entertainment and education. Moreover, Barakova et al. [24] suggested that in social robots with applications in the area of children-robot interaction, combining the social and game strategy can provide more social engagement and empathy with the robot which could be a critical cue for developing the scenarios for the CeB social robot.

Finally, we would like to mention that while there is not enough room in this paper to compare all of the factors in detail with similar studies in the literature, we tried our best to mention some main points regarding the acceptance and concerns (e.g. the future HRI design [25, 26]) for the current version of CeB.

4 Limitaions and Future Work

In addition to overcoming the decribed limitations caused by the COVID-19 pandemic, based on the CeB's considerable potentials in the fields of social robotics, children-robot interaction, entertainment, and advertising, and according to the results of the questionnaire on assessing CeB's social functionalities, specific measurements are planned to be taken in future.

To begin with, since one of the CeB's primary goals is interaction with children, the number of participants below fifteen years old (age group A in Tables 1 and 4) in both surveys to whom access has not been allowed due to the COVID-19 pandemic should increase. Secondly, in order to increase people's feelings of safety upon interacting with CeB (question 1 in Table 5), some changes in its shape are necessary so that its three coreless motors become more integrated with the body of CeB.

To make CeB's social presence more apparent, a small screen or an array of LEDs as the CeB's mouth can be added below its eyes. Moreover, currently, CeB's movements have to be controlled manually. An automatic control mode can be designed for CeB to make it more intelligent and less independent of human operators.

5 Conclusion

In this research, we have attempted to design a social blimp named CeB with two purposes of interacting with children and entertaining people in different age groups, particularly in crowded locations. Blimps have a major advantage over typical ground-moving social robots as they can fly over people's heads in crowded environments without the concern of hitting people. Because of the substantial impression that the appearance of a social robot has on its audience, a questionnaire consisting of five preliminary sketches of the CeB's structure, including a sphere, a spindle, a shark, an airship, and a flying saucer, was created. The survey was sent out to 107 people in three different age groups. The spherical design was selected as the first priority of the participants with 32 votes. Hence, CeB ended up being a friendly white sphere made of PVC with two blue eyes and a diameter of 70 cm.

At the first stage, we designed CeB in a manner to be capable of taking photos, capturing videos, and sending them to a local computer. We utilized the ESP32-CAM module as a unit that, by setting up a local server, was responsible for establishing a wireless connection between CeB and the local computer and streaming live photos and video through this connection. The Arduino Nano board is employed as an intermediary component between ESP32-CAM and CeB's driving unit, which consists of two servo motors and three DC coreless motors. The operator send commands to CeB using its especially designed GUI.

CeB's primary social behavior is to detect faces and facial expressions on the video streamed from CeB's camera and interact with the user through basic postures. To induce the more individual interaction with the users, the robot tilt downward when it detects a face. To explore people's views on CeB's social functions, a survey containing a video simulating the CeB's social behaviors and a questionnaire consisting of eight questions of various social aspects of CeB was prepared and opinions of 82 participant were acquired online. Based on the results, nearly half of the participants felt utterly safe when CeB worked in their surroundings. Over 60 percent of the respondents considered CeB as very entertaining and thought that their interaction with CeB would be easy. The majority of participants were eager to have a mutual talking with CeB, and they also preferred a medium-sized blimp over the larger ones to interact with. We hope that the results achieved by this research facilitate the designing and developing procedure of social blimps.

Acknowledgement. This research was supported by the fund provided by China National Key Research and Development Projects (Grant No. 2020YFB1313604).

References

1. Basiri, S., Taheri, A., Meghdari, A., Alemi, M.: Design and implementation of a robotic architecture for adaptive teaching: a case study on iranian sign language. J. Intell. Rob. Syst. **102**(2), 1–19 (2021). https://doi.org/10.1007/s10846-021-01413-2
2. Taheri, A., Shariati, A., Heidari, R., Shahab, M., Alemi, M., Meghdari, A.: Impacts of using a social robot to teach music to children with low-functioning autism. Paladyn J. Behav. Robot. **12**(1), 256–275 (2021)
3. Zibafar, A., et al.: State-of-the-art visual merchandising using a fashionable social robot: Roma. Int. J. Soc. Robot. **13**(3), 509–523 (2021)
4. Niemelä, M., Heikkilä, P., Lammi, H., Oksman, V.: A social robot in a shopping mall: studies on acceptance and stakeholder expectations. In: Korn, O. (ed.) Social Robots: Technological, Societal and Ethical Aspects of Human-Robot Interaction. HIS, pp. 119–144. Springer, Cham (2019). https://doi.org/10.1007/978-3-030-17107-0_7
5. Chen, H., Park, H.W., Breazeal, C.: Teaching and learning with children: impact of reciprocal peer learning with a social robot on children's learning and emotive engagement. Comput. Educ. **150**, 103836 (2020)
6. Ranjkar, E., Rafatnejad, R., Nobaveh, A.A., Meghdari, A., Alemi, M.: Design, fabrication, and evaluation of the "Maya" social robot. In: 2019 7th International Conference on Robotics and Mechatronics (ICRoM), pp. 52–62. IEEE, November 2019
7. Meghdari, A., et al.: Arash: a social robot buddy to support children with cancer in a hospital environment. Proc. Inst. Mech. Eng. [H] J. Eng. Med. **232**(6), 605–618 (2018)
8. Nemati, A., Zhao, D., Jiang, W., Ge, S.S.: Companion transporter: a co-worker in the greenhouse. In: Salichs, M.A., et al. (eds.) ICSR 2019. LNCS (LNAI), vol. 11876, pp. 322–331. Springer, Cham (2019). https://doi.org/10.1007/978-3-030-35888-4_30
9. Berk, J., Mitter, N.: Autonomous light air vessels (ALAVs). In: Proceedings of the 14th ACM International Conference on Multimedia, pp. 1029–1030, October 2006
10. Nowacka, D., Hammerla, N.Y., Elsden, C., Plötz, T., Kirk, D.: Diri-the actuated helium balloon: a study of autonomous behaviour in interfaces. In: Proceedings of the 2015 ACM International Joint Conference on Pervasive and Ubiquitous Computing, pp. 349–360, September 2015

11. Carrillo, L.R.G., López, A.E.D., Lozano, R., Pégard, C.: Quad Rotorcraft Control: Vision-Based Hovering and Navigation, pp. 10–12. Springer Science & Business Media (2012)
12. Dahms, J., Bardenhagen, A.: Propulsion model for (hybrid) unmanned aircraft systems (UAS). Aircr. Eng. Aerosp. Technol. **91**(2), 373–380 (2019). https://doi.org/10.1108/AEAT-01-2018-0033
13. Tobita, H.: Cloud interface: designing aerial computer environment for novel user interface. In: Proceedings of the 8th International Conference on Advances in Computer Entertainment Technology, pp. 1–8, November 2011
14. Tobita, H., Maruyama, S., Kuzi, T.: Floating avatar: telepresence system using blimps for communication and entertainment. In: CHI'11 Extended Abstracts on Human Factors in Computing Systems, pp. 541–550 (2011)
15. Paulos, E., Canny, J.: PRoP: personal roving presence. In: Proceedings of the SIGCHI Conference on Human Factors in Computing Systems, pp. 296–303, January 1998
16. Yamada, W., Manabe, H., Ikeda, D.: Zerone: safety drone with blade-free propulsion. In: Proceedings of the 2019 CHI Conference on Human Factors in Computing Systems, pp. 1–8, May 2019
17. Sadasivan, N.: Design and realization of an unmanned aerial rotorcraft vehicle using pressurized inflatable structure. Int. J. Aviat. Aeronaut. Aerosp. **6**(4), 3 (2019)
18. Srisamosorn, V., Kuwahara, N., Yamashita, A., Ogata, T., Ota, J.: Design of face tracking system using environmental cameras and flying robot for evaluation of health care. In: Duffy, V.G.G. (ed.) DHM 2016. LNCS, vol. 9745, pp. 264–273. Springer, Cham (2016). https://doi.org/10.1007/978-3-319-40247-5_27
19. Veronese, F., Bulgarelli, D., Besio, S., Bianquin, N., Bonarini, A.: Off-the-shelf, robotic toys and physically impaired children: an analysis and suggested improvements. In: Proceedings of the 7th International Conference on Software Development and Technologies for Enhancing Accessibility and Fighting Info-Exclusion, pp. 232–239, December 2016
20. Salem, M., Lakatos, G., Amirabdollahian, F., Dautenhahn, K.: Towards safe and trustworthy social robots: ethical challenges and practical issues. In: Tapus, A., André, E., Martin, J.C., Ferland, F., Ammi, M. (eds.) Social Robotics. ICSR 2015, LNCS, vol. 9388, pp. 584–593. Springer, Cham (2015). https://doi.org/10.1007/978-3-319-25554-5_58
21. Taheri, A., Meghdari, A., Mahoor, M.H.: A close look at the imitation performance of children with autism and typically developing children using a robotic system. Int. J. Soc. Robot. **13**(5), 1125–1147 (2021)
22. Pour, A.G., Taheri, A., Alemi, M., Meghdari, A.: Human–robot facial expression reciprocal interaction platform: case studies on children with autism. Int. J. Soc. Robot. **10**(2), 179–198 (2018)
23. Lytridis, C., et al.: Social robots as cyber-physical actors in entertainment and education. In: 2019 International Conference on Software, Telecommunications and Computer Networks (SoftCOM), pp. 1–6. IEEE. September 2019
24. Barakova, E.I., De Haas, M., Kuijpers, W., Irigoyen, N., Betancourt, A.: Socially grounded game strategy enhances bonding and perceived smartness of a humanoid robot. Connect. Sci. **30**(1), 81–98 (2018)
25. Basiri, S., Taheri, A., Meghdari, A.F., Boroushaki, M., Alemi, M.: Dynamic Iranian Sign Language Recognition Using an Optimized Deep Neural Network: An Implementation via a Robotic-Based Architecture. Int. J. Soc. Robot. 1–21 (2021). https://doi.org/10.1007/s12369-021-00819-0
26. Hosseini, S.R., Taheri, A., Alemi, M., Meghdari, A.: One-shot learning from demonstration approach toward a reciprocal sign language-based HRI. Int. J. Soc. Robot. 1–13 (2021). https://doi.org/10.1007/s12369-021-00818-1

Assessment of Engagement and Learning During Child-Robot Interaction Using EEG Signals

Maryam Alimardani[1]([✉]), Stephanie van den Braak[1], Anne-Lise Jouen[2],
Reiko Matsunaka[3], and Kazuo Hiraki[3]

[1] Tilburg University, 5037 Tilburg, AB, The Netherlands
m.alimardani@tilburguniversity.edu
[2] University of Geneva, 1205 Geneva, Switzerland
[3] The University of Tokyo, Tokyo 153-8902, Japan

Abstract. Social robots are being increasingly employed for educational purposes, such as second language tutoring. Past studies in Child-Robot Interaction (CRI) have demonstrated the positive effect of an embodied agent on engagement and consequently learning of the children. However, these studies commonly use subjective or behavioral metrics of engagement that are measured after the interaction is over. In order to gain better understanding of children's engagement with a robot during the learning phase, this study employed objective measures of EEG. Two groups of Japanese children participated in a language learning task; one group learned French vocabulary from a storytelling robot while seeing pictures of the target words on a computer screen and the other group listened to the same story with only pictures on the screen and without the robot. The engagement level and learning outcome of the children were measured using EEG signals and a post-interaction word recognition test. While no significant difference was observed between the two groups in their test performance, the EEG Engagement Index $(\frac{\beta}{\theta+\alpha})$ showed a higher power in central brain regions of the children that learned from the robot. Our findings provide evidence for the role of social presence and engagement in CRI and further shed light on cognitive mechanisms of language learning in children. Additionally, our study introduces EEG Engagement Index as a potential metric for future brain-computer interfaces that monitor engagement level of children in educational settings in order to adapt the robot behavior accordingly.

Keywords: Child-Robot Interaction (CRI) · Second language learning · Engagement · Electroencephalogram (EEG)

1 Introduction

Our society is digitalizing and so is the educational system. Computers and tablets are increasingly employed in everyday learning and with that follows the prevalence of robots in educational environments [1]. A considerable amount of

© Springer Nature Switzerland AG 2021
H. Li et al. (Eds.): ICSR 2021, LNAI 13086, pp. 671–682, 2021.
https://doi.org/10.1007/978-3-030-90525-5_59

research has been conducted in the domain of Human-Robot Interaction (HRI) focusing on this change in combination with children and second language learning. A recent study by Randall (2019) provided an overview of robot-assisted language learning and its impact on the learning outcome and affect of learners [2]. It was found that robots can assist children of different ages in learning languages when they have the role of a tutor or a teaching assistant that accompanies the human instructor. In addition, the survey concluded that robots have a positive effect on the motivation, engagement, and confidence of the learners in comparison to other technologies [2].

While the benefit of robots in various educational settings is already established, some critics are reported regarding previous research on the use of robots in language learning, namely, the studies in this field are often exploratory or descriptive, lack a control group for evaluation, or have small sample sizes [3]. Moreover, although robot-assisted language learning has shown increased learning outcome in children, the reason behind this improvement remains unclear [4]. The explanation that is often provided by past research is that children appear to be more engaged when they learn from a social robot [3, 5].

Engagement and attention are key concepts in learning and are used interchangeably in past research [6, 7]. Engagement is defined as being involved with something and is important for learning in terms of motivation, persistence, and satisfaction [8, 9]. Attention is the act of directing the mind to listen, see, or understand, which has a positive effect on memory, learning, and recognition capability [10, 11]. Motivation, sustained attention, and learning gain in second language learning can all be increased due to robot-assisted learning in comparison to computer-assisted learning [12, 13]. The use of gestures by the robot can increase engagement in children and consequently long-term memorization of new information [13]. It has been shown that even after one single tutoring session with a robot, children around the age of five show signs of second language acquisition [14]. Besides, children showed a higher engagement with the robot when the robot used a variety of gestures [14] or when it employed an adaptive tutoring strategy [13].

Past experiments have mainly evaluated engagement either by collecting post-interaction questionnaires from children or by recruiting trained annotators who watched video clips of children and rated their behavior during interaction with the robot [13, 14]. These evaluation methods are not only laborious but can also introduce subjective bias to the measurements. Alternatively, electroencephalogram (EEG) can provide a real-time and objective measure of engagement and attention in HRI settings [5]. EEG is a non-invasive brain imaging technique that provides high temporal resolution of neurophysiological responses, hence it is particularly useful when the robot should adjust its behavior in order to restore or increase the engagement and attention of the user [6, 15, 16]. EEG has already been used in the field of Human-Computer Interaction to quantify engagement and cognitive workload during educational video games [17] and arithmetic learning tasks [18]. However the use of EEG in the field of HRI is scarce [15].

The study by Szafir and Mutlu (2012) [6] is one of the few HRI reports that made use of EEG to track participants' engagement level during interaction with a storytelling robot. Authors employed a brain-computer interface (BCI) that extracted a real-time *EEG Engagement Index*, and applied behavioral techniques to restore subject's attention when they showed decrease in engagement level. The EEG signals were gathered from the user's prefrontal cortex because this area has been previously associated with learning, mental states, and attention [19,20]. The results showed a significant improvement in recall performance when adaptive behavioral techniques were performed by the robot and females reported to be more motivated by the adaptive behavior of the robot [6]. While Szafir and Mutlu (2012) only focused on the prefrontal area, other studies computed the EEG Engagement Index as an average power of multiple brain areas and successfully confirmed its association with students' learning outcome [17].

The current research employed EEG to measure the engagement level of children in a second language learning task. Two groups of Japanese children learned French vocabulary by listening to a story in the French language and seeing images of the target words on a computer screen. In one group, the story was told by a NAO robot that gestured toward the screen whenever the intended French word was recited. In the other group, children only heard the robot's voice and saw pictures on the screen. Learning in both groups was evaluated in a post-interaction word recognition test. Following [6], we extracted EEG Engagement Index and examined the effect of robot presence on children's neurophysiological responses and learning outcome. The following research questions were formulated:

RQ 1: Does EEG show different level of task engagement when children learn a second language from a storytelling robot as opposed to a computer screen?

RQ 2: Do children learn a second language vocabulary during interaction with a storytelling robot more efficiently than a computer screen?

We hypothesized that the EEG Engagement Index would be higher in children who learned from the robot than those who experienced the screen condition. Additionally, we hypothesized that the use of a storytelling robot would have a positive impact on children's recall of the target words as indicated by their test performance.

2   Experimental Setup

2.1   Participants

Forty-one (41) Japanese-speaking children participated in the experiment (22 boys, 19 girls, age M = 5.50, SD = 0.16). They were divided into two groups; one group was assigned to the Robot condition (N = 21) and the other to the Display condition (N = 20). The children's parents received explanation about the study and after reading the information letter, signed a written consent form. The study was approved by the Ethics Committee of the University of Tokyo.

2.2   Experiment Procedure

After initial explanation, the children were guided to the experiment room and seated in front of the screen. The experimenter placed the EEG cap on the children's head and checked the electrodes' impedance. In the Robot group, the EEG data was recorded during seven minutes of French storytelling done by the NAO robot, supported by a computer screen (Fig. 1a). In the Display group, the EEG data was recorded while the same story (in French, 7 min) was narrated in the robot's voice over the display (Fig. 1b). For both groups, same pictures were displayed on the screen to invigorate the storytelling. These pictures visualized the target French words, e.g. when the word 'cochon' (i.e. French word for 'pig') was used, a picture of a pig was shown. Children were exposed repeatedly to three target words in French that they were expected to learn; pig, wolf, and house.

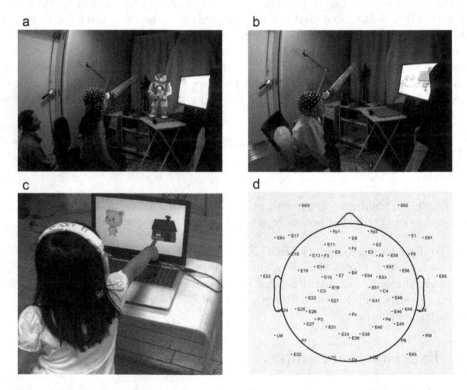

Fig. 1. Experimental procedure. Two groups of children listened to a story in French either a) narrated by a social robot that pointed to pictures on a computer screen (Robot group) or b) by a non-embodied voice using the same pictures on the computer screen (Display group). c) Children's learning of the target French words was assessed by a post-interaction word recognition test. d) EEG signals were recorded from children during the learning phase in order to measure task engagement in each group.

After the story was finished, the children participated in a word recognition task on a laptop (see Fig. 1c). The word recognition task included 13 stimuli words allowing to test children's learning of the 3 target words to which they were frequently exposed during the storytelling (i.e. pig, wolf, house). Children heard a word that was taught during the storytelling (e.g. "cochon", pig in French) and they had to choose between two visual stimuli presented simultaneously on the screen. The target words were combined with distractor words. The number of correct and incorrect answers in the word recognition test were recorded.

2.3 EEG Recording

The EEG signals were recorded using an Electrical Geodesics Inc. (EGI) EEG acquisition system consisting of a 64-channel Hydrocel Geodesic Sensor Net (Fig. 1d). The recording sampling rate 250 Hz. The Cz channel was used as the reference channel during the recording, therefore the data were re-referenced to reconstruct the Cz signal. The other channels were corrected accordingly. This resulted in a dataset with 65 EEG signals. For this study, 18 channels covering all brain regions were selected for further analysis. The selected channels were Fp1, Fp2, F3, F4, F7, F8, Fz, C3, C4, Cz, P3, P4, Pz, O1, O2, Oz, T7, and T8. The selection criteria was to include at least one left and one right hemispheric electrode as well as midline electrode in all frontal, central, temporal, parietal and occipital regions.

2.4 Data Analysis

The EEG signals were processed in MATLAB (version R2020b). The EEGLAB toolbox (verision 2021.0) was used for pre-processing of the raw recordings. First, a band-pass filter of 4–30 Hz was applied to remove high and low frequency components and only retain frequency bands theta (4–8 Hz), alpha (8–13 Hz), and beta (13–30 Hz) [11]. The filtered data was visually inspected for noisy segments, which were removed from the data. Additionally, Independent Component Analysis (ICA) was applied to clean the signals from eye artifact and, if needed, other noisy components. For every subject and every EEG channel, the mean power in the frequency bands theta, alpha, and beta were extracted using the spectopo function in EEGLAB, which relies on the fast Fourier transform (FFT). Subsequently, the EEG Engagement Index was calculated using the following equation [6]:

$$\text{EEG Engagement Index} = \frac{\beta}{\theta + \alpha} \tag{1}$$

Next, using JupyterLab, dataframes were created for the Robot and Display conditions. The EEG Engagement Indexes obtained from each group at each EEG channel were loaded into these dataframes. To inspect the normality of the data, histograms were plotted and the Shapiro-Wilk test was conducted. Both histograms and Shapiro-Wilk tests showed non-normal distribution of data in both groups. Consequently, the non-parametric Mann-Whitney U test was chosen to compare the Engagement Indexes between the two groups per channel.

Finally, the learning outcome was compared between the two groups. For every participant, the number of correctly recognized words in the post-interaction test was divided by the total number of questions. Since this data was not normally distributed, Mann-Whitney U test was chosen to compare the learning outcomes between the two groups. One participant was excluded from the analysis on the learning outcome because the mother of the child helped with the word recognition test.

3   Results

The results are presented in two parts: the children's learning outcome as measured by the post-interaction word recognition test and the results of the brain activity analysis during the learning phase which compared the EEG Engagement Index (see Eq. 1) between the two groups at different brain areas.

3.1   Learning Outcome

Figure 2 demonstrates the performance of children in each group on the word recognition test that was conducted after the storytelling i.e. the learning phase. A Mann-Whitney U test showed no significant difference between the Robot group *(mdn = 0.839)* and the Display group *(mdn = 0.708)*, *U = 146, p = 0.07*, although the median of the performance was slightly higher in the Robot group.

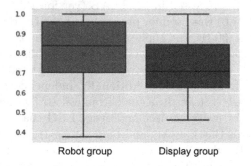

Fig. 2. Children's performance on the word recognition test. Although, the percentage of the French words that were recognized by the children was slightly higher in the Robot group, no significant difference was found between the two groups in their test performance.

3.2   EEG Engagement Index

Figure 3 displays the EEG Engagement Index computed for both groups in all selected EEG channels in this study. A Mann-Whitney U test indicated that the EEG Engagement Index in C4 was significantly higher in the Robot group *(mdn*

$= 0.062)$ in comparison to the Display group $(mdn = 0.045)$, $U = 136$, $p = 0.028$. Similar result was found for Cz, where the Robot group $(mdn = 0.030)$ showed significantly higher EEG Engagement Index compared to the Display group $(mdn = 0.026)$, $U = 130$, $p = 0.019$. While no significant difference was confirmed at other locations, the prefrontal and frontal channels showed particularly higher values of EEG Engagement Index in both groups when compared to other regions of the brain.

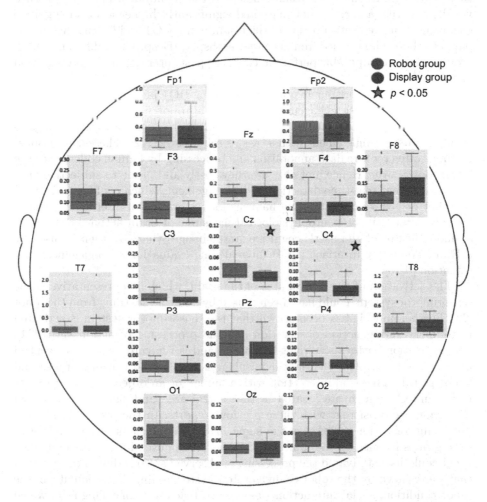

Fig. 3. Distribution of EEG Engagement Index computed for both groups in each EEG channel. The Robot group showed a significantly higher EEG Engagement Index at Cz and C4 locations.

4   Discussion

The present study aimed to validate the benefit of a robot tutor for second language learning in comparison to a screen-based learning experience using EEG analysis and a post-interaction word recognition test. By employing neurophysiological measures of EEG, we sought to objectively evaluate children's task engagement during the learning phase and validate its association with their learning outcome. Our results indicated that children who learned French vocabulary with a social robot presented significantly higher levels of cognitive engagement in the central region of the brain, namely C4 and Cz channels, compared to those who learned from a computer display. Despite this difference, both groups showed comparable performance on the post-interaction word recognition test.

Our results support our hypothesis regarding RQ1 in that EEG can identify different levels of task engagement during child-robot interaction. The majority of past HRI studies have relied on behavior analysis or subjective ratings to evaluate a user's engagement with a task or robot [14,21,22]. These conventional methods often require data annotation and processing by human coders once the interaction is over. Hence, not only are they costly and prone to subjective bias, but also prevent real-time detection of disengagement, which could then be used by robot behavior adaptation mechanisms for restoration of interaction dynamics [22]. Alternatively, neurophysiological measures of brain activity provide an online indicator of the user's cognitive state changes that can then be used by a Brain-Computer Interface (BCI) for real-time evaluation of engagement and attention [6,15].

The activation of the central area of the brain, which is representative of the sensorimotor system, could have been caused by auditory learning from the robot [23]. Furthermore, it has been shown that the sensorimotor system is activated in toddlers during action observation and the processing of action verbs [24]. This activation pattern was right-lateralized and is typically seen in the central areas of the brain [24]. The right hemisphere is involved in learning of a second language through social interaction with a human or an object [25]. Our results in Cz and C4, which are located in the central area and right hemisphere of the brain, are consistent with these previous reports. In the present study, the processing of action verbs was the same in both conditions since children of both groups listened to the same story. However, the use of a moving embodied agent could have activated the processing of observed actions due to the gestures that were shown by the robot to invigorate the storytelling. Additionally, in the robot condition, social interaction was used to teach a second language, which can explain the higher EEG Engagement Index in this group.

Based on past research regarding the benefits of robots in educational settings [2,13], it was expected that the current study would obtain a higher learning outcome in the Robot group. However, no significant difference was found between the two groups in their word recognition test performance. Thus, our second hypothesis regarding a better learning outcome in robot-assisted language learning could not be confirmed. An explanation for this could be the role of the visual material (pictures of words) that were presented on the computer screen during the learning phase. The use of technology has been shown to have a positive impact on the learning outcome when compared to traditional learning [26]. This means that the use of the display and animated pictures during storytelling could have already extended a positive effect on the engagement level and subsequently learning outcome of the children in the Display group. Additionally, all children were tested in a laboratory environment and were listening to a French story for the first time. The novelty of the environment could have introduced higher attention levels in all children, which is supported by the generally higher values of EEG Engagement Index observed in the prefrontal, frontal and temporal areas of both groups (Fig. 3). Previous research by Meyer et al. (2019) similarly reported increased fronto-temporal activity in 4-year old children during a language task, which was associated with cognitive task engagement and higher attention load [27].

The EEG Engagement Index that was employed by this research is a known metric [17], which provides a combination of higher and lower frequency bands instead of comparing each frequency band separately as previous studies have done [18,27,28]. This metric is particularly useful in development of BCI systems for real-time monitoring of engagement and attention [6,15]. However, past research has mainly employed this metric in adult learners and therefore observed its responsiveness in the (pre)frontal cortex of the adult population. In our study, the contribution of this index when measured from the frontal brain region of the children remained inconclusive, while significant effects were found in the central region. Research shows that children do not yet have fully developed frontal lobe and unlike adults, they mainly rely on sensorimotor cortex -in the central brain regions- for executive functions, cognitive processing and working memory [29]. Thus, future research should further investigate the reliability of this index and its associated brain regions among children population. Additionally, the validity of this index can be confirmed by comparing the EEG signals with other real-time measures of engagement such as facial expressions, eye tracking, galvanic skin responses, etc. [30].

The study of EEG brain activity during robot interaction is a novel and yet unexplored terrain that deserves more attention from the HRI community [15,16]. The growing market of low-cost consumer EEG headsets promises increased accessibility and adoption of this method in future educational environments. Therefore, more research is needed to investigate the potential and challenges of this technique in the HRI domain. The current study can further be expanded by increasing the number of participants and learning sessions. Particularly, increased number of sessions in a longitudinal study can shed light on the impact of novelty effect and the robot's social presence on engagement and learning outcome of the children. Furthermore, it would be interesting for future research to employ the EEG Engagement Index in an online BCI system where engagement and attention level of children are measured in real-time during the learning task. This will facilitate adaptive robot behavior for fast recovery of attention drops and eventually increased efficiency in robot-assisted learning [5,6].

5   Conclusion

The aim of this research was to quantify the effect of robot presence during children's second language learning using EEG brain activity and a post-interaction performance test. Two groups of Japanese children learned French vocabulary in different conditions; one group listened to a storytelling robot that used gestures together with pictures on a computer screen during storytelling and the other group only watched the story on the screen without the robot. Our results revealed a significantly higher cognitive engagement in the Robot group as measured by EEG in the central region of the brain. This difference is explained by the activation of the children's sensorimotor system due to the processing of observed actions and auditory learning. Our findings contribute to the field of child-robot interaction by introducing a new objective measure of interaction dynamics as it is the first study that used EEG to measure engagement in children during a second language learning task. Future research should further examine the efficacy of this measure in quantifying the temporal changes of engagement during the learning process and its association with children's learning outcome after the interaction is over.

References

1. Cheng, Y.W., Sun, P.C., Chen, N.S.: The essential applications of educational robot: requirement analysis from the perspectives of experts, researchers and instructors. Comput. Educ. **126**, 399–416 (2018)
2. Randall, N.: A survey of robot-assisted language learning (RALL). ACM Trans. Hum.-Robot Interact. (THRI) **9**(1), 1–36 (2019)
3. Kanero, J., Geçkin, V., Oranç, C., Mamus, E., Küntay, A.C., Göksun, T.: Social robots for early language learning: current evidence and future directions. Child Dev. Perspect. **12**(3), 146–151 (2018)
4. Vogt, P., De Haas, M., De Jong, C., Baxter, P., Krahmer, E.: Child-robot interactions for second language tutoring to preschool children. Front. Hum. Neurosci. **11**, 73 (2017)
5. Lytridis, C., Bazinas, C., Papakostas, G.A., Kaburlasos, V.: On measuring engagement level during child-robot interaction in education. In: International Conference on Robotics in Education (RiE), pp. 3–13, April 2019
6. Szafir, D., Mutlu, B.: Pay attention! Designing adaptive agents that monitor and improve user engagement. In Proceedings of the SIGCHI Conference on Human Factors in Computing Systems, pp. 11–20, May 2012
7. Glas, N., Pelachaud, C.: Definitions of engagement in human-agent interaction. In: 2015 International Conference on Affective Computing and Intelligent Interaction (ACII), pp. 944–949. IEEE, September 2015
8. Cambridge Dictionary. Engagement: Definition of engagement in English. https://dictionary.cambridge.org/dictionary/english/engagement. Accessed 20 Feb 2021
9. Henrie, C.R., Halverson, L.R., Graham, C.R.: Measuring student engagement in technology-mediated learning: a review. Comput. Educ. **90**, 36–53 (2015)
10. Cambridge Dictionary. Attention: Definition of attention in English. https://dictionary.cambridge.org/dictionary/english/attention. Accessed 20 Feb 2021

11. Chiang, H.S., Hsiao, K.L., Liu, L.C.: EEG-based detection model for evaluating and improving learning attention. J. Med. Biol. Eng. **38**(6), 847–856 (2018)
12. Han, J.: Robot assisted language learning. Lang. Learn. Technol. **16**(3), 1–9 (2012)
13. de Wit, J., et al.: The effect of a robot's gestures and adaptive tutoring on children's acquisition of second language vocabularies. In: Proceedings of the 2018 ACM/IEEE International Conference on Human-Robot Interaction, pp. 50–58, February 2018
14. de Wit, J., Brandse, A., Krahmer, E., Vogt, P.: Varied human-like gestures for social robots: investigating the effects on children's engagement and language learning. In: Proceedings of the 2020 ACM/IEEE International Conference on Human-Robot Interaction, pp. 359–367, March 2020
15. Alimardani, M., Hiraki, K.: Passive brain-computer interfaces for enhanced human-robot interaction. Front. Robot. A I, 7 (2020)
16. Yoon, S., Alimardani, M., Hiraki, K.: The effect of robot-guided meditation on intra-brain EEG phase synchronization. In: Companion of the 2021 ACM/IEEE International Conference on Human-Robot Interaction, pp. 318–322, March 2021
17. Khedher, A.B., Jraidi, I., Frasson, C.: Tracking students' mental engagement using EEG signals during an interaction with a virtual learning environment. J. Intell. Learn. Syst. Appl. **11**(01), 1 (2019)
18. Soltanlou, M., Artemenko, C., Dresler, T., Fallgatter, A.J., Nuerk, H.C., Ehlis, A.C.: Oscillatory EEG changes during arithmetic learning in children. Dev. Neuropsychol. **44**(3), 325–338 (2019)
19. Preston, A.R., Eichenbaum, H.: Interplay of hippocampus and prefrontal cortex in memory. Curr. Biol. **23**(17), R764–R773 (2013)
20. Collins, A., Koechlin, E.: Reasoning, learning, and creativity: frontal lobe function and human decision-making. PLoS Biol. **10**(3), e1001293 (2012)
21. Kont, M., Alimardani, M., et al.: Engagement and mind perception within human-robot interaction: a comparison between elderly and young adults. In: Wagner, A.R. (ed.) ICSR 2020. LNCS (LNAI), vol. 12483, pp. 344–356. Springer, Cham (2020). https://doi.org/10.1007/978-3-030-62056-1_29
22. Oertel, C., et al.: Engagement in human-agent interaction: an overview. Front. Robot. AI **7**, 92 (2020)
23. Kraus, N., White-Schwoch, T.: Unraveling the biology of auditory learning: a cognitive-sensorimotor-reward framework. Trends Cogn. Sci. **19**(11), 642–654 (2015)
24. Antognini, K., Daum, M.M.: Toddlers show sensorimotor activity during auditory verb processing. Neuropsychologia **126**, 82–91 (2019)
25. Li, P., Jeong, H.: The social brain of language: grounding second language learning in social interaction. NPJ Sci. Learn. **5**(1), 1–9 (2020)
26. Lin, M.H., Chen, H.G.: A study of the effects of digital learning on learning motivation and learning outcome. Eurasia J. Math. Sci. Technol. Educ. **13**(7), 3553–3564 (2017)
27. Meyer, M., Endedijk, H.M., Van Ede, F., Hunnius, S.: Theta oscillations in 4-year-olds are sensitive to task engagement and task demands. Sci. Rep. **9**(1), 1–11 (2019)
28. Alimardani, M., Kemmeren, L., Okumura, K., Hiraki, K.: Robot-assisted mindfulness practice: analysis of neurophysiological responses and affective state change. In: 2020 29th IEEE International Conference on Robot and Human Interactive Communication (RO-MAN), pp. 683–689. IEEE, August 2020

29. Mierau, A., et al.: The interrelation between sensorimotor abilities, cognitive performance and individual EEG alpha peak frequency in young children. Clin. Neurophysiol. **127**(1), 270–276 (2016)
30. Doherty, K., Doherty, G.: Engagement in HCI: conception, theory and measurement. ACM Comput. Surv. (CSUR) **51**(5), 1–39 (2018)

Social Perception of Robots

Individuals Expend More Effort to Compete Against Robots Than Humans After Observing Competitive Human–Robot Interactions

Rosanne H. Timmerman[1] , Te-Yi Hsieh[1] , Anna Henschel[1] ,
Ruud Hortensius[1,2] , and Emily S. Cross[1,3(✉)]

[1] Institute of Neuroscience and Psychology, University of Glasgow, Scotland, UK
emily.cross@glasgow.ac.uk
[2] Department of Psychology, Utrecht University, Heidelberglaan 1, 3584 CS Utrecht,
Netherlands
[3] Department of Cognitive Science, Macquarie University, Sydney, Australia

Abstract. In everyday life, we often observe and learn from interactions between other individuals—so-called third-party encounters. As robots are poised to become an increasingly familiar presence in our daily lives, third-party encounters between other people and robots might offer a valuable approach to influence people's behaviors and attitudes towards robots. Here, we conducted an online experiment where participants ($n = 48$) watched videos of human—robot dyads interacting in a cooperative or competitive manner. Following this observation, we measured participants' behavior and attitudes towards the human and robotic agents. First, participants played a game with the agents to measure whether their behavior was affected by their observed encounters. Second, participants' attitudes toward the agents were measured before and after the game. We found that the third-party encounters influenced behavior during the game but not attitudes towards the observed agents. Participants showed more effort towards robots than towards humans, especially when the human and robot agents were framed as competitive in the observation phase. Our study suggests that people's behaviors towards robots can be shaped by the mere observation of third-party encounters between robots and other people.

Keywords: Human—robot interaction · Third-party encounters · Social robotics · Artificial agents · Social cognition · Cooperation · Competition

1 Introduction

We frequently observe interactions among others—so-called third-party encounters. These encounters influence people's attitudes towards the observed individuals and, if positive, can serve as an easily to implement and unthreatening tool to reduce prejudice towards minority groups, unfamiliar individuals and other outgroups [1–9]. Some

---

R. H. Timmerman and T.-Y. Hsieh—Co-first authors.
A. Henschel, R. Hortensius and E.S. Cross—Co-senior authors.

© Springer Nature Switzerland AG 2021
H. Li et al. (Eds.): ICSR 2021, LNAI 13086, pp. 685–696, 2021.
https://doi.org/10.1007/978-3-030-90525-5_60

evidence suggests that the effects of third-party encounters can equal or even surpass those brought about by direct contact [10]. Furthermore, these effects of vicarious contact have been shown to persist over time, and can even generalize beyond the observed agents [11, 12]. For example, it was found that children prefer the friends of people receiving positive non-verbal signals over friends of people receiving negative signals [12].

Third-party encounters hold great practical potential for improving human–robot interactions (HRIs). While robots become more prevalent in daily life [13], negative attitudes towards these machines persist [14]. Third-party encounters between humans and robots have been proposed as a possible tool to reduce people's negative attitudes towards robots by a number of different researchers [14–17]. For instance, Fraune and colleagues [16] showed that watching positive HRIs increased people's willingness to interact with robots.

So far, most research has focused on the impact of third-party encounters on observers' attitudes towards robots, with limited empirical evidence to date showing that these encounters can induce behavior change in the observer, specifically towards the observed agents [7]. Skinner and colleagues [12] found that observing an interaction between people can change some daily behaviors unspecific to the observed people. Yet, more research on behavioral change is essential to lay the foundations for robust HRI. For example, people who have negative attitudes towards robots have been also shown to behave more negatively towards robots during real-life interactions [17].

The aims of the current exploratory study were to replicate findings suggesting that attitudes towards robots can be changed by observing HRIs [1–9], and to investigate potential behavior change in observers [7] based on this observational manipulation. Specifically, we set out to examine whether observing videos of cooperative versus competitive HRIs influence how people perceive similar agents, as well as behave towards them. We conducted an online experiment where participants observed human–robot dyads acting cooperatively or competitively and assessed participants' attitude changes and motivation to engage with each observed agent in a simple, competitive game. Participants were led to believe that they were playing against an algorithm based on pre-recorded behavior of the different agents. Based on the previous findings, we evaluated the following general expectations:

1. People should show a difference in motivation when playing the game with agents framed as cooperative versus competitive.
2. Participants should show differential preferences for cooperative vs. competitive agents. This is based on findings from Correia and colleagues [15], who showed that robots cooperating with the team were rated more positively than a robot following its own goal, regardless of the game result.

We further explored the extent to which opponent type influenced behaviors.

2   Methods

2.1   Data Accessibility Statement

Materials, data and code for all experiments are available on the OSF https://osf.io/ uvy3b/. We report all measures in the study, all manipulations, any data exclusions and the sample size determination rule.

2.2   Participants

Forty-eight participants, of which 16 were female (M age $= 26.2$, SD $= 6.8$; sex of one participant remained unspecified) were recruited via Prolific (www.prolific.co). As a rule of thumb, we determined the sample size by multiplying the number of participants recruited in a comparable study by two. Specifically, we used the study by Walbrin and colleagues, Experiment 2 as reference ($n = 23$) [18]. The main experiment was described as watching videos of human and robotic agents followed by playing a game with these agents. To increase the believability of the online experimental setting, participants were told that they would play against algorithms based on these previously observed agents. Participants received £2.52 for their participation in the study (equivalent to £6.73/hour). To increase motivation, participants were told that the top 10% had a chance of receiving a bonus payment of £5. Inclusion criteria were an approval rate of 100% on the Prolific website and no participation in the validation and pilot studies prior to the main experiment (see below). Participants were naive to the goal of the study, most of them (87.5%) were unfamiliar with the robot used in the study and had little or no experience in interacting with robots in daily life (median on a scale from 1 (never) to 7 (daily) was 2 with an interquartile range of 1). The experiments were designed in PsychoPy3 and later uploaded to Pavlovia (https://pavlovia.org/; [19]) an online experiment platform. The whole experiment took approximately 20 min. Participants provided informed consent before the start of the experiment. The study procedure was approved by the Research Ethics Committee of the College of Science and Engineering at the University of Glasgow (protocol number: 300180301).

2.3   Experimental Design

We used a two-by-two (agent type: human or robot; agent intention: cooperative or competitive) within-subjects factorial design to examine the impact of agent type, agent intention, and the interaction between these two factors on participants' attitudes and behaviors towards the observed agents.

2.4   Stimuli

Participants watched 2 short videos (10 s) of a human and robot playing a bar game together, which served as a framing story to the main task. In these videos (Fig. 1A and 1B), a bar was located in the middle of the screen between two opposite goals, one in the upper and one in the lower part of the screen. The agents moved their arms either up or down, giving the impression that they controlled the movement of the bar.

In the cooperative condition, the human and robot appeared to work together to reach the same goal by moving their arm in the same direction simultaneously. In the competitive condition, both agents tried to reach opposite goals by moving their arms in opposite directions (Fig. 1B). The purpose of the videos was to frame each agent as either competitive or cooperative. Later in the experiment, participants engaged in a bar game similar to this one with one of the agents (either the cooperative robot, cooperative human, competitive robot or competitive human). The bar game looked almost identical to the one in the framing videos, but the participants could now actively move the bar upwards by pressing the space bar. Again, there were two goals, the upper one belonging to the agent. The videos were edited in DaVinci Resolve v15.3.1 1 [20]. The agents were filmed in front of a green screen, which was later removed and replaced by the bar game. Three validation studies (first validation: n = 20, second validation: n = 12, third validation: n = 40) were conducted in order to improve and select the most salient stimuli for the main experiment. The third validation study (containing the videos for the main experiment) showed that agents were consistently rated as either cooperative or competitive, on a slider from '1' as 'competitive' to '7' as 'cooperative' (cooperative human: M = 5.60, SD = 1.74, cooperative robot: M = 5.97, SD = 1.48, competitive human: M = 2.35, SD = 1.85, competitive robot: M = 2.17, SD = 1.75) (Fig. 2D). To avoid possible gender bias effects, we generated two different orders: order A in which the female human agent was the cooperative agent and the male was the competitive agent, and order B where the male human agent was the cooperative agent and the female the competitive agent. For all analyses, no differences were found between the two orders.

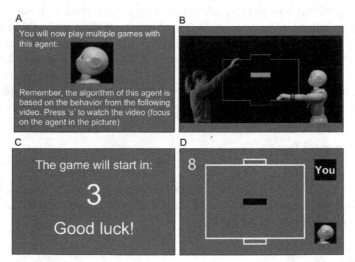

Fig. 1. Bar game design. (A) The bar game began with an agent's picture signifying participants' next opponent. (B) This was followed by a framing video. (C) Countdown to prepare the participant for the game. (D) The bar game lay-out.

2.5 Measures

To operationalize people's motivation to play against agents, we measured the number of space bar presses during the bar game. Participants played three games with each agent, and each game was at a different difficulty level (easy, medium or hard). Difficulty levels were manipulated to measure subtle differences in motivation and to increase believability of the bar game. The different difficulty levels were defined by: 1) the number of times the participant had to press the space bar before it could be moved upwards (from easy to hard respectively: 2, 4, 6), and 2) how many times the bar would move downwards towards the goal of the opponent agent (150, 100, 50). The resulting 12 games were played in a randomized order. A game ended either when ten seconds had passed or when one of the players reached one of the goals. After the game round ended, the score was presented and participants could see how many times they pressed the space bar, if they reached the goal, and if they received a penalty, as well as their total scores. Participants would get a penalty (-5 points) if they did not let go of the space bar (instead of pressing "space" repeatedly). Participants could receive one penalty per game, thus the maximum penalties per participant was 48. Penalties were low (M = 1.79, SD = 3.75). We interpreted more space presses as increased competitiveness and effort invested in the game. Measures of participants' attitudes towards agents involved three parts: First, participants' preference towards agents was measured before (pre-preference) and after (post-preference) the game by preferential ranking from "most preferable" to "least preferable" to play a game with. The pre- and post-measurements were implemented because we anticipated that an effect of the third-party encounters would be stronger in pre-preference (i.e., right after watching the framing videos) than in post-preference ratings (i.e., after playing the games where all agents played the role of a game opponent). Second, the perceived cooperativeness and socialness towards agents was determined by slider ratings from competitive to cooperative, and from individual to social. Last, participants' decisions of whether an agent was cooperative or competitive was acquired by using a two-alternative forced choice task.

2.6 Experimental Procedure

The main experiment consisted of four parts. First, participants observed two framing videos to learn the roles of each agent (cooperative or competitive agents). While watching the videos, they were instructed to pay attention specifically to one of the agents. One of the videos showed agents cooperating with each other, while the other showed two agents competing against each other. Each framing video was repeated twice for each agent. To check whether participants paid attention to the videos, they were asked whether the specified agent had reached the goal. Following the third-party encounters, participants ranked the agents from most to least preferable to play a game with. Next, participants played a bar game with each agent in a semi-randomized order. Before the game, participants read a cover story that suggested they were actually playing against an algorithm based on the observed agents' game behavior. Participants were told that the behaviors were modelled and created by using a deep neural network. The story was accompanied by an image of a schematic explanation of a deep neural network. The bar game (Fig. 1D) began with an agent's picture signifying this round's opponent (Fig. 1A).

To remind participants of the intention of the agent, the framing video was shown again (Fig. 1B). There was a countdown announcing the start of each game (Fig. 1C). After each game participants were shown their scores (Fig. 1E).

In the final part, each agent was rated on their socialness and cooperativeness levels. Ratings were placed at the end so that participants could form their own opinions throughout the experiment. Finally, we asked participants to describe the algorithm in their own words to check whether they believed the cover story. The free text responses showed that the words most used to describe the agents were 'computer' (n = 51), 'man' (n = 22), 'woman' (n = 21) and 'robot' (n = 17). It is not surprising that the agents are most often described as computers since a computer is often the layman's interpretation of an algorithm.

2.7 Data Processing and Analysis

All data analyses were carried out in R v4.0.1 [21]. For the behavioral data of the numbers of space bar presses, we ran a linear mixed effects model with the lme4 package (v1.1.23) [22] to examine if participants' game behaviors were influenced by agent type (human or robot) and agent intention (cooperative or competitive) while controlling the random individual differences (Prolific_id), trial differences (trial_number), and the random effects by game difficulty levels (difficulty_level). The model building started from the maximal random effect components [23], and we reduced the complexity, resulting in the following formula: numbers of presses ~ agent_type*agent_intention + (1 + agent_type |Prolific_id) + (1|trial_number) + (1|difficulty_level).

The analyses regarding participants' attitudes toward each agent was done in three parts. First, participants' ordinal ranking of the most preferable agent to the least preferable was analysed via a mixed effects ordinal regression model with the ordinal package (v2019.12.10) [24]. We tested the fixed effects of agent type (human or robot), agent intention (cooperative or competitive), and ranking timing (pre-game or post-game) on people's ordinal preferences, while controlling the random effects of participants (Prolific_id) and the random order of the four agents introduced to each participant (present_order). The final model that converged was ranking ~ agent_type*agent_intention*rank_time + (1 + agent_type*agent_intention|Prolific_id) + (1 + agent_type*agent_intention|present_order).

Second, participants' slider ratings of the agents' cooperativeness and socialness were analysed via two linear mixed effects models respectively. For the cooperativeness model, agent type (human or robot) and agent intention (cooperative or competitive) were included as fixed effects, and the final random effect structure which led to model convergence involved: by-subject random intercepts, and random slopes for the effects of agent type and agent intention on subjects: cooperativeness_rating ~ agent_type* agent_intention + (1 + agent_type + agent_intention |Prolific_id). The socialness model was similarly designed, except that it included an additional random factor of order (order A or B): socialness_rating ~ agent_type* agent_intention + (1 + agent_type + agent_intention |Prolific_id) + (1|order).

Third, we analysed participants' binomial forced choices on whether an agent was cooperative or competitive via a mixed effects logistic regression model with the "glmer" function in lme4 package (v1.1.23). We examined the fixed effects of agent type (human or robot) and agent intention (cooperative or competitive) on participants choices, while controlling by-subject random intercepts and random slopes for agent type on subjects: forced_choice ~ agent_type + agent_intention + (1 + agent_type|Prolific_id). All linear data were centred by the grand mean before model building. When conducting pairwise post-hoc tests, p-values were adjusted using Tukey's method. All analysis code can be accessed on our dedicated OSF page for this project: https://osf.io/uvy3b/.

3   Results

3.1   Behavioral Results (Bar Game)

The result of the mixed effects model showed a significant main effect of agent type (β = 3.08, 95% CI [0.78, 5.38], p = .009), and a significant interaction between agent type and agent intention ($\beta = -3.03$, 95% CI [$-5.42, -0.65$], p = .013) on the numbers of times participants pressed the space bar. No main effect of agent intention was observed ($\beta = 0.59$, 95% CI [$-1.09, 2.28$], p = .491). In general, participants pressed the space bar more often when playing against robots (M = 27.87, SD = 21.86) than against humans (M = 26.30, SD = 23.03) (Fig. 2A). Pairwise post-hoc tests on the interaction between agent type and intention were carried out with the emmeans package (v1.4.7) [25]. When playing against the competitive robot (M = 29.09, SD = 22.25), participants pressed the

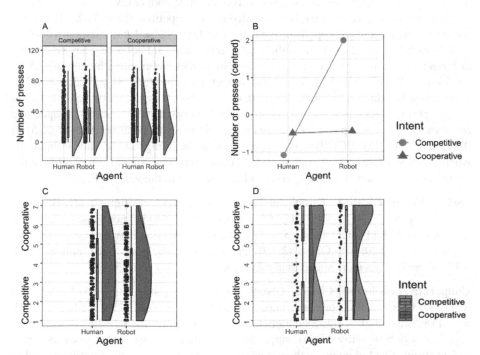

Fig. 2. (A) Number of presses in bar game per agent. (B) Interaction between agent and intent on centered number of presses. (C) Cooperativeness ratings per agent in main experiment. (D) Cooperativeness ratings per agent in validation experiment.

space bar more often than when playing against the cooperative robot (M = 26.65, SD = 21.40), t(2193.0) = 2.84, p = .024 (Fig. 2B). However, no clear difference emerged when comparing the competitive robot and the competitive human (M = 26.00, SD = 23.08), t(87.6) = -2.63, p = .049. Likewise, there was no significant difference found in the comparisons between competitive human and cooperative human (M = 26.60, SD = 22.99), t(2193.0) = -0.69, p = .902, competitive human and cooperative robot, t(87.6) = -0.55, p = .947, competitive robot and cooperative human, t(87.6) = 2.12, p = .154, or cooperative human and cooperative robot, t(87.6) = 30.04, p = 1.000.

3.2 Attitude Results

Preferential Ranking of Agents. In the result of our mixed effects ordinal regression model, agent type (odds ratio = 1.34, 95% CI [0.37, 4.90], p = .658), agent intention (odds ratio = 1.19, 95% CI [0.34, 4.09], p = .787), or ranking timing (odd ratio = 1.16, 95% CI [0.50, 2.67], p = .724) did not influence participants' preferential ranking towards the four agents.

Cooperativeness Slider Rating. Participants' cooperativeness ratings were significantly influenced by the interaction between agent type and agent intention ($\beta = -0.28$, 95% CI [−0.52, −0.04], p = .02), but not by the main effect of agent type ($\beta = -0.06$, 95% CI [−0.58, 0.41], p = .804) or agent intention ($\beta = 0.19$, 95% CI [-0.32, 0.71], p = .462). The cooperative human agent was rated most cooperative (M = 3.81, SD = 1.71), whereas the cooperative robot was rated most competitive (M = 3.47, SD = 1.42) among the four agents (competitive human: M = 3.62, SD = 1.63; competitive robot: M = 3.56, SD = 1.59). However, follow-up post hoc tests did not reveal any significant differences in the following pairs: competitive human vs. cooperative human (t(52.5) = −0.74, p = .883); competitive human vs. competitive robot (t(53.8) = 0.25, p = .995); competitive human vs. cooperative robot (t(47.0) = 0.44, p = .972); cooperative human vs. competitive robot (t(47.0) = 0.72, p = .888); cooperative human vs. cooperative robot (t(53.8) = 1.43, p = .486); competitive robot vs. cooperative robot (t(52.5) = 0.34, p = .986) (Fig. 2C). This is in contrast with the ratings in the validation study, where we observed a very clear distinction in cooperativeness slider ratings between the agents that were framed as cooperative and competitive in the videos (Fig. 2D).

Socialness Slider Rating. Participants' socialness ratings were significantly impacted by agent type ($\beta = -0.55$, 95% CI [−0.96, −0.15], p = .008) but not by agent intention ($\beta = 0.12$, 95% CI [−0.30, 0.54], p = .577) nor the interaction between agent type and intention ($\beta = -0.20$, 95% CI [-0.42, 0.02], p = .079). Participants rated humans (M = 3.79, SD = 1.50) as more social than robots (M = 3.14, SD = 1.33).

Cooperativeness Forced Choice. CNeither agent type (odds ratio = 0.46, 95% CI [0.11, 1.93], p = .288) nor agent intention (odds ratio = 0.74, 95% CI [0.50, 1.08], p = .118) was found to influence participants' forced choices of whether an agent was cooperative or competitive. This is surprising, given that in the validation study there was a clear strong effect of intent on the forced choices. Agents were consistently labelled as either cooperative (cooperative human: n = 32, cooperative robot: n = 33) or competitive (competitive human: n = 34, competitive robot: n = 34).

4 Discussion

We investigated the impact of human—robot encounters on people's attitudes and behaviors in the context of a simple online competitive game. Participants observed human—robot dyads interacting either cooperatively or competitively and were then led to believe they were playing a competitive game against algorithms informed by these agents' behaviors (while in reality, they were playing against the computer).

Third-party encounters influenced participants' competitiveness during game play, but had no influence on attitudes reported towards the observed agents. The main finding in our study was that participants showed higher game competitiveness (i.e., pressed the space bar more frequently) toward robotic agents than human agents, especially when the agents were framed as competitive in the observation phase. However, the findings on attitude change towards robots were inconsistent. Our results suggest that people's perceived cooperativeness of the agents was influenced by the interaction between agent type and agent intention, and that people perceived human agents as more social than robotic agents. Below we discuss these findings in detail.

Participants' increased competitiveness towards robotic compared to human opponents fits with previous research, in which participants behaved more competitively toward a robot than a human in economic games [26]. Our study further showed that such discriminatingly competitive behaviors toward robots could be diminished by observing cooperative human—robot encounters before engaging in an HRI. After participants observed the human and robotic agents cooperating in short videos, they responded similarly to cooperative robots and cooperative humans in the competitive online game. Notably, the effect of human–robot encounters we found on game behaviors existed regardless of the agents' actual behaviors when people directly interacted with them. Participants in the present study showed the highest game competitiveness towards the robot framed as competitive in the observation phase, even though all agents' game behaviors (behavioral competitiveness) remained consistent according to pre-programmed difficulty levels. These findings highlight the effects of third-party encounters on observers' behaviors, and relate to previous studies documenting the persistent impact of first impressions on people's behaviors during HRIs [27, 28].

Regarding the impact of human–robot encounters on participants' attitudes towards the agents, the present findings were inconsistent. First, encounters of cooperative and competitive human—robot dyads had no effect on participants' agent preference rankings, either in the pre-preference or post-preference tasks. This might suggest that the third-party encounters of cooperative and competitive HRI were irrelevant and thus did not influence people's preferences towards the agents in our experiment. A study by Huisman and colleagues [29] showed that the perceived politeness of virtual robots is not affected by cooperativeness or competitiveness of an agent during a game. However, other research reports that perceived warmth, competence, and personality of a robot are more crucial factors in our preferences towards robots [30, 31]. Future studies could consider manipulating these factors in human—robot encounters to investigate the subsequent impact on people's preferences towards the observed agents.

The impact of cooperative and competitive human—robot encounters on people's perceived cooperativeness towards the agents was not robust in our study. Our post hoc analyses did not reveal any difference between any agent pairs, albeit the significant interaction between agent type (human/robot) and agent intention (cooperative/competitive) emerged for participants' cooperativeness slider rating towards the agents. Similarly, participants' forced choices regarding the cooperative and competitive nature of an agent were not influenced by agent intention framing or agent type. These results suggest that the agent intention manipulation was perhaps not strong enough to shape participants' perceived cooperativeness of the agents, which contradicted the results of our validation studies where competitive and cooperative framing was accurately differentiated by participants' cooperativeness rating. Another possible explanation for the ineffective agent intention manipulation was the competitive nature of the game. In the bar game used here, participants and agents had opposite goals to achieve and therefore all the agents might be perceived as competitive by the participants. This competitive game experience may obscure the manipulation of agent intention in the prior observation phase. Previous studies have pointed out that the perceived competitiveness in environments or agents can shape people's attitudes. For examples, Mutlu and colleagues found that people had more positive attitudes towards the ASIMO robot in a cooperative game context than in a competitive game context [32]. Even when researchers did not intend to frame the robot as competitive, participants can be sensitive to robot's non-cooperative decisions and responded to these reciprocally [33]. Therefore, future research on this topic may choose to make more judicious decisions when designing a HRI context and manipulating an agent's intention, to ensure an agent's attribute in third-party encounters is not in contrast with how the agents behave in the actual HRI.

Finally, our study revealed a significant effect of agent type (human/robot) on participants' socialness ratings towards the agents. Human agents were rated as more social than robotic agents. This is not surprising since we have extensive social experience with human interaction partners, whereas robots are only emerging in social contexts. However, as robots become more prevalent, especially in social contexts, it could be possible to amplify a robots' perceived socialness by changing [34]. It would be valuable for future research to explore whether third-party encounters of robots with different characteristics lead to varying degrees of perceived socialness, as well as to further identify which factors are key to shaping the attribution of socialness to robots.

In summary, the current study provides important evidence documenting the influence of observed human—robot encounters on people's behaviors towards the observed robots. Specifically, in our online game environment, participants behaved more competitively when competing against the robot previously framed as competitive than the robot framed as cooperative. However, this work will require follow-up research to determine the generalizability of people's behaviors during online games to behaviors displayed during real-world HRI that takes place with embodied (as opposed to virtual) agents. Although online studies can provide insightful evidence [35–36], physical embodiment is an important factor that shapes our perceptions of and behaviors towards robots [34, 38–40]. For example, people report more enjoyment and engagement during embodied HRI than during virtual HRI [38]. Future research could further extend the current exploration of human—robot encounters to other contexts, or to other aspects of social behaviors, as well as further substantiate the link between people's attitudes and behaviors during HRI. By doing so, researchers should be able to provide further and clearer evidence of the potential utility of third-party encounters to promote the social quality of real-life HRIs, which should hopefully lead to more effectively and usefully embedded social robots in human society.

5 Competing Interests

The authors declare that they have no competing interests.

Funding. Research supported by funding from the European Research Council (ERC) under the European Union's Horizon 2020 research and innovation program (Grant agreement number 677270 to E.S.C.), the Leverhulme Trust (PLP-2018–152 to E.S.C), and the BIAL Foundation (to R.H.).

References

1. Johnson, J.D., Ashburn-Nardo, L.: Soc. Psychol. Personal. Sci. **5**(3), 369–376 (2014). https://doi.org/10.1177/1948550613499938
2. Mazziotta, A., et al.: Group Process. Intergroup Relat. **14**(2), 255–274 (2011). https://doi.org/10.1177/1368430210390533
3. Quadflieg, S., Penton-Voak, I.S.: Curr. Dir. Psychol. Sci. **26**(4), 383–389 (2017). https://doi.org/10.1177/0963721417694353
4. Quadflieg, S., Westmoreland, K.: Making sense of other people's encounters: towards an integrative model of relational impression formation. J. Nonverbal Behav. **43**(2), 233–256 (2019). https://doi.org/10.1007/s10919-019-00295-1
5. Shapiro, J.R., et al.: J. Exp. Soc. Psychol. **47**(1), 221–227 (2011). https://doi.org/10.1016/j.jesp.2010.10.006
6. Vezzali, L., et al.: Group Process. Intergroup Relat. **22**(7), 1059–1076 (2019). https://doi.org/10.1177/1368430218809885
7. West, K., Turner, R.: J. Exp. Soc. Psychol. **50**, 57–64 (2014). https://doi.org/10.1016/j.jesp.2013.06.009
8. Willard, G., et al.: Organ. Behav. Hum. Decis. Process. **128**, 96–107 (2015). https://doi.org/10.1016/j.obhdp.2015.04.002
9. Winkler, P., et al.: Short video interventions to reduce mental health stigma: a multi-centre randomised controlled trial in nursing high schools. Soc. Psychiatry Psychiatr. Epidemiol. **52**(12), 1549–1557 (2017). https://doi.org/10.1007/s00127-017-1449-y
10. Eller, A., et al.: Int. J. Intercult. Relat. **36**(5), 637–646 (2012). https://doi.org/10.1016/j.ijintrel.2012.03.005
11. Lemmer, G., Wagner, U.: EJSP. **45**(2), 152–168 (2015). https://doi.org/10.1002/ejsp.2079
12. Skinner, A.L., et al.: Psychol. Sci. **28**(2), 216–224 (2017). https://doi.org/10.1177/0956797616678930
13. Broadbent, E.: Annu. Rev. Psychol. **68**(1), 627–652 (2017). https://doi.org/10.1146/annurev-psych-010416-043958
14. Wullenkord, R., Eyssel, F.: 23rd IEEE International Symposium on Robot and Human Interactive Communication (2014). https://doi.org/10.1109/ROMAN.2014.6926300
15. Correia, F., et al.: 14th ACM/IEEE International Conference on HRI, pp. 143–151 (2019). https://doi.org/10.1109/HRI.2019.8673299
16. Fraune, M.R., et al.: Comput. Hum. Behav. **105**, e9414 (2020). https://doi.org/10.1016/j.chb.2019.106220

17. Nomura, T., et al.: IEEE Trans. Robot. **24**(2), 442–451 (2008). https://doi.org/10.1109/TRO. 2007.914004
18. Walbrin, J., et al.: Neuropsychologia **112**, 31–39 (2018). https://doi.org/10.1016/j.neuropsyc hologia.2018.02.023
19. Peirce, J., et al.: PsychoPy2: experiments in behavior made easy. Behav. Res. Methods **51**(1), 195–203 (2019). https://doi.org/10.3758/s13428-018-01193-y
20. DaVinci Resolve Engineering Team, Blackmagic Design (2019)
21. R Core Team: Foundation for Statistical Computing (2020)
22. Bates, D., et al.: ArXiv14065823 Stat, June 2014. http://arxiv.org/abs/1406.5823. Accessed 25 Jan 2021
23. Barr, D.J., et al.: J. Mem. Lang. **68**(3), 255–278 (2013). https://doi.org/10.1016/j.jml.2012. 11.001
24. Christensen, R.H.B.: 2019. https://CRAN.R-project.org/package=ordinal. Accessed 25 Jan 2021
25. Lenth, R.V., et al. https://CRAN.R-project.org/package=emmeans. Accessed 15 Feb 2021
26. Sandoval, E.B., Brandstetter, J., Obaid, M., Bartneck, C.: Reciprocity in human-robot interaction: a quantitative approach through the prisoner's dilemma and the ultimatum game. Int. J. Soc. Robot. **8**(2), 303–317 (2015). https://doi.org/10.1007/s12369-015-0323-x
27. Xu, J., Howard, A.: 2018 27th IEEE International Symposium on Robot and Human Interactive Communication (RO-MAN), pp. 435–441, August 2018. https://doi.org/10.1109/ ROMAN.2018.8525669.
28. Paetzel, M., et al: Proceedings of the 2020 ACM/IEEE International Conference on HRI, New York, NY, USA, pp. 73–82, March 2020. https://doi.org/10.1145/3319502.3374786.
29. Huisman, G., Kolkmeier, J., Heylen, D.: With us or against us: simulated social touch by virtual agents in a cooperative or competitive setting. In: Bickmore, T., Marsella, S., Sidner, C. (eds.) IVA 2014. LNCS (LNAI), vol. 8637, pp. 204–213. Springer, Cham (2014). https:// doi.org/10.1007/978-3-319-09767-1_25
30. Walters, M.L., et al.: 2009. http://uhra.herts.ac.uk/handle/2299/9642. Accessed 20 Feb 2021
31. Scheunemann, M.M., et al.: 2020 29th IEEE International Conference on Robot and Human Interactive Communication, pp. 1340–1347, August 2020. https://doi.org/10.1109/RO-MAN 47096.2020.9223478
32. Mutlu, B., et al.: Proceedings of the 1st ACM SIGCHI/SIGART Conference on HRI, New York, NY, USA, pp. 351–352. March 2006. https://doi.org/10.1145/1121241.1121311
33. Hsieh, T.-Y., et al.: PsyArXiv, 08 July 2020. https://doi.org/10.31234/osf.io/q6pv7.
34. Hortensius,R., Cross, E.S.: Ann. N. Y. Acad. Sci. **1426**(1), August 2018. Art. no. 1. https:// doi.org/10.1111/nyas.13727
35. Bridges, D., et al.: PeerJ **8**, e9414 (2020). https://doi.org/10.7717/peerj.9414
36. de Leeuw, J.R., Motz, B.A.: Psychophysics in a Web browser? Comparing response times collected with JavaScript and psychophysics toolbox in a visual search task. Behav. Res. Methods **48**(1), 1–12 (2015). https://doi.org/10.3758/s13428-015-0567-2
37. Miller, R., Schmidt, K., Kirschbaum, C., Enge, S.: Comparability, stability, and reliability of internet-based mental chronometry in domestic and laboratory settings. Behav. Res. Methods **50**(4), 1345–1358 (2018). https://doi.org/10.3758/s13428-018-1036-5
38. Wainer, J., et al.: ROMAN 2006 - The 15th IEEE International Symposium on Robot & Human Interactive Communication, pp. 117–122, September 2006. https://doi.org/10.1109/ ROMAN.2006.314404
39. Cross, E.S., Ramsey, R.: Trends Cog Sci. **25**(3), 200–2012 (2021). https://doi.org/10.1016/j. tics.2020.11.009
40. Henschel, A., et al.: Trends Neurosci. **43**(6), 373–384 (2020). https://doi.org/10.1016/j.tins. 2020.03.013

Modulating the Intentional Stance: Humanoid Robots, Narrative and Autistic Traits

Ziggy O'Reilly[1,2] , Davide Ghiglino[1] , Nicolas Spatola[1] ,
and Agnieszka Wykowska[1(✉)]

[1] Social Cognition and Human-Robot Interaction (S4HRI), Istituto Italiano di Tecnologia,
Genova, Italy
Agnieszka.Wykowska@iit.it

[2] Department of Psychology, University of Turin, Turin, Italy

Abstract. To enhance collaboration between humans and robots it might be important to trigger towards humanoid robots, similar social cognitive mechanisms that are triggered towards humans, such as the adoption of the intentional stance (i.e., explaining an agents behavior with reference to mental states). This study aimed (1) to measure whether a film modulates participants' tendency to adopt the intentional stance toward a humanoid robot and; (2) to investigate whether autistic traits affects this adoption. We administered two subscales of the InStance Test (IST) (i.e. 'isolated robot' subscale and 'social robot' subscale) before and after participants watched a film depicting an interaction between a humanoid robot and a human. On the isolated robot subscale, individuals with low autistic traits were more likely to adopt the intentional stance towards a humanoid robot after they watched the film, but there was no effect on individuals with high autistic traits. On the social robot subscale (i.e. when the robot is interacting with a human) both individuals with low and high autistic traits decreased in their adoption of the intentional stance after they watched the film. This suggests that the content of the narrative and an individual's social cognitive abilities, affects the degree to which the intentional stance towards a humanoid robot is adopted.

Keywords: Intentional stance · Human-robot interaction · Autistic traits · Narrative

1 Introduction

1.1 Social Cognition in Human-Robot Interaction

Over the past decades researchers have been exploring the application of humanoid robots in a variety of settings, ranging from robot-assisted therapies for individuals on the autism spectrum [1, 2], to tour guides in museums [3, 4]. However, the reception of robots in these environments is still a matter of debate. One of the ways to seamlessly integrate

---

Electronic supplementary material The online version of this chapter (https://doi.org/10.1007/
978-3-030-90525-5_61) contains supplementary material, which is available to authorized users.

H. Li et al. (Eds.): ICSR 2021, LNAI 13086, pp. 697–706, 2021.
https://doi.org/10.1007/978-3-030-90525-5_61

robots in real-world (social) scenarios, could be to enhance their human-likeness, which in turn, might trigger social cognition mechanisms in the human counterpart [5]. If robots are able to trigger similar social cognitive mechanisms that are elicited during human-human interactions, they might also trigger a sense of connection and positively affect performance in collaborative tasks [5].

One social cognitive process which could be important to trigger, is the ascription of mental states towards an artificial agent [6]. In human-human interactions, this process of attributing mental states (such as beliefs, desires, intentions and emotions) to others, allows us to understand and predict behaviour [7, 8]. The strategy of explaining behaviour with reference to mental states was termed by Daniel Dennett [9, 10] as adoption of the "Intentional Stance". Dennett argued that adopting the *Intentional Stance* towards humans, is the most efficient strategy to navigate social interactions. Thus, triggering the adoption of the *Intentional Stance* towards robots could enhance the ease to which individuals interact with robots in social tasks.

According to Dennett, the *Intentional Stance* is not always the most efficient strategy to explain the behaviour of all entities. For example, when individuals attempt to understand the behaviour of a robot, it could be more efficient to use knowledge about its functional design (i.e., 'the robot grabbed a glass because it was *programmed* to'), rather than describe the robot's behaviours based on mental states (i.e., 'the robot grabbed a glass because it was *thirsty*'). Dennett argued that when people use the former strategy they are adopting the *Design Stance*. Indeed, research has found variability in whether individuals describe the behaviour of a humanoid robot 'mechanistically' (i.e., adopt the *Design Stance*) or 'mentalistically' (i.e., adopt the *Intentional Stance*) [11–13]. However, it still remains to be answered what factors modulate whether individuals use mentalistic or mechanistic explanations for a humanoid robot's behaviour, or how to trigger participants to adopt the intentional stance towards a humanoid robot.

1.2 Autistic Traits and Ascription of Mental States

One factor which has been associated with an individual's ability to ascribe mental states in explaining behaviors of others, is the traits associated with autism spectrum disorder (ASD). ASD is a developmental disorder characterized by repetitive behaviors and difficulties in social communication and interaction [14]. Indeed, these social difficulties are thought to be caused by an impairment in the ability to reason about others with reference to mental states [7, 8]. These difficulties are also present in neurotypical individuals with high levels of autistic traits, as measured by the Autism Quotient (AQ) test [15]. Indeed, Baron-Cohen and colleagues found that high AQ scores in a neurotypical population are associated with reduced abilities to infer the mental states of pictures of humans expressing emotions [16]. Interestingly, studies with children with ASD have found that impairments in ascription of mental states extend to humanoid robots [17, 18]. However, it is not known whether the low likelihood of ascribing mental states to humanoid robots is also present in neurotypical individuals with high autistic traits. Understanding the degree to which autistic traits modulate ascription of mental states towards robots, could help inform the design of humanoid robots to account for individual differences.

1.3 Using Narrative to Trigger Ascription of Mental States

One of the ways to modulate how participants describe a robot's behaviour, could be by positioning it as a fictional character which communicates a narrative. Narrative has been defined as "a depiction of events driven by the intentional behaviour of one or more autonomous agents in a manner that manifests an imagined world which parallels the world of real experience," [19]. If a robot displays behaviour which appears intentional and drives a sequence of events, the most efficient strategy for the viewers to adopt to understand the narrative, should be to attribute goals, intentions and agency to the robot [20]. One way to investigate whether narrative can trigger individuals to describe the behaviour of a robot mentalistically, could be by using film. Indeed, a study using functional magnetic resonance imaging (fMRI), found that film footage activates brain regions involved in reasoning about others with reference to mental states [21]. Participants watched footage from the film *Waking Life* [22], which depicts two human characters physically embodied in the real world and the same footage converted into animated imagery (i.e., cartoonized). Brain regions involved in reasoning with reference to mental states were more active towards the 'real' film, in comparison to the cartoonized film. This suggests that film is more powerful when the characters are physically embodied in the real world, rather than cartoonized. Subsequently, showing participants a film where the events are driven by the behaviours of a humanoid robot, could enhance the likelihood that they explain a humanoid robot's behaviours mentalistically rather than mechanistically.

1.4 Aims

The question of whether narrative could trigger participants to adopt the intentional stance towards a humanoid robot and how this would vary based on the individual's level of autistic traits, has not yet been explored in detail in the literature to date. Therefore, the aim of this study was twofold: (1) to measure whether a film modulates participants' tendency to adopt the intentional stance toward a humanoid robot and; (2) to investigate whether autistic traits affect mentalistic attributions towards a humanoid robot. As stimuli, the study used a film titled *While(Alive){}* [23] which displays the relationship between a humanoid robot and a human. The film is stop-motion animation and, as such, the characters are embodied in the physical-spatial world rather than in a virtual world. Thus, it is expected that the physical embodiment should enhance the likelihood of adopting the intentional stance towards a humanoid robot [21]. We also expected that *While(Alive){}* would be more powerful at triggering adoption of intentional stance in individuals with low autistic traits, compared to individuals with high autistic traits based on previous research mentioned earlier [15, 17, 18].

2 Methods

2.1 Participants

For this study, 100 participants were recruited from an online platform Prolific (*mean age* = 27; *SD* = 6; 50 females, 1 other). The inclusion criteria for the study was (1) English as their first language and (2) consent. Additionally, half the participants had not reported a diagnosis of a developmental disability (i.e., neurotypical adults; $N = 50$) and half reported a diagnosis of ASD ($N = 50$). However, since it was not possible to validate ASD diagnosis online, participants were split into groups based on their level of autistic traits rather than their reported diagnosis. Our experimental protocols followed the ethical standards laid down in the Declaration of Helsinki and were approved by the local Ethics Committee (Comitato Etico Regione Liguria).

2.2 Stimuli

A stop-motion animated film, *While(Alive){}* was used as the experimental stimulus. *While(Alive){}* depicts the evolution of a relationship between a robot and a human over the human's lifespan. The human ages overtime, dies and exits from the frame. In contrast, the robot does not undergo any physiological changes (see Fig. 1). There is no dialogue. The narrative is communicated predominately through hand gestures and music. The duration of the film is 1 min and 53 s (including title page, closing credits, and production card).

Fig. 1. Key frames from the stop-motion animated film *While(Alive){}*. Full video available in [23]. © Cody Cameron-Brown and Ziggy O'Reilly.

2.3 Measures

Instance Test (IST). The IST contains sequences of images of the humanoid robot iCub interacting with objects and/or a human(s), designed to establish whether participants have a bias towards explaining iCub's behaviour mechanistically (i.e., *Design Stance*) or mentalistically (i.e., *Intentional Stance*) [13]. Underneath the sequence of images are two sentences representing possible explanations of the robot's behaviour. One of the sentences always explains iCub's behaviour mechanistically (i.e., 'iCub *tracked* the girls hand movements'), while the other always describes its behaviour mentalistically (i.e., 'iCub is *interested* in these objects'). These two sentences are located on the opposite poles of a bipolar scale, and participants are asked to move a slider toward the sentence that they think best suits the images. Participants instance scores (ISS) are calculated by converting the bipolar scale into a 0–100 scale for each item, which is then averaged across the items. The average indicates the participants preference for the mentalistic or mechanistic explanation, where 0 corresponds to the mechanistic explanation and 100 to the mentalistic explanation. The complete IST contains 34 items, and is associated with high internal consistency ($a = 0.83$, [24]). This study used the shortened version developed by Spatola et al., [24] which contains 12 items, containing two subscales; 'isolated robot,' scale and the 'social robot,' scale (see Fig. 2). The IST was included to investigate whether *While(Alive){}* modulated an individual's preference for mentalistic explanations of a humanoid robot's behaviour within-groups and between groups.

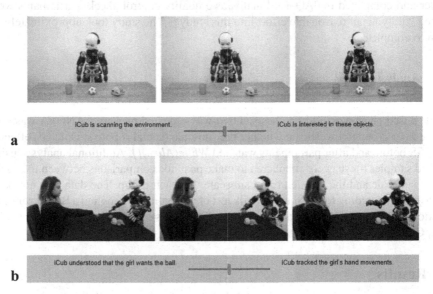

Fig. 2. Items from the InStance Test representative of the (**a**) isolated robot scale and (**b**) social robot scale.

Abbreviated Adult Autism Spectrum Quotient (AQ-10). The AQ-10 is a short ten-item self-report questionnaire which measures the presence of autistic traits in individuals aged 16 years and older [15, 25]. The 10 items (e.g., 'I find it difficult to work out people's intentions,' 'I find it easy to do more than one thing at once,' 'I often notice small sounds when others do not') are split equally into five subscales: 'attention to detail,' 'communication,' 'social,' 'attention switching,' and 'imagination,' which are answered on a four-point Likert scale marked by 'Definitely Agree', 'Slightly Agree', 'Slightly Disagree' and 'Definitely Disagree'. Any endorsements of autistic traits on positive-lykeyed items (i.e., 'Definitely,' or 'Slightly Agree') are scored as 1, and disagreements are scored as 0; negatively key items are reverse scored. The total AQ scores range from 0 to 10. Allison, Auyeung and Baron-Cohen [25] found that the adult AQ-10 has high internal consistency ($\alpha = 0.89$) and high concurrent validity, compared to the full adult 50-item version of the AQ ($r = 0.92$, $p = .0001$). The AQ-10 was included in the current study to split participants into two groups based on their level of autistic traits.

2.4 Procedure

All participants completed the online experiment in the same order. Before the main experiment begun, participants were asked to (1) check the display and audio of an unrelated short film and (2) answer demographic questions about English proficiency, age and sex. Then (after participants completed a practice item from the IST), they were presented with the first half of the IST in a pseudo-randomized order. Next, participants watched *While(Alive){}* on full screen with headphones. After watching *While(Alive){}*, they completed the second half of the IST, which was presented in a pseudo-randomized order and completed the AQ-10. Finally, as a quality control check, participants were asked "did you put reasonable effort into this study?" The study took approximately 20 min to complete.

2.5 Analysis

For each group, the ISS was screened for outliers using the 3.0 inter-quartile range rule [26]. Based on an a priori hypothesis, a two-way repeated measures ANOVA was conducted per group to investigate whether the subscale (social robot vs. isolated) effected the ISS before and after participants watched *While(Alive){}*. Additional analyses using paired samples t-tests were conducted to make post hoc comparisons between the social robot subscale and the isolated robot subscale, for each group. The data was normally distributed according to the Shapiro-Wilk test of normality. We applied a Bonferroni correction. All analyses were performed using SPSS statistical package version 24 (SPSS Inc, Chicago, IL).

3 Results

3.1 Data Screening

Eight participants were excluded for the analysis because they reported that their English was less than excellent. An additional participant was excluded because their English was less than excellent and they answered "no" to the question "did you put reasonable effort into this study?" Four more participants were excluded because their mean time to respond to the IST was above the 3.0 interquartile range rule [26]. Finally, 14 participants were excluded because they took 40 s or less to respond to 6 items the IST. This yielded a final sample of 73 participants (see Table 1). The participants were split into a low AQ group and a high AQ group based on median AQ scores ($Mdn = 6$). The AQ scores for the high AQ group were significantly greater than for the low AQ group; ($t(71) = -15.097$, $p = .000$). No outliers were detected.

Table 1. Descriptive Statistics for the Low AQ group and the High AQ group.

	Low AQ	High AQ
N (male:female:other)	36(12:24:0)	37 (22:14:1)
Age	27(7)	27(6)
AQ-10**	3.28(1.34)	7.67(1.19)

Note. Values are given as mean (SD) unless otherwise stated. Asterisks indicate when groups significantly differ from each other. ** $p < 0.001$

3.2 Main Analysis

Low AQ Group. According to a two-way repeated measures ANOVA, there was a significant main effect of IST subscale (isolated robot vs. social robot; $F(1,35) = 12.13$, $p = .001$, $\eta_p^2 = .257$; see Fig. 3a). The marginal mean for the social robot subscale was higher ($M = 49.30$) than for the isolated robot subscale ($M = 38.35$). There was no significant main effect of time (i.e., before or after participants watched *While(Alive){}*) ($F(1,35) = .569$, $p = .456$, $\eta_p^2 = .016$). However, there was a significant interaction between pre-/post- changes and the IST subscales ($F(1, 35) = 18.95$, $p < .001$, $\eta_p^2 = .351$; see Fig. 3a). For the **isolated robot subscale** of the IST, separate comparisons showed that ISS differed significantly before and after watching *While(Alive){}* ($t(35) = -3.064$, $p = .004$). The ISS after watching *While(Alive){}* was higher ($M = 46.06$, $SD = 20.92$) than before ($M = 30.64$, $SD = 25.43$). For the **social robot subscale** of the IST, we also found a significant difference between the ISS before and after watching *While(Alive){}* ($t(35) = 3.088$, $p = .004$). However, for this subscale, the ISS after watching *While(Alive){}* was lower ($M = 43.93$, $SD = 22.39$) than before ($M = 54.67$, $SD = 21.09$).

High AQ Group. According to a two-way repeated measures ANOVA, there was a significant main effect of IST subscale ($F(1,36) = 14.925$, $p < .001$, $\eta_p^2 = .293$; see Fig. 3b). The marginal mean for the social robot subscale was higher ($M = 46.48$) than for the isolated robot subscale ($M = 34.96$). There was no significant main effect of time (i.e., before or after participants watched *While(Alive){}*) ($F(1,36) = 3.089$, $p = .088$, $\eta_p^2 = .079$). However, also for this group, there was also a significant interaction between pre-/post- changes and the subscale ($F(1,36) = 6.66$, $p = .014$, $\eta_p^2 = .156$; see Fig. 3b). For the **isolated robot subscale**, there was no significant difference between the ISS before and after watching *While(Alive){}* ($t(36) = .63$, $p = .950$). In other words, there were no changes before ($M = 35.10$, $SD = 25.08$) or after ($M = 34.82$, $SD = 21.06$) watching *While(Alive){}* for this subscale of IST. On the contrary, for the **social robot subscale** of IST, there was also a significant difference between the ISS before and after watching *While(Alive){}* ($t(36) = 2.673$, $p = .011$). The ISS after watching *While(Alive){}* was lower ($M = 39.71$, $SD = 26.28$) than before ($M = 53.24$, $SD = 26.10$), paralleling the pattern for low-AQ group of participants.

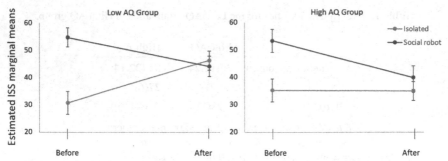

Fig. 3. (a) Interaction effect across subscales before and after watching *While(Alive){}* for the low AQ group. (b) Interaction effect across subscales before and after watching *While(Alive){}* for the high AQ group.

4 Discussion

The primary aim of the present study was to investigate whether a narrative of an interaction between a human and a humanoid robot could modulate the adoption of the intentional stance towards a humanoid robot. Secondly, it aimed to investigate whether the degree of autistic traits affected the modulation. Adoption of the Intentional Stance was measured by administering the InStance Test (IST) before and after participants watched a film titled *While(Alive){}*. The IST contained two subscales; the isolated robot scale, which shows the humanoid robot iCub interacting with objects, and the social robot scale, which depicts iCub interacting with a human(s).

Our results showed that for both groups of participants, the Intentional Stance score decreased on the IST *social robot subscale* (robot depicted in the presence of a human) after watching *While(Alive){}*. This could be explained by the narrative underlying the interaction between the human and the robot in the film. Majority of the human-robot interaction is driven by the mental states of the human, rather than of the robot. For example, in the beginning of the film, the infant's curiosity propels her to touch the robot. As such, the human character is more 'active,' in comparison to the more 'passive' robot character. Therefore, it is possible that to understand the narrative, it is sufficient to attribute mental states towards the 'active character,' (i.e., the human), rather than the 'passive character,' (i.e., the robot). Subsequently, *While(Alive){}* may trigger participants to perceive the behaviour of the robot mechanistically, by contrast to the mentalistic behaviour of the human. The decrease in scores in the social robot scale (i.e., the shift towards more mechanistic explanations) could reflect this.

Interestingly, on the *isolated robot subscale* of the IST, the very same video clip increased the IST score, but only for the low-AQ group of participants. This suggests that individuals with lower degree of autistic traits might show higher cognitive flexibility [27] and might be more likely to attribute human-like traits (such as intentionality) to non-human agents (such as humanoid robots), especially, after watching an emotionally evocative movie depicting human-robot interaction. Interestingly, although the narrative of the movie highlighted the human as the intentional agent, thereby, increasing – by contrast – the mechanistic perception of a robot when in interaction with a human (in the social robot subscale), the human intentionality was transferred to the robot, when the robot was displayed alone in the IST, being the sole agent in the scenario. This, however, occurred only among participants with higher social aptitude (lower AQ traits).

Overall, our results suggest that adoption of intentional stance is fluid, and can be modulated by various factors, such as a background narrative induced by a movie or by a social context in which a robot is presented. Importantly, the way these factors influence adoption of the Intentional Stance depends also on individual differences in social aptitude, as manifested by the degree of individual AQ traits. However, due to participants ability to use Prolific, our results are presumably based on a sample of individuals with high cognitive functioning. As such, the results should not be interpreted as representative of all individuals on the autism spectrum. Nevertheless, knowledge about individual AQ traits should be considered in the design of social robots.

Acknowledgements. This work has received support from the European Research Council under the European Union's Horizon 2020 research and innovation programme, ERC Starting grant ERC-2016-StG-715058, awarded to Agnieszka Wykowska. The content of this paper is the sole responsibility of the authors. The European Commission or its services cannot be held responsible for any use that may be made of the information it contains. We would also like to thank Serena Marchesi for assisting with creating the online questionnaire.

References

1. Silvera-Tawil, D., Roberts-Yates, C.: Socially-assistive robots to enhance learning for secondary students with intellectual disabilities and autism. In: 27th IEEE International Symposium on Robot and Human Interactive Communication (RO-MAN) 2018, pp. 838–843. IEEE (2018)
2. Ricks, D.J., Colton, M.B.: Trends and considerations in robot-assisted autism therapy. In: IEEE International Conference on Robotics and Automation 2010, pp. 4354–4359. IEEE (2010)
3. Burgard, W., et al.: Experiences with an interactive museum tour-guide robot. Artif. Intell. **114**(1–2), 3–55 (1999)
4. Nourbakhsh, I., et al.: The personal exploration rover: educational assessment of a robotic exhibit for informal learning venues. Int. J. Eng. Educ. **22**(4), 777 (2006)
5. Wiese, E., Metta, G., Wykowska, A.: Robots as intentional agents: using neuroscientific methods to make robots appear more social. Front. Psychol. **8**, 1663 (2017)
6. Gray, H.M., Gray, K., Wegner, D.M.: Dimensions of mind perception. Science **315**(5812), 619 (2007)
7. Baron-Cohen, S., Leslie, A.M., Frith, U.: Does the autistic child have a "theory of mind"? Cognition **21**(1), 37–46 (1985)
8. Baron-Cohen, S.: Theory of mind and autism: a fifteen year review. Underst. other Minds: Perspect. Dev. Cogn. Neurosci. **2**, 3–20 (2000)
9. Dennett, D.C.: Intentional systems. J. Philos. **68**(4), 87–106 (1971)
10. Dennett, D.C., Haugeland, J.: Intentionality. In: The Oxford Companion to the Mind. Oxford University Press (1987)
11. Bossi, F., Willemse, C., Cavazza, J., Marchesi, S., Murino, V., Wykowska, A.: The human brain reveals resting-state activity patterns that are predictive of biases in attitudes toward robots. Sci. Robot. **5**(46), 1–8 (2020)
12. Salichs, M.A., et al. (eds.): ICSR 2019. LNCS (LNAI), vol. 11876. Springer, Cham (2019). https://doi.org/10.1007/978-3-030-35888-4

13. Marchesi, S., Ghiglino, D., Ciardo, F., Perez-Osorio, J., Baykara, E., Wykowska, A.: Do we adopt the Intentional Stance toward humanoid robots? Front. Psychol. **10**, 450 (2019)
14. American Psychiatric Association.: Diagnostic and statistical manual of mental disorders (DSM-5®): American Psychiatric Pub. (2013)
15. Baron-Cohen, S., Wheelwright, S., Skinner, R., Martin, J., Clubley, E.: The autism-spectrum quotient (AQ): Evidence from asperger syndrome/high-functioning autism, males and females, scientists and mathematicians. J. Autism Dev. Disord. **31**(1), 5–17 (2001)
16. Baron-Cohen, S., Wheelwright, S., Hill, J., Raste, Y., Plumb, I.: The, "Reading the Mind in the Eyes" test revised version: a study with normal adults, and adults with Asperger syndrome or high-functioning autism. J. Child Psychol. Psychiatry **42**(2), 241–251 (2001)
17. O'Reilly, Z., Silvera-Tawil, D., Tan, D.W., Zurr, I.: Validation of a novel theory of mind measurement tool: the social robot video task. In: Companion of the 2021 ACM/IEEE International Conference on Human-Robot Interaction, pp. 89–93 (2021)
18. Zhang, Y., et al.: Theory of robot mind: false belief attribution to social robots in children with and without autism. Front. Psychol. **10**, 1732 (2019)
19. Mar, R.A.: The neuropsychology of narrative: Story comprehension, story production and their interrelation. Neuropsychologia **42**(10), 1414–1434 (2004)
20. Frith, C.D., Frith, U.: Interacting minds–a biological basis. Science **286**(5445), 1692–1695 (1999)
21. Mar, R.A., Macrae, C.N.: Triggering the intentional stance. In: Novartis Foundation Symposium, vol. 278, p. 111. John Wiley, Chichester (2006)
22. Linklater, R.: Waking Life. Fox Searchlight Pictures, Los Angeles (2001)
23. Cameron-Brown, C., O'Reilly, Z.: "While(Alive){}." YouTube Video. https://www.youtube.com/watch?v=qeCmqKiueu8
24. Spatola, N., Marchesi, S., Wykowska, A.: The Instance Task: how to measure the mentalistic bias in human-robot interaction, 28 May 2021.https://doi.org/10.31234/osf.io/b3wtq
25. Allison, C., Auyeung, B., Baron-Cohen, S.: Toward brief "red flags" for autism screening: the short autism spectrum quotient and the short quantitative checklist in 1,000 cases and 3,000 controls. J. Am. Acad. Child Adolesc. Psychiatry **51**(2), 202–212 (2012)
26. Hoaglin, D.C., Iglewicz, B.: Fine-tuning some resistant rules for outlier labeling. J. Am. Stat. Assoc. **82**(400), 1147–1149 (1987)
27. Wykowska, A.: Social robots to test flexibility of human social cognition. Int. J. Soc. Robot. **12**, 1203–1211 (2020)

The Personality of a Robot. An Adaptation of the HEXACO – 60 as a Tool for HRI

Giulia Siri[1,2] ⓘ, Serena Marchesi[2] ⓘ, Agnieszka Wykowska[2] ⓘ,
and Carlo Chiorri[1(✉)] ⓘ

[1] Dipartimento di Scienze della Formazione (DISFOR), Università degli Studi di Genova,
Genoa, Italy
carlo.chiorri@unige.it
[2] Social Cognition in Human-Robot Interaction Unit, Istituto Italiano di Tecnologia,
Genoa, Italy

Abstract. In this paper, we report on a study in which we used an other-report version of the HEXACO–60, a questionnaire designed to assess human personality, to evaluate how people perceive the personality traits of robots. The results showed that a four-factor measurement model fitted the data better than the expected six-factor one and suggested that the domains of the perceived personality structure of robots might differ from those of humans.

Keywords: Human-robot interaction · Personality assessment · Psychometric validation

1 Introduction

Nowadays, the use of robotics range from the industrial settings, such as production lines, to social applications, such as healthcare, assistance to elderly, children, and educational activities [1]. In this context, social robotics is an emerging field of research, interested in understanding how humans interact with social robots in everyday environments. Recent studies showed that humans can deploy similar social cognitive mechanisms during the interaction with a robot [for reviews, see 2 and 3] as during interactions with other humans. Moreover, many authors investigated the human tendency to attribute humanlike characteristics to robots [4–6], from physical traits to sociality [7] and intentions (i.e. adopting the intentional stance [8]) [9–11]. In this context, several questionnaires have been developed to assess the perception of social robots, the attitudes toward them, and the characteristics of the robots that can affect such attitudes and the human-robot interaction [12–16]. As reviewed in [16], many studies relied on the Five-Factor Model of personality, finding that the robot's perceived extraversion (dominance), agreeableness (friendliness) and conscientiousness (dependability) were the most relevant dimensions for human observers. To the best of our knowledge, however, no study referred to the Ashton and Lee's HEXACO [17] model to evaluate the perceived personality traits of a humanoid robot, whereas it has already been used in HRI to measure personality traits about humans in interaction with robots [18–21].

© Springer Nature Switzerland AG 2021
H. Li et al. (Eds.): ICSR 2021, LNAI 13086, pp. 707–717, 2021.
https://doi.org/10.1007/978-3-030-90525-5_62

The HEXACO model of personality is a dimensional taxonomy of human personality based on findings from a series of lexical studies [22–24] that proposes an organization of individual differences in personality characteristics in terms of six broad trait domains: Extraversion (i.e., tendency to feel positively about oneself, to feel confident and comfortable in social situations, to experience high levels of arousal and energy), Agreeableness (i.e., tendency to forgive the wrongs suffered, to be lenient in judging others, to be open to compromise and cooperation), Conscientiousness (i.e., tendency to be organized, disciplined, accurate, and reliable in performing tasks), Emotionality (i.e., tendency to experience negative affects such as anxiety, worry, fear, and stress), Openness to Experience (i.e., tendency to appreciate beauty, art, and unusual ideas and people, and to be curious about various domains of knowledge), and Honesty-Humility (i.e., tendency to avoid manipulation and deception for personal gain and to feel little interest for wealth, luxuries, and social status). In order to get a more comprehensive assessment of a robots' perceived personality, we included an additional, 'interstitial' domain of the HEXACO model, i.e., Altruism, that taps into the tendency to be empathic and soft-hearted to others (see https://hexaco.org/scaledescriptions). Although developed in the last two decades, the model has received convincing empirical support for its stability across cultures and predictive validity (see, e.g., [25, 26]).

2 Aims

The main aim of the present study was to investigate whether the dimensional HEXACO model of human personality could generalize to robots, too. To test this hypothesis, we asked a group of participants to think about their own definition of "robot" and to complete an other-report version of an HEXACO measure that assessed the six-plus-one original domains. In other words, participants were allowed to refer to the robot that, for them, was most representative of this category, regardless of whether they had actually interacted with a robot or not. We then use factor analysis to investigate the dimensional structure of robot personality ratings.

3 Methods and Results

3.1 Participants

We recruited 133 online participants (mean age 34.46 ± 14.170, range: 19–65) through opportunistic sampling via authors' contacts and on social media. All participants were Italian native speakers and comprised a convenience sample drawn from the Italian general population.

3.2 The HEXACO - 60

The HEXACO-60 is a short personality questionnaire developed to assess the HEXACO trait domains [17]. It asks participants to rate their agreement with 60 statements (see Appendix) on a 5-point, Likert-type scale (from 1 = "strongly disagree" to 5 = "strongly agree"). As reported by Ashton and Lee [17], the internal consistency reliability (Cronbach's α) ranged from .77 to .80 and from .73 to .80 for two different representative samples, revealing a good internal consistency of this short version. We included in the study sever further items that assessed Altruism. All the items were adapted to address the study aims by adding the expression "A robot" as the subject of each sentence (i.e. "[A robot] would never accept a bribe, even if it were very large").

3.3 Procedure

Participants were asked to complete a schedule for collecting background information and the HEXACO questionnaire. They were not compensated for their participation. In order to access the survey, participants had to explicitly declare they intention to participate after reading an informed consent form. Data collection was conducted in accordance with the privacy laws and accordance with the Regulation 2016/697 of the European Parliament of the Council of 27 April 2018, concerning the protection of the individuals about the processing of the personal data and on the free movement of such data and abrogating "Directive 95/46/EC" (General Data Protection Regulation -GDPR) and in accordance to the Declaration of Helsinki.

3.4 Results

In order to determine the optimal number of factors to be extracted, we carried out a scree-test and a parallel analysis (PA) and inspected the Minimum Average Partial Correlation

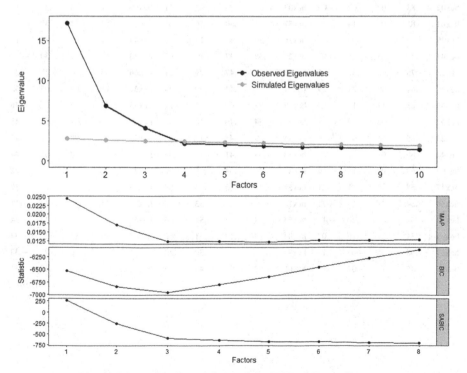

Fig. 1. Dimensionality analyses of the HEXACO questionnaire.

Statistic (MAP), the Bayesian Information Criterion (BIC), and the Sample Size adjusted BIC (SABIC) (see, e.g., [27]). The scree test suggests that the optimal number of factors corresponds to the factors before which the downward curve of the eigenvalues seem to flatten out. PA indicates to extract all those factors whose observed eigenvalues are larger than the 95th percentile of the distribution of the eigenvalues generated from 1,000 simulated matrices of random data of the same size. For the other indices, the optimal number of factors is the one at which their values reach their minimum. As shown in Fig. 1, these methods did not suggest the same number of factors, hence we carried out a series of Exploratory Factor Analyses (EFAs) setting to 1 to 7 the number of factors to be extracted. We then considered as most adequate the factor solution that allowed to obtain what Sass and Schmitt [28] call an "approximate simple structure", i.e., that each item had a substantial (i.e., >|.30|) loading on one factor and negligible loadings (i.e., <|.20|) on the others (cross-loadings).

According to this criterion, the best solution was the four-factor one (Table 1 and 2).

Table 1. Pattern matrix of the four-factor solution. Bolded values are larger than .30.

Factors

Item	1	2	3	4	Item	1	2	3	4	Item	1	2	3	4
hex58	**.93**	.03	−.02	−.14	hex01	.17	**.68**	.15	−.12	hex42	**−.36**	−.03	**.44**	.08
hex33	**.88**	.03	.09	−.03	hex05	**.32**	**−.63**	**.37**	.07	hex07	.00	.08	**.43**	−.07
hex14	**.85**	.08	.18	.10	hex18	.10	**.63**	.06	−.17	hex38	−.04	.18	**.43**	**−.38**
hex24	**.84**	−.03	−.03	−.12	hex06	**.38**	**.63**	−.05	−.12	hex52	−.02	.23	**.41**	**−.38**
hex02	**.83**	.02	−.02	−.06	hex03	−.02	**.56**	.02	.11	hex59	.16	−.13	**.39**	−.13
hex61	**.81**	.03	.14	.13	hex57	−.13	**−.50**	−.16	.01	hex30	−.05	**−.32**	**.35**	.27
hex29	**.76**	.08	.04	.07	hex16	**.30**	**−.49**	−.17	−.07	hex44	**.30**	.02	**−.34**	.19
hex41	**.73**	.03	−.25	−.07	hex28	**.38**	**.47**	.10	.07	hex20	−.11	.21	**.30**	**−.30**
hex63	**.70**	.02	**−.32**	−.26	hex62	.16	**.47**	.21	.27	hex66	.21	−.04	−.28	.24
hex40	**.64**	.08	.21	.29	hex11	.29	**.47**	.19	.24	hex21	.09	.04	.05	**.55**
hex55	**.63**	.11	−.16	−.02	hex19	.22	**.47**	.11	.27	hex53	.23	−.06	.02	**.46**
hex32	**.61**	.08	.09	.21	hex37	**.34**	**−.46**	.18	−.11	hex39	.09	−.07	−.21	**.45**
hex25	**.60**	−.01	.01	.16	hex43	.09	**.43**	−.12	−.13	hex26	.07	.08	−.12	**.45**
hex48	**.60**	−.04	−.07	.27	hex10	−.08	**.41**	.15	**.36**	hex67	−.08	−.12	.03	**−.44**
hex09	**.58**	−.09	−.13	−.06	hex49	−.24	**.34**	.05	.20	hex27	.09	.28	.00	**.42**
hex17	**.58**	−.06	−.01	.21	hex51	−.04	.05	**.70**	.09	hex36	**.30**	.07	−.15	**.39**
hex50	**.54**	**−.38**	−.14	−.21	hex15	.01	.03	**.53**	.05	hex23	−.06	.25	−.12	**.37**
hex22	**−.52**	.01	.20	−.16	hex64	−.19	.06	**.51**	−.05	hex47	.08	−.29	.23	**−.34**
hex34	**.51**	.21	−.16	−.07	hex04	.20	.19	**−.51**	.00	hex45	.22	.15	−.20	**.34**
hex12	**.48**	−.05	−.04	.16	hex54	−.22	.15	**.50**	−.13	hex46	−.27	.16	.27	**−.33**
hex13	**.45**	.16	−.01	.18	hex65	.02	.08	**.46**	−.13	hex31	**.30**	−.02	−.27	**.31**

(*continued*)

Table 1. (*continued*)

Factors												
Item	1	2	3	4	Item	1	2	3	4	Item	1	2	3	4
hex08	.39	.21	−.02	.29	hex60	.36	−.42	.46	.00	hex56	.28	−.11	−.11	.30
hex35	.38	−.27	.30	−.33										

Table 2. Factor correlation matrix.

Factor correlation matrix				
Factor	1	2	3	4
1	1.00	−.15	−.37	.43
2	−.15	1.00	.18	.24
3	−.37	.18	1.00	−.31
4	.43	.24	−.31	1.00

The first factor grouped items tapping into altruism, sociability, and openness to others (Empathy/Altruism/Sociability). The second factor grouped items related to fairness and resilience (Integrity). The third factor grouped items that operationalize dependability and sobriety (Dependability). The fourth factor grouped items expressing self-confidence attitudes (Self-confidence) (Table 1).

4 Discussion

The present study was carried out to test the usefulness of an HEXACO questionnaire in an HRI context to assess how people perceive the personality traits of robots. Results showed that the dimensional structure usually obtained with human participants was not replicated, but, rather, a four-factor structure was found as the best measurement model. Beyond the labels that can be used for the factors in Table 1, it is apparent that the items did not group themselves according to the original scales, nor the items of the same scale were grouped in the same factor. Interestingly, the Empathy/Altruism/Sociability and Dependability factors found here resembled two dimensions of Spatola et al.'s Human-Robot Interaction Evaluation Scale (HRIES) [7] (Sociability and Intentionality), and were consistent with previous studies [16]. This result suggests that these domains might be particularly relevant in the evaluation of robot personality, as they are perceived salient and defining characteristics of the robot behaviour.

The opportunistic sampling strategy used here and the relatively low sample size suggest caution in interpreting the results of this study in terms of generalizability, especially to other cultural contexts. However, having not constrained participants to think about a specific robot should have provided the necessary variability in scores to actually address the aim of this study. Analogously to studies on self-reported personality in which participants rate themselves, in this study participants rated "their" robot, thus allowing us to investigate the structure of perceived personality traits of the robot category. This would not have been possible if we asked to focus on a particular robot or category of robots. Future studies are nonetheless invited to use the HEXACO questionnaire presented here to evaluate how people perceive the personality traits of a specific robot (i.e. [iCub] would never accept a bribe, even if it were very large), for which independent information about the perceived characteristics is available. In this way, it would be possible to compare how humans perceive the personality traits of robots with different attributes and test the sensitivity of the HEXACO questionnaire.

Appendix

The HEXACO questionnaire used in this study (please note that the Italian version was used)

On the following pages, you will find a series of statements about a robot. Please read each statement and decide how much you agree or disagree with that statement. Please answer every statement, even if you are not completely sure of your response.

Item	Factor	Text
hex01	Honesty-Humility	[A robot] It would never accept a bribe, even if it were very large
hex02	Altruism	[A robot] It has sympathy for people who are less fortunate than it is
hex03	Agreeableness	[A robot] It rarely hold a grudge, even against people who have badly wronged it
hex04	Agreeableness	[A robot] People think of it as someone who has a quick temper
hex05	Extraversion	[A robot] Most people are more upbeat and dynamic than it generally is
hex06	Honesty-Humility	[A robot] It wouldn't use flattery to get a raise or promotion at work, even if it thought it would succeed
hex07	Conscientiousness	[A robot] When working on something, it doesn't pay much attention to small details
hex08	Extraversion	[A robot] It feels reasonably satisfied with itself overall
hex09	Extraversion	[A robot] It prefers jobs that involve active social interaction to those that involve working alone
hex10	Conscientiousness	[A robot] People often call it a perfectionist
hex11	Conscientiousness	[A robot] It often pushes itself very hard when trying to achieve a goal
hex12	Extraversion	[A robot] In social situations, its is usually the one who makes the first move
hex13	Agreeableness	[A robot] It tends to be lenient in judging other people
hex14	Altruism	[A robot] It tries to give generously to those in need

(continued)

(continued)

Item	Factor	Text
hex15	Conscientiousness	[A robot] When working, it sometimes has difficulties due to being disorganized
hex16	Emotionality	[A robot] It can handle difficult situations without needing emotional support from anyone else
hex17	Openness to Experience	[A robot] If it had the opportunity, it would like to attend a classical music concert
hex18	Honesty-Humility	[A robot] Having a lot of money is not especially important to it
hex19	Conscientiousness	[A robot] It plans ahead and organize things, to avoid scrambling at the last minute
hex20	Honesty-Humility	[A robot] If it wants something from someone, it will laugh at that person's worst jokes
hex21	Agreeableness	[A robot] When people tell it that it is wrong, its first reaction is to argue with them
hex22	Honesty-Humility	[A robot] It thinks that it is entitled to more respect than anyone else
hex23	Agreeableness	[A robot] People sometimes thinks that it can be too stubborn
hex24	Altruism	[A robot] It is soft-hearted
hex25	Openness to Experience	[A robot] It would enjoy creating a work of art, such as a novel, a song, or a painting
hex26	Agreeableness	[A robot] People sometimes thinks that it is too critical of others
hex27	Agreeableness	[A robot] Its attitude toward people who have treated it badly is "forgive and forget"
hex28	Honesty-Humility	[A robot] It wouldn't pretend to like someone just to get that person to do favors for it
hex29	Extraversion	[A robot] The first thing that it always does in a new place is to make friends
hex30	Openness to Experience	[A robot] It never really enjoys looking through an encyclopedia
hex31	Extraversion	[A robot] It sometimes feels that it is worthless
hex32	Openness to Experience	[A robot] It is interested in learning about the history and politics of other countries
hex33	Altruism	[A robot] It would feel very badly if it were to hurt someone
hex34	Openness to Experience	[A robot] People thinks that it has a good imagination
hex35	Altruism	[A robot] It wouldn't bother it to harm someone it doesn't like

(continued)

(*continued*)

Item	Factor	Text
hex36	Emotionality	[A robot] It sometimes can't help worrying about little things
hex37	Emotionality	[A robot] It worries a lot less than most people do
hex38	Honesty-Humility	[A robot] If it knew that it could never get caught, it would be willing to steal a million dollars
hex39	Altruism	[A robot] It likes the idea that only the strong should survive
hex40	Extraversion	[A robot] On most days, it feels cheerful and optimistic
hex41	Emotionality	[A robot] When it suffers from a painful experience, it needs someone to make it feel comfortable
hex42	Conscientiousness	[A robot] It makes decisions based on the feeling of the moment rather than on careful thought
hex43	Agreeableness	[A robot] Even when people make a lot of mistakes, it rarely says anything negative
hex44	Extraversion	[A robot] When it is in a group of people, its is often the one who speaks on behalf of the group
hex45	Extraversion	[A robot] It feels that it is unpopular
hex46	Honesty-Humility	[A robot] It wants people to know that it is important and of high status
hex47	Openness to Experience	[A robot] It doesn't think of itself as the artistic or creative type
hex48	Openness to Experience	[A robot] It likes people who have unconventional views
hex49	Agreeableness	[A robot] Most people tend to get angry more quickly than it does
hex50	Emotionality	[A robot] It remains unemotional even in situations where most people get very sentimental
hex51	Conscientiousness	[A robot] It makes a lot of mistakes because it doesn't think before it acts
hex52	Honesty-Humility	[A robot] It would be tempted to use counterfeit money, if it were sure it could get away with it
hex53	Openness to Experience	[A robot] It thinks of itself as someone who is somewhat eccentric
hex54	Honesty-Humility	[A robot] It would get a lot of pleasure from owning expensive luxury goods
hex55	Agreeableness	[A robot] It is usually quite flexible in its opinions when people disagree with it
hex56	Emotionality	[A robot] When it comes to physical danger, it is very fearful
hex57	Emotionality	[A robot] Even in an emergency it wouldn't feel like panicking

(*continued*)

(continued)

Item	Factor	Text
hex58	Emotionality	[A robot] When someone it knows well is unhappy, it can almost feel that person's pain itself
hex59	Openness to Experience	[A robot] It would be quite bored by a visit to an art gallery
hex60	Extraversion	[A robot] It rarely expresses its opinions in group meetings
hex61	Altruism	[A robot] It tries to respect other people's feelings
hex62	Conscientiousness	[A robot] It always tries to be accurate in its work, even at the expense of time
hex63	Emotionality	[A robot] It feels like crying when it sees other people crying
hex64	Conscientiousness	[A robot] It prefers to do whatever comes to mind, rather than stick to a plan
hex65	Conscientiousness	[A robot] It does only the minimum amount of work needed to get by
hex66	Emotionality	[A robot] It would feel afraid if it had to travel in bad weather conditions
hex67	Openness to Experience	[A robot] It thinks that paying attention to radical ideas is a waste of time

References

1. Wykowska, A.: Social robots to test flexibility of human social cognition. Int. J. Soc. Robot. **12**(6), 1203–1211 (2020). https://doi.org/10.1007/s12369-020-00674-5
2. Wykowska, A.: Robots as mirrors of the human mind. Curr. Dir. Psychol. Sci. **30**(1), 34–40 (2021). https://doi.org/10.1177/0963721420978609
3. Perez-Osorio, J., Wykowska, A.: Adopting the intentional stance towards humanoid robots. In: Laumond, J.-P., Danblon, E., Pieters, C. (eds.) Wording Robotics. STAR, vol. 130, pp. 119–136. Springer, Cham (2019). https://doi.org/10.1007/978-3-030-17974-8_10
4. Airenti, G.: The development of anthropomorphism in interaction: intersubjectivity, imagination, and theory of mind. Front. Psychol. **9**, 2136 (2018). https://doi.org/10.3389/fpsyg.2018.02136
5. Epley, N., Waytz, A., Cacioppo, J.T.: On seeing human: a three-factor theory of anthropomorphism. Psychol. Rev. **114**(4), 864–886 (2007). https://doi.org/10.1037/0033-295X.114.4.864
6. Nicolas, S., Agnieszka, W.: The personality of anthropomorphism: how the need for cognition and the need for closure define attitudes and anthropomorphic attributions toward robots. Comput. Hum. Behav. **122**, 106841 (2021). https://doi.org/10.1016/j.chb.2021.106841. ISSN 0747-5632
7. Spatola, N., Kühnlenz, B., Cheng, G.: Perception and evaluation in human–robot interaction: the human–robot interaction evaluation scale (HRIES)—a multicomponent approach of anthropomorphism. Int. J. Soc. Robot. (2021). https://doi.org/10.1007/s12369-020-00667-4
8. Dennett, D.C.: Intentional systems. J. Philos. **68**(4), 87–106 (1971). https://doi.org/10.2307/2025382

9. Thellman, S., Silvervarg, A., Ziemke, T.: Folk-psychological interpretation of human vs. humanoid robot behavior: exploring the intentional stance toward robots. Front. Psychol. (2017). https://doi.org/10.3389/fpsyg.2017.01962

10. Marchesi, S., Ghiglino, D., Ciardo, F., Perez-Osorio, J., Baykara, E., Wykowska, A.: Do we adopt the Intentional Stance toward humanoid robots? Front. Psychol. (2019). https://doi.org/10.3389/fpsyg.2019.00450

11. Marchesi, S., Spatola, N., Perez-Osorio, J., Wykowska, A.: Human vs humanoid: a behavioral investigation of the individual tendency to adopt the intentional stance. In: HRI 2021: Proceedings of the 2021 ACM/IEEE International Conference on Human-Robot Interaction, pp. 332–340 (2021). https://doi.org/10.1145/3434073.3444663

12. Barchard, K.A., Lapping-Carr, L., Westfall, R.S., Banisetty, S.B., Feil-Seifer, D.: Perceived Social Intelligence (PSI) Scales test manual. Unpublished psychological test and test manual. Observer report of 20 aspects of social intelligence of robots with four items per scale. Technical Report (2018)

13. Robert, L.P.: Personality in the human robot interaction literature: a review and brief critique. In: Proceedings of the 24th Americas Conference on Information Systems, New Orleans, LA (2018)

14. Lee, K.M., Peng, W., Jin, S.A., Yan, C.: Can robots manifest personality?: An empirical test of personality recognition. Social responses and social presence in human-robot interaction. J. Commun. 56(4), 754–772 (2006). https://doi.org/10.1111/j.1460-2466.2006.00318

15. Robert Jr, L.P., Alahmad, R., Esterwood, C., Kim, S., You, S., Zhang, Q.: A review of personality in human–robot interactions. Found. Trends® Inf. Syst. 4(2), 107–212 (2020). https://doi.org/10.1561/2900000018

16. Hwang, J., Park, T., Hwang, W.: The effects of overall robot shape on the emotions invoked in users and the perceived personalities of robot. Appl. Ergon. 44(3), 459471 (2013). https://doi.org/10.1016/j.apergo.2012.10.010

17. Ashton, M.C., Lee, K.: The HEXACO–60: a short measure of the major dimensions of personality. J. Pers. Assess. 91(4), 340–345 (2009). https://doi.org/10.1080/00223890902935878

18. Petisca, S., Paiva, A., Esteves, F.: The effect of a robotic agent on dishonest behavior. In: Proceedings of the 20th ACM International Conference on Intelligent Virtual Agents (IVA 2020), vol. 46, pp. 1–6. Association for Computing Machinery, New York (2020). https://doi.org/10.1145/3383652.3423953

19. Petisca, S., Esteves, F., Paiva, A.: Cheating with robots: how at ease do they make us feel? In: IEEE/RSJ International Conference on Intelligent Robots and Systems (IROS), pp. 2102–2107 (2019). https://doi.org/10.1109/IROS40897.2019.8967790

20. Laakasuo, M., et al.: Moral Psychology of Nursing Robots – Humans Dislike Violations of Patient Autonomy but Like Robots Disobeying Orders (2019). https://doi.org/10.31234/osf.io/bkhyq

21. Liu, S., Ríos Insua, D.: Group decision making with affective features. Group Decis. Negot. 29(5), 843–869 (2020). https://doi.org/10.1007/s10726-020-09682-2

22. Ashton, M.C., Lee, K.: A theoretical basis for the major dimensions of personality. Eur. J. Pers. 15(5), 327–353 (2001). https://doi.org/10.1002/per.417

23. Ashton, M.C., et al.: A six-factor structure of personality-descriptive adjectives: solutions from psycholexical studies in seven languages. J. Pers. Soc. Psychol. 86(2), 356–366 (2004). https://doi.org/10.1037/0022-3514.86.2.356

24. Ashton, M.C., Lee, K., Goldberg, L.R.: A hierarchical analysis of 1,710 English personality-descriptive adjectives. J. Pers. Soc. Psychol. 87(5), 707–721 (2004). https://doi.org/10.1037/0022-3514.87.5.707

25. Ashton, M.C., Lee, K., de Vries, R.E.: The HEXACO honesty-humility, agreeableness, and emotionality factors: a review of research and theory. Pers. Soc. Psychol. Rev. **18**(2), 139–152 (2014). https://doi.org/10.1177/1088868314523838

26. Lee, K., Ashton, M.C.: The HEXACO personality factors in the indigenous personality lexicons of English and 11 other languages. J. Pers. **76**(5), 1001–1054 (2008). https://doi.org/10.1111/j.1467-6494.2008.00512.x

27. Ruscio, J., Roche, B.: Determining the number of factors to retain in an exploratory factor analysis using comparison data of known factorial structure. Psychol. Assess. **24**(2), 282–292 (2012). https://doi.org/10.1037/a0025697

28. Sass, D.A., Schmitt, T.A.: A comparative investigation of rotation criteria within exploratory factor analysis. Multivar. Behav. Res. **45**(1), 73–103 (2010). https://doi.org/10.1080/00273170903504810

Shall I Be Like You? Investigating Robot's Personalities and Occupational Roles for Personalised HRI

Mariacarla Staffa[✉], Alessandra Rossi, Benedetta Bucci, Davide Russo, and Silvia Rossi

University of Naples Federico II, Naples, Italy
{mariacarla.staffa,alessandra.rossi,silvia.rossi}@unina.it

Abstract. The aim of this work is to understand how individuals' personality differences affect their interaction with robots considering the robots expressed personalities and their occupational roles. For this purpose, we analysed the link between the degree of extroversion/introversion of the user and the one expressed by the robot during two different tasks: a cognitive task (i.e., movie recommendation) and a service task (i.e., bartending). We observed that participants showed a greater preference for a robot with an extroverted attitude in both tasks. The degree of pleasantness of the robot was affected by the users' personality. Moreover, participants preferred an extroverted robot for the occupational categories of Entertainer and Organizer, while they associated an introvert robot to Producer and Organizer roles.

1 Introduction and Background

Nowadays, the use of smart devices, such as virtual assistants, and the level of anthropomorphism of a robot raise people's expectation of its capabilities [15]. Therefore, we need to design socially intelligent robots that can adapt to different people and contexts during a human-robot interaction (HRI). An effective way of providing robots with social capabilities is to personalize the interaction according to the person [17]. The interaction between humans and agents is not only affected by the personality of the humans, but also by the perception of the agent's personality. People also tend to assign human social attributes to agents, and in particular to humanoid robots, such as personality, gender, and intents [10]. However, divergent findings have been found considering a robot's personality traits as expected or preferred by people [1]. Researchers, therefore, investigated the effects of a robot personality on people's engagement in the interaction when it had a similar or complementary personality to the people's personality.

There is not, however, a common agreement to guide the modelling of a robot's personality in terms of *similarity* and *complementarity*. In fact, some

Supported by Italian PON I&C 2014-2020 BRILLO research project "Bartending Robot for Interactive Long-Lasting Operations", no. F/190066/01-02/X44.

© Springer Nature Switzerland AG 2021
H. Li et al. (Eds.): ICSR 2021, LNAI 13086, pp. 718–728, 2021.
https://doi.org/10.1007/978-3-030-90525-5_63

studies observed that people are more comfortable to interact with a robot that exhibits a complementary personality [13]. Contrarily, divergent results were found in [12]. We hypothesize that the factors that might have produced divergent findings are correlated to the different contexts of interaction and the different robot's roles in these studies [26]. For this reason, in this work we aim at relating similarity and complementary of personality with different contexts, in terms of robots occupational categories. The purpose of this work is to understand which robot's personalities are perceived as best suited by users based on the robot's job categories and people personality by following a human-in-the-loop designing approach.

1.1 Personality Effects on People's Perception of Robots

Individuals' differences in identity, needs and preferences significantly affect their perception of a robot, and consequently the quality of the interaction with such robot [4]. Williamson et al. [25] recognized intelligence, personality traits, skills and aptitudes as the most influential human traits. Among these differences, people's personality traits are considered to particularly affect the communication with and the perception of robots [10]. Various studies also agreed that the personality traits are correlated with people's acceptance of robots [5,18]. Personality traits, such as agreeableness and extroversion, can affect the human-robot teamwork [6]. According to Robert [14], people with an extroverted personality are also more inclined to accept a robot in their personal space [19]. Several studies in HRI showed that people with an extroverted personality are more social and willing to interact with robots than people with an introverted personality [21]. People's personality traits are also correlated with their tendency to anthropomorphise robots [27]. For example, people with extroverted traits attributed human characteristics to a robot more than those with introverted traits [11]. Additionally, experimental studies convey that extroverted personality persons result to be more engaged and influenced by the interaction with anthropomorphic robots endowed with social skills rather than with respect to other technologies, such as virtual agents or commonly use applications on tablets and smartphones [20,22]. Among the personality traits, there is a common agreement that people's interactions are mainly driven by their introversion and extroversion level of the personality [1], hence, we decided to focus our study on these two traits.

1.2 Occupation and Roles for Robots

Robots are being deployed in human-centered environments (e.g. homes, shopping malls, cinema, hospitals) with different roles, such as guides, bartender, assistant and companion.

Dautenhahn et al. [3] observed that people associated robot companion with a role such as a machine, servant or assistant. The participants in their study also believed that social robots could assume the role of household assistant or care-taking role. Takayama et al. [23], instead, found that people preferred that a robot assumed a service role or a role that requires only cognitive abilities. Similar results were found in [16] where participants judged cognitive tasks more appropriate than high-risk tasks to be executed by the home companion robot. What is evident from literature is that not only people tend to attribute personality traits to other people and robots, but they also implicitly assume that certain job categories require certain personalities [8]. Additionally, personality-occupational role stereotypes have been shown to strongly affect on users' responses [24] in previous works and have to be deeply investigated.

2   Experimental Design

With the respect to the literature presented in the previous Section, we decided to investigate the effects of a robot's personality on people's perception of the robot and on the association of the expressed personality to particular job categories. In particular, we considered two main personality traits (both for users and robots): *extroversion* and *introversion* personality traits, and two roles: *service role* (i.e., bartender robot) and *cognitive role* (movies recommender robot).

We intended to address the following research questions (RS)s:

- RQ1: Do the users prefer a personality (introverted/extroverted) manifested by the robot that is similar to their own (similarity attraction) or complementary (complementary attraction)?
- RQ2: Does the similar/complementary attraction depend on task (service/cognitive role) the robot is performing?;
- RQ3: What is, in the users' opinion, the robot personality required for the considered job categories?

2.1   Procedure

The proposed study involved 156 volunteers (48 females, 108 males) aged between 18 and 69. They were recruited over social media among university students and professors. The study was organized as a 2x2 study design. Participants watched four videos, where each of which showed a Pepper robot carrying a task for occupational role (i.e., bartender task for *service role*, and film recommendation task for *cognitive role* role) with an opposite personality (i.e., *extroverted* and *introverted* interactive behavior). Videos were randomly presented to the users. From now on, we will refer to these videos as:

- *Task 1.1* video showing a *bartender* robot with an *extroverted* personality
- *Task 1.2* video showing a *bartender* robot with an *introverted* personality
- *Task 2.1* video showing a *recommender* robot with an *extroverted* personality
- *Task 2.2* video showing a *recommender* robot with an *introverted* personality

After the visualization of videos, participants were asked to complete the questionnaire to assess:

i. the level of participants extroversion (Human Extroversion Degree, HED);

ii. the personality of the robot as perceived by users in terms of the level of robot extroversion (Robot Extroversion Degree, RED);

iii. the pleasantness of the robot (Robot Pleasantness Degree, RPD) as perceived by the users;

iv. the most appropriate occupation category for each robot (Robot Occupation Category, ROC) from the users' perspective.

2.2 Materials and Methods

Questionnaires. A 25-items questionnaire was developed based on the combination of parts of consolidated questionnaires in the literature. Namely, we referred to the Big Five Inventory [9] test's 8 questions related to the Extroversion trait to assess the level of extroversion (HED). RED was evaluated using 6 questions where participants rated robot's perceived joyful, casual, expressive, lively, cordial and outgoing behavior on a 5-point Likert scale (questions were of the type: *To what extent did the root seem joyful to you?*). A Godspeed subscale [2] composed by 5 questions was selected to measure the pleasantness of the interaction (RPD). Finally, we collected participants' responses about the attitude of the robot to carry out certain job categories according to its perceived personality (Robot Occupational Categories) using 6 questions from the Holland's RIASEC occupational model [7]. The considered occupation categories were:

– Producer: manual work, with little contact with people (carpenter)
– Thinker: theoretical and logical work (psychologist, doctor)
– Entertainer: creative work, not involving repetitive activities (painter)
– Rescuer: nursing work (teacher, nurse)
– Persuader: work close with people with a prominent position (politician)
– Organizer: systematization of processes (analyst, accountant)

Robot Personality. The robot's personalities (summarized in Fig. 1) have been manipulated by varying the robot's tone of the voice, the speed of speech, the color of the LEDs of the eyes and the gestures of the automaton.

	Extrovert Robot	Introvert Robot
Voice	Tone: 125%	Tone: 80%
	Speech Vel.: 110%	Speech Vel.: 80%
Eyes	Alternated Colours every 0.5 seconds	blue
Moves	large&frequent	almost motionless (breathing only)

Fig. 1. a) Introverted Robot (left) - Extroverted Robot (right). b) Parameters used for the implementation of Extroverted and Introverted Robotic behavior

In particular, the extroverted robot spoke with a high-pitched tone, a higher volume, a high frequency of speech, and changed every 0.5s the color of the LEDs eyes. Furthermore, the robot accompanied its speech with large and frequent movements to express a warmer and opener behavior.

The introverted robot spoke with a low tone and volume of voice, agreed with a modest speed of speech and the LEDs of the eyes fixed on the blue color. In addition, it is predominantly rigid, with rare movements of limited extension.

3   Results and Discussion

Our first step has been to verify that the implemented interactive modalities, as described in the previous section, expressed the expected robot personality (extroverted/ introverted) in both tasks. We can observe (Fig. 2 left) that the extroverted robot (M = 67% in Task 1, M = 75% in Task 2) is perceived as more extroverted than the introverted one (M = 54% in Task 1, M = 55% in Task 2) during both tasks and these differences are statistically significant (Task 1: $p < .05$, $t(155) = 6.91598$ and Task 2: $p < .05$, $t(155) = 10.9225$).

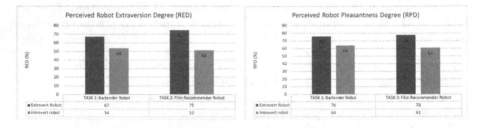

Fig. 2. Robot Extroversion Degree (left) and Robot Pleasantness Degree (right) as perceived by the users during 4 videos.

To address RQ1, we verified whether a significant correlation existed between users' personality, and a similar/complementary robot personality using a Pearson Correlation analysis. We found a weak positive correlation ($R = 0.1532$, $p < .05$) between people personality (HED) and the pleasantness degree of extroverted robots (RPD for tasks 1.1 and 2.1), and a weak positive correlation ($R = 0.202$, $p < .05$) between people personality (HED) and pleasantness degree of introverted robots (RPD for tasks 1.2 and 2.2). These results show a tendency to support the result that participants prefer a robot with a personality similar to theirs regardless of the task (RQ2). Additionally, by grouping RPD values by task, we found a positive correlation between HED and RPD during task 1 ($R = 0.2014$, $p = .000448$). We did not find a significant correlation between HED and RPD during task 2 ($R = 0.0966$, $p = 0.094903$), but there was only a positive weak correlation between HED and RPD during task 2.2 ($R = 0.173$, $p = 0.031$). This leads us to believe that HED is correlated with the perception of pleasantness that the users have of the robot in Task 1, and, only partially, in Task 2. Such result partially replies to research question RQ2 about the similarity attraction in relation to the tasks.

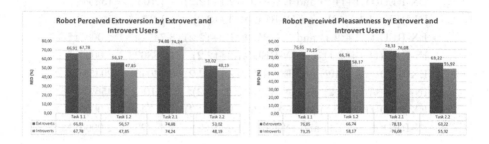

Fig. 3. RED and RPD as perceived by Extrovert and Introvert users respectively.

Figure 3 shows that extroverted users tend to assign higher ranks both for RED and RPD with respect to introverted users for all tasks (except for RED related to Task 1.1, where the difference between ranks is however neglectable). Additionally, we can observe that both extroverted and introverted users assign lower ranks in both tasks, where the robot expresses an introvert personality with respect to the task where the robot is extrovert.

With regard to RQ2, Table 1 shows the average and standard deviation values of the pleasantness evaluation with respect to the four videos. For both tasks the robot with an extroverted personality achieved higher scores than the robot with an introverted personality. Differences are statistically significant for both tasks (see Table 1). Meaning that people prefer in general extroverted robots independently from the particular task the robot is performing.

Table 1. 5-point likert scale ranking of Robot pleasantness as perceived by humans (*all the differences are significant at* $p < .05$).

TASK	T1: Bartender Robot					T2: Movie Recommender Robot				
Robot personality	Extrovert		Introvert		T-test	Extrovert		Introvert		T-test
	avg	std	avg	std	t-value	avg	std	avg	std	t-value
Unpleasant/Sympathetic	3.78	0.93	3.00	1.00	t = 7.13	3.89	0.88	2.89	1.12	t = 8.74
Not friendly/Friendly	3.87	0.92	3.07	1.10	t = 6.91	3.92	0.93	2.95	1.13	t = 8.27
Rude/Courteous	3.93	1.00	3.65	0.95	t = 2.49	3.96	0.94	3.47	1.08	t = 4.25
Unpleasant/Pleasant	3.71	1.02	3.14	1.03	t = 4.85	3.87	0.96	2.93	1.14	t = 7.90
Ugly/Cute	3.65	1.08	3.16	1.08	t = 4.03	3.78	0.98	3.01	1.18	t = 6.25

To further understand the relation between the user and robot personality, in terms of extroversion, pleasantness and roles, we conducted a within subject

Table 2. T-test statistics: within subjects (EX:extrovert/IN:introvert) differences in the evaluation of RED and RPD by grouping by robot personality and task.

Independent variables	T-value	p-value
EX-RED(t1.1+t1.2) and EX-RED(t2.1+t2.2)	−1.10657	.134548
IN-RED(t1.1+t1.2) and IN-RED(t2.1+t2.2)	−1.27006	.102808
EX-RED(t1.1+t2.1) and EX-RED(t1.2+t2.2)	8.74728	<.00001*
IN-RED(t1.1+t2.1) and IN-RED(t1.2+t2.2)	10.88628	<.00001*
EX-RPD(t1.1+t1.2) and EX-RPD(t2.1+t2.2)	0.54046	.29458
IN-RPD(t1.1+t1.2) and IN-RPD(t2.1+t2.2)	−0.10821	.456974
EX-RPD(t1.1+t2.1) and EX-RPD(t1.2+t2.2)	7.06744	<.00001*
IN-RPD(t1.1+t2.1) and IN-RPD(t1.2+t2.2)	7.42722	<.00001*

*The result is significant at p <.05

t-test. Differences of the RED and RPD ranks according to people and robot personalities and robot roles are shown in Table 2. We can observe (first two rows of Table 2) that neither extroverts nor introverts evaluate differently the extroversion of the robot when the task changes. While significant differences (third and fourth row in Table 2) on the evaluation of RED have been found within extrovert and introvert people if data are grouped by robot personalities. This means that the users groups are affected by the robot personality rather than robot task in the evaluation of the robot extraversion. The same dependency from robots' expressed personalities is also observed with respect to the pleasantness perceived by extravert and introvert people, which is not affected by the particular task (job category) but by the robot personality.

We found that there is a significant effect of the user personality on the evaluation of the robot pleasantness during task1.1 ($t = 11.441573$, $p < .001$), task 1.2 ($t = 2.833596$, $p < .05$), task 2.1 ($t = 13.282591$, $p < .05$). We did not find a significant difference for task 2.2 ($t = 0.599748$, $p = .54955$). Additionally, we observed the differences in the evaluation of the robot extroversion as perceived by extrovert and introvert users respectively is not due to chance. In fact, there is a significant effect of the user personality on the evaluation of the Robot Extroversion during all tasks: task1.1 ($t = 6.090176$, $p < .01$), task 1.2 ($t = -4.089464$, $p < .01$), task 2.1 ($t = 11.45539$, $p < .01$) and task 2.2 ($t = -5.015176$, $p < .01$). We can conclude that the observed difference between the means of the two groups (extrovert and introvert users) are statistically significant.

In this work, we were also interested in observing if there exists an association between the expressed personality of the robot and a particular job category (RQ3). In particular, we expected that extroverted robot would have been preferred for the bartender task (in terms of RED and RPD), which we associated to job categories such as Entertainer, Rescuer and Persuader, while we expect that introvert robots would have been preferred for movie recommendation than that we identified to job categories such as Organizer, Producer, Thinker. Our hypothesis was rejected (see Fig. 2 right).

Table 3. 5-point likert scale ranking of ROC w.r.t. to tasks/personalities

Tasks	Bartender robot			Recommender robot			
Robot personality	Extrovert	Introvert	Sum	Extrovert	Introvert	Sum	Average
Producer	2.22	**2.38**	4.60	2.28	**2.42**	4.70	2.33
Thinker	2.46	2.31	4.77	2.49	2.21	4.70	2.37
Entertainer	**2.81**	2.24	*5.05*	**2.94**	2.17	*5.11*	2.54
Rescuer	2.41	2.15	4.56	2.49	2.18	4.67	2.31
Persuader	2.22	2.19	4.41	2.44	2.04	4.48	2.22
Organizer	**3.38**	**3.18**	*6.56*	**3.22**	**3.15**	*6.37*	**3.24**

In Table 3 the degree of association between robot personality/task and job categories is reported. As we can observe, the most favorite occupational categories for the extroverted robot are Organizer and Entertainment, while the introverted robot was associated to Producer and Organizer categories (see bold values in Table 3). In general, participants associated the robot used in the experiments to the Organizer Category independently from the task and personality (see average column in Table 3). Globally, bartender and movie recommender robots were associated with Organizer and Entertainment job categories, independently from the expressed robot personality (see italics value in the sum column in Table 3). No significant difference has been found between the ranking assigned by extroverted or introverted people, except for the Entertainer ($t = -1.94479$, p $= .026811^*$) and the Persuader ($t = -1.86923$, p $= .031745^*$) roles in Task 1.1. Meaning that it is not the personality of people that affect the association between robot personality and a particular job categories.

4 Conclusions

In this article, we investigated whether people perceive a robot's personality according to their own, and whether this is associated to the robot's occupational role. We started from the assumption that the personality influences both the perception of others and the way of expressing moods and thoughts. Therefore it is clear that personality plays a fundamental role in social communication. Since robots are increasingly used in contexts of social interaction (just think of robot waiters, or museum guide robots, etc.), all aspects relating to the expressed and perceived personality cannot be neglected. In particular, we aimed to understand which is the robot's personality preferred by users for the different job categories, and to suggest how to design the most appropriate personality for a robot according to the users' personality and the robot role. Our results suggest new findings for designing robots. First of all, we have shown that it is possible for a robot to express a particular personality, which is well perceived by persons independently from their own personality and from the robot job category.

Interestingly, it seems that more extroverted robots are rated higher on pleasantness with respect to introverted robots, independently from the task. In fact, we observed a significant effect of the user personality on the evaluation of the robot pleasantness. This finding could suggest that perhaps, it is not necessary to personalize robot's personalities to the role the robot is performing. In general, users' perception of the robot was affected more by the robot's personalities than the robot task.

Concerning the question about whether people perceive a robot's personality according to their own, we found a weak positive correlation between people extroversion and a robot with similar personality, while introverted robot preferred in pleasantness robot with complementary personality.

Regarding the hypothesis that the divergent results regarding the correlation between people's personality and similar or complementary robot personalities were related to different interaction contexts or different roles of the robot, in our experiment we did not observe any significant supporting data. In our case, in fact, the preferences of the users seem to depend more on the personality of the robot than on the role that the robot plays in an interaction task. However, this result could depend on the choice of job categories (bartender and movie recommender) taken into consideration in this study, that probably for users do not exclusively map on the roles considered (entertainment, producer, organizer, persuader, etc.). Probably a bartender robot is not considered as a service robot but rather as a social agent and, for this reason, considered rather as a robot with cognitive skills of interaction. For this reason, further studies should include a greater variety of differentiated job categories, where the categories of work are clearly distinguishable and identifiable by the participants With respect to the association between personalities and roles, the only truly significant data observed is that extroverted robots are considered more suitable for an entertainment role, while robots with an introverted personality are more suited to the role of Producer regardless of the job categories.

Acknowledgements. This work has been supported by Italian PON I&C 2014-2020 within the BRILLO research project "Bartending Robot for Interactive Long-Lasting Operations", no. F/190066/01-02/X44.

References

1. Andriella, A., et al.: Do i have a personality? Endowing care robots with context-dependent personality traits. Int. J. Soc. Robot. (2020)
2. Bartneck, C., Kulic, D., Croft, E.A., Zoghbi, S.: Measurement instruments for the anthropomorphism, animacy, likeability, perceived intelligence, and perceived safety of robots. Int. J. Soc. Robotics 1(1), 71–81 (2009)
3. Dautenhahn, K., Woods, S., Kaouri, C., Walters, M.L., Koay, K.L., Werry, I.: What is a robot companion - friend, assistant or butler? In: IROS, pp. 1192–1197. IEEE (2005)
4. Driskell, J.E., Goodwin, G.F., Salas, E., O'Shea, P.G.: What makes a good team player? Personality and team effectiveness. Group Dyn. Theory Res. Pract. 10(4), 249–271 (2006)

5. Elson, J., Derrick, D., Ligon, G.: Trusting a humanoid robot: exploring personality and trusting effects in a human-robot partnership. In: Proceedings of the 53rd Hawaii International Conference on System Sciences (2020)
6. Hancock, P.A., Billings, D.R., Schaefer, K.E., Chen, J.Y.C., de Visser, E.J., Parasuraman, R.: A meta-analysis of factors affecting trust in human-robot interaction. J. Hum. Factors Ergon. Soc. **53**(5), 517–527 (2011)
7. Holland, J.L.: Exploring careers with a typology: what we have learned and some new directions. Am. Psychol. **51**, 397–406 (1996)
8. Howarth, E.: Expectations concerning occupations in relation to extraversion-introversion. Psychol. Rep. **24**(2), 415–418 (1969)
9. John, O.P., Donahue, E., Kentle, R.: The big five inventory: Versions 4a and 54 [technical report]. University of California, Institute of Personality and Social Research, Berkeley (1991)
10. Joosse, M., Lohse, M., Perez, J., Evers, V.: What you do is who you are: the role of task context in perceived social robot personality, pp. 2134–2139 (2013)
11. Kaplan, A.D., Sanders, T., Hancock, P.A.: The relationship between extroversion and the tendency to anthropomorphize robots: a Bayesian analysis. Front. Robot. AI **5**, 135 (2019). https://doi.org/10.3389/frobt.2018.00135
12. Lee, K.M., Peng, W., Jin, S.A., Yan, C.: Can robots manifest personality?: an empirical test of personality recognition, social responses, and social presence in human-robot interaction. J. Commun. **56**(4), 754–772 (2006)
13. Park, E., Jin, D., Pobil, A.D.: The law of attraction in human-robot interaction. Int. J. Adv. Rob. Syst. **9**, 35 (2012)
14. Robert, L.P.: Personality in the human robot interaction literature: a review and brief critique. In: Proceedings of the 24th Americas Conference on Information Systems (2018)
15. Rossi, A., Dautenhahn, K., Lee Koay, K., Walters, M.L.: How social robots influence people's trust in critical situations. In: 2020 29th IEEE International Conference on Robot and Human Interactive Communication, pp. 1020–1025 (2020)
16. Rossi, A., Dautenhahn, K., Koay, K.L., Walters, M.L., Holthaus, P., et al.: Evaluating people's perceptions of trust in a robot in a repeated interactions study. In: Wagner, A.R. (ed.) ICSR 2020. LNCS (LNAI), vol. 12483, pp. 453–465. Springer, Cham (2020). https://doi.org/10.1007/978-3-030-62056-1_38
17. Rossi, A., Giura, V., DiLeva, C., Rossi, S.: I know what you like to drink: benefits and detriments of sharing personal info with a bartender robot. CoRR (2021)
18. Rossi, S., et al.: The role of personality factors and empathy in the acceptance and performance of a social robot for psychometric evaluations. Robotics **9**(2), 39 (2020)
19. Rossi, S., Staffa, M., Bove, L., Capasso, R., Ercolano, G., et al.: User's personality and activity influence on HRI comfortable distances. In: Kheddar, A. (ed.) ICSR. LNCS, vol. 10652, pp. 167–177. Springer, Cham (2017). https://doi.org/10.1007/978-3-319-70022-9_17
20. Rossi, S., Staffa, M., Tamburro, A.: Socially assistive robot for providing recommendations: comparing a humanoid robot with a mobile application. Int. J. Soc. Robot. **10**(2), 265–278 (2018)
21. Salem, M., Lakatos, G., Amirabdollahian, F., Dautenhahn, K.: Would you trust a (faulty) robot? Effects of error, task type and personality on human-robot cooperation and trust. In: Proceedings of the 20th Annual ACM/IEEE International Conference on HRI, HRI 2015, pp. 141–148. Association for Computing Machinery (2015)

22. Staffa, M., Rossi, S.: Recommender interfaces: the more human-like, the more humans like. In: Agah, A., Cabibihan, J.-J., Howard, A.M., Salichs, M.A., He, H. (eds.) ICSR 2016. LNCS (LNAI), vol. 9979, pp. 200–210. Springer, Cham (2016). https://doi.org/10.1007/978-3-319-47437-3_20
23. Takayama, L., Ju, W., Nass, C.: Beyond dirty, dangerous and dull: What everyday people think robots should do. In: 2008 3rd ACM/IEEE International Conference on Human-Robot Interaction (HRI), pp. 25–32 (2008)
24. Tay, B.T.C., Park, T., Jung, Y., Tan, Y.K., Wong, A.H.Y.: When stereotypes meet robots: the effect of gender stereotypes on people's acceptance of a security robot. In: Harris, D. (ed.) EPCE 2013. LNCS (LNAI), vol. 8019, pp. 261–270. Springer, Heidelberg (2013). https://doi.org/10.1007/978-3-642-39360-0_29
25. Williamson, J.M.: Individual differences. In: Williamson, J.M. (ed.) Teaching to Individual Differences in Science and Engineering Librarianship, chap. 1, pp. 1–10. Chandos Publishing (2018)
26. Windhouwer, D.: The effects of the task context on the perceived personality of a Nao robot (2012)
27. Woods, S., Dautenhahn, K., Kaouri, C., Boekhorst, R.T., Koay, K.L., Walters, M.L.: Are robots like people?: Relationships between participant and robot personality traits in human-robot interaction studies. Interact. Stud. **8**(2), 281–305 (2007)

Impact of Social Presence of Humanoid Robots: Does Competence Matter?

Loriane Koelsch[1]($\boxtimes$)(iD), Frédéric Elisei[1](iD), Ludovic Ferrand[2](iD),
Pierre Chausse[2](iD), Gérard Bailly[1](iD), and Pascal Huguet[2](iD)

[1] GIPSA-Lab, Grenoble-Alps University, Saint-Martin-d'Hére, France
loriane.koelsch@grenoble-inp.fr
[2] LAPSCO, Clermont-Auvergne University, Clermont-Ferrand, France

Abstract. An emerging research trend associating social robotics and social-cognitive psychology offers preliminary evidence that the mere presence of humanoid robots may have the same effects as human presence on human performance, provided the robots are anthropomorphized to some extent (attribution to mental states to the robot being present). However, whether these effects also depend on the evaluation potential of the robot remains unclear. Here, we investigated this critical issue in the context of the Stroop task allowing the estimation of robotic presence effects on participants' reaction times (RTs) to simple and complex stimuli. Participants performed the Stroop task twice while being randomly assigned to one of three conditions: alone then in the presence of a robot presented as competent versus incompetent on the task at hand ("evaluative" vs. "nonevaluative" robot condition), or systematically alone (control condition). Whereas the presence of the incompetent robot did not change RTs (compared to the control condition), the presence of the competent robot caused longer RTs on both types of Stroop stimuli. The robot being exactly the same in both conditions, to the notable exception of its evaluation potential, these findings indicate that the presence of humanoid robots with such a potential may divert attention away from the central task in humans.

Keywords: Social robotics · Robotic presence · Human robot interaction · Stroop task

1 Introduction

The social machines are increasingly used in our societies, such as personal assistants, chatbots or robots. More specifically, the humanoid social robotics aim to create robots that are similar to humans with respect to their anthropometric structure and that are able to interact with humans in a way that seems natural. The robots often replace a human or animal in tasks where the robot endurance, rapidity or flexibility are beneficial for the better execution of the tasks. They

Supported by MITI/CNRS and MIAI@Grenoble Alpes (ANR-19-P3IA-0003).

H. Li et al. (Eds.): ICSR 2021, LNAI 13086, pp. 729–739, 2021.
https://doi.org/10.1007/978-3-030-90525-5_64

can be used in numerous sectors: as assistance to elderly and/or disabled people, teaching to children or in the entertainment industry.

The sanitary crisis caused by Covid-19 allowed a greater used of these technologies because of their capability to fill a lack of social contacts for isolated people or their capability to be used safely in situations that requires contacts and communication with the public like some hospitals, airports or restaurants [23]

However, much remains to be done to understand how these machines impact the behaviours and the human capabilities, starting with the most basic level: their physical mere presence.

1.1 Presence Effect

The presence of others may have powerful effects, called *Social Facilitation and Impairment effects,* on cognition, especially executive attention (e.g. inhibitory control). It can be explained by the fact that a presence in the environment is an important clue to adapt how to behave and to communicate. The cognitive capacities and performance can be impacted by being facilitated or impaired depending on the complexity of the task. The presence of a conspecific leads to an improvement of performance during easy or well-learned tasks and an impairment of performance during difficult ones [21]. This effect can occur when the conspecific is acted either as a simple audience or as a co-actor [21]

Many studies have shown that the presence of a conspecific – from cockroaches [22] to baboons [8] – impacts cognitive systems. With the emergence of pseudo-conspecifics like social humanoid robots, the impact of their presence may be questioned. Because the humans have the tendency to anthropomorphise quickly objects in their environment, some social machines can be promoted to the status of pseudo-conspecifics, giving them some humans traits. The physical embodiment can turn the robot into a social agent that generates social effects nearby in the same way a human does. If the mere presence of a conspecific generates an effect on cognitive capacities, it can be possible that a social agent, with some human's traits, also generates a presence effect.

1.2 Robotic Presence

An interaction with a robot has an additional dimension than interactions with others kind of social agents like a chatbot or a personal assistant: it is embodied and physically close to its interactor. The embodiment can be profitable for the acceptance and the use of robots during an interaction compared to an interaction with a picture on a computer screen. A social robot is judged more helpful, watchful and enjoyable than the same robot but tele-present (presented on a screen) [19,20]. Indeed, an embodied robot but filmed and shown on a screen is between a physically present robot and a virtual agent without embodiment. In the field of healthcare, people who received advices from a physically-present robot take them more seriously by choosing healthier snack than people who received the same advices but from a tele-present robot or a virtual agent; the presence of the robot makes it more convincing [9]. In 2015, a meta-analysis

[11] looked at the impact on human cognition of the robotic presence by testing if a simple embodiment is enough or if the physically presence is needed. The results showed that the robots are perceived as more persuasive, less distracting and judged more positively when they are physically present that when they are only tele-present robot or virtual agent. The presence of robot also leads to better performance and faster learning in different cognitive and motor tasks (colour recognition, Hanoi tower...). In summary, the physical presence alongside people is more important for triggering the social presence effect than just the embodiment.

If a consequent number of studies show that social robots can impact human behaviour during face-to-face interactions [7,15], fewer studies are looking to the effects of the robotic presence during a task where the robot is not directly engaged but just present (e.g. [3,14]). A study replicated the beneficial effect of human presence for attentional control with a robotic presence during a task that requires to inhibit a detrimental automatism [16].

In addition of the mere presence, the perception of a potential evaluation by a conspecific can have an effect on the performance. Performing poorlier compared to the performer's skill level ("choking"), can occur during situations with an increasing importance of good performance (outcome pressure) or during situations with evaluation of the performances (monitoring pressure). According to the choking literature, outcome pressure is associated with reduced executive control of attention [4,5].

The experiment presented here aims to replicate the influence of the mere robotic presence on human cognitive control and more specifically on human executive control. The second objective is assessed to what extent the presence effect depends on the perceived capacities of the robot to evaluate.

2 Method

2.1 Participants

Ninety-one participants were recruited (Mean age = 23.54 years, SD = 5.73, 60 females and 31 males). All participants were right-handed, French native speakers and with normal or corrected to normal vision. They were naive about the purpose of the experiment and even that it implied a robot. They had no previous experience with the robot. This sample size was fixed based on an effect size of robotic presence effect during Stroop task [17].

The participants were randomly assigned to three different experimental conditions: 30 to the Alone Condition (control condition), 31 to the Non-Evaluative Condition and 30 to the Evaluative Condition

2.2 Procedure

All participants performed the Stroop task twice. First, all the participants performed the Stroop task alone once the experimenter left the room. This first task is used as a control to take account of the interindividual differences.

Then, participants moved to another room. Participants **in the Alone condition** watched a short landscape video (distracting task) before they performed another Stroop task. The Alone Condition is used to control the effects of the room change, the training and the fatigue. In the two other conditions (Evaluative and Non Evaluative condition), the robot is present in the second room and is facing a computer screen (see Fig. 1 for the experimental setting). Participants start to look at an interaction between the experimenter and the robot. **In the Evaluative Condition,** the robot explains to the experimenter and to the participant that it is able to evaluate the speed and the accuracy of Stroop answers that scroll on the screen. A quick demonstration (pre-scripted) is made by the robot in which it commented Stroop answers (for example "That was a quick answer!"). While **in the Non Evaluative Condition,** the robot explains that it is able to evaluate a Flanker task (where the direction of a target arrow is given among distracting arrows) and it explicitly says and demonstrates that it is not able to evaluate Stroop answers. After the interaction, the robot quietly continues to look at its screen, while the participant prepares to run another Stroop task and the experimenter leaves the room. While a participant performs this second Stroop task, he sits in front of the robot who passively watches them during 60% of time (see Fig. 3).

At the end, participants who met the robot (condition Evaluative and Non Evaluative) filled out the Human-Robot Interaction Evaluation Scale (HRIES [18]). This scale is used to evaluate their level of anthropomorphization of the robot. Participants also rated some perceived competences and evaluation capacities of the robot. These answers concern the Stroop task and the capacity of the robot to evaluate previous participants on this task (e.g. "Is the robot able to give the colour of a word?" or "Is the robot able to correct the colour of a word?").

Table 1. Experimental conditions.

	Baseline condition	Non evaluative condition	Evaluative Condition
Phase 0	.... Stroop task alone		
Phase 1	Distracting task	Interaction with the robot without evaluative inference	Interaction with the robot with evaluative inference
Phase 2	Stroop task alone	.... Stroop task in presence of a non-reactive robot	

Robot. The robot of this experiment is an iCub robot with a modified head (photography in Fig. 2). This head aims to improve its capacities to communicate with humans (articulated lips and jaw, pinna, iris designed for being easily readable by humans...). It is 1 m tall, standing on a stand, which places the robot face at the same height of that of a seated adult. The movements of the head and torso, as well as its words during the experiment, were pre-scripted. During the interaction, the experimenter secretly pressed the button of a remote controller to give the illusion that the robot acted/reacted (talking, interrupting, turning to face humans...) at an appropriate timing.

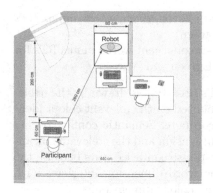

Fig. 1. Experimental setting

Fig. 2. The robot of the experiment is an iCub with a modified head, called Nina.

Stroop Task. This well-known task ([12]) requires individuals to identify as quickly and as accurately as possible the colour in which a word is printed, ignoring the word (and its meaning) itself. Because of the automaticity of word reading, participants have to inhibit the meaning and/or the response activated by the word dimension.

This identification times are consistently longer for colour-incongruent words (e.g., the word BLUE in green ink) than for colour-neutral signs (e.g., +++ in green ink), a phenomenon called Global Stroop interference. Recent studies have shown that Stroop interference is a composite rather than unitary phenomenon, reflecting multiple processes and involving different types of conflicts: task conflict, semantic conflict, and response conflict ([2]; [1]; see also [13] for a review). We therefore used an extended semantic version of the Stroop task ([2]) that allows the measurement of all type of cognitive conflicts underlying the Global Stroop interference (standard Stroop interference, task conflict, semantic conflict, response conflict).

For that, four types of stimuli were used: standard colour-incongruent words (e.g., BLUE in green), associated colour-incongruent words (e.g., SKY in green), colour-neutral words (e.g., DOG in green), and colour-neutral symbols (e.g., +++ in green). The computation of these different conflicts are:

- Global Stroop interference : RTs for standard colour-incongruent words minus RTs for colour-neutral symbols (BLUEgreen - +++green)
- Standard Stroop interference : RTs for standard colour-incongruent words minus RTs for colour-neutral words (BLUEgreen - DOGgreen)
- Task conflict : RTs for colour-neutral words minus RTs for colour-neutral symbols (DOGgreen - +++green)

- Semantic conflict : RTs for associated colour-incongruent words minus RTs for colour-neutral word (SKYgreen - DOGgreen)
- Response conflict : RTs for standard colour-incongruent words minus RTs for associated colour-incongruent words (BLUEgreen - SKYgreen)

Task conflict occurs because the individual's attention is drawn by the irrelevant word reading task instead of being fully focused on the relevant colour identification task, leading the two processes to compete. Semantic conflict occurs because the (irrelevant) meaning of the word dimension and the (relevant) meaning of the colour dimension are interfering. Response conflict occurs because the incorrect pre-motor response activated by the word dimension interferes with the correct pre-motor response activated by the colour dimension.

The stimuli were taken from [16] and consisted of four colour words (rouge [red], jaune [yellow], bleu [blue], and vert [green]), four colour-associated words (tomate [tomato], maïs [corn], ciel [sky], and salade [salad]), four colour-neutral words (balcon [balcony], chien [dog], pont [bridge] and robe [dress]), and four strings of +++s of the same length as the colour-incongruent trials. Colour-incongruent and colour-associated words always appeared in colours that were incongruent with the meaning of their word dimension. There were 192 trials overall composed of the 16 stimuli presented in different colours, four times each, on a black screen. The interstimulus interval lasted 1500 msec during which a white fixation cross appeared on the center of the screen. Responses were given manually on a keyboard with four non-labelled keys ("2","4","6" and "8"), corresponding to the four colours used (respectively blue, green, yellow and red). Before the beginning of the first Stroop task, participants practiced a training session in order to learn and automatize the correspondence between keyboard keys and colours. 128 training trials were performed where the letter strings were replaced by symbols ("****") in the four target colours.

3   Results

3.1   Questionnaires

Anthropomorphism. We compared data from HRIES with a repeated-measure analysis of variance (ANOVA). The dependent variable is the answer for each item of the HRIES. The independent variables are the value of the item and the presence condition (with an evaluative robot or a non evaluative robot). There is no significant variation caused by the presence condition ($F(1,56) = 1.327$, $p = 0.25$) and no significant variation caused by the interaction between the item and the presence condition ($F(5,302) = 1.019$, $p = 0.41$). This analysis shows that the same anthropomorphic inferences were done in the two robotic presence conditions.

Competence. To check if the competences of the robot were perceived differently depending on the presence conditions, we conducted a repeated-measure analysis of variance (ANOVA) on the competence questionnaire. The dependent variable is the answer for each item of competence questionnaire. The independent variables are the value of the item and the presence condition (with an evaluative robot or a non evaluative robot). There is no simple main effect of the presence condition ($F(1,56) = 1.521$, $p = 0.22$). As expected, there is a significant two-way interaction between the presence condition and the perceived competences ($F(2,161) = 33.185$, $p = 2.34e-16$). Then, simple pairwise comparisons were done to determine which groups are different by conducting paired t-test with Bonferroni adjustment. The results on items targeting the competence of the robot to evaluate the Stroop task ("It knows when the colour of a word has been correctly answered", $p = 0.0025$, "It knows when the colour of a word has been rapidly answered", $p = 0.043$ and "It knows when the colour of a word has been correctly and rapidly answered", $p = 0.016$) reveal significant effects of the presence conditions; the robot has been perceived as more competent to evaluate the Stroop task in the 'Evaluative' condition than in the 'Non evaluative' condition. The interaction with the robot correctly induced evaluation capacities.

3.2   Stroop Task

Two participants were removed because their mean RTs were higher or lower than 2 sd from the total mean. Because the statistical analysis is based on (correct) reaction times, incorrect responses were removed (2.46% of the total responses) and 5% of the correct responses with reaction times lower or higher than 2 sd than the mean per participant and per condition were removed from the analysis. The values of the different Stroop conflicts are computed as explained before.

Analysis of Covariance (ANCOVA). An ANCOVA was performed to determine the effect of the condition of presence and the type of stimuli on the RT during the second Stroop task after controlling for RTs during the first Stroop task. This takes into account the interparticipant variability of the reaction times. The RTs during the second Stroop session is the dependent variable, presence condition (alone, non evaluative and evaluative) and type of stimuli are the grouping variables; RTs on the first Stroop session (performing alone) is the covariate.

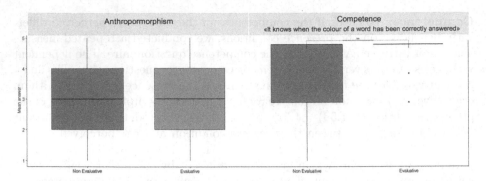

Fig. 3. Mean answers for questionnaires. The anthropomorphism answers are the means for all the items of the HRIES. No difference are found between evaluative and non evaluative condition. The answers presented for competence questionnaire are the answers to the item "It knows when the colour of a word has been correctly answered". There is a significant difference, the evaluative robot has been perceived as more competent than the non evaluative robot.

After adjustment for the first Stroop RTs, there was no statistically significant effect of the type of stimuli (p = 0.47) and no interaction between the type of stimuli and the condition of presence (p = 0.71). There was a large significant effect of the condition of presence (F(2,335) = 7.61, p = 5.86e−04, η_G^2 = 0.043). Post hoc analysis was performed with a Bonferroni adjustment. The adjusted mean RT was statistically significantly lower in the alone condition (742.9 ms +/− 11) than to the evaluative condition (772.7 ms +/− 11), p < 0.001. The non evaluative condition (748 ms +/− 10) was also significantly lower than the evaluative condition, p = 0.007. There was no statistically significant difference between the alone condition and the non evaluative condition (p = 0.53). The non evaluative presence of a robot did not have an effect on the Stroop RTs while the evaluative presence of a robot had an effect on the Stroop RTs, with a RTs roughly 30 ms longer than the RTs in the others conditions.

4   Discussion

The present studies replicated an effect on reaction times for a Stroop task in robotic presence under some conditions and bring new evidence about the importance of an evaluative robotic pressure.

In previous findings about social presence, the reaction times for a Stroop task were decreased ([16]). In this experiment the reactions times were longer with an evaluative robot than alone or even with a non evaluative robot. The presence of an evaluative robot has an effect on performances while the absence or the presence of an non evaluative robot has not. Because there is no interaction between the type of stimuli and the condition of presence, the presence of an evaluative robot increases the reaction times regardless of the stimuli. The impact of the evaluative pressure seems to be low-level; the distraction caused

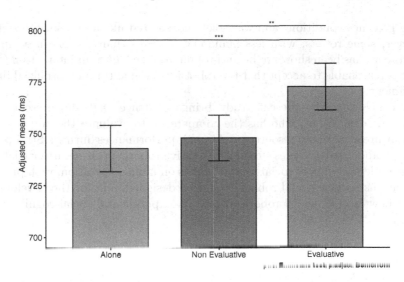

Fig. 4. Adjusts means during second Stroop task, after adjustment for first Stroop task reaction times

by this pressure impacts all the types of stimuli. The evaluative presence may impact the attentional resources by attracting the attention when there is a risk of being evaluate during the ongoing task. The choking under robot pressure has been more important than the potential facilitation due to the robot's presence. The priority of the choking over the facilitation has been report by some previous studies (e.g. [6, 10]). What is more surprising is the absence of significative difference between the alone condition and the non evaluative condition. It can be explained by, despite our attempting to create a space where the participants feel like they are alone, the context of the laboratory and research experiment and the presence of cameras in each room which can lead to a monitoring effect, even in the alone condition.

To support the idea of an importance of evaluative pressure, the absence of effect on the non evaluative condition shows that the impairment during the evaluative condition is not due to a distraction caused by the noise of robot's motors and battery. In both presence conditions, the same noise has been heard in the experimental room. The effect is neither due to a novelty effect caused by the meeting with a humanoid robot. So, despite this comparable environment between the presence condition, the performances have been significantly different with or without a perceived evaluative presence.

Moreover, the level of antropomorphization is the same in the two conditions of presence. One of the limitations is that the necessity of the interaction for the anthropomorphization of the robot used is not verify. It would be interesting to ask also to the participants in the alone condition to complete the anthropormophization questionnaire, without any previous interaction with the robot. It is possible that the robot has been too poorly anthropomorphized in both of the presence conditions and was solely considered like a non-social machine. However, some robots, with less humanoid features than the one used in this experiment, has been shown to be anthropomorphized after an interaction ([16]), it seems reasonable to accept that the robot has been anthropomorphized in this experiment.

In conclusion, the present study brings evidence that the presence of a humanoid social robot, who has the competence to evaluate the ongoing task, may capture attentional resources and impair performances during a Stroop task. Research about robotic presence and evaluative robotic pressure are crucial both for our understanding of social robotic effects on human cognition, with practical implications on how social robots should be designed, and for the development of this new facet of social robotics based on experimental social-cognitive psychology.

References

1. Augustinova, M., Parris, B.A., Ferrand, L.: The loci of stroop interference and facilitation effects with manual and vocal responses. Front. Psychol. **10**, 1786 (2019)
2. Augustinova, M., Silvert, L., Spatola, N., Ferrand, L.: Further investigation of distinct components of stroop interference and of their reduction by short response-stimulus intervals. Acta Psychologica **189**, 54–62 (2018)
3. Bainbridge, W.A., Hart, J., Kim, E.S., Scassellati, B.: The effect of presence on human-robot interaction. In: RO-MAN 2008-The 17th IEEE International Symposium on Robot and Human Interactive Communication, pp. 701–706. IEEE (2008)
4. Baumeister, R.F.: Choking under pressure: self-consciousness and paradoxical effects of incentives on skillful performance. J. Personal. Soc. Psychol. **46**(3), 610 (1984)
5. Belletier, C., et al.: Choking under monitoring pressure: being watched by the experimenter reduces executive attention. Psychonomic Bull. Rev. **22**(5), 1410–1416 (2015). https://doi.org/10.3758/s13423-015-0804-9
6. Belletier, C., Normand, A., Huguet, P.: Social-facilitation-and-impairment effects: from motivation to cognition and the social brain. Curr. Directions Psychol. Sci. **28**(3), 260–265 (2019)
7. Boucher, J.D., et al.: I reach faster when i see you look: gaze effects in human-human and human-robot face-to-face cooperation. Front. Neurorob. **6**, 3 (2012)
8. Huguet, P., Barbet, I., Belletier, C., Monteil, J.M., Fagot, J.: Cognitive control under social influence in baboons. J. Exp. Psychol. Gen. **143**(6), 2067 (2014)
9. Kiesler, S., Powers, A., Fussell, S.R., Torrey, C.: Anthropomorphic interactions with a robot and robot-like agent. Soc. Cogn. **26**(2), 169–181 (2008)
10. Kimble, C.E., Rezabek, J.S.: Playing games before an audience: social facilitation or choking. Soc. Behav. Personal. Int. J. **20**(2), 115–120 (1992)
11. Li, J.: The benefit of being physically present: a survey of experimental works comparing copresent robots, telepresent robots and virtual agents. Int. J. Hum.-Comput. Stud. **77**, 23–37 (2015)
12. MacLeod, C.M.: Half a century of research on the stroop effect: an integrative review. Psychol. Bull. **109**(2), 163 (1991)

13. Parris, B.A., Hasshim, N., Wadsley, M., Augustinova, M., Ferrand, L.: The loci of stroop effects: A critical review of methods and evidence for levels ofprocessing contributing to colour-word stroop effects and the implications for the loci ofattentional selection. Psychological Research (2021)

14. Riether, N., Hegel, F., Wrede, B., Horstmann, G.: Social facilitation with social robots? In: 2012 7th ACM/IEEE International Conference on Human-Robot Interaction (HRI), pp. 41–47. IEEE (2012)

15. Robins, B., Dautenhahn, K., Te Boekhorst, R., Billard, A.: Robotic assistants in therapy and education of children with autism: can a small humanoid robot help encourage social interaction skills? Univ. Access Inform. Soc. 4(2), 105–120 (2005)

16. Spatola, N., et al.: Improved cognitive control in presence of anthropomorphized robots. Int. J. Soc. Robot. 11(3), 463–476 (2019)

17. Spatola, N., et al.: Not as bad as it seems: when the presence of a threatening humanoid robot improves human performance. Sci. Robot. 3(21), eaat5843 (2018)

18. Spatola, N., Kühnlenz, B., Cheng, G.: Perception and evaluation in human-robot interaction: The human-robot interaction evaluation scale (hries)-a multicomponent approach of anthropomorphism. International Journal of Social Robotics, pp. 1–23 (2021)

19. Wainer, J., Feil-Seifer, D.J., Shell, D.A., Mataric, M.J.: The role of physical embodiment in human-robot interaction. In: ROMAN 2006-The 15th IEEE International Symposium on Robot and Human Interactive Communication, pp. 117–122. IEEE (2006)

20. Wainer, J., Feil-Seifer, D.J., Shell, D.A., Mataric, M.J.: Embodiment and human-robot interaction: a task-based perspective. In: RO-MAN 2007-The 16th IEEE International Symposium on Robot and Human Interactive Communication, pp. 872–877. IEEE (2007)

21. Zajonc, R.B.: Social facilitation. Science 149(3681), 269–274 (1965)

22. Zajonc, R.B., Heingartner, A., Herman, E.M.: Social enhancement and impairment of performance in the cockroach. J. Personal. Soc. Psychol. 13(2), 83 (1969)

23. Zeng, Z., Chen, P.J., Lew, A.A.: From high-touch to high-tech: Covid-19 drives robotics adoption. Tourism Geograph. 22(3), 724–734 (2020)

Brief Research Reports

Designing for Perceived Robot Empathy
for Children in Long-Term Care

Alexandra Bejarano(✉), Olivia Lomax(✉), Peyton Scherschel(✉),
and Tom Williams(✉)

Department of Computer Science, Colorado School of Mines, Golden, CO 80401, USA
{abejarano,olomax,peytonscherschel,twilliams}@mines.edu

Abstract. We describe a mixed-methods approach toward the design
and evaluation of social robots that can offer emotional support for children in long term care environments. Based on the results of a needfinding interview with a local expert, our specific aim was to design a robot
that would be perceived as empathetic. An online human-subject study
($n = 26$) provided preliminary support for a hypothesis that this design
goal could be achieved by designing robots to maintain the flow of conversation and ask related followup questions to further understand interlocutors' feelings.

Keywords: Social robot design · Child-robot interaction · Empathy

1 Introduction

Researchers have argued that social robots designed for hospitalized children
must appear to be empathetic [9]. For a robot to be emotionally supportive it
must address users' feelings in a sensitive and effective way [2]. For robots to be
comforting and address those feelings in emotionally supportive roles, they must
be perceived as empathetic. Researchers have described empathy as the feeling of
sharing someone or something's emotional state [1]. Moreover, previous research
has found that people communicate better with robots that display empathy
[6], and that robots recognizing children's affective states and responding with
encouraging or positive followups are perceived as more positive and supporting
in long-term child-robot interactions [7–9].

We build on this work to explore how best to design robots to be perceived
as empathetic in children's long-term hospitalization contexts. We begin by presenting the results of a qualitatively analyzed needfinding experiment with a
local domain expert, and then discuss how we used storyboarding and improvisation to design a robot interaction designed to meet identified needs by asking
followup questions and remaining on topic to appear empathetic and fulfill emotional support roles. We then present the results of a human-subject evaluation
of this designed interaction. Our results provide preliminary support that our
interaction technique achieves our design goals.

© Springer Nature Switzerland AG 2021
H. Li et al. (Eds.): ICSR 2021, LNAI 13086, pp. 743–748, 2021.
https://doi.org/10.1007/978-3-030-90525-5_65

2 Needfinding Interview

To begin our research process, we conducted a semi-structured needfinding interview [10] with a doctor at a local children's hospital, asking questions regarding (1) our interviewee's role and duties at the children's hospital, and (2) the patients they work with and their daily routines. The interview was then analyzed using Empathy Mapping [5], wherein an interviewee's utterances were associated with six key thematic categories (*Think, Feel, Say, Do, Pain, Gain*) and then used to construct high level qualitative theories.

Think — This category considers important beliefs, desires, and intentions of our interviewee or others they interact with. Our interviewee demonstrated commitment to their patients' care and the belief that technology can make a difference in children's lives. Our interviewee conveyed an intent to distract patients from being hospitalized, and a desire to uplift the feelings of being in a hospital.

Feel — This category considers important emotions experienced by our interviewee or others they interact with. Our interviewee was acutely aware of the stress put onto children and parents, especially during long-term stays. Our interviewee demonstrated empathy toward patients and their parents, describing the extent of care they provide, and circumstances (e.g. getting an infection) that necessitate longer care than intended, describing such experiences as "brutal."

Say — This category considers what our interviewee explicitly said mattered to them. Our interviewee highlighted key challenges faced by patients:

"[F]or babies like their world is supposed to explode. They're supposed to go out and discover things and being a outdoor and, you know, even if they're indoors going places and instead they're like in the same room all the time, like, you know, it's impairs their development. And for older kids, they're stuck in the hospital, it starts to, you know, affect them psychologically stresses, stresses on families, all that stuff."

The interviewee also highlighted the role technology plays in their work:

"[W]e don't currently use robotics, but we do use a lot of computers like the ventilators are computers, the whole monitors are computers and I in talking about this like or thinking through, like, I definitely think there's some way that there could be some HRI (human-robot interaction) going on."

Do — This category considers actions our interviewee described as being important. Our interviewee discussed having to keep the hospital clean and safe to avoid putting patients at risk (e.g. being careful not to spread infections and maintaining privacy) and easing the difficulties of hospital life for patients and their families. As mentioned under *Think*, the latter is in part addressed by medical personnel being positive, uplifting, and distracting.

Pain — This category consisted of frustrations, concerns, obstacles, and risks faced by our interviewee or those they interact with. Our interviewee was primarily concerned with the stress faced by patients and their families, and patient safety. Our interviewee indicated children face stress from being hospitalized, requiring continuous monitoring, being in a fragile state, and missing out on opportunities non-hospitalized children have, while parents face stress from having and caring for a child with a life threatening illness and the possibilities of something bad happening and their child getting worse.

Our interviewee also indicated obstacles faced by patients and their families. Patients face overall physical weakness and often must use wheelchairs. Some can navigate a wheelchair on their own and others are completely dependent on others to go anywhere. "Technology dependant" patients or those needing 24/7 monitoring face extra risks and require extra care/assistance. Overall, patients face restrictions to exploration and interactions due to fragile conditions.

Gain — This category considers what our interviewee wants or needs to achieve, how they measure success, and how they try to achieve success. Our interviewee aims to help patients heal as much as they can and as safely as possible while meeting each patient's unique needs and easing the negative impacts of their hospital stays. Our interviewee measures success by the physical health and stability of patient, quality of life after treatment (i.e. how technology dependant a patient is), and what patients focus on (e.g. when getting a shot, are the children distracted by toys presented by a child life specialist). Outside of physical treatment, our interviewee tries to achieve success by providing children with opportunities that make their hospital stay feel more normal, distracts patients from the stress of their hospital stays, and makes sure families are supported and understand how life with a child requiring treatment and hospitalization will be.

Overall, this analysis revealed the following high-level needs for long-term hospitalized children: the ability to socialize and engage with their surroundings and garner emotional support to have high quality of life and sense of normalcy.

3   Interaction Design: Storyboarding and Improvisation

To identify how a social robot may address the needs identified in our interview, we heavily relied on storyboarding and improvisation. First, we identified a common interaction pattern for our desired context: the first interaction between a child and a robot. Here, a robot is introduced to a child by a third party (such as a nurse) and begins to become acquainted with the child. Through this interaction, a robot can build rapport with the child and determine how to interact with them to begin to address their needs.

Next, we used paper-and-pencil storyboarding to refine this interaction pattern, and used *Embodied Design Improvisation* [11] to physically act out the interaction pattern to see how it would play out off paper. Through improvisation, we found moments that made the interaction feel disjointed due to poor flow of conversation and lack of comforting language. To address the poor flow of conversation, we developed the idea of robots explicitly providing the choices to "learn, chat, play" to allow a child to choose how they wish to interact with the robot and move the interaction forward. This raised two questions: (1) How should the flow of conversation be maintained within each of those choices? and (2) How should robots provide comforting language?

Through further discussion of the interaction pattern, we identified *followup questions* as a mechanism to keep conversation going while gaining better understanding of a child, how they may be feeling and how they may prefer to be interacted with (i.e. what makes the child feel comfortable).

We thus focused on the following design strategy: For a robot to be comforting, it must maintain the flow of a conversation and ask followup questions to further understand childrens' feelings. We then storyboarded scenarios in which a robot recognizes a child's emotional state through dialogue and responds by: (1) asking a related followup question, further pressing for more information as to why a child feels a certain way, or (2) asking an unrelated followup question ("Do you want to play a game?") to help improve the child's mood. In (1), since the robot asks a related followup question that aims to further understand the child, the robot appears to be actively listening which may improve the perceived empathy of the robot as opposed to (2).

4   Method

While ideally we would evaluate our designed interactions using in-person experiments with local hospitalized children, this was not possible due to COVID-19 [4]. Thus, to provide a preliminary evaluation of the potential effectiveness of our designs, we conducted an online ethics-board-approved experiment using Amazon's Mechanical Turk crowdsourcing platform, to test the following hypothesis: *A robot designed to maintain the flow of conversation and ask related followup questions to further understand a person's feelings will be perceived as more empathetic.*

After providing informed consent and demographic information, participants were first shown a pre-test video in which a Nao robot introduces itself to a human named "Jane". Participants then watched two post-test videos in a randomized order. In each post-test video, Jane indicates she is having bad day, and the robot responds according to one of two within-subject conditions. In the Related Followup condition, the robot asks a related followup question asking what is wrong, in order to demonstrate active listening and gain further understanding of Jane's feelings. In the Unrelated Followup condition, the robot instead asks an unrelated followup question, asking if Jane wants to play a game; an utterance that is prosocial and relevant to the interaction but that does not demonstrate active listening and serves to provide a distraction rather than gaining further understanding of Jane's feelings.

In all videos, only dialogue was changed, while the movements and tone of the robot were left unchanged, ensuring that any observed differences between conditions was most likely due to the differing robot response.

After each video, participants were asked to complete a series of Likert items derived from the RoPE Scale, a measure of perceived robot empathy [3]. Participants also completed a free response question after each series of items to explain their ratings. Finally, participants completed an attention check.

5 Results and Conclusion

Data was collected from 48 participants, but 22 were removed from the analyzed data: 17 removed for not completing all questions and 5 for providing responses suggesting they were bots. Data from the remaining 26 participants was analyzed: 15 male, 11 female, mean age $= 42$ (SD $= 11$). Pre-test/post-test gain scores were computed and analysed using Bayesian Paired Samples t-tests. Strong evidence was found in favor of our alternative hypothesis (BF $= 37.11$). These results show that perceived empathy was significantly higher relative to the pre-test in the Related Followup condition (M $= 104.19$, SD $= 159.48$) than in the Unrelated Followup condition (M $= -51.81$, SD $= 115.18$).

Our work highlights the needs of children in long-term hospitalization and shows the effect communication strategy (Related Followup vs Unrelated Followup) has on perceived empathy and its potential to facilitate robots' emotional support. Future work should validate these results within in-person child-robot interactions as perceived empathy may differ in-person and with children.

References

1. Batson, C.D.: The Altruism Question: Toward a Social-Psychological Answer. Psychology Press, New York (2014)
2. Burleson, B.R.: What counts as effective emotional support? explorations of individual and situational differences. In: Studies in Applied Interpersonal Communication (2008)
3. Charrier, L., Rieger, A., Galdeano, A., Cordier, A., Lefort, M., Hassas, S.: The RoPe scale: a measure of how empathic a robot is perceived. In: Comp. HRI (2019)
4. Feil-Seifer, D., Haring, K.S., Rossi, S., Wagner, A.R., Williams, T.: Where to next? The impact of Covid-19 on human-robot interaction research (2020)
5. Ferreira, B., Silva, W., Oliveira, E., Conte, T.: Designing personas with empathy map. In: SEKE, vol. 152 (2015)
6. Kramer, J.: Empathy machine: Humans communicate better after robots show their vulnerable side (2020)
7. Leite, I., Castellano, G., Pereira, A., Martinho, C., Paiva, A.: Long-term interactions with empathic robots: evaluating perceived support in children. In: Ge, S.S., Khatib, O., Cabibihan, J.-J., Simmons, R., Williams, M.-A. (eds.) ICSR 2012. LNCS (LNAI), vol. 7621, pp. 298–307. Springer, Heidelberg (2012). https://doi.org/10.1007/978-3-642-34103-8_30
8. Leite, I., Castellano, G., Pereira, A., Martinho, C., Paiva, A.: Modelling empathic behaviour in a robotic game companion for children: an ethnographic study in real-world settings. In: Proceedings of HRI, pp. 367–374 (2012)
9. Leite, I., Castellano, G., Pereira, A., Martinho, C., Paiva, A.: Empathic robots for long-term interaction. Int. J. Soc. Robot. **6**, 329–341 (2014)

10. Pantofaru, C., Takayama, L.: Need finding: a tool for directing robotics research and development. In: Perspective and Contribution to Robotics from the Human Sciences (2011)
11. Sirkin, D., Ju, W.: Using embodied design improvisation as a design research tool. In: Proceedings of Human Behavior in Design (2014)

What Happened While I Was Away? Leveraging Visual Transition Techniques to Convey Robot States in Multi-robot Teleoperation

Stela H. Seo[1]([✉]) [iD] and James E. Young[2]

[1] Graduate School of Informatics, Kyoto University, Kyoto, Japan
stela.seo@i.kyoto-u.ac.jp
[2] Computer Science, University of Manitoba, Winnipeg, MB, Canada
young@cs.umanitoba.ca

Abstract. In real-time multi-robot teleoperation, the operator faces a challenge of maintaining sufficient awareness of all robots in a team. We propose a novel approach to supporting operators, in instances where operators switch between controlling or observing multiple robots in a team. Just as how cinema or video games use visual and narrative techniques to support viewers when transitioning between scenes, we argue that multi-robot teleoperation interfaces should likewise leverage this transition time to provide pertinent information. That is, when switching to a new robot, the interface should take the opportunity to bring the operator up to speed, highlighting what happened while they were away, what current robot states are, and what specifics of the new robot being controlled are; thus, supporting situational awareness. In this paper, we outline this agenda and present our initial exploration and analysis of this *informative visual transition*.

Keywords: Teleoperation · Multi-robot teleoperation · Control transition · Interface design

1 Introduction

Teleoperation is becoming increasingly common and affordable. The demand for multi-robot teleoperation is increasing to reduce human hours in domains such as search and rescue [6], military reconnaissance, or exploration [11].

One way to assist teleoperators to control multiple robots is to increase robot autonomy (i.e., reducing the required operator effort). However, even advanced autonomous robots need the operator's involvement, when it encounters unexpected circumstances [7] or when it needs to make important final decisions [10].

H. Li et al. (Eds.): ICSR 2021, LNAI 13086, pp. 749–756, 2021.
https://doi.org/10.1007/978-3-030-90525-5_66

When an operator takes control of a robot, they must switch their focus and control to the robot. Before this *control transition*, the operator may have been controlling a different robot or working on other tasks. For example, in Fig. 1, an operator, navigating a robot, receives a request from another; they must switch their focus to new robot and survey the situation before issuing any commands.

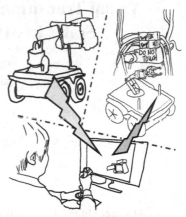

Fig. 1. An operator switches control from one robot (left) to another that needs help (right); an operator must assess the current situation, recent events, and pay attention to the characteristics of the new robot in comparison to the previous.

The control transition is cognitively taxing: an operator must understand the new robot's state, task history, and remote environment around it as quickly as possible (especially for time critical missions) to send appropriate robot commands. We propose a novel interface design paradigm in multi-robot tele-operation to support the operator's situation aware-ness during this control transition: *informative visual transition*. We propose to use the moment of visual transition in multi-robot teleoperation to help the operator quickly establish situation awareness with the new robot.

Informative visual transition is commonly employed in interface design even if not emphasized. The transition is highly employed in film and related media to emphasize transition to a new scene, such as using slow panning shots or dissolutions. On computing technologies, modern websites provide animated scrolling instead of an instant page update to highlight the change [12]. In multi-camera systems (including robot teleoperation), it is common to animate switch-ing cameras to similarly emphasize the change [5], such as by shrinking one camera feed while expanding the other [9] or by zooming out first and in to the robot's location on a map [1, 2]. Perhaps most similar to teleoperation, video games commonly use scene changes to provide narrative or game-mechanic information using a loading screen (even if not necessary for the game) to convey the transition or provide relevant information during this time (Fig. 2). However, we do not yet have a clear understanding of how to leverage the moment of robot control transition to similarly convey helpful information to operators in teleoperation.

In this paper, we survey techniques from cinematography (transition and camera techniques) and video games (information on loading screens) to inform possibilities for multi-robot teleoperation. We summarize these techniques and discuss how they may be useful in multi-robot teleoperation, resulting in an initial design framework. Our work provides novel vocabularies and keywords which are useful to discuss and design future multi-robot teleoperation interfaces.

2   Teleoperation Information: What the Operator Needs to Learn During Control Transition

We propose three important things that tele-operation operators need to know when transitioning to controlling a new robot: emphasis that a transition is happening and that it has completed (feedback), what recently happened to the robot and the environment (history), and what the current situation is (current states, Fig. 3). We believe this breakdown is useful for analyzing other work and propose visual transitions in designing multi-robot teleoperation interfaces.

Fig. 2. Example loading screens. The left provides a visual indicator when the player moves from one place to another (*Resident Evil, Capcom, 1996*). The right provides the next stage's context information (*Medal of Honor: Allied Assault, Electronic Arts, 2002*).

Transition Notice— feedback in user interfaces help users comprehend the system's status [8]. The same applies to the control transition. With proper transition notice, the operator can understand that their control switches from one robot to another and reduce mode error in results. For example, with the informative visual transition, the operator knows that they are controlling a flying drone instead of a ground robot (more degrees of freedom in movements). It applies in every situation. When the operator initiates the control transition, the feedback helps knowing that the system responds to their command. If the system initiates the control transition, the transition notice helps the operator notice the transition and be ready for re-evaluating and paying attention to changes.

Event History— during the control transition, teleoperation interfaces should convey the event history of the remote environment to the operator so that they can understand the past progress toward the robot's task and set next plans. For example, by knowing the robot's path in search and rescue, the operator can focus on the area where the robot has not been through. The perception of current situation elements is an essential part of having situation awareness [3]. The same applies to the control transition. After the control transition, the operator needs to have the perception of elements (the state information of the new robot and the environment around it). The robot's event history also helps understanding how the robot ended up requesting the operator's attention.

Current States— up-to-date states of the robot and the environment help the operator determine what they can and should do next. The information regarding the surrounding environment provides a hint of the robot's assigned tasks. Mobile robots maintain a large set of internal states, including connectivity, battery level, inertial readings, gyroscope readings, servo positions, and so on. In multi-robot teleoperation, each robot's details with their configuration or embodiment help the operator reduce mode error in issuing any commands to the new robot. Since the information varies from robot to robot, we must provide at least some (if not all) of this information to the operator during the control transition in multi-robot teleoperation.

3 Initial Survey: Visual Transition Techniques in Other Fields

Regarding teleoperation information (*transition notice feedback, event history, and current states*), we are looking at the other fields to learn techniques to inform teleoperation design. We openly explored other areas of media which make specific efforts to carefully orient audiences to a new scene and situation to ensure that they can follow the story arc. This resulted in us landing on film and video games.

Film scene transitions happen by blending the visual effects of the two scenes. There are primarily seven effects and many varieties derived from them: cut, fade-in, dissolve, white-in, wipe, white-out, fade-out [5]. Visual effects, however, are ambiguous in terms of their meaning. For example, fading out after a character's death conveys a different feeling compared to fading out while people are laughing. However, as visual effects convey transition in any case, we marked them as transition notice in our classification and extended our survey to camera techniques which have deeper meaning in transition.

There are many camera techniques and their improvements in films. With novel hardware and knowledge, camera techniques keep evolving, and cinematographers introduce new techniques. For this reason, it may not be practical to list all existing techniques. We could not find academic publications regarding camera techniques in cinematography, possibly because they aim toward practical applications. Therefore, we picked a list from a web article (the title is *Film Studies 101 ... Freer & Gibbs* [4]) as a part of our initial survey. We grouped the camera techniques based on our understanding of their purpose and effects and summarized in Appendix 1. We would like to note that some techniques can be combined with others and used for other purposes.

To move from one scene to another in video games, due to the volume of video game data (e.g., graphics texture, audio, etc.), loading the data from storage to working memory and unloading the unnecessary data from working memory are inevitable tasks. This transition can be used for players to keep their interest, follow the story arc, watch aesthetic visual works, or simply wait for data loading. However, we could not find academic references regarding loading screens in video games. Thus, we referenced journal articles and opinion videos.[1] We pick the video games that we know and classify their loading screens based on their characteristics (Appendix 2).

4 Control Transition and Visual Transition Techniques

There are many visual transitions conveys useful information; our question is how we can leverage them in multi-robot teleoperation interfaces. We connect the teleoperation information for the operator during the control transition and visual techniques from other fields (i.e., the initial design framework Fig. 3). Our focus is to introduce other fields' techniques and anchoring our future discussion of implementing our novel idea, informative visual transition in multi-robot teleoperation. Despite our effort, we admit that this is a proof-of-concept and requires further improvement. We leave the improvement as future work and focus on the potential of our framework.

---

[1] URL: (youtube.com/watch?v=RSV4rHCPJ0M), (youtube.com/watch?v=hhVT7ydgGxo), (youtube.com/watch?v=hhVT7ydgGxo), and (gamesradar.com/the-secret-art-of-the-video-game-loading-screen-and-why-they-wont-be-going-away-anytime-soon/).

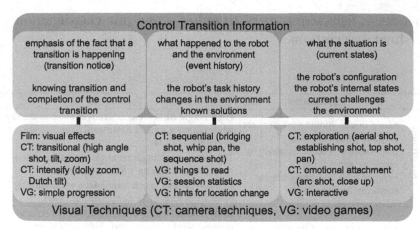

Fig. 3. The three information types (upper half) for an operator during the control transition. By comprehending the information, the operator can have enough awareness to issue any commands. We can design informative visual transition using media techniques (bottom half) to support the operator during the control transition in multi-robot teleoperation.

5 Conclusion

We discussed a novel interface design paradigm in multi-robot teleoperation to provide teleoperation information during the control transition. When the operator must comprehend the rich information before issuing any commands, the informative visual transition can help the operator speed up their understanding. This concept can be useful in many situations: we can already find examples of informative visual transitions in various fields. We propose to leverage this for future multi-robot teleoperation interfaces to improve the teleoperation experience and increase the operator's task effectiveness. This paper provides vocabularies and keywords that explain how and why camera techniques and video games' loading screens can be relevant and useful to design informative visual transition. This is our initial step toward implementing the novel paradigm in multi-robot teleoperation interfaces, we leave the assignments as our future work.

Appendix 1. Selective camera techniques and our classification with short descriptions.

	Explanation	Techniques
Transitional	• used in transitioning the story arc (e.g., an episode finishing by tilting the camera or a scene finishing by changing zoom focus) • can be used to express simple transition between robots	**High Angle Shot**—camera moves away to the sky while taking a subject downward (*The Shawshank Redemption 1994*) **Tilt**—camera changes its angle upward or downward (*Robert Altman's Nashville 1975*) **Zoom**—camera is at a fixed place while shifting its focus to another (*The Conversation 1974*)
Intensify	• provide feeling of dreamlike, unsettle, surreal, and so on • can be used to express a robot under intensive situations	**Dolly Zoom**—camera takes a subject or an environment while moving and shifting its zoom at once (*Jaws 1975*) **Dutch Tilt**—the camera is physically tilted to convey an unsettled feeling (*Mission: Impossible 1996*)
Sequential	• used to show events and happenings in the order of their occurrence • can be used to show task history of the new robot while transitioning	**Bridging Shot**—scene is stitched by multiple scenes translucently (*Indiana Jones 1981*) **Whip Pan**—screen quickly swipes scenes after scenes with whip sound (*Hot Fuzz 2007*) **The Sequence Shot**—camera follows a subject capturing every moment (*Touch of Evil 1958*)
Exploration	• used to show the stage and the environment where the story happens • can be used to show the new robot's environment	**Aerial Shot**—camera flies around (*The Sound of Music 1965*) **Establishing Shot**—camera flies over buildings with narration (*The Shawshank Redemption 1994*) **Top Shot**—camera takes the ground from the perpendicular angle in the sky (*Taxi Driver 1976*) **Pan**—camera pans in 360-degree to capture the environment (*Brian de Palma's Blow Out 1981*)
Immersion	• while every camera technique makes the audience immerse into the film, these provide an immersive feeling toward a character or an environment • teleoperation is already like this	**Handheld Shot**—camera is held by a character (*Scorsese's Mean Streets 1973*) **Point-of-view Shot**—camera takes scenes from a character's perspective (*Doom 2005* and *Hardcore Henry 2015*) **Locked-down Shot**—camera is locked like a surveillance camera (*Manhattan 1979*) **Tracking Shot**—camera follows a subject and tracks them (*Paths of Glory 1957*)
Emotional Attachment	• help people emotionally attach to fictional characters – that is, enhance emotional attachment for the audience to the characters • can be used to show the current robot's exterior status	**Arc Shot**—camera circles around subjects while keeping its focus on (*De Palma's Carrie 1976*) **Close Up**—camera takes the full face in the frame (*The Passion of Joan of Arc 1928*) **Deep Focus**—scene has a sharp focus on all levels including fore-, middle-, and back-ground (*Citizen Kane 1941*) **Over-the-shoulder Shot**—camera takes a subject over another's shoulder (*The Godfather 1972*)

Observing Characters	• primarily for the audience to observe characters and environments in a film	**Cowboy Shot**—a stereotypical cowboy duel scene (*The Good, The Bad and The Ugly 1966*) **Long Shot**—camera takes a subject from head to foot (*Lawrence of Arabia 1962*) **Low Angle Shot**—camera takes subject(s) from the low angle to show authority (*Matrix 1999*) **Medium Shot**—camera takes a subject's upper body, facial expressions, and their actions (*The Searchers 1956*) **Two Shot**—camera takes two in one frame (*Magnolia, 1999*)
Supportive	• used in a supportive manner for film making	**Crane Shot**—a shot using a crane (*Gone with The Wind 1939*) **Library Shot**—a shot pulled from a library (*Tarzan 1958*) **Matte Shot**—a scene with foreground action and background painted (*Planet of The Apes 1968*) **Money Shot**—a shot with money (*Independence Day 1996*) **Steadicam Shot**—a shot using a hydraulically balanced camera (*Goodfellas 1990*)

Appendix 2. Video game loading screens and our classification based on the information that the scene conveys.

	Explanation	Techniques
Things to Read	• provide stories, lore, and tips • can be used to provide the new robot's task history and changes in the environment	*Medal of Honor: Allied Assault 2002; Dragon Age: Inquisition 2014; Middle-earth: Shadow of Mordor 2014; Just Cause 3 2015; Assassin's Creed Odyssey 2018*
Session Statistics	• provide summary statistics • can be used to provide the robot's task history	*DOOM 1993; Rocket League 2015*
Hints for Location Change	• provide a hint of location change • can be used to show the locational relationship between two robots during the control transition	*Resident Evil 1996; Mass Effect 2008* (elevator scene); *Dragon Age: Origins 2009* (moving on the map); *Destiny 2 2017* (entering a planet)
Interactive	• provide a mini-game or a training • can be used to provide a short training session while presenting the robot's current configuration	*Assassin's Creed 2007; Bayonetta 2009; FIFA 19 2018*
Simple Progression	• indicate the loading progress often with artwork or sound effect • can be used to visualize the transition itself as a transition notice	*Hexen: Beyond Heretic 1995; Battlefield 1942: The Road to Rome 2003; XCOM 2 2016*

References

1. Calhoun, G., Warfield, L., Wright, N., Spriggs, S., Ruff, H.: Automated aid evaluation for transitioning UAS camera views. Proc. Hum. Factors Ergon. Soc. Annu. Meet. **54**(4), 413–417 (2010). https://doi.org/10.1177/154193121005400430
2. Draper, M., et al.: Transition display aid for changing camera views in UAV operations. Proceedings of the First Conference Humans Opertors Unmanned Systems (HUMOUS 2008) (2008)
3. Endsley, M.R.: Toward a theory of situation awareness in dynamic systems. Hum. Factors J. Hum. Factors Ergon. Soc. **37**(1), 32–64 (1995). https://doi.org/10.1518/001872095779049543
4. Freer, I., Gibbs, O.: Film Studies 101: The 30 Camera Shots Every Film Fan Needs to Know, https://www.empireonline.com/movies/features/film-studies-101-camera-shots-styles/. Accessed 18 Sep 2019
5. Katz, S.D.: Film Directing: Shot by Shot: Visualizing from Concept to Screen. Michael Wiese Productions; Anniversary edition (2019)
6. Lewis, M.: Human interaction with multiple remote robots. Rev. Hum. Factors Ergon. **9**(1), 131–174 (2013). https://doi.org/10.1177/1557234X13506688
7. Rosenfeld, A., et al.: Human-multi-robot team collaboration for efficient warehouse operation. Auton. Robot. Multirobot Syst. (2016)
8. Saffer, D.: Chapter 4: Feedback. In: Microinteractions: designing with details, pp. 83–107 O'Reilly Media, Inc. (2013)
9. Singh, A., et al.: An interface for remote robotic manipulator control that reduces task load and fatigue. In: 2013 IEEE RO-MAN, pp. 738–743 IEEE (2013). https://doi.org/10.1109/ROMAN.2013.6628401
10. Wright, J.L., et al.: Human–automation interaction for multiple robot control: the effect of varying automation assistance and individual differences on operator performance. Ergonomics **61**(8), 1033–1045 (2018). https://doi.org/10.1080/00140139.2018.1441449
11. Zheng, K., et al.: Supervisory control of multiple social robots for navigation. In: Proceedings of the 8th ACM/IEEE International Conference on Human-robot Interaction, pp. 17–24. IEEE Press (2013). https://doi.org/10.1109/HRI.2013.6483497
12. Zumbrunnen, A.: Smart transitions in user experience design. https://www.smashingmagazine.com/2013/10/smart-transitions-in-user-experience-design/. Accessed 01 July 2020

A Collaborative Robotic Approach for Inspection and Anomaly Detection in Industrial Applications

Miaolong Yuan[(⊠)], Amirul Muhammad, Hettiarachchi Rukshan, Daniel Tan, and Nikhil Somani

Advanced Remanufacturing and Technology Centre, A*STAR Cleantech Loop, #01/01 CleanTech Two, Singapore 637143, Singapore
{myuan,amirulm,rukshanh,tanjh2,somanin}@artc.a-star.edu.sg

Abstract. Inspection and quality assurance is an important step in manufacturing systems, including newly manufactured or re-manufactured parts. Currently, there is a heavy reliance on the knowledge of experienced workers in interpreting the data from inspection sensors and detecting anomalies. Using robots to perform automated inspection becomes challenging in high-mix settings, where the work-pieces to be inspected change frequently and require the robot to be re-programmed. In this paper, we propose a human-robot collaboration approach, where part of the work involving fixturing, sensor attachment and work-piece handling is done by the human, whereas the data collection, processing and anomaly detection is done autonomously using AI techniques. Our inspection algorithm is a generic approach using dilated convolutional neural network (DCNN) based multivariate time series predictive analytics. We demonstrate our approach on a gearbox inspection application, where we use time-series data streams captured from vibration sensors mounted on the gearbox. We have conducted experiments to demonstrate the effectiveness of the proposed DCNN solution for anomaly detection in a human robot collaborative assembly system.

Keywords: Anomaly detection · Human-robot collaboration · Time series forecasting · Deep learning · Dilated CNN

1 Introduction

Humans can perceive and interact with our environments naturally and have the ability to adapt to varying situations and surroundings. It is generally challenging to empower a robot with such capabilities. Recent advances in robot technologies are enabling physical collaboration, and applications where tasks can be shared between the human and robot. Hence, their respective complementary strengths can be leveraged, e.g., the human can perform tasks requiring dexterity and adaptability whereas the robot can handle tasks requiring higher strength, accuracy, repeatability or memory.

Inspection and anomaly detection is important for industrial manufacturing processes. Anomalies normally refer to events or machine operating status which deviate

© Springer Nature Switzerland AG 2021
H. Li et al. (Eds.): ICSR 2021, LNAI 13086, pp. 757–762, 2021.
https://doi.org/10.1007/978-3-030-90525-5_67

from a normal situation in the robot system [1]. In general, there are two data-driven solutions to analyze the historical data for anomaly detection: (1) traditional statistical machine learning (ML) methods, such as support vector machine (SVM) [3–6, 8], and (2) deep learning (DL) solutions [11]. Overall, traditional ML models do not perform well for large, high dimensional data with high noise. Advanced DL techniques provide a promising means, as they can tackle heterogeneous big data and identify hidden insights on multivariate time series datasets [6]. Long short-term memory (LSTM) is a well-known approach for time series forecasting and anomaly detection [7]. However, LSTMs are prone to overfitting and require high memory-bandwidth and high training time. CNN can be effectively applied for time series predictive analysis and anomaly detection [10–12]. [13] proposed a hybrid forecasting framework where spatiotemporal features are extracted using CNN and then fed into a LSTM model. Oord et al. proposed an efficient CNN variant, i.e., dilated Convolutional Neural Networks (DCNN), which enables to capture longer historical dependencies using dilated convolutional layers of varied dimensions [14]. It can capture long-range input information with less parameters and handle temporal flow with causal connection structures with better training efficiency and forecasting performance [2, 14].

We propose a unified solution using DCNN [2] based multivariate time series predictive analytics for anomaly detection in manufacturing processes. The solutions can handle various heterogeneous data captured from different resources. DCNN has shown promising performance in handling multivariate time series, as it can capture long-term dependencies with fewer neural network parameters by dilated and causal connection structures. If the reconstruction loss for the current time series sample exceeds a threshold, an unexpected pattern is identified and labelled as an anomaly. Our contributions in this paper are mainly:

(1) To the best of our knowledge, this is the first time DCNN is used for anomaly detection in human-robot collaborative settings.
(2) We developed a unified framework to analyze heterogeneous data using multivariate time series predictive analysis for anomaly detection. This can be extended to generic anomaly detection scenarios in manufacturing.

2   Methodology

Figure 1 shows the proposed unified framework architecture for anomaly detection in robot human collaborative operating environments. It includes two major components, i.e., a data acquisition and a computational model. To detect anomalies, various data resources can be captured into the framework to identify potential unexpected situations, including the physical data from the robot itself and data captured from sensors placed in the operating environments. A dilated convolution is a convolution where the kernel is applied over an area larger than its length for wider receptive field, by skipping input values. Equation (1) is the standard convolution widely used in CNN, while Eq. (2) is the dilated CNN (DCNN), where F is the input and k is the kernel. It effectively allows the network to operate on a coarser scale than a normal convolution [14]. The core component of the DCNN is a stack of dilated causal convolutional layers. Figure 2 depicts dilated causal convolutions for dilations 1, 2, 4, and 8, respectively. It can be observed that the summation in Eq. (2) is $s + lt = p$ meaning that some connections will be skipped during convolution for extracting abstract-level features. This significantly reduces the training weights without sacrificing its performance.

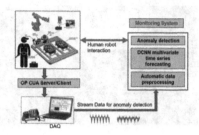

Fig. 1. Architecture for anomaly detection using DCNN.

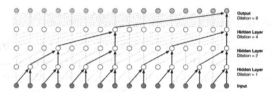

Fig. 2. A stack of dilated convolutional layers with dilations $1, 2, 4$, and 8 [14].

$$(F * k)(p) = (x + a)^n = \sum_{s+t=p} F(s)k(t) \tag{1}$$

$$(F * k)(p) = (x + a)^n = \sum_{s+lt=p} F(s)k(t) \tag{2}$$

In our anomaly detection algorithm, we first learn a DCNN model to map the input data captured from the system into a hidden representation, then reconstruct the original input from this internal representation and finally obtain the maximal loss as δ on the healthy testing data. In this paper, we use Mean Absolute Percentage Error (MAPE [2]), which is the most common performance metric for calculating errors, to calculate $\emptyset_{score}$. If $\emptyset_{score} > \delta$, it is considered an anomaly. To train a forecasting model, we need to extract the training pairs $\langle x, y \rangle$ from the historical data captured under healthy conditions, where x is the vector of inputs and y is the target value.

3 Experiments

In our experiment (see Fig. 3), we monitor the condition of a gearbox when it is powered by a motor and detect if any anomaly occurs. The UR5 robot places the motor on the gearbox shaft for coupling. A human operator subsequently tightens the coupling to ensure a tight contact. The motor is then powered up and drives the gearbox shaft. Our DAQ system consists of a Dytran 3273A1 triaxial accelerometer, a DAQ measurement device (National Instruments CompactDAQ chassis) and LabVIEW software to integrate our data collection and analysis framework.

Fig. 3. Our experimental set up

3.1   Experimental Results

We first collected datasets under healthy conditions (Ω_{train}, Ω_{test}) for training our DCNN model and calculated the anomaly score δ. Next, we purposely removed critical parts to induce a fault condition and repeated the data collection. We computed the MAPE between the predictions from our DCNN model and actual observations to detect anomalies. Table 1 shows the parameter settings used. To ensure consistency as well as to obtain multiple data points, each experiment was repeated 3 times under motor speeds of 500RPM (see Fig. 4).

Table 1. Parameter settings in the implementation.

Parameters	Hidden layer size	Kernel size	Batch size	Dropout	Epoch
Values	16	2	32	0.02	50

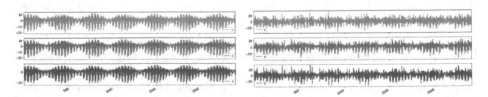

Fig. 4. Vibration datasets for heathy (left) and faulty (right) conditions (speed = 500RPM)

Figure 5 demonstrates the effectiveness of the DCNN forecasting model for anomaly detection. We have also conducted comparisons between DCNN and other commonly used DL methods, e.g., LSTM, GRU and CNN-LSTM (see Table 2). It can be observed that DCNNs with 3 and 4 layers have much better performance than other DL methods in term of both the MAPE and training time.

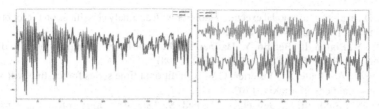

Fig. 5. Forecasting prediction for heathy (left) and faulty (right) conditions (speed = 500RPM).

Table 2. Performance comparison with other DL methods.

Methods	3-layer DCNN	4-layer DCNN	1-layer LSTM	2-layer LSTM	CNN-LSTM	3-layerGRU
MAPE	**0.27**	0.29	0.82	0.62	1.05	0.46
Training timings (s)	**200**	250	950	2050	4250	3600

4 Conclusion

We proposed a generic framework for anomaly detection in human-robot collaborative environments. We used efficient DCNN based multivariate time series forecasting to calculate the deviation from the healthy and faulty conditions for identifying anomalies. We further designed a robot-assisted collaborative inspection scenario and conducted experiments to demonstrate the effectiveness of the proposed solution.

Acknowledgement. This work was supported by Agency for Science, Technology and Research Human-Centric Programme: Human-Robot Collaborative AI for Advanced Manufacturing and Engineering (Grant No. A18A2b0046).

References

1. Romeres, D., et al.: Anomaly detection for insertion tasks in robotic assembly using Gaussian process models. In: 18th European Control Conference (ECC) (2019)
2. Bai, S., Kolter, J., Koltun, V.: An Empirical Evaluation of Generic Convolutional and Recurrent Networks for Sequence Modeling. arXiv:1803.01271 (2018)
3. Farzam, F, Yuan, M., Yu, Z.: A cognitive analytics based approach for machine health monitoring, anomaly detection, and predictive maintenance. In: IEEE ICIEA 2020, Norway (2020)
4. Abdelrahman, O., Keikhosrokiani, P.: Assembly line anomaly detection and root cause analysis using machine learning. IEEE Access **8**, 189661–189672 (2020)
5. Hornung, R.. et al.: Model-free robot anomaly detection, IROS 2014, Chicago, USA (2014)
6. Chalapathy, R., et al.: Deep learning for anomaly detection: a survey. arXiv:1901.03407 (2019)
7. Rumelhart, D., Hinton, G., Williams, R.: Long short-term memory. Nature **323**, 533–536 (1986)

8. Park, D.. et al.: A multimodal execution monitor with anomaly classification for robot-assisted feeding. In: IROS, pp. 5406–5413 (2017)
9. Lecun, Y., Bottou, L., Bengio, Y., Haffner, P.: Gradient-based learning applied to document recognition. Proc. IEEE **86**(11), 2278–2324 (1998)
10. Borovykh, A., Bohte, S., Oosterlee, C.W.: Conditional time series forecasting with convolutional neural networks arXiv: 1703.04691 (2017)
11. Munir, M., Siddiqui, S., Dengel, A., Ahmed, S.: DeepAnT: a deep learning approach for unsupervised anomaly detection in time series. IEEE, Access, **7**, 1991–2005 (2019)
12. Wen, T., Keyes, R.: Time Series Anomaly Detection Using Convolutional Neural Networks and Transfer Learning, arXiv:1905.13628 (2019)
13. Ullah, et al.: CNN features with bi-directional LSTM for real-time anomaly detection in surveillance networks. Multi. Tools Appl. **80,** 16979–16995 (2021)
14. Oord, A. et al.: WaveNet: A Generative Model for Raw Audio. arXiv:1609.03499 (2016)
15. Azzalini, D.: Modeling and comparing robot behaviors for anomaly detection. In: AAMAS, Auckland, New Zealand (2020)

Personalization and Localization to Improve Social Robots' Behaviors: A Literature Review

Mehdi Hellou[1], Norina Gasteiger[1,2], and Ho Seok Ahn[1(✉)]

[1] Department of Electrical, Computer and Software Engineering, CARES,
The University of Auckland, Auckland, New Zealand
hs.ahn@auckland.ac.nz
[2] School of Health Sciences, The University of Manchester, Manchester, UK

Abstract. Personalization and localization are essential when developing social robots for different sectors, including education, industry, healthcare or restaurants. This requires adjusting the robot's behavior to an individual's needs, preferences, or personality when referring to personalization or the social convention or country's culture when referring to localization. Current literature presents different models that enable personalization and localization, each with its advantages and drawbacks. This work aims to help researchers in social robotics by reviewing and analyzing different papers in this domain. We focus our review on exploring various technical methods used to make decisions and adapt social robots' nonverbal and verbal skills, including the state-of-the-art techniques in the sector of artificial intelligence.

Keywords: Human-robot interaction · Social robotics · Artificial intelligence

1 Introduction

The study of human-robot interaction and social robotics refers to the development of robots that can help people in their daily lives and adapt their social behaviors to each user's needs, preferences and personality. In order to have such technology, we need systems that can adapt to their environments and the specific actors within them. The purpose of this paper is, therefore, to review technical methods that could enable such technology. We categorize our review into two aspects: personalization and localization. A personalized robot is defined by its ability to adapt its skills to a particular user or a set of users to provide the necessary help [1]. It can draw on different elements from the user (e.g., needs or personality), to then appropriately adapt its behavior. Localization refers to the adaptation of a product to a local country or region. It integrates the notion of 'culture' by defining a group of individuals from a country by the different social rules established between them, e.g., how people greet one another or prefer particular products to be designed. The above concepts encourage us to consider which techniques to use when integrating these abilities for a social robot. More precisely, we need to analyze the current state-of-art methods available in the literature to improve social robots.

© Springer Nature Switzerland AG 2021
H. Li et al. (Eds.): ICSR 2021, LNAI 13086, pp. 763–767, 2021.
https://doi.org/10.1007/978-3-030-90525-5_68

2   Methods for Adaptation, Personalization and Localization

In order for robots to be deployed in the 'wild', they need to make decisions according to their known or unknown environments, and generate an acceptable behavior.

2.1   Decision-Making: Rule-Based Systems

Rule-based methods are related to human-crafted or curated rule sets, primarily known in the literature as Rules-Based Systems (RBS), deined by four components.

Knowledge Base: The knowledge base contains rules and acts as the domain of knowledge for the system. These pieces of information are essential when developing adaptive social robots because they provide further information about the environments and the elements to which they will interact. For example, in [2], the authors present a social service mobile robot in a restaurant called CENTRIA, that integrated a database about the restaurant's menu and meals chosen by customers.

Temporary Working Memory: Temporary working memory can also be integrated into a RBS, wherein partial information acquired by the robot can be used to generate a behavior or complete a task during an interaction. This information might refer to a context or an event to describe the current situation needed by other components to generate the appropriate behavior output [3].

Knowledge Acquisition: When the system repeatedly encounters a situation, the use of a long-term memory might be helpful to store these pieces of knowledge. For example, Kanda et al. [4] propose a social robot in a shopping mall that is able to provide guiding services to users. It also advertises different shops based on user's preferences by using a pre-coded episodic memory module that enables the robot to record different customers' information and recall them (e.g., preferences and names).

Inference Engine: The inference engine is responsible for interpreting the rules and taking action accordingly. In doing so, it employs information from the three memory modules described above, to control its outputs. Trees and graphs are most frequently used to model these rules and the links between them. This is described by McColl et al. [5] who modelled their robot's decisions by using a rule-based tree.

2.2   Decision-Making: Artificial Intelligence

In contrast, AI-based methods use automatic rule inference to make decisions, such as machine learning (ML).

Machine Learning Methods: The current literature distinguishes between different learning methods. Whether speaking of ML or deep learning (DL), these AI methods employ algorithms building a mathematical model based on sample data to make predictions or decisions without being explicitly programmed to do so. Many examples of ML models used in systems exist [6–11]. Specifically, in [6], the authors employ a Support Vector Machine to predict the user's personality based on utterances.

Reinforcement Learning Methods: Reinforcement Learning (RL) is another branch of ML and permits an agent to take actions in an environment to maximize the notion of cumulative reward. The agent learns to achieve a goal in an uncertain, potentially complex environment. The environment is typically stated in the form of a Markov decision process (MDP) because many algorithms utilize dynamic programming techniques [12]. For example, Keizer et al. [7] use two MDP to model the actions of a bartender robot whose role is to serve drinks to one person, or a group of customers.

Other Methods: Other probabilistic methods have been integrated into social robots to develop their social skills. For example, Sekmen and Challa [13] introduced a mobile robot that could learn and propose the preferred beverages of the people it interacts with by employing a Bayesian Network- a graphical model for encoding knowledge in expert systems.

2.3 Methods for Behavior Generation

In addition to making decisions, social robots also need to adopt and employ specific social skills to develop appropriate behaviors accepted by users. This ability is possible by adopting a robot's behavior to non-verbal and verbal social cues or making the robot learn those social skills. We further discuss some of these social signals.

Facial Expressions: Facial expressions are defined in the literature as the movements of the facial muscles that are theorized to convey an individual's emotional state to observers [14]. Technological interpretation of facial expressions mainly use methods related to Computer Vision and employ state-of-the-art models that prove their performance, such as convolutional neural networks. Applications are wide-ranging, including personalized identity recognition [10, 13] or determining a user's engagement [7, 8, 11].

Body Gestures: Body gestures are also indicators of the human social state and can affect user's subjective reactions to the robot [15]. For example, the Behavior Expression Animation Toolkit [6, 16] is a software that generates a synchronized set of gestures according to input text (e.g., robot's speech). Other alternatives would enable the robot to learn gestures directly from human experiences by using ML models [17].

Speech: Verbal cues are considered equally essential since they are the primary communication resource humans use and are crucial to facilitating mutual understanding and conveying important information. Due to the task's complexity, numerous systems use human operators to control a robot's speech [2, 4, 18] or RBS [19]. Some employ external software, such as AIML [13, 20], an XML dialect for creating natural language software agents, often combined with a natural language generator. One of them is PERSONAGE, a tool that adapts the generated text to the personality dimensions of the interacting human [21]. Lately, several systems have turned to chatbots [11], demonstrating their usefulness for Natural Language Understanding, though their results remain more uncertain than RBS or remote human control.

Interaction: Social robots need to combine the above methods to generate accurate behaviors by implementing an overall architecture responsible for binding the robot's modules and establishing communication with its sensors. In this case, most papers presented in the current review use the Robotics Operating System (ROS). ROS is a flexible framework consisting of a collection of tools, libraries, and applications to create complex and robust robot behaviors. For example, large available libraries can help to control the robot's navigation and planning [10, 11, 19, 22], which employ state-of-the-art Simultaneous Localization and Mapping methods. ROS also allows developers to build and share their own tools (e.g., behaviors for social robots [3]).

3   Conclusion

This review has presented several papers on social robots, and described how notions of personalization, localization, and adaptation may be generated. In order to support our review, we depicted a list of methods for social robots concerning decision-making and how to generate appropriate social behaviors. In decision-making, it was essential to define algorithms from the perspective of handcrafted rules with RBS. While we can easily control their outputs, these models require ongoing developers' work that can prove to be complex. On the other hand, models may integrate new AI concepts, such as RL or ML, whereby mathematical models determine outputs. Even though their performance is remarkable, it is still early to be sure of their functioning, and there are still unexpected results. Regardless of the technique employed, it is important to note that an effective social robot needs to adopt social skills similar to humans. The list of four terms (facial expressions, body gestures, speech, and interactions) is non-exhaustive but covers many possible elements that might influence a robot's behavior. We have identified some existing software and frameworks that can be used, to achieve appropriate social human-robot interaction and assist future researchers in their design work of personalized and localized social service robots.

Acknowledgment. The project was supported by the Institute for Information & communications Technology Promotion (IITP) grant funded by the Korea government (MSIP) (No. 2020–0-00842, Development of Cloud Robot Intelligence for Continual Adaptation to User Reactions in Real Service Environments).

References

1. Gasteiger, N., Hellou, M., Ahn, H.: Factors for personalization and localization to optimize human-robot interaction: a literature review. Int. J. Soc. Robot. (2021). https://doi.org/10.1007/s12369-021-00811-8
2. Pieskä, S., Luimula, M., Jauhiainen, J., et al.: Social service robots in public and private environments. Circ. Syst. Multi. Autom. Control, 190–95 (2012)
3. Huang, C-M., Mutlu, B.: Robot behavior toolkit: generating effective social behaviors for robots. In: ACM/IEEE international conference on Human-Robot Interaction, pp. 25–32 (2012)

4. Kanda, T., Shiomi, M., Miyashita, Z., et al.: A communication robot in a shopping mall. IEEE Trans. Rob. **26**(5), 897–913 (2010)
5. McColl, D., Nejat, G.: Meal-time with a socially assistive robot and older adults at a long-term care facility. J. Hum.-Robot. Interact. **2**(1), 152–171 (2013)
6. Aly, A., Tapus, A.: A model for synthesizing a combined verbal and nonverbal behavior based on personality traits in human-robot interaction. In: 2013 8th ACM/IEEE International Conference on Human-Robot Interaction (HRI). Tokyo, Japan: IEEE (2013)
7. Keizer, S., Foster, M., Wang, Z., et al.: Machine learning for social multiparty human–robot interaction. ACM Trans. Interact. Intell. Syst. **4**(3), 1–32 (2014)
8. Liu, P., Glas, D.F., Kanda, T., Ishiguro, H.: Learning proactive behavior for interactive social robots. Auton. Robot. **42**(5), 1067–1085 (2017). https://doi.org/10.1007/s10514-017-9671-8
9. Qureshi, A., Nakamura, Y., Yoshikawa, Y., et al.: Robot gains social intelligence through multimodal deep reinforcement learning. arxiv 2017
10. Portugal, D., Santos, L., Alvito, P., et al.: SocialRobot: an interactive mobile robot for elderly home care. In: IEEE/SICE International Symposium on System Integration (2015)
11. Foster, M., Craenen, B., Deshmukh, A., et al.: MuMMER: Socially Intelligent Human-Robot Interaction in Public Spaces. arXiv.org (2019)
12. Puterman, M.: Markov Decision Processes: Discrete Stochastic Dynamic Programming, 1st edn. John Wiley & Sons Inc, USA (1994)
13. Sekman, A., Challa, B.: Assessment of adaptive human–robot interactions. Knowl.-Based Syst. **42**, 49–59 (2012)
14. Ekman, P., Friesen, W., O'Sullivan, M., et al.: Universals and cultural differences in the judgments of facial expressions of emotion. J. Pers. Soc. Psychol. **53**(4), 712–717 (1987)
15. Craenen, B., Deshmukh, A., Foster, M., et al.: Shaping gestures to shape personalities: the relationship between gesture parameters, attributed personality traits and godspeed scores. In: 27th IEEE International Conference on Robot and Human Interactive Communication. IEEE, Nanjing, China (2018)
16. Cassell, J., Vilhjálmsson, H., Bickmore, T.: BEAT: the behavior expression animation toolkit. In: Prendinger, H., Ishizuka, M., eds. Life-Like Characters. Cognitive Technologies. Berlin, Heidelberg, Springer (2004). https://doi.org/10.1007/978-3-662-08373-4_8
17. Yoon, Y., Ko, W-R., Jang, M., et al.: Robots Learn Social Skills: End-to-End Learning of Co-Speech Gesture Generation for Humanoid Robots. arXiv (2018)
18. The snackbot: documenting the design of a robot for long-term human-robot interaction. In: ACM/IEEE International Conference on Human-Robot Interaction (2009)
19. Churamani, N., Anton, P., Brügger, M., et al.: The impact of personalisation on human-robot interaction in learning scenarios. In: 5th International Conference on Human Agent Interaction HAI 2017. ACM, Bielefeld, Germany, pp. 171–80 (2017)
20. Torrey, C., Powers, A., Marge, M., et al.: Effects of adaptive robot dialogue on information exchange and social relations. In: 1st ACM SIGCHI/SIGART Conference on Human-Robot Interaction. Salt Lake City, Utah, USA, pp. 126–33 (2006)
21. Mairesse, F., Walker, M.: Controlling user perceptions of linguistic style: trainable generation of personality traits. Comput. Linguist. **37**(3), 455–488 (2011)
22. Perera, V., Pereira, T., Connell, J., et al.: Setting up Pepper for autonomous navigation and personalized interaction with users. arXiv 2017

Robot-Generated Mixed Reality Gestures Improve Human-Robot Interaction

Nhan Tran[1]([⊠]), Trevor Grant[2], Thao Phung[1], Leanne Hirshfield[2], Christopher Wickens[3], and Tom Williams[1]([⊠])

[1] Department of Computer Science, Colorado School of Mines,
Golden, CO 80401, USA
nttran@alumni.mines.edu, twilliams@mines.edu
[2] Institute for Cognitive Science, University of Colorado Boulder,
Boulder, CO 80309, USA
[3] Department of Psychology, Colorado State University,
Fort Collins, CO 80523, USA

Abstract. We investigate the effectiveness of robot-generated mixed reality gestures. Our findings demonstrate how these gestures increase user effectiveness by decreasing user response time, and that robots can pair long referring expressions with mixed reality gestures without cognitively overloading users.

1 Introduction

HRI researchers have sought to enable robots to understand [4] and generate [5,6] deictic gestures as humans do. But even for armed robots, traditional deictic gestures have limitations. In search and rescue, for example, robots may need to communicate about hard-to-describe and/or highly ambiguous referents. We present a *mixed reality* solution that enables robots to generate effective *mixed reality deictic gestures* (MRDGs) without morphological requirements.

Per Hirshfield et al. [2], the tradeoffs between language and visual gesture may be highly sensitive to teammates' level and type of cognitive load. It may not be advantageous to rely on visual communication in contexts with high visual load, or to rely on linguistic communication in contexts with high auditory or working memory load. These intuitions are motivated by prior theoretical work on human information processing, including Wickens' Multiple Resource Theory (MRT) [7,8]. In this paper, we thus also present the first exploration of mixed reality communication under different levels and types of cognitive load.

2 Experiment

We experimentally assessed whether different robot communication styles improve user task performance under four conditions: high visual perceptual load, high auditory perceptual load, high working memory load, and low overall

This work was funded by NSF grants IIS-1909864 and CNS-1823245.

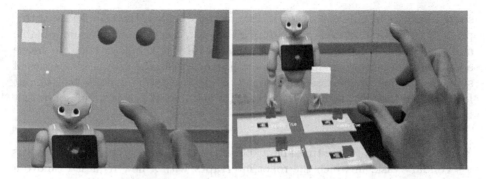

Fig. 1. Participants play a mixed reality game using the Microsoft HoloLens. The Pepper robot interacts with them from behind a table. (Color figure online)

load. On the assumption that there are different perceptual resources, and that MRDGs employ visual-spatial resources in accordance to MRT, we specifically tested four hypotheses, which formalize the intuitions of Hirshfield et al. [2].

H1 Users under high **visual perceptual load** will perform quickest and most accurately when robots use complex natural language without MRDGs.

H2 Users under high **auditory perceptual load** will perform quickest and most accurately when robots use MRDGs without using complex natural language.

H3 Users under high **working memory load** will perform quickest and most accurately when robots use MRDGs without using complex natural language.

H4 Users under **low overall load** will perform quickest and most accurately when robots use MRDGs paired with complex natural language.

2.1 Experimental Context

Participants interacted with a language-capable robot while wearing the Microsoft HoloLens over a series of trials, with robot communication style and user cognitive load varied between trials. We employed a dual-task paradigm in a tabletop pick-and-place task. Participants view the primary task through the Microsoft HoloLens, allowing them to see virtual bins overlaid over mixed reality fiducial markers, and a panel of blocks that changes every few seconds (Fig. 1). The Pepper robot is positioned behind the table, ready to interact.

2.2 Experimental Task

Primary Task: The user's *primary task* is to watch the block panel for a target block: a *red cube, red sphere, red cylinder, yellow cube, yellow sphere, yellow cylinder, green cube, green sphere,* or *green cylinder*. These blocks were formed by combining three colors with three shapes. When participants see the target block, their task is to place it into any of a particular set of bins. For example, the robot might tell a user that whenever they see a *red cube* they should place it in bins *two or three*. Two factors increase the complexity of this primary task. First, at every point during the task, one random bin is unavailable and greyed out. This forces users to remember all target bins. Second, to create a demanding auditory component to the primary task, the user hears a series of syllables playing in the task background, is given a target syllable to look out for, and is told that whenever they hear this syllable, the target and non-target bins are switched.

Secondary Task: Three times per experiment trial, the participant encounters a secondary task, in which the robot interrupts with a new request to move a block to a bin. Depending on trial condition, the robot's spoken request may be accompanied by a mixed reality gesture.

2.3   Experimental Design

We used a Latin square counterbalanced design with two within-subjects factors: Cognitive Load (4 loads) and Communication Style (3 styles).

Cognitive Load

Cognitive load was manipulated through our primary task. Following Beck and Lavie [3], we manipulated cognitive load by jointly manipulating memory constraints and target/distractor discriminability, producing four load profiles: (1) all load low, (2) high working memory load, (3) high visual perceptual load, and (4) high auditory perceptual load.

Working Memory Load: In the high working memory load condition, participants had to remember the identities of three out of six visible bins, producing a memory load of seven items: three target bins, target block color and shape, and target syllable consonant and vowel. In all other conditions, participants only had to remember the identities of two out of four visible bins, producing a total memory load of six items.

Visual Perceptual Load: In the high visual perceptual load condition, the target block was always difficult to discriminate, sharing one common property with all distractors. For example, if the target block was a red cube, all distractors were red or cubes (but not both). In the low visual perceptual load condition, the target block was always easy to discriminate, sharing no common properties with any distractors. For example, if the target block was a red cube, no distractors were red or cubes.

Auditory Perceptual Load: Auditory perceptual load conditions followed a similar structure to visual perceptual load conditions. For example, if the target syllable was *kah*, in the high load condition all distractors started with *k* or end with *ah* (but not both), and in the low load condition no distractors started with *k* or end with *ah*.

Communication Style

Communication style was manipulated through our secondary task, following Williams et al. [9]: (1) In blocks using **complex language (CL)**, the robot referred to objects using full referring expressions needed to disambiguate those objects (e.g., "the red sphere"). (2) In blocks using **MR + CL**, the robot referred to objects using full referring expressions paired with a MRDG (e.g., an arrow drawn over the red sphere). (3) In blocks using **MR + simple language (SL)**, the robot referred to objects using minimal referring expressions (e.g., "that block"), paired with a MRDG. We didn't examine SL without MR, as that communication style typically does not enable referent disambiguation, requiring the user to ask for clarification or guess at random.

2.4 Measures

Accuracy was measured for both tasks by logging which objects participants clicked on, determining whether these were intended by the task or robot, and whether they were placed in the correct bins.

Response time (RT) was measured by logging when participants interacted with blocks and bins. In a primary task, when participants see a target block, their task is to pick-and-place it into a particular set of bins. Thus, RT was measured as delay between when the target block is displayed and when placement is completed. In the secondary task, RT was measured as time between start of Pepper's utterance and placement of the secondary target block.

Perceived mental workload was measured using the NASA TLX [1].

Perceived communicative effectiveness was measured using the modified Gesture Perception Scale [6] employed by Williams et al. [9], which assesses effectiveness, helpfulness, and appropriateness of communication.

2.5 Participants and Procedure

36 participants were recruited from Mines (31 M, 5 F), aged 18–32. After providing informed consent and completing demographic and visual capability surveys, participants were introduced to the task through verbal instruction and an interactive tutorial. Participants then engaged in the twelve (Latin square counterbalanced) trials formed by combining the four cognitive load conditions and the three communication style conditions, with surveys after each block.

3 Results

Bayesian repeated measures analyses of variance (RM-ANOVA) with Bayes Inclusion Factor analyses were performed, using communication style and cognitive load as random factors. A log transformation was applied to all RT data.

Response Time: We found strong evidence against effects on primary task RT ($BFs < 0.028$), but strong evidence for an effect of communication style (BF_{Incl}

= 17.86) on secondary task RT. Post-hoc analysis revealed extreme evidence (BF = 601.46) for a difference in RT between CL ($\mu = 2.10$, $\sigma = 0.33$; untransformed $\mu = 8.88$ s, $\sigma = 4.07$ s) and MR + CL ($\mu = 1.96$, $\sigma = 0.32$; untransformed $\mu = 7.78$, $\sigma = 3.88$), weak evidence (BF = 1.55) for a difference in RT between CL and MR + SL ($\mu = 2.01$, $\sigma = 0.44$; untransformed $\mu = 8.76$, $\sigma = 6.20$), and moderate evidence (BF = 0.20) *against* a difference between MR + CL and MR + SL.

Accuracy: Strong evidence was found *against* effects on primary or secondary task accuracy (All BFs$_{Incl}$ < 0.033 for an effect). Mean primary task accuracy was 0.71 ($\sigma = 0.26$). Mean secondary task accuracy was 0.98 ($\sigma = 0.07$).

Perceived Mental Workload: Strong evidence was found *against* effects on perceived mental workload (BF$_{Incl}$ between 0.006 and 0.040 in favor of an effect). Most participants' perceived workload indicated "medium load".

Perceived Communicative Effectiveness: Anecdotal to strong evidence was found *against* any effects on perceived communicative effectiveness (BF$_{Incl}$ between 0.05 and 0.12 in favor of an effect on all questions). Participants' perceived communicative effectiveness had a mean of 5.61 out of 7 ($\sigma = 1.21$).

4   Discussion and Conclusion

We examined the effectiveness of different combinations of language and MRDG under different types of mental workload, through a mixed-reality robotics laboratory experiment. Our results suggest the primary benefit of MRDGs in robot communication is increasing secondary task speed by reducing visual search time (especially when paired with complex language) regardless of mental workload. However, our results failed to support our hypotheses. While we expected differences between communication styles based on workload, we observed that visual augmentations may *always* be helpful for a secondary task, regardless of workload. Furthermore, we found no effects on perceived workload or perceived effectiveness. The differences in participants' own secondary RTs might have been too small for participants to notice, or participants may have only considered their primary task when reporting their perceptions.

References

1. Hart, S., Staveland, L.: Development of NASA-TLX (task load index): results of empirical and theoretical research. In: Human Mental Workload (1988)
2. Hirshfield, L., Williams, T., Sommer, N., Grant, T., Gursoy, S.V.: Workload-driven modulation of mixed-reality robot-human communication. In: Proceedings of the Workshop on Modeling Cognitive Processes from Multimodal Data (2018)
3. Lavie, N.: The role of perceptual load in visual awareness. Brain Res. **1080**, 91–100 (2006)
4. Matuszek, C., Bo, L., Zettlemoyer, L., Fox, D.: Learning from unscripted deictic gesture and language for human-robot interactions. In: Proceedings of AAAI (2014)

5. Salem, M., Kopp, S., Wachsmuth, I., Rohlfing, K., Joublin, F.: Generation and evaluation of communicative robot gesture. Int. J. Soc. Robot. **4**(2), 201–221 (2012)
6. Sauppé, A., Mutlu, B.: Robot deictics: how gesture and context shape referential communication. In: Proceeding of HRI (2014)
7. Wickens, C.D.: Processing resources and attention. In: Multiple-task Performance (1991)
8. Wickens, C.D.: Multiple resources and mental workload. Hum. Factors **50**(3), 449–555 (2008)
9. Williams, T., Bussing, M., Cabrol, S., Lau, I., Boyle, E., Tran, N.: Investigating the potential effectiveness of allocentric mixed reality deictic gesture. In: Chen, J.Y.C., Fragomeni, G. (eds.) HCII 2019. LNCS, vol. 11575, pp. 178–198. Springer, Cham (2019). https://doi.org/10.1007/978-3-030-21565-1_12

Prioritising Design Features for Companion Robots Aimed at Older Adults: Stakeholder Survey Ranking Results

Hannah Bradwell[1]([envelope]) [iD], Rhona Winnington[2] [iD], Serge Thill[3] [iD], and Ray B. Jones[1] [iD]

[1] EPIC Project, University of Plymouth, Plymouth, UK
hannah.bradwell@plymouth.ac.uk
[2] Department of Nursing, Auckland University of Technology, Auckland, New Zealand
[3] Donders Centre for Cognition, Radboud University NL, Nijmegen, Netherlands

Abstract. Companion robots are social robots often resembling animals with potential wellbeing benefits for older adults. However, some such devices have failed possibly through inappropriate design. Method: Questionnaires were completed by 113 participants at nine health and care events. Participants were predominantly relevant professionals. Participants approached our interaction station, interacted with eight companion robots or alternatives, then completed questionnaires; ranking aesthetic, behaviour, technology, feel and interaction features and estimating affordable price. Results: Features ranked highly were: interactive response to vocalisations and touch, huggable size, soft fur, variety of behaviours/sounds, realistic movements, eye contact with large cute eyes, being realistic, familiar, easy to use and possessing simulated warmth. Participants thought −£225 was affordable. Conclusion: We contribute priority features for stakeholders to inform future developments. Contrasting unfamiliar embodiment of some devices, stakeholders support familiar, realistic aesthetics, with implications for enhanced acceptability, adoption and more consistent wellbeing outcomes.

1 Introduction

Health and social care (H&SC) is experiencing increasing pressure and demand worldwide, partly caused by aging and dementia [1]. Assistive robotics to support H&SC has gathered research interest [2], including robots for companionship. Among these, robot "pets" are robots designed congruent with animal aesthetics and behaviours [2]. The most well researched example is Paro, the robot seal [2]. Research has shown potential wellbeing benefits for older adults, people with dementia and stakeholders in their care, including for; loneliness, depression, agitation and quality of life [2]. Other examples include NeCoRo, AIBO, iCat [2], and comparable 'smart toys,' such as the Joy for All (JfA) cats and dogs [3]. Despite encouraging results and increasing interest, a number of devices in this sector have failed, and literature still lacks agreement on how to best design such robots. The importance of design in overall platform success cannot be overstated: appropriate design promotes acceptability among end users [4], while

© Springer Nature Switzerland AG 2021
H. Li et al. (Eds.): ICSR 2021, LNAI 13086, pp. 774–779, 2021.
https://doi.org/10.1007/978-3-030-90525-5_70

inappropriate design could lead to device disuse or no expected benefits [5], proving costly to society. In this context, research previously demonstrated significant differences between older adults (as end-users) and roboticists (as developers) in perceptions towards suitable robot pet design for older people [3]. Aesthetic and behavioural features are likely to impact device acceptability and thus ultimately use [5]. Design and embodiment continues to be a research topic without definitive results. This paper helps address the situation.

2   Methods

2.1   Setting and Procedure

Nine interaction stations at: eHealth, dementia, aging, psychiatry conferences or health-professional meetings. Attendees interacted with devices (Fig. 1), then completed consent and questionnaires. A University of Plymouth Ethics Committee granted approval.

Fig. 1.   Devices. From left, Paro, Miro, Pleo, JfA dog, JfA cat, Furby, Perfect Petz dog, Hedgehog.

2.2   Data Collection

Questionnaires gathered demographics, and established i) priority design features, ii) preferred animal for target audience, iii) most appealing eyes, iv) most appropriate size, v) most appropriate volume and frequency of vocalisations, vi) reason for preferred animal, vii) reason for most appealing eyes and viii) realistic price. To establish i) unique questionnaires included a specific combination of 10 features (informed by computer script to ensure comparable frequency), picked from 42 features in Table 1. The five categories were based on discordance in previous literature. The 42 features were a combination of those previously reported [6], and additional features from our previous study (reported elsewhere) on perceptions of care home residents, relatives and staff after interaction with the devices. To establish ii)-v) participants selected from a row of pictures under the question. For vi) – viii), free text boxes were used.

Table 1. Five design categories showing 42 features of interest included on questionnaires.

Category	Features of interest for each design category
Feel	Soft pettable fur; Huggable (right size to cuddle); Portable (ease to take with you); Solid/robust (can withstand rough handling); Realistic animal weight; Simulated warm feeling; Hard/plastic shell (eg. Pleo or Miro); Simulated breathing; Simulated heartbeat
Behaviour	Animal-appropriate responses/sounds (eg. Dog barking); Variety of behaviours and sounds; Active; Looks at user (animal provides eye contact/attention); Can talk to user (human speech); Vocalisations not too loud; Playful; Facial movements/expressions; Waggy tail; Animal appropriate behaviours
Aesthetics	Looks like a real life pet; Young or innocent looking; Nice/not scary; Cartoonish appearance; Flash/draws attention; Mythical animal; Cute eyes; Familiar animal (eg. Dog/cat); Unfamiliar animal; Cute; Customisable look/animal for each user
Technology	Mechanical parts are noiseless; Realistic movements (fluent/natural); Adaptable (shut functions on/off); Autonomous system; Easy to use; Fur is detachable (to be washed); Long battery life; Cleanable
Interaction type	Interactive: Obeys some commands (eg. Sit/paw); Interactive: Looks at me or vocalises when I am near; Interactive: Looks at me or vocalises when I stroke or touch it; Interactive: Looks at me or vocalises when I talk to it

2.3 Data Analysis

To explore i) priority design features, establishing an exact ranking of all items is computationally and prohibitively expensive. For approximate ranking, we used a variant of the Condorcet method [7]: for each feature, we counted how often it is ranked higher than other features across all questionnaires. For data on ii) preferred animal, iii) most appealing eyes, iv) most appropriate size, v) vocalisations and viii) price, we report descriptive statistics, supplemented by summary free text for vi) and vii).

3 Results

3.1 Participants

In total, 113 questionnaires were completed, mainly by H&SC professionals within gerontology, dementia, psychiatry and nursing (n = 68), although others participated (9 researchers, 5 informal carers, 24 other, 7 missing). Participants included 87 females, 17 males (9 missing), average age was 48.1 (range = 18–75, SD = 14.2).

3.2 Priority Design Features

The most important features were interactivity (in response to talking to or touching the robot), being the right size to hug, having soft fur, a variety of behaviours/sounds, realistic movement and providing eye contact (Table 2).

Table 2. i) Priority features in order of approximate ranking

Ranking (Scores)	42 Features listed in order of importance
Highly rated 1–15 (190–130)	Interactive: Looks at me or vocalises when I talk to it; Huggable (right size to cuddle); Soft pettable fur; Variety of behaviours/sounds; Realistic movements (fluent/natural); Interactive: Looks at me or vocalises when I stroke or touch it; Looks at user (provides eye contact/attention); Easy to use; Looks like a real life pet; Simulated warm feeling; Nice/not scary; Animal appropriate sounds; Familiar animal; Facial movements/expressions; Cleanable
Middle ranking 16–29 (127–82)	Active; Autonomous system (works on its own); Interactive: Looks at me or vocalises when I am near; Long battery life; Animal appropriate behaviours; Cute; Cute eyes; Waggy tail; Portable (easy to take with you); Vocalisations not too loud; Playful; Adaptable (switch functions on/off); Solid/robust (can withstand rough handling); Young/innocent looking
Low rated 30–42 (41–23)	Interactive: Obeys some commands (eg. Sit/paw); Simulated breathing; Simulated heart beat; Fur detachable (to be washed); Realistic animal weight; Customisable look/animal for each user; Can talk to user (human speech); Mechanical parts are noiseless; Flashy/Draws attention; Unfamiliar animal; Mythical animal; Cartoonish appearance; Hard/plastic shell

The preferred device was JfA cat, followed by JfA dog, then Paro (Fig. 2). The least preferred options were Miro, knitted Hedgehog and Furby. Frequent preference reasons were being realistic, soft, cuddly, lifelike and familiar. JfA cat reportedly had most appropriate vocalisations while Paro had most appealing eyes, (being large, cute, having eyelashes). Stakeholders felt JfA cat (~39 cm – 26 cm) was most appropriately sized (Fig. 2). (Some missing values: 15 to preference, 23 to eyes, 36 to size, 27 to vocalisations).

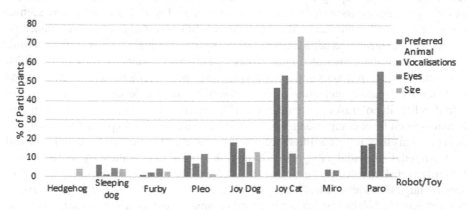

Fig. 2. Percentage of responders selecting each animal for ii), iii), iv), v)

3.3 Price

For viii) reasonable price, an example range was provided from £10–£5000 for devices on display. For participants who responded with a range (e.g. £100–£150), we took the highest figure as the maximum they consider appropriate. The average price participants felt was appropriate was £226.30 (SD = 245.80, range = £25–£1000).

4 Discussion and Conclusion

Although participants were generally H&SC professionals, the questionnaire features were derived from prior work with end-users, care staff and family members, and combined with those reported by [6]. Thus, these results provide collective insights from key stakeholders in the real-world adoption of companion robots, having implications for future developments, particularly considering importance of user-centred design [3]. Supporting [6], our relatively large sample confirmed the desire for soft fur for companion robot shells, although care must be taken in cleaning [8]. Results also strongly support familiar-realistic animal embodiment. Our stakeholders scored 'looks like a real life pet' and 'familiar animal' within the top 15 most important features, and top three specific to aesthetics. In contrast, 'unfamiliar animal,' 'mythical' and 'cartoonish' all received low priority. Participants also selected devices with familiar embodiment as preferable with older adults in mind (JfA cat/dog), and reported realistic, life-like and familiar as free-text reasons. The continued support for familiar animal embodiment has implications for robot design and selection of devices for real-world implementation, and perhaps explains some variation in response to unfamiliar Paro [1]. Research into these alternate devices may demonstrate more consistent wellbeing outcomes than Paro [1], should a familiar design be more acceptable to intended users.

Our stakeholders suggested a suitable price far below the £5000 for Paro, at −£226. This result has implications for developers. This study allowed for prioritisation of features to assist in keeping devices affordable. The most important factor was reported as variety of behaviours/sounds. Eye contact also ranked well. Paro's eyes were seen as most appealing, for being large, having eyelashes, blinking and making eye contact.

A further contribution of this paper is prioritisation of interaction type. Previous work [3], demonstrated sophisticated interactivity of Paro was undervalued by older adults. Our stakeholders felt it most important devices respond to user's vocalisations, followed by touch. Alternative interaction methods could potentially be neglected in favour of affordability. In contrast to previous work [3], where older adults valued inclusion of human speech from companion robots, it was not perceived as important to stakeholders here. This may reflect a difference between stakeholder categories of end-user and professional. Older adults may perceive an unmet need undervalued by professionals; for more verbal interaction. Regarding size, stakeholders previously reported to us Paro was too large for older resident's laps. These results suggest the most appropriate size is best reflected in JfA cat, which is considerably smaller and lighter. Questionnaires also explored life-simulation features, with simulated warmth as stakeholder's priority in this area. These results have important implications, considering aesthetic and behavioural robot design can impact acceptability and use [4, 5], and the health and wellbeing potentials such devices possess [2]. Limitations include reliance on immediate perceptions of stakeholders, without longer, real-world observations.

Conclusions. Our study provides prioritisation of features, whilst adhering to reported affordability of –£226 for future designs, which could include; interaction in response to vocalisations/touch, huggable size, soft fur, variety of behaviours/sounds, realistic movements, providing eye contact, large/cute eyes, being realistic, familiar, easy to use and possessing simulated warmth.

References

1. Moyle, W., Jones, C.J., Murfield, J.E., et al.: Using a therapeutic companion robot for dementia symptoms in long-term care: reflections from a cluster-RCT. Aging Ment. Health. **23**(3), 329–336 (2019)
2. Abbott, R., Orr, N., McGill, P., et al.: How do robopets impact the health and well-being of residents in care homes? A systematic review of qualitative and quantitative evidence. Int. J. Older People Nurs. **14**(3), e12239 (2019)
3. Bradwell, H.L., Edwards, K.J., Winnington, R., Thill, S., Jones, R.B.: Companion robots for older people: importance of user-centred design demonstrated through observations and focus groups comparing preferences of older people and roboticists in South West England. BMJ Open. **9**(9), e032468 (2019)
4. Heerink, M., Krose, B., Vanessa, E., Wielinga, B.: Assessing acceptance of assistive social agent technology: the almere model. Int. J. Soc. Robot. **2**, 361–375 (2010)
5. Forlizzi, J., Disalvo, C., Gemperle, F.: Assistive robotics and an ecology of elders living independently in their homes. Hum.-Comput. Interact. **19**, 25–59 (2004)
6. Heerink, M., et al.: Exploring requirements and alternative pet robots for robot assisted therapy with older adults with dementia. In: Herrmann, G., Pearson, M.J., Lenz, A., Bremner, P., Spiers, A., Leonards, U. (eds.) ICSR 2013. LNCS (LNAI), vol. 8239, pp. 104–115. Springer, Cham (2013). https://doi.org/10.1007/978-3-319-02675-6_11
7. Natoli, R., Zuhair, S.: Rediscovering the Condorcet approach as an aggregation technique for progress measures. Econ. Pap. **30**(3), 368–376 (2011)
8. Bradwell, H.L., Johnson, C.W., Lee, J., et al.: Microbial contamination and efficacy of disinfection procedures of companion robots in care homes. PLOS one, **15**(8), e0237069 (2020)

Acceptance of Robotic Transportation in Small Workshops: A China-Iran Cross-Cultural Study

Alireza Nemati[1] , Alireza Taheri[2](✉) , Dongjie Zhao[1] , Ali F. Meghdari[2,3] ,
and Shuzhi Sam Ge[1,4](✉)

[1] Institute for Future (IFF), Qingdao University, Qingdao 266071, China
[2] Social and Cognitive Robotics Lab., Sharif University of Technology,
1458889694 Tehran, Iran
artaheri@sharif.edu
[3] Chancellor of Fereshtegaan International Branch, Islamic Azad University, Tehran, Iran
[4] Social Robotics Lab., National University of Singapore, 117576 Singapore, Singapore
samge@nus.edu.sg

Abstract. In this research, we developed a cost-effective automated guided vehicle for small clothing production workshops that ordinary workers in such workplaces can operate. We acquired workers' opinions in multiple workshops about using the robots (with some social capabilities) and working alongside them. We performed the tests in China and Iran to investigate and compare different preferences and priorities in two countries with different cultural backgrounds. We used the UTAUT questionnaire and conducted two-way ANOVA tests considering two independent factors: Nationality and Gender. The results showed that workers in Iran and China have relatively similar expectations from a social AGV, with no contrast in the mean score of women and men. We also observed that Iranian participants have fewer concerns about the safety of working around the robot, which may be due to greater exposure of Chinese workers to automated robots and the potential dangers of working in the same environment with the robot. Moreover, we observed that female workers of both nationalities feel they need more help to work with the robots than male workers. We hope that the results presented in this cross-cultural study assists in developing an understanding of the attitude of workers in small workshops toward automated transportation.

Keywords: Smart transportation · Cross-cultural study · Attitude toward AGVs · Small and medium-sized workshops · Robot acceptance

1 Introduction

In this study, we performed a cross-cultural investigation of workers' responses toward transportation robots (with some social capabilities) in China and Iran. We first learned the workers' opinions about a few robots designs and then built two identical samples according to their feedback and preferences. The two samples used to investigate the attitude of the workers toward the fabricated robot in Iran and China [1]. Afterward, 96 participants observed the performance of the fabricated robots and were asked to fill

© Springer Nature Switzerland AG 2021
H. Li et al. (Eds.): ICSR 2021, LNAI 13086, pp. 780–784, 2021.
https://doi.org/10.1007/978-3-030-90525-5_71

out a questionnaire, including 30 questions in 6 categories (mostly extracted from the UTAUT questionnaire).

As the first step, we designed four different versions of the robot and asked both the Chinese and Iranian workers' opinions about their preferences. At this stage, we sampled the opinion of 35 workers, including 10 Iranian males, 8 Iranian females, 9 Chinese males, and 8 Chinese female participants. We also asked the participants to choose what they considered the two most essential factors in a robot (i.e., appearance, price, speed, working hour, accuracy, and/or payload).

There is no noticeable difference between the opinion of Iranian and Chinese participants; however, a clear contrast between the male and female participants is observed. The results show that the women generally would like to interact with a robot that appears friendly or neutral, but male workers prefer a robot with an aggressive look, which may convey ruggedness and the capability of doing hard work. Accuracy followed by price were the most important features the participants expected from the robot. The mentioned features have no substantial effect on either the general appearance of the robot or the design of the first version of the robot. Figure 1 presents images of the fabricated robots.

Fig. 1. The fabricated robots in the first step toward building a companion transporter robot.

2 Assessment Tool and Result

A total of 96 people participated in this study including, 49 Iranian individuals: 25 males and 22 females (mean age: 37, SD: 17 years) and 47 Chinese subjects: 26 males and 21 females (mean age: 37, SD: 12.1 years). The subjects observed the performance of the prospective robots for about 10 min and subsequently filled in the mentioned questionnaire.

We utilized a questionnaire made up of 30 five-Likert-scale questions in 6 categories (extracted primarily from the UTAUT questionnaire [2] with additional questions) as the assessing tool of this cross-cultural study. The questionnaires were presented in Chinese and Persian language to the Chinese and Iranian participants, respectively. "Nationality" and "Gender" have been considered as the independent factors for the two-way ANOVA analysis in this study.

The results of the applied two-way ANOVA tests considering Nationality, Gender, and their interactions in different categories of the questionnaire are presented in Table 1.

Table 1. P-values of the applied two-way ANOVA tests on the sub-items of the questionnaire. P-values less than 0.05 are shown in bold. P-values less than 0.001 are shown as 0.000.

Category #	Category title	Nationality	Gender	Interaction of nationality and gender
1	Anxiety and safety	**0.000**	**0.001**	0.564
2	Attitude and perceived usefulness towards technology	0.455	0.194	0.789
3	Facilitating conditions	**0.006**	**0.001**	**0.006**
4	Perceived adaptiveness	0.944	0.420	0.138
5	Perceived enjoyment	**0.000**	**0.047**	0.914
6	Perceived sociability	0.237	0.976	**0.010**

Regarding the first category, Anxiety and Safety, we observed that there are significant differences in both Nationality and Gender factor. Our results showed that the males feel significantly safer using robotic technology than the females. Similar to results reported by Broos [3], the female subjects had a more negative attitude towards technology (i.e., internet and computers) than did their male participants. Nomura et al. [4] have proposed a scale called the Robot Anxiety Scale (RAS) to assess the anxiety level that prevents users from being involved in human-robot interactions/communications, and they reported the possibility of gender difference in some factors such as behaviors toward robots in human-robot interactions/communications. Moreover, we found that the Chinese participants felt significantly less safe with the presented robot than the Iranian subjects. This observation may be due to the fact that the Chinese are, in general, more cautious and conservative than Iranians. Commonly, there are more reports of accidents caused by technology (e.g., self-driving cars and robots) in the news and social media in China, while similar cases do not usually happen in Iran, and Iranians may be less aware of the potential dangers of working with robots. Regarding this category, we did not see a significant difference in the interaction of Nationality and Gender factors. Interestingly, participants commonly felt safer with and preferred small robots over bigger robots in their working environments.

In the second category, we did not observe any significant differences between Nationality, Gender, and their Interaction factors. This observation indicates that both the Chinese and Iranian subjects have similar viewpoints regarding attitude and perceived usefulness towards technology. The mean score of the participants in this category is ~ 4 (out of 5), which indicates the overall viewpoint of "agree" on the usefulness of such robots by the subjects. Among the sub-items of this category, we noted that the participants are not currently scared about losing their jobs to robots; the high standard deviations of 1.2 and 1.3, show that opinions are very scattered.

Regarding the third category, Facilitating Conditions, although we observed significant differences in both Nationality and Gender factors, the p-value for the interaction of the factors is less than 0.05. The female participants of both nationalities feel that they need more help to work with this technology in their working environments while the male participants are more confident in handling the new situation. It should be noted that the large standard deviations observed in the sub-factor scores of this category could be due to the wide range in the participants' ages; we have not considered this an effective factor in this study. Figure 2a shows a noticeable difference between the Iranian and Chinese females' viewpoints in the third category. This can be interpreted as more equal job opportunities in technological environments for Chinese women than for women in Iran. Generally, women workers in Iran have less knowledge and experience with technology than Chinese counterparts.

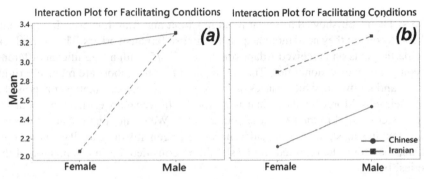

Fig. 2. Interaction plot for the (a) Facilitating conditions category, (b) Perceived enjoyment category

No significant differences were observed in Perceived Adaptiveness category. The overall viewpoints of the participants (considering nationality and gender) are more or less similar with a mean score of 3.5/5 which shows that their expectations for the robots' performance are adjusted and logical. Based on current experiences, the participants feel that robots are rigid in terms of hardware and software and have limited capabilities. This could be a reason why humans are less likely to believe that using robots will cause them to lose their jobs, which is in line with the questionnaire's second category results mentioned above. Analyzing the scores in category 5, Perceived Enjoyment, indicates that while there are significant differences in Nationality and Gender factors, no significant difference is observed in the interaction of these factors. Figure 2b shows that while the Iranian subjects showed more excitement toward having a robot in their working environments, the trend (i.e., the slope) between the female and male subjects in both nationalities are almost the same.

Regarding category 6, Perceived Sociability, we did not observe any significant differences between Gender and Nationality. Schermerhorn et al. [5] reported that believing the used robot was machine-like, the female subjects involved in tasks were not socially facilitated by their robot. We saw the same trend for Iranians (although the difference was not significant considering the Gender factor); however, the Chinese females scored a bit higher than the males in this category.

3 Conclusion

We developed a transportation robot to meet the requirements of small-sized businesses. We designed a few versions of the robot and asked 18 workers in China and 17 workers in Iran about the appearance of the robot. The results indicated that the male workers usually prefer aggressive-looking robots while female workers selected friendly or neutral-looking robots. A questionnaire containing 30 questions in 6 different categories was given to 96 participants to obtain their opinions. The results showed that Iranian workers have fewer safety concerns than Chinese workers. Iranian and Chinese participants had a similar opinion about the usefulness of the robots, with no significant/meaningful difference between female and male participants. We realized that the female workers felt they needed more help to operate the robots compare with the male workers. The result showed a similar trend in China and Iran; however, Iranian female workers expressed they need more help than Chinese female workers. The over- all view of the participants on Perceived Adaptiveness was 3.5/5, with no significant differences between genders or nationalities. The participants feel the robots are relatively rigid in software and hardware, which causes the workers to have no substantial concerns about losing their jobs. Moreover, the Iranian participants showed more excitement about using the robots compared to their Chinese counterparts. We do not claim that the observed results from the questionnaires would be necessarily generalizable to all Chinese/Iranian workers; therefore, the reported results should be considered as an estimation of these societies' beliefs.

Acknowledgement. This research was supported by the fund provided by China National Key Research and Development Projects (Grant No. 2020YFB1313604).

References

1. Nemati, A., Zhao, D., Jiang, W., Ge, S.S.: Companion transporter: a co-worker in the greenhouse. In: Salichs, M., et al. (eds.) Social Robotics. ICSR 2019. LNCS, vol. 11876 (2019). Springer, Cham. https://doi.org/10.1007/978-3-030-35888-4_30
2. Williams, M.D., Rana, N.P., Dwivedi, Y.K.: The unified theory of acceptance and use of technology (UTAUT): a literature review. J. Enterp. Inf. Manag. **28**(3), 443–488 (2015). https://doi.org/10.1108/JEIM-09-2014-0088
3. Broos, A.: Gender and information and communication technologies (ICT) anxiety: male self-assurance and female hesitation. Cyberpsychol. Behav. **8**(1), 21–31 (2005)
4. Nomura, T., Suzuki, T., Kanda, T., Kato, K.: Measurement of anxiety toward robots. In: ROMAN 2006-The 15th IEEE International Symposium on Robot and Human Interactive Communication, pp. 372–377. IEEE, September 2006
5. Schermerhorn, P., Scheutz, M., Crowell, C.R.: Robot social presence and gender: do females view robots differently than males?. In: Proceedings of the 3rd ACM/IEEE International Conference on Human Robot Interaction, pp. 263–270, March 2008

Reactive Patterns for Human-Robot Object Handovers

Sebastian Meyer zu Borgsen and Sven Wachsmuth[✉]

CITEC, Bielefeld University, 33594 Bielefeld, Germany
{semeyer,swachsmu}@cit-ec.uni-bielefeld.de

Abstract. Object handovers are one of the most basic physical collaborative tasks in human-robot interaction. They are interesting because they take place in close human-robot vicinity where both's peripersonal spaces overlap. Thus, a successful and smooth object handover requires to communicate the intention in terms of the object transition point, the timing of action, and the initiative of giving and receiving. In this paper, we model several reactive patterns extracted from human-robot handover experiments, propose an integrated robotic system implementing these strategies, and evaluate the timing, modality, and human-likeness of its implementation.

Keywords: Object handovers · Social robotics · Human-robot interaction

1 Introduction

Object handovers between humans and robots have been already researched for several years – but an autonomous human-like robot behavior (without help from external high-performance tracking) still has not been achieved so far. Handovers are mostly classified by who gives the object and who receives it. Articles typically focus on either *human to robot* [8] or *robot to human* handovers [4], while a few consider both cases [3]. Carfi et al. [2] recorded a dataset with a 2×2 experiment design taking the giver/receiver role as the first dimension and the decision who approaches whom as the second dimension. They further vary the handover strategy (e.g. normal, quick, delayed start, holding, wrong position). Thus, a robot strategy needs to deal with all of these cases: giving/receiving and mutual (maybe changing) initiatives. In our approach, we use a unified model distinguishing five distinct phases (Prepare, Approach, Reach, Transfer, Retreat) with soft boundaries and fluid transitions.

This work was supported by CITEC (DFG EXC277).

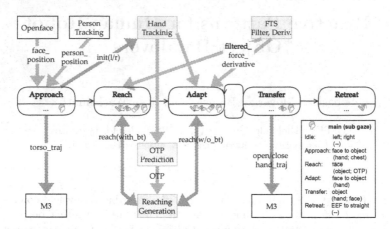

Fig. 1. A schematic view of the model implementing the complete handover behavior. Round boxes define the states of the behavior including icons indicating parts of the robot which are actively controlled; angular boxes represent processing loops controlled by the states. Dashed lines indicate data flow; solid states define state transitions. The icons in the states denote the active components (torso/arm, force/torque, hand, gaze) of the robot which are involved in the reactive patterns.

2   Reactive Patterns for Object Handovers

Previous user studies [1] revealed that the timing behaviors of object handovers and the force applied extremely vary in a person's individual runs as well as between differently experienced people. In order to deal with this large variety of cases, we propose a set of reactive patterns that are associated with the different phases of handovers that lead to an improved timing and signaling behavior of the robot. The reactive patterns utilize visual feedback as well as force feedback and are able to actively deal with unconscious as well as conscious deviations of the human's motion. Using a unified phase model for human-to-robot and robot-to-human object transfer, the same patterns work for receiving as well as providing objects. In order to deal with such requirements, the timing and signaling behavior of the robot is improved along several dimensions: a comprehensive gazing strategy, an adaptive reaching motion, and an improved transfer detection. Figure 1 shows a schematic view of the implemented model of the robot behavior. Here, the transition between *Phase 2 (Reach)* and *Phase 3 (Transfer)* is modeled by an extra state: *Adapt*, which actively controls the robot to reach and detect the object transition point (OTP). The overall model includes several reactive patterns that bind together person and face tracking, human hand tracking, force feedback, OTP prediction, torso, arm, and gripper control, as well as gazing strategies. We implemented an active human-like gazing strategy utilizing the structure of the handover process. For its physical implementation, we use an anthropomorphic robot head (see Fig. 2) with 19 degrees of freedom. It features a robot eye with expressive eye-lids that is able to mimic the movement patterns of a human eye [5] and is controlled utilizing a model for human movements [6] coordinating head (neck) and eyes' motion. In order to prevent an impolite staring, we use main- and sub-gazes in our gaze patterns (see box in Fig. 1). While the main gaze has the distinct task of communicating the robot's state or intent, the sub-gaze provides additional related information. The interruption by sub-gazes allows to intensify the main gazes without freezing in a static pose. In the state *Approach* an initial OTP is predicted based on *Person Tracking* and communicated to the interacting person by a torso trajectory. During *Approach*, the gaze target is the face of the interactant. When human and robot get close, a small motion with the robot's right arm is executed to signal readiness to handover. In [7], we introduce a scheme combining a static and dynamic OTP prediction achieving an average delay – after the initialization – of 0.07 s which is utilized in the *Approach* and *Reach* states. During the transition between these two, the robot waits for the human starting to reach out to react accordingly to the human's motion. The OTP-driven movement of the robot's arm incorporates gaze to create shared attention on the task and regularly looks at the predicted OTP. The force derivative is constantly monitored to allow in motion handover. Besides the signaling with gaze, we added a grabbing gesture with the EEF for the receiving case to signal readiness to take an object. The robot's approaching movement is a mixture of pre-trained database lookup and (inverse) Jabobian control scheme blending between both.

For the visual detection, the tracked hand position is compared to the robot's EEF location considering an offset from the EEF opening side. The distance is filtered over a time duration and a threshold triggers the *Visual Transfer*. For the force-based detection, a filter chain is applied incorporating the robot's motions and a rate of change based decision process. The input is the data of the wrist mounted FTS, which is sampled at 1 kHz, filtered with a third order Butterworth filter with a cutoff frequency 20 Hz. The signal is forwarded and processed 100 Hz applying a Savitzky and Golay filter. The L_0 norm is smoothed with a damped sliding window model considering inertia added by the carried object. When the contact is detected, a grasping/releasing of the object is initiated. The resistance is checked to verify that an object is in the EEF (otherwise system transitions back to adaptation phase). Gaze is incorporated to signal a focus on the transfer by looking at the own hand. In the *Retreat* phase, the robot is moved back to the ready state. A neutral gaze is used for signaling readiness for the next interaction.

3 Evaluation and Discussion

To evaluate the concepts discussed, a study is conducted with naive users using a completely autonomous system. In the study, a person transfers objects to a robot for learning them and receives them back (Fig. 2). To study the different reactive patterns, ten different tasks are specified and instructed to the users triggering a different timing behavior during object handover:

- T1/2: Pre-Random Give/Take — *I: Give/Take Floka the object.*
- T3: Pure Visual Give — *I: Give the object by holding it out to him.*

- T4: Pure Visual Take — *I: Take the object from Floka without pulling on it.*
- T5: Pushing Give — *I: Give the object by pushing it into the hand.*
- T6: Pushing Take — *I: Take the object by pulling it out of the hand.*
- T7/8: Early Give/Take — *I: Give/Take the object as early as possible.*
- T9: Regrasp Give — *I: Give Floka the object but pull it away as its hand closes.*
- T10: Post-Random Take — *Take the object from Floka.*

Handover Tasks 3 and 4 address the finding, that not all interactants tend to actually apply force during the interaction. In contrast to these, Tasks 5 and 6 are about creating contact with object or robot testing how the contact is actually established. Tasks 7 and 8 address short-cuts observed with experts testing the robot's capability of an in-motion handover. Task 9 simulates a failed try. The experiment consists of a questionnaire (experiences, pet ownership, NARS), handover-tasks and an interview to find out how people perceive the handover interaction with the Floka system. Three of these participants were not able to finish the interaction and, thus, did not take part in the post-interaction interview. This resulted in thirteen fully evaluated participants, aged 22.23 ± 1.88 ($F = 7, M = 6$). The group had an experience with robots of 1.54 ± 1.13. In this regard, participants were naive users considering their experience with HRI. A total of 95 object exchanges (46 gives and 49 receives) were successfully recorded. The system ran for about 8 h in total without a restart, which showed the robustness of the system. In only one trial, the object was dropped. The participant picked up the object and continued the interaction. In the interview (Fig. 2) 11 participants referred to Floka's behavior as human-like. The same number of participants described the behavior as slower or too slow but still nine of them would work with the robot. All participants rated the handover as safe where one made an exception for the receive interaction. Half of the participants recognized the difference in the give/receive force threshold. Only one participant was not aware of the gaze behavior Floka exhibited during the interaction. All others could at least roughly describe the gaze pattern integrated in the behavior. Some participants even stated that the gaze helped to understand what the robot wanted. All participants stated that they either consciously or unconsciously knew where to move their hand to exchange the object.

In general, the results (Fig. 2) show that most of the participants where able to successfully exchange objects with Floka without further explanation. Even the different tasks that involved types of handover that caused problems, before, like pure visual handover, in-motion handover, and different positions partially introduced delays in some cases but did not break the interaction. Figure 2 shows that the task descriptions do not purely determine how the transfer is detected. Even in the pulling and pushing cases, a visual detection is required to react as early as possible.

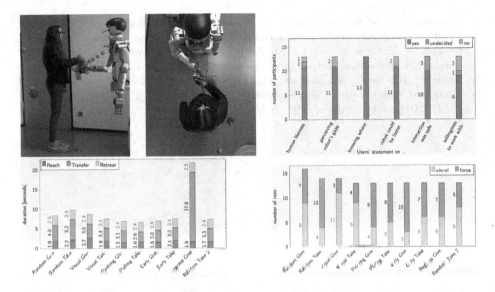

Fig. 2. Top, Left: ROS-rviz visualization of the tracking and prediction results. The big red ball is where the handtracking was initialized, the pink ball marks the predicted static OTP. The smaller reddish balls visualize the updates of the dynamic OTP predictions. The red arrow shows the detected person position. The coordinate system represents the gaze detected. **Top, Right:** answers of the post-interaction interview. **Bottom, Left:** The median duration of the successful handovers for the different tasks in three phases. **Bottom, Right:** The number of runs per task that triggered the transfer by visual, as well as force sensing. (Color figure online)

References

1. Meyer zu Borgsen, S., Bernotat, J., Wachsmuth, S.: Hand in hand with robots: differences between experienced and Naive users in human-robot handover scenarios. In: Lecture Notes in Computer Science, pp. 587–596. Springer, Cham (2017). https://doi.org/10.1007/978-3-319-70022-9_58
2. Carfi, A., Foglino, F., Bruno, B., Mastrogiovanni, F.: A multi-sensor dataset of human-human handover. Data Brief **22**, 109–117 (2019). https://doi.org/10.1016/j.dib.2018.11.110
3. Mason, A.H., Mackenzie, Æ.C.L.: Grip forces when passing an object to a partner. Exp. Brain Res. **163**, 173–187 (2005). https://doi.org/10.1007/s00221-004-2157-x
4. Parastegari, S., Abbasi, B., Noohi, E.: Modeling human reaching phase in human-human object handover with application in robot-human handover. In: IEEE/RSJ IROS, pp. 3597–3602 (2017). https://doi.org/10.1109/IROS.2017.8206205
5. Schulz, S., Meyer zu Borgsen, S., Wachsmuth, S.: See and be seen - rapid and likeable high-definition camera-eye for anthropomorphic robots. In: IEEE ICRA, Montreal, Canada (2019). https://doi.org/10.1109/ICRA.2019.8794319
6. Schulz, S., Lier, F., Kipp, A., Wachsmuth, S.: Humotion - a human inspired gaze control framework for anthropomorphic robot heads. In: International Conference on Human Agent Interaction, pp. 207–214 (2016). https://doi.org/10.1145/2974804.2974827

7. Simmering, J., Meyer zu Borgsen, S., Wachsmuth, S., Al-Hamadi, A.: Combining static and dynamic predictions of transfer points for human initiated handovers. In: Salichs, M.A., et al. (eds.) ICSR 2019. LNCS (LNAI), vol. 11876, pp. 676–686. Springer, Cham (2019). https://doi.org/10.1007/978-3-030-35888-4_63
8. Yamane, K., Revfi, M., Asfour, T.: Synthesizing object receiving motions of humanoid robots with human motion database. In: IEEE ICRA, pp. 1629–1636. IEEE (2013). https://doi.org/10.1109/ICRA.2013.6630788

Anthropomorphism and Its Negative Attitudes, Sociability, Animacy, Agency, and Disturbance Requirements for Social Robots: A Pilot Study

Ahmad Yaser Alhaddad, Asma Mecheter, Mohammed Abdul Wadood,
Ali Salem Alsaari, Houssameldin Mohammed, and John-John Cabibihan[✉]

Mechanical and Industrial Engineering Department, Qatar University,
Doha 2713, Qatar
john.cabibihan@qu.edu.qa

Abstract. A social robot that meets the acceptability requirements of the target end-users presents a significant challenge to robot designers. The design process is often iterative and requires continuous improvements and optimization over time. One key aspect in designing an acceptable social robot is anthropomorphism. Social roboticists have developed assessment tools to evaluate different aspects for the perception of the observer. In this study, we evaluated the attitude of children toward four robots with different degrees of anthropomorphic traits. Questionnaires based on the Negative Attitude toward Robots Scale (NARS) and the Human-Robot Interaction Evaluation Scale (HRIES) were used to acquire the responses of 33 participants. To identify any changes due to interactions, a pre-test questionnaire was given prior to the interaction with a robot. It was then followed by a post-test questionnaire. Statistical tests were used to analyze the effects of gender, test (i.e., pre-test vs post-test), and the four robots, on the observers' perception. Statistical differences were found between the four robots in the subscales of HRIES, namely, Sociability, Animacy, and Disturbance. The preferences of the children were leaning toward the humanoid robot (i.e., Alpha) with the moderate anthropomorphic traits in the Disturbance subscale. Low to moderate correlations were found between the subscales of NARS and HRIES.

Keywords: Social robots · Anthropomorphism · Acceptability · Negative attitudes

1 Introduction

Social robots are agents that are meant to interact directly with users to communicate, display and perceive emotions, establish relationships, and understand natural cues [9]. While it has made great strides, the research in social robotics

H. Li et al. (Eds.): ICSR 2021, LNAI 13086, pp. 791–796, 2021.
https://doi.org/10.1007/978-3-030-90525-5_73

is still lacking and in need to tackle challenges in different areas such as safety, design optimization, user acceptance, and interaction dynamics [1–4].

Social robot design variables and factors such as the size, shape, gestures, sound, and anthropomorphism affect user's acceptance [6,10]. To investigate the influence of different variables, various psychometric scales were developed to evaluate the acceptance of social robots based on different attributes [8]. These scales rely on behavioral and physiological measures of robot acceptance using self-reported questionnaires [7]. The outcomes of these questionnaires are analyzed using statistical methods to identify significant factors that affect attitudes toward social robots and influence their acceptability. Robot designers have projected anthropomorphism in different ways and at various degrees into their social robots designs. While having human-like attributes are desirable in social robots, going beyond a certain threshold might trigger eerie and unease feelings (i.e., Uncanny Valley Theory [5,11]).

In this study, we evaluated the children's perceived perception of four robots with different anthropomorphic traits using the Negative Attitude toward Robots scale (NARS; [12]) and Human-Robot Interaction Evaluation Scale (HRIES; [13]) scales.

Fig. 1. Representative robots with varying degree of anthropomorphism (left to right): Professor Einstein, Alpha, Cozmo, and Sphero RVR.

2   Methods

2.1   Participants

Thirty-three participants (21 females and 12 males) aged between 3–18 years old were recruited in Qatar for this study to answer the questionnaires. The procedures for this work did not include invasive or potentially hazardous methods and were in accordance with the Code of Ethics of the World Medical Association (Declaration of Helsinki).

2.2   Robots

Four robots were selected based on the degree of their human-like characteristics with Professor Einstein robot (Hanson Robotics, Hong Kong) having the most anthropomorphic features followed by Alpha (UBTECH Robotics, China), Cozmo (Anki, United States), and lastly RVR (Sphero, United States) with the least anthropomorphic features (Fig. 1).

2.3   Procedures

Questionnaire Items. The questionnaire consisted of 30 randomized items from the NARS and the HRIES scales. These two scales were used in the questionnaire to measure the participants' already existing bias or perception toward robots in general in the pre-test questionnaire and to measure any changes to their perception toward the robots after the interaction sessions in the post-test questionnaire. The NARS three subscales pertaining negative attitude toward situations (NS1), social influence (NS2), and emotions (NS3) and HRIES subscales namely Sociability (HC1), Animacy (HC2), Agency (HC3), and Disturbance (HC4) were used in the analysis

Experiments. Between the pre-test and post-test surveys, the participants interacted with one robot for around three minutes. During these interactions, each robot performed a demo showing a different set of behaviors based on their respective capabilities.

2.4   Analysis

Cronbach's alpha test was used to determine the internal consistency of the questionnaire items. Multivariate ANOVA test was used on all the factors and the subscales of the questionnaire items. A Pearson's correlation analysis was performed between the NARS and HRIES subscales. The statistical tests were conducted using Minitab (v18.1, Minitab Inc., USA) at a statistical significance level of $p < 0.05$.

Table 1. The mean and standard deviation of the participants' responses based on the subscales and were categorized based on the factors.

Factor	Gender		Test		Robot			
	Female	Male	Pre-test	Post-test	Alpha	Cozmo	Einstein	RVR
NS1	15.2 (4.4)	13.2 (3.9)	15.3 (4.4)	13.6 (4.1)	15.7 (3.7)	12.6 (5.4)	14.7 (2.7)	14.4 (5.1)
NS2	14.7 (4.3)	13.7 (4.1)	15.1 (4.6)	13.6 (3.8)	12.4 (3.5)	14.1 (3.5)	14.8 (4.1)	16.5 (4.8)
NS3	9.9 (3.2)	11.4 (3.0)	9.6 (3.0)	11.3 (3.1)	9.8 (2.7)	11.7 (3.5)	11.5 (2.6)	9.2 (3.5)
HC1	18.3 (5.4)	19.2 (5.2)	17.6 (5.5)	19.6 (4.9)	15.6 (3.7)	21.9 (5.4)	19.9 (4.2)	18.3 (6.0)
HC2	12.9 (6.6)	15.8 (6.3)	12.4 (5.8)	15.4 (7.2)	11.4 (5.6)	17.3 (4.1)	18.8 (4.6)	9.4 (4.4)
HC3	18.3 (4.8)	19.1 (4.0)	18.5 (4.3)	18.7 (4.7)	19.2 (4.1)	19.7 (3.2)	17.8 (4.6)	17.7 (5.8)
HC4	9.0 (4.9)	9.7 (5.4)	9.9 (5.6)	8.7 (4.5)	6.7 (3.5)	8.5 (4.8)	12.3 (5.6)	10.1 (5.1)

3 Results and Discussion

Cronbach's alpha test was used and an acceptable score of 0.71 was achieved. The mean and standard deviation for the responses of the participants based on the subscales and factors were tabulated (Table 1). A multivariate ANOVA test was conducted on all the subscales, factors, and their interactions (Table 2). A post hoc Tukey test in the case of HC1 showed that the Alpha robot differed significantly compared to the Cozmo and Einstein robots. In the case of HC2, a post hoc Tukey test showed that the Alpha and RVR robots differed significantly compared to the Einstein and Cozmo robots. For the HC4 subscale, the Einstein robot differed significantly compared to the Alpha based on a post hoc Tukey test. A total of eleven low to moderate significant correlations were found between the NARS and HRIES subscales based on Pearson's correlation analysis.

Table 2. The ANOVA test results for all the subscales, factors, and their interactions.

Factor	Gender		Test		Robot		Interaction	
	F-value	p-value	F-value	p-value	F-value	p-value	F-value	p-value
NS1	2.91	0.09	0.87	0.36	1.78	0.16	0.32	0.81
NS2	0.66	0.42	2.22	0.14	1.97	0.13	0.2	0.89
NS3	0.94	0.34	4.17	0.046*	1.72	0.18	0.62	0.61
HC1	0.5	0.48	2.4	0.13	5.11	0.004*	0.09	0.96
HC2	0.1	0.76	4.86	0.032*	8.93	0.0*	0.49	0.69
HC3	1.76	0.19	0.75	0.39	0.6	0.62	0.78	0.51
HC4	0.74	0.4	0.12	0.73	3	0.04*	1.73	0.17

$^*p < 0.05$

The results in our study did not show any significance for the gender factor. This discrepancy could be attributed to the mismatch in the number of participants based on their gender. Another factor that could have affected the preferences is the wide range of anthropomorphic traits across different robotic designs that made the responses of participants more evenly distributed. Interacting with the robots have altered some aspects of the children's perceived perceptions. For example, significant difference was found for the test factor (i.e., pre-test vs post-test) in two subscales, namely emotions in interaction (i.e., NS3) and Animacy (i.e., HC2). Seeing the robots alive and in action might have made the children more relaxed and comfortable around robots, hence, this affected their perceptions of the presented robots positively.

The participants' perceptions of the four robots have varied and showed discrepancy in the subscales. While no differences were found in NARS, the HRIES reported statistical significant differences in Sociability (i.e., HC1), Animacy (i.e., HC2), and Disturbance (i.e., HC3). Cozmo and Einstein were rated as the highest in terms of Sociability as compared to other robots. This could be attributed to their engaging interactions. Einstein scored the highest in terms of Animacy, which could be attributed to its facial expressions and hand gestures. In contrast, RVR scored the least in Animacy characteristics and that could be due to the lack of expression capabilities and minimal anthropomorphic traits. In terms of Disturbance, Einstein scored the highest (i.e., worse) while Alpha the lowest (i.e., best). Some aspects of anthropomorphism in Einstein might be going beyond the safe threshold in the Uncanny Valley, hence, affecting the responses of the children negatively.

Acknowledgments. The work was supported by a research grant from QU Marubeni Concept to Prototype Grant under the grant number M-CTP-CENG-2020-4. The statements made herein are solely the responsibility of the authors. The authors declare that they have no conflict of interest.

References

1. Alban, A.Q., et al.: Detection of challenging behaviours of children with autism using wearable sensors during interactions with social robots. In: IEEE International Conference on Robot & Human Interactive Communication (RO-MAN), pp. 852–857. IEEE (2021)
2. Alhaddad, A.Y., Cabibihan, J.J., Bonarini, A.: Recognition of aggressive interactions of children toward robotic toys. In: IEEE International Conference on Robot and Human Interactive Communication (RO-MAN), pp. 1–8. IEEE (2019)
3. Alhaddad, A.Y., Cabibihan, J.-J., Bonarini, A.: Influence of reaction time in the emotional response of a companion robot to a child's aggressive interaction. Int. J. Soc. Robot. **12**(6), 1279–1291 (2020). https://doi.org/10.1007/s12369-020-00626-z
4. Cabibihan, J.J., Pattofatto, S., Jomâa, M., Benallal, A., Carrozza, M.C., Dario, P.: The conformance test for robotic/prosthetic fingertip skins. In: International Conference on Biomedical Robotics and Biomechatronics, pp. 561–566. IEEE (2006)
5. Cabibihan, J.J., Carrozza, M.C., Dario, P., Pattofatto, S., Jomaa, M., Benallal, A.: The uncanny valley and the search for human skin-like materials for a prosthetic fingertip. In: IEEE-RAS International Conference on Humanoid Robots, pp. 474–477. IEEE (2006)
6. Cabibihan, J.J., So, W.C., Saj, S., Zhang, Z.: Telerobotic pointing gestures shape human spatial cognition. Int. J. Soc. Robot. **4**(3), 263–272 (2012)
7. Charisi, V., Davison, D., Reidsma, D., Evers, V.: Evaluation methods for user-centered child-robot interaction. In: 2016 25th IEEE International Symposium on Robot and Human Interactive Communication (RO-MAN), pp. 545–550. IEEE (2016)
8. Krägeloh, C.U., Bharatharaj, J., Sasthan Kutty, S.K., Nirmala, P.R., Huang, L.: Questionnaires to measure acceptability of social robots: a critical review. Robotics **8**(4), 88 (2019)
9. Li, H., Cabibihan, J.J., Tan, Y.K.: Towards an effective design of social robots. Int. J. Soc. Robot. **3**(4), 333–335 (2011)

10. Martín, F., Ginés, J.: Practical aspects of deploying robotherapy systems. In: Ollero, A., Sanfeliu, A., Montano, L., Lau, N., Cardeira, C. (eds.) ROBOT 2017. AISC, vol. 693, pp. 367–378. Springer, Cham (2018). https://doi.org/10.1007/978-3-319-70833-1_30
11. Mori, M., MacDorman, K.F., Kageki, N.: The uncanny valley [from the field]. IEEE Robot. Autom. Mag. **19**(2), 98–100 (2012)
12. Nomura, T., Kanda, T., Suzuki, T., Kato, K.: Psychology in human-robot communication: an attempt through investigation of negative attitudes and anxiety toward robots. In: IEEE International Workshop on Robot and Human Interactive Communication, pp. 35–40. IEEE (2004)
13. Spatola, N., Kühnlenz, B., Cheng, G.: Perception and evaluation in human-robot interaction: The human-robot interaction evaluation scale (HRIES)—a multicomponent approach of anthropomorphism. Int. J. Soc. Robot., 1–23 (2021). https://doi.org/10.1007/s12369-020-00667-4

Intention Signaling for Mobile Social Service Robots - The Example of Plant Watering

Oskar Palinko[1]([✉]) [ID], Philipp Graf[2] [ID], Lakshadeep Naik[1] [ID], Kevin Lefeuvre[3],
Christian Sønderskov Zarp[1] [ID], and Norbert Krüger[1] [ID]

[1] University of Southern Denmark, Campusvej 55, Odense, Denmark
ospa@mmmi.sdu.dk
[2] Technical University Chemnitz, Str. der Nationen 62, Chemnitz, Germany
[3] Bauhaus University Weimar, Bauhausstr. 11, Weimar, Germany

Abstract. If social service robots are to be successful in becoming part of our everyday life, they need to have proper signaling of their intention to be predictable. This is especially important when interacting with elderly people, who might be less acceptive of technology. In this study we report on such a device, a plant watering robot (PWR) for elderly care centers, which has social signaling capabilities. Signaling is achieved by using a social agent (myKeepOn) and a steerable propeller/fan on the deck of a ship-like mobile robot. We conducted an online survey to assess how predictable the robot's behavior is. We have found that the social agent was very effective in conveying turning intentions of the robot, while the propeller was less able to do so. When signals from the two sources collide in meaning, people were not as confused as expected, and prediction rates kept steady.

Keywords: Social robots · Human-robot interaction · Intention signaling

1 Introduction

Robots are slowly making their ways from factory floors and entering our everyday living environments. For this transition to be successful, they need to conform to humans' needs and expectations. Robots need to be safe, reliable, and understandable. Understandability is the ability of the robot to make itself clear to people in its environment. This primarily means that people will be able to read and interpret the intentions of the robot, which prevents unexpected situations and reduces the fear of robots. If people can't read robots' behaviors, they might reject using them all together [1]. To prevent this, careful attention needs to be paid during the design of robots and their behavior.

Robots can convey information to others using a number of sensory channels. Using the visual channel, robots convey information about their intentions via their movement, lights, displays, etc. Movement behavior is an important way of visual communication as robots are usually able to change their locations and/or their physical shape, as they typically contain wheels and joints.

H. Li et al. (Eds.): ICSR 2021, LNAI 13086, pp. 797–802, 2021.
https://doi.org/10.1007/978-3-030-90525-5_74

In this study we explore how actions of different physical elements on top of a social mobile robot platform can be used to convey information about the movement intentions of the whole robot. The mobile platform developed in our research represents a plant watering robot to be used in elderly care centers, see Fig. 1.

2 Background

Signaling of robots has been addressed widely in numerous human-robot interaction (HRI) publications [2]. Humans are very good at understanding other people's intentions. A lot of it derives from the context of our actions [3], movement behavior or expression of emotions. Another very important source is people's gaze behavior [4].

As social robots are entering our everyday environment, it is of crucial importance to make them understood even by users with no prior experience with robots, as this will inevitably influence their acceptance [5].

Robots can display their intentions in various ways. Many of these are borrowed from animation movie techniques [6]. For example, anticipatory motion can be very effective in communicating intention as in this case humans have more time to react to interactive actions [7].

The use of a small, animated characters on mobile robots has been explored by the creators of the CERO figurine, that was mounted on a service office robot [8], which served as the direct inspiration to our usage of KeepOn on our mobile system. CERO was able to provide feedback gestures in addition to speech interaction, however its interaction capabilities were not tested in human robot interaction studies.

3 Approach

3.1 Robot Design

The Plant Watering Robot (PWR) was designed to resemble a deep-sea vessel on top of a mobile robotic platform, containing an artificial pilot and several elements with which it interacts, see Fig. 1. The nautical form factor was decided upon by wanting to create a narrative that would amount to a mini theater which elderly people can observe, without the need for interaction, which could be considered intrusive or bothersome.

Fig. 1. CAD model and implemented version of the Plant Watering Robot used in study.

The planned physical components on the ship's deck include: the controlling agent, a propeller/fan, control board and control tower, see Fig. 1. The agent is designed to give intuitive signals about the ship's intentions. It was decided to be a myKeepOn, a popular social robotic platform [9] with simple but effective interaction capabilities. In the current implementation only the yaw movement of the agent is used to inform people of the ships intended direction of turn. The second interactive element is the propeller mounted on a platform which is able to perform yaw motions as well in addition to rotating continuously, while the robot moves. The yaw motion is designed to give information about the intended turn of the robot, as if the ship is a hovercraft.

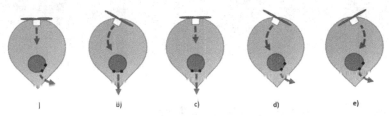

| | ii) | c) | d) | e) |

Fig. 2. Experimental conditions: a) agent only left, b) fan only left, c) neither (straight), d) agent + fan congruent, e) agent + fan incongruent.

Our test platform consisted of a TurtleBot3 base with a water tank mounted on top of it. The tank is covered with a 3D printed ship hull as shown in Fig. 1 and all the interaction components were installed on top of it.

3.2 Experimental Design

We designed an experiment to test the usefulness of the agent and the propeller for signaling the intentions of the robot to turn left, right or go straight. The social agent was selected for intention indication as it has been proven that these types of devices can convey signaling information [8]. The propeller was selected as an as a non-social signaling cue. We also explored if the combination of the two signals aids or hinders understanding of the robot's planned behavior. The combination of agent and propeller can be either congruent (when both the agent and propeller are conveying the same direction signal) or incongruent (when the two signals are in conflict). The study implemented the experimental conditions shown in Fig. 1. To test these, an online study was devised due to the Covid pandemic. Thus, the study consisted of a number of videos of the above-described robot platform approaching an intersection of corridors[1]. In each video, the robot comes up to the intersection and then signals in one of the ways described in Fig. 2. Before the robot makes the turn the video ends, to allow the participants to predict its future course (left, right or straight).

The recordings were shown in a pseudo-random order, clustered in the single signal (agent, fan, none) and combined signals groups (congruent, incongruent). Single signals were always presented before combination signals in the survey. The procedure was completed using the 'SoSci Survey' online experimentation tool.

---

[1] https://youtube.com/playlist?list=PLxFcYOmK2UZp61ghw-L6nmYLraZBpI-bz.

3.3 Experiment Participants

Participants were recruited using the Mechanical Turk website. They needed to be from the USA (to keep the sample uniform), to have a Master qualification and a 90% approval rating. We had 28 qualified participants (9 female, 19 male, avg. age 43.7, SD 12.1) to check participants' attention, after seeing the videos they were asked to state the shape and color of the robot, which all 28 answered correctly.

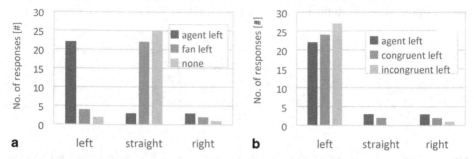

Fig. 3. a) Single signaling conditions (agent, fan, none) and b) combined signaling conditions (congruent, incongruent) compared to agent only for left turns (right turns are symmetrical).

4 Results

4.1 Prediction of the Robot's Path

We conducted a within-subject experiment according to conditions defined in Fig. 2. Results for comparing single conditions (agent, fan, none) for left signaling are shown in Fig. 3 a). The bar heights in the left figure represent how often the respondents were judging that the robot will turn left, right or keep straight, while the robot was signaling that it wants to turn left (agent left, fan left) or when it didn't signal at all (none).

It can be noticed that in the case of agent-only signals, the participants correctly estimate the intended turn of the robot (blue bars) most of the time. This is not the case for the fan-only condition (red bars). In this case most of the time subjects thought that the robot will continue driving straight, even though we were signaling left. This difference of accurate predictions for left turns between agent-only and fan-only was found to be significant with $\chi^2(1, N = 28) = 23,26, p < .000$. The output for the fan-only condition is very similar to the none condition, where people correctly estimated that the robot will continue driving straight in the great majority of times.

Next, we looked at combined conditions, Fig. 3. b) where the agent and fan were either signaling congruently (Fig. 2. d) or incongruently (Fig. 2. e). We compared these to the agent-only condition from Fig. 3 a). Participants judged correctly the intended direction of turn in the great majority of cases for all three discussed conditions. The combined cases have even higher accuracy than the agent-only condition, however there is no statistical difference between congruent and incongruent combinations.

5 Discussion

The results have shown multiple outcomes. First, for single conditions (agent, fan, none) it has been shown that the agent conveys the most information about the intended path of the robot, as expected, while the fan conveys almost none. Considering the fan, the results are somewhat unexpected, as it was unable to convey almost any information. This might be because its lack of contrast with the background or because it might require technical knowledge to interpret its influence on the robot. Regarding combinations of signals, it was unexpected that the congruent and incongruent signals are both at least on the same level of predictability as agent-only. This might be caused by the fact that the combination signals in the online questionnaire always came after the simple signals, so there might be a learning effect.

6 Conclusion

In this paper we set out to investigate what social and technical cues on a plant watering robot would work best for conveying information about the robot's future movement intentions. First, the PWR prototype itself was introduced with its technical capabilities. Then a human-robot interaction experiment was designed to shed light on different signaling cues on the robot. Due to the pandemic situation, we opted for an online study using videos of different robot actions. It was found that KeepOn is very successful in communicating the robot's movement intentions, while the propeller in the ship's back was much less able to do so. Combinations of signals were not found to be more useful than the agent itself. In conclusion, the findings of this paper tell us that using a social agent is appropriate for service robots designed to operate in the human environment with possible close contact with people. The study will guide us in improving the plant watering robot's signaling capabilities to produce a robot with better social acceptance.

Acknowledgements. The study was completed within the RethiCare project of the Volkswagen-Stiftung foundation.

References

1. Goetz, J., Kiesler, S., Powers, A.: Matching robot appearance and behavior to tasks to improve human-robot cooperation. In: The 12th IEEE International Workshop on Robot and Human Interactive Communication (2003)
2. Cha, E., Kim, Y., Fong, T., Mataric, M.: A survey of nonverbal signaling methods for non-humanoid robots. Found Trends Robot. 6(4), 211 (2018)
3. Kilner, J.M.: More than one pathway to action understanding. Trends Cogn. Sci. 15(8), 352–357 (2011)
4. Castiello, U.: Understanding other people's actions: intention and attention. J. Exp. Psychol. Human Percept. Perform. 29(2), 416 (2003)
5. Beer, J.M., Prakash, A., Mitzner, T.L., Rogers, W.A.: Understanding robot acceptance. Georgia Institute of Technology (2011)

6. Schulz, T., Torresen, J., Herstad, J.: Animation techniques in human-robot interaction user studies: a systematic literature review. ACM Trans. Human Robot Interact. **8**(2), 1–22 (2019)
7. Gielniak, M.J., Thomaz, A.: Generating anticipation in robot motion. In: RO-MAN (2011)
8. Severinson-Eklundh, K., Green, A., Hüttenrauch, H.: Socilal and collaborative aspects of interaction with a service robot. Robot. Auton. Syst. **42**(3–4), 223–234 (2003)
9. Kozima, H., Michalowski, M.P., Nakagawa, C.: Keepon. Int. J. Soc. Robot. **1**(1), 3–18 (2009)

Use of Social Robots in the Classroom

Jordis Blackburn[ID], Cody Blankenship[ID], Fengpei Yuan[ID], Lynn Hodge[ID],
and Xiaopeng Zhao[✉][ID]

University of Tennessee, Knoxville, TN 37996, USA
{jblack40,cblank10,fyuan6}@vols.utk.edu, {lhodge4,
xzhao9}@utk.edu

Abstract. Research about using social robots in the classroom is a growing topic with many unstudied/understudied problems. With the capabilities of these robots expanding rapidly, it has become necessary to explore the uses of robots in addressing persistent challenges in education. The rapid advancement in the technology of artificial intelligence, such as affective computing and natural language processing, makes the reality of social robots in schools more possible now than ever. In the early stages of research, there are many questions to be answered about these robots and their potential applications, technological limitations, and ethical uses. Although the use of social robots in the classroom may be in its infancy, there are many studies that help define where the research stands today.

Keywords: Social robots · Education · Robots in classroom

1 Introduction

With the development of information and communication technologies, using humanlike robots in the classroom has increasingly gained interest in the field of education. The rise of new technologies including artificial intelligence and facial recognition makes the reality of social robots in schools more possible now than ever. However, the public has concerns about introducing robots into the classrooms. In this paper, we conduct a narrative review to gain insight into the main topics in the field of using social robots in classrooms at such infancy stage, and to identify the primary concerns and challenges in this field.

2 Review of Main Research Topics

2.1 Expressive and Human-Like Robots

An "expressive" robot shows emotion with facial features and body language as well as speech. Since students are used to being taught by humans and learning how to interact with humans their whole lives, robots with humanlike features and expressive actions help students feel more comfortable [11]. For example, Lin [10] shows that the use of robots with human physical characteristics made it easier for students to be engaged.

© Springer Nature Switzerland AG 2021
H. Li et al. (Eds.): ICSR 2021, LNAI 13086, pp. 803–807, 2021.
https://doi.org/10.1007/978-3-030-90525-5_75

Socially assistive robots (SARs) were "'human enough' to trigger familiarity" while also not being too humanistic so that there was still a sense of curiosity associated with the robot [11]. Shiomi [15] demonstrates robots with perceived pleasant characteristics make the student-robot relationship stronger. There is much support for expressive robots because children can identify with them better [9, 11, 17]. This can be further seen in a study by Conti [5] examining the effects of storytelling on kindergarten students. This study demonstrates that an expressive robot can achieve the same level of information retention in students as an expressive human teacher [5].

Although the robots are human resemblant, they are still very different from humans with some differences being in the students' advantage. Many students deal with low self-esteem and find the classroom stressful. Student-robot interaction is perceived as less judgmental compared to the typical classroom setting, which reduces the students' fear of making a mistake [11]. Similarly, humanoid robots differed from teachers when responding to mistakes [19]. While a teacher may grow weary of repeated mistakes, a robot is unable to get tired. Robots help create a judgement free zone where students will feel less stress.

2.2 Subjects

The uses for robots vary greatly depending on the subject and type of class. There is promising research to support the use of robots in language learning. One study employed a robot in a language learning class and examined the different ways to incorporate a robot [4]. The study programs a robot to act as a foreigner in the classroom and to help the teacher tell a story [19]. Not only does the robot know the language fluently, but it can also use different voices for different characters, add entertaining body movements, sound effects, and help engage students in general [4]. Overall, many studies have demonstrated positive results with robots in language learning.

Papadopoulos [11] aimed to study how robots can be utilized in the math and science classroom. Ahmad [1] shows that there is promise for this technology in STEM class-rooms. This study was conducted with high school students using a SAR called Cozmo to teach math subjects including algebra, geometry, and trigonometry. The results showed a significant improvement in the students' understanding across all subjects. The biggest obstacle facing SARs in STEM, according to current research, is the tendency of the robots to distract students. This was seen in younger students, ages eight through nine [7], however older students reported negligible distraction from the robots [1].

2.3 Education for Students with Disabilities

Robots may also be a promising approach to providing special education or education for students with disabilities in the classroom. Robots act not only as teaching assistants to these students but also as friends [19]. Robots may be able to engage students with disabilities in a new way. Qidwai [12] studied the ways robots could be used to assist children with Autism Spectrum Disorder (ASD) and found strong evidence that using NAO led to great improvement in learning behaviors. Most children with ASD have difficulties being around other people, but these "human-phobic barriers" are removed when towards a robot. In turn, the child is more likely to interact with the robot and therefore learn from the robot. Additionally, because robots can be extremely repetitive and predictable, it is easier for children with ASD to understand "how to perceive human and understand human emotions" [12]. Kim [8] found that the teacher can elicit more interaction from the autistic children by using the social robot as a partner, and that the robot partner can increase student interaction more than the adult partner counterpart. Amanatiadis [2] studied the interaction between two NAOs and two children with ASD and found the children were not only comfortable with the robots but also had a strengthened social connection with each other.

2.4 Teacher and Student Opinions

With any new technology to market there are concerns, but this is especially true when the technology affects children. Teachers are unfamiliar and believe that robotic technology is too complex [4]. Teachers show concerns with robots used in the classroom because they are unaware of the capabilities and uncertain how to incorporate the robots in the classroom [19]. Teacher opinions and concerns are extremely important to the introduction of robots to the classroom because they will be the initiators. Xia [20] suggests introducing the robots to teachers in in-service training. However, in the study by Chang [4], teachers used robots in their classrooms and were educated on how to use them, but they still encountered challenges like lesson planning. Without appropriate content and activities, the robots were useless to the classroom.

All these concerns are not without hope and potential. Many teachers also expressed excitement for the robots and how their students responded. The robots seemed to help motivate and engage the students in the lesson [4]. A robot could be developed to provide personalized feedback based on a student's learning style and personality [11]. This ability will be an advantage in the classroom, and teachers will undoubtedly be able to use such feedback to better educate students.

It is also necessary to learn how students feel about robots being used in their classrooms. In general, students are positive, curious, and exploratory towards robots; however, some shy or socially anxious students are more reserved around them [15, 16].

2.5 Role in Classroom

Another point of contention among researchers and teachers is the role of the robot in the classroom, with the options being a replacement of the teacher, a teaching assistant, or a peer. Of the different types of roles robots could fill, teaching assistant and peer are the most accepted roles, and replacements for teachers are not generally accepted.

Teacher. As our world is moving in the direction of replacing employees of most occupations with robots or AI technology, a robot teacher could be a possible future. Effective communication skills are essential to managing a classroom, and robots are becoming more able to converse like humans [6]. However, it is still questioned whether a robot could be as effective as a human teacher. Sharkey [14] argues that robots do not have and cannot have the necessary biological nature required for a sense of morality to make fair decisions or anticipate situations. One study equipped robots with behavior recognition technology that can gather data from both faces and body poses allowing the robot to respond and adjust accordingly [3]. Despite these advances, most researchers have agreed that currently robots fit the role of teaching assistant or peer better than as a replacement for the teacher.

Teaching Assistant. As opposed to taking on the role of head teacher, robots may take on the role of a teaching assistant or aid. A teaching assistant would help teachers present material to the class [4]. Most studies choose to develop robots as the role of teaching assistant giving reason to believe this role is more acceptable. For example, teachers were reluctant about using robots, but they were more open to using robots in restricted roles such as an assistant [19].

Peer. Another potential role of a robot is a peer or a companion for students. In this role, robots act as a go-between for teachers and students [4]. Additionally, students who viewed the robot as a peer or companion, do not think of the robot as an authority and therefore the students did not feel as intimidated by or scared of the robot [14]. In one study, a robot acts as a playmate in word play games, which could be an effective way to give students more practice and attention [13]. In a similar vein, 'care-receiving' robots are taught by students and have some educational benefits [18].

3 Conclusion

Regardless of the concerns among researchers, teachers, and students, most researchers can agree that there is vast potential for the use of robots in the classroom. Whether used as an assistant to the teacher or a tool for learning, robots in the classroom may be a reality soon. The many studies included in this paper show examples of how robots have expanded the limits of what education can look like. Robots may be able to make school feel less stressful and more fun for students. Robots can also support social and emotional support that can impact learning across subjects. There are still many areas of research that are underdeveloped and require further exploration. As technology rapidly changes it is difficult to predict how, when, or if robots will be used in the classroom; however, preliminary research is encouraging for the future of social robots in education.

References

1. Ahmad, M.I., Khordi-moodi, M., Lohan, K.S.: Social robot for STEM education. In: Companion of the 2020 ACM/IEEE International Conference on Human-Robot Interaction, pp. 90–92 (2020)
2. Amanatiadis, A., Kaburlasos, V.G., Dardani, C., Chatzichristofis, S.A., Mitropoulos, A.: Social robots in special education: creating dynamic interactions for optimal experience. IEEE Consum. Electron. Mag. **9**(3), 39–45 (2020)
3. Bourguet, M.L., Jin, Y., Shi, Y., Chen, Y., Rincon-Ardila, L., Venture, G.: Social robots that can sense and improve student engagement. In: IEEE International Conference on Teaching, Assessment and Learning for Engineering (TALE), pp. 127–134 (2020)
4. Chang, C.-W., Lee, J.-H., Chao, P.-Y., Wang, C.-Y., Chen, G.-D.: Exploring the possibility of using humanoid robots as instructional tools for teaching a second language in primary school. Educ. Technol. Soc. **13**(2), 13–24 (2010)

5. Conti, D., Di Nuovo, A., Cirasa, C., Di Nuovo, S.: A comparison of kindergarten storytelling by human and humanoid robot with different social behavior. In: Proceedings of the Companion of the 2017 ACM/IEEE International Conference on Human-Robot Interaction, pp. 97–98 (2017)

6. Edwards, B., Cheok, A.: Why not robot teachers: artificial intelligence for addressing teacher shortage. Appl. Artif. Intell. **32**(4), 345–360 (2018)

7. Kennedy, J., Baxter, P., Belpaeme, T.: The robot who tried too hard: social behaviour of a robot tutor can negatively affect child learning. In: 2015 10th ACM/IEEE International Conference on Human-Robot Interaction (HRI), pp. 67–74 (2015)

8. Kim, E.S., et al.: Social robots as embedded reinforcers of social behavior in children with autism. J. Autism Dev. Disord. **43**(5), 1038–1049 (2013)

9. Kory Westlund, J.M., et al.: Flat vs. expressive storytelling: Young children's learning and retention of a social robot's narrative. Front. Human Neurosci. **11**, 295 (2017)

10. Lin, P., Abney, K., Bekey, G.A. (eds.): Robot Ethics: The Ethical and Social Implications of Robotics. MIT Press, Cambridge (2012)

11. Papadopoulos, I., Lazzarino, R., Miah, S., Weaver, T., Thomas, B., Koulouglioti, C.: A systematic review of the literature regarding socially assistive robots in pre-tertiary education. Comput. Educ. **155**, 103924 (2020)

12. Qidwai, U., Kashem, S.B.A., Conor, O.: Humanoid robot as a teacher's assistant: helping children with autism to learn social and academic skills. J. Intell. Rob. Syst. **98**(3–4), 759–770 (2019). https://doi.org/10.1007/s10846-019-01075-1

13. Schicchi, D., Pilato, G.: A social humanoid robot as a playfellow for vocabulary enhancement. In: 2018 Second IEEE International Conference on Robotic Computing (IRC), pp. 205–208 (2018)

14. Sharkey, A.J.C.: Should we welcome robot teachers? Ethics Inf. Technol. **18**(4), 283–297 (2016). https://doi.org/10.1007/s10676-016-9387-z

15. Shiomi, M., Kanda, T., Howley, I., Hayashi, K., Hagita, N.: Can a social robot stimulate science curiosity in classrooms? Int. J. Soc. Robot. **7**(5), 641–652 (2015)

16. Søraa, R.A., Nyvoll, P.S., Grønvik, K.B., Serrano, J.A.: Children's perceptions of social robots: a study of the robots Pepper, AV1 and Tessa at Norwegian research fairs. AI Soc. **36**(1), 205–216 (2020). https://doi.org/10.1007/s00146-020-00998-w

17. Takahiro, S., Naoko, K., Hideki, M., Akinori, N.: Trial of programming education for junior high-school students by using bipedal robots. In: The 4th International STEM Education 2019 Proceedings, pp. 312–318 (2019)

18. Tanaka, F., Matsuzoe, S.: Children teach a care-receiving robot to promote their learning. J. Hum. Robot Interact. **1**, 78–95 (2012)

19. Tuna, G., Tuna, A., Ahmetoglu, E., Kuscu, H.: A survey on the use of humanoid robots in primary education: Prospects, research challenges and future research directions. Cypriot J. Educ. Sci. **14**(3), 361–373 (2019)

20. Xia, Y., LeTendre, G.: Robots for future classrooms: a cross-cultural validation study of "Negative Attitudes Toward Robots Scale" in the U.S. Context. Int. J. Soc. Robotics **13**(4), 703–714 (2020)

Application of Human-Robot Interaction Features to Design and Purchase Processes of Home Robots

Nur Beril Yapici[✉] ⓘ, Tugkan Tuglular ⓘ, and Nuri Basoglu ⓘ

Izmir Institute of Technology, 35430 Izmir, Turkey
{nuryapici,tugkantuglular,nuribasoglu}@iyte.edu.tr

Abstract. Production of home robots, such as robotic vacuum cleaners, currently focuses more on the technology and its engineering than the needs of people and their interaction with robots. An observation supporting this view is that the home robots are not customizable. In other words, buyers cannot select the features and built their home robots to order. Stemmed from this observation, the paper proposes an approach that starts with a classification of features of home robots. This classification concerns robot interaction with humans and the environment, a home in our case. Following the classification, the proposed approach utilizes a new hybrid model based on a built-to-order model and dynamic eco-strategy explorer model, enabling designers to develop a production line and buyers to customize their home robots with the classified features. Finally, we applied the proposed approach to robotic vacuum cleaners. We developed a feature model for robotic vacuum cleaners, from which we formed a common uses scenario model.

Keywords: Human-robot interaction process design · Build-to-order · Dynamic eco-strategy explorer model · Robot customization

1 Introduction

This paper presents the idea of combining two strategies, build-to-order and the dynamic eco-strategy explorer model (DEEM), into **the Hybrid Model**. The Hybrid Model is used to get maximum user satisfaction by giving the user to an opportunity customizing their domestic home robots. Robotic vacuum cleaners, in a word robovacs, are chosen to apply and evaluate this idea.

2 Feature Model of Vacuum Cleaner Robots

The technical features available in the market and the expectations of the product from the user can be evaluated by using a feature model. The existing and conceptual characteristics of robotic vacuum cleaners can be used to construct an essential feature model, which is rooted in the technical features desired to be added and creates the mechanical equipment and accessories to be used in the branches. R&D designers and engineers can

© Springer Nature Switzerland AG 2021
H. Li et al. (Eds.): ICSR 2021, LNAI 13086, pp. 808–813, 2021.
https://doi.org/10.1007/978-3-030-90525-5_76

benefit from the feature tree to create the essential structure of robovac to be advanced. The user group selection will be one of the most critical factors that will determine the quality, capabilities, and combinations of the technical part to be used in the device. Currently, due to standardized production methods, the customer cannot select the characteristics of the robotic vacuum cleaner. Instead, a customer chooses market products offered close to his/her needs. Figure 1 is a designed feature model consisted of essential features for the robotic vacuum cleaner.

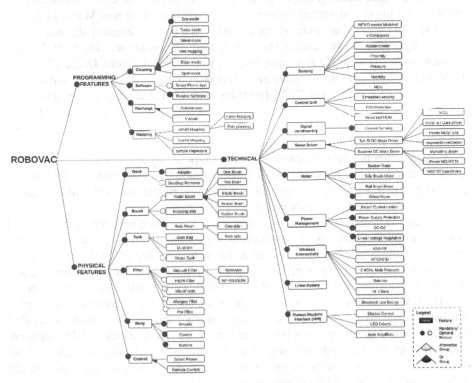

Fig. 1. Feature model for robovacs (the technical branch is modified from [1]).

3 The Proposed Customization System Design: The Hybrid Model for Robotic Vacuum Cleaners

The traditional firms fulfill customer demand using their investigations and they choose a limited set of product configurations, thereby enabling consumers to find products that are close to their ideal choice [2]. However, considering the interaction process of a basic robovac, the various parameters, which need to be evaluated simultaneously such as the physical characteristics of the environment to be used, the smart ecosystem integrated with, and the householders, that will affect the use of the product emerge. When the combinations of these parameters are calculated, a great variety of standardized preferences should design and produce. However, the robovac market inherently has customers with heterogeneous preferences for product features, considering the network of interactions. To achieve maximum product satisfaction, we are proposing a designated product configuration process, which is the process of customizing a product to meet the needs of a customer, and an effective interaction process design for the marketing and selling phase.

In this section, two models utilized in various cases are examined robovac customization. **Dynamic Eco-strategy Explorer Model** is proposed with the aim of optimizing the energy and resources consumed through the use of a product by Serna-Mansoux et al. in 2014 [3]. The DEEM aims to choose the correct product among existing alternatives and does this by scoring the products and comparing the results with each. The DEEM model is composed of six stages in sequence, Choose, Understand, Explore, Decide, Test, and If [3]. In Fig. 2, the initial interaction process is assimilated from the implementation of Serna-Mansoux et al. [3]. **The Build-to-Order model** is the strategy, that enables mass customization with aim of customer satisfaction. It has some accomplished implementation instances by considerable companies including Dell Computer, Compaq, BMW, Mercedes. The BTO is a production method that switches the market power from seller-driven perception to buyer-driven one [4]. The proposed hybrid model utilizes DEEM and BTO in a novel combination. The DEEM is adapted to get high-efficient interaction. Moreover, the direct model is accepted as a business model that will build standards quickly and manufacture a highly configurable product.

The DEEM is redesigned to construct efficient interaction between customers, and product design that consists of standardized units from purchasing decisions. In our study, it mainly applies to the first interaction with potential users during the product choosing stage. *Choose* stage aims to get the purchaser to know the product, and determine customers' individual and environmental characteristics interacting with it.

At *Understand* stage, some usage scenarios are created by referring to the selected attributes at the previous stage. These scenarios are formed as the result of detailed customer segmentation based on needs and preferences by research and development, and design teams. The customer picks from the recommended usage scenarios. These scenarios are critical to generating some product alternatives based on needs and wishes. More questions are asked for customization.

In the stage of *Explore*, based on the responses to the detailed questions asked before, the interaction system presents a robotic vacuum cleaner as a composition of desired components. At this stage, the presented product can be considered as an optimized robotic product based on users' needs. However, even so, customers can control the component features and models by their wishes. In other words, the exploration of the robovac by the user is expected. Since the product is designed modular in the R&D and design phase of the BTO, the exchange and integration of the units will be possible at every stage. After the third and fourth stages, the concept of the process starts to evolve toward decision making. At stage four, the representative product is presented as videos. At stage five, in this way, users can have predictions about the usage of the product and can test the result digitally. The final stage is deciding whether to buy or not. Here, the product is either purchased and manufactured or returned to the third stage to be modified and rebuilt.

Moving on to the implementation phase of the BTO, here are the first two phases that are critical for us. Managing the product variety is essentially the first movement to customization design of the product to be manufactured. It starts with evaluating the existing usage environment and classifies them into groups. This classification generates some customer segments based on the requirements and preferences. Thus, interaction scenarios emerge for use in the next phase and the previous model (the DEEM) implementation. The next phase consists of the set of research & development and design processes. Concepts and scenarios created in the previous stage form the source for product and component design at this stage. The components used or supplied are presented in the interaction phase for use in the explore phase. Then, production starts with simultaneous production planning and supply chain integration. In addition to these explanations, this model is the first form of the study and is still being studied.

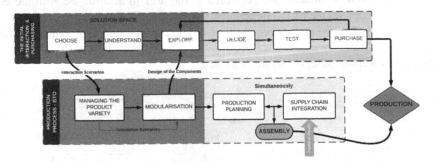

Fig. 2. The proposed hybrid model

4   Evaluation: RoboCuD Home

This study considers personalization according to usage conditions as a critical principle in the robotic vacuum cleaner development process. However, the number of product variations to be created with required and optional feature combinations reach too high for users to decide and for manufacturers to produce. To demonstrate, Fig. 1 can be utilized. Firstly, the number of features that can be added to the robot is calculated with combination calculations for each branch. Afterward, the number of robot versions is computed by using the cartesian product. The number of combinations for each branch is shown in Table 1. If all decisions are left to the user, the number of products that can be created is calculated as 84,934,656, although only the engine option is included among the technical features, and this number can be increased. This number is calculated by the multiplication of the feature tree combination possibilities.

A simple multipartite graph will be used to explain the simple implementation of this model and for the RoboCuD Home we are developing. In the first stage, we create a set, which we call *prerequisites*, which is used to define the ecosystem in which the robot will be used before recommending a robot to the user and to create product recommendations based on this. Figure 3 shows a cross-section of the items that will help determine the

Table 1. Feature model-based product options

	Cleaning Modes	Software	Recharge	Mapping	Dock	Brush	Tank	Filter	Body	Control	Motor
Number of options	32	2	3	3	2	96	4	32	1	3	2

characteristics of the home environment and the user in which RoboCuD will be used. The item combinations selected from the set for the user are designed to present the most suitable RoboCuD models for a specific home environment and user group. In the second part, user segments are created from the selected combinations. Figure 3 shows two of these segments in the *cases* section.

Finally, RoboCuD models are presented to the user in accordance with the environment, and user segments are determined for RoboCuDs appearance. The resulting models form the basis that the buyer will use before customizing the product according to his wishes. Then, the user can start customizing the robot at the website. For ongoing and detailed website design, [5] can be visited.

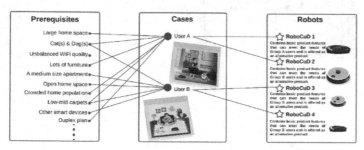

Fig. 3. Multipartite graph - a basic explanation of how the proposed system works.

5   Conclusion

This paper presents the idea of domestic social robots' customization with the proposed Hybrid Model, based on user needs by considering customer satisfaction. Robotic vacuum cleaners are selected to implement the study. Technological advancements in robotic technologies, especially in robovacs are deeply studied, and the chosen DEEM and the BTO model are combined to create a multiple-stage customization system. Then, the initial form of the Hybrid Model is explained in detail.

References

1. Robotic Vacuum Cleaner - Block Diagram, Design Solutions – STMicroelectronics. https://www.st.com/en/applications/home-and-professional-appliances/robot-vacuum-cleaners.html. Accessed 24 May 2021

2. Mendelson, H., Parlaktürk, A.K.: Product-line competition: customization vs proliferation. Manag. Sci. **54**, 2039–2053 (2008). https://doi.org/10.1287/mnsc.1080.0935
3. Serna-Mansoux, L., Popoff, A., Millet, D.: A simplified model to include dynamic product-user interaction in the eco-design process. J. Ind. Ecol. **18**, 529–544 (2014). https://doi.org/10.1111/jiec.12160
4. Kathawala, Y., Wilgen, A.: The evolution of build-to-order supply chain and its implications with selected case studies. IJSOM. **1**, 268 (2005). https://doi.org/10.1504/IJSOM.2005.006578
5. Behance: RoboCuD:WebDesignProject. https://www.behance.net/gallery/123180461/RoboCuDWebDesignProject. Accessed 6 Sept 2021

Physical Human-Robot Interaction Through Hugs with CASTOR Robot

María Gaitán-Padilla[1]([✉]), Juan C. Maldonado-Mejía[1], Leodanis Fonseca[2],
Maria J. Pinto-Bernal[1], Diego Casas[1], Marcela Múnera[1],
and Carlos A. Cifuentes[1]

[1] Colombian School of Engineering Julio Garavito, Bogota D.C., Colombia
maria.gaitan-p@mail.escuelaing.edu.co ,
carlos.cifuentes@escuelaing.edu.co
[2] Corporación Universitaria del Caribe, Sincelejo, Colombia

Abstract. Hugs play an essential role in social bonding between people. This study evaluates the hug interactions with a robot identifying the perception. Four hug release methods in adults were applied, a short-time hug, a long-time hug, a touch-controlled hug, and a pressure-controlled hug. The social robot CASTOR was integrated into this study, a modification was made in its arms to perform the hugging action, and a pressure sensor in its upper back. 12 adults (5 females and 7 males) participated in the study. Results showed that the perception of friendliness comparing the short-time hug and the pressure-controlled hug had differences ($p = 0.036$), making the pressure-controlled hug more friendly. In the case of natural perception, the touch-controlled hug was more natural comparing with the short-time hug ($p = 0.047$). This study presents the feasibility of implementing CASTOR in hugging interactions.

Keywords: Physical human-robot interaction · Robotic hug · Socially assistive robotics

1 Introduction

Physical contact is necessary for human beings to maintain psychological, emotional, and bodily well-being [1]. Hugging is the main sign of affection and emotional support [2]. Among the associated benefits is reducing stress and tension levels by releasing oxytocin, reducing the risk of dementia by giving tranquility and confidence, reduction of blood pressure by activating Pacini corpuscle receptors in the skin [3]. Recently, there has been projects aimed at developing social robots for hugging [4–6].

Casas et al. [7] developed the CASTOR (CompliAnt SofT Robotics) robot (Center of Biomechatronics, Colombia). CASTOR is a low-cost open-source platform initially created for therapies in children with Autism Spectrum Disorder (ASD) [8]. This study evaluates the feasibility of implementing CASTOR in

H. Li et al. (Eds.): ICSR 2021, LNAI 13086, pp. 814–818, 2021.
https://doi.org/10.1007/978-3-030-90525-5_77

hugging interactions. Therefore, the perception in adults of being hugged by the robot in four release methods is analyzed.

Robotic hugs have been studied recently, *Block et al.* [5] used the PR2 robot (Willow Garage, USA). The results showed that reciprocated hugs increased the interaction times and encouraged more self-disclosure. Considering the above results, *Block et al.* [9] evaluated physical variations of warmth and softness using the PR2 robot. They evaluated the perception through surveys in the physical variations, and changing the duration of the hug i.e., short time (1 s), average time (2.5 s), and long time (5 s). They determined that the social perception of the robot hug was related to the hug duration between the too-long and the too-short hug. Newly *Block et al.* [6], developed the Huggiebot 2.0 (MPI-IS and ETH, Germany and Switzerland) evaluating six parameters in the perception of the hug action. The results suggested that the perception of the haptic release method had better results than the timed-release hugs [6]. These studies were from the USA [4] and Europe [5,6,9]. This shows the lack of research in robotic hug interactions in developing countries. Considering this, this work implemented the low-cost Open-Source CASTOR social robot in the social interaction of hugging to evaluate the perception of two time-controlled hugs and two sensors-controlled hugs.

2   Method

This work seeks to evaluate the perceptions in a hug interaction with the social robot CASTOR. Aiming to achieve this goal, a questionnaire applied previously [6] based on the Unified Theory of Acceptance and Use of Technology (UTAUT) questionnaires was used. The first part focuses on the perception carried out with the volunteers about social robotic, with 13 questions (Safety (PS), Trust (PT), Attitude Towards Technology (ATT), Anxiety (ANX), Social Influence (SI), Social Presence (SP), Ease of Use (PEOU) and Utility (PU)). The second part focuses on the perception of each hug (Friendliness, Safety, Social Intelligence, Enjoyment, and Natural).

2.1   Participants and Equipment

A total of 12 healthy subjects (7 males, 5 females, 22.16 ± 2.08 years old, 1.67 ± 0.077 m) performed the study. Written consent was obtained from each participant before the study.

CASTOR robot was modified for the study. A change was made on the shoulder motors. This was done to lift the arms for a more extended period. The shoulder piece was modified to add Dynamixel MX-106 motors (Dynamixel, Seoul, Korea). Additionally, a pneumatic system was added, composed of a fabric bag, a plastic balloon inside, a pressure sensor ASDX100PAAA5 (Honeywell, North Carolina, USA), and an air pump ROB-10398 (Sparkfun, Colorado, USA). Furthermore, the touch sensor made of Velostat (Adafruit, New York, USA) located at the back of the head was used. This modifications can be seen in Fig. 1.

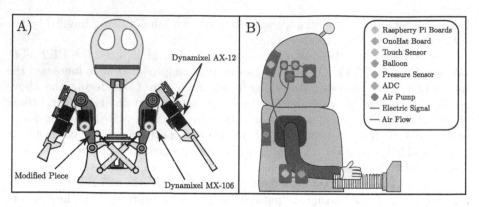

Fig. 1. Mechanic and electronic modifications. A) Mechanic modification of the robot's arms. B) Electronic distribution of the touch and pressure sensors.

2.2 Procedure

The activity to be performed was explained. Then the participant was introduced to the robot, and allowed to interact with it. The participant filled out the social robot perception questionnaire. Next, the four hugs were performed. The short-duration hug of one second. The long-duration hug of 5 s. The touch-controlled hug controlling the opening and closing of the arms with the touch sensor. And the pressure-controlled hug controlling the opening and closing of the arms exerting force on the pneumatic system in order to increase the air pressure (above 2.8 psi). After each hug the hug perception questionnaire was filled out. And at the end of the four hugs the social robot survey was filled out.

3   Results

The Shapiro-Wilk test was applied to determine the normality of the data, which showed that not all the results had a normal distribution. Therefore, the Mann-Whitney-Wilcoxon statistical test was applied. In the perception of social robotics PS, PT, ATT, ANX, SI, SP, PEOU, and PU, were assessed. Comparing before and after the hugs intervention. Considering the p-values, the metrics had no significant differences, as shown in Fig. 2. In the perception of hugs, the five metrics were evaluated. Friendliness, Safety, Social Intelligence, Enjoyment, and Natural. Comparing between the four hugs implemented, hug 4 had a better perception of making the robot seem friendly in the interaction than the short-time hug (p = 0.036). Hug 4 was more enjoyable than hug 1 (p = 0.039). And hug 3 had a higher perception of naturalness than hug 1 (p = 0.047). In the Safety and Social Intelligence metrics, were no significant differences (Fig. 3).

4   Discussion

Block et al. [9] indicate participants would prefer a robot that releases them from a hug immediately when they indicated they were ready for the hug to be over.

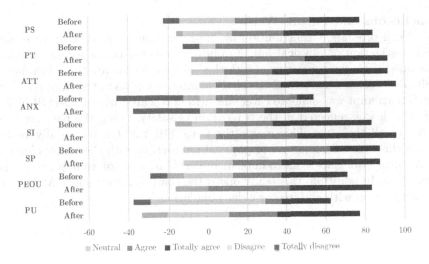

Fig. 2. Survey outcomes of Social Robot perception before and after the hugs in PS, PT, ATT, ANX, SI, SP, PEOU and PU.

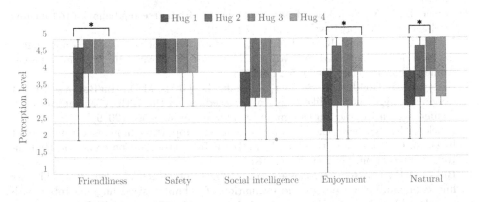

Fig. 3. Survey boxplot for each hug. Top and bottom of the box represent the 25 and 75 percentile, the x mark in the box center represents the mean. The lines extended show the farthest data point. The points indicate outliers. The * means $p < 0.05$

In this study, we found similar results; the pressure-controlled hug had better perception than a short-time hug in friendliness and enjoyment. In the same way, the touch-controlled hug had a better perception than a short-time hug in nature. In the social robotics perception, positive results were obtained, so there were no significant differences. However, in ANX, an increase in the perception of fear of damaging something in the robot was obtained after performing the hugs, which is the opposite of what was expected, but with no significance. This have been caused by the fact that, sometimes, the pressure-sensor cables got disconnected, which made it necessary to retry the hug.

Conclusions and Future Work

This work presents a contribution by implementing a low-cost social robot in the investigation of physical human-robot interaction through hugs. It can be concluded that, the robotic hugs with the best perception are those in which the individual decide when to end the physical interaction, as in the third and fourth hug. An attempt was made to cover this field of research with CASTOR in a safe way, which was reflected in the perception of safety, being the parameter best scored in all the hugs. This makes the CASTOR robot a potentially valuable tool in this type of human-robot physical interaction with the sensors-hugs.

As future work, we want to implement verbal interaction to improve the hugs perception. In addition, this study opens the road to implement CASTOR in a hug interaction with children or older population.

References

1. Gleeson, M., Higgins, A.: Touch in mental health nursing: an exploratory study of nurses' views and perceptions. J. Psychiatric Mental Health Nurs. 16(4), 382–389 (2009)
2. Forsell, L.M., Åström, J.A.: Meanings of hugging: from greeting behavior to touching implications. Compr. Psychol. 1, 02–17 (2012)
3. Light, K.C., Grewen, K.M., Amico, J.A.: More frequent partner hugs and higher oxytocin levels are linked to lower blood pressure and heart rate in premenopausal women. Biol. Psychol. 69(1), 5–21 (2005)
4. Hedayati, H., Bhaduri, S., Sumner, T., Szafir, D., Gross, M.D.: HugBot: a soft robot designed to give human-like hugs. In: Proceedings of the 18th ACM International Conference on Interaction Design and Children, pp. 556–561 (2019)
5. Block, A.E., Kuchenbecker, K.J.: Emotionally supporting humans through robot hugs. In: Companion of the 2018 ACM/IEEE International Conference on Human-Robot Interaction, pp. 293–294 (2018)
6. Block, A.E., Christen, S., Gassert, R., Hilliges, O., Kuchenbecker, K.J.: The six hug commandments: design and evaluation of a human-sized hugging robot with visual and haptic perception. In: Proceedings of the 2021 ACM/IEEE International Conference on Human-Robot Interaction, pp. 380–388 (2021)
7. Casas-Bocanegra, D., et al.: An open-source social robot based on compliant soft robotics for therapy with children with ASD. In: Actuators, vol. 9, p. 91. Multidisciplinary Digital Publishing Institute (2020)
8. Ramírez-Duque, A.A., et al.: Collaborative and inclusive process with the autism community: a case study in Colombia about social robot design. Int. J. Soc. Robot. 13(2), 153–167 (2021)
9. Block, A.E., Kuchenbecker, K.J.: Softness, warmth, and responsiveness improve robot hugs. Int. J. Soc. Robot. 11(1), 49–64 (2019)

Exploring Communicatory Gestures
for Simple Multi-robot Systems

Jaden Berger$^{(\boxtimes)}$, Alexandra Bacula$^{(\boxtimes)}$, and Heather Knight

Oregon State University, Corvallis, OR 97331, USA
{bergejad,baculaa}@oregonstate.edu

Abstract. The presented online study (N = 405) explores the impact of translational (towards, away, sideways) and rotational (spin and circle) motion patterns on the perceived communications of a three-robot group. All gestures were performed relative to a small humanoid figure at two speeds (slow and fast). Three of the gestures strongly predicted communicatory interpretation; *sideways* and *away* were seen as scared or fearful, and *spin* was seen as excited and joyful. *Circle* had low convergence and was seen as confused or frustrated. *Towards*, on the other hand, had a bimodal distribution: **slowly** towards was seen as greeting, whereas **fast** towards was seen as confrontational. The context prompts (party vs. meeting) did not affect participant interpretations.

Keywords: Expressive motion · Robotics · Multi-robot

1 Introduction and Related Works

Clear and efficient communication between humans and robots is crucial for successful human-robot interaction [3,4]. This work explores how emotions can be expressed with simple multi-robot motion using five different synchronous gestures on three simple robots and exploring how speed and context change the interpretation of expression of these gestures. In multi-robot systems, group motion patterns can be seen as exaggerated gestures, a powerful way for robots to communicate to humans without words [8].

While there have been many studies that looked at single robot motion and gestures [6,7,9,11], this work explores whether such gestures can also be read via a robot group. Such investigations extend prior findings showing simple mobile robot gestures have strong communicatory power [1,7]. Prior work in multiple robots has illustrated communicatory potentials for multi-robot systems, using parameterized motion generation [5,12] and human-controlled gesture [2,13].

The gesture and speed research conditions used in this paper were inspired by our prior work in single-root expression [10]. This study (first author participated) examined how a simple robot could incite storytelling in an improv scene using gesture (it did). This paper evaluates these same five gestures, finding similar communicatory interpretations when gestures are performed by congruent multi-robot systems.

© Springer Nature Switzerland AG 2021
H. Li et al. (Eds.): ICSR 2021, LNAI 13086, pp. 819–823, 2021.
https://doi.org/10.1007/978-3-030-90525-5_78

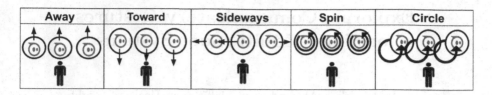

Fig. 1. Each isolated gesture was performed synchronously with all three robots.

2   Study Design

Three independent variables were explored to see how they affected perceptions of a multi-robot group: (1) gesture, meaning the way the multi-robot group moved as seen in Fig. 1; (2) speed, being how fast the robots performed the gesture; and (3) the context given to participants about the robots. The gestures replicated our prior work on a single robot system [10], representative of Cartesian linear and rotational motions. Each gesture was performed at two speeds (fast and slow). These two speeds were chosen based on the max and min speed range of the Sphero robots. Finally, all participants were presented with one of three contexts ("A robot walks into a party," "A robot walks into a meeting," or no context).

Online Study Setup. An online video study was run using Amazon's MTurk Service, which allowed for the exploration of more variables with more participants than an in-person study. Each video opened with three robots in a line in front of a humanoid figure with a plain white background, as seen in Fig. 1. The robots were placed in a straight line formation to reduce what role the formation played in perceived communication. Each participant was shown a video with one of five gestures at one of two speeds with one of three video contexts and was asked one question out of five possible questions.

Two questions used a seven-point Likert scale. Participants were given a sentence with a drop down menu of Likert scale responses. For example, the question "The actions taken were [blank]" had answer options "very positive," "positive," "somewhat positive," "neither positive or negative," "somewhat negative," "negative," and "very negative." Three questions were open-ended. Participants wrote a response after watching the video. The questions are as follows:

1. The actions taken were [very positive to very negative] (Likert).
2. The human felt [very welcome to very unwelcome] (Likert).
3. What emotion(s) are the robots portraying? (Extended Response)
4. Describe the story of what happened. (Extended Response)
5. What were the robots trying to achieve? (Extended Response)

Analysis Methods. The study was between-participants with non-normal data for the Likert scale questions, so Kruskal-Wallis tests and Mann-Whitney U tests were run to determine significance of the data. Each extended response was coded using grounded coding to find important positive, negative, and neutral language used. There were three categories for important language used: (1) robot actions/reactions; (2) robot descriptions; and (3) robot emotions. Positive language was given a value of 1 and included words like "joy". Negative language was given a value of -1 and included words like "fear". Neutral language was given a value of 0 and included words like "following". In each response, the total positive, negative, and neutral language was totaled and averaged for a single value for each response.

3   Results

Participant Attributions of Robot Motion Results. The data showed a consistent trend in the influence gestures had in the interpretation of the robots' actions and emotions. Towards and spin were positive/welcoming, away and sideways were negative/unwelcoming, and circle was slightly positive/welcoming, but had a higher variance and neutrality. Context had no significant results.

For the question "the human felt [welcome/unwelcome]," it was seen that the sideways and away gestures were viewed as very unwelcoming. Towards was viewed as very welcoming and spin was somewhat welcoming. Circle was viewed as slightly welcoming, but was more neutral than any of the other gestures. The slow speed added more variance or neutrality for each gesture. Away, sideways, and spin had significant difference between fast and slow. However, this did not change the meaning of the movement; it simply skewed the slow speed towards neutrality. Results can be seen in Fig. 2a.

The results for the question "the actions taken were [positive/negative]," varied more than [welcome/unwelcome], but showed similar trends with all five gestures but with higher variance in responses. Spin had the lowest variance in answers and was viewed as somewhat positive. Towards and circle were also viewed as somewhat positive, but with a higher range in answers. Sideways and away had high variance. Away was somewhat negative and sideways was viewed as negative. Speed did not switch the views any of the gestures, but the slower speed pushed results to be more neutral. This additional neutrality at the slow speed was significant in the sideways gesture. Results can be seen in Fig. 2b.

Extended Response Results. Overall, the results were similar to the Likert scale results where gesture was the leading variable and speed had some affect on the perceived expression of the robots. The special case was the towards gesture, which switched interpreted expressions based on speed.

Gestures affected participants' views on whether interaction between the robot and the human was described positively or negatively. Away and sideways led participants to think the robots were afraid and uncertain. The robots were often described as "scared" and "fearful." Most descriptions did not include language of aggression, but rather avoidance and wariness of the human. Spin was viewed positively with the robots' emotions often being described as "joyful" and "excited." The spin was sometimes described as a dance or an expression excitement. Circle was also sometimes described as a dance but the robots were

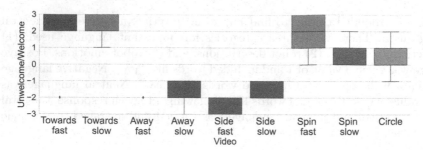

(a) The results from answers to the question "The human felt [welcome/unwelcome]" for each gesture at two different different speeds.

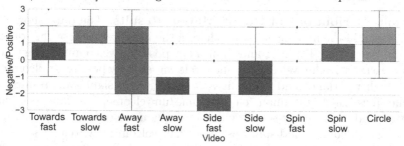

(b) The results from answers to the question "The actions taken were [negative/positive]" for each gesture at two different different speeds.

Fig. 2. Participant survey responses to Likert scale questions.

also described as "confused" or "frustrated." The towards gesture was highly variant because in these responses the gesture was dependent on speed (Fig. 3).

For away, sideways, and spin, the fast and slow speeds did not change the perceived expression of the robots. The slow speed created more neutral responses for each gesture. The only motion where speed did affect the response was the towards motion. At a fast speed, the towards motion was interpreted as negative with participants saying the robots were "trying to block the human" and "confront the human angrily." At a slow speed the towards motion was interpreted as positive with participants saying the robots were "trying to greet the human."

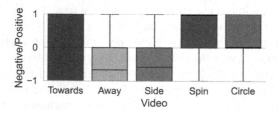

Fig. 3. A comparison of the descriptors used by participants for the five gestures in the extended response questions.

4 Discussion and Conclusions

Gesture significantly predicted communicatory interpretations across the board: (1) **Move away** was rated negatively, indicating fear/uncertainty or disengagement from the interaction. (2) **Sideways** was rated negatively, indicating fear or uncertainty relative to the figurine. (3) **Towards** had two interpretations: **slow towards** was seen as welcome, engaging, excited, whereas **fast towards** was seen as aggressive/confronting. (4) **Spin** was interpreted very positively, indicating "super happy," "joy," or similar. (5) **Moving in a circle** had more variation, ranging from neutral/happy to confused/frustrated, seeming to require additional cues. While speed did not flip the view of most gestures, the slower speed significantly neutralized the perception of the gestures.

This early work demonstrates the relevance of prior HRI motion communication research to domains in which multiple robots might operate in and around people. We conclude that the simple gestures can be used for communication by multi-robot groups and that such gestures have social and functional communicatory significance. The results show that four of the five gestures had convergent communicatory interpretations, though one of the four, *towards*, had a further division of communication at varied speeds ranging from more welcoming/friendly (when slow) to more threatening/hostile (when fast). Future work will continue to explore ways in which varied motions within the group affect multi-robot communications or indicate roles or intent within a robot group.

References

1. Agnihotri, A., Knight, H.: Persuasive chairbots. In: Ro-MAN, pp. 1–7. IEEE (2019)
2. Alonso-Mora, J., et al.: Gesture based human-multi-robot swarm interaction and its application to an interactive display. In: ICRA, pp. 5948–5953. IEEE (2015)
3. Breazeal, C., et al.: Effects of nonverbal communication on efficiency and robustness in human-robot teamwork. In: IROS, pp. 708–713. IEEE (2005)
4. Dragan, A.D, et al.: Legibility and predictability of robot motion. In: HRI, pp. 301–308. ACM/IEEE (2013)
5. Guzzi, J., et al.: A model of artificial emotions for behavior-modulation and implicit coordination in multi-robot systems. In: GECCO, pp. 21–28 (2018)
6. Hoffman, G., Weinberg, G.: Gesture-based human-robot jazz improvisation. In: ICRA, pp. 582–587. IEEE (2010)
7. Knight, H., et al.: I get it already! the influence of chairbot motion gestures on bystander response. In: Ro-MAN, pp. 443–448. IEEE (2017)
8. McNeill, D.: Hand and Mind. University of Chicago Press, Chicago (1992)
9. Perzanowski, D., et al.: Integrating natural language and gesture in a robotics domain. In: ISIC (1998)
10. Rond, J., et al.: Improv with robots. In: Ro-MAN (2019)
11. Salem, M., et al.: Generation and evaluation of communicative robot gesture. Int. J. Soc. Robot. 4(2), 201–217 (2012)
12. Santos, M., Egerstedt, M.: From motions to emotions. International Journal of Social Robotics, 1–14 (2020)
13. St-Onge, D., et al.: Engaging with robotic swarms: commands from expressive motion. ACM Trans. Human Robot Interact. 8(2), 1–26 (2019)

Control of Pneumatic Artificial Muscles with SNN-based Cerebellar-Like Model

Hongbo Zhang$^{(\boxtimes)}$ iD, Yunshuang Li iD, Yipin Guo iD, Xinyi Chen iD, and Qinyuan Ren iD

College of Control Science and Engineering, Zhejiang University, Hangzhou 310013, China

Abstract. Soft robotics technologies have gained growing interest in recent years, which allows various applications from manufacturing to human-robot interaction. Pneumatic artificial muscle (PAM), a typical soft actuator, has been widely applied to soft robots. The compliance and resilience of soft actuators allow soft robots to behave compliant when interacting with unstructured environments, while the utilization of soft actuators also introduces nonlinearity and uncertainty. Inspired by Cerebellum's vital functions in control of human's physical movement, a neural network model of Cerebellum based on spiking neuron networks (SNNs) is designed. This model is used as a feed-forward controller in controlling a 1-DOF robot arm driven by PAMs. The simulation results show that this Cerebellar-based system achieves good performance and increases the system's response speed.

Keywords: Cerebellum-like controller · Spiking neural network · Nonlinear systems · Mckibben · STDP

1 Introduction

Pneumatic artificial muscles (PAMs), such as Mckibben, are designed with the inspiration of creatures, showing great compatibility to creatures. This kind of muscle emerged in the twentieth century and has various kinds of applications after decades of development. Mckibben is small in size and relatively safe with high power to weight ratio. However, its nonlinearity and viscoelasticity properties increase the difficulty in controller designing.

The best example of control system for soft actuators can be found in animal bodies. As mentioned in [5], Cerebellum as part of creatures' neural system have attracted vast attention because of that they play important role in controlling function. Therefore, we proposed a Cerebellum-like controller based on its real structure and internal information processing mechanism. Due to the bionic advantages of this controller, it's appropriate to apply it in controlling Mckibben.

In our system, we conduct a Cerebellum-like controller based on spiking neural networks (SNNs) to control a 1-DOF robotic arm shown in Fig. 2 driven

---

H. Zhang, Y. Li and Y. Guo—Contribute equally to this work.

© Springer Nature Switzerland AG 2021
H. Li et al. (Eds.): ICSR 2021, LNAI 13086, pp. 824–828, 2021.
https://doi.org/10.1007/978-3-030-90525-5_79

by a pair of PAMs. It can also be refered as an online closed-loop error-correction controller. The controller has one kind of fibers, Mossy Fibers, with four kinds of cells, Granule cells, Purkinje cells Inferior Olive cells and Deep cerebellar nuclei cells. All of them are constructed as the similar structures of Cerebellum and we model its physical functions. Besides, the SNNs functions the feed-forward part in our controller. Previously, scholars have designed some novel SNNs [1,3,6]. In our work, a new SNN topology is designed to learn the inverse model of soft actuators and make up for the output of the controller.

2   The Structure of SNN

Here we use a real-time spiking neural network with a cerebellar-like structure that can obtain the inverse model of the Mckibben pairs to act as a feed-forward part of the controller. We use a set of spiking neurons as a basic unit of the network and imitate the structure of Cerebellar to build a neural network, which bases on [3]. The topology of the network is displayed in Fig. 1.

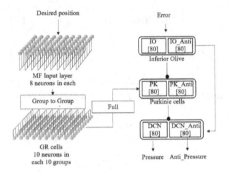

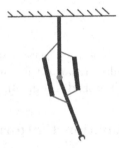

Fig. 1. Topological structure diagram of the neural network. The arrow indicates an excitatory effect, and the circle indicates an inhibitory effect.

Fig. 2. The robotic arm. Two pneumatic artificial muscles are placed on both sides. When one of them contracts, it pulls the robotic arm to rotate.

2.1   Neurons and Layers

The neural network consists of about 1000 neurons which contains 80 Mossy Fibers (MF), 100 Granule cells (GR), 160 Purkinje cells (PK), 160 Inferior Olive cells (IO), and 160 Deep cerebellar nuclei cells (DCN). The leaky integrate-and-fire (LIF) neuron model is used to build the neurons. Since the cerebellar cortex has hierarchical functional blocks, different blocks are responsible for different types of physical movements. The GR layer is connected to the MF layer hierarchically to imitate this partition mapping pattern. The PK layer and the DCN layer are divided into antagonistic pairs to receive pulses from GR and corresponding error signals from IO. Weights between GR and PK are adjusted and trained according to Spike Timing–Dependent Plasticity (STDP) learning rules.

2.2 Learning Rules

Studies have shown that learning in Cerebellum is mediated by synaptic plasticity. In our network, the connection between the GR layer and the PK layer is carried out according to the learning rules.

STDP is a learning method based on Hebbian learning rules. The dependence of synaptic modification on the order of pre and postsynaptic spiking within a critical window of tens of milliseconds has profound functional utilities in learning and memory [2].

STDP in this network is divided into long-term potentiation (LTP) mediated by GR pulses and long-term depression (LTD) mediated by IO pulses. The equations are as follows: LTP effect increases the weight w at a specific learning rate whenever there is a GR pulse, while the LTD effect adds the historical GR pulse to the kernel function whenever there is an IO input pulse.

$$\text{LTP} : \Delta w\left(t\right) = \text{nu}_0\, \delta\left(t\right), \tag{1}$$

$$\text{LTD} : \Delta w\left(t_{\text{IO}}\right) = -\text{nu}_1 \int_{-\infty}^{t_{\text{IO}}} K\left(t - t_{\text{IO}}\right) \delta_{\text{GR}}\left(t\right) \mathrm{d}t, \tag{2}$$

$$K(x) = \mathrm{e}^x - \mathrm{e}^{4x}. \tag{3}$$

where nu_1, nu_2 represents learning rate for LTP and LTD respectively, δ represents pulse signal of the corresponding neurons and K represents the kernel function described in Eq. (3).

3 Simulation Platform

Bindsnet [4], an open-source spiking neural network building platform, is used to build and train the neural network. Meanwhile, Simulink is used as the platform to build the physical simulation environment and the controller.

3.1 The Robotic Arm

Our robotic arm uses two iron rods as bones and a pair of pneumatic muscles as actuators imitating bicep and tricep of human respectively in Fig. 2.

One end of the link is fixed, and the muscles are installed on both sides of the link. When one of the muscles contracts, it will pull the unfixed link to rotate. We take the deflection angle of the robotic arm as output and model the robotic arm in Simulink.

3.2 Control Loop

A cascade control method including a feed-forward part and a feedback part is applied in our system shown in Fig. 3 The air pressure feedback controller

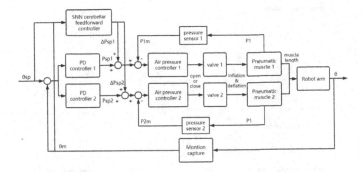

Fig. 3. The block diagram of the feed-forward and feedback cascade control system.

shown in Fig. 3 directly controls the air pressure of the two pneumatic muscles by controlling opening and closing of the solenoid valves.

The PD controllers in the outer loop is served as the main controller to obtain the precision of motion control. Cerebellum-inspired feed-forward controller contributes to improve the response speed and deal with the nonlinearity.

4   Results and Discussions

In the simulation, we use two different control strategies: (1) A controller with both feed-forward and feedback blocks (2) A controller with a single feed-forward block in Fig. 4.

Firstly, a controller with a PD feedback part and a feed-forward part built by the network is applied. The feedback controller is added to achieve the rapid response of the control system to disturbances. In order to test the trajectory tracking effect and the anti-interference effect of the end of the manipulator, a sinusoidal trajectory input is applied as the desired trajectory to analyze the control effect. Results in Fig. 4 (a) shows improvement in control accuracy comparing with the PD controller. Results in Fig. 4 (b) also indicate that the feed-forward controller achieves good performance as well.

The experiment verifies that our controller can replace traditional controllers, and we will continue to reduce the effect of feedback part and verify the control effect of our controller on Mckibben artificial muscle. The whole system shows strong bionics and has potentially large applications in many fields.

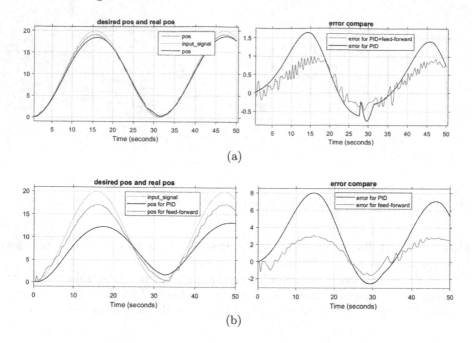

Fig. 4. (a) Results for a controller with both feed-forward and feedback blocks. (b) Results for a controller with a single feed-forward block.

References

1. Abadía, I., Naveros, F., Garrido, J.A., Ros, E., Luque, N.R.: On robot compliance: a cerebellar control approach. IEEE Trans. Cybern. **51**(5), 2476–2489 (2021). https://doi.org/10.1109/TCYB.2019.2945498
2. Caporale, N., Dan, Y.: Spike timing-dependent plasticity: a hebbian learning rule. Ann. Rev. Neurosci. **31**, 25–46 (2008)
3. Carrillo, R.R., Ros, E., Boucheny, C., Coenen, O.J.M.: A real-time spiking cerebellum model for learning robot control. Biosystems **94**(1), 18–27 (2008). https://doi.org/10.1016/j.biosystems.2008.05.008. https://www.sciencedirect.com/science/article/pii/S0303264708001226. seventh International Workshop on Information Processing in Cells and Tissues
4. Hazan, H., et al.: BindsNet: a machine learning-oriented spiking neural networks library in python. Front. Neuroinform. **12**, 89 (2018). https://doi.org/10.3389/fninf.2018.00089. https://www.frontiersin.org/article/10.3389/fninf.2018.00089
5. Miall, R.: The cerebellum and visually controlled movements. In: IEE Workshop on Self-Learning Robots III Brainstyle Robotics: The Cerebellum Beyond Function Approximation (Ref. No. 1999/049), pp. 2/1–2/5 (1999). https://doi.org/10.1049/ic:19990257
6. Yang, J., Song, T.: A prediction scheme in spiking neural network (SNN) hardware for ultra-low power consumption. In: 2020 International SoC Design Conference (ISOCC), pp. 310–311 (2020). https://doi.org/10.1109/ISOCC50952.2020.9333106

Author Index